literature

The Human Experience

LiTERATURE The Human Experience

RICHARD ABCARIAN AND MARVIN KLOTZ, EDITORS

California State University, Northridge

St. Martin's Press   New York

ACKNOWLEDGMENTS

ANTIOCH REVIEW: "Advice to My Son" by J. Peter Meinke. From *Antioch Review,* Vol. XXV, 1965, p. 374. Reprinted by permission of the publisher.

ATHENEUM PUBLISHERS, INC.: "The Dover Bitch" from *The Hard Hours* by Anthony Hecht. Copyright © 1960 by Anthony E. Hecht. Appeared originally in *Transatlantic Review.* Reprinted by permission of Atheneum Publishers.

JONATHAN CAPE LTD.: "Naming of Parts" and "Judging Distances" from *A Map of Verona* by Henry Reed. Reprinted by permission of Jonathan Cape Ltd.

CHATTO AND WINDUS LTD.: "The Last Laugh" and "Dulce et Decorum Est" from *The Collected Poems of Wilfred Owen* edited by C. Day-Lewis, together with the draft version of "Last Words" by Wilfred Owen. Reprinted by permission of The Executors of Harold Owen's Estate and Chatto and Windus Ltd.

CONTINENTAL TOTAL MEDIA PROJECT, INC.: "Suzanne," words and music by Leonard Cohen. Published by Continental Total Media Project Inc., 515 Madison Ave., New York, N.Y. 10022. Reprinted by permission of the publisher.

CATHERINE DAVIS: "After a Time" by Catherine Davis. Reprinted by permission of the author.

J. M. DENT & SONS LTD.: "Everyman" (Anonymous) edited by A. C. Cawley, Everyman's Library text. Reprinted by permission of J. M. Dent & Sons, Ltd.

The Secret Sharer by Joseph Conrad. Reprinted by permission of J. M. Dent & Sons, Ltd. and the Trustees of the Joseph Conrad Estate.

"An Enemy of the People" by Henrik Ibsen, translated by R. Farquharson Sharp, Everyman's Library series. Reprinted by permission of J. M. Dent & Sons, Ltd.

"Fern Hill," "Do Not Go Gentle into That Good Night" and "I Have Longed to Move Away" from *Collected Poems* by Dylan Thomas. Reprinted by permission of J. M. Dent & Sons Ltd. and the Trustees for the Copyrights of the late Dylan Thomas.

THE DIAL PRESS: "Going to Meet the Man," Copyright © 1965 by James Baldwin. From the book *Going to Meet the Man* by James Baldwin. Reprinted by permission of the publisher, The Dial Press.

DODD, MEAD & COMPANY: "We Wear the Mask" by Paul Laurence Dunbar. Reprinted by permission of Dodd, Mead & Company, Inc. from *The Complete Poems of Paul Laurence Dunbar.*

Major Barbara by George Bernard Shaw. Copyright 1907, 1913, 1930, 1941, George Bernard Shaw. Copyright 1957, The Public Trustee as Executor of the Estate of George Bernard Shaw. Reprinted by permission of Dodd, Mead & Company, Inc. and The Society of Authors as Agent for the Estate of George Bernard Shaw.

DOUBLEDAY & COMPANY, INC.: "Dolor," copyright 1943 by Modern Poetry Association, Inc., and "Elegy for Jane," copyright 1944 by Theodore Roethke from the book *Collected Poems of Theodore Roethke.* Reprinted by permission of Doubleday & Company, Inc.

E. P. DUTTON & CO., INC.: "Everyman" (Anonymous). From the book *Everyman and Medieval Miracle Plays.* Edited and with an Introduction by A. C. Cawley. Published by E. P. Dutton & Co., Inc. in a paperback edition and used with their permission.

"An Enemy of the People" from the book *Ghosts; An Enemy of the People; The Warriors at Helgeland* by Henrik Ibsen. Trans. by R. Farquharson Sharp. Everyman's Library edition. Published by E. P. Dutton & Co., Inc. and used with their permission.

"In a Spring Still Not Written Of" from the book *Views from a Ferris Wheel* by Robert Wallace. Copyright © 1965 by Robert Wallace. Published by E. P. Dutton & Co., Inc. and used with their permission.

"People" from the book *Selected Poems* by Yevgeny Yevtushenko. Trans. by Robin Milner-Gulland and Peter Levi. Copyright © 1962 by Robin Milner-Gulland and Peter Levi. Published by E. P. Dutton & Co., Inc. and used with their permission.

HARLAN ELLISON: " 'Repent, Harlequin!' Said the Ticktockman," by Harlan Ellison, copyright © 1965 by Galaxy Publishing Corporation. All rights reassigned, 1966, to the Author. Reprinted by permission of the Author and the Author's agent, Robert P. Mills, Ltd.

FABER AND FABER LTD.: "In Memory of W. B. Yeats," "That Night when Joy Began" (from *Five Songs*), and "The Unknown Citizen" by W. H. Auden. Reprinted by permission of Faber and Faber Ltd. from *Collected Shorter Poems 1927–1957.*

"The Love Song of J. Alfred Prufrock" by T. S. Eliot. Reprinted by permission of Faber and Faber Ltd. from *Collected Poems 1909–1962.*

"Innocence" by Thom Gunn. Reprinted by permission of Faber and Faber Ltd. from *My Sad Captains.*

"Relic" by Ted Hughes. Reprinted by permission of Faber and Faber Ltd. from *Lupercal.*

FARRAR, STRAUS & GIROUX, INC.: "Death of the Ball Turret Gunner" and "Losses" by Randall Jarrell, from *The Complete Poems* by Randall Jarrell, copyright © 1945, 1948, 1969 by Mrs. Randall Jarrell.

"Benito Cereno" by Robert Lowell. Reprinted with the permission of Farrar, Straus & Giroux, Inc. from *The Old Glory* by Robert Lowell, copyright © 1964, 1965, 1968 by Robert Lowell.

"Idiots First" from *Idiots First* by Bernard Malamud, copyright © 1961, 1963 by Bernard Malamud. Reprinted with the permission of Farrar, Straus & Giroux, Inc.

HARCOURT BRACE JOVANOVICH, INC.: "nobody loses all the time" copyright, 1926, by Horace Liveright, copyright, 1954, by E. E. Cummings; "if everything happens that can't be done" copyright, 1944, by E. E. Cummings; "the Cambridge ladies" copyright, 1923, 1951, by E. E. Cummings; "i sing of Olaf" copyright, 1931, 1959, by E. E. Cummings. All reprinted from his volume *Poems 1923–1954* by permission of Harcourt Brace Jovanovich, Inc.

"The Love Song of J. Alfred Prufrock" from *Collected Poems 1909–1962* by T. S. Eliot, copyright, 1936, by Harcourt Brace Jovanovich, Inc.; copyright © 1963, 1964, by T. S. Eliot. Reprinted by permission of the publisher.

Molière's *The Misanthrope* translated by Richard Wilbur, copyright © 1954, 1955, by Richard Wilbur. Reprinted by permission of Harcourt Brace Jovanovich, Inc. CAUTION: Professionals and amateurs are hereby warned that this translation, being fully protected under the copyright laws of the United States of America, the British Empire, including the Dominion of

THE MODERN POETRY ASSOCIATION: "The Calamity" by Richard Schramm. First appeared in *Poetry,* copyright 1972 by The Modern Poetry Association. Reprinted by permission of the Editor of *Poetry* and the author.

NEW DIRECTIONS PUBLISHING CORP.: "In Goya's Greatest Scenes" by Lawrence Ferlinghetti, *A Coney Island of the Mind.* Copyright © 1958 by Lawrence Ferlinghetti. Reprinted by permission of New Directions Publishing Corporation.

"Patriotism" by Yukio Mishima, translated by Geoffrey W. Sargent. From Yukio Mishima, *Death in Midsummer and Other Stories.* Copyright © 1966 by New Directions Publishing Corporation. Reprinted by permission of New Directions Publishing Corporation.

"The Last Laugh," "Last Words," and "Dulce et Decorum Est" by Wilfred Owen, *Collected Poems.* Copyright Chatto & Windus, Ltd. 1946, © 1963. Reprinted by permission of New Directions Publishing Corporation.

"Hugh Selwyn Mauberley," Sections IV and V, by Ezra Pound, *Personae.* Copyright 1926 by Ezra Pound. Reprinted by permission of New Directions Publishing Corporation.

"Fern Hill," "Do Not Go Gentle into That Good Night," and "I Have Longed to Move Away" by Dylan Thomas, *The Poems of Dylan Thomas.* Copyright 1939, 1946 by New Directions Publishing Corporation. Copyright 1952 by Dylan Thomas. Reprinted by permission of New Directions Publishing Corporation.

"Tract" by William Carlos Williams, *Collected Earlier Poems.* Copyright 1938 by William Carlos Williams. Reprinted by permission of New Directions Publishing Corporation.

HAROLD OBER ASSOCIATES, INC.: "I Want to Know Why" by Sherwood Anderson, from *The Triumph of the Egg.* Reprinted by permission of Harold Ober Associates Incorporated. Copyright 1921 by B. W. Huebsch. Renewed 1948 by Eleanor C. Anderson.

"Same in Blues" by Langston Hughes, from *Montage of a Dream Deferred.* Reprinted by permission of Harold Ober Associates Incorporated. Copyright 1951 by Langston Hughes.

OXFORD UNIVERSITY PRESS: "Spring and Fall: To a Young Child" and "Thou Art Indeed Just, Lord" by Gerard M. Hopkins, published by Oxford University Press.

"The Death of Iván Ilých" from *Iván Ilých, Hadji Murad and Other Stories* by Leo Tolstoy, translated by Louise and Aylmer Maude and published by Oxford University Press.

A. D. PETERS & CO.: Excerpts from *My Oedipus Complex* by Frank O'Connor. Reprinted by permission of A. D. Peters and Company.

RANDOM HOUSE, INC.: "In Memory of W. B. Yeats," copyright 1940, renewed 1968 by W. H. Auden; Stanza II from "Five Songs" (previously titled "That Night When Joy Began"), copyright 1937, renewed 1965 by W. H. Auden; "The Unknown Citizen," copyright 1940, renewed 1968 by W. H. Auden. All reprinted from *Collected Shorter Poems 1927–1957,* by W. H. Auden, by permission of Random House, Inc.

"Dry September," copyright 1930, renewed 1958 by William Faulkner. Reprinted from *Selected Short Stories of William Faulkner,* by permission of Random House, Inc.

"The Conscientious Objector," copyright 1947 by Karl Shapiro. Reprinted from *Selected Poems of Karl Shapiro,* by permission of Random House, Inc.

PAUL R. REYNOLDS, INC.: "The Man Who Lived Underground" by Richard Wright. Copyright 1944 by L. B. Fischer Publishing Corp. Reprinted by permission of Paul R. Reynolds, Inc., 599 Fifth Avenue, New York, N.Y. 10017.

SCHOCKEN BOOKS INC.: "A Hunger Artist" by Franz Kafka. Reprinted by permission of Schocken Books Inc. from *The Penal Colony* by Franz Kafka. Copyright © 1948 by Schocken Books Inc.

SCORPION PRESS: "Five Ways to Kill a Man" by Edwin Brock, from *With Love From Judas.* Reprinted by permission of Scorpion Press.

CHARLES SCRIBNER'S SONS: "Speaking of Poetry" is reprinted by permission of Charles Scribner's Sons from *The Collected Poems of John Peale Bishop* edited by Allen Tate. Copyright 1948 Charles Scribner's Sons.

"A Marriage" is reprinted by permission of Charles Scribner's Sons from *For Love* by Robert Creeley. Copyright © 1962 Robert Creeley.

"Richard Cory" is reprinted by permission of Charles Scribner's Sons from *The Children of the Night* by Edwin Arlington Robinson (1897). "How Annandale Went Out" (Copyright 1910 Charles Scribner's Sons; renewal copyright 1938) and "Miniver Cheevy" (Copyright 1907 Charles Scribner's Sons; renewal copyright 1935) are reprinted by permission of Charles Scribner's Sons from *The Town Down the River* by Edwin Arlington Robinson.

SIMON & SCHUSTER, INC.: "Seventh Seal" by Ingmar Bergman, from *Four Screen Plays of Ingmar Bergman*. Copyright © 1960, by Ingmar Bergman. Reprinted by permission of Simon and Schuster.

SIQUOMB PUBLISHING CORP.: "Songs to Aging Children Come" words and music by Joni Mitchell. Copyright © 1967 by Siquomb Publishing Corp. Reprinted by permission of the publishers, Siquomb Publishing Corp. All rights reserved.

THE SOCIETY OF AUTHORS: "To an Athlete Dying Young" and "When I Was One-and-Twenty" by A. E. Housman. Reprinted by permission of The Society of Authors as the literary representative of the Estate of A. E. Housman, and Jonathan Cape Ltd., publishers of A. E. Housman's *Collected Poems*.

Major Barbara by George Bernard Shaw. Reprinted by permission of The Society of Authors on behalf of the Bernard Shaw Estate.

THE UNIVERSITY OF CHICAGO PRESS: "Innocence" from *My Sad Captains*, © 1961 by Thom Gunn. Reprinted by permission of the author and the University of Chicago Press.

THE UNIVERSITY OF MICHIGAN PRESS: "The Widow of Ephesus" from William Arrowsmith's translation of Petronius, *The Satyricon*. Copyright © by William Arrowsmith 1959. Reprinted by permission of the University of Michigan Press.

THE VIKING PRESS INC.: "Araby" from *Dubliners* by James Joyce. Copyright © 1967 by The Estate of James Joyce. Reprinted by permission of The Viking Press, Inc.

"The Horse Dealer's Daughter" from *The Complete Short Stories*—D. H. Lawrence. Copyright 1922 by Thomas B. Seltzer Inc., 1950 by Frieda Lawrence. Reprinted by permission of The Viking Press, Inc.

"The Messenger" from *The Weathercock* by Ann Stanford. Copyright © 1964 by Ann Stanford. Originally appeared in *Poetry Magazine*. Reprinted by permission of The Viking Press, Inc.

A. P. WATT & SON: "Among School Children," "No Second Troy," "The Old Men Admiring Themselves in the Water," and "Sailing to Byzantium" by William Butler Yeats. All from *The Collected Poems of W. B. Yeats*. Reprinted by permission of A. P. Watt & Son, M. B. Yeats, and the Macmillan Company of Canada.

PICTURE CREDITS

Innocence and Experience

Color opening, p. xxxiv: "Snake Charmer," 1953 by Henri Rousseau. Oil on canvas. Permission SPADEM 1973 by French Reproduction Rights, Inc. Transparency courtesy of GIRAUDON, Paris.

Fiction, p. 2: "Blind Minotaur," 1934 by Pablo Picasso. Aquatint and etching, 9 3/8" x 11 3/4". Collection, The Museum of Modern Art, New York. Abby Aldrich Rockefeller Fund. Permission SPADEM 1973 by French Reproduction Rights, Inc.

Poetry, p. 78: "Adam and Eve" by Hans Baldung Grien. Courtesy of The Metropolitan Museum of Art, Harris Brisbane Dick Fund, 1927.

Drama, p. 116: "Seated Woman," c. 1885 by Georges-Pierre Seurat. Conte crayon, 18 7/8" x 12 3/8". Collection, The Museum of Modern Art, New York. Bequest of Abby Aldrich Rockefeller.

Conformity and Rebellion

Color opening, p. 226: "Frieze of protective figures from the Tomb of Tutankhamen," The British Museum. Transparency courtesy of Mr. William MacQuilty, Motemount, Highwood Hill, Mill Hill, London N.W. 7.

Fiction, p. 230: "Current," 1964 by Bridget Riley. Synthetic polymer paint on composition board, 58 3/8" x 58 7/8". Collection, The Museum of Modern Art, New York. Gift of Philip Johnson.

Poetry, p. 320: "New York," 1953 by Franz Kline. Oil on canvas. Courtesy of the Albright-Knox Art Gallery, Buffalo, New York. Gift of Seymour H. Knox.

Drama, p. 352: "El Grito (The Cry)," 1967 by Juan Genoves. Oil on canvas. Collection Joseph Bernstein, Louisiana. Photograph courtesy of Marlborough Gallery, New York.

Love and Hate

Color opening, p. 454: "La Vie," 1881 by Pablo Picasso. Oil on canvas. Courtesy of the Cleveland Museum of Art, Gift of Hanna Fund, 1945. Permission SPADEM 1973 by French Reproduction Rights, Inc.

Fiction, p. 460: "The Love of Jupiter and Semele," 1930 by Pablo Picasso. Illustration for Ovid: *Metamorphoses*. Etching, published by Albert Skira, Lausanne, 1931. Collection, The Museum of Modern Art, New York. Permission SPADEM 1973 by French Reproduction Rights, Inc.

Poetry, p. 504: Detail of "The Creation of Adam" by Michelangelo. Rome The Sistine Chapel. Photograph by Anderson-Giraudon.

Drama, p. 538. "Young Couple," 1917 by Emil Nolde. Woodcut painted in black, 12 5/8" x 9 1/16". Collection, The Museum of Modern Art, New York. Purchase.

The Presence of Death

Color opening, p. 682. "Masks Confronting Death (Masques devant la mort)," 1888 by James Ensor. Oil on canvas, 32" x 39 1/2". Collection, The Museum of Modern Art, New York. Mrs. Simon Guggenheim Fund.

Fiction, p. 686: "Liberation of the Peon," 1931 by Diego Rivera. Fresco. Courtesy of the Philadelphia Museum of Art. Photograph by A. J. Wyatt, Staff Photographer.

Poetry, p. 788: "Girl Held in the Lap of Death," 1934–36 by Kathe Kollwitz. Lithograph. Collection, The Museum of Modern Art, New York.

Drama, p. 828: "Tirant Sin," from the Progress of Sin. 1744. N.Y. Public Library picture collection.

Appendices

Opening picture, p. 898: "The Wind Man," c. 1953 by Yasuji Morita. Brush and ink, 53 1/2" x 27 1/2". Japanese House Fund. Collection, The Museum of Modern Art.

pp. 926–927: The Globe Theatre, 1953; Interior of the Globe Theatre in the days of Shakespeare; and A French theatre during Molière's management: Courtesy of The Bettman Archive, Inc. Interior of the Swan Theatre, London, 1596: Courtesy of Culver Pictures. The Greek theatre at Epidaurus: Courtesy of the Greek National Tourist Office.

For Dan, Dave, Jennifer, Peter, Rick, Robin, and Sara

PREFACE The short stories, poems, and plays in *Literature: The Human Experience* represent literary traditions ranging from 400 B.C. to the present and reflect widely diverse cultures. In choosing the selections we have been governed by a belief that the first task of an introductory anthology of literature is to engage the reader's interest, to make the experience of literature an immediate and exciting one. A corollary of that belief is our conviction that a genuine interest in literary history or the formal analysis of literature arises out of the experience of being engaged by particular works. Thus, we have selected works not primarily because they illustrate critical definitions or lend themselves to a particular approach but because we find them exciting and believe that students will, too.

The arrangement of the works in four thematic groups provides opportunities to explore diverse attitudes toward the same powerful human tendencies and experiences and to contrast formal treatments as well. Within each thematic section, the works are arranged by genre—fiction, poetry, drama—chronologically. Each section is introduced by a short essay that examines some of the crucial human issues embodied in the works that follow. These essays are deliberately polemical, and, no doubt, readers will sometimes take exception to them. This is all to the good, for we believe that our proper mission as editors is to provide the groundwork for discussion and debate, not to promulgate "truths" for the edification of students.

We should perhaps say a word about the questions—rarely more than two or three—that we have placed after about half of the stories, most of the poems, and all of the plays. We believe that too often students are prevented from responding to a work as fully as they might because they are immediately asked questions that require them to confront formal problems. But there are certain kinds of questions, our students have convinced us, that can be helpful by opening works that might otherwise prove difficult. The questions in this book are intended to serve this purpose. At the end of each of the four thematic sections we have provided a number of general questions, each alluding to several works in the section. We have found that these questions are especially useful as starting points for student writing.

The first appendix, The Poet and His Craft, presents three poems in both early draft and published versions. A student who compares the two versions of each poem will, we think, gain some insight into the ways in which poems are created.

Although the emphasis throughout this book is on the values of literature as a means to enjoyment and, indeed, to a better understanding of our own humanity, it is of course true that the fullest appreciation of literary achievement requires a certain facility in formal matters and some acquaintance with literary history as well. The essays Reading Fiction, Reading Poetry, and Reading Drama acquaint readers with some formal concepts and historical considerations that are basic to the study of the major genres of literary art. The essay on drama also includes a discussion of some of the less obvious differences between live performance and film art.

In the final essay, Three Critical Approaches: Formalist, Sociological, Psychoanalytic, we develop, for one story and one poem, three critical readings that emphasize different aspects of the works and reflect the diversity of response that may occur when readers bring different expectations and attitudes to literature. Seeing that a variety of critical approaches may all illuminate a work, and complement one another, helps to free students, we believe, from a timid acquiescence to some "correct" received view and enables them to respond to literature more honestly and openly.

The Glossary of Literary Terms includes brief excerpts to illustrate the definitions presented there and also makes specific reference to selections in the anthology.

Finally, we have provided sources of recordings and a list of available films of many of the selections.

We would like to acknowledge our debt to our colleagues Robert apRoberts and Wallace Graves for their invaluable comments and criticism and to Fred Lopez, who helped us prepare the manuscript. None of them, of course, is to blame for our blunders.

Richard Abcarian
Marvin Klotz

Northridge, California
January 16, 1973

CONTENTS

Innocence and Experience

Love and Hate

The Presence of Death   684

FICTION   687

POETRY   789

Appendices   899

Alternate Table of Contents
(arranged by genre)

FICTION

POETRY

DRAMA

innocence and experience

Snake Charmer, Henri Rousseau

INNOCENCE AND EXPERIENCE

Man strives to give order and meaning to his life, to reduce the mystery and unpredictability that constantly threaten him. Life is infinitely more complex and surprising than we imagine, and the categories we establish to give it order and meaning are, for the most part, "momentary stays against confusion." At any time, the equilibrium of our lives, the comfortable image of ourselves and the world around us, may be disrupted suddenly by something new, forcing us into painful reevaluation. These disruptions create pain, anxiety, terror—but also wisdom and awareness.

The works in this section deal generally with the movement of a central character from moral simplicities and certainties into a more complex and problematic world. Though these works frequently issue in awareness, even wisdom, their central figures rarely act decisively; the protagonist is more often a passive figure who learns the difference between the ideal world he imagines and the injurious real world. If he survives the ordeal (and he doesn't always, either emotionally or physically), he will doubtless be a better human—better equipped to wrest some satisfaction from a bleak and threatening world. It is no accident, of course, that so many of the works here deal with the passage from childhood to adulthood, for childhood is a time of simplicities and certainties that must give way to the complexities and uncertainties of adult life.

Almost universally, innocence is associated with childhood and youth, as experience is with age. We teach the young about an ideal world, without explaining that it has not yet been and may never be achieved. As innocents, they are terribly vulnerable to falsehood, to intrusive sexuality, to the machinations of the wicked who, despite all the moral tales, often do triumph. We know, if we have not already forgotten what the innocence of childhood celebrates, that time and experience will disabuse them.

But the terms *innocence* and *experience* range widely in meaning, and that range is reflected here. Innocence may be defined almost biologically, as illustrated by the sexual innocence of the young boy in Sherwood Anderson's "I Want to Know Why." Innocence may be social—the innocence of Robin in Nathaniel Hawthorne's "My Kinsman, Major Molineux" or the young boy in Frank O'Connor's "My Oedipus Complex." Or innocence may be seen as the child's ignorance of his own mortality, as in Gerard Manley Hopkins' "Spring and Fall" and Dylan Thomas' "Fern Hill."

Innocence almost always reflects a foolishness based on ignorance; sometimes, as well, it is the occasion for arrogance. The narrator of Joseph Conrad's "The Secret Sharer," at the beginning of his account, asserts confidently that "the sea was not likely to keep any special surprises expressly for my discomfiture" and explains that he is attracted to the sea because of its "great security" and "the singleness of its purpose." The events of the story markedly change his attitudes about himself and the moral universe in which he operates. In such works as Robert Lowell's *Benito Cereno* and Robert Browning's "My Last Duchess," one discovers the tragic and violent consequences of an innocence that is blind. And in George Bernard Shaw's *Major Barbara*, Barbara, our innocent, learns that, despite all the sentimental moral postures associated with Christian charity on the one hand and munitions manufacturers on the other, her father's ability to create a just and responsive social system far exceeds that of the Salvation Army.

The contrast between what we thought in our youth and what we have come to know, painfully, as adults stands as an emblem of the passage from innocence to experience. Yet, all of us remain, to one degree or another, innocent throughout life, since we never, except with death, stop learning from experience. Looked at in this way, experience is the ceaseless assault life makes upon our innocence, moving us to a greater wisdom about ourselves and the world around us.

FICTION

My Kinsman, Major Molineux[*]

NATHANIEL HAWTHORNE [1804-1864]

AFTER the kings of Great Britain had assumed the right of appointing the colonial governors, the measures of the latter seldom met with the ready and generous approbation which had been paid to those of their predecessors, under the original charters. The people looked with most jealous scrutiny to the exercise of power which did not emanate from themselves, and they usually rewarded their rulers with slender gratitude for the compliances by which, in softening their instructions from beyond the sea, they had incurred the reprehension of those who gave them. The annals of Massachusetts Bay will inform us, that of six governors in the space of about forty years from the surrender of the old charter, under James II., two were imprisoned by a popular insurrection; a third, as Hutchinson inclines to believe, was driven from the province by the whizzing of a musket-ball; a fourth, in the opinion of the same historian, was hastened to his grave by continual bickerings with the House of Representatives; and the remaining two, as well as their successors, till the Revolution, were favored with few and brief intervals of peaceful sway. The inferior members of the court party, in times of high political excitement, led scarcely a more desirable life. These remarks may serve as a preface to the following adventures, which chanced upon a summer night, not far from a hundred years ago. The reader, in order to avoid a long and dry detail of colonial affairs, is requested to dispense with an account of the train of circumstances that had caused much temporary inflammation of the popular mind.

It was near nine o'clock of a moonlight evening, when a boat crossed the ferry with a single passenger, who had obtained his conveyance at that unusual hour by the promise of an extra fare. While he stood on the landing-place, searching in either pocket for the means of fulfilling his agreement, the ferryman lifted a lantern, by the aid of which, and the newly risen moon, he took a very accurate survey of the stranger's figure. He was a youth of

---

[*] This story is considered in detail in the essay "Three Critical Approaches: Formalist, Sociological, Psychoanalytic" at the end of the book.

barely eighteen years, evidently country-bred, and now, as it should seem, upon his first visit to town. He was clad in a coarse gray coat, well worn, but in excellent repair; his under garments were durably constructed of leather, and fitted tight to a pair of serviceable and well-shaped limbs; his stockings of blue yarn were the incontrovertible work of a mother or a sister; and on his head was a three-cornered hat, which in its better days had perhaps sheltered the graver brow of the lad's father. Under his left arm was a heavy cudgel formed of an oak sapling, and retaining a part of the hardened root; and his equipment was completed by a wallet, not so abundantly stocked as to incommode the vigorous shoulders on which it hung. Brown, curly hair, well-shaped features, and bright, cheerful eyes were nature's gifts, and worth all that art could have done for his adornment.

The youth, one of whose names was Robin, finally drew from his pocket the half of a little province bill of five shillings, which, in the depreciation in that sort of currency, did but satisfy the ferryman's demand, with the surplus of a sexangular piece of parchment, valued at three pence. He then walked forward into the town, with as light a step as if his day's journey had not already exceeded thirty miles, and with as eager an eye as if he were entering London city, instead of the little metropolis of a New England colony. Before Robin had proceeded far, however, it occurred to him that he knew not whither to direct his steps; so he paused, and looked up and down the narrow street, scrutinizing the small and mean wooden buildings that were scattered on either side.

"This low hovel cannot be my kinsman's dwelling," thought he, "nor yonder old house, where the moonlight enters at the broken casement; and truly I see none hereabouts that might be worthy of him. It would have been wise to inquire my way of the ferryman, and doubtless he would have gone with me, and earned a shilling from the Major for his pains. But the next man I meet will do as well."

He resumed his walk, and was glad to perceive that the street now became wider, and the houses more respectable in their appearance. He soon discerned a figure moving on moderately in advance, and hastened his steps to overtake it. As Robin drew nigh, he saw that the passenger was a man in years, with a full periwig of gray hair, a wide-skirted coat of dark cloth, and silk stockings rolled above his knees. He carried a long and polished cane, which he struck down perpendicularly before him at every step; and at regular intervals he uttered two successive hems, of a peculiarly solemn and sepulchral intonation. Having made these observations, Robin laid hold of the skirt of the old man's coat, just when the light from the open door and windows of a barber's shop fell upon both their figures.

"Good evening to you, honored sir," said he, making a low bow, and still retaining his hold of the skirt. "I pray you tell me whereabouts is the dwelling of my kinsman, Major Molineux."

The youth's question was uttered very loudly; and one of the barbers, whose razor was descending on a well-soaped chin, and another who was dressing a Ramillies wig, left their occupations, and came to the door. The citizen, in the mean time, turned a long-favored countenance upon Robin, and answered him in a tone of excessive anger and annoyance. His two sepulchral hems, however, broke into the very centre of his rebuke, with most singular effect, like a thought of the cold grave obtruding among wrathful passions.

"Let go my garment, fellow! I tell you, I know not the man you speak of. What! I have authority, I have—hem, hem—authority; and if this be the respect you show for your betters, your feet shall be brought acquainted with the stocks by daylight, tomorrow morning!"

Robin released the old man's skirt, and hastened away, pursued by an ill-mannered roar of laughter from the barber's shop. He was at first considerably surprised by the result of his question, but, being a shrewd youth, soon thought himself able to account for the mystery.

"This is some country representative," was his conclusion, "who has never seen the inside of my kinsman's door, and lacks the breeding to answer a stranger civilly. The man is old, or verily—I might be tempted to turn back and smite him on the nose. Ah, Robin, Robin! even the barber's boys laugh at you for choosing such a guide! You will be wiser in time, friend Robin."

He now became entangled in a succession of crooked and narrow streets, which crossed each other, and meandered at no great distance from the water-side. The smell of tar was obvious to his nostrils, the masts of vessels pierced the moonlight above the tops of the buildings, and the numerous signs, which Robin paused to read, informed him that he was near the centre of business. But the streets were empty, the shops were closed, and lights were visible only in the second stories of a few dwelling-houses. At length, on the corner of a narrow lane, through which he was passing, he beheld the broad countenance of a British hero swinging before the door of an inn, whence proceeded the voices of many guests. The casement of one of the lower windows was thrown back, and a very thin curtain permitted Robin to distinguish a party at supper, round a well-furnished table. The fragrance of the good cheer steamed forth into the outer air, and the youth could not fail to recollect that the last remnant of his travelling stock of provision had yielded to his morning appetite, and that noon had found and left him dinnerless.

"Oh, that a parchment three-penny might give me a right to sit down at yonder table!" said Robin, with a sigh. "But the Major will make me welcome to the best of his victuals; so I will even step boldly in, and inquire my way to his dwelling."

He entered the tavern, and was guided by the murmur of voices and the fumes of tobacco to the public-room. It was a long and low apartment, with oaken walls, grown dark in the continual smoke, and a floor which was thickly sanded, but of no immaculate purity. A number of persons—the larger part of whom appeared to be mariners, or in some way connected with the sea—occupied the wooden benches, or leather-bottomed chairs, conversing on various matters, and occasionally lending their attention to some topic of general interest. Three or four little groups were draining as many bowls of punch, which the West India trade had long since made a familiar drink in the colony. Others, who had the appearance of men who lived by regular and laborious handicraft, preferred the insulated bliss of an unshared potation, and became more taciturn under its influence. Nearly all, in short, evinced a predilection for the Good Creature in some of its various shapes, for this is a vice to which, as Fast Day sermons of a hundred years ago will testify, we have a long hereditary claim. The only guests to whom Robin's sympathies inclined him were two or three sheepish country-men, who were using the inn somewhat after the fashion of a Turkish cara-vansary; they had gotten themselves into the darkest corner of the room, and heedless of the Nicotian atmosphere, were supping on the bread of their own ovens, and the bacon cured in their own chimney-smoke. But though Robin felt a sort of brotherhood with these strangers, his eyes were attracted from them to a person who stood near the door, holding whispered con-versation with a group of ill-dressed associates. His features were separately striking almost to grotesqueness, and the whole face left a deep impression on the memory. The forehead bulged out into a double prominence, with a vale between; the nose came boldly forth in an irregular curve, and its bridge was of more than a finger's breadth; the eyebrows were deep and shaggy, and the eyes glowed beneath them like fire in a cave.

While Robin deliberated of whom to inquire respecting his kinsman's dwelling, he was accosted by the innkeeper, a little man in a stained white apron, who had come to pay his professional welcome to the stranger. Being in the second generation from a French Protestant, he seemed to have in-herited the courtesy of his parent nation; but no variety of circumstances was ever known to change his voice from the one shrill note in which he now ad-dressed Robin.

"From the country, I presume, sir?" said he, with a profound bow. "Beg leave to congratulate you on your arrival, and trust you intend a long stay with us. Fine town here, sir, beautiful buildings, and much that may in-terest a stranger. May I hope for the honor of your commands in respect to supper?"

"The man sees a family likeness! the rogue has guessed that I am re-lated to the Major!" thought Robin, who had hitherto experienced little superfluous civility.

All eyes were now turned on the country lad, standing at the door, in his worn three-cornered hat, gray coat, leather breeches, and blue yarn stock-ings, leaning on an oaken cudgel, and bearing a wallet on his back.

Robin replied to the courteous innkeeper, with such an assumption of confidence as befitted the Major's relative. "My honest friend," he said, "I shall make it a point to patronize your house on some occasion, when"—here he could not help lowering his voice—"when I may have more than a parchment three-pence in my pocket. My present business," continued he, speaking with lofty confidence, "is merely to inquire my way to the dwelling of my kinsman, Major Molineux."

There was a sudden and general movement in the room, which Robin interpreted as expressing the eagerness of each individual to become his guide. But the innkeeper turned his eyes to a written paper on the wall, which he read, or seemed to read, with occasional recurrences to the young man's figure.

"What have we here?" said he, breaking his speech into little dry fragments. " 'Left the house of the subscriber, bounden servant, Hezekiah Mudge, —had on, when he went away, gray coat, leather breeches, master's third-best hat. One pound currency reward to whosoever shall lodge him in any jail of the providence.' Better trudge, boy; better trudge!"

Robin had begun to draw his hand towards the lighter end of the oak cudgel, but a strange hostility in every countenance induced him to relinquish his purpose of breaking the courteous innkeeper's head. As he turned to leave the room, he encountered a sneering glance from the bold-featured personage whom he had before noticed, and no sooner was he beyond the door, than he heard a general laugh, in which the innkeeper's voice might be distinguished, like the dropping of small stones into a kettle.

"Now, is it not strange," thought Robin, with his usual shrewdness,— "is it not strange that the confession of an empty pocket should outweigh the name of my kinsman, Major Molineux? Oh, if I had one of those grinning rascals in the woods, where I and my oak sapling grew up together, I would teach him that my arm is heavy though my purse be light!"

On turning the corner of the narrow lane, Robin found himself in a spacious street, with an unbroken line of lofty houses on each side, and a steepled building at the upper end, whence the ringing of a bell announced the hour of nine. The light of the moon, and the lamps from the numerous shop-windows, discovered people promenading on the pavement, and amongst them Robin had hoped to recognize his hitherto inscrutable relative. The result of his former inquiries made him unwilling to hazard another, in a scene of such publicity, and he determined to walk slowly and silently up the street, thrusting his face close to that of every elderly gentleman, in search of the Major's lineaments. In his progress, Robin encountered many gay and gallant figures. Embroidered garments of showy colors, enormous periwigs, gold-laced hats, and silver-hilted swords glided past him and dazzled his optics. Travelled youths, imitators of the European fine gentlemen of the period, trod jauntily along, half dancing to the fashionable tunes which they hummed, and making poor Robin ashamed of his quiet and natural gait. At length, after many pauses to examine the gorgeous display of goods in the shop-windows, and after suffering some rebukes for the impertinence of his scrutiny into people's faces, the Major's kinsman found himself near the steepled building, still unsuccessful in his search. As yet, however, he had seen only one side of the thronged street; so Robin crossed, and continued the same sort of inquisition down the opposite pavement, with stronger hopes than the philosopher seeking an honest man, but with no better fortune. He had arrived about midway towards the lower end, from which his course began, when he overheard the approach of some one who struck down a cane on the flag-stones at every step, uttering at regular intervals, two sepulchral hems.

"Mercy on us!" quoth Robin, recognizing the sound.

Turning a corner, which chanced to be close at his right hand, he hastened to pursue his researches in some other part of the town. His patience now was wearing low, and he seemed to feel more fatigue from his rambles since he crossed the ferry, than from his journey of several days on the other side. Hunger also pleaded loudly within him, and Robin began to balance the propriety of demanding, violently, and with lifted cudgel, the necessary guidance from the first solitary passenger whom he should meet. While a resolution to this effect was gaining strength, he entered a street of mean appearance, on either side of which a row of ill-built houses was straggling towards the harbor. The moonlight fell upon no passenger along the whole extent, but in the third domicile which Robin passed there was a half-opened door, and his keen glance detected a woman's garment within.

"My luck may be better here," said he to himself.

Accordingly, he approached the door, and beheld it shut closer as he did so; yet an open space remained, sufficing for the fair occupant to observe the stranger, without a corresponding display on her part. All that Robin could discern was a strip of scarlet petticoat, and the occasional sparkle of an eye, as if the moonbeams were trembling on some bright thing.

"Pretty mistress," for I may call her so with a good conscience, thought the shrewd youth, since I know nothing to the contrary,—"my sweet pretty mistress, will you be kind enough to tell me whereabouts I must seek the dwelling of my kinsman, Major Molineux?"

Robin's voice was plaintive and winning, and the female, seeing nothing to be shunned in the handsome country youth, thrust open the door, and came forth into the moonlight. She was a dainty little figure, with a white neck, round arms, and a slender waist, at the extremity of which her scarlet petticoat jutted out over a hoop, as if she were standing in a balloon. Moreover, her face was oval and pretty, her hair dark beneath the little cap, and her bright eyes possessed a sly freedom, which triumphed over those of Robin.

"Major Molineux dwells here," said this fair woman.

Now, her voice was the sweetest Robin had heard that night, yet he could not help doubting whether that sweet voice spoke Gospel truth. He looked up and down the mean street, and then surveyed the house before which they stood. It was a small, dark edifice of two stories, the second of which projected over the lower floor, and the front apartment had the aspect of a shop for petty commodities.

"Now, truly, I am in luck," replied Robin, cunningly, "and so indeed is my kinsman, the Major, in having so pretty a housekeeper. But I prithee trouble him to step to the door; I will deliver him a message from his friends in the country, and then go back to my lodgings at the inn."

"Nay, the Major has been abed this hour or more," said the lady of the scarlet petticoat; "and it would be to little purpose to disturb him to-night, seeing his evening draught was of the strongest. But he is a kind-hearted man, and it would be as much as my life's worth to let a kinsman of his turn away from the door. You are the good old gentleman's very picture, and I could swear that was his rainy-weather hat. Also he has garments very much resembling those leather small-clothes. But come in, I pray, for I bid you hearty welcome in his name."

So saying, the fair and hospitable dame took our hero by the hand; and the touch was light, and the force was gentleness, and though Robin read in her eyes what he did not hear in her words, yet the slender-waisted woman in the scarlet petticoat proved stronger than the athletic country youth. She had drawn his half-willing footsteps nearly to the threshold, when the opening of a door in the neighborhood startled the Major's housekeeper, and, leaving the Major's kinsman, she vanished speedily into her own domicile. A heavy yawn preceded the appearance of a man, who, like the Moonshine of Pyramus and Thisbe,[1] carried a lantern, needlessly aiding his sister luminary in the heavens. As he walked sleepily up the street, he turned his broad, dull face on Robin, and displayed a long staff, spiked at the end.

"Home, vagabond, home!" said the watchman, in accents that seemed to fall asleep as soon as they were uttered. "Home, or we'll set you in the stocks by peep of day!"

"This is the second hint of the kind," thought Robin. "I wish they would end my difficulties, by setting me there to-night."

Nevertheless, the youth felt an instinctive antipathy towards the guardian of midnight order, which at first prevented him from asking his usual question. But just when the man was about to vanish behind the corner, Robin resolved not to lose the opportunity, and shouted lustily after him,—

"I say, friend! will you guide me to the house of my kinsman, Major Molineux?"

The watchman made no reply, but turned the corner and was gone; yet Robin seemed to hear the sound of drowsy laughter stealing along the solitary street. At that moment, also, a pleasant titter saluted him from the open window above his head; he looked up, and caught the sparkle of a saucy eye; a round arm beckoned to him, and next he heard light footsteps descending the staircase within. But Robin, being of the household of a New England clergyman, was a good youth, as well as a shrewd one; so he resisted temptation, and fled away.

He now roamed desperately, and at random, through the town, almost ready to believe that a spell was on him, like that by which a wizard of his country had once kept three pursuers wandering, a whole winter night,

---

1. In Shakespeare's *A Midsummer-Night's Dream*, Act V, Scene 1, the moon is represented by a man carrying a lantern in the comic performance of the tragic love story of Pyramus and Thisbe.

within twenty paces of the cottage which they sought. The streets lay before him, strange and desolate, and the lights were extinguished in almost every house. Twice, however, little parties of men, among whom Robin distinguished individuals in outlandish attire, came hurrying along; but, though on both occasions, they paused to address him, such intercourse did not at all enlighten his perplexity. They did but utter a few words in some language of which Robin knew nothing, and perceiving his inability to answer, bestowed a curse upon him in plain English and hastened away. Finally, the lad determined to knock at the door of every mansion that might appear worthy to be occupied by his kinsman, trusting that perseverance would overcome the fatality that had hitherto thwarted him. Firm in this resolve, he was passing beneath the walls of a church, which formed the corner of two streets, when, as he turned into the shade of its steeple, he encountered a bulky stranger, muffled in a cloak. The man was proceeding with the speed of earnest business, but Robin planted himself full before him, holding the oak cudgel with both hands across his body as a bar to further passage.

"Halt, honest man, and answer me a question," said he, very resolutely. "Tell me, this instant, whereabouts is the dwelling of my kinsman, Major Molineux!"

"Keep your tongue between your teeth, fool, and let me pass!" said a deep, gruff voice, which Robin partly remembered. "Let me pass, or I'll strike you to the earth!"

"No, no, neighbor!" cried Robin, flourishing his cudgel, and then thrusting its larger end close to the man's muffled face. "No, no, I'm not the fool you take me for, nor do you pass till I have an answer to my question. Whereabouts is the dwelling of my kinsman, Major Molineux?"

The stranger, instead of attempting to force his passage, stepped back into the moonlight, unmuffled his face, and stared full into that of Robin.

"Watch here an hour, and Major Molineux will pass by," said he.

Robin gazed with dismay and astonishment on the unprecedented physiognomy of the speaker. The forehead with its double prominence, the broad hooked nose, the shaggy eyebrows, and fiery eyes were those which he had noticed at the inn, but the man's complexion had undergone a singular, or, more properly, a twofold change. One side of the face blazed an intense red, while the other was black as midnight, the division line being in the broad bridge of the nose; and a mouth which seemed to extend from ear to ear was black or red, in contrast to the color of the cheek. The effect was as if two individual devils, a fiend of fire and a fiend of darkness, had united themselves to form this infernal visage. The stranger grinned in Robin's face, muffled his party-colored features, and was out of sight in a moment.

"Strange things we travellers see!" ejaculated Robin.

He seated himself, however, upon the steps of the church-door, resolving to wait the appointed time for his kinsman. A few moments were consumed in philosophical speculations upon the species of man who had just left him; but having settled this point shrewdly, rationally, and satisfactorily, he was compelled to look elsewhere for his amusement. And first he threw his eyes along the street. It was of more respectable appearance than most of those into which he had wandered; and the moon, creating, like the imaginative power, a beautiful strangeness in familiar objects, gave something of romance to a scene that might not have possessed it in the light of day. The irregular and often quaint architecture of the houses, some of whose roofs were broken into numerous little peaks, while others ascended, steep and narrow, into a single point, and others again were square; the pure snow-white of some of their complexions, the aged darkness of others, and the thousand sparklings, reflected from bright substances in the walls of many; these matters engaged Robin's attention for a while, and then began to grow wearisome. Next he endeavored to define the forms of distant objects, starting away, with almost ghostly indistinctness, just as his eye appeared to grasp them; and finally he took a minute survey of an edifice which stood on the opposite side of the street, directly in front of the church-door, where he was stationed. It was a large, square mansion, distinguished from its neighbors by a balcony, which rested on tall pillars, and by an elaborate Gothic window, communicating therewith.

"Perhaps this is the very house I have been seeking," thought Robin.

Then he strove to speed away the time, by listening to a murmur which swept continually along the street, yet was scarcely audible, except to an unaccustomed ear like his; it was a low, dull, dreamy sound, compounded of many noises, each of which was at too great a distance to be separately heard. Robin marvelled at this snore of a sleeping town, and marvelled more whenever its continuity was broken by now and then a distant shout, apparently loud where it originated. But altogether it was a sleep-inspiring sound, and, to shake off its drowsy influence, Robin arose, and climbed a window-frame, that he might view the interior of the church. There the moonbeams came trembling in, and fell down upon the deserted pews, and extended along the quiet aisles. A fainter yet more awful radiance was hovering around the pulpit, and one solitary ray had dared to rest upon the open page of the great Bible. Had nature, in that deep hour, become a worshipper in the house which man had builded? Or was that heavenly light the visible sanctity of the place,—visible because no earthly and impure feet were within the walls? The scene made Robin's heart shiver with a sensation of loneliness stronger than he had ever felt in the remotest depths of his native woods; so he turned away and sat down again before the door. There were graves around the church, and now an uneasy thought obtruded into Robin's breast. What if the object of his search, which had been so often and so strangely thwarted, were all the time mouldering in his shroud? What if his kinsman should glide through yonder gate, and nod and smile to him in dimly passing by?

"Oh that any breathing thing were here with me!" said Robin.

Recalling his thoughts from this uncomfortable track, he sent them over forest, hill, and stream, and attempted to imagine how that evening of ambiguity and weariness had been spent by his father's household. He pictured them assembled at the door, beneath the tree, the great old tree, which had been spared for its huge twisted trunk and venerable shade, when a thousand leafy brethren fell. There, at the going down of the summer sun, it was his father's custom to perform domestic worship, that the neighbors might come and join with him like brothers of the family, and that the wayfaring man might pause to drink at that fountain, and keep his heart pure by freshening the memory of home. Robin distinguished the seat of every individual of the little audience; he saw the good man, in the midst, holding the Scriptures in the golden light that fell from the western clouds; he beheld him close the book and all rise up to pray. He heard the old thanksgivings for daily mercies, the old supplications for their continuance, to which he had so often listened in weariness, but which were now among his dear remembrances. He perceived the slight inequality of his father's voice when he came to speak of the absent one; he noted how his mother turned her face to the broad and knotted trunk; how his elder brother scorned, because the beard was rough upon his upper lip, to permit his features to be moved; how the younger sister drew down a low hanging branch before her eyes; and how the little one of all, whose sports had hitherto broken the decorum of the scene, understood the prayer for her playmate, and burst into clamorous grief. Then he saw them go in at the door; and when Robin would have entered also, the latch tinkled into its place, and he was excluded from his home.

"Am I here, or there?" cried Robin, starting; for all at once, when his thoughts had become visible and audible in a dream, the long, wide, solitary street shone out before him.

He aroused himself, and endeavored to fix his attention steadily upon the large edifice which he had surveyed before. But still his mind kept vibrating between fancy and reality; by turns, the pillars of the balcony lengthened into the tall, bare stems of pines, dwindled down to human figures, settled again into their true shape and size, and then commenced a new succession of changes. For a single moment, when he deemed himself awake, he could have sworn that a visage—one which he seemed to remember, yet could not absolutely name as his kinsman's—was looking towards him from the Gothic window. A deeper sleep wrestled with and nearly overcame him, but fled at the sound of footsteps along the opposite pavement. Robin rubbed his eyes, discerned a man passing at the foot of the balcony, and addressed him in a loud, peevish, and lamentable cry.

"Hallo, friend! must I wait here all night for my kinsman, Major Molineux?"

The sleeping echoes awoke, and answered the voice; and the passenger, barely able to discern a figure sitting in the oblique shade of the steeple, traversed the street to obtain a nearer view. He was himself a gentleman in his prime, of open, intelligent, cheerful, and altogether prepossessing countenance. Perceiving a country youth, apparently homeless and without friends, he accosted him in a tone of real kindness, which had become strange to Robin's ears.

"Well, my good lad, why are you sitting here?" inquired he. "Can I be of service to you in any way?"

"I am afraid not, sir," replied Robin, despondingly; "yet I shall take it kindly, if you'll answer me a single question. I've been searching, half the night, for one Major Molineux; now, sir, is there really such a person in these parts, or am I dreaming?"

"Major Molineux! The name is not altogether strange to me," said the gentleman, smiling. "Have you any objection to telling me the nature of your business with him?"

Then Robin briefly related that his father was a clergyman, settled on a small salary, at a long distance back in the country, and that he and Major Molineux were brothers' children. The Major, having inherited riches, and acquired civil and military rank, had visited his cousin, in great pomp, a year or two before; had manifested much interest in Robin and an elder brother, and, being childless himself, had thrown out hints respecting the future establishment of one of them in life. The elder brother was destined to succeed to the farm which his father cultivated in the interval of sacred duties; it was therefore determined that Robin should profit by his kinsman's generous intentions, especially as he seemed to be rather the favorite, and was thought to possess other necessary endowments.

"For I have the name of being a shrewd youth," observed Robin, in this part of his story.

"I doubt not you deserve it," replied his new friend, good-naturedly; "but pray proceed."

"Well, sir, being nearly eighteen years old, and well grown, as you see," continued Robin, drawing himself up to his full height, "I thought it high time to begin in the world. So my mother and sister put me in handsome trim, and my father gave me half the remnant of his last year's salary, and five days ago I started for this place, to pay the Major a visit. But, would you believe it, sir! I crossed the ferry a little after dark, and have yet found nobody that would show me the way to his dwelling; only, an hour or two since, I was told to wait here, and Major Molineux would pass by."

"Can you describe the man who told you this?" inquired the gentleman.

"Oh, he was a very ill-favored fellow, sir," replied Robin, "with two great bumps on his forehead, a hook nose, fiery eyes; and, what struck me as the strangest, his face was of two different colors. Do you happen to know such a man, sir?"

"Not intimately," answered the stranger, "but I chanced to meet him a little time previous to your stopping me. I believe you may trust his word, and that the Major will very shortly pass through this street. In the mean time, as I have a singular curiosity to witness your meeting, I will sit down here upon the steps and bear you company."

He seated himself accordingly, and soon engaged his companion in animated discourse. It was but of brief continuance, however, for a noise of shouting, which had long been remotely audible, drew so much nearer that Robin inquired its cause.

"What may be the meaning of this uproar?" asked he. "Truly, if your town be always as noisy, I shall find little sleep while I am an inhabitant."

"Why, indeed, friend Robin, there do appear to be three or four riotous fellows abroad to-night," replied the gentleman. "You must not expect all the stillness of your native woods here in our streets. But the watch will shortly be at the heels of these lads and"—

"Ay, and set them in the stocks by peep of day," interrupted Robin, recollecting his own encounter with the drowsy lantern-bearer. "But, dear sir, if I may trust my ears, an army of watchmen would never make head against such a multitude of rioters. There were at least a thousand voices went up to make that one shout.'

"May not a man have several voices, Robin, as well as two complexions?" said his friend.

"Perhaps a man may; but Heaven forbid that a woman should!" responded the shrewd youth, thinking of the seductive tones of the Major's housekeeper.

The sounds of a trumpet in some neighboring street now became so evident and continual, that Robin's curiosity was strongly excited. In addition to the shouts, he heard frequent bursts from many instruments of discord, and a wild and confused laughter filled up the intervals. Robin rose from the steps, and looked wistfully towards a point whither people seemed to be hastening.

"Surely some prodigious merry-making is going on," exclaimed he. "I have laughed very little since I left home, sir, and should be sorry to lose an opportunity. Shall we step round the corner by that darkish house, and take our share of the fun?"

"Sit down again, sit down, good Robin," replied the gentleman, laying his hand on the skirt of the gray coat. "You forget that we must wait here for your kinsman; and there is reason to believe that he will pass by, in the course of a very few moments."

The near approach of the uproar had now disturbed the neighborhood; windows flew open on all sides; and many heads, in the attire of the pillow, and confused by sleep suddenly broken, were protruded to the gaze of whoever had leisure to observe them. Eager voices hailed each other from house to house, all demanding the explanation, which not a soul could give. Half-dressed men hurried towards the unknown commotion, stumbling as they went over the stone steps that thrust themselves into the narrow footwalk. The shouts, the laughter, and the tuneless bray, the antipodes of music, came onwards with increasing din, till scattered individuals, and then denser bodies, began to appear round a corner at the distance of a hundred yards.

"Will you recognize your kinsman, if he passes in this crowd?" inquired the gentleman.

"Indeed, I can't warrant it, sir; but I'll take my stand here, and keep a bright lookout," answered Robin, descending to the outer edge of the pavement.

A mighty stream of people now emptied into the street, and came rolling slowly towards the church. A single horseman wheeled the corner in the midst of them, and close behind him came a band of fearful wind-instruments, sending forth a fresher discord now that no intervening buildings kept it from the ear. Then a redder light disturbed the moonbeams, and a dense multitude of torches shone along the street, concealing, by their glare, whatever object they illuminated. The single horseman, clad in a military dress, and bearing a drawn sword, rode onward as the leader, and, by his fierce and variegated countenance, appeared like war personified; the red of one cheek was an emblem of fire and sword; the blackness of the other betokened the mourning that attends them. In his train were wild figures in the Indian dress, and many fantastic shapes without a model, giving the whole march a visionary air, as if a dream had broken forth from some feverish brain, and were sweeping visibly through the midnight streets. A mass of people, inactive, except as applauding spectators, hemmed the procession in; and several women ran along the sidewalk, piercing the confusion of heavier sounds with their shrill voices of mirth or terror.

"The double-faced fellow has his eye upon me," muttered Robin, with an indefinite but an uncomfortable idea that he was himself to bear a part in the pageantry.

The leader turned himself in the saddle, and fixed his glance full upon the country youth, as the steed went slowly by. When Robin had freed his eyes from those fiery ones, the musicians were passing before him, and the torches were close at hand; but the unsteady brightness of the latter formed a veil which he could not penetrate. The rattling of wheels over the stones sometimes found its way to his ear, and confused traces of a human form appeared at intervals, and then melted into the vivid light. A moment more, and the leader thundered a command to halt: the trumpets vomited a horrid breath, and then held their peace; the shouts and laughter of the people died away, and there remained only a universal hum, allied to silence. Right before Robin's eyes was an uncovered cart. There the torches blazed the brightest, there the moon shone out like day, and there, in tar-and-feathery dignity, sat his kinsman, Major Molineux!

He was an elderly man, of large and majestic person, and strong, square features betokening a steady soul; but steady as it was, his enemies had found means to shake it. His face was pale as death, and far more ghastly; the broad forehead was contracted in his agony, so that his eyebrows formed one grizzled line; his eyes were red and wild, and the foam hung white upon his quivering lip. His whole frame was agitated by a quick and continual tremor, which his pride strove to quell, even in those circumstances of overwhelming humiliation. But perhaps the bitterest pang of all was when his eyes met those of Robin; for he evidently knew him on the instant, as the youth stood witnessing the foul disgrace of a head grown gray in honor.

They stared at each other in silence, and Robin's knees shook, and his hair bristled, with a mixture of pity and terror. Soon, however, a bewildering excitement began to seize upon his mind; the preceding adventures of the night, the unexpected appearance of the crowd, the torches, the confused din and the hush that followed, the spectre of his kinsman reviled by that great multitude,—all this, and, more than all, a perception of tremendous ridicule in the whole scene, affected him with a sort of mental inebriety. At that moment a voice of sluggish merriment saluted Robin's ears; he turned instinctively, and just behind the corner of the church stood the lantern-bearer, rubbing his eyes, and drowsily enjoying the lad's amazement. Then he heard a peal of laughter like the ringing of silvery bells; a woman twitched his arm, a saucy eye met his, and he saw the lady of the scarlet petticoat. A sharp, dry cachinnation appealed to his memory, and standing on tiptoe in the crowd, with his white apron over his head, he beheld the courteous little innkeeper. And lastly, there sailed over the heads of the multitude a great, broad laugh, broken in the midst by two sepulchral hems; thus, "Haw, haw, haw,—hem, hem,—haw, haw, haw, haw!"

The sound proceeded from the balcony of the opposite edifice, and thither Robin turned his eyes. In front of the Gothic window stood the old citizen, wrapped in a wide gown, his gray periwig exchanged for a nightcap, which was thrust back from his forehead, and his silk stockings hanging about his legs. He supported himself on his polished cane in a fit of convulsive merriment, which manifested itself on his solemn old features like a funny inscription on a tombstone. Then Robin seemed to hear the voices of the barbers, of the guests of the inn, and of all who had made sport of him that night. The contagion was spreading among the multitude, when all at once, it seized upon Robin, and he sent forth a shout of laughter that echoed through the street,—every man shook his sides, every man emptied his lungs, but Robin's shout was the loudest there. The cloud-spirits peeped from their silvery islands, as the congregated mirth went roaring up the sky! The Man in the Moon heard the far bellow. "Oho," quoth he, "the old earth is frolicsome to-night!"

When there was a momentary calm in that tempestuous sea of sound, the leader gave the sign, the procession resumed its march. On they went, like fiends that throng in mockery around some dead potentate, mighty no more, but majestic still in his agony. On they went, in counterfeited pomp, in senseless uproar, in frenzied merriment, trampling all on an old man's heart. On swept the tumult, and left a silent street behind.

●　●　●　●　●　●

"Well, Robin, are you dreaming?" inquired the gentleman, laying his hand on the youth's shoulder.

Robin started, and withdrew his arm from the stone post to which he had instinctively clung, as the living stream rolled by him. His cheek was somewhat pale, and his eye not quite as lively as in the earlier part of the evening.

"Will you be kind enough to show me the way to the ferry?" said he, after a moment's pause.

"You have, then, adopted a new subject of inquiry?" observed his companion, with a smile.

"Why, yes, sir," replied Robin, rather dryly. "Thanks to you, and to my other friends, I have at last met my kinsman, and he will scarce desire to see my face again. I begin to grow weary of a town life, sir. Will you show me the way to the ferry?"

"No, my good friend Robin,—not to-night, at least," said the gentleman. "Some few days hence, if you wish it, I will speed you on your journey. Or, if you prefer to remain with us, perhaps, as you are a shrewd youth, you may rise in the world without the help of your kinsman, Major Molineux."

The Secret Sharer

JOSEPH CONRAD [1857–1924]

I

ON my right hand there were lines of fishing stakes resembling a mysterious system of half-submerged bamboo fences, incomprehensible in its division of the domain of tropical fishes, and crazy of aspect as if abandoned forever by some nomad tribe of fishermen now gone to the other end of the ocean; for there was no sign of human habitation as far as the eye could reach. To the left a group of barren islets, suggesting ruins of stone walls, towers, and blockhouses, had its foundations set in a blue sea that itself looked solid, so still and stable did it lie below my feet; even the track of light from the westering sun shone smoothly, without that animated glitter which tells of an imperceptible ripple. And when I turned my head to take a parting glance at the tug which had just left us anchored outside the bar, I saw the straight line of the flat shore joined to the stable sea, edge to edge, with a perfect and unmarked closeness, in one leveled floor half brown, half blue under the enormous dome of the sky. Corresponding in their insignificance to the islets of the sea, two small clumps of trees, one on each side of the only fault in the impeccable joint, marked the mouth of the river Meinam we had just left on the first preparatory stage of our homeward journey; and, far back on the inland level, a larger and loftier mass, the grove surrounding the great Paknam pagoda, was the only thing on which the eye could rest from the vain task of exploring the monotonous sweep of the horizon. Here and there gleams as of a few scattered pieces of silver marked the windings of the great river; and on the nearest of them, just within the bar, the tug steaming right into the land become lost to my sight, hull and funnel and masts, as though the impassive earth had swallowed her up without an effort, without a tremor. My eye followed the light cloud of her smoke, now here, now there, above the plain, according to the devious curves of the stream, but always fainter and farther away, till I lost it at last behind the miter-shaped hill of the great pagoda. And then I was left alone with my ship, anchored at the head of the Gulf of Siam.

She floated at the starting point of a long journey, very still in an immense stillness, the shadows of her spars flung far to the eastward by the setting sun. At that moment I was alone on her decks. There was not a sound in her—and around us nothing moved, nothing lived, not a canoe on the water, not a bird in the air, not a cloud in the sky. In this breathless pause at the threshold of a long passage we seemed to be measuring our fitness for a long and arduous enterprise, the appointed task of both our existences to be carried out, far from all human eyes, with only sky and sea for spectators and for judges.

There must have been some glare in the air to interfere with one's sight, because it was only just before the sun left us that my roaming eyes made out beyond the highest ridge of the principal islet of the group something which did away with the solemnity of perfect solitude. The tide of darkness flowed on swiftly; and with tropical suddenness a swarm of stars came out above the shadowy earth, while I lingered yet, my hand resting lightly on my ship's rail as if on the shoulder of a trusted friend. But, with all that multitude of celestial bodies staring down at one, the comfort of quiet communion with her was gone for good. And there were also disturbing sounds by this time—voices, footsteps forward; the steward flitted along the main deck, a busily ministering spirit; a hand bell tinkled urgently under the poop deck. . . .

I found my two officers waiting for me near the supper table, in the lighted cuddy. We sat down at once, and as I helped the chief mate, I said:

"Are you aware that there is a ship anchored inside the islands? I saw her mastheads above the ridge as the sun went down."

He raised sharply his simple face, overcharged by a terrible growth of whisker, and emitted his usual ejaculations: "Bless my soul, sir! You don't say so!"

My second mate was a sound-cheeked, silent young man, grave beyond his years, I thought; but as our eyes happened to meet I detected a slight quiver on his lips. I looked down at once. It was not my part to encourage sneering on board my ship. It must be said, too, that I knew very little of my officers. In consequence of certain events of no particular significance, except to myself, I had been appointed to the command only a fortnight before. Neither did I know much of the hands forward. All these people had been together for eighteen months or so, and my position was that of the only stranger on board. I mention this because it has some bearing on what is to follow. But what I felt most was my being a stranger to the ship; and if truth must be told, I was somewhat of a stranger to myself. The youngest man on board (barring the second mate), and untried as yet by a position of the fullest responsibility, I was willing to take the adequacy of the others for granted. They had simply to be equal to their tasks: but I wondered how far I should turn out faithful to that ideal conception of one's own personality every man sets up for himself secretly.

Meantime the chief mate, with an almost visible effect of collaboration on the part of his round eyes and frightful whiskers, was trying to evolve a theory of the anchored ship. His dominant trait was to take all things into earnest consideration. He was of a painstaking turn of mind. As he used to say, he "liked to account to himself" for practically everything that came in his way, down to a miserable scorpion he had found in his cabin a week before. The why and the wherefore of that scorpion—how it got on board and came to select his room rather than the pantry (which was a dark place and more what a scorpion would be partial to), and how on earth it managed to drown itself in the inkwell of his writing desk—had exercised him infinitely. The ship within the islands was much more easily accounted for; and just as we were about to rise from the table he made his pronouncement. She was, he doubted not, a ship from home lately arrived. Probably she drew too much water to cross the bar except at the top of spring tides. Therefore she went into that natural harbor to wait for a few days in preference to remaining in an open roadstead.

"That's so," confirmed the second mate, suddenly, in his slightly hoarse voice. "She draws over twenty feet. She's the Liverpool ship *Sephora* with a cargo of coal. Hundred and twenty-three days from Cardiff."

We looked at him in surprise.

"The tugboat skipper told me when he came on board for your letters, sir," explained the young man. "He expects to take her up the river the day after tomorrow."

After thus overwhelming us with the extent of his information he slipped out of the cabin. The mate observed regretfully that he "could not account for that young fellow's whims." What prevented him telling us all about it at once, he wanted to know.

I detained him as he was making a move. For the last two days the crew had had plenty of hard work, and the night before they had very little sleep. I felt painfully that I—a stranger—was doing something unusual when I directed him to let all hands turn in without setting an anchor watch. I proposed to keep on deck myself till one o'clock or thereabouts. I would get the second mate to relieve me at that hour.

"He will turn out the cook and the steward at four," I concluded, "and then give you a call. Of course at the lightest sign of any sort of wind we'll have the hands up and make a start at once."

He concealed his astonishment. "Very well, sir." Outside the cuddy he put his head in the second mate's door to inform him of my unheard-of caprice to take a five hours' anchor watch on myself. I heard the other raise his voice incredulously: "What? The captain himself?" Then a few more murmurs, a door closed, then another. A few moments later I went on deck.

My strangeness, which had made me sleepless, had prompted that unconventional arrangement, as if I had expected in those solitary hours of the night to get on terms with the ship of which I knew nothing, manned by men of whom I knew very little more. Fast alongside a wharf, littered like any ship in port with a tangle of unrelated things, invaded by unrelated shore people, I had hardly seen her yet properly. Now, as she lay cleared for sea, the stretch of her main deck seemed to me very fine under the stars. Very fine, very roomy for her size, and very inviting. I descended the poop and paced the waist, my mind picturing to myself the coming passage through the Malay Archipelago, down the Indian Ocean, and up the Atlantic. All its phases were familiar enough to me, every characteristic, all the alternatives which were likely to face me on the high seas—everything! . . . except the novel responsibility of command. But I took heart from the reasonable thought that the ship was like other ships, the men like other men, and that the sea was not likely to keep any special surprises expressly for my discomfiture.

Arrived at that comforting conclusion, I bethought myself of a cigar and went below to get it. All was still down there. Everybody at the after end of the ship was sleeping profoundly. I came out again on the quarter-deck, agreeably at ease in my sleeping suit on that warm breathless night, barefooted, a glowing cigar in my teeth, and, going forward, I was met by the profound silence of the fore end of the ship. Only as I passed the door of the forecastle I heard a deep, quiet, trustful sigh of some sleeper inside. And suddenly I rejoiced in the great security of the sea as compared with the unrest of the land, in my choice of that untempted life presenting no disquieting problems, invested with an elementary moral beauty by the absolute straightforwardness of its appeal and by the singleness of its purpose.

The riding light in the fore-rigging burned with a clear, untroubled, as if symbolic, flame, confident and bright in the mysterious shades of the night. Passing on my way aft along the other side of the ship, I observed that the rope side ladder, put over, no doubt, for the master of the tug when he came to fetch away our letters, had not been hauled in as it should have been. I became annoyed at this, for exactitude in small matters is the very soul of discipline. Then I reflected that I had myself peremptorily dismissed my officers from duty, and by my own act had prevented the anchor watch being formally set and things properly attended to. I asked myself whether it was wise ever to interfere with the established routine of duties even from the kindest of motives. My action might have made me appear eccentric. Goodness only knew how that absurdly whiskered mate would "account" for my conduct, and what the whole ship thought of that informality of their new captain. I was vexed with myself.

Not from compunction certainly, but, as it were mechanically, I proceeded to get the ladder in myself. Now a side ladder of that sort is a light affair and comes in easily, yet my vigorous tug, which should have brought it flying on board, merely recoiled upon my body in a totally unexpected jerk. What the devil! . . . I was so astounded by the immovableness of that ladder that I remained stock-still, trying to account for it to myself like that imbecile mate of mine. In the end, of course, I put my head over the rail.

The side of the ship made an opaque belt of shadow on the darkling glassy shimmer of the sea. But I saw at once something elongated and pale floating very close to the ladder. Before I could form a guess a faint flash of phosphorescent light, which seemed to issue suddenly from the naked body of a man, flickered in the sleeping water with the elusive, silent play of summer lightning in a night sky. With a gasp I saw revealed to my stare a pair of feet, the long legs, a broad livid back immersed right up to the neck in a greenish cadaverous glow. One hand, awash, clutched the bottom rung of the ladder. He was complete but for the head. A headless corpse! The cigar dropped out of my gaping mouth with a tiny plop and a short hiss quite audible in the absolute stillness of all things under heaven. At that I suppose he raised up his face, a dimly pale oval in the shadow of the ship's side. But even then I could only barely make out down there the shape of his black-haired head. However, it was enough for the horrid, frost-bound sensation which had gripped me about the chest to pass off. The moment of vain exclamations was past, too. I only climbed on the spare spar and leaned over the rail as far as I could, to bring my eyes nearer to that mystery floating alongside.

As he hung by the ladder, like a resting swimmer, the sea lightning played about his limbs at every stir; and he appeared in it ghastly, silvery, fishlike. He remained as mute as a fish, too. He made no motion to get out of the water, either. It was inconceivable that he should not attempt to come on board, and strangely troubling to suspect that perhaps he did not want to. And my first words were prompted by just that troubled incertitude.

"What's the matter?" I asked in my ordinary tone, speaking down to the face upturned exactly under mine.

"Cramp," it answered, no louder. Then slightly anxious, "I say, no need to call anyone."

"I was not going to," I said.

"Are you alone on deck?"

"Yes."

I had somehow the impression that he was on the point of letting go the ladder to swim away beyond my ken—mysterious as he came. But, for the moment, this being appearing as if he had risen from the bottom of the sea (it was certainly the nearest land to the ship) wanted only to know the time. I told him. And he, down there, tentatively:

"I suppose your captain's turned in?"

"I am sure he isn't," I said.

He seemed to struggle with himself, for I heard something like the low, bitter murmur of doubt. "What's the good?" His next words came out with a hesitating effort.

"Look here, my man. Could you call him out quietly?"

I thought the time had come to declare myself.

"I am the captain."

I heard a "By Jove!" whispered at the level of the water. The phosphorescence flashed in the swirl of the water all about his limbs, his other hand seized the ladder.

"My name's Leggatt."

The voice was calm and resolute. A good voice. The self-possession of that man had somehow induced a corresponding state in myself. It was very quietly that I remarked:

"You must be a good swimmer."

"Yes. I've been in the water practically since nine o'clock. The question for me now is whether I am to let go this ladder and go on swimming till I sink from exhaustion, or—to come on board here."

I felt this was no mere formula of desperate speech, but a real alternative in the view of a strong soul. I should have gathered from this that he was young; indeed, it is only the young who are ever confronted by such clear issues. But at this time it was pure intuition on my part. A mysterious communication was established already between us two—in the face of that silent darkened tropical sea. I was young, too; young enough to make no comment. The man in the water began suddenly to climb up the ladder, and I hastened away from the rail to fetch some clothes.

Before entering the cabin I stood still, listening in the lobby at the foot of the stairs. A faint snore came through the closed door of the chief mate's room. The second mate's door was on the hook, but the darkness in there was absolutely soundless. He, too, was young and could sleep like a stone. Remained the steward, but he was not likely to wake up before he was called. I got a sleeping suit out of my room and, coming back on deck, saw the naked man from the sea sitting on the main hatch, glimmering white in the darkness, his elbows on his knees and his head in his hands. In a moment he had concealed his damp body in a sleeping suit of the same gray-stripe pattern as the one I was wearing and followed me like my double on the poop. Together we moved right aft, barefooted, silent.

"What is it?" I asked in a deadened voice, taking the lighted lamp out of the binnacle, and raising it to his face.

"An ugly business."

He had rather regular features; a good mouth; light eyes under somewhat heavy, dark eyebrows; a smooth, square forehead; no growth on his cheeks; a small, brown mustache, and a well-shaped, round chin. His expression was concentrated, meditative, under the inspecting light of the lamp I held up to his face; such as a man thinking hard in solitude might wear. My sleeping suit was just right for his size. A well-knit young fellow of twenty-five at most. He caught his lower lip with the edge of white, even teeth.

"Yes," I said, replacing the lamp in the binnacle. The warm, heavy tropical night closed upon his head again.

"There's a ship over there," he murmured.

"Yes, I know. The *Sephora*. Did you know of us?"

"Hadn't the slightest idea. I am the mate of her—" He paused and corrected himself. "I should say I *was*."

"Aha! Something wrong?"

"Yes. Very wrong indeed. I've killed a man."

"What do you mean? Just now?"

"No, on the passage. Weeks ago. Thirty-nine south. When I say a man—"

"Fit of temper," I suggested, confidently.

The shadowy, dark head, like mine, seemed to nod imperceptibly above the ghostly gray of my sleeping suit. It was, in the night, as though I had been faced by my own reflection in the depths of a somber and immense mirror.

"A pretty thing to have to own up to for a Conway boy," murmured my double, distinctly.

"You're a Conway boy?"

"I am," he said, as if startled. Then, slowly . . . "Perhaps you too—"

It was so; but being a couple of years older I had left before he joined. After a quick interchange of dates a silence fell; and I thought suddenly of my absurd mate with his terrific whiskers and the "Bless my soul—you don't say so" type of intellect. My double gave me an inkling of his thoughts by saying:

"My father's a parson in Norfolk. Do you see me before a judge and jury on that charge? For myself I can't see the necessity. There are fellows that an angel from heaven—And I am not that. He was one of those creatures that are just simmering all the time with a silly sort of wickedness. Miserable devils that have no business to live at all. He wouldn't do his duty and wouldn't let anybody else do theirs. But what's the good of talking! You know well enough the sort of ill-conditioned snarling cur—"

He appealed to me as if our experiences had been as identical as our clothes. And I knew well enough the pestiferous danger of such a character where there are no means of legal repression. And I knew well enough also that my double there was no homicidal ruffian. I did not think of asking him for details, and he told me the story roughly in brusque, disconnected sentences. I needed no more. I saw it all going on as though I were myself inside that other sleeping suit.

"It happened while we were setting a reefed foresail, at dusk. Reefed foresail! You understand the sort of weather. The only sail we had left to keep the ship running; so you may guess what it had been like for days. Anxious sort of job, that. He gave me some of his cursed insolence at the sheet. I tell you I was overdone with this terrific weather that seemed to have no end to it. Terrific, I tell you—and a deep ship. I believe the fellow himself was half crazed with funk. It was no time for gentlemanly reproof, so I turned round and felled him like an ox. He up and at me. We closed just as an awful sea made for the ship. All hands saw it coming and took to the rigging, but I had him by the throat, and went on shaking him like a rat, the men above us yelling, 'Look out! look out!' Then a crash as if the sky had fallen on my head. They say that for over ten minutes hardly anything was to be seen of the ship—just the three masts and a bit of the forecastle head and of the poop all awash driving along in a smother of foam. It was a miracle that they found us, jammed together behind the forebits. It's clear that I meant business, because I was holding him by the throat still when they picked us up. He was black in the face. It was too much for them. It seems they rushed us aft together, gripped as we were, screaming 'Murder!' like a lot of lunatics, and broke into the cuddy. And the ship running for her life, touch and go all the time, any minute her last in a sea fit to turn your hair gray only a-looking at it. I understand that the skipper, too, started raving like the rest of them. The man had been deprived of sleep for more than a week, and to have this sprung on him at the height of a furious gale nearly drove him out of his mind. I wonder they didn't fling me overboard after getting the carcass of their precious shipmate out of my fingers. They had rather a job to separate us, I've been told. A sufficiently fierce story to make an old judge and a respectable jury sit up a bit. The first thing I heard when I came to myself was the maddening howling of that endless gale, and on that the voice of the old man. He was hanging on to my bunk, staring into my face out of his sou'wester.

" 'Mr. Leggatt, you have killed a man. You can act no longer as chief mate of this ship.' "

His care to subdue his voice made it sound monotonous. He rested a hand on the end of the skylight to steady himself with, and all that time did not stir a limb, so far as I could see. "Nice little tale for a quiet tea party," he concluded in the same tone.

One of my hands, too, rested on the end of the skylight; neither did I stir a limb, so far as I knew. We stood less than a foot from each other. It occurred to me that if old "Bless my soul—you don't say so" were to put his head up the companion and catch sight of us, he would think he was seeing double, or imagine himself come upon a scene of weird witchcraft; the strange captain having a quiet confabulation by the wheel with his own gray ghost. I became very much concerned to prevent anything of the sort. I heard the other's soothing undertone.

"My father's a parson in Norfolk," it said. Evidently he had forgotten he had told me this important fact before. Truly a nice little tale.

"You had better slip down into my stateroom now," I said, moving off stealthily. My double followed my movements; our bare feet made no sound; I let him in, closed the door with care, and, after giving a call to the second mate, returned on deck for my relief.

"Not much sign of any wind yet," I remarked when he approached.

"No, sir. Not much," he assented, sleepily, in his hoarse voice, with just enough deference, no more, and barely suppressing a yawn.

"Well, that's all you have to look out for. You have got your orders."

"Yes, sir."

I paced a turn or two on the poop and saw him take up his position face forward with his elbow in the rat-lines of the mizzen-rigging before I went below. The mate's faint snoring was still going on peacefully. The cuddy lamp was burning over the table on which stood a vase with flowers, a polite attention from the ships' provision merchant—the last flowers we should see for the next three months at the very least. Two bunches of bananas hung from the beam symmetrically, one on each side of the rudder casing. Everything was as before in the ship—except that two of her captain's sleeping suits were simultaneously in use, one motionless in the cuddy, the other keeping very still in the captain's stateroom.

It must be explained here that my cabin had the form of the capital letter L, the door being within the angle and opening into the short part of the letter. A couch was to the left, the bed-place to the right; my writing desk and the chronometers' table faced the door. But anyone opening it, unless he stepped right inside, had no view of what I call the long (or vertical) part of the letter. It contained some lockers surmounted by a bookcase; and a few clothes, a thick jacket or two, caps, oilskin coat, and such like, hung on hooks. There was at the bottom of that part a door opening into my bathroom, which could be entered also directly from the saloon. But that way was never used.

The mysterious arrival had discovered the advantage of this particular shape. Entering my room, lighted strongly by a big bulkhead lamp swung on gimbals above my writing desk, I did not see him anywhere till he stepped out quietly from behind the coats hung in the recessed part.

"I heard somebody moving about, and went in there at once," he whispered.

I, too, spoke under my breath.

"Nobody is likely to come in here without knocking and getting permission."

He nodded. His face was thin and the sunburn faded, as though he had been ill. And no wonder. He had been, I heard presently, kept under arrest in his cabin for nearly seven weeks. But there was nothing sickly in his eyes or in his expression. He was not a bit like me, really; yet, as we stood leaning over my bed-place, whispering side by side, with our dark heads together and our backs to the door, anybody bold enough to open it stealthily would have been treated to the uncanny sight of a double captain busy talking in whispers with his other self.

"But all this doesn't tell me how you came to hang on to our side ladder," I inquired, in the hardly audible murmurs we used, after he had told me something more of the proceedings on board the *Sephora* once the bad weather was over.

"When we sighted Java Head I had had time to think all those matters out several times over. I had six weeks of doing nothing else, and with only an hour or so every evening for a tramp on the quarter-deck."

He whispered, his arms folded on the side of my bed-place, staring through the open port. And I could imagine perfectly the manner of this thinking out—a stubborn if not a steadfast operation; something of which I should have been perfectly incapable.

"I reckoned it would be dark before we closed with the land," he continued, so low that I had to strain my hearing, near as we were to each other, shoulder touching shoulder almost. "So I asked to speak to the old man. He always seemed very sick when he came to see me—as if he could not look me in the face. You know, that foresail saved the ship. She was too deep to have run long under bare poles. And it was I that managed to set it for him. Anyway, he came. When I had him in my cabin—he stood by the door looking at me as if I had the halter around my neck already—I asked him right away to leave my cabin door unlocked at night while the ship was going through Sunda Straits. There would be the Java coast within two or three miles, off Angier Point. I wanted nothing more. I've had a prize for swimming my second year in the Conway."

"I can believe it," I breathed out.

"God only knows why they locked me in every night. To see some of their faces you'd have thought they were afraid I'd go about at night strangling people. Am I a murdering brute? Do I look it? By Jove! if I had been he wouldn't have trusted himself like that into my room. You'll say I might have chucked him aside and bolted out, there and then—it was dark already. Well, no. And for the same reason I wouldn't think of trying to smash the door. There would have been a rush to stop me at the noise, and I did not mean to get into a confounded scrimmage. Somebody else might have got killed—for I would not have broken out only to get chucked back, and I did not want any more of that work. He refused, looking more sick than ever. He was afraid of the men, and also of that old second mate of his who had been sailing with him for years—a gray-headed old humbug; and his steward, too, had been with him devil knows how long—seventeen years or more—a dogmatic sort of loafer who hated me like poison, just because I was the chief mate. No chief mate ever made more than one voyage in the *Sephora,* you know. Those two old chaps ran the ship. Devil only knows what the skipper wasn't afraid of (all his nerve went to pieces altogether in that hellish spell of bad weather we had)—of what the law would do to him—of his wife, perhaps. Oh, yes! she's on board. Though I don't think she would have meddled. She would have been only too glad to have me out of the ship in any way. The 'brand of Cain' business, don't you see. That's all right. I was ready enough to go off wandering on the face of the earth—and that was price enough to pay for an Abel of that sort. Anyhow, he wouldn't listen to me. 'This thing must take its course. I represent the law here.' He was shaking life a leaf. 'So you won't?' 'No!' 'Then I hope you will be able to sleep on that,' I said, and turned my back on him. 'I wonder that *you* can,' cries he, and locks the door.

"Well, after that, I couldn't. Not very well. That was three weeks ago. We have had a slow passage through the Java Sea; drifted about Carimata for ten days. When we anchored here they thought, I suppose, it was all right. The nearest land (and that's five miles) is the ship's destination; the consul would soon set about catching me; and there would have been no object in bolting to these islets there. I don't suppose there's a drop of water on them. I don't know how it was, but tonight that steward, after bringing me my supper, went out to let me eat it, and left the door unlocked. And I ate it—all there was, too. After I had finished I strolled out on the quarter-deck. I don't know that I meant to do anything. A breath of fresh air was all I wanted, I believe. Then a sudden temptation came over me. I kicked off my slippers and was in the water before I had made up my mind fairly. Somebody heard the splash and they raised an awful hullabaloo. 'He's gone! Lower the boats! He's committed suicide! No, he's swimming.' Certainly I was swimming. It's not so easy for a swimmer like me to commit suicide by drowning. I landed on the nearest islet before the boat left the ship's side. I heard them pulling about in the dark, hailing, and so on, but after a bit they gave up. Everything quieted down and the anchorage became as still as death. I sat down on a stone and began to think. I felt certain they would start searching for me at daylight. There was no place to hide on those stony things—and if there had been, what would have been the good? But now I was clear of that ship, I was not going back. So after a while I took off all my clothes, tied them up in a bundle with a stone inside, and dropped them in the deep water on the outer side of the islet. That was suicide enough for me. Let them think what they liked, but I didn't mean to drown myself. I meant to swim till I sank—but that's not the same thing. I struck out for another of these little islands, and it was from that one that I first saw your riding light. Something to swim for. I went on easily, and on the way I came upon a flat rock a foot or two above water. In the daytime, I dare say, you might make it out with a glass from your poop. I scrambled up on it and rested myself for a bit. Then I made another start. That last spell must have been over a mile."

His whisper was getting fainter and fainter, and all the time he stared straight out through the porthole, in which there was not even a star to be seen. I had not interrupted him. There was something that made comment impossible in his narrative, or perhaps in himself; a sort of feeling, a quality, which I can't find a name for. And when he ceased, all I found was a futile whisper: "So you swam for our light?"

"Yes—straight for it. It was something to swim for. I couldn't see any stars low down because the coast was in the way, and I couldn't see the land, either. The water was like glass. One might have been swimming in a confounded thousand-feet deep cistern with no place for scrambling out anywhere; but what I didn't like was the notion of swimming round and round like a crazed bullock before I gave out; and as I didn't mean to go back ... No. Do you see me being hauled back, stark naked, off one of these little islands by the scruff of the neck and fighting like a wild beast? Somebody would have got killed for certain, and I did not want any of that. So I went on. Then your ladder—"

"Why didn't you hail the ship?" I asked, a little louder.

He touched my shoulder lightly. Lazy footsteps came right over our heads and stopped. The second mate had crossed from the other side of the poop and might have been hanging over the rail, for all we knew.

"He couldn't hear us talking—could he?" My double breathed into my very ear, anxiously.

His anxiety was an answer, a sufficient answer, to the question I had put to him. An answer containing all the difficulty of that situation. I closed the porthole quietly, to make sure. A louder word might have been overheard.

"Who's that?" he whispered then.

"My second mate. But I don't know much more of the fellow than you do."

And I told him a little about myself. I had been appointed to take charge while I least expected anything of the sort, not quite a fortnight ago. I didn't know either the ship or the people. Hadn't had the time in port to look about me or size anybody up. And as to the crew, all they knew was that

I was appointed to take the ship home. For the rest, I was almost as much of a stranger on board as himself, I said. And at the moment I felt it most acutely. I felt that it would take very little to make me a suspect person in the eyes of the ship's company.

He had turned about meantime; and we, the two strangers in the ship, faced each other in identical attitudes.

"Your ladder—" he murmured, after a silence. "Who'd have thought of finding a ladder hanging over at night in a ship anchored out here! I felt just then a very unpleasant faintness. After the life I've been leading for nine weeks, anybody would have got out of condition. I wasn't capable of swimming round as far as your rudder chains. And, lo and behold! there was a ladder to get hold of. After I gripped it I said to myself, 'What's the good?' When I saw a man's head looking over I thought I would swim away presently and leave him shouting—in whatever language it was. I didn't mind being looked at. I—I liked it. And then you speaking to me so quietly—as if you had expected me—made me hold on a little longer. It had been a confounded lonely time—I don't mean while swimming. I was glad to talk a little to somebody that didn't belong to the *Sephora*. As to asking for the captain, that was a mere impulse. It could have been no use, with all the ship knowing about me and the other people pretty certain to be round here in the morning. I don't know—I wanted to be seen, to talk with somebody, before I went on. I don't know what I would have said. . . . 'Fine night, isn't it?' or something of the sort."

"Do you think they will be round here presently?" I asked with some incredulity.

"Quite likely," he said, faintly.

He looked extremely haggard all of a sudden. His head rolled on his shoulders.

'H'm. We shall see then. Meantime get into that bed," I whispered. "Want help? There."

It was a rather high bed-place with a set of drawers underneath. This amazing swimmer really needed the lift I gave him by seizing his leg. He tumbled in, rolled over on his back, and flung one arm across his eyes. And then, with his face nearly hidden, he must have looked exactly as I used to look in that bed. I gazed upon my other self for a while before drawing across carefully the two green serge curtains which ran on a brass rod. I thought for a moment of pinning them together for greater safety, but I sat down on the couch, and once there I felt unwilling to rise and hunt for a pin. I would do it in a moment. I was extremely tired, in a peculiarly intimate way, by the strain of stealthiness, by the effort of whispering and the general secrecy of this excitement. It was three o'clock by now and I had been on my feet since nine, but I was not sleepy; I could not have gone to sleep. I sat there, fagged out, looking at the curtains, trying to clear my mind of the confused sensation of being in two places at once, and greatly bothered by an exasperating knocking in my head. It was a relief to discover suddenly that it was not in my head at all, but on the outside of the door. Before I

JOSEPH CONRAD   29

could collect myself the words "Come in" were out of my mouth, and the steward entered with a tray, bringing in my morning coffee. I had slept, after all, and I was so frightened that I shouted, "This way! I am here, steward," as though he had been miles away. He put down the tray on the table next the couch and only then said, very quietly, "I can see you are here, sir." I felt him give me a keen look, but I dared not meet his eyes just then. He must have wondered why I had drawn the curtains of my bed before going to sleep on the couch. He went out, hooking the door open as usual.

I heard the crew washing decks above me. I knew I would have been told at once if there had been any wind. Calm, I thought, and I was doubly vexed. Indeed, I felt dual more than ever. The steward reappeared suddenly in the doorway. I jumped up from the couch so quickly that he gave a start.

"What do you want here?"

Close your port, sir—they are washing decks."

"It is closed," I said, reddening.

"Very well, sir." But he did not move from the doorway and returned my stare in an extraordinary, equivocal manner for a time. Then his eyes wavered, all his expression changed, and in a voice unusually gentle, almost coaxingly:

"May I come in to take the empty cup away, sir?"

"Of course!" I turned my back on him while he popped in and out. Then I unhooked and closed the door and even pushed the bolt. This sort of thing could not go on very long. The cabin was as hot as an oven, too. I took a peep at my double, and discovered that he had not moved, his arm was still over his eyes; but his chest heaved; his hair was wet; his chin glistened with perspiration. I reached over him and opened the port.

"I must show myself on deck," I reflected.

Of course, theoretically, I could do what I liked, with no one to say nay to me within the whole circle of the horizon; but to lock my cabin door and take the key away I did not dare. Directly I put my head out of the companion I saw the group of my two officers, the second mate barefooted, the chief mate in long india-rubber boots, near the break of the poop, and the steward halfway down the poop ladder talking to them eagerly. He happened to catch sight of me and dived, the second ran down on the main deck shouting some order or other, and the chief mate came to meet me, touching his cap.

There was a sort of curiosity in his eye that I did not like. I don't know whether the steward had told them that I was "queer" only, or downright drunk, but I know the man meant to have a good look at me. I watched him coming with a smile which, as he got into point-blank range, took effect and froze his very whiskers. I did not give him time to open his lips.

"Square the yards by lifts and braces before the hands go to breakfast."

It was the first particular order I had given on board that ship; and I stayed on deck to see it executed, too. I had felt the need of asserting myself without loss of time. That sneering young cub got taken down a peg or two on that occasion, and I also seized the opportunity of having a good look at the face of every foremast man as they filed past me to go to the after braces. At breakfast time, eating nothing myself, I presided with such frigid dignity that the two mates were only too glad to escape from the cabin as soon as decency permitted; and all the time the dual working of my mind distracted me almost to the point of insanity. I was constantly watching myself, my secret self, as dependent on my actions as my own personality, sleeping in that bed, behind that door which faced me as I sat at the head of the table. It was very much like being mad, only it was worse because one was aware of it.

I had to shake him for a solid minute, but when at last he opened his eyes it was in the full possession of his senses, with an inquiring look.

"All's well so far," I whispered. "Now you must vanish into the bathroom."

He did so, as noiseless as a ghost, and I then rang for the steward, and facing him boldly, directed him to tidy up my stateroom while I was having my bath— "and be quick about it." As my tone admitted of no excuses, he said, "Yes, sir," and ran off to fetch his dustpan and brushes. I took a bath and did most of my dressing, splashing, and whistling softly for the steward's edification, while the secret sharer of my life stood drawn up bolt upright in that little space, his face looking very sunken in daylight, his eyelids lowered under the stern, dark line of his eyebrows drawn together by a slight frown.

When I left him there to go back to my room the steward was finished dusting. I sent for the mate and engaged him in some insignificant conversation. It was, as it were, trifling with the terrific character of whiskers; but my object was to give him an opportunity for a good look at my cabin. And then I could at last shut, with a clear conscience, the door of my stateroom and get my double back into the recessed part. There was nothing else for it. He had to sit still on a small folding stool, half smothered by the heavy coats hanging there. We listened to the steward going into the bathroom out of the saloon, filling the water bottles there, scrubbing the bath, setting things to rights, whisk, bang, clatter—out again into the saloon—turn the key—click. Such was my scheme for keeping my second self invisible. Nothing better could be contrived under the circumstances. And there we sat; I at my writing desk ready to appear busy with some papers, he behind me, out of sight of the door. It would not have been prudent to talk in daytime; and I could not have stood the excitement of that queer sense of whispering to myself. Now and then, glancing over my shoulder, I saw him far back there, sitting rigidly on the low stool, his bare feet close together, his arms folded, his head hanging on his breast—and perfectly still. Anybody would have taken him for me.

I was fascinated by it myself. Every moment I had to glance over my shoulder. I was looking at him when a voice outside the door said:

"Beg pardon, sir."

"Well!" ... I kept my eyes on him, and so, when the voice outside the door announced, "There's a ship's boat coming our way, sir," I saw him give a start—the first movement he had made for hours. But he did not raise his bowed head.

"All right. Get the ladder over."

I hesitated. Should I whisper something to him? But what? His immobility seemed to have been never disturbed. What could I tell him he did not know already? . . . Finally I went on deck.

II

THE skipper of the *Sephora* had a thin red whisker all round his face, and the sort of complexion that goes with hair of that color; also the particular, rather smeary shade of blue in the eyes. He was not exactly a showy figure; his shoulders were high, his stature but middling—one leg slightly more bandy than the other. He shook hands, looking vaguely around. A spiritless tenacity was his main characteristic, I judged. I behaved with a politeness which seemed to disconcert him. Perhaps he was shy. He mumbled to me as if he were ashamed of what he was saying; gave his name (it was something like Archbold—but at this distance of years I hardly am sure), his ship's name, and a few other particulars of that sort, in the manner of a criminal making a reluctant and doleful confession. He had had terrible weather on the passage out—terrible—terrible—wife aboard, too.

By this time we were seated in the cabin and the steward brought in a tray with a bottle and glasses. "Thanks! No." Never took liquor. Would have some water, though. He drank two tumblerfuls. Terrible thirsty work. Ever since daylight had been exploring the islands round his ship.

"What was that for—fun?" I asked, with an appearance of polite interest.

"No!" He sighed. "Painful duty."

As he persisted in his mumbling and I wanted my double to hear every word, I hit upon the notion of informing him that I regretted to say I was hard of hearing.

"Such a young man, too!" he nodded, keeping his smeary blue, unintelligent eyes fastened upon me. What was the cause of it—some disease? he inquired, without the least sympathy and as if he thought that, if so, I'd got no more than I deserved.

"Yes; disease," I admitted in a cheerful tone which seemed to shock him. But my point was gained, because he had to raise his voice to give me his tale. It is not worth while to record that version. It was just over two months since all this had happened, and he had thought so much about it that he seemed completely muddled as to its bearings, but still immensely impressed.

"What would you think of such a thing happening on board your own ship? I've had the *Sephora* for these fifteen years. I am a well-known shipmaster."

He was densely distressed—and perhaps I should have sympathized with him if I had been able to detach my mental vision from the unsuspected sharer of my cabin as though he were my second self. There he was on the other side of the bulkhead, four or five feet from us, no more, as we sat in the saloon. I looked politely at Captain Archbold (if that was his name), but it was the other I saw, in a gray sleeping suit, seated on a low stool, his bare feet close together, his arms folded, and every word said between us falling into the ears of his dark head bowed on his chest.

"I have been at sea now, man and boy, for seven-and-thirty years, and I've never heard of such a thing happening in an English ship. And that it should be my ship. Wife on board, too."

I was hardly listening to him.

"Don't you think," I said, "that the heavy sea which, you told me, came aboard just then might have killed the man? I have seen the sheer weight of a sea kill a man very neatly, by simply breaking his neck."

"Good God!" he uttered, impressively, fixing his smeary blue eyes on me. "The sea! No man killed by the sea ever looked like that." He seemed positively scandalized at my suggestion. And as I gazed at him, certainly not prepared for anything original on his part, he advanced his head close to mine and thrust his tongue out at me so suddenly that I couldn't help starting back.

After scoring over my calmness in this graphic way he nodded wisely. If I had seen the sight, he assured me, I would never forget it as long as I lived. The weather was too bad to give the corpse a proper sea burial. So next day at dawn they took it up on the poop, covering its face with a bit of bunting; he read a short prayer, and then, just as it was, in its oilskins and long boots, they launched it amongst those mountainous seas that seemed ready every moment to swallow up the ship herself and the terrified lives on board of her.

"That reefed foresail saved you," I threw in.

"Under God—it did," he exclaimed fervently. "It was by a special mercy, I firmly believe, that it stood some of those hurricane squalls."

"It was the setting of that sail which—" I began.

"God's own hand in it," he interrupted me. "Nothing less could have done it. I don't mind telling you that I hardly dared give the order. It seemed impossible that we could touch anything without losing it, and then our last hope would have been gone."

The terror of that gale was on him yet. I let him go on for a bit, then said, casually—as if returning to a minor subject:

"You were very anxious to give up your mate to the shore people, I believe?"

He was. To the law. His obscure tenacity on that point had in it something incomprehensible and a little awful; something, as it were, mystical, quite apart from his anxiety that he should not be suspected of "countenancing any doings of that sort." Seven-and-thirty virtuous years at sea, of which over twenty of immaculate command, and the last fifteen in the *Sephora,* seemed to have laid him under some pitiless obligation.

"And you know," he went on, groping shamefacedly amongst his feelings, "I did not engage that young fellow. His people had some interest with my owners. I was in a way forced to take him on. He looked very smart, very gentlemanly, and all that. But do you know—I never liked him, somehow. I am a plain man. You see, he wasn't exactly the sort for the chief mate of a ship like the *Sephora*."

I had become so connected in thoughts and impressions with the secret sharer of my cabin that I felt as if I, personally, were being given to understand that I, too, was not the sort that would have done for the chief mate of a ship like the *Sephora*. I had no doubt of it in my mind.

"Not at all the style of man. You understand," he insisted, superfluously, looking hard at me.

I smiled urbanely. He seemed at a loss for a while.

"I suppose I must report a suicide."

"Beg pardon?"

"Sui-cide! That's what I'll have to write to my owners directly I get in."

"Unless you manage to recover him before tomorrow," I assented, dispassionately. . . . "I mean, alive."

He mumbled something which I really did not catch, and I turned my ear to him in a puzzled manner. He fairly bawled:

"The land—I say, the mainland is at least seven miles off my anchorage."

"About that."

My lack of excitement, of curiosity, of surprise, of any sort of pronounced interest, began to arouse his distrust. But except for the felicitous pretense of deafness I had not tried to pretend anything. I had felt utterly incapable of playing the part of ignorance properly, and therefore was afraid to try. It is also certain that he had brought some ready-made suspicions with him, and that he viewed my politeness as a strange and unnatural phenomenon. And yet how else could I have received him? Not heartily! That was impossible for psychological reasons, which I need not state here. My only object was to keep off his inquiries. Surlily? Yes, but surliness might have provoked a point-blank question. From its novelty to him and from its nature, punctilious courtesy was the manner best calculated to restrain the man. But there was the danger of his breaking through my defense bluntly. I could not, I think, have met him by a direct lie, also for psychological (not moral) reasons. If he had only known how afraid I was of his putting my feeling of identity with the other to the test! But, strangely enough—(I thought of it only afterward)—I believe that he was not a little disconcerted by the reverse side of that weird situation, by something in me that reminded him of the man he was seeking—suggested a mysterious similitude to the young fellow he had distrusted and disliked from the first.

However that might have been, the silence was not very prolonged. He took another oblique step.

"I reckon I had no more than a two-mile pull to your ship. Not a bit more."

"And quite enough, too, in this awful heat," I said.

Another pause full of mistrust followed. Necessity, they say, is mother of invention, but fear, too, is not barren of ingenious suggestions. And I was afraid he would ask me point-blank for news of my other self.

"Nice little saloon, isn't it?" I remarked, as if noticing for the first time the way his eyes roamed from one closed door to the other. "And very well fitted out, too. Here, for instance," I continued reaching over the back of my seat negligently and flinging the door open, "is my bathroom."

He made an eager movement, but hardly gave it a glance. I got up, shut the door of the bathroom, and invited him to have a look round, as if I were very proud of my accommodation. He had to rise and be shown round, but he went through the business without any raptures whatever.

"And now we'll have a look at my stateroom," I declared, in a voice as loud as I dared to make it, crossing the cabin to the starboard side with purposely heavy steps.

He followed me in and gazed around. My intelligent double had vanished. I played my part.

"Very convenient—isn't it?"

"Very nice. Very comf . . ." He didn't finish, and went out brusquely as if to escape from some unrighteous wiles of mine. But it was not to be. I had been too frightened not to feel vengeful; I felt I had him on the run, and I meant to keep him on the run. My polite insistence must have had something menacing in it, because he gave in suddenly. And I did not let him off a single item; mate's room, pantry, storerooms, the very sail locker which was also under the poop—he had to look into them all. When at last I showed him out on the quarter-deck he drew a long, spiritless sigh, and mumbled dismally that he must really be going back to his ship now. I desired my mate, who had joined us, to see to the captain's boat.

The man of whiskers gave a blast on the whistle which he used to wear hanging round his neck, and yelled, "*Sephora* away!" My double down there in my cabin must have heard, and certainly could not feel more relieved than I. Four fellows came running out from somewhere forward and went over the side, while my own men, appearing on deck too, lined the rail. I escorted my visitor to the gangway ceremoniously, and nearly overdid it. He was a tenacious beast. On the very ladder he lingered, and in that unique, guiltily conscientious manner of sticking to the point:

"I say . . . you . . . you don't think that—"

I covered his voice loudly:

"Certainly not. . . . I am delighted. Good-by."

I had an idea of what he meant to say, and just saved myself by the privilege of defective hearing. He was too shaken generally to insist, but my mate, close witness of that parting, looked mystified and his face took on a thoughtful cast. As I did not want to appear as if I wished to avoid all communication with my officers, he had the opportunity to address me.

"Seems a very nice man. His boat's crew told our chaps a very extraordinary story, if what I am told by the steward is true. I suppose you had it from the captain, sir?"

"Yes. I had a story from the captain."

"A very horrible affair—isn't it, sir?"

"It is."

"Beats all these tales we hear about murders in Yankee ships."

"I don't think it beats them. I don't think it resembles them in the least."

"Bless my soul—you don't say so! But of course I've no acquaintance whatever with American ships, not I, so I couldn't go against your knowledge. It's horrible enough for me. . . . But the queerest part is that these fellows seemed to have some idea the man was hidden aboard here. They had really. Did you ever hear of such a thing?"

"Preposterous—isn't it?"

We were walking to and fro athwart the quarter-deck. No one of the crew forward could be seen (the day was Sunday), and the mate pursued:

"There was some little dispute about it. Our chaps took offense. 'As if we would harbor a thing like that,' they said. 'Wouldn't you like to look for him in our coal hole?' Quite a tiff. But they made it up in the end. I suppose he did drown himself. Don't you, sir?"

"I don't suppose anything."

"You have no doubt in the matter, sir?"

"None whatever."

I left him suddenly. I felt I was producing a bad impression, but with my double down there it was most trying to be on deck. And it was almost as trying to be below. Altogether a nerve-trying situation. But on the whole I felt less torn in two when I was with him. There was no one in the whole ship whom I dared take into my confidence. Since the hands had got to know his story, it would have been impossible to pass him off for anyone else, and an accidental discovery was to be dreaded now more than ever. . . .

The steward being engaged in laying the table for dinner, we could talk only with our eyes when I first went down. Later in the afternoon we had a cautious try at whispering. The Sunday quietness of the ship was against us; the stillness of air and water around her was against us; the elements, the men were against us—everything was against us in our secret partnership; time itself—for this could not go on forever. The very trust in Providence was, I suppose, denied to his guilt. Shall I confess that this thought cast me down very much? And as to the chapter of accidents which counts for so much in the book of success, I could only hope that it was closed. For what favorable accident could be expected?

"Did you hear everything?" were my first words as soon as we took up our position side by side, leaning over my bed-place.

He had. And the proof of it was his earnest whisper, "The man told you he hardly dared to give the order."

I understood the reference to be to that saving foresail.

"Yes. He was afraid of it being lost in the setting."

"I assure you he never gave the order. He may think he did, but he never gave it. He stood there with me on the break of the poop after the maintopsail blew away, and whimpered about our last hope—positively whimpered about it and nothing else—and the night coming on! To hear one's skipper go on like that in such weather was enough to drive any fellow out of his mind. It worked me up into a sort of desperation. I just took it into my hands and went away from him, boiling, and—But what's the use telling you? *You* know! . . . Do you think that if I had not been pretty fierce with them I should have got the men to do anything? Not it! The bosun perhaps? Perhaps! It wasn't a heavy sea—it was a sea gone mad! I suppose the end of the world will be something like that; and a man may have the heart to see it coming once and be done with it—but to have to face it day after day—I don't blame anybody. I was precious little better than the rest. Only— I was an officer of that old coal-wagon, anyhow—"

"I quite understand," I conveyed that sincere assurance into his ear. He was out of breath with whispering; I could hear him pant slightly. It was all very simple. The same strung-up force which had given twenty-four men a chance, at least, for their lives, had, in a sort of recoil, crushed an unworthy mutinous existence.

But I had no leisure to weigh the merits of the matter—footsteps in the saloon, a heavy knock. "There's enough wind to get under way with, sir." Here was the call of a new claim upon my thoughts and even upon my feelings.

"Turn the hands up," I cried through the door. "I'll be on deck directly."

I was going out to make the acquaintance of my ship. Before I left the cabin our eyes met—the eyes of the only two strangers on board. I pointed to the recessed part where the little campstool awaited him and laid my finger on my lips. He made a gesture—somewhat vague—a little mysterious, accompanied by a faint smile, as if of regret.

This is not the place to enlarge upon the sensations of a man who feels for the first time a ship move under his feet to his own independent word. In my case they were not unalloyed. I was not wholly alone with my command; for there was that stranger in my cabin. Or rather, I was not completely and wholly with her. Part of me was absent. That mental feeling of being in two places at once affected me physically as if the mood of secrecy had penetrated my very soul. Before an hour had elapsed since the ship had begun to move, having occasion to ask the mate (he stood by my side) to take a compass bearing of the Pagoda, I caught myself reaching up to his ear in whispers. I say I caught myself, but enough had escaped to startle the man. I can't describe it otherwise than by saying that he shied. A grave, preoccupied manner, as though he were in possession of some perplexing intelligence, did not leave him henceforth. A little later I moved away from the rail to look at the compass with such a stealthy gait that the helmsman noticed it—and I could not help noticing the unusual roundness of his eyes. These are trifling instances, though it's to no commander's advantage to be suspected of ludicrous eccentricities. But I was also more seriously affected. There are to a seaman certain words, gestures, that should in given conditions come as naturally, as instinctively as the winking of a menaced eye. A certain order should spring on to his lips without thinking; a certain sign should get itself made, so to speak, without reflection. But all unconscious alertness had abandoned me. I had to make an effort of will to recall myself back (from the cabin) to the conditions of the moment. I felt that I was appearing an irresolute commander to those people who were watching me more or less critically.

And, besides, there were the scares. On the second day out, for instance, coming off the deck in the afternoon (I had straw slippers on my bare feet) I stopped at the open pantry door and spoke to the steward. He was doing something there with his back to me. At the sound of my voice he nearly jumped out of his skin, as the saying is, and incidentally broke a cup.

"What on earth's the matter with you?" I asked, astonished.

He was extremely confused. "Beg your pardon, sir. I made sure you were in your cabin."

"You see I wasn't."

"No, sir. I could have sworn I had heard you moving in there not a moment ago. It's most extraordinary . . . very sorry, sir."

I passed on with an inward shudder. I was so identified with my secret double that I did not even mention the fact in those scanty, fearful whispers we exchanged. I suppose he had made some slight noise of some kind or other. It would have been miraculous if he hadn't at one time or another. And yet, haggard as he appeared, he looked always perfectly self-controlled, more than calm—almost invulnerable. On my suggestion he remained almost entirely in the bathroom, which, upon the whole, was the safest place. There could be really no shadow of an excuse for anyone ever wanting to go in there, once the steward had done with it. It was a very tiny place. Sometimes he reclined on the floor, his legs bent, his head sustained on one elbow. At others I would find him on the campstool, sitting in his gray sleeping suit and with his cropped dark hair like a patient, unmoved convict. At night I would smuggle him into my bed-place, and we would whisper together, with the regular footfalls of the officer of the watch passing and repassing over our heads. It was an infinitely miserable time. It was lucky that some tins of fine preserves were stowed in a locker in my stateroom; hard bread I could always get hold of; and so he lived on stewed chicken, paté de foie gras, asparagus, cooked oysters, sardines—on all sorts of abominable sham delicacies out of tins. My early morning coffee he always drank; and it was all I dared do for him in that respect.

Every day there was the horrible maneuvering to go through so that my room and then the bathroom should be done in the usual way. I came to hate the sight of the steward, to abhor the voice of that harmless man. I felt that it was he who would bring on the disaster of discovery. It hung like a sword over our heads.

The fourth day out, I think (we were working down the east side of the Gulf of Siam, tack for tack, in light winds and smooth water)—the fourth day, I say, of this miserable juggling with the unavoidable, as we sat at our evening meal, that man, whose slightest movement I dreaded, after putting down the dishes ran up on deck busily. This could not be dangerous. Presently he came down again; and then it appeared that he had remembered a coat of mine which I had thrown over a rail to dry after having been wetted in a shower which had passed over the ship in the afternoon. Sitting stolidly at the head of the table I became terrified at the sight of the garment on his arm. Of course he made for my door. There was no time to lose.

"Steward," I thundered. My nerves were so shaken that I could not govern my voice and conceal my agitation. This was the sort of thing that made my terrifically whiskered mate tap his forehead with his forefinger. I had detected him using that gesture while talking on deck with a confidential air to the carpenter. It was too far to hear a word, but I had no doubt that this pantomime could only refer to the strange new captain.

"Yes, sir," the pale-faced steward turned resignedly to me. It was this maddening course of being shouted at, checked without rhyme or reason, arbitrarily chased out of my cabin, suddenly called into it, sent flying out of his pantry on incomprehensible errands, that accounted for the growing wretchedness of his expression.

"Where are you going with that coat?"

"To your room, sir."

"Is there another shower coming?"

"I'm sure I don't know, sir. Shall I go up again and see, sir?"

"No! never mind."

My object was attained, as of course my other self in there would have heard everything that passed. During this interlude my two officers never raised their eyes off their respective plates; but the lip of that confounded cub, the second mate, quivered visibly.

I expected the steward to hook my coat on and come out at once. He was very slow about it; but I dominated my nervousness sufficiently not to shout after him. Suddenly I became aware (it could be heard plainly enough) that the fellow for some reason or other was opening the door of the bathroom. It was the end. The place was literally not big enough to swing a cat in. My voice died in my throat and I went stony all over. I expected to hear a yell of surprise and terror, and made a movement, but had not the strength to get on my legs. Everything remained still. Had my second self taken the poor wretch by the throat? I don't know what I would have done next moment if I had not seen the steward come out of my room, close the door, and then stand quietly by the sideboard.

Saved, I thought. But, no! Lost! Gone! He was gone!

I laid my knife and fork down and leaned back in my chair. My head swam. After a while, when sufficiently recovered to speak in a steady voice, I instructed my mate to put the ship round at eight o'clock himself.

"I won't come on deck," I went on. "I think I'll turn in, and unless the wind shifts I don't want to be disturbed before midnight. I feel a bit seedy."

"You did look middling bad a little while ago," the chief mate remarked without showing any great concern.

They both went out, and I stared at the steward clearing the table. There was nothing to be read on that wretched man's face. But why did he avoid my eyes I asked myself. Then I thought I should like to hear the sound of his voice.

"Steward!"

"Sir!" Startled as usual.

"Where did you hang up that coat?"

"In the bathroom, sir." The usual anxious tone. "It's not quite dry yet, sir."

For some time longer I sat in the cuddy. Had my double vanished as he had come? But of his coming there was an explanation, whereas his disappearance would be inexplicable. . . . I went slowly into my dark room, shut the door, lighted the lamp, and for a time dared not turn round. When at last I did I saw him standing bolt upright in the narrow recessed part. It would not be true to say I had a shock, but an irresistible doubt of his bodily existence flitted through my mind. Can it be, I asked myself, that he is not visible to other eyes than mine? It was like being haunted. Motionless, with a grave face, he raised his hands slightly at me in a gesture which meant clearly, "Heavens! what a narrow escape!" Narrow indeed. I think I had come creeping quietly as near insanity as any man who has not actually gone over the border. That gesture restrained me, so to speak.

The mate with the terrific whiskers was now putting the ship on the other tack. In the moment of profound silence which follows upon the hands going to their stations I heard on the poop his raised voice: "Hard alee!" and the distant shout of the order repeated on the maindeck. The sails, in that light breeze, made but a faint fluttering noise. It ceased. The ship was coming round slowly; I held my breath in the renewed stillness of expectation; one wouldn't have thought that there was a single living soul on her decks. A sudden brisk shout, "Mainsail haul!" broke the spell, and in the noisy cries and rush overhead of the men running away with the main brace we two, down in my cabin, came together in our usual position by the bed-place.

He did not wait for my question. "I heard him fumbling here and just managed to squat myself down in the bath," he whispered to me. "The fellow only opened the door and put his arm in to hang the coat up. All the same—"

"I never thought of that," I whispered back, even more appalled than before at the closeness of the shave, and marveling at that something unyielding in his character which was carrying him through so finely. There was no agitation in his whisper. Whoever was being driven distracted, it was not he. He was sane. And the proof of his sanity was continued when he took up the whispering again.

"It would never do for me to come to life again."

It was something that a ghost might have said. But what he was alluding to was his old captain's reluctant admission of the theory of suicide. It would obviously serve his turn—if I had understood at all the view which seemed to govern the unalterable purpose of his action.

"You must maroon me as soon as ever you can get amongst these islands off the Cambodje shore," he went on.

"Maroon you! We are not living in a boy's adventure tale," I protested. His scornful whispering took me up.

"We aren't indeed! There's nothing of a boy's tale in this. But there's nothing else for it. I want no more. You don't suppose I am afraid of what can be done to me? Prison or gallows or whatever they may please. But you don't see me coming back to explain such things to an old fellow in a wig and twelve respectable tradesmen, do you? What can they know whether I am guilty or not—or of *what* I am guilty, either? That's my affair. What does the Bible say? 'Driven off the face of the earth.' Very well. I am off the face of the earth now. As I came at night so I shall go."

"Impossible!" I murmured. "You can't."

"Can't?... Not naked like a soul on the Day of Judgment. I shall freeze on to this sleeping suit. The Last Day is not yet—and . . . you have understood thoroughly. Didn't you?"

I felt suddenly ashamed of myself. I may say truly that I understood—and my hesitation in letting that man swim away from my ship's side had been a mere sham sentiment, a sort of cowardice.

"It can't be done now till next night," I breathed out. "The ship is on the offshore tack and the wind may fail us."

"As long as I know that you understand," he whispered. "But of course you do. It's a great satisfaction to have got somebody to understand. You seem to have been there on purpose." And in the same whisper, as if we two whenever we talked had to say things to each other which were not fit for the world to hear, he added, "It's very wonderful."

We remained side by side talking in our secret way—but sometimes silent or just exchanging a whispered word or two at long intervals. And as usual he stared through the port. A breath of wind came now and again into our faces. The ship might have been moored in dock, so gently and on an even keel she slipped through the water, that did not murmur even at our passage, shadowy and silent like a phantom sea.

At midnight I went on deck, and to my mate's great surprise put the ship round on the other tack. His terrible whiskers flitted round me in silent criticism. I certainly should not have done it if it had been only a question of getting out of that sleepy gulf as quickly as possible. I believe he told the second mate, who relieved him, that it was a great want of judgment. The other only yawned. That intolerable cub shuffled about so sleepily and lolled against the rails in such a slack, improper fashion that I came down on him sharply.

"Aren't you properly awake yet?"

"Yes, sir! I am awake."

"Well, then, be good enough to hold yourself as if you were. And keep a lookout. If there's any current we'll be closing with some islands before daylight."

The east side of the gulf is fringed with islands, some solitary, others in groups. On the blue background of the high coast they seem to float on silvery patches of calm water, arid and gray, or dark green and rounded like clumps of evergreen bushes, with the larger ones, a mile or two long, show-ing the outlines of ridges, ribs of gray rock under the dark mantle of matted leafage. Unknown to trade, to travel, almost to geography, the manner of life they harbor is an unsolved secret. There must be villages—settlements of fishermen at least—on the largest of them, and some communication with the world is probably kept up by native craft. But all forenoon, as we headed for them, fanned along by the faintest of breezes, I saw no sign of man or canoe in the field of the telescope I kept on pointing at the scattered group.

At noon I gave no orders for a change of course, and the mate's whiskers became much concerned and seemed to be offering themselves unduly to my notice. At last I said:

"I am going to stand right in. Quite in—as far as I can take her."

The stare of extreme surprise imparted an air of ferocity also to his eyes, and he looked truly terrific for a moment.

"We're not doing well in the middle of the gulf," I continued, casually. "I am going to look for the land breezes tonight."

"Bless my soul! Do you mean, sir, in the dark amongst the lot of all them islands and reefs and shoals?"

"Well—if there are any regular land breezes at all on this coast one must get close inshore to find them, mustn't one?"

"Bless my soul!" he exclaimed again under his breath. All that after-noon he wore a dreamy, contemplative appearance which in him was a mark of perplexity. After dinner I went into my stateroom as if I meant to take some rest. There we two bent our dark heads over a half-unrolled chart lying on my bed.

"There," I said. "It's got to be Koh-ring. I've been looking at it ever since sunrise. It has got two hills and a low point. It must be inhabited. And on the coast opposite there is what looks like the mouth of a biggish river—with some town, no doubt, not far up. It's the best chance for you that I can see.

"Anything. Koh-ring let it be."

He looked thoughtfully at the chart as if surveying chances and dis-tances from a lofty height—and following with his eyes his own figure wan-dering on the blank land of Cochin China, and then passing off that piece of paper clean out of sight into uncharted regions. And it was as if the ship had two captains to plan her course for her. I had been so worried and restless running up and down that I had not had the patience to dress that day. I had remained in my sleeping suit, with straw slippers and a soft floppy hat. The closeness of the heat in the gulf had been most oppressive, and the crew were used to see me wandering in that airy attire.

"She will clear the south point as she heads now," I whispered into his ear. "Goodness only knows when, though, but certainly after dark. I'll edge her in to half a mile, as far as I may be able to judge in the dark—"

"Be careful," he murmured, warningly—and I realized suddenly that all my future, the only future for which I was fit, would perhaps go irretrievably to pieces in any mishap to my first command.

I could not stop a moment longer in the room. I motioned him to get out of sight and made my way on the poop. That unplayful cub had the watch. I walked up and down for a while thinking things out, then beckoned him over.

"Send a couple of hands to open the two quarter-deck ports," I said, mildly.

He actually had the impudence, or else so forgot himself in his wonder at such an incomprehensible order, as to repeat:

"Open the quarter-deck ports! What for, sir?"

"The only reason you need concern yourself about is because I tell you to do so. Have them open wide and fastened properly."

He reddened and went off, but I believe made some jeering remark to the carpenter as to the sensible practice of ventilating a ship's quarter-deck. I know he popped into the mate's cabin to impart the fact to him because the whiskers came on deck, as it were by chance, and stole glances at me from below—for signs of lunacy or drunkenness, I suppose.

A little before supper, feeling more restless than ever, I rejoined, for a moment, my second self. And to find him sitting so quietly was surprising, like something against nature, inhuman.

I developed my plan in a hurried whisper.

"I shall stand in as close as I dare and then put her round. I shall presently find means to smuggle you out of here into the sail locker, which communicates with the lobby. But there is an opening, a sort of square for hauling the sails out, which gives straight on the quarter-deck and which is never closed in fine weather, so as to give air to the sails. When the ship's way is deadened in stays and all the hands are aft at the main braces you shall have a clear road to slip out and get overboard through the open quarter-deck port. I've had them both fastened up. Use a rope's end to lower yourself into the water so as to avoid a splash—you know. It could be heard and cause some beastly complication."

He kept silent for a while, then whispered, "I understand."

"I won't be there to see you go," I began with an effort. "The rest . . . I only hope I have understood, too."

"You have. From first to last," and for the first time there seemed to be a faltering, something strained in his whisper. He caught hold of my arm, but the ringing of the supper bell made me start. He didn't, though; he only released his grip.

After supper I didn't come below again till well past eight o'clock. The faint, steady breeze was loaded with dew; and the wet, darkened sails held all there was of propelling power in it. The night, clear and starry, sparkled darkly, and the opaque, lightless patches shifting slowly against the low stars were the drifting islets. On the port bow there was a big one more distant and shadowily imposing by the great space of sky it eclipsed.

On opening the door I had a back view of my very own self looking at a chart. He had come out of the recess and was standing near the table.

"Quite dark enough," I whispered.

He stepped back and leaned against my bed with a level, quiet glance.

I sat on the couch. We had nothing to say to each other. Over our heads the officer of the watch moved here and there. Then I heard him move quickly. I knew what that meant. He was making for the companion; and presently his voice was outside my door.

"We are drawing in pretty fast, sir. Land looks rather close."

"Very well," I answered. "I am coming on deck directly."

I waited till he was gone out of the cuddy, then rose. My double moved too. The time had come to exchange our last whispers, for neither of us was ever to hear each other's natural voice.

"Look here!" I opened a drawer and took out three sovereigns. "Take this, anyhow. I've got six and I'd give you the lot, only I must keep a little money to buy some fruit and vegetables for the crew from native boats as we go through Sunda Straits."

He shook his head.

"Take it," I urged him, whispering desperately. "No one can tell what—"

He smiled and slapped meaningly the only pocket of the sleeping jacket. It was not safe, certainly. But I produced a large old silk handkerchief of mine, and tying the three pieces of gold in a corner, pressed it on him. He was touched, I suppose, because he took it at last and tied it quickly round his waist under the jacket, on his bare skin.

Our eyes met; several seconds elapsed, till, our glances still mingled, I extended my hand and turned the lamp out. Then I passed through the cuddy, leaving the door of my room wide open. . . . "Steward!"

He was still lingering in the pantry in the greatness of his zeal, giving a rub-up to a plated cruet stand the last thing before going to bed. Being careful not to wake up the mate, whose room was opposite, I spoke in an undertone.

He looked round anxiously. "Sir!"

"Can you get me a little hot water from the galley?"

"I am afraid, sir, the galley fire's been out for some time now."

"Go and see."

He fled up the stairs.

"Now," I whispered, loudly, into the saloon—too loudly, perhaps, but I was afraid I couldn't make a sound. He was by my side in an instant—the double captain slipped past the stairs—through the tiny dark passage . . . a sliding door. We were in the sail locker, scrambling on our knees over the sails. A sudden thought struck me. I saw myself wandering barefooted, bareheaded, the sun beating on my dark poll. I snatched off my floppy hat and tried hurriedly in the dark to ram it on my other self. He dodged and fended off silently. I wonder what he thought had come to me before he understood and suddenly desisted. Our hands met gropingly, lingered united in a steady, motionless clasp for a second. . . . No word was breathed by either of us when they separated.

I was standing quietly by the pantry door when the steward returned.

"Sorry, sir. Kettle barely warm. Shall I light the spirit lamp?"

"Never mind."

I came out on deck slowly. It was now a matter of conscience to shave the land as close as possible—for now he must go overboard whenever the ship was put in stays. Must! There could be no going back for him. After a moment I walked over to leeward and my heart flew into my mouth at the nearness of the land on the bow. Under any other circumstances I would not have held on a minute longer. The second mate had followed me anxiously.

I looked on till I felt I could command my voice.

"She will weather," I said then in a quiet tone.

"Are you going to try that, sir?" he stammered out incredulously.

I took no notice of him and raised my tone just enough to be heard by the helmsman.

"Keep her good full."

"Good full, sir."

The wind fanned my cheek, the sails slept, the world was silent. The strain of watching the dark loom of the land grow bigger and denser was too much for me. I had shut my eyes—because the ship must go closer. She must! The stillness was intolerable. Were we standing still?

When I opened my eyes the second view started my heart with a thump. The black southern hill of Koh-ring seemed to hang right over the ship like a towering fragment of the everlasting night. On that enormous mass of blackness there was not a gleam to be seen, not a sound to be heard. It was gliding irresistibly toward us and yet seemed already within reach of the hand. I saw the vague figures of the watch grouped in the waist, gazing in awed silence.

"Are you going on, sir?" inquired an unsteady voice at my elbow.

I ignored it. I had to go on.

"Keep her full. Don't check her way. That won't do now," I said warningly.

"I can't see the sails very well," the helmsman answered me, in strange, quavering tones.

Was she close enough? Already she was, I won't say in the shadow of the land, but in the very blackness of it, already swallowed up as it were, gone too close to be recalled, gone from me altogether.

"Give the mate a call," I said to the young man who stood at my elbow still as death. "And turn all hands up."

My tone had a borrowed loudness reverberated from the height of the land. Several voices cried out together: "We are all on deck, sir."

Then stillness again, with the great shadow gliding closer, towering higher, without a light, without a sound. Such a hush had fallen on the ship that she might have been a bark of the dead floating in slowly under the very gate of Erebus.

"My God! Where are we?"

It was the mate moaning at my elbow. He was thunderstruck, and as it were deprived of the moral support of his whiskers. He clapped his hands and absolutely cried out, "Lost!"

"Be quiet," I said sternly.

He lowered his tone, but I saw the shadowy gesture of his despair. "What are we doing here?"

"Looking for the land wind."

He made as if to tear his hair, and addressed me recklessly.

"She will never get out. You have done it, sir. I knew it'd end in something like this. She will never weather, and you are too close now to stay. She'll drift ashore before she's round. O my God!"

I caught his arm as he was raising it to batter his poor devoted head, and shook it violently.

"She's ashore already," he wailed, trying to tear himself away.

"Is she? . . . Keep good full there!"

"Good full, sir," cried the helmsman in a frightened, thin, childlike voice.

I hadn't let go the mate's arm and went on shaking it. "Ready about, do you hear? You go forward"—shake—"and stop there"—shake—"and hold your noise"—shake—"and see these head sheets properly overhauled" —shake, shake—shake.

And all the time I dared not look toward the land lest my heart should fail me. I released my grip at last and he ran forward as if fleeing for dear life.

I wondered what my double there in the sail locker thought of this commotion. He was able to hear everything—and perhaps he was able to understand why, on my conscience, it had to be thus close—no less. My first order "Hard alee!" re-echoed ominously under the towering shadow of Koh-ring as if I had shouted in a mountain gorge. And then I watched the land intently. In that smooth water and light wind it was impossible to feel the ship coming-to. No! I could not feel her. And my second self was making now ready to slip out and lower himself overboard. Perhaps he was gone already . . . ?

The great black mass brooding over our very mastheads began to pivot away from the ship's side silently. And now I forgot the secret stranger ready to depart, and remembered only that I was a total stranger to the ship. I did not know her. Would she do it? How was she to be handled?

I swung the mainyard and waited helplessly. She was perhaps stopped, and her very fate hung in the balance, with the black mass of Koh-ring like the gate of the everlasting night towering over her taffrail. What would she do now? Had she way on her yet? I stepped to the side swiftly, and on the shadowy water I could see nothing except a faint phosphorescent flash revealing the glassy smoothness of the sleeping surface. It was impossible to tell—and I had not learned yet the feel of my ship. Was she moving? What I needed was something easily seen, a piece of paper, which I could throw overboard and watch. I had nothing on me. To run down for it I didn't dare. There was no time. All at once my strained, yearning stare distinguished a white object floating within a yard of the ship's side. White on the black water. A phosphorescent flash passed under it. What was that thing? . . . I recognized my own floppy hat. It must have fallen off his head . . . and he didn't bother. Now I had what I wanted—the saving mark for my eyes. But I hardly thought of my other self, now gone from the ship, to be hidden forever from all friendly faces, to be a fugitive and a vagabond on the earth, with no brand of the curse on his sane forehead to stay a slaying hand ... too proud to explain.

And I watched the hat—the expression of my sudden pity for his mere flesh. It had been meant to save his homeless head from the dangers of the sun. And now—behold—it was saving the ship, by serving me for a mark to help out the ignorance of my strangeness. Ha! It was drifting forward, warning me just in time that the ship had gathered sternway.

"Shift the helm," I said in a low voice to the seaman standing still like a statue.

The man's eyes glistened wildly in the binnacle light as he jumped round to the other side and spun round the wheel.

I walked to the break of the poop. On the overshadowed deck all hands stood by the forebraces waiting for my order. The stars ahead seemed to be gliding from right to left. And all was so still in the world that I heard the quiet remark "She's round," passed in a tone of intense relief between two seamen.

"Let go and haul."

The foreyards ran round with a great noise, amidst cheery cries. And now the frightful whiskers made themselves heard giving various orders. Already the ship was drawing ahead. And I was alone with her. Nothing! no one in the world should stand now between us, throwing a shadow on the way of silent knowledge and mute affection, the perfect communion of a seaman with his first command.

Walking to the taffrail, I was in time to make out, on the very edge of a darkness thrown by a towering black mass like the very gateway of Erebus— yes, I was in time to catch an evanescent glimpse of my white hat left behind to mark the spot where the secret sharer of my cabin and of my thoughts, as though he were my second self, had lowered himself into the water to take his punishment: a free man, a proud swimmer striking out for a new destiny.

Questions

1. *"And suddenly I rejoiced in the great security of the sea as compared with the unrest of the land, in my choice of that untempted life presenting no disquieting problems, invested with an elementary moral beauty by the absolute straightforwardness of its appeal and by the singleness of its purpose" (p. 21). Do the events of the story justify these early musings of the captain? Explain. Who in the story might represent elementary morality? Can that elementary morality be described as "beautiful"? Why or why not?* 2. *When the frightened mate cries out that the ship will founder, the captain catches his arm. "I hadn't let go the mate's arm and went on shaking it. 'Ready about, do you hear? You go forward'—shake—'and stop there'—shake—'and hold your noise'—shake—'and see these head sheets properly overhauled'—shake, shake— shake" (p. 46). What is the significance of the captain's behavior?* 3. *Why does the captain sail closer to the land than even he feels is necessary to ensure Leggatt's escape?* 4. *If the captain is "innocent" at the outset, in what way is he "experienced" at the conclusion?*

The Bride Comes to Yellow Sky

STEPHEN CRANE [1871–1900]

I

THE great Pullman was whirling onward with such dignity of motion that a glance from the window seemed simply to prove that the plains of Texas were pouring eastward. Vast flats of green grass, dull-hued spaces of mesquit and cactus, little groups of frame houses, woods of light and tender trees, all were sweeping into the east, sweeping over the horizon, a precipice.

A newly married pair had boarded this coach at San Antonio. The man's face was reddened from many days in the wind and sun, and a direct result of his new black clothes was that his brick-coloured hands were constantly performing in a most conscious fashion. From time to time he looked down respectfully at his attire. He sat with a hand on each knee, like a man waiting in a barber's shop. The glances he devoted to other passengers were furtive and shy.

The bride was not pretty, nor was she very young. She wore a dress of blue cashmere, with small reservations of velvet here and there, and with steel buttons abounding. She continually twisted her head to regard her puff sleeves, very stiff, straight, and high. They embarrassed her. It was quite apparent that she had cooked, and that she expected to cook, dutifully. The blushes caused by the careless scrutiny of some passengers as she had entered the car were strange to see upon this plain, under-class countenance, which was drawn in placid, almost emotionless lines.

They were evidently very happy. "Ever been in a parlour-car before?" he asked, smiling with delight.

"No," she answered; "I never was. It's fine, ain't it?"

"Great! And then after a while we'll go forward to the diner, and get a big lay-out. Finest meal in the world. Charge a dollar."

"Oh, do they?" cried the bride. "Charge a dollar? Why, that's too much —for us—ain't it, Jack?"

"Not this trip, anyhow," he answered bravely. "We're going to go the whole thing."

Later he explained to her about the trains. "You see, it's a thousand miles from one end of Texas to the other; and this train runs right across it, and never stops but four times." He had the pride of an owner. He pointed out to her the dazzling fittings of the coach; and in truth her eyes opened wider as she contemplated the sea-green figured velvet, the shining brass, silver, and glass, the wood that gleamed as darkly brilliant as the surface of a pool of oil.

At one end a bronze figure sturdily held a support for a separated chamber, and at convenient places on the ceiling were frescos in olive and silver.

To the minds of the pair, their surroundings reflected the glory of their marriage that morning in San Antonio; this was the environment of their new estate; and the man's face in particular beamed with an elation that made him appear ridiculous to the negro porter. This individual at times surveyed them from afar with an amused and superior grin. On other occasions he bullied them with skill in ways that did not make it exactly plain to them that they were being bullied. He subtly used all the manners of the most unconquerable kind of snobbery. He oppressed them; but of this oppression they had small knowledge, and they speedily forgot that infrequently a number of travellers covered them with stares of derisive enjoyment. Historically there was supposed to be something infinitely humorous in their situation.

"We are due in Yellow Sky at 3:42," he said, looking tenderly into her eyes.

"Oh, are we?" she said, as if she had not been aware of it. To evince surprise at her husband's statement was part of her wifely amiability. She took from a pocket a little silver watch; and as she held it before her, and stared at it with a frown of attention, the new husband's face shone.

"I bought it in San Anton' from a friend of mine," he told her gleefully.

"It's seventeen minutes past twelve," she said, looking up at him with a kind of shy and clumsy coquetry. A passenger, noting this play, grew excessively sardonic, and winked at himself in one of the numerous mirrors.

At last they went to the dining-car. Two rows of negro waiters, in glowing white suits, surveyed their entrance with the interest, and also the equanimity, of men who had been forewarned. The pair fell to the lot of a waiter who happened to feel pleasure in steering them through their meal. He viewed them with the manner of a fatherly pilot, his countenance radiant with benevolence. The patronage, entwined with the ordinary deference, was not plain to them. And yet, as they returned to their coach, they showed in their faces a sense of escape.

To the left, miles down a long purple slope, was a little ribbon of mist where moved the keening Rio Grande. The train was approaching it at an angle, and the apex was Yellow Sky. Presently it was apparent that, as the distance from Yellow Sky grew shorter, the husband became commensurately restless. His brick-red hands were more insistent in their prominence. Occasionally he was even rather absent-minded and far-away when the bride leaned forward and addressed him.

As a matter of truth, Jack Potter was beginning to find the shadow of a deed weigh upon him like a leaden slab. He, the town marshal of Yellow Sky, a man known, liked, and feared in his corner, a prominent person, had gone to San Antonio to meet a girl he believed he loved, and there, after the usual prayers, had actually induced her to marry him, without consulting Yellow Sky for any part of the transaction. He was now bringing his bride before an innocent and unsuspecting community.

Of course people in Yellow Sky married as it pleased them, in accordance with a general custom; but such was Potter's thought of his duty to his friends, or of their idea of his duty, or of an unspoken form which does not control men in these matters, that he felt he was heinous. He had committed an extraordinary crime. Face to face with this girl in San Antonio, and spurred by his sharp impulse, he had gone headlong over all the social hedges. At San Antonio he was like a man hidden in the dark. A knife to sever any friendly duty, any form, was easy to his hand in that remote city. But the hour of Yellow Sky—the hour of daylight—was approaching.

He knew full well that his marriage was an important thing to his town. It could only be exceeded by the burning of the new hotel. His friends could not forgive him. Frequently he had reflected on the advisability of telling them by telegraph, but a new cowardice had been upon him. He feared to do it. And now the train was hurrying him toward a scene of amazement, glee, and reproach. He glanced out of the window at the line of haze swinging slowly in toward the train.

Yellow Sky had a kind of brass band, which played painfully, to the delight of the populace. He laughed without heart as he thought of it. If the citizens could dream of his prospective arrival with his bride, they would parade the band at the station and escort them, amid cheers and laughing congratulations, to his adobe home.

He resolved that he would use all the devices of speed and plainscraft in making the journey from the station to his house. Once within that safe citadel, he could issue some sort of vocal bulletin, and then not go among the citizens until they had time to wear off a little of their enthusiasm.

The bride looked anxiously at him. "What's worrying you, Jack?"

He laughed again. "I'm not worrying, girl; I'm only thinking of Yellow Sky."

She flushed in comprehension.

A sense of mutual guilt invaded their minds and developed a finer tenderness. They looked at each other with eyes softly aglow. But Potter often laughed the same nervous laugh; the flush upon the bride's face seemed quite permanent.

The traitor to the feelings of Yellow Sky narrowly watched the speeding landscape. "We're nearly there," he said.

Presently the porter came and announced the proximity of Potter's home. He held a brush in his hand, and, with all his airy superiority gone, he brushed Potter's new clothes as the latter slowly turned this way and that way. Potter fumbled out a coin and gave it to the porter, as he had seen others do. It was a heavy and muscle-bound business, as that of a man shoeing his first horse.

The porter took their bag, and as the train began to slow they moved forward to the hooded platform of the car. Presently the two engines and their string of coaches rushed into the station of Yellow Sky.

"They have to take water here," said Potter, from a constricted throat and in mournful cadence, as one announcing death. Before the train stopped his eye had swept the length of the platform, and he was glad and astonished to see there was none upon it but the station-agent, who, with a slightly hurried and anxious air, was walking toward the water-tanks. When the train had halted, the porter alighted first, and placed in position a little temporary step.

"Come on, girl," said Potter, hoarsely. As he helped her down they each laughed on a false note. He took the bag from the negro, and bade his wife cling to his arm. As they slunk rapidly away, his hang-dog glance perceived that they were unloading the two trunks, and also that the station-agent, far ahead near the baggage-car, had turned and was running toward him, making gestures. He laughed, and groaned as he laughed, when he noted the first effect of his marital bliss upon Yellow Sky. He gripped his wife's arm firmly to his side, and they fled. Behind them the porter stood, chuckling fatuously.

II

THE California express on the Southern Railway was due at Yellow Sky in twenty-one minutes. There were six men at the bar of the Weary Gentleman saloon. One was a drummer who talked a great deal and rapidly; three were Texans who did not care to talk at that time; and two were Mexican sheepherders, who did not talk as a general practice in the Weary Gentleman saloon. The barkeeper's dog lay on the board walk that crossed in front of the door. His head was on his paws, and he glanced drowsily here and there with the constant vigilance of a dog that is kicked on occasion. Across the sandy street were some vivid green grass-plots, so wonderful in appearance, amid the sands that burned near them in a blazing sun, that they caused a doubt in the mind. They exactly resembled the grass mats used to represent lawns on the stage. At the cooler end of the railway station, a man without a coat sat in a tilted chair and smoked his pipe. The fresh-cut bank of the Rio Grande circled near the town, and there could be seen beyond it a great plum-coloured plain of mesquit.

Save for the busy drummer and his companions in the saloon, Yellow Sky was dozing. The new-comer leaned gracefully upon the bar, and recited many tales with the confidence of a bard who has come upon a new field.

"—and at the moment that the old man fell downstairs with the bureau in his arms, the old woman was coming up with two scuttles of coal, and of course—"

The drummer's tale was interrupted by a young man who suddenly appeared in the open door. He cried: "Scratchy Wilson's drunk, and has turned loose with both hands." The two Mexicans at once set down their glasses and faded out of the rear entrance of the saloon.

The drummer, innocent and jocular, answered: "All right, old man. S'pose he has? Come in and have a drink, anyhow."

But the information had made such a obvious cleft in every skull in the room that the drummer was obliged to see its importance. All had become instantly solemn. "Say," said he, mystified, "what is this?" His three companions made the introductory gesture of eloquent speech; but the young man at the door forestalled them.

"It means, my friend," he answered, as he came into the saloon, "that for the next two hours this town won't be a health resort."

The barkeeper went to the door, and locked and barred it; reaching out of the window, he pulled in heavy wooden shutters, and barred them. Immediately a solemn, chapel-like gloom was upon the place. The drummer was looking from one to another.

"But say," he cried, "what is this, anyhow? You don't mean there is going to be a gun-fight?"

"Don't know whether there'll be a fight or not," answered one man, grimly; "but there'll be some shootin'—some good shootin'."

The young man who had warned them waved his hand. "Oh, there'll be a fight fast enough, if any one wants it. Anybody can get a fight out there in the street. There's a fight just waiting."

The drummer seemed to be swayed between the interest of a foreigner and a perception of personal danger.

"What did you say his name was?" he asked.

"Scratchy Wilson," they answered in chorus.

"And will he kill anybody? What are you going to do? Does this happen often? Does he rampage around like this once a week or so? Can he break in that door?"

"No; he can't break down that door," replied the barkeeper. "He's tried it three times. But when he comes you'd better lay down on the floor, stranger. He's dead sure to shoot at it, and a bullet may come through."

Thereafter the drummer kept a strict eye upon the door. The time had not yet been called for him to hug the floor, but, as a minor precaution, he sidled near to the wall. "Will he kill anybody?" he said again.

The men laughed low and scornfully at the question.

"He's out to shoot, and he's out for trouble. Don't see any good in experimentin' with him."

"But what do you do in a case like this? What do you do?"

A man responded: "Why, he and Jack Potter—"

"But," in chorus the other men interrupted, "Jack Potter's in San Anton'."

"Well, who is he? What's he got to do with it?"

"Oh, he's the town marshal. He goes out and fights Scratchy when he gets on one of these tears."

"Wow!" said the drummer, mopping his brow. "Nice job he's got."

The voices had toned away to mere whisperings. The drummer wished to ask further questions, which were born of an increasing anxiety and bewilderment; but when he attempted them, the men merely looked at him in irritation and motioned him to remain silent. A tense waiting hush was upon them. In the deep shadows of the room their eyes shone as they listened for sounds from the street. One man made three gestures at the barkeeper; and the latter, moving like a ghost, handed him a glass and a bottle. The man poured a full glass of whisky, and set down the bottle noiselessly. He gulped the whisky in a swallow, and turned again toward the door in immovable silence. The drummer saw that the barkeeper, without a sound, had taken a Winchester from beneath the bar. Later he saw this individual beckoning to him, so he tiptoed across the room.

"You better come with me back of the bar."

"No, thanks," said the drummer, perspiring; "I'd rather be where I can make a break for the back door."

Whereupon the man of bottles made a kindly but peremptory gesture. The drummer obeyed it, and, finding himself seated on a box with his head below the level of the bar, balm was laid upon his soul at sight of various zinc and copper fittings that bore a resemblance to armour-plate. The barkeeper took a seat comfortably upon an adjacent box.

"You see," he whispered, "this here Scratchy Wilson is a wonder with a gun—a perfect wonder; and when he goes on the war-trail, we hunt our holes —naturally. He's about the last one of the old gang that used to hang out along the river here. He's a terror when he's drunk. When he's sober he's all right— kind of simple—wouldn't hurt a fly—nicest fellow in town. But when he's drunk—whoo!"

There were periods of stillness. "I wish Jack Potter was back from San Anton'," said the barkeeper. "He shot Wilson up once—in the leg—and he would sail in and pull out the kinks in this thing."

Presently they heard from a distance the sound of a shot, followed by three wild yowls. It instantly removed a bond from the men in the darkened saloon. There was a shuffling of feet. They looked at each other. "Here he comes," they said.

III

A man in a maroon-coloured flannel shirt, which had been pur-chased for purposes of decoration, and made principally by some Jewish women on the East Side of New York, rounded a corner and walked into the middle of the main street of Yellow Sky. In either hand the man held a long, heavy, blue-black revolver. Often he yelled, and these cries rang through a semblance of a deserted village, shrilly flying over the roofs in a volume that seemed to have no relation to the ordinary vocal strength of a man. It was as if the surrounding stillness formed the arch of a tomb over him. These cries of ferocious challenge rang against walls of silence. And his boots had red tops with gilded imprints, of the kind beloved in winter by little sledding boys on the hillsides of New England.

The man's face flamed in a rage begot of whisky. His eyes, rolling, and yet keen for ambush, hunted the still doorways and windows. He walked with the creeping movement of the midnight cat. As it occurred to him, he roared menacing information. The long revolvers in his hands were as easy as straws; they were moved with an electric swiftness. The little fingers of each hand played sometimes in a musician's way. Plain from the low collar of the shirt, the cords of his neck straightened and sank, straightened and sank, as passion moved him. The only sounds were his terrible invitations. The calm adobes preserved their demeanour at the passing of this small thing in the middle of the street.

There was no offer of fight—no offer of fight. The man called to the sky. There were no attractions. He bellowed and fumed and swayed his revolvers here and everywhere.

The dog of the barkeeper of the Weary Gentleman saloon had not appreciated the advance of events. He yet lay dozing in front of his master's door. At sight of the dog, the man paused and raised his revolver humorously. At sight of the man, the dog sprang up and walked diagonally away, with a sullen head, and growling. The man yelled, and the dog broke into a gallop. As it was about to enter an alley, there was a loud noise, a whistling, and something spat the ground directly before it. The dog screamed, and, wheeling in terror, galloped headlong in a new direction. Again there was a noise, a whistling, and sand was kicked viciously before it. Fear-stricken, the dog turned and flurried like an animal in a pen. The man stood laughing, his weapons at his hips.

Ultimately the man was attracted by the closed door of the Weary Gentleman saloon. He went to it and, hammering with a revolver, demanded drink.

The door remaining imperturbable, he picked a bit of paper from the walk, and nailed it to the framework with a knife. He then turned his back contemptuously upon this popular resort and, walking to the opposite side of the street and spinning there on his heel quickly and lithely, fired at the bit of paper. He missed it by a half-inch. He swore at himself, and went away. Later he comfortably fusilladed the windows of his most intimate friend. The man was playing with this town; it was a toy for him.

But still there was no offer of fight. The name of Jack Potter, his ancient antagonist, entered his mind, and he concluded that it would be a glad thing if he should go to Potter's house, and by bombardment induce him to come out and fight. He moved in the direction of his desire, chanting Apache scalp-music.

When he arrived at it, Potter's house presented the same still front as had the other adobes. Taking up a strategic position, the man howled a challenge. But this house regarded him as might a great stone god. It gave no sign. After a decent wait, the man howled further challenges, mingling with them wonderful epithets.

Presently there came the spectacle of a man churning himself into deepest rage over the immobility of a house. He fumed at it as the winter wind attacks a prairie cabin in the North. To the distance there should have gone the sound of a tumult like the fighting of two hundred Mexicans. As necessity bade him, he paused for breath or to reload his revolvers.

IV

POTTER and his bride walked sheepishly and with speed. Sometimes they laughed together shamefacedly and low.

"Next corner, dear," he said finally.

They put forth the efforts of a pair walking bowed against a strong wind. Potter was about to raise a finger to point the first appearance of the new home when, as they circled the corner, they came face to face with a man in a maroon-coloured shirt, who was feverishly pushing cartridges into a large revolver. Upon the instant the man dropped his revolver to the ground and, like lightning, whipped another from its holster. The second weapon was aimed at the bridegroom's chest.

There was a silence. Potter's mouth seemed to be merely a grave for his tongue. He exhibited an instinct to at once loosen his arm from the woman's grip, and he dropped the bag to the sand. As for the bride, her face had gone as yellow as old cloth. She was a slave to hideous rites, gazing at the apparitional snake.

The two men faced each other at a distance of three paces. He of the revolver smiled with a new and quiet ferocity.

"Tried to sneak up on me," he said. "Tried to sneak up on me!" His eyes grew more baleful. As Potter made a slight movement, the man thrust his revolver venomously forward. "No; don't you do it, Jack Potter. Don't you move a finger toward a gun just yet. Don't you move an eyelash. The time has come for me to settle with you, and I'm goin' to do it my own way, and loaf along with no interferin'. So if you don't want a gun bent on you, just mind what I tell you."

Potter looked at his enemy. "I ain't got a gun on me, Scratchy," he said. "Honest, I ain't." He was stiffening and steadying, but yet somewhere at the back of his mind a vision of the Pullman floated: the sea-green figured velvet, the shining brass, silver, and glass, the wood that gleamed as darkly brilliant as the surface of a pool of oil—all the glory of the marriage, the environment of the new estate. "You know I fight when it comes to fighting, Scratchy Wilson; but I ain't got a gun on me. You'll have to do all the shootin' yourself."

His enemy's face went livid. He stepped forward, and lashed his weapon to and fro before Potter's chest. "Don't you tell me you ain't got no gun on you, you whelp. Don't tell me no lie like that. There ain't a man in Texas ever seen you without no gun. Don't take me for no kid." His eyes blazed with light, and his throat worked like a pump.

"I ain't takin' you for no kid," answered Potter. His heels had not moved an inch backward. "I'm takin' you for a damn fool. I tell you I ain't got a gun, and I ain't. If you're goin' to shoot me up, you better begin now; you'll never get a chance like this again."

So much enforced reasoning had told on Wilson's rage; he was calmer. "If you ain't got a gun, why ain't you got a gun?" he sneered. "Been to Sunday-school?"

"I ain't got a gun because I've just come from San Anton' with my wife. I'm married," said Potter. "And if I'd thought there was going to be any galoots like you prowling around when I brought my wife home, I'd had a gun, and don't you forget it."

"Married!" said Scratchy, not at all comprehending.

"Yes, married. I'm married," said Potter, distinctly.

"Married?" said Scratchy. Seemingly for the first time, he saw the drooping, drowning woman at the other man's side. "No!" he said. He was like a creature allowed a glimpse of another world. He moved a pace backward, and his arm, with the revolver, dropped to his side. "Is this the lady?" he asked.

"Yes; this is the lady," answered Potter.

There was another period of silence.

"Well," said Wilson at last, slowly, "I s'pose it's all off now."

"It's all off if you say so, Scratchy. You know I didn't make the trouble." Potter lifted his valise.

"Well, I 'low it's off, Jack," said Wilson. He was looking at the ground. "Married!" He was not a student of chivalry; it was merely that in the presence of this foreign condition he was a simple child of the earlier plains. He picked up his starboard revolver, and, placing both weapons in their holsters, he went away. His feet made funnel-shaped tracks in the heavy sand.

Questions

1. Scratchy is described in the final paragraph as "a simple child of the earlier plains." In the context of the story what does this mean? Was Potter ever a simple child of the earlier plains? **2.** Early in the story we read that ". . . Jack Potter was beginning to find the shadow of a deed weigh upon him like a leaden slab. He, the town marshal of Yellow Sky, a man known, liked, and feared in his corner, a prominent person, had gone to San Antonio to meet a girl he believed he loved, and there, after the usual prayers, had actually induced her to marry him, without consulting Yellow Sky for any part of the transaction. He was now bringing his bride before an innocent and unsuspecting community." Jack Potter, like any man, has a right to marry. How do you account for his feelings as described in this passage? **3.** How would you characterize Scratchy's behavior? How does it relate to the "myth of the west" preserved in films and western novels? How does the description of Scratchy's shirt at the beginning of part III affect that view of the west? **4.** A drummer is a traveling salesman. What effect does his presence have on the "myth of the west"? **5.** Why is Scratchy disconsolate at the end?

I Want to Know Why

SHERWOOD ANDERSON [1876–1941]

W<small>E</small> got up at four in the morning, that first day in the east. On the evening before we had climbed off a freight train at the edge of town, and with the true instinct of Kentucky boys had found our way across town and to the race track and the stables at once. Then we knew we were all right. Hanley Turner right away found a nigger we knew. It was Bildad Johnson who in the winter works at Ed Becker's livery barn in our home town, Beckersville. Bildad is a good cook as almost all our niggers are and of course he, like everyone in our part of Kentucky who is anyone at all, likes the horses. In the spring Bildad begins to scratch around. A nigger from our country can flatter and wheedle anyone into letting him do most anything he wants. Bildad wheedles the stable men and the trainers from the horse farms in our country around Lexington. The trainers come into town in the evening to stand around and talk and maybe get into a poker game. Bildad gets in with them. He is always doing little favors and telling about things to eat, chicken browned in a pan, and how is the best way to cook sweet potatoes and corn bread. It makes your mouth water to hear him.

When the racing season comes on and the horses go to the races and there is all the talk on the streets in the evenings about the new colts, and everyone says when they are going over to Lexington or to the spring meeting at Churchill Downs or to Latonia, and the horsemen that have been down to New Orleans or maybe at the winter meeting at Havana in Cuba come home to spend a week before they start out again, at such a time when everything talked about in Beckersville is just horses and nothing else and the outfits start out and horse racing is in every breath of air you breathe, Bildad shows up with a job as cook for some outfit. Often when I think about it, his always going all season to the races and working in the livery barn in the winter where horses are and where men like to come and talk about horses, I wish I was a nigger. It's a foolish thing to say, but that's the way I am about being around horses, just crazy. I can't help it.

Well, I must tell you about what we did and let you in on what I'm talking about. Four of us boys from Beckersville, all whites and sons of men who live in Beckersville regular, made up our minds we were going to the races, not just to Lexington or Louisville, I don't mean, but to the big eastern track we were always hearing our Beckersville men talk about, to Saratoga. We were all pretty young then. I was just turned fifteen and I was the oldest of the four. It was my scheme. I admit that and I talked the others into trying it. There was Hanley Turner and Henry Rieback and Tom Tumberton and myself. I had thirty-seven dollars I had earned during the winter working nights and Saturdays in Enoch Myer's grocery. Henry Rieback had eleven dollars and the others, Hanley and Tom, had only a dollar or two each. We fixed it all up and laid low until the Kentucky spring meetings were over and some of our men, the sportiest ones, the ones we envied the most, had cut out—then we cut out too.

I won't tell you the trouble we had beating our way on freights and all. We went through Cleveland and Buffalo and other cities and saw Niagara Falls. We bought things there, souvenirs and spoons and cards and shells with pictures of the falls on them for our sisters and mothers, but thought we had better not send any of the things home. We didn't want to put the folks on our trail and maybe be nabbed.

We got into Saratoga as I said at night and went to the track. Bildad fed us up. He showed us a place to sleep in hay over a shed and promised to keep still. Niggers are all right about things like that. They won't squeal on you. Often a white man you might meet, when you had run away from home like that, might appear to be all right and give you a quarter or a half-dollar or something, and then go right and give you away. White men will do that, but not a nigger. You can trust them. They are squarer with kids. I don't know why.

At the Saratoga meeting that year there were a lot of men from home. Dave Williams and Arthur Mulford and Jerry Myers and others. Then there was a lot from Louisville and Lexington Henry Rieback knew but I didn't. They were professional gamblers and Henry Rieback's father is one too. He is what is called a sheet writer and goes away most of the year to tracks. In the winter when he is home in Beckersville he don't stay there much but goes away to cities and deals faro. He is a nice man and generous, is always sending Henry presents, a bicycle and a gold watch and a boy scout suit of clothes and things like that.

My own father is a lawyer. He's all right, but don't make much money and can't buy me things and anyway I'm getting so old now I don't expect it. He never said nothing to me against Henry, but Hanley Turner and Tom Tumberton's fathers did. They said to their boys that money so come by is no good and they didn't want their boys brought up to hear gamblers' talk and be thinking about such things and maybe embrace them.

That's all right and I guess the men know what they are talking about, but I don't see what it's got to do with Henry or with horses either. That's what I'm writing this story about. I'm puzzled. I'm getting to be a man and want to think straight and be O.K., and there's something I saw at the race meeting at the eastern track I can't figure out.

I can't help it, I'm crazy about thoroughbred horses. I've always been that way. When I was ten years old and saw I was growing to be big and couldn't be a rider I was so sorry I nearly died. Harry Hellinfinger in Beckersville, whose father is Postmaster, is grown up and too lazy to work, but liked to stand around in the street and get up jokes on boys like sending them to a hardware store for a gimlet to bore square holes and other jokes like that. He played one on me. He told me that if I would eat a half a cigar I would be stunted and not grow any more and maybe could be a rider. I did it. When father wasn't looking I took a cigar out of his pocket and gagged it down some way. It made me awful sick and the doctor had to be sent for, and then it did no good. I kept right on growing. It was a joke. When I told what I had done and why most fathers would have whipped me but mine didn't.

Well, I didn't get stunted and didn't die. It serves Harry Hellinfinger right. Then I made up my mind I would like to be a stable boy, but had to give that up too. Mostly niggers do that work and I knew father wouldn't let me go into it. No use to ask him.

If you've never been crazy about thoroughbreds it's because you've never been around where they are much and don't know any better. They're beautiful. There isn't anything so lovely and clean and full of spunk and honest and everything as some race horses. On the big horse farms that are all around our town Beckersville there are tracks and the horses run in the early morning. More than a thousand times I've got out of bed before day-light and walked two or three miles to the tracks. Mother wouldn't of let me go but father always says, "Let him alone." So I got some bread out of the bread box and some butter and jam, gobbled it and lit out.

At the tracks you sit on the fence with men, whites and niggers, and they chew tobacco and talk, and then the colts are brought out. It's early and the grass is covered with shiny dew and in another field a man is plowing and they are frying things in a shed where the track niggers sleep, and you know how a nigger can giggle and laugh and say things that make you laugh. A white man can't do it and some niggers can't but a track nigger can every time.

And so the colts are brought out and some are just galloped by stable boys, but almost every morning on a big track owned by a rich man who lives maybe in New York, there are always, nearly every morning, a few colts and some of the old race horses and geldings and mares that are cut loose.

It brings a lump up into my throat when a horse runs. I don't mean all horses but some. I can pick them nearly every time. It's in my blood like in the blood of race track niggers and trainers. Even when they just go slob-jogging along with a little nigger on their backs I can tell a winner. If my throat hurts and it's hard for me to swallow, that's him. He'll run like Sam Hill when you let him out. If he don't win every time it'll be a wonder and because they've got him in a pocket behind another or he was pulled or got off bad at the post or something. If I wanted to be a gambler like Henry Rieback's father I could get rich. I know I could and Henry says so, too. All I would have to do is to wait 'til that hurt comes when I see a horse and then bet every cent. That's what I could do if I wanted to be a gambler, but I don't.

When you're at the tracks in the morning—not the race tracks but the training tracks around Beckersville—you don't see a horse the kind I've been talking about, very often, but it's nice anyway. Any thoroughbred, that is sired right and out of a good mare and trained by a man that knows how, can run. If he couldn't what would he be there for and not pulling a plow?

Well, out of the stables they come and the boys are on their backs and it's lovely to be there. You hunch down on top of the fence and itch inside you. Over in the sheds the niggers giggle and sing. Bacon is being fried and coffee made. Everything smells lovely. Nothing smells better than coffee and manure and horses and niggers and bacon frying and pipes being smoked out of doors on a morning like that. It just gets you, that's what it does.

But about Saratoga. We was there six days and not a soul from home seen us and everything came off just as we wanted it to, fine weather and horses and races and all. We beat our way home and Bildad gave us a basket with fried chicken and bread and other eatables in, and I had eighteen dollars when we got back to Beckersville. Mother jawed and cried but Pop didn't say much. I told everything we done except one thing. I did and saw that alone. That's what I'm writing about. It got me upset. I think about it at night. Here it is.

At Saratoga we laid up nights in the hay in the shed Bildad had showed us and ate with the niggers early and at night when the race people had all gone away. The men from home stayed mostly in the grandstand and betting field, and didn't come out around the places where the horses are kept except to the paddocks just before a race when the horses are saddled. At Saratoga they don't have paddocks under an open shed as at Lexington and Churchill Downs and other tracks down in our country, but saddle the horses right out in an open place under trees on a lawn as smooth and nice as Banker Bohon's front yard here in Beckersville. It's lovely. The horses are sweaty and nervous and shine and the men come out and smoke cigars and look at them and the trainers are there and the owners, and your heart thumps so you can hardly breathe.

Then the bugle blows for post and the boys that ride come running out with their silk clothes on and you run to get a place by the fence with the niggers.

I always am wanting to be a trainer or owner, and at the risk of being seen and caught and sent home I went to the paddocks before every race. The other boys didn't but I did.

We got to Saratoga on a Friday and on Wednesday the next week the big Mullford Handicap was to be run. Middlestride was in it and Sunstreak. The weather was fine and the track fast. I couldn't sleep the night before.

What had happened was that both these horses are the kind it makes my throat hurt to see. Middlestride is long and looks awkward and is a gelding. He belongs to Joe Thompson, a little owner from home who only has a half-dozen horses. The Mullford Handicap is for a mile and Middlestride can't untrack fast. He goes away slow and is always way back at the half, then he begins to run and if the race is a mile and a quarter he'll just eat up everything and get there.

Sunstreak is different. He is a stallion and nervous and belongs on the biggest farm we've got in our country, the Van Riddle place that belongs to Mr. Van Riddle of New York. Sunstreak is like a girl you think about sometimes but never see. He is hard all over and lovely too. When you look at his head you want to kiss him. He is trained by Jerry Tillford who knows me and has been good to me lots of times, lets me walk into a horse's stall to look at him close and other things. There isn't anything as sweet as that horse. He stands at the post quiet and not letting on, but he is just burning up inside. Then when the barrier goes up he is off like his name, Sunstreak. It makes you ache to see him. It hurts you. He just lays down and runs like a bird dog. There can't anything I ever see run like him except Middlestride when he gets untracked and stretches himself.

Gee! I ached to see that race and those two horses run, ached and dreaded it too. I didn't want to see either of our horses beaten. We had never sent a pair like that to the races before. Old men in Beckersville said so and the niggers said so. It was a fact.

Before the race I went over to the paddocks to see. I looked a last look at Middlestride, who isn't such a much standing in a paddock that way, then I went to see Sunstreak.

It was his day. I knew when I see him. I forgot all about being seen myself and walked right up. All the men from Beckersville were there and no one noticed me except Jerry Tillford. He saw me and something happened. I'll tell you about that.

I was standing looking at that horse and aching. In some way, I can't tell how, I knew just how Sunstreak felt inside. He was quiet and letting the niggers rub his legs and Mr. Van Riddle himself put the saddle on, but he was just a raging torrent inside. He was like the water in the river at Niagara Falls just before it goes plunk down. That horse wasn't thinking about running. He don't have to think about that. He was just thinking about holding himself back 'til the time for the running came. I knew that. I could just in a way see right inside him. He was going to do some awful running and I knew it. He wasn't bragging or letting on much or prancing or making a fuss, but just waiting. I knew it and Jerry Tillford his trainer knew. I looked up and then that man and I looked into each other's eyes. Something happened to me. I guess I loved the man as much as I did the horse because he knew what I knew. Seemed to me there wasn't anything in the world but that man and the horse and me. I cried and Jerry Tillford had a shine in his eyes. Then I came away to the fence to wait for the race. The horse was better than me, more steadier, and now I know better than Jerry. He was the quietest and he had to do the running.

Sunstreak ran first of course and he busted the world's record for a mile. I've seen that if I never see anything more. Everything came out just as I expected. Middlestride got left at the post and was way back and closed up to be second, just as I knew he would. He'll get a world's record too some day. They can't skin the Beckersville country on horses.

I watched the race calm because I knew what would happen. I was sure.

Hanley Turner and Henry Rieback and Tom Tumberton were all more excited than me.

A funny thing had happened to me. I was thinking about Jerry Tillford the trainer and how happy he was all through the race. I liked him that afternoon even more than I ever liked my own father. I almost forgot the horses thinking that way about him. It was because of what I had seen in his eyes as he stood in the paddocks beside Sunstreak before the race started. I knew he had been watching and working with Sunstreak since the horse was a baby colt, had taught him to run and be patient and when to let himself out and not to quit, never. I knew that for him it was like a mother seeing her child do something brave or wonderful. It was the first time I ever felt for a man like that.

After the race that night I cut out from Tom and Hanley and Henry. I wanted to be by myself and I wanted to be near Jerry Tillford if I could work it. Here is what happened.

The track in Saratoga is near the edge of town. It is all polished up and trees around, the evergreen kind, and grass and everything painted and nice. If you go past the track you get to a hard road made of asphalt for automobiles, and if you go along this for a few miles there is a road turns off to a little rummy-looking farm house set in a yard.

That night after the race I went along that road because I had seen Jerry and some other men go that way in an automobile. I didn't expect to find them. I walked for a ways and then sat down by a fence to think. It was the direction they went in. I wanted to be as near Jerry as I could. I felt close to him. Pretty soon I went up the side road—I don't know why—and came to the rummy farm house. I was just lonesome to see Jerry, like wanting to see your father at night when you are a young kid. Just then an automobile came along and turned in. Jerry was in it and Henry Rieback's father, and Arthur Bedford from home, and Dave Williams and two other men I didn't know. They got out of the car and went into the house, all but Henry Rieback's father who quarreled with them and said he wouldn't go. It was only about nine o'clock, but they were all drunk and the rummy-looking farm house was a place for bad women to stay in. That's what it was. I crept up along a fence and looked through a window and saw.

It's what give me the fantods. I can't make it out. The women in the house were all ugly mean-looking women, not nice to look at or be near. They were homely too, except one who was tall and looked a little like the gelding Middlestride, but not clean like him, but with a hard ugly mouth. She had red hair. I saw everything plain. I got up by an old rose bush by an open window and looked. The women had on loose dresses and sat around in chairs. The men came in and some sat on the women's laps. The place smelled rotten and there was rotten talk, the kind a kid hears around a livery stable in a town like Beckersville in the winter but don't ever expect to hear talked when there are women around. It was rotten. A nigger wouldn't go into such a place.

I looked at Jerry Tillford. I've told you how I had been feeling about him on account of his knowing what was going on inside of Sunstreak in the minute before he went to the post for the race in which he made a world's record.

Jerry bragged in that bad woman house as I know Sunstreak wouldn't never have bragged. He said that he made that horse, that it was him that won the race and made the record. He lied and bragged like a fool. I never heard such silly talk.

And then, what do you suppose he did! He looked at the woman in there, the one that was lean and hard-mouthed and looked a little like the gelding Middlestride, but not clean like him, and his eyes began to shine just as they did when he looked at me and at Sunstreak in the paddocks at the track in the afternoon. I stood there by the window—gee!—but I wished I hadn't gone away from the tracks, but had stayed with the boys and the niggers and the horses. The tall rotten-looking woman was between us just as Sunstreak was in the paddocks in the afternoon.

Then, all of a sudden, I began to hate that man. I wanted to scream and rush in the room and kill him. I never had such a feeling before. I was so mad clean through that I cried and my fists were doubled up so my finger nails cut my hands.

And Jerry's eyes kept shining and he waved back and forth, and then he went and kissed that woman and I crept away and went back to the tracks and to bed and didn't sleep hardly any, and then next day I got the other kids to start home with me and never told them anything I seen.

I been thinking about it ever since. I can't make it out. Spring has come again and I'm nearly sixteen and go to the tracks mornings same as always, and I see Sunstreak and Middlestride and a new colt named Strident I'll bet will lay them all out, but no one thinks so but me and two or three niggers.

But things are different. At the tracks the air don't taste as good or smell as good. It's because a man like Jerry Tillford, who knows what he does, could see a horse like Sunstreak run, and kiss a woman like that the same day. I can't make it out. Darn him, what did he want to do like that for? I keep thinking about it and it spoils looking at horses and smelling things and hearing niggers laugh and everything. Sometimes I'm so mad about it I want to fight someone. It gives me the fantods. What did he do it for? I want to know why.

Araby*

JAMES JOYCE [1882–1941]

NORTH Richmond Street, being blind, was a quiet street except at the hour when the Christian Brothers' School set the boys free. An uninhabited house of two storeys stood at the blind end, detached from its neighbours in a square ground. The other houses of the street, conscious of decent lives within them, gazed at one another with brown imperturbable faces.

The former tenant of our house, a priest, had died in the back drawing-room. Air, musty from having been long enclosed, hung in all the rooms, and the waste room behind the kitchen was littered with old useless papers. Among these I found a few paper-covered books, the pages of which were curled and damp: *The Abbot*, by Walter Scott, *The Devout Communicant* and *The Memoirs of Vidocq*. I liked the last best because its leaves were yellow. The wild garden behind the house contained a central apple-tree and a few straggling bushes under one of which I found the late tenant's rusty bicycle-pump. He had been a very charitable priest; in his will he had left all his money to institutions and the furniture of his house to his sister.

When the short days of winter came dusk fell before we had well eaten our dinners. When we met in the street the houses had grown sombre. The space of sky above us was the colour of ever-changing violet and towards it the lamps of the street lifted their feeble lanterns. The cold air stung us and we played till our bodies glowed. Our shouts echoed in the silent street. The career of our play brought us through the dark muddy lanes behind the houses where we ran the gauntlet of the rough tribes from the cottages, to the back doors of the dark dripping gardens where odours arose from the ashpits, to the dark odorous stables where a coachman smoothed and combed the horse or shook music from the buckled harness. When we returned to the street light from the kitchen windows had filled the areas. If my uncle was seen turning the corner we hid in the shadow until we had seen him safely housed. Or if Mangan's sister came out on the doorstep to call her brother in to his tea we watched her from our shadow peer up and down the street. We waited to see whether she would remain or go in and, if she remained, we left our shadow and walked up to Mangan's steps resignedly. She was waiting for us, her figure defined by the light from the half-opened door. Her brother always teased her before he obeyed and I stood by the railings looking at her. Her dress swung as she moved her body and the soft rope of her hair tossed from side to side.

*This story is considered in the essay "Reading Fiction" at the end of the book.

Every morning I lay on the floor in the front parlour watching her door. The blind was pulled down to within an inch of the sash so that I could not be seen. When she came out on the doorstep my heart leaped. I ran to the hall, seized my books and followed her. I kept her brown figure always in my eye and, when we came near the point at which our ways diverged, I quickened my pace and passed her. This happened morning after morning. I had never spoken to her, except for a few casual words, and yet her name was like a summons to all my foolish blood.

Her image accompanied me even in places the most hostile to romance. On Saturday evenings when my aunt went marketing I had to go to carry some of the parcels. We walked through the flaring streets, jostled by drunken men and bargaining women, amid the curses of labourers, the shrill litanies of shop-boys who stood on guard by the barrels of pigs' cheeks, the nasal chanting of street-singers, who sang a *come-all-you*[1] about O'Donovan Rossa, or a ballad about the troubles in our native land. These noises converged in a single sensation of life for me: I imagined that I bore my chalice safely through a throng of foes. Her name sprang to my lips at moments in strange prayers and praises which I myself did not understand. My eyes were often full of tears (I could not tell why) and at times a flood from my heart seemed to pour itself out into my bosom. I thought little of the future. I did not know whether I would ever speak to her or not or, if I spoke to her, how I could tell her of my confused adoration. But my body was like a harp and her words and gestures were like fingers running upon the wires.

One evening I went into the back drawing-room in which the priest had died. It was a dark rainy evening and there was no sound in the house. Through one of the broken panes I heard the rain impinge upon the earth, the fine incessant needles of water playing in the sodden beds. Some distant lamp or lighted window gleamed below me. I was thankful that I could see so little. All my senses seemed to desire to veil themselves and, feeling that I was about to slip from them, I pressed the palms of my hands together until they trembled, murmuring: "*O love! O love!*" many times.

At last she spoke to me. When she addressed the first words to me I was so confused that I did not know what to answer. She asked me was I going to *Araby.* I forgot whether I answered yes or no. It would be a splendid bazaar, she said she would love to go.

"And why can't you?" I asked.

While she spoke she turned a silver bracelet round and round her wrist. She could not go, she said, because there would be a retreat that week in her convent. Her brother and two other boys were fighting for their caps and I was alone at the railings. She held one of the spikes, bowing her head towards me. The light from the lamp opposite our door caught the white curve of her neck, lit up her hair that rested there and, falling, lit up the hand

---

1. A street ballad beginning with these words. This one is about Jeremiah Donovan, a nineteenth-century Irish nationalist popularly known as O'Donovan Rossa.

upon the railing. It fell over one side of her dress and caught the white border of a petticoat, just visible as she stood at ease.

"It's well for you," she said.

"If I go," I said, "I will bring you something."

What innumerable follies laid waste my waking and sleeping thoughts after that evening! I wished to annihilate the tedious intervening days. I chafed against the work of school. At night in my bedroom and by day in the classroom her image came between me and the page I strove to read. The syllables of the word *Araby* were called to me through the silence in which my soul luxuriated and cast an Eastern enchantment over me. I asked for leave to go to the bazaar on Saturday night. My aunt was surprised and hoped it was not some Freemason affair. I answered few questions in class. I watched my master's face pass from amiability to sternness; he hoped I was not beginning to idle. I could not call my wandering thoughts together. I had hardly any patience with the serious work of life which, now that it stood between me and my desire, seemed to me child's play, ugly monotonous child's play.

On Saturday morning I reminded my uncle that I wished to go to the bazaar in the evening. He was fussing at the hallstand, looking for the hat-brush, and answered me curtly:

"Yes, boy, I know."

As he was in the hall I could not go into the front parlour and lie at the window. I left the house in bad humour and walked slowly towards the school. The air was pitilessly raw and already my heart misgave me.

When I came home to dinner my uncle had not yet been home. Still it was early. I sat staring at the clock for some time and, when its ticking began to irritate me, I left the room. I mounted the staircase and gained the upper part of the house. The high cold empty gloomy rooms liberated me and I went from room to room singing. From the front window I saw my companions playing below in the street. Their cries reached me weakened and indistinct and, leaning my forehead against the cool glass, I looked over at the dark house where she lived. I may have stood there for an hour, seeing nothing but the brown-clad figure cast by my imagination, touched discreetly by the lamplight at the curved neck, at the hand upon the railings and at the border below the dress.

When I came downstairs again I found Mrs. Mercer sitting at the fire. She was an old garrulous woman, a pawnbroker's widow, who collected used stamps for some pious purpose. I had to endure the gossip of the tea-table. The meal was prolonged beyond an hour and still my uncle did not come. Mrs. Mercer stood up to go: she was sorry she couldn't wait any longer, but it was after eight o'clock and she did not like to be out late, as the night air was bad for her. When she had gone I began to walk up and down the room, clenching my fists. My aunt said:

"I'm afraid you may put off your bazaar for this night of Our Lord."

At nine o'clock I heard my uncle's latchkey in the halldoor. I heard him talking to himself and heard the hallstand rocking when it had received the weight of his overcoat. I could interpret these signs. When he was midway through his dinner I asked him to give me the money to go to the bazaar. He had forgotten.

"The people are in bed and after their first sleep now," he said.

I did not smile. My aunt said to him energetically:

"Can't you give him the money and let him go? You've kept him late enough as it is."

My uncle said he was very sorry he had forgotten. He said he believed in the old saying: "All work and no play makes Jack a dull boy." He asked me where I was going and, when I had told him a second time he asked me did I know *The Arab's Farewell to his Steed*. When I left the kitchen he was about to recite the opening lines of the piece to my aunt.

I held a florin tightly in my hand as I strode down Buckingham Street towards the station. The sight of the streets thronged with buyers and glaring with gas recalled to me the purpose of my journey. I took my seat in a third-class carriage of a deserted train. After an intolerable delay the train moved out of the station slowly. It crept onward among ruinous houses and over the twinkling river. At Westland Row Station a crowd of people pressed to the carriage doors; but the porters moved them back, saying that it was a special train for the bazaar. I remained alone in the bare carriage. In a few minutes the train drew up beside an improvised wooden platform. I passed out on to the road and saw by the lighted dial of a clock that it was ten minutes to ten. In front of me was a large building which displayed the magical name.

I could not find any sixpenny entrance and, fearing that the bazaar would be closed, I passed in quickly through a turnstile, handing a shilling to a weary-looking man. I found myself in a big hall girdled at half its height by a gallery. Nearly all the stalls were closed and the greater part of the hall was in darkness. I recognised a silence like that which pervades a church after a service. I walked into the centre of the bazaar timidly. A few people were gathered about the stalls which were still open. Before a curtain, over which the words *Café Chantant* were written in coloured lamps, two men were counting money on a salver. I listened to the fall of the coins.

Remembering with difficulty why I had come I went over to one of the stalls and examined porcelain vases and flowered tea-sets. At the door of the stall a young lady was talking and laughing with two young gentlemen. I remarked their English accents and listened vaguely to their conversation.

"O, I never said such a thing!"

"O, but you did!"

"O, but I didn't!"

"Didn't she say that?"

"Yes. I heard her."

"O, there's a ... fib!"

Observing me the young lady came over and asked me did I wish to buy anything. The tone of her voice was not encouraging; she seemed to have spoken to me out of a sense of duty. I looked humbly at the great jars that stood like eastern guards at either side of the dark entrance to the stall and murmured:

"No, thank you."

The young lady changed the position of one of the vases and went back to the two young men. They began to talk of the same subject. Once or twice the young lady glanced at me over her shoulder.

I lingered before her stall, though I knew my stay was useless, to make my interest in her wares seem the more real. Then I turned away slowly and walked down the middle of the bazaar. I allowed the two pennies to fall against the sixpence in my pocket. I heard a voice call from one end of the gallery that the light was out. The upper part of the hall was now completely dark.

Gazing up into the darkness I saw myself as a creature driven and derided by vanity; and my eyes burned with anguish and anger.

My Oedipus Complex

FRANK O'CONNOR [1903–1966]

FATHER was in the army all through the war—the first war, I mean—so, up to the age of five, I never saw much of him, and what I saw did not worry me. Sometimes I woke and there was a big figure in khaki peering down at me in the candlelight. Sometimes in the early morning I heard the slamming of the front door and the clatter of nailed boots down the cobbles of the lane. These were Father's entrances and exits. Like Santa Claus he came and went mysteriously.

In fact, I rather liked his visits, though it was an uncomfortable squeeze between Mother and him when I got into the big bed in the early morning. He smoked, which gave him a pleasant musty smell, and shaved, an operation of astounding interest. Each time he left a trail of souvenirs—model tanks and Gurkha knives with handles made of bullet cases, and German helmets and cap badges and button-sticks, and all sorts of military equipment—carefully stowed away in a long box on top of the wardrobe, in case they ever came in handy. There was a bit of the magpie about Father; he expected everything to come in handy. When his back was turned, Mother let me get a chair and rummage through his treasures. She didn't seem to think so highly of them as he did.

The war was the most peaceful period of my life. The window of my attic faced southeast. My mother had curtained it, but that had small effect. I always woke with the first light and, with all the responsibilities of the previous day melted, feeling myself rather like the sun, ready to illumine and rejoice. Life never seemed so simple and clear and full of possibilities as then. I put my feet out from under the clothes—I called them Mrs. Left and Mrs. Right—and invented dramatic situations for them in which they discussed the problems of the day. At least Mrs. Right did; she was very demonstrative, but I hadn't the same control of Mrs. Left, so she mostly contented herself with nodding agreement.

They discussed what Mother and I should do during the day, what Santa Claus should give a fellow for Christmas, and what steps should be taken to brighten the home. There was that little matter of the baby, for instance. Mother and I could never agree about that. Ours was the only house in the terrace without a new baby, and Mother said we couldn't afford one till Father came back from the war because they cost seventeen and six. That showed how simple she was. The Geneys up the road had a baby, and everyone knew they couldn't afford seventeen and six. It was probably a cheap baby, and Mother wanted something really good, but I felt she was too exclusive. The Geneys' baby would have done us fine.

Having settled my plans for the day, I got up, put a chair under the attic window, and lifted the frame high enough to stick out my head. The window overlooked the front gardens of the terrace behind ours, and beyond these it looked over a deep valley to the tall, red-brick houses terraced up the opposite hillside, which were all still in shadow, while those at our side of the valley were all lit up, though with long strange shadows that made them seem unfamiliar; rigid and painted.

After that I went into Mother's room and climbed into the big bed. She woke and I began to tell her of my schemes. By this time, though I never seem to have noticed it, I was petrified in my nightshirt, and I thawed as I talked until, the last frost melted, I fell asleep beside her and woke again only when I heard her below in the kitchen, making the breakfast.

After breakfast we went into town; heard Mass at St. Augustine's and said a prayer for Father, and did the shopping. If the afternoon was fine we either went for a walk in the country or a visit to Mother's great friend in the convent, Mother St. Dominic. Mother had them all praying for Father, and every night, going to bed, I asked God to send him back safe from the war to us. Little, indeed, did I know what I was praying for!

One morning, I got into the big bed, and there, sure enough, was Father in his usual Santa Claus manner, but later, instead of uniform, he put on his best blue suit, and Mother was as pleased as anything. I saw nothing to be pleased about, because, out of uniform, Father was altogether less interesting, but she only beamed, and explained that our prayers had been answered, and off we went to Mass to thank God for having brought Father safely home.

The irony of it! That very day when he came in to dinner he took off his boots and put on his slippers, donned the dirty old cap he wore about the house to save him from colds, crossed his legs, and began to talk gravely to Mother, who looked anxious. Naturally, I disliked her looking anxious, because it destroyed her good looks, so I interrupted him.

"Just a moment, Larry!" she said gently.

This was only what she said when we had boring visitors, so I attached no importance to it and went on talking.

"Do be quiet, Larry!" she said impatiently. "Don't you hear me talking to Daddy?"

This was the first time I had heard those ominous words, "talking to Daddy," and I couldn't help feeling that if this was how God answered prayers, he couldn't listen to them very attentively.

"Why are you talking to Daddy?" I asked with as great a show of indifference as I could muster.

"Because Daddy and I have business to discuss. Now, don't interrupt again!"

In the afternoon, at Mother's request, Father took me for a walk. This time we went into town instead of out to the country, and I thought at first, in my usual optimistic way, that it might be an improvement. It was nothing of the sort. Father and I had quite different notions of a walk in town. He had no proper interest in trams, ships, and horses, and the only thing that seemed to divert him was talking to fellows as old as himself. When I wanted to stop he simply went on, dragging me behind him by the hand; when he wanted to stop I had no alternative but to do the same. I noticed that it seemed to be a sign that he wanted to stop for a long time whenever he leaned against a wall. The second time I saw him do it I got wild. He seemed to be settling himself forever. I pulled him by the coat and trousers, but, unlike Mother who, if you were too persistent, got into a wax and said: "Larry, if you don't behave yourself, I'll give you a good slap," Father had an extraordinary capacity for amiable inattention. I sized him up and wondered would I cry, but he seemed to be too remote to be annoyed even by that. Really, it was like going for a walk with a mountain! He either ignored the wrenching and pummeling entirely, or else glanced down with a grin of amusement from his peak. I had never met anyone so absorbed in himself as he seemed.

At teatime, "talking to Daddy" began again, complicated this time by the fact that he had an evening paper, and every few minutes he put it down and told Mother something new out of it. I felt this was foul play. Man for man, I was prepared to compete with him any time for Mother's attention, but when he had it all made up for him by other people it left me no chance. Several times I tried to change the subject without success.

"You must be quiet while Daddy is reading, Larry," Mother said impatiently.

It was clear that she either genuinely liked talking to Father better than talking to me, or else that he had some terrible hold on her which made her afraid to admit the truth.

"Mummy," I said that night when she was tucking me up, "do you think if I prayed hard God would send Daddy back to the war?"

She seemed to think about that for a moment.

"No, dear," she said with a smile. "I don't think he would."

"Why wouldn't he, Mummy?"

"Because there isn't a war any longer, dear."

"But, Mummy, couldn't God make another war, if he liked?"

"He wouldn't like to, dear. It's not God who makes wars, but bad people."

"Oh!" I said.

I was disappointed about that. I began to think that God wasn't quite what he was cracked up to be.

Next morning I woke at my usual hour, feeling like a bottle of champagne. I put out my feet and invented a long conversation in which Mrs. Right talked of the trouble she had with her own father till she put him in the Home. I didn't quite know what the Home was but it sounded the right place for Father. Then I got my chair and stuck my head out of the attic window. Dawn was just breaking, with a guilty air that made me feel I had caught it in the act. My head bursting with stories and schemes, I stumbled in next door, and in the half-darkness scrambled into the big bed. There was no room at

Mother's side so I had to get between her and Father. For the time being I had forgotten about him, and for several minutes I sat bolt upright, racking my brains to know what I could do with him. He was taking up more than his fair share of the bed, and I couldn't get comfortable, so I gave him several kicks that made him grunt and stretch. He made room all right, though. Mother waked and felt for me. I settled back comfortably in the warmth of the bed with my thumb in my mouth.

"Mummy!" I hummed, loudly and contentedly.

"Sssh! dear," she whispered. "Don't wake Daddy!"

This was a new development, which threatened to be even more serious than "talking to Daddy." Life without my early-morning conferences was unthinkable.

"Why?" I asked severely.

"Because poor Daddy is tired."

This seemed to me a quite inadequate reason, and I was sickened by the sentimentality of her "poor Daddy." I never liked that sort of gush; it always struck me as insincere.

"Oh!" I said lightly. Then in my most winning tone: "Do you know where I want to go with you today, Mummy?"

"No, dear," she sighed.

"I want to go down the Glen and fish for thornybacks with my new net, and then I want to go out to the Fox and Hounds, and—"

"Don't-wake-Daddy!" she hissed angrily, clapping her hand across my mouth.

But it was too late. He was awake, or nearly so. He grunted and reached for the matches. Then he stared incredulously at his watch.

"Like a cup of tea, dear?" asked Mother in a meek, hushed voice I had never heard her use before. It sounded almost as though she were afraid.

"Tea?" he exclaimed indignantly. "Do you know what the time is?"

"And after that I want to go up the Rathcooney Road," I said loudly, afraid I'd forget something in all those interruptions.

"Go to sleep at once, Larry!" she said sharply.

I began to snivel. I couldn't concentrate, the way that pair went on, and smothering my early-morning schemes was like burying a family from the cradle.

Father said nothing, but lit his pipe and sucked it, looking out into the shadows without minding Mother or me. I knew he was mad. Every time I made a remark Mother hushed me irritably. I was mortified. I felt it wasn't fair; there was even something sinister in it. Every time I had pointed out to her the waste of making two beds when we could both sleep in one, she had told me it was healthier like that, and now here was this man, this stranger, sleeping with her without the least regard for her health!

He got up early and made tea, but though he brought Mother a cup he brought none for me.

"Mummy," I shouted, "I want a cup of tea, too."

"Yes, dear," she said patiently. "You can drink from Mummy's saucer."

That settled it. Either Father or I would have to leave the house. I didn't want to drink from Mother's saucer; I wanted to be treated as an equal in my own home, so, just to spite her, I drank it all and left none for her. She took that quietly, too.

But that night when she was putting me to bed she said gently: "Larry, I want you to promise me something."

"What is it?" I asked.

"Not to come in and disturb poor Daddy in the morning. Promise?"

"Poor Daddy" again! I was becoming suspicious of everything involving that quite impossible man.

"Why?" I asked.

"Because poor Daddy is worried and tired and he doesn't sleep well."

"Why doesn't he, Mummy?"

"Well, you know, don't you, that while he was at the war Mummy got the pennies from the Post Office?"

"From Miss MacCarthy?"

"That's right. But now, you see, Miss MacCarthy hasn't any more pennies, so Daddy must go out and find us some. You know what would happen if he couldn't?"

"No," I said, "tell us."

"Well, I think we might have to go out and beg for them like the poor old woman on Fridays. We wouldn't like that, would we?"

"No," I agreed. "We wouldn't."

"So you'll promise not to come in and wake him?"

"Promise."

Mind you, I meant that. I knew pennies were a serious matter, and I was all against having to go out and beg like the old woman on Fridays. Mother laid out all my toys in a complete ring round the bed so that, whatever way I got out, I was bound to fall over one of them.

When I woke I remembered my promise all right. I got up and sat on the floor and played—for hours, it seemed to me. Then I got my chair and looked out the attic window for more hours. I wished it was time for Father to wake; I wished someone would make me a cup of tea. I didn't feel in the least like the sun; instead, I was bored and so very, very cold! I simply longed for the warmth and depth of the big featherbed.

At last I could stand it no longer. I went into the next room. As there was still no room at Mother's side I climbed over her and she woke with a start.

"Larry," she whispered, gripping my arm very tightly, "what did you promise?"

"But I did, Mummy," I wailed, caught in the very act. "I was quiet for ever so long."

"Oh, dear, and you're perished!" she said sadly, feeling me all over. "Now, if I let you stay will you promise not to talk?"

"But I want to talk, Mummy," I wailed.

"That has nothing to do with it," she said with a firmness that was new to me. "Daddy wants to sleep. Now, do you understand that?"

I understood it only too well. I wanted to talk, he wanted to sleep—whose house was it, anyway?

"Mummy," I said with equal firmness, "I think it would be healthier for Daddy to sleep in his own bed."

That seemed to stagger her, because she said nothing for a while.

"Now, once for all," she went on, "you're to be perfectly quiet or go back to your own bed. Which is it to be?"

The injustice of it got me down. I had convicted her out of her own mouth of inconsistency and unreasonableness, and she hadn't even attempted to reply. Full of spite, I gave Father a kick, which she didn't notice but which made him grunt and open his eyes in alarm.

"What time is it?" he asked in a panic-stricken voice, not looking at Mother but the door, as if he saw someone there.

"It's early yet," she replied soothingly. "It's only the child. Go to sleep again.... Now, Larry," she added, getting out of bed, "you've wakened Daddy and you must go back."

This time, for all her quiet air, I knew she meant it, and knew that my principal rights and privileges were as good as lost unless I asserted them at once. As she lifted me, I gave a screech, enough to wake the dead, not to mind Father. He groaned.

"That damn child! Doesn't he ever sleep?"

"It's only a habit, dear," she said quietly, though I could see she was vexed.

"Well, it's time he got out of it," shouted Father, beginning to heave in the bed. He suddenly gathered all the bedclothes about him, turned to the wall, and then looked back over his shoulder with nothing showing only two small, spiteful, dark eyes. The man looked very wicked.

To open the bedroom door, Mother had to let me down, and I broke free and dashed for the farthest corner, screeching. Father sat bolt upright in bed.

"Shut up, you little puppy!" he said in a choking voice.

I was so astonished that I stopped screeching. Never, never had anyone spoken to me in that tone before. I looked at him incredulously and saw his face convulsed with rage. It was only then that I fully realized how God had codded me, listening to my prayers for the safe return of this monster.

"Shut up, you!" I bawled, beside myself.

"What's that you said?" shouted Father, making a wild leap out of bed.

"Mick, Mick!" cried Mother. "Don't you see the child isn't used to you?"

"I see he's better fed than taught," snarled Father, waving his arms wildly. "He wants his bottom smacked."

All his previous shouting was as nothing to these obscene words referring to my person. They really made my blood boil.

"Smack your own!" I screamed hysterically. "Smack your own! Shut up! Shut up!"

At this he lost his patience and let fly at me. He did it with the lack of conviction you'd expect of a man under Mother's horrified eyes, and it ended up as a mere tap, but the sheer indignity of being struck at all by a stranger, a total stranger who had cajoled his way back from the war into our big bed as a result of my innocent intercession, made me completely dotty. I shrieked and shrieked, and danced in my bare feet, and Father, looking awkward and hairy in nothing but a short grey army shirt, glared down at me like a mountain out for murder. I think it must have been then that I realized he was jealous too. And there stood Mother in her nightdress, looking as if her heart was broken between us. I hoped she felt as she looked. It seemed to me that she deserved it all.

From that morning out my life was a hell. Father and I were enemies, open and avowed. We conducted a series of skirmishes against one another, he trying to steal my time with Mother and I his. When she was sitting on my bed, telling me a story, he took to looking for some pair of old boots which he alleged he had left behind him at the beginning of the war. While he talked to Mother I played loudly with my toys to show my total lack of concern. He created a terrible scene one evening when he came in from work and found me at his box, playing with his regimental badges, Gurkha knives and button-sticks. Mother got up and took the box from me.

"You mustn't play with Daddy's toys unless he lets you, Larry," she said severely. "Daddy doesn't play with yours."

For some reason Father looked at her as if she had struck him and then turned away with a scowl.

"Those are not toys," he growled, taking down the box again to see had I lifted anything. "Some of those curios are very rare and valuable."

But as time went on I saw more and more how he managed to alienate Mother and me. What made it worse was that I couldn't grasp his method or see what attraction he had for Mother. In every possible way he was less winning than I. He had a common accent and made noises at his tea. I thought for a while that it might be the newspapers she was interested in, so I made up bits of news of my own to read to her. Then I thought it might be the smoking, which I personally thought attractive, and took his pipes and went round the house dribbling into them till he caught me. I even made noises at my tea, but Mother only told me I was disgusting. It all seemed to hinge round that unhealthy habit of sleeping together, so I made a point of dropping into their bedroom and nosing round, talking to myself, so that they wouldn't know I was watching them, but they were never up to anything that I could see. In the end it beat me. It seemed to depend on being grown-up and giving people rings, and I realized I'd have to wait.

But at the same time I wanted him to see that I was only waiting, not giving up the fight. One evening when he was being particularly obnoxious, chattering away well above my head, I let him have it.

"Mummy," I said, "do you know what I'm going to do when I grow up?"

"No, dear," she replied. "What?"

"I'm going to marry you," I said quietly.

Father gave a great guffaw out of him, but he didn't take me in. I knew it must only be pretense. And Mother, in spite of everything, was pleased. I felt she was probably relieved to know that one day Father's hold on her would be broken.

"Won't that be nice?" she said with a smile.

"It'll be very nice," I said confidently. "Because we're going to have lots and lots of babies."

"That's right, dear," she said placidly. "I think we'll have one soon, and then you'll have plenty of company."

I was no end pleased about that because it showed that in spite of the way she gave in to Father she still considered my wishes. Besides, it would put the Geneys in their place.

It didn't turn out like that, though. To begin with, she was very pre-occupied—I supposed about where she would get the seventeen and six—and though Father took to staying out late in the evenings it did me no particular good. She stopped taking me for walks, became as touchy as blazes, and smacked me for nothing at all. Sometimes I wished I'd never mentioned the confounded baby—I seemed to have a genius for bringing calamity on myself.

And calamity it was! Sonny arrived in the most appalling hullabaloo—even that much he couldn't do without a fuss—and from the first moment I disliked him. He was a difficult child—so far as I was concerned he was always difficult—and demanded far too much attention. Mother was simply silly about him, and couldn't see when he was only showing off. As company he was worse than useless. He slept all day, and I had to go round the house on tiptoe to avoid waking him. It wasn't any longer a question of not waking Father. The slogan now was "Don't-wake-Sonny!" I couldn't understand why the child wouldn't sleep at the proper time, so whenever Mother's back was turned I woke him. Sometimes to keep him awake I pinched him as well. Mother caught me at it one day and gave me a most unmerciful flaking.

One evening, when Father was coming from work, I was playing trains in the front garden. I let on not to notice him; instead, I pretended to be talking to myself, and said in a loud voice: "If another bloody baby comes into this house, I'm going out."

Father stopped dead and looked at me over his shoulder.

"What's that you said?" he asked sternly.

"I was only talking to myself," I replied, trying to conceal my panic. "It's private."

He turned and went in without a word. Mind you, I intended it as a solemn warning, but its effect was quite different. Father started being quite nice to me. I could understand that, of course. Mother was quite sickening about Sonny. Even at mealtimes she'd get up and gawk at him in the cradle with an idiotic smile, and tell Father to do the same. He was always polite about it, but he looked so puzzled you could see he didn't know what she was talking about. He complained of the way Sonny cried at night, but she only got cross and said that Sonny never cried except when there was something up with him—which was a flaming lie, because Sonny never had anything up with him, and only cried for attention. It was really painful to see how simple-minded she was. Father wasn't attractive, but he had a fine intelligence. He saw through Sonny, and now he knew that I saw through him as well.

One night I woke with a start. There was someone beside me in the bed. For one wild moment I felt sure it must be Mother, having come to her senses and left Father for good, but then I heard Sonny in convulsions in the next room, and Mother saying: "There! There! There!" and I knew it wasn't she. It was Father. He was lying beside me, wide awake, breathing hard and apparently as mad as hell.

After a while it came to me what he was mad about. It was his turn now. After turning me out of the big bed, he had been turned out himself. Mother had no consideration now for anyone but that poisonous pup, Sonny. I couldn't help feeling sorry for Father. I had been through it all myself, and even at that age I was magnanimous. I began to stroke him down and say: "There! There!" He wasn't exactly responsive.

"Aren't you asleep either?" he snarled.

"Ah, come on and put your arm around us, can't you?" I said, and he did, in a sort of way. Gingerly, I suppose, is how you'd describe it. He was very bony but better than nothing.

At Christmas he went out of his way to buy me a really nice model railway.

Questions

1. *Is the story narrated from the point of view of a young child or a mature man?* 2. *Note that the narrator's most ardent wishes—for the return of his father and for a new baby in the house—are granted. What are the consequences for him?* 3. *What specific details in the story contribute to the appropriateness of its title?* 4. *With whom does the reader sympathize? How does the author control those sympathies?*

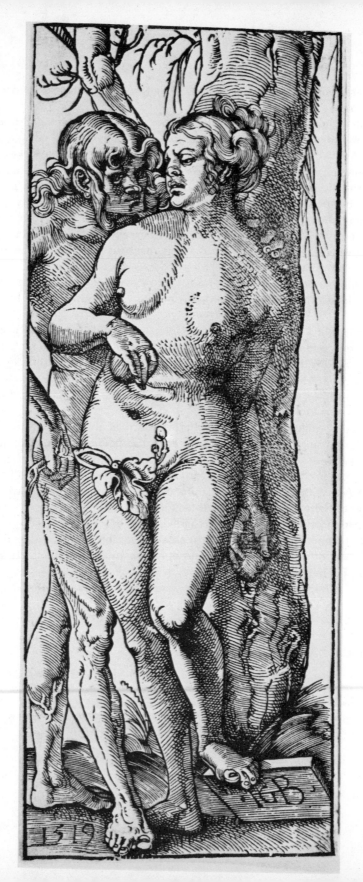

POETRY

The Chimney Sweeper

WILLIAM BLAKE   [1757–1827]

When my mother died I was very young,
And my Father sold me while yet my tongue
Could scarcely cry " 'weep! 'weep! 'weep! 'weep!"
So your chimneys I sweep, and in soot I sleep.

There's little Tom Dacre, who cried when his head,
That curled like a lamb's back, was shaved: so I said,
"Hush, Tom! never mind it, for when your head's bare
You know that the soot cannot spoil your white hair."

And so he was quiet and that very night
As Tom was a-sleeping, he had such a sight!   10
That thousands of sweepers, Dick, Joe, Ned, and Jack,
Were all of them locked up in coffins of black.

And by came an Angel who had a bright key,
And he opened the coffins and set them all free;
Then down a green plain leaping, laughing, they run,
And wash in a river, and shine in the Sun.

Then naked and white, all their bags left behind,
They rise upon clouds and sport in the wind;
And the Angel told Tom, if he'd be a good boy,
He'd have God for his father, and never want joy.   20

And so Tom awoke; and we rose in the dark,
And got with our bags and our brushes to work.
Though the morning was cold, Tom was happy and warm;
So if all do their duty they need not fear harm.

The Garden of Love

WILLIAM BLAKE [1757-1827]

I went to the Garden of Love,
And saw what I never had seen:
A Chapel was built in the midst,
Where I used to play on the green.

And the gates of this Chapel were shut,
And "Thou shalt not" writ over the door;
So I turn'd to the Garden of Love,
That so many sweet flowers bore,

And I saw it was filled with graves,
And tomb-stones where flowers should be: 10
And Priests in black gowns were walking their rounds,
And binding with briars my joys & desires.

1. What meanings does the word "love" have in this poem? 2. What is Blake's judgment on established religion? 3. Explain the meaning of "chapel" (l. 3) and of "briars" (l. 12).

To a Mouse
ON TURNING HER UP IN HER NEST WITH THE PLOUGH,
NOVEMBER, 1785

ROBERT BURNS [1759-1796]

Wee, sleekit,° cow'rin, tim'rous beastie,   *sleek*
O, what a panic's in thy breastie!
Thou need na start awa sae hasty,
          Wi' bickering° brattle!°   *hurried/scamper*
I wad be laith to rin an' chase thee,
          Wi' murd'ring pattle!°   *plowstaff*

I'm truly sorry man's dominion
Has broken Nature's social union,
An' justifies that ill opinion
          Which makes thee startle   10

At me, thy poor earth-born companion,
        An' fellow-mortal!

I doubt na, whiles,° but thou may thieve;   *sometimes*
What then? poor beastie, thou maun° live!   *must*
A daimen° icker° in a thrave°   *occasional/corn-ear/shock*
        'S a sma' request:
I'll get a blessin wi' the lave,°   *rest*
        And never miss't!

Thy wee bit housie, too, in ruin!
Its silly wa's the win's are strewin!   *20*
An' naething, now, to big° a new ane,   *build*
        O' foggage° green!   *mosses*
An' bleak December's winds ensuin,
        Baith snell° an' keen!   *bitter*

Thou saw the fields laid bare and waste,
An' weary winter comin fast,
An' cozie here, beneath the blast,
        Thou thought to dwell,
Till crash! the cruel coulter° past   *plowshare*
        Out thro' thy cell.   *30*

That wee bit heap o' leaves an' stibble
Has cost thee mony a weary nibble!
Now thou's turned out, for a' thy trouble,
        But° house or hald,   *without*
To thole° the winter's sleety dribble,   *endure*
        An' cranreuch° cauld!   *hoarfrost*

But, Mousie, thou art no thy lane°   *not alone*
In proving foresight may be vain:
The best laid schemes o' mice an' men   *39*
        Gang° aft a-gley.°   *go / awry*
An' lea'e us nought but grief an' pain
        For promised joy.

Still thou art blest, compared wi' me!
The present only toucheth thee:
But och! I backward cast my e'e
        On prospects drear!
An' forward, tho' I canna see,
        I guess an' fear!

Lines[1]

COMPOSED A FEW MILES ABOVE TINTERN ABBEY
ON REVISITING THE BANKS OF THE WYE
DURING A TOUR. JULY 13, 1798

WILLIAM WORDSWORTH [1770–1850]

Five years have passed;[2] five summers, with the length
Of five long winters! and again I hear
These waters, rolling from their mountain-springs
With a soft inland murmur. Once again
Do I behold these steep and lofty cliffs,
That on a wild secluded scene impress
Thoughts of more deep seclusion; and connect
The landscape with the quiet of the sky.
The day is come when I again repose
Here, under this dark sycamore, and view   10
These plots of cottage ground, these orchard tufts,
Which at this season, with their unripe fruits,
Are clad in one green hue, and lose themselves
'Mid groves and copses. Once again I see
These hedgerows, hardly hedgerows, little lines
Of sportive wood run wild; these pastoral farms,
Green to the very door; and wreaths of smoke
Sent up, in silence, from among the trees!
With some uncertain notice, as might seem
Of vagrant dwellers in the houseless woods,   20
Or of some Hermit's cave, where by his fire
The Hermit sits alone.

                These beauteous forms,
Through a long absence, have not been to me
As is a landscape to a blind man's eye;
But oft, in lonely rooms, and 'mid the din
Of towns and cities, I have owed to them,
In hours of weariness, sensations sweet,
Felt in the blood, and felt along the heart;
And passing even into my purer mind,
With tranquil restoration—feelings too   30
Of unremembered pleasure; such, perhaps,
As have no slight or trivial influence
On that best portion of a good man's life,

---

1. Wordsworth wrote this poem during a four- or five-day walking tour through the Wye valley with his sister Dorothy.
2. The poet had visited the region on a solitary walking tour in August of 1793 when he was twenty-three years old.

His little, nameless, unremembered, acts
Of kindness and of love. Nor less, I trust,
To them I may have owed another gift,
Of aspect more sublime; that blessed mood,
In which the burthen of the mystery,
In which the heavy and the weary weight
Of all this unintelligible world,   40
Is lightened—that serene and blessed mood,
In which the affections gently lead us on—
Until, the breath of this corporeal frame
And even the motion of our human blood
Almost suspended, we are laid asleep
In body, and become a living soul;
While with an eye made quiet by the power
Of harmony, and the deep power of joy,
We see into the life of things.

                              If this
Be but a vain belief, yet, oh! how oft—   50
In darkness and amid the many shapes
Of joyless daylight; when the fretful stir
Unprofitable, and the fever of the world,
Have hung upon the beatings of my heart—
How oft, in spirit, have I turned to thee,
O sylvan Wye! thou wanderer through the woods,
How often has my spirit turned to thee!

   And now, with gleams of half-extinguished thought
With many recognitions dim and faint,
And somewhat of a sad perplexity,   60
The picture of the mind revives again;
While here I stand, not only with the sense
Of present pleasure, but with pleasing thoughts
That in this moment there is life and food
For future years. And so I dare to hope,
Though changed, no doubt, from what I was when first
I came among these hills; when like a roe
I bounded o'er the mountains, by the sides
Of the deep rivers, and the lonely streams,
Wherever nature led—more like a man   70
Flying from something that he dreads than one
Who sought the thing he loved. For nature then
(The coarser pleasures of my boyish days,
And their glad animal movements all gone by)
To me was all in all.—I cannot paint
What then I was. The sounding cataract
Haunted me like a passion; the tall rock,
The mountain, and the deep and gloomy wood,
Their colors and their forms, were then to me
An appetite; a feeling and a love,   80

That had no need of a remoter charm,
By thought supplied, nor any interest
Unborrowed from the eye.—That time is past,
And all its aching joys are now no more,
And all its dizzy raptures. Not for this
Faint[3] I, nor mourn nor murmur; other gifts
Have followed; for such loss, I would believe,
Abundant recompense. For I have learned
To look on nature, not as in the hour
Of thoughtless youth; but hearing oftentimes   90
The still, sad music of humanity,
Nor harsh nor grating, though of ample power
To chasten and subdue. And I have felt
A presence that disturbs me with the joy
Of elevated thoughts; a sense sublime
Of something far more deeply interfused,
Whose dwelling is the light of setting suns,
And the round ocean and the living air,
And the blue sky, and in the mind of man:
A motion and a spirit, that impels   100
All thinking things, all objects of all thought,
And rolls through all things. Therefore am I still
A lover of the meadows and the woods,
And mountains; and of all that we behold
From this green earth; of all the mighty world
Of eye, and ear—both what they half create,
And what perceive; well pleased to recognize
In nature and the language of the sense
The anchor of my purest thoughts, the nurse,
The guide, the guardian of my heart, and soul   110
Of all my moral being.

                                        Nor perchance,
If I were not thus taught, should I the more
Suffer my genial spirits to decay:
For thou art with me here upon the banks
Of this fair river; thou my dearest Friend,[4]
My dear, dear Friend; and in thy voice I catch
The language of my former heart, and read
My former pleasures in the shooting lights
Of thy wild eyes. Oh! yet a little while
May I behold in thee what I was once,   120
My dear, dear Sister! and this prayer I make,
Knowing that Nature never did betray
The heart that loved her; 'tis her privilege,
Through all the years of this our life, to lead

---

3. Lose heart.
4. The poet addresses his sister Dorothy.

From joy to joy: for she can so inform
The mind that is within us, so impress
With quietness and beauty, and so feed
With lofty thoughts, that neither evil tongues,
Rash judgments, nor the sneers of selfish men,
Nor greetings where no kindness is, nor all   130
The dreary intercourse of daily life,
Shall e'er prevail against us, or disturb
Our cheerful faith, that all which we behold
Is full of blessings. Therefore let the moon
Shine on thee in thy solitary walk;
And let the misty mountain winds be free
To blow against thee: and, in after years,
When these wild ecstasies shall be matured
Into a sober pleasure; when thy mind
Shall be a mansion for all lovely forms,   140
Thy memory be as a dwelling place
For all sweet sounds and harmonies; oh! then,
If solitude, or fear, or pain, or grief
Should be thy portion, with what healing thoughts
Of tender joy wilt thou remember me,
And these my exhortations! Nor, perchance—
If I should be where I no more can hear
Thy voice, nor catch from thy wild eyes these gleams
Of past existence[5]—wilt thou then forget
That on the banks of this delightful stream   150
We stood together; and that I, so long
A worshiper of Nature, hither came
Unwearied in that service; rather say
With warmer love—oh! with far deeper zeal
Of holier love. Nor wilt thou then forget,
That after many wanderings, many years
Of absence, these steep woods and lofty cliffs,
And this green pastoral landscape, were to me
More dear, both for themselves and for thy sake!

1. In this poem the poet distinguishes between two important periods in his life: the first is described in lines 65–83, and the second is described in lines 83–111. How does he characterize these two periods?   **2.** The poem describes a visit to a familiar scene of the poet's youth and includes a meditation upon the changes that have occurred. Are the changes in the poet, the scene itself, or both?

---

5.   I.e., the poet's past experience. Note lines 116–119.

My Last Duchess

ROBERT BROWNING   [1812–1889]

FERRARA

That's my last Duchess painted on the wall,
Looking as if she were alive. I call
That piece a wonder, now: Frà Pandolf's⁶ hands
Worked busily a day, and there she stands.
Will't please you sit and look at her? I said
"Frà Pandolf" by design, for never read
Strangers like you that pictured countenance,
The depth and passion of its earnest glance,
But to myself they turned (since none puts by
The curtain I have drawn for you, but I)   10
And seemed as they would ask me, if they durst,
How such a glance came there; so, not the first
Are you to turn and ask thus. Sir, 'twas not
Her husband's presence only, called that spot
Of joy into the Duchess' cheek: perhaps
Frà Pandolf chanced to say "Her mantle laps
"Over my lady's wrist too much," or "Paint
"Must never hope to reproduce the faint
"Half-flush that dies along her throat": such stuff
Was courtesy, she thought, and cause enough   20
For calling up that spot of joy. She had
A heart—how shall I say?—too soon made glad,
Too easily impressed; she liked whate'er
She looked on, and her looks went everywhere.
Sir, 'twas all one! My favor at her breast,
The dropping of the daylight in the West,
The bough of cherries some officious fool
Broke in the orchard for her, the white mule
She rode with round the terrace—all and each
Would draw from her alike the approving speech,   30
Or blush, at least. She thanked men—good! but thanked
Somehow—I know not how—as if she ranked
My gift of a nine-hundred-years-old name
With anybody's gift. Who'd stoop to blame
This sort of trifling? Even had you skill
In speech—which I have not—to make your will
Quite clear to such an one, and say, "Just this
"Or that in you disgusts me; here you miss,
"Or there exceed the mark"—and if she let
Herself be lessoned so, nor plainly set

---

6. Frà Pandolf and Claus of Innsbruck (mentioned in the last line) are imaginary artists.

Her wits to yours, forsooth, and made excuse,   40
—E'en then would be some stooping; and I choose
Never to stoop. Oh sir, she smiled, no doubt,
Whene'er I passed her; but who passed without
Much the same smile? This grew; I gave commands;
Then all smiles stopped together. There she stands
As if alive. Will't please you rise? We'll meet
The company below, then. I repeat,
The Count your master's known munificence
Is ample warrant that no just pretense   50
Of mine for dowry will be disallowed;
Though his fair daughter's self, as I avowed
At starting, is my object. Nay, we'll go
Together down, sir. Notice Neptune, though,
Taming a sea-horse, thought a rarity,
Which Claus of Innsbruck cast in bronze for me!

1. To whom is the duke speaking and what is the occasion?   2. Is the duke an admirable character? Do you share his judgment of his last duchess? Explain.   3. Contrast the duke's moral and aesthetic sensibility.   4. Note that this poem employs the same prevailing meter and rhyme scheme as Pope's "An Essay on Man" (p.322), but that the effect is very different. Can you suggest why?

Out of the Cradle Endlessly Rocking

WALT WHITMAN   [1819–1892]

Out of the cradle endlessly rocking,
Out of the mocking-bird's throat, the musical shuttle,
Out of the Ninth-month[7] midnight,
Over the sterile sands and the fields beyond, where the child leaving his bed
     wander'd alone, bareheaded, barefoot,
Down from the shower'd halo,
Up from the mystic play of shadows twining and twisting as if they were alive,
Out from the patches of briers and blackberries,
From the memories of the bird that chanted to me,
From your memories sad brother, from the fitful risings and fallings I heard,
From under that yellow half-moon late-risen and swollen as if with tears,   10
From those beginning notes of yearning and love there in the mist,
From the thousand responses of my heart never to cease,
From the myriad thence-arous'd words,

---

7.   Quaker designation for September.

From the word stronger and more delicious than any,
From such as now they start the scene revisiting,
As a flock, twittering, rising, or overhead passing,
Borne hither, ere all eludes me, hurriedly,
A man, yet by these tears a little boy again,
Throwing myself on the sand, confronting the waves,
I, chanter of pains and joys, uniter of here and hereafter, 20
Taking all hints to use them, but swiftly leaping beyond them,
A reminiscence sing.

Once Paumanok,[8]
When the lilac-scent was in the air and Fifth-month grass was growing,
Up this seashore in some briers,
Two feather'd guests from Alabama, two together,
And their nest, and four light-green eggs spotted with brown,
And every day the he-bird to and fro near at hand,
And every day the she-bird crouch'd on her nest, silent, with bright eyes,
And every day I, a curious boy, never too close, never disturbing them, 30
Cautiously peering, absorbing, translating.

Shine! shine! shine!
Pour down your warmth, great sun!
While we bask, we two together.

Two together!
Winds blow south, or winds blow north,
Day come white, or night come black,
Home, or rivers and mountains from home,
Singing all time, minding no time,
While we two keep together. 40

Till of a sudden,
May-be kill'd, unknown to her mate,
One forenoon the she-bird crouch'd not on the nest,
Nor return'd that afternoon, nor the next,
Nor ever appear'd again.

And thenceforward all summer in the sound of the sea,
And at night under the full of the moon in calmer weather,
Over the hoarse surging of the sea,
Or flitting from brier to brier by day,
I saw, I heard at intervals the remaining one, the he-bird, 50
The solitary guest from Alabama.

Blow! blow! blow!
Blow up sea-winds along Paumanok's shore;
I wait and I wait till you blow my mate to me.

---

8. Paumanok is the Indian name of Long Island, where the poet was born and grew up.

Yes, when the stars glisten'd,
All night long on the prong of a moss-scallop'd stake,
Down almost amid the slapping waves,
Sat the lone singer wonderful causing tears.

He call'd on his mate,
He pour'd forth the meanings which I of all men know.   60

Yes my brother I know,
The rest might not, but I have treasur'd every note,
For more than once dimly down to the beach gliding,
Silent, avoiding the moonbeams, blending myself with the shadows,
Recalling now the obscure shapes, the echoes, the sounds and sights after
     their sorts,
The white arms out in the breakers tirelessly tossing,
I, with bare feet, a child, the wind wafting my hair,
Listen'd long and long.

Listen'd to keep, to sing, now translating the notes,
Following you my brother.   70

Soothe! soothe! soothe!
Close on its wave soothes the wave behind,
And again another behind embracing and lapping, every one close,
But my love soothes not me, not me.

Low hangs the moon, it rose late,
It is lagging—O I think it is heavy with love, with love.

O madly the sea pushes upon the land,
With love, with love.

O night! do I not see my love fluttering out among the breakers?
What is that little black thing I see there in the white?   80

Loud! loud! loud!
Loud I call to you, my love!

High and clear I shoot my voice over the waves,
Surely you must know who is here, is here,
You must know who I am, my love.

Low-hanging moon!
What is that dusky spot in your brown yellow?
O it is the shape, the shape of my mate!
O moon do not keep her from me any longer.

Land! land! O land!   90
Whichever way I turn, O I think you could give me my mate back again if you
     only would,
For I am almost sure I see her dimly whichever way I look.

O rising stars!
Perhaps the one I want so much will rise, will rise with some of you.

O throat! O trembling throat!
Sound clearer through the atmosphere!
Pierce the woods, the earth,
Somewhere listening to catch you must be the one I want.

Shake out carols!
Solitary here, the night's carols!   100
Carols of lonesome love! death's carols!
Carols under that lagging, yellow, waning moon!
O under that moon where she droops almost down into the sea!
O reckless despairing carols.

But soft! sink low!
Soft! let me just murmur,
And do you wait a moment you husky-nois'd sea,
For somewhere I believe I heard my mate responding to me,
So faint, I must be still, be still to listen,
But not altogether still, for then she might not come immediately to me.   110

Hither my love!
Here I am! here!
With this just-sustain'd note I announce myself to you,
This gentle call is for you my love, for you.

Do not be decoy'd elsewhere,
That is the whistle of the wind, it is not my voice,
That is the fluttering, the fluttering of the spray,
Those are the shadows of leaves.

O darkness! O in vain!
O I am very sick and sorrowful.   120

O brown halo in the sky near the moon, drooping upon the sea!
O troubled reflection in the sea!
O throat! O throbbing heart!
And I singing uselessly, uselessly all the night.

O past! O happy life! O songs of joy!
In the air, in the woods, over fields,
Loved! loved! loved! loved! loved!
But my mate no more, no more with me!
We two together no more.

The aria sinking, 130
All else continuing, the stars shining,
The winds blowing, the notes of the bird continuous echoing,
With angry moans the fierce old mother incessantly moaning,
On the sands of Paumanok's shore gray and rustling,
The yellow half-moon enlarged, sagging down, drooping, the face of the sea
almost touching,
The boy ecstatic, with his bare feet the waves, with his hair the atmosphere
dallying,
The love in the heart long pent, now loose, now at last tumultuously bursting,
The aria's meaning, the ears, the soul, swiftly depositing,
The strange tears down the cheeks coursing,
The colloquy there, the trio, each uttering, 140
The undertone, the savage old mother incessantly crying,
To the boy's soul's questions sullenly timing, some drown'd secret hissing,
To the outsetting bard.

Demon or bird! (said the boy's soul,)
Is it indeed toward your mate you sing? or is it really to me?
For I, that was a child, my tongue's use sleeping, now I have heard you,
Now in a moment I know what I am for, I awake,
And already a thousand singers, a thousand songs, clearer, louder and more
sorrowful than yours,
A thousand warbling echoes have started to life within me, never to die.

O you singer solitary, singing by yourself, projecting me, 150
O solitary me listening, never more shall I cease perpetuating you,
Never more shall I escape, never more the reverberations,
Never more the cries of unsatisfied love be absent from me,
Never again leave me to be the peaceful child I was before what there in the
night,
By the sea under the yellow and sagging moon,
The messenger there arous'd, the fire, the sweet hell within,
The unknown want, the destiny of me.

O give me the clew! (it lurks in the night here somewhere,)
O if I am to have so much, let me have more!

A word then, (for I will conquer it,) 160
The word final, superior to all,
Subtle, sent up—what is it?—I listen;
Are you whispering it, and have been all the time, you sea-waves?
Is that it from your liquid rims and wet sands?

Whereto answering, the sea,
Delaying not, hurrying not,
Whisper'd me through the night, and very plainly before daybreak,
Lisp'd to me the low and delicious word death,
And again death, death, death, death,
Hissing melodious, neither like the bird nor like my arous'd child's heart, 170

But edging near as privately for me rustling at my feet,
Creeping thence steadily up to my ears and laving me softly all over,
Death, death, death, death, death.

Which I do not forget,
But fuse the song of my dusky demon and brother,
That he sang to me in the moonlight on Paumanok's gray beach,
With the thousand responsive songs at random,
My own songs awaked from that hour,
And with them the key, the word up from the waves,
The word of the sweetest song and all songs,   180
That strong and delicious word which, creeping to my feet,
(Or like some old crone rocking the cradle, swathed in sweet garments, bend-
    ing aside,)
The sea whisper'd me.

1. *In this poem Whitman reminisces about an event that proved crucial to him. What was the event? What awareness did it generate in the young boy?* **2.** *In what way does the young boy emulate the bird? (See ll. 114–157.)* **3.** *This poem utilizes neither rhyme nor metrical regularity. What poetic devices and patterns distinguish it from prose?*

The Ruined Maid

THOMAS HARDY [1840–1928]

"O'Melia, my dear, this does everything crown!
Who could have supposed I should meet you in Town?
And whence such fair garments, such prosperi-ty?"
"O didn't you know I'd been ruined?" said she.

"You left us in tatters, without shoes or socks,
Tired of digging potatoes, and spudding up docks;°   *digging herbs*
And now you've gay bracelets and bright feathers three!"
"Yes: that's how we dress when we're ruined," said she.

"At home in the barton° you said 'thee' and 'thou,'   *farmyard*
And 'thik onn,' and 'theäs oon,' and 't'other; but now   10
Your talking quite fits 'ee for high compa-ny!"
"Some polish is gained with one's ruin," said she.

"Your hands were like paws then, your face blue and bleak
But now I'm bewitched by your delicate cheek,
And your little gloves fit as on any la-dy!"
"We never do work when we're ruined," said she.

"You used to call home-life a hag-ridden dream,
And you'd sigh, and you'd sock; but at present you seem
To know not of megrims° or melancho-ly!"   *sick headaches*
"True. One's pretty lively when ruined," said she.   20

"I wish I had feathers, a fine sweeping gown,
And a delicate face, and could strut about Town!"
"My dear—a raw country girl, such as you be,
Cannot quite expect that. You ain't ruined," said she.

Spring and Fall

TO A YOUNG CHILD

GERARD MANLEY HOPKINS [1844–1889]

Márgarét, áre you gríeving
Over Goldengrove unleaving?°   *losing leaves*
Leáves, líke the things of man, you
With your fresh thoughts care for, can you?
Áh! ás the heart grows older
It will come to such sights colder
By and by, nor spare a sigh
Though worlds of wanwood leafmeal[9] lie;
And yet you wíll weep and know why.
Now no matter, child, the name: 10
Sórrow's spríngs are the same.
Nor mouth had, no nor mind, expressed
What heart heard of, ghost° guessed: *soul*
It ís the blight man was born for,
It is Margaret you mourn for.

1. *In this poem Margaret grieves over the passing of spring and the coming of fall. What does the coming of fall symbolize?* **2.** *Why, when Margaret grows older, will she not sigh over the coming of fall?* **3.** *What are "Sorrow's springs" (l. 11)?*

---

9. Pale woods littered with mouldering leaves.

When I Was One-and-Twenty

A. E. HOUSMAN [1859–1936]

When I was one-and-twenty
    I heard a wise man say,
"Give crowns and pounds and guineas
    But not your heart away;
Give pearls away and rubies
    But keep your fancy free."
But I was one-and-twenty,
    No use to talk to me.

When I was one-and-twenty
    I heard him say again,
"The heart out of the bosom
    Was never given in vain;
'Tis paid with sighs a plenty
    And sold for endless rue."
And I am two-and-twenty,
    And oh, 'tis true, 'tis true.

Leda and the Swan [10]

WILLIAM BUTLER YEATS [1865–1939]

A sudden blow: the great wings beating still
Above the staggering girl, her thighs caressed
By the dark webs, her nape caught in his bill;
He holds her helpless breast upon his breast.

How can those terrified vague fingers push
The feathered glory from her loosening thighs?
And how can body, laid in that white rush,
But feel the strange heart beating where it lies?

---

10. In Greek myth, Zeus, in the form of a swan, rapes Leda. As a consequence, Helen and Clytemnestra are born. Each sister marries the king of a city-state; Helen marries Menelaus and Clytemnestra marries Agamemnon. Helen, the most beautiful woman on earth, elopes with Paris, a prince of Troy, an act that precipitates the Trojan War in which Agamemnon commands the combined Greek armies. The war ends with the destruction of Troy. Agamemnon, when he returns to his home, is murdered by his unfaithful wife.

A shudder in the loins engenders there
The broken wall, the burning roof and tower   *10*
And Agamemnon dead.
              Being so caught up,
So mastered by the brute blood of the air,
Did she put on his knowledge with his power
Before the indifferent beak could let her drop?

Among School Children

WILLIAM BUTLER YEATS   [1865–1939]

1

I walk through the long schoolroom questioning;
A kind old nun in a white hood replies;
The children learn to cipher and to sing,
To study reading-books and histories,
To cut and sew, be neat in everything
In the best modern way—the children's eyes
In momentary wonder stare upon
A sixty-year-old smiling public man.

2

I dream of a Ledaean body,[11] bent
Above a sinking fire, a tale that she   *10*
Told of a harsh reproof, or trivial event
That changed some childish day to tragedy—
Told, and it seemed that our two natures blent
Into a sphere from youthful sympathy,
Or else, to alter Plato's parable,
Into the yolk and white of the one shell.[12]

3

And thinking of that fit of grief or rage
I look upon one child or t'other there
And wonder if she stood so at that age—
For even daughters of the swan can share   *20*
Something of every paddler's heritage—

---

11. I.e., beautiful, evoking Leda, the mother of Helen of Troy. Yeats is recalling a woman he knew and loved.
12. In Plato's Symposium, one speaker advances the theory that originally humans were spherical creatures with four arms and four legs. Zeus cut them into two and, ever since, the separated parts have struggled to reunite. This is the "parable" Yeats changes in order to make it into a metaphor for communion between two people.

And had that color upon cheek or hair,
And thereupon my heart is driven wild:
She stands before me as a living child.

4

Her present image floats into the mind—
Did Quattrocento finger[13] fashion it
Hollow of cheek as though it drank the wind
And took a mess of shadows for its meat?
And I though never of Ledaean kind
Had pretty plumage once—enough of that,   30
Better to smile on all that smile, and show
There is a comfortable kind of old scarecrow.

5

What youthful mother, a shape upon her lap
Honey of generation had betrayed,
And that must sleep, shriek, struggle to escape
As recollection or the drug decide,[14]
Would think her son, did she but see that shape
With sixty or more winters on its head,
A compensation for the pang of his birth,   40
Or the uncertainty of his setting forth?

6

Plato thought nature but a spume that plays
Upon a ghostly paradigm of things;
Solider Aristotle played the taws
Upon the bottom of a king of kings;
World-famous golden-thighed Pythagoras
Fingered upon a fiddle-stick or strings
What a star sang and careless Muses heard.
Old clothes upon old sticks to scare a bird.[15]

---

13. Literally, four hundred. The word refers to the 1400's, the period of the Italian Renaissance.
14. Yeats alludes to an essay by Porphyry (c. 232–305) on the Thirteenth Book of Homer's *Odyssey*. The sweetness of honey describes the pleasure of copulation ("generation"), but the honey acts as a drug which expels the child from the happiness and security of the womb. Hence the infant is "betrayed" into the world and denied the memory of prenatal happiness. He then either sleeps, shrieks, or struggles to escape back into that prenatal bliss, depending on whether or not the drug successfully blanks his recollection.
15. In this stanza Yeats comments on three great Greek thinkers. Plato taught that everything in the world is an imperfect replica of an ideal form. Aristotle believed that natural objects are real (hence he is "solider"). He tutored Alexander the Great (a king of kings) and disciplined him with a strap (taws). Pythagoras, a sixth-century B.C. Greek philosopher-mathematician, explored the mathematical relationships of musical overtones. His followers venerated him, and legend asserts that he had a golden thigh. The last line sums up the collective accomplishments of these thinkers contemptuously. The poet moves in the next stanza to the objects that teachers and mothers worship, objects which contrast markedly with the preoccupations of ancient Greek philosophers.

7

Both nuns and mothers worship images,
But those the candles light are not as those
That animate a mother's reveries, 50
But keep a marble or a bronze repose.
And yet they too break hearts—O Presences
That passion, piety or affection knows,
And that all heavenly glory symbolize—
O self-born mockers of man's enterprise;

8

Labor is blossoming or dancing where
The body is not bruised to pleasure soul,
Nor beauty born out of its own despair, 60
Nor blear-eyed wisdom out of midnight oil.
O chestnut-tree, great-rooted blossomer,
Are you the leaf, the blossom or the bole?
O body swayed to music, O brightening glance,
How can we know the dancer from the dance?

1. *In this poem Yeats (who had been an Irish senator—i.e., a "public man") describes a visit to a classroom. Among the school children, he dreams of a woman he loved and imagines her as a young girl in just such a classroom. His dreaming leads him to a contemplation of old age and the value of life. He alludes to ancient teachers and calls them scarecrows. He returns to the present and suggests that nuns, like mothers, are vulnerable to the heartbreak of disappointed expectations. The second half of stanza 7 and all of stanza 8 distill abstractions from the preceding verses. Can you suggest what "Presences" (l. 53) refers to? What are the "mockers of man's enterprise" (l. 56), and why are they "self-born?"* **2.** *Explain the relationship between the first four lines and last four lines of stanza 8.*

Lapis Lazuli [16]

(FOR HARRY CLIFTON)

WILLIAM BUTLER YEATS [1865–1939]

I have heard that hysterical women say
They are sick of the palette and fiddle-bow,
Of poets that are always gay,
For everybody knows or else should know
That if nothing drastic is done
Aeroplane and Zeppelin will come out,

---

16. An azure blue, semiprecious stone, often carved in bas relief.

Pitch like King Billy[17] bomb-balls in
Until the town lie beaten flat.

All perform their tragic play,
There struts Hamlet, there is Lear,   *10*
That's Ophelia, that Cordelia;
Yet they, should the last scene be there,
The great stage curtain about to drop,
If worthy their prominent part in the play,
Do not break up their lines to weep.
They know that Hamlet and Lear are gay;
Gaiety transfiguring all that dread.
All men have aimed at, found and lost;
Black out; Heaven blazing into the head:
Tragedy wrought to its uttermost.   *20*
Though Hamlet rambles and Lear rages,
And all the drop-scenes drop at once
Upon a hundred thousand stages,
It cannot grow by an inch or an ounce.

On their own feet they came, or on shipboard,
Camelback, horseback, ass-back, mule-back,
Old civilizations put to the sword.
Then they and their wisdom went to rack:
No handiwork of Callimachus,[18]   *30*
Who handled marble as if it were bronze,
Made draperies that seemed to rise
When sea-wind swept the corner, stands;
His long lamp-chimney shaped like the stem
Of a slender palm, stood but a day;
All things fall and are built again,
And those that build them again are gay.

Two Chinamen, behind them a third,
Are carved in lapis lazuli,
Over them flies a long-legged bird,
A symbol of longevity;
The third, doubtless a serving-man,   *40*
Carries a musical instrument.

Every discoloration of the stone,
Every accidental crack or dent,
Seems a water-course or an avalanche,
Or lofty slope where it still snows
Though doubtless plum or cherry-branch

---

17. William III, the Protestant king of England, defeated the forces of the deposed Catholic king,
James II, on July 1, 1690, at the Battle of Boyne. Ever since, William III has been a prototypical villain in
Catholic Ireland.
18. A fifth-century B.C. Greek sculptor.

Sweetens the little half-way house
Those Chinamen climb towards, and I
Delight to imagine them seated there;   50
There, on the mountain and the sky,
On all the tragic scene they stare.
One asks for mournful melodies;
Accomplished fingers begin to play.
Their eyes mid many wrinkles, their eyes,
Their ancient, glittering eyes, are gay.

1. *What do "palette" and "fiddle-bow" refer to (l. 2)? Why are the women hysterical?*
2. *What "cannot grow by an inch or an ounce" (l. 24)? Since they are central to great tragedies, how do you interpret the paradoxical "Hamlet and Lear are gay" (l. 16)? In what way does the third stanza suggest answers to these questions?* **3.** *This poem was published on the eve of World War II. What function is served by its movement from the present to Shakespearean England, to classical Greece, and finally to ancient China?*

Birches

ROBERT FROST   [1874–1963]

When I see birches bend to left and right
Across the lines of straighter darker trees,
I like to think some boy's been swinging them.
But swinging doesn't bend them down to stay.
Ice-storms do that. Often you must have seen them
Loaded with ice a sunny winter morning
After a rain. They click upon themselves
As the breeze rises, and turn many-colored
As the stir cracks and crazes their enamel.
Soon the sun's warmth makes them shed crystal shells   10
Shattering and avalanching on the snow-crust—
Such heaps of broken glass to sweep away
You'd think the inner dome of heaven had fallen.
They are dragged to the withered bracken by the load,
And they seem not to break; though once they are bowed
So low for long, they never right themselves:
You may see their trunks arching in the woods
Years afterwards, trailing their leaves on the ground
Like girls on hands and knees that throw their hair
Before them over their heads to dry in the sun.   20
But I was going to say when Truth broke in
With all her matter-of-fact about the ice-storm
I should prefer to have some boy bend them
As he went out and in to fetch the cows—
Some boy too far from town to learn baseball,
Whose only play was what he found himself,

Summer or winter, and could play alone.
One by one he subdued his father's trees
By riding them down over and over again
Until he took the stiffness out of them,   30
And not one but hung limp, not one was left
For him to conquer. He learned all there was
To learn about not launching out too soon
And so not carrying the tree away
Clear to the ground. He always kept his poise
To the top branches, climbing carefully
With the same pains you use to fill a cup
Up to the brim, and even above the brim.
Then he flung outward, feet first, with a swish,
Kicking his way down through the air to the ground.   40
So was I once myself a swinger of birches.
And so I dream of going back to be.
It's when I'm weary of considerations,
And life is too much like a pathless wood
Where your face burns and tickles with the cobwebs
Broken across it, and one eye is weeping
From a twig's having lashed across it open.
I'd like to get away from earth awhile
And then come back to it and begin over.
May no fate willfully misunderstand me   50
And half grant what I wish and snatch me away
Not to return. Earth's the right place for love:
I don't know where it's likely to go better.
I'd like to go by climbing a birch tree,
And climb black branches up a snow-white trunk
Toward heaven, till the tree could bear no more,
But dipped its top and set me down again.
That would be good both going and coming back.
One could do worse than be a swinger of birches.

Provide, Provide

ROBERT FROST [1874–1963]

The witch that came (the withered hag)
To wash the steps with pail and rag,
Was once the beauty Abishag,[19]

---

19. "Now King David was old and advanced in years; and although they covered him with clothes, he could not get warm. Therefore his servants said to him, 'Let a young maiden be sought for my lord the king, and let her wait upon the king, and be his nurse; let her lie in your bosom, that my lord the king may be warm.' So they sought for a beautiful maiden throughout all the territory of Israel, and found Abishag, the Shunammite, and brought her to the king. The maiden was very beautiful. . . ."—I Kings 1:1–4.

The picture pride of Hollywood.
Too many fall from great and good
For you to doubt the likelihood.

Die early and avoid the fate.
Or if predestined to die late,
Make up your mind to die in state.

Make the whole stock exchange your own!　　　　　　　10
If need be occupy a throne,
Where nobody can call *you* crone.

Some have relied on what they knew;
Others on being simply true.
What worked for them might work for you.

No memory of having starred
Atones for later disregard,
Or keeps the end from being hard.

Better to go down dignified
With boughten friendship at your side　　　　　　　20
Than none at all. Provide, provide!

Peter Quince at the Clavier[20]

WALLACE STEVENS　[1879–1955]

1
Just as my fingers on these keys
Make music, so the selfsame sounds
On my spirit make a music, too.

Music is feeling, then, not sound;
And thus it is that what I feel,
Here in this room, desiring you,

---

20. A clavier is a keyboard instrument. The title is probably a whimsical reference to Peter Quince of Shakespeare's *A Midsummer Night's Dream*, who directs the mechanics' production of the "most cruel death of Pyramus and Thisby" to be performed at the king's wedding festival. One of the actors, Bottom, advises the director, "First, good Peter Quince, say what the play treats on, then read the names of the actors, and so grow on to a point." Peter Quince, here a musician, seems to follow that advice.

Thinking of your blue-shadowed silk,
Is music. It is like the strain
Waked in the elders by Susanna.[21]

Of a green evening, clear and warm,   10
She bathed in her still garden, while
The red-eyed elders watching, felt

The basses of their beings throb
In witching chords, and their thin blood
Pulse pizzicati of Hosanna.[22]

2

In the green water, clear and warm,
Susanna lay.
She searched
The touch of springs,
And found   20
Concealed imaginings.
She sighed,
For so much melody.

Upon the bank, she stood
In the cool
Of spent emotions.
She felt, among the leaves,
The dew
Of old devotions.

She walked upon the grass,   30
Still quavering.
The winds were like her maids,
On timid feet,
Fetching her woven scarves,
Yet wavering.

A breath upon her hand
Muted the night.
She turned—
A cymbal crashed,
And roaring horns.   40

3

Soon, with a noise like tambourines,
Came her attendant Byzantines.[23]

---

21. The Old Testament Apocrypha includes the story of Susanna, who is saved by the wisdom of
Daniel from a death sentence for adultery based on the perjured testimony of the "elders."
22. Pizzicati notes are produced by plucking the strings rather than bowing. Hosanna is a cry of
acclamation and adoration.
23. From Byzantium (now Istanbul). The attendants are slaves.

They wondered why Susanna cried
Against the elders by her side;

And as they whispered, the refrain
Was like a willow swept by rain.

Anon, their lamps' uplifted flame
Revealed Susanna and her shame.

And then, the simpering Byzantines
Fled, with a noise like tambourines.   50

4
Beauty is momentary in the mind—
The fitful tracing of a portal;
But in the flesh it is immortal.

The body dies; the body's beauty lives.
So evenings die, in their green going,
A wave, interminably flowing.
So gardens die, their meek breath scenting
The cowl of winter, done repenting.
So maidens die, to the auroral
Celebration of a maiden's choral.   60

Susanna's music touched the bawdy strings
Of those white elders; but, escaping,
Left only Death's ironic scraping.
Now, in its immortality, it plays
On the clear viol of her memory,
And makes a constant sacrament of praise.

1. *Trace the relationship of the narrative in lines 10–50 to lines 1–9 and to section IV.* **2.** *Is the statement contained in lines 51–54 self-contradictory? Explain.* **3.** *This poem is famous for its sound patterns. What are the dominating consonant and vowel sounds in lines 1–11? What sounds dominate lines 12–15? Can you suggest some formal reasons for the change?*

Table Talk

WALLACE STEVENS   [1879–1955]

Granted, we die for good.
Life, then, is largely a thing
Of happens to like, not should.

And that, too, granted, why
Do I happen to like red bush,
Gray grass and green-gray sky?

What else remains? But red,
Gray, green, why those of all?
That is not what I said:

Not those of all. But those.   10
One likes what one happens to like.
One likes the way red grows.

It cannot matter at all.
Happens to like is one
Of the ways things happen to fall.

Speaking of Poetry

JOHN PEALE BISHOP   [1892–1944]

The ceremony must be found
That will wed Desdemona to the huge Moor.[24]

                                   It is not enough—
To win the approval of the Senator
Or to outwit his disapproval; honest Iago
Can manage that: it is not enough. For then,
Though she may pant again in his black arms
(His weight resilient as a Barbary stallion's)
She will be found
When the ambassadors of the Venetian state arrive   10
Again smothered. These things have not been changed,
Not in three hundred years

                              (Tupping° is still tupping   *copulating*
Though that particular word is obsolete.
Naturally, the ritual would not be in Latin.)

For though Othello had his blood from kings
His ancestry was barbarous, his ways African,

---

24. This poem is based on Shakespeare's *Othello* (p. 539).

His speech uncouth. It must be remembered
That though he valued an embroidery—
Three mulberries proper on a silk like silver—   20
It was not for the subtlety of the stitches,
But for the magic in it. Whereas, Desdemona
Once contrived to imitate in needlework
Her father's shield, and plucked it out
Three times, to begin again, each time
With diminished colors. This is a small point
But indicative.

     Desdemona was small and fair,
Delicate as a grasshopper
At the tag-end of summer: a Venetian   30
To her noble finger-tips.

      O, it is not enough
That they should meet, naked, at dead of night
In a small inn on a dark canal. Procurers
Less expert than Iago can arrange as much.

The ceremony must be found

Traditional, with all its symbols
Ancient as the metaphors in dreams;
Strange, with never before heard music; continuous
Until the torches deaden at the bedroom door.   40

1. *What fundamental difference separates the nature of Othello from the nature of Desdemona?* 2. *Is it possible that "the ceremony" to wed them exists? If not, why not? If
so, of what would it consist?* 3. *What does Bishop see as the major theme of Shakespeare's Othello? Do you agree with his reading of the play?*

Incident

COUNTEE CULLEN [1903–1946]

Once riding in old Baltimore,
 Heart-filled, head-filled with glee,
I saw a Baltimorean
 Keep looking straight at me.

Now I was eight and very small,
 And he was no whit bigger,

And so I smiled, but he poked out
    His tongue and called me, "Nigger."

I saw the whole of Baltimore
    From May until December: 10
Of all the things that happened there
    That's all that I remember.

Fern Hill

DYLAN THOMAS   [1914–1953]

Now as I was young and easy under the apple boughs
About the lilting house and happy as the grass was green,
      The night above the dingle° starry,   *small wooded valley*
        Time let me hail and climb
      Golden in the heydays of his eyes,
And honored among wagons I was prince of the apple towns
And once below a time I lordly had the trees and leaves
        Trail with daisies and barley
      Down the rivers of the windfall light.

And as I was green and carefree, famous among the barns   10
About the happy yard and singing as the farm was home,
      In the sun that is young once only,
        Time let me play and be
      Golden in the mercy of his means,
And green and golden I was huntsman and herdsman, the calves
Sang to my horn, the foxes on the hills barked clear and cold,
        And the sabbath rang slowly
      In the pebbles of the holy streams.

All the sun long it was running, it was lovely, the hay
Fields high as the house, the tunes from the chimneys, it was air   20
      And playing, lovely and watery
      And fire green as grass.
      And nightly under the simple stars
As I rode to sleep the owls were bearing the farm away,
All the moon long I heard, blessed among stables, the nightjars[25]
      Flying with the ricks, and the horses
        Flashing into the dark.

---

25. Nightjars are harsh-sounding nocturnal birds.

And then to awake, and the farm, like a wanderer white
With the dew, come back, the cock on his shoulder: it was all
    Shining, it was Adam and maiden,   30
        The sky gathered again
    And the sun grew round that very day.
So it must have been after the birth of the simple light
In the first, spinning place, the spellbound horses walking warm
    Out of the whinnying green stable
        On to the fields of praise.

And honored among foxes and pheasants by the gay house
Under the new made clouds and happy as the heart was long,
    In the sun born over and over,
        I ran my heedless ways,   40
    My wishes raced through the house high hay
And nothing I cared, at my sky blue trades, that time allows
In all his tuneful turning so few and such morning songs
    Before the children green and golden
        Follow him out of grace,

Nothing I cared, in the lamb white days, that time would take me
Up to the swallow thronged loft by the shadow of my hand,
    In the moon that is always rising,
        Nor that riding to sleep
    I should hear him fly with the high fields   50
And wake to the farm forever fled from the childless land.
Oh as I was young and easy in the mercy of his means,
        Time held me green and dying
    Though I sang in my chains like the sea.

1. *Lines 17–18, 25, 30–36, and 45–46 incorporate religious language and biblical allusion. What function do they serve?* **2.** *What emotional impact does the color imagery in the poem provide?* **3.** *Trace the behavior of "time" in the poem.* **4.** *Fairy tales often begin with the words "once upon a time." Why does Thomas alter that formula in line 7?* **5.** *Explain the paradox in line 53.*

Curiosity

ALASTAIR REID [b. 1926]

may have killed the cat; more likely
the cat was just unlucky, or else curious
to see what death was like, having no cause
to go on licking paws, or fathering
litter on litter of kittens, predictably.

Nevertheless, to be curious
is dangerous enough. To distrust
what is always said, what seems,
to ask odd questions, interfere in dreams,
leave home, smell rats, have hunches
does not endear him to those doggy circles
where well-smelt baskets, suitable wives, good lunches
are the order of things, and where prevails
much wagging of incurious heads and tails.

      Face it. Curiosity
will not cause him to die—
only lack of it will.
Never to want to see
the other side of the hill,
or that improbable country
where living is an idyll
(although a probable hell)
would kill us all.
Only the curious
have, if they live, a tale
worth telling at all.

      Dogs say he loves too much, is irresponsible,
is changeable, marries too many wives,
deserts his children, chills all dinner tables
with tales of his nine lives.
Well, he is lucky. Let him be
nine-lived and contradictory,
curious enough to change, prepared to pay
the cat price, which is to die
and die again and again,
each time with no less pain.
A cat minority of one
is all that can be counted on
to tell the truth. And what he has to tell
on each return from hell
is this: that dying is what the living do,
that dying is what the loving do,
and that dead dogs are those who do not know
that hell is where, to live, they have to go.

April Inventory

W. D. SNODGRASS [b. 1926]

The green catalpa tree has turned
All white; the cherry blooms once more.

In one whole year I haven't learned
A blessed thing they pay you for.
The blossoms snow down in my hair;
The trees and I will soon be bare.

The trees have more than I to spare.
The sleek, expensive girls I teach,
Younger and pinker every year,
Bloom gradually out of reach.
The pear tree lets its petals drop
Like dandruff on a tabletop.

The girls have grown so young by now
I have to nudge myself to stare.
This year they smile and mind me how
My teeth are falling with my hair.
In thirty years I may not get
Younger, shrewder, or out of debt.

The tenth time, just a year ago,
I made myself a little list
Of all the things I'd ought to know;
Then told my parents, analyst,
And everyone who's trusted me
I'd be substantial, presently.

I haven't read one book about
A book or memorized one plot.
Or found a mind I didn't doubt.
I learned one date. And then forgot.
And one by one the solid scholars
Get the degrees, the jobs, the dollars.

And smile above their starchy collars.
I taught my classes Whitehead's notions;
One lovely girl, a song of Mahler's.
Lacking a source-book or promotions,
I showed one child the colors of
A luna moth and how to love.

I taught myself to name my name,
To bark back, loosen love and crying;
To ease my woman so she came,
To ease an old man who was dying.
I have not learned how often I
Can win, can love, but choose to die.

I have not learned there is a lie
Love shall be blonder, slimmer, younger;
That my equivocating eye
Loves only by my body's hunger;
That I have poems, true to feel,
Or that the lovely world is real.

W. D. SNODGRASS   109

While scholars speak authority
And wear their ulcers on their sleeves,
My eyes in spectacles shall see   50
These trees procure and spend their leaves.
There is a value underneath
The gold and silver in my teeth.

Though trees turn bare and girls turn wives,
We shall afford our costly seasons;
There is a gentleness survives
That will outspeak and has its reasons.
There is a loveliness exists,
Preserves us. Not for specialists.   60

1. *What do the words "I have not learned" (ll. 41, 43) mean in the context of the poem?*
2. *In what way does the tone of the first four stanzas differ from the tone of the last two?*
3. *What is the meaning of "specialists" in the last line?* 4. *What is the speaker's conception of teaching?*

Innocence

FOR TONY WHITE

THOM GUNN [b. 1929]

He ran the course and as he ran he grew,
And smelt his fragrance in the field. Already,
Running he knew the most he ever knew,
The egotism of a healthy body.

Ran into manhood, ignorant of the past:
Culture of guilt and guilt's vague heritage,
Self-pity and the soul; what he possessed
Was rich, potential, like the bud's tipped rage.

The Corps developed, it was plain to see,
Courage, endurance, loyalty and skill
To a morale firm as morality,   10
Hardening him to an instrument, until

The finitude of virtues that were there
Bodied within the swarthy uniform
A compact innocence, child-like and clear,
No doubt could penetrate, no act could harm.

When he stood near the Russian partisan
Being burned alive, he therefore could behold
The ribs wear gently through the darkening skin
And sicken only at the Northern cold,   20

Could watch the fat burn with a violet flame

And feel disgusted only at the smell,
And judge that all pain finishes the same
As melting quietly by his boots it fell.

Advice to My Son

J. PETER MEINKE [b. 1932]

The trick is, to live your days
as if each one may be your last
(for they go fast, and young men lose their lives
in strange and unimaginable ways)
but at the same time, plan long range
(for they go slow: if you survive
the shattered windshield and the bursting shell
you will arrive
at our approximation here below
of heaven or hell).   10

To be specific, between the peony and the rose
plant squash and spinach, turnips and tomatoes;
beauty is nectar
and nectar, in a desert, saves—
but the stomach craves stronger sustenance
than the honied vine.
Therefore, marry a pretty girl
after seeing her mother;
show your soul to one man,
work with another;   20
and always serve bread with your wine.

But, son,
always serve wine.

1. *The advice of the first stanza seems contradictory. In what ways does the second stanza attempt to resolve the contradiction or explain "The trick" (l. 1)? What do the various plants and the bread and wine symbolize?* **2.** *Explain how the advice of lines 17–21 is logically related to the preceding lines.* **3.** *What do the final two lines tell the reader about the speaker?*

In a Spring Still Not Written Of

ROBERT WALLACE [b. 1932]

This morning
with a class of girls outdoors, I saw
how frail poems are

in a world burning up with flowers,
in which, overhead,
the great elms
—green, and tall—
stood carrying leaves in their arms.

The girls listened equally
to my drone, reading, and to the bees'   10
ricocheting
among them for the blossom on the bone,
or gazed off at a distant mower's
astronomies of green
and clover, flashing,
threshing in the new, untarnished sunlight.

And all the while, dwindling,
tinier, the voices—Yeats, Marvell, Donne—
sank drowning
in a spring still not written of,   20
as only the sky
clear above the brick bell-tower
—blue, and white—
was shifting toward the hour.

Calm, indifferent, cross-legged
or on elbows half-lying in the grass—
how should the great dead
tell them of dying?
They will come to time for poems at last,
when they have found they are no more   30
the beautiful and young
all poems are for.

1. *Explain the paradox developed in this poem.* **2.** *What is the speaker's attitude toward the "class of girls" he is teaching? Toward his job as a teacher?* **3.** *Explain the meaning of the title.* **4.** *Explain the various meanings of "drone" (l. 10).*

Suzanne

LEONARD COHEN [b. 1934]

Suzanne takes you down
to her place near the river,
you can hear the boats go by
you can stay the night beside her.
And you know that she's half crazy
but that's why you want to be there
and she feeds you tea and oranges
that come all the way from China.
Just when you mean to tell her

that you have no gifts to give her,
she gets you on her wave-length
and she lets the river answer
that you've always been her lover.
   And you want to travel with her,
   you want to travel blind
   and you know that she can trust you
   because you've touched her perfect body
   with your mind.

Jesus was a sailor
when he walked upon the water
and he spent a long time watching
from a lonely wooden tower
and when he knew for certain
only drowning men could see him
he said All men will be sailors then
until the sea shall free them,
but he himself was broken
long before the sky would open,
forsaken, almost human,
he sank beneath your wisdom like a stone.
   And you want to travel with him,
   you want to travel blind
   and you think maybe you'll trust him
   because he touched your perfect body
   with his mind.

Suzanne takes your hand
and she leads you to the river,
she is wearing rags and feathers
from Salvation Army counters.
The sun pours down like honey
on our lady of the harbour
as she shows you where to look
among the garbage and the flowers,
there are heroes in the seaweed
there are children in the morning,
they are leaning out for love
they will lean that way forever
while Suzanne she holds the mirror.
   And you want to travel with her
   and you want to travel blind
   and you're sure that she can find you
   because she's touched her perfect body
   with her mind.

10

20

30

40

50

1. *In what ways is Suzanne associated with Jesus? What is the significance of that association?* **2.** *What statement does the poem make about the ancient distinction between
body and mind? Does the poem assert the superiority of one over the other?* **3.** *Why
is Suzanne described as "wearing rags and feathers"? (l. 38) Compare this with "the
garbage and the flowers" (l. 43). What do these rather surprising contrasts suggest about
the nature of Suzanne and the values she embodies?*

My Mother

ROBERT MEZEY [b. 1935]

My mother writes from Trenton,
a comedian to the bone
but underneath, serious
and all heart. "Honey," she says,
"be a mensch[26] and Mary too,
its no good to worry, you
are doing the best you can
your Dad and everyone
thinks you turned out very well
as long as you pay your bills   10
nobody can say a word
you can tell them to drop dead
so save a dollar it can't
hurt—remember Frank you went
to highschool with? he still lives
with his wife's mother, his wife
works while he writes his books and
did he ever sell a one
the four kids run around naked
36 and he's never had,   20
you'll forgive my expression
even a pot to piss in
or a window to throw it,
such a smart boy he couldn't
read the footprints on the wall
honey you think you know all
the answers you dont, please try
to put some money away
believe me it wouldn't hurt
artist shmartist life's too short   30
for that kind of, forgive me,
horseshit, I know what you want
better than you, all that counts
is to make a good living
and the best of everything,
as Sholem Aleichem said
he was a great writer did
you ever read his books dear,
you should make what he makes a year
anyway he says some place   40
Poverty is no disgrace
but its no honor either
that's what I say,
                     love,
                          Mother"

---

26. Man, in the sense of "human being."

Songs to Aging Children Come

JONI MITCHELL [b. 1943]

Through the windless wells of wonder
By the throbbing light machine
In a tea leaf trance or under
Orders from the king and queen

Songs to aging children come
Aging children, I am one

People hurry by so quickly
Don't they hear the melodies
In the chiming and the clicking
And the laughing harmonies   10

Songs to aging children come
Aging children, I am one

Some come dark and strange like dying
Crows and ravens whistling
Lines of weeping, strings of crying
So much said in listening

Songs to aging children come
Aging children, I am one

Does the moon play only silver
When it strums the galaxy   20
Dying roses will they will their
Perfumed rhapsodies to me

Songs to aging children come
This is one

1. *What is the meaning of "songs"?* 2. *What different kinds of experiences or life styles are suggested by "tea leaf trance" and "Orders from the king and queen" in the first stanza?* 3. *Explain the paradox of line 16.* 4. *The seventh stanza utilizes the conventional images of the silver moon and roses that are associated, especially in popular songs, with youthful love. How has the poet altered the conventional meaning of those images?* 5. *What does "This" in the last line refer to?*

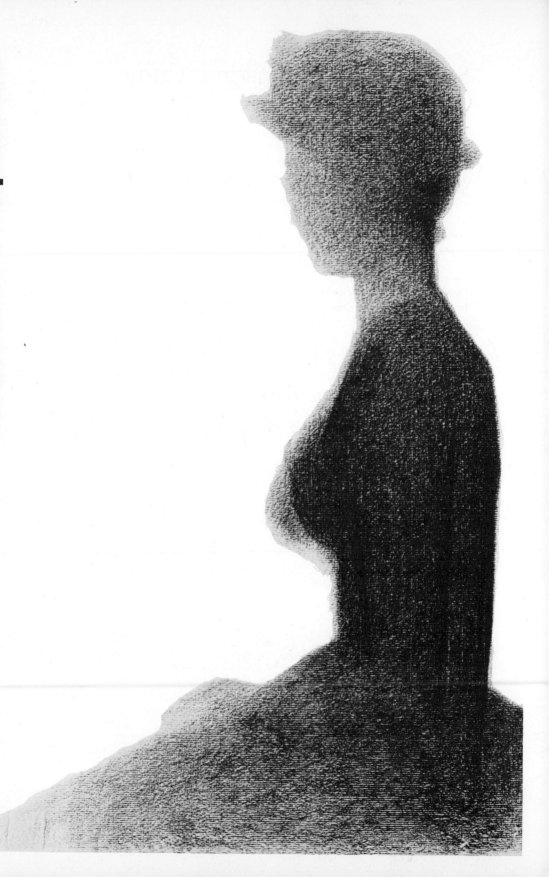

iNNOCENCE ANd EXPERiENCE

DRAMA

Major Barbara

GEORGE BERNARD SHAW [1856–1950]

CHARACTERS

Stephen Undershaft, *son of* **Andrew Undershaft** *and* **Lady Britomart**

Lady Britomart, *daughter of the* **Earl of Stevenage** *and wife of* **Andrew Under-** shaft

Barbara Undershaft, *daughter of* **Andrew Undershaft** *and* **Lady Britomart;** *a Major in the Salvation Army*

Sarah Undershaft, *daughter of* **Andrew Undershaft** *and* **Lady Britomart**

Adolphus Cusins, *fiancé of* **Barbara Undershaft**

Charles Lomax, *fiancé of* **Sarah Undershaft**

Morrison, **Lady Britomart's** *butler*

Andrew Undershaft, *husband of* **Lady Britomart;** *head of Undershaft and Lazarus, munitions makers*

Rummy (Romola) Mitchens, } *Regulars at the West Ham*
Snobby (Bronterre O'Brien) Price, } *Salvation Army shelter*

Peter Shirley, *a discharged workman, poor but honest*

Jenny Hill, *a Salvation Army lass*

Bill Walker, *a young tough*

Mrs. Baines, *a Salvation Army Commissioner*

Bilton, *a foreman in Undershaft and Lazarus*

Act One

It is after dinner in January 1906, in the library in Lady Britomart Undershaft's house in Wilton Crescent. A large and comfortable settee is in the middle of the room, upholstered in dark leather. A person sitting on it (it is vacant at present) would have, on his right, Lady Britomart's writing table, with the lady herself busy at it; a smaller writing table behind him on his left; the door behind him on Lady Britomart's side; and a window with a window seat directly on his left. Near the window is an armchair.

Lady Britomart is a woman of fifty or thereabouts, well dressed and yet careless of her dress, well bred and quite reckless of her breeding, well mannered and yet appallingly outspoken and indifferent to the opinion of her interlocutors, amiable and yet peremptory, arbitrary, and high-tempered to the last bearable degree, and withal a very typical managing matron of the upper class, treated as a naughty child until she grew into a scolding mother, and finally settling down with plenty of practical ability and worldly experience, limited in the oddest way with domestic and class limitations, conceiving the universe exactly as if it were a large house in Wilton Crescent, though handling her corner of it very effectively on that assumption, and being quite enlightened and liberal as to the books in the library, the pictures on the walls, the music in the portfolios, and the articles in the papers.

Her son, Stephen, comes in. He is a gravely correct young man under 25, taking himself very seriously, but still in some awe of his mother, from childish habit and bachelor shyness rather than from any weakness of character.

Stephen. Whats the matter?
Lady Britomart. Presently, Stephen.

Stephen submissively walks to the settee and sits down. He takes up a Liberal weekly called The Speaker.

Lady Britomart. Dont begin to read, Stephen. I shall require all your attention.
Stephen. It was only while I was waiting—
Lady Britomart. Dont make excuses, Stephen. (He puts down The Speaker). Now! (She finishes her writing; rises; and comes to the settee). I have not kept you waiting very long, I think.
Stephen. Not at all, mother.
Lady Britomart. Bring me my cushion. (He takes the cushion from the chair at the desk and arranges it for her as she sits down on the settee). Sit down. (He sits down and fingers his tie nervously). Dont fiddle with your tie, Stephen: there is nothing the matter with it.
Stephen. I beg your pardon. (He fiddles with his watch chain instead).
Lady Britomart. Now are you attending to me, Stephen?
Stephen. Of course, mother.
Lady Britomart. No: it's not of course. I want something much more than your everyday matter-of-course attention. I am going to speak to you very seriously, Stephen. I wish you would let that chain alone.
Stephen (hastily relinquishing the chain). Have I done anything to annoy you, mother? If so, it was quite unintentional.
Lady Britomart (astonished). Nonsense! (With some remorse) My poor boy, did you think I was angry with you?

Stephen. What is it, then, mother? You are making me very uneasy.

Lady Britomart (*squaring herself at him rather aggressively*). Stephen: may I ask how soon you intend to realize that you are a grown-up man, and that I am only a woman?

Stephen (*amazed*). Only a—

Lady Britomart. Dont repeat my words, please: it is a most aggravating habit. You must learn to face life seriously, Stephen. I really cannot bear the whole burden of our family affairs any longer. You must advise me: you must assume the responsibility.

Stephen. I!

Lady Britomart. Yes, you, of course. You were 24 last June. Youve been at Harrow and Cambridge. Youve been to India and Japan. You must know a lot of things, now; unless you have wasted your time most scandalously. Well, advise me.

Stephen (*much perplexed*). You know I have never interfered in the household—

Lady Britomart. No: I should think not. I dont want you to order the dinner.

Stephen. I mean in our family affairs.

Lady Britomart. Well, you must interfere now; for they are getting quite beyond me.

Stephen (*troubled*). I have thought sometimes that perhaps I ought; but really, mother, I know so little about them; and what I do know is so painful! it is so impossible to mention some things to you—(*he stops, ashamed*).

Lady Britomart. I suppose you mean your father.

Stephen (*almost inaudibly*). Yes.

Lady Britomart. My dear: we cant go on all our lives not mentioning him. Of course you were quite right not to open the subject until I asked you to; but you are old enough now to be taken into my confidence, and to help me to deal with him about the girls.

Stephen. But the girls are all right. They are engaged.

Lady Britomart (*complacently*). Yes: I have made a very good match for Sarah. Charles Lomax will be a millionaire at 35. But that is ten years ahead; and in the meantime his trustees cannot under the terms of his father's will allow him more than £800 a year.

Stephen. But the will says also that if he increases his income by his own exertions, they may double the increase.

Lady Britomart. Charles Lomax's exertions are much more likely to decrease his income than to increase it. Sarah will have to find at least another £800 a year for the next ten years; and even then they will be as poor as church mice. And what about Barbara? I thought Barbara was going to make the most brilliant career of all of you. And what does she do? Joins the Salvation Army; discharges her maid; lives on a pound a week; and walks in one evening with a professor of Greek whom she has picked up in the street, and who pretends to be a Salvationist, and actually plays the big drum for her in public because he has fallen head over ears in love with her.

Stephen. I was certainly rather taken aback when I heard they were engaged. Cusins is a very nice fellow, certainly: nobody would ever guess that he was born in Australia; but—

Lady Britomart. Oh, Adolphus Cusins will make a very good husband. After all, nobody can say a word against Greek: it stamps a man at once as an educated gentleman. And my family, thank Heaven, is not a pig-headed Tory one. We are Whigs, and believe in liberty. Let snobbish people say what they please: Barbara shall marry, not the man they like, but the man *I* like.

Stephen. Of course I was thinking only of his income. However, he is not likely to be extravagant.

Lady Britomart. Dont be too sure of that, Stephen. I know your quiet, simple, refined, poetic people like Adolphus: quite content with the best of everything! They cost more than your extravagant people, who are always as mean as they are second rate. No: Barbara will need at least £2000 a year. You see it means two additional households. Besides, my dear, you must marry soon. I dont approve of the present fashion of philandering bachelors and late marriages; and I am trying to arrange something for you.

Stephen. It's very good of you, mother; but perhaps I had better arrange that for myself.

Lady Britomart. Nonsense! you are much too young to begin matchmaking: you would be taken in by some pretty little nobody. Of course I dont mean that you are not to be consulted: you know that as well as I do. *(Stephen closes his lips and is silent).* Now dont sulk, Stephen.

Stephen. I am not sulking, mother. What has all this got to do with—with—with my father?

Lady Britomart. My dear Stephen: where is the money to come from? It is easy enough for you and the other children to live on my income as long as we are in the same house; but I cant keep four families in four separate houses. You know how poor my father is: he has barely seven thousand a year now; and really, if he were not the Earl of Stevenage, he would have to give up society. He can do nothing for us. He says, naturally enough, that it is absurd that he should be asked to provide for the children of a man who is rolling in money. You see, Stephen, your father must be fabulously wealthy, because there is always a war going on somewhere.

Stephen. You need not remind me of that, mother. I have hardly ever opened a newspaper in my life without seeing our name in it. The Undershaft torpedo! The Undershaft quick firers! The Undershaft ten inch! the Undershaft disappearing rampart gun! the Undershaft submarine! and now the Undershaft aerial battleship! At Harrow they called me the Woolwich Infant. At Cambridge it was the same. A little brute at King's who was always trying to get up revivals, spoilt my Bible—your first birth-day present to me—by writing under my name, 'Son and heir to Under-shaft and Lazarus, Death and Destruction Dealers: address Christendom and Judea.' But that was not so bad as the way I was kowtowed to every-where because my father was making millions by selling cannons.

Lady Britomart.   It is not only the cannons, but the war loans that Lazarus ar-ranges under cover of giving credit for the cannons. You know, Stephen, it's perfectly scandalous. Those two men, Andrew Undershaft and Laz-arus, positively have Europe under their thumbs. That is why your father is able to behave as he does. He is above the law. Do you think Bismarck or Gladstone or Disraeli could have openly defied every social and moral obligation all their lives as your father has? They simply wouldnt have dared. I asked Gladstone to take it up. I asked The Times to take it up. I asked the Lord Chamberlain to take it up. But it was just like asking them to declare war on the Sultan. They wouldnt. They said they couldnt touch him. I believe they were afraid.

Stephen.   What could they do? He does not actually break the law.

Lady Britomart.   Not break the law! He is always breaking the law. He broke the law when he was born: his parents were not married.

Stephen.   Mother! Is that true?

Lady Britomart.   Of course it's true: that was why we separated.

Stephen.   He married without letting you know this!

Lady Britomart (rather taken aback by this inference).   Oh no. To do An-drew justice, that was not the sort of thing he did. Besides, you know the Undershaft motto: Unashamed. Everybody knew.

Stephen.   But you said that was why you separated.

Lady Britomart.   Yes, because he was not content with being a foundling him-self: he wanted to disinherit you for another foundling. That was what I couldnt stand.

Stephen (ashamed).   Do you mean for—for—for—

Lady Britomart.   Dont stammer, Stephen. Speak distinctly.

Stephen.   But this is so frightful to me, mother. To have to speak to you about such things!

Lady Britomart.   It's not pleasant for me, either, especially if you are still so childish that you must make it worse by a display of embarrassment. It is only in the middle classes, Stephen, that people get into a state of dumb helpless horror when they find that there are wicked people in the world. In our class, we have to decide what is to be done with wicked people; and nothing should disturb our self-possession. Now ask your question properly.

Stephen.   Mother: have you no consideration for me? Either treat me as a child, as you always do, and tell me nothing at all; or tell me everything and let me take it as best I can.

Lady Britomart.   Treat you as a child! What do you mean? It is most unkind and ungrateful of you to say such a thing. You know I have never treated any of you as children. I have always made you my companions and friends, and allowed you perfect freedom to do and say whatever you liked, so long as you liked what I could approve of.

Stephen *(desperately).* I daresay we have been the very imperfect children of a very perfect mother; but I do beg you to let me alone for once, and tell me about this horrible business of my father wanting to set me aside for another son.

Lady Britomart *(amazed).* Another son! I never said anything of the kind. I never dreamt of such a thing. This is what comes of interrupting me.

Stephen. But you said—

Lady Britomart *(cutting him short).* Now be a good boy, Stephen, and listen to me patiently. The Undershafts are descended from a foundling in the parish of St Andrew Undershaft in the city. That was long ago, in the reign of James the First. Well, this foundling was adopted by an armorer and gun-maker. In the course of time the foundling succeeded to the business; and from some notion of gratitude, or some vow or something, he adopted another foundling, and left the business to him. And that foundling did the same. Ever since that, the cannon business has always been left to an adopted foundling named Andrew Undershaft.

Stephen. But did they never marry? Were there no legitimate sons?

Lady Britomart. Oh yes: they married just as your father did; and they were rich enough to buy land for their own children and leave them well provided for. But they always adopted and trained some foundling to succeed them in the business; and of course they always quarrelled with their wives furiously over it. Your father was adopted in that way; and he pretends to consider himself bound to keep up the tradition and adopt somebody to leave the business to. Of course I was not going to stand that. There may have been some reason for it when the Undershafts could only marry women in their own class, whose sons were not fit to govern great estates. But there could be no excuse for passing over my son.

Stephen *(dubiously).* I am afraid I should make a poor hand of managing a cannon foundry.

Lady Britomart. Nonsense! you could easily get a manager and pay him a salary.

Stephen. My father evidently had no great opinion of my capacity.

Lady Britomart. Stuff, child! you were only a baby: it had nothing to do with your capacity. Andrew did it on principle, just as he did every perverse and wicked thing on principle. When my father remonstrated, Andrew actually told him to his face that history tells us of only two successful institutions: one the Undershaft firm, and the other the Roman Empire under the Antonines. That was because the Antonine emperors all adopted their successors. Such rubbish! The Stevenages are as good as the Antonines, I hope; and you are a Stevenage. But that was Andrew all over. There you have the man! Always clever and unanswerable when he was defending nonsense and wickedness: always awkward and sullen when he had to behave sensibly and decently!

Stephen.   Then it was on my account that your home life was broken up, mother. I am sorry.

Lady Britomart.   Well, dear, there were other differences. I really cannot bear an immoral man. I am not a Pharisee, I hope; and I should not have minded his merely doing wrong things: we are none of us perfect. But your father didnt exactly do wrong things: he said them and thought them: that was what was so dreadful. He really had a sort of religion of wrongness. Just as one doesnt mind men practising immorality so long as they own that they are in the wrong by preaching morality; so I couldnt forgive Andrew for preaching immorality while he practised morality. You would all have grown up without principles, without any knowledge of right and wrong, if he had been in the house. You know, my dear, your father was a very attractive man in some ways. Children did not dislike him; and he took advantage of it to put the wickedest ideas into their heads, and make them quite unmanageable. I did not dislike him myself: very far from it; but nothing can bridge over moral disagreement.

Stephen.   All this simply bewilders me, mother. People may differ about matters of opinion, or even about religion; but how can they differ about right and wrong? Right is right; and wrong is wrong; and if a man cannot distinguish them properly, he is either a fool or a rascal: thats all.

Lady Britomart *(touched)*.   Thats my own boy *(she pats his cheek)!* Your father never could answer that: he used to laugh and get out of it under cover of some affectionate nonsense. And now that you understand the situation, what do you advise me to do?

Stephen.   Well, what can you do?

Lady Britomart.   I must get the money somehow.

Stephen.   We cannot take money from him. I had rather go and live in some cheap place like Bedford Square or even Hampstead than take a farthing of his money.

Lady Britomart.   But after all, Stephen, our present income comes from Andrew.

Stephen *(shocked)*.   I never knew that.

Lady Britomart.   Well, you surely didnt suppose your grandfather had anything to give me. The Stevenages could not do everything for you. We gave you social position. Andrew had to contribute something. He had a very good bargain, I think.

Stephen *(bitterly)*.   We are utterly dependent on him and his cannons, then?

Lady Britomart.   Certainly not: the money is settled. But he provided it. So you see it is not a question of taking money from him or not: it is simply a question of how much. I dont want any more for myself.

Stephen.   Nor do I.

Lady Britomart.   But Sarah does; and Barbara does. That is, Charles Lomax and Adolphus Cusins will cost them more. So I must put my pride in my pocket and ask for it, I suppose. That is your advice, Stephen, is it not?

Stephen. No.

Lady Britomart *(sharply)*. Stephen!

Stephen. Of course if you are determined—

Lady Britomart. I am not determined: I ask your advice; and I am waiting for it. I will not have all the responsibility thrown on my shoulders.

Stephen *(obstinately)*. I would die sooner than ask him for another penny.

Lady Britomart *(resignedly)*. You mean that *I* must ask him. Very well, Stephen: it shall be as you wish. You will be glad to know that your grandfather concurs. But he thinks I ought to ask Andrew to come here and see the girls. After all, he must have some natural affection for them.

Stephen. Ask him here!!!

Lady Britomart. Do not repeat my words, Stephen. Where else can I ask him?

Stephen. I never expected you to ask him at all.

Lady Britomart. Now dont tease, Stephen. Come! you see that it is necessary that he should pay us a visit, dont you?

Stephen *(reluctantly)*. I suppose so, if the girls cannot do without his money.

Lady Britomart. Thank you, Stephen: I knew you would give me the right advice when it was properly explained to you. I have asked your father to come this evening. *(Stephen bounds from his seat)*. Dont jump, Stephen: it fidgets me.

Stephen *(in utter consternation)*. Do you mean to say that my father is coming here tonight—that he may be here at any moment?

Lady Britomart *(looking at her watch)*. I said nine. *(He gasps. She rises)*. Ring the bell, please. *(Stephen goes to the smaller writing table! presses a button on it; and sits at it with his elbows on the table and his head in his hands, outwitted and overwhelmed)*. It is ten minutes to nine yet; and I have to prepare the girls. I asked Charles Lomax and Adolphus to dinner on purpose that they might be here. Andrew had better see them in case he should cherish any delusions as to their being capable of supporting their wives. *(The butler enters: Lady Britomart goes behind the settee to speak to him)*. Morrison: go up to the drawing room and tell everybody to come down here at once. *(Morrison withdraws. Lady Britomart turns to Stephen)*. Now remember, Stephen: I shall need all your countenance and authority. *(He rises and tries to recover some vestige of these attributes)*. Give me a chair, dear. *(He pushes a chair forward from the wall to where she stands, near the smaller writing table. She sits down; and he goes to the armchair, into which he throws himself)*. I dont know how Barbara will take it. Ever since they made her a major in the Salvation Army she has developed a propensity to have her own way and order people about which quite cows me sometimes. It's not ladylike: I'm sure I dont know where she picked it up. Anyhow, Barbara shant bully me; but still it's just as well that your father should be here before she has time to refuse to meet him or make a fuss. Dont look nervous, Stephen: it will only encourage Barbara to make difficulties. *I* am nervous enough, goodness knows; but I dont shew it.

Sarah and Barbara come in with their respective young men, Charles Lomax and Adolphus Cusins. Sarah is slender, bored, and mundane. Barbara is robuster, jollier, much more energetic. Sarah is fashionably dressed: Barbara is in Salvation Army uniform. Lomax, a young man about town, is like many other young men about town. He is afflicted with a frivolous sense of humor which plunges him at the most inopportune moments into paroxysms of imperfectly suppressed laughter. Cusins is a spectacled student, slight, thin haired, and sweet voiced, with a more complex form of Lomax's complaint. His sense of humor is intellectual and subtle, and is complicated by an appalling temper. The lifelong struggle of a benevolent temperament and a high conscience against impulses of inhuman ridicule and fierce impatience has set up a chronic strain which has visibly wrecked his constitution. He is a most implacable, determined, tenacious, intolerant person who by mere force of character presents himself as—and indeed actually is—considerate, gentle, explanatory, even mild and apologetic, capable possibly of murder, but not of cruelty or coarseness. By the operation of some instinct which is not merciful enough to blind him with the illusions of love, he is obstinately bent on marrying Barbara. Lomax likes Sarah and thinks it will be rather a lark to marry her. Consequently he has not attempted to resist Lady Britomart's arrangements to that end.

All four look as if they had been having a good deal of fun in the drawing room. The girls enter first, leaving the swains outside. Sarah comes to the settee. Barbara comes in after her and stops at the door.

Barbara. Are Cholly and Dolly to come in?

Lady Britomart *(forcibly).* Barbara: I will not have Charles called Cholly: the vulgarity of it positively makes me ill.

Barbara. It's all right, mother: Cholly is quite correct nowadays. Are they to come in?

Lady Britomart. Yes, if they will behave themselves.

Barbara *(through the door).* Come in, Dolly; and behave yourself.

Barbara comes to her mother's writing table. Cusins enters smiling, and wanders towards Lady Britomart.

Sarah *(calling).* Come in, Cholly. *(Lomax enters, controlling his features very imperfectly, and places himself vaguely between Sarah and Barbara).*

Lady Britomart *(peremptorily).* Sit down, all of you. *(They sit. Cusins crosses to the window and seats himself there. Lomax takes a chair. Barbara sits at the writing table and Sarah on the settee).* I dont in the least know what you are laughing at, Adolphus. I am surprised at you, though I expected nothing better from Charles Lomax.

Cusins (in a remarkably gentle voice).   Barbara has been trying to teach me the West Ham Salvation March.

Lady Britomart.   I see nothing to laugh at in that; nor should you if you are really converted.

Cusins (sweetly).   You were not present. It was really funny, I believe.

Lomax.   Ripping.

Lady Britomart.   Be quiet, Charles. Now listen to me, children. Your father is coming here this evening.

General stupefaction. Lomax, Sarah, and Barbara rise: Sarah scared, and Barbara amused and expectant.

Lomax (remonstrating).   Oh I say!

Lady Britomart.   You are not called on to say anything, Charles.

Sarah.   Are you serious, mother?

Lady Britomart.   Of course I am serious. It is on your account, Sarah, and also on Charles's. (Silence. Sarah sits, with a shrug. Charles looks painfully unworthy). I hope you are not going to object, Barbara.

Barbara.   I! why should I! My father has a soul to be saved like anybody else. He's quite welcome as far as I am concerned. (She sits on the table, and softly whistles 'Onward Christian Soldiers').

Lomax (still remonstrant).   But really, dont you know! Oh I say!

Lady Britomart (frigidly).   What do you wish to convey, Charles?

Lomax.   Well, you must admit that this is a bit thick.

Lady Britomart (turning with ominous suavity to Cusins).   Adolphus: you are a professor of Greek. Can you translate Charles Lomax's remarks into reputable English for us?

Cusins (cautiously).   If I may say so, Lady Brit, I think Charles has rather happily expressed what we all feel. Homer, speaking of Autolycus, uses the same phrase. πυκινὸν δόμον ἐλθεῖν means a bit thick.

Lomax (handsomely).   Not that I mind, you know, if Sarah dont. (He sits).

Lady Britomart (crushingly).   Thank you. Have I your permission, Adolphus, to invite my own husband to my own house?

Cusins (gallantly).   You have my unhesitating support in everything you do.

Lady Britomart.   Tush! Sarah: have you nothing to say?

Sarah.   Do you mean that he is coming regularly to live here?

Lady Britomart.   Certainly not. The spare room is ready for him if he likes to stay for a day or two and see a little more of you; but there are limits.

Sarah.   Well, he cant eat us, I suppose. *I* dont mind.

Lomax (chuckling).   I wonder how the old man will take it.

Lady Britomart.   Much as the old woman will, no doubt, Charles.

Lomax (abashed).   I didnt mean—at least—

Lady Britomart.   You didnt think, Charles. You never do; and the result is, you never mean anything. And now please attend to me, children. Your father will be quite a stranger to us.

Lomax.   I suppose he hasnt seen Sarah since she was a little kid.

Lady Britomart. Not since she was a little kid, Charles, as you express it with that elegance of diction and refinement of thought that seem never to desert you. Accordingly—er—*(impatiently)* Now I have forgotten what I was going to say. That comes of your provoking me to be sarcastic, Charles. Adolphus: will you kindly tell me where I was.

Cusins *(sweetly)*. You were saying that as Mr Undershaft has not seen his children since they were babies, he will form his opinion of the way you have brought them up from their behavior tonight, and that therefore you wish us all to be particularly careful to conduct ourselves well, especially Charles.

Lady Britomart *(with emphatic approval)*. Precisely.

Lomax. Look here, Dolly: Lady Brit didnt say that.

Lady Britomart *(vehemently)*. I did, Charles. Adolphus's recollection is perfectly correct. It is most important that you should be good; and I do beg you for once not to pair off into opposite corners and giggle and whisper while I am speaking to your father.

Barbara. All right, mother. We'll do you credit. *(She comes off the table, and sits in her chair with ladylike elegance)*.

Lady Britomart. Remember, Charles, that Sarah will want to feel proud of you instead of ashamed of you.

Lomax. Oh I say! theres nothing to be exactly proud of, dont you know.

Lady Britomart. Well, try and look as if there was.

Morrison, pale and dismayed, breaks into the room in unconcealed disorder.

Morrison. Might I speak a word to you, my lady?

Lady Britomart. Nonsense! Shew him up.

Morrison. Yes, my lady. *(He goes)*.

Lomax. Does Morrison know who it is?

Lady Britomart. Of course. Morrison has always been with us.

Lomax. It must be a regular corker for him, dont you know.

Lady Britomart. Is this a moment to get on my nerves, Charles, with your outrageous expressions?

Lomax. But this is something out of the ordinary, really—

Morrison *(at the door)*. The—er—Mr Undershaft. *(He retreats in confusion)*.

Andrew Undershaft comes in. All rise. Lady Britomart meets him in the middle of the room behind the settee.

Andrew is, on the surface, a stoutish, easygoing elderly man, with kindly patient manners, and an engaging simplicity of character. But he has a watchful, deliberate, waiting, listening face, and formidable reserves of power, both bodily and mental, in his capacious chest and long head. His gentleness is partly that of a strong man who has learnt by experience that his natural grip hurts ordinary people unless he handles them very carefully, and partly the mellowness of age and success. He is also a little shy in his present very delicate situation.

Lady Britomart. Good evening, Andrew.

Undershaft. How d'ye do, my dear.

Lady Britomart. You look a good deal older.

Undershaft *(apologetically).* I am somewhat older. *(Taking her hand with a touch of courtship)* Time has stood still with you.

Lady Britomart *(throwing away his hand).* Rubbish! This is your family.

Undershaft *(surprised).* Is it so large? I am sorry to say my memory is failing very badly in some things. *(He offers his hand with paternal kindness to Lomax).*

Lomax *(jerkily shaking his hand).* Ahdedoo.

Undershaft. I can see you are my eldest. I am very glad to meet you again, my boy.

Lomax *(remonstrating).* No, but look here dont you know—*(Overcome)* Oh I say!

Lady Britomart *(recovering from momentary speechlessness).* Andrew: do you mean to say that you dont remember how many children you have?

Undershaft. Well, I am afraid I—. They have grown so much—er. Am I making any ridiculous mistake? I may as well confess: I recollect only one son. But so many things have happened since, of course—er—

Lady Britomart *(decisively).* Andrew: you are talking nonsense. Of course you have only one son.

Undershaft. Perhaps you will be good enough to introduce me, my dear.

Lady Britomart. That is Charles Lomax, who is engaged to Sarah.

Undershaft. My dear sir, I beg your pardon.

Lomax. Notatall. Delighted, I assure you.

Lady Britomart. This is Stephen.

Undershaft *(bowing).* Happy to make your acquaintance, Mr. Stephen. *(Taking Cusins' hands in his)* How are you, my young friend? *(To Lady Britomart)* He is very like you, my love.

Cusins. You flatter me, Mr Undershaft. My name is Cusins: engaged to Barbara. *(Very explicitly)* That is Major Barbara Undershaft, of the Salvation Army. That is Sarah, your second daughter. This is Stephen Undershaft, your son.

Undershaft. My dear Stephen, I beg your pardon.

Stephen. Not at all.

Undershaft. Mr. Cusins: I am much indebted to you for explaining so precisely. *(Turning to Sarah)* Barbara, my dear—

Sarah *(prompting him).* Sarah.

Undershaft. Sarah, of course. *(They shake hands. He goes over to Barbara)* Barbara—I am right this time, I hope?

Barbara. Quite right. *(They shake hands).*

Lady Britomart *(resuming command).* Sit down, all of you. Sit down, Andrew. *(She comes forward and sits on the setee. Cusins also brings his chair forward on her left. Barbara and Stephen resume their seats. Lomax gives his chair to Sarah and goes for another).*

Undershaft.   Thank you, my love.

Lomax *(conversationally, as he brings a chair forward between the writing table and the settee, and offers it to Undershaft).*   Takes you some time to find out exactly where you are, dont it?

Undershaft *(accepting the chair, but remaining standing).*   That is not what embarrasses me, Mr Lomax. My difficulty is that if I play the part of a father, I shall produce the effect of an intrusive stranger; and if I play the part of a discreet stranger, I may appear a callous father.

Lady Britomart.   There is no need for you to play any part at all, Andrew. You had much better be sincere and natural.

Undershaft *(submissively).*   Yes, my dear: I daresay that will be best. *(He sits down comfortably).* Well, here I am. Now what can I do for you all?

Lady Britomart.   You need not do anything, Andrew. You are one of the family. You can sit with us and enjoy yourself.

A painfully conscious pause. Barbara makes a face at Lomax, whose too long suppressed mirth immediately explodes in agonized neighings.

Lady Britomart *(outraged).*   Charles Lomax: if you can behave yourself, behave yourself. If not, leave the room.

Lomax.   I'm awfully sorry, Lady Brit; but really you know, upon my soul! *(He sits on the settee between Lady Britomart and Undershaft, quite overcome).*

Barbara.   Why dont you laugh if you want to, Cholly? It's good for your inside.

Lady Britomart.   Barbara: you have had the education of a lady. Please let your father see that; and dont talk like a street girl.

Undershaft.   Never mind me, my dear. As you know, I am not a gentleman; and I was never educated.

Lomax *(encouragingly).*   Nobody'd know it, I assure you. You look all right, you know.

Cusins.   Let me advise you to study Greek, Mr Undershaft. Greek scholars are privileged men. Few of them know Greek; and none of them know anything else; but their position is unchallengeable. Other languages are the qualifications of waiters and commercial travellers: Greek is to a man of position what the hallmark is to silver.

Barbara.   Dolly: dont be insincere. Cholly: fetch your concertina and play something for us.

Lomax *(jumps up eagerly, but checks himself to remark doubtfully to Undershaft).*   Perhaps that sort of thing isnt in your line, eh?

Undershaft.   I am particularly fond of music.

Lomax *(delighted).*   Are you? Then I'll get it. *(He goes upstairs for the instrument).*

Undershaft.   Do you play, Barbara?

Barbara.   Only the tambourine. But Cholly's teaching me the concertina.

Undershaft.   Is Cholly also a member of the Salvation Army?

Barbara.   No: he says it's bad form to be a dissenter. But I dont despair of Cholly. I made him come yesterday to a meeting at the dock gates, and take the collection in his hat.

Undershaft *(looks whimsically at his wife)*!!

Lady Britomart.   It is not my doing, Andrew. Barbara is old enough to take her own way. She has no father to advise her.

Barbara.   Oh yes she has. There are no orphans in the Salvation Army.

Undershaft.   Your father there has a great many children and plenty of experience, eh?

Barbara *(looking at him with quick interest and nodding)*.   Just so. How did you come to understand that? *(Lomax is heard at the door trying the concertina).*

Lady Britomart.   Come in, Charles. Play us something at once.

Lomax.   Righto! *(He sits down in his former place, and preludes).*

Undershaft.   One moment, Mr. Lomax. I am rather interested in the Salvation Army. Its motto might be my own: Blood and Fire.

Lomax *(shocked)*.   But not your sort of blood and fire, you know.

Undershaft.   My sort of blood cleanses: my sort of fire purifies.

Barbara.   So do ours. Come down tomorrow to my shelter—the West Ham shelter—and see what we're doing. We're going to march to a great meeting in the Assembly Hall at Mile End. Come and see the shelter and then march with us: it will do you a lot of good. Can you play anything?

Undershaft.   In my youth I earned pennies, and even shillings occasionally, in the streets and in public house parlors by my natural talent for step-dancing. Later on, I became a member of the Undershaft orchestral society, and performed passably on the tenor trombone.

Lomax *(scandalized—putting down the concertina)*.   Oh I say!

Barbara.   Many a sinner has played himself into heaven on the trombone, thanks to the Army.

Lomax *(to Barbara, still rather shocked)*.   Yes; but what about the cannon business, dont you know? *(To Undershaft)* Getting into heaven is not exactly in your line, is it?

Lady Britomart.   Charles!!!

Lomax.   Well; but it stands to reason, dont it? The cannon business may be necessary and all that: we cant get on without cannons; but it isnt right, you know. On the other hand, there may be a certain amount of tosh about the Salvation Army—I belong to the Established Church myself—but still you cant deny that it's religion; and you cant go against religion, can you? At least unless youre downright immoral, dont you know.

Undershaft.   You hardly appreciate my position, Mr. Lomax—

Lomax *(hastily)*.   I'm not saying anything against you personally—

Undershaft.   Quite so, quite so. But consider for a moment. Here I am, a profiteer in mutilation and murder. I find myself in a specially amiable humor just now because, this morning, down at the foundry, we blew twenty-seven dummy soldiers into fragments with a gun which formerly destroyed only thirteen.

Lomax (*leniently*). Well, the more destructive war becomes, the sooner it will be abolished, eh?

Undershaft. Not at all. The more destructive war becomes the more fascinating we find it. No, Mr. Lomax: I am obliged to you for making the usual excuse for my trade; but I am not ashamed of it. I am not one of those men who keep their morals and their business in watertight compartments. All the spare money my trade rivals spend on hospitals, cathedrals, and other receptacles for conscience money, I devote to experiments and researches in improved methods of destroying life and property. I have always done so; and I always shall. Therefore your Christmas card moralities of peace on earth and goodwill among men are of no use to me. Your Christianity, which enjoins you to resist not evil, and to turn the other cheek, would make me a bankrupt. My morality—my religion—must have a place for cannons and torpedoes in it.

Stephen (*coldly—almost sullenly*). You speak as if there were half a dozen moralities and religions to choose from, instead of one true morality and one true religion.

Undershaft. For me there is only one true morality; but it might not fit you, as you do not manufacture aerial battleships. There is only one true morality for every man; but every man has not the same true morality.

Lomax (*overtaxed*). Would you mind saying that again? I didn't quite follow it.

Cusins. It's quite simple. As Euripides says, one man's meat is another man's poison morally as well as physically.

Undershaft. Precisely.

Lomax. Oh, that! Yes, yes, yes. True. True.

Stephen. In other words, some men are honest and some are scoundrels.

Barbara. Bosh! There are no scoundrels.

Undershaft. Indeed? Are there any good men?

Barbara. No. Not one. There are neither good men nor scoundrels: there are just children of one Father; and the sooner they stop calling one another names the better. You neednt talk to me: I know them. Ive had scores of them through my hands: scoundrels, criminals, infidels, philanthropists, missionaries, county councillors, all sorts. Theyre all just the same sort of sinner; and theres the same salvation ready for them all.

Undershaft. May I ask have you ever saved a maker of cannons?

Barbara. No. Will you let me try?

Undershaft. Well, I will make a bargain with you. If I go to see you tomorrow in your Salvation Shelter, will you come the day after to see me in my cannon works?

Barbara. Take care. It may end in your giving up the cannons for the sake of the Salvation Army.

Undershaft. Are you sure it will not end in your giving up the Salvation Army for the sake of the cannons?

Barbara. I will take my chance of that.

Undershaft. And I will take my chance of the other. *(They shake hands on it).* Where is your shelter?

Barbara. In West Ham. At the sign of the cross. Ask anybody in Canning Town. Where are your works?

Undershaft. In Perivale St. Andrews. At the sign of the sword. Ask anybody in Europe.

Lomax. Hadnt I better play something?

Barbara. Yes. Give us Onward, Christian Soldiers.

Lomax. Well, thats rather a strong order to begin with, dont you know. Suppose I sing Thourt passing hence, my brother. It's much the same tune.

Barbara. It's too melancholy. You get saved, Cholly; and youll pass hence, my brother, without making such a fuss about it.

Lady Britomart. Really, Barbara, you go on as if religion were a pleasant subject. Do have some sense of propriety.

Undershaft. I do not find it an unpleasant subject, my dear. It is the only one that capable people really care for.

Lady Britomart *(looking at her watch).* Well, if you are determined to have it, I insist on having it in a proper and respectable way. Charles: ring for prayers.

General amazement. Stephen rises in dismay.

Lomax *(rising).* Oh I say!

Undershaft *(rising).* I am afraid I must be going.

Lady Britomart. You cannot go now, Andrew: it would be most improper. Sit down. What will the servants think?

Undershaft. My dear: I have conscientious scruples. May I suggest a compromise? If Barbara will conduct a little service in the drawing room, with Mr. Lomax as organist, I will attend it willingly. I will even take part, if a trombone can be procured.

Lady Britomart. Dont mock, Andrew.

Undershaft *(shocked—to Barbara).* You dont think I am mocking, my love, I hope.

Barbara. No, of course not; and it wouldnt matter if you were: half the Army came to their first meeting for a lark. *(Rising)* Come along. *(She throws her arm round her father and sweeps him out, calling to the others from the threshold)* Come, Dolly. Come, Cholly.

Cusins rises.

Lady Britomart. I will not be disobeyed by everybody. Adolphus: sit down. *(He does not).* Charles: you may go. You are not fit for prayers: you cannot keep your countenance.

Lomax. Oh I say! *(He goes out).*

Lady Britomart *(continuing).* But you, Adolphus, can behave yourself if you choose to. I insist on your staying.

Cusins. My dear Lady Brit: there are things in the family prayer book that I couldnt bear to hear you say.

Lady Britomart. What things, pray?

Cusins. Well, you would have to say before all the servants that we have done things we ought not to have done, and left undone things we ought to have done, and that there is no health in us. I cannot bear to hear you doing yourself such an injustice, and Barbara such an injustice. As for myself, I flatly deny it: I have done my best. I shouldnt dare to marry Barbara—I couldnt look you in the face—if it were true. So I must go to the drawing room.

Lady Britomart *(offended).* Well, go. *(He starts for the door).* And remember this, Adolphus *(he turns to listen):* I have a very strong suspicion that you went to the Salvation Army to worship Barbara and nothing else. And I quite appreciate the very clever way in which you systematically humbug me. I have found you out. Take care Barbara doesnt. Thats all.

Cusins *(with unruffled sweetness).* Dont tell on me. *(He steals out).*

Lady Britomart. Sarah: if you want to go, go. Anything's better than to sit there as if you wished you were a thousand miles away.

Sarah *(languidly).* Very well, mamma. *(She goes).*

Lady Britomart, with a sudden flounce, gives way to a little gust of tears.

Stephen *(going to her).* Mother: whats the matter?

Lady Britomart *(swishing away her tears with her handkerchief).* Nothing. Foolishness. You can go with him, too, if you like, and leave me with the servants.

Stephen. Oh, you mustnt think that, mother. I—I dont like him.

Lady Britomart. The others do. That is the injustice of a woman's lot. A woman has to bring up her children; and that means to restrain them, to deny them things they want, to set them tasks, to punish them when they do wrong, to do all the unpleasant things. And then the father, who has nothing to do but pet them and spoil them, comes in when all her work is done and steals their affection from her.

Stephen. He has not stolen our affection from you. It is only curiosity.

Lady Britomart *(violently).* I wont be consoled, Stephen. There is nothing the matter with me. *(She rises and goes towards the door).*

Stephen. Where are you going, mother?

Lady Britomart. To the drawing room, of course. *(She goes out. Onward, Christian Soldiers, on the concertina, with tambourine accompaniment, is heard when the door opens).* Are you coming, Stephen?

Stephen. No. Certainly not. *(She goes. He sits down on the settee, with compressed lips and an expression of strong dislike).*

Act Two

The yard of the West Ham shelter of the Salvation Army is a cold place on a January morning. The building itself, an old warehouse, is newly whitewashed. Its gabled end projects into the yard in the middle, with a door on the ground floor, and another in the loft above it without any balcony or ladder, but with a pulley rigged over it for hoisting sacks. Those who come from this central gable end into the yard have the gateway leading to the street on their left, with a stone horsetrough just beyond it, and, on the right, a penthouse shielding a table from the weather. There are forms at the table; and on them are seated a man and a woman, both much down on their luck, finishing a meal of bread (one thick slice each, with margarine and golden syrup) and diluted milk.

The man, a workman out of employment, is young, agile, a talker, a poser, sharp enough to be capable of anything in reason except honesty or altruistic considerations of any kind. The woman is a commonplace old bundle of poverty and hard-worn humanity. She looks sixty and probably is forty-five. If they were rich people, gloved and muffed and well wrapped up in furs and overcoats, they would be numbed and miserable; for it is a grindingly cold raw January day; and a glance at the background of grimy warehouses and leaden sky visible over the whitewashed walls of the yard would drive any idle rich person straight to the Mediterranean. But these two, being no more troubled with visions of the Mediterranean than of the moon, and being compelled to keep more of their clothes in the pawnshop, and less on their persons, in winter than in summer, are not depressed by the cold: rather are they stung into vivacity, to which their meal has just now given an almost jolly turn. The man takes a pull at his mug, then gets up and moves about the yard with his hands deep in his pockets, occasionally breaking into a step-dance.

The Woman.   Feel better arter your meal, sir?

The Man.   No. Call that a meal! Good enough for you, praps; but wot is it to me, an intelligent workin man.

The Woman.   Workin man! Wot are you?

The Man.   Painter.

The Woman (*sceptically*).   Yus, I dessay.

The Man.   Yus, you dessay! I know. Every loafer that cant do nothink calls isself a painter. Well, I'm a real painter: grainer, finisher, thirty-eight bob a week when I can get it.

The Woman.   Then why dont you go and get it?

The Man.   I'll tell you why. Fust: I'm intelligent—fffff! it's rotten cold here (*he dances a step or two*)—yes: intelligent beyond the station o life into which it has pleased the capitalists to call me; and they dont like a man that sees through em. Second, an intelligent bein needs a doo share of appiness;

so I drink somethink cruel when I get the chawnce. Third, I stand by my class and do as little as I can so's to leave arf the job for me fellow workers. Fourth, I'm fly enough to know wots inside the law and wots outside it; and inside I do as the capitalists do: pinch wot I can lay me ands on. In a proper state of society I am sober, industrious and honest: in Rome, so to speak, I do as the Romans do. Wots the consequence? When trade is bad—and it's rotten bad just now—and the employers az to sack arf their men, they generally start on me.

The Woman. Whats your name?

The Man. Price. Bronterre O'Brien Price. Usually called Snobby Price, for short.

The Woman. Snobby's a carpenter, aint it? You said you was a painter.

Price. Not that kind of snob, but the genteel sort. I'm too uppish, owing to my intelligence, and my father being a Chartist and a reading, thinking man: a stationer, too. I'm none of your common hewers of wood and drawers of water; and dont you forget it. (*He returns to his seat at the table, and takes up his mug*). Wots your name?

The Woman. Rummy Mitchens, sir.

Price (*quaffing the remains of his milk to her*). Your elth, Miss Mitchens.

Rummy (*correcting him*). Missis Mitchens.

Price. Wot! Oh Rummy, Rummy! Respectable married woman, Rummy, gittin rescued by the Salvation Army by pretendin to be a bad un. Same old game!

Rummy. What am I to do? I cant starve. Them Salvation lasses is dear good girls; but the better you are, the worse they likes to think you were before they rescued you. Why shouldnt they av a bit o credit, poor loves? theyre worn to rags by their work. And where would they get the money to rescue us if we was to let on we're no worse than other people? You know what ladies and gentlemen are.

Price. Thievin swine! Wish I ad their job, Rummy, all the same. Wot does Rummy stand for? Pet name praps?

Rummy. Short for Romola.

Price. For wot!?

Rummy. Romola. It was out of a new book. Somebody me mother wanted me to grow up like.

Price. We're companions in misfortune, Rummy. Both on us got names that nobody cawnt pronounce. Consequently I'm Snobby and youre Rummy because Bill and Sally wasnt good enough for our parents. Such is life!

Rummy. Who saved you, Mr Price? Was it Major Barbara?

Price. No: I come here on my own. I'm going to be Bronterre O'Brien Price, the converted painter. I know wot they like. I'll tell em how I blasphemed and gambled and wopped my poor old mother—

Rummy (*shocked*). Used you to beat your mother?

Price. Not likely. She used to beat me. No matter: you come and listen to the converted painter, and youll hear how she was a pious woman that taught me prayers at er knee, an how I used to come home drunk and drag her out o bed be er snow white airs, an lam into er with the poker.

Rummy. Thats whats so unfair to us women. Your confessions is just as big lies as ours: you dont tell what you really done no more than us; but you men can tell your lies right out at the meetins and be made much of for it; while the sort o confessions we az to make az to be wispered to one lady at a time. It aint right, spite of all their piety.

Price. Right! Do you spose the Army'd be allowed if it went and did right? Not much. It combs our air and makes us good little blokes to be robbed and put upon. But I'll play the game as good as any of em. I'll see somebody struck by lightnin, or hear a voice sayin 'Snobby Price: where will you spend eternity?' I'll av a time of it, I tell you.

Rummy. You wont be let drink, though.

Price. I'll take it out in gorspellin, then. I dont want to drink if I can get fun enough any other way.

Jenny Hill, a pale, overwrought, pretty Salvation lass of 18, comes in through the yard gate, leading Peter Shirley, a half hardened, half worn-out elderly man, weak with hunger.

Jenny *(supporting him).* Come! pluck up. I'll get you something to eat. Youll be all right then.

Price *(rising and hurrying officiously to take the old man off Jenny's hands).* Poor old man! Cheer up, brother: youll find rest and peace and appiness ere. Hurry up with the food, miss: e's fair done. *(Jenny hurries into the shelter).* Ere, buck up, daddy! she's fetchin y'a thick slice of breadn treacle, an a mug o skyblue. *(He seats him at the corner of the table).*

Rummy *(gaily).* Keep up your old art! Never say die!

Shirley. I'm not an old man. I'm ony 46. I'm as good as ever I was. The grey patch come in my hair before I was thirty. All it wants is three pennorth o hair dye: am I to be turned on the streets to starve for it? Holy God! Ive worked ten to twelve hours a day since I was thirteen, and paid my way all through; and now am I to be thrown into the gutter and my job given to a young man that can do it no better than me because Ive black hair that goes white at the first change?

Price *(cheerfully).* No good jawrin about it. Your ony a jumped-up, jerked-off, orspittle-turned-out incurable of an ole workin man: who cares about you? Eh? Make the thievin swine give you a meal: theyve stole many a one from you. Get a bit o your own back. *[Jenny returns with the usual meal].* There you are, brother. Awsk a blessin an tuck that into you.

Shirley *(looking at it ravenously but not touching it, and crying like a child).* I never took anything before.

Jenny *(petting him).* Come, come! the Lord sends it to you: he wasnt above taking bread from his friends; and why should you be? Besides, when we find you a job you can pay us for it if you like.

Shirley *(eagerly).* Yes, yes: thats true. I can pay you back: it's only a loan.

(Shivering) Oh Lord! oh Lord! *(He turns to the table and attacks the meal ravenously).*

Jenny. Well, Rummy, are you more comfortable now?

Rummy. God bless you, lovey! youve fed my body and saved my soul, havnt you? *(Jenny, touched, kisses her).* Sit down and rest a bit: you must be ready to drop.

Jenny. Ive been going hard since morning. But theres more work than we can do. I mustnt stop.

Rummy. Try a prayer for just two minutes. Youll work all the better after.

Jenny *(her eyes lighting up).* Oh isnt it wonderful how a few minutes prayer revives you! I was quite lightheaded at twelve o'clock, I was so tired; but Major Barbara just sent me to pray for five minutes; and I was able to go on as if I had only just begun. *(To Price)* Did you have a piece of bread?

Price *(with unction).* Yes, miss; but Ive got the piece that I value more; and thats the peace that passeth hall hannerstennin.

Rummy *(fervently).* Glory Hallelujah!

Bill Walker, a rough customer of about 25, appears at the yard gate and looks malevolently at Jenny.

Jenny. That makes me so happy. When you say that, I feel wicked for loitering here. I must get to work again.

She is hurrying to the shelter, when the newcomer moves quickly up to the door and intercepts her. His manner is so threatening that she retreats as he comes at her truculently, driving her down the yard.

Bill. Aw knaow. Youre the one that took awy maw girl. Youre the one that set er agen me. Well, I'm gowin to ev er aht. Not that Aw care a carse for er or you: see? Bat Aw'll let er knaow; and Aw'll let you knaow. Aw'm gowing to give her a doin thatll teach er to cat awy from me. Nah in wiv you and tell er to cam aht afore Aw cam in and kick er aht. Tell er Bill Walker wants er. She'll knaow wot thet means; and if she keeps me witin itll be worse. You stop to jawr beck at me; and Aw'll stawt on you: d'ye eah? Theres your wy. In you gow. *(He takes her by the arm and slings her towards the door of the shelter. She falls on her hand and knee. Rummy helps her up again).*

Price *(rising, and venturing irresolutely towards Bill).* Easy there, mate. She aint doin you no arm.

Bill. Oo are you callin mite? *(Standing over him threateningly)* Youre goin to stend ap for er, aw yer? Put ap your ends.

Rummy *(running indignantly to him to scold him).* Oh, you great brute— *(He instantly swings his left hand back against her face. She screams and reels back to the trough, where she sits down, covering her bruised face with her hands and rocking herself and moaning with pain).*

Jenny *(going to her).* Oh, God forgive you! How could you strike an old woman like that?

Bill *(seizing her by the hair so violently that she also screams, and tearing her away from the old woman).*   You Gawd forgimme again an Aw'll Gawd forgive you one on the jawr thetll stop you pryin for a week. *(Holding her and turning fiercely on Price)* Ev you ennything to sy agen it?

Price *(intimidated).*   No, matey: she aint anything to do with me.

Bill.   Good job for you! Aw'd pat two meals into you and fawt you with one finger arter, you stawved cur. [*To Jenny*] Nah are you gowin to fetch aht Mog Ebbijem; or em Aw to knock your fice off you and fetch her meself?

Jenny *(writhing in his grasp).*   Oh please someone go in and tell Major Barbara—*(she screams again as he wrenches her head down; and Price and Rummy flee into the shelter).*

Bill.   You want to gow in and tell your Mijor of me, do you?

Jenny.   Oh please dont drag my hair. Let me go.

Bill.   Do you or downt you? *(She stifles a scream).* Yus or nao?

Jenny.   God give me strength—

Bill *(striking her with his fist in the face).*   Gow an shaow her thet, and tell her if she wants one lawk it to cam and interfere with me. *(Jenny, crying with pain, goes into the shed. He goes to the form and addresses the old man).* Eah: finish your mess; an git aht o maw wy.

Shirley *(springing up and facing him fiercely, with the mug in his hand).*   You take a liberty with me, and I'll smash you over the face with the mug and cut your eye out. Aint you satisfied—young whelps like you—with takin the bread out o the mouths of your elders that have brought you up and slaved for you, but you must come shovin and cheekin and bullyin in here, where the bread o charity is sickenin in our stummicks?

Bill *(contemptuously, but backing a little).*   Wot good are you, you aold palsy mag? Wot good are you?

Shirley.   As good as you and better. I'll do a day's work agen you or any fat young soaker of your age. Go and take my job at Horrockses, where I worked for ten year. They want young men there: they cant afford to keep men over forty-five. Theyre very sorry—give you a character and happy to help you to get anything suited to your years—sure a steady man wont be long out of a job. Well, let em try you. Theyll find the differ. What do you know? Not as much as how to beeyave yourself—layin your dirty fist across the mouth of a respectable woman!

Bill.   Downt provowk me to ly it acrost yours: d'ye eah?

Shirley *(with blighting contempt).*   Yes: you like an old man to hit, dont you, when youve finished with the women. I aint seen you hit a young one yet.

Bill *(stung).*   You loy, you aold soupkitchener, you. There was a yang menn eah. Did Aw offer to itt him or did Aw not?

Shirley.   Was he starvin or was he not? Was he a man or only a crosseyed thief an a loafer? Would you hit my son-in-law's brother?

Bill.   Oo's ee?

Shirley.   Todger Fairmile o Balls Pond. Him that won £20 off the Japanese wrastler at the music hall by standin out 17 minutes 4 seconds agen him.

Bill *(sullenly).* Aw'm nao music awl wrastler. Ken he box?

Shirley. Yes: an you cant.

Bill. Wot! Aw cawnt, cawnt Aw? Wots thet you sy *(threatening him)*?

Shirley *(not budging an inch).* Will you box Todger Fairmile if I put him on to you? Say the word.

Bill *(subsiding with a slouch).* Aw'll stend ap to enny menn alawv, if he was ten Todger Fairmawls. But Aw dont set ap to be a perfeshnal.

Shirley *(looking down on him with unfathomable disdain).* You box! Slap an old woman with the back o your hand! You hadnt even the sense to hit her where a magistrate couldnt see the mark of it, you silly young lump of conceit and ignorance. Hit a girl in the jaw and ony make her cry! If Todger Fairmile'd done it, she wouldnt a got up inside o ten minutes, no more than you would if he got on to you. Yah! I'd set about you myself if I had a week's feedin in me instead o two months' starvation. *(He turns his back on him and sits down moodily at the table).*

Bill *(following him and stooping over him to drive the taunt in).* You loy! youve the bread and treacle in you that you cam eah to beg.

Shirley *(bursting into tears).* Oh God! it's true: I'm only an old pauper on the scrap heap. *(Furiously)* But youll come to it yourself; and then youll know. Youll come to it sooner than a teetotaller like me, fillin yourself with gin at this hour o the mornin!

Bill. Aw'm nao gin drinker, you oald lawr; bat wen Aw want to give my girl a bloomin good awdin Aw lawk to ev a bit o devil in me: see? An eah emm, talkin to a rotten aold blawter like you sted o givin her wot for. *(Working himself into a rage)* Aw'm gowin in there to fetch her aht. *(He makes vengefully for the shelter door).*

Shirley. Youre going to the station on a stretcher, more likely; and theyll take the gin and the devil out of you there when they get you inside. You mind what youre about: the major here is the Earl o Stevenage's grand-daughter.

Bill *(checked).* Garn!

Shirley. Youll see.

Bill *(his resolution oozing).* Well, Aw aint dan nathin to er.

Shirley. Spose she said you did! who'd believe you?

Bill *(very uneasy, skulking back to the corner of the penthouse).* Gawd! theres no jastice in this cantry. To think wot them people can do! Aw'm as good as er.

Shirley. Tell her so. It's just what a fool like you would do.

Barbara, brisk and businesslike, comes from the shelter with a note book, and addresses herself to Shirley. Bill, cowed, sits down in the corner on a form, and turns his back on them.

Barbara. Good morning.

Shirley *(standing up and taking off his hat).* Good morning, miss.

Barbara. Sit down: make yourself at home. *(He hesitates; but she puts a* *friendly hand on his shoulder and makes him obey).* Now then! since youve made friends with us, we want to know all about you. Names and addresses and trades.

Shirley. Peter Shirley. Fitter. Chucked out two months ago because I was too old.

Barbara *(not at all surprised).* Youd pass still. Why didnt you dye your hair?

Shirley. I did. Me age come out at a coroner's inquest on me daughter.

Barbara. Steady?

Shirley. Teetotaller. Never out of a job before. Good worker. And sent to the knackers like an old horse!

Barbara. No matter: if you did your part God will do his.

Shirley *(suddenly stubborn).* My religion's no concern of anybody but myself.

Barbara *(guessing).* I know. Secularist?

Shirley *(hotly).* Did I offer to deny it?

Barbara. Why should you? My own father's a Secularist, I think. Our Father —yours and mine—fulfils himself in many ways; and I daresay he knew what he was about when he made a Secularist of you. So buck up, Peter! we can always find a job for a steady man like you. *(Shirley, disarmed and a little bewildered touches his hat. She turns from him to Bill).* Whats your name?

Bill *(insolently).* Wots thet to you?

Barbara *(calmly making a note).* Afraid to give his name. Any trade?

Bill. Oo's afride to give is nime? *(Doggedly, with a sense of heroically defying the House of Lords in the person of Lord Stevenage)* If you want to bring a chawge agen me, bring it. *(She waits, unruffled).* Moy nime's Bill Walker.

Barbara *(as if the name were familiar: trying to remember how.)* Bill Walker? *(Recollecting)* Oh, I know: youre the man that Jenny Hill was praying for inside just now. *(She enters his name in her note book).*

Bill. Oo's Jenny Ill? And wot call as she to pry for me?

Barbara. I dont know. Perhaps it was you that cut her lip.

Bill *(defiantly).* Yus, it was me that cat her lip. Aw aint afride o you.

Barbara. How could you be, since youre not afraid of God? Youre a brave man, Mr. Walker. It takes some pluck to do our work here; but none of us dare lift our hand against a girl like that, for fear of her father in heaven.

Bill *(sullenly).* I want nan o your kentin jawr. I spowse you think Aw cam eah to beg from you, like this demmiged lot eah. Not me. Aw downt want your bread and scripe and ketlep. Aw dont blieve in your Gawd, no more than you do yourself.

Barbara *(sunnily apologetic and ladylike, as on a new footing with him).* Oh, I beg your pardon for putting your name down, Mr. Walker. I didnt understand. I'll strike it out.

Bill *(taking this as a slight, and deeply wounded by it).* Eah! you let maw nime alown. Aint it good enaff to be in your book?

Barbara *(considering).* Well, you see, theres no use putting down your name unless I can do something for you, is there? Whats your trade?

Bill *(still smarting).* Thets nao concern o yours.

Barbara. Just so. *(Very businesslike)* I'll put you down as *(writing)* the man who—struck—poor little Jenny Hill—in the mouth.

Bill *(rising threateningly).* See eah. Awve ed enaff o this.

Barbara *(quite sunny and fearless).* What did you come to us for?

Bill. Aw cam for maw gel, see? Aw cam to tike her aht o this and to brike er jawr for er.

Barbara *(complacently).* You see I was right about your trade. *(Bill, on the point of retorting furiously, finds himself, to his great shame and terror, in danger of crying instead. He sits down again suddenly).* Whats her name?

Bill *(dogged).* Er nime's Mog Ebbijem: thets wot her nime is.

Barbara. Mog Habbijam! Oh, she's gone to Canning Town, to our barracks there.

Bill *(fortified by his resentment of Mog's perfidy).* Is she? *(Vindictively)* Then Aw'm gowin to Kennintahn arter her. *(He crosses to the gate; hesitates; finally comes back at Barbara).* Are you loyin to me to git shat o me?

Barbara. I dont want to get shut of you. I want to keep you here and save your soul. Youd better stay: youre going to have a bad time today, Bill.

Bill. Oo's gowin to give it to me? You, preps?

Barbara. Someone you dont believe in. But youll be glad afterwards.

Bill *(slinking off).* Aw'll gow to Kennintahn to be aht o reach o your tangue. *(Suddenly turning on her with intense malice)* And if Aw downt fawnd Mog there, Aw'll cam beck and do two years for you, selp me Gawd if Aw downt!

Barbara *(a shade kindlier, if possible).* It's no use, Bill. She's got another bloke.

Bill Wot!

Barbara. One of her own converts. He fell in love with her when he saw her with her soul saved, and her face clean, and her hair washed.

Bill *(surprised).* Wottud she wash it for, the carroty slat? It's red.

Barbara. It's quite lovely now, because she wears a new look in her eyes with it. It's a pity youre too late. The new bloke has put your nose out of joint, Bill.

Bill. Aw'll put his nowse aht o joint for him. Not that Aw care a carse for er, mawnd thet. But Aw'll teach her to drop me as if Aw was dirt. And Aw'll teach him to meddle with maw judy. Wots iz bleedin nime?

Barbara. Sergeant Todger Fairmile.

Shirley *(rising with grim joy).* I'll go with him, miss. I want to see them two meet. I'll take him to the infirmary when it's over.

Bill *(to Shirley, with undissembled misgiving).* Is thet im you was speakin on?

Shirley. Thats him.

Bill. Im that wrastled in the music awl?

Shirley. The competitions at the National Sportin Club was worth nigh a hundred a year to him. He's gev em up now for religion; so he's a bit fresh for want of the exercise he was accustomed to. He'll be glad to see you. Come along.

Bill. Wots is wight?

Shirley. Thirteen four. *(Bill's last hope expires).*

Barbara. Go and talk to him, Bill. He'll convert you.

Shirley. He'll convert your head into a mashed potato.

Bill *(sullenly).* Aw aint afride of im. Aw aint afride of ennybody. Bat e can lick me. She's dan me. *(He sits down moodily on the edge of the horse trough).*

Shirley. You aint going. I thought not. *(He resumes his seat).*

Barbara *(calling).* Jenny!

Jenny *(appearing at the shelter door with a plaster on the corner of her mouth).* Yes, Major.

Barbara. Send Rummy Mitchens out to clear away here.

Jenny. I think she's afraid.

Barbara *(her resemblance to her mother flashing out for a moment).* Nonsense! she must do as she's told.

Jenny *(calling into the shelter).* Rummy: the Major says you must come.

Jenny comes to Barbara, purposely keeping on the side next Bill, lest he should suppose that she shrank from him or bore malice.

Barbara. Poor little Jenny! Are you tired? *(Looking at the wounded cheek)* Does it hurt?

Jenny. No: it's all right now. It was nothing.

Barbara *(critically).* It was as hard as he could hit, I expect. Poor Bill! You dont feel angry with him, do you?

Jenny. Oh no, no, no: indeed I dont, Major, bless his poor heart! *(Barbara kisses her; and she runs away merrily into the shelter. Bill writhes with an agonizing return of his new and alarming symptoms, but says nothing. Rummy Mitchens comes from the shelter).*

Barbara *(going to meet Rummy).* Now Rummy, bustle. Take in those mugs and plates to be washed; and throw the crumbs about for the birds.

Rummy takes the three plates and mugs; but Shirley takes back his mug from her, as there is till some milk left in it.

Rummy. There aint any crumbs. This aint a time to waste good bread on birds.

Price *(appearing at the shelter door).* Gentleman come to see the shelter, Major. Says he's your father.

Barbara. All right. Coming. *(Snobby goes back into the shelter, followed by Barbara).*

Rummy *(stealing across to Bill and addressing him in a subdued voice, but with intense conviction).* I'd av the lor of you, you flat eared pignosed potwalloper, if she'd let me. Youre no gentleman, to hit a lady in the face. *(Bill, with greater things moving in him, takes no notice).*

Shirley *(following her).* Here! in with you and dont get yourself into more trouble by talking.

Rummy *(with hauteur).* I aint ad the pleasure o being hintroduced to you, as I can remember. *(She goes into the shelter with the plates).*

Shirley. Thats the—

Bill *(savagely).* Downt you talk to me, d'ye eah? You lea me alown, or Aw'll do you a mischief. Aw'm not dirt under your feet, ennywy.

Shirley *(calmly).* Dont you be afeered. You aint such prime company that you need expect to be sought after. *(He is about to go into the shelter when Barbara comes out, with Undershaft on her right).*

Barbara. Oh, there you are, Mr Shirley! *(Between them)* This is my father: I told you he was a Secularist, didnt I? Perhaps youll be able to comfort one another.

Undershaft *(startled).* A Secularist! Not the least in the world: on the contrary, a confirmed mystic.

Barbara. Sorry, I'm sure. By the way, papa, what is your religion? in case I have to introduce you again.

Undershaft. My religion? Well, my dear, I am a Millionaire. That is my religion.

Barbara. Then I'm afraid you and Mr Shirley wont be able to comfort one another after all. Youre not a Millionaire, are you, Peter?

Shirley. No; and proud of it.

Undershaft *(gravely).* Poverty, my friend, is not a thing to be proud of.

Shirley *(angrily).* Who made your millions for you? Me and my like. Whats kep us poor? Keepin you rich. I wouldnt have your conscience, not for all your income.

Undershaft. I wouldnt have your income, not for all your conscience, Mr Shirley. *(He goes to the penthouse and sits down on a form).*

Barbara *(stopping Shirley adroitly as he is about to retort).* You wouldnt think he was my father, would you, Peter? Will you go into the shelter and lend the lasses a hand for a while: we're worked off our feet.

Shirley *(bitterly).* Yes: I'm in their debt for a meal, aint I?

Barbara. Oh, not because youre in their debt, but for love of them, Peter, for love of them. *(He cannot understand, and is rather scandalized)* There! dont stare at me. In with you; and give that conscience of yours a holiday *(bustling him into the shelter).*

Shirley *(as he goes in).* Ah! it's a pity you never was trained to use your reason, miss. Youd have been a very taking lecturer on Secularism.

Barbara turns to her father.

Undershaft. Never mind me, my dear. Go about your work; and let me watch it for a while.

Barbara. All right.

Undershaft. For instance, whats the matter with that outpatient over there?

Barbara *(looking at Bill, whose attitude has never changed, and whose expression of brooding wrath has deepened).* Oh, we shall cure him in no time. Just watch. *(She goes over to Bill and waits. He glances up at her and casts his eyes down again, uneasy, but grimmer than ever).* It would be nice to just stamp on Mog Habbijam's face, wouldnt it, Bill?

Bill *(starting up from the trough in consternation).* It's a loy: Aw never said so. *(She shakes her head).* Oo taold you wot was in moy mawnd?

Barbara. Only your new friend.

Bill. Wot new friend?

Barbara. The devil, Bill. When he gets round people they get miserable, just like you.

Bill *(with a heartbreaking attempt at devil-may-care cheerfulness).* Aw aint miserable. *(He sits down again, and stretches his legs in an attempt to seem indifferent).*

Barbara. Well, if youre happy, why dont you look happy, as we do?

Bill *(his legs curling back in spite of him).* Aw'm eppy enaff, Aw tell you. Woy cawnt you lea me alown? Wot ev I dan to you? Aw aint smashed your fice, ev Aw?

Barbara *(softly: wooing his soul).* It's not me thats getting at you, Bill.

Bill. Oo else is it?

Barbara. Somebody that doesnt intend you to smash women's faces, I suppose. Somebody or something that wants to make a man of you.

Bill *(blustering).* Mike a menn o me! Aint Aw a menn? eh? Oo sez Aw'm not a menn?

Barbara. Theres a man in you somewhere, I suppose. But why did he let you hit poor little Jenny Hill? That wasnt very manly of him, was it?

Bill *(tormented).* Ev dan wiv it, Aw tell you. Chack it. Aw'm sick o your Jenny Ill and er silly little fice.

Barbara. Then why do you keep thinking about it? Why does it keep coming up against you in your mind? Youre not getting converted, are you?

Bill *(with conviction).* Not ME. Not lawkly.

Barbara. Thats right, Bill. Hold out against it. Put out your strength. Dont lets get you cheap. Todger Fairmile said he wrestled for three nights against his salvation harder than he ever wrestled with the Jap at the music hall. He gave in to the Jap when his arm was going to break. But he didnt give in to his salvation until his heart was going to break. Perhaps youll escape that. You havnt any heart, have you?

Bill. Wot d'ye mean? Woy aint Aw got a awt the sime as ennybody else?

Barbara. A man with a heart wouldnt have bashed poor little Jenny's face, would he?

Bill *(almost crying).* Ow, will you lea me alown? Ev Aw ever offered to meddle with you, that you cam neggin and provowkin me lawk this? *(He writhes convulsively from his eyes to his toes).*

Barbara *(with a steady soothing hand on his arm and a gentle voice that never* *lets him go).* It's your soul thats hurting you, Bill, and not me. Weve been through it all ourselves. Come with us, Bill. *(He looks wildly round).* To brave manhood on earth and eternal glory in heaven. *(He is on the point of breaking down).* Come. *(A drum is heard in the shelter; and Bill, with a gasp, escapes from the spell as Barbara turns quickly. Adolphus enters from the shelter with a big drum).* Oh! there you are, Dolly. Let me introduce a new friend of mine, Mr Bill Walker. This is my bloke, Bill: Mr Cusins. *(Cusins salutes with his drumstick).*

Bill.   Gowin to merry im?

Barbara.   Yes.

Bill *(fervently).*   Gawd elp im! Gaw-aw-aw-awd elp im!

Barbara.   Why? Do you think he wont be happy with me?

Bill.   Awve aony ed to stend it for a mawnin: e'll ev to stend it for a lawftawm.

Cusins.   That is a frightful reflection, Mr Walker. But I cant tear myself away from her.

Bill.   Well, Aw ken. *(To Barbara)* Eah! do you knaow where Aw'm gowin to, and wot Aw'm gowin to do?

Barbara.   Yes: youre going to heaven; and youre coming back here before the week's out to tell me so.

Bill.   You loy. Aw'm gowin to Kennintahn, to spit in Todger Fairmawl's eye. Aw beshed Jenny Ill's fice; an nar Aw'll git me aown fice beshed and cam beck and shaow it to er. Ee'll itt me ardern Aw itt her. Thatll mike us square. *(To Adolphus)* Is thet fair or is it not? Youre a genlmn: you oughter knaow.

Barbara.   Two black eyes wont make one white one, Bill.

Bill.   Aw didnt awst you. Cawnt you never keep your mahth shat? Oy awst the genlmn.

Cusins *(reflectively).*   Yes: I think youre right, Mr Walker. Yes: I should do it. It's curious: it's exactly what an ancient Greek would have done.

Barbara.   But what good will it do?

Cusins.   Well, it will give Mr. Fairmile some exercise; and it will satisfy Mr Walker's soul.

Bill.   Rot! there aint nao sach a thing as a saoul. Ah kin you tell wevver Awve a saoul or not? You never seen it.

Barbara.   Ive seen it hurting you when you went against it.

Bill *(with compressed aggravation).*   If you was maw gel and took the word aht o me mahth lawk thet, Aw'd give you sathink youd feel urtin, Aw would. *(To Adolphus)* You tike maw tip, mite. Stop er jawr; or youll doy afoah your tawm *(With intense expression)* Wore aht: thets wot youll be: wore aht. *(He goes away through the gate).*

Cusins *(looking after him).*   I wonder!

Barbara.   Dolly! *(indignant, in her mother's manner).*

Cusins.   Yes, my dear, it's very wearing to be in love with you. If it lasts, I quite think I shall die young.

Barbara.   Should you mind?

Cusins. Not at all. *(He is suddenly softened, and kisses her over the drum, evidently not for the first time, as people cannot kiss over a big drum without practice. Undershaft coughs).*

Barbara. It's all right, papa, weve not forgotten you. Dolly: explain the place to papa: I havnt time. *(She goes busily into the shelter).*

Undershaft and Adolphus now have the yard to themselves. Undershaft, seated on a form, and still keenly attentive, looks hard at Adolphus. Adolphus looks hard at him.

Undershaft. I fancy you guess something of what is in my mind, Mr Cusins. *(Cusins flourishes his drumsticks as if in the act of beating a lively rataplan, but makes no sound).* Exactly so. But suppose Barbara finds you out!

Cusins. You know, I do not admit that I am imposing on Barbara. I am quite genuinely interested in the views of the Salvation Army. The fact is, I am a sort of collector of religions; and the curious thing is that I find I can believe them all. By the way, have you any religion?

Undershaft. Yes.

Cusins. Anything out of the common?

Undershaft. Only that there are two things necessary to Salvation.

Cusins *(disappointed, but polite).* Ah, the Church Catechism. Charles Lomax also belongs to the Established Church.

Undershaft. The two things are—

Cusins. Baptism and—

Undershaft. No. Money and gunpowder.

Cusins *(surprised, but interested).* That is the general opinion of our governing classes. The novelty is in hearing any man confess it.

Undershaft. Just so.

Cusins. Excuse me: is there any place in your religion for honor, justice, truth, love, mercy and so forth?

Undershaft. Yes: they are the graces and luxuries of a rich, strong, and safe life.

Cusins. Suppose one is forced to choose between them and money or gunpowder?

Undershaft. Choose money and gunpowder; for without enough of both you cannot afford the others.

Cusins. That is your religion?

Undershaft. Yes.

The cadence of this reply makes a full close in the conversation, Cusins twists his face dubiously and contemplates Undershaft. Undershaft contemplates him.

Cusins. Barbara wont stand that. You will have to choose between your religion and Barbara.

Undershaft. So will you, my friend. She will find out that that drum of yours is hollow.

Cusins. Father Undershaft: you are mistaken: I am a sincere Salvationist. You do not understand the Salvation Army. It is the army of joy, of love, of courage: it has banished the fear and remorse and despair of the old hell-ridden evangelical sects: it marches to fight the devil with trumpet and drum, with music and dancing, with banner and palm, as becomes a sally from heaven by its happy garrison. It picks the waster out of the public house and makes a man of him: it finds a worm wriggling in a back kitchen, and lo! a woman! Men and women of rank too, sons and daughters of the Highest. It takes the poor professor of Greek, the most artificial and self-suppressed of human creatures, from his meal of roots, and lets loose the rhapsodist in him; reveals the true worship of Dionysos to him; sends him down the public street drumming dithyrambs (*he plays a thundering flourish on the drum*).

Undershaft. You will alarm the shelter.

Cusins. Oh, they are accustomed to these sudden ecstasies. However, if the drum worries you—(*he pockets the drumsticks; unhooks the drum; and stands it on the ground opposite the gateway*).

Undershaft. Thank you.

Cusins. You remember what Euripides says about your money and gunpowder?

Undershaft. No.

Cusins (*declaiming*).

> One and another
> In money and guns may outpass his brother;
> And men in their millions float and flow
> And seethe with a million hopes as leaven;
> And they win their will; or they miss their will;
> And their hopes are dead or are pined for still;
> But who'er can know
> As the long days go
> That to live is happy, has found his heaven.

My translation: what do you think of it?

Undershaft. I think, my friend, that if you wish to know, as the long days go, that to live is happy, you must first acquire money enough for a decent life, and power enough to be your own master.

Cusins. You are damnably discouraging. (*He resumes his declamation*).

> Is it so hard a thing to see
> That the spirit of God—whate'er it be—
> The law that abides and changes not, ages long,
> The Eternal and Nature-born: these things be strong?
> What else is Wisdom? What of Man's endeavor,
> Or God's high grace so lovely and so great?
> To stand from fear set free? to breathe and wait?
> To hold a hand uplifted over Fate?
> And shall not Barbara be loved for ever?

Undershaft. Euripides mentions Barbara, does he?

Cusins. It is a fair translation. The word means Loveliness.

Undershaft. May I ask—as Barbara's father—how much a year she is to be loved for ever on?

Cusins. As for Barbara's father, that is more your affair than mine. I can feed her by teaching Greek: that is about all.

Undershaft. Do you consider it a good match for her?

Cusins (with polite obstinacy). Mr Undershaft: I am in many ways a weak, timid, ineffectual person; and my health is far from satisfactory. But whenever I feel that I must have anything, I get it, sooner or later. I feel that way about Barbara. I dont like marriage: I feel intensely afraid of it; and I dont know what I shall do with Barbara or what she will do with me. But I feel that I and nobody else must marry her. Please regard that as settled.—Not that I wish to be arbitrary; but why should I waste your time in discussing what is inevitable?

Undershaft. You mean that you will stick at nothing: not even the conversion of the Salvation Army to the worship of Dionysos.

Cusins. The business of the Salvation Army is to save, not to wrangle about the name of the pathfinder. Dionysos or another: what does it matter?

Undershaft (rising and approaching him). Professor Cusins: you are a young man after my own heart.

Cusins. Mr Undershaft: you are, as far as I am able to gather, a most infernal old rascal; but you appeal very strongly to my sense of ironic humor.

Undershaft mutely offers his hand. They shake.

Undershaft (suddenly concentrating himself). And now to business.

Cusins. Pardon me. We are discussing religion. Why go back to such an uninteresting and unimportant subject as business?

Undershaft. Religion is our business at present, because it is through religion alone that we can win Barbara.

Cusins. Have you, too, fallen in love with Barbara?

Undershaft. Yes, with a father's love.

Cusins. A father's love for a grown-up daughter is the most dangerous of all infatuations. I apologize for mentioning my own pale, coy, mistrustful fancy in the same breath with it.

Undershaft. Keep to the point. We have to win her; and we are neither of us Methodists.

Cusins. That doesnt matter. The power Barbara wields here—the power that wields Barbara herself—is not Calvinism, not Presbyterianism, not Methodism—

Undershaft. Not Greek Paganism either, eh?

Cusins. I admit that. Barbara is quite original in her religion.

Undershaft (triumphantly). Aha! Barbara Undershaft would be. Her inspiration comes from within herself.

Cusins.   How do you suppose it got there?

Undershaft *(in towering excitement)*.   It is the Undershaft inheritance. I shall hand on my torch to my daughter. She shall make my converts and preach my gospel—

Cusins.   What! Money and gunpowder!

Undershaft.   Yes, money and gunpowder. Freedom and power. Command of life and command of death.

Cusins *(urbanely: trying to bring him down to earth)*.   This is extremely interesting, Mr Undershaft. Of course you know that you are mad.

Undershaft *(with redoubled force)*.   And you?

Cusins.   Oh, mad as a hatter. You are welcome to my secret since I have discovered yours. But I am astonished. Can a madman make cannons?

Undershaft.   Would anyone else than a madman make them? And now *(with surging energy)* Question for question. Can a sane man translate Euripides?

Cusins.   No.

Undershaft *(seizing him by the shoulder)*.   Can a sane woman make a man of a waster or a woman of a worm?

Cusins *(reeling before the storm)*.   Father Colossus—Mammoth Millionaire—

Undershaft *(pressing him)*.   Are there two mad people or three in this Salvation shelter today?

Cusins.   You mean Barbara is as mad as we are?

Undershaft *(pushing him lightly off and resuming his equanimity suddenly and completely)*.   Pooh, Professor! let us call things by their proper names. I am a millionaire; you are a poet: Barbara is a savior of souls. What have we three to do with the common mob of slaves and idolators? *(He sits down again with a shrug of contempt for the mob)*.

Cusins.   Take care! Barbara is in love with the common people. So am I. Have you never felt the romance of that love?

Undershaft *(cold and sardonic)*   Have you ever been in love with Poverty, like St Francis? Have you ever been in love with Dirt, like St Simeon! Have you ever been in love with disease and suffering, like our nurses and philanthropists? Such passions are not virtues, but the most unnatural of all the vices. This love of the common people may please an earl's granddaughter and a university professor; but I have been a common man and a poor man; and it has no romance for me. Leave it to the poor to pretend that poverty is a blessing: leave it to the coward to make a religion of his cowardice by preaching humility: we know better than that. We three must stand together above the common people: how else can we help their children to climb up beside us? Barbara must belong to us, not to the Salvation Army.

Cusins.   Well, I can only say that if you think you will get her away from the Salvation Army by talking to her as you have been talking to me, you dont know Barbara.

Undershaft. My friend: I never ask for what I can buy.

Cusins *(in a white fury).* Do I understand you to imply that you can buy Barbara?

Undershaft. No; but I can buy the Salvation Army.

Cusins. Quite impossible.

Undershaft. You shall see. All religious organizations exist by selling themselves to the rich.

Cusins. Not the Army. That is the Church of the poor.

Undershaft. All the more reason for buying it.

Cusins. I dont think you quite know what the Army does for the poor.

Undershaft. Oh yes I do. It draws their teeth: that is enough for me as a man of business.

Cusins. Nonsense! It makes them sober—

Undershaft. I prefer sober workmen. The profits are larger.

Cusins. —honest—

Undershaft. Honest workmen are the most economical.

Cusins. —attached to their homes—

Undershaft. So much the better: they will put up with anything sooner than change their shop.

Cusins. —happy—

Undershaft. An invaluable safeguard against revolution.

Cusins. —unselfish—

Undershaft. Indifferent to their own interests, which suits me exactly.

Cusins. —with their thoughts on heavenly things—

Undershaft *(rising).* And not on Trade Unionism nor Socialism. Excellent.

Cusins *(revolted).* You really are an infernal old rascal.

Undershaft *(indicating Peter Shirley, who has just come from the shelter and strolled dejectedly down the yard between them).* And this is an honest man!

Shirley. Yes; and what av I got by it? *(he passes on bitterly and sits on the form, in the corner of the penthouse).*

Snobby Price, beaming sanctimoniously, and Jenny Hill, with a tambourine full of coppers, come from the shelter and go to the drum, on which Jenny begins to count the money.

Undershaft *(replying to Shirley).* Oh, your employers must have got a good deal by it from first to last. *(He sits on the table, with one foot on the side form, Cusins, overwhelmed, sits down on the same form nearer the shelter. Barbara comes from the shelter to the middle of the yard. She is excited and a little overwrought).*

Barbara. Weve just had a splendid experience meeting at the other gate in Cripps's lane. Ive hardly ever seen them so much moved as they were by your confession, Mr Price.

Price. I could amost be glad of my past wickedness if I could believe that it would elp to keep hathers stright.

Barbara. So it will, Snobby. How much, Jenny?

Jenny. Four and tenpence, Major.

Barbara. Oh Snobby, if you had given your poor mother just one more kick, we should have got the whole five shillings!

Price. If she heard you say that, miss, she'd be sorry I didnt. But I'm glad. Oh what a joy it will be to her when she hears I'm saved!

Undershaft. Shall I contribute the odd twopence, Barbara? The millionaire's mite, eh? *(He takes a couple of pennies from his pocket).*

Barbara. How did you make that twopence?

Undershaft. As usual. By selling cannons, torpedoes, submarines, and my new patent Grand Duke hand grenade.

Barbara. Put it back in your pocket. You cant buy your salvation here for two-pence: you must work it out.

Undershaft. Is twopence not enough? I can afford a little more, if you press me.

Barbara. Two million millions would not be enough. There is bad blood on your hands; and nothing but good blood can cleanse them. Money is no use. Take it away. *(She turns to Cusins).* Dolly: you must write another letter for me to the papers *(He makes a wry face).* Yes: I know you dont like it; but it must be done. The starvation this winter is beating us: everybody is unemployed. The General says we must close this shelter if we cant get more money. I force the collections at the meetings until I am ashamed: dont I, Snobby?

Price. It's a fair treat to see you work it, miss. The way you got them up from three-and-six to four-and-ten with that hymn, penny by penny and verse by verse, was a caution. Not a Cheap Jack on Mile End Waste could touch you at it.

Barbara. Yes; but I wish we could do without it. I am getting at last to think more of the collection than of the people's souls. And what are those hatfuls of pence and halfpence? We want thousands! I want to convert people, not to be always begging for the Army in a way I'd die sooner than beg for myself.

Undershaft *(in profound irony).* Genuine unselfishness is capable of anything, my dear.

Barbara *(unsuspectingly, as she turns away to take the money from the drum and put it in a cash bag she carries).* Yes, isnt it? *(Undershaft looks sardonically at Cusins).*

Cusins *(aside to Undershaft).* Mephistopheles! Machiavelli!

Barbara *(tears coming into her eyes as she ties the bag and pockets it).* How are we to feed them? I cant talk religion to a man with bodily hunger in his eyes. *(Almost breaking down)* It's frightful.

Jenny *(running to her).* Major, dear—

Barbara *(rebounding).* No: dont comfort me. It will be all right. We shall get the money.

Undershaft. How?

Jenny. By praying for it, of course. Mrs Baines says she prayed for it last night; and she has never prayed for it in vain: never once. *(She goes to the gate and looks out into the street).*

Barbara. *(who has dried her eyes and regained her composure).* By the way, dad, Mrs Baines has come to march with us to our big meeting this afternoon; and she is very anxious to meet you, for some reason or other. Perhaps she'll convert you.

Undershaft. I shall be delighted, my dear.

Jenny *(at the gate: excitedly).* Major! Major! heres that man back again.

Barbara. What man?

Jenny. The man that hit me. Oh, I hope he's coming back to join us.

Bill Walker, with frost on his jacket, comes through the gate, his hands deep in his pockets and his chin sunk between his shoulders, like a cleaned-out gambler. He halts between Barbara and the drum.

Barbara. Hullo, Bill! Back already!

Bill *(nagging at her).* Bin talkin ever sence, ev you?

Barbara. Pretty nearly. Well, has Todger paid you out for poor Jenny's jaw?

Bill. Nao e aint.

Barbara. I thought your jacket looked a bit snowy.

Bill. Sao it is snaowy. You want to knaow where the snaow cam from, downt you?

Barbara. Yes.

Bill. Well, it cam from orf the grahnd in Pawkinses Corner in Kennintahn. It got rabbed orf be maw shaoulders: see?

Barbara. Pity you didnt rub some off with your knees, Bill! That would have done you a lot of good.

Bill *(with sour mirthless humor).* Aw was sivin anather menn's knees at the tawm. E was kneelin on moy ed, e was.

Jenny. Who was kneeling on your head?

Bill. Todger was. E was pryin for me: pryin camfortable wiv me as a cawpet. Sow was Mog. Sao was the aol bloomin meetin. Mog she sez 'Ow Lawd brike is stabborn sperrit; bat downt urt is dear art.' Thet was wot she said. 'Downt urt is dear art'! An er blowk—thirteen stun four!—kneelin wiv all is wight on me. Fanny, aint it?

Jenny. Oh no. We're so sorry, Mr Walker.

Barbara *(enjoying it frankly).* Nonsense! of course it's funny. Served you right, Bill! You must have done something to him first.

Bill *(doggedly).* Aw did wot Aw said Aw'd do. Aw spit in is eye. E looks ap at the skoy and sez, 'Ow that Aw should be fahnd worthy to be spit upon for the gospel's sike!' e sez; an Mog sez 'Glaory Allelloolier!'; and then e called me Braddher, an dahned me as if Aw was a kid and e was me mather worshin me a Setterda nawt. Aw ednt jast nao shaow wiv im at all. Arf the street pryed; and the tather arf larfed fit to split theirselves. *(To Barbara)* There! are you settisfawd nah?

Barbara *(her eyes dancing).* Wish I'd been there, Bill.

Bill. Yus: youd a got in a hextra bit o talk on me, wouldnt you?

Jenny. I'm so sorry, Mr Walker.

Bill *(fiercely).* Downt you gow being sorry for me: youve no call. Listen eah. Aw browk your jawr.

Jenny. No, it didnt hurt me: indeed it didnt, except for a moment. It was only that I was frightened.

Bill. Aw downt want to be forgiven be you, or be ennybody. Wot Aw did Aw'll py for. Aw trawd to gat me aown jawr browk to settisfaw you—

Jenny *(distressed).* Oh no—

Bill *(impatiently).* Tell y' Aw did: cawnt you listen to wots bein taold you? All Aw got be it was bein mide a sawt of in the pablic street for me pines. Well, if Aw cawnt settisfaw you one wy, Aw ken anather. Listen eah! Aw ed two quid sived agen the frost; and Awve a pahnd of it left. A mite o mawn last week ed words with the judy e's gowing to merry. E give er wot-for; an e's bin fawnd fifteen bob. E ed a rawt to itt er cause they was gowin to be merrid; but Aw ednt nao rawt to itt you; sao put anather fawv bob on an call it a pahnd's worth. *(He produces a sovereign).* Eahs the manney. Tike it; and lets ev no more o your forgivin an pryin and your Mijor jawrin me. Let wot Aw dan be dan an pide for; and let there be a end of it.

Jenny. Oh, I couldnt take it, Mr Walker. But if you would give a shilling or two to poor Rummy Mitchens! you really did hurt her; and she's old.

Bill *(contemptuously).* Not lawkly. Aw'd give her anather as soon as look at er. Let her ev the lawr o me as she threatened! She aint forgiven me: not mach. Wot Aw dan to er is not on me mawnd—wot she *(indicating Barbara)* mawt call on me conscience—no more than stickin a pig. It's this Christian gime o yours that Aw wownt ev plyed agen me: this bloomin forgivin an neggin an jawrin that mikes a menn thet sore that iz lawf's a burdn to im. Aw wownt ev it, Aw tell you; sao tike your manney and stop thraowin your silly beshed fice hap agen me.

Jenny. Major: may I take a little of it for the Army?

Barbara. No: the Army is not to be bought. We want your soul, Bill; and we'll take nothing less.

Bill *(bitterly).* Aw knaow. Me an maw few shillins is not good enaff for you. Youre a earl's grendorter, you are. Nathink less than a andered pahnd for you.

Undershaft. Come, Barbara! you could do a great deal of good with a hundred pounds. If you will set this gentleman's mind at ease by taking his pound, I will give the other ninety-nine.

Bill, dazed by such opulence, instinctively touches his cap.

Barbara. Oh, youre too extravagant, papa. Bill offers twenty pieces of silver. All you need offer is the other ten. That will make the standard price to buy anybody who's for sale. I'm not; and the Army's not. *(To Bill)* Youll never have another quiet moment, Bill, until you come round to us. You cant stand out against your salvation.

Bill (*sullenly*).   Aw cawnt stend aht agen music awl wrastlers and awtful tangued women. Awve offered to py. Aw can do no more. Tike it or leave it. There it is. (*He throws the sovereign on the drum, and sits down on the horsetrough. The coin fascinates Snobby Price, who takes an early opportunity of dropping his cap on it*).

Mrs Baines comes from the shelter. She is dressed as a Salvation Army Commissioner. She is an earnest looking woman of about 40, with a caressing, urgent voice, and an appealing manner.

Barbara.   This is my father, Mrs Baines. (*Undershaft comes from the table, taking his hat off with marked civility*). Try what you can do with him. He wont listen to me, because he remembers what a fool I was when I was a baby. (*She leaves them together and chats with Jenny*).

Mrs Baines.   Have you been shewn over the shelter, Mr Undershaft? You know the work we're doing, of course.

Undershaft (*very civilly*).   The whole nation knows it, Mrs Baines.

Mrs Baines.   No, sir: the whole nation does not know it, or we should not be crippled as we are for want of money to carry our work through the length and breadth of the land. Let me tell you that there would have been rioting this winter in London but for us.

Undershaft.   You really think so?

Mrs Baines.   I know it. I remember 1886, when you rich gentlemen hardened your hearts against the cry of the poor. They broke the windows of your clubs in Pall Mall.

Undershaft (*gleaming with approval of their method.*).   And the Mansion House Fund went up next day from thirty thousand pounds to seventy-nine thousand! I remember quite well.

Mrs Baines.   Well, wont you help me to get at the people? They wont break windows then. Come here, Price. Let me shew you to this gentleman (*Price comes to be inspected*). Do you remember the window breaking?

Price.   My ole father thought it was the revolution, maam.

Mrs Baines.   Would you break windows now?

Price.   Oh no, maam. The windows of eaven ave bin opened to me. I know now that the rich man is a sinner like myself.

Rummy (*appearing above at the loft door*).   Snobby Price!

Snobby.   Wot is it?

Rummy.   Your mother's askin for you at the other gate in Cripps's Lane. She's heard about your confession (*Price turns pale*).

Mrs Baines.   Go, Mr Price; and pray with her.

Jenny.   You can go through the shelter, Snobby.

Price (*to Mrs Baines*).   I couldnt face her now, maam, with all the weight of my sins fresh on me. Tell her she'll find her son at ome, waitin for her in prayer. (*He skulks off through the gate, incidentally stealing the sovereign on his way out by picking up his cap from the drum*).

Mrs Baines (*with swimming eyes*).   You see how we take the anger and the bitterness against you out of their hearts, Mr Undershaft.

Undershaft.   It is certainly most convenient and gratifying to all large employers of labor, Mrs Baines.

Mrs Baines.   Barbara: Jenny: I have good news: most wonderful news. (*Jenny runs to her*). My prayers have been answered. I told you they would, Jenny, didnt I?

Jenny.   Yes, yes.

Barbara (*moving nearer to the drum*).   Have we got money enough to keep the shelter open?

Mrs Baines.   I hope we shall have enough to keep all the shelters open. Lord Saxmundham has promised us five thousand pounds—

Barbara.   Hooray!

Jenny.   Glory!

Mrs Baines.   —if—

Barbara.   'If!' If what?

Mrs Baines.   —if five other gentlemen will give a thousand each to make it up to ten thousand.

Barbara.   Who is Lord Saxmundham? I never heard of him.

Undershaft (*who has pricked up his ears at the peer's name, and is now watching Barbara curiously*).   A new creation, my dear. You have heard of Sir Horace Bodger?

Barbara.   Bodger! Do you mean the distiller? Bodger's whisky!

Undershaft.   That is the man. He is one of the greatest of our public benefactors. He restored the cathedral at Hakington. They made him a baronet for that. He gave half a million to the funds of his party: they made him a baron for that.

Shirley.   What will they give him for the five thousand?

Undershaft.   There is nothing left to give him. So the five thousand, I should think, is to save his soul.

Mrs Baines.   Heaven grant it may! Oh Mr Undershaft, you have some very rich friends. Cant you help us towards the other five thousand? We are going to hold a great meeting this afternoon at the Assembly Hall in the Mile End Road. If I could only announce that one gentleman had come forward to support Lord Saxmundham, others would follow. Dont you know somebody? couldnt you? wouldnt you? (*her eyes fill with tears*) oh, think of those poor people, Mr Undershaft: think of how much it means to them, and how little to a great man like you.

Undershaft (*sardonically gallant*).   Mrs Baines: you are irresistible. I cant disappoint you; and I cant deny myself the satisfaction of making Bodger pay up. You shall have your five thousand pounds.

Mrs Baines.   Thank God!

Undershaft.   You dont thank me?

Mrs Baines.   Oh sir, dont try to be cynical: dont be ashamed of being a good man. The Lord will bless you abundantly; and our prayers will be like a strong fortification round you all the days of your life. (*With a touch of* *caution)* You will let me have the cheque to shew at the meeting, wont you? Jenny: go in and fetch a pen and ink. *(Jenny runs to the shelter door).*

Undershaft. Do not disturb Miss Hill: I have a fountain pen *(Jenny halts. He sits at the table writes the cheque. Cusins rises to make room for him. They all watch him silently).*

Bill *(cynically, aside to Barbara, his voice and accent horribly debased).* Wot prawce selvytion nah?

Barbara. Stop. *(Undershaft stops writing: they all turn to her in surprise).* Mrs Baines: are you really going to take this money?

Mrs Baines *(astonished).* Why not, dear?

Barbara. Why not! Do you know what my father is? Have you forgotten that Lord Saxmundham is Bodger the whisky man? Do you remember how we implored the County Council to stop him from writing Bodger's Whisky in letters of fire against the sky; so that the poor drink-ruined creatures on the Embankment could not wake up from their snatches of sleep without being reminded of their deadly thirst by that wicked sky sign? Do you know that the worst thing I have had to fight here is not the devil, but Bodger, Bodger, Bodger, with his whisky, his distilleries, and his tied houses? Are you going to make our shelter another tied house for him, and ask me to keep it?

Bill. Rotten dranken whisky it is too.

Mrs Baines. Dear Barbara: Lord Saxmundham has a soul to be saved like any of us. If heaven has found the way to make a good use of his money, are we to set ourselves up against the answer to our prayers?

Barbara. I know he has a soul to be saved. Let him come down here; and I'll do my best to help him to his salvation. But he wants to send his cheque down to buy us, and go on being as wicked as ever.

Undershaft *(with a reasonableness which Cusins alone perceives to be ironical).* My dear Barbara: alcohol is a very necessary article. It heals the sick—

Barbara. It does nothing of the sort.

Undershaft. Well, it assists the doctor: that is perhaps a less questionable way of putting it. It makes life bearable to millions of people who could not endure their existence if they were quite sober. It enables Parliament to do things at eleven at night that no sane person would do at eleven in the morning. Is it Bodger's fault that this inestimable gift is deplorably abused by less than one per cent of the poor? *(He turns again to the table; signs the cheque; and crosses it).*

Mrs Baines. Barbara: will there be less drinking or more if all those poor souls we are saving come tomorrow and find the doors of our shelters shut in their faces? Lord Saxmundham gives us the money to stop drinking—to take his own business from him.

Cusins *(impishly).* Pure self-sacrifice on Bodger's part, clearly! Bless dear Bodger! *(Barbara almost breaks down as Adolphus, too, fails her).*

Undershaft (*tearing out the cheque and pocketing the book as he rises and goes past Cusins to Mrs Baines*). I also, Mrs Baines, may claim a little disinterestedness. Think of my business! think of the widows and orphans! the men and lads torn to pieces with shrapnel and poisoned with lyddite! (*Mrs Baines shrinks; but he goes on remorselessly*) the oceans of blood, not one drop of which is shed in a really just cause! the ravaged crops! The peaceful peasants forced, women and men, to till their fields under the fire of opposing armies on pain of starvation! the bad blood of the fierce little cowards at home who egg on others to fight for the gratification of their national vanity! All this makes money for me: I am never richer, never busier than when the papers are full of it. Well, it is your work to preach peace on earth and good will to men. (*Mrs Baines's face lights up again*). Every convert you make is a vote against war. (*Her lips move in prayer*). Yet I give you this money to help you to hasten my own commercial ruin. (*He give her the cheque*).

Cusins (*mounting the form in an ecstasy of mischief*). The millennium will be inaugurated by the unselfishness of Undershaft and Bodger. Oh be joyful! (*He takes the drumsticks from his pocket and flourishes them*).

Mrs Baines (*taking the cheque*). The longer I live the more proof I see that there is an Infinite Goodness that turns everything to the work of salvation sooner or later. Who would have thought that any good could have come out of war and drink? And yet their profits are brought today to the feet of salvation to do its blessed work. (*She is affected to tears*).

Jenny (*running to Mrs Baines and throwing her arms round her*). Oh dear! how blessed, how glorious it all is!

Cusins (*in a convulsion of irony*). Let us seize this unspeakable moment. Let us march to the great meeting at once. Excuse me just an instant. (*He rushes into the shelter. Jenny takes her tambourine from the drum head*).

Mrs Baines. Mr Undershaft: have you ever seen a thousand people fall on their knees with one impulse and pray? Come with us to the meeting. Barbara shall tell them that the Army is saved, and saved through you.

Cusins (*returning impetuously from the shelter with a flag and a trombone, and coming between Mrs Baines and Undershaft*). You shall carry the flag down the first street, Mrs Baines (*he gives her the flag*). Mr Undershaft is a gifted trombonist: he shall intone an Olympian diapason to the West Ham Salvation March. (*Aside to Undershaft, as he forces the trombone on him*) Blow, Machiavelli, blow.

Undershaft (*aside to him, as he takes the trombone*). The trumpet in Zion! (*Cusins rushes to the drum, which he takes up and puts on. Undershaft continues, aloud*) I will do my best. I could vamp a bass if I knew the tune.

Cusins. It is a wedding chorus from one of Donizetti's operas; but we have converted it. We convert everything to good here, including Bodger. You remember the chorus. 'For thee immense rejoicing—immenso giubilo—immenso giubilo.' (*With drum obbligato*) Rum tum ti tum tum, tum tum ti ta—

Barbara. Dolly: you are breaking my heart.

Cusins. What is a broken heart more or less here? Dionysos Undershaft has descended. I am possessed.

Mrs Baines. Come, Barbara: I must have my dear Major to carry the flag with me.

Jenny. Yes, yes, Major darling.

Cusins (*snatches the tambourine out of Jenny's hand and mutely offers it to Barbara*).

Barbara (*coming forward a little as she puts the offer behind her with a shudder, whilst Cusins recklessly tosses the tambourine back to Jenny and goes to the gate*). I cant come.

Jenny. Not come!

Mrs Baines (*with tears in her eyes*). Barbara: do you think I am wrong to take the money?

Barbara (*impulsively going to her and kissing her*). No, no: God help you, dear, you must: you are saving the Army. Go; and may you have a great meeting!

Jenny. But arnt you coming?

Barbara. No. (*She begins taking off the silver S brooch from her collar*).

Mrs Baines. Barbara: what are you doing?

Jenny. Why are you taking your badge off? You cant be going to leave us, Major.

Barbara (*quietly*). Father: come here.

Undershaft (*coming to her*). My dear! (*Seeing that she is going to pin the badge on his collar, he retreats to the penthouse in some alarm*).

Barbara (*following him*). Dont be frightened. (*She pins the badge on and steps back towards the table, shewing him to the others*) There! It's not much for £5000, is it?

Mrs Baines. Barbara: if you wont come and pray with us, promise me you will pray for us.

Barbara. I cant pray now. Perhaps I shall never pray again.

Mrs Baines. Barbara!

Jenny. Major!

Barbara (*almost delirious*). I cant bear any more. Quick march!

Cusins (*calling to the procession in the street outside*). Off we go. Play up, there! Immenso giubilo. (*He gives the time with his drum; and the band strikes up the march, which rapidly becomes more distant as the procession moves briskly away*).

Mrs Baines. I must go, dear. Youre overworked: you will be all right tomorrow. We'll never lose you. Now Jenny: step out with the old flag. Blood and Fire! (*She marches out through the gate with her flag*).

Jenny. Glory Hallelujah! (*flourishing her tambourine and marching*).

Undershaft (*to Cusins, as he marches out past him easing the slide of his trombone*). 'My ducats and my daughter'!

Cusins (*following him out*). Money and gunpowder!

Barbara. Drunkenness and Murder! My God: why hast thou forsaken me?

She sinks on the form with her face buried in her hands. The march passes away into silence. Bill Walker steals across to her.

Bill *(taunting)*. Wot prawce selvytion nah?

Shirley. Dont you hit her when she's down.

Bill. She itt me wen aw wiz dahn. Waw shouldnt Aw git a bit o me aown beck?

Barbara *(raising her head)*. I didnt take your money, Bill. *(She crosses the yard to the gate and turns her back on the two men to hide her face from them).*

Bill *(sneering after her)*. Naow, it warnt enaff for you. *(Turning to the drum, he misses the money)* Ellow! If you aint took it sammun else ez. Weres it gorn? Bly me if Jenny Ill didnt tike it arter all!

Rummy *(screaming at him from the loft)*. You lie, you dirty blackguard! Snobby Price pinched it off the drum when he took up his cap. I was up here all the time an see im do it.

Bill. Wot! Stowl maw manney! Waw didnt you call thief on him, you silly aold macker you?

Rummy. To serve you aht for ittin me acrost the fice. It's cost y'pahnd, that az. *(Raising a paean of squalid triumph)* I done you. I'm even with you. Uve ad it aht o y—*(Bill snatches up Shirley's mug and hurls it at her. She slams the loft door and vanishes. The mug smashes against the door and falls in fragments).*

Bill *(beginning to chuckle)*. Tell us, aol menn, wot o'clock this mawnin was it wen im as they call Snobby Prawce was sived?

Barbara *(turning to him more composedly, and with unspoiled sweetness)*. About half past twelve, Bill. And he pinched your pound at a quarter to two. *I* know. Well, you cant afford to lose it. I'll send it to you.

Bill *(his voice and accent suddenly improving)*. Not if Aw wiz to stawve for it. Aw aint to be bought.

Shirley. Aint you? Youd sell yourself to the devil for a pint o beer; only there aint no devil to make the offer.

Bill *(unashamed)*. Sao Aw would, mite, and often ev, cheerful. But she cawnt baw me. *(Approaching Barbara)* You wanted maw saoul, did you? Well, you aint got it.

Barbara. I nearly got it, Bill. But weve sold it back to you for ten thousand pounds.

Shirley. And dear at the money!

Barbara. No, Peter: it was worth more than money.

Bill *(salvationproof)*. It's nao good: you cawnt get rahnd me nah. Aw downt blieve in it; and Awve seen tody that Aw was rawt. *(Going)* Sao long, aol soupkitchener! Ta, ta, Mijor Earl's Grendorter! *(Turning at the gate)* Wot Prawce selvytion nah? Snobby Prawce! Ha! ha!

Barbara *(offering her hand)*. Goodbye, Bill.

Bill *(taken aback, half plucks his cap off; then shoves it on again defiantly)*. Git aht. *(Barbara drops her hand, discouraged. He has a twinge of re-*

morse). But thets aw rawt, you knaow. Nathink pasnl. Naow mellice, Sao long, Judy. *(He goes).*

Barbara.   No malice. So long, Bill.

Shirley *(shaking his head).*   You make too much of him, miss, in your innocence.

Barbara *(going to him).*   Peter: I'm like you now. Cleaned out, and lost my job.

Shirley.   Youve youth an hope. Thats two better than me.

Barbara.   I'll get you a job, Peter. Thats hope for you: the youth will have to be enough for me *(She counts her money).* I have just enough left for two teas at Lockharts, a Rowton doss for you, and my tram and bus home. *(He frowns and rises with offended pride. She takes his arm).* Dont be proud, Peter: it's sharing between friends. And promise me youll talk to me and not let me cry. *(She draws him towards the gate).*

Shirley.   Well, I'm not accustomed to talk to the like of you—

Barbara *(urgently).*   Yes, yes: you must talk to me. Tell me about Tom Paine's books and Bradlaugh's lectures. Come along.

Shirley.   Ah, if you would only read Tom Paine in the proper spirit, miss! *(They go out through the gate together).*

Act Three

Next day after lunch Lady Britomart is writing in the library in Wilton Crescent. Sarah is reading in the armchair near the window. Barbara, in ordinary fashionable dress, pale and brooding, is on the settee. Charles Lomax enters. He starts on seeing Barbara fashionably attired and in low spirits.

Lomax.   Youve left off your uniform!

Barbara says nothing; but an expression of pain passes over her face.

Lady Britomart *(warning him in low tones to be careful).*   Charles!

Lomax *(much concerned, coming behind the settee and bending sympathetically over Barbara).*   I'm awfully sorry, Barbara. You know I helped you all I could with the concertina and so forth. *(Momentously)* Still, I have never shut my eyes to the fact that there is a certain amount of tosh about the Salvation Army. Now the claims of the Church of England—

Lady Britomart.   Thats enough, Charles. Speak of something suited to your mental capacity.

Lomax.   But surely the Church of England is suited to all our capacities.

Barabara *(pressing his hand).*   Thank you for your sympathy, Cholly. Now go and spoon with Sarah.

Lomax *(dragging a chair from the writing table and seating himself affectionately by Sarah's side).*   How is my ownest today?

Sarah. I wish you wouldnt tell Cholly to do things, Barbara. He always comes straight and does them. Cholly: we're going to the works this afternoon.

Lomax. What works?

Sarah. The cannon works.

Lomax. What? your governor's shop!

Sarah. Yes.

Lomax. Oh I say!

Cusins enters in poor condition. He also starts visibly when he sees Barbara without her uniform.

Barbara. I expected you this morning, Dolly. Didnt you guess that?

Cusins (*sitting down beside her*). I'm sorry. I have only just breakfasted.

Sarah. But weve just finished lunch.

Barbara. Have you had one of your bad nights?

Cusins. No: I had rather a good night: in fact, one of the most remarkable nights I have ever passed.

Barbara. The meeting?

Cusins. No: after the meeting.

Lady Britomart. You should have gone to bed after the meeting. What were you doing?

Cusins. Drinking.

Lady Britomart.	Adolphus!
Sarah.	Dolly!
Barbara.	Dolly!
Lomax.	Oh I say!

Lady Britomart. What were you drinking, may I ask?

Cusins. A most devilish kind of Spanish burgundy, warranted free from added alcohol: a Temperance burgundy in fact. Its richness in natural alcohol made any addition superfluous.

Barbara. Are you joking, Dolly?

Cusins (*patiently*). No. I have been making a night of it with the nominal head of this household: that is all.

Lady Britomart. Andrew made you drunk!

Cusins. No: he only provided the wine. I think it was Dionysos who made me drunk. (*To Barbara*) I told you I was possessed.

Lady Britomart. Youre not sober yet. Go home to bed at once.

Cusins. I have never before ventured to reproach you, Lady Brit; but how could you marry the Prince of Darkness?

Lady Britomart. It was much more excusable to marry him than to get drunk with him. That is a new accomplishment of Andrew's, by the way. He usent to drink.

Cusins. He doesnt now. He only sat there and completed the wreck of my moral basis, the rout of my convictions, the purchase of my soul. He cares for you, Barbara. That is what makes him so dangerous to me.

Barbara. That has nothing to do with it, Dolly. There are larger loves and diviner dreams than the fireside ones. You know that, dont you?

Cusins. Yes: that is our understanding. I know it. I hold to it. Unless he can win me on that holier ground he may amuse me for a while; but he can get no deeper hold, strong as he is.

Barbara. Keep to that; and the end will be right. Now tell me what happened at the meeting?

Cusins. It was an amazing meeting. Mrs Baines almost died of emotion. Jenny Hill simply gibbered with hysteria. The Prince of Darkness played his trombone like a madman: its brazen roarings were like the laughter of the damned. 117 conversions took place then and there. They prayed with the most touching sincerity and gratitude for Bodger, and for the anonymous donor of the £5000. Your father would not let his name be given.

Lomax. That was rather fine of the old man, you know. Most chaps would have wanted the advertisement.

Cusins. He said all the charitable institutions would be down on him like kites on a battlefield if he gave his name.

Lady Britomart. Thats Andrew all over. He never does a proper thing without giving an improper reason for it.

Cusins. He convinced me that I have all my life been doing improper things for proper reasons.

Lady Britomart. Adolphus: now that Barbara has left the Salvation Army, you had better leave it too. I will not have you playing that drum in the streets.

Cusins. Your orders are already obeyed, Lady Brit.

Barbara. Dolly: were you ever really in earnest about it? Would you have joined if you had never seen me?

Cusins (*disingenuously*). Well—er—well, possibly, as a collector of religions—

Lomax (*cunningly*). Not as a drummer, though, you know. You are a very clearheaded brainy chap, Dolly; and it must have been apparent to you that there is a certain amount of tosh about—

Lady Britomart. Charles: if you must drivel, drivel like a grown-up man and not like a schoolboy.

Lomax (*out of countenance*). Well, drivel is drivel, dont you know, whatever a man's age.

Lady Britomart. In good society in England, Charles, men drivel at all ages by repeating silly formulas with an air of wisdom. Schoolboys make their own formulas out of slang, like you. When they reach your age, and get political private secretaryships and things of that sort, they drop slang and get their formulas out of the Spectator or The Times. You had better confine yourself to The Times. You will find that there is a certain amount of tosh about The Times; but at least its language is reputable.

Lomax (*overwhelmed*). You are so awfully strong-minded, Lady Brit—

Lady Britomart. Rubbish! *(Morrison comes in).* What is it?

Morrison. If you please, my lady, Mr Undershaft has just drove up to the door.

Lady Britomart. Well, let him in. *(Morrison hesitates).* Whats the matter with you?

Morrison. Shall I announce him, my lady; or is he at home here, so to speak, my lady?

Lady Britomart. Announce him.

Morrison. Thank you, my lady. You wont mind my asking, I hope. The occasion is in a manner of speaking new to me.

Lady Britomart. Quite right. Go and let him in.

Morrison. Thank you, my lady. *(He withdraws).*

Lady Britomart. Children: go and get ready. *(Sarah and Barbara go upstairs for their out-of-door wraps).* Charles: go and tell Stephen to come down here in five minutes: you will find him in the drawing room. *(Charles goes).* Adolphus: tell them to send round the carriage in about fifteen minutes. *(Adolphus goes).*

Morrison *(at the door).* Mr Undershaft.

Undershaft comes in. Morrison goes out.

Undershaft. Alone! How fortunate!

Lady Britomart *(rising).* Dont be sentimental, Andrew. Sit down. *(She sits on the settee: he sits beside her, on her left. She comes to the point before he has time to breathe).* Sarah must have £800 a year until Charles Lomax comes into his property. Barbara will need more, and need it permanently, because Adolphus hasnt any property.

Undershaft *(resignedly).* Yes, my dear: I will see to it. Anything else? for yourself, for instance?

Lady Britomart. I want to talk to you about Stephen.

Undershaft *(rather wearily).* Dont, my dear. Stephen doesnt interest me.

Lady Britomart. He does interest me. He is our son.

Undershaft. Do you really think so? He has induced us to bring him into the world; but he chose his parents very incongruously, I think. I see nothing of myself in him, and less of you.

Lady Britomart. Andrew: Stephen is an excellent son, and a most steady, capable, high-minded young man. You are simply trying to find an excuse for disinheriting him.

Undershaft. My dear Biddy: the Undershaft tradition disinherits him. It would be dishonest of me to leave the cannon foundry to my son.

Lady Britomart. It would be most unnatural and improper of you to leave it to anyone else, Andrew. Do you suppose this wicked and immoral tradition can be kept up for ever? Do you pretend that Stephen could not carry on the foundry just as well as all the other sons of the big business houses?

Undershaft. Yes: he could learn the office routine without understanding the business, like all the other sons; and the firm would go on by its own momentum until the real Undershaft—probably an Italian or a German—would invent a new method and cut him out.

Lady Britomart. There is nothing that any Italian or German could do that Stephen could not do. And Stephen at least has breeding.

Undershaft. The son of a foundling! Nonsense!

Lady Britomart. My son, Andrew! And even you may have good blood in your veins for all you know.

Undershaft. True. Probably I have. That is another argument in favour of a foundling.

Lady Britomart. Andrew: dont be aggravating. And dont be wicked. At present you are both.

Undershaft. This conversation is part of the Undershaft tradition, Biddy. Every Undershaft's wife has treated him to it ever since the house was founded. It is a mere waste of breath. If the tradition be ever broken it will be for an abler man than Stephen.

Lady Britomart *(pouting).* Then go away.

Undershaft *(deprecatory).* Go away!

Lady Britomart. Yes: go away. If you will do nothing for Stephen, you are not wanted here. Go to your foundling, whoever he is; and look after him.

Undershaft. The fact is, Biddy—

Lady Britomart. Dont call me Biddy. I dont call you Andy.

Undershaft. I will not call my wife Britomart: it is not good sense. Seriously, my love, the Undershaft tradition has landed me in a difficulty. I am getting on in years; and my partner Lazarus has at last made a stand and insisted that the succession must be settled one way or the other; and of course he is quite right. You see, I havent found a fit successor yet.

Lady Britomart *(obstinately).* There is Stephen.

Undershaft. Thats just it: all the foundlings I can find are exactly like Stephen.

Lady Britomart. Andrew!!

Undershaft. I want a man with no relations and no schooling: that is, a man who would be out of the running altogether if he were not a strong man. And I cant find him. Every blessed foundling nowadays is snapped up in his infancy by Barnardo homes, or School Board officers, or Boards of Guardians; and if he shews the least ability he is fastened on by schoolmasters; trained to win scholarships like a racehorse; crammed with secondhand ideas; drilled and disciplined in docility and what they call good taste; and lamed for life so that he is fit for nothing but teaching. If you want to keep the foundry in the family, you had better find an eligible foundling and marry him to Barbara.

Lady Britomart. Ah! Barbara! Your pet! You would sacrifice Stephen to Barbara.

Undershaft. Cheerfully. And you, my dear, would boil Barbara to make soup for Stephen.

Lady Britomart. Andrew: this is not a question of our likings and dislikings: it is a question of duty. It is your duty to make Stephen your successor.

Undershaft. Just as much as it is your duty to submit to your husband. Come, Biddy! these tricks of the governing class are of no use with me. I am one of the governing class myself; and it is waste of time giving tracts to a missionary. I have the power in this matter; and I am not to be humbugged into using it for your purposes.

Lady Britomart. Andrew: you can talk my head off; but you cant change wrong into right. And your tie is all on one side. Put it straight.

Undershaft (disconcerted). It wont stay unless it's pinned (he fumbles at it with childish grimaces)—

Stephen comes in.

Stephen (at the door). I beg your pardon (about to retire).

Lady Britomart. No: come in, Stephen. (Stephen comes forward to his mother's writing table).

Undershaft (not very cordially). Good afternoon.

Stephen (coldly). Good afternoon.

Undershaft (to Lady Britomart). He knows all about the tradition, I suppose?

Lady Britomart. Yes. (To Stephen) It is what I told you last night, Stephen.

Undershaft (sulkily). I understand you want to come into the cannon business.

Stephen. I go into trade! Certainly not.

Undershaft (opening his eyes, greatly eased in mind and manner). Oh! in that case—

Lady Britomart. Cannons are not trade, Stephen. They are enterprise.

Stephen. I have no intention of becoming a man of business in any sense. I have no capacity for business and no taste for it. I intend to devote myself to politics.

Undershaft (rising). My dear boy: this is an immense relief to me. And I trust it may prove an equally good thing for the country. I was afraid you would consider yourself disparaged and slighted. (He moves towards Stephen as if to shake hands with him).

Lady Britomart (rising and interposing). Stephen: I cannot allow you to throw away an enormous property like this.

Stephen (stiffly). Mother: there must be an end of treating me as a child, if you please. (Lady Britomart recoils, deeply wounded by his tone). Until last night I did not take your attitude seriously, because I did not think you meant it seriously. But I find now that you left me in the dark as to matters which you should have explained to me years ago. I am extremely hurt and offended. Any further discussion of my intentions had better take place with my father, as between one man and another.

Lady Britomart. Stephen! (She sits down again, her eyes filling with tears).

Undershaft (with grave compassion). You see, my dear, it is only the big men who can be treated as children.

Stephen. I am sorry, mother, that you have forced me—

Undershaft (*stopping him*). Yes, yes, yes, yes: thats all right, Stephen. She wont interfere with you any more: your independence is achieved: you have won your latchkey. Dont rub it in; and above all, dont apologize. (*He resumes his seat*). Now what about your future, as between one man and another—I beg your pardon, Biddy: as between two men and a woman.

Lady Britomart (*who has pulled herself together strongly*). I quite understand, Stephen. By all means go your own way if you feel strong enough. (*Stephen sits down magisterially in the chair at the writing table with an air of affirming his majority*).

Undershaft. It is settled that you do not ask for the succession to the cannon business.

Stephen. I hope it is settled that I repudiate the cannon business.

Undershaft. Come, come! dont be so devilishly sulky: it's boyish. Freedom should be generous. Besides, I owe you a fair start in life in exchange for disinheriting you. You cant become prime minister all at once. Havnt you a turn for something? What about literature, art, and so forth?

Stephen. I have nothing of the artist about me, either in faculty or character, thank Heaven!

Undershaft. A philosopher, perhaps? Eh?

Stephen. I make no such ridiculous pretension.

Undershaft. Just so. Well, there is the army, the navy, the Church, the Bar. The Bar requires some ability. What about the Bar?

Stephen. I have not studied law. And I am afraid I have not the necessary push—I believe that is the name barristers give to their vulgarity—for success in pleading.

Undershaft. Rather a difficult case, Stephen. Hardly anything left but the stage, is there? (*Stephen makes an impatient movement*). Well, come! is there anything you know or care for?

Stephen (*rising and looking at him steadily*). I know the difference between right and wrong.

Undershaft (*hugely tickled*). You dont say so! What! no capacity for business, no knowledge of law, no sympathy with art, no pretension to philosophy; only a simple knowledge of the secret that has puzzled all the philosophers, baffled all the lawyers, muddled all the men of business, and ruined most of the artists: the secret of right and wrong. Why, man, youre a genius, a master of masters, a god! At twenty-four, too!

Stephen (*keeping his temper with difficulty*). You are pleased to be facetious. I pretend to be nothing more than any honorable English gentleman claims as his birthright (*he sits down angrily*).

Undershaft. Oh, thats everybody's birthright. Look at poor little Jenny Hill, the Salvation lassie! she would think you were laughing at her if you asked her to stand up in the street and teach grammar or geography or mathematics or even drawing room dancing; but it never occurs to her to doubt that she can teach morals and religion. You are all alike, you respectable people. You cant tell me the bursting strain of a ten-inch gun, which is a very simple matter; but you all think you can tell me the bursting strain of a man under temptation. You darent handle high explosives; but youre all ready to handle honesty and truth and justice and the whole duty of man, and kill one another at that game. What a country! What a world!

Lady Britomart *(uneasily).* What do you think he had better do, Andrew?

Undershaft. Oh, just what he wants to do. He knows nothing and he thinks he knows everything. That points clearly to a political career. Get him a private secretaryship to someone who can get him an Under Secretaryship; and then leave him alone. He will find his natural and proper place in the end on the Treasury Bench.

Stephen *(springing up again).* I am sorry, sir, that you force me to forget the respect due to you as my father. I am an Englishman and I will not hear the Government of my country insulted. *(He thrusts his hands in his pockets, and walks angrily across to the window).*

Undershaft *(with a touch of brutality).* The government of your country! *I* am the government of your country: I, and Lazarus. Do you suppose that you and half a dozen amateurs like you, sitting in a row in that foolish gabble shop, can govern Undershaft and Lazarus? No, my friend: you will do what pays us. You will make war when it suits us, and keep peace when it doesnt. You will find out that trade requires certain measures when we have decided on those measures. When I want anything to keep my dividends up, you will discover that my want is a national need. When other people want something to keep my dividends down, you will call out the police and military. And in return you shall have the support and applause of my newspapers, and the delight of imagining that you are a great statesman. Government of your country! Be off with you, my boy, and play with your caucuses and leading articles and historic parties and great leaders and burning questions and the rest of your toys. *I* am going back to my counting-house to pay the piper and call the tune.

Stephen *(actually smiling, and putting his hand on his father's shoulder with indulgent patronage).* Really, my dear father, it is impossible to be angry with you. You dont know how absurd all this sounds to me. You are very properly proud of having been industrious enough to make money; and it is greatly to your credit that you have made so much of it. But it has kept you in circles where you are valued for your money and deferred to for it, instead of in the doubtless very old-fashioned and behind-the-times public school and university where I formed my habits of mind. It is natural for you to think that money governs England; but you must allow me to think I know better.

Undershaft. And what does govern England, pray?

Stephen. Character, father, character.

Undershaft. Whose character? Yours or mine?

Stephen. Neither yours nor mine, father, but the best elements in the English national character.

Undershaft. Stephen: Ive found your profession for you. Youre a born journalist. I'll start you with a high-toned weekly review. There!

Before Stephen can reply Sarah, Barbara, Lomax, and Cusins come in ready for walking. Barbara crosses the room to the window and looks out. Cusins drifts amiably to the armchair. Lomax remains near the door, whilst Sarah comes to her mother.

Stephen goes to the smaller writing table and busies himself with his letters.

Sarah. Go and get ready, mamma: the carriage is waiting. *(Lady Britomart leaves the room).*

Undershaft *(to Sarah).* Good day, my dear. Good afternoon, Mr Lomax.

Lomax *(vaguely).* Ahdedoo.

Undershaft *(to Cusins).* Quite well after last night, Euripides, eh?

Cusins. As well as can be expected.

Undershaft. Thats right. *(To Barbara)* So you are coming to see my death and devastation factory, Barbara?

Barabara *(at the window).* You came yesterday to see my salvation factory. I promised you a return visit.

Lomax *(coming forward between Sarah and Undershaft).* Youll find it awfully interesting. Ive been through the Woolwich Arsenal; and it gives you a ripping feeling of security, you know, to think of the lot of beggars we could kill if it came to fighting. *(To Undershaft, with sudden solemnity)* Still, it must be rather an awful reflection for you, from the religious point of view as it were. Youre getting on, you know, and all that.

Sarah. You dont mind Cholly's imbecility, papa, do you?

Lomax *(much taken aback).* Oh I say!

Undershaft. Mr Lomax looks at the matter in a very proper spirit, my dear.

Lomax. Just so. Thats all I meant, I assure you.

Sarah. Are you coming, Stephen?

Stephen. Well, I am rather busy—er—*(Magnanimously)* Oh well, yes: I'll come. That is, if there is room for me.

Undershaft. I can take two with me in a little motor I am experimenting with for field use. You wont mind its being rather unfashionable. It's not painted yet; but it's bullet proof.

Lomax *(appalled at the prospect of confronting Wilton Crescent in an unpainted motor).* Oh I say!

Sarah. The carriage for me, thank you. Barbara doesnt mind what she's seen in.

Lomax. I say, Dolly, old chap: do you really mind the car being a guy? Because of course if you do I'll go in it. Still—

Cusins. I prefer it.

Lomax. Thanks awfully, old man. Come, my ownest. *(He hurries out to secure his seat in the carriage. Sarah follows him).*

Cusins *(moodily walking across to Lady Britomart's writing table).* Why are we two coming to this Works Department of Hell? that is what I ask myself.

Barbara. I have always thought of it as a sort of pit where lost creatures with blackened faces stirred up smoky fires and were driven and tormented by my father? Is it like that, dad?

Undershaft *(scandalized).* My dear! It is a spotlessly clean and beautiful hillside town.

Cusins. With a Methodist chapel? Oh do say theres a Methodist chapel.

Undershaft. There are two: a Primitive one and a sophisticated one. There is even an Ethical Society; but it is not much patronized, as my men are all strongly religious. In the High Explosives Sheds they object to the presence of Agnostics as unsafe.

Cusins. And yet they dont object to you!

Barbara. Do they obey all your orders?

Undershaft. I never give them any orders. When I speak to one of them it is 'Well, Jones, is the baby doing well? and has Mrs Jones made a good recovery?' 'Nicely, thank you, sir.' And thats all.

Cusins. But Jones has to be kept in order. How do you maintain discipline among your men?

Undershaft. I dont. They do. You see, the one thing Jones wont stand is any rebellion from the man under him, or any assertion of social equality between the wife of the man with 4 shillings a week less than himself, and Mrs Jones! Of course they all rebel against me, theoretically. Practically, every man of them keeps the man just below him in his place. I never meddle with them. I never bully them. I dont even bully Lazarus. I say that certain things are to be done; but I dont order anybody to do them. I dont say, mind you, that there is no ordering about and snubbing and even bullying. The men snub the boys and order them about; the carmen snub the sweepers; the artisans snub the unskilled laborers; the foremen drive and bully both the laborers and artisans; the assistant engineers find fault with the foremen; the chief engineers drop on the assistants; the departmental managers worry the chiefs; and the clerks have tall hats and hymnbooks and keep up the social tone by refusing to associate on equal terms with anybody. The result is a colossal profit, which comes to me.

Cusins *(revolted).* You really are a—well, what I was saying yesterday.

Barbara. What was he saying yesterday?

Undershaft. Never mind, my dear. He thinks I have made you unhappy. Have I?

Barbara. Do you think I can be happy in this vulgar silly dress? I! who have worn the uniform. Do you understand what you have done to me? Yesterday I had a man's soul in my hand. I set him in the way of life with his face to salvation. But when we took your money he turned back to drunkenness and derision. *(With intense conviction)* I will never forgive you that. If I had a child, and you destroyed its body with your explosives—if you murdered Dolly with your horrible guns—I could forgive you if my forgiveness would open the gates of heaven to you. But to take a human soul from me, and turn it into the soul of a wolf! that is worse than any murder.

Undershaft. Does my daughter despair so easily? Can you strike a man to the heart and leave no mark on him?

Barbara *(her face lighting up).* Oh, you are right: he can never be lost now: where was my faith?

Cusins. Oh, clever clever devil!

Barbara. You may be a devil; but God speaks through you sometimes. *(She takes her father's hands and kisses them).* You have given me back my happiness: I feel it deep down now, though my spirit is troubled.

Undershaft. You have learnt something. That always feels at first as if you had lost something.

Barbara. Well, take me to the factory of death; and let me learn something more. There must be some truth or other behind all this frightful irony. Come, Dolly. *(She goes out).*

Cusins. My guardian angel! *(To Undershaft)* Avaunt! *(He follows Barbara).*

Stephen *(quietly, at the writing table).* You must not mind Cusins, father. He is a very amiable good fellow; but he is a Greek scholar and naturally a little eccentric.

Undershaft. Ah, quite so, Thank you, Stephen. Thank you. *(He goes out).*

Stephen smiles patronizingly; buttons his coat responsibly; and crosses the room to the door. Lady Britomart, dressed for out-of-doors, opens it before he reaches it. She looks round for others; looks at Stephen; and turns to go without a word.

Stephen *(embarrassed).* Mother—

Lady Britomart. Dont be apologetic, Stephen. And dont forget that you have outgrown your mother. *(She goes out).*

Perivale St Andrews lies between two Middlesex hills, half climbing the northern one. It is an almost smokeless town of white walls, roofs of narrow green slates or red tiles, tall trees, domes, campaniles, and slender chimney shafts, beautifully situated and beautiful in itself. The best view of it is obtained from the crest of a slope about half a mile to the east, where the high explosives are dealt with. The foundry lies hidden in the depths between, the tops of its chimneys sprouting like huge skittles into the middle distance. Across the crest runs an emplacement of concrete, with a firestep, and a parapet which suggests a fortification, because there is a huge cannon of the obsolete Woolwich Infant pattern peering across it at the town. The can-

non is mounted on an experimental gun carriage: possibly the original model of the Undershaft disappearing rampart gun alluded to by Stephen. The firestep, being a convenient place to sit, is furnished here and there with straw disc cushions; and at one place there is the additional luxury of a fur rug.

Barbara is standing on the firestep, looking over the parapet towards the town. On her right is the cannon; on her left the end of a shed raised on piles, with a ladder of three or four steps up to the door, which opens outwards and has a little wooden landing at the threshold, with a fire bucket in the corner of the landing. Several dummy soldiers more or less mutilated, with straw protruding from their gashes, have been shoved out of the way under the landing. A few others are nearly upright against the shed; and one has fallen forward and lies, like a grotesque corpse, on the emplacement. The parapet stops short of the shed, leaving a gap which is the beginning of the path down the hill through the foundry to the town. The rug is on the firestep near this gap. Down on the emplacement behind the cannon is a trolley carrying a huge conical bombshell with a red band painted on it. Further to the right is the door of an office, which, like the sheds, is of the lightest possible construction.

Cusins arrives by the path from the town.

Barbara. Well?
Cusins. Not a ray of hope. Everything perfect! wonderful! real! It only needs a cathedral to be a heavenly city instead of a hellish one.
Barbara. Have you found out whether they have done anything for old Peter Shirley?
Cusins. They have found him a job as gatekeeper and timekeeper. He's frightfully miserable. He calls the time-keeping brainwork, and says he isnt used to it; and his gate lodge is so splendid that he's ashamed to use the rooms, and skulks in the scullery.
Barbara. Poor Peter!

Stephen arrives from town. He carries a fieldglass.

Stephen (enthusiastically). Have you two seen the place? Why did you leave us?
Cusins. I wanted to see everything I was not intended to see; and Barbara wanted to make the men talk.
Stephen. Have you found anything discreditable?
Cusins. No. They call him Dandy Andy and are proud of his being a cunning old rascal; but it's all horribly, frightfully, immorally, unanswerably perfect.

Sarah arrives.

Sarah. Heavens! what a place! *(She crosses to the trolley).* Did you see the nursing home!? *(She sits down on the shell).*

Stephen. Did you see the libraries and schools!?

Sarah. Did you see the ball room and the banqueting chamber in the Town Hall!?

Stephen. Have you gone into the insurance fund, the pension fund, the building society, the various applications of cooperation!?

Undershaft comes from the office, with a sheaf of telegrams in his hand.

Undershaft. Well, have you seen everything? I'm sorry I was called away. *(Indicating the telegrams)* Good news from Manchuria.

Stephen. Another Japanese victory?

Undershaft. Oh, I dont know. Which side wins does not concern us here. No: the good news is that the aerial battleship is a tremendous success. At the first trial it has wiped out a fort with three hundred soldiers in it.

Cusins *(from the platform).* Dummy soldiers?

Undershaft *(striding across to Stephen and kicking the prostrate dummy brutally out of his way).* No: the real thing.

Cusins and Barbara exchange glances. Then Cusins sits on the step and buries his face in his hands. Barbara gravely lays her hand on his shoulder. He looks up at her in whimsical desperation.

Undershaft. Well, Stephen, what do you think of the place?

Stephen. Oh, magnificent. A perfect triumph of modern industry. Frankly, my dear father, I have been a fool: I had no idea of what it all meant: of the wonderful forethought, the power of organization, the administrative capacity, the financial genius, the colossal capital it represents. I have been repeating to myself as I came through your streets 'Peace hath her victories no less renowned than War.' I have only one misgiving about it all.

Undershaft. Out with it.

Stephen. Well, I cannot help thinking that all this provision for every want of your workmen may sap their independence and weaken their sense of responsibility. And greatly as we enjoyed our tea at that splendid restaurant—how they gave us all that luxury and cake and jam and cream for threepence I really cannot imagine!—still you must remember that restaurants break up home life. Look at the continent, for instance! Are you sure so much pampering is really good for the men's characters?

Undershaft. Well you see, my dear boy, when you are organizing civilization you have to make up your mind whether trouble and anxiety are good things or not. If you decide that they are, then, I take it, you simply dont organize civilization; and there you are, with trouble and anxiety enough to make us all angels! But if you decide the other way, you may as well go through with it. However, Stephen, our characters are safe here. A sufficient dose of anxiety is always provided by the fact that we may be blown to smithereens at any moment.

Sarah. By the way, papa, where do you make the explosives?

Undershaft. In separate little sheds, like that one. When one of them blows up, it costs very little; and only the people quite close to it are killed.

Stephen, who is quite close to it, looks at it rather scaredly, and moves away quickly to the cannon. At the same moment the door of the shed is thrown abruptly open; and a foreman in overalls and list slippers comes out on the little landing and holds the door for Lomax, who appears in the doorway.

Lomax *(with studied coolness).* My good fellow: you neednt get into a state of nerves. Nothing's going to happen to you; and I suppose it wouldnt be the end of the world if anything did. A little bit of British pluck is what you want, old chap. *(He descends and strolls across to Sarah).*

Undershaft *(to the foreman).* Anything wrong, Bilton?

Bilton *(with ironic calm).* Gentleman walked into the high explosives shed and lit a cigaret, sir: thats all.

Undershaft. Ah, quite so. *(Going over to Lomax)* Do you happen to remember what you did with the match?

Lomax. Oh come! I'm not a fool. I took jolly good care to blow it out before I chucked it away.

Bilton. The top of it was red hot inside, sir.

Lomax. Well, suppose it was! I didn't chuck it into any of your messes.

Undershaft. Think no more of it, Mr Lomax. By the way, would you mind lending me your matches.

Lomax *(offering his box).* Certainly.

Undershaft. Thanks. *(He pockets the matches).*

Lomax *(lecturing to the company generally).* You know, these high explosives dont go off like gunpowder, except when theyre in a gun. When theyre spread loose, you can put a match to them without the least risk: they just burn quietly like a bit of paper. *(Warming to the scientific interest of the subject)* Did you know that, Undershaft? Have you ever tried?

Undershaft. Not on a large scale, Mr Lomax. Bilton will give you a sample of gun cotton when you are leaving if you ask him. You can experiment with it at home. *(Bilton looks puzzled).*

Sarah. Bilton will do nothing of the sort, papa. I suppose it's your business to blow up the Russians and Japs; but you might really stop short of blowing up poor Cholly. *(Bilton gives it up and retires into the shed).*

Lomax. My ownest, there is no danger. *(He sits beside her on the shell).*

Lady Britomart arrives from the town with a bouquet.

Lady Britomart *(impetuously).* Andrew: you shouldnt have let me see this place.

Undershaft. Why, my dear?

Lady Britomart.   Never mind why: you shouldnt have: thats all. To think of all that *(indicating the town)* being yours! and that you have kept it to yourself all these years!

Undershaft.   It does not belong to me. I belong to it. It is the Undershaft inheritance.

Lady Britomart.   It is not. Your ridiculous cannons and that noisy banging foundry may be the Undershaft inheritance; but all that plate and linen, all that furniture and those houses and orchards and gardens belong to us. They belong to me: they are not a man's business. I wont give them up. You must be out of your senses to throw them all away; and if you persist in such folly, I will call in a doctor.

Undershaft *(stooping to smell the bouquet)*.   Where did you get the flowers, my dear?

Lady Britomart.   Your men presented them to me in your William Morris Labor Church.

Cusins.   Oh! It needed only that. A Labor Church! *(he mounts the firestep distractedly, and leans with his elbows on the parapet, turning his back to them)*.

Lady Britomart.   Yes, with Morris's words in mosaic letters ten feet high round the dome. NO MAN IS GOOD ENOUGH TO BE ANOTHER MAN'S MASTER. The cynicism of it!

Undershaft.   It shocked the men at first, I am afraid. But now they take no more notice of it than of the ten commandments in church.

Lady Britomart.   Andrew: you are trying to put me off the subject of the inheritance by profane jokes. Well, you shant. I dont ask it any longer for Stephen: he has inherited far too much of your perversity to be fit for it. But Barbara has rights as well as Stephen. Why should not Adolphus succeed to the inheritance? I could manage the town for him; and he can look after the cannons, if they are really necessary.

Undershaft.   I should ask nothing better if Adolphus were a foundling. He is exactly the sort of new blood that is wanted in English business. But he's not a foundling; and theres an end of it. *(He makes for the office door)*.

Cusins *(turning to them)*.   Not quite. *(They all turn and stare at him)*. I think —Mind! I am not committing myself in any way as to my future course— but I think the foundling difficulty can be got over. *(He jumps down to the emplacement)*.

Undershaft *(coming back to him)*.   What do you mean?

Cusins.   Well, I have something to say which is in the nature of a confession.

Sarah.

Lady Britomart.

Barbara.   } Confession!

Stephen.

Lomax.   Oh I say!

Cusins.   Yes, a confession. Listen, all. Until I met Barbara I thought myself in the main an honorable, truthful man, because I wanted the approval of my conscience more than I wanted anything else. But the moment I saw Barbara, I wanted her far more than the approval of my conscience.

Lady Britomart.   Adolphus!

Cusins.   It is true. You accused me yourself, Lady Brit, of joining the Army to worship Barbara; and so I did. She bought my soul like a flower at a street corner; but she bought it for herself.

Undershaft.   What! Not for Dionysos or another?

Cusins.   Dionysos and all the others are in herself. I adored what was divine in her, and was therefore a true worshipper. But I was romantic about her too. I thought she was a woman of the people, and that a marriage with a professor of Greek would be far beyond the wildest social ambitions of her rank.

Lady Britomart.   Adolphus!!

Lomax.   Oh I say!!!

Cusins.   When I learnt the horrible truth—

Lady Britomart.   What do you mean by the horrible truth, pray?

Cusins.   That she was enormously rich; that her grandfather was an earl; that her father was the Prince of Darkness—

Undershaft.   Chut!

Cusins.   —and that I was only an adventurer trying to catch a rich wife, then I stooped to deceive her about my birth.

Barbara (*rising*).   Dolly!

Lady Britomart.   Your birth! Now Adolphus, dont dare to make up a wicked story for the sake of these wretched cannons. Remember: I have seen photographs of your parents; and the Agent General for South Western Australia knows them personally and has assured me that they are most respectable married people.

Cusins.   So they are in Australia; but here they are outcasts. Their marriage is legal in Australia, but not in England. My mother is my father's deceased wife's sister; and in this island I am consequently a foundling. (*Sensation*).

Barbara.   Silly! (*She climbs to the cannon, and leans, listening, in the angle it makes with the parapet*).

Cusins.   Is the subterfuge good enough, Machiavelli?

Undershaft (*thoughtfully*).   Biddy: this may be a way out of the difficulty.

Lady Britomart.   Stuff! A man cant make cannons any the better for being his own cousin instead of his proper self (*she sits down on the rug with a bounce that expresses her downright contempt for their casuistry*).

Undershaft (*to Cusins*).   You are an educated man. That is against the tradition.

Cusins.   Once in ten thousand times it happens that the schoolboy is a born master of what they try to teach him. Greek has not destroyed my mind: it has nourished it. Besides, I did not learn it at an English public school.

Undershaft. Hm! Well, I cannot afford to be too particular: you have cornered the foundling market. Let it pass. You are eligible, Euripides: you are eligible.

Barbara. Dolly: yesterday morning, when Stephen told us all about the tradition, you became very silent; and you have been strange and excited ever since. Were you thinking of your birth then?

Cusins. When the finger of Destiny suddenly points at a man in the middle of his breakfast, it makes him thoughtful.

Undershaft. Aha! You have had your eye on the business, my young friend, have you?

Cusins. Take care! There is an abyss of moral horror between me and your accursed aerial battleships.

Undershaft. Never mind the abyss for the present. Let us settle the practical details and leave your final decision open. You know that you will have to change your name. Do you object to that?

Cusins. Would any man named Adolphus—any man called Dolly!—object to be called something else?

Undershaft. Good. Now, as to money! I propose to treat you handsomely from the beginning. You shall start at a thousand a year.

Cusins (with sudden heat, his spectacles twinkling with mischief). A thousand! You dare offer a miserable thousand to the son-in-law of a millionaire! No, by Heavens, Machiavelli! you shall not cheat me. You cannot do without me; and I can do without you. I must have two thousand five hundred a year for two years. At the end of that time, if I am a failure, I go. But if I am a success, and stay on, you must give me the other five thousand.

Undershaft. What other five thousand?

Cusins. To make the two years up to five thousand a year. The two thousand five hundred is only half pay in case I should turn out a failure. The third year I must have ten per cent on the profits.

Undershaft (take aback). Ten per cent! Why, man, do you know what my profits are?

Cusins. Enormous, I hope: otherwise I shall require twenty-five percent.

Undershaft. But, Mr Cusins, this is a serious matter of business. You are not bringing any capital into the concern.

Cusins. What! no capital! Is my mastery of Greek no capital? Is my access to the subtlest thought, the loftiest poetry yet attained by humanity, no capital? My character! my intellect! my life! my career! what Barbara calls my soul! are these no capital? Say another word; and I double my salary.

Undershaft. Be reasonable—

Cusins (peremptorily). Mr Undershaft: you have my terms. Take them or leave them.

Undershaft (recovering himself). Very well. I note your terms; and I offer you half.

Cusins (*disgusted*).   Half!

Undershaft (*firmly*).   Half.

Cusins.   You call yourself a gentleman; and you offer me half!!

Undershaft.   I do not call myself a gentleman; but I offer you half.

Cusins.   This to your future partner! your successor! your son-in-law!

Barbara.   You are selling your own soul, Dolly, not mine. Leave me out of the bargain, please.

Undershaft.   Come! I will go a step further for Barbara's sake. I will give you three fifths; but that is my last word.

Cusins.   Done!

Lomax.   Done in the eye! Why, *I* get only eight hundred, you know.

Cusins.   By the way, Mac, I am a classical scholar, not an arithmetical one. Is three fifths more than half or less?

Undershaft.   More, of course.

Cusins.   I would have taken two hundred and fifty. How you can succeed in business when you are willing to pay all that money to a University don who is obviously not worth a junior clerk's wages!—well! What will Lazarus say?

Undershaft.   Lazarus is a gentle romantic Jew who cares for nothing but string quartets and stalls at fashionable theatres. He will be blamed for your rapacity in money matters, poor fellow! as he has hitherto been blamed for mine. You are a shark of the first order, Euripides. So much the better for the firm!

Barbara.   Is the bargain closed, Dolly? Does your soul belong to him now?

Cusins.   No: the price is settled: that is all. The real tug of war is still to come. What about the moral question?

Lady Britomart.   There is no moral question in the matter at all, Adolphus. You must simply sell cannons and weapons to people whose cause is right and just, and refuse them to foreigners and criminals.

Undershaft (*determinedly*).   No: none of that. You must keep the true faith of an Armorer, or you dont come in here.

Cusins.   What on earth is the true faith of an Armorer?

Undershaft.   To give arms to all men who offer an honest price for them, without respect of persons or principles: to aristocrat and republican, to Nihilist and Tsar, to Capitalist and Socialist, to Protestant and Catholic, to burglar and policeman, to black man, white man and yellow man, to all sorts and conditions, all nationalities, all faiths, all follies, all causes and all crimes. The first Undershaft wrote up in his shop IF GOD GAVE THE HAND, LET NOT MAN WITHHOLD THE SWORD. The second wrote up ALL HAVE THE RIGHT TO FIGHT: NONE HAVE THE RIGHT TO JUDGE. The third wrote up TO MAN THE WEAPON: TO HEAVEN THE VICTORY. The fourth had no literary turn; so he did not write up anything; but he sold cannons to Napoleon under the nose of George the Third. The fifth wrote up PEACE SHALL NOT PREVAIL SAVE WITH A SWORD IN HER HAND. The sixth, my master, was the best of all. He wrote up NOTHING IS EVER DONE IN THIS WORLD UNTIL

MEN ARE PREPARED TO KILL ONE ANOTHER IF IT IS NOT DONE. After that, there was nothing left for the seventh to say. So he wrote up, simply, UNASHAMED.

Cusins. My good Machiavelli, I shall certainly write something up on the wall; only, as I shall write it in Greek, you wont be able to read it. But as to your Armorer's faith, if I take my neck out of the noose of my own morality I am not going to put it into the noose of yours. I shall sell cannons to whom I please and refuse them to whom I please. So there!

Undershaft. From the moment when you become Andrew Undershaft, you will never do as you please again. Dont come here lusting for power, young man.

Cusins. If power were my aim I should not come here for it. You have no power.

Undershaft. None of my own, certainly.

Cusins. I have more power than you, more will. You do not drive this place: it drives you. And what drives the place?

Undershaft (enigmatically). A will of which I am a part.

Barbara (startled). Father! Do you know what you are saying; or are you laying a snare for my soul?

Cusins. Dont listen to his metaphysics, Barbara. The place is driven by the most rascally part of society, the money hunters, the pleasure hunters, the military promotion hunters; and he is their slave.

Undershaft. Not necessarily. Remember the Armorer's Faith. I will take an order from a good man as cheerfully as from a bad one. If you good people prefer preaching and shirking to buying my weapons and fighting the rascals, dont blame me. I can make cannons: I cannot make courage and conviction. Bah! you tire me, Euripides, with your morality mongering. Ask Barbara: she understands. (He suddenly reaches up and takes Barbara's hands, looking powerfully into her eyes) Tell him, my love, what power really means.

Barbara (hypnotized). Before I joined the Salvation Army, I was in my own power; and the consequence was that I never knew what to do with myself. When I joined it, I had not time enough for all the things I had to do.

Undershaft (approvingly). Just so. And why was that, do you suppose?

Barbara. Yesterday I should have said, because I was in the power of God. (She resumes her self-possession, withdrawing her hands from his with a power equal to his own). But you came and shewed me that I was in the power of Bodger and Undershaft. Today I feel—oh! how can I put it into words? Sarah: do you remember the earthquake at Cannes, when we were little children?—how little the surprise of the first shock mattered compared to the dread and horror of waiting for the second? That is how I feel in this place today. I stood on the rock I thought eternal; and without a word of warning it reeled and crumbled under me. I was safe with an infinite wisdom watching me, an army marching to Salvation with me; and in a moment, at a stroke of your pen in a cheque book, I stood alone; and the heavens were empty. That was the first shock of the earthquake: I am waiting for the second.

Undershaft. Come, come, my daughter! dont make too much of your little tinpot tragedy. What do we do here when we spend years of work and thought and thousands of pounds of solid cash on a new gun or an aerial battleship that turns out just a hairsbreadth wrong after all? Scrap it. Scrap it without wasting another hour or another pound on it. Well, you have made for yourself something that you call a morality or a religion or what not. It doesnt fit the facts. Well, scrap it. Scrap it and get one that does fit. That is what is wrong with the world at present. It scraps its obsolete steam engines and dynamos; but it wont scrap its old prejudices and its old moralities and its old religions and its old political constitutions. Whats the result? In machinery it does very well; but in morals and religion and politics it is working at a loss that brings it nearer bankruptcy every year. Dont persist in that folly. If your old religion broke down yesterday, get a newer and a better one for tomorrow.

Barbara. Oh how gladly I would take a better one to my soul! But you offer me a worse one. (*Turning on him with sudden vehemence*). Justify yourself: shew me some light through the darkness of this dreadful place, with its beautifully clean workshops, and respectable workmen, and model homes.

Undershaft. Cleanliness and respectability do not need justification, Barbara: they justify themselves. I see no darkness here, no dreadfulness. In your Salvation shelter I saw poverty, misery, cold and hunger. You gave them bread and treacle and dreams of heaven. I give from thirty shillings a week to twelve thousand a year. They find their own dreams; but I look after the drainage.

Barbara. And their souls?

Undershaft. I save their souls just as I saved yours.

Barbara (*revolted*). You saved my soul! What do you mean?

Undershaft. I fed you and clothed you and housed you. I took care that you should have money enough to live handsomely—more than enough; so that you could be wasteful, careless, generous. That saved your soul from the seven deadly sins.

Barbara (*bewildered*). The seven deadly sins!

Undershaft. Yes, the deadly seven. (*Counting on his fingers*) Food, clothing, firing, rent, taxes, respectability and children. Nothing can lift those seven millstones from Man's neck but money; and the spirit cannot soar until the mill stones are lifted. I lifted them from your spirit. I enabled Barbara to become Major Barbara; and I saved her from the crime of poverty.

Cusins. Do you call poverty a crime?

Undershaft. The worst of crimes. All the other crimes are virtues beside it: all the other dishonors are chivalry itself by comparison. Poverty blights whole cities; spreads horrible pestilences; strikes dead the very souls of all who come within sight, sound, or smell of it. What you call crime is nothing: a murder here and a theft there, a blow now and a curse then: what do they matter? they are only the accidents and illnesses of life: there are not fifty genuine professional criminals in London. But there are millions of poor people, abject people, dirty people, ill fed, ill clothed people. They poison us morally and physically: they kill the happiness of society: they force us to do away with our own liberties and to organize unnatural cruelties for fear they should rise against us and drag us down into their abyss. Only fools fear crime: we all fear poverty. Pah! (turning on Barbara) you talk of your half-saved ruffian in West Ham: you accuse me of dragging his soul back to perdition. Well, bring him to me here; and I will drag his soul back again to salvation for you. Not by words and dreams; but by thirty-eight shillings a week, a sound house in a handsome street, and a permanent job. In three weeks he will have a fancy waistcoat; in three months a tall hat and a chapel sitting; before the end of the year he will shake hands with a duchess at a Primrose League meeting, and join the Conservative Party.

Barbara. And will he be the better for that?

Undershaft. You know he will. Dont be a hypocrite, Barbara. He will be better fed, better housed, better clothed, better behaved; and his children will be pounds heavier and bigger. That will be better than an American cloth mattress in a shelter, chopping firewood, eating bread and treacle, and being forced to kneel down from time to time to thank heaven for it: knee drill, I think you call it. It is cheap work converting starving men with a Bible in one hand and a slice of bread in the other. I will undertake to convert West Ham to Mahometanism on the same terms. Try your hand on my men: their souls are hungry because their bodies are full.

Barbara. And leave the east end to starve?

Undershaft (his energetic tone dropping into one of bitter and brooding remembrance). I was an east ender. I moralized and starved until one day I swore that I would be a full-fed free man at all costs; that nothing should stop me except a bullet, neither reason nor morals nor the lives of other men. I said 'Thou shalt starve ere I starve'; and with that word I became free and great. I was a dangerous man until I had my will: now I am a useful, beneficent, kindly person. That is the history of most self-made millionaires, I fancy. When it is the history of every Englishman we shall have an England worth living in.

Lady Britomart. Stop making speeches, Andrew. This is not the place for them.

Undershaft (punctured). My dear: I have no other means of conveying my ideas.

Lady Britomart. Your ideas are nonsense. You got on because you were selfish and unscrupulous.

Undershaft. Not at all. I had the strongest scruples about poverty and starvation. Your moralists are quite unscrupulous about both: they make virtues of them. I had rather be a thief than a pauper. I had rather be a murderer than a slave. I dont want to be either; but if you force the alternative on me, then, by Heaven, I'll chose the braver and more moral one. I hate poverty and slavery worse than any other crimes whatsoever. And let me tell you this. Poverty and slavery have stood up for centuries to your sermons and leading articles: they will not stand up to my machine guns. Dont preach at them: dont reason with them. Kill them.

Barbara. Killing. Is that your remedy for everything?

Undershaft. It is the final test of conviction, the only lever strong enough to overturn a social system, the only way of saying Must. Let six hundred and seventy fools loose in the streets; and three policemen can scatter them. But huddle them together in a certain house in Westminster; and let them go through certain ceremonies and call themselves certain names until at last they get the courage to kill; and your six hundred and seventy fools become a government. Your pious mob fills up ballot papers and imagines it is governing its masters; but the ballot paper that really governs is the paper that has a bullet wrapped up in it.

Cusins. That is perhaps why, like most intelligent people, I never vote.

Undershaft. Vote! Bah! When you vote, you only change the names of the cabinet. When you shoot, you pull down governments, inaugurate new epochs, abolish old orders and set up new. Is that historically true, Mr Learned Man, or is it not?

Cusins. It is historically true. I loathe having to admit it. I repudiate your sentiments. I abhor your nature. I defy you in every possible way. Still, it is true. But it ought not to be true.

Undershaft. Ought! ought! ought! ought! ought! Are you going to spend your life saying ought, like the rest of our moralists? Turn your oughts into shalls, man. Come and make explosives with me. Whatever can blow men up can blow society up. The history of the world is the history of those who had courage enough to embrace this truth. Have you the courage to embrace it, Barbara?

Lady Britomart. Barbara: I positively forbid you to listen to your father's abominable wickedness. And you, Adolphus, ought to know better than to go about saying that wrong things are true. What does it matter whether they are true if they are wrong?

Undershaft. What does it matter whether they are wrong if they are true?

Lady Britomart (rising). Children: come home instantly. Andrew: I am exceedingly sorry I allowed you to call on us. You are wickeder than ever. Come at once.

Barbara (shaking her head). It's no use running away from wicked people, mamma.

Lady Britomart. It is every use. It shews your disapprobation of them.

Barbara. It does not save them.

Lady Britomart. I can see that you are going to disobey me. Sarah: are you coming home or are you not?

Sarah. I daresay it's very wicked of papa to make cannons; but I dont think I shall cut him on that account.

Lomax *(pouring oil on the troubled waters).* The fact is, you know, there is a certain amount of tosh about this notion of wickedness. It doesnt work. You must look at facts. Not that I would say a word in favor of anything wrong; but then, you see, all sorts of chaps are always doing all sorts of things; and we have to fit them in somehow, dont you know. What I mean is that you cant go cutting everybody; and thats about what it comes to. *(Their rapt attention to his eloquence makes him nervous).* Perhaps I dont make myself clear.

Lady Britomart. You are lucidity itself, Charles. Because Andrew is successful and has plenty of money to give to Sarah, you will flatter him and encourage him in his wickedness.

Lomax *(unruffled).* Well, where the carcase is, there will the eagles be gathered, dont you know. *(To Undershaft)* Eh? What?

Undershaft. Precisely. By the way, may I call you Charles?

Lomax. Delighted. Cholly is the usual ticket.

Undershaft *(to Lady Britomart).* Biddy—

Lady Britomart *(violently).* Dont dare call me Biddy. Charles Lomax: you are a fool. Adolphus Cusins: you are a Jesuit. Stephen: you are a prig. Barbara: you are a lunatic. Andrew: you are a vulgar tradesman. Now you all know my opinion; and my conscience is clear, at all events *(she sits down with a vehemence that the rug fortunately softens).*

Undershaft. My dear: you are the incarnation of morality. *(She snorts).* Your conscience is clear and your duty done when you have called everybody names. Come, Euripides! it is getting late; and we all want to go home. Make up your mind.

Cusins. Understand this, you old demon—

Lady Britomart. Adolphus!

Undershaft. Let him alone, Biddy. Proceed, Euripides.

Cusins. You have me in a horrible dilemma. I want Barbara.

Undershaft. Like all young men, you greatly exaggerate the difference between one young woman and another.

Barbara. Quite true, Dolly.

Cusins. I also want to avoid being a rascal.

Undershaft *(with biting contempt).* You lust for personal righteousness, for self-approval, for what you call a good conscience, for what Barbara calls salvation, for what I call patronizing people who are not so lucky as yourself.

Cusins. I do not: all the poet in me recoils from being a good man. But there are things in me that I must reckon with. Pity—

Undershaft. Pity! The scavenger of misery.

Cusins. Well, love.

Undershaft. I know. You love the needy and the outcast: you love the oppressed races, the negro, the Indian ryot, the underdog everywhere. Do you love the Japanese? Do you love the French? Do you love the English?

Cusins. No. Every true Englishman detests the English. We are the wickedest nation on earth; and our success is a moral horror.

Undershaft. That is what comes of your gospel of love, is it?

Cusins. May I not love even my father-in-law?

Undershaft. Who wants your love, man? By what right do you take the liberty of offering it to me? I will have your due heed and respect, or I will kill you. But your love! Damn your impertinence!

Cusins (grinning). I may not be able to control my affections, Mac.

Undershaft. You are fencing, Euripides. You are weakening: your grip is slipping. Come! try your last weapon. Pity and love have broken in your hand: forgiveness is still left.

Cusins. No: forgiveness is a beggar's refuge. I am with you there: we must pay our debts.

Undershaft. Well said. Come! you will suit me. Remember the words of Plato.

Cusins (starting). Plato! You dare quote Plato to me!

Undershaft. Plato says, my friend, that society cannot be saved until either the Professors of Greek take to making gunpowder, or else the makers of gunpowder become Professors of Greek.

Cusins. Oh, tempter, cunning tempter!

Undershaft. Come! choose, man, choose.

Cusins. But perhaps Barbara will not marry me if I make the wrong choice.

Barbara. Perhaps not.

Cusins (desperately perplexed). You hear!

Barbara. Father: do you love nobody?

Undershaft. I love my best friend.

Lady Britomart. And who is that, pray?

Undershaft. My bravest enemy. That is the man who keeps me up to the mark.

Cusins. You know, the creature is really a sort of poet in his way. Suppose he is a great man, after all!

Undershaft. Suppose you stop talking and make up your mind, my young friend.

Cusins. But you are driving me against my nature. I hate war.

Undershaft. Hatred is the coward's revenge for being intimidated. Dare you make war on war? Here are the means: my friend Mr Lomax is sitting on them.

Lomax (springing up). Oh I say! You dont mean that this thing is loaded, do you? My ownest: come off it.

Sarah *(sitting placidly on the shell).* If I am to be blown up, the more thoroughly it is done the better. Dont fuss, Cholly.

Lomax *(to Undershaft, strongly remonstrant).* Your own daughter, you know!

Undershaft. So I see. *(To Cusins).* Well, my friend, may we expect you here at six tomorrow morning?

Cusins *(firmly).* Not on any account. I will see the whole establishment blown up with its own dynamite before I will get up at five. My hours are healthy, rational hours: eleven to five.

Undershaft. Come when you please: before a week you will come at six and stay until I turn you out for the sake of your health. *(Calling)* Bilton! *(He turns to Lady Britomart, who rises).* My dear: let us leave these two young people to themselves for a moment. *(Bilton comes from the shed).* I am going to take you through the gun cotton shed.

Bilton *(barring the way).* You cant take anything explosive in here, sir.

Lady Britomart. What do you mean? Are you alluding to me?

Bilton *(unmoved).* No, maam. Mr Undershaft has the other gentleman's matches in his pocket.

Lady Britomart *(abruptly).* Oh! I beg your pardon. *(She goes into the shed).*

Undershaft. Quite right, Bilton, quite right: here you are. *(He gives Bilton the box of matches).* Come Stephen. Come, Charles. Bring Sarah. *(He passes into the shed).*

Bilton opens the box and deliberately drops the matches into the fire-bucket.

Lomax. Oh! I Say *(Bilton stolidly hands him the empty box).* Infernal nonsense! Pure scientific ignorance! *(He goes in).*

Sarah. Am I all right, Bilton?

Bilton. Youll have to put on list slippers, miss: that's all. Weve got em inside. *(She goes in).*

Stephen *(very seriously to Cusins).* Dolly, old fellow, think. Think before you decide. Do you feel that you are a sufficiently practical man? It is a huge undertaking, an enormous responsibility. All this mass of business will be Greek to you.

Cusins. Oh, I think it will be much less difficult than Greek.

Stephen. Well, I just want to say this before I leave you to yourselves. Dont let anything I have said about right and wrong prejudice you against this great chance in life. I have satisfied myself that the business is one of the highest character and a credit to our country. *(Emotionally)* I am very proud of my father. I—*(Unable to proceed, he presses Cusins' hand and goes hastily into the shed, followed by Bilton). Barbara and Cusins, left alone together, look at one another silently.*

Cusins. Barbara: I am going to accept this offer.

Barbara. I thought you would.

Cusins. You understand, dont you, that I had to decide without consulting you. If I had thrown the burden of the choice on you, you would sooner or later have despised me for it.

Barbara. Yes: I did not want you to sell your soul for me any more than for this inheritance.

Cusins. It is not the sale of my soul that troubles me: I have sold it too often to care about that. I have sold it for a professorship. I have sold it for an income. I have sold it to escape being imprisoned for refusing to pay taxes for hangmen's ropes and unjust wars and things that I abhor. What is all human conduct but the daily and hourly sale of our souls for trifles? What I am now selling it for is neither money nor position nor comfort, but for reality and for power.

Barbara. You know that you will have no power, and that he has none.

Cusins. I know. It is not for myself alone. I want to make power for the world.

Barbara. I want to make power for the world too; but it must be spiritual power.

Cusins. I think all power is spiritual: these cannons will not go off by themselves. I have tried to make spiritual power by teaching Greek. But the world can never be really touched by a dead language and a dead civilization. The people must have power; and the people cannot have Greek. Now the power that is made here can be wielded by all men.

Barbara. Power to burn women's houses down and kill their sons and tear their husbands to pieces.

Cusins. You cannot have power for good without having power for evil too. Even mother's milk nourishes murderers as well as heroes. This power which only tears men's bodies to pieces has never been so horribly abused as the intellectual power, the imaginative power, the poetic, religious power that can enslave men's souls. As a teacher of Greek I gave the intellectual man weapons against the common man. I now want to give the common man weapons against the intellectual man. I love the common people. I want to arm them against the lawyers, the doctors, the priests, the literary men, the professors, the artists, and the politicians, who, once in authority, are more disastrous and tyrannical than all the fools, rascals, and impostors. I want a power simple enough for common men to use, yet strong enough to force the intellectual oligarchy to use its genius for the general good.

Barbara. Is there no higher power than that *(pointing to the shell)?*

Cusins. Yes; but that power can destroy the higher powers just as a tiger can destroy a man: therefore Man must master that power first. I admitted this when the Turks and Greeks were last at war. My best pupil went out to fight for Hellas. My parting gift to him was not a copy of Plato's Republic, but a revolver and a hundred Undershaft cartridges. The blood of every Turk he shot—if he shot any—is on my head as well as on Undershaft's. That act committed me to this place for ever. Your father's challenge has beaten me. Dare I make war on war? I must. I will. And now, is it all over between us?

Barbara *(touched by his evident dread of her answer).* Silly baby Dolly! How could it be!

Cusins (*overjoyed*).   Then you—you—you—Oh for my drum! (*He flourishes imaginery drumsticks*).

Barbara (*angered by his levity*).   Take care, Dolly, take care. Oh, if only I could get away from you and from father and from it all! if I could have the wings of a dove and fly away to heaven!

Cusins.   And leave me!

Barbara.   Yes, you, and all the other naughty mischievous children of men. But I cant. I was happy in the Salvation Army for a moment. I escaped from the world into a paradise of enthusiasm and prayer and soul saving; but the moment our money ran short, it all came back to Bodger: it was he who saved our people: he, and the Prince of Darkness, my papa. Undershaft and Bodger: their hands stretch everywhere: when we feed a starving fellow creature, it is with their bread, because there is no other bread; when we tend the sick, it is in the hospitals they endow; if we turn from the churches they build, we must kneel on the stones of the streets they pave. As long as that lasts, there is no getting away from them. Turning our backs on Bodger and Undershaft is turning our backs on life.

Cusins.   I thought you were determined to turn you back on the wicked side of life.

Barbara.   There is no wicked side: life is all one. And I never wanted to shirk my share in whatever evil must be endured, whether it be sin or suffering. I wish I could cure you of middle-class ideas, Dolly.

Cusins (*gasping*).   Middle cl—! A snub! A social snub to me! from the daughter of a foundling!

Barbara.   That is why I have no class, Dolly: I come straight out of the heart of the whole people. If I were middle-class I should turn my back on my father's business; and we should both live in an artistic drawing room, with you reading the reviews in one corner, and I in the other at the piano, playing Schumann: both very superior persons, and neither of us a bit of use. Sooner than that, I would sweep out the guncotton shed, or be one of Bodger's barmaids. Do you know what would have happened if you had refused papa's offer?

Cusins.   I wonder!

Barbara.   I should have given you up and married the man who accepted it. After all, my dear old mother has more sense than any of you. I felt like her when I saw this place—felt that I must have it—that never, never, never could I let it go; only she thought it was the houses and the kitchen ranges and the linen and china, when it was really all the human souls to be saved: not weak souls in starved bodies, sobbing with gratitude for a scrap of bread and treacle, but fullfed, quarrelsome, snobbish, uppish creatures, all standing on their little rights and dignities, and thinking that my father ought to be greatly obliged to them for making so much money for him—and so he ought. That is where salvation is really wanted. My father shall never throw it in my teeth again that my converts were bribed with bread. *(She is transfigured).* I have got rid of the bribe of bread. I have got rid of the bribe of heaven. Let God's work be done for its own sake: the work he had to create us to do because it cannot be done except by living men and women. When I die, let him be in my debt, not I in his; and let me forgive him as becomes a woman of my rank.

Cusins. Then the way of life lies through the factory of death?

Barbara. Yes, through the raising of hell to heaven and of man to God, through the unveiling of an eternal light in the Valley of The Shadow. *(Seizing him with both hands)* Oh, did you think my courage would never come back? did you believe that I was a deserter? that I, who have stood in the streets, and taken my people to my heart, and talked of the holiest and greatest things with them, could ever turn back and chatter foolishly to fashionable people about nothing in a drawing room? Never, never, never, never: Major Barbara will die with the colors. Oh! and I have my dear little Dolly boy still; and he has found me my place and my work. Glory Hallelujah! *(She kisses him).*

Cusins. My dearest: consider my delicate health. I cannot stand as much happiness as you can.

Barbara. Yes: it is not easy work being in love with me, is it? But its good for you. *(She runs to the shed, and calls, childlike)* Mamma! Mamma! *(Bilton comes out of the shed, followed by Undershaft).* I want Mamma.

Undershaft. She is taking off her list slippers, dear. *(He passes on to Cusins).* Well? What does she say?

Cusins. She has gone right up into the skies.

Lady Britomart *(coming from the shed and stopping on the steps, obstructing Sarah, who follows with Lomax. Barbara clutches like a baby at her mother's skirt).* Barbara: when will you learn to be independent and to act and think for yourself? I know as well as possible what that cry of 'Mamma, Mamma,' means. Always running to me!

Sarah *(touching Lady Britomart's ribs with her finger tips and imitating a bicycle horn).* Pip! pip!

Lady Britomart *(highly indignant).* How dare you say Pip! pip! to me, Sarah? You are both very naughty children. What do you want, Barbara?

Barbara. I want a house in the village to live in with Dolly. *(Dragging at the skirt)* Come and tell me which one to take.

Undershaft *(to Cusins).* Six o'clock tomorrow morning, Euripides.

THE END

Questions

1. *What commonly held social, political, moral, and religious attitudes does Undershaft attack in this play? Justify or refute his position.* **2.** *What different viewpoints are represented by Lady Britomart, Stephen, and Charles Lomax? How, in the creation of* these characters, does Shaw manipulate the audience's response to those points of view?   **3.** What function does the episode involving Bill Walker serve in the play? In what way does he differ from Snobby Price?   **4.** In Act III Stephen tells his father that he knows "the difference between right and wrong." Why does Undershaft ridicule that assertion? Does Undershaft know the difference between right and wrong? Explain. **5.** Undershaft quotes the Undershaft maxims in Act III (p. 177). Do you accept or reject the underlying ethical principles they illustrate? Explain.   **6.** If Undershaft represents power and Barbara represents religion, what does Cusins represent in the play? Do you find Cusins' decision to become Undershaft's successor satisfying? Explain.

Benito Cereno

ROBERT LOWELL   [b. 1917]

CHARACTERS

Captain Amasa Delano
John Perkins
Don Benito Cereno
Babu
Atufal
Francesco
American Sailors
Spanish Sailors
Negro Slaves

THE SCENE: *About the year 1800, an American sealing vessel, the President Adams, at anchor in an island harbor off the coast of Trinidad. The stage is part of the ship's deck. Everything is unnaturally clean, bare and ship-shape. To one side, a polished, coal-black cannon. The American captain, Amasa Delano from Duxbury, Massachusetts, sits in a cane chair. He is a strong, comfortable looking man in his early thirties who wears a spotless blue coat and white trousers. Incongruously, he has on a straw hat and smokes a corncob pipe. Beside him stands John Perkins, his bosun, a very stiff, green young man, a relative of Delano's. Three Sailors, one carrying an American flag, enter. Everyone stands at attention and salutes with machinelike exactitude. Then the Three Sailors march off-stage. Delano and Perkins are alone.*

Delano.   There goes the most beautiful woman in South America.
Perkins.   We never see any women, Sir;
   just this smothering, overcast Equator,
   a seal or two,
   the flat dull sea,
   and a sky like a gray wasp's nest.
Delano.   I wasn't talking about women,
   I was calling your attention to the American flag.
Perkins.   Yes, Sir! I wish we were home in Duxbury.
Delano.   We are home. America is wherever her flag flies.
   My own deck is the only place in the world
   where I feel at home.
Perkins.   That's too much for me, Captain Delano.
   I mean I wish I were home with my wife;
   these world cruises are only for bachelors.

Delano. Your wife will keep. You should smoke, Perkins.
Smoking turns men into philosophers
and swabs away their worries.
I can see my wife and children or not see them
in each puff of blue smoke.

Perkins. You are always tempting me, Sir!
I try to keep fit,
I want to return to my wife as fit as I left her.

Delano. You're much too nervous, Perkins.
Travel will shake you up. You should let
a little foreign dirt rub off on you.
I've taught myself to speak Spanish like a Spaniard.
At each South American port, they mistake me for a
Castilian Don.

Perkins: Aren't you lowering yourself a little, Captain?
Excuse me, Sir, I have been wanting to ask you a question.
Don't you think our President, Mr. Jefferson, is lowering himself
by being so close to the French?
I'd feel a lot safer in this unprotected place
if we'd elected Mr. Adams instead of Mr. Jefferson.

Delano. The better man ran second!
Come to think of it, he rather let us down
by losing the election just after we had named this ship,
the *President Adams*. Adams is a nervous dry fellow.
When you've travelled as much as I have,
you'll learn that that sort doesn't export, Perkins.
Adams didn't get a vote outside New England!

Perkins. He carried every New England state;
that was better than winning the election.
I'm afraid I'm a dry fellow, too, Sir.

Delano. Not when I've educated you!
When I am through with you, Perkins,
you'll be as worldly as the Prince Regent of England,
only you'll be a first class American officer.
I'm all for Jefferson, he has the popular touch.
Of course he's read too many books,
but I've always said an idea or two won't sink our Republic.
I'll tell you this, Perkins,
Mr. Jefferson is a gentleman and an American.

Perkins. They say he has two illegitimate Negro children.

Delano: The more the better! That's the quickest way
to raise the blacks to our level.
I'm surprised you swallow such Federalist bilge, Perkins!
I told you Mr. Jefferson is a gentleman and an American;
when a man's in office, Sir, we all pull behind him!

Perkins.   Thank God our Revolution ended where the French one began.

Delano.   Oh the French! They're like the rest of the Latins,
   they're hardly white people,
   they start with a paper republic
   and end with a toy soldier, like Bonaparte.

Perkins.   Yes, Sir. I see a strange sail making for the harbor.
   They don't know how to sail her.

Delano.   Hand me my telescope.

Perkins.   Aye, aye, Sir!

Delano [*With telescope*].   I see an ocean undulating in long scoops of swells;
   it's set like the beheaded French Queen's high wig;
   the sleek surface is like waved lead,
   cooled and pressed in the smelter's mould.
   I see flights of hurried gray fowl,
   patches of fluffy fog.
   They skim low and fitfully above the decks,
   like swallows sabering flies before a storm.
   This gray boat foreshadows something wrong.

Perkins.   It does, Sir!
   They don't know how to sail her!

Delano.   I see a sulphurous haze above her cabin,
   the new sun hangs like a silver dollar to her stern;
   low creeping clouds blow on from them to us.

Perkins.   What else, Sir?

Delano.   The yards are woolly
   the ship is furred with fog.
   On the cracked and rotten head-boards,
   the tarnished, gilded letters say, the *San Domingo*.
   A rat's nest messing up the deck,
   black faces in white sheets are fussing with the ropes.
   I think it's a cargo of Dominican monks.

Perkins.   Dominican monks, Sir! God help us,
   I thought they were outlawed in the new world.

Delano.   No, it's nothing. I see they're only slaves.
   the boat's transporting slaves.

Perkins.   Do you believe in slavery, Captain Delano?

Delano.   In a civilized country, Perkins,
   everyone disbelieves in slavery,
   everyone disbelieves in slavery and wants slaves.
   We have the perfect uneasy answer;
   in the North, we don't have them and want them;
   Mr. Jefferson has them and fears them.

Perkins.   Is that how you answer, Sir,
   when a little foreign dirt has rubbed off on you?

Delano. Don't ask me such intense questions.
   You should take up smoking, Perkins.
   There was a beautiful, dumb English actress—
   I saw her myself in London.
   They wanted her to look profound,
   so she read Plato and the Bible and Benjamin Franklin,
   and thought about them every minute.
   She still looked like a moron.
   Then they told her to think about nothing.
   She thought about nothing, and looked like Socrates.
   That's smoking, Perkins, you think about nothing and look deep.

Perkins. I don't believe in slavery, Sir.

Delano. You don't believe in slavery or Spaniards
   or smoking or long cruises or monks or Mr. Jefferson!
   You are a Puritan, all faith and fire.

Perkins. Yes, Sir.

Delano. God save America from Americans!

[*Takes up the telescope*]

   I see octogonal network bagging out
   from her heavy top like decayed beehives.
   The battered forecastle looks like a raped Versailles.
   On the stern-piece, I see the fading arms of Spain.
   There's a masked satyr, or something
   with it's foot on a big white goddess.
   She has quite a figure.

Perkins. They oughtn't to be allowed on the ocean!

Delano. Who oughtn't? Goddesses?

Perkins. I mean Spaniards, who cannot handle a ship,
   and mess up its hull with immoral statues.

Delano. You're out of step. You're much too dry.
   Bring me my three-cornered hat.
   Order some men to clear a whaleboat.
   I am going to bring water and fresh fish to the *San Domingo*.
   These people have had some misfortune, Perkins!

Perkins. Aye, aye, Sir.

Delano. Spaniards? The name gets you down,
   you think their sultry faces and language
   make them Zulus.
   You take the name *Delano*—
   I've always thought it has some saving
   Italian or Spanish virtue in it.

Perkins. Yes, Sir.

Delano. A Spaniard isn't a negro under the skin,
   particularly a Spaniard from Spain—

these South American ones mix too much with the Indians.
Once you get inside a Spaniard,
he talks about as well as your wife in Duxbury.
Perkins [*Shouting*].   A boat for the captain! A whaleboat for Captain Delano!

[*A bosun's whistle is heard, the lights dim. When they come up, we are on the deck of the San Domingo, the same set, identical except for litter and disorder. Three American Sailors climb on board. They are followed by Perkins and Delano, now wearing a three-cornered hat. Once on board, the American Sailors salute Delano and stand stiffly at attention like toys. Negroes from the San Domingo drift silently and furtively forward*]

Delano.   I see a wen of barnacles hanging to the waterline of this ship.
It sticks out like the belly of a pregnant woman.
Have a look at our dory Bosun.
Perkins.   Aye, aye, Sir!

[*By now, about twenty blacks and two Spanish sailors have drifted in. They look like some gaudy, shabby, unnautical charade, and pay no attention to the Americans, until an unseen figure in the rigging calls out a single sharp warning in an unknown tongue. Then they all rush forward, shouting, waving their arms and making inarticulate cries like birds. Three shrill warnings come from the rigging. Dead silence. The men from the San Domingo press back in a dense semicircle. One by one, individuals come forward, make showy bows to Delano, and speak*]

First Negro.   Scurvy, Master Yankee!
Second Negro.   Yellow fever, Master Yankee!
Third Negro.   Two men knocked overboard rounding Cape Horn,
Master Yankee!
Fourth Negro.   Nothing to eat, Master Yankee!
Negro Woman.   Nothing to drink, Master Yankee!
Second Negro Woman.   Our mouths are dead wood, Master Yankee!
Delano.   You see, Perkins,
these people have had some misfortune.

[*General hubbub, muttering, shouts, gestures, ritual and dumbshow of distress. The rigging, hitherto dark, lightens, as the sun comes out of a cloud, and shows Three Old Negroes, identical down to their shabby patches. They perch on cat's-heads; their heads are grizzled like dying willow tops; each is picking bits of unstranded rope for oakum. It is they who have been giving the warnings that control the people below. Everyone, Delano along with the rest, looks up. Delano turns aside and speaks to Perkins*]

It is like a Turkish bazaar.
Perkins.   They are like gypsies showing themselves for money
at a county fair, Sir.

Delano. This is enchanting after the blank gray roll of the ocean!
Go tell the Spanish captain I am waiting for him.

[*Perkins goes off. Sharp warnings from the Oakum-Pickers. A big black spread of canvas is pulled creakingly and ceremoniously aside. Six Figures stand huddled on a platform about four feet from the deck. They look like weak old invalids in bathrobes and nightcaps until they strip to the waist and turn out to be huge, shining young negroes. Saying nothing, they set to work cleaning piles of rusted hatchets. From time to time, they turn and clash their hatchets together with a rhythmic shout. Perkins returns*]

Perkins. Their captain's name is Don Benito Cereno,
he sends you his compliments, Sir.
He looks more like a Mexican planter than a seaman.
He's put his fortune on his back:
he doesn't look as if he had washed since they left port.
Delano. Did you tell him I was waiting for him?
A captain should be welcomed by his fellow-captain.
I can't understand this discourtesy.
Perkins. He's coming, but there's something wrong with him.

[*Benito Cereno, led by his negro servant, Babu, enters. Benito, looking sick and dazed, is wearing a sombrero and is dressed with a singular but shabby richness. Head bent to one side, he leans in a stately coma against the rail, and stares unseeingly at Delano. Babu, all in scarlet, and small and quick, keeps whispering, pointing and pulling at Benito's sleeve. Delano walks over to them*]

Delano. Your hand, Sir. I am Amasa Delano,
captain of the *President Adams,*
a sealing ship from the United States.
This is your lucky day,
the sun is out of hiding for the first time in two weeks,
and here I am aboard your ship
like the Good Samaritan with fresh food and water.
Benito. The Good Samaritan? Yes, yes,
we mustn't use the Scriptures lightly.
Welcome, Captain. It is the end of the day.
Delano. The end? It's only morning.
I loaded and lowered a whaleboat
as soon as I saw how awkwardly your ship was making for the harbor.
Benito. Your whaleboat's welcome, Captain.
I am afraid I am still stunned by the storm.
Delano. Buck up. Each day is a new beginning.
Assign some sailors to help me dole out my provisions.
Benito. I have no sailors.
Babu. [*In a quick sing-song*]. Scurvy, yellow fever,

ten men knocked off on the Horn,
doldrums, nothing to eat, nothing to drink!
By feeding us, you are feeding the King of Spain.
Delano. Sir, your slave has a pretty way of talking.
What do you need?

[*Delano waits for Benito to speak. When nothing more is said, he shifts awkwardly from foot to foot, then turns to his Sailors*]

Stand to, men!

[*The American Sailors, who have been lounging and gaping, stand in a row, as if a button had been pressed*]

Lay our fish and water by the cabin!

[*The Sailors arrange the watercans and baskets of fish by the cabin. A sharp whistle comes from the Oakum-Pickers. Almost instantly, the provisions disappear*]

Captain Cereno, you are surely going to taste my water!
Benito. A captain is a servant, almost a slave, Sir.
Delano. No, a captain's a captain.
I am sending for more provisions.
Stand to!

[*The American Sailors stand to*]

Row back to the ship. When you get there,
take on five hogsheads of fresh water,
and fifty pounds of soft bread.

[*First Sailor salutes and goes down the ladder*]

Bring all our remaining pumpkins!

[*Second and Third Sailors salute and go down the ladder*]

My bosun and I will stay on board.
until our boat returns.
I imagine you can use us.
Benito. Are you going to stay here alone?
Won't your ship be lost without you?
Won't you be lost without your ship?
Babu. Listen to Master!
He is the incarnation of courtesy, Yankee Captain.
Your ship doesn't need you as much as we do.
Delano. Oh, I've trained my crew.
I can sail my ship in my sleep.

[*Leaning over the railing and calling*]

Men, bring me a box of lump sugar,
and six bottles of my best cider.

[*Turning to Benito*]

Cider isn't my favorite drink, Don Benito,
but it's a New England specialty;
I'm ordering six bottles for your table.

[*Babu whispers and gestures to Don Benito, who is exhausted and silent*]

Babu.   *Une bouteille du vin* [*To Negroes*]
My master wishes to give you a bottle
of the oldest wine in Seville.

[*He whistles. A negro woman rushes into the cabin and returns with a dusty beribboned bottle, which she holds like a baby*]

[*Babu ties a rope around the bottle*]

Babu.   I am sending this bottle of wine to your cabin.
When you drink it, you will remember us.
Do you see these ribbons? The crown of Spain is tied to one.
Forgive me for tying a rope around the King of Spain's neck.

[*Lowers the wine on the rope to the whaleboat*]

Delano.   [*Shouting to his Sailors*]

Pick up your oars!
Sailors.   Aye, aye, Sir!
Delano.   We're New England Federalists;
we can drink the King of Spain's health.

[*Benito stumbles off-stage on Babu's arm*]

Perkins.   Captain Cereno hasn't travelled as much as you have;
I don't think he knew what you meant by the New England
Federalists.
Delano [*Leaning comfortably on the rail; half to himself and half to Perkins*].
The wind is dead. We drift away.
We will be left alone all day,
here in this absentee empire.
Thank God, I know my Spanish!
Perkins.   You'll have to watch them, Sir.
Brown men in charge of black men—
it doesn't add up to much!
This Babu, I don't trust him!
Why doesn't he talk with a Southern accent,
Like Mr. Jefferson? They're out of hand, Sir!
Delano.   Nothing relaxes order more than misery.

They need severe superior officers.
They haven't one.
Now, if this Benito were a man of energy . . .
a Yankee . . .

Perkins. How can a Spaniard sail?

Delano. Some can. There was Vasco da Gama and Columbus . . .
No, I guess they were Italians. Some can,
but this captain is tubercular.

Perkins. Spaniards and Negroes have no business on a ship.

Delano. Why is this captain so indifferent to me?
If only I could stomach his foreign reserve!
This absolute dictator of his ship
only gives orders through his slaves!
He is like some Jesuit-haunted Hapsburg king
about to leave the world and hope the world will end.

Perkins. He said he was lost in the storm.

Delano. Perhaps it's only policy,
a captain's icy dignity
obliterating all democracy—

Perkins. He's like someone walking in his sleep.

Delano. Ah, slumbering dominion!
He is so self-conscious in his imbecility . . .
No, he's sick. He sees his men no more than me.
This ship is like a crowded immigration boat;
it needs severe superior officers,
the friendly arm of a strong mate.
Perhaps, I ought to take it over by force.
No, they're sick, they've been through the plague.
I'll go and speak and comfort my fellow captain.
I think you can help me, Captain. I'm feeling useless.
My own thoughts oppress me, there's so much to do.
I wonder if you would tell me the whole sad story of your voyage.
Talk to me as captain to captain.
We have sailed the same waters.
Please tell me your story.

Benito. A story? A story! That's out of place.
When I was a child, I used to beg for stories back in Lima.
Now my tongue's tied and my heart is bleeding.

[*Stops talking, as if his breath were gone. He stares for a few moments, then looks up at the rigging, as if he were counting the ropes one by one. Delano turns abruptly to Perkins*]

Delano. Go through the ship, Perkins,
and see if you can find me a Spaniard who can talk.

Benito. You must be patient, Captain Delano;

      if we only see with our eyes,
      sometimes we cannot see at all.
Delano.   I stand corrected, Captain;
      tell me about your voyage.
Benito.   It's now a hundred and ninety days . . .
      This ship, well manned, well officered, with several cabin passengers,
      carrying a cargo of Paraguay tea and Spanish cutlery.
      That parcel of Negro slaves, less than four score now,
      was once three hundred souls.
      Ten sailors and three officers fell from the mainyard off the Horn;
      part of our rigging fell overboard with them,
      as they were beating down the icy sail.
      We threw away all our cargo,
      Broke our waterpipes,
      Lashed them on deck,
      this was the chief cause of our suffering.
Delano.   I must interrupt you, Captain.
      How did you happen to have three officers on the mainyard?
      I never heard of such a disposal,
      it goes against all seamanship.
Babu.   Our officers never spared themselves;
      if there was any danger, they rushed in
      to save us without thinking.
Delano.   I can't understand such an oversight.
Babu.   There was no oversight. My master had a hundred eyes.
      He had an eye for everything.
      Sometimes the world falls on a man.
      The sea wouldn't let Master act like a master,
      yet he saved himself and many lives.
      He is still a rich man, and he saved the ship.
Benito.   Oh my God, I wish the world had fallen on me,
      and the terrible cold sea had drowned me;
      that would have been better than living through what I've
      lived through!
Babu.   He is a good man, but his mind is off;
      he's thinking about the fever when the wind stopped—
      poor, poor Master!
      Be patient, Yankee Captain, these fits are short,
      Master will be the master once again.
Benito.   The scurvy was raging through us.
      We were on the Pacific. We were invalids
      and couldn't man our mangled spars.
      A hurricane blew us northeast through the fog.
      Then the wind died.
      We lay in irons fourteen days in unknown waters,

     our black tongues stuck through our mouths,
     but we couldn't mend our broken waterpipes.

Babu.   Always those waterpipes,
     he dreams about them like a pile of snakes!

Benito.   Yellow fever followed the scurvy,
     the long heat thickened in the calm,
     my Spaniards turned black and died like slaves,
     The blacks died too. I am my only officer left.

Babu.   Poor, poor Master! He had a hundred eyes,
     he lived our lives for us.
     He is still a rich man.

Benito.   In the smart winds beating us northward,
     our torn sails dropped like sinkers in the sea;
     each day we dropped more bodies.
     Almost without a crew, canvas, water, or a wind,
     we were bounced about by the opposing waves
     through cross-currents and the weedy calms,
     and dropped our dead.
     Often we doubled and redoubled on our track
     like children lost in jungle. The thick fog
     hid the Continent and our only port from us.

Babu.   We were poor kidnapped jungle creatures.
     We only lived on what he could give us.
     He had a hundred eyes, he was the master.

Benito.   These Negroes saved me, Captain.
     Through the long calamity,
     they were as gentle as their owner, Don Aranda, promised.
     Don Aranda took away their chains before he died.

Babu.   Don Aranda saved our lives, but we couldn't save his.
     Even in Africa I was a slave.
     He took away my chains.

Benito.   I gave them the freedom of my ship.
     I did not think they were crates or cargo or cannibals.
     But it was Babu—under God, I swear I owe my life to Babu!
     He calmed his ignorant, wild brothers,
     never left me, saved the *San Domingo*.

Babu.   Poor, poor Master. He is still a rich man.
     Don't speak of Babu. Babu is dirt under your feet.
     He did his best.

Delano.   You are a good fellow, Babu.
     You are the salt of the earth. I envy you, Don Benito;
     he is no slave, Sir, but your friend.

Benito.   Yes, he is salt in my wounds.
     I can never repay him, I mean.

Excuse me, Captain, my strength is gone.
I have done too much talking. I want to rest.

[*Babu leads Benito to a shabby straw chair at the side. Benito sits. Babu fans him with his sombrero*]

Perkins. He's a fine gentleman, but no seaman.
A cabin boy would have known better
than to send his three officers on the mainyard.
Delano [*Paying no attention*].
A terrible story. I would have been unhinged myself.

[*Looking over toward Babu and Benito*]

There's a true servant. They do things better
in the South and in South America—
trust in return for trust!
The beauty of that relationship is unknown
in New England. We're too much alone
in Massachusetts, Perkins.
How do our captains and our merchants live,
each a republic to himself.
Even Sam Adams had no friends and only loved the mob.
Perkins. Sir, you are forgetting that
New England seamanship brought them their slaves.
Delano. Oh, just our Southern slaves;
we had nothing to do with these fellows.
Perkins. The ocean would be a different place
if every Spaniard served an apprenticeship on an American ship
before he got his captain's papers.
Delano. This captain's a gentleman, not a sailor.
His little yellow hands
got their command before they held a rope—
in by the cabin-window, not the hawse-hole!
Do you want to know why
they drifted hog-tied in those easy calms—
inexperience, sickness, impotence and aristocracy!
Perkins. Here comes Robinson Crusoe and his good man Friday.
Delano. We don't beat a man when he's down.

[*Benito advances uncertainly on Babu's arm*]

I am glad to see you on your feet again,
That's the only place for a Captain, sir!
I have the cure for you, I have decided
to bring you medicine and a sufficient supply of water.
A first class deck officer, a man from Salem,
shall be stationed on your quarter deck,

a temporary present from my owners.
We shall refit your ship and clear this mess.
Benito.   You will have to clear away the dead.
Babu.   This excitement is bad for him, Yankee Master.
He's lived with death. He lives on death still;
this sudden joy will kill him. You've heard
how thirsty men die from overdrinking!
His heart is with his friend, our owner, Don Aranda.
Benito.   I am the only owner.

[*He looks confused and shaken. Babu scurries off and brings up the straw chair. Benito sits*]

Delano.   Your friend is dead? He died of fever?
Benito.   He died very slowly and in torture.
He was the finest man in Lima.
We were brought up together,
I am lost here.
Delano.   Pardon me, Sir. You are young at sea.
My experience tells me what your trouble is:
this is the first body you have buried in the ocean.
I had a friend like yours, a warm honest fellow,
who would look you in the eye—
we had to throw him to the sharks.
Since then I've brought embalming gear on board.
Each man of mine shall have a Christian grave on land.
You wouldn't shake so, if Don Aranda were on board,
I mean, if you'd preserved the body.
Benito.   If he were on board this ship?
If I had preserved his body?
Babu.   Be patient, Master!
We still have the figurehead.
Delano.   You have the figurehead?
Babu.   You see that thing wrapped up in black cloth?
It's a figurehead Don Aranda bought us in Spain.
It was hurt in the storm. It's very precious.
Master takes comfort in it,
he is going to give it to Don Aranda's widow.
It's time for the pardon ceremony, Master.

[*Sound of clashing hatchets*]

Delano.   I am for these hatchet-cleaners.
They are saving cargo. They make
an awful lot of pomp and racket though
about a few old, rusty knives.
Benito.   They think steel is worth its weight in gold.

[*A slow solemn march is sounded on the gongs and other instruments. A gigantic coal-black Negro comes up the steps. He wears a spiked iron collar to which a chain is attached that goes twice around his arms and ends padlocked to a broad band of iron. The Negro comes clanking forward and stands dumbly and like a dignitary in front of Benito. Two small black boys bring Benito a frail rattan cane and a silver ball, which they support on a velvet cushion. Benito springs up, holds the ball, and raises the cane rigidly above the head of the Negro in chains. For a moment, he shows no trace of sickness. The assembled blacks sing, "Evviva, Benito!" three times*]

Babu [*At one side with the Americans, but keeping an eye on Benito*].
    You are watching the humiliation of King Atufal,
    once a ruler in Africa. He ruled as much land there as your President.
    Poor Babu was a slave even in Africa,
    a black man's slave, and now a white man's.
Benito [*In a loud, firm voice*].
    Former King Atufal, I call on you to kneel!
    Say, "My sins are black as night,
    I ask the King of Spain's pardon.
    through his servant, Don Benito."

[*Pause. Atufal doesn't move*]

Negroes.   Your sins are black as night, King Atufal!
    Your sins are black as night, King Atufal!
Delano.   What has King Atufal done?
Babu.   I will tell you later, Yankee Captain.
Benito.   Ask pardon, former King Atufal.
    If you will kneel,
    I will strike away your chains.

[*Atufal slowly raises his chained arms and lets them drop*]

    Ask pardon!
Woman Slave.   Ask pardon, King Atufal.
Benito.   Go!

[*Sound of instruments. The Black Boys take Benito's ball and cane. The straw chair is brought up. Benito sits. Francesco then leads him off-stage*]

Babu.   Francesco!
    I will be with you in a moment, Master.
    You mustn't be afraid,
    Francesco will serve you like a second Babu.
Benito.   Everyone serves me alike here,
    but no one can serve me as you have.
Babu.   I will be with you in a moment.
    The Yankee master is at sea on our ship.
    He wants me to explain our customs.

[*Benito is carried off-stage*]

> You would think Master's afraid of dying,
> if Babu leaves him!

Delano. I can imagine your tenderness during his sickness.
> You were part of him,
> you were almost a wife.

Babu. You say such beautiful things,
> the United States must be a paradise for people like Babu.

Delano. I don't know.
> We have our faults. We have many states,
> some of them could stand improvement.

Babu. The United States must be heaven.

Delano. I suppose we have fewer faults than other countries.
> What did King Atufal do?

Babu. He used the Spanish flag for toilet paper.

Delano. That's treason.
> Did Atufal know what he was doing?
> Perhaps the flag was left somewhere it shouldn't have been.
> Things aren't very strict here.

Babu. I never thought of that.
> I will go and tell Master.

Delano. Oh, no, you mustn't do that!
> I never interfere with another man's ship.
> Don Benito is your lord and dictator.
> How long has this business with King Atufal been going on?

Babu. Ever since the yellow fever,
> and twice a day.

Delano. He did a terrible thing, but he looks like a royal fellow.
> You shouldn't call him a king, though,
> it puts ideas into his head.

Babu. Atufal had gold wedges in his ears in Africa;
> now he wears a padlock and Master bears the key.

Delano. I see you have a feeling for symbols of power.
> You had better be going now,
> Don Benito will be nervous about you.

[*Babu goes off*]

> That was a terrible thing to do with a flag;
> everything is untidy and unravelled here—
> this sort of thing would never happen on the *President Adams*.

Perkins. Your ship is as shipshape as our country, Sir.

Delano. I wish people wouldn't take me as representative of our country:
> America's one thing, I am another;
> we shouldn't have to bear one another's burdens.

Perkins. You are a true American for all your talk, Sir;
   I can't believe you were mistaken for a Castilian Don.
Delano. No one would take me for Don Benito.
Perkins. I wonder if he isn't an imposter, some traveling
   actor from a circus?
Delano. No, Cereno is a great name in Peru, like Winthrop or Adams with us.
   I recognize the family features in our captain.

[*An old Spanish Sailor, grizzled and dirty, is seen crawling on all fours with an armful of knots toward the Americans. He points to where Benito and Babu have disappeared and whistles. He holds up the knots as though he were in chains, then throws them out loosely on the deck in front of him. A Group of Negroes forms a circle around him, holding hands and singing childishly. Then, laughing, they carry the Spaniard off-stage on their shoulders*]

   These blacks are too familiar!
   We are never alone!

[*Sound of gongs. Full minute's pause, as if time were passing. Delano leans on the railing. The sun grows brighter*]

   This ship is strange.
   These people are too spontaneous—all noise and show,
   no character!
   Real life is a simple monotonous thing.
   I wonder about that story about the calms;
   it doesn't stick.
   Don Benito hesitated himself in telling it.
   No one could run a ship so stupidly,
   and place three officers on one yard.

[*Benito and Babu return*]

   A captain has unpleasant duties;
   I am sorry for you, Don Benito.
Benito. You find my ship unenviable, Sir?
Delano. I was talking about punishing Atufal;
   he acted like an animal!
Benito. Oh, yes, I was forgetting . . .
   He was a King,
   How long have you lain in at this island, Sir?
Delano. Oh, a week today.
Benito. What was your last port, Sir?
Delano. Canton.
Benito. You traded seal-skins and American muskets
   for Chinese tea and silks, perhaps?
Delano. We took in some silks.
Benito. A little gold and silver too?

Delano. Just a little silver. We are only merchants.
    We take in a dollar here and there. We have no Peru,
    or a Pizarro who can sweat gold out of the natives.
Benito. You'll find things have changed
    a little in Peru since Pizarro, Captain.

[*Starts to move away. Babu whispers to him, and he comes back abruptly, as if he had forgotten something important*]

    How many men have you on board, Sir?
Delano. Some twenty-five, Sir. Each man is at his post.
Benito. They're all on board, Sir, now?
Delano. They're all on board. Each man is working.
Benito. They'll be on board tonight, Sir?
Delano. Tonight? Why do you ask, Don Benito?
Benito. Will they be on board tonight, Captain?
Delano. They'll be on board for all I know.

[*Perkins makes a sign to Delano*]

    Well, no, to tell the truth, today's our Independence Day.
    A gang is going ashore to see the village.
    A little diversion improves their efficiency,
    a little regulated corruption.
Benito. You North Americans take no chances. Generally, I suppose,
    even your merchant ships go more or less armed?
Delano. A rack full of muskets, sealing spears and cutlasses.
    Oh, and a six-pounder or two; we are a sealing ship,
    but with us each merchant is a privateer—
    only in case of oppression, of course.
    You've heard about how we shoot pirates.
Babu. Boom, boom, come Master.

[*Benito walks away on Babu's arm and sits down, almost off-stage in his straw chair. They whisper. Meanwhile, a Spanish Sailor climbs the rigging furtively, spread-eagles his arms and shows a lace shirt under his shabby jacket. He points to Benito and Babu and winks. At a cry from One of the Oakum Pickers, Three Negroes help the Spaniard down with servile, ceremonious attentions*]

Perkins. Did you see that sailor's lace shirt, Sir?
    He must have robbed one of the cabin passengers.
    I hear that people strip the dead
    in these religious countries.
Delano. No, you don't understand the Spaniards.
    In these old Latin countries,
    each man's a beggar or a noble, often both;
    they have no middle class. With them it's customary

to sew a mess of gold and pearls on rags—
that's how an aristocracy that's going to the dogs
keeps up its nerve.

Delano.   It's odd though,
that Spanish sailor seemed to want to tell me something.
He ought to dress himself properly and speak his mind.
That's what we do. That's why we're strong:
everybody trusts us. Nothing gets done
when every man's a noble. I wonder why
the captain asked me all those questions?

Perkins.   He was passing the time of day, Sir;
It's a Latin idleness.

Delano.   It's strange. Did you notice how Benito stopped rambling?
He was conventional . . . consecutive for the first time since we met him.
Something's wrong. Perhaps, they've men below the decks,
a sleeping volcano of Spanish infantry. The Malays do it,
play sick and cut your throat.
A drifting boat, a dozen doped beggars on deck,
two hundred sweating murderers packed below like sardines—
that's rot! Anyone can see these people are really sick,
sicker than usual. Our countries are at peace.
I wonder why he asked me all those questions?

Perkins.   Just idle curiosity. I hear
the gentlemen of Lima sit at coffee-tables from sun to sun
and gossip. They don't even have women to look at;
they're all locked up with their aunts.

Delano.   Their sun is going down. These old empires go.
They are much too familiar with their blacks.
I envy them though, they have no character,
they feel no need to stand alone.
We stand alone too much,
that's why no one can touch us for sailing a ship;
When a country loses heart, it's easier to live.
Ah, Babu! I suppose Don Benito's indisposed again!
Tell him I want to talk to his people;
there's nothing like a well man to help the sick.

Babu.   Master is taking his siesta, Yankee Master.
His siesta is sacred, I am afraid to disturb it.
Instead, let me show you our little entertainment.

Delano.   Let's have your entertainment;
if you know a man's pleasure
you know his measure.

Babu.   We are a childish people. Our pleasures are childish.
No one helped us, we know nothing
about your important amusements,
such as killing seals and pirates.

Delano.   I'm game. Let's have your entertainment.

[*Babu signals. The gong sounds ten times and the canvas is pulled from the circular structure. Enclosed in a triangular compartment, an Old Spanish Sailor is dipping naked white dolls in a tar-pot*]

Babu.   This little amusement keeps him alive, Yankee Master.
He is especially fond of cleaning the dolls
after he has dirtied them.

[*The Old Spanish Sailor laughs hysterically, and then smears his whole face with tar*]

Old Spanish Sailor.   My soul is white!
Babu.   The yellow fever destroyed his mind.
Delano.   Let's move on. This man's brain,
as well as his face, is defiled with pitch!
Babu.   He says his soul is white.

[*The structure is pushed around and another triangular compartment appears. A Negro Boy is playing chess against a splendid Spanish doll with a crown on its head. He stops and holds two empty wine bottles to his ears*]

This boy is deaf.
The yellow fever destroyed his mind.
Delano.   Why is he holding those bottles to his ears?
Babu.   He is trying to be a rabbit,
or listening to the ocean, his mother—
who knows?
Delano.   If he's deaf, how can he hear the ocean?
Anyway, he can't hear me.
I pass, let's move on.

[*The structure is pushed around to a third compartment. A Spanish Sailor is holding a big armful of rope*]

What are you knotting there, my man?
Spanish Sailor.   The knot.
Delano.   So I see, but what's it for?
Spanish Sailor.   For someone to untie. Catch!

[*Throws the knot to Delano*]

Babu [*Snatching the knot from Delano*].
It's dirty, it will dirty your uniform.
Delano.   Let's move on. Your entertainment
is rather lacking in invention, Babu.
Babu.   We have to do what we can.
We are just beginners at acting.
This next one will be better.

[*The structure is pushed around and shows a beautiful Negro Woman. She is dressed and posed as the Virgin Mary. A Christmas crèche is arranged around her. A Very White Spaniard dressed as Saint Joseph stands behind her. She holds a Christ-child, the same crowned doll, only black, the Negro Boy was playing chess against*]

She is the Virgin Mary. That man is not the father.

Delano.   I see. I suppose her son is the King of Spain.

Babu.   The Spaniards taught us everything,
there's nothing we can learn from you, Yankee Master.
When they took away our country, they gave us a better world.
Things do not happen in that world as they do here.

Delano.   That's a very beautiful,
though unusual Virgin Mary.

Babu.   Yes, the Bible says, "I am black not white."
When Don Aranda was dying,
we wanted to give him the Queen of Heaven
because he took away our chains.

Perkins.   The Spaniards must have taught them everything;
they're all mixed up, they don't even know their religion.

Delano.   No, no! The Catholic Church doesn't just teach,
it knows how to take from its converts.

Babu.   Do you want to shake hands with the Queen of Heaven, Yankee Master?

Delano.   No, I'm not used to royalty.
Tell her I believe in freedom of religion,
if people don't take liberties.
Let's move on.

Babu [*Kneeling to the Virgin Mary*].
I present something Your Majesty has never seen,
a white man who doesn't believe in taking liberties,
Your Majesty.

[*The structure is pushed around and shows Atufal in chains but with a crown on his head*]

Babu.   This is the life we believe in.

The Negroes All Together.   Ask pardon, King Atufal!
Kiss the Spanish flag!

Delano.   Please don't ask me to shake hands with King Atufal!

[*The canvas is put back on the structure*]

Babu.   You look tired and serious, Yankee Master.
We have to have what fun we can.
We never would have lived through the deadly calms
without a little amusement.

[*Bows and goes off*]

[The Negroes gradually drift away. Delano sighs with relief]

Delano. Well, that wasn't much!
   I suppose Shakespeare started that way.
Perkins. Who cares?
   I see a speck on the blue sea, Sir,
   our whaleboat is coming.
Delano. A speck? My eyes are speckled.
   I seem to have been dreaming. What's solid?

[Touches the ornate railing; a piece falls onto the deck]

   This ship is nothing, Perkins!
   I dreamed someone was trying to kill me!
   How could he? Jack-of-the-beach,
   they used to call me on the Duxbury shore.
   Carrying a duck-satchel in my hand, I used to paddle
   along the waterfront from a hulk to school.
   I didn't learn much there. I was always shooting duck
   or gathering huckleberries along the marsh with Cousin Nat!
   I like nothing better than breaking myself on the surf.
   I used to track the seagulls down the five-mile stretch of beach for eggs.
   How can I be killed now at the ends of the earth
   by this insane Spaniard?
   Who could want to murder Amasa Delano?
   My conscience is clear. God is good.
   What am I doing on board this nigger-pirate ship?
Perkins. You're not talking like a skipper, Sir.
   Our boat's a larger spot now.
Delano. I am childish.
   I am doddering and drooling into my second childhood.
   God help me, nothing's solid!
Perkins. Don Benito, Sir. Touch him,
   he's as solid as his ship.
Delano. Don Benito? He's a walking ghost!

[Benito comes up to Delano. Babu is a few steps behind him]

Benito. I am the ghost of myself, Captain.
   Excuse me, I heard you talking about dreams and childhood.
   I was a child, too, once, I have dreams about it.
Delano [*Starting*]. I'm sorry.
   This jumping's just a nervous habit.
   I thought you were part of my dreams.
Benito. I was taking my siesta,
   I dreamed I was a boy back in Lima.
   I was with my brothers and sisters,

and we were dressed for the festival of Corpus Christi
like people at our Bourbon court.
We were simple children, but something went wrong;
little black men came on us with beetle backs.
They had caterpillar heads and munched away on our fine clothes.
They made us lick their horned and varnished insect legs.
Our faces turned brown from their spit,
we looked like bugs, but nothing could save our lives!
Delano.   Ha, ha, Captain. We are like two dreams meeting head-on.
My whaleboat's coming,
we'll both feel better over a bottle of cider.

[*Babu blows a bosun's whistle. The gongs are sounded with descending notes. The Negroes assemble in ranks*]

Babu.   It's twelve noon, Master Yankee.
Master wants his midday shave.
All the Negroes.   Master wants his shave! Master wants his shave!
Benito.   Ah, yes, the razor! I have been talking too much.
You can see how badly I need a razor.
I must leave you, Captain.
Babu.   No, Don Amasa wants to talk.
Come to the cabin, Don Amasa.
Don Amasa will talk, Master will listen.
Babu will lather and strop.
Delano.   I want to talk to you about navigation.
I am new to these waters.
Benito.   Doubtless, doubtless, Captain Delano.
Perkins.   I think I'll take my siesta, Sir.

[*He walks off*]

[*Benito, Babu and Delano walk toward the back of the stage. A scrim curtain lifts, showing a light deck cabin that forms a sort of attic. The floor is matted, partitions that still leave splintered traces have been knocked out. To one side, a small table screwed to the floor; on it, a dirty missal; above it, a small crucifix, rusty crossed muskets on one side, rusty crossed cutlasses on the other. Benito sits down in a broken throne-like and gilded chair. Babu begins to lather. A magnificent array of razors, bottles and other shaving equipment lies on a table beside him. Behind him, a hammock with a pole in it and a dirty pillow*]

Delano.   So this is where you took your siesta.
Benito.   Yes, Captain, I rest here when my fate will let me.
Delano.   This seems like a sort of dormitory, sitting-room,
sail-loft, chapel, armory, and private bedroom all together.
Benito.   Yes, Captain: events have not been favorable
to much order in my personal arrangements.

[*Babu moves back and opens a locker. A lot of flags, torn shirts and socks tumble out. He takes one of the flags, shakes it with a flourish, and ties it around Benito's neck*]

Babu. Master needs more protection.
    I do everything I can to save his clothes.
Delano. The Castle and the Lion of Spain.
    Why, Don Benito, this is the flag of Spain you're using!
    It's well it's only I and not the King of Spain who sees this!
    All's one, though, I guess, in this carnival world.
    I see you like gay colors as much as Babu.
Babu [*Giggling*].
    The bright colors draw the yellow fever
    from Master's mind.

[*Raises the razor. Benito begins to shake*]

    Now, Master, now, Master!
Benito. You are talking while you hold the razor.
Babu. You mustn't shake so, Master.
    Look, Don Amasa, Master always shakes when I shave him,
    though he is braver than a lion and stronger than a castle.
    Master knows Babu has never yet drawn blood.
    I may, though, sometime, if he shakes so much.
    Now, Master!
    Come, Don Amasa, talk to Master about the gales and calms,
    he'll answer and forget to shake.
Delano. Those calms, the more I think of them the more I wonder.
    You say you were two months sailing here;
    I made that stretch in less than a week.
    We never met with any calms.
    If I'd not heard your story from your lips,
    and seen your ruined ship,
    I would have said something was missing,
    I would have said this was a mystery ship.
Benito. For some men the whole world is a mystery;
    they cannot believe their senses.

[*Benito shakes, the razor gets out of hand and cuts his cheek*]

    Santa Maria!
Babu. Poor, poor Master, see, you shook so;
    this is Babu's first blood.
    Please answer Don Amasa, while I wipe
    this ugly blood from the razor and strop it again.
Benito. The sea was like the final calm of the world,
    On, on it went. It sat on us and drank our strength,
    crosscurrents eased us out to sea,
    the yellow fever changed our blood to poison.

Babu. You stood by us. Some of us stood by you!

Benito. Yes, my Spanish crew was weak and surly, but the blacks,
the blacks were angels. Babu has kept me in this world.
I wonder what he is keeping me for?
You belong to me. I belong to you forever.

Babu. Ah, Master, spare yourself.
Forever is a very long time;
nothing's forever.

[*With great expertness, delicacy and gentleness, Babu massages Benito's cheeks, shakes out the flag, pours lotion from five bottles on Benito's hair, cleans the shaving materials, and stands off admiring his work*]

Master looks just like a statue.
He's like a figurehead, Don Amasa!

[*Delano looks, then starts to walk out leaving Benito and Babu. The curtain drops upon them. Delano rejoins Perkins, lounging at the rail*]

Perkins. Our boat is coming.

Delano [*Gaily*]. I know!
I don't know how I'll explain this pomp
and squalor to my own comfortable family of a crew.
Even shaving here is like a High Mass.
There's something in a Negro, something
that makes him fit to have around your person.
His comb and brush are castanets.
What tact Babu had!
What noiseless, gliding briskness!

Perkins. Our boat's about along side, Sir.

Delano. What's more, the Negro has a sense of humor.
I don't mean their boorish giggling and teeth-showing,
I mean his easy cheerfulness in every glance and gesture.
You should have seen Babu toss that Spanish flag like a juggler,
and change it to a shaving napkin!

Perkins. The boat's here, Sir.

Delano. We need inferiors, Perkins,
more manners, more docility, no one has an inferior mind in America.

Perkins. Here is your crew, Sir.

[*Babu runs out from the cabin. His cheek is bleeding*]

Delano. Why, Babu, what has happened?

Babu. Master will never get better from his sickness.
His bad nerves and evil fever made him use me so.
I gave him one small scratch by accident,
the only time I've nicked him, Don Amasa.
He cut me with his razor. Do you think I will die?
I'd rather die than bleed to death!

Delano.   It's just a pinprick, Babu. You'll live.

Babu.   I must attend my master.

[*Runs back into cabin*]

Delano.   Just a pinprick, but I wouldn't have thought
Don Benito had the stuff to swing a razor.
Up north we use our fists instead of knives.
I hope Benito's not dodging around some old grindstone
in the hold, and sharpening a knife for me.
Here, Perkins, help our men up the ladder.

[*Two immaculate American Sailors appear carrying great casks of water. Two more follow carrying net baskets of wilted pumpkins. The Negroes begin to crowd forward, shouting, "We want Yankee food, we want Yankee drink!" Delano grandiosely holds up a pumpkin; an Old Negro rushes forward, snatches at the pumpkin, and knocks Delano off-balance into Perkins's arms. Delano gets up and knocks the Negro down with his fist. All is tense and quiet. The Six Hatchet-Cleaners lift their hatchets above their heads*]

Delano [*Furious*]. Americans, stand by me! Stand by your captain!

[*Like lightning, the Americans unsling their muskets, fix bayonets, and kneel with their guns pointing at the Negroes*]

Don Benito, Sir, call your men to order!

Babu.   We're starving, Yankee Master. We mean no harm;
we've never been so scared.

Delano.   You try my patience, Babu.
I am talking to Captain Cereno;
call your men to order, Sir.

Benito.   Make them laugh, Babu. The Americans aren't going to shoot.

[*Babu airily waves a hand. The Negroes smile. Delano turns to Benito*]

You mustn't blame them too much; they're sick and hungry.
We have kept them cooped up for ages.

Delano [*As the Negroes relax*]. Form them in lines, Perkins!
Each man shall have his share.
That's how we run things in the States—
to each man equally, no matter what his claims.

Negroes [*Standing back, bleating like sheep*].
Feed me, Master Yankee! Feed me, Master Yankee!

Delano.   You are much too close.
Here, Perkins, take the provisions aft.
You'll save lives by giving each as little as you can,
Be sure to keep a tally.

[*Francesco, a majestic, yellow-colored mulatto, comes up to Delano*]

Francesco.   My master requests your presence at dinner, Don Amasa.

Delano.   Tell him I have indigestion.
Tell him to keep better order on his ship.

It's always the man of good will that gets hurt;
my fist still aches from hitting that old darky.

Francesco. My master has his own methods of discipline
that are suitable for our unfortunate circumstances.
Will you come to dinner, Don Amasa?

Delano. I'll come. When in Rome, do as the Romans.
Excuse my quick temper, Sir.
It's better to blow up than to smoulder.

[*The scrim curtain is raised. In the cabin, a long table loaded with silver has
been laid out. The locker has been closed and the Spanish flag hangs on
the wall. Don Benito is seated, Babu stands behind him. As soon as Delano
sits down, Francesco begins serving with great dignity and agility*]

Francesco. A finger bowl, Don Amasa.

[*After each statement, he moves about the table*]

A napkin, Don Amasa.
A glass of American water, Don Amasa.
A slice of American pumpkin, Don Amasa.
A goblet of American cider, Don Amasa.

[*Delano drinks a great deal of cider, Benito hardly touches his*]

Delano. This is very courtly for a sick ship, Don Benito.
The Spanish Empire will never go down, if she keeps her chin up.

Benito. I'm afraid I shan't live long enough to enjoy your prophecy.

Delano. I propose a toast to the Spanish Empire
on which the sun never sets;
may you find her still standing, when you land, Sir!

Benito. Our Empire has lasted three hundred years,
I suppose she will last another month.
I wish I could say the same for myself. My sun is setting,
I hear the voices of the dead in this calm.

Delano. You hear the wind lifting;
it's bringing our two vessels together.
We are going to take you into port, Don Benito.

Benito. You are either too late or too early with your good works.
Our yellow fever may break out again.
You aren't going to put your men in danger, Don Amasa?

Delano. My boys are all healthy, sir.

Benito. Health isn't God, I wouldn't trust it.

Francesco. May I fill your glass, Don Amasa?

Babu. New wine in new bottles,
that's the American spirit, Yankee Master.
They say all men are created equal in North America.

Delano. We prefer merit to birth, boy.

[*Babu motions imperiously for Francesco to leave. As he goes, bowing to the
Captains, Four Negroes play the Marseillaise*]

Why are they playing the *Marseillaise?*

Babu.   His uncle is supposed to have been in the French Convention,
and voted for the death of the French King.

Delano.   This polite and royal fellow is no anarchist!

Babu.   Francesco is very *ancien regime,*
he is even frightened of the Americans.
He doesn't like the way you treated King George.
Babu is more liberal.

Delano.   A royal fellow,
this usher of yours, Don Benito!
He is as yellow as a goldenrod.
He is a king, a king of kind hearts.
What a pleasant voice he has!

Benito [*Glumly*]. Francesco is a good man.

Delano.   As long as you've known him,
he's been a worthy fellow, hasn't he?
Tell me, I am particularly curious to know.

Benito.   Francesco is a good man.

Delano.   I'm glad to hear it, I am glad to hear it!
You refute the saying of a planter friend of mine.
He said, "When a mulatto has a regular European face,
look out for him, he is a devil."

Benito.   I've heard your planter's remark applied
to intermixtures of Spaniards and Indians;
I know nothing about mulattoes.

Delano.   No, no, my friend's refuted;
if we're so proud of our white blood,
surely a little added to the blacks improves their breed.
I congratulate you on your servants, Sir.

Babu.   We've heard that Jefferson, the King of your Republic,
would like to free his slaves.

Delano.   Jefferson has read too many books, boy,
but you can trust him. He's a gentleman and an American!
He's not lifting a finger to free his slaves.

Babu.   We hear you have a new capital modelled on Paris,
and that your President is going to set up
a guillotine on the Capitol steps.

Delano.   Oh, Paris! I told you you could trust Mr. Jefferson, boy,
he stands for law and order like your mulatto.
Have you been to Paris, Don Benito?

Benito.   I'm afraid I'm just a provincial Spaniard, Captain.

Delano.   Let me tell you about Paris.
You know what French women are like—
nine parts sex and one part logic.
Well, one of them in Paris heard
that my ship was the *President Adams.* She said,

"You are descended from Adam, Captain,
you must know everything,
tell me how Adam and Eve learned to sleep together."
Do you know what I said?

Benito.   No, Captain.

Delano.   I said, "I guess Eve was a Frenchwoman,
the first Frenchwoman."
Do you know what she answered?

Benito.   No, Captain Delano.

Delano.   She said, "I was trying to provoke a philosophical discussion, Sir."
A philosophical discussion, ha, ha!
You look serious, Sir. You know, something
troubles me.

Benito.   Something troubles you, Captain Delano?

Delano.   I still can't understand those calms,
but let that go. The scurvy,
why did it kill off three Spaniards in every four,
and only half the blacks?
Negroes are human, but surely you couldn't have favored them
before your own flesh and blood!

Benito.   This is like the Inquisition, Captain Delano.
I have done the best I could.

[*Babu dabs Benito's forehead with cider*]

Babu.   Poor, poor Master; since Don Aranda died,
he trusts no one except Babu.

Delano.   Your Babu is an uncommonly intelligent fellow;
you are right to trust him, Sir.
Sometimes I think we overdo our talk of freedom.
If you looked into our hearts, we all want slaves.

Benito.   Disease is a mysterious thing;
it takes one man, and leaves his friend.
Only the unfortunate can understand misfortune.

Delano.   I must return to my bosun;
he's pretty green to be left alone here.
Before I go I want to propose a last toast to you!
A good master deserves good servants!

[*He gets up. As he walks back to Perkins, the scrim curtain falls, concealing Benito and Babu*]

That captain must have jaundice,
I wish he kept better order.
I don't like hitting menials.

Perkins.   I've done some looking around, Sir. I've used my eyes.

Delano.   That's what they're for, I guess. You have to watch your step,
this hulk, this rotten piece of finery,
will fall apart. This old world needs new blood

and Yankee gunnery to hold it up.
You shouldn't mess around, though, it's their ship;
you're breaking all the laws of the sea.

Perkins. Do you see that man-shaped thing in canvas?

Delano. I see it.

Perkins. Behind the cloth, there's a real skeleton,
a man dressed up like Don Benito.

Delano. They're Catholics, and worship bones.

Perkins. There's writing on its coat. It says,
"I am Don Aranda," and, "Follow your leader."

Delano. Follow your leader?

Perkins. I saw two blacks unfurling a flag,
a black skull and crossbones on white silk.

Delano. That's piracy. We've been ordered
to sink any ship that flies that flag.
Perhaps they were playing.

Perkins. I saw King Atufal throw away his chains,
He called for food, the Spaniards served him two pieces of pumpkin,
and a whole bottle of your cider.

Delano. Don Benito has the only key to Atufal's padlock.
My cider was for the captain's table.

Perkins. Atufal pointed to the cabin where you were dining,
and drew a finger across his throat.

Delano. Who could want to kill Amasa Delano?

Perkins. I warned our men to be ready for an emergency.

Delano. You're a mind reader,
I couldn't have said better myself;
but we're at peace with Spain.

Perkins. I told them to return with loaded muskets
and fixed bayonets.

Delano. Here comes Benito. Watch how I'll humor him
and sound him out.

[*Babu brings out Benito's chair. Benito sits in it*]
It's good to have you back on deck, Captain.
Feel the breeze! It holds and will increase.
My ship is moving nearer. Soon we will be together.
We have seen you through your troubles.

Benito. Remember, I warned you about the yellow fever.
I am surprised you haven't felt afraid.

Delano. Oh, that will blow away.
Everything is going to go better and better;
the wind's increasing, soon you'll have no cares.
After the long voyage, the anchor drops into the harbor.
It's a great weight lifted from the captain's heart.
We are getting to be friends, Don Benito.
My ship's in sight, the *President Adams!*

How the wind braces a man up!
I have a small invitation to issue to you.
Benito. An invitation?
Delano. I want you to take a cup of coffee
with me on my quarter deck tonight.
The Sultan of Turkey never tasted such coffee
as my old steward makes. What do you say, Don Benito?
Benito. I cannot leave my ship.
Delano. Come, come, you need a change of climate.
The sky is suddenly blue, Sir,
my coffee will make a man of you.
Benito. I cannot leave my ship.
Even now, I don't think you understand my position here.
Delano. I want to speak to you alone.
Benito. I am alone, as much as I ever am.
Delano. In America, we don't talk about money
in front of servants and children.
Benito. Babu is not my servant.
You spoke of money—since the yellow fever,
he has had a better head for figures than I have.
Delano. You embarrass me, Captain,
but since circumstances are rather special here,
I will proceed.
Benito. Babu takes an interest in all our expenses.
Delano. Yes, I am going to talk to you about your expenses.
I am responsible to my owners for all
the sails, ropes, food and carpentry I give you.
You will need a complete rerigging, almost a new ship, in fact,
You shall have our services at cost.
Benito. I know, you are a merchant.
I suppose I ought to pay you for our lives.
Delano. I envy you, Captain. You are the only owner
of the *San Domingo,* since Don Aranda died.
I am just an employee. Our owners would sack me,
if I followed my better instincts.
Benito. You can give your figures to Babu, Captain.
Delano. You are very offhand about money, Sir;
I don't think you realize the damage that has been done to your ship.
Ah, you smile. I'm glad you're loosening up.
Look, the water gurgles merrily, the wind is high,
a mild light is shining. I sometimes think
such a tropical light as this must have shone
on the tents of Abraham and Isaac.
It seems as if Providence were watching over us.
Perkins. There are things that need explaining here, Sir.
Delano. Yes, Captain, Perkins saw some of your men

    unfurling an unlawful flag,
    a black skull and crossbones.
Benito.   You know my only flag is the Lion and Castle of Spain.
Delano.   No, Perkins says he saw a skull and crossbones.
    That's piracy. I trust Perkins.
    You've heard about how my government blew
    the bowels out of the pirates at Tripoli?
Benito.   Perhaps my Negroes . . .
Delano.   My government doesn't intend
    to let you play at piracy!
Benito.   Perhaps my Negroes were playing.
    When you take away their chains . . .
Delano.   I'll see that you are all put back in chains,
    if you start playing pirates!
Perkins.   There's something else he can explain, Sir.
Delano.   Yes, Perkins saw Atufal throw off his chains
    and order dinner.
Babu.   Master has the key, Yankee Master.
Benito.   I have the key.
    You can't imagine how my position exhausts me, Captain.
Delano.   I can imagine. Atufal's chains are fakes.
    You and he are in cahoots, Sir!
Perkins.   They don't intend to pay for our sails and service.
    They think America is Santa Claus.
Delano.   The United States are death on pirates and debtors.
Perkins.   There's one more thing for him to explain, Sir.
Delano.   Do you see that man-shaped thing covered with
    black cloth, Don Benito?
Benito.   I always see it.
Delano.   Take away the cloth. I order you to take away the cloth!
Benito.   I cannot. Oh, Santa Maria, have mercy!
Delano.   Of course, you can't. It's no Virgin Mary.
    You have done something terrible to your friend, Don Aranda.
    Take away the cloth, Perkins!

[*As Perkins moves forward, Atufal suddenly stands chainless and with folded arms, blocking his way*]

Babu [*Dancing up and down and beside himself*].
    Let them see it! Let them see it!
    I can't stand any more of their insolence;
    the Americans treat us like their slaves!

[*Babu and Perkins meet at the man-shaped object and start pulling away the cloth. Benito rushes between them, and throws them back and sprawling on the deck. Babu and Perkins rise, and stand hunched like wrestlers, about to close in on Benito, who draws his sword with a great gesture. It is only a hilt. He runs at Babu and knocks him down. Atufal throws off his chains and* signals to the Hatchet-Cleaners. They stand behind Benito with raised hatchets. The Negroes shout ironically, "Evviva Benito!"]

> You too, Yankee Captain!
> If you shoot, we'll kill you.

Delano. If a single American life is lost,
> I will send this ship to the bottom,
> and all Peru after it.
> Do you hear me, Don Benito?

Benito. Don't you understand? I am as powerless as you are!

Babu. He is as powerless as you are.

Benito. Don't you understand? He has been holding a knife at my back.
> I have been talking all day to save your life.

Babu [*Holding a whip*].
> Do you see this whip? When Don Aranda was out of temper,
> he used to snap pieces of flesh off us with it.
> Now I hold the whip.
> When I snap it, Don Benito jumps!

[*Snaps the whip. Don Benito flinches*]

Delano [*Beginning to understand*].
> It's easy to terrorize the defenseless.

Babu. That's what we thought when Don Aranda held the whip.

Delano. You'll find I am made of tougher stuff than your Spaniards.

Atufal. We want to kill you.

Negroes. We want to kill you, Yankee Captain.

Delano. Who could want to kill Amasa Delano?

Babu. Of course. We want to keep you alive.
> We want you to sail us back to Africa.
> Has anyone told you how much you are worth, Captain?

Delano. I have another course in mind.

Babu. Yes, there's another course if you don't like Africa, there's another
> course.
> King Atufal, show the Yankee captain
> the crew that took the other course!

[*Three dead Spanish Sailors are brought on stage*]

Atufal. Look at Don Aranda?

Babu. Yes, you are hot-tempered and discourteous, Captain.
> I am going to introduce you to Don Aranda.
> You have a new command, Captain. You must
> meet your new owner.

[*The black cloth is taken from the man-shaped object and shows a chalk-white skeleton dressed like Don Benito*]

> Don Amasa, Don Aranda!
> You can see that Don Aranda was a white man like you,
> because his bones are white.

Negroes.   He is a white because his bones are white!
   He is a white because his bones are white!
Atufal [*Pointing to the ribbon on the skeleton's chest*].
   Do you see that ribbon?
   It says, "Follow the leader."
   We wrote it in his blood.
Babu.   He was a white man
   even though his blood was red as ours.
Negroes.   He is white because his bones are white!
Babu.   Don Aranda is our figurehead,
   we are going to chain him to the bow of our ship
   to scare off devils.
Atufal.   This is the day of Jubilee,
   I am raising the flag of freedom!
Negroes.   Freedom! Freedom! Freedom!

[*The black skull and crossbones is raised on two poles. The Negroes form two lines, leading up to the flag, and leave an aisle. Each man is armed with some sort of weapon*]

Babu.   Spread out the Spanish flag!

[*The Lion and Castle of Spain is spread out on the deck in front of the skull and crossbones*]

   The Spanish flag is the road to freedom.
   Don Benito mustn't hurt his white feet on the splinters.

[*Kneeling in front of Benito*]

   Your foot, Master!

[*Benito holds out his foot. Babu takes off Benito's shoes*]

   Give Don Benito back his sword!

[*The sword-hilt is fastened back in Benito's scabbard*]

   Load him with chains!

[*Two heavy chains are draped on Benito's neck. The cane and ball are handed to him*]

   Former Captain Benito Cereno, kneel!
   Ask pardon of man!
Benito [*Kneeling*]. I ask pardon for having been born a Spaniard.
   I ask pardon for having enslaved my fellow man.
Babu.   Strike off the oppressor's chain!

[*One of Benito's chains is knocked off, then handed to Atufal, who dashes it to the deck*]

   Former Captain Benito Cereno,
   you must kiss the flag of freedom.

[*Points to Don Aranda*]

Kiss the mouth of the skull!

[*Benito walks barefoot over the Spanish flag and kisses the mouth of Don Aranda*]

Negroes.   *Evviva Benito! Evviva Benito!*

[*Sounds are heard from Perkins, whose head has been covered with the sack*]

Atufal.   The bosun wants to kiss the mouth of freedom.

Babu.   March over the Spanish flag, Bosun.

[*Perkins starts forward*]

Delano.   You are dishonoring your nation, Perkins!
    Don't you stand for anything?

Perkins.   I have only one life, Sir.

[*Walks over the Spanish flag and kisses the mouth of the skull*]

Negroes.   *Evviva Bosun! Evviva Bosun!*

Delano.   You are no longer an American, Perkins!

Perkins.   He was free to choose freedom, Captain.

Atufal.   Captain Delano wants to kiss the mouth of freedom.

Babu.   He is jealous of the bosun.

Atufal.   In the United States, all men are created equal.

Babu.   Don't you want to kiss the mouth of freedom, Captain?

Delano [*Lifting his pocket and pointing the pistol*].
    Do you see what I have in my hand?

Babu.   A pistol.

Delano.   I am unable to miss at this distance.

Babu.   You must take your time, Yankee Master.
    You must take your time.

Delano.   I am unable to miss.

Babu.   You stand there like a block of wood
    as long as you want to, Yankee Master.
    You will drop asleep, then we will tie you up,
    and make you sail us back to Africa.

[*General laughter. Suddenly, there's a roar of gunfire. Several Negroes, mostly women, fall. American Seamen in spotless blue and white throw themselves in a lying position on deck. More kneel above them, then More stand above these. All have muskets and fixed bayonets. The First Row fires. More Negroes fall. They start to retreat. The Second Row fires. More Negroes fall. They retreat further. The Third Row fires. The Three American Lines march forward, but all the Negroes are either dead or in retreat. Don Benito has been wounded. He staggers over to Delano and shakes his hand*]

Benito.   You have saved my life.
    I thank you for my life.

Delano.   A man can only do what he can,
    We have saved American lives.

Perkins [*Pointing to Atufal's body*].
    We have killed King Atufal,
    we have killed their ringleader.

[*Babu jumps up. He is unwounded*]

Babu.   I was the King. Babu, not Atufal
    was the king, who planned, dared and carried out
    the seizure of this ship, the *San Domingo*.
    Untouched by blood myself, I had all
    the most dangerous and useless Spaniards killed.
    I freed my people from their Egyptian bondage.
    The heartless Spaniards slaved for me like slaves.

[*Babu steps back, and quickly picks up a crown from the litter*]

    This is my crown.

[*Puts crown on his head. He snatches Benito's rattan cane*]

    This is my rod.

[*Picks up silver ball*]

    This is the earth.

[*Holds the ball out with one hand and raises the cane*]

    This is the arm of the angry God.

[*Smashes the ball*]

Perkins.   Let him surrender. Let him surrender.
    We want to save someone.
Benito.   My God how little these people understand!
Babu [*Holding a white handkerchief and raising both his hands*].
    Yankee Master understand me. The future is with us.
Delano [*Raising his pistol*].   This is your future.

[*Babu falls and lies still. Delano pauses, then slowly empties the five remaining barrels of his pistol into the body. Lights dim*]

CURTAIN

Questions

1. In the opening speeches of the play, before the San Domingo is sighted, Delano and Perkins converse. What is the function of those speeches? What political and racial attitudes are defined?   **2.** This play is one of a trilogy collectively called **The Old Glory**. Each of the plays makes use of flag symbolism. Trace the allusions to flags (both American and Spanish) in the play. What function does the flag symbolism serve? **3.** Who is the hero of the play, Benito Cereno, Babu, or Amasa Delano? Upon what conception of heroism is your choice based?   **4.** What emotional impact is conveyed by the mechanical precision of the American sailors?   **5.** In what sense are Delano and Perkins "ugly Americans"?   **6.** What ironic import is contained in Delano's remark, "Who would want to kill Amasa Delano?" That is, how does his self-conception differ from Babu's conception of him and the audience's conception of him?   **7.** Is the play a tragedy or a comedy?

iNNOCENCE ANd EXpERiENCE

QUESTIONS FOR FURTHER ANALYSIS

1. What support do the works in this section provide for Thomas Gray's well-known observation that "where ignorance is bliss,/'Tis folly to be wise?"

2. In such poems as Robert Burns' "To a Mouse," William Wordsworth's "Lines Composed a Few Miles Above Tintern Abbey," Robert Frost's "Birches," and Joni Mitchell's "Songs to Aging Children Come," growing up is seen as a growing away from a kind of truth and reality; in other poems, such as Walt Whitman's "Out of the Cradle Endlessly Rocking," Gerard Manley Hopkins' "Spring and Fall," Dylan Thomas' "Fern Hill," and Robert Wallace's "In a Spring Still Not Written of," growing up is seen as growing into truth and reality. Do these two groups of poems embody contradictory and mutually exclusive conceptions of childhood? Explain.

3. Consider the meaning of innocence in Thomas Hardy's "The Ruined Maid," Thom Gunn's "Innocence," and Robert Lowell's *Benito Cereno*. What are the sources of innocence in these works? What are the effects?

4. An eighteenth-century novelist wrote: "O Innocence, how glorious and happy a portion art thou to the breast that possesses thee! thou fearest neither the eyes nor the tongues of men. Truth, the most powerful of all things, is thy strongest friend; and the brighter the light is in which thou art displayed, the more it discovers thy transcendent beauties." Are there works in this section that support this assessment of innocence? Are there works that contradict it? How would you characterize the relationship between "truth" and "innocence" in the fiction and the drama presented here?

5. A certain arrogance is associated with the innocence of Barbara in Shaw's *Major Barbara* and Amasa Delano in Lowell's *Benito Cereno*. On what is the arrogance based? Is that arrogance finally destroyed in either case? How?

6. Robin, in Hawthorne's "My Kinsman, Major Molineux," and the captain in Conrad's "The Secret Sharer" also exhibit a certain arrogance. On what is their arrogance based, and how is it modified?

7. Which poems in this section depend largely on irony for their force? Can you suggest why irony is a particularly useful device in literature that portrays innocence and experience?

CONFORMITY AND REBELLION

Frieze of Protective Figures from
the Tomb of Tutankhamen

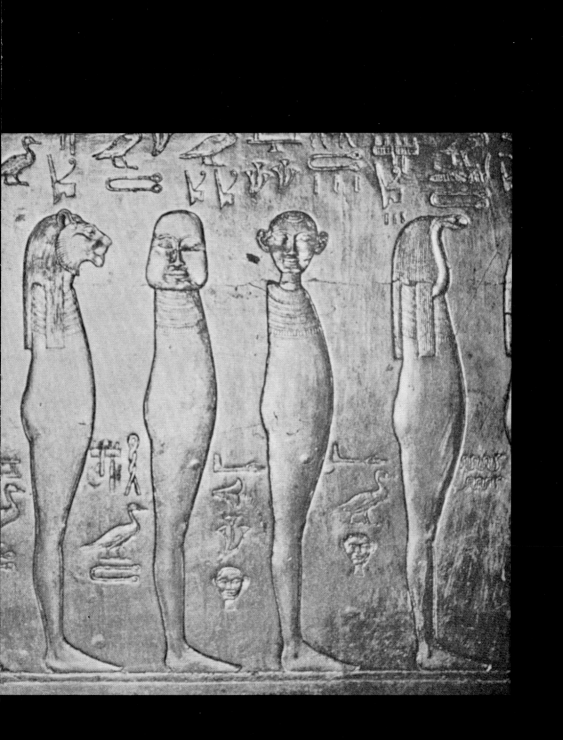

CONFORMITY ANd RebEllION

Although the works in this section, like those in Innocence and Experience, may also feature a violation of innocence, the events are usually based on the clash between two well-articulated positions; the rebel, on principle, confronts and struggles with established authority. Central in these works is the sense of tremendous external forces—the state, the church, tradition—which can be obeyed only at the expense of conscience and humanity. At the most general level, these works confront a dilemma older than Antigone's Thebes: the very organizations men establish to protect and nurture the individual demand—on pain of economic ruin, social ostracism, even death, spiritual or physical—that he violate his most deeply cherished beliefs. When the individual refuses such a demand, he translates his awareness of a hostile social order into action against it and precipitates a crisis. In *Antigone*, the issue is drawn with utter clarity: Antigone must obey either the state (Creon) or the gods. In *An Enemy of the People*, Dr. Stockmann learns how costly a sense of honesty and social responsibility can be when it conflicts with powerful economic forces in his village.

Many of the works in this section, particularly the poems, do not treat the theme of conformity and rebellion quite so explicitly and dramatically. Some, like "Eleanor Rigby," describe a world devoid of human communion and community without directly accounting for it; others, like W. H. Auden's "The Unknown Citizen," tell us that the price exacted for total conformity to the industrial superstate is spiritual death. In "Easter, 1916," William Butler Yeats meditates upon the awesome meaning of the lives and deaths of political revolutionaries, and in "Harlem," Langston Hughes warns that an in-flexible and constricting social order will generate explosion.

Two basic modes, then, inform the literary treatment of conformity and rebellion. While in many of the works, notably the plays and stories, the individual is caught up in a crisis that forces him into rebellion, in other works, especially the poems, the focus may be on the individual's failure to move from awareness into action, as in Amy Lowell's "Patterns." Indeed, the por-traits of Auden's unknown citizen and of Cummings' Cambridge ladies affirm the necessity for rebellion by rendering so effectively the hollow life of mind-less conformity.

However diverse in treatment and technique, all the works in this sec-tion are about individuals trapped by complex sets of external forces that regulate and define their lives. The social being, man, sometimes submits to these forces, but it is always an uneasy submission, for their purpose is to curb and control him. He may recognize that he must be controlled for some larger good; yet he is aware that established social power is often abusive. The tendency of power, at its best, is to act as a conserving force that brakes the disruptive impulse to abandon and destroy old ways and ideas. At its worst, power is self-serving. The individual must constantly judge which tendency power is enhancing. And since the power of the individual is neg-ligible beside that of frequently abusive social forces, it is not surprising that many artists since the advent of the great nation-states have found a funda-mental human dignity in the resistance of the individual to organized society. One of man's ancient and profound recognitions, after all, is that the impulse of a Creon is always to make unknown citizens of us all.

conformity and rebellion

FICTION

Bartleby the Scrivener
A Story of Wall Street

HERMAN MELVILLE [1819–1891]

I AM a rather elderly man. The nature of my avocations, for the last thirty years, has brought me into more than ordinary contact with what would seem an interesting and somewhat singular set of men, of whom, as yet, nothing, that I know of, has ever been written—I mean, the law-copyists, or scriveners. I have known very many of them, professionally and privately, and, if I pleased, could relate divers histories, at which good-natured gentlemen might smile, and sentimental souls might weep. But I waive the biographies of all other scriveners, for a few passages in the life of Bartleby, who was a scrivener, the strangest I ever saw, or heard of. While, of other law-copyists, I might write the complete life, of Bartleby nothing of that sort can be done. I believe that no materials exist for a full and satisfactory biography of this man. It is an irreparable loss to literature. Bartleby was one of those beings of whom nothing is ascertainable, except from the original sources, and, in his case, those are very small. What my own astonished eyes saw of Bartleby, *that* is all I know of him, except, indeed, one vague report, which will appear in the sequel.

Ere introducing the scrivener, as he first appeared to me, it is fit I make some mention of myself, my employees, my business, my chambers, and general surroundings; because some such description is indispensable to an adequate understanding of the chief character about to be presented. Imprimis: I am a man who, from his youth upwards, has been filled with a profound conviction that the easiest way of life is the best. Hence, though I belong to a profession proverbially energetic and nervous, even to turbulence, at times, yet nothing of that sort have I ever suffered to invade my peace. I am one of those unambitious lawyers who never addresses a jury, or in any way draws down public applause; but, in the cool tranquillity of a snug retreat, do a snug business among rich men's bonds, and mortgages, and title-deeds. All who know me, consider me an eminently *safe* man. The late John Jacob Astor,[1]

---

1. A poor immigrant who rose to become one of the great business tycoons of the nineteenth century.

a personage little given to poetic enthusiasm, had no hesitation in pronouncing my first grand point to be prudence; my next, method. I do not speak it in vanity, but simply record the fact, that I was not unemployed in my profession by the late John Jacob Astor; a name which, I admit, I love to repeat; for it hath a rounded and orbicular sound to it, and rings like unto bullion. I will freely add, that I was not insensible to the late John Jacob Astor's good opinion.

Some time prior to the period at which this little history begins, my avocations had been largely increased. The good old office, now extinct in the State of New York, of a Master in Chancery,[2] had been conferred upon me. It was not a very arduous office, but very pleasantly remunerative. I seldom lose my temper; much more seldom indulge in dangerous indignation at wrongs and outrages; but, I must be permitted to be rash here, and declare that I consider the sudden and violent abrogation of the office of Master in Chancery, by the new Constitution, as a—premature act; inasmuch as I had counted upon a life-lease of the profits, whereas I only received those of a few short years. But this is by the way.

My chambers were up stairs, at No.____ Wall Street. At one end, they looked upon the white wall of the interior of a spacious sky-light shaft, penetrating the building from top to bottom.

This view might have been considered rather tame than otherwise, deficient in what landscape painters call "life." But, if so, the view from the other end of my chambers offered, at least, a contrast, if nothing more. In that direction, my windows commanded an unobstructed view of a lofty brick wall, black by age and everlasting shade; which wall required no spyglass to bring out its lurking beauties, but, for the benefit of all near-sighted spectators, was pushed up to within ten feet of my window panes. Owing to the great height of the surrounding buildings, and my chambers being on the second floor, the interval between this wall and mine not a little resembled a huge square cistern.

At the period just preceding the advent of Bartleby, I had two persons as copyists in my employment, and a promising lad as an office-boy. First, Turkey; second, Nippers; third, Ginger Nut. These may seem names, the like of which are not usually found in the Directory. In truth, they were nicknames, mutually conferred upon each other by my three clerks, and were deemed expressive of their respective persons or characters. Turkey was a short, pursy Englishman, of about my own age—that is, somewhere not far from sixty. In the morning, one might say, his face was of a fine florid hue, but after twelve o'clock, meridian—his dinner hour—it blazed like a grate full of Christmas coals; and continued blazing—but, as it were, with a gradual wane—till six o'clock P.M., or thereabouts; after which, I saw no more of the proprietor of the face, which, gaining its meridian with the sun, seemed to set with it, to rise, culminate, and decline the following day, with the like

---

2. Courts of Chancery often adjudicated business disputes.

regularity and undiminished glory. There are many singular coincidences I have known in the course of my life, not the least among which was the fact, that, exactly when Turkey displayed his fullest beams from his red and radiant countenance, just then, too, at that critical moment, began the daily period when I considered his business capacities as seriously disturbed for the remainder of the twenty-four hours. Not that he was absolutely idle, or averse to business, then; far from it. The difficulty was, he was apt to be altogether too energetic. There was a strange, inflamed, flurried, flighty recklessness of activity about him. He would be incautious in dipping his pen into his inkstand. All his blots upon my documents were dropped there after twelve o'clock meridian. Indeed, not only would he be reckless, and sadly given to making blots in the afternoon, but, some days, he went further, and was rather noisy. At such times, too, his face flamed with augmented blazonry, as if cannel coal had been heaped on anthracite. He made an unpleasant racket with his chair; spilled his sand-box; in mending his pens, impatiently split them all to pieces, and threw them on the floor in a sudden passion; stood up, and leaned over his table, boxing his papers about in a most indecorous manner, very sad to behold in an elderly man like him. Nevertheless, as he was in many ways a most valuable person to me, and all the time before twelve o'clock meridian, was the quickest, steadiest creature, too, accomplishing a great deal of work in a style not easily to be matched—for these reasons, I was willing to overlook his eccentricities, though, indeed, occasionally, I remonstrated with him. I did this very gently, however, because, though the civilest, nay, the blandest and most reverential of men in the morning, yet, in the afternoon, he was disposed, upon provocation, to be slightly rash with his tongue—in fact, insolent. Now, valuing his morning services as I did, and resolved not to lose them—yet, at the same time, made uncomfortable by his inflamed ways after twelve o'clock—and being a man of peace, unwilling by my admonitions to call forth unseemly retorts from him, I took upon me, one Saturday noon (he was always worse on Saturdays) to hint to him, very kindly, that, perhaps, now that he was growing old, it might be well to abridge his labors; in short, he need not come to my chambers after twelve o'clock, but, dinner over, had best go home to his lodgings, and rest himself till tea-time. But no; he insisted upon his afternoon devotions. His countenance became intolerably fervid, as he oratorically assured me—gesticulating with a long ruler at the other end of the room—that if his services in the morning were useful, how indispensable, then, in the afternoon?

"With submission, sir," said Turkey, on this occasion, "I consider myself your right-hand man. In the morning I but marshal and deploy my columns; but in the afternoon I put myself at their head, and gallantly charge the foe, thus"—and he made a violent thrust with the ruler.

"But the blots, Turkey," intimated I.

"True; but, with submission, sir, behold these hairs! I am getting old. Surely, sir, a blot or two of a warm afternoon is not to be severely urged against gray hairs. Old age—even if it blot the page—is honorable. With submission, sir, we *both* are getting old."

This appeal to my fellow-feeling was hardly to be resisted. At all events, I saw that go he would not. So, I made up my mind to let him stay, resolving, nevertheless, to see to it that, during the afternoon, he had to do with my less important papers.

Nippers, the second on my list, was a whiskered, sallow, and, upon the whole, rather piratical-looking young man, of about five and twenty. I always deemed him the victim of two evil powers—ambition and indigestion. The ambition was evinced by a certain impatience of the duties of a mere copyist, an unwarrantable usurpation of strictly professional affairs, such as the original drawing up of legal documents. The indigestion seemed betokened in an occasional nervous testiness and grinning irritability, causing the teeth to audibly grind together over mistakes committed in copying; unnecessary maledictions, hissed, rather than spoken, in the heat of business; and especially by a continual discontent with the height of the table where he worked. Though of a very ingenious, mechanical turn, Nippers could never get this table to suit him. He put chips under it, blocks of various sorts, bits of pasteboard, and at last went so far as to attempt an exquisite adjustment, by final pieces of folded blotting-paper. But no invention would answer. If, for the sake of easing his back, he brought the table lid at a sharp angle well up towards his chin, and wrote there like a man using the steep roof of a Dutch house for his desk, then he declared that it stopped the circulation in his arms. If now he lowered the table to his waistbands, and stooped over it in writing, then there was a sore aching in his back. In short, the truth of the matter was, Nippers knew not what he wanted. Or, if he wanted anything, it was to be rid of a scrivener's table altogether. Among the manifestations of his diseased ambition was a fondness he had for receiving visits from certain ambiguous-looking fellows in seedy coats, whom he called his clients. Indeed, I was aware that not only was he, at times, considerable of a ward-politician, but he occasionally did a little business at the Justices' courts, and was not unknown on the steps of the Tombs.[3] I have good reason to believe, however, that one individual who called upon him at my chambers, and who, with a grand air, he insisted was his client, was no other than a dun, and the alleged title-deed, a bill. But, with all his failings, and the annoyances he caused me, Nippers, like his compatriot Turkey, was a very useful man to me; wrote a neat, swift hand; and, when he chose, was not deficient in a gentlemanly sort of deportment. Added to this, he always dressed in a gentlemanly sort of way; and so, incidentally, reflected credit upon my chambers. Whereas, with respect to Turkey, I had much ado to keep him from being a reproach to me. His clothes were apt to look oily, and smell of eating-houses. He wore his pantaloons very loose and baggy in summer. His coats were

---

3. A prison in New York City.

execable; his hat not to be handled. But while the hat was a thing of indifference to me, inasmuch as his natural civility and deference, as a dependent Englishman, always led him to doff it the moment he entered the room, yet his coat was another matter. Concerning his coats, I reasoned with him; but with no effect. The truth was, I suppose, that a man with so small an income could not afford to sport such a lustrous face and a lustrous coat at one and the same time. As Nippers once observed, Turkey's money went chiefly for red ink. One winter day, I presented Turkey with a highly respectable-looking coat of my own—a padded gray coat, of a most comfortable warmth, and which buttoned straight up from the knee to the neck. I thought Turkey would appreciate the favor, and abate his rashness and obstreperousness of afternoons. But no; I verily believe that buttoning himself up in so downy and blanket-like a coat had a pernicious effect upon him—upon the same principle that too much oats are bad for horses. In fact, precisely as a rash, restive horse is said to feel his oats, so Turkey felt his coat. It made him insolent. He was a man whom prosperity harmed.

Though, concerning the self-indulgent habits of Turkey, I had my own private surmises, yet, touching Nippers, I was well persuaded that, whatever might be his faults in other respects, he was, at least, a temperate young man. But, indeed, nature herself seemed to have been his vintner, and, at his birth, charged him so thoroughly with an irritable, brandy-like disposition, that all subsequent potations were needless. When I consider how, amid the stillness of my chambers, Nippers would sometimes impatiently rise from his seat, and stooping over his table, spread his arms wide apart, seize the whole desk, and move it, and jerk it, with a grim, grinding motion on the floor, as if the table were a perverse voluntary agent and vexing him, I plainly perceive that, for Nippers, brandy-and-water were altogether superfluous.

It was fortunate for me that, owing to its peculiar cause—indigestion— the irritability and consequent nervousness of Nippers were mainly observable in the morning, while in the afternoon he was comparatively mild. So that, Turkey's paroxysms only coming on about twelve o'clock, I never had to do with their eccentricities at one time. Their fits relieved each other, like guards. When Nippers's was on, Turkey's was off; and *vice versa*. This was a good natural arrangement, under the circumstances.

Ginger Nut, the third on my list, was a lad, some twelve years old. His father was a car-man, ambitious of seeing his son on the bench instead of a cart, before he died. So he sent him to my office, as student at law, errand-boy, cleaner and sweeper, at the rate of one dollar a week. He had a little desk to himself; but he did not use it much. Upon inspection, the drawer exhibited a great array of the shells of various sorts of nuts. Indeed, to this quick-witted youth, the whole noble science of the law was contained in a nutshell. Not the least among the employments of Ginger Nut, as well as one which he discharged with the most alacrity, was his duty as cake and apple purveyor for Turkey and Nippers. Copying law-papers being proverbially a dry, husky sort of business, my two scriveners were fain to moisten their mouths very often with Spitzenbergs,[4] to be had at the numerous stalls nigh the Custom House and Post Office. Also, they sent Ginger Nut very frequently for that peculiar cake—small, flat, round, and very spicy—after which he had been named by them. Of a cold morning, when business was but dull, Turkey would gobble up scores of these cakes, as if they were mere wafers—indeed, they sell them at the rate of six or eight for a penny—the scrape of his pen blending with the crunching of the crisp particles in his mouth. Rashest of all the fiery afternoon blunders and flurried rashnesses of Turkey, was his once moistening a ginger-cake between his lips, and clapping it on to a mortgage, for a seal. I came within an ace of dismissing him then. But he mollified me by making an oriental bow, and saying—

"With submission, sir, it was generous of me to find you in stationery on my own account."

Now my original business—that of a conveyancer and title hunter, and drawer-up of recondite documents of all sorts—was considerably increased by receiving the master's office. There was now great work for scriveners. Not only must I push the clerks already with me, but I must have additional help.

In answer to my advertisement, a motionless young man one morning stood upon my office threshold, the door being open, for it was summer. I can see that figure now—pallidly neat, pitiably respectable, incurably forlorn! It was Bartleby.

After a few words touching his qualifications, I engaged him, glad to have among my corps of copyists a man of so singularly sedate an aspect, which I thought might operate beneficially upon the flighty temper of Turkey, and the fiery one of Nippers.

I should have stated before that ground glass folding-doors divided my premises into two parts, one of which was occupied by my scriveners, the other by myself. According to my humor, I threw open these doors, or closed them. I resolved to assign Bartleby a corner by the folding-doors, but on my side of them, so as to have this quiet man within easy call, in case any trifling thing was to be done. I placed his desk close up to a small side-window in that part of the room, a window which originally had afforded a lateral view of certain grimy backyards and bricks, but which, owing to subsequent erections, commanded at present no view at all, though it gave some light. Within three feet of the panes was a wall, and the light came down from far above, between two lofty buildings, as from a very small opening in a dome. Still further to a satisfactory arrangement, I procured a high green folding screen, which might entirely isolate Bartleby from my sight, though not remove him from my voice. And thus, in a manner, privacy and society were conjoined.

At first, Bartleby did an extraordinary quantity of writing. As if long famishing for something to copy, he seemed to gorge himself on my documents. There was no pause for digestion. He ran a day and night line, copy-

---

4. A variety of apple.

ing by sun-light and by candle-light. I should have been quite delighted with his application, had he been cheerfully industrious. But he wrote on silently, palely, mechanically.

It is, of course, an indispensable part of a scrivener's business to verify the accuracy of his copy, word by word. Where there are two or more scriveners in an office, they assist each other in this examination, one reading from the copy, the other holding the original. It is a very dull, wearisome, and lethargic affair. I can readily imagine that, to some sanguine temperaments, it would be altogether intolerable. For example, I cannot credit that the mettlesome poet, Byron, would have contentedly sat down with Bartleby to examine a law document of, say five hundred pages, closely written in a crimpy hand.

Now and then, in the haste of business, it had been my habit to assist in comparing some brief document myself, calling Turkey or Nippers for this purpose. One object I had, in placing Bartleby so handy to me behind the screen, was to avail myself of his services on such trivial occasions. It was on the third day, I think, of his being with me, and before any necessity had arisen for having his own writing examined, that, being much hurried to complete a small affair I had in hand, I abruptly called to Bartleby. In my haste and natural expectancy of instant compliance, I sat with my head bent over the original on my desk, and my right hand sideways, and somewhat nervously extended with the copy, so that, immediately upon emerging from his retreat, Bartleby might snatch it and proceed to business without the least delay.

In this very attitude did I sit when I called to him, rapidly stating what it was I wanted him to do—namely, to examine a small paper with me. Imagine my surprise, nay, my consternation, when, without moving from his privacy, Bartleby, in a singularly mild, firm voice, replied, "I would prefer not to."

I sat awhile in perfect silence, rallying my stunned faculties. Immediately it occurred to me that my ears had deceived me, or Bartleby had entirely misunderstood my meaning. I repeated my request in the clearest tone I could assume; but in quite as clear a one came the previous reply, "I would prefer not to."

"Prefer not to," echoed I, rising in high excitement, and crossing the room with a stride. "What do you mean? Are you moon-struck? I want you to help me compare this sheet here—take it," and I thrust it towards him.

"I would prefer not to," said he.

I looked at him steadfastly. His face was leanly composed; his gray eye dimly calm. Not a wrinkle of agitation rippled him. Had there been the least uneasiness, anger, impatience, or impertinence in his manner; in other words, had there been any thing ordinarily human about him, doubtless I should have violently dismissed him from the premises. But as it was, I should have as soon thought of turning my pale plaster-of-paris bust of Cicero out of doors. I stood gazing at him awhile, as he went on with his own writing, and then reseated myself at my desk. This is very strange, thought I. What had one best do? But my business hurried me. I concluded to forget the matter for the present, reserving it for my future leisure. So calling Nippers from the other room, the paper was speedily examined.

A few days after this, Bartleby concluded four lengthy documents, being quadruplicates of a week's testimony taken before me in my High Court of Chancery. It became necessary to examine them. It was an important suit, and great accuracy was imperative. Having all things arranged, I called Turkey, Nippers, and Ginger Nut from the next room, meaning to place the four copies in the hands of my four clerks, while I should read from the original. Accordingly, Turkey, Nippers, and Ginger Nut had taken their seats in a row, each with his document in his hand, when I called to Bartleby to join this interesting group.

"Bartleby! quick, I am waiting."

I heard a slow scrape of his chair legs on the uncarpeted floor, and soon he appeared standing at the entrance of his hermitage.

"What is wanted?" said he, mildly.

"The copies, the copies," said I, hurriedly. "We are going to examine them. There—" and I held towards him the fourth quadruplicate.

"I would prefer not to," he said, and gently disappeared behind the screen.

For a few moments I was turned into a pillar of salt, standing at the head of my seated column of clerks. Recovering myself, I advanced towards the screen, and demanded the reason for such extraordinary conduct.

"*Why* do you refuse?"

"I would prefer not to."

With any other man I should have flown outright into a dreadful passion, scorned all further words, and thrust him ignominiously from my presence. But there was something about Bartleby that not only strangely disarmed me, but in a wonderful manner, touched and disconcerted me. I began to reason with him.

"These are your own copies we are about to examine. It is labor saving to you, because one examination will answer for your four papers. It is common usage. Every copyist is bound to help examine his copy. Is it not so? Will you not speak? Answer!"

"I prefer not to," he replied in a flutelike tone. It seemed to me that, while I had been addressing him, he carefully revolved every statement that I made; fully comprehended the meaning; could not gainsay the irresistible conclusion; but, at the same time, some paramount consideration prevailed with him to reply as he did.

"You are decided, then, not to comply with my request—a request made according to common usage and common sense?"

He briefly gave me to understand, that on that point my judgment was sound. Yes: his decision was irreversible.

It is not seldom the case that, when a man is browbeaten in some unprecedented and violently unreasonable way, he begins to stagger in his own plainest faith. He begins, as it were, vaguely to surmise that, wonderful as it may be, all the justice and all the reason is on the other side. Accordingly, if any disinterested persons are present, he turns to them for some reinforcement of his own faltering mind.

"Turkey," said I, "what do you think of this? Am I not right?"

"With submission, sir," said Turkey, in his blandest tone, "I think that you are."

"Nippers," said I, "what do *you* think of it?"

"I think I should kick him out of the office."

(The reader, of nice perceptions, will here perceive that, it being morning, Turkey's answer is couched in polite and tranquil terms, but Nippers replies in ill-tempered ones. Or, to repeat a previous sentence, Nippers's ugly mood was on duty, and Turkey's off.)

"Ginger Nut," said I, willing to enlist the smallest suffrage in my behalf, "what do *you* think of it?"

"I think, sir, he's a little *luny*," replied Ginger Nut, with a grin.

"You hear what they say," said I, turning towards the screen, "come forth and do your duty."

But he vouchsafed no reply. I pondered a moment in sore perplexity. But once more business hurried me. I determined again to postpone the consideration of this dilemma to my future leisure. With a little trouble we made out to examine the papers without Bartleby, though at every page or two Turkey deferentially dropped his opinion, that this proceeding was quite out of the common; while Nippers, twitching in his chair with a dyspeptic nervousness, ground out, between his set teeth, occasional hissing maledictions against the stubborn oaf behind the screen. And for his (Nippers's) part, this was the first and the last time he would do another man's business without pay.

Meanwhile Bartleby sat in his hermitage, oblivious to everything but his own peculiar business there.

Some days passed, the scrivener being employed upon another lengthy work. His late remarkable conduct led me to regard his ways narrowly. I observed that he never went to dinner; indeed, that he never went anywhere. As yet I had never, of my personal knowledge, known him to be outside of my office. He was a perpetual sentry in the corner. At about eleven o'clock though, in the morning, I noticed that Ginger Nut would advance toward the opening in Bartleby's screen, as if silently beckoned thither by a gesture invisible to me where I sat. The boy would then leave the office, jingling a few pence, and reappear with a handful of ginger-nuts, which he delivered in the hermitage, receiving two of the cakes for his trouble.

He lives, then, on ginger-nuts, thought I; never eats a dinner, properly speaking; he must be a vegetarian, then; but no; he never eats even vegetables; he eats nothing but ginger-nuts. My mind then ran on in reveries concerning the probable effects upon the human constitution of living entirely on ginger-nuts. Ginger-nuts are so called, because they contain ginger as one of their peculiar constituents, and the final flavoring one. Now, what was ginger? A hot, spicy thing. Was Bartleby hot and spicy? Not at all. Ginger, then, had no effect upon Bartleby. Probably he preferred it should have none.

Nothing so aggravates an earnest person as a passive resistance. If the individual so resisted be of a not inhumane temper, and the resisting one perfectly harmless in his passivity, then, in the better moods of the former, he will endeavor charitably to construe to his imagination what proves impossible to be solved by his judgment. Even so, for the most part, I regarded Bartleby and his ways. Poor fellow! thought I, he means no mischief; it is plain he intends no insolence; his aspect sufficiently evinces that his eccentricities are involuntary. He is useful to me. I can get along with him. If I turn him away, the chances are he will fall in with some less-indulgent employer, and then he will be rudely treated, and perhaps driven forth miserably to starve. Yes. Here I can cheaply purchase a delicious self-approval. To befriend Bartleby; to humor him in his strange willfulness, will cost me little or nothing, while I lay up in my soul what will eventually prove a sweet morsel for my conscience. But this mood was not invariable with me. The passiveness of Bartleby sometimes irritated me. I felt strangely goaded on to encounter him in new opposition—to elicit some angry spark from him answerable to my own. But, indeed, I might as well have essayed to strike fire with my knuckles against a bit of Windsor soap. But one afternoon the evil impulse in me mastered me, and the following little scene ensued:

"Bartleby," said I, "when those papers are all copied, I will compare them with you."

"I would prefer not to."

"How? Surely you do not mean to persist in that mulish vagary?"

No answer.

I threw open the folding-doors near by, and, turning upon Turkey and Nippers, exclaimed:

"Bartleby a second time says, he won't examine his papers. What do you think of it, Turkey?"

It was afternoon, be it remembered. Turkey sat glowing like a brass boiler; his bald head steaming; his hands reeling among his blotted papers.

"Think of it?" roared Turkey; "I think I'll just step behind his screen, and black his eyes for him!"

So saying, Turkey rose to his feet and threw his arms into a pugilistic position. He was hurrying away to make good his promise, when I detained him, alarmed at the effect of incautiously rousing Turkey's combativeness after dinner.

"Sit down, Turkey," said I, "and hear what Nippers has to say. What do you think of it, Nippers? Would I not be justified in immediately dismissing Bartleby?"

"Excuse me, that is for you to decide, sir. I think his conduct quite unusual, and, indeed, unjust, as regards Turkey and myself. But it may only be a passing whim."

"Ah," exclaimed I, "you have strangely changed your mind, then—you speak very gently of him now."

"All beer," cried Turkey; "gentleness is effects of beer—Nippers and I dined together to-day. You see how gentle *I* am, sir. Shall I go and black his eyes?"

"You refer to Bartleby, I suppose. No, not to-day, Turkey," I replied; "pray, put up your fists."

I closed the doors, and again advanced towards Bartleby. I felt additional incentives tempting me to my fate. I burned to be rebelled against again. I remembered that Bartleby never left the office.

"Bartleby," said I, "Ginger Nut is away; just step around to the Post Office, won't you? (it was but a three minutes' walk), and see if there is anything for me."

"I would prefer not to."

"You *will* not?"

"I *prefer* not."

I staggered to my desk, and sat there in a deep study. My blind inveteracy returned. Was there any other thing in which I could procure myself to be ignominiously repulsed by this lean, penniless wight?—my hired clerk? What added thing is there, perfectly reasonable, that he will be sure to refuse to do? "Bartleby!"

No answer.

"Bartleby," in a louder tone.

No answer.

"Bartleby," I roared.

Like a very ghost, agreeably to the laws of magical invocation, at the third summons, he appeared at the entrance of his hermitage.

"Go to the next room, and tell Nippers to come to me."

"I prefer not to," he respectfully and slowly said and mildly disappeared.

"Very good, Bartleby," said I, in a quiet sort of serenely-severe, self-possessed tone, intimating the unalterable purpose of some terrible retribution very close at hand. At the moment I half intended something of the kind. But upon the whole, as it was drawing towards my dinner-hour, I thought it best to put on my hat and walk home for the day, suffering much from perplexity and distress of mind.

Shall I acknowledge it? The conclusion of this whole business was, that it soon became a fixed fact of my chambers, that a pale young scrivener, by the name of Bartleby, had a desk there; that he copied for me at the usual rate of four cents a folio (one hundred words); but he was permanently exempt from examining the work done by him, that duty being transferred to Turkey and Nippers, out of compliment, doubtless, to their superior acuteness; moreover, said Bartleby was never, on any account, to be dispatched on the most trivial errand of any sort; and that even if entreated to take upon him such a matter, it was generally understood that he would "prefer not to" —in other words, that he would refuse point-blank.

As days passed on, I became considerably reconciled to Bartleby. His steadiness, his freedom from all dissipation, his incessant industry (except when he chose to throw himself into a standing revery behind his screen), his great stillness, his unalterableness of demeanor under all circumstances, made him a valuable acquisition. One prime thing was this—*he was always there*—first in the morning, continually through the day, and the last at night. I had a singular confidence in his honesty. I felt my most precious papers perfectly safe in his hands. Sometimes, to be sure, I could not, for the very soul of me, avoid falling into sudden spasmodic passions with him. For it was exceeding difficult to bear in mind all the time those strange peculiarities, privileges, and unheard of exemptions, forming the tacit stipulations on Bartleby's part under which he remained in my office. Now and then, in the eagerness of dispatching pressing business, I would inadvertently summon Bartleby, in a short, rapid tone, to put his finger, say, on the incipient tie of a bit of red tape with which I was about compressing some papers. Of course, from behind the screen the usual answer, "I prefer not to," was sure to come; and then, how could a human creature, with the common infirmities of our nature, refrain from bitterly exclaiming upon such perverseness—such unreasonableness. However, every added repulse of this sort which I received only tended to lessen the probability of my repeating the inadvertence.

Here it must be said, that according to the custom of most legal gentlemen occupying chambers in densely-populated law buildings, there were several keys to my door. One was kept by a woman residing in the attic, which person weekly scrubbed and daily swept and dusted my apartments. Another was kept by Turkey for convenience sake. The third I sometimes carried in my own pocket. The fourth I knew not who had.

Now, one Sunday morning I happened to go to Trinity Church, to hear a celebrated preacher, and finding myself rather early on the ground I thought I would walk around to my chambers for a while. Luckily I had my key with me; but upon applying it to the lock, I found it resisted by something inserted from the inside. Quite surprised, I called out; when to my consternation a key was turned from within; and thrusting his lean visage at me, and holding the door ajar, the apparition of Bartleby appeared, in his shirt sleeves, and otherwise in a strangely tattered *déshabillé*, saying quietly that he was sorry, but he was deeply engaged just then, and—preferred not admitting me at present. In a brief word or two, he moreover added, that perhaps I had better walk around the block two or three times, and by that time he would probably have concluded his affairs.

Now, the utterly unsurmised appearance of Bartleby, tenanting my law-chambers of a Sunday morning, with his cadaverously gentlemanly *nonchalance*, yet withal firm and self-possessed, had such a strange effect upon me, that incontinently I slunk away from my own door, and did as desired. But not without sundry twinges of impotent rebellion against the mild effrontery of this unaccountable scrivener. Indeed, it was his wonderful mildness chiefly, which not only disarmed me, but unmanned me as it were. For I consider that one, for the time, is somehow unmanned when he tranquilly permits his hired clerk to dictate to him, and order him away from his own premises. Furthermore, I was full of uneasiness as to what Bartleby could possibly be doing in my office in his shirt sleeves, and in an otherwise dismantled condition of a Sunday morning. Was anything amiss going on? Nay, that was out of the question. It was not to be thought of for a moment that Bartleby was an immoral person. But what could he be doing there?—copying? Nay again, whatever might be his eccentricities, Bartleby was an eminently decorous person. He would be the last man to sit down to his desk in any state approaching to nudity. Besides, it was Sunday; and there was something about Bartleby that forbade the supposition that he would by any secular occupation violate the proprieties of the day.

Nevertheless, my mind was not pacified; and full of a restless curiosity, at last I returned to the door. Without hindrance I inserted my key, opened it, and entered. Bartleby was not to be seen. I looked round anxiously, peeped behind his screen; but it was very plain that he was gone. Upon more closely examining the place, I surmised that for an indefinite period Bartleby must have eaten, dressed, and slept in my office, and that, too, without plate, mirror, or bed. The cushioned seat of a rickety old sofa in one corner bore the faint impress of a lean, reclining form. Rolled away under his desk, I found a blanket; under the empty grate, a blacking box and brush; on a chair, a tin basin, with soap and a ragged towel; in a newspaper a few crumbs of ginger-nuts and a morsel of cheese. Yes, thought I, it is evident enough that Bartleby has been making his home here, keeping bachelor's hall all by himself. Immediately then the thought came sweeping across me, what miserable friendlessness and loneliness are here revealed! His poverty is great; but his solitude, how horrible! Think of it. Of a Sunday, Wall Street is deserted as Petra[5] ; and every night of every day it is an emptiness. This building, too, which of week-days hums with industry and life, at nightfall echoes with sheer vacancy, and all through Sunday is forlorn. And here Bartleby makes his home; sole spectator of a solitude which he has seen all populous—a sort of innocent and transformed Marius brooding among the ruins of Carthage![6]

For the first time in my life a feeling of over-powering stinging melancholy seized me. Before, I had never experienced aught but a not unpleasing sadness. The bond of a common humanity now drew me irresistibly to gloom. A fraternal melancholy! For both I and Bartleby were sons of Adam. I remembered the bright silks and sparkling faces I had seen that day, in gala trim, swan-like sailing down the Mississippi of Broadway; and I contrasted them with the pallid copyist, and thought to myself, Ah, happiness courts the light, so we deem the world is gay; but misery hides aloof, so we deem that

---

5. A city in Palestine found by explorers in 1812. It had been deserted and lost for centuries.
6. Caius Marius (155–86 B.C.), a plebeian general who was forced to flee from Rome. Nineteenth-century democratic literature sometimes pictured him old and alone among the ruins of Carthage.

misery there is none. These sad fancyings—chimeras, doubtless, of a sick and silly brain—led on to other and more special thoughts, concerning the eccentricities of Bartleby. Presentiments of strange discoveries hovered round me. The scrivener's pale form appeared to me laid out, among uncaring strangers, in its shivering winding sheet.

Suddenly I was attracted by Bartleby's closed desk, the key in open sight left in the lock.

I mean no mischief, seek the gratification of no heartless curiosity, thought I; besides, the desk is mine, and its contents, too, so I will make bold to look within. Everything was methodically arranged, the papers smoothly placed. The pigeon holes were deep, and removing the files of documents, I groped into their recesses. Presently I felt something there, and dragged it out. It was an old bandanna handkerchief, heavy and knotted. I opened it, and saw it was a savings bank.

I now recalled all the quiet mysteries which I had noted in the man. I remembered that he never spoke but to answer; that, though at intervals he had considerable time to himself, yet I had never seen him reading—no, not even a newspaper; that for long periods he would stand looking out, at his pale window behind the screen, upon the dead brick wall; I was quite sure he never visited any refectory or eating house; while his pale face clearly indicated that he never drank beer like Turkey, or tea and coffee even, like other men; that he never went anywhere in particular that I could learn; never went out for a walk, unless, indeed, that was the case at present; that he had declined telling who he was, or whence he came, or whether he had any relatives in the world; that though so thin and pale, he never complained of ill health. And more than all, I remembered a certain unconscious air of pallid—how shall I call it?—of pallid haughtiness, say, or rather an austere reserve about him, which had positively awed me into my tame compliance with his eccentricities, when I had feared to ask him to do the slightest incidental thing for me, even though I might know, from his long-continued motionlessness, that behind his screen he must be standing in one of those dead-wall reveries of his.

Revolving all these things, and coupling them with the recently discovered fact, that he made my office his constant abiding place and home, and not forgetful of his morbid moodiness; revolving all these things, a prudential feeling began to steal over me. My first emotions had been those of pure melancholy and sincerest pity; but just in proportion as the forlornness of Bartleby grew and grew to my imagination, did that same melancholy merge into fear, that pity into repulsion. So true it is, and so terrible, too, that up to a certain point the thought or sight of misery enlists our best affections; but, in certain special cases, beyond that point it does not. They err who would assert that invariably this is owing to the inherent selfishness of the human heart. It rather proceeds from a certain hopelessness of remedying excessive and organic ill. To a sensitive being, pity is not seldom pain. And when at last it is perceived that such pity cannot lead to effectual succor, common sense bids the soul be rid of it. What I saw that morning persuaded me that the scrivener was the victim of innate and incurable disorder. I might give alms to his body; but his body did not pain him; it was his soul that suffered, and his soul I could not reach.

I did not accomplish the purpose of going to Trinity Church that morning. Somehow, the things I had seen disqualified me for the time from church-going. I walked homeward, thinking what I would do with Bartleby. Finally, I resolved upon this—I would put certain calm questions to him the next morning, touching his history, etc., and if he declined to answer them openly and unreservedly (and I supposed he would prefer not), then to give him a twenty dollar bill over and above whatever I might owe him, and tell him his services were no longer required; but that if in any other way I could assist him, I would be happy to do so, especially if he desired to return to his native place, wherever that might be, I would willingly help to defray the expenses. Moreover, if, after reaching home, he found himself at any time in want of aid, a letter from him would be sure of a reply.

The next morning came.

"Bartleby," said I, gently calling to him behind his screen.

No reply.

"Bartleby," said I, in a still gentler tone, "come here; I am not going to ask you to do anything you would prefer not to do—I simply wish to speak to you."

Upon this he noiselessly slid into view.

"Will you tell me, Bartleby, where you were born?"

"I would prefer not to."

"Will you tell me *anything* about yourself?"

"I would prefer not to."

"But what reasonable objection can you have to speak to me? I feel friendly towards you."

He did not look at me while I spoke, but kept his glance fixed upon my bust of Cicero, which, as I then sat, was directly behind me, some six inches above my head.

"What is your answer, Bartleby," said I, after waiting a considerable time for a reply, during which his countenance remained immovable, only there was the faintest conceivable tremor of the white attenuated mouth.

"At present I prefer to give no answer," he said, and retired into his hermitage.

It was rather weak in me I confess, but his manner, on this occasion, nettled me. Not only did there seem to lurk in it a certain calm disdain, but his perverseness seemed ungrateful, considering the undeniable good usage and indulgence he had received from me.

Again I sat ruminating what I should do. Mortified as I was at his behavior, and resolved as I had been to dismiss him when I entered my office, nevertheless I strangely felt something superstitious knocking at my heart, and forbidding me to carry out my purpose, and denouncing me for a villain if I dared to breathe one bitter word against this forlornest of mankind. At last, familiarly drawing my chair behind his screen, I sat down and said: "Bartleby, never mind, then, about revealing your history; but let me entreat you, as a friend, to comply as far as may be with the usages of this office. Say now, you will help to examine papers to-morrow or next day: in short, say now, that in a day or two you will begin to be a little reasonable:—say so, Bartleby."

"At present I would prefer not to be a little reasonable," was his mildly cadaverous reply.

Just then the folding-doors opened, and Nippers approached. He seemed suffering from an unusually bad night's rest, induced by severer indigestion than common. He overheard those final words of Bartleby.

"*Prefer not*, eh?" gritted Nippers—"I'd *prefer* him, if I were you, sir," addressing me—"I'd *prefer* him; I'd give him preferences, the stubborn mule! What is it, sir, pray, that he *prefers* not to do now?"

Bartleby moved not a limb.

"Mr. Nippers," said I, "I'd prefer that you would withdraw for the present."

Somehow, of late, I had got into the way of involuntarily using this word "prefer" upon all sorts of not exactly suitable occasions. And I trembled to think that my contact with the scrivener had already and seriously affected me in a mental way. And what further and deeper aberration might it not yet produce? This apprehension had not been without efficacy in determining me to summary measures.

As Nippers, looking very sour and sulky, was departing, Turkey blandly and deferentially approached.

"With submission, sir," said he, "yesterday I was thinking about Bartleby here, and I think that if he would but prefer to take a quart of good ale every day, it would do much towards mending him, and enabling him to assist in examining his papers."

"So you have got the word, too," said I, slightly excited.

"With submission, what word, sir," asked Turkey, respectfully crowding himself into the contracted space behind the screen, and by so doing, making me jostle the scrivener. "What word, sir?"

"I would prefer to be left alone here," said Bartleby, as if offended at being mobbed in his privacy.

"*That's* the word, Turkey," said I—"*that's* it."

"Oh, *prefer?* oh yes—queer word. I never use it myself. But, sir, as I was saying, if he would but prefer—"

"Turkey," interrupted I, "you will please withdraw."

"Oh certainly, sir, if you prefer that I should."

As he opened the folding-door to retire, Nippers at his desk caught a glimpse of me, and asked whether I would prefer to have a certain paper copied on blue paper or white. He did not in the least roguishly accent the word prefer. It was plain that it involuntarily rolled from his tongue. I thought to myself, surely I must get rid of a demented man, who already has in some degree turned the tongues, if not the heads of myself and clerks. But I thought it prudent not to break the dismission at once.

The next day I noticed that Bartleby did nothing but stand at his window in his dead-wall revery. Upon asking him why he did not write, he said that he had decided upon doing no more writing.

"Why, how now? what next?" exclaimed I, "do no more writing?"

"No more."

"And what is the reason?"

"Do you not see the reason for yourself," he indifferently replied.

I looked steadfastly at him, and perceived that his eyes looked dull and glazed. Instantly it occurred to me, that his unexampled diligence in copying by his dim window for the first few weeks of his stay with me might have temporarily impaired his vision.

I was touched. I said something in condolence with him. I hinted that of course he did wisely in abstaining from writing for a while; and urged him to embrace that opportunity of taking wholesome exercise in the open air. This, however, he did not do. A few days after this, my other clerks being absent, and being in a great hurry to dispatch certain letters by the mail, I thought that, having nothing else earthly to do, Bartleby would surely be less inflexible than usual, and carry these letters to the post-office. But he blankly declined. So, much to my inconvenience, I went myself.

Still added days went by. Whether Bartleby's eyes improved or not, I could not say. To all appearance I thought they did. But when I asked him if they did, he vouchsafed no answer. At all events, he would do no copying. At last, in reply to my urgings, he informed me that he had permanently given up copying.

"What!" exclaimed I; "suppose your eyes should get entirely well— better than ever before—would you not copy then?"

"I have given up copying," he answered, and slid aside.

He remained as ever, a fixture in my chamber. Nay—if that were possible—he became still more of a fixture than before. What was to be done? He would do nothing in the office; why should he stay there? In plain fact, he had now become a millstone to me, not only useless as a necklace, but afflictive to bear. Yet I was sorry for him. I speak less than truth when I say that, on his own account, he occasioned me uneasiness. If he would but have named a single relative or friend, I would instantly have written, and urged their taking the poor fellow away to some convenient retreat. But he seemed alone, absolutely alone in the universe. A bit of wreck in the mid Atlantic. At length, necessities connected with my business tyrannized over all other considerations. Decently as I could, I told Bartleby that in six days time he must unconditionally leave the office. I warned him to take measures, in the interval, for procuring some other abode. I offered to assist him in his endeavor, if he himself would but take the first step towards a removal. "And when you finally quit me, Bartleby," added I, "I shall see that you go not away entirely unprovided. Six days from this hour, remember."

At the expiration of that period, I peeped behind the screen, and lo! Bartleby was there.

I buttoned up my coat, balanced myself; advanced slowly towards him, touched his shoulder, and said, "The time has come; you must quit this place; I am sorry for you; here is money; but you must go."

"I would prefer not," he replied, with his back still towards me.

"You *must*."

He remained silent.

Now I had an unbounded confidence in this man's common honesty. He had frequently restored to me sixpences and shillings carelessly dropped upon the floor, for I am apt to be very reckless in such shirt-button affairs. The proceeding, then, which followed will not be deemed extraordinary.

"Bartleby," said I, "I owe you twelve dollars on account; here are thirty-two; the odd twenty are yours—Will you take it?" and I handed the bills towards him.

But he made no motion.

"I will leave them here, then," putting them under a weight on the table. Then taking my hat and cane and going to the door, I tranquilly turned and added—"After you have removed your things from these offices, Bartleby, you will of course lock the door—since every one is now gone for the day but you—and if you please, slip your key underneath the mat, so that I may have it in the morning. I shall not see you again; so good-by to you. If, hereafter, in your new place of abode, I can be of any service to you, do not fail to advise me by letter. Good-by, Bartleby, and fare you well.

But he answered not a word; like the last column of some ruined temple, he remained standing mute and solitary in the middle of the otherwise deserted room.

As I walked home in a pensive mood, my vanity got the better of my pity. I could not but highly plume myself on my masterly management in getting rid of Bartleby. Masterly I call it, and such it must appear to any dispassionate thinker. The beauty of my procedure seemed to consist in its perfect quietness. There was no vulgar bullying, no bravado of any sort, no choleric hectoring, and striding to and fro across the apartment, jerking out vehement commands for Bartleby to bundle himself off with his beggarly traps. Nothing of the kind. Without loudly bidding Bartleby depart—as an inferior genius might have done—I *assumed* the ground that depart he must; and upon that assumption built all I had to say. The more I thought over my procedure, the more I was charmed with it. Nevertheless, next morning, upon awakening, I had my doubts—I had somehow slept off the fumes of vanity. One of the coolest and wisest hours a man has, is just after he awakes in the morning. My procedure seemed as sagacious as ever—but only in theory. How it would prove in practice—there was the rub. It was truly a beautiful thought to have assumed Bartleby's departure; but, after all, that assumption was simply my own, and none of Bartleby's. The great point was, not whether I had assumed that he would quit me, but whether he would prefer so to do. He was more a man of preferences than assumptions.

After breakfast, I walked down town, arguing the probabilities *pro* and *con*. One moment I thought it would prove a miserable failure, and Bartleby would be found all alive at my office as usual; the next moment it seemed certain that I should find his chair empty. And so I kept veering about. At the corner of Broadway and Canal Street, I saw quite an excited group of people standing in earnest conversation.

"I'll take odds he doesn't," said a voice as I passed.

"Doesn't go?—done!" said I; "put up your money."

I was instinctively putting my hand in my pocket to produce my own, when I remembered that this was an election day. The words I had overheard bore no reference to Bartleby, but to the success or non-success of some candidate for the mayoralty. In my intent frame of mind, I had, as it were, imagined that all Broadway shared in my excitement, and were debating the same question with me. I passed on, very thankful that the uproar of the street screened my momentary absent-mindedness.

As I had intended, I was earlier than usual at my office door. I stood listening for a moment. All was still. He must be gone. I tried the knob. The door was locked. Yes, my procedure had worked to a charm; he indeed must be vanished. Yet a certain melancholy mixed with this: I was almost sorry for my brilliant success. I was fumbling under the door mat for key, which Bartleby was to have left there for me, when accidentally my knee knocked against a panel, producing a summoning sound, and in response a voice came to me from within—"Not yet; I am occupied."

It was Bartleby.

I was thunderstruck. For an instant I stood like the man who, pipe in mouth, was killed one cloudless afternoon long ago in Virginia, by summer lightning; at his own warm open window he was killed, and remained leaning out there upon the dreamy afternoon, till some one touched him, when he fell.

"Not gone!" I murmured at last. But again obeying that wondrous ascendancy which the inscrutable scrivener had over me, and from which ascendancy, for all my chafing, I could not completely escape, I slowly went down stairs and out into the street, and while walking round the block, considered what I should next do in this unheard-of perplexity. Turn the man out by an actual thrusting I could not; to drive him away by calling him hard names would not do; calling in the police was an unpleasant idea; and yet, permit him to enjoy his cadaverous triumph over me—this, too, I could not think of. What was to be done? or, if nothing could be done, was there anything further that I could *assume* in the matter? Yes, as before I had prospectively assumed that Bartleby would depart, so now I might retrospectively assume that departed he was. In the legitimate carrying out of this assumption, I might enter my office in a great hurry, and pretending not to see Bartleby at all, walk straight against him as if he were air. Such a proceeding would in a singular degree have the appearance of a home-thrust. It was hardly possible that Bartleby could withstand such an application of the doctrine of assumptions. But upon second thoughts the success of the plan seemed rather dubious. I resolved to argue the matter over with him again.

"Bartleby," said I, entering the office, with a quietly severe expression, "I am seriously displeased. I am pained, Bartleby. I had thought better of you. I had imagined you of such a gentlemanly organization, that in any delicate dilemma a slight hint would suffice—in short, an assumption. But it appears I am deceived. Why," I added, unaffectedly starting, "you have not even touched that money yet," pointing to it, just where I had left it the evening previous.

He answered nothing.

"Will you, or will you not, quit me?" I now demanded in a sudden passion, advancing close to him.

"I would prefer *not* to quit you," he replied, gently emphasizing the *not*.

"What earthly right have you to stay here? Do you pay any rent? Do you pay my taxes? Or is this property yours?"

He answered nothing.

"Are you ready to go on and write now? Are your eyes recovered? Could you copy a small paper for me this morning? or help examine a few lines? or step round to the post-office? In a word, will you do anything at all, to give a coloring to your refusal to depart the premises?"

He silently retired into his hermitage.

I was now in such a state of nervous resentment that I thought it but prudent to check myself at present from further demonstrations. Bartleby and I were alone. I remembered the tragedy of the unfortunate Adams and the still more unfortunate Colt in the solitary office of the latter; and how poor Colt, being dreadfully incensed by Adams, and imprudently permitting himself to get wildly excited, was at unawares hurried into his fatal act—an act which certainly no man could possibly deplore more than the actor himself.[7] Often it had occurred to me in my ponderings upon the subject, that had that altercation taken place in the public street, or at a private residence, it would not have terminated as it did. It was the circumstance of being alone in a solitary office, up stairs, of a building entirely unhallowed by humanizing domestic associations—an uncarpeted office, doubtless, of a dusty, haggard sort of appearance—this it must have been, which greatly helped to enhance the irritable desperation of the hapless Colt.

But when this old Adam of resentment rose in me and tempted me concerning Bartleby, I grappled him and threw him. How? Why, simply by

---

7. A sensational homicide case in which Colt murdered Adams in a fit of passion.

recalling the divine injunction: "A new commandment give I unto you, that ye love one another." Yes, this it was that saved me. Aside from higher considerations, charity often operates as a vastly wise and prudent principle—a great safeguard to its possessor. Men have committed murder for jealousy's sake, and anger's sake, and hatred's sake, and selfishness' sake, and spiritual pride's sake; but no man, that ever I heard of, ever committed a diabolical murder for sweet charity's sake. Mere self-interest, then, if no better motive can be enlisted, should, especially with high-tempered men, prompt all beings to charity and philanthropy. At any rate, upon the occasion in question, I strove to drown my exasperated feelings towards the scrivener by benevolently construing his conduct. Poor fellow, poor fellow! thought I, he don't mean anything; and besides, he has seen hard times, and ought to be indulged.

I endeavored, also, immediately to occupy myself, and at the same time to comfort my despondency. I tried to fancy, that in the course of the morning, at such time as might prove agreeable to him, Bartleby, of his own free accord, would emerge from his hermitage and take up some decided line of march in the direction of the door. But no. Half-past twelve o'clock came; Turkey began to glow in the face, overturn his inkstand, and become generally obstreperous; Nippers abated down into quietude and courtesy; Ginger Nut munched his noon apple; and Bartleby remained standing at his window in one of his profoundest dead-wall reveries. Will it be credited? Ought I to acknowledge it? That afternoon I left the office without saying one further word to him.

Some days now passed, during which, at leisure intervals I looked a little into "Edwards on the Will," and "Priestly on Necessity."[8] Under the circumstances, those books induced a salutary feeling. Gradually I slid into the persuasion that these troubles of mine, touching the scrivener, had been all predestinated from eternity, and Bartleby was billeted upon me for some mysterious purpose of an all-wise Providence, which it was not for a mere mortal like me to fathom. Yes, Bartleby, stay there behind your screen, thought I; I shall persecute you no more; you are harmless and noiseless as any of these old chairs; in short, I never feel so private as when I know you are here. At last I see it, I feel it; I penetrate to the predestinated purpose of my life. I am content. Others may have loftier parts to enact; but my mission in this world, Bartleby, is to furnish you with office-room for such period as you may see fit to remain.

I believe that this wise and blessed frame of mind would have continued with me, had it not been for the unsolicited and uncharitable remarks obtruded upon me by my professional friends who visited the rooms. But thus it often is, that the constant friction of illiberal minds wears out at last the best resolves of the more generous. Though to be sure, when I re-

---

8. Jonathan Edwards (1703–1758), American theologian, and Joseph Priestly (1733–1804), English clergyman and chemist, both held that man's life was predetermined.

flected upon it, it was not strange that people entering my office should be struck by the peculiar aspect of the unaccountable Bartleby, and so be tempted to throw out some sinister observations concerning him. Sometimes an attorney, having business with me, and calling at my office, and finding no one but the scrivener there, would undertake to obtain some sort of precise information from him touching my whereabouts; but without heeding his idle talk, Bartleby would remain standing immovable in the middle of the room. So after contemplating him in that position for a time, the attorney would depart, no wiser than he came.

Also, when a reference was going on, and the room full of lawyers and witnesses, and business driving fast, some deeply-occupied legal gentleman present, seeing Bartleby wholly unemployed, would request him to run round to his (the legal gentleman's) office and fetch some papers for him. Thereupon, Bartleby would tranquilly decline, and yet remain idle as before. Then the lawyer would give a great stare, and turn to me. And what could I say? At last I was made aware that all through the circle of my professional acquaintance, a whisper of wonder was running round, having reference to the strange creature I kept at my office. This worried me very much. And as the idea came upon me of his possibly turning out a long-lived man, and keep occupying my chambers, and denying my authority; and perplexing my visitors; and scandalizing my professional reputation; and casting a general gloom over the premises; keeping soul and body together to the last upon his savings (for doubtless he spent but half a dime a day), and in the end perhaps outlive me, and claim possession of my office by right of his perpetual occupancy: as all these dark anticipations crowded upon me more and more, and my friends continually intruded their relentless remarks upon the apparition in my room; a great change was wrought in me. I resolved to gather all my faculties together, and forever rid me of this intolerable incubus.

Ere revolving any complicated project, however, adapted to this end, I first simply suggested to Bartleby the propriety of his permanent departure. In a calm and serious tone, I commended the idea to his careful and mature consideration. But, having taken three days to meditate upon it, he apprised me, that his original determination remained the same; in short, that he still preferred to abide with me.

What shall I do? I now said to myself, buttoning up my coat to the last button. What shall I do? what ought I to do? what does conscience say I *should* do with this man, or, rather, ghost. Rid myself of him, I must; go, he shall. But how? You will not thrust him, the poor, pale, passive mortal—you will not thrust such a helpless creature out of your door? you will not dishonor yourself by such cruelty? No, I will not, I cannot do that. Rather would I let him live and die here, and then mason up his remains in the wall. What, then, will you do? For all your coaxing, he will not budge. Bribes he leaves under your own paper-weight on your table; in short, it is quite plain that he prefers to cling to you.

Then something severe, something unusual must be done, What! surely you will not have him collared by a constable, and commit his innocent pallor to the common jail? And upon what ground could you procure such a thing to be done?—a vagrant, is he? What! he a vagrant, a wanderer, who refuses to budge? It is because he will *not* be a vagrant, then, that you seek to count him as a vagrant. This is too absurd. No visible means of support: there I have him. Wrong again: for indubitably he *does* support himself, and that is the only unanswerable proof that any man can show of his possessing the means so to do. No more, then. Since he will not quit me, I must quit him. I will change my offices; I will move elsewhere, and give him fair notice, that if I find him on my new premises I will then proceed against him as a common trespasser.

Acting accordingly, next day I thus addressed him: "I find these chambers too far from the City Hall; the air is unwholesome. In a word, I propose to remove my offices next week, and shall no longer require your services. I tell you this now, in order that you may seek another place."

He made no reply; and nothing more was said.

On the appointed day I engaged carts and men, proceeded to my chambers, and, having but little furniture, everything was removed in a few hours. Throughout, the scrivener remained standing behind the screen, which I directed to be removed the last thing. It was withdrawn; and, being folded up like a huge folio, left him the motionless occupant of a naked room. I stood in the entry watching him a moment, while something from within me upbraided me.

I re-entered, with my hand in my pocket—and—and my heart in my mouth.

"Good-by, Bartleby; I am going—good-by, and God some way bless you; and take that," slipping something in his hand. But it dropped upon the floor, and then—strange to say—I tore myself from him whom I had so longed to be rid of.

Established in my new quarters, for a day or two I kept the door locked, and started at every footfall in the passages. When I returned to my rooms, after any little absence, I would pause at the threshold for an instant, and attentively listen, ere applying my key. But these fears were needless. Bartleby never came nigh me.

I thought all was going well, when a perturbed-looking stranger visited me, inquiring whether I was the person who had recently occupied rooms at No. ____ Wall Street.

Full of forebodings, I replied that I was.

"Then, sir," said the stranger, who proved a lawyer, "you are responsible for the man you left there. He refuses to do any copying; he refuses to do anything; he says he prefers not to; and he refuses to quit the premises."

"I am very sorry, sir," said I, with assumed tranquillity, but an inward tremor, "but, really, the man you allude to is nothing to me—he is no relation or apprentice of mine, that you should hold me responsible for him."

"In mercy's name, who is he?"

"I certainly cannot inform you. I know nothing about him. Formerly I employed him as a copyist; but he has done nothing for me now for some time past."

"I shall settle him, then—good morning, sir."

Several days passed, and I heard nothing more; and, though I often felt a charitable prompting to call at the place and see poor Bartleby, yet a certain squeamishness, of I know not what, withheld me.

All is over with him, by this time, thought I, at last, when, through another week, no further intelligence reached me. But, coming to my room the day after, I found several persons waiting at my door in a high state of nervous excitement.

"That's the man—here he comes," cried the foremost one, whom I recognized as the lawyer who had previously called upon me alone.

"You must take him away, sir, at once," cried a portly person among them, advancing upon me, and whom I knew to be the landlord of No.____ Wall Street. "These gentlemen, my tenants, cannot stand it any longer; Mr. B—," pointing to the lawyer, "has turned him out of his room, and he now persists in haunting the building generally, sitting upon the banisters of the stairs by day, and sleeping in the entry by night. Everybody is concerned; clients are leaving the offices; some fears are entertained of a mob; something you must do, and that without delay."

Aghast at this torrent, I fell back before it, and would fain have locked myself in my new quarters. In vain I persisted that Bartleby was nothing to me—no more than to any one else. In vain—I was the last person known to have anything to do with him, and they held me to the terrible account. Fearful, then, of being exposed in the papers (as one person present obscurely threatened), I considered the matter, and, at length, said, that if the lawyer would give me a confidential interview with the scrivener, in his (the lawyer's) own room, I would, that afternoon, strive my best to rid them of the nuisance they complained of.

Going up stairs to my old haunt, there was Bartleby silently sitting upon the banister at the landing.

"What are you doing here, Bartleby?" said I.

"Sitting upon the banister," he mildly replied.

I motioned him into the lawyer's room, who then left us.

"Bartleby," said I, "are you aware that you are the cause of great tribulation to me, by persisting in occupying the entry after being dismissed from the office?"

No answer.

"Now one of two things must take place. Either you must do something, or something must be done to you. Now what sort of business would you like to engage in? Would you like to re-engage in copying for some one?"

"No; I would prefer not to make any change."

"Would you like a clerkship in a dry-goods store?"

"There is too much confinement about that. No, I would not like a clerkship; but I am not particular."

"Too much confinement," I cried, "why you keep yourself confined all the time!"

"I would prefer not to take a clerkship," he rejoined, as if to settle that little item at once.

"How would a bar-tender's business suit you? There is no trying of the eye-sight in that."

"I would not like it at all; though, as I said before, I am not particular."

His unwonted wordiness inspirited me. I returned to the charge.

"Well, then, would you like to travel through the country collecting bills for the merchants? That would improve your health."

"No, I would prefer to be doing something else."

"How, then, would going as a companion to Europe, to entertain some young gentleman with your conversation—how would that suit you?"

"Not at all. It does not strike me that there is anything definite about that. I like to be stationary. But I am not particular."

"Stationary you shall be, then," I cried, now losing all patience, and, for the first time in all my exasperating connection with him, fairly flying into a passion. "If you do not go away from these premises before night, I shall feel bound—indeed, I *am* bound—to—to—to quit the premises myself!" I rather absurdly concluded, knowing not with what possible threat to try to frighten his immobility into compliance. Despairing of all further efforts, I was precipitately leaving him, when a final thought occurred to me—one which had not been wholly unindulged before.

"Bartleby," said I, in the kindest tone I could assume under such exciting circumstances, "will you go home with me now—not to my office, but my dwelling—and remain there till we can conclude upon some convenient arrangement for you at our leisure? Come, let us start now, right away."

"No: at present I would prefer not to make any change at all."

I answered nothing; but, effectually dodging every one by the suddenness and rapidity of my flight, rushed from the building, ran up Wall Street towards Broadway, and, jumping into the first omnibus, was soon removed from pursuit. As soon as tranquillity returned, I distinctly perceived that I had now done all that I possibly could, both in respect to the demands of the landlord and his tenants, and with regard to my own desire and sense of duty, to benefit Bartleby, and shield him from rude persecution. I now strove to be entirely care-free and quiescent; and my conscience justified me in the attempt; though, indeed, it was not so successful as I could have wished. So fearful was I of being again hunted out by the incensed landlord and his exasperated tenants, that, surrendering my business to Nippers, for a few days, I drove about the upper part of the town and through the suburbs, in my rockaway; crossed over to Jersey City and Hoboken, and paid fugitive visits to Manhattanville and Astoria. In fact, I almost lived in my rockaway for the time.

When again I entered my office, lo, a note from the landlord lay upon the desk. I opened it with trembling hands. It informed me that the writer had sent to the police, and had Bartleby removed to the Tombs as a vagrant. Moreover, since I knew more about him than any one else, he wished me to appear at that place, and make a suitable statement of the facts. These tidings had a conflicting effect upon me. At first I was indignant; but, at last, almost approved. The landlord's energetic, summary disposition, had led him to adopt a procedure which I do not think I would have decided upon myself; and yet, as a last resort, under such peculiar circumstances, it seemed the only plan.

As I afterwards learned, the poor scrivener, when told that he must be conducted to the Tombs, offered not the slightest obstacle, but, in his pale, unmoving way, silently acquiesced.

Some of the compassionate and curious bystanders joined the party; and headed by one of the constables arm in arm with Bartleby, the silent procession filed its way through all the noise, and heat, and joy of the roaring thoroughfares at noon.

The same day I received the note, I went to the Tombs, or, to speak more properly, the Halls of Justice. Seeking the right officer, I stated the purpose of my call, and was informed that the individual I described was, indeed, within. I then assured the functionary that Bartleby was a perfectly honest man, and greatly to be compassionated, however unaccountably eccentric. I narrated all I knew, and closed by suggesting the idea of letting him remain in as indulgent confinement as possible, till something less harsh might be done—though, indeed, I hardly knew what. At all events, if nothing else could be decided upon, the alms-house must receive him. I then begged to have an interview.

Being under no disgraceful charge, and quite serene and harmless in all his ways, they had permitted him freely to wander about the prison, and, especially, in the inclosed grass-platted yards thereof. And so I found him there, standing all alone in the quietest of the yards, his face towards a high wall, while all around, from the narrow slits of the jail windows, I thought I saw peering out upon him the eyes of murderers and thieves.

"Bartleby!"

"I know you," he said, without looking round—"and I want nothing to say to you."

"It was not I that brought you here, Bartleby," said I, keenly pained at his implied suspicion. "And to you, this should not be so vile a place. Nothing reproachful attaches to you by being here. And see, it is not so sad a place as one might think. Look, there is the sky, and here is the grass."

"I know where I am," he replied, but would say nothing more, and so I left him.

As I entered the corridor again, a broad meat-like man, in an apron, accosted me, and, jerking his thumb over his shoulder, said—"Is that your friend?"

"Yes."

"Does he want to starve? If he does, let him live on the prison fare, that's all."

"Who are you?" asked I, not knowing what to make of such an unofficially speaking person in such a place.

"I am the grub-man. Such gentlemen as have friends here, hire me to provide them with something good to eat."

"Is this so?" said I, turning to the turnkey.

He said it was.

"Well, then," said I, slipping some silver into the grub-man's hands (for so they called him), "I want you to give particular attention to my friend there; let him have the best dinner you can get. And you must be as polite to him as possible."

"Introduce me, will you?" said the grub-man, looking at me with an expression which seemed to say he was all impatience for an opportunity to give a specimen of his breeding.

Thinking it would prove of benefit to the scrivener, I acquiesced; and, asking the grub-man his name, went up with him to Bartleby.

"Bartleby, this is a friend; you will find him very useful to you."

"Your sarvant, sir, your sarvant," said the grub-man, making a low salutation behind his apron. "Hope you find it pleasant here, sir; nice grounds—cool apartments—hope you'll stay with us sometime—try to make it agreeable. What will you have for dinner to-day?"

"I prefer not to dine to-day," said Bartleby, turning away. "It would disagree with me; I am unused to dinners." So saying, he slowly moved to the other side of the inclosure, and took up a position fronting the dead-wall.

"How's this?" said the grub-man, addressing me with a stare of astonishment." He's odd, ain't he?"

"I think he is a little deranged," said I, sadly.

"Deranged? deranged is it? Well, now, upon my word, I thought that friend of yourn was a gentleman forger; they are always pale and genteel-like, them forgers. I can't help pity 'em—can't help it, sir. Did you know Monroe Edwards?" he added, touchingly, and paused. Then, laying his hand piteously on my shoulder, sighed, "he died of consumption at Sing-Sing.[9] So you weren't acquainted with Monroe?"

"No, I was never socially acquainted with any forgers. But I cannot stop longer. Look to my friend yonder. You will not lose by it. I will see you again."

---

9. The state prison near Ossining, New York.

Some few days after this, I again obtained admission to the Tombs, and went through the corridors in quest of Bartleby; but without finding him.

"I saw him coming from his cell not long ago," said a turnkey, "may be he's gone to loiter in the yards."

So I went in that direction.

"Are you looking for the silent man?" said another turnkey, passing me. "Yonder he lies—sleeping in the yard there. 'Tis not twenty minutes since I saw him lie down."

The yard was entirely quiet. It was not accessible to the common prisoners. The surrounding walls of amazing thickness, kept off all sounds behind them. The Egyptian character of the masonry weighed upon me with its gloom. But a soft imprisoned turf grew under foot. The heart of the eternal pyramids, it seemed, wherein, by some strange magic, through the clefts, grass-seed, dropped by birds, had sprung.

Strangely huddled at the base of the wall, his knees drawn up, and lying on his side, his head touching the cold stones, I saw the wasted Bartleby. But nothing stirred. I paused; then went close up to him; stooped over, and saw that his dim eyes were open; otherwise he seemed profoundly sleeping. Something prompted me to touch him. I felt his hand, when a tingling shiver ran up my arm and down my spine to my feet.

The round face of the grub-man peered upon me now. "His dinner is ready. Won't he dine to-day, either? Or does he live without dining?"

"Lives without dining," said I, and closed the eyes.

"Eh!—He's asleep, ain't he?"

"With kings and counselors," murmured I.

•   •   •   •   •

There would seem little need for proceeding further in this history. Imagination will readily supply the meagre recital of poor Bartleby's interment. But, ere parting with the reader, let me say, that if this little narrative has sufficiently interested him, to awaken curiosity as to who Bartleby was, and what manner of life he led prior to the present narrator's making his acquaintance, I can only reply, that in such curiosity I fully share, but am wholly unable to gratify it. Yet here I hardly know whether I should divulge one little item of rumor, which came to my ear a few months after the scrivener's decease. Upon what basis it rested, I could never ascertain; and hence, how true it is I cannot now tell. But, inasmuch as this vague report has not been without a certain suggestive interest to me, however said, it may prove the same with some others; and so I will briefly mention it. The report was this: that Bartleby had been a subordinate clerk in the Dead Letter Office at Washington, from which he had been suddenly removed by a change in the administration. When I think over this rumor, hardly can I express the emotions which seize me. Dead letters! does it not sound like dead men? Conceive a man by nature and misfortune prone to a pallid hopelessness, can any business seem more fitted to heighten it than that of continually handling these dead letters, and assorting them for the flames? For by the cart-load they are annually burned. Some times from out the folded paper the pale clerk takes a ring—the finger it was meant for, perhaps, moulders in the grave; a bank-note sent in swiftest charity—he whom it would relieve, nor eats nor hungers any more; pardon for those who died despairing; hope for those who died unhoping; good tidings for those who died stifled by unrelieved calamities. On errands of life, these letters speed to death.

Ah, Bartleby! Ah, humanity!

Questions

1. *Readers differ as to whether this is the story of Bartleby or the story of the lawyer-narrator. What is your view?* 2. *What is it about Bartleby that so intrigues and fascinates the narrator? Why does the narrator continue to feel a moral obligation to an employee who refuses to work and curtly rejects kindly offers of help?* 3. *Why does Melville allow the narrator (and the reader) to discover so little about Bartleby and the causes of his behavior? All that we learn of Bartleby's past is contained in the next-to-last paragraph. What, if anything, in this paragraph establishes a link between Bartleby and the narrator?* 4. *With his final utterance, "Ah, Bartleby! Ah, humanity!" the narrator apparently penetrates the mystery of Bartleby. The comments seem to suggest that for the narrator Bartleby is a representative of humanity. In what sense might the narrator come to see Bartleby in this light?* 5. *What functions do Turkey and Nippers serve?* 6. *Would it be fair to describe Bartleby as a rebel without a cause, as a young man who refuses to participate in a comfortable and well-ordered business world but fails to offer any alternative way of life? Justify your answer.*

A Hunger Artist*

FRANZ KAFKA   [1883–1924]

DURING these last decades the interest in professional fasting has markedly diminished. It used to pay very well to stage such great performances under one's own management, but today that is quite impossible. We live in a different world now. At one time the whole town took a lively interest in the hunger artist; from day to day of his fast the excitement mounted; everybody wanted to see him at least once a day; there were people who bought season tickets for the last few days and sat from morning till night in front of his small barred cage; even in the nighttime there were visiting hours, when the whole effect was heightened by torch flares; on fine days the cage was set out in the open air, and then it was the children's special treat to see the hunger artist; for their elders he was often just a joke that happened to be in fashion, but the children stood open-mouthed, holding each other's hands for greater security, marveling at him as he sat there pallid in black tights, with his ribs sticking out so prominently, not even on a seat but down among straw on the ground, sometimes giving a courteous nod, answering questions with a constrained smile, or perhaps stretching an arm through the bars so that one might feel how thin it was, and then again withdrawing deep into himself, paying no attention to anyone or anything, not even to the all-important striking of the clock that was the only piece of furniture in his cage, but merely staring into vacancy with half-shut eyes, now and then taking a sip from a tiny glass of water to moisten his lips.

Besides casual onlookers there were also relays of permanent watchers selected by the public, usually butchers, strangely enough, and it was their task to watch the hunger artist day and night, three of them at a time, in case he should have some secret recourse to nourishment. This was nothing but a formality, instituted to reassure the masses, for the initiates knew well enough that during his fast the artist would never in any circumstances, not even under forcible compulsion, swallow the smallest morsel of food; the honor of his profession forbade it. Not every watcher, of course, was capable of understanding this, there were often groups of night watchers who were very lax in carrying out their duties and deliberately huddled together in a retired corner to play cards with great absorption, obviously intending to give the hunger artist the chance of a little refreshment, which they supposed he could draw from some private hoard. Nothing annoyed the artist more than such watchers; they made him miserable; they made his fast seem unendurable; sometimes he mastered his feebleness sufficiently to sing during their watch

---

*Translated by Edwin and Willa Muir.

for as long as he could keep going, to show them how unjust their suspicions were. But that was of little use; they only wondered at his cleverness in being able to fill his mouth even while singing. Much more to his taste were the watchers who sat close up to the bars, who were not content with the dim night lighting of the hall but focused him in the full glare of the electric pocket torch given them by the impresario. The harsh light did not trouble him at all, in any case he could never sleep properly, and he could always drowse a little, whatever the light, at any hour, even when the hall was thronged with noisy onlookers. He was quite happy at the prospect of spending a sleepless night with such watchers; he was ready to exchange jokes with them, to tell them stories out of his nomadic life, anything at all to keep them awake and demonstrate to them again that he had no eatables in his cage and that he was fasting as not one of them could fast. But his happiest moment was when the morning came and an enormous breakfast was brought them, at his expense, on which they flung themselves with the keen appetite of healthy men after a weary night of wakefulness. Of course there were people who argued that this breakfast was an unfair attempt to bribe the watchers, but that was going rather too far, and when they were invited to take on a night's vigil without a breakfast, merely for the sake of the cause, they made themselves scarce, although they stuck stubbornly to their suspicions.

Such suspicions, anyhow, were a necessary accompaniment to the profession of fasting. No one could possibly watch the hunger artist continuously, day and night, and so no one could produce first-hand evidence that the fast had really been rigorous and continuous; only the artist himself could know that, he was therefore bound to be the sole completely satisfied spectator of his own fast. Yet for other reasons he was never satisfied; it was not perhaps mere fasting that had brought him to such skeleton thinness that many people had regretfully to keep away from his exhibitions, because the sight of him was too much for them, perhaps it was dissatisfaction with himself that had worn him down. For he alone knew, what no other initiate knew, how easy it was to fast. It was the easiest thing in the world. He made no secret of this, yet people did not believe him, at the best they set him down as modest, most of them, however, thought he was out for publicity or else was some kind of cheat who found it easy to fast because he had discovered a way of making it easy, and then had the impudence to admit the fact, more or less. He had to put up with all that, and in the course of time had got used to it, but his inner dissatisfaction always rankled, and never yet, after any term of fasting—this must be granted to his credit—had he left the cage of his own free will. The longest period of fasting was fixed by his impresario at forty days, beyond that term he was not allowed to go, not even in great cities, and there was good reason for it, too. Experience had proved that for about forty days the interest of the public could be stimulated by a steadily increasing pressure of advertisement, but after that the town began to lose interest, sympathetic support began notably to fall off; there were of course local variations as between one town and another or one country and another, but as a general rule forty days marked the limit. So on the fortieth day the flower bedecked cage was opened, enthusiastic spectators filled the hall, a military band played, two doctors entered the cage to measure the results of the fast, which were announced through a megaphone, and finally two young ladies appeared, blissful at having been selected for the honor, to help the hunger artist down the few steps leading to a small table on which was spread a carefully chosen invalid repast. And at this very moment the artist always turned stubborn. True, he would entrust his bony arms to the outstretched helping hands of the ladies bending over him, but stand up he would not. Why stop fasting at this particular moment, after forty days of it? He had held out for a long time, an illimitably long time; why stop now, when he was in his best fasting form, or rather, not yet quite in his best fasting form? Why should he be cheated of the fame he would get for fasting longer, for being not only the record hunger artist of all time, which presumably he was already, but for beating his own record by a performance beyond human imagination, since he felt that there were no limits to his capacity for fasting? His public pretended to admire him so much, why should it have so little patience with him; if he could endure fasting longer, why shouldn't the public endure it? Besides, he was tired, he was comfortable sitting in the straw, and now he was supposed to lift himself to his full height and go down to a meal the very thought of which gave him a nausea that only the presence of the ladies kept him from betraying, and even that with an effort. And he looked up into the eyes of the ladies who were apparently so friendly and in reality so cruel, and shook his head, which felt too heavy on its strengthless neck. But then there happened yet again what always happened. The impresario came forward, without a word—for the band made speech impossible—lifted his arms in the air above the artist, as if inviting Heaven to look down upon its creature here in the straw, this suffering martyr, which indeed he was, although in quite another sense; grasped him round the emaciated waist, with exaggerated caution, so that the frail condition he was in might be appreciated; and committed him to the care of the blenching ladies, not without secretly giving him a shaking so that his legs and body tottered and swayed. The artist now submitted completely; his head lolled on his breast as if it had landed there by chance; his body was hollowed out; his legs in a spasm of self-preservation clung close to each other at the knees, yet scraped on the ground as if it were not really solid ground, as if they were only trying to find solid ground; and the whole weight of his body, a feather-weight after all, relapsed onto one of the ladies, who, looking round for help and panting a little—this post of honor was not at all what she had expected it to be—first stretched her neck as far as she could to keep her face at least free from contact with the artist, when finding this impossible, and her more fortunate companion not coming to her aid but merely holding extended on her own trembling hand the little bunch of knucklebones that was the artist's, to the great delight of the spectators burst into tears and had to be replaced by an attendant who had long been stationed in readiness. Then came the food, a little of which the impresario managed to get between the artist's lips, while he sat in a kind of half-fainting trance, to the accompaniment of cheerful patter designed to distract the public's attention from the artist's condition; after that, a toast was drunk to the public, supposedly prompted by a whisper from the artist in the impresario's ear; the band confirmed it with a mighty flourish, the spectators melted away, and no one had any cause to be dissatisfied with the proceedings, no one except the hunger artist himself, he only, as always.

So he lived for many years, with small regular intervals of recuperation, in visible glory, honored by the world, yet in spite of that troubled in spirit, and all the more troubled because no one would take his trouble seriously. What comfort could he possibly need? What more could he possibly wish for? And if some good-natured person, feeling sorry for him, tried to console him by pointing out that his melancholy was probably caused by fasting, it could happen, especially when he had been fasting for some time, that he reacted with an outburst of fury and to the general alarm began to shake the bars of his cage like a wild animal. Yet the impresario had a way of punishing these outbreaks which he rather enjoyed putting into operation. He would apologize publicly for the artist's behavior, which was only to be excused, he admitted, because of the irritability caused by fasting; a condition hardly to be understood by well-fed people; then by natural transition he went on to mention the artist's equally incomprehensible boast that he could fast for much longer than he was doing; he praised the high ambition, the good will, the great self-denial undoubtedly implicit in such a statement; and then quite simply countered it by bringing out photographs, which were also on sale to the public, showing the artist on the fortieth day of a fast lying in bed almost dead from exhaustion. This perversion of the truth, familiar to the artist though it was, always unnerved him afresh and proved too much for him. What was a consequence of the premature ending of his fast was here presented as the cause of it! To fight against this lack of understanding, against a whole world of non-understanding, was impossible. Time and again in good faith he stood by the bars listening to the impresario, but as soon as the photographs appeared he always let go and sank with a groan back on to his straw, and the reassured public could once more come close and gaze at him.

A few years later when the witnesses of such scenes called them to mind, they often failed to understand themselves at all. For meanwhile the aforementioned change in public interest had set in; it seemed to happen almost overnight; there may have been profound causes for it, but who was going to bother about that; at any rate the pampered hunger artist suddenly found himself deserted one fine day by the amusement seekers, who went streaming past him to other more favored attractions. For the last time the impresario hurried him over half Europe to discover whether the old interest might still survive here and there; all in vain; everywhere, as if by secret agreement, a positive revulsion from professional fasting was in evidence. Of course it could not really have sprung up so suddenly as all that, and many premonitory symptoms which had not been sufficiently remarked or suppressed during the rush and glitter of success now came retrospectively to mind, but it was now too late to take any countermeasures. Fasting would surely come into fashion again at some future date, yet that was no comfort for those living in the present. What, then, was the hunger artist to do? He had been applauded by thousands in his time and could hardly come down to showing himself in a street booth at village fairs, and as for adopting another profession, he was not only too old for that but too fanatically devoted to fasting. So he took leave of the impresario, his partner in an unparalleled career, and hired himself to a large circus; in order to spare his own feelings he avoided reading the conditions of his contract.

A large circus with its enormous traffic in replacing and recruiting men, animals and apparatus can always find a use for people at any time, even for a hunger artist, provided of course that he does not ask too much, and in this particular case anyhow it was not only the artist who was taken on but his famous and long-known name as well, indeed considering the peculiar nature of his performance, which was not impaired by advancing age, it could not be objected that here was an artist past his prime, no longer at the height of his professional skill, seeking a refuge in some quiet corner of a circus; on the contrary, the hunger artist averred that he could fast as well as ever, which was entirely credible, he even alleged that if he were allowed to fast as he liked, and this was at once promised him without more ado, he could astound the world by establishing a record never yet achieved, a statement which certainly provoked a smile among the other professionals, since it left out of account the change in public opinion, which the hunger artist in his zeal conveniently forgot.

He had not, however, actually lost his sense of the real situation and took it as a matter of course that he and his cage should be stationed, not in the middle of the ring as a main attraction, but outside, near the animal cages, on a site that was after all easily accessible. Large and gaily painted placards made a frame for the cage and announced what was to be seen inside it. When the public came thronging out in the intervals to see the animals, they could hardly avoid passing the hunger artist's cage and stopping there for a moment, perhaps they might even have stayed longer had not those pressing behind them in the narrow gangway, who did not understand why they should be held up on their way toward the excitements of the menagerie, made it impossible for anyone to stand gazing quietly for any length of time. And that was the reason why the hunger artist, who had of course been looking forward to these visiting hours as the main achievement of his life, began instead to shrink from them. At first he could hardly wait for the intervals; it was exhilarating to watch the crowds come streaming his way, until only too soon—not even the most obstinate self-deception, clung to almost consciously, could hold out against the fact—the conviction was borne in upon him that these people, most of them, to judge from their actions, again and again, without exception, were all on their way to the menagerie. And the first sight of them from the distance remained the best. For when they reached his cage he was at once deafened by the storm of shouting and abuse that arose from the two contending factions, which renewed themselves continuously, of those who wanted to stop and stare at him—he soon began to dislike them more than the others—not out of real interest but only out of obstinate self-assertiveness, and those who wanted to go straight on to the animals. When the first great rush was past, the stragglers came along, and these, whom nothing could have prevented from stopping to look at him as long as they had breath, raced past with long strides, hardly even glancing at him, in their haste to get to the menagerie in time. And all too rarely did it happen that he had a stroke of luck, when some father of a family fetched up before him with his children, pointed a finger at the hunger artist and explained at length what the phenomenon meant, telling stories of earlier years when he himself had watched similar but much more thrilling performances, and the children, still rather uncomprehending, since neither inside nor outside school had they been sufficiently prepared for this lesson—what did they care about fasting?—yet showed by the brightness of their intent eyes that new and better times might be coming. Perhaps, said the hunger artist to himself many a time, things would be a little better if his cage were set not quite so near the menagerie. That made it too easy for people to make their choice, to say nothing of what he suffered from the stench of the menagerie, the animals' restlessness by night, the carrying past of raw lumps of flesh for the beasts of prey, the roaring at feeding times, which depressed him continually. But he did not dare to lodge a complaint with the management; after all, he had the animals to thank for the troops of people who passed his cage, among whom there might always be one here and there to take an interest in him, and who could tell where they might seclude him if he called attention to his existence and thereby to the fact that, strictly speaking, he was only an impediment on the way to the menagerie.

A small impediment, to be sure, one that grew steadily less. People grew familiar with the strange idea that they could be expected, in times like these, to take an interest in a hunger artist, and with this familiarity the verdict went out against him. He might fast as much as he could, and he did so; but nothing could save him now, people passed him by. Just try to explain to anyone the art of fasting! Anyone who has no feeling for it cannot be made to understand it. The fine placards grew dirty and illegible, they were torn down; the little notice board telling the number of fast days achieved, which at first was changed carefully every day, had long stayed at the same figure, for after the first few weeks even this small task seemed pointless to the staff; and so the artist simply fasted on and on, as he had once dreamed of doing, and it was no trouble to him, just as he had always foretold, but no one counted the days, no one, not even the artist himself, knew what records he was already breaking, and his heart grew heavy. And when once in a time some leisurely passer-by stopped, made merry over the old figure on the board and spoke of swindling, that was in its way the stupidest lie ever invented by indifference and inborn malice, since it was not the hunger artist who was cheating; he was working honestly, but the world was cheating him of his reward.

M ANY more days went by, however, and that too came to an end. An overseer's eye fell on the cage one day and asked the attendants why this perfectly good cage should be left standing there unused with dirty straw inside it; nobody knew, until one man, helped out by the notice board, remembered about the hunger artist. They poked into the straw with sticks and found him in it. "Are you still fasting?" asked the overseer. "When on earth do you mean to stop?" "Forgive me, everybody," whispered the hunger artist; only the overseer, who had his ear to the bars, understood him. "Of course," said the overseer, and tapped his forehead with a finger to let the attendants know what state the man was in, "we forgive you." "I always wanted you to admire my fasting," said the hunger artist. "We do admire it," said the overseer, affably. "But you shouldn't admire it," said the hunger artist. "Well, then we don't admire it," said the overseer, "but why shouldn't we admire it?" "Because I have to fast, I can't help it," said the hunger artist. "What a fellow you are," said the overseer, "and why can't you help it?" "Because," said the hunger artist, lifting his head a little and speaking, with his lips pursed, as if for a kiss, right into the overseer's ear, so that no syllable might be lost, "because I couldn't find the food I liked. If I had found it, believe me, I should have made no fuss and stuffed myself like you or anyone else." These were his last words, but in his dimming eyes remained the firm though no longer proud persuasion that he was still continuing to fast.

"Well, clear this out now!" said the overseer, and they buried the hunger artist, straw and all. Into the cage they put a young panther. Even the most insensitive felt it refreshing to see this wild creature leaping around the cage that had so long been dreary. The panther was all right. The food he liked was brought him without hesitation by the attendants; he seemed not even to miss his freedom; his noble body, furnished almost to the bursting point with all that it needed, seemed to carry freedom around with it too; somewhere in his jaws it seemed to lurk; and the joy of life streamed with such ardent passion from his throat that for the onlookers it was not easy to stand the shock of it. But they braced themselves, crowded round the cage, and did not want ever to move away.

Questions

1. *Many readers interpret this story as a parable of the artist in the modern world, while others see it as a religious parable. What evidence do you find in the story to support either reading? Why would Kafka select an expert in fasting rather than someone (say, a singer or a priest) whose profession would make the story clearer?* 2. *What is the hunger artist's relationship to his audiences? Even though his greatest achievements involve a deep inwardness and withdrawal, why does he nevertheless seem to need the audiences?* 3. *How does Kafka manage to achieve such a bizarre and dreamlike effect with dry and factual prose?* 4. *Should the hunger artist be admired for his passionate and single-minded devotion to his art or condemned for his withdrawal from humanity and his sickness of will? Why? In this connection, what is the significance of the panther put in the cage after the artist's death?*

The Man Who Lived Underground

RICHARD WRIGHT   [1908–1960]

I'VE got to hide, he told himself. His chest heaved as he waited, crouching in a dark corner of the vestibule. He was tired of running and dodging. Either he had to find a place to hide, or he had to surrender. A police car swished by through the rain, its siren rising sharply. They're looking for me all over . . . He crept to the door and squinted through the fogged plate glass. He stiffened as the siren rose and died in the distance. Yes, he had to hide, but where? He gritted his teeth. Then a sudden movement in the street caught his attention. A throng of tiny columns of water snaked into the air from the perforations of a manhole cover. The columns stopped abruptly, as though the perforations had become clogged; a gray spout of sewer water jutted up from underground and lifted the circular metal cover, juggled it for a moment, then let it fall with a clang.

He hatched a tentative plan: he would wait until the siren sounded far off, then he would go out. He smoked and waited, tense. At last the siren gave him his signal; it wailed, dying, going away from him. He stepped to the sidewalk, then paused and looked curiously at the open manhole, half expecting the cover to leap up again. He went to the center of the street and stooped and peered into the hole, but could see nothing. Water rustled in the black depths.

He started with terror; the siren sounded so near that he had the idea that he had been dreaming and had awakened to find the car upon him. He dropped instinctively to his knees and his hands grasped the rim of the manhole. The siren seemed to hoot directly above him and with a wild gasp of exertion he snatched the cover far enough off to admit his body. He swung his legs over the opening and lowered himself into watery darkness. He hung for an eternal moment to the rim by his finger tips, then he felt rough metal prongs and at once he knew that sewer workmen used these ridges to lower themselves into manholes. Fist over fist, he let his body sink until he could feel no more prongs. He swayed in dank space; the siren seemed to howl at the very rim of the manhole. He dropped and was washed violently into an ocean of warm, leaping water. His head was battered against a wall and he wondered if this were death. Frenziedly his fingers clawed and sank into a crevice. He steadied himself and measured the strength of the current with his own muscular tension. He stood slowly in water that dashed past his knees with fearful velocity.

He heard a prolonged scream of brakes and the siren broke off. Oh, God! They had found him! Looming above his head in the rain a white face hovered over the hole. "How did this damn thing get off?" he heard a policeman ask. He saw the steel cover move slowly until the hole looked like a quarter moon turned black. "Give me a hand here," someone called. The cover clanged into place, muffling the sights and sounds of the upper world. Knee-deep in the pulsing current, he breathed with aching chest, filling his lungs with the hot stench of yeasty rot.

From the perforations of the manhole cover, delicate lances of hazy violet sifted down and wove a mottled pattern upon the surface of the streaking current. His lips parted as a car swept past along the wet pavement overhead, its heavy rumble soon dying out, like the hum of a plane speeding through a dense cloud. He had never thought that cars could sound like that; everything seemed strange and unreal under here. He stood in darkness for a long time, knee-deep in rustling water, musing.

The odor of rot had become so general that he no longer smelled it. He got his cigarettes, but discovered that his matches were wet. He searched and found a dry folder in the pocket of his shirt and managed to strike one; it flared weirdly in the wet gloom, glowing greenishly, turning red, orange, then yellow. He lit a crumpled cigarette; then, by the flickering light of the match, he looked for support so that he would not have to keep his muscles flexed against the pouring water. His pupils narrowed and he saw to either side of him two steaming walls that rose and curved inward some six feet above his head to form a dripping, mouse-colored dome. The bottom of the sewer was a sloping V-trough. To the left, the sewer vanished in ashen fog. To the right was a steep down-curve into which water plunged.

He saw now that had he not regained his feet in time, he would have been swept to death, or had he entered any other manhole he would have probably drowned. Above the rush of the current he heard sharper juttings of water; tiny streams were spewing into the sewer from smaller conduits. The match died; he struck another and saw a mass of debris sweep past him and clog the throat of the down-curve. At once the water begain rising rapidly. Could he climb out before he drowned? A long hiss sounded and the debris was sucked from sight; the current lowered. He understood now what had made the water toss the manhole cover; the down-curve had become tempo-rarily obstructed and the perforations had become clogged.

He was in danger; he might slide into a down-curve; he might wander with a lighted match into a pocket of gas and blow himself up; or he might contract some horrible disease . . . Though he wanted to leave, an irrational impulse held him rooted. To the left, the convex ceiling swooped to a height of less than five feet. With cigarette slanting from pursed lips, he waded with taut muscles, his feet sloshing over the slimy bottom, his shoes sinking into spongy slop, the slate-colored water cracking in creamy foam against his knees. Pressing his flat left palm against the lowered ceiling, he struck another match and saw a metal pole nestling in a niche of the wall. Yes, some sewer workman had left it. He reached for it, then jerked his head away as a whisper of scurrying life whisked past and was still. He held the match close and saw a huge rat, wet with slime, blinking beady eyes and baring tiny fangs. The light blinded the rat and the frizzled head moved aimlessly. He grabbed the pole and let it fly against the rat's soft body; there was shrill piping and the grizzly body splashed into the dun-colored water and was snatched out of sight, spinning in the scuttling stream.

He swallowed and pushed on, following the curve of the misty cavern, sounding the water with the pole. By the faint light of another manhole cover he saw, amid loose wet brick, a hole with walls of damp earth leading into blackness. Gingerly he poked the pole into it; it was hollow and went beyond the length of the pole. He shoved the pole before him, hoisted himself upward, got to his hands and knees, and crawled. After a few yards he paused, struck to wonderment by the silence; it seemed that he had traveled a million miles away from the world. As he inched forward again he could sense the bottom of the dirt tunnel becoming dry and lowering slightly. Slowly he rose and to his astonishment he stood erect. He could not hear the rustling of the water now and he felt confoundingly alone, yet lured by the darkness and silence.

He crept a long way, then stopped, curious, afraid. He put his right foot forward and it dangled in space; he drew back in fear. He thrust the pole outward and it swung in emptiness. He trembled, imagining the earth crumbling and burying him alive. He scratched a match and saw that the dirt floor sheered away steeply and widened into a sort of cave some five feet below him. An old sewer, he muttered. He cocked his head, hearing a feathery cadence which he could not identify. The match ceased to burn.

Using the pole as a kind of ladder, he slid down and stood in darkness. The air was a little fresher and he could still hear vague noises. Where was he? He felt suddenly that someone was standing near him and he turned sharply, but there was only darkness. He poked cautiously and felt a brick wall; he followed it and the strange sounds grew louder. He ought to get out of here. This was crazy. He could not remain here for any length of time; there was no food and no place to sleep. But the faint sounds tantalized him; they were strange but familiar. Was it a motor? A baby crying? Music? A siren? He groped on, and the sounds came so clearly that he could feel the pitch and timbre of human voices. Yes, singing! That was it! He listened with open mouth. It was a church service. Enchanted, he groped toward the waves of melody.

> *Jesus, take me to your home above*
> *And fold me in the bosom of Thy love . . .*

The singing was on the other side of the brick wall. Excited, he wanted to watch the service without being seen. Whose church was it? He knew most of the churches in this area above ground, but the singing sounded too strange and detached for him to guess. He looked to the left, to the right, down to the black dirt, then upward and was startled to see a bright sliver of light slicing the darkness like the blade of a razor. He struck one of his two remaining matches and saw rusty pipes running along an old concrete ceiling. Photographically he located the exact position of the pipes in his mind. The match flame sank and he sprang upward; his hands clutched a pipe. He swung his legs and tossed his body onto the bed of pipes and they creaked, swaying up and down; he thought that the tier was about to crash, but nothing happened. He edged to the crevice and saw a segment of black men and women, dressed in white robes, singing, holding tattered songbooks in their black palms. His first impulse was to laugh, but he checked himself.

What was he doing? He was crushed with a sense of guilt. Would God strike him dead for that? The singing swept on and he shook his head, disagreeing in spite of himself. They oughtn't to do that, he thought. But he could think of no reason *why* they should not do it. Just singing with the air of the sewer blowing in on them . . . He felt that he was gazing upon something abysmally obscene, yet he could not bring himself to leave.

After a long time he grew numb and dropped to the dirt. Pain throbbed in his legs and a deeper pain, induced by the sight of those black people groveling and begging for something they could never get, churned in him. A vague conviction made him feel that those people should stand unrepentant and yield no quarter in singing and praying, yet *he* had run away from the police, had pleaded with them to believe in *his* innocence. He shook his head, bewildered.

How long had he been down here? He did not know. This was a new kind of living for him; the intensity of feelings he had experienced when looking at the church people sing made him certain that he had been down here a long time, but his mind told him that the time must have been short. In this darkness the only notion he had of time was when a match flared and measured time by its fleeting light. He groped back through the hole toward the sewer and the waves of song subsided and finally he could not hear them at all. He came to where the earth hole ended and he heard the noise of the current and time lived again for him, measuring the moments by the wash of the water.

The rain must have slackened, for the flow of water had lessened and came only to his ankles. Ought he to go up into the streets and take his chances on hiding somewhere else? But they would surely catch him. The mere thought of dodging and running again from the police made him tense. No, he would stay and plot how to elude them. But what could he do down here? He walked forward into the sewer and came to another manhole cover; he stood beneath it, debating. Fine pencils of gold spilled suddenly from the little circles in the manhole cover and trembled on the surface of the current. Yes, street lamps . . . It must be night . . .

He went forward for about a quarter of an hour, wading aimlessly, poking the pole carefully before him. Then he stopped, his eyes fixed and intent. What's that? A strangely familiar image attracted and repelled him. Lit by the yellow stems from another manhole cover was a tiny nude body of a baby snagged by debris and half-submerged in water. Thinking that the baby was alive, he moved impulsively to save it, but his roused feelings told him that it was dead, cold, nothing, the same nothingness he had felt while watching the men and women singing in the church. Water blossomed about the tiny legs, the tiny arms, the tiny head, and rushed onward. The eyes were closed, as though in sleep; the fists were clenched, as though in protest; and the mouth gaped black in a soundless cry.

He straightened and drew in his breath, feeling that he had been staring for all eternity at the ripples of veined water skimming impersonally over the shriveled limbs. He felt as condemned as when the policemen had accused him. Involuntarily he lifted his hand to brush the vision away, but his arm fell listlessly to his side. Then he acted; he closed his eyes and reached forward slowly with the soggy shoe of his right foot and shoved the dead baby from where it had been lodged. He kept his eyes closed, seeing the little body twisting in the current as it floated from sight. He opened his eyes, shivered, placed his knuckles in the sockets, hearing the water speed in the somber shadows.

He tramped on, sensing at times a sudden quickening in the current as he passed some conduit whose waters were swelling the stream that slid by his feet. A few minutes later he was standing under another manhole cover, listening to the faint rumble of noises above ground. Streetcars and trucks, he mused. He looked down and saw a stagnant pool of gray-green sludge; at intervals a balloon pocket rose from the scum, glistening a bluish-purple, and burst. Then another. He turned, shook his head, and tramped back to the dirt cave by the church, his lips quivering.

Back in the cave, he sat and leaned his back against a dirt wall. His body was trembling slightly. Finally his senses quieted and he slept. When he awakened he felt stiff and cold. He had to leave this foul place, but leaving meant facing those policemen who had wrongly accused him. No, he could not go back aboveground. He remembered the beating they had given him and how he had signed his name to a confession, a confession which he had not even read. He had been too tired when they had shouted at him, demanding that he sign his name; he had signed it to end his pain.

He stood and groped about in the darkness. The church singing had stopped. How long had he slept? He did not know. But he felt refreshed and hungry. He doubled his fist nervously, realizing that he could not make a decison. As he walked about he stumbled over an old rusty iron pipe. He picked it up and felt a jagged edge. Yes, there was a brick wall and he could dig into it. What would he find? Smiling, he groped to the brick wall, sat, and began digging idly into damp cement. I can't make any noise, he cautioned himself. As time passed he grew thirsty, but there was no water. He had to kill time or go aboveground. The cement came out of the wall easily; he extracted four bricks and felt a soft draft blowing into his face. He stopped, afraid. What was beyond? He waited a long time and nothing happened; then he began digging again, soundlessly, slowly; he enlarged the hole and crawled through into a dark room and collided with another wall. He felt his way to the right; the wall ended and his fingers toyed in space, like the antennae of an insect.

He fumbled on and his feet struck something hollow, like wood. What's this? He felt with his fingers. Steps . . . He stooped and pulled off his shoes and mounted the stairs and saw a yellow chink of light shining and heard a low voice speaking. He placed his eye to a keyhole and saw the nude waxen figure of a man stretched out upon a white table. The voice, low-pitched and vibrant, mumbled indistinguishable words, neither rising nor falling. He craned his neck and squinted to see the man who was talking, but he could not locate him. Above the naked figure was suspended a huge glass container filled with a blood-red liquid from which a white rubber tube dangled. He crouched closer to the door and saw the tip end of a black object lined with pink satin. A coffin, he breathed. This is an undertaker's establishment . . . A fine-spun lace of ice covered his body and he shuddered. A throaty chuckle sounded in the depths of the yellow room.

He turned to leave. Three steps down it occurred to him that a light switch should be nearby; he felt along the wall, found an electric button, pressed it, and a blinding glare smote his pupils so hard that he was sightless, defenseless. His pupils contracted and he wrinkled his nostrils at a peculiar odor. At once he knew that he had been dimly aware of this odor in the darkness, but the light had brought it sharply to his attention. Some kind of stuff they use to embalm, he thought. He went down the steps and saw piles of lumber, coffins, and a long workbench. In one corner was a tool chest. Yes, he could use tools, could tunnel through walls with them. He lifted the lid of the chest and saw nails, a hammer, a crowbar, a screwdriver, a light bulb, and a long length of electric wire. Good! He would lug these back to his cave.

He was about to hoist the chest to his shoulders when he discovered a door behind the furnace. Where did it lead? He tried to open it and found it securely bolted. Using the crowbar so as to make no sound, he pried the door open; it swung on creaking hinges, outward. Fresh air came to his face and he caught the faint roar of faraway sound. Easy now, he told himself. He widened the door and a lump of coal rattled toward him. A coalbin . . . Evidently the door led into another basement. The roaring noise was louder now, but he could not identify it. Where was he? He groped slowly over the coal pile, then ranged in darkness over a gritty floor. The roaring noise seemed to come from above him, then below. His fingers followed a wall until he touched a wooden ridge. A door, he breathed.

The noise died to a low pitch; he felt his skin prickle. It seemed that he was playing a game with an unseen person whose intelligence outstripped his. He put his ear to the flat surface of the door. Yes, voices . . . Was this a prize fight stadium? The sound of the voices came near and sharp, but he could not tell if they were joyous or despairing. He twisted the knob until he heard a soft click and felt the springy weight of the door swinging toward him. He was afraid to open it, yet captured by curiosity and wonder. He jerked the door wide and saw on the far side of the basement a furnace glowing red. Ten feet away was still another door, half ajar. He crossed and peered through the door into an empty, high-ceilinged corridor that terminated in a dark complex of shadow. The belling voices rolled about him and his eagerness mounted. He stepped into the corridor and the voices swelled louder. He crept on and came to a narrow stairway leading circularly upward; there was no question but that he was going to ascend those stairs.

Mounting the spiraled staircase, he heard the voices roll in a steady wave, then leap to crescendo, only to die away, but always remaining audible. Ahead of him glowed red letters: E—X—I—T. At the top of the steps he paused in front of a black curtain that fluttered uncertainly. He parted the folds and looked into a convex depth that gleamed with clusters of shimmering lights. Sprawled below him was a stretch of human faces, tilted upward, chanting, whistling, screaming, laughing. Dangling before the faces, high upon a screen of silver, were jerking shadows. A movie, he said with slow laughter breaking from his lips.

He stood in a box in the reserved section of a movie house and the impulse he had had to tell the people in the church to stop their singing seized him. These people were laughing at their lives, he thought with amazement. They were shouting and yelling at the animated shadows of themselves. His compassion fired his imagination and he stepped out of the box, walked out upon thin air, walked on down to the audience; and, hovering in the air just above them, he stretched out his hand to touch them . . . His tension snapped and he found himself back in the box, looking down into the sea of faces. No; it could not be done; he could not awaken them. He sighed. Yes, these people were children, sleeping in their living, awake in their dying.

He turned away, parted the black curtain, and looked out. He saw no one. He started down the white stone steps and when he reached the bottom he saw a man in trim blue uniform coming toward him. So used had he become to being underground that he thought that he could walk past the man, as though he were a ghost. But the man stopped. And he stopped.

"Looking for the men's room, sir?" the man asked, and, without waiting for an answer, he turned and pointed. "This way, sir. The first door to your right."

He watched the man turn and walk up the steps and go out of sight. Then he laughed. What a funny fellow! He went back to the basement and stood in the red darkness, watching the glowing embers in the furnace. He went to the sink and turned the faucet and the water flowed in a smooth silent stream that looked like a spout of blood. He brushed the mad image from his mind and began to wash his hands leisurely, looking about for the usual bar of soap. He found one and rubbed it in his palms until a rich lather bloomed in his cupped fingers, like a scarlet sponge. He scrubbed and rinsed his hands meticulously, then hunted for a towel; there was none. He shut off the water, pulled off his shirt, dried his hands on it; when he put it on again he was grateful for the cool dampness that came to his skin.

Yes, he was thirsty; he turned on the faucet again, bowled his fingers and when the water bubbled over the brim of his cupped palms, he drank in long, slow swallows. His bladder grew tight; he shut off the water, faced the wall, bent his head, and watched a red stream strike the floor. His nostrils wrinkled against acrid wisps of vapor; though he had tramped in the waters of the sewer, he stepped back from the wall so that his shoes, wet with sewer slime, would not touch his urine.

He heard footsteps and crawled quickly into the coalbin. Lumps rattled noisily. The footsteps came into the basement and stopped. Who was it? Had someone heard him and come down to investigate? He waited, crouching, sweating. For a long time there was silence, then he heard the clang of metal and a brighter glow lit the room. Somebody's tending the furnace, he thought. Footsteps came closer and he stiffened. Looming before him was a white face lined with coal dust, the face of an old man with watery blue eyes. Highlights spotted his gaunt cheekbones, and he held a huge shovel. There was a screechy scrape of metal against stone, and the old man lifted a shovelful of coal and went from sight.

The room dimmed momentarily, then a yellow glare came as coal flared at the furnace door. Six times the old man came to the bin and went to the furnace with shovels of coal, but not once did he lift his eyes. Finally he dropped the shovel, mopped his face with a dirty handkerchief, and sighed: "Wheeew!" He turned slowly and trudged out of the basement, his footsteps dying away.

He stood, and lumps of coal clattered down the pile. He stepped from the bin and was startled to see the shadowy outline of an electric bulb hanging above his head. Why had not the old man turned it on? Oh, yes . . . He understood. The old man had worked here for so long that he had no need for light; he had learned a way of seeing in his dark world, like those sightless worms that inch along underground by a sense of touch.

His eyes fell upon a lunch pail and he was afraid to hope that it was full. He picked it up; it was heavy. He opened it. *Sandwiches!* He looked guiltily around; he was alone. He searched farther and found a folder of matches and a half-empty tin of tobacco; he put them eagerly into his pocket and clicked off the light. With the lunch pail under his arm, he went through the door, groped over the pile of coal, and stood again in the lighted basement of the undertaking establishment. I've got to get those tools, he told himself. And turn off that light. He tiptoed back up the steps and switched off the light; the invisible voice still droned on behind the door. He crept down and, seeing with his fingers, opened the lunch pail and tore off a piece of paper bag and brought out the tin and spilled grains of tobacco into the makeshift concave. He rolled it and wet it with spittle, then inserted one end into his mouth and lit it: he sucked smoke that bit his lungs. The nicotine reached his brain, went out along his arms to his finger tips, down to his stomach, and over all the tired nerves of his body.

He carted the tools to the hole he had made in the wall. Would the noise of the falling chest betray him? But he would have to take a chance; he had to have those tools. He lifted the chest and shoved it; it hit the dirt on the other side of the wall with a loud clatter. He waited, listening; nothing happened. Head first, he slithered through and stood in the cave. He grinned, filled with a cunning idea. Yes, he would now go back into the basement of the undertaking establishment and crouch behind the coal pile and dig another hole. Sure! Fumbling, he opened the tool chest and extracted a crowbar, a screwdriver, and a hammer; he fastened them securely about his person.

With another lumpish cigarette in his flexed lips, he crawled back through the hole and over the coal pile and sat, facing the brick wall. He jabbed with the crowbar and the cement sheered away; quicker than he thought, a brick came loose. He worked an hour; the other bricks did not come easily. He sighed, weak from effort. I ought to rest a little, he thought. I'm hungry. He felt his way back to the cave and stumbled along the wall till he came to the tool chest. He sat upon it, opened the lunch pail, and took out two thick sandwiches. He smelled them. Pork chops . . . His mouth watered. He closed his eyes and devoured a sandwich, savoring the smooth rye bread and juicy meat. He ate rapidly, gulping down lumpy mouthfuls that made him long for water. He ate the other sandwich and found an apple and gobbled that up too, sucking the core till the last trace of flavor was drained from it. Then, like a dog, he ground the meat bones with his teeth, enjoying the salty, tangy marrow. He finished and stretched out full length on the ground and went to sleep. . . .

. . . His body was washed by cold water that gradually turned warm and he was buoyed upon a stream and swept out to sea where waves rolled gently and suddenly he found himself walking upon the water how strange and delightful to walk upon the water and he came upon a nude woman holding a nude baby in her arms and the woman was sinking into the water holding the baby above her head and screaming *help* and he ran over the water to the woman and he reached her just before she went down and he took the baby from her hands and stood watching the breaking bubbles where the woman sank and he called *lady* and still no answer yes dive down there and rescue that woman but he could not take this baby with him and he stooped and laid the baby tenderly upon the surface of the water expecting it to sink but it floated and he leaped into the water and held his breath and strained his eyes to see through the gloomy volume of water but there was no woman and he opened his mouth and called *lady* and the water bubbled and his chest ached and his arms were tired but he could not see the woman and he called again *lady lady* and his feet touched sand at the bottom of the sea and his chest felt as though it would burst and he bent his knees and propelled himself upward and water rushed past him and his head bobbed out and he breathed deeply and looked around where was the baby the baby was gone and he rushed over the water looking for the baby calling *where is it* and the empty sky and sea threw back his voice *where is it* and he began to doubt that he could stand upon the water and then he was sinking and as he struggled the water rushed him downward spinning dizzily and he opened his mouth to call for help and water surged into his lungs and he choked . . .

He groaned and leaped erect in the dark, his eyes wide. The images of terror that thronged his brain would not let him sleep. He rose, made sure that the tools were hitched to his belt, and groped his way to the coal pile and found the rectangular gap from which he had taken the bricks. He took out the crowbar and hacked. Then dread paralyzed him. How long had he slept? Was it day or night now? He had to be careful. Someone might hear him if it were day. He hewed softly for hours at the cement, working silently. Faintly quivering in the air above him was the dim sound of yelling voices. Crazy people, he muttered. They're still there in that movie . . .

Having rested, he found the digging much easier. He soon had a dozen bricks out. His spirits rose. He took out another brick and his fingers fluttered in space. Good! What lay ahead of him? Another basement? He made the hole larger, climbed through, walked over an uneven floor and felt a metal surface. He lighted a match and saw that he was standing behind a furnace in a basement; before him, on the far side of the room, was a door. He crossed and opened it; it was full of odds and ends. Daylight spilled from a window above his head.

Then he was aware of a soft, continuous tapping. What was it? A clock? No, it was louder than a clock and more irregular. He placed an old empty box beneath the window, stood upon it, and looked into an areaway. He eased the window up and crawled through; the sound of the tapping came clearly now. He glanced about; he was alone. Then he looked upward at a series of window ledges. The tapping identified itself. That's a typewriter, he said to himself. It seemed to be coming from just above. He grasped the ridges of a rain pipe and lifted himself upward; through a half-inch opening of window he saw a door-knob about three feet away. No, it was not a doorknob; it was a small circular disk made of stainless steel with many fine markings upon it. He held his breath; an eerie white hand, seemingly detached from its arm, touched the metal knob and whirled it, first to the left, then to the right. It's a safe! . . . Suddenly he could see the dial no more; a huge metal door swung slowly toward him and he was looking into a safe filled with green wads of paper money, rows of coins wrapped in brown paper, and glass jars and boxes of various sizes. His heart quickened. Good Lord! The white hand went in and out of the safe, taking wads of bills and cylinders of coins. The hand vanished and he heard the muffled click of the big door as it closed. Only the steel dial was visible now. The typewriter still tapped in his ears, but he could not see it. He blinked, wondering if what he had seen was real. There was more money in that safe than he had seen in all his life.

As he clung to the rain pipe, a daring idea came to him and he pulled the screwdriver from his belt. If the white hand twirled that dial again, he would be able to see how far to left and right it spun and he would have the combination! His blood tingled. I can scratch the numbers right here, he thought. Holding the pipe with one hand, he made the sharp edge of the screwdriver bite into the brick wall. Yes, he could do it. Now, he was set. Now, he had a reason for staying here in the underground. He waited for a long time, but the white hand did not return. Goddamn! Had he been more alert, he could have counted the twirls and he would have had the combination. He got down and stood in the areaway, sunk in reflection.

How could he get into that room? He climbed back into the basement and saw wooden steps leading upward. Was that the room where the safe stood? Fearing that the dial was now being twirled, he clambered through the window, hoisted himself up the rain pipe, and peered; he saw only the naked gleam of the steel dial. He got down and doubled his fists. Well, he would explore the basement. He returned to the basement room and mounted the steps to the door and squinted through the keyhole; all was dark, but the tapping was still somewhere near, still faint and directionless. He pushed the door in; along one wall of a room was a table piled with radios and electrical equipment. A radio shop, he muttered.

Well, he could rig up a radio in his cave. He found a sack, slid the radio into it, and slung it across his back. Closing the door, he went down the steps and stood again in the basement, disappointed. He had not solved the problem of the steel dial and he was irked. He set the radio on the floor and again hoisted himself through the window and up the rain pipe and squinted; the metal door was swinging shut. Goddamn! He's worked the combination again. If I had been patient, I'd have had it! How could he get into that room? He *had* to get into it. He could jimmy the window, but it would be much better if he could get in without any traces. To the right of him, he calculated, should be the basement of the building that held the safe; therefore, if he dug a hole right *here,* he ought to reach his goal.

He began a quiet scraping; it was hard work, for the bricks were not damp. He eventually got one out and lowered it softly to the floor. He had to be careful; perhaps people were beyond this wall. He extracted a second layer of brick and found still another. He gritted his teeth, ready to quit. I'll dig one more, he resolved. When the next brick came out he felt air blowing into his face. He waited to be challenged, but nothing happened.

He enlarged the hole and pulled himself through and stood in quiet darkness. He scratched a match to flame and saw steps; he mounted and peered through a keyhole; Darkness . . . He strained to hear the typewriter, but there was only silence. Maybe the office had closed? He twisted the knob and swung the door in; a frigid blast made him shiver. In the shadows before him were halves and quarters of hogs and lambs and steers hanging from metal hooks on the low ceiling, red meat encased in folds of cold white fat. Fronting him was frost-coated glass from behind which came indistinguishable sounds. The odor of fresh raw meat sickened him and he backed away. A meat market, he whispered.

He ducked his head, suddenly blinded by light. He narrowed his eyes; the red-white rows of meat were drenched in yellow glare. A man wearing a crimson spotted jacket came in and took down a bloody meat cleaver. He eased the door to, holding it ajar just enough to watch the man, hoping that the darkness in which he stood would keep him from being seen. The man took down a hunk of steer and placed it upon a bloody wooden block and bent forward and whacked with the cleaver. The man's face was hard, square, grim; a jet of mustache smudged his upper lip and a glistening cowlick of hair fell over his left eye. Each time he lifted the cleaver and brought it down upon the meat, he let out a short, deep-chested grunt. After he had cut the meat, he wiped blood off the wooden block with a sticky wad of gunny sack and hung the cleaver upon a hook. His face was proud as he placed the chunk of meat in the crook of his elbow and left.

The door slammed and the light went off; once more he stood in shadow. His tension ebbed. From behind the frosted glass he heard the man's voice: "Forty-eight cents a pound, ma'am." He shuddered, feeling that there was something he had to do. But what? He stared fixedly at the cleaver, then he sneezed and was terrified for fear that the man had heard him. But the door did not open. He took down the cleaver and examined the sharp edge smeared with cold blood. Behind the ice-coated glass a cash register rang with a vibrating, musical tinkle.

Absent-mindedly holding the meat cleaver, he rubbed the glass with his thumb and cleared a spot that enabled him to see into the front of the store. The shop was empty, save for the man who was now putting on his hat and coat. Beyond the front window a wan sun shone in the streets; people passed and now and then a fragment of laughter or the whir of a speeding auto came to him. He peered closer and saw on the right counter of the shop a mosquito netting covering pears, grapes, lemons, oranges, bananas, peaches, and plums. His stomach contracted.

The man clicked out the light and he gritted his teeth, muttering, Don't lock the icebox door . . . The man went through the door of the shop and locked it from the outside. Thank God! Now, he would eat some more! He waited, trembling. The sun died and its rays lingered on in the sky, turning the streets to dusk. He opened the door and stepped inside the shop. In reverse letters across the front window was: NICK'S FRUITS AND MEATS. He laughed, picked up a soft ripe yellow pear and bit into it; juice squirted; his mouth ached as his saliva glands reacted to the acid of the fruit. He ate three pears, gobbled six bananas, and made away with several oranges, taking a bite out of their tops and holding them to his lips and squeezing them as he hungrily sucked the juice.

He found a faucet, turned it on, laid the cleaver aside, pursed his lips under the stream until his stomach felt about to burst. He straightened and belched, feeling satisfied for the first time since he had been underground. He sat upon the floor, rolled and lit a cigarette, his bloodshot eyes squinting against the film of drifting smoke. He watched a patch of sky turn red, then purple; night fell and he lit another cigarette, brooding. Some part of him was trying to remember the world he had left, and another part of him did not want to remember it. Sprawling before him in his mind was his wife, Mrs. Wooten for whom he worked, the three policemen who had picked him up . . . He possessed them now more completely than he had ever possessed them when he had lived aboveground. How this had come about he could not say, but he had no desire to go back to them. He laughed, crushed the cigarette, and stood up.

He went to the front door and gazed out. Emotionally he hovered between the world aboveground and the world underground. He longed to go out, but sober judgment urged him to remain here. Then impulsively he pried the lock loose with one swift twist of the crowbar; the door swung outward. Through the twilight he saw a white man and a white woman coming toward him. He held himself tense, waiting for them to pass; but they came directly to the door and confronted him.

"I want to buy a pound of grapes," the woman said.

Terrified, he stepped back into the store. The white man stood to one side and the woman entered.

"Give me a pound of dark ones," the woman said.

The white man came slowly forward, blinking his eyes.

"Where's Nick?" the man asked.

"Were you just closing?" the woman asked.

"Yes, ma'am," he mumbled. For a second he did not breathe, then he mumbled again: "Yes, ma'am."

"I'm sorry," the woman said.

The street lamps came on, lighting the store somewhat. Ought he run? But that would raise an alarm. He moved slowly, dreamily, to a counter and lifted up a bunch of grapes and showed them to the woman.

"Fine," the woman said. "But isn't that more than a pound?"

He did not answer. The man was staring at him intently.

"Put them in a bag for me," the woman said, fumbling with her purse.

"Yes, ma'am."

He saw a pile of paper bags under a narrow ledge; he opened one and put the grapes in.

"Thanks," the woman said, taking the bag and placing a dime in his dark palm.

"Where's Nick?" the man asked again. "At supper?"

"Sir? Yes, sir," he breathed.

They left the store and he stood trembling in the doorway. When they were out of sight, he burst out laughing and crying. A trolley car rolled noisily past and he controlled himself quickly. He flung the dime to the pavement with a gesture of contempt and stepped into the warm night air. A few shy stars trembled above him. The look of things was beautiful, yet he felt a lurking threat. He went to an unattended newsstand and looked at a stack of papers. He saw a headline: HUNT NEGRO FOR MURDER.

He felt that someone had slipped up on him from behind and was stripping off his clothes; he looked about wildly, went quickly back into the store, picked up the meat cleaver where he had left it near the sink, then made his way through the icebox to the basement. He stood for a long time, breathing heavily. They know I didn't do anything, he muttered. But how could he prove it? He had signed a confession. Though innocent, he felt guilty, condemned. He struck a match and held it near the steel blade, fascinated and repelled by the dried blotches of blood. Then his fingers gripped the handle of the cleaver with all the strength of his body, he wanted to fling the cleaver from him, but he could not. The match flame wavered and fled; he struggled through the hole and put the cleaver in the sack with the radio. He was determined to keep it, for what purpose he did not know.

He was about to leave when he remembered the safe. Where was it? He wanted to give up, but felt that he ought to make one more try. Opposite the last hole he had dug, he tunneled again, plying the crowbar. Once he was so exhausted that he lay on the concrete floor and panted. Finally he made another hole. He wriggled through and his nostrils filled with the fresh smell of coal. He struck a match; yes, the usual steps led upward. He tiptoed to a door and eased it open. A fair-haired white girl stood in front of a steel cabinet, her blue eyes wide upon him. She turned chalky and gave a high-pitched scream. He bounded down the steps and raced to his hole and clambered through, replacing the bricks with nervous haste. He paused, hearing loud voices.

"What's the matter, Alice?"

"A man . . ."

"What man? Where?"

"A man was at that door . . ."

"Oh, nonsense!"

"He was looking at me through the door!"

"Aw, you're dreaming."

"I *did* see a man!"

The girl was crying now.

"There's nobody here."

Another man's voice sounded.

"What is it, Bob?"

"Alice says she saw a man in here, in that door!"

"Let's take a look."

He waited, poised for flight. Footsteps descended the stairs.

"There's nobody down here."

"The window's locked."

"And there's no door."

"You ought to fire that dame."

"Oh, I don't know. Women are that way."

"She's too hysterical."

The men laughed. Footsteps sounded again on the stairs. A door slammed. He sighed, relieved that he had escaped. But he had not done what he had set out to do; his glimpse of the room had been too brief to determine if the safe was there. He had to know. Boldly he groped through the hole once more; he reached the steps and pulled off his shoes and tip-toed up and peered through the keyhole. His head accidentally touched the door and it swung silently in a fraction of an inch; he saw the girl bent over the cabinet, her back to him. Beyond her was the safe. He crept back down the steps, thinking exultingly: I found it!

Now he had to get the combination. Even if the window in the areaway was locked and bolted, he could gain entrance when the office closed. He scoured through the holes he had dug and stood again in the basement where he had left the radio and the cleaver. Again he crawled out of the window and lifted himself up the rain pipe and peered. The steel dial showed lonely and bright, reflecting the yellow glow of an unseen light. Resigned to a long wait, he sat and leaned against the wall. From far off came the faint sounds of life aboveground; once he looked with a baffled expression at the dark sky. Frequently he rose and climbed the pipe to see the white hand spin the dial, but nothing happened. He bit his lip with impatience. It was not the money that was luring him, but the mere fact that he could get it with impunity. Was the hand now twirling the dial? He rose and looked, but the white hand was not in sight.

Perhaps it would be better to watch continuously? Yes; he clung to the pipe and watched the dial until his eyes thickened with tears. Exhausted, he stood again in the areaway. He heard a door being shut and he clawed up the pipe and looked. He jerked tense as a vague figure passed in front of him. He stared unblinkingly, hugging the pipe with one hand and holding the screwdriver with the other, ready to etch the combination upon the wall. His ears caught: *Dong . . . Dong . . . Dong . . . Dong . . . Dong . . . Dong . . . Dong . . .* Seven o'clock, he whispered. Maybe they were closing now? What kind of a store would be open as late as this? he wondered. Did anyone live in the rear? Was there a night watchman? Perhaps the safe was *already* locked for the night! Goddamn! While he had been eating in that shop, they had locked up everything . . . Then, just as he was about to give up, the white hand touched the dial and turned it once to the right and stopped at six. With quivering fingers, he etched 1—R—6 upon the brick wall with the tip of the screwdriver. The hand twisted the dial twice to the left and stopped at two, and he engraved 2—L—2 upon the wall. The dial was spun four times to the right and stopped at six again; he wrote 4—R—6. The dial rotated three times to the left and was centered straight up and down; he wrote 3—L—0. The door swung open and again he saw the piles of green money and the rows of wrapped coins. I got it, he said grimly.

Then he was stone still, astonished. There were two hands now. A right hand lifted a wad of green bills and deftly slipped it up the sleeve of the left arm. The hands trembled; again the right hand slipped a packet of bills up the left sleeve. He's stealing he said to himself. He grew indignant, as if the money belonged to him. Though *he* had planned to steal the money, he despised and pitied the man. He felt that his stealing the money and the man's stealing were two entirely different things. He wanted to steal the money merely for the sensation involved in getting it, and he had no intention whatever of spending a penny of it; but he knew that the man who was now stealing it was going to spend it, perhaps for pleasure. The huge steel door closed with a soft click.

Though angry, he was somewhat satisfied. The office would close soon. I'll clean the place out, he mused. He imagined the entire office staff cringing with fear; the police would question everyone for a crime they had not committed, just as they had questioned him. And they would have no idea of how the money had been stolen until they discovered the holes he had tunneled in the walls of the basements. He lowered himself and laughed mischievously, with the abandoned glee of an adolescent.

He flattened himself against the wall as the window above him closed with rasping sound. He looked; somebody was bolting the window securely with a metal screen. That won't help you, he snickered to himself. He clung to the rain pipe until the yellow light in the office went out. He went back into the basement, picked up the sack containing the radio and cleaver, and crawled through the two holes he had dug and groped his way into the basement of the building that held the safe. He moved in slow motion, breathing softly. Be careful now, he told himself. There might be a night watchman ... In his memory was the combination written in bold white characters as upon a blackboard. Eel-like he squeezed through the last hole and crept up the steps and put his hand on the knob and pushed the door in about three inches. Then his courage ebbed; his imagination wove dangers for him.

Perhaps the night watchman was waiting in there, ready to shoot. He dangled his cap on a forefinger and poked it past the jamb of the door. If anyone fired, they would hit his cap; but nothing happened. He widened the door, holding the crowbar high above his head, ready to beat off an assailant. He stood like that for five minutes; the rumble of a streetcar brought him to himself. He entered the room. Moonlight floated in from a side window. He confronted the safe, then checked himself. Better take a look around first . . . He stepped about and found a closed door. Was the night watchman in there? He opened it and saw a washbowl, a faucet, and a commode. To the left was still another door that opened into a huge dark room that seemed empty; on the far side of that room he made out the shadow of still another door. Nobody's here, he told himself.

He turned back to the safe and fingered the dial; it spun with ease. He laughed and twirled it just for fun. Get to work, he told himself. He turned the dial to the figures he saw on the blackboard of his memory; it was so easy that he felt that the safe had not been locked at all. The heavy door eased loose and he caught hold of the handle and pulled hard, but the door swung open with a slow momentum of its own. Breathless, he gaped at wads of green bills, rows of wrapped coins, curious glass jars full of white pellets, and many oblong green metal boxes. He glanced guiltily over his shoulder; it seemed impossible that someone should not call to him to stop.

They'll be surprised in the morning, he thought. He opened the top of the sack and lifted a wad of compactly tied bills; the money was crisp and new. He admired the smooth, cleancut edges. The fellows in Washington sure know how to make this stuff, he mused. He rubbed the money with his fingers, as though expecting it to reveal hidden qualities. He lifted the wad to his nose and smelled the fresh odor of ink. Just like any other paper, he mumbled. He dropped the wad into the sack and picked up another. Holding the bag, he thought and laughed.

There was in him no sense of possessiveness; he was intrigued with the form and color of the money, with the manifold reactions which he knew that men aboveground held toward it. The sack was one-third full when it occurred to him to examine the denominations of the bills; without realizing it, he had put many wads of one-dollar bills into the sack. Aw, nuts, he said in disgust. Take the big ones . . . He dumped the one-dollar bills onto the floor and swept all the hundred-dollar bills he could find into the sack, then he raked in rolls of coins with crooked fingers.

He walked to a desk upon which sat a typewriter, the same machine which the blond girl had used. He was fascinated by it; never in his life had he used one of them. It was a queer instrument of business, something beyond the rim of his life. Whenever he had been in an office where a girl was typing, he had almost always spoken in whispers. Remembering vaguely what he had seen others do, he inserted a sheet of paper into the machine; it went in lop-sided and he did not know how to straighten it. Spelling in a soft diffident voice, he pecked out his name on the keys: *freddaniels.* He looked at it and laughed. He would learn to type correctly one of these days.

Yes, he would take the typewriter too. He lifted the machine and placed it atop the bulk of money in the sack. He did not feel that he was stealing, for the cleaver, the radio, the money, and the typewriter were all on the same level of value, all meant the same thing to him. They were the serious toys of the men who lived in the dead world of sunshine and rain he had left, the world that had condemned him, branded him guilty.

But what kind of a place is this? He wondered. What was in that dark room to his rear? He felt for his matches and found that he had only one left. He leaned the sack against the safe and groped forward into the room, en-countering smooth, metallic objects that felt like machines. Baffled, he touched a wall and tried vainly to locate an electric switch. Well, he *had* to strike his last match. He knelt and struck it, cupping the flame near the floor with his palms. The place seemed to be a factory, with benches and tables. There were bulbs with green shades spaced about the tables; he turned on a light and twisted it low so that the glare was limited. He saw a half-filled packet of cigarettes and appropriated it. There were stools at the benches and he con-cluded that men worked here at some trade. He wandered and found a few half-used folders of matches. If only he could find more cigarettes! But there were none.

But what kind of a place was this? On a bench he saw a pad of paper captioned: PEER'S—MANUFACTURING JEWELERS. His lips formed an "O," then he snapped off the light and ran back to the safe and lifted one of the glass jars and stared at the tiny white pellets. Gingerly he picked up one and found that it was wrapped in tissue paper. He peeled the paper and saw a glit-tering stone that looked like glass, glinting white and blue sparks. Diamonds, he breathed.

Roughly he tore the paper from the pellets and soon his palm quivered with precious fire. Trembling, he took all four glass jars from the safe and put them into the sack. He grabbed one of the metal boxes, shook it, and heard a tinny rattle. He pried off the lid with the screwdriver. Rings! Hundreds of them . . . Were they worth anything? He scooped up a handful and jets of fire shot fitfully from the stones. These are diamonds too, he said. He pried open another box. Watches! A chorus of soft, metallic ticking filled his ears. For a moment he could not move, then he dumped all the boxes into the sack.

He shut the safe door, then stood looking around, anxious not to over- look anything. Oh! He had seen a door in the room where the machines were. What was in there? More valuables? He re-entered the room, crossed the floor, and stood undecided before the door. He finally caught hold of the knob and pushed the door in; the room beyond was dark. He advanced cau- tiously inside and ran his fingers along the wall for the usual switch, then he was stark still. *Something had moved in the room!* What was it? Ought he to creep out, taking the rings and diamonds and money? Why risk what he al- ready had? He waited and the ensuing silence gave him confidence to ex- plore further. Dare he strike a match? Would not a match flame make him a good target? He tensed again as he heard a faint sigh; he was now convinced that there was something alive near him, something that lived and breathed. On tiptoe he felt slowly along the wall, hoping that he would not collide with anything. Luck was with him; he found the light switch.

No; don't turn the light on . . . Then suddenly he realized that he did not know in what direction the door was. Goddamn! He had to turn the light on or strike a match. He fingered the switch for a long time, then thought of an idea. He knelt upon the floor, reached his arm up to the switch and flicked the button, hoping that if anyone shot, the bullet would go above his head. The moment the light came on he narrowed his eyes to see quickly. He sucked in his breath and his body gave a violent twitch and was still. In front of him, so close that it made him want to bound up and scream, was a human face.

He was afraid to move lest he touch the man. If the man had opened his eyes at that moment, there was no telling what he might have done. The man—long and rawboned—was stretched out on his back upon a little cot, sleeping in his clothes, his head cushioned by a dirty pillow; his face, clouded by a dark stubble of beard, looked straight up to the ceiling. The man sighed, and he grew tense to defend himself; the man mumbled and turned his face away from the light. I've got to turn off that light, he thought. Just as he was about to rise, he saw a gun and cartridge belt on the floor at the man's side. Yes, he would take the gun and cartridge belt, not to use them, but just to keep them, as one takes a memento from a country fair. He picked them up and was about to click off the light when his eyes fell upon a photograph perched upon a chair near the man's head; it was the picture of a woman, smiling, shown against a background of open fields; at the woman's side were two young children, a boy and a girl. He smiled indulgently; he could send a bullet into that man's brain and time would be over for him . . .

He clicked off the light and crept silently back into the room where the safe stood; he fastened the cartridge belt about him and adjusted the holster at his right hip. He strutted about the room on tiptoe, lolling his head non-chalantly, then paused, abruptly pulled the gun, and pointed it with grim face toward an imaginary foe. "Boom!" he whispered fiercely. Then he bent forward with silent laughter. That's just like they do it in the movies, he said.

He contemplated his loot for a long time, then got a towel from the washroom and tied the sack securely. When he looked up he was momentarily frightened by his shadow looming on the wall before him. He lifted the sack, dragged it down the basement steps, lugged it across the basement, gasping for breath. After he had struggled through the hole, he clumsily replaced the bricks, then tussled with the sack until he got it to the cave. He stood in the dark, wet with sweat, brooding about the diamonds, the rings, the watches, the money; he remembered the singing in the church, the people yelling in the movie, the dead baby, the nude man stretched out upon the white table ... He saw these items hovering before his eyes and felt that some dim meaning linked them together, that some magical relationship made them kin. He stared with vacant eyes, convinced that all of these images, with their tongueless reality, were striving to tell him something ...

Later, seeing with his fingers, he untied the sack and set each item neatly upon the dirt floor. Exploring, he took the bulb, the socket, and the wire out of the tool chest; he was elated to find a double socket at one end of the wire. He crammed the stuff into his pockets and hoisted himself upon the rusty pipes and squinted into the church; it was dim and empty. Somewhere in this wall were live electric wires; but where? He lowered himself, groped and tapped the wall with the butt of the screwdriver, listening vainly for hollow sounds. I'll just take a chance and dig, he said.

For an hour he tried to dislodge a brick, and when he struck a match, he found that he had dug a depth of only an inch! No use in digging here, he sighed. By the flickering light of a match, he looked upward, then lowered his eyes, only to glance up again, startled. Directly above his head, beyond the pipes, was a wealth of electric wiring. I'll be damned, he snickered.

He got an old dull knife from the chest and, seeing again with his fingers, separated the two strands of wire and cut away the insulation. Twice he received a slight shock. He scraped the wiring clean and managed to join the two twin ends, then screwed in the bulb. The sudden illumination blinded him and he shut his lids to kill the pain in his eyeballs. I've got that much done, he thought jubilantly.

He placed the bulb on the dirt floor and the light cast a blatant glare on the bleak clay walls. Next he plugged one end of the wire that dangled from the radio into the light socket and bent down and switched on the button; almost at once there was the harsh sound of static, but no words or music. Why won't it work? he wondered. Had he damaged the mechanism in any way? Maybe it needed grounding? Yes ... He rummaged in the tool chest and found another length of wire, fastened it to the ground of the radio, and then tied the opposite end to a pipe. Rising and growing distinct, a slow strain of music entranced him with its measured sound. He sat upon the chest, deliriously happy.

Later he searched again in the chest and found a half-gallon can of glue; he opened it and smelled a sharp odor. Then he recalled that he had not even looked at the money. He took a wad of green bills and weighed it in his palm, then broke the seal and held one of the bills up to the light and studied it closely. *The United States of America will pay to the bearer on demand one hundred dollars,* he read in slow speech; then: *This note is legal tender for all debts, public and private . . .* He broke into a musing laugh, feeling that he was reading of the doings of people who lived on some far-off planet. He turned the bill over and saw on the other side of it a delicately beautiful building gleaming with paint and set amidst green grass. He had no desire whatever to count the money; it was what it stood for—the various currents of life swirling aboveground—that captivated him. Next he opened the rolls of coins and let them slide from their paper wrappings to the ground; the bright, new gleaming pennies and nickles and dimes piled high at his feet, a glowing mound of shimmering copper and silver. He sifted them through his fingers, listening to their tinkle as they struck the conical heap.

Oh, yes! He had forgotten. He would now write his name on the typewriter. He inserted a piece of paper and poised his fingers to write. But what was his name? He stared, trying to remember. He stood and glared about the dirt cave, his name on the tip of his lips. But it would not come to him. Why was he here? Yes, he had been running away from the police. But why? His mind was blank. He bit his lips and sat again, feeling a vague terror. But why worry? He laughed, then pecked slowly: *itwasalonghotday.* He was determined to type the sentence without making any mistakes. How did one make capital letters? He experimented and luckily discovered how to lock the machine for capital letters and then shift it back to lower case. Next he discovered how to make spaces, then he wrote neatly and correctly: *It was a long hot day.* Just why he selected that sentence he did not know; it was merely the ritual of performing the thing that appealed to him. He took the sheet out of the machine and looked around with stiff neck and hard eyes and spoke to an imaginary person:

"Yes, I'll have the contracts ready tomorrow."

He laughed. That's just the way they talk, he said. He grew weary of the game and pushed the machine aside. His eyes fell upon the can of glue, and a mischievous idea bloomed in him, filling him with nervous eagerness. He leaped up and opened the can of glue, then broke the seals on all the wads of money. I'm going to have some wallpaper, he said with a luxurious, physical laugh that made him bend at the knees. He took the towel with which he had tied the sack and balled it into a swab and dipped it into the can of glue and dabbed glue onto the wall; then he pasted one green bill by the side of another. He stepped back and cocked his head. Jesus! That's funny . . . He slapped his thighs and guffawed. He had triumphed over the world aboveground! He was free! If only people could see this! He wanted to run from this cave and yell his discovery to the world.

He swabbed all the dirt walls of the cave and pasted them with green bills; when he had finished the walls blazed with a yellow-green fire. Yes, this room would be his hide-out; between him and the world that had branded him guilty would stand this mocking symbol. He had not stolen the money; he had simply picked it up, just as a man would pick up firewood in a forest. And that was how the world aboveground now seemed to him, a wild forest filled with death.

The walls of money finally palled on him and he looked about for new interests to feed his emotions. The cleaver! He drove a nail into the wall and hung the bloody cleaver upon it. Still another idea welled up. He pried open the metal boxes and lined them side by side on the dirt floor. He grinned at the gold and fire. From one box he lifted up a fistful of ticking gold watches and dangled them by their gleaming chains. He stared with an idle smile, then began to wind them up; he did not attempt to set them at any given hour, for there was no time for him now. He took a fistful of nails and drove them into the papered walls and hung the watches upon them, letting them swing down by their glittering chains, trembling and ticking busily against the backdrop of green with the lemon sheen of the electric light shining upon the metal watch casings, converting the golden disks into blobs of liquid yellow. Hardly had he hung up the last watch than the idea extended itself; he took more nails from the chest and drove them into the green paper and took the boxes of rings and went from nail to nail and hung up the golden bands. The blue and white sparks from the stones filled the cave with brittle laughter, as though enjoying his hilarious secret. People certainly can do some funny things, he said to himself.

He sat upon the tool chest, alternately laughing and shaking his head soberly. Hours later he became conscious of the gun sagging at his hip and he pulled it from the holster. He had seen men fire guns in movies, but somehow his life had never led him into contact with firearms. A desire to feel the sensation others felt in firing came over him. But someone might hear . . . Well, what if they did? They would not know where the shot had come from. Not in their wildest notions would they think that it had come from under the streets! He tightened his fingers on the trigger; there was a deafening report and it seemed that the entire underground had caved in upon his eardrums; and in the same instant there flashed an orange-blue spurt of flame that died quickly but lingered on as a vivid after-image. He smelled the acrid stench of burnt powder filling his lungs and he dropped the gun abruptly.

The intensity of his feelings died and he hung the gun and cartridge belt upon the wall. Next he lifted the jars of diamonds and turned them bottom up-ward, dumping the white pellets upon the ground. One by one he picked them up and peeled the tissue paper from them and piled them in a neat heap. He wiped his sweaty hands on his trousers, lit a cigarette, and commenced playing another game. He imagined that he was a rich man who lived aboveground in the obscene sunshine and he was strolling through a park of a summer morning, smiling, nodding to his neighbors, sucking an after-breakfast cigar. Many times he crossed the floor of the cave, avoiding the diamonds with his feet, yet subtly gauging his footsteps so that his shoes, wet with sewer slime, would strike the diamonds at some undetermined moment. After twenty minutes of sauntering, his right foot smashed into the heap and diamonds lay scattered in all directions, glinting with a million tiny chuckles of icy laughter. Oh, shucks, he mumbled in mock regret, intrigued by the damage he had wrought. He continued walking, ignoring the brittle fire. He felt that he had a glorious victory locked in his heart.

He stooped and flung the diamonds more evenly over the floor and they showered rich sparks, collaborating with him. He went over the floor and trampled the stones just deeply enough for them to be faintly visible, as though they were set deliberately in the prongs of a thousand rings. A ghostly light bathed the cave. He sat on the chest and frowned. Maybe *anything's* right, he mumbled. Yes, if the world as men had made it was right, then anything else was right, any act a man took to satisfy himself, murder, theft, torture.

He straightened with a start. What was happening to him? He was drawn to these crazy thoughts, yet they made him feel vaguely guilty. He would stretch out upon the ground, then get up; he would want to crawl again through the holes he had dug, but would restrain himself; he would think of going again up into the streets, but fear would hold him still. He stood in the middle of the cave, surrounded by green walls and a laughing floor, trembling. He was going to do something, but what? Yes, he was afraid of himself, afraid of doing some nameless thing.

To control himself, he turned on the radio. A melancholy piece of music rose. Brooding over the diamonds on the floor was like looking up into a sky full of restless stars; then the illusion turned into its opposite: he was high up in the air looking down at the twinkling lights of a sprawling city. The music ended and a man recited news events. In the same attitude in which he had contemplated the city, so now, as he heard the cultivated tone, he looked down upon land and sea as men fought, as cities were razed, as planes scattered death upon open towns, as long lines of trenches wavered and broke. He heard the names of generals and the names of mountains and the names of countries and the names and numbers of divisions that were in action on different battle fronts. He saw black smoke billowing from the stacks of warships as they neared each other over wastes of water and he heard their huge thunder as red-hot shells screamed across the surface of night seas. He saw hundreds of planes wheeling and droning in the sky and heard the clatter of machine guns as they fought each other and he saw planes falling in plumes of smoke and blaze of fire. He saw steel tanks rumbling across fields of ripe wheat to meet other tanks and there was a loud clang of steel as numberless tanks collided. He saw troops with fixed bayonets charging in waves against other troops who held fixed bayonets and men groaned as steel ripped into their bodies and they went down to die . . . The voice of the radio faded and he was staring at the diamonds on the floor at his feet.

He shut off the radio, fighting an irrational compulsion to act. He walked aimlessly about the cave, touching the walls with his finger tips. Suddenly he stood still. *What was the matter with him?* Yes, he knew . . . It was these walls; these crazy walls were filling him with a wild urge to climb out into the dark sunshine aboveground. Quickly he doused the light to banish the shouting walls, then sat again upon the tool chest. Yes, he was trapped. His muscles were flexed taut and sweat ran down his face. He knew now that he could not stay here and he could not go out. He lit a cigarette with shaking fingers; the match flame revealed the green-papered walls with militant distinctness; the purple on the gun barrel glinted like a threat; the meat cleaver brooded with its eloquent splotches of blood; the mound of silver and copper smoldered angrily; the diamonds winked at him from the floor, and the gold watches ticked and trembled, crowning time the king of consciousness, defining the limits of living . . . The match blaze died and he bolted from where he stood and collided brutally with the nails upon the walls. The spell was broken. He shuddered, feeling that, in spite of his fear, sooner or later he would go up into that dead sunshine and somehow say something to somebody about all this.

He sat again upon the tool chest. Fatigue weighed upon his forehead and eyes. Minutes passed and he relaxed. He dozed, but his imagination was alert. He saw himself rising, wading again in the sweeping water of the sewer; he came to a manhole and climbed out and was amazed to discover that he hoisted himself into a room filled with armed policemen who were watching him intently. He jumped awake in the dark; he had not moved. He sighed, closed his eyes, and slept again; this time his imagination designed a scheme of protection for him. His dreaming made him feel that he was standing in a room watching over his own nude body lying stiff and cold upon a white table. At the far end of the room he saw a crowd of people huddled in a corner, afraid of his body. Though lying dead upon the table, he was standing in some mysterious way at his side, warding off the people, guarding his body, and laughing to himself as he observed the situation. They're scared of me, he thought.

He awakened with a start, leaped to his feet, and stood in the center of the black cave. It was a full minute before he moved again. He hovered between sleeping and waking, unprotected, a prey of wild fears. He could neither see nor hear. One part of him was asleep; his blood coursed slowly and his flesh was numb. On the other hand he was roused to a strange, high pitch of tension. He lifted his fingers to his face, as though about to weep. Gradually his hands lowered and he struck a match, looking about, expecting to see a door through which he could walk to safety; but there was no door, only the green walls and the moving floor. The match flame died and it was dark again.

Five minutes later he was still standing when the thought came to him that he had been asleep. Yes . . . But he was not yet fully awake; he was still queerly blind and deaf. How long had he slept? Where was he? Then suddenly he recalled the green-papered walls of the cave and in the same instant he heard loud singing coming from the church beyond the wall. Yes, they woke me up, he muttered. He hoisted himself and lay atop the bed of pipes and brought his face to the narrow slit. Men and women stood here and there between pews. A song ended and a young black girl tossed back her head and closed her eyes and broke plaintively into another hymn:

> Glad, glad, glad, oh, so glad
> I got Jesus in my soul . . .

Those few words were all she sang, but what her words did not say, her emotions said as she repeated the lines, varying the mood and tempo, making her tone express meanings which her conscious mind did not know. Another woman melted her voice with the girl's, and then an old man's voice merged with that of the two women. Soon the entire congregation was singing:

> Glad, glad, glad, oh, so glad
> I got Jesus in my soul . . .

They're wrong, he whispered in the lyric darkness. He felt that their search for a happiness they could never find made them feel that they had committed some dreadful offense which they could not remember or understand. He was now in possession of the feeling that had gripped him when he had first come into the underground. It came to him in a series of questions: Why was this sense of guilt so seemingly innate, so easy to come by, to think, to feel, so verily physical? It seemed that when one felt this guilt one was retracing in one's feelings a faint pattern designed long before; it seemed that one was always trying to remember a gigantic shock that had left a haunting impression upon one's body which one could not forget or shake off, but which had been forgotten by the conscious mind, creating in one's life a state of eternal anxiety.

He had to tear himself away from this; he got down from the pipes. His nerves were so taut that he seemed to feel his brain pushing through his skull. He felt that he had to do something, but he could not figure out what it was. Yet he knew that if he stood here until he made up his mind, he would never move. He crawled through the hole he had made in the brick wall and the exertion afforded him respite from tension. When he entered the basement of the radio store, he stopped in fear, hearing loud voices.

"Come on, boy! Tell us what you did with the radio!"

"Mister, I didn't steal the radio! I swear!"

He heard a dull thumping sound and he imagined a boy being struck violently.

"Please, mister!"

"Did you take it to a pawn shop?"

"No, sir! I didn't steal the radio! I got a radio at home," the boy's voice pleaded hysterically. "Go to my home and look!"

There came to his ears the sound of another blow. It was so funny that he had to clap his hand over his mouth to keep from laughing out loud. They're beating some poor boy, he whispered to himself, shaking his head. He felt a sort of distant pity for the boy and wondered if he ought to bring back the radio and leave it in the basement. No. Perhaps it was a good thing that they were beating the boy; perhaps the beating would bring to the boy's attention, for the first time in his life, the secret of his existence, the guilt that he could never get rid of.

Smiling, he scampered over a coal pile and stood again in the basement of the building where he had stolen the money and jewelry. He lifted himself into the areaway, climbed the rain pipe, and squinted through a two-inch opening of window. The guilty familiarity of what he saw made his muscles tighten. Framed before him in a bright tableau of daylight was the night watchman sitting upon the edge of a chair, stripped to the waist, his head sagging forward, his eyes red and puffy. The watchman's face and shoulders were stippled with red and black welts. Back of the watchman stood the safe, the steel door wide open showing the empty vault. Yes, they think he did it, he mused.

Footsteps sounded in the room and a man in a blue suit passed in front of him, then another, then still another. Policemen, he breathed. Yes, they were trying to make the watchman confess, just as they had once made him confess to a crime he had not done. He stared into the room, trying to recall something. Oh . . . Those were the same policemen who had beaten him, had made him sign that paper when he had been too tired and sick to care. Now, they were doing the same thing to the watchman. His heart pounded as he saw one of the policemen shake a finger into the watchman's face.

"Why don't you admit it's an inside job, Thompson?" the policeman said.

"I've told you all I know," the watchman mumbled through swollen lips.

"But nobody was here but you!" the policeman shouted.

"I was sleeping," the watchman said. "It was wrong, but I was sleeping all that night!"

"Stop telling us that lie!"

"It's the truth!"

"When did you get the combination?"

"I don't know how to open the safe," the watchman said.

He clung to the rain pipe, tense; he wanted to laugh, but he controlled himself. He felt a great sense of power; yes, he could go back to the cave, rip the money off the walls, pick up the diamonds and rings, and bring them here and write a note, telling them where to look for their foolish toys. No . . . What good would that do? It was not worth the effort. The watchman was guilty; although he was not guilty of the crime of which he had been accused, he was guilty, had always been guilty. The only thing that worried him was that the man who had been really stealing was not being accused. But he consoled himself: they'll catch him sometime during his life.

He saw one of the policemen slap the watchman across the mouth.

"Come clean, you bastard!"

"I've told you all I know," the watchman mumbled like a child.

One of the police went to the rear of the watchman's chair and jerked it from under him; the watchman pitched forward upon his face.

"Get up!" a policeman said.

Trembling, the watchman pulled himself up and sat limply again in the chair.

"Now, are you going to talk?"

"I've told you all I know," the watchman gasped.

"Where did you hide the stuff?"

"I didn't take it!"

"Thompson, your brains are in your feet," one of the policemen said. "We're going to string you up and get them back into your skull."

He watched the policemen clamp handcuffs on the watchman's wrists and ankles; then they lifted the watchman and swung him upside-down and hoisted his feet to the edge of a door. The watchman hung, head down, his eyes bulging. They're crazy, he whispered to himself as he clung to the ridges of the pipe.

"You going to talk?" a policeman shouted into the watchman's ear.

He heard the watchman groan.

"We'll let you hang there till you talk, see?"

He saw the watchman close his eyes.

"Let's take 'im down. He passed out," a policeman said.

He grinned as he watched them take the body down and dump it carelessly upon the floor. The policeman took off the handcuffs.

"Let 'im come to. Let's get a smoke," a policeman said.

The three policemen left the scope of his vision. A door slammed. He had an impulse to yell to the watchman that he could escape through the hole in the basement and live with him in the cave. But he wouldn't understand, he told himself. After a moment he saw the watchman rise and stand, swaying from weakness. He stumbled across the room to a desk, opened a drawer, and took out a gun. He's going to kill himself, he thought, intent, eager, detached, yearning to see the end of the man's actions. As the watchman stared vaguely about he lifted the gun to his temple; he stood like that for some minutes, biting his lips until a line of blood etched its way down a corner of his chin. No, he oughtn't do that, he said to himself in a mood of pity.

"Don't!" he half whispered and half yelled.

The watchman looked wildly about; he had heard him. But it did not help; there was a loud report and the watchman's head jerked violently and he fell like a log and lay prone, the gun clattering over the floor.

The three policemen came running into the room with drawn guns. One of the policemen knelt and rolled the watchman's body over and stared at a ragged, scarlet hole in the temple.

"Our hunch was right," the kneeling policeman said. "He was guilty, all right."

"Well, this ends the case," another policeman said.

"He knew he was licked," the third one said with grim satisfaction.

He eased down the rain pipe, crawled back through the holes he had made, and went back into his cave. A fever burned in his bones. He had to act, yet he was afraid. His eyes stared in the darkness as though propped open by invisible hands, as though they had become lidless. His muscles were rigid and he stood for what seemed to him a thousand years.

WHEN he moved again his actions were informed with precision, his muscular system reinforced from a reservoir of energy. He crawled through the hole of earth, dropped into the gray sewer current, and sloshed ahead. When his right foot went forward at a street intersection, he fell backward and shot down into water. In a spasm of terror his right hand grabbed the concrete ledge of a down-curve and he felt the streaking water tugging violently at his body. The current reached his neck and for a moment he was still. He knew if he moved clumsily he would be sucked under. He held onto the ledge with both hands and slowly pulled himself up. He sighed, standing once more in the sweeping water, thankful that he had missed death.

He waded on through sludge, moving with care, until he came to a web of light sifting down from a manhole cover. He saw steel hooks running up the side of the sewer wall; he caught hold and lifted himself and put his shoulder to the cover and moved it an inch. A crash of sound came to him as he looked into a hot glare of sunshine through which blurred shapes moved. Fear scalded him and he dropped back into the pallid current and stood paralyzed in the shadows. A heavy car rumbled past overhead, jarring the pavement, warning him to stay in his world of dark light, knocking the cover back into place with an imperious clang.

He did not know how much fear he felt, for fear claimed him completely; yet it was not a fear of the police or of people, but a cold dread at the thought of the actions he knew he would perform if he went out into that cruel sunshine. His mind said no; his body said yes; and his mind could not understand his feelings. A low whine broke from him and he was in the act of uncoiling. He climbed upward and heard the faint honking of auto horns. Like a frantic cat clutching a rag, he clung to the steel prongs and heaved his shoulder against the cover and pushed it off halfway. For a split second his eyes were drowned in the terror of yellow light and he was in a deeper darkness than he had ever known in the underground.

Partly out of the hole, he blinked, regaining enough sight to make out meaningful forms. An odd thing was happening: No one was rushing forward to challenge him. He had imagined the moment of his emergence as a desperate tussle with men who wanted to cart him off to be killed; instead, life froze about him as the traffic stopped. He pushed the cover aside, stood, swaying in a world so fragile that he expected it to collapse and drop him into some deep void. But nobody seemed to pay him heed. The cars were now swerving to shun him and the gaping hole.

"Why in hell don't you put up a red light, dummy?" a raucous voice yelled.

He understood; they thought that he was a sewer workman. He walked toward the sidewalk, weaving unsteadily through the moving traffic.

"Look where you're going, nigger!"

"That's right! Stay there and get killed!"

"You blind, you bastard?"

"Go home and sleep your drunk off!"

A policeman stood at the curb, looking in the opposite direction. When he passed the policeman, he feared that he would be grabbed, but nothing happened. Where was he? Was this real? He wanted to look about to get his bearings, but felt that something awful would happen to him if he did. He wandered into a spacious doorway of a store that sold men's clothing and saw his reflection in a long mirror: his cheekbones protruded from a hairy black face; his greasy cap was perched askew upon his head and his eyes were red and glassy. His shirt and trousers were caked with mud and hung loosely. His hands were gummed with a black stickiness. He threw back his head and laughed so loudly that passers-by stopped and stared.

He ambled on down the sidewalk, not having the merest notion of where he was going. Yet, sleeping within him, was the drive to go somewhere and say something to somebody. Half an hour later his ears caught the sound of spirited singing.

The Lamb, the Lamb, the Lamb
I hear thy voice a-calling
The Lamb, the Lamb, the Lamb
I feel thy grace a-falling

A church! He exclaimed. He broke into a run and came to brick steps leading downward to a subbasement. This is it! The church into which he had peered. Yes, he was going in and tell them. What? He did not know; but, once face to face with them, he would think of what to say. Must be Sunday, he mused. He ran down the steps and jerked the door open; the church was crowded and a deluge of song swept over him.

The Lamb, the Lamb, the Lamb
Tell me again your story
The Lamb, the Lamb, the Lamb
Flood my soul with your glory

He stared at the singing faces with a trembling smile.

"Say!" he shouted.

Many turned to look at him, but the song rolled on. His arm was jerked violently.

"I'm sorry, Brother, but you can't do that in here," a man said.

"But, mister!"

"You can't act rowdy in God's house," the man said.

"He's filthy," another man said.

"But I want to tell 'em," he said loudly.

"He stinks," someone muttered.

The song had stopped, but at once another one began.

> Oh, wondrous sight upon the cross
>   Vision sweet and divine
> Oh, wondrous sight upon the cross
>   Full of such love sublime

He attempted to twist away, but other hands grabbed him and rushed him into the doorway.

"Let me alone!" he screamed, struggling.

"Get out!"

"He's drunk," somebody said. "He ought to be ashamed!"

"He acts crazy!"

He felt that he was failing and he grew frantic.

"But, mister, let me tell—"

"Get away from this door, or I'll call the police!"

He stared, his trembling smile fading in a sense of wonderment.

"The police," he repeated vacantly.

"Now, get!"

He was pushed toward the brick steps and the door banged shut. The waves of song came.

> Oh, wondrous sight, wondrous sight
>   Lift my heavy heart above
> Oh, wondrous sight, wondrous sight
>   Fill my weary soul with love

He was smiling again now. Yes, the police . . . That was it! Why had he not thought of it before? The idea had been deep down in him, and only now did it assume supreme importance. He looked up and saw a street sign: COURT STREET—HARTSDALE AVENUE. He turned and walked northward, his mind filled with the image of the police station. Yes, that was where they had beaten him, accused him, and had made him sign a confession of his guilt. He would go there and clear up everything, make a statement. What statement?

He did not know. He was the statement, and since it was all so clear to him, surely he would be able to make it clear to others.

He came to the corner of Hartsdale Avenue and turned westward. Yeah, there's the station . . . A policeman came down the steps and walked past him without a glance. He mounted the stone steps and went through the door, paused; he was in a hallway where several policemen were standing, talking, smoking. One turned to him.

"What do you want, boy?"

He looked at the policeman and laughed.

"What in hell are you laughing about?" the policeman asked.

He stopped laughing and stared. His whole being was full of what he wanted to say to them, but he could not say it.

"Are you looking for the Desk Sergeant?"

"Yes, sir," he said quickly; then: "Oh, no, sir."

"Well, make up your mind, now."

Four policemen grouped themselves around him.

"I'm looking for the men," he said.

"What men?"

Peculiarly, at that moment he could not remember the names of the policemen; he recalled their beating him, the confession he had signed, and how he had run away from them. He saw the cave next to the church, the money on the walls, the guns, the rings, the cleaver, the watches, and the diamonds on the floor.

"They brought me here," he began.

"When?"

His mind flew back over the blur of the time lived in the underground blackness. He had no idea of how much time had elapsed, but the intensity of what had happened to him told him that it could not have transpired in a short space of time, yet his mind told him that time must have been brief.

"It was a long time ago." He spoke like a child relating a dimly remembered dream. "It was a long time," he repeated, following the promptings of his emotions. "They beat me . . . I was scared . . . I ran away."

A policeman raised a finger to his temple and made a derisive circle.

"Nuts," the policeman said.

"Do you know what place this is, boy?"

"Yes, sir. The police station," he answered sturdily, almost proudly.

"Well, who do you want to see?"

"The men," he said again, feeling that surely they knew the men. "You know the men," he said in a hurt tone.

"What's your name?"

He opened his lips to answer and no words came. He had forgotten. But what did it matter if he had? It was not important.

"Where do you live?"

Where did he live? It had been so long ago since he had lived up here in this strange world that he felt it was foolish even to try to remember. Then for a moment the old mood that had dominated him in the underground surged back. He leaned forward and spoke eagerly.

"They said I killed the woman."

"What woman?" a policeman asked.

"And I signed a paper that said I was guilty," he went on, ignoring their questions. "Then I ran off . . ."

"Did you run off from an institution?"

"No, sir," he said, blinking and shaking his head. "I came from under the ground. I pushed off the manhole cover and climbed out . . ."

"All right, now," a policeman said, placing an arm about his shoulder. "We'll send you to the psycho and you'll be taken care of."

"Maybe he's a Fifth Columnist!" a policeman shouted.

There was laughter and, despite his anxiety, he joined in. But the laughter lasted so long that it irked him.

"I got to find those men," he protested mildly.

"Say, boy, what have you been drinking?"

"Water," he said. "I got some water in a basement."

"Were the men you ran away from dressed in white, boy?"

"No, sir," he said brightly. "They were men like you."

An elderly policeman caught hold of his arm.

"Try and think hard. Where did they pick you up?"

He knotted his brows in an effort to remember, but he was blank inside. The policeman stood before him demanding logical answers and he could no longer think with his mind; he thought with his feelings and no words came.

"I was guilty," he said. "Oh, no, sir. I wasn't then, I mean, mister!"

"Aw, talk sense. Now, where did they pick you up?"

He felt challenged and his mind began reconstructing events in reverse; his feelings ranged back over the long hours and he saw the cave, the sewer, the bloody room where it was said that a woman had been killed.

"Oh, yes, sir," he said, smiling. "I was coming from Mrs. Wooten's."

"Who is she?"

"I work for her."

"Where does she live?"

"Next door to Mrs. Peabody, the woman who was killed."

The policemen were very quiet now, looking at him intently.

"What do you know about Mrs. Peabody's death, boy?"

"Nothing, sir. But they said I killed her. But it doesn't make any difference, I'm guilty!"

"What are you talking about, boy?"

His smile faded and he was possessed with memories of the underground; he saw the cave next to the church and his lips moved to speak. But how could he say it? The distance between what he felt and what these men meant was vast. Something told him, as he stood there looking into their faces, that he would never be able to tell them, that they would never believe him even if he told them.

"All the people I saw was guilty," he began slowly.

"Aw, nuts," a policeman muttered.

"Say," another policeman said, "that Peabody woman was killed over on Winewood. That's Number Ten's beat."

"Where's Number Ten?" a policeman asked.

"Upstairs in the swing room," someone answered.

"Take this boy up, Sam," a policeman ordered.

"O.K. Come along, boy."

An elderly policeman caught hold of his arm and led him up a flight of wooden stairs, down a long hall, and to a door.

"Squad Ten!" the policeman called through the door.

"What?" a gruff voice answered.

"Someone to see you!"

"About what?"

The old policeman pushed the door in and then shoved him into the room.

He stared, his lips open, his heart barely beating. Before him were the three policemen who had picked him up and had beaten him to extract the confession. They were seated about a small table, playing cards. The air was blue with smoke and sunshine poured through a high window, lighting up fantastic smoke shapes. He saw one of the policemen look up; the policeman's face was tired and a cigarette drooped limply from one corner of his mouth and both of his fat, puffy eyes were squinting and his hands gripped his cards.

"Lawson!" the man exclaimed.

The moment the man's name sounded he remembered the names of all of them: Lawson, Murphy, and Johnson. How simple it was. He waited, smiling, wondering how they would react when they knew that he had come back.

"Looking for me?" the man who had been called Lawson mumbled, sorting his cards. "For what?"

So far only Murphy, the red-headed one, had recognized him.

"Don't you-all remember me?" he blurted, running to the table.

All three of the policemen were looking at him now. Lawson, who seemed the leader, jumped to his feet.

"Where in hell have you been?"

"Do you know 'im, Lawson?" the old policeman asked.

"Huh?" Lawson frowned. "Oh, yes. I'll handle 'im." The old policeman left the room and Lawson crossed to the door and turned the key in the lock. "Come here, boy," he ordered in a cold tone.

He did not move; he looked from face to face. Yes, he would tell them about his cave.

"He looks batty to me," Johnson said, the one who had not spoken before.

"Why in hell did you come back here?" Lawson said.

"I—I just didn't want to run away no more," he said. "I'm all right, now." He paused; the men's attitude puzzled him.

"You've been hiding, huh?" Lawson asked in a tone that denoted that he had not heard his previous words. "You told us you were sick, and when we left you in the room, you jumped out of the window and ran away."

Panic filled him. Yes, they were indifferent to what he would say! They were waiting for him to speak and they would laugh at him. He had to rescue himself from this bog; he had to force the reality of himself upon them.

"Mister, I took a sackful of money and pasted it on the walls . . ." he began.

"I'll be damned," Lawson said.

"Listen," said Murphy, "let me tell you something for your own good. We don't want you, see? You're free, free as air. Now go home and forget it. It was all a mistake. We caught the guy who did the Peabody job. He wasn't colored at all. He was an Eyetalian."

"Shut up!" Lawson yelled. "Have you no sense!"

"But I want to tell 'im," Murphy said.

"We can't let this crazy fool go," Lawson exploded. "He acts nuts, but this may be a stunt . . ."

"I was down in the basement," he began in a childlike tone, as though repeating a lesson learned by heart; "and I went into a movie . . ." His voice failed. He was getting ahead of his story. First, he ought to tell them about the singing in the church, but what words could he use? He looked at them appealingly. "I went into a shop and took a sackful of money and diamonds and watches and rings . . . I didn't steal 'em, I'll give 'em all back. I just took 'em to play with . . . " He paused, stunned by their disbelieving eyes.

Lawson lit a cigarette and looked at him coldly.

"What did you do with the money?" he asked in a quiet, waiting voice.

"I pasted the hundred-dollar bills on the walls."

"What walls?" Lawson asked.

"The walls of the dirt room," he said, smiling, "the room next to the church. I hung up the rings and the watches and I stamped the diamonds into the dirt . . ." He saw that they were not understanding what he was saying. He grew frantic to make them believe, his voice tumbled on eagerly. "I saw a dead baby and a dead man . . ."

"Aw, you're nuts," Lawson snarled, shoving him into a chair.

"But mister . . ."

"Johnson, where's the paper he signed?" Lawson asked.

"What paper?"

"The confession, fool!"

Johnson pulled out his billfold and extracted a crumpled piece of paper.

"Yes, sir, mister," he said, stretching forth his hand. "That's the paper I signed . . ."

Lawson slapped him and he would have toppled had his chair not struck a wall behind him. Lawson scratched a match and held the paper over the flame; the confession burned down to Lawson's finger-tips.

He stared, thunderstruck; the sun of the underground was fleeting and the terrible darkness of the day stood before him. They did not believe him, but he *had* to make them believe him!

"But mister . . ."

"It's going to be all right, boy," Lawson said with a quiet, soothing laugh. "I've burned your confession, see? You didn't sign anything." Lawson came close to him with the black ashes cupped in his palm. "You don't remember a thing about this, do you?"

"Don't you-all be scared of me," he pleaded, sensing their uneasiness. "I'll sign another paper, if you want me to. I'll show you the cave."

"What's your game, boy?" Lawson asked suddenly.

"What are you trying to find out?" Johnson asked.

"Who sent you here?" Murphy demanded.

"Nobody sent me, mister," he said. "I just want to show you the room . . ."

"Aw, he's plumb bats," Murphy said. "Let's ship 'im to the psycho."

"No," Lawson said. "He's playing a game and I wish to God I knew what it was."

There flashed through his mind a definite way to make them believe him; he rose from the chair with nervous excitement.

"Mister, I saw the night watchman blow his brains out because you accused him of stealing," he told them. "But he didn't steal the money and diamonds. I took 'em."

Tigerishly Lawson grabbed his collar and lifted him bodily.

"Who told you about that?"

"Don't get excited, Lawson," Johnson said. "He read about it in the papers."

Lawson flung him away.

"He couldn't have," Lawson said, pulling papers from his pocket. "I haven't turned in the reports yet."

"Then how *did* he find out?" Murphy asked.

"Let's get out of here," Lawson said with quick resolution. "Listen, boy, we're going to take you to a nice, quiet place, see?"

"Yes, sir," he said. "And I'll show you the underground."

"Goddamn," Lawson muttered, fastening the gun at his hip. He narrowed his eyes at Johnson and Murphy. "Listen," he spoke just above a whisper, "say nothing about this, you hear?"

"O.K.," Johnson said.

"Sure," Murphy said.

Lawson unlocked the door and Johnson and Murphy led him down the stairs. The hallway was crowded with policemen.

"What have you got there, Lawson?"

"What did he do, Lawson?"

"He's psycho, ain't he, Lawson?"

Lawson did not answer; Johnson and Murphy led him to the car parked at the curb, pushed him into the back seat. Lawson got behind the steering wheel and the car rolled forward.

"What's up, Lawson?" Murphy asked.

"Listen," Lawson began slowly, "we tell the papers that he spilled about the Peabody job, then he escapes. The Wop is caught and we tell the papers that we steered them wrong to trap the real guy, see? Now this dope shows up and acts nuts. If we let him go, he'll squeal that we framed him, see?"

"I'm all right, mister," he said, feeling Murphy's and Johnson's arms locked rigidly into his. "I'm guilty . . . I'll show you everything in the underground. I laughed and laughed . . ."

"Shut that fool up!" Lawson ordered.

Johnson tapped him across the head with a blackjack and he fell back against the seat cushion, dazed.

"Yes, sir," he mumbled. "I'm all right."

The car sped along Hartsdale Avenue, then swung onto Pine Street and rolled to State Street, then turned south. It slowed to a stop, turned in the middle of a block, and headed north again.

"You're going around in circles, Lawson," Murphy said.

Lawson did not answer; he was hunched over the steering wheel. Finally he pulled the car to a stop at a curb.

"Say, boy, tell us the truth," Lawson asked quietly. "Where did you hide?"

"I didn't hide, mister."

The three policemen were staring at him now; he felt that for the first time they were willing to understand him.

"Then what happened?"

"Mister, when I looked through all of those holes and saw how people were living, I loved 'em . . ."

"Cut out that crazy talk!" Lawson snapped. "Who sent you back here?"

"Nobody, mister."

"Maybe he's talking straight," Johnson ventured.

"All right," Lawson said. "Nobody hid you. Now, tell us *where* you hid."

"I went underground . . ."

"What goddamn underground do you keep talking about?"

"I just went . . ." He paused and looked into the street, then pointed to a manhole cover. "I went down in there and stayed."

"In the *sewer?*"

"Yes, sir."

The policemen burst into a sudden laugh and ended quickly. Lawson swung the car around and drove to Woodside Avenue; he brought the car to a stop in front of a tall apartment building.

"What're we going to do, Lawson?" Murphy asked.

"I'm taking him up to my place," Lawson said. "We've got to wait until night. There's nothing we can do now."

They took him out of the car and led him into a vestibule.

"Take the steps," Lawson muttered.

They led him up four flights of stairs and into the living room of a small apartment. Johnson and Murphy let go of his arms and he stood uncertainly in the middle of the room.

"Now, listen, boy," Lawson began, "forget those wild lies you've been telling us. Where did you hide?"

"I just went underground, like I told you."

The room rocked with laughter. Lawson went to a cabinet and got a bottle of whisky; he placed glasses for Johnson and Murphy. The three of them drank.

He felt that he could not explain himself to them. He tried to muster all the sprawling images that floated in him; the images stood out sharply in his mind, but he could not make them have the meaning for others that they had for him. He felt so helpless that he began to cry.

"He's nuts, all right," Johnson said. "All nuts cry like that."

Murphy crossed the room and slapped him.

"Stop that raving!"

A sense of excitement flooded him; he ran to Murphy and grabbed his arm.

"Let me show you the cave," he said. "Come on, and you'll see!"

Before he knew it a sharp blow had clipped him on the chin; darkness covered his eyes. He dimly felt himself being lifted and laid out on the sofa. He heard low voices and struggled to rise, but hard hands held him down. His brain was clearing now. He pulled to a sitting posture and stared with glazed eyes. It had grown dark. How long had he been out?

"Say, boy," Lawson said soothingly, "will you show us the underground?"

His eyes shone and his heart swelled with gratitude. Lawson believed him! He rose, glad; he grabbed Lawson's arm, making the policeman spill whisky from the glass to his shirt.

"Take it easy, goddammit," Lawson said.

"Yes, sir."

"O.K. We'll take you down. But you'd better be telling us the truth, you hear?"

He clapped his hands in wild joy.

"I'll show you everything!"

He had triumphed at last! He would now do what he had felt was compelling him all along. At last he would be free of his burden.

"Take 'im down," Lawson ordered.

They led him down to the vestibule; when he reached the side-walk he saw that it was night and a fine rain was falling.

"It's just like when I went down," he told them.

"What?" Lawson asked.

"The rain," he said, sweeping his arm in a wide arc. "It was raining when I went down. The rain made the water rise and lift the cover off."

"Cut it out," Lawson snapped.

They did not believe him now, but they would. A mood of high selflessness throbbed in him. He could barely contain his rising spirits. They would see what he had seen; they would feel what he had felt. He would lead them through all the holes he had dug and . . . He wanted to make a hymn, prance about in physical ecstasy, throw his arm about the policemen in fellowship.

"Get into the car," Lawson ordered.

He climbed in and Johnson and Murphy sat at either side of him; Lawson slid behind the steering wheel and started the motor.

"Now, tell us where to go," Lawson said.

"It's right around the corner from where the lady was killed," he said.

The car rolled slowly and he closed his eyes, remembering the song he had heard in the church, the song that had wrought him to such a high pitch of terror and pity. He sang softly, lolling his head:

> Glad, glad, glad, oh, so glad
> I got Jesus in my soul . . .

"Mister," he said, stopping his song, "you ought to see how funny the rings look on the wall." He giggled. "I fired a pistol, too. Just once, to see how it felt."

"What do you suppose he's suffering from?" Johnson asked.

"Delusions of grandeur, maybe," Murphy said.

"Maybe it's because he lives in a white man's world," Lawson said.

"Say, boy, what did you eat down there?" Murphy asked, prodding Johnson anticipatorily with his elbow.

"Pears, oranges, bananas, and pork chops," he said.

The car filled with laughter.

"You didn't eat any watermelon?" Lawson asked, smiling.

"No, sir," he answered calmly. "I didn't see any."

The three policemen roared harder and louder.

"Boy, you're sure some case," Murphy said, shaking his head in wonder.

The car pulled to a curb.

"All right, boy," Lawson said. "Tell us where to go."

He peered through the rain and saw where he had gone down. The streets, save for a few dim lamps glowing softly through the rain, were dark and empty.

"Right there, mister," he said, pointing.

"Come on; let's take a look," Lawson said.

"Well, suppose he did hide down there," Johnson said, "what is that supposed to prove?"

"I don't believe he hid down there," Murphy said.

"It won't hurt to look," Lawson said. "Leave things to me."

Lawson got out of the car and looked up and down the street.

He was eager to show them the cave now. If he could show them what he had seen, then they would feel what he had felt and they in turn would show it to others and those others would feel as they had felt, and soon everybody would be governed by the same impulse of pity.

"Take 'im out," Lawson ordered.

Johnson and Murphy opened the door and pushed him out; he stood trembling in the rain, smiling. Again Lawson looked up and down the street; no one was in sight. The rain came down hard, slanting like black wires across the wind-swept air.

"All right," Lawson said. "Show us."

He walked to the center of the street, stopped and inserted a finger in one of the tiny holes of the cover and tugged, but he was too weak to budge it.

"Did you really go down in there, boy?" Lawson asked; there was a doubt in his voice.

"Yes, sir. Just a minute. I'll show you."

"Help 'im get that damn thing off," Lawson said.

Johnson stepped forward and lifted the cover; it clanged against the wet pavement. The hole gaped round and black.

"I went down in there," he announced with pride.

Lawson gazed at him for a long time without speaking, then he reached his right hand to his holster and drew his gun.

"Mister, I got a gun just like that down there," he said, laughing and looking into Lawson's face. "I fired it once then hung it on the wall. I'll show you."

"Show us how you went down," Lawson said quietly.

"I'll go down first, mister, and then you-all can come after me, hear?" he spoke like a little boy playing a game.

"Sure, sure," Lawson said soothingly. "Go ahead. We'll come."

He looked brightly at the policemen; he was bursting with happiness. He bent down and placed his hands on the rim of the hole and sat on the edge, his feet dangling into watery darkness. He heard the familiar drone of the gray current. He lowered his body and hung for a moment by his fingers, then he went downward on the steel prongs, hand over hand, until he reached the last rung. He dropped and his feet hit the water and he felt the stiff current trying to suck him away. He balanced himself quickly and looked back upward at the policemen.

"Come on, you-all!" he yelled, casting his voice above the rustling at his feet.

The vague forms that towered above him in the rain did not move. He laughed, feeling that they doubted him. But, once they saw the things he had done, they would never doubt again.

"Come on! The cave isn't far!" he yelled. "But be careful when your feet hit the water, because the current's pretty rough down here!"

Lawson still held the gun. Murphy and Johnson looked at Lawson quizzically.

"What are we going to do, Lawson?" Murphy asked.

"We are not going to follow that crazy nigger down into that sewer, are we?" Johnson asked.

"Come on, you-all!" he begged in a shout.

He saw Lawson raise the gun and point it directly at him. Lawson's face twitched, as though he were hesitating.

Then there was a thunderous report and a streak of fire ripped through his chest. He was hurled into the water, flat on his back. He looked in amazement at the blurred white faces looming above him. They shot me, he said to himself. The water flowed past him, blossoming in foam about his arms, his legs, and his head. His jaw sagged and his mouth gaped soundless. A vast pain gripped his head and gradually squeezed out consciousness. As from a great distance he heard hollow voices.

"What did you shoot him for, Lawson?"

"I had to."

"Why?"

"You've got to shoot his kind. They'd wreck things."

As though in a deep dream, he heard a metallic clank; they had replaced the manhole cover, shutting out forever the sound of wind and rain. From overhead came the muffled roar of a powerful motor and the swish of a speeding car. He felt the strong tide pushing him slowly into the middle of the sewer, turning him about. For a split second there hovered before his eyes the glittering cave, the shouting walls, and the laughing floor . . . Then his mouth was full of thick, bitter water. The current spun him around. He sighed and closed his eyes, a whirling object rushing alone in the darkness, veering, tossing, lost in the heart of the earth.

Questions

1. Fred Daniels goes underground to escape punishment for a crime he did not commit. He is a black man, and the underground is an appropriate metaphor for the position white America has accorded blacks. The underground is more than a place of escape for him, however; it is a place where he comes to understand what the society he lives in, black and white, is about. How do various episodes—the discovery of the dead baby, the funeral parlor, the meat market, the black church—contribute to this understanding? **2.** What is the significance of Fred Daniels' pecking out his own name on the typewriter? **3.** What significance do you see in the fact that Daniels tries to communicate his joyous feelings at a church and a police station? What is it that he wants to communicate? **4.** The police officer who kills Daniels sees him as a dangerous rebel, as the kind who'd "wreck things." In what sense could Daniels be seen as a rebel?

Hands*

YURI DANIEL [b. 1925]

Hᴇʀᴇ then, Sergey, you're an intellectual—polite. Therefore, you're silent; you ask nothing. But our factory boys come right out and ask you: "What is it?" they say. "Has Vaska turned into an outright drunkard, drinking his hands off?" This is what they say about my hands. Do you think I didn't notice that you glanced at my hands and turned away? And even now you're still trying to glance past my hands. Yes, indeed, I understand everything— you're doing this out of politeness, in order not to embarrass me. But look, look at them. It's all right. I won't be offended. I'm sure you won't see a thing like this every day. This, my dear friend, is not from drunkenness. I seldom drink—mostly in company or on some occasion, like for instance when I'm with you. We can't not drink to our meeting. I, dear fellow, remember everything: how we were scouting, and how you spoke French with the White officer,[1] and how we took Yaroslavl. Do you remember the speech you made at the meeting? You took me by the hand—I happened to be next to you—and you said: "With these hands . . ." you said. Ye-es. Well, Sergey, start pouring. Or else I'll just spill it. I forget the medical term for the shakes. Good, I have it written down, I'll show it to you later. . . . Well then—why did all that happen to me? There was an incident. But speaking chronologically, I'll tell you: When we were demobilized, after the victory in '21, I immediately returned to my old factory. There, of course, as expected, I was honored and respected as a revolutionary hero. Moreover, I was a member of the Party and a conscientious worker. Of course, it didn't happen without my having to straighten out somebody's mind. All kinds of talk began, like: "Well, you've fought, and what have you managed to accomplish—you have neither bread nor water. . . ." Such words I'd cut short. I was always very strict. You couldn't fool me with this Menshevik nonsense. Well, there, pour it, don't wait. But I had been working longer than a year when they called me to the District Office. "Here you are, Malinin," they told me, "your trip-ticket. The Party," they said, "is mobilizing you, Malinin Vasily Semyonovich, into the ranks of the glorious Special Committee to fight against the counter-revolutionaries. We wish you," they said, "the best of luck in your fight with the world bourgeoisie, and please give our humble greetings to Comrade Dzerzhinsky, if you see him." And I—what did I

---

*Translated by Vera von Wiren-Garczynski.
1.   The narrator recalls events that occurred during his service with the Bolshevik forces during and after the Russian revolution of 1917. The White officer was anti-communist, the enemy here. After the revolution a struggle developed between the Menshevik party and the Bolshevik party, which the Bolsheviks eventually won. Dzerzhinsky was the first head of the Cheka, a secret police force established to combat any counter-revolutionary movement.

do? Of course, I was a Party man. "Ye-es sir, I accept the order of our Party." I took my trip-ticket, went to the factory, said good-by to my comrades, and was on my way. Off I went, and I could already imagine how mercilessly I'd catch all the counter-revolutionaries, so they wouldn't be able to contaminate our Soviet government. . . . And so I arrived, and indeed met Dzerzhinsky. I repeated the wishes of our district comrades. He shook my hand, thanked me, and later he took all of us who were present, and there were about thirty of us there mobilized by the Party, and lined us up, and told us that one cannot build a house on mud, and that one has to dry the mud up first, and that in that process many an animal like a frog and a snake has to be destroyed, and therefore, he said, an iron will is required. And for this job, he said, we all have to put our hands together. . . . He said it, of course, in the form of an anecdote or fable, but, of course, it was clear. He himself was strict, never smiled. Later they started to classify us. Who is who, from where. "What is your education?" they asked. You know what my education consists of—the German and Civil wars—besides my work behind the workbench, that's my education. Two grades of elementary school I had. . . . And so they assigned me to special ser- vice—speaking frankly—to execution. This job one wouldn't call difficult, but one couldn't call it easy, either. It has an effect on one's heart. It's one thing at the front line, you know: either you get him or he gets you. But here. . . . Well, of course, I got used to it. You step behind him in the courtyard, and you say to yourself: "You must do it Vasily, you M-U-S-T. If you don't finish him off now, he'll corrupt the whole Soviet Republic." I got used to it. I started to drink, of course, couldn't get along without it. They gave us liquor. As regards to some "special rations," it's all nonsense, bourgeois inventions, that Cheka members eat white rolls and chocolate. Our rations were the same as a soldier's—bread, grain, and fat. Liquor, indeed, that we got. You had to have it, you understand. Yes sir, I worked this way for about seven months, and that's when it hap- pened. We received an order to exterminate a number of priests. For counter- revolutionary agitation. For their provocations. They aroused their pa- rishioners. Because of Tikhon,[2] I think. Or due to their anti-socialism—I don't know. In other words, they were considered enemies. There were twelve of them. Our boss gave the order: "You," he said to me, "Malinin, will take three of them, you, Vlasenko, you, Golovchiner, and you. . . ." I forgot the name of the fourth; he was a Latvian—some strange name, not like ours. He and Golov- chiner went first. We had it arranged in the following manner: the guard- house was right in the middle. On one side, that is, was a room, where they kept the condemned, and on the other side was the exit to the courtyard. We took them one by one. You'd finish off one in the yard, then drag him to the side and go back for the next. You had to drag them away to the side, or else when you entered with the next, if he saw the dead one, he'd start tearing himself away. The trouble sometime was endless. But, of course, this is under-

2.   Bishop Tikhon, patriarch of the Russian Church, who called on his fellow churchmen to openly resist the Bolshevik government's attacks on the church. He was arrested and removed from the leadership of the church.

standable. It was better when they were silent. And so, that Golovchiner and that Latvian finished off their victims and then it was my turn. Before that I had a few drinks. It's not that I was scared or a sort of religious person. No. I was a Party member, tough, I didn't believe in all that nonsense—gods of various sorts, angels, archangels,—no, I didn't—and yet I felt kind of strange. It was easy for Golovchiner, he was a Jew; they, I heard, don't even have icons. I don't know if it's true, but there I sat and drank, and all kinds of nonsense came to my mind: how my deceased mother back in the village would take me to church, and how I would kiss Father Vasily's hand, and how the old man would call me brother by name. . . . Ye-es, indeed. And so I went to get the first one, took him out. Came back, had a smoke, took out the next. Came back, had a drink—and became nauseous. "Wait a second, fellows," I said, "I'll be right back." I put the gun on the table and went out. I'm drunk, I thought. I'll shove a finger in my mouth, get some relief and I'll feel much better. And so I did what I had to, but I didn't feel any better. All right, I thought, I'll finish everything I'm supposed to do—and off to bed. I took my gun and went to get the third one. The third was a young stout fellow, such a healthy chunk of a priest, good-looking. I take him down the corridor, and I see how he raises his long robe over the threshhold, and I began to feel miserable, I don't know why myself. Out we went into the yard. And up he looks at the sky and raises his beard. "Go ahead, father, don't look back. You yourself have prayed for this kind of heaven." I wanted to joke, to raise my spirits. Why, I don't know myself. Never did I talk to the prisoners before. And so I let him walk three steps ahead of me, as required, I placed the gun between his shoulders and fired. As you know—a Mauser fires like a cannon! And it kicks back so strong that it almost tears your arm out of your shoulder. But all of a sudden, what do I see? My victim turns around and comes at me. Of course, sometimes there are complications: some are knocked off immediately, some swirl on the ground, sometimes they even take a few steps and swing as if they were drunk. But this one comes straight at me with small steps, as if he was swimming in his cassock, as if I never shot him. "Stop, father, I say stop!" And again I put the gun against him—his chest. He tore his robe at the chest, a chest full of curly hair, then goes and screams at the top of his lungs: "Go ahead, shoot," he screams, "go ahead you anti-christ! Go ahead, kill me, kill your Christ!" I got all confused, and shot once more and once again. But he keeps on coming at me! Neither blood nor a wound anywhere, he goes and prays: "O Lord, You have stopped the bullet from black hands! For You will I endure all tortures! . . . do not kill a living soul!" And something else. . . . I don't remember anymore, I know that I must have shot him—I couldn't have missed, I shot straight where I aimed. There he stands in front of me and his eyes burn like a wolf's, his chest bare, and around his head there seems to be a halo—later I realized that he stood sheltering the rays of the sun from my eyes, it was right before sunset. "Your hands," he screams, "are full of blood! Look at your hands!" I threw my gun down, ran into the guard-house, knocked somebody off his feet at the door, ran in, the fellows looked at me as if I were a psychopath and roared. I grabbed the gun from the pile and yelled: "I'll finish you off if you don't take me immediately to Dzerzhinsky!" They grabbed the gun away from me and took me in a hurry. I entered the drawing room, got loose from my comrades, and in a stuttering voice I told him: "Go ahead shoot me, Felix Edmundovich, I can't kill a priest!" I said that, and fell on the ground, I don't remember a thing more. I came to in a hospital. The doctors said: "Nervous breakdown." They treated me well, I must say, with care. The care, the cleanliness, and the food, for those times, were pretty decent. They cured everything, but my hands, as you can see for yourself, they always tremble. Probably the shock passed into them. I was discharged from the Cheka, of course. They need different kind of hands there. Of course, I couldn't go back to the workbench either. I was assigned work in the factory supply-room. There, of course, I do my business well. True, I can't write all those reports myself, my hands can't. I have an assistant for that purpose, a smart little girl. That's the way I live now, my fellow. What happened with the priest? I found out later. There was nothing divine about it. Our boys, when I went out to vomit, took out the real bullets and put in empty shells instead. They tried to make a joke. Well, I am not mad at them—it was a youthful prank, they didn't have it easy either, so they thought of a joke. No, I don't blame them. But my hands now . . . are no good to work with.

"Repent, Harlequin!" Said the Ticktockman

HARLAN ELLISON [b. 1934]

THERE are always those who ask, what is it all about? For those who need to ask, for those who need points sharply made, who need to know "where it's at," this:

"The mass of men serve the state thus, not as men mainly, but as machines, with their bodies. They are the standing army, and the militia, jailors, constables, posse comitatus, etc. In most cases there is no free exercise whatever of the judgment or of the moral sense; but they put themselves on a level with wood and earth and stones; and wooden men can perhaps be manufactured that will serve the purposes as well. Such command no more respect than men of straw or a lump of dirt. They have the same sort of worth only as horses and dogs. Yet such as these even are commonly esteemed good citizens. Others—as most legislators, politicians, lawyers, ministers, and office-holders—serve the state chiefly with their heads; and, as they rarely make any moral distinctions, they are as likely to serve the Devil, without intending it, as God. A very few, as heroes, patriots, martyrs, reformers in the great sense, and *men*, serve the state with their consciences also, and so necessarily resist it for the most part; and they are commonly treated as enemies by it."

> Henry David Thoreau,
> "Civil Disobedience"

That is the heart of it. Now begin in the middle, and later learn the beginning; the end will take care of itself.

BUT because it was the very world it was, the very world they had allowed it to *become*, for months his activities did not come to the alarmed attention of The Ones Who Kept The Machine Functioning Smoothly, the ones who poured the very best butter over the cams and mainsprings of the culture. Not until it had become obvious that somehow, someway, he had become a notoriety, a celebrity, perhaps even a hero for (what Officialdom inescapably tagged) "an emotionally disturbed segment of the populace," did they turn it over to the Ticktockman and his legal machinery. But by then, because it was the very world it was, and they had no way to predict he would happen— possibly a strain of disease long-defunct, now, suddenly, reborn in a system where immunity had been forgotten, had lapsed—he had been allowed to become too real. Now he had form and substance.

He had become a *personality*, something they had filtered out of the system many decades ago. But there it was, and there *he* was, a very definitely imposing personality. In certain circles—middle-class circles—it was thought disgusting. Vulgar ostentation. Anarchistic. Shameful. In others, there was only sniggering, those strata where thought is subjugated to form and ritual, niceties, proprieties. But down below, ah, down below, where the people always needed their saints and sinners, their bread and circuses, their heroes and villains, he was considered a Bolivar; a Napoleon; a Robin Hood; a Dick Bong (Ace of Aces); a Jesus; a Jomo Kenyatta.

And at the top—where, like socially-attuned Shipwreck Kellys, every tremor and vibration threatens to dislodge the wealthy, powerful and titled from their flagpoles—he was considered a menace; a heretic; a rebel; a disgrace; a peril. He was known down the line, to the very heartmeat core, but the important reactions were high above and far below. At the very top, at the very bottom.

So his file was turned over, along with his time-card and his cardioplate, to the office of the Ticktockman.

The Ticktockman: very much over six feet tall, often silent, a soft purring man when things went timewise. The Ticktockman.

Even in the cubicles of the hierarchy, where fear was generated, seldom suffered, he was called the Ticktockman. But no one called him that to his mask.

You don't call a man a hated name, not when that man, behind his mask, is capable of revoking the minutes, the hours, the days and nights, the years of your life. He was called the Master Timekeeper to his mask. It was safer that way.

"This is *what* he is," said the Ticktockman with genuine softness, "but not *who* he is? This time-card I'm holding in my left hand has a name on it, but it is the name of *what* he is, not *who* he is. This cardioplate here in my right hand is also named, but not whom named, merely what named. Before I can exercise proper revocation, I have to know who this what is."

To his staff, all the ferrets, all the loggers, all the finks, all the commex, even the mineez, he said, "Who is this Harlequin?"

He was not purring smoothly. Timewise, it was jangle.

However, it *was* the longest single speech they had ever heard him utter at one time, the staff, the ferrets, the loggers, the finks, the commex, but not the mineez, who usually weren't around to know, in any case. But even they scurried to find out.

Who is the Harlequin?

HIGH above the third level of the city, he crouched on the humming aluminum-frame platform of the air-boat (foof! air-boat, indeed! swizzleskid is what it was, with a tow-rack jerry-rigged) and stared down at the neat Mondrian arrangement of the buildings.

Somewhere nearby, he could hear the metronomic left-right-left of the

2:47 P.M. shift, entering the Timkin roller-bearing plant in their sneakers. A minute later, precisely, he heard the softer right-left-right of the 5:00 A.M. formation, going home.

An elfish grin spread across his tanned features, and his dimples appeared for a moment. Then, scratching at his thatch of auburn hair, he shrugged within his motley, as though girding himself for what came next, and threw the joystick forward, and bent into the wind as the air-boat dropped. He skimmed over a slidewalk, purposely dropping a few feet to crease the tassels of the ladies of fashion, and—inserting thumbs in large ears—he stuck out his tongue, rolled his eyes and went wugga-wugga-wugga. It was a minor diversion. One pedestrian skittered and tumbled, sending parcels every-whichway, another wet herself, a third keeled slantwise and the walk was stopped automatically by the servitors till she could be resuscitated. It was a minor diversion.

Then he swirled away on a vagrant breeze, and was gone. Hi-ho.

As he rounded the cornice of the Time-Motion Study Building, he saw the shift, just boarding the slidewalk. With practiced motion and an absolute conservation of movement, they sidestepped up onto the slowstrip and (in a chorus line reminiscent of a Busby Berkeley film of the antediluvian 1930's) advanced across the strips ostrich-walking till they were lined up on the express-trip.

Once more, in anticipation, the elfin grin spread, and there was a tooth missing back there on the left side. He dipped, skimmed, and swooped over them; and then, scrunching about on the air-boat, he released the holding pins that fastened shut the ends of the home-made pouring troughs that kept his cargo from dumping prematurely. And as he pulled the trough-pins, the air-boat slid over the factory workers and one hundred and fifty thousand dollars worth of jelly beans cascaded down on the expresstrip.

Jelly beans! Millons and billions of purples and yellows and greens and licorice and grape and raspberry and mint and round and smooth and crunchy outside and soft-mealy inside and sugary and bouncing jouncing tumbling clittering clattering skittering fell on the heads and shoulders and hard-hats and carapaces of the Timkin workers, tinkling on the slidewalk and bouncing away and rolling about underfoot and filling the sky on their way down with all the colors of joy and childhood and holidays, coming down in a steady rain, a solid wash, a torrent of color and sweetness out of the sky from above, and entering a universe of sanity and metronomic order with quite-mad coocoo newness. Jelly beans!

The shift workers howled and laughed and were pelted, and broke ranks, and the jelly beans managed to work their way into the mechanism of the slidewalks after which there was a hideous scraping as the sound of a million fingernails rasped down a quarter of a million blackboards, followed by a coughing and a sputtering, and then the slidewalks all stopped and everyone was dumped thisawayandthataway in a jackstraw tumble, and still laughing and popping little jelly bean eggs of childish color into their mouths.

It was a holiday, and a jollity, an absolute insanity, a giggle. But . . .

The shift was delayed seven minutes.

They did not get home for seven minutes.

The master schedule was thrown off by seven minutes.

Quotas were delayed by inoperative slidewalks for seven minutes.

He had tapped the first domino in the line, and one after another, like chik chik chik, the others had fallen.

The System had been seven minutes worth of disrupted. It was a tiny matter, one hardly worthy of note, but in a society where the single driving force was order and unity and promptness and clocklike precision and attention to the clock, reverence of the gods of the passage of time, it was a disaster of major importance.

So he was ordered to appear before the Ticktockman. It was broadcast across every channel of the communications web. He was ordered to be *there* at 7:00 dammit on time. And they waitĕd, and they waited, but he didn't show up till almost ten-thirty, at which time he merely sang a little song about moonlight in a place no one had ever heard of, called Vermont, and vanished again. But they had all been waiting since seven, and it wrecked *hell* with their schedules. So the question remained: Who is the Harlequin?

But the *unasked* question (more important of the two) was: how did we get *into* this position, where a laughing, irresponsible japer of jabberwocky and jive could disrupt our entire economic and cultural life with a hundred and fifty thousand dollars worth of jelly beans . . .

Jelly for God's sake *beans!* This is madness! Where did he get the money to buy a hundred and fifty thousand dollars worth of jelly beans? (They knew it would have cost that much, because they had a team of Situation Analysts pulled off another assignment, and rushed to the slidewalk scene to sweep up and count the candies, and produce findings, which disrupted *their* schedules and threw their entire branch at least a day behind.) Jelly beans! Jelly . . . *beans?* Now wait a second—a second accounted for—no one has manufactured jelly beans for over a hundred years. Where did he get jelly beans?

That's another good question. More than likely it will never be answered to your complete satisfaction. But then, how many questions ever are?

THE middle you know. Here is the beginning. How it starts:

A desk pad. Day for day, and turn each day. 9:00—open the mail. 9:45—appointment with planning commission board. 10:30—discuss installation progress charts with J.L. 11:15—pray for rain. 12:00—lunch. *And so it goes.*

"I'm sorry, Miss Grant, but the time for interviews was set at 2:30, and it's almost five now. I'm sorry you're late, but those are the rules. You'll have to wait till next year to submit application for this college again." *And so it goes.*

The 10:00 local stops at Cresthaven, Galesville, Tonawanda Junction, Selby and Farnhurst, but not at Indiana City, Lucasville and Colton, except on

Sunday. The 10:35 express stops at Galesville, Selby and Indiana City, except on Sundays & Holidays, at which time it stops at . . . *and so it goes.*

"I couldn't wait, Fred. I had to be at Pierre Cartain's by 3:00, and you said you'd meet me under the clock in the terminal at 2:45, and you weren't there, so I had to go on. You're always late, Fred. If you'd been there, we could have sewed it up together, but as it was, well, I took the order alone . . ." *And so it goes.*

Dear Mr. and Mrs. Atterley: in reference to your son Gerold's constant tardiness, I am afraid we will have to suspend him from school unless some more reliable method can be instituted guaranteeing he will arrive at his classes on time. Granted he is an exemplary student, and his marks are high, his constant flouting of the schedules of this school makes it impractical to maintain him in a system where the other children seem capable of getting where they are supposed to be on time *and so it goes.*

YOU CANNOT VOTE UNLESS YOU APPEAR AT 8:45 A.M.

"I don't care if the script is *good,* I need it Thursday!"

CHECK-OUT TIME IS 2:00 P.M.

"You got here late. The job's taken. Sorry."

YOUR SALARY HAS BEEN DOCKED FOR TWENTY MINUTES TIME LOST.

"God, what time is it, I've gotta run!"

And so it goes. And so it goes. And so it goes. And so it goes goes goes goes goes tick tock tick tock tick tock and one day we no longer let time serve us, we serve time and we are slaves of the schedule, worshippers of the sun's passing, bound into a life predicated on restrictions because the system will not function if we don't keep the schedule tight.

Until it becomes more than a minor inconvenience to be late. It becomes a sin. Then a crime. Then a crime punishable by this:

EFFECTIVE 15 JULY 2389, 12:00:00 midnight, the office of the Master Timekeeper will require all citizens to submit their time-cards and cardio-plates for processing. In accordance with Statute 555-7-SGH-999 governing the revocation of time per capita, all cardioplates will be keyed to the individual holder and—

What they had done, was devise a method of curtailing the amount of life a person could have. If he was ten minutes late, he lost ten minutes of his life. An hour was proportionately worth more revocation. If someone was consistently tardy, he might find himself, on a Sunday night, receiving a communique from the Master Timekeeper that his time had run out, and he would be "turned off" at high noon on Monday, please straighten your affairs, sir.

And so, by this simple scientific expedient (utilizing a scientific process held dearly secret by the Ticktockman's office) the System was maintained. It was the only expedient thing to do. It was, after all, patriotic. The schedules had to be met. After all, there *was* a war on!

But, wasn't there always?

Now that is really disgusting," the Harlequin said, when pretty Alice showed him the wanted poster. "Disgusting and *highly* improbable. After all, this isn't the days of desperadoes. A *wanted* poster!"

"You know," Alice noted, "you speak with a great deal of inflection."

"I'm sorry," said the Harlequin, humbly.

"No need to be sorry. You're always saying 'I'm sorry.' You have such massive guilt, Everett, it's really very sad."

"I'm sorry," he repeated, then pursed his lips so the dimples appeared momentarily. He hadn't wanted to say that at all. "I have to go out again. I have to *do* something."

Alice slammed her coffee-bulb down on the counter. "Oh for God's *sake*, Everett, can't you stay home just *one* night! Must you always be out in that ghastly clown suit, running around annoying people?"

"I'm—" he stopped, and clapped the jester's hat onto his auburn thatch with a tiny tingling of bells. He rose, rinsed out his coffee-bulb at the tap, and put it into the drier for a moment. "I have to go."

She didn't answer. The faxbox was purring, and she pulled a sheet out, read it, threw it toward him on the counter. "It's about you. Of course. You're ridiculous."

He read it quickly. It said the Ticktockman was trying to locate him. He didn't care, he was going to be late again. At the door, dredging for an exit line, he hurled back petulantly, "Well, *you* speak with inflection, *too*!"

Alice rolled her pretty eyes heavenward. "You're ridiculous." The Harlequin stalked out, slamming the door, which sighed shut softly, and locked itself.

There was a gentle knock, and Alice got up with an exhalation of exasperated breath, and opened the door. He stood there. "I'll be back about ten-thirty, okay?"

She pulled a rueful face. "Why do you tell me that? Why? You *know* you'll be late! You *know* it! You're *always* late, so why do you tell me these dumb things?" She closed the door.

On the other side, the Harlequin nodded to himself. *She's right. She's always right. I'll be late. I'm always late. Why do I tell her these dumb things?*

He shrugged again, and went off to be late once more.

He had fired off the firecracker rockets that said: I will attend the 115th annual International Medical Association Invocation at 8:00 P.M. precisely. I do hope you will all be able to join me.

The words had burned in the sky, and of course the authorities were there, lying in wait for him. They assumed, naturally, that he would be late. He arrived twenty minutes early, while they were setting up the spiderwebs to trap and hold him, and blowing a large bullhorn, he frightened and unnerved them so, their own moisturized encirclement webs sucked closed, and they were hauled up, kicking and shrieking, high above the amphitheatre's floor. The Harlequin laughed and laughed, and apologized profusely. The physicians, gathered in solemn conclave, roared with laughter, and accepted the Harlequin's apologies with exaggerated bowing and posturing, and a merry time was had by all, who thought the Harlequin was a regular foofaraw in fancy pants; all, that is, but the authorities, who had been sent out by the office of the Ticktockman, who hung there like so much dockside cargo, hauled up above the floor of the amphitheatre in a most unseemly fashion.

(In another part of the same city where the Harlequin carried on his "activities," totally unrelated in every way to what concerns here, save that it illustrates the Ticktockman's power and import, a man named Marshall Delahanty received his turn-off notice from the Ticktockman's office. His wife received the notification from the grey-suited minee who delivered it, with the traditional "look of sorrow" plastered hideously across his face. She knew what it was, even without unsealing it. It was a billet-doux of immediate recognition to everyone these days. She gasped, and held it as though it were a glass slide tinged with botulism, and prayed it was not for her. Let it be for Marsh, she thought, brutally, realistically, or one of the kids, but not for me, please dear God, not for me. And then she opened it, and it *was* for Marsh, and she was at one and the same time horrified and relieved. The next trooper in the line had caught the bullet. "Marshall," she screamed, "Marshall! Termination, Marshall! OhmiGod, Marshall, whattl we do, whattl we do, Marshall omigodmarshall . . ." and in their home that night was the sound of tearing paper and fear, and the stink of madness went up the flue and there was nothing, absolutely nothing they could do about it.

(But Marshall Delahanty tried to run. And early the next day, when turn-off time came, he was deep in the forest two hundred miles away, and the office of the Ticktockman blanked his cardioplate, and Marshall Delahanty keeled over, running, and his heart stopped, and the blood dried up on its way to his brain, and he was dead that's all. One light went out on his sector map in the office of the Master Timekeeper, while notification was entered for fax reproduction, and Georgette Delahanty's name was entered on the dole roles till she could re-marry. Which is the end of the footnote, and all the point that need be made, except don't laugh, because that is what would happen to the Harlequin if ever the Ticktockman found out his real name. It isn't funny.)

The shopping level of the city was thronged with the Thursday-colors of the buyers. Women in canary yellow chitons and men in pseudo-Tyrolean outfits that were jade and leather and fit very tightly, save for the balloon pants.

When the Harlequin appeared on the still-being-constructed shell of the new Efficiency Shopping Center, his bullhorn to his elfishly-laughing lips, everyone pointed and stared, and he berated them:

"Why let them order you about? Why let them tell you to hurry and scurry like ants or maggots? Take your time! Saunter a while! Enjoy the sunshine, enjoy the breeze, let life carry you at your own pace! Don't be slaves of time, it's a helluva way to die, slowly, by degrees ... down with the Ticktockman!"

Who's the nut? most of the shoppers wanted to know. Who's the nut oh wow I'm gonna be late I gotta run ...

And the construction gang on the Shopping Center received an urgent order from the office of the Master Timekeeper that the dangerous criminal known as the Harlequin was atop their spire, and their aid was urgently needed in apprehending him. The work crew said no, they would lose time on their construction schedule, but the Ticktockman managed to pull the proper threads of governmental webbing, and they were told to cease work and catch that nitwit up there on the spire with the bullhorn. So a dozen and more burly workers began climbing into their construction platforms, releasing the a-grav plates, and rising toward the Harlequin.

After the debacle (in which, through the Harlequin's attention to personal safety, no one was seriously injured), the workers tried to re-assemble, and assault him again, but it was too late. He had vanished. It had attracted quite a crowd, however, and the shopping cycle was thrown off by hours, simply hours. The purchasing needs of the system were therefore falling behind, and so measures were taken to accelerate the cycle for the rest of the day, but it got bogged down and speeded up and they sold too many float-valves and not nearly enough wegglers, which meant that the popli ratio was off, which made it necessary to rush cases and cases of spoiling Smash-O to stores that usually needed a case only every three or four hours. The shipments were bollixed, the trans-shipments were mis-routed, and in the end, even the swizzleskid industries felt it.

"Don't come back till you have him!" the Ticktockman said, very quietly, very sincerely, extremely dangerously.

They used dogs. They used probes. They used cardioplate crossoffs. They used feepers. They used bribery. They used stiktytes. They used intimidation. They used torment. They used torture. They used finks. They used cops. They used search&seizure. They used fallaron. They used betterment incentive. They used fingerprints. They used Bertillon. They used cunning. They used guile. They used treachery. They used Raoul Mitgong, but he didn't help much. They used applied physics. They used techniques of criminology.

And what the hell: they caught him.

After all, his name was Everett C. Marm, and he wasn't much to begin with, except a man who had no sense of time.

"REPENT, Harlequin!" said the Ticktockman.

"Get stuffed!" the Harlequin replied, sneering.

"You've been late a total of sixty-three years, five months, three weeks, two days, twelve hours, forty-one minutes, fifty-nine seconds, point oh three six one one one microseconds. You've used up everything you can, and more. I'm going to turn you off."

"Scare someone else. I'd rather be dead than live in a dumb world with a bogey man like you."

"It's my job."

"You're full of it. You're a tyrant. You have no right to order people around and kill them if they show up late."

"You can't adjust. You can't fit in."

"Unstrap me, and I'll fit my fist into your mouth."

"You're a non-conformist."

"That didn't used to be a felony."

"It is now. Live in the world around you."

"I hate it. It's a terrible world."

"Not everyone thinks so. Most people enjoy order."

"I don't, and most of the people I know don't."

"That's not true. How do you think we caught you?"

"I'm not interested."

"A girl named pretty Alice told us who you were."

"That's a lie."

"It's true. You unnerve her. She wants to belong, she wants to conform, I'm going to turn you off."

"Then do it already, and stop arguing with me."

"I'm not going to turn you off."

"You're an idiot!"

"Repent, Harlequin!" said the Ticktockman.

"Get stuffed."

So they sent him to Coventry. And in Coventry they worked him over. It was just like what they did to Winston Smith in "1984", which was a book none of them knew about, but the techniques are really quite ancient, and so they did it to Everett C. Marm, and one day quite a long time later, the Harlequin appeared on the communications web, appearing elfish and dimpled and bright-eyed, and not at all brainwashed, and he said he had been wrong, that it was a good, a very good thing indeed, to belong, and be right on time hip-ho and away we go, and everyone stared up at him on the public screens that covered an entire city block, and they said to themselves, well, you see, he was just a nut after all, and if that's the way the system is run, then let's do it that way, because it doesn't pay to fight city hall, or in this case, the Ticktockman. So Everett C. Marm was destroyed, which was a loss, because of what Thoreau said earlier, but you can't make an omelet without breaking a few eggs, and in every revolution, a few die who shouldn't, but they have to, because that's the way it happens, and if you make only a little change, then it seems to be worthwhile. Or, to make the point lucidly:

"UH, excuse me, sir, I, uh, don't know how to uh, to uh, tell you this, but you were three minutes late. The schedule is a little, uh, bit off."

He grinned sheepishly.

"That's ridiculous!" murmured the Ticktockman behind his mask. "Check your watch." And then he went into his office, going mrmee, mrmee, mrmee, mrmee.

conformity and rebellion

POETRY

from
Paradise Lost[1]

JOHN MILTON   [1608–1674]

"Is this the region, this the soil, the clime,"
Said then the lost archangel, "this the seat
That we must change for Heaven? this mournful gloom
For that celestial light? Be it so, since he
Who now is sovereign can dispose and bid
What shall be right: farthest from him is best,
Whom reason hath equaled, force hath made supreme
Above his equals. Farewell, happy fields,
Where joy forever dwells! Hail, horrors! hail,
Infernal world! and thou, profoundest Hell,   10
Receive thy new possessor, one who brings
A mind not to be changed by place or time.
The mind is its own place, and in itself
Can make a Heaven of Hell, a Hell of Heaven.
What matter where, if I be still the same,
And what I should be, all but° less than he   *only*
Whom thunder hath made greater? Here at least
We shall be free; th' Almighty hath not built
Here for his envy, will not drive us hence:
Here we may reign secure; and, in my choice,   20
To reign is worth ambition, though in Hell:
Better to reign in Hell than serve in Heaven.
But wherefore let we then our faithful friends,
Th' associates and copartners of our loss,
Lie thus astonished on th' oblivious pool,
And call them not to share with us their part
In this unhappy mansion, or once more
With rallied arms to try what may be yet
Regained in Heaven, or what more lost in Hell?"

1. *Is the statement in line 22 a logical extension of the statement in lines 13–14? Explain.* **2.** *Is the rebellious Satan heroic or ignoble? Defend your answer.* **3.** *What are the political implications of Satan's analysis of power (ll. 4–8)?*

---

1.   The first part of *Paradise Lost*, a poem on the expulsion of Adam and Eve from the Garden of Eden, tells the story of Satan's rebellion against God, his defeat and expulsion from heaven. In this passage, Satan surveys the infernal region to which God has banished him.

from
An Essay on Man

ALEXANDER POPE [1688–1744]

Cease then, nor ORDER imperfection name:
Our proper bliss depends on what we blame.
Know thy own point: this kind, this due degree
Of blindness, weakness, Heaven bestows on thee.
Submit—In this, or any other sphere,
Secure to be as blest as thou canst bear:
Safe in the hand of one disposing Power,
Or in the natal, or the mortal hour.
All Nature is but art, unknown to thee;
All chance, direction, which thou canst not see;   10
All discord, harmony not understood;
All partial evil, universal good:
And, spite of pride, in erring reason's spite,
One truth is clear: Whatever IS, is RIGHT.

The World Is Too Much with Us

WILLIAM WORDSWORTH [1770–1850]

The world is too much with us; late and soon,
Getting and spending, we lay waste our powers;
Little we see in Nature that is ours;
We have given our hearts away, a sordid boon!
This Sea that bares her bosom to the moon,
The winds that will be howling at all hours,
And are up-gathered now like sleeping flowers,
For this, for everything, we are out of tune;
It moves us not.—Great God! I'd rather be
A Pagan suckled in a creed outworn;   10
So might I, standing on this pleasant lea,
Have glimpses that would make me less forlorn;
Have sight of Proteus rising from the sea;
Or hear Old Triton blow his wreathèd horn.[2]

1. What does "world" mean in line 1? **2.** What does Wordsworth complain of in the first four lines? **3.** In lines 4–8 Wordsworth tells us what we have lost; in the concluding lines he suggests a remedy. What is that remedy? What do Proteus and Triton symbolize?

---

2. Proteus and Triton are both figures from Greek mythology. Proteus had the power to assume different forms; Triton was often represented as blowing on a conch shell.

Ulysses[3]

ALFRED, LORD TENNYSON [1809–1892]

It little profits that an idle king,
By this still hearth, among these barren crags,
Matched with an aged wife, I mete and dole
Unequal laws unto a savage race,
That hoard, and sleep, and feed, and know not me.
    I cannot rest from travel; I will drink
Life to the lees. All times I have enjoyed
Greatly, have suffered greatly, both with those
That loved me, and alone; on shore, and when
Through scudding drifts the rainy Hyades[4]   *10*
Vexed the dim sea. I am become a name;
For always roaming with a hungry heart
Much have I seen and known—cities of men
And manners, climates, councils, governments,
Myself not least, but honored of them all—
And drunk delight of battle with my peers,
Far on the ringing plains of windy Troy.
I am a part of all that I have met;
Yet all experience is an arch wherethrough
Gleams that untraveled world whose margin fades   *20*
Forever and forever when I move.
How dull it is to pause, to make an end,
To rust unburnished, not to shine in use!
As though to breathe were life! Life piled on life
Were all too little, and of one to me
Little remains; but every hour is saved
From that eternal silence, something more,
A bringer of new things; and vile it were
For some three suns to store and hoard myself,
And this gray spirit yearning in desire   *30*
To follow knowledge like a sinking star,
Beyond the utmost bound of human thought.

    This is my son, mine own Telemachus,
To whom I leave the scepter and the isle—
Well-loved of me, discerning to fulfill
This labor, by slow prudence to make mild
A rugged people, and through soft degrees

---

3. Ulysses, according to Greek legend, was the king of Ithaca and a hero of the Trojan War. Tennyson represents him as eager to resume the life of travel and adventure.
4. A group of stars in the constellation Taurus. According to Greek mythology, the rising of these stars with the sun foretold rain.

Subdue them to the useful and the good.
Most blameless is he, centered in the sphere
Of common duties, decent not to fail   40
In offices of tenderness, and pay
Meet° adoration to my household gods,   *proper*
When I am gone. He works his work, I mine.

    There lies the port; the vessel puffs her sail;
There gloom the dark, broad seas. My mariners,
Souls that have toiled, and wrought, and thought with me—
That ever with a frolic welcome took
The thunder and the sunshine, and opposed
Free hearts, free foreheads—you and I are old;
Old age hath yet his honor and his toil.   50
Death closes all; but something ere the end,
Some work of noble note, may yet be done,
Not unbecoming men that strove with Gods.
The lights begin to twinkle from the rocks;
The long day wanes; the slow moon climbs; the deep
Moans round with many voices. Come, my friends,
'Tis not too late to seek a newer world.
Push off, and sitting well in order smite
The sounding furrows; for my purpose holds
To sail beyond the sunset, and the baths   60
Of all the western stars, until I die.
It may be that the gulfs will wash us down;
It may be we shall touch the Happy Isles,[5]
And see the great Achilles, whom we knew.
Though much is taken, much abides; and though
We are not now that strength which in old days
Moved earth and heaven, that which we are, we are—
One equal temper of heroic hearts,
Made weak by time and fate, but strong in will
To strive, to seek, to find, and not to yield.   70

1. *Is Ulysses' desire to abdicate his duties as king irresponsible? Defend your answer.*
2. *At the conclusion of the poem Ulysses is determined not to yield. Yield to what?*
3. *Contrast Ulysses with his son Telemachus as the latter is described in lines 33–43. Is Telemachus admirable? Explain.*

---

5. The Islands of the Blessed (also Elysium), thought to be in the far western oceans, where those favored by the gods, such as Achilles, enjoyed life after death.

Lucifer in Starlight

GEORGE MEREDITH [1828–1909]

On a starred night Prince Lucifer uprose.
Tired of his dark dominion, swung the fiend
Above the rolling ball, in cloud part screened,
Where sinners hugged their specter of repose.
Poor prey to his hot fit of pride were those.
And now upon his western wing he leaned,
Now his huge bulk o'er Afric's sands careened,
Now the black planet shadowed Arctic snows.
Soaring through wider zones that pricked his scars
With memory of the old revolt from Awe,[6]   10
He reached a middle height, and at the stars,
Which are the brain of heaven, he looked, and sank.
Around the ancient track° marched, rank on rank,   *celestial orbits*
The army of unalterable law.

1. *What is the object of Lucifer's journey?* **2.** *If the "sinners" are "poor prey" to Lucifer's "fit of pride" (l. 5), what is a worthy prey?* **3.** *Why does the sight of the stars cause Lucifer to sink?*

Much Madness Is Divinest Sense

EMILY DICKINSON [1830–1886]

Much Madness is divinest Sense—
To a discerning Eye—
Much Sense—the starkest Madness—
'Tis the Majority
In this, as All, prevail—
Assent—and you are sane—
Demur—you're straightway dangerous—
And handled with a Chain—

---

6. The sky reminds Satan of the wounds he received when he revolted against God and was cast out of heaven.

Thou Art Indeed Just, Lord

GERARD MANLEY HOPKINS [1844–1889]

> *Justus quidem tu es, Domine, si disputem tecum: verumtamen*
> *justa loquar ad te: Quare via impiorum prosperatur? & c.*[7]

Thou art indeed just, Lord, if I contend
With thee; but, sir, so what I plead is just.
Why do sinners' ways prosper? and why must
Disappointment all I endeavour end?
    Wert thou my enemy, O thou my friend,
How wouldst thou worse, I wonder, than thou dost
Defeat, thwart me? Oh, the sots and thralls of lust
Do in spare hours more thrive than I that spend,
Sir, life upon thy cause. See, banks and brakes
Now, leavèd how thick! lacèd they are again   10
With fretty chervil,° look, and fresh wind shakes   *parsley*
Them; birds build—but not I build; no, but strain,
Time's eunuch, and not breed one work that wakes.
Mine, O thou lord of life, send my roots rain.

1. Summarize the debate in this poem. What implications about divine justice emerge from the poet's questions in lines 3 and 4? **2.** *How is the nature imagery used to indicate the speaker's plight?* **3.** *How would you characterize the poet's attitude toward God?*

The Scholars

WILLIAM BUTLER YEATS [1865–1939]

Bald heads forgetful of their sins,
Old, learned, respectable bald heads
Edit and annotate the lines
That young men, tossing on their beds,
Rhymed out in love's despair
To flatter beauty's ignorant ear.

---

7. The first three lines of the poem translate the Latin epigraph.

All shuffle there; all cough in ink;
All wear the carpet with their shoes;
All think what other people think;
All know the man their neighbor knows.　　　　　　　　　　*10*
Lord, what would they say
Did their Catullus[8] walk that way?

Easter 1916[9]

WILLIAM BUTLER YEATS　[1865–1939]

I have met them at close of day
Coming with vivid faces
From counter or desk among grey
Eighteenth-century houses.
I have passed with a nod of the head
Or polite meaningless words,
Or have lingered awhile and said
Polite meaningless words,
And thought before I had done
Of a mocking tale or a gibe　　　　　　　　　　*10*
To please a companion
Around the fire at the club,
Being certain that they and I
But lived where motley is worn:
All changed, changed utterly:
A terrible beauty is born.

That woman's days were spent
In ignorant good-will,
Her nights in argument
Until her voice grew shrill.　　　　　　　　　　*20*
What voice more sweet than hers
When, young and beautiful,
She rode to harriers?
This man had kept a school
And rode our wingéd horse;[10]
This other his helper and friend
Was coming into his force;

8.　Roman lyric poet, author of many erotic poems.
9.　On Easter Sunday of 1916, a group of Irish nationalists seized key points in Ireland, including the Dublin Post Office, from which they proclaimed an independent Irish Republic. At first, most Irishmen were indifferent to the nationalists' futile and heroic gesture, but as the rebellion was crushed and the leaders executed, they became heroes in their countrymen's eyes. Some of those leaders are alluded to in the second stanza and are named in lines 75 and 76.
10.　In Greek mythology, a winged horse is associated with poetic inspiration.

He might have won fame in the end,
So sensitive his nature seemed,
So daring and sweet his thought.
This other man I had dreamed   30
A drunken, vainglorious lout.
He had done most bitter wrong
To some who are near my heart,
Yet I number him in the song;
He, too, has resigned his part
In the casual comedy;
He, too, has been changed in his turn,
Transformed utterly:
A terrible beauty is born.   40

Hearts with one purpose alone
Through summer and winter seem
Enchanted to a stone
To trouble the living stream.
The horse that comes from the road,
The rider, the birds that range
From cloud to tumbling cloud,
Minute by minute they change;
A shadow of cloud on the stream
Changes minute by minute;   50
A horse-hoof slides on the brim,
And a horse plashes within it;
The long-legged moor-hens dive,
And hens to moor-cocks call;
Minute by minute they live:
The stone's in the midst of all.

Too long a sacrifice
Can make a stone of the heart.
O when may it suffice?
That is Heaven's part, our part   60
To murmur name upon name,
As a mother names her child
When sleep at last has come
On limbs that had run wild.
What is it but nightfall?
No, no, not night but death;
Was it needless death after all?
For England may keep faith
For all that is done and said.
We know their dream; enough   70
To know they dreamed and are dead;
And what if excess of love
Bewildered them till they died?
I write it out in a verse—

MacDonagh and MacBride
And Connolly and Pearse
Now and in time to be,
Wherever green is worn,
Are changed, changed utterly:
A terrible beauty is born.   *80*

1. *In the first stanza the attitude of the poet toward the people he is describing is indifferent, even contemptuous. How is that attitude modified in the rest of the poem?* **2.** *What does "they" in line 55 refer to? What does the "stone" in lines 43 and 56 symbolize? What is Yeats contrasting?* **3.** *How does the poet answer the question he asks in line 67?* **4.** *What is "changed utterly," and in what sense can beauty be "terrible"?*

Miniver Cheevy

EDWIN ARLINGTON ROBINSON   [1869–1935]

Miniver Cheevy, child of scorn,
    Grew lean while he assailed the seasons;
He wept that he was ever born,
    And he had reasons.

Miniver loved the days of old
    When swords were bright and steeds were prancing;
The vision of a warrior bold
    Would set him dancing.

Miniver sighed for what was not,
    And dreamed, and rested from his labors;   *10*
He dreamed of Thebes and Camelot,
    And Priam's neighbors.[11]

Miniver mourned the ripe renown
    That made so many a name so fragrant;
He mourned Romance, now on the town,
    And Art, a vagrant.

Miniver loved the Medici,[12]
    Albeit he had never seen one;

---

11.   Thebes was an ancient Greek city, famous in history and legend; Camelot was the site of the legendary King Arthur's court; Priam was king of Troy during the Trojan War.
12.   A family of bankers and statesmen, notorious for their cruelty, who ruled Florence for nearly two centuries during the Italian Renaissance.

He would have sinned incessantly
    Could he have been one.

20

Miniver cursed the commonplace
    And eyed a khaki suit with loathing;
He missed the medieval grace
    Of iron clothing.

Miniver scorned the gold he sought,
    But sore annoyed was he without it;
Miniver thought, and thought, and thought,
    And thought about it.

Miniver Cheevy, born too late,
    Scratched his head and kept on thinking;
Miniver coughed, and called it fate,
    And kept on drinking.

30

We Wear the Mask

PAUL LAURENCE DUNBAR [1872–1906]

We wear the mask that grins and lies,
It hides our cheeks and shades our eyes—
This debt we pay to human guile;
With torn and bleeding hearts we smile,
And mouth with myriad subtleties.

Why should the world be over-wise,
In counting all our tears and sighs?
Nay, let them only see us, while
    We wear the mask.

We smile, but, O great Christ, our cries
To thee from tortured souls arise.
We sing, but oh the clay is vile
Beneath our feet, and long the mile;
But let the world dream otherwise,
    We wear the mask!

10

Patterns

AMY LOWELL [1874–1925]

I walk down the garden-paths,
And all the daffodils
Are blowing, and the bright blue squills.
I walk down the patterned garden-paths
In my stiff, brocaded gown.
With my powdered hair and jeweled fan,
I too am a rare
Pattern. As I wander down
The garden-paths.

My dress is richly figured, 10
And the train
Makes a pink and silver stain
On the gravel, and the thrift
Of the borders.
Just a plate of current fashion,
Tripping by in high-heeled, ribboned shoes.
Not a softness anywhere about me,
Only whalebone and brocade.
And I sink on a seat in the shade
Of a lime tree. For my passion 20
Wars against the stiff brocade.
The daffodils and squills
Flutter in the breeze
As they please.
And I weep;
For the lime-tree is in blossom
And one small flower has dropped upon my bosom.

And the plashing of waterdrops
In the marble fountain
Comes down the garden-paths. 30
The dripping never stops.
Underneath my stiffened gown
Is the softness of a woman bathing in a marble basin,
A basin in the midst of hedges grown
So thick, she cannot see her lover hiding,
But she guesses he is near,
And the sliding of the water
Seems the stroking of a dear
Hand upon her.
What is Summer in a fine brocaded gown! 40

I should like to see it lying in a heap upon the ground.
All the pink and silver crumpled up on the ground.

I would be the pink and silver as I ran along the paths,
And he would stumble after,
Bewildered by my laughter.
I should see the sun flashing from his sword-hilt and the buckles on his shoes.
I would choose
To lead him in a maze along the patterned paths,
A bright and laughing maze for my heavy-booted lover.
Till he caught me in the shade,   50
And the buttons of his waistcoat bruised my body as he clasped me,
Aching, melting, unafraid.
With the shadows of the leaves and the sundrops,
All about us in the open afternoon—
I am very like to swoon
With the weight of this brocade,
For the sun sifts through the shade.

Underneath the fallen blossom
In my bosom
Is a letter I have hid.   60
It was brought to me this morning by a rider from the Duke.
"Madam, we regret to inform you that Lord Hartwell
Died in action Thursday se'nnight."
As I read it in the white, morning sunlight,
The letters squirmed like snakes.
"Any answer, Madam," said my footman.
"No," I told him.
"See that the messenger takes some refreshment.
No, no answer."   70
And I walked into the garden,
Up and down the patterned paths,
In my stiff, correct brocade.
The blue and yellow flowers stood up proudly in the sun,
Each one.
I stood upright too,
Held rigid to the pattern
By the stiffness of my gown;
Up and down I walked,
Up and down.   80

In a month he would have been my husband.
In a month, here, underneath this lime,
We would have broke the pattern;
He for me, and I for him,
He as Colonel, I as Lady,
On this shady seat.
He had a whim

That sunlight carried blessing.
And I answered, "It shall be as you have said."
Now he is dead.

In Summer and in Winter I shall walk
Up and down
The patterned garden-paths
In my stiff, brocaded gown.
The squills and daffodils
Will give place to pillared roses, and to asters, and to snow.
I shall go
Up and down
In my gown.
Gorgeously arrayed,
Boned and stayed.
And the softness of my body will be guarded from embrace
By each button, hook, and lace.
For the man who should loose me is dead,
Fighting with the Duke in Flanders,
In a pattern called a war.
Christ! What are patterns for?

A Roadside Stand

ROBERT FROST [1874–1963]

The little old house was out with a little new shed
In front at the edge of the road where the traffic sped,
A roadside stand that too pathetically pled,
It would not be fair to say for a dole of bread,
But for some of the money, the cash, whose flow supports
The flower of cities from sinking and withering faint.
The polished traffic passed with a mind ahead,
Or if ever aside a moment, then out of sorts
At having the landscape marred with the artless paint
Of signs that with N turned wrong and S turned wrong
Offered for sale wild berries in wooden quarts,
Or crook-necked golden squash with silver warts,
Or beauty rest in a beautiful mountain scene.
You have the money, but if you want to be mean,
Why, keep your money (this crossly) and go along.
The hurt to the scenery wouldn't be my complaint
So much as the trusting sorrow of what is unsaid:
Here far from the city we make our roadside stand

And ask for some city money to feel in hand
To try if it will not make our being expand,   *20*
And give us the life of the moving-pictures' promise
That the party in power is said to be keeping from us.

It is in the news that all these pitiful kin
Are to be bought out and mercifully gathered in
To live in villages, next to the theater and store,
Where they won't have to think for themselves anymore;
While greedy good-doers, beneficent beasts of prey,
Swarm over their lives enforcing benefits
That are calculated to soothe them out of their wits,
And by teaching them how to sleep the sleep all day,   *30*
Destroy their sleeping at night the ancient way.

Sometimes I feel myself I can hardly bear
The thought of so much childish longing in vain,
The sadness that lurks near the open window there,
That waits all day in almost open prayer
For the squeal of brakes, the sound of a stopping car,
Of all the thousand selfish cars that pass,
Just one to inquire what a farmer's prices are.
And one did stop, but only to plow up grass
In using the yard to back and turn around;   *40*
And another to ask the way to where it was bound;
And another to ask could they sell it a gallon of gas
They couldn't (this crossly): they had none, didn't it see?

No, in country money, the country scale of gain,
The requisite lift of spirit has never been found,
Or so the voice of the country seems to complain.
I can't help owning the great relief it would be
To put these people at one stroke out of their pain.
And then next day as I come back into the sane,
I wonder how I should like you to come to me   *50*
And offer to put me gently out of my pain.

1. *Welfare legislation during the great depression of the 1930's provoked this response
from Frost. What are Frost's objections to public welfare?* 2. *What is Frost's attitude
toward human misery in this poem?* 3. *What assumptions underlie such expressions as
"greedy good-doers" and "beneficent beasts of prey" (l. 27)?* 4. *Does Frost finally offer
some solution to the problem he perceives?*

Departmental

ROBERT FROST [1874–1963]

An ant on the table cloth
Ran into a dormant moth
Of many times his size.
He showed not the least surprise.
His business wasn't with such.
He gave it scarcely a touch,
And was off on his duty run.
Yet if he encountered one
Of the hive's enquiry squad
Whose work is to find out God   10
And the nature of time and space,
He would put him onto the case.
Ants are a curious race;
One crossing with hurried tread
The body of one of their dead
Isn't given a moment's arrest—
Seems not even impressed.
But he no doubt reports to any
With whom he crosses antennae,
And they no doubt report   20
To the higher up at court.
Then word goes forth in Formic:
"Death's come to Jerry McCormic,
Our selfless forager Jerry.
Will the special Janizary
Whose office it is to bury
The dead of the commissary
Go bring him home to his people.
Lay him in state on a sepal.
Wrap him for shroud in a petal.   30
Embalm him with ichor of nettle.
This is the word of your Queen."
And presently on the scene
Appears a solemn mortician;
And taking formal position
With feelers calmly atwiddle,
Seizes the dead by the middle,
And heaving him high in air,
Carries him out of there.
No one stands round to stare.   40
It is nobody else's affair.

It couldn't be called ungentle.
But how thoroughly departmental.

1. What comment does this poem make on human society? Is ant society a good meta-phor for human society? Explain.   2. How do the diction and rhyme help establish the tone?   3. Does the tone of the poem indicate approval or disapproval of the society pic-tured? Indicate specific words that convey that tone.

A High-Toned Old Christian Woman

WALLACE STEVENS   [1879-1955]

Poetry is the supreme fiction, madame.
Take the moral law and make a nave of it
And from the nave build haunted heaven. Thus,
The conscience is converted into palms,
Like windy citherns hankering for hymns.
We agree in principle. That's clear. But take
The opposing law and make a peristyle,
And from the peristyle project a masque
Beyond the planets. Thus, our bawdiness,
Unpurged by epitaph, indulged at last,   10
Is equally converted into palms,
Squiggling like saxophones. And palm for palm,
Madame, we are where we began. Allow,
Therefore, that in the planetary scene
Your disaffected flagellants, well-stuffed,
Smacking their muzzy bellies in parade,
Proud of such novelties of the sublime,
Such tink and tank and tunk-a-tunk-tunk,
May, merely may, madame, whip from themselves
A jovial hullabaloo among the spheres.   20
This will make widows wince. But fictive things
Wink as they will. Wink most when widows wince.

1. Stevens speaks of the "moral law" (l. 2) and the "opposing law" (l. 7). How are these two laws characterized? Is one superior to the other?   2. Why is the poem addressed to a high-toned old Christian woman?   3. Why might the flagellants (ll. 15–20) be objects of mirth?

from

Hugh Selwyn Mauberley

EZRA POUND   [1885–1972]

IV
These fought in any case,
and some believing,
                    pro domo,[13] in any case . . .

Some quick to arm,
some for adventure,
some from fear of weakness,
some from fear of censure,
some for love of slaughter, in imagination,
learning later . . .
some in fear, learning love of slaughter;   10

Died some, pro patria,[14]
                    non 'dulce' non 'et decor' . . .
walked eye-deep in hell
believing in old men's lies, then unbelieving
came home, home to a lie,
home to many deceits,
home to old lies and new infamy;
usury age-old and age-thick
and liars in public places.

Daring as never before, wastage as never before.   20
Young blood and high blood,
fair cheeks, and fine bodies;

fortitude as never before

frankness as never before,
disillusions as never told in the old days,
hysterias, trench confessions,
laughter out of dead bellies.

          V
          There died a myriad,
          And of the best, among them,

---

13. Latin, meaning "for home."
14. Latin, meaning "for country." This, with the following line, plays upon the famous statement of
the Latin poet Horace, *Dulce et decorum est pro patria mori*, "It is sweet and fitting to die for one's
country."

For an old bitch gone in the teeth,
For a botched civilization,

Charm, smiling at the good mouth,
Quick eyes gone under earth's lid,

For two gross of broken statues,
For a few thousand battered books.

i sing of Olaf glad and big

E. E. CUMMINGS   [1894–1962]

i sing of Olaf glad and big
whose warmest heart recoiled at war:
a conscientious object-or

his wellbelovéd colonel(trig
westpointer most succinctly bred)
took erring Olaf soon in hand;
but—though an host of overjoyed
noncoms(first knocking on the head
him)do through icy waters roll
that helplessness which others stroke
with brushes recently employed
anent this muddy toiletbowl,
while kindred intellects evoke
allegiance per blunt instruments—
Olaf(being to all intents
a corpse and wanting any rag
upon what God unto him gave)
responds,without getting annoyed
"I will not kiss your f.ing flag"

straightway the silver bird looked grave
(departing hurriedly to shave)

but—though all kinds of officers
(a yearning nation's blueeyed pride)
their passive prey did kick and curse
until for wear their clarion
voices and boots were much the worse,
and egged the firstclassprivates on
his rectum wickedly to tease
by means of skilfully applied

30

10

20

bayonets roasted hot with heat— 30
Olaf(upon what were once knees)
does almost ceaselessly repeat
"there is some s. I will not eat"

our president,being of which
assertions duly notified
threw the yellowsonofabitch
into a dungeon,where he died

Christ(of His mercy infinite)
i pray to see;and Olaf, too

preponderatingly because 40
unless statistics lie he was
more brave than me:more blond than you.

1. *What function do such words as "anent" (l. 12), "per" (l. 14), and "duly notified" (l. 35) serve?* 2. *Who are the "kindred intellects" (l. 13)?* 3. *In what sense do statistics (l. 41) prove that Olaf was braver than the speaker?* 4. *The first half of the last line is clear. What does the second half mean? (Consider ll. 22–23.)*

the Cambridge ladies
who live in furnished souls

E. E. CUMMINGS [1894–1962]

the Cambridge ladies who live in furnished souls
are unbeautiful and have comfortable minds
(also, with the church's protestant blessings
daughters, unscented shapeless spirited)
they believe in Christ and Longfellow, both dead,
are invariably interested in so many things—
at the present writing one still finds
delighted fingers knitting for the is it Poles?
perhaps. While permanent faces coyly bandy
scandal of Mrs. N and Professor D 10
. . . . the Cambridge ladies do not care, above
Cambridge if sometimes in its box of
sky lavender and cornerless, the
moon rattles like a fragment of angry candy

1. *What images does the poet use to describe the Cambridge ladies? What do the images suggest?* 2. *What is the effect of the interruption "is it" in line 8?* 3. *In the final lines the moon seems to protest against the superficiality of these ladies. What is the effect of comparing the moon to a fragment of candy?*

Harlem

LANGSTON HUGHES   [1902–1967]

What happens to a dream deferred?

    Does it dry up
    like a raisin in the sun?
    Or fester like a sore—
    And then run?
    Does it stink like rotten meat?
    Or crust and sugar over—
    like a syrupy sweet?

    Maybe it just sags
    like a heavy load.   10

    Or does it explode?

Same in Blues

LANGSTON HUGHES   [1902–1967]

I said to my baby,
Baby, take it slow.
I can't, she said, I can't!
I got to go!

    There's a certain
    amount of traveling
    in a dream deferred.

Lulu said to Leonard,
I want a diamond ring.
Leonard said to Lulu,
You won't get a goddam thing!   10

    A certain
    amount of nothing
    in a dream deferred.

Daddy, daddy, daddy,
All I want is you.
You can have me, baby—
but my lovin' days is through.

   A certain
   amount of impotence   20
   in a dream deferred.

Three parties
On my party line—
But that third party,
Lord, ain't mine!

   There's liable
   to be confusion
   in a dream deferred.

From river to river
Uptown and down,   30
There's liable to be confusion
when a dream gets kicked around.

The Unknown Citizen

(To JS/07/M/378 This Marble Monument Is Erected by the State)

W. H. AUDEN   **[b. 1907]**

He was found by the Bureau of Statistics to be
One against whom there was no official complaint,
And all the reports on his conduct agree
That, in the modern sense of an old-fashioned word, he was a saint,
For in everything he did he served the Greater Community.
Except for the War till the day he retired
He worked in a factory and never got fired,
But satisfied his employers, Fudge Motors Inc.
Yet he wasn't a scab or odd in his views,
For his Union reports that he paid his dues,   10
(Our report on his Union shows it was sound)
And our Social Psychology workers found
That he was popular with his mates and liked a drink.
The Press are convinced that he bought a paper every day
And that his reactions to advertisements were normal in every way.
Policies taken out in his name prove that he was fully insured,

And his Health-card shows he was once in hospital but left it cured.
Both Producers Research and High-Grade Living declare
He was fully sensible to the advantages of the Installment Plan
And had everything necessary to the Modern Man, 20
A phonograph, a radio, a car and a frigidaire.
Our researchers into Public Opinion are content
That he held the proper opinions for the time of year;
When there was peace, he was for peace; when there was war, he went.
He was married and added five children to the population,
Which our Eugenist says was the right number for a parent of his generation,
And our teachers report that he never interfered with their education.
Was he free? Was he happy? The question is absurd:
Had anything been wrong, we should certainly have heard. 30

Dolor

THEODORE ROETHKE   [1908–1963]

I have known the inexorable sadness of pencils,
Neat in their boxes, dolor of pad and paper-weight,
All the misery of manilla folders and mucilage,
Desolation in immaculate public places,
Lonely reception room, lavatory, switchboard,
The unalterable pathos of basin and pitcher,
Ritual of multigraph, paper-clip, comma,
Endless duplication of lives and objects.
And I have seen dust from the walls of institutions,
Finer than flour, alive, more dangerous than silica, 10
Sift, almost invisible, through long afternoons of tedium,
Dropping a fine film on nails and delicate eyebrows,
Glazing the pale hair, the duplicate grey standard faces.

The Conscientious Objector

KARL SHAPIRO   [b. 1913]

The gates clanged and they walked you into jail
More tense than felons but relieved to find
The hostile world shut out, flags that dripped
From every mother's windowpane, obscene
The bloodlust sweating from the public heart,

The dog authority slavering at your throat.
A sense of quiet, of pulling down the blind
Possessed you. Punishment you felt was clean.

The decks, the catwalks, and the narrow light
Composed a ship. This was a mutinous crew   10
Troubling the captains for plain decencies,
A *Mayflower* brim with pilgrims headed out
To establish new theocracies to west,
A Noah's ark coasting the topmost seas
Ten miles above the sodomites and fish.
These inmates loved the only living doves.

Like all men hunted from the world you made
A good community, voyaging the storm
To no safe Plymouth or green Ararat;
Trouble or calm, the men with Bibles prayed,   20
The gaunt politicals construed our hate.
The opposite of all armies, you were best
Opposing uniformity and yourselves;
Prison and personality were your fate.

You suffered not so physically but knew
Maltreatment, hunger, ennui of the mind.
Well might the soldier kissing the hot beach
Erupting in his face damn all your kind.
Yet you who saved neither yourselves nor us
Are equally with those who shed the blood   30
The heroes of our cause. Your conscience is
What we come back to in the armistice.

1. *Who is the speaker of this poem, and what are his assumptions about "good citizenship"?* **2.** *Why does the conscientious objector feel that punishment is clean (l. 8)?* **3.** *The prison is compared to the Mayflower and Noah's ark. Do you find the allusive comparisons between the prisoners and the occupants of the Mayflower and the ark effective? Explain.* **4.** *What, finally, are the differences between the man described here and Auden's unknown citizen? Is the conscientious objector "free"? "Happy"? Is he an unknown citizen?*

I Have Longed to Move Away

DYLAN THOMAS [1914–1953]

I have longed to move away
From the hissing of the spent lie

And the old terrors' continual cry
Growing more terrible as the day
Goes over the hill into the deep sea;
I have longed to move away
From the repetition of salutes,
For there are ghosts in the air
And ghostly echoes on paper,
And the thunder of calls and notes.   10

I have longed to move away but am afraid;
Some life, yet unspent, might explode
Out of the old lie burning on the ground
And, crackling into the air, leave me half-blind.
Neither by night's ancient fear,
The parting of hat from hair,
Pursed lips at the receiver,
Shall I fall to death's feather.
By these I would not care to die,
Half convention and half lie.

1. *What life style is suggested by the things from which the poet has "longed to move away"?* **2.** *What three attitudes toward death are expressed by lines 15–18?* **3.** *Explain the final couplet.*

Naming of Parts

HENRY REED [b. 1914]

Today we have naming of parts. Yesterday,
We had daily cleaning. And tomorrow morning,
We shall have what to do after firing. But today,
Today we have naming of parts. Japonica
Glistens like coral in all of the neighboring gardens,
    And today we have naming of parts.

This is the lower sling swivel. And this
Is the upper sling swivel, whose use you will see,
When you are given your slings. And this is the piling swivel,
Which in your case you have not got. The branches   10
Hold in the gardens their silent, eloquent gestures,
    Which in our case we have not got.

This is the safety-catch, which is always released
With an easy flick of the thumb. And please do not let me

See anyone using his finger. You can do it quite easy
If you have any strength in your thumb. The blossoms
Are fragile and motionless, never letting anyone see
　　　Any of them using their finger.

And this you can see is the bolt. The purpose of this
Is to open the breech, as you see. We can slide it　　　　　　　*20*
Rapidly backwards and forwards: we call this
Easing the spring. And rapidly backwards and forwards
The early bees are assaulting and fumbling the flowers:
　　　They call it easing the Spring.

They call it easing the Spring: it is perfectly easy
If you have any strength in your thumb: like the bolt,
And the breech, and the cocking-piece, and the point of balance,
Which in our case we have not got; and the almond-blossom
Silent in all of the gardens and the bees going backwards and forwards,
　　　For today we have naming of parts.　　　　　　　　　　*30*

1. *The poem has two speakers. Identify their speeches, and characterize the speakers.* 2. *The poem incorporates a subtle underlying sexuality. Trace the language that generates it. What function does that sexuality serve in the poem?* 3. *The last line of each stanza repeats a phrase from within the stanza. What is the effect of the repetition?*

Judging Distances

HENRY REED　[b. 1914]

Not only how far away, but the way that you say it
Is very important. Perhaps you may never get
The knack of judging a distance, but at least you know
How to report on a landscape: the central sector,
The right of arc and that, which we had last Tuesday,
　　　And at least you know

That maps are of time, not place, so far as the army
Happens to be concerned—the reason being,
Is one which need not delay us. Again, you know
There are three kinds of tree, three only, the fir and the poplar,　　　*10*
And those which have bushy tops to; and lastly
　　　That things only seem to be things.

A barn is not called a barn, to put it more plainly,
Or a field in the distance, where sheep may be safely grazing.
You must never be over-sure. You must say, when reporting:

At five o'clock in the central sector is a dozen
Of what appear to be animals; whatever you do,
    Don't call the bleeders *sheep.*

I am sure that's quite clear; and suppose, for the sake of example,
The one at the end, asleep, endeavors to tell us   20
What he sees over there to the west, and how far away,
After first having come to attention. There to the west,
On the fields of summer the sun and the shadows bestow
    Vestments of purple and gold.

The still white dwellings are like a mirage in the heat,
And under the swaying elms a man and a woman
Lie gently together. Which is, perhaps, only to say
That there is a row of houses to the left of arc,
And that under some poplars a pair of what appear to be humans
    Appear to be loving.   30

Well that, for an answer, is what we might rightly call
Moderately satisfactory only, the reason being,
Is that two things have been omitted, and those are important.
The human beings, now: in what direction are they,
And how far away, would you say? And do not forget
    There may be dead ground[15] in between.

There may be dead ground in between; and I may not have got
The knack of judging a distance; I will only venture
A guess that perhaps between me and the apparent lovers,
(Who, incidentally, appear by now to have finished,)   40
At seven o'clock from the houses, is roughly a distance
    Of about one year and a half.

1. *Identify and characterize the two speakers.* **2.** *Maps are of time (l. 7) because direction is indicated by such expressions as "at seven o'clock from the houses" (l. 41). What is the effect, then, of the last stanza?* **3.** *What devices are used to establish the central contrast of the poem? Why is the poet's judgment so clear to the reader?*

from

The Children of the Poor

GWENDOLYN BROOKS [b. 1917]

4
First fight. Then fiddle. Ply the slipping string
With feathery sorcery; muzzle the note

---

15. A military term describing space that cannot be reached by a given weapon.

With hurting love, the music that they wrote
Bewitch, bewilder. Qualify to sing
Threadwise. Devise no salt, no hempen thing
For the dear instrument to bear. Devote
The bow to silks and honey. Be remote
A while from malice and from murdering.
But first to arms, to armor. Carry hate
In front of you and harmony behind.   10
Be deaf to music and to beauty blind.
Win war. Rise bloody, maybe not too late
For having first to civilize a space
Wherein to play your violin with grace.

5
When my dears die, the festival-colored brightness
That is their motion and mild repartee
Enchanted, a macabre mockery
Charming the rainbow radiance into tightness
And into a remarkable politeness
That is not kind and does not want to be,
May not they in the crisp encounter see
Something to recognize and read as rightness?
I say they may, so granitely discreet,
The little crooked questionings inbound,   10
Concede themselves on most familiar ground,
Cold an old predicament of the breath:
Adroit, the shapely prefaces complete,
Accept the university of death.

II
Life for my child is simple, and is good.
He knows his wish. Yes, but that is not all.
Because I know mine too.
And we both want joy of undeep and unabiding things,
Like kicking over a chair or throwing blocks out of a window
Or tipping over an icebox pan
Or snatching down curtains or fingering an electric outlet
Or a journey or a friend or an illegal kiss.
No. There is more to it than that.
It is that he has never been afraid.   10
Rather, he reaches out and lo the chair falls with a beautiful crash,
And the blocks fall, down on the people's heads,
And the water comes slooshing sloppily out across the floor.
And so forth.
Not that success, for him, is sure, infallible.
But never has he been afraid to reach.
His lesions are legion.
But reaching is his rule.

1. *In sonnet 4, the poet advises the children: "First fight, Then fiddle." The meaning of "fight" is clear. What does "fiddle" symbolize?* 2. *Why does the poet advocate violence?* 3. *In sonnet 5, contrast the images that describe the children alive with those that describe them dead. What is the relationship suggested between the children in life and the children after death?* 4. *In sonnet 5, "university" (l. 14) is a pun. Explain its meanings.* 5. *Is the child described in poem II different from the children addressed in sonnet 4 and described in sonnet 5?* 6. *Explain the meaning of line 4 in poem II.* 7. *What does "reaching" in the last line mean?*

In Goya's Greatest Scenes

LAWRENCE FERLINGHETTI   [b. 1919]

In Goya's greatest scenes[16] we seem to see
                                 the people of the world
       exactly at the moment when
         they first attained the title of
                    'suffering humanity'
       They writhe upon the page
              in a veritable rage
                    of adversity
       Heaped up
          groaning with babies and bayonets   10
                  under cement skies
      in an abstract landscape of blasted trees
        bent statues bats wings and beaks
          slippery gibbets
        cadavers and carnivorous cocks
     and all the final hollering monsters
       of the
            'imagination of disaster'
     they are so bloody real
             it is as if they really still existed   20

   And they do

      Only the landscape is changed

 They still are ranged along the roads
     plagued by legionaires
          false windmills and demented roosters

 They are the same people
        only further from home

---

16.   Francisco Jose de Goya (1764-1828), famous Spanish artist, celebrated for his representations of "suffering humanity."

on freeways fifty lanes wide
                    on a concrete continent
                              spaced with bland billboards   *30*
                    illustrating imbecile illusions of happiness

The scene shows fewer tumbrils[17]
                    but more maimed citizens
                                        in painted cars
          and they have strange license plates
          and engines
                    that devour America

1. *To whom does the word "they" refer in line 26?* **2.** *What is responsible for the "suffering" of modern American "humanity"?*

Poetry of Departures

PHILIP LARKIN [b. 1922]

Sometimes you hear, fifth-hand,
As epitaph:
He chucked up everything
And just cleared off,
And always the voice will sound
Certain you approve
This audacious, purifying,
Elemental move.

And they are right, I think.
We all hate home   *10*
And having to be there:
I detest my room,
Its specially-chosen junk,
The good books, the good bed,
And my life, in perfect order:
So to hear it said

He walked out on the whole crowd
Leaves me flushed and stirred,
Like *Then she undid her dress*
Or *Take that you bastard;*   *20*
Surely I can, if he did?
And that helps me stay
Sober and industrious.
But I'd go today,

---

17. Carts in which prisoners were conducted to the place of execution.

Yes, swagger the nut-strewn roads,
Crouch in the fo'c'sle
Stubbly with goodness, if
It weren't so artificial,
Such a deliberate step backwards
To create an object: 30
Books; china; a life
Reprehensibly perfect.

1. What motivates the kind of person who "chucked up everything and just cleared off"? Why might such an action be characterized as "purifying" and "elemental"?   **2.** In what sense is the simile of lines 16–20 appropriate? What function does it serve?   **3.** Why does the poet conclude that departing is "artificial" (l. 28) and that perfection is "reprehensible" (l. 32)?

Counting Small-Boned Bodies

ROBERT BLY [b. 1926]

Let's count the bodies over again.

If we could only make the bodies smaller,
The size of skulls,
We could make a whole plain white with skulls in the moonlight!

If we could only make the bodies smaller,
Maybe we could get
A whole year's kill in front of us on a desk!

If we could only make the bodies smaller,
We could fit
A body into a finger-ring, for a keepsake forever.   10

Eleanor Rigby

JOHN LENNON [b. 1940] and **PAUL McCARTNEY** [b. 1942]

Ah, look at all the lonely people!
Ah, look at all the lonely people!
Eleanor Rigby picks up the rice
    in the church
Where a wedding has been.

Lives in a dream.
Waits at the window, wearing the face
    that she keeps in a jar by the door.
Who is it for?

All the lonely people,   10
    where do they all come from?
All the lonely people,
    where do they all belong?

Father McKenzie writing the words
    of a sermon that no one will hear—
No one comes near. Look at him
    working, darning his socks in the night
    when there's nobody there.

All the lonely people,
    where do they all come from?   20
All the lonely people.
    where do they all belong?

Ah, look at all the lonely people!
Ah, look at all the lonely people!
Eleanor Rigby died in the church and
    was buried along with her name.
Nobody came.
Father McKenzie wiping the dirt from
    his hands as he walks from the grave.
No one was saved.   30

All the lonely people,
    where do they all come from?
All the lonely people,
    where do they all belong?

---

1. *How does the first stanza establish Eleanor Rigby's character? What is the meaning of lines 7–8?* **2.** *What does the portrait of Father McKenzie contribute to our understanding of the theme of the lyric?* **3.** *What signifiance has the juxtaposition of Father McKenzie's writing "a sermon that no one will hear" and "darning his socks in the night" (stanza 3)?* **4.** *What is the significance of Eleanor Rigby's dying in the church? Why was "No one saved" (l. 30)?* **5.** *What answers, if any, does the poem suggest to the questions in the last stanza?*

conformity and rebellion

DRAMA

Antigone*

SOPHOCLES (496?–406 B.C.)

CHARACTERS

Antigonê	**Teiresias**
Ismenê	**A Sentry**
Eurydicê	**A Messenger**
Creon	**Chorus**
Haimon	

SCENE. *Before the Palace of Creon, King of Thebes. A central double door, and two lateral doors. A platform extends the length of the façade, and from this platform three steps lead down into the "orchestra," or chorus-ground.*

TIME. *Dawn of the day after the repulse of the Argive army from the assault on Thebes.*

Prologue

[*Antigonê and Ismenê enter from the central door of the Palace.*]

Antigonê. Ismenê, dear sister,
    You would think that we had already suffered enough
    For the curse on Oedipus:
    I cannot imagine any grief
    That you and I have not gone through. And now—
    Have they told you of the new decree of our King Creon?
Ismenê. I have heard nothing: I know
    That two sisters lost two brothers, a double death
    In a single hour; and I know that the Argive army
    Fled in the night; but beyond this, nothing.

---

*Translated by Dudley Fitts and Robert Fitzgerald.

Antigonê. I thought so. And that is why I wanted you
To come out here with me. There is something we must do.
Ismenê. Why do you speak so strangely?
Antigonê. Listen, Ismenê:
Creon buried our brother Eteoclês
With military honors, gave him a soldier's funeral,
And it was right that he should; but Polyneicês,
Who fought as bravely and died as miserably,—
They say that Creon has sworn
No one shall bury him, no one mourn for him,
But his body must lie in the fields, a sweet treasure
For carrion birds to find as they search for food.
That is what they say, and our good Creon is coming here
To announce it publicly; and the penalty—
Stoning to death in the public square!

                             There it is,
And now you can prove what you are:
A true sister, or a traitor to your family.
Ismenê. Antigonê, you are mad! What could I possibly do?
Antigonê. You must decide whether you will help me or not.
Ismenê. I do not understand you. Help you in what?
Antigonê. Ismenê, I am going to bury him. Will you come?
Ismenê. Bury him! You have just said the new law forbids it.
Antigonê. He is my brother. And he is your brother, too.
Ismenê. But think of the danger! Think what Creon will do!
Antigonê. Creon is not strong enough to stand in my way.
Ismenê. Ah sister!
Oedipus died, everyone hating him
For what his own search brought to light, his eyes
Ripped out by his own hand; and Iocastê died,
His mother and wife at once: she twisted the cords
That strangled her life; and our two brothers died,
Each killed by the other's sword. And we are left:
But oh, Antigonê,
Think how much more terrible than these
Our own death would be if we should go against Creon
And do what he has forbidden! We are only women,
We cannot fight with men, Antigonê!
The law is strong, we must give in to the law
In this thing, and in worse. I beg the Dead
To forgive me, but I am helpless: I must yield
To those in authority. And I think it is dangerous business
To be always meddling.
Antigonê.   If that is what you think,
I should not want you, even if you asked to come.
You have made your choice, you can be what you want to be.
But I will bury him; and if I must die,
I say that this crime is holy: I shall lie down

With him in death, and I shall be as dear
To him as he to me.
                                It is the dead,
Not the living, who make the longest demands:
We die for ever . . .
                                You may do as you like,
Since apparently the laws of the gods mean nothing to you.

Ismenê.   They mean a great deal to me; but I have no strength
To break laws that were made for the public good.

Antigonê.   That must be your excuse, I suppose. But as for me,
I will bury the brother I love.

Ismenê.   Antigonê,
I am so afraid for you!

Antigonê.   You need not be:
You have yourself to consider, after all.

Ismenê.   But no one must hear of this, you must tell no one!
I will keep it a secret, I promise!

Antigonê.   Oh tell it! Tell everyone!
Think how they'll hate you when it all comes out
If they learn that you knew about it all the time!

Ismenê.   So fiery! You should be cold with fear.

Antigonê.   Perhaps. But I am doing only what I must.

Ismenê.   But can you do it? I say that you cannot.

Antigonê.   Very well: when my strength gives out, I shall do no more.

Ismenê.   Impossible things should not be tried at all.

Antigonê.   Go away, Ismenê:
I shall be hating you soon, and the dead will too,
For your words are hateful. Leave me my foolish plan:
I am not afraid of the danger; if it means death,
It will not be the worst of deaths—death without honor.

Ismenê.   Go then, if you feel that you must.
You are unwise,
But a loyal friend indeed to those who love you.

[*Exit into the Palace. Antigonê goes off, L. Enter the Chorus.*]

Párodos

Chorus.   Now the long blade of the sun, lying   [*Strophe 1*]
Level east to west, touches with glory
Thebes of the Seven Gates. Open, unlidded
Eye of golden day! O marching light
Across the eddy and rush of Dircê's stream,
Striking the white shields of the enemy
Thrown headlong backward from the blaze of morning!

Choragos.   Polyneicês their commander
Roused them with windy phrases,
He the wild eagle screaming

        Insults above our land,
        His wings their shields of snow,
        His crest their marshalled helms.

Chorus.   Against our seven gates in a yawning ring   *[Antistrophe I]*
        The famished spears came onward in the night;
        But before his jaws were sated with our blood,
        Or pinefire took the garland of our towers,
        He was thrown back; and as he turned, great Thebes—
        No tender victim for his noisy power—
        Rose like a dragon behind him, shouting war.
Choragos.   For God hates utterly
        The bray of bragging tongues;
        And when he beheld their smiling,
        Their swagger of golden helms,
        The frown of his thunder blasted
        Their first man from our walls.

Chorus.   We heard his shout of triumph high in the air   *[Strophe 2]*
        Turn to a scream; far out in a flaming arc
        He fell with his windy torch, and the earth struck him.
        And others storming in fury no less than his
        Found shock of death in the dusty joy of battle.
Choragos.   Seven captains at seven gates
        Yielded their clanging arms to the god
        That bends the battle-line and breaks it.
        These two only, brothers in blood,
        Face to face in matchless rage,
        Mirroring each the other's death,
        Clashed in long combat.

Chorus.   But now in the beautiful morning of victory   *[Antistrophe 2]*
        Let Thebes of the many chariots sing for joy!
        With hearts for dancing we'll take leave of war:
        Our temples shall be sweet with hymns of praise,
        And the long night shall echo with our chorus.

SCENE I

Choragos.   But now at last our new King is coming:
        Creon of Thebes, Menoikeus' son.
        In this auspicious dawn of his reign
        What are the new complexities
        That shifting Fate has woven for him?
        What is his counsel? Why has he summoned
        The old men to hear him?

[*Enter Creon from the Palace, C. He addresses the Chorus from the top
step.*]

Creon. Gentlemen: I have the honor to inform you that our Ship of State, which recent storms have threatened to destroy, has come safely to harbor at last, guided by the merciful wisdom of Heaven. I have summoned you here this morning because I know that I can depend upon you: your devotion to King Laïos was absolute; you never hesitated in your duty to our late ruler Oedipus; and when Oedipus died, your loyalty was transferred to his children. Unfortunately, as you know, his two sons, the princes Eteoclês and Polyneicês, have killed each other in battle; and I, as the next in blood, have succeeded to the full power of the throne.

I am aware, of course, that no Ruler can expect complete loyalty from his subjects until he has been tested in office. Nevertheless, I say to you at the very outset that I have nothing but contempt for the kind of Governor who is afraid, for whatever reason, to follow the course that he knows is best for the State; and as for the man who sets private friendship above the public welfare,—I have no use for him, either. I call God to witness that if I saw my country headed for ruin, I should not be afraid to speak out plainly; and I need hardly remind you that I would never have any dealings with an enemy of the people. No one values friendship more highly than I; but we must remember that friends made at the risk of wrecking our Ship are not real friends at all.

These are my principles, at any rate, and that is why I have made the following decision concerning the sons of Oedipus: Eteoclês, who died as a man should die, fighting for his country, is to be buried with full military honors, with all the ceremony that is usual when the greatest heroes die; but his brother Polyneicês, who broke his exile to come back with fire and sword against his native city and the shrines of his fathers' gods, whose one idea was to spill the blood of his blood and sell his own people into slavery—Polyneicês, I say, is to have no burial: no man is to touch him or say the least prayer for him; he shall lie on the plain, unburied; and the birds and the scavenging dogs can do with him whatever they like.

This is my command, and you can see the wisdom behind it. As long as I am King, no traitor is going to be honored with the loyal man. But whoever shows by word and deed that he is on the side of the State,—he shall have my respect while he is living and my reverence when he is dead.

Choragos. If that is your will, Creon son of Menoikeus,
You have the right to enforce it: we are yours.

Creon. That is my will. Take care that you do your part.

Choragos. We are old men: let the younger ones carry it out.

Creon. I do not mean that: the sentries have been appointed.

Choragos. Then what is it that you would have us do?

Creon. You will give no support to whoever breaks this law.

Choragos. Only a crazy man is in love with death!

Creon. And death it is; yet money talks, and the wisest
Have sometimes been known to count a few coins too many.

[*Enter Sentry from L.*]

Sentry. I'll not say that I'm out of breath from running, King, because every time I stopped to think about what I have to tell you, I felt like going back. And all the time a voice kept saying, "You fool, don't you know you're walking straight into trouble?"; and then another voice: "Yes, but if you let somebody else get the news to Creon first, it will be even worse than that for you!" But good sense won out, at least I hope it was good sense, and here I am with a story that makes no sense at all; but I'll tell it anyhow, because, as they say, what's going to happen's going to happen, and—

Creon. Come to the point. What have you to say?

Sentry. I did not do it. I did not see who did it. You must not punish me for what someone else has done.

Creon. A comprehensive defense! More effective, perhaps,
If I knew its purpose. Come: what is it?

Sentry. A dreadful thing . . . I don't know how to put it—

Creon. Out with it!

Sentry.   Well, then;
The dead man—
                    Polyneicês—

[*Pause. The Sentry is overcome, fumbles for words. Creon waits impassively.*]

                    out there—
                              someone,—
New dust on the slimy flesh!

[*Pause. No sign from Creon.*]

Someone has given it burial that way, and
Gone . . .

[*Long pause. Creon finally speaks with deadly control.*]

Creon. And the man who dared do this?

Sentry.   I swear I
Do not know! You must believe me!
                              Listen:
The ground was dry, not a sign of digging, no,
Not a wheeltrack in the dust, no trace of anyone.
It was when they relieved us this morning: and one of them,
The corporal, pointed to it.
                              There it was,
The strangest—
          Look:
The body, just mounded over with light dust: you see?
Not buried really, but as if they'd covered it
Just enough for the ghost's peace. And no sign
Of dogs or any wild animal that had been there.

And then what a scene there was! Every man of us
Accusing the other: we all proved the other man did it,
We all had proof that we could not have done it.
We were ready to take hot iron in our hands,
Walk through fire, swear by all the gods,

It was not I!
I do not know who it was, but it was not I!

[*Creon's rage has been mounting steadily, but the Sentry is too intent upon his story to notice it.*]

And then, when this came to nothing, someone said
A thing that silenced us and made us stare
Down at the ground: you had to be told the news,
And one of us had to do it! We threw the dice,
And the bad luck fell to me. So here I am,
No happier to be here than you are to have me:
Nobody likes the man who brings bad news.

Choragos.   I have been wondering, King: can it be that the gods have done this?

Creon.   Stop!   [*Furiously.*]
Must you doddering wrecks
Go out of your heads entirely? "The gods!"
Intolerable!
The gods favor this corpse? Why? How had he served them?
Tried to loot their temples, burn their images,
Yes, and the whole State, and its laws with it!
Is it your senile opinion that the gods love to honor bad men?
A pious thought!—
                    No, from the very beginning
There have been those who have whispered together,
Stiff-necked anarchists, putting their heads together,
Scheming against me in alleys. These are the men,
And they have bribed my own guard to do this thing.
Money!   [*Sententiously.*]
There's nothing in the world so demoralizing as money.
Down go your cities,
Homes gone, men gone, honest hearts corrupted,
Crookedness of all kinds, and all for money!

                                                    [*To Sentry.*]
                    But you—!
I swear by God and by the throne of God,
The man who has done this thing shall pay for it!
Find that man, bring him here to me, or your death
Will be the least of your problems: I'll string you up
Alive, and there will be certain ways to make you
Discover your employer before you die;
And the process may teach you a lesson you seem to have missed:
The dearest profit is sometimes all too dear:
That depends on the source. Do you understand me?
A fortune won is often misfortune.

Sentry.   King, may I speak?
Creon.   Your very voice distresses me.
Sentry.   Are you sure that it is my voice, and not your conscience?
Creon.   By God, he wants to analyze me now!

Sentry.   It is not what I say, but what has been done, that hurts you.
Creon.   You talk too much.
Sentry.   Maybe; but I've done nothing.
Creon.   Sold your soul for some silver: that's all you've done.
Sentry.   How dreadful it is when the right judge judges wrong!
Creon.   Your figures of speech
    May entertain you now; but unless you bring me the man,
    You will get little profit from them in the end.

[Exit Creon into the Palace.]

Sentry.   "Bring me the man"—!
    I'd like nothing better than bringing him the man!
    But bring him or not, you have seen the last of me here.
    At any rate, I am safe!   *[Exit Sentry.]*

Ode I

Chorus.   Numberless are the world's wonders, but none   *[Strophe 1]*
    More wonderful than man; the stormgray sea
    Yields to his prows, the huge crests bear him high;
    Earth, holy and inexhaustible, is graven
    With shining furrows where his plows have gone
    Year after year, the timeless labor of stallions.

    The lightboned birds and beasts that cling to cover,   *[Antistrophe 1]*
    The lithe fish lighting their reaches of dim water,
    All are taken, tamed in the net of his mind;
    The lion on the hill, the wild horse windy-maned,
    Resign to him; and his blunt yoke has broken
    The sultry shoulders of the mountain bull.

    Words also, and thought as rapid as air,   *[Strophe 2]*
    He fashions to his good use; statecraft is his,
    And his the skill that deflects the arrows of snow,
    The spears of winter rain: from every wind
    He has made himself secure—from all but one:
    In the late wind of death he cannot stand.

    O clear intelligence, force beyond all measure!   *[Antistrophe 2]*
    O fate of man, working both good and evil!
    When the laws are kept, how proudly his city stands!
    When the laws are broken, what of his city then?
    Never may the anárchic man find rest at my hearth,
    Never be it said that my thoughts are his thoughts.

SCENE II

[*Re-enter Sentry leading Antigonê.*]

Choragos.   What does this mean? Surely this captive woman
Is the Princess, Antigonê. Why should she be taken?
Sentry.   Here is the one who did it! We caught her
In the very act of burying him.—Where is Creon?
Choragos.   Just coming from the house.

[Enter Creon, C.]

Creon.   What has happened?
Why have you come back so soon?
Sentry.   O King,   [*Expansively.*]
A man should never be too sure of anything:
I would have sworn
That you'd not see me here again: your anger
Frightened me so, and the things you threatened me with;
But how could I tell then
That I'd be able to solve the case so soon?
No dice-throwing this time: I was only too glad to come!

Here is this woman. She is the guilty one:
We found her trying to bury him.
Take her, then; question her; judge her as you will.
I am through with the whole thing now, and glád óf it.
Creon.   But this is Antigonê! Why have you brought her here?
Sentry.   She was burying him, I tell you!

[*Severely.*]

Creon.   Is this the truth?
Sentry.   I saw her with my own eyes. Can I say more?
Creon.   The details: come, tell me quickly!
Sentry.   It was like this:
After those terrible threats of yours, King,
We went back and brushed the dust away from the body.
The flesh was soft by now, and stinking,
So we sat on a hill to windward and kept guard.
No napping this time! We kept each other awake.
But nothing happened until the white round sun
Whirled in the center of the round sky over us:
Then, suddenly,
A storm of dust roared up from the earth, and the sky
Went out, the plain vanished with all its trees
In the stinging dark. We closed our eyes and endured it.
The whirlwind lasted a long time, but it passed;
And then we looked, and there was Antigonê!
I have seen
A mother bird come back to a stripped nest, heard
Her crying bitterly a broken note or two
For the young ones stolen. Just so, when this girl

Found the bare corpse, and all her love's work wasted,
She wept, and cried on heaven to damn the hands
That had done this thing.

And then she brought more dust
And sprinkled wine three times for her brother's ghost.

We ran and took her at once. She was not afraid,
Not even when we charged her with what she had done.
She denied nothing.

And this was a comfort to me,
And some uneasiness: for it is a good thing
To escape from death, but it is no great pleasure
To bring death to a friend.

Yet I always say
There is nothing so comfortable as your own safe skin!

Creon.   And you, Antigonê,   [*Slowly, dangerously*]
You with your head hanging,—do you confess this thing?

Antigonê.   I do. I deny nothing.

[*To Sentry:*]

Creon.   You may go.

[*Exit Sentry. To Antigonê:*]

Tell me, tell me briefly:
Had you heard my proclamation touching this matter?

Antigonê.   It was public. Could I help hearing it?

Creon.   And yet you dared defy the law.

Antigonê.   I dared.
It was not God's proclamation. That final Justice
That rules the world below makes no such laws.

Your edict, King, was strong,
But all your strength is weakness itself against
The immortal unrecorded laws of God.
They are not merely now: they were, and shall be,
Operative for ever, beyond man utterly.

I knew I must die, even without your decree:
I am only mortal. And if I must die
Now, before it is my time to die,
Surely this is no hardship: can anyone
Living, as I live, with evil all about me,
Think Death less than a friend? This death of mine
Is of no importance; but if I had left my brother
Lying in death unburied, I should have suffered.
Now I do not.

You smile at me. Ah Creon,
Think me a fool, if you like; but it may well be
That a fool convicts me of folly.

Choragos.   Like father, like daughter: both headstrong, deaf to reason!
She has never learned to yield.

Creon.   She has much to learn.
  The inflexible heart breaks first, the toughest iron
  Cracks first, and the wildest horses bend their necks
  At the pull of the smallest curb.
                                    Pride? In a slave?
  This girl is guilty of a double insolence,
  Breaking the given laws and boasting of it.
  Who is the man here,
  She or I, if this crime goes unpunished?
  Sister's child, or more than sister's child,
  Or closer yet in blood—she and her sister
  Win bitter death for this!

                                                      [*To servants:*]

                        Go, some of you,
  Arrest Ismenê. I accuse her equally.
  Bring her: you will find her sniffling in the house there.

  Her mind's a traitor: crimes kept in the dark
  Cry for light, and the guardian brain shudders;
  But how much worse than this
  Is brazen boasting of barefaced anarchy!
Antigonê.   Creon, what more do you want than my death?
Creon.   Nothing.
  That gives me everything.
Antigonê.   Then I beg you: kill me.
  This talking is a great weariness: your words
  Are distasteful to me, and I am sure that mine
  Seem so to you. And yet they should not seem so:
  I should have praise and honor for what I have done.
  All these men here would praise me
  Were their lips not frozen shut with fear of you.

                                                      [*Bitterly.*]

  Ah the good fortune of kings,
  Licensed to say and do whatever they please!
Creon.   You are alone here in that opinion.
Antigonê.   No, they are with me. But they keep their tongues in leash.
Creon.   Maybe. But you are guilty, and they are not.
Antigonê.   There is no guilt in reverence for the dead.
Creon.   But Eteoclês—was he not your brother too?
Antigonê.   My brother too.
Creon.   And you insult his memory?
Antigonê.   The dead man would not say that I insult it.   [*Softly.*]
Creon.   He would: for you honor a traitor as much as him.
Antigonê.   His own brother, traitor or not, and equal in blood.
Creon.   He made war on his country. Eteoclês defended it.
Antigonê.   Nevertheless, there are honors due all the dead.
Creon.   But not the same for the wicked as for the just.
Antigonê.   Ah Creon, Creon,
  Which of us can say what the gods hold wicked?

Creon.   An enemy is an enemy, even dead.

Antigonê.   It is my nature to join in love, not hate.

Creon.   Go join them, then; if you must have your love,

[*Finally losing patience.*]

Find it in hell!

Choragos.   But see, Ismenê comes:

[*Enter Ismenê, guarded.*]

Those tears are sisterly, the cloud
That shadows her eyes rains down gentle sorrow.

Creon.   You too, Ismenê,
Snake in my ordered house, sucking my blood
Stealthily—and all the time I never knew
That these two sisters were aiming at my throne!

Ismenê,
Do you confess your share in this crime, or deny it?
Answer me.

Ismenê.   Yes, if she will let me say so. I am guilty.

Antigonê.   No, Ismenê. You have no right to say so.   [*Coldly.*]
You would not help me, and I will not have you help me.

Ismenê.   But now I know what you meant; and I am here
To join you, to take my share of punishment.

Antigonê.   The dead man and the gods who rule the dead
Know whose act this was. Words are not friends.

Ismenê.   Do you refuse me, Antigonê? I want to die with you:
I too have a duty that I must discharge to the dead.

Antigonê.   You shall not lessen my death by sharing it.

Ismenê.   What do I care for life when you are dead?

Antigonê.   Ask Creon. You're always hanging on his opinions.

Ismenê.   You are laughing at me. Why, Antigonê?

Antigonê.   It's a joyless laughter, Ismenê.

Ismenê.   But can I do nothing?

Antigonê.   Yes. Save yourself. I shall not envy you.
There are those who will praise you; I shall have honor, too.

Ismenê.   But we are equally guilty!

Antigonê.   No more, Ismenê.
You are alive, but I belong to Death.

Creon.   Gentlemen, I beg you to observe these girls: [*To the Chorus:*]
One has just now lost her mind; the other,
It seems, has never had a mind at all.

Ismenê.   Grief teaches the steadiest minds to waver, King.

Creon.   Yours certainly did, when you assumed guilt with the guilty!

Ismenê.   But how could I go on living without her?

Creon.   You are.
She is already dead.

Ismenê.   But your own son's bride!

Creon.   There are places enough for him to push his plow.
I want no wicked women for my sons!

Ismenê.   O dearest Haimon, how your father wrongs you!

Creon.   I've had enough of your childish talk of marriage!

Choragos. Do you really intend to steal this girl from your son?
Creon. No; Death will do that for me.
Choragos.   Then she must die?
Creon. You dazzle me.   [*Ironically.*]
                    —But enough of this talk!

                                                                    [*To Guards:*]

You there, take them away and guard them well:
For they are but women, and even brave men run
When they see Death coming.

                              [*Exeunt Ismenê, Antigonê, and Guards.*]

Ode II

Chorus. Fortunate is the man who has never tasted   [*Strophe 1*]
              God's vengeance!
Where once the anger of heaven has struck, that house is shaken
For ever: damnation rises behind each child
Like a wave cresting out of the black northeast,
When the long darkness under sea roars up
And bursts drumming death upon the windwhipped sand.

I have seen this gathering sorrow from time long past   [*Antistrophe 1*]
Loom upon Oedipus' children: generation from generation
Takes the compulsive rage of the enemy god.
So lately this last flower of Oedipus' line
Drank the sunlight! but now a passionate word
And a handful of dust have closed up all its beauty.

              What mortal arrogance   [*Strophe 2*]
              Transcends the wrath of Zeus?
Sleep cannot lull him, nor the effortless long months
Of the timeless gods: but he is young for ever,
And his house is the shining day of high Olympos.
              All that is and shall be,
              And all the past, is his.
No pride on earth is free of the curse of heaven.

The straying dreams of men   [*Antistrophe 2*]
              May bring them ghosts of joy:
But as they drowse, the waking embers burn them;
Or they walk with fíxed éyes, as blind men walk.
But the ancient wisdom speaks for our own time:
              Fate works most for woe
              With Folly's fairest show.
Man's little pleasure is the spring of sorrow.

SCENE III

Choragos. But here is Haimon, King, the last of all your sons.

Is it grief for Antigonê that brings him here,
And bitterness at being robbed of his bride?

[*Enter Haimon.*]

Creon.   We shall soon see, and no need of diviners.

                                              —Son,
You have heard my final judgment on that girl:
Have you come here hating me, or have you come
With deference and with love, whatever I do?

Haimon.   I am your son, father. You are my guide.
You make things clear for me, and I obey you.
No marriage means more to me than your continuing wisdom.

Creon.   Good. That is the way to behave: subordinate
Everything else, my son, to your father's will.
This is what a man prays for, that he may get
Sons attentive and dutiful in his house,
Each one hating his father's enemies,
Honoring his father's friends. But if his sons
Fail him, if they turn out unprofitably,
What has he fathered but trouble for himself
And amusement for the malicious?

                                    So you are right
Not to lose your head over this woman.
Your pleasure with her would soon grow cold, Haimon,
And then you'd have a hellcat in bed and elsewhere.
Let her find her husband in Hell!
Of all the people in this city, only she
Has had contempt for my law and broken it.

Do you want me to show myself weak before the people?
Or to break my sworn word? No, and I will not.
The woman dies.
I suppose she'll plead "family ties." Well, let her.
If I permit my own family to rebel,
How shall I earn the world's obedience?
Show me the man who keeps his house in hand,
He's fit for public authority.

                              I'll have no dealings
With law-breakers, critics of the government:
Whoever is chosen to govern should be obeyed—
Must be obeyed, in all things, great and small,
Just and unjust! O Haimon,
The man who knows how to obey, and that man only,
Knows how to give commands when the time comes.
You can depend on him, no matter how fast
The spears come: he's a good soldier, he'll stick it out.

Anarchy, anarchy! Show me a greater evil!
This is why cities tumble and the great houses rain down,
This is what scatters armies!

No, no: good lives are made so by discipline.
We keep the laws then, and the lawmakers,
And no woman shall seduce us. If we must lose,
Let's lose to a man, at least! Is a woman stronger than we?

Choragos.   Unless time has rusted my wits,
What you say, King, is said with point and dignity.

Haimon.   Father: [*Boyishly earnest.*]
Reason is God's crowning gift to man, and you are right
To warn me against losing mine. I cannot say—
I hope that I shall never want to say!—that you
Have reasoned badly. Yet there are other men
Who can reason, too; and their opinions might be helpful.
You are not in a position to know everything
That people say or do, or what they feel:
Your temper terrifies them—everyone
Will tell you only what you like to hear.
But I, at any rate, can listen; and I have heard them
Muttering and whispering in the dark about this girl.
They say no woman has ever, so unreasonably,
Died so shameful a death for a generous act:
"She covered her brother's body. Is this indecent?
She kept him from dogs and vultures. Is this a crime?
Death?—She should have all the honor that we can give her!"

This is the way they talk out there in the city.

You must believe me:
Nothing is closer to me than your happiness.
What could be closer? Must not any son
Value his father's fortune as his father does his?
I beg you, do not be unchangeable:
Do not believe that you alone can be right.
The man who thinks that,
The man who maintains that only he has the power
To reason correctly, the gift to speak, the soul—
A man like that, when you know him, turns out empty.

It is not reason never to yield to reason!

In flood time you can see how some trees bend,
And because they bend, even their twigs are safe,
While stubborn trees are torn up, roots and all.
And the same thing happens in sailing:
Make your sheet fast, never slacken,—and over you go,
Head over heels and under: and there's your voyage.
Forget you are angry! Let yourself be moved!
I know I am young; but please let me say this:
The ideal condition
Would be, I admit, that men should be right by instinct;

But since we are all too likely to go astray,
The reasonable thing is to learn from those who can teach.
Choragos.   You will do well to listen to him, King,
If what he says is sensible. And you, Haimon,
Must listen to your father.—Both speak well.
Creon.   You consider it right for a man of my years and experience
To go to school to a boy?
Haimon.   It is not right
If I am wrong. But if I am young, and right,
What does my age matter?
Creon.   You think it right to stand up for an anarchist?
Haimon.   Not at all. I pay no respect to criminals.
Creon.   Then she is not a criminal?
Haimon.   The City would deny it, to a man.
Creon.   And the City proposes to teach me how to rule?
Haimon.   Ah. Who is it that's talking like a boy now?
Creon.   My voice is the one voice giving orders in this City!
Haimon.   It is no City if it takes orders from one voice.
Creon.   The State is the King!
Haimon.   Yes, if the State is a desert.

[*Pause.*]

Creon.   This boy, it seems, has sold out to a woman.
Haimon.   If you are a woman: my concern is only for you.
Creon.   So? Your "concern"! In a public brawl with your father!
Haimon.   How about you, in a public brawl with justice?
Creon.   With justice, when all that I do is within my rights?
Haimon.   You have no right to trample on God's right.
Creon.   Fool, adolescent fool! Taken in by a woman!

[*Completely out of control.*]

Haimon.   You'll never see me taken in by anything vile.
Creon.   Every word you say is for her!
Haimon.   And for you.   [*Quietly, darkly.*]
And for me. And for the gods under the earth.
Creon.   You'll never marry her while she lives.
Haimon.   Then she must die.—But her death will cause another.
Creon.   Another?
Have you lost your senses? It this an open threat?
Haimon.   There is no threat in speaking to emptiness.
Creon.   I swear you'll regret this superior tone of yours!
You are the empty one!
Haimon.   If you were not my father,
I'd say you were perverse.
Creon.   You girlstruck fool, don't play at words with me!
Haimon.   I am sorry. You prefer silence.
Creon.   Now, by God—!
I swear, by all the gods in heaven above us,
You'll watch it, I swear you shall!

[*To the Servants:*]

                                Bring her out!
        Bring the woman out! Let her die before his eyes!
        Here, this instant, with her bridegroom beside her!
Haimon.   Not here, no; she will not die here, King.
        And you will never see my face again.
        Go on raving as long as you've a friend to endure you.

                                                            [*Exit Haimon.*]

Choragos.   Gone, gone.
        Creon, a young man in a rage is dangerous!
Creon.   Let him do, or dream to do, more than a man can.
        He shall not save these girls from death.
Choragos.   These girls?
        You have sentenced them both?
Creon.   No, you are right.
        I will not kill the one whose hands are clean.
Choragos.   But Antigonê?
Creon.   I will carry her far away   [*Somberly.*]
        Out there in the wilderness, and lock her
        Living in a vault of stone. She shall have food,
        As the custom is, to absolve the State of her death.
        And there let her pray to the gods of hell:
        They are her only gods:
        Perhaps they will show her an escape from death,
        Or she may learn,
                          though late,
        That piety shown the dead is pity in vain.

                                                            [*Exit Creon.*]

Ode III

Chorus.   Love, unconquerable   [*Strophe*]
        Waster of rich men, keeper
        Of warm lights and all-night vigil
        In the soft face of a girl:
        Sea-wanderer, forest-visitor!
        Even the pure Immortals cannot escape you,
        And mortal man, in his one day's dusk,
        Trembles before your glory.

        Surely you swerve upon ruin   [*Antistrophe*]
        The just man's consenting heart,
        As here you have made bright anger
        Strike between father and son—
        And none has conquered but Love!
        A girl's glance working the will of heaven:
        Pleasure to her alone who mocks us,
        Merciless Aphroditê.

SCENE IV

Choragos. But I can no longer   [*As Antigonê enters guarded.*]
          stand in awe of this,
    Nor, seeing what I see, keep back my tears.
    Here is Antigonê, passing to that chamber
    Where all find sleep at last.

Antigonê.   Look upon me, friends, and pity me   [*Strophe 1*]
    Turning back at the night's edge to say
    Good-by to the sun that shines for me no longer;
    Now sleepy Death
    Summons me down to Acheron, that cold shore:
    There is no bridesong there, nor any music.
Chorus.   Yet not unpraised, not without a kind of honor,
    You walk at last into the underworld;
    Untouched by sickness, broken by no sword.
    What woman has ever found your way to death?

Antigonê.   How often I have heard the story of Niobê,   [*Antistrophe 1*]
    Tantalos' wretched daughter, how the stone
    Clung fast about her, ivy-close: and they say
    The rain falls endlessly
    And sifting soft snow; her tears are never done.
    I feel the loneliness of her death in mine.
Chorus.   But she was born of heaven, and you
    Are woman, woman-born. If her death is yours,
    A mortal woman's, is this not for you
    Glory in our world and in the world beyond?
Antigonê.   You laugh at me. Ah, friends, friends,
    Can you not wait until I am dead? O Thebes,
    O men many-charioted, in love with Fortune,
    Dear springs of Dircê, sacred Theban grove,
    Be witnesses for me, denied all pity,
    Unjustly judged! and think a word of love
    For her whose path turns
    Under dark earth, where there are no more tears.
Chorus.   You have passed beyond human daring and come at last
    Into a place of stone where Justice sits.
    I cannot tell
    What shape of your father's guilt appears in this.

Antigonê.   You have touched it at last: that bridal bed   [*Antistrophe 2*]
    Unspeakable, horror of son and mother mingling:
    Their crime, infection of all our family!
    O Oedipus, father and brother!
    Your marriage strikes from the grave to murder mine.
    I have been a stranger here in my own land:

All my life
The blasphemy of my birth has followed me.
Chorus.   Reverence is a virtue, but strength
Lives in established law: that must prevail.
You have made your choice,
Your death is the doing of your conscious hand.

Antigonê.   Then let me go, since all your words are bitter,   [*Epode*]
And the very light of the sun is cold to me.
Lead me to my vigil, where I must have
Neither love nor lamentation; no song, but silence.

[*Creon interrupts impatiently.*]

Creon.   If dirges and planned lamentations could put off death,
Men would be singing for ever.

[*To the Servants:*]

Take her, go!
You know your orders: take her to the vault
And leave her alone there. And if she lives or dies,
That's her affair, not ours: our hands are clean.

Antigonê.   O tomb, vaulted bride-bed in eternal rock,
Soon I shall be with my own again
Where Persephonê welcomes the thin ghosts underground:
And I shall see my father again, and you, mother,
And dearest Polyneicês—
                              dearest indeed
To me, since it was my hand
That washed him clean and poured the ritual wine:
And my reward is death before my time!

And yet, as men's hearts know, I have done no wrong,
I have not sinned before God. Or if I have,
I shall know the truth in death. But if the guilt
Lies upon Creon who judged me, then, I pray,
May his punishment equal my own.
Choragos.   O passionate heart,
Unyielding, tormented still by the same winds!
Creon.   Her guards shall have good cause to regret their delaying.
Antigonê.   Ah! That voice is like the voice of death!
Creon.   I can give you no reason to think you are mistaken.
Antigonê.   Thebes, and you my fathers' gods,
And rulers of Thebes, you see me now, the last
Unhappy daughter of a line of kings,
Your kings, led away to death. You will remember
What things I suffer, and at what men's hands,
Because I would not transgress the laws of heaven.

[*To the Guards, simply:*]

Come: let us wait no longer.

[*Exit Antigonê, L., guarded.*]

Ode IV

Chorus. All Danaê's beauty was locked away   [Strophe 1]
    In a brazen cell where the sunlight could not come:
    A small room, still as any grave, enclosed her.
    Yet she was a princess too,
    And Zeus in a rain of gold poured love upon her.
    O child, child,
    No power in wealth or war
    Or tough sea-blackened ships
    Can prevail against untiring Destiny!

    And Dryas' son also, that furious king,   *[Antistrophe 1]*
    Bore the god's prisoning anger for his pride:
    Sealed up by Dionysos in deaf stone,
    His madness died among echoes.
    So at the last he learned what dreadful power
    His tongue had mocked:
    For he had profaned the revels,
    And fired the wrath of the nine
    Implacable Sisters that love the sound of the flute.

    And old men tell a half-remembered tale   *[Strophe 2]*
    Of horror where a dark ledge splits the sea
    And a double surf beats on the gráy shóres:
    How a king's new woman, sick
    With hatred for the queen he had imprisoned,
    Ripped out his two sons' eyes with her bloody hands
    While grinning Arês watched the shuttle plunge
    Four times: four blind wounds crying for revenge,

    Crying, tears and blood mingled.—Piteously born,   *[Antistrophe 2]*
    Those sons whose mother was of heavenly birth!
    Her father was the god of the North Wind
    And she was cradled by gales,
    She raced with young colts on the glittering hills
    And walked untrammeled in the open light:
    But in her marriage deathless Fate found means
    To build a tomb like yours for all her joy.

SCENE V

[Enter blind Teiresias, led by a boy. The opening speeches of Teiresias should be in singsong contrast to the realistic lines of Creon.]

Teiresias. This is the way the blind man comes, Princes, Princes,
    Lock-step, two heads lit by the eyes of one.
Creon. What new thing have you to tell us, old Teiresias?
Teiresias. I have much to tell you: listen to the prophet, Creon.

Creon. I am not aware that I have ever failed to listen.

Teiresias. Then you have done wisely, King, and ruled well.

Creon. I admit my debt to you. But what have you to say?

Teiresias. This, Creon: you stand once more on the edge of fate.

Creon. What do you mean? Your words are a kind of dread.

Teiresias. Listen, Creon:
  I was sitting in my chair of augury, at the place
  Where the birds gather about me. They were all a-chatter,
  As is their habit, when suddenly I heard
  A strange note in their jangling, a scream, a
  Whirring fury; I knew that they were fighting,
  Tearing each other, dying
  In a whirlwind of wings clashing. And I was afraid.
  I began the rites of burnt-offering at the altar,
  But Hephaistos failed me: instead of bright flame,
  There was only the sputtering slime of the fat thigh-flesh
  Melting: the entrails dissolved in gray smoke;
  The bare bone burst from the welter. And no blaze!

  This was a sign from heaven. My boy described it,
  Seeing for me as I see for others.

  I tell you, Creon, you yourself have brought
  This new calamity upon us. Our hearths and altars
  Are stained with the corruption of dogs and carrion birds
  That glut themselves on the corpse of Oedipus' son.
  The gods are deaf when we pray to them, their fire
  Recoils from our offering, their birds of omen
  Have no cry of comfort, for they are gorged
  With the thick blood of the dead.
                              O my son,
  These are no trifles! Think: all men make mistakes,
  But a good man yields when he knows his course is wrong,
  And repairs the evil. The only crime is pride.

  Give in to the dead man, then: do not fight with a corpse—
  What glory is it to kill a man who is dead?
  Think, I beg you:
  It is for your own good that I speak as I do.
  You should be able to yield for your own good.

Creon. It seems that prophets have made me their especial province.
  All my life long
  I have been a kind of butt for the dull arrows
  Of doddering fortune-tellers!
                              No, Teiresias:
  If your birds—if the great eagles of God himself
  Should carry him stinking bit by bit to heaven,
  I would not yield. I am not afraid of pollution:
  No man can defile the gods.

                                            Do what you will,
          Go into business, make money, speculate
          In India gold or that synthetic gold from Sardis,
          Get rich otherwise than by my consent to bury him.
          Teiresias, it is a sorry thing when a wise man
          Sells his wisdom, lets out his words for hire!
Teiresias. Ah Creon! Is there no man left in the world—
Creon. To do what?—Come, let's have the aphorism!
Teiresias. No man who knows that wisdom outweighs any wealth?
Creon. As surely as bribes are baser than any baseness.
Teiresias. You are sick, Creon! You are deathly sick!
Creon. As you say: it is not my place to challenge a prophet.
Teiresias. Yet you have said my prophecy is for sale.
Creon. The generation of prophets has always loved gold.
Teiresias. The generation of kings has always loved brass.
Creon. You forget yourself! You are speaking to your King.
Teiresias. I know it. You are a king because of me.
Creon. You have a certain skill; but you have sold out.
Teiresias. King, you will drive me to words that—
Creon.   Say them, say them!
          Only remember: I will not pay you for them.
Teiresias. No, you will find them too costly.
Creon.   No doubt. Speak:
          Whatever you say, you will not change my will.
Teiresias. Then take this, and take it to heart!
          The time is not far off when you shall pay back
          Corpse for corpse, flesh of your own flesh.
          You have thrust the child of this world into living night,
          You have kept from the gods below the child that is theirs:
          The one in a grave before her death, the other,
          Dead, denied the grave. This is your crime:
          And the Furies and the dark gods of Hell
          Are swift with terrible punishment for you.

          Do you want to buy me now, Creon?

                                       Not many days,
          And your house will be full of men and women weeping,
          And curses will be hurled at you from far
          Cities grieving for sons unburied, left to rot
          Before the walls of Thebes.

          These are my arrows, Creon: they are all for you.

                                                              [*To Boy:*]

          But come, child: lead me home.
          Let him waste his fine anger upon younger men.
          Maybe he will learn at last
          To control a wiser tongue in a better head.

                                                    [*Exit Teiresias.*]

Choragos. The old man has gone, King, but his words
  Remain to plague us. I am old, too,
  But I cannot remember that he was ever false.
Creon. That is true. . . . It troubles me.
  Oh it is hard to give in! but it is worse
  To risk everything for stubborn pride.
Choragos. Creon: take my advice.
Creon.   What shall I do?
Choragos. Go quickly: free Antigonê from her vault
  And build a tomb for the body of Polyneicês.
Creon. You would have me do this?
Choragos.   Creon, yes!
  And it must be done at once: God moves
  Swiftly to cancel the folly of stubborn men.
Creon. It is hard to deny the heart! But I
  Will do it: I will not fight with destiny.
Choragos. You must go yourself, you cannot leave it to others.
Creon. I will go.
          —Bring axes, servants:
  Come with me to the tomb. I buried her, I
  Will set her free.
              Oh quickly!
  My mind misgives—
  The laws of the gods are mighty, and a man must serve them
  To the last day of his life!

                                        [*Exit Creon.*]

Paean

Choragos. God of many names   [*Strophe 1*]
Chorus.   O Iacchos
                              son
  of Kadmeian Sémelê
                    O born of the Thunder!
  Guardian of the West
                    Regent
  of Eleusis' plain
                    O Prince of maenad Thebes
  and the Dragon Field by rippling Ismenos:

Choragos. God of many names   [*Antistrophe 1*]
Chorus.   the flame of torches
  flares on our hills
                    the nymphs of Iacchos
  dance at the spring of Castalia:
  from the vine-close mountain
                              come ah come in ivy:
  Evohé evohé! sings through the streets of Thebes

Choragos.   God of many names   [*Strophe 2*]
Chorus.   Iachos of Thebes
   heavenly Child
        of Sémelê bride of the Thunderer!
   The shadow of plague is upon us:
            come
  with clement feet
        oh come from Parnasos
  down the long slopes
        across the lamenting water

Choragos.   Iô Fire! Chorister of the throbbing stars!   [*Antistrophe 2*]
  O purest among the voices of the night!
  Thou son of God, blaze for us!
Chorus.   Come with choric rapture of circling Maenads
  Who cry *Iô Iacche!*
      God of many names!

Exodos

[*Enter Messenger, L.*]

Messenger.   Men of the line of Kadmos, you who live
  Near Amphion's citadel:
          I cannot say
  Of any condition of human life "This is fixed,
  This is clearly good, or bad." Fate raises up,
  And Fate casts down the happy and unhappy alike:
  No man can foretell his Fate.
          Take the case of Creon:
  Creon was happy once, as I count happiness:
  Victorious in battle, sole governor of the land,
  Fortunate father of children nobly born.
  And now it has all gone from him! Who can say
  That a man is still alive when his life's joy fails?
  He is a walking dead man. Grant him rich,
  Let him live like a king in his great house:
  If his pleasure is gone, I would not give
  So much as the shadow of smoke for all he owns.
Choragos.   Your words hint at sorrow: what is your news for us?
Messenger.   They are dead. The living are guilty of their death.
Choragos.   Who is guilty? Who is dead? Speak!
Messenger.   Haimon.
  Haimon is dead; and the hand that killed him
  Is his own hand.
Choragos.   His father's? or his own?
Messenger.   His own, driven mad by the murder his father had done.

Choragos. Teiresias, Teiresias, how clearly you saw it all!

Messenger. This is my news: you must draw what conclusions you can from
                  it.

Choragos. But look: Eurydicê, our Queen:
                  Has she overheard us?

                                     [*Enter Eurydicê from the Palace, C.*]

Eurydicê. I have heard something, friends:
                  As I was unlocking the gate of Pallas' shrine,
                  For I needed her help today, I heard a voice
                  Telling of some new sorrow. And I fainted
                  There at the temple with all my maidens about me.
                  But speak again: whatever it is, I can bear it:
                  Grief and I are no strangers.

Messenger.   Dearest Lady,
                  I will tell you plainly all that I have seen.
                  I shall not try to comfort you: what is the use,
                  Since comfort could lie only in what is not true?
                  The truth is always best.

                                     I went with Creon
                  To the outer plain where Polyneicês was lying,
                  No friend to pity him, his body shredded by dogs.
                  We made our prayers in that place to Hecatê
                  And Pluto, that they would be merciful. And we bathed
                  The corpse with holy water, and we brought
                  Fresh-broken branches to burn what was left of it,
                  And upon the urn we heaped up a towering barrow
                  Of the earth of his own land.

                                     When we were done, we ran
                  To the vault where Antigonê lay on her couch of stone.
                  One of the servants had gone ahead,
                  And while he was yet far off he heard a voice
                  Grieving within the chamber, and he came back
                  And told Creon. And as the King went closer,
                  The air was full of wailing, the words lost,
                  And he begged us to make all haste. "Am I a prophet?"
                  He said, weeping, "And must I walk this road,
                  The saddest of all that I have gone before?
                  My son's voice calls me on. Oh quickly, quickly!
                  Look through the crevice there, and tell me
                  If it is Haimon, or some deception of the gods!"

                  We obeyed; and in the cavern's farthest corner
                  We saw her lying:
                  She had made a noose of her fine linen veil
                  And hanged herself. Haimon lay beside her,
                  His arms about her waist, lamenting her,
                  His love lost under ground, crying out
                  That his father had stolén her away from him.

                                                         SOPHOCLES   377

When Creon saw him the tears rushed to his eyes
And he called to him: "What have you done, child? Speak to me.
What are you thinking that makes your eyes so strange?
O my son, my son, I come to you on my knees!"
But Haimon spat in his face. He said not a word,
Staring—
        And suddenly drew his sword
And lunged. Creon shrank back, the blade missed; and the boy,
Desperate against himself, drove it half its length
Into his own side, and fell. And as he died
He gathered Antigonê close in his arms again,
Choking, his blood bright red on her white cheek.
And now he lies dead with the dead, and she is his
At last, his bride in the houses of the dead.

                                    [Exit Eurydicê into the Palace.]

Choragos.   She has left us without a word. What can this mean?
Messenger.   It troubles me, too; yet she knows what is best,
    Her grief is too great for public lamentation,
    And doubtless she has gone to her chamber to weep
    For her dead son, leading her maidens in his dirge.
Choragos.   It may be so: but I fear this deep silence.   *[Pause.]*
Messenger.   I will see what she is doing. I will go in.

                               [Exit Messenger into the Palace.]
                  [Enter Creon with attendants, bearing Haimon's body.]

Choragos.   But here is the King himself: oh look at him,
    Bearing his own damnation in his arms.
Creon.   Nothing you say can touch me any more.
    My own blind heart has brought me
    From darkness to final darkness. Here you see
    The father murdering, the murdered son—
    And all my civic wisdom!

    Haimon my son, so young, so young to die,
    I was the fool, not you; and you died for me.
Choragos.   That is the truth; but you were late in learning it.
Creon.   This truth is hard to bear. Surely a god
    Has crushed me beneath the hugest weight of heaven,
    And driven me headlong a barbaric way
    To trample out the thing I held most dear.

    The pains that men will take to come to pain!

                                [Enter Messenger from the Palace.]

Messenger.   The burden you carry in your hands is heavy,
    But it is not all: you will find more in your house.
Creon.   What burden worse than this shall I find there?

Messenger.   The Queen is dead.

Creon.   O port of death, deaf world,
    Is there no pity for me? And you, Angel of evil,
    I was dead, and your words are death again.
    Is it true, boy? Can it be true?
    Is my wife dead? Has death bred death?

Messenger.   You can see for yourself.

[*The doors are opened, and the body of Eurydicê is disclosed within.*]

Creon.   Oh pity!
    All true, all true, and more than I can bear!
    O my wife, my son!

Messenger.   She stood before the altar, and her heart
    Welcomed the knife her own hand guided,
    And a great cry burst from her lips for Megareus dead,
    And for Haimon dead, her sons; and her last breath
    Was a curse for their father, the murderer of her sons,
    And she fell, and the dark flowed in through her closing eyes.

Creon.   O God, I am sick with fear.
    Are there no swords here? Has no one a blow for me?

Messenger.   Her curse is upon you for the deaths of both.

Creon.   It is right that it should be. I alone am guilty.
    I know it, and I say it. Lead me in,
    Quickly, friends.
    I have neither life nor substance. Lead me in.

Choragos.   You are right, if there can be right in so much wrong.
    The briefest way is best in a world of sorrow.

Creon.   Let it come,
    Let death come quickly, and be kind to me.
    I would not ever see the sun again.

Choragos.   All that will come when it will; but we, meanwhile,
    Have much to do. Leave the future to itself.

Creon.   All my heart was in that prayer!

Choragos.   Then do not pray any more: the sky is deaf.

Creon.   Lead me away. I have been rash and foolish.
    I have killed my son and my wife.
    I look for comfort; my comfort lies here dead.
    Whatever my hands have touched has come to nothing.
    Fate has brought all my pride to a thought of dust.

[*As Creon is being led into the house, the Choragos advances and speaks
directly to the audience.*]

Choragos.   There is no happiness where there is no wisdom;
    No wisdom but in submission to the gods.
    Big words are always punished,
    And proud men in old age learn to be wise.

Questions

1. Critics have traditionally divided over the question of whether Antigone or Creon is the protagonist in the play. How does the answer to this question affect one's interpretation of the play? **2.** How does the Prologue establish the mood and theme of the play? **3.** Does the character of Antigone change during the course of the play? **4.** Does the action of the play prepare us for the change in Creon—that is, for his realization that he has been wrong? **5.** Can *Antigone* be read as a justification for civil disobedience? Explain. **6.** Is there any justification for Antigone's cold refusal to allow Ismene to share her martyrdom? Explain. **7.** To what extent and in what ways does the Chorus contribute to the dramatic development and tension of the play?

An Enemy of the People[*]

HENRIK IBSEN   [1828–1906]

DRAMATIS PERSONAE

Dr. Thomas Stockmann,   *Medical Officer of the Municipal Baths.*
Mrs. Stockmann,   *his wife.*
Petra,   *their daughter, a teacher.*
Ejlif
Morten   } *their sons (aged 13 and 10 respectively).*
Peter Stockmann,   *the Doctor's elder brother; Mayor of the Town and Chief Constable, Chairman of the Baths' Committee, etc., etc.*
Morten Kiil,   *a tanner (Mrs. Stockmann's adoptive father).*
Hovstad,   *editor of the "People's Messenger."*
Billing,   *sub-editor.*
Captain Horster.
Aslaksen,   *a printer.*
Men of various conditions and occupations, some few women, and a troop of schoolboys—the audience at a public meeting.

The action takes place in a coast town in southern Norway.

Act I

(SCENE.   *Dr. Stockmann's sitting-room. It is evening. The room is plainly but neatly appointed and furnished. In the right-hand wall are two doors; the farther leads out to the hall, the nearer to the doctor's study. In the left-hand wall, opposite the door leading to the hall, is a door leading to the other rooms occupied by the family. In the middle of the same wall stands the stove, and, further forward, a couch with a looking-glass hanging over it and an oval table in front of it. On the table, a lighted lamp, with a lampshade. At the back of the room, an open door leads to the dining-room. Billing is seen sitting at the dining table, on which a lamp is burning. He has a napkin tucked under his chin, and Mrs. Stockmann is standing by the table handing him a large plate-full of roast beef. The other places at the table are empty, and the table somewhat in disorder, a meal having evidently recently been finished.)*

---

*Translated by R. Farquharson Sharp.

Mrs. Stockmann. You see, if you come an hour late, Mr. Billing, you have to put up with cold meat.

Billing (*as he eats*). It is uncommonly good, thank you—remarkably good.

Mrs. Stockmann. My husband makes such a point of having his meals punctually, you know—

Billing. That doesn't affect me a bit. Indeed, I almost think I enjoy a meal all the better when I can sit down and eat all by myself and undisturbed.

Mrs. Stockmann. Oh well, as long as you are enjoying it—. (*Turns to the hall door, listening.*) I expect that is Mr. Hovstad coming too.

Billing. Very likely.

(*Peter Stockmann comes in. He wears an overcoat and his official hat, and carries a stick.*)

Peter Stockmann. Good evening, Katherine.

Mrs. Stockmann (*coming forward into the sitting-room*). Ah, good evening—is it you? How good of you to come up and see us!

Peter Stockmann. I happened to be passing, and so—(*looks into the dining-room*). But you have company with you, I see.

Mrs. Stockmann (*a little embarrassed*). Oh, no—it was quite by chance he came in. (*Hurriedly.*) Won't you come in and have something, too?

Peter Stockmann. I! No, thank you. Good gracious—hot meat at night! Not with my digestion.

Mrs. Stockmann. Oh, but just once in a way—

Peter Stockmann. No, no, my dear lady; I stick to my tea and bread and butter. It is much more wholesome in the long run—and a little more economical, too.

Mrs. Stockmann (*smiling*). Now you mustn't think that Thomas and I are spendthrifts.

Peter Stockmann. Not you, my dear; I would never think that of you. (*Points to the Doctor's study.*) Is he not at home?

Mrs. Stockmann. No, he went for a little turn after supper—he and the boys.

Peter Stockmann. I doubt if that is a wise thing to do. (*Listens.*) I fancy I hear him coming now.

Mrs. Stockmann. No, I don't think it is he. (*A knock is heard at the door.*) Come in! (*Hovstad comes in from the hall.*) Oh, it is you, Mr. Hovstad!

Hovstad. Yes, I hope you will forgive me, but I was delayed at the printers. Good evening, Mr. Mayor.

Peter Stockmann (*bowing a little distantly*). Good evening. You have come on business, no doubt.

Hovstad. Partly. It's about an article for the paper.

Peter Stockmann. So I imagined. I hear my brother has become a prolific contributor to the "People's Messenger."

Hovstad. Yes, he is good enough to write in the "People's Messenger" when he has any home truths to tell.

Mrs. Stockmann (*to Hovstad*). But won't you—? (*Points to the dining-room.*)

Peter Stockmann. Quite so, quite so. I don't blame him in the least, as a writer, for addressing himself to the quarters where he will find the readiest sympathy. And, besides that, I personally have no reason to bear any ill will to your paper, Mr. Hovstad.

Hovstad. I quite agree with you.

Peter Stockmann. Taking one thing with another, there is an excellent spirit of toleration in the town—an admirable municipal spirit. And it all springs from the fact of our having a great common interest to unite us—an interest that is in an equally high degree the concern of every right-minded citizen—

Hovstad. The Baths, yes.

Peter Stockmann. Exactly—our fine, new, handsome Baths. Mark my words, Mr. Hovstad—the Baths will become the focus of our municipal life! Not a doubt of it!

Mrs. Stockmann. That is just what Thomas says.

Peter Stockmann. Think how extraordinarily the place has developed within the last year or two! Money has been flowing in, and there is some life and some business doing in the town. Houses and landed property are rising in value every day.

Hovstad. And unemployment is diminishing.

Peter Stockmann. Yes, that is another thing. The burden of the poor rates has been lightened, to the great relief of the propertied classes; and that relief will be even greater if only we get a really good summer this year, and lots of visitors—plenty of invalids, who will make the Baths talked about.

Hovstad. And there is a good prospect of that, I hear.

Peter Stockmann. It looks very promising. Enquiries about apartments and that sort of thing are reaching us every day.

Hovstad. Well, the doctor's article will come in very suitably.

Peter Stockmann. Has he been writing something just lately?

Hovstad. This is something he wrote in the winter; a recommendation of the Baths—an account of the excellent sanitary conditons here. But I held the article over, temporarily.

Peter Stockmann. Ah,—some little difficulty about it, I suppose?

Hovstad. No, not at all; I thought it would be better to wait till the spring, because it is just at this time that people begin to think seriously about their summer quarters.

Peter Stockmann. Quite right; you were perfectly right, Mr. Hovstad.

Hovstad. Yes, Thomas is really indefatigable when it is a question of the Baths.

Peter Stockmann. Well—remember, he is the Medical Officer to the Baths.

Hovstad. Yes, and what is more, they owe their existence to him.

Peter Stockmann. To him? Indeed! It is true I have heard from time to time that some people are of that opinion. At the same time I must say I imagined that I took a modest part in the enterprise.

Mrs. Stockmann. Yes, that is what Thomas is always saying.

Hovstad. But who denies it, Mr. Stockmann? You set the thing going and made a practical concern of it; we all know that. I only meant that the idea of it came first from the doctor.

Peter Stockmann. Oh, ideas—yes! My brother has had plenty of them in his time—unfortunately. But when it is a question of putting an idea into practical shape, you have to apply to a man of different mettle, Mr. Hovstad. And I certainly should have thought that in this house at least—

Mrs. Stockmann. My dear Peter—

Hovstad. How can you think that—?

Mrs. Stockmann. Won't you go in and have something, Mr. Hovstad? My husband is sure to be back directly.

Hovstad. Thank you, perhaps just a morsel. (*Goes into the dining-room.*)

Peter Stockmann (*lowering his voice a little*). It is a curious thing that these farmers' sons never seem to lose their want of tact.

Mrs. Stockmann. Surely it is not worth bothering about! Cannot you and Thomas share the credit as brothers?

Peter Stockmann. I should have thought so; but apparently some people are not satisfied with a share.

Mrs. Stockmann. What nonsense! You and Thomas get on so capitally together. (*Listens.*) There he is at last, I think. (*Goes out and opens the door leading to the hall.*)

Dr. Stockmann (*laughing and talking outside*). Look here—here is another guest for you, Katherine. Isn't that jolly! Come in, Captain Horster; hang your coat upon this peg. Ah, you don't wear an overcoat. Just think, Katherine; I met him in the street and could hardly persuade him to come up! (*Captain Horster comes into the room and greets Mrs. Stockmann. He is followed by Dr. Stockmann.*) Come along in, boys. They are ravenously hungry again, you know. Come along, Captain Horster; you must have a slice of beef. (*Pushes Horster into the dining-room. Ejlif and Morten go in after them.*)

Mrs. Stockmann. But, Thomas, don't you see—?

Dr. Stockmann (*turning in the doorway*). Oh, is it you, Peter? (*Shakes hands with him.*) Now that is very delightful.

Peter Stockmann. Unfortunately I must go in a moment—

Dr. Stockmann. Rubbish! There is some toddy just coming in. You haven't forgotten the toddy, Katherine?

Mrs. Stockmann. Of course not; the water is boiling now. (*Goes into the dining-room.*)

Peter Stockmann. Toddy too!

Dr. Stockmann. Yes, sit down and we will have it comfortably.

Peter Stockmann. Thanks, I never care about an evening's drinking.

Dr. Stockmann. But this isn't an evening's drinking.

Peter Stockmann. It seems to me—. (*Looks towards the dining-room.*) It is extraordinary how they can put away all that food.

Dr. Stockmann (*rubbing his hands*).   Yes, isn't it splendid to see young people eat? They have always got an appetite, you know! That's as it should be. Lots of food—to build up their strength! They are the people who are going to stir up the fermenting forces of the future, Peter.

Peter Stockmann.   May I ask what they will find here to "stir up," as you put it?

Dr. Stockmann.   Ah, you must ask the young people that—when the time comes. We shan't be able to see it, of course. That stands to reason—two old fogies, like us—

Peter Stockmann.   Really, really! I must say that is an extremely odd expression to—

Dr. Stockmann.   Oh, you mustn't take me too literally, Peter. I am so heartily happy and contented, you know. I think it is such an extraordinary piece of good fortune to be in the middle of all this growing, germinating life. It is a splendid time to live in! It is as if a whole new world were being created around one.

Peter Stockmann.   Do you really think so?

Dr. Stockmann.   Ah, naturally you can't appreciate it as keenly as I. You have lived all your life in these surroundings, and your impressions have got blunted. But I, who have been buried all these years in my little corner up north, almost without ever seeing a stranger who might bring new ideas with him—well, in my case it has just the same effect as if I had been transported into the middle of a crowded city.

Peter Stockmann.   Oh, a city—!

Dr. Stockmann.   I know, I know; it is all cramped enough here, compared with many other places. But there is life here—there is promise—there are innumerable things to work for and fight for; and that is the main thing. (*Calls.*) Katherine, hasn't the postman been here?

Mrs. Stockmann (*from the dining-room*).   No.

Dr. Stockmann.   And then to be comfortably off, Peter! That is something one learns to value, when one has been on the brink of starvation, as we have.

Peter Stockmann.   Oh, surely—

Dr. Stockmann.   Indeed I can assure you we have often been very hard put to it, up there. And now to be able to live like a lord! To-day, for instance, we had roast beef for dinner—and, what is more, for supper too. Won't you come and have a little bit? Or let me show it you, at any rate? Come here—

Peter Stockmann.   No, no—not for worlds!

Dr. Stockmann.   Well, but just come here then. Do you see, we have got a table-cover?

Peter Stockmann.   Yes, I noticed it.

Dr. Stockmann.   And we have got a lamp-shade too. Do you see? All out of Katherine's savings! It makes the room so cosy. Don't you think so? Just stand here for a moment—no, no, not there—just here, that's it! Look now, when you get the light on it altogether—I really think it looks very nice, doesn't it?

Peter Stockmann. Oh, if you can afford luxuries of this kind—

Dr. Stockmann. Yes, I can afford it now. Katherine tells me I earn almost as much as we spend.

Peter Stockmann. Almost—yes!

Dr. Stockmann. But a scientific man must live in a little bit of style. I am quite sure an ordinary civil servant spends more in a year than I do.

Peter Stockmann. I daresay. A civil servant—a man in a well-paid position—

Dr. Stockmann. Well, any ordinary merchant, then! A man in that position spends two or three times a much as—

Peter Stockmann. It just depends on circumstances.

Dr. Stockmann. At all events I assure you I don't waste money unprofitably. But I can't find it in my heart to deny myself the pleasure of entertaining my friends. I need that sort of thing, you know. I have lived for so long shut out of it all, that it is a necessity of life to me to mix with young, eager, ambitious men, men of liberal and active minds; and that describes every one of those fellows who are enjoying their supper in there. I wish you knew more of Hovstad—

Peter Stockmann. By the way, Hovstad was telling me he was going to print another article of yours.

Dr. Stockmann. An article of mine?

Peter Stockmann. Yes, about the Baths. An article you wrote in the winter.

Dr. Stockmann. Oh, that one! No, I don't intend that to appear just for the present.

Peter Stockmann. Why not? It seems to me that this would be the most opportune moment.

Dr. Stockmann. Yes, very likely—under normal conditions. (*Crosses the room.*)

Peter Stockmann (*following him with his eyes*). Is there anything abnormal about the present conditions?

Dr. Stockmann (*standing still*). To tell you the truth, Peter, I can't say just at this moment—at all events not tonight. There may be much that is very abnormal about the present conditions—and it is possible there may be nothing abnormal about them at all. It is quite possible it may be merely my imagination.

Peter Stockmann. I must say it all sounds most mysterious. Is there something going on that I am to be kept in ignorance of? I should have imagined that I, as Chairman of the governing body of the Baths—

Dr. Stockmann. And I should have imagined that I—. Oh, come, don't let us fly out at one another, Peter.

Peter Stockmann. Heaven forbid! I am not in the habit of flying out at people, as you call it. But I am entitled to request most emphatically that all arrangements shall be made in a business-like manner, through the proper channels, and shall be dealt with by the legally constituted authorities. I can allow no going behind our backs by any roundabout means.

Dr. Stockmann. Have I ever at any time tried to go behind your backs!

Peter Stockmann. You have an ingrained tendency to take your own way, at all events; and that is almost equally inadmissible in a well ordered community. The individual ought undoubtedly to acquiesce in subordinating himself to the community—or, to speak more accurately, to the authorities who have the care of the community's welfare.

Dr. Stockmann. Very likely. But what the deuce has all this got to do with me?

Peter Stockmann. That is exactly what you never appear to be willing to learn, my dear Thomas. But, mark my words, some day you will have to suffer for it—sooner or later. Now I have told you. Good-bye.

Dr. Stockmann. Have you taken leave of your senses? You are on the wrong scent altogether.

Peter Stockmann. I am not usually that. You must excuse me now if I—(*calls into the dining-room*). Good night, Katherine. Good night, gentlemen. (*Goes out.*)

Mrs. Stockmann (*coming from the dining-room*). Has he gone?

Dr. Stockmann. Yes, and in such a bad temper.

Mrs. Stockmann. But, dear Thomas, what have you been doing to him again?

Dr. Stockmann. Nothing at all. And, anyhow, he can't oblige me to make my report before the proper time.

Mrs. Stockmann. What have you got to make a report to him about?

Dr. Stockmann. Hm! Leave that to me, Katherine.—It is an extraordinary thing that the postman doesn't come.

(*Hovstad, Billing, and Horster have got up from the table and come into the sitting-room. Ejlif and Morten come in after them.*)

Billing (*stretching himself*). Ah!—one feels a new man after a meal like that.

Hovstad. The mayor wasn't in a very sweet temper tonight, then.

Dr. Stockmann. It is his stomach; he has a wretched digestion.

Hovstad. I rather think it was us two of the "People's Messenger" that he couldn't digest.

Mrs. Stockmann. I thought you came out of it pretty well with him.

Hovstad. Oh yes; but it isn't anything more than a sort of truce.

Billing. That is just what it is! That word sums up the situation.

Dr. Stockmann. We must remember that Peter is a lonely man, poor chap. He has no home comforts of any kind; nothing but everlasting business. And all that infernal weak tea wash that he pours into himself! Now then, my boys, bring chairs up to the table. Aren't we going to have that toddy, Katherine?

Mrs. Stockmann (*going into the dining-room*). I am just getting it.

Dr. Stockmann. Sit down here on the couch beside me, Captain Horster. We so seldom see you—. Please sit down, my friends. (*They sit down at the* *table. Mrs. Stockmann brings a tray, with a spirit-lamp, glasses, bottles, etc., upon it.)*

Mrs. Stockmann. There you are! This is arrack, and this is rum, and this one is the brandy. Now everyone must help themselves.

Dr. Stockmann (*taking a glass*). We will. (*They all mix themselves some toddy.*) And let us have the cigars. Ejlif, you know where the box is. And you, Morten, can fetch my pipe. (*The two boys go into the room on the right.*) I have a suspicion that Ejlif pockets a cigar now and then!—but I take no notice of it. (*Calls out.*) And my smoking-cap too, Morten. Katherine, you can tell him where I left it. Ah, he has got it. (*The boys bring the various things.*) Now, my friends. I stick to my pipe, you know. This one has seen plenty of bad weather with me up north. (*Touches glasses with them.*) Your good health! Ah, it is good to be sitting snug and warm here.

Mrs. Stockmann (*who sits knitting*). Do you sail soon, Captain Horster?

Horster. I expect to be ready to sail next week.

Mrs. Stockmann. I suppose you are going to America?

Horster. Yes, that is the plan.

Mrs. Stockmann. Then you won't be able to take part in the coming election.

Horster. Is there going to be an election?

Billing. Didn't you know?

Horster. No, I don't mix myself up with those things.

Billing. But do you not take an interest in public affairs?

Horster. No, I don't know anything about politics.

Billing. All the same, one ought to vote, at any rate.

Horster. Even if one doesn't know anything about what is going on?

Billing. Doesn't know! What do you mean by that? A community is like a ship; every one ought to be prepared to take the helm.

Horster. Maybe that is all very well on shore; but on board ship it wouldn't work.

Hovstad. It is astonishing how little most sailors care about what goes on on shore.

Billing. Very extraordinary.

Dr. Stockmann. Sailors are like birds of passage; they feel equally at home in any latitude. And that is only an additional reason for our being all the more keen, Hovstad. Is there to be anything of public interest in tomorrow's "Messenger"?

Hovstad. Nothing about municipal affairs. But the day after to-morrow I was thinking of printing your article—

Dr. Stockmann. Ah, devil take it—my article! Look here, that must wait a bit.

Hovstad. Really? We had just got convenient space for it, and I thought it was just the opportune moment—

Dr. Stockmann. Yes, yes, very likely you are right; but it must wait all the same. I will explain to you later. (*Petra comes in from the hall, in hat and cloak and with a bundle of exercise books under her arm.*)

Petra.   Good evening.

Dr. Stockmann.   Good evening, Petra; come along. (*Mutual greetings; Petra takes off her things and puts them down on a chair by the door.*)

Petra.   And you have all been sitting here enjoying yourselves, while I have been out slaving!

Dr. Stockmann.   Well, come and enjoy yourself too!

Billing.   May I mix a glass for you?

Petra (*coming to the table*).   Thanks, I would rather do it; you always mix it too strong. But I forgot, father—I have a letter for you. (*Goes to the chair where she has laid her things.*)

Dr. Stockmann.   A letter? From whom?

Petra (*looking in her coat pocket*).   The postman gave it to me just as I was going out—

Dr. Stockmann (*getting up and going to her*).   And you only give to me now!

Petra.   I really had not time to run up again. There it is!

Dr. Stockmann (*seizing the letter*).   Let's see, let's see, child! (*Looks at the address.*) Yes, that's all right!

Mrs. Stockmann.   Is it the one you have been expecting so anxiously, Thomas?

Dr. Stockmann.   Yes, it is. I must go to my room now and—. Where shall I get a light, Katherine? Is there no lamp in my room again?

Mrs. Stockmann.   Yes, your lamp is all ready lit on your desk.

Dr. Stockmann.   Good, good. Excuse me for a moment—. (*Goes into his study.*)

Petra.   What do you suppose it is, mother?

Mrs. Stockmann.   I don't know; for the last day or two he has always been asking if the postman has not been.

Billing.   Probably some country patient.

Petra.   Poor old dad!—he will overwork himself soon. (*Mixes a glass for herself.*) There, that will taste good!

Hovstad.   Have you been teaching in the evening school again to-day?

Petra (*sipping from her glass*).   Two hours.

Billing.   And four hours of school in the morning—

Petra.   Five hours.

Mrs. Stockmann.   And you have still got exercises to correct, I see.

Petra.   A whole heap, yes.

Horster.   You are pretty full up with work too, it seems to me.

Petra.   Yes—but that is good. One is so delightfully tired after it.

Billing.   Do you like that?

Petra.   Yes, because one sleeps so well then.

Morten.   You must be dreadfully wicked, Petra.

Petra.   Wicked?

Morten.   Yes, because you work so much. Mr. Rörlund says work is a punishment for our sins.

Ejlif.   Pooh, what a duffer you are, to believe a thing like that!

Mrs. Stockmann.   Come, come, Ejlif!

Billing (*laughing*).   That's capital!

Hovstad.   Don't you want to work as hard as that, Morten?

Morten.   No, indeed I don't.

Hovstad.   What do you want to be, then?

Morten.   I should like best to be a Viking.

Ejlif.   You would have to be a pagan then.

Morten.   Well, I could become a pagan, couldn't I?

Billing.   I agree with you, Morten! My sentiments, exactly.

Mrs. Stockmann (*signalling to him*).   I am sure that is not true, Mr. Billing.

Billing.   Yes, I swear it is! I am a pagan, and I am proud of it. Believe me, before long we shall all be pagans.

Morten.   And then shall we be allowed to anything we like?

Billing.   Well, you see, Morten—.

Mrs. Stockmann.   You must go to your room now, boys; I am sure you have some lessons to learn for to-morrow.

Ejlif.   I should like so much to stay a little longer—

Mrs. Stockmann.   No, no; away you go, both of you. (*The boys say good night and go into the room on the left.*)

Hovstad.   Do you really think it can do the boys any harm to hear such things?

Mrs. Stockmann.   I don't know; but I don't like it.

Petra.   But you know, mother, I think you really are wrong about it.

Mrs. Stockmann.   Maybe, but I don't like it—not in our own home.

Petra.   There is so much falsehood both at home and at school. At home one must not speak, and at school we have to stand and tell lies to the children.

Horster.   Tell lies?

Petra.   Yes, don't you suppose we have to teach them all sorts of things that we don't believe?

Billing.   That is perfectly true.

Petra.   If only I had the means I would start a school of my own, and it would be conducted on very different lines.

Billing.   Oh, bother the means—!

Horster.   Well if you are thinking of that, Miss Stockmann, I shall be delighted to provide you with a schoolroom. The great big old house my father left me is standing almost empty; there is an immense dining-room downstairs—

Petra (*laughing*).   Thank you very much; but I am afraid nothing will come of it.

Hovstad.   No, Miss Petra is much more likely to take to journalism, I expect. By the way, have you had time to do anything with that English story you promised to translate for us?

Petra.   No, not yet; but you shall have it in good time.

(*Dr. Stockmann comes in from his room with an open letter in his hand.*)

Dr. Stockmann (*waving the letter*). Well, now the town will have something new to talk about, I can tell you!

Billing. Something new?

Mrs. Stockmann. What is this?

Dr. Stockmann. A great discovery, Katherine.

Hovstad. Really?

Mrs. Stockmann. A discovery of yours?

Dr. Stockmann. A discovery of mine. (*Walks up and down.*) Just let them come saying, as usual, that it is all fancy and a crazy man's imagination! But they will be careful what they say this time, I can tell you!

Petra. But, father, tell us what it is.

Dr. Stockmann. Yes, yes—only give me time, and you shall know all about it. If only I had Peter here now! It just shows how we men can go about forming our judgments, when in reality we are as blind as any moles—

Hovstad. What are you driving at, Doctor?

Dr. Stockmann (*standing still by the table*). Isn't it the universal opinion that our town is a healthy spot?

Hovstad. Certainly.

Dr. Stockmann. Quite an unusually healthy spot, in fact—a place that deserves to be recommended in the warmest possible manner either for invalids or for people who are well—

Mrs. Stockmann. Yes, but my dear Thomas—

Dr. Stockmann. And we have been recommending it and praising it—I have written and written, both in the "Messenger" and in pamphlets—

Hovstad. Well, what then?

Dr. Stockmann. And the Baths—we have called them the "main artery of the town's life-blood," the "nerve-centre of our town," and the devil knows what else—

Billing. "The town's pulsating heart" was the expression I once used on an important occasion—

Dr. Stockmann. Quite so. Well, do you know what they really are, these great, splendid, much praised Baths, that have cost so much money—do you know what they are?

Hovstad. No, what are they?

Mrs. Stockmann. Yes, what are they?

Dr. Stockmann. The whole place is a pesthouse!

Petra. The Baths, father?

Mrs. Stockmann (*at the same time*). Our Baths!

Hovstad. But, Doctor—

Billing. Absolutely incredible!

Dr. Stockmann. The whole Bath establishment is a whited, poisoned sepulchre, I tell you—the gravest possible danger to the public health! All the nastiness up at Mölledal, all that stinking filth, is infecting the water in the conduit-pipes leading to the reservoir; and the same cursed, filthy poison oozes out on the shore too—

Horster. Where the bathing-place is?

Dr. Stockmann. Just there.

Hovstad. How do you come to be so certain of all this, Doctor?

Dr. Stockmann. I have investigated the matter most conscientiously. For a long time past I have suspected something of the kind. Last year we had some very strange cases of illness among the visitors—typhoid cases, and cases of gastric fever—

Mrs. Stockmann. Yes, that is quite true.

Dr. Stockmann. At the time, we supposed the visitors had been infected before they came; but later on, in the winter, I began to have a different opinion; and so I set myself to examine the water, as well as I could.

Mrs. Stockmann. Then that is what you have been so busy with?

Dr. Stockmann. Indeed I have been busy, Katherine. But here I had none of the necessary scientific apparatus; so I sent samples, both of the drinking-water and of the sea-water, up to the University, to have an accurate analysis made by a chemist.

Hovstad. And have you got that?

Dr. Stockmann (*showing him the letter*). Here it is! It proves the presence of decomposing organic matter in the water—it is full of infusoria. The water is absolutely dangerous to use, either internally or externally.

Mrs. Stockmann. What a mercy you discovered it in time.

Dr. Stockmann. You may well say so.

Hovstad. And what do you propose to do now, Doctor?

Dr. Stockmann. To see the matter put right—naturally.

Hovstad. Can that be done?

Dr. Stockmann. It must be done. Otherwise the Baths will be absolutely useless and wasted. But we need not anticipate that; I have a very clear idea what we shall have to do.

Mrs. Stockmann. But why have you kept this all so secret, dear?

Dr. Stockmann. Do you suppose I was going to run about the town gossiping about it, before I had absolute proof? No, thank you. I am not such a fool.

Petra. Still, you might have told us—

Dr. Stockmann. Not a living soul. But to-morrow you may run around to the old Badger—

Mrs. Stockmann. Oh, Thomas! Thomas!

Dr. Stockmann. Well, to your grandfather, then. The old boy will have something to be astonished at! I know he thinks I am cracked—and there are lots of other people think so too, I have noticed. But now these good folks shall see—they shall just see—! (*Walks about, rubbing his hands.*) There will be a nice upset in the town, Katherine; you can't imagine what it will be. All the conduit-pipes will have to be relaid.

Hovstad (*getting up*). All the conduit-pipes—?

Dr. Stockmann. Yes, of course. The intake is too low down; it will have to be lifted to a position much higher up.

Petra. Then you were right after all.

Dr. Stockmann. Ah, you remember, Petra—I wrote opposing the plans before the work was begun. But at that time no one would listen to me. Well, I am going to let them have it, now! Of course I have prepared a report for the Baths Committee; I have had it ready for a week, and was only waiting for this to come. (*Shows the letter.*) Now it shall go off at once. (*Goes into his room and comes back with some papers.*) Look at that! Four closely written sheets!—and the letter shall go with them. Give me a bit of paper, Katherine—something to wrap them up in. That will do! Now give it to—to—(*stamps his foot*)—what the deuce is her name?—give it to the maid, and tell her to take it at once to the Mayor.

(*Mrs. Stockmann takes the packet and goes out through the dining-room.*)

Petra. What do you think uncle Peter will say, father?
Dr. Stockmann. What is there for him to say? I should think he would be very glad that such an important truth has been brought to light.
Hovstad. Will you let me print a short note about your discovery in the "Messenger"?
Dr. Stockmann. I shall be very much obliged if you will.
Hovstad. It is very desirable that the public should be informed of it without delay.
Dr. Stockmann. Certainly.
Mrs. Stockmann (*coming back*). She has just gone with it.
Billing. Upon my soul, Doctor, you are going to be the foremost man in the town!
Dr. Stockmann (*walking about happily*). Nonsense! As a matter of fact I have done nothing more than my duty. I have only made a lucky find—that's all. Still, all the same—
Billing. Hovstad, don't you think the town ought to give Dr. Stockmann some sort of testimonial?
Hovstad. I will suggest it, anyway.
Billing. And I will speak to Aslaksen about it.
Dr. Stockmann. No, my good friends, don't let us have any of that nonsense. I won't hear of anything of the kind. And if the Baths Committee should think of voting me an increase of salary, I will not accept it. Do you hear, Katherine?—I won't accept it.
Mrs. Stockmann. You are quite right, Thomas.
Petra (*lifting her glass*). Your health, father!
Hovstad and Billing. Your health, Doctor! Good health!
Horster (*touches glasses with Dr. Stockmann*). I hope it will bring you nothing but good luck.
Dr. Stockmann. Thank you, thank you, my dear fellows! I feel tremendously happy! It is a splendid thing for a man to be able to feel that he has done a service to his native town and to his fellow-citizens. Hurrah, Katherine! (*He puts his arms round her and whirls her round and round, while she protests with laughing cries. They all laugh, clap their hands, and cheer*

the Doctor. The boys put their heads in at the door to see what is going on.)

Act II

(SCENE.   The same. The door into the dining-room is shut. It is morning. Mrs. Stockmann, with a sealed letter in her hand, comes in from the dining-room, goes to the door of the Doctor's study, and peeps in.)

Mrs. Stockmann.   Are you in, Thomas?

Dr. Stockmann (*from within his room*).   Yes, I have just come in. (*Comes into the room.*) What is it?

Mrs. Stockmann.   A letter from your brother.

Dr. Stockmann.   Aha, let us see! (*Opens the letter and reads:*) "I return herewith the manuscript you sent me"—(*reads on in a low murmur*) Hm!—

Mrs. Stockmann.   What does he say?

Dr. Stockmann (*putting the papers in his pocket*).   Oh, he only writes that he will come up here himself about midday.

Mrs. Stockmann.   Well, try and remember to be at home this time.

Dr. Stockmann.   That will be all right; I have got through all my morning visits.

Mrs. Stockmann.   I am extremely curious to know how he takes it.

Dr. Stockmann.   You will see he won't like its having been I, and not he, that made the discovery.

Mrs. Stockmann.   Aren't you a little nervous about that?

Dr. Stockmann.   Oh, he really will be pleased enough, you know. But, at the same time, Peter is so confoundedly afraid of anyone's doing any service to the town except himself.

Mrs. Stockmann.   I will tell you what, Thomas—you should be good natured, and share the credit of this with him. Couldn't you make out that it was he who set you on the scent of this discovery?

Dr. Stockmann.   I am quite willing. If only I can get the thing set right. I—

(*Morten Kiil puts his head in through the door leading from the hall, looks round in an enquiring manner, and chuckles.*)

Morten Kiil (*slyly*).   Is it—is it true?

Mrs. Stockmann (*going to the door*).   Father!—is it you?

Dr. Stockmann.   Ah, Mr. Kiil—good morning, good morning!

Mrs. Stockmann.   But come along in.

Morten Kiil.   If it is true, I will; if not, I am off.

Dr. Stockmann.   If what is true?

Morten Kiil.   This tale about the water supply. Is it true?

Dr. Stockmann.   Certainly it is true. But how did you come to hear it?

Morten Kiil (*coming in*).   Petra ran in on her way to the school—

Dr. Stockmann.   Did she?

Morten Kiil.   Yes; and she declares that—. I thought she was only making a fool of me, but it isn't like Petra to do that.

Dr. Stockmann.   Of course not. How could you imagine such a thing!

Morten Kiil.   Oh well, it is better never to trust anybody; you may find you have been made a fool of before you know where you are. But it is really true, all the same?

Dr. Stockmann.   You can depend upon it that it is true. Won't you sit down? (*Settles him on the couch.*) Isn't it a real bit of luck for the town—

Morten Kiil (*suppressing his laughter*).   A bit of luck for the town?

Dr. Stockmann.   Yes, that I made the discovery in good time.

Morten Kiil (*as before*).   Yes, yes, yes!—But I should never have thought you the sort of man to pull your own brother's leg like this!

Dr. Stockmann.   Pull his leg!

Mrs. Stockmann.   Really, father dear—

Morten Kiil (*resting his hands and his chin on the handle of his stick and winking slyly at the Doctor*).   Let me see, what was the story? Some kind of beast that had got into the water-pipes, wasn't it?

Dr. Stockmann.   Infusoria—yes.

Morten Kiil.   And a lot of these beasts had got in, according to Petra—a tremendous lot.

Dr. Stockmann.   Certainly; hundreds of thousands of them, probably.

Morten Kiil.   But no one can see them—isn't that so?

Dr. Stockmann.   Yes; you can't see them.

Morten Kiil (*with a quiet chuckle*).   Damme—it's the finest story I have ever heard!

Dr. Stockmann.   What do you mean?

Morten Kiil.   But you will never get the Mayor to believe a thing like that.

Dr. Stockmann.   We shall see.

Morten Kiil.   Do you think he will be fool enough to—?

Dr. Stockmann.   I hope the whole town will be fools enough.

Morten Kiil.   The whole town! Well, it wouldn't be a bad thing. It would just serve them right, and teach them a lesson. They think themselves so much cleverer than we old fellows. They hounded me out of the council; they did, I tell you—they hounded me out. Now they shall pay for it. You pull their legs too, Thomas!

Dr. Stockmann.   Really, I—

Morten Kiil.   You pull their legs! (*Gets up.*) If you can work it so that the Mayor and his friends all swallow the same bait, I will give ten pounds to a charity—like a shot!

Dr. Stockmann.   That is very kind of you.

Morten Kiil.   Yes, I haven't got much money to throw away, I can tell you; but if you can work this, I will give five pounds to a charity at Christmas.

(*Hovstad comes in by the hall door.*)

Hovstad.   Good morning! (*Stops.*) Oh, I beg your pardon—

Dr. Stockmann.   Not at all; come in.

Morten Kiil (*with another chuckle*).   Oho!—is he in this too?

Hovstad.   What do you mean?

Dr. Stockmann.   Certainly he is.

Morten Kiil.   I might have known it! It must get into the papers. You know how to do it, Thomas! Set your wits to work. Now I must go.

Dr. Stockmann.   Won't you stay a little while?

Morten Kiil.   No, I must be off now. You keep up this game for all it is worth; you won't repent it, I'm damned if you will!

(*He goes out; Mrs. Stockmann follows him into the hall.*)

Dr. Stockmann (*laughing*).   Just imagine—the old chap doesn't believe a word of all this about the water supply.

Hovstad.   Oh that was it, then?

Dr. Stockmann.   Yes, that was what we were talking about. Perhaps it is the same thing that brings you here?

Hovstad.   Yes, it is. Can you spare me a few minutes, Doctor?

Dr. Stockmann.   As long as you like, my dear fellow.

Hovstad.   Have you heard from the Mayor yet?

Dr. Stockmann.   Not yet. He is coming here later.

Hovstad.   I have given the matter a great deal of thought since last night.

Dr. Stockmann.   Well?

Hovstad.   From your point of view, as a doctor and a man of science, this affair of the water-supply is an isolated matter. I mean, you do not realise that it involves a great many other things.

Dr. Stockmann.   How, do you mean?—Let us sit down, my dear fellow. No, sit here on the couch. (*Hovstad sits down on the couch, Dr. Stockmann on a chair on the other side of the table.*) Now then. You mean that—?

Hovstad.   You said yesterday that the pollution of the water was due to impurities in the soil.

Dr. Stockmann.   Yes, unquestionably it is due to that poisonous morass up at Mölledal.

Hovstad.   Begging your pardon, doctor, I fancy it is due to quite another morass altogether.

Dr. Stockmann.   What morass?

Hovstad.   The morass that the whole life of our town is built on and is rotting in.

Dr. Stockmann.   What the deuce are you driving at, Hovstad?

Hovstad.   The whole of the town's interests have, little by little, got into the hands of a pack of officials.

Dr. Stockmann.   Oh, come!—they are not all officials.

Hovstad.   No, but those that are not officials are at any rate the officials' friends and adherents; it is the wealthy folk, the old families in the town, that have got us entirely in their hands.

Dr. Stockmann. Yes, but after all they are men of ability and knowledge.

Hovstad. Did they show any ability or knowledge when they laid the conduit-pipes where they are now?

Dr. Stockmann. No, of course that was a great piece of stupidity on their part. But that is going to be set right now.

Hovstad. Do you think that will be all such plain sailing?

Dr. Stockmann. Plain sailing or no, it has got to be done, anyway.

Hovstad. Yes, provided the press takes up the question.

Dr. Stockmann. I don't think that will be necessary, my dear fellow, I am certain my brother—

Hovstad. Excuse me, doctor; I feel bound to tell you I am inclined to take the matter up.

Dr. Stockmann. In the paper?

Hovstad. Yes. When I took over the "People's Messenger" my idea was to break up this ring of self-opinionated old fossils who had got hold of all the influence.

Dr. Stockmann. But you know you told me yourself what the result had been; you nearly ruined your paper.

Hovstad. Yes, at the time we were obliged to climb down a peg or two, it is quite true; because there was a danger of the whole project of the Baths coming to nothing if they failed us. But now the scheme has been carried through, and we can dispense with these grand gentlemen.

Dr. Stockmann. Dispense with them, yes; but we owe them a great debt of gratitude.

Hovstad. That shall be recognised ungrudgingly. But a journalist of my democratic tendencies cannot let such an opportunity as this slip. The bubble of official infallibility must be pricked. This superstition must be destroyed, like any other.

Dr. Stockmann. I am whole-heartedly with you in that, Mr. Hovstad; if it is a superstition, away with it!

Hovstad. I should be very reluctant to bring the Mayor into it, because he is your brother. But I am sure you will agree with me that truth should be the first consideration.

Dr. Stockmann. That goes without saying. (*With sudden emphasis.*) Yes, but—but—

Hovstad. You must not misjudge me. I am neither more self-interested nor more ambitious than most men.

Dr. Stockmann. My dear fellow—who suggests anything of that kind?

Hovstad. I am of humble origin, as you know; and that has given me opportunities of knowing what is the most crying need in the humbler ranks of life. It is that they should be allowed some part in the direction of public affairs, Doctor. That is what will develop their faculties and intelligence and self respect—

Dr. Stockmann. I quite appreciate that.

Hovstad. Yes—and in my opinion a journalist incurs a heavy responsibility if he neglects a favourable opportunity of emancipating the masses—the humble and oppressed. I know well enough that in exalted circles I shall be called an agitator, and all that sort of thing; but they may call what they like. If only my conscience doesn't reproach me, then—

Dr. Stockmann. Quite right! Quite right, Mr. Hovstad, But all the same—devil take it! (*A knock is heard at the door.*) Come in!

(*Aslaksen appears at the door. He is poorly but decently dressed, in black, with a slightly crumpled white neckcloth; he wears gloves and has a felt hat in his hand.*)

Aslaksen (*bowing*).   Excuse my taking the liberty, Doctor—

Dr. Stockmann (*getting up*).   Ah, it is you, Aslaksen!

Aslaksen.   Yes, Doctor.

Hovstad (*standing up*).   Is it me you want, Aslaksen?

Aslaksen.   No; I didn't know I should find you here. No, it was the Doctor I—

Dr. Stockmann.   I am quite at your service. What is it?

Aslaksen.   Is what I heard from Mr. Billing true, sir—that you mean to improve our water-supply?

Dr. Stockmann.   Yes, for the Baths.

Aslaksen.   Quite so, I understand. Well, I have come to say that I will back that up by every means in my power.

Hovstad (*to the Doctor*).   You see!

Dr. Stockmann.   I shall be very grateful to you, but—

Aslaksen.   Because it may be no bad thing to have us small tradesmen at your back. We form, as it were, a compact majority in the town—if we choose. And it is always a good thing to have the majority with you, Doctor.

Dr. Stockmann.   This is undeniably true; but I confess I don't see why such unusual precautions should be necessary in this case. It seems to me that such a plain, straightforward thing—

Aslaksen.   Oh, it may be very desirable, all the same. I know our local authorities so well; officials are not generally very ready to act on proposals that come from other people. That is why I think it would not be at all amiss if we made a little demonstration.

Hovstad.   That's right.

Dr. Stockmann.   Demonstration, did you say? What on earth are you going to make a demonstration about?

Aslaksen.   We shall proceed with the greatest moderation, Doctor. Moderation is always my aim; it is the greatest virtue in a citizen—at least, I think so.

Dr. Stockmann.   It is well known to be a characteristic of yours, Mr. Aslaksen.

Aslaksen.   Yes, I think I may pride myself on that. And this matter of the water-supply is of the greatest importance to us small tradesmen. The Baths promise to be a regular gold-mine for the town. We shall all make our living out of them, especially those of us who are householders. That is why we will back up the project as strongly as possible. And as I am at present Chairman of the Householders' Association—

Dr. Stockmann. Yes—?

Aslaksen. And, what is more, local secretary of the Temperance Society—you know, sir, I suppose, that I am a worker in the temperance cause?

Dr. Stockmann. Of course, of course.

Aslaksen. Well, you can understand that I come into contact with a great many people. And as I have the reputation of a temperate and law-abiding citizen—like yourself, Doctor—I have a certain influence in the town, a little bit of power, if I may be allowed to say so.

Dr. Stockmann. I know that quite well, Mr. Aslaksen.

Aslaksen. So you see it would be an easy matter for me to set on foot some testimonial, if necessary.

Dr. Stockmann. A testimonial?

Aslaksen. Yes, some kind of an address of thanks from the townsmen for your share in a matter of such importance to the community. I need scarcely say that it would have to be drawn up with the greatest regard to moderation, so as not to offend the authorities—who, after all, have the reins in their hands. If we pay strict attention to that, no one can take it amiss, I should think!

Hovstad. Well, and even supposing they didn't like it—

Aslaksen. No, no, no; there must be no discourtesy to the authorities, Mr. Hovstad. It is no use falling foul of those upon whom our welfare so closely depends. I have done that in my time, and no good ever comes of it. But no one can take exception to a reasonable and frank expression of a citizen's views.

Dr. Stockmann (*shaking him by the hand*). I can't tell you, dear Mr. Aslaksen, how extremely pleased I am to find such hearty support among my fellow-citizens. I am delighted—delighted! Now, you will take a small glass of sherry, eh?

Aslaksen. No, thank you; I never drink alcohol of that kind.

Dr. Stockmann. Well, what do you say to a glass of beer, then?

Aslaksen. Nor that either, thank you, Doctor. I never drink anything as early as this. I am going into town now to talk this over with one or two householders, and prepare the ground.

Dr. Stockmann. It is tremendously kind of you, Mr. Aslaksen; but I really cannot understand the necessity for all these precautions. It seems to me that the thing should go of itself.

Aslaksen. The authorities are somewhat slow to move, Doctor. Far be it from me to seem to blame them—

Hovstad. We are going to stir them up in the paper tomorrow, Aslaksen.

Aslaksen. But not violently, I trust, Mr. Hovstad. Proceed with moderation, or you will do nothing with them. You may take my advice; I have gathered my experience in the school of life. Well, I must say good-bye, Doctor. You know now that we small tradesmen are at your back at all events, like a solid wall. You have the compact majority on your side, Doctor.

Dr. Stockmann. I am very much obliged, dear Mr. Aslaksen. (*Shakes hands with him.*) Good-bye, good-bye.

Aslaksen. Are you going my way, towards the printing-office, Mr. Hovstad?

Hovstad. I will come later; I have something to settle up first.

Aslaksen. Very well. (*Bows and goes out; Stockmann follows him into the hall.*)

Hovstad (*as Stockmann comes in again*). Well, what do you think of that, Doctor? Don't you think it is high time we stirred a little life into all this slackness and vacillation and cowardice?

Dr. Stockmann. Are you referring to Aslaksen?

Hovstad. Yes, I am. He is one of those who are floundering in a bog—decent enough fellow though he may be, otherwise. And most of the people here are in just the same case—see-sawing and edging first to one side and then to the other, so overcome with caution and scruple that they never dare to take any decided step.

Dr. Stockmann. Yes, but Aslaksen seemed to me so thoroughly well-intentioned.

Hovstad. There is one thing I esteem higher than that; and that is for a man to be self-reliant and sure of himself.

Dr. Stockmann. I think you are perfectly right there.

Hovstad. That is why I want to seize this opportunity, and try if I cannot manage to put a little virility into these well-intentioned people for once. The idol of Authority must be shattered in this town. This gross and inexcusable blunder about the water-supply must be brought home to the mind of every municipal voter.

Dr. Stockmann. Very well; if you are of opinion that it is for the good of the community, so be it. But not until I have had a talk with my brother.

Hovstad. Anyway, I will get a leading article ready; and if the Mayor refuses to take the matter up—

Dr. Stockmann. How can you suppose such a thing possible?

Hovstad. It is conceivable. And in that case—

Dr. Stockmann. In that case I promise you—. Look here, in that case you may print my report—every word of it.

Hovstad. May I? Have I your word for it?

Dr. Stockmann (*giving him the MS.*). Here it is; take it with you. It can do no harm for you to read it through, and you can give it back to me later on.

Hovstad. Good, good! That is what I will do. And now good-bye, Doctor.

Dr. Stockmann. Good-bye, good-bye. You will see everything will run quite smoothly, Mr. Hovstad—quite smoothly.

Hovstad. Hm!—we shall see. (*Bows and goes out.*)

Dr. Stockmann (*opens the dining-room door and looks in*). Katherine! Oh, you are back, Petra?

Petra (*coming in*). Yes, I have just come from the school.

Mrs. Stockmann (*coming in*). Has he not been here yet?

Dr. Stockmann. Peter? No. But I have had a long talk with Hovstad. He is quite excited about my discovery. I find it has a much wider bearing than I at first imagined. And he has put his paper at my disposal if necessity should arise.

Mrs. Stockmann. Do you think it will?

Dr. Stockmann. Not for a moment. But at all events it makes me feel proud to know that I have the liberal-minded independent press on my side. Yes, and—just imagine—I have had a visit from the Chairman of the Householders' Association!

Mrs. Stockmann. Oh! What did he want?

Dr. Stockmann. To offer me his support too. They will support me in a body if it should be necessary. Katherine—do you know what I have got behind me?

Mrs. Stockmann. Behind you? No, what have you got behind you?

Dr. Stockmann. The compact majority.

Mrs. Stockmann. Really? Is that a good thing for you, Thomas?

Dr. Stockmann. I should think it was a good thing. (*Walks up and down rubbing his hands.*) By Jove, it's a fine thing to feel this bond of brotherhood between oneself and one's fellow citizens!

Petra. And to be able to do so much that is good and useful, father!

Dr. Stockmann. And for one's own native town into the bargain, my child!

Mrs. Stockmann. That was a ring at the bell.

Dr. Stockmann. It must be he, then. (*A knock is heard at the door.*) Come in!

Peter Stockmann (*comes in from the hall*). Good morning.

Dr. Stockmann. Glad to see you, Peter!

Mrs. Stockmann. Good morning, Peter. How are you?

Peter Stockmann. So so, thank you. (*To Dr. Stockmann.*) I received from you yesterday, after office hours, a report dealing with the condition of the water at the Baths.

Dr. Stockmann. Yes. Have you read it?

Peter Stockmann. Yes, I have.

Dr. Stockmann. And what have you to say to it?

Peter Stockmann (*with a sidelong glance*). Hm!—

Mrs. Stockmann. Come along, Petra. (*She and Petra go into the room on the left.*)

Peter Stockmann (*after a pause*). Was it necessary to make all these investigations behind my back?

Dr. Stockmann. Yes, because until I was absolutely certain about it—

Peter Stockmann. Then you mean that you are absolutely certain now?

Dr. Stockmann. Surely you are convinced of that.

Peter Stockmann. Is it your intention to bring this document before the Baths Committee as a sort of official communication?

Dr. Stockmann. Certainly. Something must be done in the matter—and that quickly.

Peter Stockmann. As usual, you employ violent expressions in your report. You say, amongst other things, that what we offer visitors in our Baths is a permanent supply of poison.

Dr. Stockmann. Well, can you describe it any other way, Peter? Just think— water that is poisonous, whether you drink it or bathe in it! And this we offer to the poor sick folk who come to us trustfully and pay us at an exorbitant rate to be made well again!

Peter Stockmann. And your reasoning leads you to this conclusion, that we must build a sewer to draw off the alleged impurities from Mölledal and must relay the water-conduits.

Dr. Stockmann. Yes. Do you see any other way out of it? I don't.

Peter Stockmann. I made a pretext this morning to go and see the town engineer, and, as if only half seriously, broached the subject of these proposals as a thing we might perhaps have to take under consideration some time later on.

Dr. Stockmann. Some time later on!

Peter Stockmann. He smiled at what he considered to be my extravagance, naturally. Have you taken the trouble to consider what your proposed alterations would cost? According to the information I obtained, the expenses would probably mount up to fifteen or twenty thousand pounds.

Dr. Stockmann. Would it cost so much?

Peter Stockmann. Yes; and the worst part of it would be that the work would take at least two years.

Dr. Stockmann. Two years? Two whole years?

Peter Stockmann. At least. And what are we to do with the Baths in the meantime? Close them? Indeed we should be obliged to. And do you suppose any one would come near the place after it had got about that the water was dangerous?

Dr. Stockmann. Yes, but, Peter, that is what it is.

Peter Stockmann. And all this at this juncture—just as the Baths are beginning to be known. There are other towns in the neighbourhood with qualifications to attract visitors for bathing purposes. Don't you suppose they would immediately strain every nerve to divert the entire stream of strangers to themselves? Unquestionably they would; and then where should we be? We should probably have to abandon the whole thing, which has cost us so much money—and then you would have ruined your native town.

Dr. Stockmann. I—should have ruined—!

Peter Stockmann. It is simply and solely through the Baths that the town has before it any future worth mentioning. You know that just as well as I.

Dr. Stockmann. But what do you think ought to be done, then?

Peter Stockmann. Your report has not convinced me that the condition of the water at the Baths is as bad as you represent it to be.

Dr. Stockmann. I tell you it is even worse!—or at all events it will be in summer, when the warm weather comes.

Peter Stockmann. As I said, I believe you exaggerate the matter considerably. A capable physician ought to know what measures to take—he ought to be capable of preventing injurious influences or of remedying them if they become obviously persistent.

Dr. Stockmann. Well? What more?

Peter Stockmann. The water supply for the Baths is now an established fact, and in consequence must be treated as such. But probably the Committee, at its discretion, will not be disinclined to consider the question of how far it might be possible to introduce certain improvements consistently with a reasonable expenditure.

Dr. Stockmann. And do you suppose that I will have anything to do with such a piece of trickery as that?

Peter Stockmann. Trickery!!

Dr. Stockmann. Yes, it would be a trick—a fraud, a lie, a downright crime towards the public, towards the whole community!

Peter Stockmann. I have not, as I remarked before, been able to convince myself that there is actually any imminent danger.

Dr. Stockmann. You have! It is impossible that you should not be convinced. I know I have represented the facts absolutely truthfully and fairly. And you know it very well, Peter, only you won't acknowledge it. It was owing to your action that both the Baths and the water-conduits were built where they are; and that is what you won't acknowledge—that damnable blunder of yours. Pooh!—do you suppose I don't see through you?

Peter Stockmann. And even if that were true? If I perhaps guard my reputation somewhat anxiously, it is in the best interests of the town. Without moral authority I am powerless to direct public affairs as seems, to my judgment, to be best for the common good. And on that account—and for various other reasons too—it appears to me to be a matter of importance that your report should not be delivered to the Committee. In the interests of the public, you must withhold it. Then, later on, I will raise the question and we will do our best, privately; but nothing of this unfortunate affair—not a single word of it—must come to the ears of the public.

Dr. Stockmann. I am afraid you will not be able to prevent that now, my dear Peter.

Peter Stockmann. It must and shall be prevented.

Dr. Stockmann. It is no use, I tell you. There are too many people that know about it.

Peter Stockmann. That know about it? Who? Surely you don't mean those fellows on the "People's Messenger"?

Dr. Stockmann. Yes, they know. The liberal-minded independent press is going to see that you do your duty.

Peter Stockmann (*after a short pause*). You are an extraordinarily independent man, Thomas. Have you given no thought to the consequences this may have for yourself?

Dr. Stockmann. Consequences?—for me?

Peter Stockmann. For you and yours, yes.

Dr. Stockmann. What the deuce do you mean?

Peter Stockmann. I believe I have always behaved in a brotherly way to you—have always been ready to oblige or to help you?

Dr. Stockmann. Yes, you have, and I am grateful to you for it.

Peter Stockmann. There is no need. Indeed, to some extent I was forced to do so—for my own sake. I always hoped that, if I helped to improve your financial position, I should be able to keep some check on you.

Dr. Stockmann. What!! Then it was only for your own sake—!

Peter Stockmann. Up to a certain point, yes. It is painful for a man in an official position to have his nearest relative compromising himself time after time.

Dr. Stockmann. And do you consider that I do that?

Peter Stockmann. Yes, unfortunately, you do, without even being aware of it. You have a restless, pugnacious, rebellious disposition. And then there is that disastrous propensity of yours to want to write about every sort of possible and impossible thing. The moment an idea comes into your head, you must needs go and write a newspaper article or a whole pamphlet about it.

Dr. Stockmann. Well, but is it not the duty of a citizen to let the public share in any new ideas he may have?

Peter Stockmann. Oh, the public doesn't require any new ideas. The public is best served by the good, old-established ideas it already has.

Dr. Stockmann. And that is your honest opinion?

Peter Stockmann. Yes, and for once I must talk frankly to you. Hitherto I have tried to avoid doing so, because I know how irritable you are; but now I must tell you the truth, Thomas. You have no conception what an amount of harm you do yourself by your impetuosity. You complain of the authorities, you even complain of the government—you are always pulling them to pieces; you insist that you have been neglected and persecuted. But what else can such a cantankerous man as you expect?

Dr. Stockmann. What next! Cantankerous, am I?

Peter Stockmann. Yes, Thomas, you are an extremely cantankerous man to work with—I know that to my cost. You disregard everything that you ought to have consideration for. You seem completely to forget that it is me you have to thank for your appointment here as medical officer to the Baths—

Dr. Stockmann. I was entitled to it as a matter of course!—I and nobody else! I was the first person to see that the town could be made into a flourishing watering-place, and I was the only one who saw it at that time. I had to fight single-handed in support of the idea for many years; and I wrote and wrote—

Peter Stockmann. Undoubtedly. But things were not ripe for the scheme then—though, of course, you could not judge of that in your out-of-the-way corner up north. But as soon as the opportune moment came I—and the others—took the matter into our hands—

Dr. Stockmann. Yes, and made this mess of all my beautiful plan. It is pretty obvious now what clever fellows you were!

Peter Stockmann. To my mind the whole thing only seems to mean that you are seeking another outlet for your combativeness. You want to pick a quarrel with your superiors—an old habit of yours. You cannot put up with any authority over you. You look askance at anyone who occupies a superior official position; you regard him as a personal enemy, and then any stick is good enough to beat him with. But now I have called your attention to the fact that the town's interests are at stake—and, incidentally, my own too. And therefore I must tell you, Thomas, that you will find me inexorable with regard to what I am about to require you to do.

Dr. Stockmann. And what is that?

Peter Stockmann. As you have been so indiscreet as to speak of this delicate matter to outsiders, despite the fact that you ought to have treated it as entirely official and confidential, it is obviously impossible to hush it up now. All sorts of rumours will get about directly, and everybody who has a grudge against us will take care to embellish these rumours. So it will be necessary for you to refute them publicly.

Dr. Stockmann. I! How? I don't understand.

Peter Stockmann. What we shall expect is that, after making further investigations, you will come to the conclusion that the matter is not by any means as dangerous or as critical as you imagined in the first instance.

Dr. Stockmann. Oho!—so that is what you expect!

Peter Stockmann. And, what is more, we shall expect you to make public profession of your confidence in the Committee and in their readiness to consider fully and conscientiously what steps may be necessary to remedy any possible defects.

Dr. Stockmann. But you will never be able to do that by patching and tinkering at it—never! Take my word for it, Peter; I mean what I say, as deliberately and emphatically as possible.

Peter Stockmann. As an officer under the Committee, you have no right to any individual opinion.

Dr. Stockmann (*amazed*). No right?

Peter Stockmann. In your official capacity, no. As a private person, it is quite another matter. But as a subordinate member of the staff of the Baths, you have no right to express any opinion which runs contrary to that of your superiors.

Dr. Stockmann. This is too much! I, a doctor, a man of science, have no right to—!

Peter Stockmann. The matter in hand is not simply a scientific one. It is a complicated matter, and has its economic as well as its technical side.

Dr. Stockmann. I don't care what it is! I intend to be free to express my opinion on any subject under the sun.

Peter Stockmann. As you please—but not on any subject concerning the Baths. That we forbid.

Dr. Stockmann (*shouting*). You forbid—! You! A pack of—

Peter Stockmann. *I* forbid it—I, your chief; and if I forbid it, you have to obey.

Dr. Stockmann (*controlling himself*).   Peter—if you were not my brother—

Petra (*throwing open the door*).   Father, you shan't stand this!

Mrs. Stockmann (*coming in after her*).   Petra, Petra!

Peter Stockmann.   Oh, so you have been eavesdropping.

Mrs. Stockmann.   You were talking so loud, we couldn't help—

Petra.   Yes, I was listening.

Peter Stockmann.   Well, after all, I am very glad—

Dr. Stockmann (*going up to him*).   You were saying something about forbidding and obeying?

Peter Stockmann.   You obliged me to take that tone with you.

Dr. Stockmann.   And so I am to give myself the lie, publicly?

Peter Stockmann.   We consider it absolutely necessary that you should make some such public statement as I have asked for.

Dr. Stockmann.   And if I do not—obey?

Peter Stockmann.   Then we shall publish a statement ourselves to reassure the public.

Dr. Stockmann.   Very well; but in that case I shall use my pen against you. I stick to what I have said; I will show that I am right and that you are wrong. And what will you do then?

Peter Stockmann.   Then I shall not be able to prevent your being dismissed.

Dr. Stockmann.   What—?

Petra.   Father—dismissed!

Mrs. Stockmann.   Dismissed!

Peter Stockmann.   Dismissed from the staff of the Baths. I shall be obliged to propose that you shall immediately be given notice, and shall not be allowed any further participation in the Baths' affairs.

Dr. Stockmann.   You would dare to do that!

Peter Stockmann.   It is you that are playing the daring game.

Petra.   Uncle, that is a shameful way to treat a man like father!

Mrs. Stockmann.   Do hold your tongue, Petra!

Peter Stockmann (*looking at Petra*).   Oh, so we volunteer our opinions already, do we? Of course. (*To Mrs. Stockmann.*) Katherine, I imagine you are the most sensible person in this house. Use any influence you may have over your husband, and make him see what this will entail for his family as well as—

Dr. Stockmann.   My family is my own concern and nobody else's!

Peter Stockmann.   —for his own family, as I was saying, as well as for the town he lives in.

Dr. Stockmann.   It is I who have the real good of the town at heart! I want to lay bare the defects that sooner or later must come to the light of day. I will show whether I love my native town.

Peter Stockmann.   You, who in your blind obstinacy want to cut off the most important source of the town's welfare?

Dr. Stockmann.   The source is poisoned, man! Are you mad? We are making our living by retailing filth and corruption! The whole of our flourishing municipal life derives its sustenance from a lie!

Peter Stockmann. All imagination—or something even worse. The man who can throw out such offensive insinuations about his native town must be an enemy to our community.

Dr. Stockmann (*going up to him*). Do you dare to—!

Mrs. Stockmann (*throwing herself between them*). Thomas!

Petra (*catching her father by the arm*). Don't lose your temper, father!

Peter Stockmann. I will not expose myself to violence. Now you have had a warning; so reflect on what you owe to yourself and your family. Good-bye. (*Goes out.*)

Dr. Stockmann (*walking up and down*). Am I to put up with such treatment as this? In my own house, Katherine! What do you think of that!

Mrs. Stockmann. Indeed it is both shameful and absurd, Thomas—

Petra. If only I could give uncle a piece of my mind—

Dr. Stockmann. It is my own fault. I ought to have flown out at him long ago!—shown my teeth!—bitten! To hear him call me an enemy to our community! Me! I shall not take that lying down, upon my soul!

Mrs. Stockmann. But, dear Thomas, your brother has power on his side—

Dr. Stockmann. Yes, but I have right on mine, I tell you.

Mrs. Stockmann. Oh yes, right—right. What is the use of having right on your side if you have not got might?

Petra. Oh, mother!—how can you say such a thing!

Dr. Stockmann. Do you imagine that in a free country it is no use having right on your side? You are absurd, Katherine. Besides, haven't I got the liberal-minded independent press to lead the way, and the compact majority behind me? That is might enough, I should think!

Mrs. Stockmann. But, good heavens, Thomas, you don't mean to—?

Dr. Stockmann. Don't mean to what?

Mrs. Stockmann. To set yourself up in opposition to your brother.

Dr. Stockmann. In God's name, what else do you suppose I should do but take my stand on right and truth?

Petra. Yes, I was just going to say that.

Mrs. Stockmann. But it won't do you any earthly good. If they won't do it, they won't.

Dr. Stockmann. Oho, Katherine! Just give me time, and you will see how I will carry the war into their camp.

Mrs. Stockmann. Yes, you carry the war into their camp, and you get your dismissal—that is what you will do.

Dr. Stockmann. In any case I shall have done my duty towards the public—towards the community. I, who am called its enemy!

Mrs. Stockmann. But towards your family, Thomas? Towards your own home! Do you think that is doing your duty towards those you have to provide for?

Petra. Ah, don't think always first of us, mother.

Mrs. Stockmann. Oh, it is easy for you to talk; you are able to shift for yourself, if need be. But remember the boys, Thomas; and think a little too of yourself, and of me—

Dr. Stockmann. I think you are out of your senses, Katherine! If I were to be such a miserable coward as to go on my knees to Peter and his damned crew, do you suppose I should ever know an hour's peace of mind all my life afterwards?

Mrs. Stockmann. I don't know anything about that; but God preserve us from the peace of mind we shall have, all the same, if you go on defying him! You will find yourself again without the means of subsistence, with no income to count upon. I should think we had had enough of that in the old days. Remember that, Thomas; think what that means.

Dr. Stockmann (*collecting himself with a struggle and clenching his fists*). And this is what this slavery can bring upon a free, honourable man! Isn't it horrible, Katherine?

Mrs. Stockmann. Yes, it is sinful to treat you so, it is perfectly true. But, good heavens, one has to put up with so much injustice in this world.—There are the boys, Thomas! Look at them! What is to become of them? Oh, no, you can never have the heart—. (*Ejlif and Morten have come in while she was speaking, with their school books in their hands.*)

Dr. Stockmann. The boys—! (*Recovers himself suddenly.*) No, even if the whole world goes to pieces, I will never bow my neck to this yoke! (*Goes towards his room.*)

Mrs. Stockmann (*following him*). Thomas—what are you going to do!

Dr. Stockmann (*at his door*). I mean to have the right to look my sons in the face when they are grown men. (*Goes into his room.*)

Mrs. Stockmann (*bursting into tears*). God help us all!

Petra. Father is splendid! He will not give in.

(*The boys look on in amazement; Petra signs to them not to speak.*)

Act III

(**SCENE.** *The editorial office of the "People's Messenger." The entrance door is on the left-hand side of the back wall; on the right-hand side is another door with glass panels through which the printing-room can be seen. Another door in the right-hand wall. In the middle of the room is a large table covered with papers, newspapers and books. In the foreground on the left a window, before which stands a desk and a high stool. There are a couple of easy chairs by the table, and other chairs standing along the wall. The room is dingy and uncomfortable; the furniture is old, the chairs stained and torn. In the printing-room the compositors are seen at work, and a printer is working a hand-press. Hovstad is sitting at the desk, writing. Billing comes in from the right with Dr. Stockmann's manuscript in his hand.*)

Billing. Well, I must say!

Hovstad (*still writing*). Have you read it through?

Billing (*laying the MS. on the desk*). Yes, indeed I have.

Hovstad. Don't you think the Doctor hits them pretty hard?

Billing. Hard? Bless my soul, he's crushing! Every word falls like—how shall I put it?—like the blow of a sledge-hammer.

Hovstad. Yes, but they are not the people to throw up the sponge at the first blow.

Billing. That is true; and for that reason we must strike blow upon blow until the whole of this aristocracy tumbles to pieces. As I sat there reading this, I almost seemed to see a revolution in being.

Hovstad (*turning round*). Hush!—Speak so that Aslaksen cannot hear you.

Billing (*lowering his voice*). Aslaksen is a chicken-hearted chap, a coward; there is nothing of the man in him. But this time you will insist on your own way, won't you? You will put the Doctor's article in?

Hovstad. Yes, and if the Mayor doesn't like it—

Billing. That will be the devil of a nuisance.

Hovstad. Well, fortunately we can turn the situation to good account, whatever happens. If the Mayor will not fall in with the Doctor's project, he will have all the small tradesmen down on him—the whole of the Householders' Association and the rest of them. And if he does fall in with it, he will fall out with the whole crowd of large shareholders in the Baths, who up to now have been his most valuable supporters—

Billing. Yes, because they will certainly have to fork out a pretty penny—

Hovstad. Yes, you may be sure they will. And in this way the ring will be broken up, you see, and then in every issue of the paper we will enlighten the public on the Mayor's incapability on one point and another, and make it clear that all the positions of trust in the town, the whole control of municipal affairs, ought to be put in the hands of the Liberals.

Billing. That is perfectly true! I see it coming—I see it coming; we are on the threshold of a revolution!

(*A knock is heard at the door.*)

Hovstad. Hush! (*Calls out.*) Come in! (*Dr. Stockmann comes in by the street door. Hovstad goes to meet him.*) Ah, it is you, Doctor! Well?

Dr. Stockmann. You may set to work and print it, Mr. Hovstad!

Hovstad. Has it come to that, then?

Billing. Hurrah!

Dr. Stockmann. Yes, print away. Undoubtedly it has come to that. Now they must take what they get. There is going to be a fight in the town, Mr. Billing!

Billing. War to the knife, I hope! We will get our knives to their throats, Doctor!

Dr. Stockmann. This article is only a beginning. I have already got four or five more sketched out in my head. Where is Aslaksen?

Billing (*calls into the printing-room*). Aslaksen, just come here for a minute!

Hovstad. Four or five more articles, did you say? On the same subject?

Dr. Stockmann. No—far from it, my dear fellow. No, they are about quite another matter. But they all spring from the question of the water-supply and the drainage. One thing leads to another, you know. It is like beginning to pull down an old house, exactly.

Billing. Upon my soul, it's true; you find you are not done till you have pulled all the old rubbish down.

Aslaksen (*coming in*). Pulled down? You are not thinking of pulling down the Baths surely, Doctor?

Hovstad. Far from it, don't be afraid.

Dr. Stockmann. No, we meant something quite different. Well, what do you think of my article, Mr. Hovstad?

Hovstad. I think it is simply a masterpiece—

Dr. Stockmann. Do you really think so? Well, I am very pleased, very pleased.

Hovstad. It is so clear and intelligible. One need have no special knowledge to understand the bearing of it. You will have every enlightened man on your side.

Aslaksen. And every prudent man too, I hope?

Billing. The prudent and the imprudent—almost the whole town.

Aslaksen. In that case we may venture to print it.

Dr. Stockmann. I should think so!

Hovstad. We will put it in to-morrow morning.

Dr. Stockmann. Of course—you must not lose a single day. What I wanted to ask you, Mr. Aslaksen, was if you would supervise the printing of it yourself.

Aslaksen. With pleasure.

Dr. Stockmann. Take care of it as if it were a treasure! No misprints—every word is important. I will look in again a little later; perhaps you will be able to let me see a proof. I can't tell you how eager I am to see it in print, and see it burst upon the public—

Billing. Burst upon them—yes, like a flash of lightning!

Dr. Stockmann. —and to have it submitted to the judgment of my intelligent fellow-townsmen. You cannot imagine what I have gone through to-day. I have been threatened first with one thing and then with another; they have tried to rob me of my most elementary rights as a man—

Billing. What! Your rights as a man!

Dr. Stockmann. —they have tried to degrade me, to make a coward of me, to force me to put personal interests before my most sacred convictions—

Billing. That is too much—I'm damned if it isn't.

Hovstad. Oh, you mustn't be surprised at anything from that quarter.

Dr. Stockmann. Well, they will get the worst of it with me; they may assure themselves of that. I shall consider the "People's Messenger" my sheet-anchor now, and every single day I will bombard them with one article after another, like bomb-shells—

Aslaksen. Yes, but—

Billing. Hurrah!—it is war, it is war!

Dr. Stockmann. I shall smite them to the ground—I shall crush them—I shall break down all their defences, before the eyes of the honest public! That is what I shall do!

Aslaksen. Yes, but in moderation, Doctor—proceed with moderation—

Billing. Not a bit of it, not a bit of it! Don't spare the dynamite!

Dr. Stockmann. Because it is not merely a question of water-supply and drains now, you know. No—it is the whole of our social life that we have got to purify and disinfect—

Billing. Spoken like a deliverer!

Dr. Stockmann. All the incapables must be turned out, you understand—and that in every walk of life! Endless vistas have opened themselves to my mind's eye to-day. I cannot see it all quite clearly yet, but I shall in time. Young and vigorous standard-bearers—those are what we need and must seek, my friends; we must have new men in command at all our outposts.

Billing. Hear, hear!

Dr. Stockmann. We only need to stand by one another, and it will all be perfectly easy. The revolution will be launched like a ship that runs smoothly off the stocks. Don't you think so?

Hovstad. For my part I think we have now a prospect of getting the municipal authority into the hands where it should lie.

Aslaksen. And if only we proceed with moderation, I cannot imagine that there will be any risk.

Dr. Stockmann. Who the devil cares whether there is any risk or not! What I am doing, I am doing in the name of truth and for the sake of my conscience.

Hovstad. You are a man who deserves to be supported, Doctor.

Aslaksen. Yes, there is no denying that the Doctor is a true friend to the town—a real friend to the community, that he is.

Billing. Take my word for it, Aslaksen, Dr. Stockmann is a friend of the people.

Aslaksen. I fancy the Householders' Association will make use of that expression before long.

Dr. Stockmann (*affected, grasps their hands*). Thank you, thank you, my dear staunch friends. It is very refreshing to me to hear you say that; my brother called me something quite different. By Jove, he shall have it back, with interest! But now I must be off to see a poor devil—. I will come back, as I said. Keep a very careful eye on the manuscript, Aslaksen, and don't for worlds leave out any of my notes of exclamation! Rather put one or two more in! Capital, capital! Well, good-bye for the present—good-bye, good-bye!

(*They show him to the door, and bow him out.*)

Hovstad. He may prove an invaluably useful man to us.

Aslaksen. Yes, so long as he confines himself to this matter of the Baths. But if he goes farther afield, I don't think it would be advisable to follow him.

Hovstad. Hm!—that all depends—

Billing. You are so infernally timid, Aslaksen!

Aslaksen. Timid? Yes, when it is a question of the local authorities, I am timid, Mr. Billing; it is a lesson I have learnt in the school of experience, let me tell you. But try me in higher politics, in matters that concern the government itself, and then see if I am timid.

Billing. No, you aren't, I admit. But this is simply contradicting yourself.

Aslaksen. I am a man with a conscience, and that is the whole matter. If you attack the government, you don't do the community any harm, anyway; those fellows pay no attention to attacks, you see—they go on just as they are, in spite of them. But *local* authorities are different; they *can* be turned out, and then perhaps you may get an ignorant lot into office who may do irreparable harm to the householders and everybody else.

Hovstad. But what of the education of citizens by self-government—don't you attach any importance to that?

Aslaksen. When a man has interests of his own to protect, he cannot think of everything, Mr. Hovstad.

Hovstad. Then I hope I shall never have interests of my own to protect!

Billing. Hear, hear!

Aslaksen (*with a smile*). Hm! (*Points to the desk.*) Mr. Sheriff Stensgaard was your predecessor at that editorial desk.

Billing (*spitting*). Bah! That turncoat.

Hovstad. I am not a weathercock—and never will be.

Aslaksen. A politician should never be too certain of anything, Mr. Hovstad. And as for you, Mr. Billing, I should think it is time for you to be taking in a reef or two in your sails, seeing that you are applying for the post of secretary to the Bench.

Billing. I—!

Hovstad. Are you, Billing?

Billing. Well, yes—but you must clearly understand I am only doing it to annoy the bigwigs.

Aslaksen. Anyhow, it is no business of mine. But if I am to be accused of timidity and of inconsistency in my principles, this is what I want to point out: my political past is an open book. I have never changed, except to become a little more moderate, you see. My heart is still with the people; but I don't deny that my reason has a certain bias towards the authorities—the local ones, I mean. (*Goes into the printing-room.*)

Billing. Oughtn't we to try and get rid of him, Hovstad?

Hovstad. Do you know anyone else who will advance the money for our paper and printing bill?

Billing. It is an infernal nuisance that we don't possess some capital to trade on.

Hovstad (*sitting down at his desk*). Yes, if we only had that, then—

Billing. Suppose you were to apply to Dr. Stockmann?

Hovstad (*turning over some papers*). What is the use? He has got nothing.

Billing. No, but he has got a warm man in the background, old Morten Kiil—"the Badger," as they call him.

Hovstad (*writing*).   Are you so sure *he* has got anything?

Billing.   Good Lord, of course he has! And some of it must come to the Stock-manns. Most probably he will do something for the children, at all events.

Hovstad (*turning half round*).   Are you counting on that?

Billing.   Counting on it? Of course I am not counting on anything.

Hovstad.   That is right. And I should not count on the secretaryship to the Bench either, if I were you; for I can assure you—you won't get it.

Billing.   Do you think I am not quite aware of that? My object is precisely *not* to get it. A slight of that kind stimulates a man's fighting power—it is like getting a supply of fresh bile—and I am sure one needs that badly enough in a hole-and-corner place like this, where it is so seldom anything happens to stir one up.

Hovstad (*writing*).   Quite so, quite so.

Billing.   Ah, I shall be heard of yet!—Now I shall go and write the appeal to the Householders' Association. (*Goes into the room on the right.*)

Hovstad (*sitting at his desk, biting his penholder, says slowly*).   Hm!—that's it, is it. (*A knock is heard.*) Come in! (*Petra comes in by the outer door. Hovstad gets up.*) What, you!—here?

Petra.   Yes, you must forgive me—

Hovstad (*pulling a chair forward*).   Won't you sit down?

Petra.   No, thank you; I must go again in a moment.

Hovstad.   Have you come with a message from your father, by any chance?

Petra.   No, I have come on my own account. (*Takes a book out of her coat pocket.*) Here is the English story.

Hovstad.   Why have you brought it back?

Petra.   Because I am not going to translate it.

Hovstad.   But you promised me faithfully—

Petra.   Yes, but then I had not read it. I don't suppose you have read it either?

Hovstad.   No, you know quite well I don't understand English; but—

Petra.   Quite so. That is why I wanted to tell you that you must find something else. (*Lays the book on the table.*) You can't use this for the "People's Messenger."

Hovstad.   Why not?

Petra.   Because it conflicts with all your opinions.

Hovstad.   Oh, for that matter—

Petra.   You don't understand me. The burden of this story is that there is a supernatural power that looks after the so-called good people in this world and makes everything happen for the best in their case—while all the so-called bad people are punished.

Hovstad.   Well, but that is all right. That is just what our readers want.

Petra.   And are you going to be the one to give it to them? For myself, I do not believe a word of it. You know quite well that things do not happen so in reality.

Hovstad.   You are perfectly right; but an editor cannot always act as he would prefer. He is often obliged to bow to the wishes of the public in unimportant matters. Politics are the most important thing in life—for a newspaper, anyway; and if I want to carry my public with me on the path that leads to liberty and progress, I must not frighten them away. If they find a moral tale of this sort in the serial at the bottom of the page, they will be all the more ready to read what is printed above it; they feel more secure, as it were.

Petra. For shame! You would never go and set a snare like that for your readers; you are not a spider!

Hovstad (*smiling*). Thank you for having such a good opinion of me. No; as a matter of fact that is Billing's idea and not mine.

Petra. Billing's!

Hovstad. Yes; anyway he propounded that theory here one day. And it is Billing who is so anxious to have that story in the paper; I don't know anything about the book.

Petra. But how can Billing, with his emancipated views—

Hovstad. Oh, Billing is a many-sided man. He is applying for the post of secretary to the Bench, too, I hear.

Petra. I don't believe it, Mr. Hovstad. How could he possibly bring himself to do such a thing?

Hovstad. Ah, you must ask him that.

Petra. I should never have thought it of him.

Hovstad (*looking more closely at her*). No? Does it really surprise you so much?

Petra. Yes. Or perhaps not altogether. Really, I don't quite know—

Hovstad. We journalists are not much worth, Miss Stockmann.

Petra. Do you really mean that?

Hovstad. I think so sometimes.

Petra. Yes, in the ordinary affairs of everyday life, perhaps; I can understand that. But now, when you have taken a weighty matter in hand—

Hovstad. This matter of your father's, you mean?

Petra. Exactly. It seems to me that now you must feel you are a man worth more than most.

Hovstad. Yes, to-day I do feel something of that sort.

Petra. Of course you do, don't you? It is a splendid vocation you have chosen—to smooth the way for the march of unappreciated truths, and new and courageous lines of thought. If it were nothing more than because you stand fearlessly in the open and take up the cause of an injured man—

Hovstad. Especially when that injured man is—ahem!—I don't rightly know how to—

Petra. When that man is so upright and so honest, you mean?

Hovstad (*more gently*). Especially when he is your father, I meant.

Petra (*suddenly checked*). That?

Hovstad. Yes, Petra—Miss Petra.

Petra. Is it *that*, that is first and foremost with you? Not the matter itself? Not the truth?—not my father's big generous heart?

Hovstad. Certainly—of course—that too.

Petra. No, thank you; you have betrayed yourself, Mr. Hovstad, and now I shall never trust you again in anything.

Hovstad. Can you really take it so amiss in me that it is mostly for your sake—?

Petra. What I am angry with you for, is for not having been honest with my father. You talked to him as if the truth and the good of the community were what lay nearest to your heart. You have made fools of both my father and me. You are not the man you made yourself out to be. And that I shall never forgive you—never!

Hovstad. You ought not to speak so bitterly, Miss Petra—least of all now.

Petra. Why not now, especially?

Hovstad. Because your father cannot do without my help.

Petra (*looking him up and down*).   Are you that sort of man too? For shame!

Hovstad. No, no, I am not. This came upon me so unexpectedly—you must believe that.

Petra. I know what to believe. Good-bye.

Aslaksen (*coming from the printing-room, hurriedly and with an air of mystery*).   Damnation, Hovstad!—(*Sees Petra.*) Oh, this is awkward—

Petra. There is the book; you must give it to some one else. (*Goes towards the door.*)

Hovstad (*following her*).   But, Miss Stockmann—

Petra. Good-bye. (*Goes out.*)

Aslaksen. I say—Mr. Hovstad—

Hovstad. Well, well!—what is it?

Aslaksen. The Mayor is outside in the printing-room.

Hovstad. The Mayor, did you say?

Aslaksen. Yes, he wants to speak to you. He came in by the back door— didn't want to be seen, you understand.

Hovstad. What can he want? Wait a bit—I will go myself. (*Goes to the door of the printing-room, opens it, bows and invites Peter Stockmann in.*) Just see, Aslaksen, that no one—

Aslaksen. Quite so. (*Goes into the printing-room.*)

Peter Stockmann. You did not expect to see me here, Mr. Hovstad?

Hovstad. No, I confess I did not.

Peter Stockmann (*looking round*).   You are very snug in here—very nice indeed.

Hovstad. Oh—

Peter Stockmann. And here I come, without any notice, to take up your time!

Hovstad. By all means, Mr. Mayor. I am at your service. But let me relieve you of your— (*takes Stockmann's hat and stick and puts them on a chair*). Won't you sit down?

Peter Stockmann (*sitting down by the table*).   Thank you. (*Hovstad sits down.*) I have had an extremely annoying experience to-day, Mr. Hovstad.

Hovstad. Really? Ah well, I expect with all the various business you have to attend to—

Peter Stockmann. The Medical Officer of the Baths is responsible for what happened to-day.

Hovstad. Indeed? The Doctor?

Peter Stockmann. He has addressed a kind of report to the Baths Committee on the subject of certain supposed defects in the Baths.

Hovstad. Has he indeed?

Peter Stockmann. Yes—has he not told you? I thought he said—

Hovstad. Ah, yes—it is true he did mention something about—

Aslaksen (*coming from the printing-room*). I ought to have that copy—

Hovstad (*angrily*). Ahem!—there it is on the desk.

Aslaksen (*taking it*). Right.

Peter Stockmann. But look there—that is the thing I was speaking of!

Aslaksen. Yes, that is the Doctor's article, Mr. Mayor.

Hovstad. Oh, is *that* what you were speaking about?

Peter Stockmann. Yes, that is it. What do you think of it?

Hovstad. Oh, I am only a layman—and I have only taken a very cursory glance at it.

Peter Stockmann. But you are going to print it?

Hovstad. I cannot very well refuse a distinguished man—

Aslaksen. I have nothing to do with editing the paper, Mr. Mayor—

Peter Stockmann. I understand.

Aslaksen. I merely print what is put into my hands.

Peter Stockmann. Quite so.

Aslaksen. And so I must— (*moves off towards the printing-room*).

Peter Stockmann. No, wait a moment, Mr. Aslaksen. You will allow me, Mr. Hovstad?

Hovstad. If you please, Mr. Mayor.

Peter Stockmann. You are a discreet and thoughtful man, Mr. Aslaksen.

Aslaksen. I am delighted to hear you think so, sir.

Peter Stockmann. And a man of very considerable influence.

Aslaksen. Chiefly among the small tradesmen, sir.

Peter Stockmann. The small tax-payers are the majority—here as everywhere else.

Aslaksen. That is true.

Peter Stockmann. And I have no doubt you know the general trend of opinion among them, don't you?

Aslaksen. Yes, I think I may say I do, Mr. Mayor.

Peter Stockmann. Yes. Well, since there is such a praiseworthy spirit of self-sacrifice among the less wealthy citizens of our town—

Aslaksen. What?

Hovstad. Self-sacrifice?

Peter Stockmann. It is pleasing evidence of a public-spirited feeling, extremely pleasing evidence. I might almost say I hardly expected it. But you have a closer knowledge of public opinion than I.

Aslaksen. But, Mr. Mayor—

Peter Stockmann. And indeed it is no small sacrifice that the town is going to make.

Hovstad. The town?

Aslaksen. But I don't understand. Is it the Baths—?

Peter Stockmann. At a provisional estimate, the alterations that the Medical Officer asserts to be desirable will cost somewhere about twenty thousand pounds.

Aslaksen. That is a lot of money, but—

Peter Stockmann. Of course it will be necessary to raise a municipal loan.

Hovstad (*getting up*). Surely you don't mean that the town must pay—?.

Aslaksen. Do you mean that it must come out of the municipal funds?—out of the ill-filled pockets of the small tradesmen?

Peter Stockmann. Well, my dear Mr. Aslaksen, where else is the money to come from?

Aslaksen. The gentlemen who own the Baths ought to provide that.

Peter Stockmann. The proprietors of the Baths are not in a position to incur any further expense.

Aslaksen. Is that absolutely certain, Mr. Mayor?

Peter Stockmann. I have satisfied myself that it is so. If the town wants these very extensive alterations, it will have to pay for them.

Aslaksen. But, damn it all—I beg your pardon—this is quite another matter, Mr. Hovstad!

Hovstad. It is, indeed.

Peter Stockmann. The most fatal part of it is that we shall be obliged to shut the Baths for a couple of years.

Hovstad. Shut them? Shut them altogether?

Aslaksen. For two years?

Peter Stockmann. Yes, the work will take as long as that—at least.

Aslaksen. I'm damned if we will stand that, Mr. Mayor! What are we householders to live upon in the meantime?

Peter Stockmann. Unfortunately that is an extremely difficult question to answer, Mr. Aslaksen. But what would you have us do? Do you suppose we shall have a single visitor in the town, if we go about proclaiming that our water is polluted, that we are living over a plague spot, that the entire town—

Aslaksen. And the whole thing is merely imagination?

Peter Stockmann. With the best will in the world, I have not been able to come to any other conclusion.

Aslaksen. Well then I must say it is absolutely unjustifiable of Dr. Stockmann—I beg your pardon, Mr. Mayor—

Peter Stockmann. What you say is lamentably true, Mr. Aslaksen. My brother has unfortunately always been a headstrong man.

Aslaksen. After this, do you mean to give him your support, Mr. Hovstad?

Hovstad. Can you suppose for a moment that I—?

Peter Stockmann. I have drawn up a short *résume* of the situation as it appears from a reasonable man's point of view. In it I have indicated how certain possible defects might suitably be remedied without out-running the resources of the Baths Committee.

Hovstad.   Have you got it with you, Mr. Mayor?

Peter Stockmann (*fumbling in his pocket*).   Yes, I brought it with me in case you should—

Aslaksen.   Good Lord, there he is!

Peter Stockmann.   Who? My brother?

Hovstad.   Where? Where?

Aslaksen.   He has just gone through the printing-room.

Peter Stockmann.   How unlucky! I don't want to meet him here, and I had still several things to speak to you about.

Hovstad (*pointing to the door on the right*).   Go in there for the present.

Peter Stockmann.   But—?

Hovstad.   You will only find Billing in there.

Aslaksen.   Quick, quick, Mr. Mayor—he is just coming.

Peter Stockmann.   Yes, very well; but see that you get rid of him quickly. (*Goes out through the door on the right, which Aslaksen opens for him and shuts after him.*)

Hovstad.   Pretend to be doing something, Aslaksen. (*Sits down and writes. Aslaksen begins foraging among a heap of newspapers that are lying on a chair.*)

Dr. Stockmann (*coming in from the printing-room*).   Here I am again. (*Puts down his hat and stick.*)

Hovstad (*writing*).   Already, Doctor? Hurry up with what we were speaking about, Aslaksen. We are very pressed for time to-day.

Dr. Stockmann (*to Aslaksen*).   No proof for me to see yet, I hear.

Aslaksen (*without turning round*).   You couldn't expect it yet, Doctor.

Dr. Stockmann.   No, no; but I am impatient, as you can understand. I shall not know a moment's peace of mind till I see it in print.

Hovstad.   Hm!—It will take a good while yet, won't it, Aslaksen?

Aslaksen.   Yes, I am almost afraid it will.

Dr. Stockmann.   All right, my dear friends; I will come back. I do not mind coming back twice if necessary. A matter of such great importance—the welfare of the town at stake—it is no time to shirk trouble. (*Is just going, but stops and comes back.*). Look here—there is one thing more I want to speak to you about.

Hovstad.   Excuse me, but could it not wait till some other time?

Dr. Stockmann.   I can tell you in half a dozen words. It is only this. When my article is read to-morrow and it is realised that I have been quietly working the whole winter for the welfare of the town—

Hovstad.   Yes but, Doctor—

Dr. Stockmann.   I know what you are going to say. You don't see how on earth it was any more than my duty—my obvious duty as a citizen. Of course it wasn't; I know that as well as you. But my fellow citizens, you know—! Good Lord, think of all the good souls who think so highly of me—!

Aslaksen. Yes, our townsfolk have had a very high opinion of you so far, Doctor.

Dr. Stockmann. Yes, and that is just why I am afraid they—. Well, this is the point; when this reaches them, especially the poorer classes, and sounds in their ears like a summons to take the town's affairs into their own hands for the future—

Hovstad (*getting up*). Ahem! Doctor, I won't conceal from you the fact—

Dr. Stockmann. Ah!—I knew there was something in the wind! But I won't hear a word of it. If anything of that sort is being set on foot—

Hovstad. Of what sort?

Dr. Stockmann. Well, whatever it is—whether it is a demonstration in my honour, or a banquet, or a subscription list for some presentation to me—whatever it is, you most promise me solemnly and faithfully to put a stop to it. You too, Mr. Aslaksen; do you understand?

Hovstad. You must forgive me, Doctor, but sooner or later we must tell you the plain truth—

(*He is interrupted by the entrance of Mrs. Stockmann, who comes in from the street door.*).

Mrs. Stockmann (*seeing her husband*). Just as I thought!

Hovstad (*going towards her*). You too, Mrs. Stockmann?

Dr. Stockmann. What on earth do *you* want here, Katherine?

Mrs. Stockmann. I should think you know very well what I want.

Hovstad. Won't you sit down? Or perhaps—

Mrs. Stockmann. No, thank you; don't trouble. And you must not be offended at my coming to fetch my husband; I am the mother of three children, you know.

Dr. Stockmann. Nonsense!—we know all about that.

Mrs. Stockmann. Well, one would not give you credit for much thought for your wife and the children to-day; if you had had that, you would not have gone and dragged us all into misfortune.

Dr. Stockmann. Are you out of your senses, Katherine! Because a man has a wife and children, is he not to be allowed to do a service to his native town!

Mrs. Stockmann. Yes, Thomas—in reason.

Aslaksen. Just what I say. Moderation in everything.

Mrs. Stockmann. And that is why you wrong us, Mr. Hovstad, in enticing my husband away from his home and making a dupe of him in all this.

Hovstad. I certainly am making a dupe of no one—

Dr. Stockmann. Making a dupe of me! Do you suppose *I* should allow myself to be duped!

Mrs. Stockmann. It is just what you do. I know quite well you have more brains than anyone in the town, but you are extremely easily duped,

Thomas. (*To Hovstad.*) Please realise that he loses his post at the Baths if you print what he has written—

Aslaksen. What?

Hovstad. Look here, Doctor—

Dr. Stockmann (*laughing*). Ha—ha!—just let them try! No, no—they will take good care not to. I have got the compact majority behind me, let me tell you!

Mrs. Stockmann. Yes, that is just the worst of it—your having any such horrid thing behind you.

Dr. Stockmann. Rubbish, Katherine!—Go home and look after your house and leave me to look after the community. How can you be so afraid, when I am so confident and happy? (*Walks up and down, rubbing his hands.*) Truth and the People will win the fight, you may be certain! I see the whole of the broad-minded middle class marching like a victorious army—! (*Stops beside a chair.*). What the deuce is that lying there?

Aslaksen. Good Lord!

Hovstad. Ahem!

Dr. Stockmann. Here we have the topmost pinnacle of authority! (*Takes the Mayor's official hat carefully between his finger-tips and holds it up in the air.*)

Mrs. Stockmann. The Mayor's hat!

Dr. Stockmann. And here is the staff of office too. How in the name of all that's wonderful—?

Hovstad. Well, you see—

Dr. Stockmann. Oh, I understand. He has been here trying to talk you over. Ha—ha!—he made rather a mistake there! And as soon as he caught sight of me in the printing-room—. (*Bursts out laughing.*) Did he run away, Mr. Aslaksen?

Aslaksen (*hurriedly*). Yes, he ran away, Doctor.

Dr. Stockmann. Ran away without his stick or his—. Fiddlesticks! Peter doesn't run away and leave his belongings behind him. But what the deuce have you done with him? Ah!—in there, of course. Now you shall see, Katherine!

Mrs. Stockmann. Thomas—please don't—!

Aslaksen. Don't be rash, Doctor.

(*Dr. Stockmann has put on the Mayor's hat and taken his stick in his hand. He goes up to the door, opens it, and stands with his hand to his hat at the salute. Peter Stockmann comes in, red with anger. Billing follows him.*)

Peter Stockmann. What does this tomfoolery mean?

Dr. Stockmann. Be respectful, my good Peter. I am the chief authority in the town now. (*Walks up and down.*)

Mrs. Stockmann (*almost in tears*). Really, Thomas!

Peter Stockmann (*following him about*). Give me my hat and stick.

Dr. Stockmann (*in the same tone as before*). If you are chief constable, let me tell you that I am the Mayor—I am the master of the whole town, please understand!

Peter Stockmann. Take off my hat, I tell you. Remember it is part of an official uniform.

Dr. Stockmann. Pooh! Do you think the newly awakened lion-hearted people are going to be frightened by an official hat? There is going to be a revolution in the town to-morrow, let me tell you. You thought you could turn me out; but now I shall turn you out—turn you out of all your various offices. Do you think I cannot? Listen to me. I have triumphant social forces behind me. Hovstad and Billing will thunder in the "People's Messenger," and Aslaksen will take the field at the head of the whole Householders' Association—

Aslaksen. That I won't, Doctor.

Dr. Stockmann. Of course you will—

Peter Stockmann. Ah!—may I ask then if Mr. Hovstad intends to join this agitation.

Hovstad. No, Mr. Mayor.

Aslaksen. No, Mr. Hovstad is not such a fool as to go and ruin his paper and himself for the sake of an imaginary grievance.

Dr. Stockmann (*looking round him*). What does this mean?

Hovstad. You have represented your case in a false light, Doctor, and therefore I am unable to give you my support.

Billing. And after what the Mayor was so kind as to tell me just now, I—

Dr. Stockmann. A false light! Leave that part of it to me. Only print my article; I am quite capable of defending it.

Hovstad. I am not going to print it. I cannot and will not and dare not print it.

Dr. Stockmann. You dare not? What nonsense!—you are the editor; and an editor controls his paper, I suppose!

Aslaksen. No, it is the subscribers, Doctor.

Peter Stockmann. Fortunately, yes.

Aslaksen. It is public opinion—the enlightened public—householders and people of that kind; they control the newspapers.

Dr. Stockmann (*composedly*). And I have all these influences against me?

Aslaksen. Yes, you have. It would mean the absolute ruin of the community if your article were to appear.

Dr. Stockmann. Indeed.

Peter Stockmann. My hat and stick, if you please. (*Dr. Stockmann takes off the hat and lays it on the table with the stick. Peter Stockmann takes them up.*) Your authority as mayor has come to an untimely end.

Dr. Stockmann. We have not got to the end yet. (*To Hovstad.*) Then it is quite impossible for you to print my article in the "People's Messenger"?

Hovstad. Quite impossible—out of regard for your family as well.

Mrs. Stockmann. You need not concern yourself about his family, thank you, Mr. Hovstad.

Peter Stockmann (*taking a paper from his pocket*). It will be sufficient, for the guidance of the public, if this appears. It is an official statement. May I trouble you?

Hovstad (*taking the paper*).   Certainly; I will see that it is printed.

Dr. Stockmann.   But not mine. Do you imagine that you can silence me and stifle the truth! You will not find it so easy as you suppose. Mr. Aslaksen, kindly take my manuscript at once and print it as a pamphlet—at my expense. I will have four hundred copies—no, five—six hundred.

Aslaksen.   If you offered me its weight in gold, I could not lend my press for any such purpose, Doctor. It would be flying in the face of public opinion. You will not get it printed anywhere in the town.

Dr. Stockmann.   Then give it back to me.

Hovstad (*giving him the MS.*).   Here it is.

Dr. Stockmann (*taking his hat and stick*).   It shall be made public all the same. I will read it out at a mass meeting of the townspeople. All my fellow-citizens shall hear the voice of truth!

Peter Stockmann.   You will not find any public body in the town that will give you the use of their hall for such a purpose.

Aslaksen.   Not a single one, I am certain.

Billing.   No, I'm damned if you will find one.

Mrs. Stockmann.   But this is too shameful! Why should every one turn against you like that?

Dr. Stockmann (*angrily*).   I will tell you why. It is because all the men in this town are old women—like you; they all think of nothing but their families, and never of the community.

Mrs. Stockmann (*putting her arm into his*).   Then I will show them that an—an old woman can be a man for once. I am going to stand by you, Thomas!

Dr. Stockmann.   Bravely said, Katherine! It shall be made public—as I am a living soul! If I can't hire a hall, I shall hire a drum, and parade the town with it and read it at every street-corner.

Peter Stockmann.   You are surely not such an arrant fool as that!   '

Dr. Stockmann.   Yes, I am.

Aslaksen.   You won't find a single man in the whole town to go with you.

Billing.   No, I'm damned if you will.

Mrs. Stockmann.   Don't give in, Thomas. I will tell the boys to go with you.

Dr. Stockmann.   That is a splendid idea!

Mrs. Stockmann.   Morten will be delighted; and Ejlif will do whatever he does.

Dr. Stockmann.   Yes, and Petra!—and you too, Katherine!

Mrs. Stockmann.   No, I won't do that; but I will stand at the window and watch you, that's what I will do.

Dr. Stockmann (*puts his arms round her and kisses her*).   Thank you, my dear! Now you and I are going to try a fall, my fine gentlemen! I am going to see whether a pack of cowards can succeed in gagging a patriot who wants to purify society! (*He and his wife go out by the street door.*)

Peter Stockmann (*shaking his head seriously*).   Now he has sent *her* out of her senses, too.

Act IV

(SCENE.—*A big old-fashioned room in Captain Horster's house. At the back folding-doors, which are standing open, lead to an ante-room. Three windows in the left-hand wall. In the middle of the opposite wall a platform has been erected. On this is a small table with two candles, a water-bottle and glass, and a bell. The room is lit by lamps placed between the windows. In the foreground on the left there is a table with candles and a chair. To the right is a door and some chairs standing near it. The room is nearly filled with a crowd of townspeople of all sorts, a few women and schoolboys being amongst them. People are still streaming in from the back, and the room is soon filled.*)

1st Citizen (*meeting another*). Hullo, Lamstad! You here too?

2nd Citizen. I go to every public meeting, I do.

3rd Citizen. Brought your whistle too, I expect!

2nd Citizen. I should think so. Haven't you?

3rd Citizen. Rather! And old Evensen said he was going to bring a cow-horn, he did.

2nd Citizen. Good old Evensen! (*Laughter among the crowd.*)

4th Citizen (*coming up to them*). I say, tell me what is going on here to-night.

2nd Citizen. Dr. Stockmann is going to deliver an address attacking the Mayor.

4th Citizen. But the Mayor is his brother.

1st Citizen. That doesn't matter; Dr. Stockmann's not the chap to be afraid.

3rd Citizen. But he is in the wrong; it said so in the "People's Messenger."

2nd Citizen. Yes, I expect he must be in the wrong this time, because neither the Householders' Association nor the Citizens' Club would lend him their hall for his meeting.

1st Citizen. He couldn't even get the loan of the hall at the Baths.

2nd Citizen. No, I should think not.

A Man in another part of the crowd. I say—who are we to back up in this?

Another Man, beside him. Watch Aslaksen, and do as he does.

Billing (*pushing his way through the crowd, with a writing-case under his arm*). Excuse me, gentlemen—do you mind letting me through? I am reporting for the "People's Messenger." Thank you very much! (*He sits down at the table on the left.*)

A Workman. Who was that?

Second Workman. Don't you know him? It's Billing, who writes for Aslaksen's paper.

(*Captain Horster brings in Mrs. Stockmann and Petra through the door on the right. Ejlif and Morten follow them in.*)

Horster. I thought you might all sit here; you can slip out easily from here, if things get too lively.

Mrs. Stockmann. Do you think there will be a disturbance?

Horster. One can never tell—with such a crowd. But sit down, and don't be uneasy.

Mrs. Stockmann (*sitting down*).   It was extremely kind of you to offer my husband the room.

Horster.   Well, if nobody else would—

Petra (*who has sat down beside her mother*).   And it was a plucky thing to do, Captain Horster.

Horster.   Oh, it is not such a great matter as all that.

(*Hovstad and Aslaksen make their way through the crowd.*)

Aslaksen (*going up to Horster*).   Has the Doctor not come yet?

Horster.   He is waiting in the next room. (*Movement in the crowd by the door at the back.*)

Hovstad.   Look—here comes the Mayor!

Billing.   Yes, I'm damned if he hasn't come after all!

(*Peter Stockmann makes his way gradually through the crowd, bows courteously, and takes up a position by the wall on the left. Shortly afterwards Dr. Stockmann comes in by the right-hand door. He is dressed in a black frock-coat, with a white tie. There is a little feeble applause, which is hushed down. Silence is obtained.*)

Dr. Stockmann (*in an undertone*).   How do you feel, Katherine?

Mrs. Stockmann.   All right, thank you. (*Lowering her voice.*) Be sure not to lose your temper, Thomas.

Dr. Stockmann.   Oh, I know how to control myself. (*Looks at his watch, steps on to the platform, and bows.*) It is a quarter past—so I will begin. (*Takes his MS. out of his pocket.*)

Aslaksen.   I think we ought to elect a chairman first.

Dr. Stockmann.   No, it is quite unnecessary.

Some of the Crowd.   Yes—yes!

Peter Stockmann.   I certainly think too that we ought to have a chairman.

Dr. Stockmann.   But I have called this meeting to deliver a lecture, Peter.

Peter Stockmann.   Dr. Stockmann's lecture may possibly lead to a considerable conflict of opinion.

Voices in the Crowd.   A chairman! A chairman!

Hovstad.   The general wish of the meeting seems to be that a chairman should be elected.

Dr. Stockmann (*restraining himself*).   Very well—let the meeting have its way.

Aslaksen.   Will the Mayor be good enough to undertake the task?

Three Men (*clapping their hands*).   Bravo! Bravo!

Peter Stockmann.   For various reasons, which you will easily understand, I must beg to be excused. But fortunately we have amongst us a man who I think will be acceptable to you all. I refer to the President of the Householders' Association, Mr. Aslaksen!

Several voices.   Yes—Aslaksen! Bravo Aslaksen!

(Dr. Stockmann takes up his MS. and walks up and down the platform.)

Aslaksen. Since my fellow-citizens choose to entrust me with this duty, I cannot refuse.

(Loud applause. Aslaksen mounts the platform.)

Billing *(writing)*. "Mr. Aslaksen was elected with enthusiasm."

Aslaksen. And now, as I am in this position, I should like to say a few brief words. I am a quiet and peaceable man, who believes in discreet moderation, and—and—in moderate discretion. All my friends can bear witness to that.

Several Voices. That's right! That's right, Aslaksen!

Aslaksen. I have learnt in the school of life and experience that moderation is the most valuable virtue a citizen can possess—

Peter Stockmann. Hear, hear!

Aslaksen. —And moreover that discretion and moderation are what enable a man to be of most service to the community. I would therefore suggest to our esteemed fellow-citizen, who has called this meeting, that he should strive to keep strictly within the bounds of moderation.

A Man by the Door. Three cheers for the Moderation Society!

A Voice. Shame!

Several Voices. Sh!—Sh!

Aslaksen. No interruptions, gentlemen, please! Does anyone wish to make any remarks?

Peter Stockmann. Mr. Chairman.

Aslaksen. The Mayor will address the meeting.

Peter Stockmann. In consideration of the close relationship in which, as you all know, I stand to the present Medical Officer of the Baths, I should have preferred not to speak this evening. But my official position with regard to the Baths and my solicitude for the vital interests of the town compel me to bring forward a motion. I venture to presume that there is not a single one of our citizens present who considers it desirable that unreliable and exaggerated accounts of the sanitary condition of the Baths and the town should be spread abroad.

Several Voices. No, no! Certainly not! We protest against it!

Peter Stockmann. Therefore I should like to propose that the meeting should not permit the Medical Officer either to read or to comment on his proposed lecture.

Dr. Stockmann *(impatiently)*. Not permit—! What the devil—!

Mrs. Stockmann *(coughing)*. Ahem!—ahem!

Dr. Stockmann *(collecting himself)*. Very well. Go ahead!

Peter Stockmann. In my communication to the "People's Messenger," I have put the essential facts before the public in such a way that every fair-minded citizen can easily form his own opinion. From it you will see that the main result of the Medical Officer's proposals—apart from their constituting a vote of censure on the leading men of the town—would be to saddle the ratepayers with an unnecessary expenditure of at least some thousands of pounds.

(*Sounds of disapproval among the audience, and some cat-calls.*)

Aslaksen (*ringing his bell*).   Silence, please, gentlemen! I beg to support the Mayor's motion. I quite agree with him that there is something behind this agitation started by the Doctor. He talks about the Baths; but it is a revolution he is aiming at—he wants to get the administration of the town put into new hands. No one doubts the honesty of the Doctor's intentions—no one will suggest that there can be any two opinions as to that. I myself am a believer in self-government for the people, provided it does not fall too heavily on the ratepayers. But that would be the case here; and that is why I will see Dr. Stockmann damned—I beg your pardon—before I go with him in the matter. You can pay too dearly for a thing sometimes; that is my opinion.

(*Loud applause on all sides.*)

Hovstad.   I, too, feel called upon to explain my position. Dr. Stockmann's agitation appeared to be gaining a certain amount of sympathy at first, so I supported it as impartially as I could. But presently we had reason to suspect that we had allowed ourselves to be misled by misrepresentation of the state of affairs—

Dr. Stockmann.   Misrepresentation—!

Hovstad.   Well, let us say a not entirely trustworthy representation. The Mayor's statement has proved that. I hope no one here has any doubt as to my liberal principles; the attitude of the "People's Messenger" towards important political questions is well known to every one. But the advice of experienced and thoughtful men has convinced me that in purely local matters a newspaper ought to proceed with a certain caution.

Aslaksen.   I entirely agree with the speaker.

Hovstad.   And, in the matter before us, it is now an undoubted fact that Dr. Stockmann has public opinion against him. Now, what is an editor's first and most obvious duty, gentlemen? Is it not to work in harmony with his readers? Has he not received a sort of tacit mandate to work persistently and assiduously for the welfare of those whose opinions he represents? Or is it possible I am mistaken in that?

Voices from the crowd.   No, No! You are quite right!

Hovstad.   It has cost me a severe struggle to break with a man in whose house I have been lately a frequent guest—a man who till to-day has been able to pride himself on the undivided goodwill of his fellow-citizens—a man whose only, or at all events whose essential failing, is that he is swayed by his heart rather than his head.

A few scattered voices.   That is true! Bravo, Stockmann!

Hovstad.   But my duty to the community obliged me to break with him. And there is another consideration that impels me to oppose him, and, as far as possible, to arrest him on the perilous course he has adopted; that is, consideration for his family—

Dr. Stockmann. Please stick to the water-supply and drainage!

Hovstad. —consideration, I repeat, for his wife and his children for whom he has made no provision.

Morten. Is that us, mother?

Mrs. Stockmann. Hush!

Aslaksen. I will now put the Mayor's proposition to the vote.

Dr. Stockmann. There is no necessity! To-night I have no intention of dealing with all that filth down at the Baths. No; I have something quite different to say to you.

Peter Stockmann (*aside*). What is coming now?

A Drunken Man (*by the entrance door*). I am a rate-payer! And therefore I have a right to speak too! And my entire—firm—inconceivable opinion is—

A number of voices. Be quiet, at the back there!

Others. He is drunk! Turn him out! (*They turn him out.*)

Dr. Stockmann. Am I allowed to speak?

Aslaksen (*ringing his bell*). Dr. Stockmann will address the meeting.

Dr. Stockmann. I should like to have seen anyone, a few days ago, dare to attempt to silence me as has been done to-night! I would have defended my sacred rights as a man, like a lion! But now it is all one to me; I have something of even weightier importance to say to you. (*The crowd presses nearer to him, Morten Kiil conspicuous among them.*)

Dr. Stockmann (*continuing*). I have thought and pondered a great deal, these last few days—pondered over such a variety of things that in the end my head seemed too full to hold them—

Peter Stockmann (*with a cough*). Ahem!

Dr. Stockmann.—but I got them clear in my mind at last, and then I saw the whole situation lucidly. And that is why I am standing here to-night. I have a great revelation to make to you, my fellow-citizens! I will impart to you a discovery of a far wider scope than the trifling matter that our water-supply is poisoned and our medicinal Baths are standing on pestiferous soil.

A number of voices (*shouting*). Don't talk about the Baths! We won't hear you! None of that!

Dr. Stockmann. I have already told you that what I want to speak about is the great discovery I have made lately—the discovery that all the sources of our *moral* life are poisoned and that the whole fabric of our civic community is founded on the pestiferous soil of falsehood.

Voices of disconcerted Citizens. What is that he says?

Peter Stockmann. Such an insinuation—!

Aslaksen (*with his hand on his bell*). I call upon the speaker to moderate his language.

Dr. Stockmann. I have always loved my native town as a man only can love the home of his youthful days. I was not old when I went away from here; and exile, longing and memories cast as it were an additional halo over both the town and its inhabitants. (*Some clapping and applause.*) And there I stayed, for many years, in a horrible hole far away up north. When I came into contact with some of the people that lived scattered about among the rocks, I often thought it would have been more service to the poor half-starved creatures if a veterinary doctor had been sent up there, instead of a man like me. (*Murmurs among the crowd.*)

Billing (*laying down his pen*).   I'm damned if I have ever heard—!

Hovstad.   It is an insult to a respectable population!

Dr. Stockmann.   Wait a bit! I do not think anyone will charge me with having forgotten my native town up there. I was like one of the eider-ducks brooding on its nest, and what I hatched was—the plans for these Baths. (*Applause and protests.*) And then when fate at last decreed for me the great happiness of coming home again—I assure you, gentlemen, I thought I had nothing more in the world to wish for. Or rather, there was one thing I wished for—eagerly, untiringly, ardently—and that was to be able to be of service to my native town and the good of the community.

Peter Stockmann (*looking at the ceiling*).   You chose a strange way of doing it—ahem!

Dr. Stockmann.   And so, with my eyes blinded to the real facts, I revelled in happiness. But yesterday morning—no, to be precise, it was yesterday afternoon—the eyes of my mind were opened wide, and the first thing I realised was the colossal stupidity of the authorities—. (*Uproar, shouts and laughter. Mrs. Stockmann coughs persistently.*)

Peter Stockmann.   Mr. Chairman!

Aslaksen (*ringing his bell*).   By virtue of my authority—!

Dr. Stockmann.   It is a pretty thing to catch me up on a word, Mr. Aslaksen. What I mean is only that I got scent of the unbelievable piggishness our leading men had been responsible for down at the Baths. I can't stand leading men at any price!—I have had enough of such people in my time. They are like billy-goats in a young plantation; they do mischief everywhere. They stand in a free man's way, whichever way he turns, and what I should like best would be to see them exterminated like any other vermin—. (*Uproar.*)

Peter Stockmann.   Mr. Chairman, can we allow such expressions to pass?

Aslaksen (*with his hand on his bell*).   Doctor—!

Dr. Stockmann.   I cannot understand how it is that I have only now acquired a clear conception of what these gentry are, when I had almost daily before my eyes in this town such an excellent specimen of them—my brother Peter—slow-witted and hide-bound in prejudice—. (*Laughter, uproar and hisses. Mrs. Stockmann sits coughing assiduously. Aslaksen rings his bell violently.*)

The Drunken Man (*who has got in again*).   Is it me he is talking about? My name's Petersen, all right—but devil take me if I—

Angry Voices. Turn out that drunken man! Turn him out. (*He is turned out again.*)

Peter Stockmann. Who was that person?

1st Citizen. I don't know who he is, Mr. Mayor.

2nd Citizen. He doesn't belong here.

3rd Citizen. I expect he is a navvy from over at—(*the rest is inaudible*).

Aslaksen. He had obviously had too much beer.—Proceed, Doctor; but please strive to be moderate in your language.

Dr. Stockmann. Very well, gentlemen, I will say no more about our leading men. And if anyone imagines, from what I have just said, that my object is to attack these people this evening, he is wrong—absolutely wide of the mark. For I cherish the comforting conviction that these parasites—all these venerable relics of a dying school of thought—are most admirably paving the way for their own extinction; they need no doctor's help to hasten their end. Nor is it folk of that kind who constitute the most pressing danger to the community. It is not they who are most instrumental in poisoning the sources of our moral life and infecting the ground on which we stand. It is not they who are the most dangerous enemies of truth and freedom amongst us.

Shouts from all sides. Who then? Who is it? Name! Name!

Dr. Stockmann. You may depend upon it I shall name them! That is precisely the great discovery I made yesterday. (*Raises his voice.*) The most dangerous enemy of truth and freedom amongst us is the compact majority—yes, the damned compact Liberal majority—that is it! Now you know!

(*Tremendous uproar. Most of the crowd are shouting, stamping and hissing. Some of the older men among them exchange stolen glances and seem to be enjoying themselves. Mrs. Stockmann gets up, looking anxious. Ejlif and Morten advance threateningly upon some schoolboys who are playing pranks. Aslaksen rings his bell and begs for silence. Hovstad and Billing both talk at once, but are inaudible. At last quiet is restored.*)

Aslaksen. As chairman, I call upon the speaker to withdraw the ill-considered expressions he has just used.

Dr. Stockmann. Never, Mr. Aslaksen! It is the majority in our community that denies me my freedom and seeks to prevent my speaking the truth.

Hovstad. The majority always has right on its side.

Billing. And truth too, by God!

Dr. Stockmann. The majority *never* has right on its side. Never, I say! That is one of these social lies against which an independent, intelligent man must wage war. Who is it that constitute the majority of the population in a country? Is it the clever folk or the stupid? I don't imagine you will dispute the fact that at present the stupid people are in an absolutely overwhelming majority all the world over. But, good Lord!—you can never pretend that it is right that the stupid folk should govern the clever ones! (*Uproar and cries.*) Oh, yes—you can shout me down, I know! but you cannot answer me. The majority has *might* on its side—unfortunately; but *right* it has *not*. I am in the right—I and a few other scattered individuals. The minority is always in the right. (*Renewed uproar.*)

Hovstad. Aha!—so Dr. Stockmann has become an aristocrat since the day before yesterday!

Dr. Stockmann. I have already said that I don't intend to waste a word on the puny, narrow-chested, short-winded crew whom we are leaving astern. Pulsating life no longer concerns itself with them. I am thinking of the few, the scattered few amongst us, who have absorbed new and vigorous truths. Such men stand, as it were, at the outposts, so far ahead that the compact majority has not yet been able to come up with them; and there they are fighting for truths that are too newly-born into the world of consciousness to have any considerable number of people on their side as yet.

Hovstad. So the Doctor is a revolutionary now!

Dr. Stockmann. Good heavens—of course I am, Mr. Hovstad! I propose to raise a revolution against the lie that the majority has the monopoly on the truth. What sort of truths are they that the majority usually supports? They are truths that are of such advanced age that they are beginning to break up. And if a truth is as old as that, it is also in a fair way to become a lie, gentlemen. (*Laughter and mocking cries.*) Yes, believe me or not, as you like; but truths are by no means as long-lived at Methuselah—as some folks imagine. A normally constituted truth lives, let us say, as a rule seventeen or eighteen, or at most twenty years; seldom longer. But truths as aged as that are always worn frightfully thin, and nevertheless it is only then that the majority recognises them and recommends them to the community as wholesome moral nourishment. There is no great nutritive value in that sort of fare, I can assure you; and, as a doctor, I ought to know. These "majority truths" are like last year's cured meat—like rancid, tainted ham; and they are the origin of the moral scurvy that is rampant in our communities.

Aslaksen. It appears to me that the speaker is wandering a long way from his subject.

Peter Stockmann. I quite agree with the Chairman.

Dr. Stockmann. Have you gone clean out of your senses, Peter? I am sticking as closely to my subject as I can; for my subject is precisely this, that it is the masses, the majority—this infernal compact majority—that poisons the sources of our moral life and infects the ground we stand on.

Hovstad. And all this because the great, broad-minded majority of the people is prudent enough to show deference only to well-ascertained and well-approved truths?

Dr. Stockmann. Ah, my good Mr. Hovstad, don't talk nonsense about well-ascertained truths! The truths of which the masses now approve are the very truths that the fighters at the outposts held to in the days of our grandfathers. We fighters at the outposts nowadays no longer approve of them; and I do not believe there is any other well-ascertained truth except this, that no community can live a healthy life if it is nourished only on such old marrowless truths.

Hovstad. But instead of standing there using vague generalities, it would be interesting if you would tell us what these old marrowless truths are, that we are nourished on.

(*Applause from many quarters.*)

Dr. Stockmann. Oh, I could give you a whole string of such abominations; but to begin with I will confine myself to one well-approved truth, which at bottom is a foul lie, but upon which nevertheless Mr. Hovstad and the "People's Messenger" and all the "Messenger's" supporters are nourished.

Hovstad. And that is—?

Dr. Stockmann. That is, the doctrine you have inherited from your forefathers and proclaim thoughtlessly far and wide—the doctrine that the public, the crowd, the masses, are the essential part of the population—that they constitute the People—that the common folk, the ignorant and incomplete element in the community, have the same right to pronounce judgment and to approve, to direct and to govern, as the isolated, intellectually superior personalities in it.

Billing. Well, damn me if ever I—

Hovstad (*at the same time, shouting out*). Fellow-citizens, take good note of that!

A number of voices (*angrily*). Oho!—we are not the People! Only the superior folk are to govern, are they!

A Workman. Turn the fellow out, for talking such rubbish!

Another. Out with him!

Another (*calling out*). Blow your horn, Evensen!

(*A horn is blown loudly, amidst hisses and an angry uproar.*)

Dr. Stockmann (*when the noise has somewhat abated*). Be reasonable! Can't you stand hearing the voice of truth for once? I don't in the least expect you to agree with me all at once; but I must say I did expect Mr. Hovstad to admit I was right, when he had recovered his composure a little. He claims to be a freethinker—

Voices (*in murmurs of astonishment*). Freethinker, did he say? Is Hovstad a freethinker?

Hovstad (*shouting*). Prove it, Dr. Stockmann! When have I said so in print?

Dr. Stockmann (*reflecting*). No, confound it, you are right!—you have never had the courage to. Well, I won't put you in a hole, Mr. Hovstad. Let us say it is I that am the freethinker, then. I am going to prove to you, scientifically, that the "People's Messenger" leads you by the nose in a shameful manner when it tells you that you—that the common people, the crowd, the masses, are the real essence of the People. That is only a newspaper lie, I tell you! The common people are nothing more than the raw material of which a People is made. (*Groans, laughter and uproar.*) Well, isn't that the case? Isn't there an enormous difference between a well-bred and an ill-bred strain of animals? Take, for instance, a common barn-door hen. What sort of eating do you get from a shrivelled up old scrag of a fowl like that? Not much, do you! And what sort of eggs does it lay? A fairly good crow or a raven can lay pretty nearly as good an egg. But take a well-bred Spanish or Japanese hen, or a good pheasant or a turkey—then you will see the difference. Or take the case of dogs, with whom we humans are on such intimate terms. Think first of an ordinary common cur—I mean one of the horrible, coarse-haired, low-bred curs that do nothing but run about the streets and befoul the walls of the houses. Compare one of these curs with a poodle whose sires for many generations have been bred in a gentleman's house, where they have had the best of food and had the opportunity of hearing soft voices and music. Do you not think that the poodle's brain is developed to quite a different degree from that of the cur? Of course it is. It is puppies of well-bred poodles like that, that showmen train to do incredibly clever tricks—things that a common cur could never learn to do even if it stood on its head. (*Uproar and mocking cries.*)

A Citizen (*calls out*).   Are you going to make out we are dogs, now?

Another Citizen.   We are not animals, Doctor!

Dr. Stockmann.   Yes, but, bless my soul, we *are*, my friend! It is true we are the finest animals anyone could wish for; but, even amongst us, exceptionally fine animals are rare. There is a tremendous difference between poodle-men and cur-men. And the amusing part of it is, that Mr. Hovstad quite agrees with me as long as it is a question of four-footed animals—

Hovstad.   Yes, it is true enough as far as they are concerned.

Dr. Stockmann.   Very well. But as soon as I extend the principle and apply it to two-legged animals, Mr. Hovstad stops short. He no longer dares to think independently, or to pursue his ideas to their logical conclusion; so he turns the whole theory upside down and proclaims in the "People's Messenger" that it is the barn-door hens and street curs that are the finest specimens in the menagerie. But that is always the way, as long as a man retains the traces of common origin and has not worked his way up to intellectual distinction.

Hovstad.   I lay no claim to any sort of distinction. I am the son of humble countryfolk, and I am proud that the stock I come from is rooted deep among the common people he insults.

Voices.   Bravo, Hovstad! Bravo! Bravo!

Dr. Stockmann.   The kind of common people I mean are not only to be found low down in the social scale; they crawl and swarm all around us—even in the highest social positions. You have only to look at your own fine, distinguished Mayor! My brother Peter is every bit as plebian as anyone that walks in two shoes—(*laughter and hisses*).

Peter Stockmann. I protest against personal allusions of this kind.

Dr. Stockmann (*imperturbably*).—and that, not because he is, like myself, descended from some old rascal of a pirate from Pomerania or thereabouts—because that is who we are descended from—

Peter Stockmann. An absurd legend. I deny it!

Dr. Stockmann. —but because he thinks what his superiors think and holds the same opinions as they. People who do that are, intellectually speaking, common people; and that is why my magnificent brother Peter is in reality so very far from any distinction—and consequently also so far from being liberal-minded.

Peter Stockmann. Mr. Chairman—!

Hovstad. So it is only the distinguished men that are liberal-minded in this country? We are learning something quite new! (*Laughter.*)

Dr. Stockmann. Yes, that is part of my new discovery too. And another part of it is that broad-mindedness is almost precisely the same thing as morality. That is why I maintain that it is absolutely inexcusable in the "People's Messenger" to proclaim, day in and day out, the false doctrine that it is the masses, the crowd, the compact majority, that have the monopoly of broad-mindedness and morality—and that vice and corruption and every kind of intellectual depravity are the result of culture, just as all the filth that is draining into our Baths is the result of the tanneries up at Mölledal! (*Uproar and interruptions. Dr. Stockmann is undisturbed, and goes on, carried away by his ardour, with a smile.*) And yet this same "People's Messenger" can go on preaching that the masses ought to be elevated to higher conditions of life! But, bless my soul, if the "Messenger's" teaching is to be depended upon, this very raising up the masses would mean nothing more or less than setting them straightway upon the paths of depravity! Happily the theory that culture demoralises is only an old falsehood that our forefathers believed in and we have inherited. No, it is ignorance, poverty, ugly conditions of life, that do the devil's work! In a house which does not get aired and swept every day—my wife Katherine maintains that the floor ought to be scrubbed as well, but that is a debatable question—in such a house, let me tell you, people will lose within two or three years the power of thinking or acting in a moral manner. Lack of oxygen weakens the conscience. And there must be a plentiful lack of oxygen in very many houses in this town, I should think, judging from the fact that the whole compact majority can be unconscientious enough to wish to build the town's prosperity on a quagmire of falsehood and deceit.

Aslaksen. We cannot allow such a grave accusation to be flung at a citizen community.

A Citizen. I move that the Chairman direct the speaker to sit down.

Voices (*angrily*). Hear, hear! Quite right! Make him sit down!

Dr. Stockmann (*losing his self-control*). Then I will go and shout the truth at every street corner! I will write it in other towns' newspapers! The whole country shall know what is going on here!

Hovstad. It almost seems as if Dr. Stockmann's intention were to ruin the town.

Dr. Stockmann. Yes, my native town is so dear to me that I would rather ruin it than see it flourishing upon a lie.

Aslaksen. This is really serious. (*Uproar and cat-calls. Mrs. Stockmann coughs, but to no purpose; her husband does not listen to her any longer.*)

Hovstad (*shouting above the din*). A man must be a public enemy to wish to ruin a whole community!

Dr. Stockmann (*with growing fervour*). What does the destruction of a community matter, if it lives on lies! It ought to be razed to the ground, I tell you! All who live by lies ought to be exterminated like vermin! You will end by infecting the whole country; you will bring about such a state of things that the whole country will deserve to be ruined. And if things come to that pass, I shall say from the bottom of my heart: Let the whole country perish, let all these people be exterminated!

Voices from the crowd. That is talking like an out-and-out enemy of the people!

Billing. There sounded the voice of the people, by all that's holy!

The whole crowd (*shouting*). Yes, yes! He is an enemy of the people! He hates his country! He hates his own people!

Aslaksen. Both as a citizen and as an individual, I am profoundly disturbed by what we have had to listen to. Dr. Stockmann has shown himself in a light I should never have dreamed of. I am unhappily obliged to subscribe to the opinion which I have just heard my estimable fellow-citizens utter; and I propose that we should give expression to that opinion in a resolution. I propose a resolution as follows: "This meeting declares that it considers Dr. Thomas Stockmann, Medical Officer of the Baths, to be an enemy of the people." (*A storm of cheers and applause. A number of men surround the Doctor and hiss him. Mrs. Stockmann and Petra have got up from their seats. Morten and Ejlif are fighting the other schoolboys for hissing; some of their elders separate them.*)

Dr. Stockmann (*to the men who are hissing him*). Oh, you fools! I tell you that—

Aslaksen (*ringing his bell*). We cannot hear you now, Doctor. A formal vote is about to be taken; but, out of regard for personal feelings, it shall be by ballot and not verbal. Have you any clean paper, Mr. Billing?

Billing. I have both blue and white here.

Aslaksen (*going to him*). That will do nicely; we shall get on more quickly that way. Cut it up into small strips—yes, that's it. (*To the meeting.*) Blue means no; white means yes. I will come round myself and collect votes. (*Peter Stockmann leaves the hall. Aslaksen and one or two others go round the room with the slips of paper in their hats.*)

1st Citizen (*to Hovstad*). I say, what has come to the Doctor? What are we to think of it?

Hovstad, Oh, you know how headstrong he is.

2nd Citizen (*to Billing*).   Billing, you go to their house—have you ever noticed if the fellow drinks?

Billing.   Well I'm hanged if I know what to say. There are always spirits on the table when you go.

3rd Citizen.   I rather think he goes quite off his head sometimes.

1st Citizen.   I wonder if there is any madness in his family?

Billing.   I shouldn't wonder if there were.

4th Citizen.   No, it is nothing more than sheer malice; he wants to get even with somebody for something or other.

Billing.   Well certainly he suggested a rise in his salary on one occasion lately, and did not get it.

The Citizens (*together*).   Ah!—then it is easy to understand how it is!

The Drunken Man (*who has got amongst the audience again*).   I want a blue one, I do! And I want a white one too!

Voices.   It's that drunken chap again! Turn him out!

Morten Kiil (*going up to Dr. Stockmann*).   Well, Stockmann, do you see what these monkey tricks of yours lead to?

Dr. Stockmann.   I have done my duty.

Morten Kiil.   What was that you said about the tanneries at Mölledal?

Dr. Stockmann.   You heard well enough. I said they were the source of all the filth.

Morten Kiil.   My tannery too?

Dr. Stockmann.   Unfortunately your tannery is by far the worst.

Morten Kiil.   Are you going to put that in the papers?

Dr. Stockmann.   I shall conceal nothing.

Morten Kiil.   That may cost you dear, Stockmann. (*Goes out.*)

A Stout Man (*going up to Captain Horster, without taking any notice of the ladies*).   Well, Captain, so you lend your house to enemies of the people?

Horster.   I imagine I can do what I like with my own possessions, Mr. Vik.

The Stout Man.   Then you can have no objection to my doing the same with mine.

Horster.   What do you mean, sir?

The Stout Man.   You shall hear from me in the morning. (*Turns his back on him and moves off.*)

Petra.   Was that not your owner, Captain Horster?

Aslaksen (*with the voting-papers in his hands, gets up on to the platform, and rings his bell*).   Gentlemen, allow me to announce the result. By the votes of every one here except one person—

A Young Man.   That is the drunk chap!

Aslaksen.   By the votes of every one here except a tipsy man, this meeting of citizens declares Dr. Thomas Stockmann to be an enemy of the people. (*Shouts and applause.*) Three cheers for our ancient and honourable citizen community! (*Renewed applause.*) Three cheers for our able and energetic Mayor, who has so loyally suppressed the promptings of family feeling! (*Cheers.*) The meeting is dissolved. (*Gets down.*)

Billing.   Three cheers for the Chairman!

The whole crowd. Three cheers for Aslaksen! Hurrah!

Dr. Stockmann. My hat and coat, Petra! Captain, have you room on your ship for passengers to the New World?

Horster. For you and yours we will make room, Doctor.

Dr. Stockmann (*as Petra helps him into his coat*). Good. Come, Katherine! Come, boys!

Mrs. Stockmann (*in an undertone*). Thomas, dear, let us go out by the back way.

Dr. Stockmann. No back ways for me, Katherine. (*Raising his voice.*) You will hear more of this enemy of the people, before he shakes the dust off his shoes upon you! I am not so forgiving as a certain Person; I do not say: "I forgive you, for ye know not what ye do."

Aslaksen (*shouting*). That is a blasphemous comparison, Dr. Stockmann!

Billing. It is, by God! It's dreadful for an earnest man to listen to.

A Coarse Voice. Threatens us now, does he!

Other Voices (*excitedly*). Let's go and break his windows! Duck him in the fjord!

Another Voice. Blow your horn, Evensen! Pip, pip!

(*Horn-blowing, hisses, and wild cries. Dr. Stockmann goes out through the hall with his family, Horster elbowing a way for them.*)

The Whole Crowd (*howling after them as they go*). Enemy of the People! Enemy of the People!

Billing (*as he puts his papers together*). Well, I'm damned if I go and drink toddy with the Stockmanns to-night!

(*The crowd press towards the exit. The uproar continues outside; shouts of "Enemy of the People!" are heard from without.*)

Act V

(SCENE.—*Dr. Stockmann's study. Bookcases, and cabinets containing specimens, line the walls. At the back is a door leading to the hall; in the foreground on the left, a door leading to the sitting-room. In the right-hand wall are two windows, of which all the panes are broken. The Doctor's desk, littered with books and papers, stands in the middle of the room, which is in disorder. It is morning. Dr. Stockmann in dressing-gown, slippers and a smoking-cap, is bending down and raking with an umbrella under one of the cabinets. After a little while he rakes out a stone.*)

Dr. Stockmann (*calling through the open sitting-room door*). Katherine, I have found another one.

Mrs. Stockmann (*from the sitting-room*). Oh, you will find a lot more yet, I expect.

Dr. Stockmann (*adding the stone to a heap of others on the table*). I shall treasure these stones as relics. Ejlif and Morten shall look at them every day, and when they are grown up they shall inherit them as heirlooms. (*Rakes about under a bookcase.*) Hasn't—what the deuce is her name?—the girl, you know—hasn't she been to fetch the glazier yet?

Mrs. Stockmann (*coming in*). Yes, but he said he didn't know if he would be able to come to-day.

Dr. Stockmann. You will see he won't dare to come.

Mrs. Stockmann. Well, that is just what Randine thought—that he didn't dare to, on account of the neighbours. (*Calls into the sitting-room*). What is it you want, Randine? Give it to me. (*Goes in, and comes out again directly.*) Here is a letter for you, Thomas.

Dr. Stockmann. Let me see it. (*Opens and reads it.*) Ah!—of course.

Mrs. Stockmann. Who is it from?

Dr. Stockmann. From the landlord. Notice to quit.

Mrs. Stockmann. Is it possible? Such a nice man—

Dr. Stockmann (*looking at the letter*). Does not dare do otherwise, he says. Doesn't like doing it, but dare not do otherwise—on account of his fellow-citizens—out of regard for public opinion. Is in a dependent position—dare not offend certain influential men—

Mrs. Stockmann. There, you see, Thomas!

Dr. Stockmann. Yes, yes, I see well enough; the whole lot of them in the town are cowards; not a man among them dares do anything for fear of the others. (*Throws the letter on to the table.*) But it doesn't matter to us, Katherine. We are going to sail away to the New World, and—

Mrs. Stockmann. But, Thomas, are you sure we are well advised to take this step?

Dr. Stockmann. Are you suggesting that I should stay here, where they have pilloried me as an enemy of the people—branded me—broken my windows! And just look here, Katherine—they have torn a great rent in my black trousers too!

Mrs. Stockmann. Oh, dear!—and they are the best pair you have got!

Dr. Stockmann. You should never wear your best trousers when you go out to fight for freedom and truth. It is not that I care so much about the trousers, you know; you can always sew them up again for me. But that the common herd should dare to make this attack on me, as if they were my equals—that is what I cannot, for the life of me, swallow!

Mrs. Stockmann. There is no doubt they have behaved very ill to you, Thomas; but is that sufficient reason for our leaving our native country for good and all?

Dr. Stockmann. If we went to another town, do you suppose we should not find the common people just as insolent as they are here? Depend upon it, there is not much to choose between them. Oh, well, let the curs snap—that is not the worst part of it. The worst is that, from one end of this country to the other, every man is the slave of his Party. Although, as far as that goes, I daresay it is not much better in the free West either; the compact majority, and liberal public opinion, and all that infernal old bag of tricks are probably rampant there too. But there things are done on a larger scale, you see. They may kill you, but they won't put you to death by slow torture. They don't squeeze a free man's soul in a vice, as they do here. And, if need be, one can live in solitude. (*Walks up and down.*) If only I knew where there was a virgin forest or a small South Sea island for sale, cheap—

Mrs. Stockmann.   But think of the boys, Thomas!

Dr. Stockmann (*standing still*).   What a strange woman you are, Katherine! Would you prefer to have the boys grow up in a society like this? You saw for yourself last night that half the population are out of their minds; and if the other half have not lost their senses, it is because they are mere brutes, with no sense to lose.

Mrs. Stockmann.   But, Thomas dear, the imprudent things you said had something to do with it, you know.

Dr. Stockmann.   Well, isn't what I said perfectly true? Don't they turn every idea topsy-turvy? Don't they make a regular hotch-potch of right and wrong? Don't they say that the things I know are true, are lies? The craziest part of it all is the fact of these "liberals," men of full age, going about in crowds imagining that they are the broad-minded party! Did you ever hear anything like it, Katherine!

Mrs. Stockmann.   Yes, yes, it's mad enough of them, certainly; but—(*Petra comes in from the sitting-room*). Back from school already?

Petra.   Yes. I have been given notice of dismissal.

Mrs. Stockmann.   Dismissal?

Dr. Stockmann.   You too?

Petra.   Mrs. Busk gave me my notice; so I thought it was best to go at once.

Dr. Stockmann.   You were perfectly right, too!

Mrs. Stockmann.   Who would have thought Mrs. Busk was a woman like that!

Petra.   Mrs. Busk isn't a bit like that, mother; I saw quite plainly how it hurt her to do it. But she didn't dare do otherwise, she said; and so I got my notice.

Dr. Stockmann (*laughing and rubbing his hands*).   She didn't dare do otherwise, either! It's delicious!

Mrs. Stockmann.   Well, after the dreadful scenes last night—

Petra.   It was not only that. Just listen to this, father!

Dr. Stockmann.   Well?

Petra.   Mrs. Busk showed me no less than three letters she received this morning—

Dr. Stockmann.   Anonymous, I suppose?

Petra.   Yes.

Dr. Stockmann.   Yes, because they didn't dare to risk signing their names, Katherine!

Petra.   And two of them were to the effect that a man, who has been our guest here, was declaring last night at the Club that my views on various subjects are extremely emancipated—

Dr. Stockmann. You did not deny that, I hope?

Petra. No, you know I wouldn't. Mrs. Busk's own views are tolerably emancipated, when we are alone together; but now that this report about me is being spread, she dare not keep me on any longer.

Mrs. Stockmann. And someone who had been a guest of ours! That shows you the return you get for your hospitality, Thomas!

Dr. Stockmann. We won't live in such a disgusting hole any longer. Pack up as quickly as you can, Katherine; the sooner we can get away, the better.

Mrs. Stockmann. Be quiet—I think I hear someone in the hall. See who it is, Petra.

Petra (*opening the door*). Oh, it's you, Captain Horster! Do come in.

Horster (*coming in*). Good morning. I thought I would just come in and see how you were.

Dr. Stockmann (*shaking his hand*). Thanks—that is really kind of you.

Mrs. Stockmann. And thank you, too, for helping us through the crowd, Captain Horster.

Petra. How did you manage to get home again?

Horster. Oh, somehow or other. I am fairly strong, and there is more sound than fury about these folk.

Dr. Stockmann. Yes, isn't their swinish cowardice astonishing? Look here, I will show you something! There are all the stones they have thrown through my windows. Just look at them! I'm hanged if there are more than two decently large bits of hardstone in the whole heap; the rest are nothing but gravel—wretched little things. And yet they stood out there bawling and swearing that they would do me some violence; but as for *doing* anything—you don't see much of that in this town.

Horster. Just as well for you this time, Doctor!

Dr. Stockmann. True enough. But it makes one angry all the same; because if some day it should be a question of a national fight in real earnest, you will see that public opinion will be in favor of taking to one's heels, and the compact majority will turn tail like a flock of sheep, Captain Horster. That is what is so mournful to think of; it gives me so much concern, that—. No, devil take it, it is ridiculous to care about it! They have called me an enemy of the people, so an enemy of the people let me be!

Mrs. Stockmann. You will never be that, Thomas.

Dr. Stockmann. Don't swear to that, Katherine. To be called an ugly name may have the same effect as a pin-scratch in the lung. And that hateful name—I can't get quit of it. It is sticking here in the pit of my stomach, eating into me like a corrosive acid. And no magnesia will remove it.

Petra. Bah!—you should only laugh at them, father.

Horster. They will change their minds some day, Doctor.

Mrs. Stockmann. Yes, Thomas, as sure as you are standing here.

Dr. Stockmann. Perhaps, when it is too late. Much good may it do them!

They may wallow in their filth then and rue the day when they drove a patriot into exile. When do you sail, Captain Horster?

Horster. Hm!—that was just what I had come to speak about—

Dr. Stockmann. Why, has anything gone wrong with the ship?

Horster. No; but what has happened is that I am not to sail in it.

Petra. Do you mean that you have been dismissed from your command?

Horster (*smiling*). Yes, that's just it.

Petra. You too.

Mrs. Stockmann. There, you see, Thomas!

Dr. Stockmann. And that for the truth's sake! Oh, if I had thought such a thing possible—

Horster. You mustn't take it to heart; I shall be sure to find a job with some ship-owner or other, elsewhere.

Dr. Stockmann. And that is this man Vik—a wealthy man, independent of everyone and everything—! Shame on him!

Horster. He is quite an excellent fellow otherwise; he told me himself he would willingly have kept me on, if only he had dared—

Dr. Stockmann. But he didn't dare? No, of course not.

Horster. It is not such an easy matter, he said, for a party man—

Dr. Stockmann. The worthy man spoke the truth. A party is like a sausage machine; it mashes up all sorts of heads together into the same mincemeat—fatheads and blockheads, all in one mash!

Mrs. Stockmann. Come, come, Thomas dear!

Petra (*to Horster*). If only you had not come home with us, things might not have come to this pass.

Horster. I do not regret it.

Petra (*holding out her hand to him*). Thank you for that!

Horster (*to Dr. Stockmann*). And so what I came to say was that if you are determined to go away, I have thought of another plan—

Dr. Stockmann. That's splendid!—if only we can get away at once.

Mrs. Stockmann. Hush!—wasn't that someone knocking?

Petra. That is uncle, surely.

Dr. Stockmann. Aha! (*Calls out.*). Come in!

Mrs. Stockmann. Dear Thomas, promise me definitely—.

(*Peter Stockmann comes in from the hall.*)

Peter Stockmann. Oh, you are engaged. In that case, I will—

Dr. Stockmann. No, no, come in.

Peter Stockmann. But I wanted to speak to you alone.

Mrs. Stockmann. We will go into the sitting-room in the meanwhile.

Horster. And I will look in again later.

Dr. Stockmann. No, go in there with them, Captain Horster; I want to hear more about—.

Horster. Very well, I will wait, then. (*He follows Mrs. Stockmann and Petra into the sitting-room.*)

Dr. Stockmann. I daresay you find it rather draughty here to-day. Put your hat on.

Peter Stockmann. Thank you, if I may. (*Does so.*) I think I caught cold last night; I stood and shivered—

Dr. Stockmann. Really? I found it warm enough.

Peter Stockmann. I regret that it was not in my power to prevent those excesses last night.

Dr. Stockmann. Have you anything particular to say to me besides that?

Peter Stockmann (*taking a big letter from his pocket*). I have this document for you, from the Baths Committee.

Dr. Stockmann. My dismissal?

Peter Stockmann. Yes, dating from to-day. (*Lays the letter on the table.*) It gives us pain to do it; but, to speak frankly, we dared not do otherwise on account of public opinion.

Dr. Stockmann (*smiling*). Dared not? I seem to have heard that word before, to-day.

Peter Stockmann. I must beg you to understand your position clearly. For the future you must not count on any practice whatever in the town.

Dr. Stockmann. Devil take the practice! But why are you so sure of that?

Peter Stockmann. The Householders' Association is circulating a list from house to house. All right-minded citizens are being called upon to give up employing you; and I can assure you that not a single head of a family will risk refusing his signature. They simply dare not.

Dr. Stockmann. No, no; I don't doubt it. But what then?

Peter Stockmann. If I might advise you, it would be best to leave the place for a little while—

Dr. Stockmann. Yes, the propriety of leaving the place *has* occurred to me.

Peter Stockmann. Good. And then, when you have had six months to think things over, if, after mature consideration, you can persuade yourself to write a few words of regret, acknowledging your error—

Dr. Stockmann. I might have my appointment restored to me, do you mean?

Peter Stockmann. Perhaps. It is not at all impossible.

Dr. Stockmann. But what about public opinion, then? Surely you would not dare to do it on account of public feeling.

Peter Stockmann. Public opinion is an extremely mutable thing. And, to be quite candid with you, it is a matter of great importance to us to have some admission of that sort from you in writing.

Dr. Stockmann. Oh, that's what you are after, is it! I will just trouble you to remember what I said to you lately about foxy tricks of that sort!

Peter Stockmann. Your position was quite different then. At that time you had reason to suppose you had the whole town at your back—

Dr. Stockmann. Yes, and now I feel I have the whole town *on* my back— (*flaring up*). I would not do it if I had the devil and his dam on my back—! Never—never, I tell you!

Peter Stockmann. A man with a family has no right to behave as you do. You have no right to do it, Thomas.

Dr. Stockmann. I have no right! There is only one single thing in the world a free man has no right to do. Do you know what that is?

Peter Stockmann. No.

Dr. Stockmann. Of course you don't, but I will tell you. A free man has no right to soil himself with filth; he has no right to behave in a way that would justify his spitting in his own face.

Peter Stockmann. This sort of thing sounds extremely plausible, of course; and if there were no other explanation for your obstinacy—. But as it happens that there is.

Dr. Stockmann. What do you mean?

Peter Stockmann. You understand very well what I mean. But, as your brother and as a man of discretion, I advise you not to build too much upon expectations and prospects that may so very easily fail you.

Dr. Stockmann. What in the world is all this about?

Peter Stockmann. Do you really ask me to believe that you are ignorant of the terms of Mr. Kiil's will?

Dr. Stockmann. I know that the small amount he possesses is to go to an institution for indigent old workpeople. How does that concern me?

Peter Stockmann. In the first place, it is by no means a small amount that is in question. Mr. Kiil is a fairly wealthy man.

Dr. Stockmann. I had no notion of that!

Peter Stockmann. Hm!—hadn't you really? Then I suppose you had no notion, either, that a considerable portion of his wealth will come to your children, you and your wife having a life-rent of the capital. Has he never told you so?

Dr. Stockmann. Never, on my honour! Quite the reverse; he has consistently done nothing but fume at being so unconscionably heavily taxed. But are you perfectly certain of this, Peter?

Peter Stockmann. I have it from an absolutely reliable source.

Dr. Stockmann. Then, thank God, Katherine is provided for—and the children too! I must tell her this at once—(*calls out*) Katherine, Katherine!

Peter Stockmann (*restraining him*). Hush, don't say a word yet!

Mrs. Stockmann (*opening the door*). What is the matter?

Dr. Stockmann. Oh, nothing, nothing; you can go back. (*She shuts the door. Dr. Stockmann walks up and down in his excitement*). Provided for!— Just think of it, we are all provided for! And for life! What a blessed feeling it is to know one is provided for!

Peter Stockmann. Yes, but that is just exactly what you are not. Mr. Kiil can alter his will any day he likes.

Dr. Stockmann. But he won't do that, my dear Peter. The "Badger" is much too delighted at my attack on you and your wise friends.

Peter Stockmann (*starts and looks intently at him*). Ah, that throws a light on various things.

Dr. Stockmann. What things?

Peter Stockmann. I see that the whole thing was a combined manœuvre on your part and his. These violent, reckless attacks that you have made against the leading men of the town, under the pretence that it was in the name of truth—

Dr. Stockmann. What about them?

Peter Stockmann. I see that they were nothing else than the stipulated price for that vindictive old man's will.

Dr. Stockmann (*almost speechless*). Peter—you are the most disgusting plebeian I have ever met in all my life.

Peter Stockmann. All is over between us. Your dismissal is irrevocable—we have a weapon against you now. (*Goes out.*)

Dr. Stockmann. For shame! For shame! (*Calls out.*) Katherine, you must have the floor scrubbed after him! Let—what's her name—devil take it, the girl who has always got soot on her nose—

Mrs. Stockmann (*in the sitting-room*). Hush, Thomas, be quiet!

Petra (*coming to the door*). Father, grandfather is here, asking if he may speak to you alone.

Dr. Stockmann. Certainly he may. (*Going to the door.*) Come in, Mr. Kiil. (*Morten Kiil comes in. Dr. Stockmann shuts the door after him.*) What can I do for you? Won't you sit down?

Morten Kiil. I won't sit. (*Looks around.*) You look very comfortable here to-day, Thomas.

Dr. Stockmann. Yes, don't we!

Morten Kiil. Very comfortable—plenty of fresh air. I should think you have got enough to-day of that oxygen you were talking about yesterday. Your conscience must be in splendid order to-day, I should think.

Dr. Stockmann. It is.

Morten Kiil. So I should think. (*Taps his chest.*) Do you know what I have got here?

Dr. Stockmann. A good conscience, too, I hope.

Morten Kiil. Bah!—No, it is something better than that. (*He takes a thick pocket-book from his breast-pocket, opens it, and displays a packet of papers.*)

Dr. Stockmann (*looking at him in astonishment*). Shares in the Baths?

Morten Kiil. They were not difficult to get to-day.

Dr. Stockmann. And you have been buying—?

Morten Kiil. As many as I could pay for.

Dr. Stockmann. But, my dear Mr. Kiil—consider the state of the Baths' affairs!

Morten Kiil. If you behave like a reasonable man, you can soon set the Baths on their feet again.

Dr. Stockmann. Well, you can see for yourself that I have done all I can, but—. They are all mad in this town!

Morten Kiil. You said yesterday that the worst of this pollution came from my tannery. If that is true, then my grandfather and my father before me, and

I myself, for many years past, have been poisoning the town like three destroying angels. Do you think I am going to sit quiet under that reproach?

Dr. Stockmann. Unfortunately I am afraid you will have to.

Morten Kiil. No, thank you. I am jealous of my name and reputation. They call me "the Badger," I am told. A badger is a kind of pig, I believe; but I am not going to give them the right to call me that. I mean to live and die a clean man.

Dr. Stockmann. And how are you going to set about it?

Morten Kiil. You shall cleanse me, Thomas.

Dr. Stockmann. I!

Morten Kiil. Do you know what money I have bought these shares with? No, of course you can't know—but I will tell you. It is the money that Katherine and Petra and the boys will have when I am gone. Because I have been able to save a little bit after all, you know.

Dr. Stockmann (*flaring up*). And you have gone and taken Katherine's money for *this*!

Morten Kiil. Yes, the whole of the money is invested in the Baths now. And now I just want to see whether you are quite stark, staring mad, Thomas! If you still make out that these animals and other nasty things of that sort come from my tannery, it will be exactly as if you were to flay broad strips of skin from Katherine's body, and Petra's, and the boys'; and no decent man would do that—unless he were mad.

Dr. Stockmann (*walking up and down*). Yes, but I *am* mad; I *am* mad!

Morten Kiil. You cannot be so absurdly mad as all that, when it is a question of your wife and children.

Dr. Stockmann (*standing still in front of him*). Why couldn't you consult me about it, before you went and bought all that trash?

Morten Kiil. What is done cannot be undone.

Dr. Stockmann (*walks about uneasily*). If only I were not so certain about it—! But I am absolutely convinced that I am right.

Morten Kiil (*weighing the pocket-book in his hand*). If you stick to your mad idea, this won't be worth much, you know. (*Puts the pocket-book in his pocket.*).

Dr. Stockmann. But, hang it all! it might be possible for science to discover some prophylactic, I should think—or some antidote of some kind—

Morten Kiil. To kill these animals, do you mean?

Dr. Stockmann. Yes, or to make them innocuous.

Morten Kiil. Couldn't you try some rat's-bane?

Dr. Stockmann. Don't talk nonsense! They all say it is only imagination, you know. Well, let it go at that! Let them have their own way about it! Haven't the ignorant, narrow-minded curs reviled me as an enemy of the people?—and haven't they been ready to tear the clothes off my back too?

Morten Kiil. And broken all your windows to pieces!

Dr. Stockmann. And then there is my duty to my family. I must talk it over with Katherine; she is great on those things.

Morten Kiil. That is right; be guided by a reasonable woman's advice.

Dr. Stockmann (*advancing towards him*). To think you could do such a preposterous thing! Risking Katherine's money in this way, and putting me in such a horribly painful dilemma! When I look at you, I think I see the devil himself—.

Morten Kiil. Then I had better go. But I must have an answer from you before two o'clock—yes or no. If it is no, the shares go to a charity, and that this very day.

Dr. Stockmann. And what does Katherine get?

Morten Kiil. Not a halfpenny. (*The door leading to the hall opens, and Hovstad and Aslaksen make their appearance.*) Look at those two!

Dr. Stockmann (*staring at them*). What the devil!—have *you* actually the face to come into my house?

Hovstad. Certainly.

Aslaksen. We have something to say to you, you see.

Morten Kiil (*in a whisper*). Yes or no—before two o'clock.

Aslaksen (*glancing at Hovstad*). Aha! (*Morten Kiil goes out.*)

Dr. Stockmann. Well, what do you want with me? Be brief.

Hovstad. I can quite understand that you are annoyed with us for our attitude at the meeting yesterday—

Dr. Stockmann. Attitude, do you call it? Yes, it was a charming attitude! I call it weak, womanish—damnably shameful!

Hovstad. Call it what you like, we could not do otherwise.

Dr. Stockmann. You *dared* not do otherwise—isn't that it?

Hovstad. Well, if you like to put it that way.

Aslaksen. But why did you not let us have word of it beforehand?—just a hint to Mr. Hovstad or to me?

Dr. Stockmann. A hint? Of what?

Aslaksen. Of what was behind it all.

Dr. Stockmann. I don't understand you in the least.

Aslaksen (*with a confidential nod*). Oh yes, you do, Dr. Stockmann.

Hovstad. It is no good making a mystery of it any longer.

Dr. Stockmann (*looking first at one of them and then at the other*). What the devil do you both mean?

Aslaksen. May I ask if your father-in-law is not going round the town buying up all the shares in the Baths?

Dr. Stockmann. Yes, he has been buying Baths shares to-day; but—

Aslaksen. It would have been more prudent to get someone else to do it— someone less nearly related to you.

Hovstad. And you should not have let your name appear in the affair. There was no need for anyone to know that the attack on the Baths came from you. You ought to have consulted me, Dr. Stockmann.

Dr. Stockmann (*looks in front of him; then a light seems to dawn on him and* *he says in amazement:*) Are such things conceivable? Are such things possible?

Aslaksen (*with a smile*). Evidently they are. But it is better to use a little *finesse*, you know.

Hovstad. And it is much better to have several persons in a thing of that sort; because the responsibility of each individual is lessened, when there are others with him.

Dr. Stockmann (*composedly*). Come to the point, gentlemen. What do you want?

Aslaksen. Perhaps Mr. Hovstad had better—

Hovstad. No, you tell him, Aslaksen.

Aslaksen. Well, the fact is that, now we know the bearings of the whole affair, we think we might venture to put the "People's Messenger" at your disposal.

Dr. Stockmann. Do you dare do that now? What about public opinion? Are you not afraid of a storm breaking upon our heads?

Hovstad. We will try to weather it.

Aslaksen. And you must be ready to go off quickly on a new tack, Doctor. As soon as your invective has done its work—

Dr. Stockmann. Do you mean, as soon as my father-in-law and I have got hold of the shares at a low figure?

Hovstad. Your reasons for wishing to get the control of the Baths are mainly scientific, I take it.

Dr. Stockmann. Of course; it was for scientific reasons that I persuaded the old "Badger" to stand in with me in the matter. So we will tinker at the conduit-pipes a little, and dig up a little bit of the shore, and it shan't cost the town a sixpence. That will be all right—eh?

Hovstad. I think so—if you have the "People's Messenger" behind you.

Aslaksen. The Press is a power in a free community, Doctor.

Dr. Stockmann. Quite so. And so is public opinion. And you, Mr. Aslaksen—I suppose you will be answerable for the Householders' Association?

Aslaksen. Yes, and for the Temperance Society. You may rely on that.

Dr. Stockmann. But, gentlemen—I really am ashamed to ask the question— but, what return do you—?

Hovstad. We should prefer to help you without any return whatever, believe me. But the "People's Messenger" is in rather a shaky condition; it doesn't go really well; and I should be very unwilling to suspend the paper now, when there is so much work to do here in the political way.

Dr. Stockmann. Quite so; that would be a great trial to such a friend of the people as you are. (*Flares up.*) But I am an enemy of the people, remember! (*Walks about the room.*) Where have I put my stick? Where the devil is my stick?

Hovstad. What's that?

Aslaksen. Surely you never mean—?

Dr. Stockmann (*standing still*).   And suppose I don't give you a single penny of all I get out of it? Money is not very easy to get out of us rich folk, please to remember!

Hovstad.   And you please to remember that this affair of the shares can be represented in two ways!

Dr. Stockmann.   Yes, and you are just the man to do it. If I don't come to the rescue of the "People's Messenger," you will certainly take an evil view of the affair; you will hunt me down, I can well imagine—pursue me—try to throttle me as a dog does a hare.

Hovstad.   It is a natural law; every animal must fight for its own livelihood.

Aslaksen.   And get its food where it can, you know.

Dr. Stockmann (*walking about the room*).   Then you go and look for yours in the gutter; because I am going to show you which is the strongest animal of us three! (*Finds an umbrella and brandishes it above his head.*) Ah, now—!

Hovstad.   You are surely not going to use violence!

Aslaksen.   Take care what you are doing with that umbrella.

Dr. Stockmann.   Out of the window with you, Mr. Hovstad!

Hovstad (*edging to the door*).   Are you quite mad!

Dr. Stockmann.   Out of the window, Mr. Aslaksen! Jump, I tell you! You will have to do it, sooner or later.

Aslaksen (*running round the writing-table*).   Moderation, Doctor—I am a delicate man—I can stand so little—(*calls out*) help, help!

(*Mrs. Stockmann, Petra and Horster come in from the sitting-room.*)

Mrs. Stockmann.   Good gracious, Thomas! What is happening?

Dr. Stockmann (*brandishing the umbrella*).   Jump out, I tell you! Out into the gutter!

Hovstad.   An assault on an unoffending man! I call you to witness, Captain Horster. (*Hurries out through the hall.*)

Aslaksen (*irresolutely*).   If only I knew the way about here—. (*Steals out through the sitting-room*).

Mrs. Stockmann (*holding her husband back*).   Control yourself, Thomas!

Dr. Stockmann (*throwing down the umbrella*).   Upon my soul, they have escaped after all.

Mrs. Stockmann.   What did they want you to do?

Dr. Stockmann.   I will tell you later on; I have something else to think about now. (*Goes to the table and writes something on a calling-card*). Look there, Katherine; what is written there?

Mrs. Stockmann.   Three big *Noes*; what does that mean?

Dr. Stockmann.   I will tell you that too, later on. (*Holds out the card to Petra.*) There, Petra; tell sooty-face to run over to the "Badger's" with that, as quick as she can. Hurry up! (*Petra takes the card and goes out to the hall.*)

Dr. Stockmann.   Well, I think I have had a visit from every one of the devil's messengers to-day! But now I am going to sharpen my pen till they can feel its point; I shall dip it in venom and gall; I shall hurl my ink-pot at their heads!

Mrs. Stockmann.   Yes, but we are going away, you know, Thomas.

(*Petra comes back.*)

Dr. Stockmann.   Well?

Petra.   She has gone with it.

Dr. Stockmann.   Good.—Going away, did you say? No, I'll be hanged if we are going away! We are going to stay where we are, Katherine!

Petra.   Stay here?

Mrs. Stockmann.   Here, in the town?

Dr. Stockmann.   Yes, here. This is the field of battle—this is where the fight will be. This is where I shall triumph! As soon as I have had my trousers sewn up I shall go out and look for another house. We must have a roof over our heads for the winter.

Horster.   That you shall have in my house.

Dr. Stockmann.   Can I?

Horster.   Yes, quite well. I have plenty of room, and I am almost never at home.

Mrs. Stockmann.   How good of you, Captain Horster!

Petra.   Thank you!

Dr. Stockmann (*grasping his hand*).   Thank you, thank you! That is one trouble over! Now I can set to work in earnest at once. There is an endless amount of things to look through here, Katherine! Luckily I shall have all my time at my disposal; because I have been dismissed from the Baths, you know.

Mrs. Stockmann (*with a sigh*).   Oh yes, I expected that.

Dr. Stockmann.   And they want to take my practice away from me too. Let them! I have got the poor people to fall back upon, anyway—those that don't pay anything! and, after all, they need me most, too. But, by Jove, they will have to listen to me; I shall preach to them in season and out of season, as it says somewhere.

Mrs. Stockmann.   But, dear Thomas, I should have thought events had showed you what use it is to preach.

Dr. Stockmann.   You are really ridiculous, Katherine. Do you want me to let myself be beaten off the field by public opinion and the compact majority and all that deviltry? No, thank you! And what I want to do is so simple and clear and straightforward. I only want to drum into the heads of these curs the fact that the liberals are the most insidious enemies of freedom— that party programmes strangle every young and vigorous truth—that considerations of expediency turn morality and justice upside down—and that they will end by making life here unbearable. Don't you think, Captain Horster, that I ought to be able to make people understand that?

Horster. Very likely; I don't know much about such things myself.

Dr. Stockmann. Well, look here—I will explain! It is the party leaders that must be exterminated. A party leader is like a wolf, you see—like a voracious wolf. He requires a certain number of smaller victims to prey upon every year, if he is to live. Just look at Hovstad and Aslaksen! How many smaller victims have they not put an end to—or at any rate maimed and mangled until they are fit for nothing except to be householders or subscribers to the "People's Messenger"! (*Sits down on the edge of the table.*) Come here, Katherine—look how beautifully the sun shines to-day! And this lovely spring air I am drinking in!

Mrs. Stockmann. Yes, if only we could live on sunshine and spring air, Thomas.

Dr. Stockmann. Oh, you will have to pinch and save a bit—then we shall get along. That gives me very little concern. What is much worse is, that I know of no one who is liberal-minded and high-minded enough to venture to take up my work after me.

Petra. Don't think about that, father; you have plenty of time before you.— Hullo, here are the boys already!

(*Ejlif and Morten come in from the sitting-room.*)

Mrs. Stockmann. Have you got a holiday?

Morten. No; but we were fighting with the other boys between lessons—

Ejlif. That isn't true; it was the other boys were fighting with us.

Morten. Well, and then Mr. Rörlund said we had better stay at home for a day or two.

Dr. Stockmann (*snapping his fingers and getting up from the table*). I have it! I have it, by Jove! You shall never set foot in the school again!

The Boys. No more school!

Mrs. Stockmann. But, Thomas—

Dr. Stockmann. Never, I say. I will educate you myself; that is to say, you shan't learn a blessed thing—

Morten. Hooray!

Dr. Stockmann. —but I will make liberal-minded and high-minded men of you. You must help me with that, Petra.

Petra. Yes, father, you may be sure I will.

Dr. Stockmann. And my school shall be in the room where they insulted me and called me an enemy of the people. But we are too few as we are; I must have at least twelve boys to begin with.

Mrs. Stockmann. You will certainly never get them in this town.

Dr. Stockmann. We shall. (*To the boys.*) Don't you know any street urchins— regular ragamuffins—?

Morten. Yes, father, I know lots!

Dr. Stockmann. That's capital! Bring me some specimens of them. I am going to experiment with curs, just for once; there may be some exceptional heads amongst them.

Morten. And what are we going to do, when you have made liberal-minded and high-minded men of us?

Dr. Stockmann. Then you shall drive all the wolves out of the country, my boys!

(*Ejlif looks rather doubtful about it; Morten jumps about crying "Hurrah!"*)

Mrs. Stockmann. Let us hope it won't be the wolves that will drive you out of the country, Thomas.

Dr. Stockmann. Are you out of your mind, Katherine? Drive me out! Now— when I am the strongest man in the town!

Mrs. Stockmann. The strongest—now?

Dr. Stockmann. Yes, and I will go so far as to say that now I am the strongest man in the whole world.

Morten. I say!

Dr. Stockmann (*lowering his voice*). Hush! You mustn't say anything about it yet; but I have made a great discovery.

Mrs. Stockmann. Another one?

Dr. Stockmann. Yes. (*Gathers them round him, and says confidentially:*) It is this, let me tell you—that the strongest man in the world is he who stands most alone.

Mrs. Stockmann (*smiling and shaking her head*). Oh, Thomas, Thomas!

Petra (*encouragingly, as she grasps her father's hands*). Father!

Questions

1. In Act I Peter Stockmann says to his brother, "You have an ingrained tendency to take your own way, at all events; and that is almost equally inadmissible in a well ordered community. The individual ought undoubtedly to acquiesce in subordinating himself to the community—or to speak more accurately, to the authorities who have the care of the community's welfare." How does this speech serve to characterize the mayor? What does Peter Stockmann mean by "community"? **2.** What political position do Hovstad and Billing represent? Why do they support Dr. Stockmann in Act I? What political position does Aslaksen represent? Why does he switch sides in the course of the action? **3.** How do Petra's reasons for refusing to translate an English story for the newspaper (Act III) relate to the main action of the play? **4.** At the public meeting in Act IV, Dr. Stockmann says, "The majority never has right on its side. Never, I say! That is one of these social lies against which an independent, intelligent man must wage war. Who is it that constitute the majority of the population in a country? Is it the clever folk or the stupid? I don't imagine you will dispute the fact that at present the stupid people are in an absolutely overwhelming majority all the world over. But, good Lord!—you can never pretend that it is right that the stupid folk should govern the clever ones! . . . The minority is always in the right." In what way does this speech embody the theme of the play? Contrast it with Peter Stockmann's speech quoted in question 1. Are the brothers' positions antagonistic or parallel? Explain. **5.** In Act V Morten Kiil buys stock in the

Baths and tells Dr. Stockmann he has purchased the shares with Mrs. Stockmann's inheritance. What function does this event serve in the play?   **6.** Is Dr. Stockmann's optimism at the end of the play justified? Why? Is his determination to establish a school to educate street "curs" a logical extension of the position he asserts in the speech quoted in question 4? Explain.   **7.** Dr. Stockmann's final words are "the strongest man in the world is he who stands alone." Does the play vindicate this position? In any case, do you agree with Stockmann's statement? Explain.

CONFORMITY AND REbELLION

QUESTIONS FOR FURTHER ANALYSIS

1. What answers do the works in this section provide to the question posed by Albert Camus in the following passage:

> The present interest of the problem of rebellion only springs from the fact that nowadays whole societies have wanted to discard the sacred. We live in an unsacrosanct moment in history. Insurrection is certainly not the sum total of human experience. But history today, with all its storm and strife, compels us to say that rebellion is one of the essential dimensions of man. It is our historic reality. Unless we choose to ignore reality, we must find our values in it. Is it possible to find a rule of conduct outside the realm of religion and its absolute values? That is the question raised by rebellion.

2. Examine some of the representatives of established order—Creon, Peter Stockmann, Bartleby's employer, the Ticktockman—and discuss what attitudes they share and how effectively they function as spokesmen for law and order.

3. What support do the works in this section offer for Emily Dickinson's assertion that "Much Madness Is Divinest Sense"?

4. Which works in this section can be criticized on the grounds that while they attack the established order they fail to provide any alternatives?

5. In a number of these works, the result of rebellion is defeat and death. Are these works therefore pessimistic and despairing? If not, then what is the purpose of the rebellions, and why do the authors choose to bring their characters to such ends?

6. Do any of the works in this section offer support to the idea that a single individual or a small minority can have a decisive effect on the larger society? Discuss.

7. Amy Lowell's "Patterns," Ezra Pound's "Hugh Selwyn Mauberley," E. E. Cummings' "i sing of Olaf glad and big," Karl Shapiro's "The Conscientious Objector," Lawrence Ferlinghetti's "In Goya's Greatest Scenes," Henry Reed's "Naming of Parts" and "Judging Distances," and Robert Bly's "Counting Small-Boned Bodies" are, in different ways, antiwar poems. May one argue validly that while they condemn war, none of them examines the specific reasons that a nation may be obliged to fight—self-defense and national self-interest, for example—and consequently, they are irresponsible? Explain.

8. Most of us live out our lives in the ordinary and humdrum world that is rejected in such poems as Wordsworth's "The World Is Too Much with Us," Tennyson's "Ulysses," Auden's "The Unknown Citizen," Thomas' "I Have Longed to Move Away," and Lennon and McCartney's "Eleanor Rigby." Can it be said that these poems are counsels to social irresponsibility? In this respect, contrast these poems with Philip Larkin's "Poetry of Departures."

LOVE AND HATE

Love and death, it is often noted, are the two great themes of literature. Much of the literary art we have placed in the sections on Innocence and Experience and Conformity and Rebellion speaks of love and death as well. But in those works other thematic interests dominate. In this section we gather a number of works in which love and hate are thematically central.

The rosy conception of love presented in many popular and sentimental stories ill prepares us for the complicated reality we will face. We know that the course of true love never runs smooth, but in those popular stories the obstacles that hinder the lovers are simple and external. If the young lover can land the high-paying job or convince his beloved's parents that he is worthy despite social differences, all will be well. Those stories end, obstacles overcome, in a glowing marriage, the lovers riding off, whether by horse, auto, or jet, into a brilliant sunset. But love in life is rarely that simple. The external obstacles may be insuperable, or the obstacles may lie deep within the personality. The major obstacle may very well be an individual's difficult and painful effort to understand that he has been deceived by an immature and sentimental conception of love.

In this age of psychoanalytic awareness, the claims of the flesh are well recognized. But psychoanalytic theory teaches us, as well, to recognize the aggressive aspect of the human condition. The omnipresent selfishness that civilization attempts to check may be aggressively violent as well as lustful. Remarkably, many literary treatments of love envision the lovers sometimes as victims of the chaos that seems to surround them and sometimes as serene and safe in the midst of violence. Petronius' little sketch of the widow of Ephesus and D. H. Lawrence's "The Horse Dealer's Daughter" are embroidered on a fabric of violence and chaos. William Faulkner in "Dry September" and James Baldwin in "Going to Meet the Man" both recognize the erotic sources of certain kinds of violence in stories ostensibly about hate. And Matthew Arnold in "Dover Beach" finds love the only refuge from a chaotic world in which "ignorant armies clash by night."

The cliché has it that love and hate are closely related, and much evidence supports this proposition. But why should love and hate, seeming opposites, lie so close together in the emotional lives of men and women? We are all egos, separate from each other. And as separate individuals, we develop elaborate behavior mechanisms which defend us from each other. Self-esteem is terribly important, and threats to self-esteem must somehow be neutralized. But the erotic love relationship differs from other relationships in that it may be defined as a rejection of separateness. The common metaphor speaks of two lovers as joining, as merging into one. That surrender of the "me" to join in an "us" leaves the lovers uniquely vulnerable to psychic injury. In short, the defenses are down, and the self-esteem of each of the lovers depends importantly on the behavior of the other. If the lover is betrayed by his beloved, the emotional consequences are uniquely disastrous—hence the peculiarly close relationship of passionate hatred with erotic love.

Words like *love* and *hate* are so general that poets rarely use them except as one term in a metaphor designed to project sharply some aspect of emotional life. The simple sexuality in such poems as Marvell's "To His Coy Mistress," Marlowe's "The Passionate Shepherd to His Love," and Campion's "I Care Not for These Ladies" may be juxtaposed with the hatred and violence generated in Othello by sexual jealousy or with the quick reprisal of the slighted Barbara Allen. And Shakespeare's description of lust in "The Expense of Spirit in a Waste of Shame" notes an aspect of love quite overlooked by Sir John Suckling and Edmund Waller in their songs. Molière's comic misanthrope, who, finally, is unwilling to let down his defenses despite his feeling for his lady, handles his jealousy quite differently from Othello.

Perhaps more than anything, the works in this section celebrate the elemental impulses of man that run counter to those rational formulations by which we govern our lives. We pursue Othello's love for Desdemona and Iago's hate for Othello and arrive at an irreducible mystery, for neither Othello's love nor Iago's hate yields satisfactorily to rational explanation. Reason does not tell us why Othello and Desdemona love one another or why Iago hates rather than honors Othello. Alceste in Molière's *The Misanthrope* comes, for seemingly plausible and rational reasons, to hate mankind, and yet he persists, paradoxically, in his love for the coquettish Célimène.

Love is an act of faith springing from man's deep-seated need to join with another human being not only in physical nakedness but in emotional and spiritual nakedness as well. While hate is a denial of that faith and, therefore, a retreat into spiritual isolation, love is an attempt to break out of the isolation. And, as Erich Fromm writes in *The Art of Loving*:

> The basic need to fuse with another person so as to transcend the prison of one's separateness is closely related to another specifically human desire, that to know the "secret of man." While life in its merely biological aspects is a miracle and a secret, man in his human aspects is an unfathomable secret to himself—and to his fellow man. We know ourselves, and yet even with all the efforts we may make, we do not know ourselves. We know our fellow man, and yet we do not know him, because we are not a thing, and our fellow man is not a thing. The further we reach into the depth of our being, or someone else's being, the more the goal of knowledge eludes us. Yet we cannot help desiring to penetrate into the secret of man's soul, into the innermost nucleus which is "he."
>
> There is one way, a desperate one, to know the secret: it is that of complete power over another person; the power which makes him do what we want, feel what we want, think what we want; which transforms him into a thing, our thing, our possession. The ultimate degree of this attempt to know lies in the extremes of sadism, the desire and ability to make a human being suffer; to torture him, to force him to betray his secret in his suffering. In this craving for penetrating man's secret, his and hence our own, lies an essential motivation for the depth and intensity of cruelty and destructiveness. . . .
>
> The other path to knowing "the secret" is love. Love is active penetration of the other person, in which my desire to know is stilled by union. In the act of fusion I know you, I know myself, I know everybody—and I "know" nothing. I know in the only way knowledge of that which is alive is possible for man—by experience of union—not by any knowledge our thought can give. Sadism is motivated by the wish to know the secret, yet I remain as ignorant as I was before. I have torn the other being apart limb from limb, yet all I have done is to destroy him. Love is the only way of knowledge, which in the act of union answers my quest. In the act of loving, of giving myself, in the act of penetrating the other person, I find myself, I discover myself, I discover us both, I discover man.

FICTION

from The Satyricon
The Widow of Ephesus*

PETRONIUS [1st. **CENTURY A.D.**]

"ONCE upon a time there was a certain married woman in the city of Ephesus whose fidelity to her husband was so famous that the women from all the neighboring towns and villages used to troop into Ephesus merely to stare at this prodigy. It happened, however, that her husband one day died. Finding the normal custom of following the cortege with hair unbound and beating her breast in public quite inadequate to express her grief, the lady insisted on following the corpse right into the tomb, an underground vault of the Greek type, and there set herself to guard the body, weeping and wailing night and day. Although in her extremes of grief she was clearly courting death from starvation, her parents were utterly unable to persuade her to leave, and even the magistrates, after one last supreme attempt, were rebuffed and driven away. In short, all Ephesus had gone into mourning for this extraordinary woman, all the more since the lady was now passing her fifth consecutive day without once tasting food. Beside the failing woman sat her devoted maid, sharing her mistress' grief and relighting the lamp whenever it flickered out. The whole city could speak, in fact, of nothing else: here at last, all classes alike agreed, was the one true example of conjugal fidelity and love.

"In the meantime, however, the governor of the province gave orders that several thieves should be crucified in a spot close by the vault where the lady was mourning her dead husband's corpse. So, on the following night, the soldier who had been assigned to keep watch on the crosses so that nobody could remove the thieves' bodies for burial suddenly noticed a light blazing among the tombs and heard the sounds of groaning. And prompted by a natural human curiosity to know who or what was making those sounds, he descended into the vault.

"But at the sight of a strikingly beautiful woman, he stopped short in

---

*Translated by William Arrowsmith.

terror, thinking he must be seeing some ghostly apparition out of hell. Then, observing the corpse and seeing the tears on the lady's face and the scratches her fingernails had gashed in her cheeks, he realized what it was: a widow, in inconsolable grief. Promptly fetching his little supper back down to the tomb, he implored the lady not to persist in her sorrow or break her heart with useless mourning. All men alike, he reminded her, have the same end; the same resting place awaits us all. He used, in short, all those platitudes we use to comfort the suffering and bring them back to life. His consolations, being unwelcome, only exasperated the widow more; more violently than ever she beat her breast, and tearing out her hair by the roots, scattered it over the dead man's body. Undismayed, the soldier repeated his arguments and pressed her to take some food, until the little maid, quite overcome by the smell of the wine, succumbed and stretched out her hand to her tempter. Then, restored by the food and wine, she began herself to assail her mistress' obstinate refusal.

" 'How will it help you,' she asked the lady, 'if you faint from hunger? Why should you bury yourself alive, and go down to death before the Fates have called you? What does Vergil say?—

> Do you suppose the shades and ashes of the dead are by such sorrow touched?

No, begin your life afresh. Shake off these woman's scruples; enjoy the light while you can. Look at that corpse of your poor husband: doesn't it tell you more eloquently than any words that you should live?'

"None of us, of course, really dislikes being told that we must eat, that life is to be lived. And the lady was no exception. Weakened by her long days of fasting, her resistance crumbled at last, and she ate the food the soldier offered her as hungrily as the little maid had eaten earlier.

"Well, you know what temptations are normally aroused in a man on a full stomach. So the soldier, mustering all those blandishments by means of which he had persuaded the lady to live, now laid determined siege to her virtue. And chaste though she was, the lady found him singularly attractive and his arguments persuasive. As for the maid, she did all she could to help the soldier's cause, repeating like a refrain the appropriate line of Vergil:

> If love is pleasing, lady, yield yourself to love.

To make the matter short, the lady's body soon gave up the struggle; she yielded and our happy warrior enjoyed a total triumph on both counts. That very night their marriage was consummated, and they slept together the second and the third night too, carefully shutting the door of the tomb so that any passing friends or stranger would have thought the lady of famous chastity had at last expired over her dead husband's body.

"As you can perhaps imagine, our soldier was a very happy man, utterly delighted with his lady's ample beauty and that special charm that a secret love confers. Every night, as soon as the sun had set, he bought what few provisions his slender pay permitted and smuggled them down to the tomb. One night, however, the parents of one of the crucified thieves, noticing that the watch was being badly kept, took advantage of our hero's absence to remove their son's body and bury it. The next morning, of course, the soldier was horror-struck to discover one of the bodies missing from its cross, and ran to tell his mistress of the horrible punishment which awaited him for neglecting his duty. In the circumstances, he told her, he would not wait to be tried and sentenced, but would punish himself then and there with his own sword. All he asked of her was that she make room for another corpse and allow the same gloomy tomb to enclose husband and lover together.

"Our lady's heart, however, was no less tender than pure. 'God forbid,' she cried, 'that I should have to see at one and the same time the dead bodies of the only two men I have ever loved. No, better far, I say, to hang the dead than kill the living.' With these words, she gave orders that her husband's body should be taken from its bier and strung up on the empty cross. The soldier followed this good advice, and the next morning the whole city wondered by what miracle the dead man had climbed up on the cross."

Questions

1. *This tale is told in* The Satyricon *to illustrate one character's conviction that all women are fickle. Does the story succeed in making that point? Should the widow behave differently? On what set of underlying attitudes about love and fidelity and death is your answer based?* **2.** *Presumably the woman's behavior at the beginning of the story publicly displays the virtues of chastity and fidelity. What does her behavior at the end of the story display?* **3.** *The narrator, in the course of his recitation, makes numerous judgments about the human condition. Do you find those judgments convincing? Why?*

The Horse Dealer's Daughter

D. H. LAWRENCE [1885–1930]

"WELL, Mabel, and what are you going to do with yourself?" asked Joe, with foolish flippancy. He felt quite safe himself. Without listening for an answer, he turned aside, worked a grain of tobacco to the tip of his tongue, and spat it out. He did not care about anything, since he felt safe himself.

The three brothers and the sister sat round the desolate breakfast table, attempting some sort of desultory consultation. The morning's post had given the final tap to the family fortune, and all was over. The dreary dining-room itself, with its heavy mahogany furniture, looked as if it were waiting to be done away with.

But the consultation amounted to nothing. There was a strange air of ineffectuality about the three men, as they sprawled at table, smoking and reflecting vaguely on their own condition. The girl was alone, a rather short, sullen-looking young woman of twenty-seven. She did not share the same life as her brothers. She would have been good-looking, save for the impassive fixity of her face, "bull-dog," as her brothers called it.

There was a confused tramping of horses' feet outside. The three men all sprawled round in their chairs to watch. Beyond the dark hollybushes that separated the strip of lawn from the high-road, they could see a cavalcade of shire horses swinging out of their own yard, being taken for exercise. This was the last time. These were the last horses that would go through their hands. The young men watched with critical, callous look. They were all frightened at the collapse of their lives, and the sense of disaster in which they were involved left them no inner freedom.

Yet they were three fine, well-set fellows enough. Joe, the eldest, was a man of thirty-three, broad and handsome in a hot, flushed way. His face was red, he twisted his black moustache over a thick finger, his eyes were shallow and restless. He had a sensual way of uncovering his teeth when he laughed, and his bearing was stupid. Now he watched the horses with a glazed look of helplessness in his eyes, a certain stupor of downfall.

The great draught-horses swung past. They were tied head to tail, four of them, and they heaved along to where a lane branched off from the high-road, planting their great hoofs floutingly in the fine black mud, swinging their great rounded haunches sumptuously, and trotting a few sudden steps as they were led into the lane, round the corner. Every movement showed a massive, slumbrous strength, and a stupidity which held them in subjection. The groom at the head looked back, jerking the leading rope. And the cavalcade moved out of sight up the lane, the tail of the last horse bobbed up tight and stiff, held out taut from the swinging great haunches as they rocked behind the hedges in a motion like sleep.

Joe watched with glazed hopeless eyes. The horses were almost like his own body to him. He felt he was done for now. Luckily he was engaged to a woman as old as himself, and therefore her father, who was steward of a neighbouring estate, would provide him with a job. He would marry and go into harness. His life was over, he would be a subject animal now.

He turned uneasily aside, the retreating steps of the horses echoing in his ears. Then, with foolish restlessness, he reached for the scraps of bacon-rind from the plates, and making a faint whistling sound, flung them to the terrier that lay against the fender. He watched the dog swallow them, and waited till the creature looked into his eyes. Then a faint grin came on his face, and in a high, foolish voice he said:

"You won't get much more bacon, shall you, you little bitch?"

The dog faintly and dismally wagged its tail, then lowered its haunches, circled round, and lay down again.

There was another helpless silence at the table. Joe sprawled uneasily in his seat, not willing to go till the family conclave was dissolved. Fred Henry, the second brother, was erect, clean-limbed, alert. He had watched the passing of the horses with more sangfroid. If he was an animal, like Joe, he was an animal which controls, not one which is controlled. He was master of any horse, and he carried himself with a well-tempered air of mastery. But he was not master of the situations of life. He pushed his coarse brown moustache upwards, off his lip, and glanced irritably at his sister, who sat impassive and inscrutable.

"You'll go and stop with Lucy for a bit, shan't you?" he asked. The girl did not answer.

"I don't see what else you can do," persisted Fred Henry.

"Go as a skivvy," Joe interpolated laconically.

The girl did not move a muscle.

"If I was her, I should go in for training for a nurse," said Malcolm, the youngest of them all. He was the baby of the family, a young man of twenty-two, with a fresh, jaunty *museau*.[1]

But Mabel did not take any notice of him. They had talked at her and round her for so many years, that she hardly heard them at all.

The marble clock on the mantelpiece softly chimed the half-hour, the dog rose uneasily from the hearthrug and looked at the party at the breakfast table. But still they sat on in ineffectual conclave.

"Oh, all right," said Joe suddenly, apropos of nothing. "I'll get a move on."

He pushed back his chair, straddled his knees with a downward jerk, to get them free, in horsey fashion, and went to the fire. Still he did not go out of the room; he was curious to know what the others would do or say. He began

---

1. Nose.

to charge his pipe, looking down at the dog and saying, in a high, affected voice:

"Going wi' me? Going wi' me are ter? Tha'rt goin' further than tha counts on just now, dost hear?"

The dog faintly wagged its tail, the man stuck out his jaw and covered his pipe with his hands, and puffed intently, losing himself in the tobacco, looking down all the while at the dog with an absent brown eye. The dog looked up at him in mournful distrust. Joe stood with his knees stuck out, in real horsey fashion.

"Have you had a letter from Lucy?" Fred Henry asked of his sister.

"Last week," came the neutral reply.

"And what does she say?"

There was no answer.

"Does she *ask* you to go and stop there?" persisted Fred Henry.

"She says I can if I like."

"Well, then, you'd better. Tell her you'll come on Monday."

This was received in silence.

"That's what you'll do then, is it?" said Fred Henry, in some exasperation.

But she made no answer. There was a silence of futility and irritation in the room. Malcolm grinned fatuously.

"You'll have to make up your mind between now and next Wednesday," said Joe loudly, "or else find yourself lodgings on the kerbstone."

The face of the young woman darkened, but she sat on immutable.

"Here's Jack Fergusson!" exclaimed Malcolm, who was looking aimlessly out of the window.

"Where?" exclaimed Joe, loudly.

"Just gone past."

"Coming in?"

Malcolm craned his neck to see the gate.

"Yes," he said.

There was a silence. Mabel sat on like one condemned, at the head of the table. Then a whistle was heard from the kitchen. The dog got up and barked sharply. Joe opened the door and shouted:

"Come on."

After a moment a young man entered. He was muffled up in overcoat and a purple woollen scarf, and his tweed cap, which he did not remove, was pulled down on his head. He was of medium height, his face was rather long and pale, his eyes looked tired.

"Hello, Jack! Well, Jack!" exclaimed Malcolm and Joe. Fred Henry merely said, "Jack."

"What's doing?" asked the newcomer, evidently addressing Fred Henry.

"Same. We've got to be out by Wednesday. Got a cold?"

"I have—got it bad, too."

"Why don't you stop in?"

"Me stop in? When I can't stand on my legs, perhaps I shall have a chance." The young man spoke huskily. He had a slight Scotch accent.

"It's a knock-out, isn't it," said Joe, boisterously, "if a doctor goes round croaking with a cold. Looks bad for the patients, doesn't it?"

The young doctor looked at him slowly.

"Anything the matter with you, then?" he asked sarcastically.

"Not as I know of. Damn your eyes, I hope not. Why?"

"I thought you were very concerned about the patients, wondered if you might be one yourself."

"Damn it, no, I've never been patient to no flaming doctor, and hope I never shall be," returned Joe.

At this point Mabel rose from the table, and they all seemed to become aware of her existence. She began putting the dishes together. The young doctor looked at her, but did not address her. He had not greeted her. She went out of the room with the tray, her face impassive and unchanged.

"When are you off then, all of you?" asked the doctor.

"I'm catching the eleven-forty," replied Malcolm. "Are you goin' down wi' th' trap, Joe?"

"Yes, I've told you I am going down wi' th' trap, haven't I?"

"We'd better be getting her in then. So long, Jack, if I don't see you before I go," said Malcolm, shaking hands.

He went out, followed by Joe, who seemed to have his tail between his legs.

"Well, this is the devil's own," exclaimed the doctor, when he was left alone with Fred Henry. "Going before Wednesday, are you."

"That's the orders," replied the other.

"Where, to Northampton?"

"That's it."

"The devil!" exclaimed Fergusson, with quiet chagrin.

And there was silence between the two.

"All settled up, are you?" asked Fergusson.

"About."

There was another pause.

"Well, I shall miss yer, Freddy, boy," said the young doctor.

"And I shall miss thee, Jack," returned the other.

"Miss you like hell," mused the doctor.

Fred Henry turned aside. There was nothing to say. Mabel came in again, to finish clearing the table.

"What are you going to do, then, Miss Pervin?" asked Fergusson. "Going to your sister's, are you?"

Mabel looked at him with her steady, dangerous eyes, that always made him uncomfortable, unsettling his superficial ease.

"No," she said.

"Well, what in the name of fortune are *you* going to do? Say what you mean to do," cried Fred Henry, with futile intensity.

But she only averted her head, and continued her work. She folded the white table-cloth, and put on the chenille cloth.

"The sulkiest bitch that ever trod!" muttered her brother.

But she finished her task with perfectly impassive face, the young doctor watching her interestedly all the while. Then she went out.

Fred Henry stared after her, clenching his lips, his blue eyes fixing in sharp antagonism, as he made a grimace of sour exasperation.

"You could bray her into bits, and that's all you'd get out of her," he said in a small, narrowed tone.

The doctor smiled faintly.

"What's she *going* to do, then?" he asked.

"Strike me if I know!" returned the other.

There was a pause. Then the doctor stirred.

"I'll be seeing you to-night, shall I?" he said to his friend.

"Ay—where's it to be? Are we going over to Jessdale?"

"I don't know. I've got such a cold on me. I'll come round to the Moon and Stars, anyway."

"Let Lizzie and May miss their night for once, eh?"

"That's it—if I feel as I do now."

"All's one—"

The two young men went through the passage and down to the back door together. The house was large, but it was servantless now, and desolate. At the back was a small bricked house-yard, and beyond that a big square, gravelled fine and red, and having stables on two sides. Sloping, dank, winter-dark fields stretched away on the open sides.

But the stables were empty. Joseph Pervin, the father of the family, had been a man of no education, who had become a fairly large horse dealer. The stables had been full of horses, there was a great turmoil and come-and-go of horses and of dealers and grooms. Then the kitchen was full of servants. But of late things had declined. The old man had married a second time, to retrieve his fortunes. Now he was dead and everything was gone to the dogs, there was nothing but debt and threatening.

For months, Mabel had been servantless in the big house, keeping the home together in penury for her ineffectual brothers. She had kept house for ten years. But previously it was with unstinted means. Then, however brutal and coarse everything was, the sense of money had kept her proud, confident. The men might be foul-mouthed, the women in the kitchen might have bad reputations, her brothers might have illegitimate children. But so long as there was money, the girl felt herself established and brutally proud, reserved.

No company came to the house, save dealers and coarse men. Mabel had no associates of her own sex, after her sister went away. But she did not mind. She went regularly to church, she attended to her father. And she lived in the memory of her mother, who had died when she was fourteen, and whom she had loved. She had loved her father, too, in a different way, depending upon him, and feeling secure in him, until at the age of fifty-four he married again. And then she had set hard against him. Now he had died and left them all hopelessly in debt.

She had suffered badly during the period of poverty. Nothing, however, could shake the curious sullen, animal pride that dominated each member of the family. Now, for Mabel, the end had come. Still she would not cast about her. She would follow her own way just the same. She would always hold the keys of her own situation. Mindless and persistent, she endured from day to day. What should she think? Why should she answer anybody? It was enough that this was the end and there was no way out. She need not pass any more darkly along the main street of the small town, avoiding every eye. She need not demean herself any more, going into the shops and buying the cheapest food. This was at an end. She thought of nobody, not even of herself. Mindless and persistent, she seemed in a sort of ecstasy to be coming nearer to her fulfilment, her own glorification, approaching her dead mother, who was glorified.

In the afternoon she took a little bag, with shears and sponge and a small scrubbing brush, and went out. It was a grey, wintry day, with saddened, dark green fields and an atmosphere blackened by the smoke of foundries not far off. She went quickly, darkly along the causeway, heeding nobody, through the town to the churchyard.

There she always felt secure, as if no one could see her, although as a matter of fact she was exposed to the stare of every one who passed along under the churchyard wall. Nevertheless, once under the shadow of the great looming church, among the graves, she felt immune from the world, reserved within the thick churchyard wall as in another country.

Carefully she clipped the grass from the grave, and arranged the pinky white, small chrysanthemums in the tin cross. When this was done, she took an empty jar from a neighbouring grave, brought water, and carefully, most scrupulously sponged the marble head-stone and the coping-stone.

It gave her sincere satisfaction to do this. She felt in immediate contact with the world of her mother. She took minute pains, went through the park in a state bordering on pure happiness, as if in performing this task she came into a subtle, intimate connection with her mother. For the life she followed here in the world was far less real than the world of death she inherited from her mother.

The doctor's house was just by the church. Fergusson, being a mere hired assistant, was slave to the country-side. As he hurried now to attend to the out-patients in the surgery, glancing across the graveyard with his quick eye, he saw the girl at her task at the grave. She seemed so intent and remote, it was like looking into another world. Some mystical element was touched in him. He slowed down as he walked, watching her as if spell-bound.

She lifted her eyes, feeling him looking. Their eyes met. And each looked away again at once, each feeling, in some way, found out by the other.

He lifted his cap and passed on down the road. There remained distinct in his consciousness, like a vision, the memory of her face, lifted from the tombstone in the churchyard, and looking at him with slow, large, portentous eyes. It *was* portentous, her face. It seemed to mesmerize him. There was a heavy power in her eyes which laid hold of his whole being, as if he had drunk some powerful drug. He had been feeling weak and done before. Now the life came back into him, he felt delivered from his own fretted, daily self.

He finished his duties at the surgery as quickly as might be, hastily filling up the bottle of the waiting people with cheap drugs. Then, in perpetual haste, he set off again to visit several cases in another part of his round, before tea-time. At all times he preferred to walk if he could, but particularly when he was not well. He fancied the motion restored him.

The afternoon was falling. It was grey, deadened, and wintry, with a slow, moist, heavy coldness sinking in and deadening all the faculties. But why should he think or notice? He hastily climbed the hill and turned across the dark green fields, following the black cinder-track. In the distance, across a shallow dip in the country, the small town was clustered like smouldering ash, a tower, a spire, a heap of low, raw, extinct houses. And on the nearest fringe of the town, sloping into the dip, was Oldmeadow, the Pervins' house. He could see the stables and the outbuildings distinctly, as they lay towards him on the slope. Well, he would not go there many more times! Another resource would be lost to him, another place gone: the only company he cared for in the alien, ugly little town he was losing. Nothing but work, drudgery, constant hastening from dwelling to dwelling among the colliers and the ironworkers. It wore him out, but at the same time he had a craving for it. It was a stimulant to him to be in the homes of the working people, moving as it were through the innermost body of their life. His nerves were excited and gratified. He could come so near, into the very lives of the rough, inarticulate, powerfully emotional men and women. He grumbled, he said he hated the hellish hole. But as a matter of fact it excited him, the contact with the rough, strongly-feeling people was a stimulant applied direct to his nerves.

Below Oldmeadow, in the green, shallow, soddened hollow of fields lay a square, deep pond. Roving across the landscape, the doctor's quick eye detected a figure in black passing through the gate of the field, down towards the pond. He looked again. It would be Mabel Pervin. His mind suddenly became alive and attentive.

Why was she going down there? He pulled up on the path on the slope above, and stood staring. He could just make sure of the small black figure moving in the hollow of the failing day. He seemed to see her in the midst of such obscurity, that he was like a clairvoyant, seeing rather with the mind's eye than with ordinary sight. Yet he could see her positively enough, whilst he kept his eye attentive. He felt, if he looked away from her, in the thick, ugly falling dusk, he would lose her altogether.

He followed her minutely as she moved, direct and intent, like something transmitted rather than stirring in voluntary activity, straight down the field towards the pond. There she stood on the bank for a moment. She never raised her head. Then she waded slowly into the water.

He stood motionless as the small black figure walked slowly and deliberately towards the centre of the pond, very slowly, gradually moving deeper into the motionless water, and still moving forward as the water got up to her breast. Then he could see her no more in the dusk of the dead afternoon.

"There!" he exclaimed. "Would you believe it?"

And he hastened straight down, running over the wet, soddened fields, pushing through the hedges, down into the depression of callous wintry obscurity. It took him several minutes to come to the pond. He stood on the bank, breathing heavily. He could see nothing. His eyes seemed to penetrate the dead water. Yes, perhaps that was the dark shadow of her black clothing beneath the surface of the water.

He slowly ventured into the pond. The bottom was deep, soft clay, he sank in, and the water clasped dead cold round his legs. As he stirred he could smell the cold, rotten clay that fouled up into the water. It was objectionable in his lungs. Still, repelled and yet not heeding, he moved deeper into the pond. The cold water rose over his thighs, over his loins, upon his abdomen. The lower part of his body was all sunk in the hideous cold element. And the bottom was so deeply soft and uncertain, he was afraid of pitching with his mouth underneath. He could not swim, and was afraid.

He crouched a little, spreading his hands under the water and moving them round, trying to feel for her. The dead cold pond swayed upon his chest. He moved again, a little deeper, and again, with his hands underneath, he felt all around under the water. And he touched her clothing. But it evaded his fingers. He made a desperate effort to grasp it.

And so doing he lost his balance and went under, horribly, suffocating in the foul earthy water, struggling madly for a few moments. At last, after what seemed an eternity, he got his footing, rose again into the air and looked around. He gasped, and knew he was in the world. Then he looked at the water. She had risen near him. He grasped her clothing, and drawing her nearer, turned to take his way to land again.

He went very slowly, carefully, absorbed in the slow progress. He rose higher, climbing out of the pond. The water was now only about his legs; he was thankful, full of relief to be out of the clutches of the pond. He lifted her and staggered on to the bank, out of the horror of wet, grey clay.

He laid her down on the bank. She was quite unconscious and running with water. He made the water come from her mouth, he worked to restore her. He did not have to work very long before he could feel the breathing begin again in her; she was breathing naturally. He worked a little longer. He could feel her live beneath his hands; she was coming back. He wiped her face, wrapped her in his overcoat, looked round into the dim, dark grey world, then lifted her and staggered down the bank and across the fields.

It seemed an unthinkably long way, and his burden so heavy he felt he would never get to the house. But at last he was in the stable-yard, and then in the house-yard. He opened the door and went into the house. In the kitchen he laid her down on the hearth-rug, and called. The house was empty. But the fire was burning in the grate.

Then again he kneeled to attend to her. She was breathing regularly, her eyes were wide open and as if conscious, but there seemed something missing in her look. She was conscious in herself, but unconscious of her surroundings.

He ran upstairs, took blankets from a bed, and put them before the fire to warm. Then he removed her saturated, earthy-smelling clothing, rubbed her dry with a towel, and wrapped her naked in the blankets. Then he went into the dining-room, to look for spirits. There was a little whisky. He drank a gulp himself, and put some into her mouth.

The effect was instantaneous. She looked full into his face, as if she had been seeing him for some time, and yet had only just become conscious of him.

"Dr. Fergusson?" she said.

"What?" he answered.

He was divesting himself of his coat, intending to find some dry clothing upstairs. He could not bear the smell of the dead, clayey water, and he was mortally afraid for his own health.

"What did I do?" she asked.

"Walked into the pond," he replied. He had begun to shudder like one sick, and could hardly attend to her. Her eyes remained full on him, he seemed to be going dark in his mind, looking back at her helplessly. The shuddering became quieter in him, his life came back in him, dark and unknowing, but strong again.

"Was I out of my mind?" she asked, while her eyes were fixed on him all the time.

"Maybe, for the moment," he replied. He felt quiet, because his strength had come back. The strange fretful strain had left him.

"Am I out of my mind now?" she asked.

"Are you?" he reflected a moment. "No," he answered truthfully. "I don't see that you are." He turned his face aside. He was afraid now, because he felt dazed, and felt dimly that her power was stronger than his, in this issue. And she continued to look at him fixedly all the time. "Can you tell me where I shall find some dry things to put on?" he asked.

"Did you dive into the pond for me?" she asked.

"No," he answered. "I walked in. But I went in overhead as well."

There was silence for a moment. He hesitated. He very much wanted to go upstairs to get into dry clothing. But there was another desire in him. And she seemed to hold him. His will seemed to have gone to sleep, and left him, standing there slack before her. But he felt warm inside himself. He did not shudder at all, though his clothes were sodden on him.

"Why did you?" she asked.

"Because I didn't want you to do such a foolish thing," he said.

"It wasn't foolish," she said, still gazing at him as she lay on the floor, with a sofa cushion under her head. "It was the right thing to do. *I* knew best, then."

"I'll go and shift these wet things," he said. But still he had not the power to move out of her presence, until she sent him. It was as if she had the life of his body in her hands, and he could not extricate himself. Or perhaps he did not want to.

Suddenly she sat up. Then she became aware of her own immediate condition. She felt the blankets about her, she knew her own limbs. For a moment it seemed as if her reason were going. She looked round, with wild eye, as if seeking something. He stood still with fear. She saw her clothing lying scattered.

"Who undressed me?" she asked, her eyes resting full and inevitable on his face.

"I did," he replied, "to bring you round."

For some moments she sat and gazed at him awfully, her lips parted.

"Do you love me, then?" she asked.

He only stood and stared at her, fascinated. His soul seemed to melt.

She shuffled forward on her knees, and put her arms round him, round his legs, as he stood there, pressing her breasts against his knees and thighs, clutching him with strange, convulsive certainty, pressing his thighs against her, drawing him to her face, her throat, as she looked up at him with flaring, humble eyes of transfiguration, triumphant in first possession.

"You love me," she murmured, in strange transport, yearning and triumphant and confident. "You love me. I know you love me, I know."

And she was passionately kissing his knees, through the wet clothing, passionately and indiscriminately kissing his knees, his legs, as if unaware of everything.

He looked down at the tangled wet hair, the wild, bare, animal shoulders. He was amazed, bewildered, and afraid. He had never thought of loving her. He had never wanted to love her. When he rescued her and restored her, he was a doctor, and she was a patient. He had had no single personal thought of her. Nay, this introduction of the personal element was very distasteful to him, a violation of his professional honour. It was horrible to have her there embracing his knees. It was horrible. He revolted from it, violently. And yet— and yet—he had not the power to break away.

She looked at him again, with the same supplication of powerful love, and that same transcendent, frightening light of triumph. In view of the delicate flame which seemed to come from her face like a light, he was powerless. And yet he had never intended to love her. He had never intended. And something stubborn in him could not give way.

"You love me," she repeated, in a murmur of deep rhapsodic assurance. "You love me."

Her hands were drawing him, drawing him down to her. He was afraid, even a little horrified. For he had, really, no intention of loving her. Yet her hands were drawing him towards her. He put out his hand quickly to steady himself, and grasped her bare shoulder. A flame seemed to burn the hand that grasped her soft shoulder. He had no intention of loving her: his whole will was against his yielding. It was horrible. And yet wonderful was the touch of her shoulders, beautiful the shining of her face. Was she perhaps mad? He had a horror of yielding to her. Yet something in him ached also.

He had been staring away at the door, away from her. But his hand remained on her shoulder. She had gone suddenly very still. He looked down at her. Her eyes were now wide with fear, with doubt, the light was dying from her face, a shadow of terrible greyness was returning. He could not bear the touch of her eyes' question upon him, and the look of death behind the question.

With an inward groan he gave way, and let his heart yield towards her. A sudden gentle smile came on his face. And her eyes, which never left his face, slowly, slowly filled with tears. He watched the strange water rise in her eyes, like some slow fountain coming up. And his heart seemed to burn and melt away in his breast.

He could not bear to look at her any more. He dropped on his knees and caught her head with his arms and pressed her face against his throat. She was very still. His heart, which seemed to have broken, was burning with a kind of agony in his breast. And he felt her slow, hot tears wetting his throat. But he could not move.

He felt the hot tears wet his neck and the hollows of his neck, and he remained motionless, suspended through one of man's eternities. Only now it had become indispensable to him to have her face pressed close to him; he could never let her go again. He could never let her head go away from the close clutch of his arm. He wanted to remain like that for ever, with his heart hurting him in a pain that was also life to him. Without knowing, he was looking down on her damp, soft brown hair.

Then, as it were suddenly, he smelt the horrid stagnant smell of that water. And at the same moment she drew away from him and looked at him. Her eyes were wistful and unfathomable. He was afraid of them, and he fell to kissing her, not knowing what he was doing. He wanted her eyes not to have that terrible, wistful, unfathomable look.

When she turned her face to him again, a faint delicate flush was glowing, and there was again dawning that terrible shining of joy in her eyes, which really terrified him, and yet which he now wanted to see, because he feared the look of doubt still more.

"You love me?" she said, rather faltering.

"Yes." The word cost him a painful effort. Not because it wasn't true. But because it was too newly true, the *saying* seemed to tear open again his newly-torn heart. And he hardly wanted it to be true, even now.

She lifted her face to him, and he bent forward and kissed her on the mouth, gently, with the one kiss that is an eternal pledge. And as he kissed her his heart strained again in his breast. He never intended to love her. But now it was over. He had crossed over the gulf to her, and all that he had left behind had shrivelled and become void.

After the kiss, her eyes again slowly filled with tears. She sat still, away from him, with her face drooped aside, and her hands folded in her lap. The tears fell very slowly. There was complete silence. He too sat there motionless and silent on the hearthrug. The strange pain of his heart that was broken seemed to consume him. That he should love her? That this was love! That he should be ripped open in this way! Him, a doctor! How they would all jeer if they knew! It was agony to him to think they might know.

In the curious naked pain of the thought he looked again to her. She was sitting there drooped into a muse. He saw a tear fall, and his heart flared hot. He saw for the first time that one of her shoulders was quite uncovered, one arm bare, he could see one of her small breasts; dimly, because it had become almost dark in the room.

"Why are you crying?" he asked, in an altered voice.

She looked up at him, and behind her tears the consciousness of her situation for the first time brought a dark look of shame to her eyes.

"I'm not crying, really," she said, watching him half frightened.

He reached his hand, and softly closed it on her bare arm.

"I love you! I love you!" he said in a soft, low vibrating voice, unlike himself.

She shrank, and dropped her head. The soft, penetrating grip of his hand on her arm distressed her. She looked up at him.

"I want to go," she said. "I want to go and get you some dry things."

"Why?" he said. "I'm all right."

"But I want to go," she said. "And I want you to change your things."

He released her arm, and she wrapped herself in the blanket, looking at him rather frightened. And still she did not rise.

"Kiss me," she said wistfully.

He kissed her, but briefly, half in anger.

Then, after a second, she rose nervously, all mixed up in the blanket. He watched her in her confusion, as she tried to extricate herself and wrap herself up so that she could walk. He watched her relentlessly, as she knew. And as she went, the blanket trailing, and as he saw a glimpse of her feet and her white leg, he tried to remember her as she was when he had wrapped her in the blanket. But then he didn't want to remember, because she had been nothing to him then, and his nature revolted from remembering her as she was when she was nothing to him.

A tumbling, muffled noise from within the dark house startled him. Then he heard her voice:—"There are clothes." He rose and went to the foot of the stairs, and gathered up the garments she had thrown down. Then he came back to the fire, to rub himself down and dress. He grinned at his own appearance when he had finished.

The fire was sinking, so he put on coal. The house was now quite dark, save for the light of a street-lamp that shone in faintly from beyond the holly trees. He lit the gas with matches he found on the mantelpiece. Then he emptied the pockets of his own clothes, and threw all his wet things in a heap into the scullery. After which he gathered up her sodden clothes, gently, and put them in a separate heap on the copper-top in the scullery.

It was six o'clock on the clock. His own watch had stopped. He ought to go back to the surgery. He waited, and still she did not come down. So he went to the foot of the stairs and called:

"I shall have to go."

Almost immediately he heard her coming down. She had on her best dress of black voile, and her hair was tidy, but still damp. She looked at him— and in spite of herself, smiled.

"I don't like you in those clothes," she said.

"Do I look a sight?" he answered.

They were shy of one another.

"I'll make you some tea," she said.

"No, I must go."

"Must you?" And she looked at him again with the wide, strained, doubtful eyes. And again, from the pain of his breast, he knew how he loved her. He went and bent to kiss her, gently, passionately, with his heart's painful kiss.

"And my hair smells so horrible," she murmured in distraction. "And I'm so awful, I'm so awful! Oh, no, I'm too awful." And she broke into bitter, heart-broken sobbing. "You can't want to love me, I'm horrible."

"Don't be silly, don't be silly," he said, trying to comfort her, kissing her, holding her in his arms. "I want you, I want to marry you, we're going to be married, quickly, quickly—tomorrow if I can."

But she only sobbed terribly, and cried:

"I feel awful. I feel awful. I feel I'm horrible to you."

"No, I want you, I want you," was all he answered, blindly, with that terrible intonation which frightened her almost more than her horror lest he should *not* want her.

Questions

1. The central episode in the story is Mabel's attempted suicide. What symbolic qualities do the events at the pond have?   2. In what way does Mabel's character change? In what way does Jack Fergusson's?   3. Why does Fergusson resist the attraction he feels toward Mabel? Why does he finally yield?   4. What function is served by the presence of Mabel's brothers in the first third of the story?

Theater

JEAN TOOMER [1894–1967]

LIFE of nigger alleys, of pool rooms and restaurants and near-beer saloons soaks into the walls of Howard Theater and sets them throbbing jazz songs. Black-skinned, they dance and shout above the tick and trill of white-walled buildings. At night, they open doors to people who come in to stamp their feet and shout. At night, road-shows volley songs into the mass-heart of black people. Songs soak the walls and seep out to the nigger life of alleys and near-beer saloons, of the Poodle Dog and Black Bear cabarets. Afternoons, the house is dark, and the walls are sleeping singers until rehearsal begins. Or until John comes within them. Then they start throbbing to a subtle syncopation. And the space-dark air grows softly luminous.

John is the manager's brother. He is seated at the center of the theater, just before rehearsal. Light streaks down upon him from a window high above. One half his face is orange in it. One half his face is in shadow. The soft glow of the house rushes to, and compacts about, the shaft of light. John's mind coincides with the shaft of light. Thoughts rush to, and compact about it. Life of the house and of the slowly awakening stage swirls to the body of John, and thrills it. John's body is separate from the thoughts that pack his mind.

Stage-lights, soft, as if they shine through clear pink fingers. Beneath them, hid by the shadow of a set, Dorris. Other chorus girls drift in. John feels them in the mass. And as if his own body were the mass-heart of a black audience listening to them singing, he wants to stamp his feet and shout. His mind, contained above desires of his body, singles the girls out, and tries to trace origins and plot destinies.

A pianist slips into the pit and improvises jazz. The walls awake. Arms of the girls, and their limbs, which . . . jazz, jazz . . . by lifting up their tight street skirts they set free, jab the air and clog the floor in rhythm to the music. (Lift your skirts, Baby, and talk t papa!) Crude, individualized, and yet . . . monotonous. . . .

John: Soon the director will herd you, my full-lipped, distant beauties, and tame you, and blunt your sharp thrusts in loosely suggestive movements, appropriate to Broadway. (O dance!) Soon the audience will paint your dusk faces white, and call you beautiful. (O dance!) Soon I. . . . (O dance!) I'd like . . .

Girls laugh and shout. Sing discordant snatches of other jazz songs. Whirl with loose passion into the arms of passing show-men.

John: Too thick. Too easy. Too monotonous. Her whom I'd love I'd

leave before she knew that I was with her. Her? Which? (O dance!) I'd like to
. . .

Girls dance and sing. Men clap. The walls sing and press inward. They press the men and girls, they press John towards a center of physical ecstasy. Go to it, Baby! Fan yourself, and feed your papa! Put . . . nobody lied . . . and take . . . when they said I cried over you. No lie! The glitter and color of stacked scenes, the gilt and brass and crimson of the house, converge towards a center of physical ecstasy. John's feet and torso and his blood press in. He wills thought to rid his mind of passion.

"All right, girls. Alaska. Miss Reynolds, please."

The director wants to get the rehearsal through with.

The girls line up. John sees the front row: dancing ponies. The rest are in shadow. The leading lady fits loosely in the front. Lack-life, monotonous. "One, two, three—" Music starts. The song is somewhere where it will not strain the leading lady's throat. The dance is somewhere where it will not strain the girls. Above the staleness, one dancer throws herself into it. Dorris. John sees her. Her hair, crisp-curled, is bobbed. Bushy, black hair bobbing about her lemon-colored face. Her lips are curiously full, and very red. Her limbs in silk purple stockings are lovely. John feels them. Desires her. Holds off.

John: Stage-door johnny; chorus-girl. No, that would be all right. Dictie,[1] educated, stuck-up; show-girl. Yep. Her suspicion would be stronger than her passion. It wouldnt work. Keep her loveliness. Let her go.

Dorris sees John and knows that he is looking at her. Her own glowing is too rich a thing to let her feel the slimness of his diluted passion.

"Who's that?" she asks her dancing partner.

"Th manager's brother. Dictie. Nothin doin, hon."

Dorris tosses her head and dances for him until she feels she has him. Then, withdrawing disdainfully, she flirts with the director.

Dorris: Nothin doin? How come? Aint I as good as him? Couldnt I have got an education if I'd wanted one? Dont I know respectable folks, lots of em, in Philadelphia and New York and Chicago? Aint I had men as good as him? Better. Doctors an lawyers. Whats a manager's brother, anyhow?

Two steps back, and two steps front.

"Say, Mame, where do you get that stuff?"

"Whatshmean, Dorris?"

"If you two girls cant listen to what I'm telling you, I know where I can get some who can. Now listen."

Mame: Go to hell, you black bastard.

Dorris: Whats eatin at him, anyway?

"Now follow me in this, you girls. Its three counts to the right, three counts to the left, and then you shimmy—"

John: —and then you shimmy. I'll bet she can. Some good cabaret, with rooms upstairs. And what in hell do you think you'd get from it? Youre going

---

1. A snob.

wrong. Here's right: get her to herself—(Christ, but how she'd bore you after the first five minutes)—not if you get her right she wouldnt. Touch her, I mean. To herself—in some room perhaps. Some cheap, dingy bedroom. Hell no. Cant be done. But the point is, brother John, it can be done. Get her to herself somewhere, anywhere. Go down in yourself—and she'd be calling you all sorts of asses while you were in the process of going down. Hold em, bud. Cant be done. Let her go. (Dance and I'll love you!) And keep her loveliness.

"All right now, Chicken Chaser. Dorris and girls. Where's Dorris? I told you to stay on the stage, didnt I? Well? Now thats enough. All right. All right there, Professor?[2] All right. One, two, three—"

Dorris swings to the front. The line of girls, four deep, blurs within the shadow of suspended scenes. Dorris wants to dance. The director feels that and steps to one side. He smiles, and picks her for a leading lady, one of these days. Odd ends of stage-men emerge from the wings, and stare and clap. A crap game in the alley suddenly ends. Black faces crowd the rear stage doors. The girls, catching joy from Dorris, whip up within the footlights' glow. They forget set steps; they find their own. The director forgets to bawl them out. Dorris dances.

John: Her head bobs to Broadway. Dance from yourself. Dance! O just a little more.

Dorris' eyes burn across the space of seats to him.

Dorris: I bet he can love. Hell, he cant love. He's too skinny. His lips are too skinny. He wouldnt love me anyway, only for that. But I'd get a pair of silk stockings out of it. Red silk. I got purple. Cut it, kid. You cant win him to respect you that away. He wouldnt anyway. Maybe he would. Maybe he'd love. I've heard em say that men who look like him (what does he look like?) will marry if they love. O will you love me? And give me kids, and a home, and everything? (I'd like to make your nest, and honest, hon, I wouldnt run out on you.) You will if I make you. Just watch me.

Dorris dances. She forgets her tricks. She dances.

Glorious songs are the muscles of her limbs.

And her singing is of canebrake loves and mangrove feastings.

The walls press in, singing. Flesh of a throbbing body, they press close to John and Dorris. They close them in. John's heart beats tensely against her dancing body. Walls press his mind within his heart. And then, the shaft of light goes out the window high above him. John's mind sweeps up to follow it. Mind pulls him upward into dream. Dorris dances. . . John dreams:

> Dorris is dressed in a loose black gown splashed with lemon ribbons. Her feet taper long and slim from trim ankles. She waits for him just inside the stage door. John, collar and tie colorful and flaring, walks towards the stage door. There are no trees in the alley. But his feet feel as though they step on autumn leaves whose rustle has been pressed

---

2. A piano player.

out of them by the passing of a million satin slippers. The air is sweet with roasting chestnuts, sweet with bonfires of old leaves. John's melancholy is a deep thing that seals all senses but his eyes, and makes him whole.

Dorris knows that he is coming. Just at the right moment she steps from the door, as if there were no door. Her face is tinted like the autumn alley. Of old flowers, or of a southern canefield, her perfume. "Glorious Dorris." So his eyes speak. And their sadness is too deep for sweet untruth. She barely touches his arm. They glide off with footfalls softened on the leaves, the old leaves powdered by a million satin slippers.

They are in a room. John knows nothing of it. Only, that the flesh and blood of Dorris are its walls. Singing walls. Lights, soft, as if they shine through clear pink fingers. Soft lights, and warm.

John reaches for a manuscript of his, and reads. Dorris, who has no eyes, has eyes to understand him. He comes to a dancing scene. The scene is Dorris. She dances. Dorris dances. Glorious Dorris. Dorris whirls, whirls, dances. . . .

Dorris dances. The pianist crashes a bumper chord. The whole stage claps. Dorris, flushed, looks quick at John. His whole face is in shadow. She seeks for her dance in it. She finds it a dead thing in the shadow which is his dream. She rushes from the stage. Falls down the steps into her dressing-room. Pulls her hair. Her eyes, over a floor of tears, stare at the whitewashed ceiling. (Smell of dry paste, and paint, and soiled clothing.) Her pal comes in. Dorris flings herself into the old safe arms, and cries bitterly.

"I told you nothin doing," is what Mame says to comfort her.

Questions

1. State the nature of the conflict in John. **2.** How does Toomer achieve dramatic conflict between John and Dorris even though they do not speak to each other? **3.** How does the opening paragraph establish the mood and the values of the story?

Dry September

WILLIAM FAULKNER [1897–1962]

I

THROUGH the bloody September twilight, aftermath of sixty-two rainless days, it had gone like a fire in dry grass—the rumor, the story, whatever it was. Something about Miss Minnie Cooper and a Negro. Attacked, insulted, frightened: none of them, gathered in the barber shop on that Saturday evening where the ceiling fan stirred, without freshening it, the vitiated air, sending back upon them, in recurrent surges of stale pomade and lotion, their own stale breath and odors, knew exactly what had happened.

"Except it wasn't Will Mayes," a barber said. He was a man of middle age; a thin, sand-colored man with a mild face, who was shaving a client. "I know Will Mayes. He's a good nigger. And I know Miss Minnie Cooper, too."

"What do you know about her?" a second barber said.

"Who is she?" the client said. "A young girl?"

"No," the barber said. "She's about forty, I reckon. She aint married. That's why I dont believe—"

"Believe, hell!" a hulking youth in a sweat-stained silk shirt said. "Wont you take a white woman's word before a nigger's?"

"I dont believe Will Mayes did it," the barber said. "I know Will Mayes."

"Maybe you know who did it, then. Maybe you already got him out of town, you damn niggerlover."

"I dont believe anybody did anything. I dont believe anything happened. I leave it to you fellows if them ladies that get old without getting married dont have notions that a man cant—"

"Then you are a hell of a white man," the client said. He moved under the cloth. The youth had sprung to his feet.

"You dont?" he said. "Do you accuse a white woman of lying?"

The barber held the razor poised above the half-risen client. He did not look around.

"It's this durn weather," another said. "It's enough to make a man do anything. Even to her."

Nobody laughed. The barber said in his mild, stubborn tone: "I aint accusing nobody of nothing. I just know and you fellows know how a woman that never—"

"You damn niggerlover!" the youth said.

"Shut up, Butch," another said. "We'll get the facts in plenty of time to act."

"Who is? Who's getting them?" the youth said. "Facts, hell! I—"

"You're a fine white man," the client said. "Aint you?" In his frothy beard he looked like a desert rat in the moving pictures. "You tell them, Jack," he said to the youth. "If there aint any white men in this town, you can count on me, even if I aint only a drummer and a stranger."

"That's right, boys," the barber said. "Find out the truth first. I know Will Mayes."

"Well, by God!" the youth shouted. "To think that a white man in this town—"

"Shut up, Butch," the second speaker said. "We got plenty of time."

The client sat up. He looked at the speaker. "Do you claim that anything excuses a nigger attacking a white woman? Do you mean to tell me you are a white man and you'll stand for it? You better go back North where you came from. The South dont want your kind here."

"North what?" the second said. "I was born and raised in this town."

"Well, by God!" the youth said. He looked about with a strained, baffled gaze, as if he was trying to remember what it was he wanted to say or to do. He drew his sleeve across his sweating face. "Damn if I'm going to let a white woman—"

"You tell them, Jack," the drummer said. "By God, if they—"

The screen door crashed open. A man stood in the door, his feet apart and his heavy-set body poised easily. His white shirt was open at the throat; he wore a felt hat. His hot, bold glance swept the group. His name was McLendon. He had commanded troops at the front in France and had been decorated for valor.

"Well," he said, "are you going to sit there and let a black son rape a white woman on the streets of Jefferson?"

Butch sprang up again. The silk of his shirt clung flat to his heavy shoulders. At each armpit was a dark halfmoon. "That's what I been telling them! That's what I—"

"Did it really happen?" a third said. "This aint the first man scare she ever had, like Hawkshaw says. Wasn't there something about a man on the kitchen roof, watching her undress, about a year ago?"

"What?" the client said. "What's that?" The barber had been slowly forcing him back into the chair; he arrested himself reclining, his head lifted, the barber still pressing him down.

McLendon whirled on the third speaker. "Happen? What the hell difference does it make? Are you going to let the black sons get away with it until one really does it?"

"That's what I'm telling them!" Butch shouted. He cursed, long and steady, pointless.

"Here, here," a fourth said. "Not so loud. Dont talk so loud."

"Sure," McLendon said; "no talking necessary at all. I've done my talking. Who's with me?" He poised on the balls of his feet, roving his gaze.

The barber held the drummer's face down, the razor poised. "Find out the facts first, boys. I know Willy Mayes. It wasn't him. Let's get the sheriff and do this thing right."

McLendon whirled upon him his furious, rigid face. The barber did not look away. They looked like men of different races. The other barbers had ceased also above their prone clients. "You mean to tell me," McLendon said, "that you'd take a nigger's word before a white woman's? Why, you damn niggerloving—"

The third speaker rose and grasped McLendon's arm; he too had been a soldier, "Now, now. Let's figure this thing out. Who knows anything about what really happened?"

"Figure out hell!" McLendon jerked his arm free. "All that're with me get up from there. The ones that aint—" He roved his gaze, dragging his sleeve across his face.

Three men rose. The drummer in the chair sat up. "Here," he said, jerking at the cloth about his neck; "get this rag off me. I'm with him. I dont live here, but by God, if our mothers and wives and sisters—" He smeared the cloth over his face and flung it to the floor. McLendon stood in the floor and cursed the others. Another rose and moved toward him. The remainder sat uncomfortable, not looking at one another, then one by one they rose and joined him.

The barber picked the cloth from the floor. He began to fold it neatly. "Boys, dont do that. Will Mayes never done it. I know."

"Come on," McLendon said. He whirled. From his hip pocket protruded the butt of a heavy automatic pistol. They went out. The screen door crashed behind them reverberant in the dead air.

The barber wiped the razor carefully and swiftly, and put it away, and ran to the rear, and took his hat from the wall. "I'll be back as soon as I can," he said to the other barbers. "I cant let—" He went out, running. The two other barbers followed him to the door and caught it on the rebound, leaning out and looking up the street after him. The air was flat and dead. It had a metallic taste at the base of the tongue.

"What can he do?" the first said. The second one was saying "Jees Christ, Jees Christ" under his breath. "I'd just as lief be Will Mayes as Hawk, if he gets McLendon riled."

"Jees Christ, Jees Christ," the second whispered.

"You reckon he really done it to her?" the first said.

II

SHE was thirty-eight or thirty-nine. She lived in a small frame house with her invalid mother and a thin, sallow, unflagging aunt, where each morning between ten and eleven she would appear on the porch in a lace-trimmed boudoir cap, to sit swinging in the porch swing until noon. After dinner she lay down for a while, until the afternoon began to cool. Then, in one of the three or four new voile dresses which she had each summer, she would go downtown to spend the afternoon in the stores with the other ladies, where they would handle the goods and haggle over the prices in cold, immediate voices, without any intention of buying.

She was of comfortable people—not the best in Jefferson, but good people enough—and she was still on the slender side of ordinary looking, with a bright, faintly haggard manner and dress. When she was young she had had a slender, nervous body and a sort of hard vivacity which had enabled her for a time to ride upon the crest of the town's social life as exemplified by the high school party and church social period of her contemporaries while still children enough to be unclassconscious.

She was the last to realize that she was losing ground; that those among whom she had been a little brighter and louder flame than any other were beginning to learn the pleasure of snobbery—male—and retaliation—female. That was when her face began to wear that bright, haggard look. She still carried it to parties on shadowy porticoes and summer lawns, like a mask or a flag, with that bafflement of furious repudiation of truth in her eyes. One evening at a party she heard a boy and two girls, all schoolmates, talking. She never accepted another invitation.

She watched the girls with whom she had grown up as they married and got homes and children, but no man ever called on her steadily until the children of the other girls had been calling her "aunty" for several years, the while their mothers told them in bright voices about how popular Aunt Minnie had been as a girl. Then the town began to see her driving on Sunday afternoons with the cashier in the bank. He was a widower of about forty—a high-colored man, smelling always faintly of the barber shop or of whisky. He owned the first automobile in town, a red runabout; Minnie had the first motoring bonnet and veil the town ever saw. Then the town began to say: "Poor Minnie." "But she is old enough to take care of herself," others said. That was when she began to ask her old schoolmates that their children call her "cousin" instead of "aunty."

It was twelve years now since she had been relegated into adultery by public opinion, and eight years since the cashier had gone to a Memphis bank, returning for one day each Christmas, which he spent at an annual bachelors' party at a hunting club on the river. From behind their curtains the neighbors would see the party pass, and during the over-the-way Christmas day visiting they would tell her about him, about how well he looked, and how they heard that he was prospering in the city, watching with bright, secret eyes her haggard, bright face. Usually by that hour there would be the scent of whisky on her breath. It was supplied her by a youth, a clerk at the soda fountain: "Sure; I buy it for the old gal. I reckon she's entitled to a little fun."

Her mother kept to her room altogether now; the gaunt aunt ran the house. Against that background Minnie's bright dresses, her idle and empty days, had a quality of furious unreality. She went out in the evenings only with women now, neighbors, to the moving pictures. Each afternoon she dressed in one of the new dresses and went downtown alone, where her young "cousins" were already strolling in the late afternoons with their delicate, silken heads and thin, awkward arms and conscious hips, clinging to one another or shrieking and giggling with paired boys in the soda fountain when she passed and went on along the serried store fronts, in the doors of which the sitting and lounging men did not even follow her with their eyes any more.

III

THE barber went swiftly up the street where the sparse lights, insect-swirled, glared in rigid and violent suspension in the lifeless air. The day had died in a pall of dust; above the darkened square, shrouded by the spent dust, the sky was as clear as the inside of a brass bell. Below the east was a rumor of the twice-waxed moon.

When he overtook them McLendon and three others were getting into a car parked in an alley. McLendon stooped his thick head, peering out beneath the top. "Changed your mind, did you?" he said. "Damn good thing; by God, tomorrow when this town hears about how you talked tonight—"

"Now, now," the other ex-soldier said. "Hawkshaw's all right. Come on, Hawk; jump in."

"Will Mayes never done it, boys," the barber said. "If anybody done it. Why, you all know well as I do there aint any town where they got better niggers than us. And you know how a lady will kind of think things about men when there aint any reason to, and Miss Minnie anyway—"

"Sure, sure," the soldier said. "We're just going to talk to him a little; that's all."

"Talk hell!" Butch said. "When we're through with the—"

"Shut up, for God's sake!" the soldier said. "Do you want everybody in town—"

"Tell them, by God!" McLendon said. "Tell every one of the sons that'll let a white woman—"

"Let's go; let's go: here's the other car." The second car slid squealing out of a cloud of dust at the alley mouth. McLendon started his car and took the lead. Dust lay like fog in the street. The street lights hung nimbused as in water. They drove on out of town.

A rutted lane turned at right angles. Dust hung above it too, and above all the land. The dark bulk of the ice plant, where the Negro Mayes was night watchman, rose against the sky. "Better stop here, hadn't we?" the soldier said. McLendon did not reply. He hurled the car up and slammed to a stop, the headlights glaring on the blank wall.

"Listen here, boys," the barber said; "if he's here, dont that prove he never done it? Dont it? If it was him, he would run. Dont you see he would?" The second car came up and stopped. McLendon got down; Butch sprang down beside him. "Listen, boys," the barber said.

"Cut the lights off!" McLendon said. The breathless dark rushed down. There was no sound in it save their lungs as they sought air in the parched dust in which for two months they had lived; then the diminishing crunch of McLendon's and Butch's feet, and a moment later McLendon's voice:

"Will! . . . Will!"

Below the east the wan hemorrhage of the moon increased. It heaved above the ridge, silvering the air, the dust, so that they seemed to breathe, live, in a bowl of molten lead. There was no sound of nightbird nor insect, no sound save their breathing and a faint ticking of contracting metal about the cars. Where their bodies touched one another they seemed to sweat dryly, for no more moisture came. "Christ!" a voice said; "let's get out of here."

But they didn't move until vague noises began to grow out of the darkness ahead; then they got out and waited tensely in the breathless dark. There was another sound: a blow, a hissing expulsion of breath and McLendon cursing in undertone. They stood a moment longer, then they ran forward. They ran in a stumbling clump, as though they were fleeing something. "Kill him, kill the son," a voice whispered. McLendon flung them back.

"Not here," he said. "Get him into the car." "Kill him, kill the black son!" the voice murmured. They dragged the Negro to the car. The barber had waited beside the car. He could feel himself sweating and he knew he was going to be sick at the stomach.

"What is it, captains?" the Negro said. "I aint done nothing. 'Fore God, Mr John." Someone produced handcuffs. They worked busily about the Negro as though he were a post, quiet, intent, getting in one another's way. He submitted to the handcuffs, looking swiftly and constantly from dim face to dim face. "Who's here, captains?" he said, leaning to peer into the faces until they could feel his breath and smell his sweaty reek. He spoke a name or two. "What you all say I done, Mr John?"

McLendon jerked the car door open. "Get in!" he said.

The Negro did not move. "What you all going to do with me, Mr John? I aint done nothing. White folks, captains, I aint done nothing: I swear 'fore God." He called another name.

"Get in!" McLendon said. He struck the Negro. The others expelled their breath in a dry hissing and struck him with random blows and he whirled and cursed them, and swept his manacled hands across their faces and slashed the barber upon the mouth, and the barber struck him also. "Get him in there," McLendon said. They pushed at him. He ceased struggling and got in and sat quietly as the others took their places. He sat between the barber and the soldier, drawing his limbs in so as not to touch them, his eyes going swiftly and constantly from face to face. Butch clung to the running board. The car moved on. The barber nursed his mouth with his handkerchief.

"What's the matter, Hawk?" the soldier said.

"Nothing," the barber said. They regained the highroad and turned away from town. The second car dropped back out of the dust. They went on, gaining speed; the final fringe of houses dropped behind.

"Goddamn, he stinks!" the soldier said.

"We'll fix that," the drummer in front beside McLendon said. On the running board Butch cursed into the hot rush of air. The barber leaned suddenly forward and touched McLendon's arm.

"Let me out, John," he said.

"Jump out, niggerlover," McLendon said without turning his head. He drove swiftly. Behind them the sourceless lights of the second car glared in the dust. Presently McLendon turned into a narrow road. It was rutted with disuse. It led back to an abandoned brick kiln—a series of reddish mounds and weed- and vine-choked vats without bottom. It had been used for pasture once, until one day the owner missed one of his mules. Although he prodded carefully in the vats with a long pole, he could not even find the bottom of them.

"John," the barber said.

"Jump out, then," McLendon said, hurling the car along the ruts. Beside the barber the Negro spoke:

"Mr Henry."

The barber sat forward. The narrow tunnel of the road rushed up and past. Their motion was like an extinct furnace blast: cooler, but utterly dead. The car bounded from rut to rut.

"Mr Henry," the Negro said.

The barber began to tug furiously at the door. "Look out, there!" the soldier said, but the barber had already kicked the door open and swung onto the running board. The soldier leaned across the Negro and grasped at him, but he had already jumped. The car went on without checking speed.

The impetus hurled him crashing through dust-sheathed weeds, into the ditch. Dust puffed about him, and in a thin, vicious crackling of sapless stems he lay choking and retching until the second car passed and died away. Then he rose and limped on until he reached the highroad and turned toward town, brushing at his clothes with his hands. The moon was higher, riding high and clear of the dust at last, and after a while the town began to glare beneath the dust. He went on, limping. Presently he heard cars and the glow of them grew in the dust behind him and he left the road and crouched again in the weeds until they passed. McLendon's car came last now. There were four people in it and Butch was not on the running board.

They went on; the dust swallowed them; the glare and the sound died away. The dust of them hung for a while, but soon the eternal dust absorbed it again. The barber climbed back onto the road and limped on toward town.

IV

As she dressed for supper on that Saturday evening, her own flesh felt like fever. Her hands trembled among the hooks and eyes, and her eyes had a feverish look, and her hair swirled crisp and crackling under the comb.

While she was still dressing the friends called for her and sat while she donned her sheerest underthings and stockings and a new voile dress. "Do you feel strong enough to go out?" they said, their eyes bright too, with a dark glitter. "When you have had time to get over the shock, you must tell us what happened. What he said and did; everything."

In the leafed darkness, as they walked toward the square, she began to breathe deeply, something like a swimmer preparing to dive, until she ceased trembling, the four of them walking slowly because of the terrible heat and out of solicitude for her. But as they neared the square she began to tremble again, walking with her head up, her hands clenched at her sides, their voices about her murmurous, also with that feverish, glittering quality of their eyes.

They entered the square, she in the center of the group, fragile in her fresh dress. She was trembling worse. She walked slower and slower, as children eat ice cream, her head up and her eyes bright in the haggard banner of her face, passing the hotel and the coatless drummers in chairs along the curb looking around at her: "That's the one: see? The one in pink in the middle." "Is that her? What did they do with the nigger? Did they—?" "Sure. He's all right." "All right, is he?" "Sure. He went on a little trip." Then the drug store, where even the young men lounging in the doorway tipped their hats and followed with their eyes the motion of her hips and legs when she passed.

They went on, passing the lifted hats of the gentlemen, the suddenly ceased voices, deferent, protective. "Do you see?" the friends said. Their voices sounded like long, hovering sighs of hissing exultation. "There's not a Negro on the square. Not one."

They reached the picture show. It was like a miniature fairyland with its lighted lobby and colored lithographs of life caught in its terrible and beautiful mutations. Her lips began to tingle. In the dark, when the picture began, it would be all right; she could hold back the laughing so it would not waste away so fast and so soon. So she hurried on before the turning faces, the undertones of low astonishment, and they took their accustomed places where she could see the aisle against the silver glare and the young men and girls coming in two and two against it.

The lights flicked away; the screen glowed silver, and soon life began to unfold, beautiful and passionate and sad, while still the young men and girls entered, scented and sibilant in the half dark, their paired backs in silhouette delicate and sleek, their slim, quick bodies awkward, divinely young, while beyond them the silver dream accumulated, inevitably on and on. She began to laugh. In trying to suppress it, it made more noise than ever; heads began to turn. Still laughing, her friends raised her and led her out, and she stood at the curb, laughing on a high, sustained note, until the taxi came up and they helped her in.

They removed the pink voile and the sheer underthings and the stockings, and put her to bed, and cracked ice for her temples, and sent for the doctor. He was hard to locate, so they ministered to her with hushed ejaculations, renewing the ice and fanning her. While the ice was fresh and cold she stopped laughing and lay still for a time, moaning only a little. But soon the laughing welled again and her voice rose screaming.

"Shhhhhhhhhhh! Shhhhhhhhhhhhhhh!" they said, freshening the ice-pack, smoothing her hair, examining it for gray; "poor girl!" Then to one another: "Do you suppose anything really happened?" their eyes darkly aglitter, secret and passionate. "Shhhhhhhhhh! Poor girl! Poor Minnie!"

V

IT was midnight when McLendon drove up to his neat new house. It was trim and fresh as a birdcage and almost as small, with its clean, green-and-white paint. He locked the car and mounted the porch and entered. His wife rose from a chair beside the reading lamp. McLendon stopped in the floor and stared at her until she looked down.

"Look at that clock," he said, lifting his arm, pointing. She stood before him, her face lowered, a magazine in her hands. Her face was pale, strained, and weary-looking. "Haven't I told you about sitting up like this, waiting to see when I come in?"

"John," she said. She laid the magazine down. Poised on the balls of his feet, he glared at her with his hot eyes, his sweating face.

"Didn't I tell you?" He went toward her. She looked up then. He caught her shoulder. She stood passive, looking at him.

"Don't, John. I couldn't sleep ... The heat; something. Please, John. You're hurting me."

"Didn't I tell you?" He released her and half struck, half flung her across the chair, and she lay there and watched him quietly as he left the room.

He went on through the house, ripping off his shirt, and on the dark, screened porch at the rear he stood and mopped his head and shoulders with the shirt and flung it away. He took the pistol from his hip and laid it on the table beside the bed, and sat on the bed and removed his shoes, and rose and slipped his trousers off. He was sweating again already, and he stooped and hunted furiously for the shirt. At last he found it and wiped his body again, and, with his body pressed against the dusty screen, he stood panting. There was no movement, no sound, not even an insect. The dark world seemed to lie stricken beneath the cold moon and the lidless stars.

Going to Meet the Man

JAMES BALDWIN [b. 1924]

W HAT'S the matter?" she asked.

"I don't know," he said, trying to laugh, "I guess I'm tired."

"You've been working too hard," she said. "I keep telling you."

"Well, goddammit, woman," he said, "it's not my fault!" He tried again; he wretchedly failed again. Then he just lay there, silent, angry, and helpless. Excitement filled him just like a toothache, but it refused to enter his flesh. He stroked her breast. This was his wife. He could not ask her to do just a little thing for him, just to help him out, just for a little while, the way he could ask a nigger girl to do it. He lay there, and he sighed. The image of a black girl caused a distant excitement in him, like a far-away light; but, again, the excitement was more like pain; instead of forcing him to act, it made action impossible.

"Go to sleep," she said, gently, "you got a hard day tomorrow."

"Yeah," he said, and rolled over on his side, facing her, one hand still on one breast. "Goddamn the niggers. The black stinking coons. You'd think they'd learn. Wouldn't you think they'd learn? I mean, *wouldn't* you?"

"They going to be out there tomorrow," she said, and took his hand away, "get some sleep."

He lay there, one hand between his legs, staring at the frail sanctuary of his wife. A faint light came from the shutters; the moon was full. Two dogs, far away, were barking at each other, back and forth, insistently, as though they were agreeing to make an appointment. He heard a car coming north on the road and he half sat up, his hand reaching for his holster, which was on a chair near the bed, on top of his pants. The lights hit the shutters and seemed to travel across the room and then went out. The sound of the car slipped away, he heard it hit gravel, then heard it no more. Some liver-lipped students, probably, heading back to that college—but coming from where? His watch said it was two in the morning. They could be coming from anywhere, from out of state most likely, and they would be at the court-house tomorrow. The niggers were getting ready. Well, they would be ready, too.

He moaned. He wanted to let whatever was in him out; but it wouldn't come out. Goddamn! he said aloud, and turned again, on his side, away from Grace, staring at the shutters. He was a big, healthy man and he had never had any trouble sleeping. And he wasn't old enough yet to have any trouble getting it up—he was only forty-two. And he was a good man, a God-fearing man, he had tried to do his duty all his life, and he had been a deputy sheriff for several years. Nothing had ever bothered him before, certainly not getting it up. Sometimes, sure, like any other man, he knew that he wanted a little more spice than Grace could give him and he would drive over yonder and pick up a black piece or arrest her, it came to the same thing, but he couldn't do that now, no more. There was no telling what might happen once your ass was in the air. And they were low enough to kill a man then, too, everyone of them, or the girl herself might do it, right while she was making believe you made her feel so good. The niggers. What had the good Lord Almighty had in mind when he made the niggers? Well. They were pretty good at that, all right. Damn. Damn. Goddamn.

This wasn't helping him to sleep. He turned again, toward Grace again, and moved close to her warm body. He felt something he had never felt before. He felt that he would like to hold her, hold her, hold her, and be buried in her like a child and never have to get up in the morning again and go downtown to face those faces, good Christ, they were ugly! and never have to enter that jail house again and smell that smell and hear that singing; never again feel that filthy, kinky, greasy hair under his hand, never again watch those black breasts leap against the leaping cattle prod, never hear those moans again or watch that blood run down or the fat lips split or the sealed eyes struggle open. They were animals, they were no better than animals, what could be done with people like that? Here they had been in a civilized country for years and they still lived like animals. Their houses were dark, with oil cloth or cardboard in the windows, the smell was enough to make you puke your guts out, and there they sat, a whole tribe, pumping out kids, it looked like, every damn five minutes, and laughing and talking and playing music like they didn't have a care in the world, and he reckoned they didn't, neither, and coming to the door, into the sunlight, just standing there, just looking foolish, not thinking of anything but just getting back to what they were doing, saying, Yes suh, Mr. Jesse. I surely will, Mr. Jesse. Fine weather, Mr. Jesse. Why, I thank you, Mr. Jesse. He had worked for a mail-order house for a while and it had been his job to collect the payments for the stuff they bought. They were too dumb to know that they were being cheated blind, but that was no skin off his ass—he was just supposed to do his job. They would be late—they didn't have the sense to put money aside; but it was easy to scare them, and he never really had any trouble. Hell, they all liked him, the kids used to smile when he came to the door. He gave them candy, sometimes, or chewing gum, and rubbed their rough bullet heads—maybe the candy should have been poisoned. Those kids were grown now. He had had trouble with one of them today.

"There was this nigger today," he said; and stopped; his voice sounded peculiar. He touched Grace. "You awake?" he asked. She mumbled something, impatiently, she was probably telling him to go to sleep. It was all right. He knew that he was not alone.

"What a funny time," he said, "to be thinking about a thing like that— you listening?" She mumbled something again. He rolled over on his back. "This nigger's one of the ringleaders. We had trouble with him before. We must have had him out there at the work farm three or four times. Well, Big Jim C. and some of the boys really had to whip that nigger's ass today." He looked over at Grace; he could not tell whether she was listening or not; and he was afraid to ask again. "They had this line you know, to register"—he laughed, but she did not—"and they wouldn't stay where Big Jim C. wanted them, no, they had to start blocking traffic all around the court house so couldn't nothing or nobody get through, and Big Jim C. told them to disperse and they wouldn't move, they just kept up that singing, and Big Jim C. figured that the others would move if this nigger would move, him being the ring-leader, but he wouldn't move and he wouldn't let the others move, so they had to beat him and a couple of the others and they threw them in the wagon —but *I* didn't see this nigger till I got to the jail. They were still singing and I was supposed to make them stop. Well, I couldn't make them stop for me but I knew he could make them stop. He was lying on the ground jerking and moaning, they had threw him in a cell by himself, and blood was coming out his ears from where Big Jim C. and his boys had whipped him. Wouldn't you think they'd learn? I put the prod to him and he jerked some more and he kind of screamed—but he didn't have much voice left. "You make them stop that singing," I said to him, "you hear me? You make them stop that singing." He acted like he didn't hear me and I put it to him again, under his arms, and he just rolled around on the floor and blood started coming from his mouth. He'd pissed his pants already." He paused. His mouth felt dry and his throat was as rough as sandpaper; as he talked, he began to hurt all over with that peculiar excitement which refused to be released. "You all are going to stop your singing, I said to him, and you are going to stop coming down to the court house and disrupting traffic and molesting the people and keeping us from our duties and keeping doctors from getting to sick white women and getting all them Northerners in this town to give our town a bad name—!" As he said this, he kept prodding the boy, sweat pouring from beneath the helmet he had not yet taken off. The boy rolled around in his own dirt and water and blood and tried to scream again as the prod hit his testicles, but the scream did not come out, only a kind of rattle and a moan. He stopped. He was not supposed to kill the nigger. The cell was filled with a terrible odor. The boy was still. "You hear me?" he called. "You had enough?" The singing went on. "You had enough?" His foot leapt out, he had not known it was going to, and caught the boy flush on the jaw. *Jesus*, he thought, *this ain't no nigger, this is a goddamn bull*, and he screamed again, "You had enough? You going to make them stop that singing now?"

But the boy was out. And now he was shaking worse than the boy had been shaking. He was glad no one could see him. At the same time, he felt very close to a very peculiar, particular joy; something deep in him and deep in his memory was stirred, but whatever was in his memory eluded him. He took off his helmet. He walked to the cell door.

"White man," said the boy, from the floor, behind him.

He stopped. For some reason, he grabbed his privates.

"You remember Old Julia?"

The boy said, from the floor, with his mouth full of blood, and one eye, barely open, glaring like the eye of a cat in the dark, "My grandmother's name was Mrs. Julia Blossom. *Mrs.* Julia Blossom. You going to call our women by their right names yet.—And those kids ain't going to stop singing. We going to keep on singing until every one of you miserable white mothers go stark raving out of your minds. Then he closed the one eye; he spat blood; his head fell back against the floor.

He looked down at the boy, whom he had been seeing, off and on, for more than a year, and suddenly remembered him: Old Julia had been one of his mail-order customers, a nice old woman. He had not seen her for years, he supposed that she must be dead.

He had walked into the yard, the boy had been sitting in a swing. He had smiled at the boy, and asked, "Old Julia home?"

The boy looked at him for a long time before he answered. "Don't no Old Julia live here."

"This is her house. I know her. She's lived here for years."

The boy shook his head. "You might know a Old Julia someplace else, white man. But don't nobody by that name live here."

He watched the boy; the boy watched him. The boy certainly wasn't more than ten. *White man.* He didn't have time to be fooling around with some crazy kid. He yelled, "Hey! Old Julia!"

But only silence answered him. The expression on the boy's face did not change. The sun beat down on them both, still and silent; he had the feeling that he had been caught up in a nightmare, a nightmare dreamed by a child; perhaps one of the nightmares he himself had dreamed as a child. It had that feeling—everything familiar, without undergoing any other change, had been subtly and hideously displaced: the trees, the sun, the patches of grass in the yard, the leaning porch and the weary porch steps and the cardboard in the windows and the black hole of the door which looked like the entrance to a cave, and the eyes of the pickaninny, all, all, were charged with malevolence. *White man.* He looked at the boy. "She's gone out?"

The boy said nothing.

"Well," he said, "tell her I passed by and I'll pass by next week." He started to go; he stopped. "You want some chewing gum?"

The boy got down from the swing and started for the house. He said, "I don't want nothing you got, white man." He walked into the house and closed the door behind him.

Now the boy looked as though he were dead. Jesse wanted to go over to him and pick him up and pistol whip him until the boy's head burst open like a melon. He began to tremble with what he believed was rage, sweat, both cold and hot, raced down his body, the singing filled him as though it were a weird, uncontrollable, monstrous howling rumbling up from the depths of his own belly, he felt an icy fear rise in him and raise him up, and he shouted, he howled, "You lucky we *pump* some white blood into you every once in a while—your women! Here's what I got for all the black bitches in the world—!" Then he was, abruptly, almost too weak to stand; to his bewilderment, his horror, beneath his own fingers, he felt himself violently stiffen—with no warning at all; he dropped his hands and he stared at the boy and he left the cell.

"All that singing they do," he said. "All that singing." He could not remember the first time he had heard it; he had been hearing it all his life. It was the sound with which he was most familiar—though it was also the sound of which he had been least conscious—and it had always contained an obscure comfort. They were singing to God. They were singing for mercy and they hoped to go to heaven, and he had even sometimes felt, when looking into the eyes of some of the old women, a few of the very old men, that they were singing for mercy for his soul, too. Of course he had never thought of their heaven or of what God was, or could be, for them; God was the same for everyone, he supposed, and heaven was where good people went—he supposed. He had never thought much about what it meant to be a good person. He tried to be a good person and treat everybody right: it wasn't his fault if the niggers had taken it into their heads to fight against God and go against the rules laid down in the Bible for everyone to read! Any preacher would tell you that. He was only doing his duty: protecting white people from the niggers and the niggers from themselves. And there were still lots of good niggers around—he had to remember that; they weren't all like that boy this afternoon; and the good niggers must be mighty sad to see what was happening to their people. They would thank him when this was over. In that way they had, the best of them, not quite looking him in the eye, in a low voice, with a little smile: We surely thanks you, Mr. Jesse. From the bottom of our hearts, we thanks you. He smiled. They hadn't all gone crazy. This trouble would pass.—He knew that the young people had changed some of the words to the songs. He had scarcely listened to the words before and he did not listen to them now; but he knew that the words were different; he could hear that much. He did not know if the faces were different, he had never, before this trouble began, watched them as they sang, but he certainly did not like what he saw now. They hated him, and this hatred was blacker than their hearts, blacker than their skins, redder than their blood, and harder, by far, then his club. Each day, each night, he felt worn out, aching, with their smell in his nostrils and filling his lungs, as though he were drowning—drowning in niggers; and it was all to be done again when he awoke. It would never end. It would never end. Perhaps this was what the singing had meant all along. They had not been singing black folks into heaven, they had been singing white folks into hell.

Everyone felt this black suspicion in many ways, but no one knew how to express it. Men much older than he, who had been responsible for law and order much longer than he, were now much quieter than they had been, and the tone of their jokes, in a way that he could not quite put his finger on, had changed. These men were his models, they had been friends to his father, and they had taught him what it meant to be a man. He looked to them for courage now. It wasn't that he didn't know that what he was doing was right—he knew that, nobody had to tell him that; it was only that he missed the ease of former years. But they didn't have much time to hang out with each other these days. They tended to stay close to their families every free minute because nobody knew what might happen next. Explosions rocked the night of their tranquil town. Each time each man wondered silently if perhaps this time the dynamite had not fallen into the wrong hands. They thought that they knew where all the guns were; but they could not possibly know every move that was made in that secret place where the darkies lived. From time to time it was suggested that they form a posse and search the home of every nigger, but they hadn't done it yet. For one thing, this might have brought the bastards from the North down on their backs; for another, although the niggers were scattered throughout the town—down in the hollow near the railroad tracks, way west near the mills, up on the hill, the well-off ones, and some out near the college—nothing seemed to happen in one part of town without the niggers immediately knowing it in the other. This meant that they could not take them by surprise. They rarely mentioned it, but they *knew* that some of the niggers had guns. It stood to reason, as they said, since, after all, some of them had been in the Army. There were niggers in the Army right now and God knows they wouldn't have had any trouble stealing this half-assed government blind—the whole world was doing it, look at the European countries and all those countries in Africa. They made jokes about it—bitter jokes; and they cursed the government in Washington, which had betrayed them; but they had not yet formed a posse. Now, if their town had been laid out like some towns in the North, where all the niggers lived together in one locality, they could have gone down and set fire to the houses and brought about peace that way. If the niggers had all lived in one place, they could have kept the fire in one place. But the way this town was laid out, the fire could hardly be controlled. It would spread all over town—and the niggers would probably be helping it to spread. Still, from time to time, they spoke of doing it, anyway; so that now there was a real fear among them that somebody might go crazy and light the match.

They rarely mentioned anything not directly related to the war that they were fighting, but this had failed to establish between them the unspoken communication of soldiers during a war. Each man, in the thrilling silence which sped outward from their exchanges, their laughter, and their anecdotes, seemed wrestling, in various degrees of darkness, with a secret which he could not articulate to himself, and which, however directly it related to the war, related yet more surely to his privacy and his past. They could no longer be sure, after all, that they had all done the same things. They had never dreamed that their privacy could contain any element of terror, could threaten, that is, to reveal itself, to the scrutiny of a judgment day, while remaining unreadable and inaccessible to themselves; nor had they dreamed that the past, while certainly refusing to be forgotten, could yet so stubbornly refuse to be remembered. They felt themselves mysteriously set at naught, as no longer entering into the real concerns of other people—while here they were, outnumbered, fighting to save the civilized world. They had thought that people would care—people didn't care; not enough, anyway, to help them. It would have been a help, really, or at least a relief, even to have been forced to surrender. Thus they had lost, probably forever, their old and easy connection with each other. They were forced to depend on each other more and, at the same time, to trust each other less. Who could tell when one of them might not betray them all, for money, or for the ease of confession? But no one dared imagine what there might be to confess. They were soldiers fighting a war, but their relationship to each other was that of accomplices in a crime. They all had to keep their mouths shut.

I stepped in the river at Jordan.

Out of the darkness of the room, out of nowhere, the line came flying up at him, with the melody and the beat. He turned wordlessly toward his sleeping wife. *I stepped in the river at Jordan.* Where had he heard that song?

"Grace," he whispered. "You awake?"

She did not answer. If she was awake, she wanted him to sleep. Her breathing was slow and easy, her body slowly rose and fell.

I stepped in the river at Jordan.
The water came to my knees.

He began to sweat. He felt an overwhelming fear, which yet contained a curious and dreadful pleasure.

I stepped in the river at Jordan.
The water came to my waist.

It had been night, as it was now, he was in the car between his mother and his father, sleepy, his head in his mother's lap, sleepy, and yet full of excitement. The singing came from far away, across the dark fields. There were no lights anywhere. They had said good-bye to all the others and turned off on this dark dirt road. They were almost home.

I stepped in the river at Jordan,
The water came over my head,
I looked way over to the other side,
He was making up my dying bed!

"I guess they singing for him," his father said, seeming very weary and subdued now. "Even when they're sad, they sound like they just about to go and tear off a piece." He yawned and leaned across the boy and slapped his wife lightly on the shoulder, allowing his hand to rest there for a moment. "Don't they?"

"Don't talk that way," she said.

"Well, that's what we going to do," he said, "you can make up your mind to that." He started whistling. "You see? When I begin to feel it, I gets kind of musical, too."

Oh, Lord! Come on and ease my troubling mind!

He had a black friend, his age, eight, who lived nearby. His name was Otis. They wrestled together in the dirt. Now the thought of Otis made him sick. He began to shiver. His mother put her arm around him.

"He's tired," she said.

"We'll be home soon," said his father. He began to whistle again.

"We didn't see Otis this morning," Jesse said. He did not know why he said this. His voice, in the darkness of the car, sounded small and accusing.

"You haven't seen Otis for a couple of mornings," his mother said.

That was true. But he was only concerned about *this* morning.

"No," said his father, "I reckon Otis's folks was afraid to let him show himself this morning."

"But Otis didn't do nothing!" Now his voice sounded questioning.

"Otis *can't* do nothing," said his father, "he's too little." The car lights picked up their wooden house, which now solemnly approached them, the lights falling around it like yellow dust. Their dog, chained to a tree, began to bark.

"We just want to make sure Otis *don't* do nothing," said his father, and stopped the car. He looked down at Jesse. "And you tell him what your Daddy said, you hear?"

"Yes sir," he said.

His father switched off the lights. The dog moaned and pranced, but they ignored him and went inside. He could not sleep. He lay awake, hearing the night sounds, the dog yawning and moaning outside, the sawing of the crickets, the cry of the owl, dogs barking far away, then no sounds at all, just the heavy, endless buzzing of the night. The darkness pressed on his eyelids like a scratchy blanket. He turned, he turned again. He wanted to call his mother, but he knew his father would not like this. He was terribly afraid. Then he heard his father's voice in the other room, low, with a joke in it; but this did not help him, it frightened him more, he knew what was going to happen. He put his head under the blanket, then pushed his head out again, for fear, staring at the dark window. He heard his mother's moan, his father's sigh; he gritted his teeth. Then their bed began to rock. His father's breathing seemed to fill the world.

That morning, before the sun had gathered all its strength, men and women, some flushed and some pale with excitement, came with news.

Jesse's father seemed to know what the news was before the first jalopy stopped in the yard, and he ran out, crying, "They got him, then? They got him?"

The first jalopy held eight people, three men and two women and three children. The children were sitting on the laps of the grown-ups. Jesse knew two of them, the two boys; they shyly and uncomfortably greeted each other. He did not know the girl.

"Yes, they got him," said one of the women, the older one, who wore a wide hat and a fancy, faded blue dress. "They found him early this morning."

"How far had he got?" Jesse's father asked.

"He hadn't got no further than Harkness," one of the men said. "Look like he got lost up there in all them trees—or maybe he just got so scared he couldn't move." They all laughed.

"Yes, and you know it's near a graveyard, too," said the younger woman, and they laughed again.

"Is that where they got him now?" asked Jesse's father.

By this time there were three cars piled behind the first one, with everyone looking excited and shining, and Jesse noticed that they were carrying food. It was like a Fourth of July picnic.

"Yeah, that's where he is," said one of the men, "declare, Jesse, you going to keep us here all day long, answering your damn fool questions. Come on, we ain't got no time to waste."

"Don't bother putting up no food," cried a woman from one of the other cars, "we got enough. Just come on."

"Why, thank you," said Jesse's father, "we be right along, then."

"I better get a sweater for the boy," said his mother, "in case it turns cold."

Jesse watched his mother's thin legs cross the yard. He knew that she also wanted to comb her hair a little and maybe put on a better dress, the dress she wore to church. His father guessed this, too, for he yelled behind her, "Now don't you go trying to turn yourself into no movie star. You just come on." But he laughed as he said this, and winked at the men; his wife was younger and prettier than most of the other women. He clapped Jesse on the head and started pulling him toward the car. "You all go on," he said, "I'll be right behind you. Jesse, you go tie up that there dog while I get this car started."

The cars sputtered and coughed and shook; the caravan began to move; bright dust filled the air. As soon as he was tied up, the dog began to bark. Jesse's mother came out of the house, carrying a jacket for his father and a sweater for Jesse. She had put a ribbon in her hair and had an old shawl around her shoulders.

"Put these in the car, son," she said, and handed everything to him. She bent down and stroked the dog, looked to see if there was water in his bowl, then went back up the three porch steps and closed the door.

"Come on," said his father, "ain't nothing in there for nobody to steal." He was sitting in the car, which trembled and belched. The last car of the caravan had disappeared but the sound of singing floated behind them.

Jesse got into the car, sitting close to his father, loving the smell of the car, and the trembling, and the bright day, and the sense of going on a great and unexpected journey. His mother got in and closed the door and the car began to move. Not until then did he ask, "Where are we going? Are we going on a picnic?"

He had a feeling that he knew where they were going, but he was not sure.

"That's right," his father said, "we're going on a picnic. You won't ever forget *this* picnic—!"

"Are we," he asked, after a moment, "going to see the bad nigger—the one that knocked down old Miss Standish?"

"Well, I reckon," said his mother, "that we *might* see him."

He started to ask, *Will a lot of niggers be there? Will Otis be there?*—but he did not ask his question, to which, in a strange and uncomfortable way, he already knew the answer. Their friends, in the other cars, stretched up the road as far as he could see; other cars had joined them; there were cars behind them. They were singing. The sun seemed, suddenly, very hot, and he was at once very happy and a little afraid. He did not quite understand what was happening, and he did not know what to ask—he had no one to ask. He had grown accustomed, for the solution of such mysteries, to go to Otis. He felt that Otis knew everything. But he could not ask Otis about this. Anyway, he had not seen Otis for two days; he had not seen a black face anywhere for more than two days; and he now realized, as they began chugging up the long hill which eventually led to Harkness, that there were no black faces on the road this morning, no black people anywhere. From the houses in which they lived, all along the road, no smoke curled, no life stirred—maybe one or two chickens were to be seen, that was all. There was no one at the windows, no one in the yard, no one sitting on the porches, and the doors were closed. He had come this road many a time and seen women washing in the yard (there were no clothes on the clotheslines) men working in the fields, children playing in the dust; black men passed them on the road other mornings, other days, on foot, or in wagons, sometimes in cars, tipping their hats, smiling, joking, their teeth a solid white against their skin, their eyes as warm as the sun, the blackness of their skin like dull fire against the white of the blue or the grey of their torn clothes. They passed the nigger church—dead-white, desolate, locked up; and the graveyard, where no one knelt or walked, and he saw no flowers. He wanted to ask, *Where are they? Where are they all?* But he did not dare. As the hill grew steeper, the sun grew colder. He looked at his mother and his father. They looked straight ahead, seeming to be listening to the singing which echoed and echoed in this graveyard silence. They were strangers to him now. They were looking at something he could not see. His father's lips had a strange, cruel curve, he wet his lips from time to time, and swallowed. He was terribly aware of his father's tongue, it was as though he had never seen it before. And his father's body suddenly seemed immense, bigger than a mountain. His eyes, which were grey-green, looked yellow in the sunlight; or at least there was a light in them which he had never seen before. His mother patted her hair and adjusted the ribbon, leaning forward to look into the car mirror. "You look all right," said his father, and laughed. "When that nigger looks at you, he's going to swear he throwed his life away for nothing. Wouldn't be surprised if he don't come back to haunt you." And he laughed again.

The singing now slowly began to cease; and he realized that they were nearing their destination. They had reached a straight, narrow, pebbly road, with trees on either side. The sunlight filtered down on them from a great height, as though they were under-water; and the branches of the trees scraped against the cars with a tearing sound. To the right of them, and beneath them, invisible now, lay the town; and to the left, miles of trees which led to the high mountain range which his ancestors had crossed in order to settle in this valley. Now, all was silent, except for the bumping of the tires against the rocky road, the sputtering of motors, and the sound of a crying child. And they seemed to move more slowly. They were beginning to climb again. He watched the cars ahead as they toiled patiently upward, disappearing into the sunlight of the clearing. Presently, he felt their vehicle also rise, heard his father's changed breathing, the sunlight hit his face, the trees moved away from them, and they were there. As their car crossed the clearing, he looked around. There seemed to be millions, there were certainly hundreds of people in the clearing, staring toward something he could not see. There was a fire. He could not see the flames, but he smelled the smoke. Then they were on the other side of the clearing, among the trees again. His father drove off the road and parked the car behind a great many other cars. He looked down at Jesse.

"You all right?" he asked.

"Yes sir," he said.

"Well, come on, then," his father said. He reached over and opened the door on his mother's side. His mother stepped out first. They followed her into the clearing. At first he was aware only of confusion, of his mother and father greeting and being greeted, himself being handled, hugged, and patted, and told how much he had grown. The wind blew the smoke from the fire across the clearing into his eyes and nose. He could not see over the backs of the people in front of him. The sounds of laughing and cursing and wrath—and something else—rolled in waves from the front of the mob to the back. Those in front expressed their delight at what they saw, and this delight rolled backward, wave upon wave, across the clearing, more acrid than the smoke. His father reached down suddenly and sat Jesse on his shoulders.

Now he saw the fire—of twigs and boxes, piled high; flames made pale orange and yellow and thin as a veil under the steadier light of the sun; grey-blue smoke rolled upward and poured over their heads. Beyond the shifting curtain of fire and smoke, he made out first only a length of gleaming chain, attached to a great limb of the tree; then he saw that this chain bound two black hands together at the wrist, dirty yellow palm facing dirty yellow palm. The smoke poured up; the hands dropped out of sight; a cry went up from the crowd. Then the hands slowly came into view again, pulled upward by the chain. This time he saw the kinky, sweating, bloody head—he had never before seen a head with so much hair on it, hair so black and so tangled that it seemed like another jungle. The head was hanging. He saw the forehead, flat and high, with a kind of arrow of hair in the center, like he had, like his father had; they called it a widow's peak; and the mangled eye brows, the wide nose, the closed eyes, and the glinting eye lashes and the hanging lips, all streaming with blood and sweat. His hands were straight above his head. All his weight pulled downward from his hands; and he was a big man, a bigger man than his father, and black as an African jungle cat, and naked. Jesse pulled upward; his father's hands held him firmly by the ankles. He wanted to say something, he did not know what, but nothing he said could have been heard, for now the crowd roared again as a man stepped forward and put more wood on the fire. The flames leapt up. He thought he heard the hanging man scream, but he was not sure. Sweat was pouring from the hair in his armpits, poured down his sides, over his chest, into his navel and his groin. He was lowered again; he was raised again. Now Jesse knew that he heard him scream. The head went back, the mouth wide open, blood bubbling from the mouth; the veins of the neck jumped out; Jesse clung to his father's neck in terror as the cry rolled over the crowd. The cry of all the people rose to answer the dying man's cry. He wanted death to come quickly. They wanted to make death wait: and it was they who held death, now, on a leash which they lengthened little by little. *What did he do?* Jesse wondered. *What did the man do? What did he do?*—but he could not ask his father. He was seated on his father's shoulders, but his father was far away. There were two older men, friends of his father's, raising and lowering the chain; everyone, indiscriminately, seemed to be responsible for the fire. There was no hair left on the nigger's privates, and the eyes, now, were wide open, as white as the eyes of a clown or a doll. The smoke now carried a terrible odor across the clearing, the odor of something burning which was both sweet and rotten.

He turned his head a little and saw the field of faces. He watched his mother's face. Her eyes were very bright, her mouth was open: she was more beautiful than he had ever seen her, and more strange. He began to feel a joy he had never felt before. He watched the hanging, gleaming body, the most beautiful and terrible object he had ever seen till then. One of his father's friends reached up and in his hands he held a knife: and Jesse wished that he had been that man. It was a long, bright knife and the sun seemed to catch it, to play with it, to caress it—it was brighter than the fire.

And a wave of laughter swept the crowd. Jesse felt his father's hands on his ankles slip and tighten. The man with the knife walked toward the crowd, smiling slightly; as though this were a signal, silence fell; he heard his mother cough. Then the man with the knife walked up to the hanging body. He turned and smiled again. Now there was a silence all over the field. The hanging head looked up. It seemed fully conscious now, as though the fire had burned out terror and pain. The man with the knife took the nigger's privates in his hand, one hand, still smiling, as though he were weighing them. In the cradle of the one white hand, the nigger's privates seemed as remote as meat being weighed in the scales; but seemed heavier, too, much heavier, and Jesse felt his scrotum tighten; and huge, huge, much bigger than his father's, flaccid, hairless, the largest thing he had ever seen till then, and the blackest. The white hand stretched them, cradled them, caressed them. Then the dying man's eyes looked straight into Jesse's eyes—it could not have been as long as a second, but it seemed longer than a year. Then Jesse screamed, and the crowd screamed as the knife flashed, first up, then down cutting the dreadful thing away, and the blood came roaring down. Then the crowd rushed forward, tearing at the body with their hands, with knives, with rocks, with stones, howling and cursing. Jesse's head, of its own weight, fell downward toward his father's head. Someone stepped forward and drenched the body with kerosene. Where the man had been, a great sheet of flame appeared. Jesse's father lowered him to the ground.

"Well, I told you," said his father, "you wasn't never going to forget *this* picnic." His father's face was full of sweat, his eyes were very peaceful. At that moment Jesse loved his father more than he had ever loved him. He felt that his father had carried him through a mighty test, had revealed to him a great secret which would be the key to his life forever.

"I reckon," he said. "I reckon."

Jesse's father took him by the hand and, with his mother a little behind them, talking and laughing with the other women, they walked through the crowd, across the clearing. The black body was on the ground, the chain which had held it was being rolled up by one of his father's friends. Whatever the fire had left undone, the hands and the knives and the stones of the people had accomplished. The head was caved in, one eye was torn out, one ear was hanging. But one had to look carefully to realize this, for it was, now, merely, a black charred object on the black, charred ground. He lay spread-eagled with what had been a wound between what had been his legs.

"They going to leave him here, then?" Jesse whispered.

"Yeah," said his father, "they'll come and get him by and by. I reckon we better get over there and get some of that food before it's all gone."

"I reckon," he muttered now to himself, "I reckon." Grace stirred and touched him on the thigh: the moonlight covered her like glory. Something bubbled up in him, his nature again returned to him. He thought of the boy in the cell; he thought of the man in the fire; he thought of the knife and grabbed himself and stroked himself and a terrible sound, something between a high laugh and a howl, came out of him and dragged his sleeping wife up on one elbow. She stared at him in a moonlight which had now grown cold as ice. He thought of the morning and grabbed her, laughing and crying, crying and laughing, and he whispered, as he stroked her, as he took her, "Come on, sugar, I'm going to do you like a nigger, just like a nigger, come on, sugar, and love me just like you'd love a nigger." He thought of the morning as he labored and she moaned, thought of morning as he labored harder than he ever had before, and before his labors had ended, he heard the first cock crow and the dogs begin to bark, and the sound of tires on the gravel road.

Questions

1. What is Jesse's failure at the beginning of the story? How does it relate to the rest of the story? **2.** Under what circumstances was the young leader of the black demonstrators arrested? Why was he beaten? What does Jesse experience after he beats the prisoner? **3.** Why did the young black leader, as a ten-year-old boy, tell Jesse on one occasion, "Don't no Old Julia live here"? **4.** Why is Jesse so determined to stop the prisoners from singing? **5.** Is Jesse a totally evil and depraved man? Upon what details in the narrative do you base your answer? **6.** Baldwin and Faulkner (in "Dry September") juxtapose murderous violence and sexual excitement. Is that juxtaposition justified? Explain.

POETRY

Bonny Barbara Allan

ANONYMOUS

It was in and about the Martinmas[1] time,
    When the green leaves were a falling,
That Sir John Graeme, in the West Country,
    Fell in love with Barbara Allan.

He sent his man down through the town,
    To the place where she was dwelling:
"O haste and come to my master dear,
    Gin° ye be Barbara Allan."   *if*

O hooly,° hooly rose she up,   *slowly*
    To the place where he was lying,   10
And when she drew the curtain by:
    "Young man, I think you're dying."

"O it's I'm sick, and very, very sick,
    And 'tis a' for Barbara Allan."
"O the better for me ye s'° never be,   *ye shall*
    Though your heart's blood were a-spilling.

"O dinna° ye mind,° young man," said she,   *don't/remember*
    "When ye was in the tavern a drinking,
That ye made the healths gae° round and round,   *go*
    And slighted Barbara Allan?"   20

He turned his face unto the wall,
    And death was with him dealing:
"Adieu, adieu, my dear friends all,
    And be kind to Barbara Allan."

And slowly, slowly raise she up,
    And slowly, slowly left him,
And sighing said, she could not stay,
    Since death of life had reft him.

---

1. November 11.

She had not gane a mile but twa,
    When she heard the dead-bell ringing,
And every jow° that the dead-bell geid,°   30
    It cried, "Woe to Barbara Allan!"   *stroke/gave*

"O mother, mother, make my bed!
    O make it saft and narrow!
Since my love died for me to-day,
    I'll die for him to-morrow."

They Flee from Me

SIR THOMAS WYATT   [1503?–1542]

They flee from me, that sometime did me seek,[2]
With naked foot stalking in my chamber.
I have seen them, gentle, tame, and meek,
That now are wild, and do not remember
That sometime they put themselves in danger
To take bread at my hand; and now they range,
Busily seeking with a continual change.

Thanked be Fortune, it hath been otherwise
Twenty times better; but once in special,
In thin array, after a pleasant guise,   10
When her loose gown from her shoulders did fall,
And she me caught in her arms long and small,°   *slender*
And therewith all sweetly did me kiss
And softly said, "Dear heart, how like you this?"

It was no dream, I lay broad waking.
But all is turned, thorough my gentleness,
Into a strange fashion of forsaking;
And I have leave to go, of her goodness,
And she also to use newfangleness.°   *fickleness*
But since that I so kindely[3] am served,   20
I fain would know what she hath deserved.

1. *"They" in line 1 apparently refers to animals or birds. What creatures do you see and for what might they be a metaphor?* **2.** *What sort of relationship is described in the last stanza? How does the poet feel about it?* **3.** *How does the first stanza serve to introduce the theme of the poem?*

---

2.   That is, formerly pursued me.
3.   That is, served in kind. The pun on the modern meaning of *kindly* is intended.

from

The Faerie Queen

EDMUND SPENSER   [1552?–1599]

74
The whiles some one did chaunt this lovely lay:
    "Ah see, who faire thing doest faine to see
    In springing flowre the image of thy day;
    Ah see the Virgin Rose, how sweetly shee
    Doth first peepe forth with bashfull modestee
    That fairer seemes, the lesse ye see her may
    Lo see soone after, how more bold and free
    Her baréd bosome she doth broad display;
Loe see soone after, how she fades, and falles away.

75
"So passeth, in the passing of a day,
    Of mortall life the leafe, the bud, the flowre,
    Ne more doth flourish after first decay,
    That earst was sought to decke both bed and bowre,
    Of many a Ladie, and many a Paramowre:
    Gather therefore the Rose, whilest yet is prime
    For soone comes age, that will her pride deflowre
    Gather the Rose of love, whilest yet is time,
Whilest loving thou mayst lovéd be with equal crime."

Since There's No Help, Come Let Us Kiss and Part

MICHAEL DRAYTON   [1563–1631]

Since there's no help, come let us kiss and part;
Nay, I have done, you get no more of me,
And I am glad, yea glad with all my heart
That thus so cleanly I myself can free;
Shake hands forever, cancel all our vows,
And when we meet at any time again,
Be it not seen in either of our brows
That we one jot of former love retain.
Now at the last gasp of love's latest breath,

When, his pulse failing, passion speechless lies,   *10*
When faith is kneeling by his bed of death,
And innocence is closing up his eyes,
    Now if thou wouldst, when all have given him over,
    From death to life thou mightst him yet recover.

1. *Describe the scene in lines 9-12. Why is "innocence" described as closing "love's" eyes?* 2. *How might the lady save love from death?*

The Passionate Shepherd
to His Love

CHRISTOPHER MARLOWE [1564–1593]

Come live with me and be my love,
And we will all the pleasures prove
That valleys, groves, hills, and fields,
Woods, or steepy mountain yields.

And we will sit upon the rocks,
Seeing the shepherds feed their flocks,
By shallow rivers to whose falls
Melodious birds sing madrigals.

And I will make thee beds of roses
And a thousand fragrant posies,   *10*
A cap of flowers, and a kirtle°   skirt
Embroidered all with leaves of myrtle;

A gown made of the finest wool
Which from our pretty lambs we pull;
Fair lined slippers for the cold,
With buckles of the purest gold;

A belt of straw and ivy buds,
With coral clasps and amber studs:
And if these pleasures may thee move,
Come live with me, and be my love.   *20*

The shepherds' swains shall dance and sing
For thy delight each May morning:
If these delights thy mind may move,
Then live with me and be my love.

The Nymph's Reply to the Shepherd

SIR WALTER RALEGH [1552?–1618]

If all the world and love were young,
And truth in every shepherd's tongue,
These pretty pleasures might me move
To live with thee and be thy love.

Time drives the flocks from field to fold
When rivers rage and rocks grow cold,
And Philomel° becometh dumb;   *the nightingale*
The rest complains of cares to come.

The flowers do fade, and wanton fields
To wayward winter reckoning yields;   10
A honey tongue, a heart of gall,
Is fancy's spring, but sorrow's fall.

Thy gowns, thy shoes, thy beds of roses,
Thy cap, thy kirtle, and thy posies
Soon break, soon wither, soon forgotten—
In folly ripe, in reason rotten.

Thy belt of straw and ivy buds,
Thy coral clasps and amber studs,
All these in me no means can move
To come to thee and be thy love.   20

But could youth last and love still breed,
Had joys no date° nor age no need,   *end*
Then these delights my mind might move
To live with thee and be thy love.

Sonnets

WILLIAM SHAKESPEARE [1564–1616]

18

Shall I compare thee to a summer's day?
Thou art more lovely and more temperate:
Rough winds do shake the darling buds of May,

And summer's lease hath all too short a date:
Sometime too hot the eye of heaven shines,
And often is his gold complexion dimmed;
And every fair from fair sometimes declines,
By chance or nature's changing course untrimmed;
But thy eternal summer shall not fade,
Nor lose possession of that fair thou ow'st;°   ownest 10
Nor shall death brag thou wander'st in his shade,
When in eternal lines to time thou grow'st:
    So long as men can breathe, or eyes can see,
    So long lives this, and this gives life to thee.

1. *Why does the poet argue that "a summer's day" is an inappropriate metaphor for his beloved?*   **2.** *What is "this" in line 14?*

29

When, in disgrace with fortune and men's eyes,
I all alone beweep my outcast state
And trouble deaf heaven with my bootless cries
And look upon myself and curse my fate,
Wishing me like to one more rich in hope,
Featured like him, like him with friends possessed,
Desiring this man's art and that man's scope,
With what I most enjoy contented least;
Yet in these thoughts myself almost despising,
Haply I think on thee, and then my state,   10
Like to the lark at break of day arising
From sullen earth, sings hymns at heaven's gate;
    For thy sweet love remembered such wealth brings
    That then I scorn to change my state with kings.

129

Th' expense of spirit in a waste of shame
Is lust in action; and till action, lust
Is perjured, murderous, bloody, full of blame,
Savage, extreme, rude, cruel, not to trust;
Enjoyed no sooner but despisèd straight;
Past reason hunted; and no sooner had,
Past reason hated, as a swallowed bait,
On purpose laid to make the taker mad:
Mad in pursuit, and in possession so;
Had, having, and in quest to have, extreme;   10
A bliss in proof,° and proved, a very woe;   experience
Before, a joy proposed; behind, a dream.
    All this the world well knows; yet none knows well
    To shun the heaven that leads men to this hell.

1. *Paraphrase "Th' expense of spirit in a waste of shame / Is lust in action."* **2.** *Describe the sound patterns and metrical variations in lines 3 and 4. What do they contribute to the "sense" of the lines?* **3.** *Explain the paradox in the final couplet.*

130

My mistress' eyes are nothing like the sun;
Coral is far more red than her lips' red;
If snow be white, why then her breasts are dun;
If hairs be wires, black wires grow on her head.
I have seen roses damasked,° red and white,   *variegated*
But no such roses see I in her cheeks;
And in some perfumes is there more delight
Than in the breath that from my mistress reeks.
I love to hear her speak, yet well I know
That music hath a far more pleasing sound;   10
I grant I never saw a goddess go;
My mistress, when she walks, treads on the ground.
    And yet, by heaven, I think my love as rare
    As any she belied with false compare.[4]

I Care Not for These Ladies

THOMAS CAMPION   [1567–1620]

I care not for these ladies,
That must be wooed and prayed:
Give me kind Amaryllis,[5]
The wanton country maid.
Nature art disdaineth,
Her beauty is her own.
    Her when we court and kiss,
    She cries, "Forsooth, let go!"
    But when we come where comfort is,
    She never will say no.   10

If I love Amaryllis,
She gives me fruit and flowers:
But if we love these ladies,
We must give golden showers.
Give them gold, that sell love,
Give me the nut-brown lass,
    Who, when we court and kiss,
    She cries, "Forsooth, let go!"

---

4. That is, as any woman misrepresented with false comparisons.
5. A conventional name for a country girl in pastoral poetry.

But when we come where comfort is,
She never will say no.   20

These ladies must have pillows,
And beds by strangers wrought;
Give me a bower of willows,
Of moss and leaves unbought,
And fresh Amaryllis,
With milk and honey fed;
    Who, when we court and kiss,
    She cries, "Forsooth, let go!"
    But when we come where comfort is,
    She never will say no.   30

The Flea

JOHN DONNE [1572–1631]

Mark but this flea, and mark in this,
How little that which thou deniest me is;
It sucked me first, and now sucks thee,
And in this flea our two bloods mingled be;
Thou know'st that this cannot be said
A sin, nor shame, nor loss of maidenhead,
    Yet this enjoys before it woo,
    And pampered swells with one blood made of two,
    And this, alas, is more than we would do.

Oh stay, three lives in one flea spare,   10
Where we almost, yea more than married, are.
This flea is you and I, and this
Our marriage bed and marriage temple is;
Though parents grudge, and you, we are met,
And cloistered in these living walls of jet,
    Though use° make you apt to kill me   *custom*
    Let not to that, self-murder added be,
    And sacrilege, three sins in killing three.

Cruel and sudden, hast thou since
Purpled thy nail, in blood of innocence?   20
Wherein could this flea guilty be,
Except in that drop which it sucked from thee?
Yet thou triumph'st, and say'st that thou
Find'st not thy self nor me the weaker now;
    'Tis true, then learn how false fears be;
    Just so much honor, when thou yield'st to me,
    Will waste, as this flea's death took life from thee.

A Valediction: Forbidding Mourning

JOHN DONNE   [1572–1631]

As virtuous men pass mildly away,
    And whisper to their souls to go,
Whilst some of their sad friends do say
    The breath goes now, and some say, No;

So let us melt, and make no noise,
    No tear-floods, nor sigh-tempests move,
'Twere profanation of our joys
    To tell the laity our love.

Moving of th' earth° brings harms and fears,   *earthquake*
    Men reckon what it did and meant;   10
But trepidation of the spheres,
    Though greater far, is innocent.[6]

Dull sublunary° lovers' love   *under the moon*
    (Whose soul is sense) cannot admit
Absence, because it doth remove
    Those things which elemented it.

But we by a love so much refined
    That our selves know not what it is,
Inter-assurèd of the mind,
    Care less, eyes, lips, and hands to miss.   20

Our two souls therefore, which are one,
    Though I must go, endure not yet
A breach, but an expansion,
    Like gold to airy thinness beat.

If they be two, they are two so
    As stiff twin compasses are two;
Thy soul, the fixed foot, makes no show
    To move, but doth, if th' other do.

And though it in the center sit,
    Yet when the other far doth roam,   30
It leans and harkens after it,
    And grows erect, as that comes home.

6. The movement of the heavenly spheres is harmless.

Such wilt thou be to me, who must
    Like th' other foot, obliquely run;
Thy firmness makes my circle just,
    And makes me end where I begun.

1. Two kinds of love are described in this poem—spiritual and physical. How does the simile drawn in the first two stanzas help define the differences between them? 2. How does the contrast between earthquakes and the movement of the spheres in stanza three further develop the contrast between the two types of lovers? 3. Explain the comparison between a drawing compass and the lovers in the last three stanzas.

Corinna's Going A-Maying

ROBERT HERRICK [1591–1674]

Get up! get up for shame! the blooming morn
Upon her wings presents the god unshorn.
    See how Aurora[7] throws her fair
    Fresh-quilted colors through the air:
    Get up, sweet slug-a-bed, and see
    The dew bespangling herb and tree.
Each flower has wept and bowed toward the east
Above an hour since, yet you not dressed;
    Nay, not so much as out of bed?
    When all the birds have matins said,   *10*
    And sung their thankful hymns, 'tis sin,
    Nay, profanation to keep in,
Whenas a thousand virgins on this day
Spring, sooner than the lark, to fetch in May.

Rise, and put on your foliage, and be seen
To come forth, like the springtime, fresh and green,
    And sweet as Flora.[8] Take no care
    For jewels for your gown or hair;
    Fear not; the leaves will strew
    Gems in abundance upon you;   *20*
Besides, the childhood of the day has kept,
Against you come, some orient pearls unwept;
    Come and receive them while the light
    Hangs on the dew-locks of the night,
    And Titan° on the eastern hill   *the sun*
    Retires himself, or else stands still

---

7. Aurora is the goddess of the morning. The god unshorn is Apollo, god of the sun.
8. Flora is the goddess of flowers.

Till you come forth. Wash, dress, be brief in praying:
Few beads° are best when once we go a-Maying.   *prayers*

Come, my Corinna, come; and, coming mark
How each field turns a street, each street a park   30
    Made green and trimmed with trees; see how
    Devotion gives each house a bough
    Or branch: each porch, each door ere this,
    An ark, a tabernacle is,
Made up of whitethorn neatly interwove,
As if here were those cooler shades of love.
    Can such delights be in the street
    And open fields, and we not see 't?
    Come, we'll abroad; and let's obey
    The proclamation made for May,   40
And sin no more, as we have done, by staying;
But, my Corinna, come, let's go a-Maying.

There's not a budding boy or girl this day
But is got up and gone to bring in May;
    A deal of youth, ere this, is come
    Back, and with whitethorn laden home.
    Some have dispatched their cakes and cream
    Before that we have left to dream;
And some have wept, and wooed, and plighted troth,
And chose their priest, ere we can cast off sloth.   50
    Many a green-gown° has been given,   *grass-stained gown*
    Many a kiss, both odd and even,
    Many a glance, too, has been sent
    From out the eye, love's firmament;
Many a jest told of the keys betraying
This night, and locks picked; yet we're not a-Maying.

Come, let us go while we are in our prime,
And take the harmless folly of the time.
    We shall grow old apace, and die
    Before we know our liberty.   60
    Our life is short, and our days run
    As fast away as does the sun;
And, as a vapor or a drop of rain
Once lost, can ne'er be found again;
    So when or you or I are made
    A fable, song, or fleeting shade,
    All love, all liking, all delight
    Lies drowned with us in endless night.
Then while time serves, and we are but decaying,
Come, my Corinna, come, let's go a-Maying.   70

1. Note that the poem alludes to pagan and to Christian elements, especially in the first three stanzas. How are these religious allusions used? Does the language introduce an ironic reversal of common Christian attitudes? **2.** Mayday celebrations reflect pagan spring fertility rites designed to ensure increase in crops, herds, and population. Trace the sexual aspects of the Mayday celebration in the poem. Is the poem a frank invitation to sexual union (like Marlowe's "The Passionate Shepherd to His Love"), or does the language of the last stanza raise some questions, by implication, about the claims of the flesh?

Go, Lovely Rose!

EDMUND WALLER   [1606–1687]

    Go, lovely rose!
Tell her that wastes her time and me
    That now she knows,
When I resemble° her to thee,   *compare*
How sweet and fair she seems to be.

    Tell her that's young,
And shuns to have her graces spied,
    That hadst thou sprung
In deserts, where no men abide,
Thou must have uncommended died.   10

    Small is the worth
Of beauty from the light retired;
    Bid her come forth,
Suffer herself to be desired,
And not blush so to be admired.

    Then die! that she
The common fate of all things rare
    May read in thee;
How small a part of time they share
That are so wondrous sweet and fair!   20

Why So Pale and Wan, Fond Lover?

SIR JOHN SUCKLING [1609–1642]

Why so pale and wan, fond lover?
    Prithee, why so pale?
Will, when looking well can't move her,
    Looking ill prevail?
    Prithee, why so pale?

Why so dull and mute, young sinner?
    Prithee, why so mute?
Will, when speaking well can't win her,
    Saying nothing do 't?
    Prithee, why so mute?   10

Quit, quit, for shame; this will not move,
    This cannot take her.
If of herself she will not love,
    Nothing can make her:
    The devil take her!

Out upon It!

SIR JOHN SUCKLING [1609–1642]

Out upon it! I have loved
    Three whole days together;
And am like to love three more,
    If it prove fair weather.

Time shall molt away his wings,
    Ere he shall discover
In the whole wide world again
    Such a constant lover.

But the spite on 't is, no praise
    Is due at all to me: 10
Love with me had made no stays
    Had it any been but she.

Had it any been but she,
  And that very face,
There had been at least ere this
  A dozen dozen in her place.

1. *State the central irony in the poem.* **2.** *Is this poem a compliment to the speaker's beloved? Explain.*

To His Coy Mistress

ANDREW MARVELL [1621–1678]

      Had we but world enough, and time,
This coyness, lady, were no crime.
We would sit down, and think which way
To walk, and pass our long love's day.
Thou by the Indian Ganges' side
Shouldst rubies find; I by the tide
Of Humber would complain. I would
Love you ten years before the flood,
And you should, if you please, refuse
Till the conversion of the Jews.   10
My vegetable love should grow
Vaster than empires and more slow;
An hundred years should go to praise
Thine eyes, and on thy forehead gaze;
Two hundred to adore each breast,
But thirty thousand to the rest;
An age at least to every part,
And the last age should show your heart.
For, lady, you deserve this state,
Nor would I love at lower rate.   20
      But at my back I always hear
Time's wingéd chariot hurrying near;
And yonder all before us lie
Deserts of vast eternity.
Thy beauty shall no more be found,
Nor, in thy marble vault, shall sound
My echoing song; then worms shall try
That long-preserved virginity,
And your quaint honor turn to dust,
And into ashes all my lust: 30
The grave's a fine and private place,
But none, I think, do there embrace.

Now therefore, while the youthful hue
Sits on thy skin like morning dew,
And while thy willing soul transpires
At every pore with instant fires,
Now let us sport us while we may,
And now, like amorous birds of prey,
Rather at once our time devour   39
Than languish in his slow-chapped° power.   *slow-jawed*
Let us roll all our strength and all
Our sweetness up into one ball,
And tear our pleasures with rough strife
Thorough the iron gates of life:
Thus, though we cannot make our sun
Stand still, yet we will make him run.

1. *State the argument of the poem (see II. 1–2, 21–22, 33–34).* **2.** *Compare the figures of speech in the first verse paragraph with those in the last. How do they differ?* **3.** *Characterize the attitude toward life recommended by the poet.*

A Poison Tree

WILLIAM BLAKE [1757–1827]

I was angry with my friend:
I told my wrath, my wrath did end.
I was angry with my foe:
I told it not, my wrath did grow.

And I watered it in fears,
Night & morning with my tears;
And I sunnèd it with smiles,
And with soft deceitful wiles.

And it grew both day and night,
Till it bore an apple bright.   10
And my foe beheld it shine,
And he knew that it was mine,

And into my garden stole,
When the night had veil'd the pole;
In the morning glad I see
My foe outstretched beneath the tree.

1. Is anything gained from the parallel readers might draw between this tree and the tree in the Garden of Eden? Explain. 2. Can you articulate what the "poison" is? 3. Does your own experience verify the first stanza of the poem?

A Red, Red Rose

ROBERT BURNS [1759–1796]

O My Luve's like a red, red rose,
    That's newly sprung in June;
O My Luve's like the melodie
    That's sweetly played in tune.

As fair art thou, my bonnie lass,
    So deep in luve am I;
And I will luve thee still, my dear,
    Till a' the seas gang dry.

Till a' the seas gang dry, my dear,
    And the rocks melt wi' the sun: 10
O I will love thee still, my dear,
    While the sands o' life shall run.

And fare thee weel, my only luve,
    And fare thee weel awhile!
And I will come again, my luve,
    Though it were ten thousand mile.

Written After Swimming from Sestos to Abydos[9]

GEORGE GORDON, LORD BYRON   [1788–1824]

1
If in the month of dark December,
    Leander, who was nightly wont
(What maid will not the tale remember?)
    To cross thy stream, broad Hellespont!

---

9.   Abydos, in Asia, is separated from Sestos, in Greece, by the Hellespont (now called the Dardanelles), a narrow strait of water. In Greek legend, Leander used to swim from Abydos to visit his sweetheart Hero at Sestos. Leander drowned when he made the attempt during a storm. Byron made the swim himself on May 3, 1810, and left this verse record.

2

If, when the wintry tempest roared,
    He sped to Hero, nothing loath,
And thus of old thy current poured,
    Fair Venus! how I pity both!

3

For *me*, degenerate modern wretch,
    Though in the genial month of May,   10
My dripping limbs I faintly stretch,
    And think I've done a feat today.

4

But since he crossed the rapid tide,
    According to the doubtful story,
To woo—and—Lord knows what beside,
    And swam for Love, as I for Glory;

5

'Twere hard to say who fared the best:
    Sad mortals! thus the gods still plague you!
He lost his labor, I my jest;
    For he was drowned, and I've the ague.°   *chills and fever*

Give All to Love

RALPH WALDO EMERSON   [1803–1882]

Give all to love;
Obey thy heart;
Friends, kindred, days,
Estate, good-fame,
Plans, credit and the Muse,—
Nothing refuse.

'T is a brave master;
Let it have scope:
Follow it utterly,
Hope beyond hope: 10
High and more high
It dives into noon,
With wing unspent,

Untold intent;
But it is a god,
Knows its own path
And the outlets of the sky.

It was never for the mean;
It requireth courage stout.
Souls above doubt,   20
Valor unbending,
It will reward,—
They shall return
More than they were,
and ever ascending.

Leave all for love;
Yet, hear me, yet,
One word more thy heart behoved,
One pulse more of firm endeavor,—
Keep thee to-day,   30
To-morrow, forever,
Free as an Arab
Of thy beloved.

Cling with life to the maid;
But when the surprise,
First vague shadow of surmise
Flits across her bosom young,
Of a joy apart from thee,
Free be she, fancy-free;
Nor thou detain her vesture's hem,   40
Nor the palest rose she flung
From her summer diadem.

Though thou loved her as thyself,
As a self of purer clay,
Though her parting dims the day,   45
Stealing grace from all alive;
Heartily know,
When half-gods go,
The gods arrive.

1. *What popular conception of love is implied by the first three stanzas? State the paradox developed by the last three stanzas.*   2. *Explain the last three lines.*

Soliloquy of the Spanish Cloister

ROBERT BROWNING   [1812–1889]

1

Gr-r-r—there go, my heart's abhorrence!
    Water your damned flower-pots, do!
If hate killed men, Brother Lawrence,
    God's blood, would not mine kill you!
What? your myrtle-bush wants trimming?
    Oh, that rose has prior claims—
Needs its leaden vase filled brimming?
    Hell dry you up with its flames!

2

At the meal we sit together:
    Salve tibi!° I must hear   *Hail to thee!*   9
Wise talk of the kind of weather,
    Sort of season, time of year:
Not a plenteous cork-crop: scarcely
    Dare we hope oak-galls,[10] *I doubt:*
What's the Latin name for "parsley"?
    What's the Greek name for Swine's Snout?

3

Whew! We'll have our platter burnished,
    Laid with care on our own shelf!
With a fire-new spoon we're furnished,
    And a goblet for ourself,   20
Rinsed like something sacrificial
    Ere 'tis fit to touch our chaps—
Marked with L for our initial!
    (He-he! There his lily snaps!)

4

Saint, forsooth! While brown Dolores
    Squats outside the Convent bank
With Sanchicha, telling stories,
    Steeping tresses in the tank,
Blue-black, lustrous, thick like horsehairs,
    —Can't I see his dead eye glow,   30
Bright as 'twere a Barbary corsair's?[11]
    (That is, if he'd let it show!)

---

10. Abnormal outgrowths on oak trees, used in the tanning process.
11. North African pirates, renowned for ferocity and lust.

5

When he finishes refection,°   *dinner*
    Knife and fork he never lays
Cross-wise, to my recollection,
    As do I, in Jesu's praise.
I the Trinity illustrate,
    Drinking watered orange-pulp—
In three sips the Arian[12] frustrate;
    While he drains his at one gulp.   40

6

Oh, those melons? If he's able
    We're to have a feast! so nice!
One goes to the Abbot's table,
    All of us get each a slice.
How go on your flowers? None double?
    Not one fruit-sort can you spy?
Strange! And I, too, at such trouble,
    Keep them close-nipped on the sly!

7

There's a great text in Galatians,[13]
    Once you trip on it, entails   50
Twenty-nine distinct damnations,
    One sure, if another fails:
If I trip him just a-dying,
    Sure of heaven as sure can be,
Spin him around and send him flying
    Off to hell, a Manichee?[14]

8

Or, my scrofulous French novel
    On grey paper with blunt type!
Simply glance at it, you grovel
    Hand and foot in Belial's[15] gripe: 60
If I double down its pages
    At the woeful sixteenth print,
When he gathers his greengages,
    Ope a sieve and slip it in't?

---

12. Followers of the heretic Arius (256–336) who denied the doctrine of the Trinity.
13. This probably refers to Galatians 5:15–23 where St. Paul lists a number of "works of the flesh" that lead to damnation.
14. A believer in the Manichean heresy which held that the world was ruled by two equally strong forces—one good, one evil.
15. One of the names of the devil.

9

Or, there's Satan! one might venture
    Pledge one's soul to him, yet leave
Such a flaw in the indenture
    As he'd miss till, past retrieve,
Blasted lay that rose-acacia
    We're so proud of! *Hy, Zy, Hine*[16] . . .   70
'St, there's vespers! *Plena gratiâ*
    Ave, Virgo![17] Gr-r-r—you swine!

1. *Characterize the speaker of this dramatic monologue.* **2.** *Is it possible to characterize Brother Lawrence as well? Can you suggest reasons for the speaker's hatred?* **3.** *Show how the speaker, in his own imprecations and actions, specifically violates each part of the threefold monastic vow of poverty, chastity, and obedience. (See stanzas 3, 4, and 6.)*

Dover Beach[*]

MATTHEW ARNOLD [1822–1888]

The sea is calm tonight.
The tide is full, the moon lies fair
Upon the straits; on the French coast the light
Gleams and is gone; the cliffs of England stand,
Glimmering and vast, out in the tranquil bay.
Come to the window, sweet is the night-air!
Only, from the long line of spray
Where the sea meets the moon-blanched land,
Listen! you hear the grating roar
Of pebbles which the waves draw back, and fling,   10
At their return, up the high strand,
Begin, and cease, and then again begin,
With tremulous cadence slow, and bring
The eternal note of sadness in.

Sophocles long ago
Heard it on the Aegean, and it brought
Into his mind the turbid ebb and flow
Of human misery; we
Find also in the sound a thought,
Hearing it by this distant northern sea.   20

---

16. Possibly the beginning of a conjuration of the devil; possibly a response to the ringing of the bells that signal vespers.
17. Hail Virgin, full of grace.
*This poem is considered in detail in the essay "Three Critical Approaches: Formalist, Sociological, Psychoanalytic" at the end of the book.

The Sea of Faith
Was once, too, at the full, and round earth's shore
Lay like the folds of a bright girdle furled.
But now I only hear
Its melancholy, long, withdrawing roar,
Retreating, to the breath
Of the night-wind, down the vast edges drear
And naked shingles° of the world.   *pebble beaches*

Ah, love, let us be true
To one another! for the world, which seems   30
To lie before us like a land of dreams,
So various, so beautiful, so new,
Hath really neither joy, nor love, nor light,
Nor certitude, nor peace, nor help for pain;
And we are here as on a darkling plain
Swept with confused alarms of struggle and flight,
Where ignorant armies clash by night.

from

Modern Love

GEORGE MEREDITH [1828–1909]

17
At dinner, she is hostess, I am host.
Went the feast ever cheerfuller? She keeps
The Topic over intellectual deeps
In buoyancy afloat. They see no ghost.
With sparkling surface-eyes we ply the ball:
It is in truth a most contagious game:
HIDING THE SKELETON, shall be its name.
Such play as this the devils might appall!
But here's the greater wonder: in that we,
Enamored of an acting naught can tire,   10
Each other, like true hypocrites, admire;
Warm-lighted looks, Love's ephemeridae,°   *short-lived insects*
Shoot gayly o'er the dishes and the wine.
We waken envy of our happy lot.
Fast, sweet, and golden, shows the marriage knot.
Dear guests, you now have seen Love's corpse-light[18] shine.

---

18. I.e., corpse-candle, a soft light which, when seen in church-yards, portends a funeral.

1. What, precisely, is "Love's corpse-light" (l. 16) a metaphor for in this poem?   2. Is the "marriage knot" really "fast, sweet, and golden" (l. 15)? Explain.

Mine Enemy Is Growing Old

EMILY DICKINSON   [1830–1886]

Mine Enemy is growing old—
I have at last Revenge—
The Palate of the Hate departs—
If any would avenge

Let him be quick—the Viand flits—
It is a faded Meat—
Anger as soon as fed is dead—
'Tis starving makes it fat—

1. Explain the paradox contained in the last two lines.

A Birthday

CHRISTINA ROSSETTI   [1830–1894]

My heart is like a singing bird
    Whose nest is in a watered shoot:
My heart is like an apple tree
    Whose boughs are bent with thickset fruit;
My heart is like a rainbow shell
    That paddles in a halcyon sea;
My heart is gladder than all these
    Because my love is come to me.

Raise me a dais of silk and down;
    Hang it with vair° and purple dyes;   9   squirrel fur
Carve it in doves and pomegranates,
    And peacocks with a hundred eyes;
Work it in gold and silver grapes,
    In leaves and silver fleurs-de-lys;
Because the birthday of my life
    Is come, my love is come to me.

No Second Troy

WILLIAM BUTLER YEATS   [1865–1939]

Why should I blame her[19] that she filled my days
With misery, or that she would of late
Have taught to ignorant men most violent ways,
Or hurled the little streets upon the great,
Had they but courage equal to desire?
What could have made her peaceful with a mind
That nobleness made simple as a fire,
With beauty like a tightened bow, a kind
That is not natural in an age like this,
Being high and solitary and most stern?   10
Why, what could she have done, being what she is?
Was there another Troy for her to burn?

1. Describe the speaker's attitude toward the woman in the poem. Does the speaker, in fact, "blame" her? **2.** What literal event does the figure "hurled the little streets upon the great" (l. 4) describe?

The Love Song of J. Alfred Prufrock

T. S. ELIOT   [1888–1965]

*S'io credesse che mia risposta fosse
A persona che mai tornasse al mondo,
Questa fiamma staria senza piu scosse.
Ma perciocche giammai di questo fondo
Non torno vivo alcun, s'i'odo il vero,
Senza tema d' infamia ti rispondo.*[20]

Let us go then, you and I,
When the evening is spread out against the sky
Like a patient etherized upon a table;
Let us go, through certain half-deserted streets,

---

19.   Yeats speaks of Maud Gonne, the woman he loved for many years, who was devoted to the cause of Irish nationalism. He compares her, here, to Helen of Troy.

20.   From Dante, *Inferno,* XXVII, 61–66. The speaker is Guido de Montefeltro, who is imprisoned in a flame in the level of Hell reserved for false counselors. He tells Dante and Virgil, "If I thought my answer were given to one who might return to the world, this flame would stay without further movement. But since from this depth none has ever returned alive, if what I hear is true, I answer you without fear of infamy."

The muttering retreats
Of restless nights in one-night cheap hotels
And sawdust restaurants with oyster shells:
Streets that follow like a tedious argument
Of insidious intent
To lead you to an overwhelming question . . .   10
Oh, do not ask, "What is it?"
Let us go and make our visit.

In the room the women come and go
Talking of Michelangelo.

The yellow fog that rubs its back upon the windowpanes,
The yellow smoke that rubs its muzzle on the windowpanes
Licked its tongue into the corners of the evening,
Lingered upon the pools that stand in drains,
Let fall upon its back the soot that falls from chimneys,
Slipped by the terrace, made a sudden leap,   20
And seeing that it was a soft October night,
Curled once about the house, and fell asleep.

And indeed there will be time
For the yellow smoke that slides along the street,
Rubbing its back upon the windowpanes;
There will be time, there will be time
To prepare a face to meet the faces that you meet;
There will be time to murder and create,
And time for all the works and days of hands
That lift and drop a question on your plate;   30
Time for you and time for me,
And time yet for a hundred indecisions,
And for a hundred visions and revisions,
Before the taking of a toast and tea.

In the room the women come and go
Talking of Michelangelo.

And indeed there will be time
To wonder, "Do I dare?" and, "Do I dare?"
Time to turn back and descend the stair,
With a bald spot in the middle of my hair—   40
(They will say: "How his hair is growing thin!")
My morning coat, my collar mounting firmly to the chin,
My necktie rich and modest, but asserted by a simple pin—
(They will say: "But how his arms and legs are thin!")
Do I dare
Disturb the universe?
In a minute there is time
For decisions and revisions which a minute will reverse.

For I have known them all already, known them all—
Have known the evenings, mornings, afternoons,   50
I have measured out my life with coffee spoons;
I know the voices dying with a dying fall
Beneath the music from a farther room.
     So how should I presume?

And I have known the eyes already, known them all—
The eyes that fix you in a formulated phrase,
And when I am formulated, sprawling on a pin,
When I am pinned and wriggling on the wall,
Then how should I begin
To spit out all the butt-ends of my days and ways?   60
     And how should I presume?

And I have known the arms already, known them all—
Arms that are braceleted and white and bare
(But in the lamplight, downed with light brown hair!)
Is it perfume from a dress
That makes me so digress?
Arms that lie along a table, or wrap about a shawl.
     And should I then presume?
     And how should I begin?

        . . . . .

Shall I say, I have gone at dusk through narrow streets   70
And watched the smoke that rises from the pipes
Of lonely men in shirt-sleeves, leaning out of windows? . . .

I should have been a pair of ragged claws
Scuttling across the floors of silent seas.

        . . . . .

And the afternoon, the evening, sleeps so peacefully!
Smoothed by long fingers,
Asleep . . . tired . . . or it malingers,
Stretched on the floor, here beside you and me.
Should I, after tea and cakes and ices,
Have the strength to force the moment to its crisis?   80
But though I have wept and fasted, wept and prayed,
Though I have seen my head (grown slightly bald) brought in upon a platter,[21]
I am no prophet—and here's no great matter;
I have seen the moment of my greatness flicker,
And I have seen the eternal Footman hold my coat, and snicker,
And in short, I was afraid.

---

21. Like the head of John the Baptist. See Matthew 14:3–12.

And would it have been worth it, after all,
After the cups, the marmalade, the tea,
Among the porcelain, among some talk of you and me,
Would it have been worth while,   *90*
To have bitten off the matter with a smile,
To have squeezed the universe into a ball
To roll it toward some overwhelming question,
To say: "I am Lazarus,²² come from the dead,
Come back to tell you all, I shall tell you all"—
If one, settling a pillow by her head,
        Should say: "That is not what I meant at all.
        That is not it, at all."

And would it have been worth it, after all,
Would it have been worth while,   *100*
After the sunsets and the dooryards and the sprinkled streets,
After the novels, after the teacups, after the skirts that trail along the floor—
And this, and so much more?—
It is impossible to say just what I mean!
But as if a magic lantern threw the nerves in patterns on a screen:
Would it have been worth while
If one, settling a pillow or throwing off a shawl,
And turning toward the window, should say:
        "That is not it at all,
        That is not what I meant, at all."   *110*

                    .   .   .   .   .

No! I am not Prince Hamlet, nor was meant to be;
Am an attendant lord, one that will do
To swell a progress,° start a scene or two,   *state journey*
Advise the prince; no doubt, an easy tool,
Deferential, glad to be of use,
Politic, cautious, and meticulous;
Full of high sentence,° but a bit obtuse;   *sententiousness*
At times, indeed, almost ridiculous—
Almost, at times, the Fool.

I grow old . . . I grow old . . .   *120*
I shall wear the bottoms of my trousers rolled.°   *cuffed*

Shall I part my hair behind? Do I dare to eat a peach?
I shall wear white flannel trousers, and walk upon the beach.
I have heard the mermaids singing, each to each.

I do not think that they will sing to me.

---

22. See John 11:1–44, and Luke 16:19–26.

I have seen them riding seaward on the waves
Combing the white hair of the waves blown back
When the wind blows the water white and black.

We have lingered in the chambers of the sea
By sea-girls wreathed with seaweed red and brown   *130*
Till human voices wake us, and we drown.

1. *This poem may be understood as a stream of consciousness passing through the mind of Prufrock. The "you and I" of line 1 may be different aspects of his personality. Or perhaps the "you and I" is parallel to Guido who speaks the epigraph and Dante to whom he tells the story that resulted in his damnation—hence, "you" is the reader and "I" is Prufrock. Apparently Prufrock is on his way to a tea, and is pondering his relationship with a certain lady. The poem is disjointed because it proceeds by psychological rather than logical stages. To what social class does Prufrock belong? How does Prufrock respond to the attitudes and values of his class?* **2.** *Line 92 provides a good example of literary allusion (see the last stanza of Marvell, "To His Coy Mistress," especially ll. 41–42). How does an awareness of the allusion contribute to the reader's response to the stanza here?* **3.** *What might the song of the mermaids (l. 124) signify, and why does Prufrock think they will not sing to him (l. 125)?* **4.** *T. S. Eliot once said that some poetry "can communicate without being understood." Is this such a poem?**

if everything happens that can't be done

E. E. CUMMINGS   [1894–1962]

if everything happens that can't be done
(and anything's righter
than books
could plan)
the stupidest teacher will almost guess
(with a run
skip
around we go yes)
there's nothing as something as one

one hasn't a why or because or although   *10*
(and buds know better
than books
don't grow)
one's anything old being everything new
(with a what
which
around we come who)
one's everyanything so

so world is a leaf so tree is a bough
(and birds sing sweeter   20
than books
tell how)
so here is away and so your is a my
(with a down
up
around again fly)
forever was never till now

now i love you and you love me
(and books are shuter
than books   30
can be)
and deep in the high that does nothing but fall
(with a shout
each
around we go all)
there's somebody calling who's we

we're anything brighter than even the sun
(we're everything greater
than books
might mean)   40
we're everyanything more than believe
(with a spin
leap
alive we're alive)
we're wonderful one times one

1. *What fundamental contrast is stated by the poem?* 2. *Lines 2–4 and 6–8 of each stanza could be printed as single lines. Why do you think Cummings decided to print them as he does?* 3. *What common attitude toward lovers is expressed by the last lines of the stanzas?* 4. *Is the poem free verse or formal verse?*

from
Five Songs

W. H. AUDEN [b. 1907]

That night when joy began
Our narrowest veins to flush,
We waited for the flash
Of morning's levelled gun.

But morning let us pass,
And day by day relief
Outgrew his nervous laugh,
Grows credulous of peace.

As mile by mile is seen
No trespasser's reproach,   10
And love's best glasses reach
No fields but are his own.

1. *Describe the sound relationships among the last words in the lines of each stanza.* **2.** *What is the controlling metaphor in the poem? Is it appropriate for a love poem?* **3.** *If it were suggested that the poem describes a homosexual relationship, would your response to the poem's figurative language change?*

The Messenger

ANN STANFORD [b. 1916]

I don't deny that I believe in ghosts
Myself being one. No, not the ultimate last
Spirit, I mean, but this a messenger.
Soft, soft, last night half falling into sleep
I rose like smoke, up, curving past the window
Floating, a gray cloud seaward, slow and pale.

And then, the wings!

Did you hear the birds piling against your window?
A snow of wings, crowding and gentle, crying
Over and over, each with the single errand   10
Light cannot bring, nor ever my tongue would say.
Archaic doves, rustling your sleep, and calling
Crowding upon you, drifting and crying love.

1. *Who or what is the messenger?* **2.** *Why is a messenger necessary?*

The Dover Bitch

A CRITICISM OF LIFE

ANTHONY HECHT [b. 1922]

So there stood Matthew Arnold and this girl
With the cliffs of England crumbling away behind them,

And he said to her, "Try to be true to me,
And I'll do the same for you, for things are bad
All over, etc., etc."
Well now, I knew this girl. It's true she had read
Sophocles in a fairly good translation
And caught that bitter allusion to the sea,
But all the time he was talking she had in mind
The notion of what his whiskers would feel like   10
On the back of her neck. She told me later on
That after a while she got to looking out
At the lights across the channel, and really felt sad,
Thinking of all the wine and enormous beds
And blandishments in French and the perfumes.
And then she got really angry. To have been brought
All the way down from London, and then be addressed
As sort of a mournful cosmic last resort
Is really tough on a girl, and she was pretty.
Anyway, she watched him pace the room   20
And finger his watch-chain and seem to sweat a bit,
And then she said one or two unprintable things.
But you mustn't judge her by that. What I mean to say is,
She's really all right. I still see her once in a while
And she always treats me right. We have a drink
And I give her a good time, and perhaps it's a year
Before I see her again, but there she is,
Running to fat, but dependable as they come,
And sometimes I bring her a bottle of *Nuit d'Amour*.

1. *This poem is a response to Matthew Arnold's "Dover Beach," which appears earlier in this section. What is the fundamental difference between the speaker's conception of love in Arnold's poem and the girl's conception of love as reported in this poem?* **2.** *Arnold's poem is often read as a pained response to the breakdown of religious tradition and social and political order in the mid-nineteenth century. Is this poem, in contrast, optimistic? Is the relationship between the speaker and the girl at the end of the poem admirable? Explain.* **3.** *Do you suppose Hecht was moved to write this poem out of admiration for "Dover Beach"? Explain.*

Prothalamion

MAXINE KUMIN [b. 1925]

The far court opens for us all July.
Your arm, flung up like an easy sail bellying,
comes down on the serve in a blue piece of sky
barely within reach, and you following
tip forward on the smash. The sun sits still

on the hard white linen lip of the net. Five-love.
Salt runs behind my ears at thirty-all.
At game I see the sweat that you're made of.
We improve each other, quickening so by noon
that the white game moves itself, the universe   10
contracted to the edge of the dividing line
you toe against, limbering for your service,
arm up, swiping the sun time after time,
and the square I live in, measured out with lime.

1. What literal circumstances are described by the figurative tennis match? (Note the title.) **2.** *Compare this poem with Shakespeare's sonnet "Shall I Compare Thee to a Summer's Day" and Meredith's sonnet from Modern Love. Which of the three poems most tellingly describes the relationship between lovers?*

A Marriage

ROBERT CREELEY   [b. 1926]

The first retainer
he gave to her
was a golden
wedding ring.

The second—late at night
he woke up,
leaned over on an elbow,
and kissed her.

The third and the last—
he died with   10
and gave up loving
and lived with her.

The Calamity

RICHARD SCHRAMM   [b. 1934]

On the last day
after the vendors boarded over
their shops I took a few things
wrapped in a child's drawing

earth from the garden warmth
from our bed a measure of salt

I did not want to stay
to the end I could not watch
so I climbed around in the sunlight
full of their voices looking   10
in the wrong places

At the top of the escarpment
I took off my shoes my clothes
everything I had saved I folded
just in case

When I realized it didn't matter
any longer I dropped off pieces
of my body
fingers feet a whole arm
I brushed off an ear and one side   20
of the world went numb I listened
to the soft rendings of my legs
and saw them fall in branches

The other arm I left wedged
in a cleft of stone a flag
for my last encampment

I remember your calling Come in
but the child was not listening
Come in before

and I scraped the side of my head   30
not to hear watching the animals
toy with a hand and the teeth
carrying my heart
through the tensed forest

1. What emotional state does "a measure of salt" (l. 6) connote? What does "just in case" (l. 15) refer to?   2. What might the "animals" and the "tensed forest" of the last stanza symbolize?   3. Would the poem be more effective if the poet had defined the calamity clearly? Explain.

DRAMA

Othello

WILLIAM SHAKESPEARE [1564–1616]

CHARACTERS

Duke of Venice
Brabantio, *a Senator*
Senators
Gratiano, *Brother to Brabantio*
Lodovico, *Kinsman to Brabantio*
Othello, *a noble Moor; in the service of the Venetian State*
Cassio, *his Lieutenant*
Iago, *his Ancient*
Roderigo, *a Venetian Gentleman*
Montano, *Othello's predecessor in the Government of Cyprus*
Clown, *Servant to Othello*
Desdemona, *Daughter to Brabantio, and Wife to Othello*
Emilia, *Wife to Iago*
Bianca, *Mistress to Cassio*
Sailor, Officers, Gentlemen, Messengers, Musicians, Heralds, Attendants

SCENE. *For the first Act, in Venice; during the rest of the Play, at a Sea-port in Cyprus*

Act I

SCENE 1. *Venice. A Street.*

(*Enter Roderigo and Iago.*)

Roderigo.   Tush! Never tell me; I take it much unkindly
That thou, Iago, who hast had my purse

As if the strings were thine, shouldst know of this.[1]

Iago. 'Sblood,[2] but you will not hear me:
    If ever I did dream of such a matter,
    Abhor me.

Roderigo.   Thou told'st me thou didst hold him[3] in thy hate.

Iago.   Despise me if I do not. Three great ones of the city,
    In personal suit to make me his lieutenant,
    Off-capp'd[4] to him; and, by the faith of man,
    I know my price, I am worth no worse a place;
    But he, as loving his own pride and purposes,
    Evades them, with a bombast circumstance[5]
    Horribly stuff'd with epithets of war;
    And, in conclusion,
    Nonsuits[6] my mediators;[7] for, 'Certes,'[8] says he,
    'I have already chosen my officer.'
    And what was he?
    Forsooth, a great arithmetician,
    One Michael Cassio, A Florentine,
    A fellow almost damn'd in a fair wife;[9]
    That never set a squadron in the field,
    Nor the division of a battle knows
    More than a spinster; unless[10] the bookish theoric,[11]
    Wherein the toged consuls can propose
    As masterly as he: mere prattle, without practice,
    Is all his soldiership. But he, sir, had the election;
    And I—of whom his eyes had seen the proof
    At Rhodes, at Cyprus, and on other grounds
    Christian and heathen—must be be-lee'd[12] and calm'd
    By debitor and creditor; this counter-caster,[13]
    He, in good time, must his lieutenant be,
    And I—God bless the mark!—his Moorship's ancient.[14]

Roderigo.   By heaven, I rather would have been his hangman.

Iago.   Why, there's no remedy: 'tis the curse of the service,
    Preferment goes by letter and affection,
    Not by the old gradation,[15] where each second
    Stood heir to the first. Now, sir, be judge yourself,
    Whe'r[16] I in any just term am affin'd[17]
    To love the Moor.

---

1. *I.e.,* Othello's successful courtship of Desdemona.   2. By God's blood.   3. *I.e.,* Othello.   4. Took off their caps.   5. Pompous wordiness, circumlocution. 6. Turns down.   7. Spokesmen.   8. In truth.   9. A much debated phrase. In the Italian source the Captain (*i.e.,* Cassio) was married, and it may be that Shakespeare originally intended Bianca to be Cassio's wife but later changed his mind and failed to alter the phrase here accordingly. Or perhaps Iago simply sneers at Cassio as a notorious ladies' man.   10. Except. 11. Theory.   12. Left without wind for my sails.   13. Bookkeeper (cf. "arithmetician" above).   14. Ensign (but Iago's position in the play seems to be that of Othello's aide-de-camp).   15. Seniority.   16. Whether.   17. Obliged.

Roderigo. I would not follow him then.

Iago. O! sir, content you;
I follow him to serve my turn upon him;
We cannot all be masters, nor all masters
Cannot be truly follow'd. You shall mark
Many a duteous and knee-crooking knave,
That, doting on his own obsequious bondage,
Wears out his time, much like his master's ass,
For nought but provender, and when he's old, cashier'd;
Whip me such honest knaves. Others there are
Who, trimm'd in forms and visages of duty,
Keep yet their hearts attending on themselves,
And, throwing but shows of service on their lords,
Do well thrive by them, and when they have lin'd their coats
Do themselves homage: these fellows have some soul;
And such a one do I profess myself. For, sir,
It is as sure as you are Roderigo,
Were I the Moor, I would not be Iago:
In following him, I follow but myself;
Heaven is my judge, not I for love and duty,
But seeming so, for my peculiar end:
For when my outward action doth demonstrate
The native act and figure of my heart
In compliment extern,[18] 'tis not long after
But I will wear my heart upon my sleeve
For daws to peck at: I am not what I am.

Roderigo. What a full fortune does the thick-lips owe,[19]
If he can carry 't thus!

Iago. Call up her father;
Rouse him, make after him, poison his delight,
Proclaim him in the streets, incense her kinsmen,
And, though he in a fertile climate dwell,[20]
Plague him with flies; though that his joy be joy,
Yet throw such changes of vexation on 't
As it may lose some colour.

Roderigo. Here is her father's house; I'll call aloud.

Iago. Do; with like timorous[21] accent and dire yell
As when, by night and negligence, the fire
Is spied in populous cities.

Roderigo. What, ho! Brabantio: Signior Brabantio, ho!

Iago. Awake! what, ho! Brabantio! thieves! thieves! thieves!
Look to your house, your daughter, and your bags!
Thieves! thieves!

---

18. External show.   19. Own.   20. *I.e.*, is fortunate.   21. Frightening.

(Enter Brabantio, above, at a window.)

Brabantio. What is the reason of this terrible summons?
  What is the matter there?
Roderigo. Signior, is all your family within?
Iago. Are your doors lock'd?
Brabantio. Why? wherefore ask you this?
Iago. 'Zounds!²² sir, you're robb'd; for shame, put on your gown;
  Your heart is burst, you have lost half your soul;
  Even now, now, very now, an old black ram
  Is tupping²³ your white ewe. Arise, arise!
  Awake the snorting²⁴ citizens with the bell,
  Or else the devil will make a grandsire of you.
  Arise, I say.
Brabantio. What! have you lost your wits?
Roderigo. Most reverend signior, do you know my voice?
Brabantio. Not I, what are you?
Roderigo. My name is Roderigo.
Brabantio. The worser welcome:
  I have charg'd thee not to haunt about my doors:
  In honest plainness thou hast heard me say
  My daughter is not for thee; and now, in madness,
  Being full of supper and distempering draughts,
  Upon malicious knavery dost thou come
  To start my quiet.
Roderigo. Sir, sir, sir!
Brabantio. But thou must needs be sure
  My spirit and my place²⁵ have in them power
  To make this bitter to thee.
Roderigo. Patience, good sir.
Brabantio. What tell'st thou me of robbing? this is Venice;
  My house is not a grange.²⁶
Roderigo. Most grave Brabantio,
  In simple and pure soul I come to you.
Iago. 'Zounds! sir, you are one of those that will not serve God if the devil bid
  you. Because we come to do you service and you think we are ruffians,
  you'll have your daughter covered with a Barbary horse; you'll have your
  nephews neigh to you; you'll have coursers for cousins and gennets²⁷ for
  germans.²⁸
Brabantio. What profane wretch art thou?
Iago. I am one, sir, that comes to tell you, your daughter and the Moor are
  now making the beast with two backs.

---

22. By God's wounds.   23. Copulating.   24. Snoring.   25. Position.
26. Isolated farm house.   27. Spanish horses.   28. Blood relations.

Brabantio. Thou art a villain.

Iago. You are—a senator.

Brabantio. This thou shalt answer; I know thee, Roderigo.

Roderigo. Sir, I will answer any thing. But, I beseech you,
    If 't be your pleasure and most wise consent,—
    As partly, I find, it is,—that your fair daughter,
    At this odd-even[29] and dull watch o' the night,
    Transported with no worse nor better guard
    But with a knave of common hire, a gondolier,
    To the gross clasps of a lascivious Moor,—
    If this be known to you, and your allowance,[30]
    We then have done you bold and saucy wrongs;
    But if you know not this, my manners tell me
    We have your wrong rebuke. Do not believe
    That, from[31] the sense of all civility,
    I thus would play and trifle with your reverence:
    Your daughter, if you have not given her leave,
    I say again, hath made a gross revolt;
    Tying her duty, beauty, wit and fortunes
    In[32] an extravagant[33] and wheeling stranger
    Of here and every where. Straight satisfy yourself:
    If she be in her chamber or your house,
    Let loose on me the justice of the state
    For thus deluding you.

Brabantio: Strike on the tinder, ho!
    Give me a taper! call up all my people!
    This accident[34] is not unlike my dream;
    Belief of it oppresses me already.
    Light, I say! light!   *(Exit, from above.)*

Iago. Farewell, for I must leave you:
    It seems not meet nor wholesome to my place
    To be produc'd,[35] as, if I stay, I shall,
    Against the Moor; for I do know the state,
    However this may gall him with some check,[36]
    Cannot with safety cast him; for he's embark'd
    With such loud reason to the Cyprus wars,—
    Which even now stand in act,—that, for their souls,
    Another of his fathom[37] they have none,
    To lead their business; in which regard,
    Though I do hate him as I do hell-pains,
    Yet, for necessity of present life,

---

29. Between night and morning.   30. By your approval.   31. Away from.
32. To.   33. Expatriate.   34. Happening.   35. *I.e.,* as a witness.   36. Restraining adversity.   37. Caliber, ability.

I must show out a flag and sign of love,
Which is indeed but sign. That you shall surely find him,
Lead to the Sagittary[38] the raised search;
And there will I be with him. So, farewell.   (*Exit.*)

(*Enter below, Brabantio, and servants with torches.*)

Brabantio.   It is too true an evil: gone she is,
And what 's to come of my despised time
Is nought but bitterness. Now, Roderigo,
Where didst thou see her? O, unhappy girl!
With the Moor, sayst thou? Who would be a father!
How didst thou know 'twas she? O, she deceives me
Past thought. What said she to you? Get more tapers!
Raise all my kindred! Are they married, think you?
Roderigo.   Truly, I think they are.
Brabantio.   O heaven! How got she out? O treason of the blood:
Fathers, from hence trust not your daughters' minds
By what you see them act. Are there not charms
By which the property of youth and maidhood
May be abus'd? Have you not read, Roderigo,
Of some such thing?
Roderigo.   Yes, sir, I have indeed.
Brabantio.   Call up my brother. O! that you had had her.
Some one way, some another! Do you know
Where we may apprehend her and the Moor?
Roderigo.   I think I can discover him, if you please
To get good guard and go along with me.
Brabantio.   Pray you, lead on. At every house I'll call;
I may command at most. Get weapons, ho!
And raise some special officers of night.
On, good Roderigo; I'll deserve[39] your pains.   (*Exeunt.*)

SCENE 2.   *Another street.*

(*Enter Othello, Iago, and Attendants, with torches.*)

Iago.   Though in the trade of war I have slain men,
Yet do I hold it very stuff o' the conscience
To do no contriv'd murder: I lack iniquity
Sometimes to do me service. Nine or ten times
I had thought to have yerk'd[40] him here under the ribs.

---

38.   The name of an inn (?).   39.   *I.e.*, reward.   40.   Stabbed.

Othello. 'Tis better as it is.

Iago. Nay, but he prated,
And spoke such scurvy and provoking terms
Against your honour
That, with the little godliness I have,
I did full hard forbear him. But, I pray, sir,
Are you fast married? Be assur'd of this,
That the magnifico[41] is much belov'd,
And hath in his effect a voice potential
As double[42] as the duke's; he will divorce you,
Or put upon you what restraint and grievance
The law—with all his might to enforce it on—
Will give him cable.[43]

Othello. Let him do his spite:
My services which I have done the signiory[44]
Shall out-tongue his complaints. 'Tis yet to know,[45]
Which when I know that boasting is an honour
I shall promulgate, I fetch my life and being
From men of royal siege, and my demerits[46]
May speak unbonneted[47] to as proud a fortune
As this[48] that I have reach'd; for know, Iago,
But that I love the gentle Desdemona,
I would not my unhoused[49] free condition
Put into circumscription and confine
For the sea's worth. But, look! what lights come yond?

Iago. Those are the raised[50] father and his friends:
You were best[51] go in.

Othello. Not I; I must be found:
My parts, my title, and my perfect[52] soul
Shall manifest me rightly. Is it they?

Iago. By Janus,[53] I think no.

(*Enter Cassio and certain Officers, with torches.*)

Othello. The servants of the duke, and my lieutenant.
The goodness of the night upon you, friends!
What is the news?

Cassio. The duke does greet you, general,
And he requires your haste-post-haste appearance,
Even on the instant.

---

41. One of the grandees, or rulers, of Venice; here, Brabantio.   42. Iago means that Brabantio's influence equals that of the Doge's, with his double vote.   43. *I.e.,* scope.
44. The Venetian government.   45. *I.e.,* the signiory does not as yet know.
46. Merits.   47. *I.e.,* as equals.   48. *I.e.,* that of Desdemona's family.   49. Unconfined.   50. Aroused.   51. Had better.   52. Untroubled by a bad conscience.
53. The two-faced Roman god of portals and doors and (hence) of beginnings and ends.

Othello. What is the matter, think you?

Cassio. Something from Cyprus, as I may divine.
It is a business of some heat;[54] the galleys
Have sent a dozen sequent[55] messengers
This very night at one another's heels,
And many of the consuls,[56] rais'd and met,
Are at the duke's already. You have been hotly call'd for;
When, being not at your lodging to be found,
The senate hath sent about three several[57] quests
To search you out.

Othello. 'Tis well I am found by you.
I will but spend a word here in the house,
And go with you.

Cassio. Ancient, what makes he here?   (*Exit.*)

Iago. Faith, he to-night hath boarded a land carrack;[58]
If it prove lawful prize, he's made for ever.

Cassio. I do not understand.

Iago. He's married.

Cassio. To who?

(*Re-enter Othello.*)

Iago. Marry,[59] to—Come, captain, will you go?

Othello. Have with you.

Cassio. Here comes another troop to seek for you.

Iago. It is Brabantio. General, be advis'd;
He comes to bad intent.

(*Enter Brabantio, Roderigo, and Officers, with torches and weapons.*)

Othello. Holla! stand there!

Roderigo. Signior, it is the Moor.

Brabantio. Down with him, thief!

(*They draw on both sides.*)

Iago. You, Roderigo! Come, sir, I am for you.[60]

Othello. Keep up your bright swords, for the dew will rust them.
Good signior, you shall more command with years
Than with your weapons.

Brabantio. O thou foul thief! where hast thou stow'd my daughter?
Damn'd as thou art, thou hast enchanted her;

---

54. Urgency.   55. Following one another.   56. *I.e.,* senators.   57. Separate.
58. Treasure ship.   59. By the Virgin Mary.   60. Let you and me fight.

For I'll refer me to all things of sense,
If she in chains of magic were not bound,
Whether a maid so tender, fair, and happy,
So opposite to marriage that she shunn'd
The wealthy curled darlings of our nation,
Would ever have, to incur a general mock,
Run from her guardage to the sooty bosom
Of such a thing as thou; to fear, not to delight.
Judge me the world, if 'tis not gross in sense[61]
That thou hast practis'd on her with foul charms,
Abus'd her delicate youth with drugs or minerals
That weaken motion:[62] I'll have 't disputed on;
'Tis probable, and palpable to thinking.
I therefore apprehend and do attach[63] thee
For an abuser of the world, a practiser
Of arts inhibited and out of warrant.[64]
Lay hold upon him: if he do resist,
Subdue him at his peril.

Othello.   Hold your hands,
Both you of my inclining,[65] and the rest:
Were it my cue to fight, I should have known it
Without a prompter. Where will you that I go
To answer this your charge?

Brabantio.   To prison; till fit time
Of law and course of direct session[66]
Call thee to answer.

Othello.   What if I do obey?
How may the duke be therewith satisfied,
Whose messengers are here about my side,
Upon some present[67] business of the state
To bring me to him?

Officer.   'Tis true, most worthy signior;
The duke's in council, and your noble self,
I am sure, is sent for.

Brabantio.   How! the duke in council!
In this time of the night! Bring him away.
Mine's not an idle cause: the duke himself,
Or any of my brothers of the state.[68]
Cannot but feel this wrong as 'twere their own;
For if such actions may have passage free,
Bond-slaves and pagans shall our statesmen be.   (*Exeunt.*)

---

61. Obvious.   62. Normal reactions.   63. Arrest.   64. Prohibited and illegal.
65. Party.   66. Normal process of law.   67. Immediate, pressing.   68. Fellow senators.

SCENE 3.   *A Council Chamber.*

(The Duke and Senators sitting at a table. Officers attending.)

Duke.   There is no composition[69] in these news
      That gives them credit.
First Senator.   Indeed, they are disproportion'd;
      My letters say a hundred and seven galleys.
Duke.   And mine, a hundred and forty.
Second Senator.   And mine, two hundred:
      But though they jump[70] not on a just[71] account,—
      As in these cases, where the aim[72] reports,
      'Tis oft with difference,—yet do they all confirm
      A Turkish fleet, and bearing up to Cyprus.
Duke.   Nay, it is possible enough to judgment:
      I do not so secure me in[73] the error,
      But the main article[74] I do approve[75]
      In fearful sense.
Sailor (*within*).   What, ho! what, ho! what, ho!
Officer.   A messenger from the galleys.

(Enter a Sailor.)

Duke.   Now, what's the business?
Sailor.   The Turkish preparation makes for Rhodes;
      So was I bid report here to the state
      By Signior Angelo.
Duke.   How say you by this change?
First Senator.   This cannot be
      By no[76] assay[77] of reason; 'tis a pageant[78]
      To keep us in false gaze.[79] When we consider
      The importancy of Cyprus to the Turk,
      And let ourselves again but understand,
      That as it more concerns the Turk than Rhodes,
      So may he with more facile question bear[80] it,
      For that it stands not in such warlike brace,[81]
      But altogether lacks the abilities
      That Rhodes is dress'd in: if we make thought of this,
      We must not think the Turk is so unskilful
      To leave that latest which concerns him first,

---

69. Consistency, agreement.   70. Coincide.   71. Exact.   72. Conjecture.
73. Draw comfort from.   74. Substance.   75. Believe.   76. Any.   77. Test.
78. (Deceptive) show.   79. Looking in the wrong direction.   80. More easily capture.
81. State of defense.

Neglecting an attempt of ease and gain,
To wake and wage a danger profitless.

Duke. Nay, in all confidence, he's not for Rhodes.

Officer. Here is more news.

(*Enter a Messenger.*)

Messenger. The Ottomites,[82] reverend and gracious,
Steering with due course toward the isle of Rhodes,
Have there injointed[83] them with an after fleet.[84]

First Senator. Ay, so I thought. How many, as you guess?

Messenger. Of thirty sail; and now they do re-stem[85]
Their backward course, bearing with frank appearance
Their purposes toward Cyprus. Signior Montano,
Your trusty and most valiant servitor,
With his free duty[86] recommends[87] you thus,
And prays you to believe him.

Duke. 'Tis certain then, for Cyprus.
Marcus Luccicos, is not he in town?

First Senator. He's now in Florence.

Duke. Write from us to him; post-post-haste dispatch.

First Senator. Here comes Brabantio and the valiant Moor.

(*Enter Brabantio, Othello, Iago, Roderigo, and Officers.*)

Duke. Valiant Othello, we must straight employ you
Against the general enemy Ottoman.
(*To Brabantio*) I did not see you; welcome, gentle signior;
We lack'd your counsel and your help to-night.

Brabantio. So did I yours. Good your Grace, pardon me;
Neither my place nor aught I heard of business
Hath rais'd me from my bed, nor doth the general care
Take hold of me, for my particular grief
Is of so flood-gate[88] and o'erbearing nature
That it engluts and swallows other sorrows
And it is still itself.

Duke. Why, what's the matter?

Brabantio. My daughter! O! my daughter.

Duke. ⎫
Senators. ⎬ Dead?

Brabantio. Ay, to me;
She is abus'd, stol'n from me, and corrupted
By spells and medicines bought of mountebanks;

---

82. Turks.   83. Joined.   84. Fleet that followed after.   85. Steer again.
86. Unqualified expressions of respect.   87. Informs.   88. Torrential.

For nature so preposterously to err,
Being not deficient, blind, or lame of sense,
Sans[89] witchcraft could not.

Duke.   Whoe'er he be that in this foul proceeding
Hath thus beguil'd your daughter of herself
And you of her, the bloody book of law
You shall yourself read in the bitter letter
After your own sense; yea, though our proper[90] son
Stood[91] in your action.[92]

Brabantio.   Humbly I thank your Grace.
Here is the man, this Moor; whom now, it seems,
Your special mandate for the state affairs
Hath hither brought.

Duke.
Senators. }   We are very sorry for it.

Duke (to Othello).   What, in your own part, can you say to this?

Brabantio.   Nothing, but this is so.

Othello.   Most potent, grave, and reverend signiors,
My very noble and approv'd[93] good masters,
That I have ta'en away this old man's daughter,
It is most true; true, I have married her:
The very head and front of my offending
Hath this extent, no more. Rude am I in my speech,
And little bless'd with the soft phrase of peace;
For since these arms of mine had seven years' pith,[94]
Till now some nine moons wasted,[95] they have us'd
Their dearest action in the tented field;
And little of this great world can I speak,
More than pertains to feats of broil and battle;
And therefore little shall I grace my cause
In speaking for myself. Yet, by your gracious patience,
I will a round[96] unvarnish'd tale deliver
Of my whole course of love; what drugs, what charms,
What conjuration, and what mighty magic,
For such proceeding I am charg'd withal,
I won his daughter.

Brabantio.   A maiden never bold;
Of spirit so still and quiet, that her motion
Blush'd at herself;[97] and she, in spite of nature,
Of years, of country, credit, every thing,

---

89. Without.   90. Own.   91. Were accused.   92. Suit.   93. Tested (by past experience).   94. Strength.   95. Past.   96. Blunt.   97. *I.e.*, (her modesty was such that) she blushed at her own emotions; or: could not move without blushing.

To fall in love with what she fear'd to look on!
It is a judgment maim'd and most imperfect
That will confess[98] perfection so could err
Against all rules of nature, and must be driven
To find out practices of cunning hell,
Why this should be. I therefore vouch again
That with some mixtures powerful o'er the blood,
Or with some dram conjur'd to this effect,
He wrought upon her.

Duke.   To vouch this, is no proof,
Without more certain and more overt test
Than these thin habits[99] and poor likelihoods
Of modern[100] seeming do prefer against him.

First Senator.   But, Othello, speak:
Did you by indirect and forced courses
Subdue and poison this young maid's affections;
Or came it by request and such fair question[101]
As soul to soul affordeth?

Othello.   I do beseech you;
Send for the lady to the Sagittary,
And let her speak of me before her father:
If you do find me foul in her report,
The trust, the office I do hold of you,
Not only take away, but let your sentence
Even fall upon my life.

Duke.   Fetch Desdemona hither.

Othello.   Ancient, conduct them; you best know the place.

(*Exeunt Iago and Attendants.*)

And, till she come, as truly as to heaven
I do confess the vices of my blood,
So justly to your grave ears I'll present
How I did thrive in this fair lady's love,
And she in mine.

Duke.   Say it, Othello.

Othello.   Her father lov'd me; oft invited me;
Still[102] question'd me the story of my life
From year to year, the battles, sieges, fortunes
That I have pass'd.
I ran it through, even from my boyish days
To the very moment that he bade me tell it;

---

98. Assert.   99. Weak appearances.   100. Commonplace.   101. Conversation.
102. Always, regularly.

Wherein I spake of most disastrous chances,
Of moving accidents by flood and field,
Of hair-breadth 'scapes i' the imminent deadly breach,
Of being taken by the insolent foe
And sold to slavery, of my redemption thence
And portance[103] in my travel's history;
Wherein of antres[104] vast and deserts idle,[105]
Rough quarries, rocks, and hills whose heads touch heaven,
It was my hint[106] to speak, such was the process;
And of the Cannibals that each other eat,
The Anthropophagi,[107] and men whose heads
Do grow beneath their shoulders. This to hear
Would Desdemona seriously incline;
But still the house-affairs would draw her thence;
Which ever as she could with haste dispatch,
She'd come again, and with a greedy ear
Devour up my discourse. Which I observing,
Took once a pliant[108] hour, and found good means
To draw from her a prayer of earnest heart
That I would all my pilgrimage dilate,[109]
Whereof by parcels[110] she had something heard,
But not intentively:[111] I did consent;
And often did beguile her of her tears,
When I did speak of some distressful stroke
That my youth suffer'd. My story being done,
She gave me for my pains a world of sighs:
She swore, in faith, 'twas strange, 'twas passing[112] strange;
'Twas pitiful, 'twas wondrous pitiful:
She wish'd she had not heard it, yet she wish'd
That heaven had made her[113] such a man; she thank'd me,
And bade me, if I had a friend that lov'd her,
I should but teach him how to tell my story,
And that would woo her. Upon this hint I spake.
She lov'd me for the dangers I had pass'd,
And I lov'd her that she did pity them.
This only is the witchcraft I have us'd:
Here comes the lady; let her witness it.

(*Enter Desdemona, Iago, and Attendants.*)

Duke. I think this tale would win my daughter too.
Good Brabantio,

---

103. Behavior. 104. Caves. 105. Empty, sterile. 106. Opportunity.
107. Man-eaters. 108. Suitable. 109. Relate in full. 110. Piecemeal.
111. In sequence. 112. Surpassing. 113. Direct object; not "for her."

Take up this mangled matter at the best;
Men do their broken weapons rather use
Than their bare hands.

Brabantio. I pray you, hear her speak:
If she confess that she was half the wooer,
Destruction on my head, if my bad blame
Light on the man! Come hither, gentle mistress:
Do you perceive in all this noble company
Where most you owe obedience?

Desdemona. My noble father,
I do perceive here a divided duty:
To you I am bound for life and education;
My life and education both do learn[114] me
How to respect you; you are the lord of duty,
I am hitherto your daughter: but here's my husband;
And so much duty as my mother show'd
To you, preferring you before her father,
So much I challenge[115] that I may profess
Due to the Moor my lord.

Brabantio. God be with you! I have done.
Please it your Grace, on to the state affairs:
I had rather to adopt a child than get it.
Come hither, Moor:
I here do give thee that with all my heart
Which, but thou hast[116] already, with all my heart
I would keep from thee. For your sake,[117] jewel,
I am glad at soul I have no other child;
For thy escape would teach me tyranny,
To hang clogs on them. I have done, my lord.

Duke. Let me speak like yourself and lay a sentence,[118]
Which as a grize[119] or step, may help these lovers
Into your favour.
When remedies are past, the griefs are ended
By seeing the worst, which[120] late on hopes depended.
To mourn a mischief that is past and gone
Is the next way to draw new mischief on.
What cannot be preserv'd when Fortune takes,
Patience her injury a mockery makes.[121]
The robb'd that smiles steals something from the thief;
He robs himself that spends a bootless grief.

---

114. Teach.   115. Claim as right.   116. Didn't you have it.   117. Because of
you.   118. Provide a maxim.   119. Step.   120. The antecedent is "griefs."
121. To suffer an irreparable loss patiently is to make light of injury (*i.e.*, to triumph over adversity).

Brabantio. So let the Turk of Cyprus us beguile;
　　We lose it not so long as we can smile.
　　He bears the sentence[122] well that nothing bears
　　But the free comfort which from thence he hears;
　　But he bears both the sentence and the sorrow
　　That, to pay grief, must of poor patience borrow.
　　These sentences, to sugar, or to gall,
　　Being strong on both sides, are equivocal:[123]
　　But words are words: I never yet did hear
　　That the bruis'd heart was pierced[124] through the ear.
　　I humbly beseech you, proceed to the affairs of state.

Duke. The Turk with a most mighty preparation makes for Cyprus. Othello, the fortitude[125] of the place is best known to you; and though we have there a substitute of most allowed sufficiency,[126] yet opinion, a sovereign mistress of effects, throws a more safer voice on you:[127] you must therefore be content to slubber[128] the gloss of your new fortunes with this more stubborn[129] and boisterous expedition.

Othello. The tyrant custom, most grave senators,
　　Hath made the flinty and steel couch of war
　　My thrice-driven[130] bed of down: I do agnize[131]
　　A natural and prompt alacrity
　　I find in hardness, and do undertake
　　These present wars against the Ottomites.
　　Most humbly therefore bending to your state,[132]
　　I crave fit disposition[133] for my wife,
　　Due reference of place and exhibition,[134]
　　With such accommodation and besort[135]
　　As levels with[136] her breeding.

Duke. If you please,
　　Be 't at her father's.

Brabantio. I'll not have it so.

Othello. Nor I.

Desdemona. Nor I; I would not there reside,
　　To put my father in impatient thoughts
　　By being in his eye. Most gracious duke,
　　To my unfolding[137] lend your gracious ear;
　　And let me find a charter[138] in your voice
　　To assist my simpleness.

---

122. (1) Verdict, (2) Maxim.　　123. Sententious comfort (like the Duke's trite maxims) can hurt as well as soothe.　　124. (1) Lanced (*i.e.*, cured), (2) Wounded.　　125. Strength. 126. Admitted competence.　　127. General opinion, which mainly determines action, thinks Cyprus safer with you in command.　　128. Besmear.　　129. Rough.　　130. Made as soft as possible.　　131. Recognize.　　132. Submitting to your authority. 133. Disposal.　　134. Provision.　　135. Fitness.　　136. Is proper to. 137. Explanation.　　138. Permission.

Duke.   What would you, Desdemona?

Desdemona.   That I did love the Moor to live with him,
My downright violence and storm of fortunes
May trumpet to the world; my heart's subdu'd
Even to the very quality of my lord;[139]
I saw Othello's visage in his mind,
And to his honours and his valiant parts
Did I my soul and fortunes consecrate.
So that, dear lords, if I be left behind,
A moth of peace, and he go to the war,
The rites[140] for which I love him are bereft me,
And I a heavy interim shall support[141]
By his dear[142] absence. Let me go with him.

Othello.   Let her have your voices.
Vouch with me, heaven, I therefore beg it not
To please the palate of my appetite,
Nor to comply with heat,—the young affects[143]
In me defunct,—and proper satisfaction,
But to be free and bounteous to her mind;
And heaven defend[144] your good souls that you think
I will your serious and great business scant
For[145] she is with me. No, when light-wing'd toys
Of feather'd Cupid seel[146] with wanton dulness
My speculative and offic'd instruments,[147]
That[148] my disports corrupt and taint my business,
Let housewives make a skillet of my helm,
And all indign[149] and base adversities
Make head against my estimation![150]

Duke.   Be it as you shall privately determine,
Either for her stay or going. The affair cries haste,
And speed must answer it.

First Senator.   You must away to-night.

Othello.   With all my heart.

Duke.   At nine i' the morning here we'll meet again.
Othello, leave some officer behind,
And he shall our commission bring to you;
With such things else of quality and respect
As doth import you.[151]

---

139. *I.e.*, I have become a soldier, like Othello.   140. *I.e.*, of marriage, or of war, or of both.
141. Endure.   142. Closely concerning (*i.e.*, Desdemona).   143. The passions of
youth (hence, here, *immoderate* sexual passion).   144. Forbid.   145. Because.
146. Blind (v.) by sewing up the eyelids (a term from falconry).   147. Reflective and execu-
tive faculties and organs.   148. So that.   149. Shameful.   150. Reputation.
151. Concern.

Othello. So please your Grace, my ancient;
A man he is of honesty and trust:
To his conveyance I assign my wife,
With what else needful your good grace shall think
To be sent after me.

Duke. Let it be so.
Good-night to every one. (*To Brabantio*) And, noble signior,
If virtue no delighted[152] beauty lack,
Your son-in-law is far more fair than black.

First Senator. Adieu, brave Moor! use Desdemona well.

Brabantio. Look to her, Moor, if thou hast eyes to see:
She has deceiv'd her father, and may thee.

(*Exeunt Duke, Senators, Officers, &c.*)

Othello. My life upon her faith! Honest Iago,
My Desdemona must I leave to thee:
I prithee, let thy wife attend on her;
And bring them after in the best advantage.[153]
Come, Desdemona; I have but an hour
Of love, of worldly matters and direction,
To spend with thee: we must obey the time.

(*Exeunt Othello and Desdemona.*)

Roderigo. Iago!

Iago. What sayst thou, noble heart?

Roderigo. What will I do, think'st thou?

Iago. Why, go to bed, and sleep.

Roderigo. I will incontinently[154] drown myself.

Iago. Well, if thou dost, I shall never love thee after.
Why, thou silly gentleman!

Roderigo. It is silliness to live when to live is torment; and then have we a
prescription to die when death is our physician.

Iago. O! villanous; I have looked upon the world for four times seven years,
and since I could distinguish betwixt a benefit and an injury, I never found
man that knew how to love himself. Ere I would say, I would drown myself
for the love of a guinea-hen, I would change my humanity with a baboon.

Roderigo. What should I do? I confess it is my shame to be so fond;[155] but it is
not in my virtue[156] to amend it.

Iago. Virtue! a fig! 'tis in ourselves that we are thus, or thus. Our bodies are
our gardens, to the which our wills are gardeners; so that if we will plant
nettles or sow lettuce, set hyssop and weed up thyme, supply it with one

---

152. Delightful.   153. Opportunity.   154. Forthwith.   155. Infatuated.
156. Strength.

gender[157] of herbs or distract it with many, either to have it sterile with id-leness or manured with industry, why, the power and corrigible[158] au-thority of this lies in our wills. If the balance of our lives had not one scale of reason to poise another of sensuality, the blood and baseness of our na-tures would conduct us to most preposterous conclusions; but we have reason to cool our raging motions, our carnal stings, our unbitted[159] lusts, whereof I take this that you call love to be a sect or scion.[160]

Roderigo. It cannot be.

Iago. It is merely a lust of the blood and a permission of the will. Come, be a man. Drown thyself! drown cats and blind puppies. I have professed me thy friend, and I confess me knit to thy deserving with cables of per-durable toughness; I could never better stead thee than now. Put money in thy purse; follow these wars; defeat thy favour[161] with a usurped[162] beard; I say, put money in thy purse. It cannot be that Desdemona should long continue her love to the Moor,—put money in thy purse,—nor he his to her. It was a violent commencement in her, and thou shalt see an an-swerable sequestration;[163] put but money in thy purse. These Moors are changeable in their wills;—fill thy purse with money:—the food that to him now is as luscious as locusts,[164] shall be to him shortly as bitter as colo-quintida.[165] She must change for youth: when she is sated with his body, she will find the error of her choice. She must have change, she must: therefore put money in thy purse. If thou wilt needs damn thyself, do it a more delicate way than drowning. Make all the money thou canst. If sanctimony and a frail vow betwixt an erring[166] barbarian and a super-subtle[167] Venetian be not too hard for my wits and all the tribe of hell, thou shalt enjoy her; therefore make money. A pox of drowning thyself! it is clean out of the way: seek thou rather to be hanged in compassing thy joy than to be drowned and go without her.

Roderigo. Wilt thou be fast to my hopes, if I depend on the issue?[168]

Iago. Thou art sure of me: go, make money. I have told thee often, and I re-tell thee again and again, I hate the Moor; my cause is hearted; thine hath no less reason. Let us be conjunctive[169] in our revenge against him; if thou canst cuckold him, thou dost thyself a pleasure, me a sport. There are many events in the womb of time which will be delivered. Traverse;[170] go: provide thy money. We will have more of this to-morrow. Adieu.

Roderigo. Where shall we meet i' the morning?

Iago. At my lodging.

Roderigo. I'll be with thee betimes.

---

157. Kind.   158. Corrective.   159. *I.e.,* uncontrolled.   160. Offshoot.
161. Change thy appearance (for the worse?).   162. Assumed.   163. Estrangement.
164. Sweet-tasting fruits (perhaps the carob, the edible seed-pod of an evergreen tree in the Mediterranean area).   165. Purgative derived from a bitter apple.   166. Vagabond.
167. Exceedingly refined.   168. Rely on the outcome.   169. Allied.   170. March.

Iago. Go to: farewell. Do you hear, Roderigo?

Roderigo. What say you?

Iago. No more of drowning, do you hear?

Roderigo. I am changed. I'll sell all my land.

Iago. Go to; farewell! put money enough in your purse.   (*Exit Roderigo.*)
> Thus do I ever make my fool my purse;
> For I mine own gain'd knowledge should profane,
> If I would time expend with such a snipe[171]
> But for my sport and profit. I hate the Moor,
> And it is thought abroad[172] that 'twixt my sheets
> He has done my office: I know not if 't be true,
> But I, for mere suspicion in that kind,
> Will do as if for surety.[173] He holds me well;[174]
> The better shall my purpose work on him.
> Cassio's a proper[175] man; let me see now:
> To get his place; and to plume up[176] my will
> In double knavery; how, how? Let's see:
> After some time to abuse Othello's ear
> That he[177] is too familiar with his wife:
> He hath a person and a smooth dispose[178]
> To be suspected; framed[179] to make women false,
> The Moor is of a free and open nature,
> That thinks men honest that but seem to be so,
> And will as tenderly be led by the nose
> As asses are.
> I have't; it is engender'd: hell and night
> Must bring this monstrous birth to the world's light.   (*Exit.*)

Act II

SCENE 1. *A Sea-port Town in Cyprus. An open place near the Quay.*

(*Enter Montano and two Gentlemen.*)

Montano. What from the cape can you discern at sea?

First Gentleman. Nothing at all: it is a high-wrought flood;
> I cannot 'twixt the heaven and the main[180]
> Descry a sail.

Montano. Methinks the wind hath spoke aloud at land;

---

171. Dupe.   172. People think.   173. As if it were certain.   174. In high regard.
175. Handsome.   176. Make ready.   177. *I.e.,* Cassio.   178. Bearing.
179. Designed, apt.   180. Ocean.

A fuller blast ne'er shook our battlements;
If it hath ruffian'd so upon the sea,
What ribs of oak, when mountains melt on them,
Can hold the mortise?[181] what shall we hear of this?

Second Gentleman. A segregation[182] of the Turkish fleet;
For do but stand upon the foaming shore,
The chidden billow seems to pelt the clouds;
The wind-shak'd surge, with high and monstrous mane,
Seems to cast water on the burning bear[183]
And quench the guards of the ever-fixed pole:[184]
I never did like[185] molestation view
On the enchafed[186] flood.

Montano. If that[187] the Turkish fleet
Be not enshelter'd and embay'd, they are drown'd;
It is impossible they bear it out.

(Enter a Third Gentleman.)

Third Gentleman. News, lad! our wars are done.
The desperate tempest hath so bang'd the Turks
That their designment halts;[188] a noble ship of Venice
Hath seen a grievous wrack and suffrance[189]
On most part of their fleet.

Montano. How! is this true?

Third Gentleman. The ship is here put in,
A Veronesa;[190] Michael Cassio,
Lieutenant to the warlike Moor Othello,
Is come on shore: the Moor himself's at sea,
And is in full commission here for Cyprus.

Montano. I am glad on 't; 'tis a worthy governor.

Third Gentleman. But this same Cassio, though he speak of comfort
Touching the Turkish loss, yet he looks sadly
And prays the Moor be safe; for they were parted
With foul and violent tempest.

Montano. Pray heaven he be;
For I have serv'd him, and the man commands
Like a full soldier. Let's to the sea-side, ho!
As well to see the vessel that's come in
As to throw out our eyes for brave Othello,

---

181. Hold the joints together.   182. Scattering.   183. Ursa Minor (the Little Dipper).
184. Polaris, the North Star, almost directly above the Earth's axis, is part of the constellation of the Little Bear, or Dipper.   185. Similar.   186. Agitated.   187. If.   188. Plan is stopped.   189. Damage.   190. Probably a *type* of ship, rather than a ship from Verona —not only because Verona is an inland city but also because of "a noble ship of Venice" above.

Even till we make the main and the aerial blue
An indistinct regard.[191]
Third Gentleman. Come, let's do so;
For every minute is expectancy
Of more arrivance.

(*Enter Cassio.*)

Cassio. Thanks, you the valiant of this warlike isle,
That so approve the Moor. O! let the heavens
Give him defence against the elements,
For I have lost him on a dangerous sea.
Montano. Is he well shipp'd?
Cassio. His bark is stoutly timber'd, and his pilot
Of very expert and approv'd allowance;[192]
Therefore my hopes, not surfeited to death,[193]
Stand in bold cure.[194]

(*Within,* 'A sail!—a sail!—a sail!' *Enter a Messenger.*)

Cassio. What noise?
Messenger. The town is empty; on the brow o' the sea
Stand ranks of people, and they cry 'A sail!'
Cassio. My hopes do shape him for the governor.

(*Guns heard.*)

Second Gentleman. They do discharge their shot of courtesy;
Our friends at least.
Cassio. I pray you, sir, go forth.
And give us truth who 'tis that is arriv'd.
Second Gentleman. I shall.   (*Exit.*)
Montano. But, good lieutenant, is your general wiv'd?
Cassio. Most fortunately: he hath achiev'd a maid
That paragons[195] description and wild fame;
One that excels the quirks[196] of blazoning pens,
And in th' essential vesture of creation[197]
Does tire the ingener.[198]

(*Re-enter Second Gentleman.*)

How now! who has put in?
Second Gentleman. 'Tis one Iago, ancient to the general.

---

191. Till our (straining) eyes can no longer distinguish sea and sky.   192. Admitted and
proven to be expert.   193. Over indulged.   194. With good chance of being fulfilled.
195. Exceeds, surpasses.   196. Ingenuities.   197. *I.e.,* just as God made her; or: (even
in) the (mere) essence of human nature.   198. Inventor (*i.e.,* of her praises?).

Cassio.   He has had most favourable and happy speed:
    Tempests themselves, high seas, and howling winds,
    The gutter'd[199] rocks, and congregated sands,
    Traitors ensteep'd[200] to clog the guiltless keel,
    As having sense of beauty, do omit
    Their mortal[201] natures, letting go safely by
    The divine Desdemona.
Montano.   What is she?
Cassio.   She that I spake of, our great captain's captain,
    Left in the conduct of the bold Iago,
    Whose footing[202] here anticipates our thoughts
    A se'nnight's[203] speed. Great Jove, Othello guard,
    And swell his sail with thine own powerful breath,
    That he may bless this bay with his tall[204] ship,
    Make love's quick pants in Desdemona's arms,
    Give renew'd fire to our extinced spirits,
    And bring all Cyprus comfort!

(*Enter Desdemona, Emilia, Iago, Roderigo, and Attendants.*)

    O! behold,
    The riches of the ship is come on shore.
    Ye men of Cyprus, let her have your knees.
    Hail to thee, lady! and the grace of heaven,
    Before, behind thee, and on every hand,
    Enwheel thee round!
Desdemona.   I thank you, valiant Cassio
    What tidings can you tell me of my lord?
Cassio.   He is not yet arriv'd; nor know I aught
    But that he's well, and will be shortly here.
Desdemona.   O! but I fear—How lost you company?
Cassio.   The great contention of the sea and skies
    Parted our fellowship. But hark! a sail.

(*Cry within,* 'A sail—a sail!' *Guns heard.*)

Second Gentleman.   They give their greeting to the citadel:
    This likewise is a friend.
Cassio.   See for the news!   (*Exit Gentleman.*)
    Good ancient, you are welcome:—(*To Emilia*) welcome, mistress.
    Let it not gall your patience, good Iago,
    That I extend my manners; 'tis my breeding
    That gives me this bold show of courtesy.   (*Kissing her.*)

---

199. Jagged;   or: submerged.   200. Submerged.   201. Deadly.   202. Landing.
203. Week's.   204. Brave.

Iago.   Sir, would she give you so much of her lips
As of her tongue she oft bestows on me,
You'd have enough.

Desdemona.   Alas! she has no speech.

Iago.   In faith, too much;
I find it still when I have list[205] to sleep:
Marry, before your ladyship, I grant,
She puts her tongue a little in her heart,
And chides with thinking.[206]

Emilia.   You have little cause to say so.

Iago.   Come on, come on; you are pictures[207] out of doors,
Bells[208] in your parlours, wild cats in your kitchens,
Saints in your injuries, devils being offended,
Players[209] in your housewifery,[210] and housewives[211] in your beds.

Desdemona.   O! fie upon thee, slanderer.

Iago.   Nay, it is true, or else I am a Turk:
You rise to play and go to bed to work.

Emilia.   You shall not write my praise.

Iago.   No, let me not.

Desdemona.   What wouldst thou write of me, if thou shouldst praise me?

Iago.   O gentle lady, do not put me to 't,
For I am nothing if not critical,

Desdemona.   Come on; assay. There's one gone to the harbour?

Iago.   Ay, madam.

Desdemona.   I am not merry, but I do beguile
The thing I am by seeming otherwise.
Come, how wouldst thou praise me?

Iago.   I am about it; but indeed my invention
Comes from my pate[212] as birdlime does from frize;[213]
It plucks out brains and all: but my muse labours
And thus she is deliver'd.
If she be fair and wise, fairness and wit,
The one's for use, the other useth it.

Desdemona.   Well prais'd! How if she be black and witty?

Iago.   If she be black,[214] and thereto have a wit,
She'll find a white that shall her blackness fit.

Desdemona.   Worse and worse.

Emilia.   How if fair and foolish?

Iago.   She never yet was foolish that was fair,
For even her folly[215] help'd to an heir.

---

205. Wish.   206. *I.e.,* without words.   207. *I.e.,* made up, "painted."   208. *I.e.,* jangly.   209. Triflers, wastrels.   210. Housekeeping.   211. (1) Hussies, (2) (unduly) frugal with their sexual favors, (3) businesslike, serious.   212. Head.   213. Coarse cloth.   214. Brunette, dark haired.   215. Here also, wantonness.

Desdemona. These are old fond[216] paradoxes to make fools laugh i' the alehouse. What miserable praise hast thou for her that's foul and foolish?

Iago. There's none so foul and foolish thereunto,
But does foul pranks which fair and wise ones do.

Desdemona. O heavy ignorance! thou praisest the worst best. But what praise couldst thou bestow on a deserving woman indeed, one that, in the authority of her merit, did justly put on the vouch[217] of very malice itself?

Iago. She that was ever fair and never proud,
Had tongue at will and yet was never loud,
Never lack'd gold and yet went never gay,
Fled from her wish and yet said 'Now I may,'
She that being anger'd, her revenge being nigh,
Bade her wrong stay and her displeasure fly,
She that in wisdom never was so frail
To change the cod's head for the salmon's tail,[218]
She that could think and ne'er disclose her mind,
See suitors following and not look behind,
She was a wight, if ever such wight were,—

Desdemona. To do what?

Iago. To suckle fools and chronicle small beer.[219]

Desdemona. O most lame and impotent conclusion! Do not learn of him, Emilia, though he be thy husband. How say you, Cassio? Is he not a most profane and liberal[220] counsellor?

Cassio. He speaks home,[221] madam; you may relish him more in the soldier than in[222] the scholar.

Iago (*aside*). He takes her by the palm: ay, well said, whisper; with as little a web as this will I ensnare as great a fly as Cassio. Ay, smile upon her, do; I will gyve[223] thee in thine own courtship. You say true, 'tis so, indeed. If such tricks as these strip you out of your lieutenantry, it had been better you had not kissed your three fingers so oft, which now again you are most apt to play the sir[224] in. Very good; well kissed! an excellent courtesy! 'tis so, indeed. Yet again your fingers to your lips? would they were clyster-pipes[225] for your sake! (*A trumpet heard.*) The Moor! I know his trumpet.[226]

Cassio. 'Tis truly so.

Desdemona. Let's meet him and receive him.

Cassio. Lo! where he comes.

(*Enter Othello and Attendants.*)

---

216. Foolish.   217. Compel the approval.   218. To make a foolish exchange (a bawdy secondary meaning is probable).   219. *I.e.,* keep petty household accounts. 220. Free-spoken, licentious.   221. To the mark, aptly.   222. As . . . as.   223. Entangle.   224. Gentleman.   225. Syringes, enema pipes.   226. *I.e.,* Othello's distinctive trumpet call.

Othello. O my fair warrior!

Desdemona. My dear Othello!

Othello. It gives me wonder great as my content
To see you here before me. O my soul's joy!
If after every tempest come such calms,
May the winds blow till they have waken'd death!
And let the labouring bark climb hills of seas
Olympus-high, and duck again as low
As hell's from heaven! If it were now to die,
'Twere now to be most happy, for I fear
My soul hath her content so absolute
That not another comfort like to this
Succeeds in unknown fate.

Desdemona. The heavens forbid
But that our loves and comforts should increase
Even as our days do grow!

Othello. Amen to that, sweet powers!
I cannot speak enough of this content;
It stops me here; it is too much of joy:
And this, and this, the greatest discords be   (*Kissing her.*)
That e'er our hearts shall make!

Iago (*aside*). O! you are well tun'd now,
But I'll set down[227] the pegs that make this music,
As honest as I am.

Othello. Come, let us to the castle.
News, friends; our wars are done, the Turks are drown'd.
How does my old acquaintance of this isle?
Honey, you shall be well desir'd[228] in Cyprus;
I have found great love amongst them. O my sweet,
I prattle out of fashion, and I dote
In mine own comforts. I prithee, good Iago,
Go to the bay and disembark my coffers.
Bring thou the master to the citadel;
He is a good one, and his worthiness
Does challenge much respect. Come, Desdemona,
Once more well met at Cyprus.

(*Exeunt all except Iago and Roderigo.*)

Iago. Do thou meet me presently at the harbour. Come hither. If thou be'st valiant, as they say base men being in love have then a nobility in their natures more than is native to them, list[229] me. The lieutenant to-night watches on the court of guard:[230] first, I must tell thee this, Desdemona is directly in love with him.

---

227. Loosen.   228. Welcomed.   229. Listen to.   230. Guardhouse.

Roderigo. With him! Why, 'tis not possible.

Iago. Lay thy finger thus, and let thy soul be instructed. Mark me with what violence she first loved the Moor but for bragging and telling her fantastical lies; and will she love him still for prating? let not thy discreet heart think it. Her eye must be fed; and what delight shall she have to look on the devil? When the blood is made dull with the act of sport, there should be, again to inflame it, and to give satiety a fresh appetite, loveliness in favour, sympathy in years, manners, and beauties; all which the Moor is defective in. Now, for want of these required conveniences, her delicate tenderness will find itself abused, begin to heave the gorge,[231] disrelish and abhor the Moor; very nature will instruct her in it, and compel her to some second choice. Now, sir, this granted, as it is a most pregnant[232] and unforced position, who stands so eminently in the degree of this fortune as Cassio does? a knave very voluble, no further conscionable[233] than in putting on the mere form of civil and humane seeming, for the better compassing of his salt[234] and most hidden loose affection? why, none; why, none: a slipper[235] and subtle knave, a finder-out of occasions, that has an eye can stamp and counterfeit advantages, though true advantage never present itself; a devilish knave! Besides, the knave is handsome, young, and hath all those requisites in him that folly and green minds look after; a pestilent complete knave! and the woman hath found him already.

Roderigo. I cannot believe that in her; she is full of most blessed condition.

Iago. Blessed fig's end! the wine she drinks is made of grapes;[236] if she had been blessed she would never have loved the Moor; blessed pudding! Didst thou not see her paddle with the palm of his hand? didst not mark that?

Roderigo. Yes, that I did; but that was but courtesy.

Iago. Lechery, by this hand! an index[237] and obscure prologue to the history of lust and foul thoughts. They met so near with their lips, that their breaths embraced together. Villanous thoughts, Roderigo! when these mutualities so marshal the way, hard at hand comes the master and main exercise, the incorporate[238] conclusion. Pish![239] But, sir, be you ruled by me: I have brought you from Venice. Watch you to-night; for the command, I'll lay 't upon you: Cassio knows you not. I'll not be far from you: do you find some occasion to anger Cassio, either by speaking too loud, or tainting[240] his discipline; or from what other course you please, which the time shall more favourably minister.

Roderigo. Well.

Iago. Sir, he is rash and very sudden in choler, and haply may strike at you: provoke him, that he may; for even out of that will I cause these of Cyprus

---

231. Vomit. 232. Obvious. 233. Conscientious. 234. Lecherous.
235. Slippery. 236. *I.e.*, she is only flesh and blood. 237. Pointer. 238. Carnal. 239. Exclamation of disgust. 240. Disparaging.

to mutiny, whose qualification[241] shall come into no true taste again but by the displanting of Cassio. So shall you have a shorter journey to your desires by the means I shall then have to prefer[242] them; and the impediment most profitably removed, without the which there were no expectation of our prosperity.

Roderigo. I will do this, if I can bring it to any opportunity.

Iago. I warrant thee. Meet me by and by at the citadel: I must fetch his necessaries ashore. Farewell.

Roderigo. Adieu.   (*Exit.*)

Iago.   That Cassio loves her, I do well believe it;
That she loves him, 'tis apt,[243] and of great credit:[244]
The Moor, howbeit that I endure him not,
Is of a constant, loving, noble nature;
And I dare think he'll prove to Desdemona
A most dear[245] husband. Now, I do love her too;
Not out of absolute lust,—though peradventure[246]
I stand accountant[247] for as great a sin,—
But partly led to diet my revenge,
For that I do suspect the lusty Moor
Hath leap'd into my seat; the thought whereof
Doth like a poisonous mineral gnaw my inwards;
And nothing can or shall content my soul
Till I am even'd with him, wife for wife;
Or failing so, yet that I put the Moor
At least into a jealousy so strong
That judgment cannot cure. Which thing to do,
If this poor trash[248] of Venice, whom I trash[249]
For his quick hunting, stand the putting-on,[250]
I'll have our Michael Cassio on the hip;
Abuse him to the Moor in the rank garb,[251]
For I fear Cassio with my night-cap too,
Make the Moor thank me, love me, and reward me
For making him egregiously an ass
And practising upon his peace and quiet
Even to madness. 'Tis here, but yet confus'd:
Knavery's plain face is never seen till us'd.   (*Exit.*)

---

241. Appeasement.   242. Advance.   243. Natural, probable.   244. Easily believable.   245. A pun on the word in the sense of: expensive.   246. Perchance, perhaps.   247. Accountable.   248. *I.e.*, Roderigo.   249. Check, control.   250. Inciting.   251. Gross manner.

SCENE 2.   *A Street.*

(Enter a Herald with a proclamation; people following.)

Herald.   It is Othello's pleasure, our noble and valiant general, that, upon certain tidings now arrived, importing the mere[252] perdition of the Turkish fleet, every man put himself into triumph; some to dance, some to make bonfires, each man to what sport and revels his addiction leads him; for, besides these beneficial news, it is the celebration of his nuptial. So much was his pleasure should be proclaimed. All offices[253] are open, and there is full liberty of feasting from this present hour of five till the bell have told eleven. Heaven bless the isle of Cyprus and our noble general Othello!   *(Exeunt.)*

SCENE 3.   *A Hall in the Castle.*

(Enter Othello, Desdemona, Cassio, and Attendants.)

Othello.   Good Michael, look you to the guard to-night:
Let's teach ourselves that honourable stop,[254]
Not to outsport discretion.
Cassio.   Iago hath direction what to do:
But, notwithstanding, with my personal[255] eye
Will I look to 't.
Othello.   Iago is most honest.
Michael, good-night; to-morrow with your earliest
Let me have speech with you. (*To Desdemona.*) Come, my dear love,
The purchase made, the fruits are to ensue;
That profit's yet to come 'twixt me and you.
Good-night.

(Exeunt Othello, Desdemona, and Attendants.)

(Enter Iago.)

Cassio.   Welcome, Iago; we must to the watch.
Iago.   Not this hour, lieutenant; 'tis not yet ten o' the clock. Our general casts us thus early for the love of his Desdemona, who let us not therefore blame; he hath not yet made wanton the night with her, and she is sport for Jove.
Cassio.   She's a most exquisite lady.
Iago.   And, I'll warrant her, full of game.

---

252. Utter.   253. Kitchens and storehouses.   254. Discipline.   255. Own.

Cassio. Indeed, she is a most fresh and delicate creature.

Iago. What an eye she has! methinks it sounds a parley[256] of provocation.

Cassio. An inviting eye: and yet methinks right modest.

Iago. And when she speaks, is it not an alarum[257] to love?

Cassio. She is indeed perfection.

Iago. Well, happiness to their sheets! Come, lieutenant, I have a stoup of wine, and here without are a brace[258] of Cyprus gallants that would fain have a measure to the health of black Othello.

Cassio. Not to-night, good Iago: I have very poor and unhappy brains for drinking: I could well wish courtesy would invent some other custom of entertainment.

Iago. O! they are our friends; but one cup: I'll drink for you.

Cassio. I have drunk but one cup to-night, and that was craftily qualified[259] too, and, behold, what innovation[260] it makes here: I am unfortunate in the infirmity, and dare not task my weakness with any more.

Iago. What, man! 'tis a night of revels; the gallants desire it.

Cassio. Where are they?

Iago. Here at the door; I pray you, call them in.

Cassio. I'll do 't; but it dislikes me.   (*Exit.*)

Iago. If I can fasten but one cup upon him,
With that which he hath drunk to-night already,
He'll be as full of quarrel and offence
As my young mistress' dog. Now, my sick fool Roderigo,
Whom love has turn'd almost the wrong side out,
To Desdemona hath to-night carous'd
Potations pottle-deep;[261] and he's to watch.
Three lads of Cyprus, noble swelling spirits,
That hold their honours in a wary distance,[262]
The very elements[263] of this warlike isle,
Have I to-night fluster'd with flowing cups,
And they watch too. Now, 'mongst this flock of drunkards,
Am I to put our Cassio in some action
That may offend the isle. But here they come.
If consequence[264] do but approve my dream,
My boat sails freely, both with wind and stream.

(*Re-enter Cassio, with him Montano, and Gentlemen. Servant following with wine.*)

Cassio. 'Fore God, they have given me a rouse[265] already.

Montano. Good faith, a little one; not past a pint, as I am a soldier.

Iago. Some wine, ho!

---

256. Conference.   257. Call-to-arms.   258. Pair.   259. Diluted.
260. Change, revolution.   261. Bottoms-up.   262. Take offense easily.
263. Types.   264. Succeeding events.   265. Drink.

(*Sings*)   And let me the canakin[266] clink, clink;
            And let me the canakin clink:
            A soldier's a man;
            A life's but a span;
            Why then let a soldier drink.

    Some wine, boys!

Cassio.   'Fore God, an excellent song.

Iago.   I learned it in England, where indeed they are most potent in potting; your Dane, your German, and your swag-bellied[267] Hollander,—drink, ho!—are nothing to your English.

Cassio.   Is your Englishman so expert in his drinking?

Iago.   Why, he drinks you[268] with facility your Dane dead drunk; he sweats not to overthrow your Almain;[269] he gives your Hollander a vomit ere the next pottle can be filled.

Cassio.   To the health of our general!

Montano.   I am for it, lieutenant; and I'll do you justice.

Iago.   O sweet England!

(*Sings*)   King Stephen was a worthy peer,
                His breeches cost him but a crown;
            He held them sixpence all too dear,
                With that he call'd the tailor lown.[270]
            He was a wight of high renown,
                And thou art but of low degree:
            'Tis pride that pulls the country down,
                Then take thine auld cloak about thee.

    Some wine, ho!

Cassio.   Why, this is a more exquisite song than the other.

Iago.   Will you hear 't again?

Cassio.   No; for I hold him to be unworthy of his place that does those things. Well, God's above all; and there be souls must be saved, and there be souls must not be saved.

Iago.   It's true, good lieutenant.

Cassio.   For mine own part,—no offence to the general, nor any man of quality,—I hope to be saved.

Iago.   And so do I too, lieutenant.

Cassio.   Ay; but, by your leave, not before me; the lieutenant is to be saved before the ancient. Let's have no more of this; let's to our affairs. God forgive us our sins! Gentlemen, let's look to our business. Do not think, gentlemen, I am drunk: this is my ancient; this is my right hand, and this is my left hand. I am not drunk now; I can stand well enough, and speak well enough.

All.   Excellent well.

---

266. Small cup. see that he drinks.   267. With a pendulous belly.   268. The "ethical" dative, *i.e.*, you'll   269. German.   270. Lout, rascal.

Cassio. Why, very well, then; you must not think then that I am drunk. (*Exit.*)

Montano. To the platform, masters; come, let's set the watch.

Iago. You see this fellow that is gone before;
 He is a soldier fit to stand by Caesar
 And give direction; and do but see his vice;
 'Tis to his virtue a just equinox,[271]
 The one as long as the other; 'tis pity of him.
 I fear the trust Othello puts him in,
 On some odd time of his infirmity,
 Will shake this island.

Montano. But is he often thus?

Iago. 'Tis evermore the prologue to his sleep;
 He'll watch the horologe a double set,[272]
 If drink rock not his cradle.

Montano. It were well
 The general were put in mind of it.
 Perhaps he sees it not; or his good nature
 Prizes the virtue that appears in Cassio,
 And looks not on his evils. Is not this true?

(*Enter Roderigo.*)

Iago (*aside to him*). How now, Roderigo!
I pray you, after the lieutenant; go.   (*Exit Roderigo*)

Montano. And 'tis great pity that the noble Moor
 Should hazard such a place as his own second
 With one of an ingraft[273] infirmity;
 It were an honest action to say
 So to the Moor.

Iago. Not I, for this fair island:
 I do love Cassio well, and would do much
 To cure him of this evil. But hark! what noise?

(*Cry within, 'Help! Help!' Re-enter Cassio, driving in Roderigo.*)

Cassio. You rogue! you rascal!

Montano. What's the matter, lieutenant?

Cassio. A knave teach me my duty!
 I'll beat the knave into a twiggen[274] bottle.

Roderigo. Beat me!

Cassio. Dost thou prate, rogue?

(*Striking Roderigo.*)

---

271. Equivalent.   272. Stand watch twice twelve hours.   273. Ingrained.
274. Wicker.

Montano (*staying him*).   Nay, good lieutenant;
    I pray you, sir, hold your hand.
Cassio.   Let me go, sir,
    Or I'll knock you o'er the mazzard.[275]
Montano.   Come, come; you're drunk.
Cassio.   Drunk!

(*They fight.*)

Iago (*aside to Roderigo*).   Away, I say! go out, and cry a mutiny.
                                    (*Exit Roderigo.*)

    Nay, good lieutenant! God's will, gentlemen!
    Help, ho! Lieutenant! sir! Montano! sir!
    Help, masters! Here's a goodly watch indeed!

(*Bell rings.*)

    Who's that that rings the bell? Diablo, ho!
    The town will rise: God's will! lieutenant, hold!
    You will be sham'd for ever.

(*Re-enter Othello and Attendants.*)

Othello.   What is the matter here?
Montano.   'Zounds! I bleed still; I am hurt to the death.

(*He faints.*)

Othello.   Hold, for your lives!
Iago.   Hold, ho, lieutenant! Sir! Montano! gentlemen!
    Have you forgot all sense of place and duty?
    Hold! the general speaks to you; hold for shame!
Othello.   Why, how now, ho! from whence ariseth this?
    Are we turn'd Turks, and to ourselves do that
    Which heaven hath forbid the Ottomites?
    For Christian shame put by this barbarous brawl;
    He that stirs next to carve for his own rage
    Holds his soul light; he dies upon his motion.
    Silence that dreadful bell! it frights the isle
    From her propriety. What is the matter, masters?
    Honest Iago, that look'st dead with grieving,
    Speak, who began this? On thy love, I charge thee.
Iago.   I do not know; friends all but now, even now,
    In quarter[276] and in terms like bride and groom
    Devesting[277] them for bed; and then, but now,—
    As if some planet had unwitted men,—

---

275. Head.   276. On duty.   277. Undressing.

Swords out, and tilting one at other's breast,
In opposition bloody. I cannot speak
Any beginning to this peevish odds,[278]
And would in action glorious I had lost
Those legs that brought me to a part of it!

Othello. How comes it, Michael, you are thus forgot?

Cassio. I pray you, pardon me; I cannot speak.

Othello. Worthy Montano, you were wont be civil;
The gravity and stillness of your youth
The world hath noted, and your name is great
In mouths of wisest censure:[279] what's the matter,
That you unlace[280] your reputation thus
And spend your rich opinion[281] for the name
Of a night-brawler? give me answer to it.

Montano. Worthy Othello, I am hurt to danger;
Your officer, Iago, can inform you,
While I spare speech, which something now offends[282] me,
Of all that I do know; nor know I aught
By me that 's said or done amiss this night,
Unless self-charity be sometimes a vice,
And to defend ourselves it be a sin
When violence assails us.

Othello. Now, by heaven,
My blood begins my safer guides to rule,
And passion, having my best judgment collied,[283]
Assays to lead the way. If I once stir,
Or do but lift this arm, the best of you
Shall sink in my rebuke. Give me to know
How this foul rout began, who set it on;
And he that is approv'd[284] in this offence,
Though he had twinn'd with me—both at a birth—
Shall lose me. What! in a town of war,
Yet wild, the people's hearts brimful of fear,
To manage private and domestic quarrel,
In night, and on the court and guard of safety!
'Tis monstrous. Iago, who began 't?

Montano. If partially affin'd,[285] or leagu'd in office,
Thou dost deliver more or less than truth,
Thou art no soldier.

Iago. Touch me not so near;
I had rather[286] have this tongue cut from my mouth

---

278. Silly quarrel.   279. Judgment.   280. Undo.   281. High reputation.
282. Pains, harms.   283. Clouded.   284. Proved (i.e., guilty).   285. Favorably
biased (by ties of friendship, or as Cassio's fellow officer).   286. More quickly.

Than it should do offence to Michael Cassio;
Yet, I persuade myself, to speak the truth
Shall nothing wrong him. Thus it is, general.
Montano and myself being in speech,
There comes a fellow crying out for help,
And Cassio following with determin'd sword
To execute upon him. Sir, this gentleman
Steps in to Cassio, and entreats his pause;
Myself the crying fellow did pursue,
Lest by his clamour, as it so fell out,
The town might fall in fright; he, swift of foot,
Outran my purpose, and I return'd the rather
For that I heard the clink and fall of swords,
And Cassio high in oath, which till to-night
I ne'er might say before. When I came back,—
For this was brief,—I found them close together,
At blow and thrust, even as again they were
When you yourself did part them.
More of this matter can I not report:
But men are men; the best sometimes forget:
Though Cassio did some little wrong to him,
As men in rage strike those that wish them best,
Yet, surely Cassio, I believe, receiv'd
From him that fled some strange indignity,
Which patience could not pass.

Othello.   I know, Iago.
Thy honesty and love doth mince[287] this matter,
Making it light to Cassio. Cassio, I love thee;
But never more be officer of mine.

(*Enter Desdemona, attended.*)

Look! if my gentle love be not rais'd up;
(*To Cassio.*)   I'll make thee an example.

Desdemona.   What's the matter?

Othello.   All's well now, sweeting; come away to bed.
Sir, for your hurts, myself will be your surgeon.
Lead him off.   (*Montano is led off.*)
Iago, look with care about the town,
And silence those whom this vile brawl distracted.
Come, Desdemona; 'tis the soldier's life,
To have their balmy slumbers wak'd with strife.

(*Exeunt all but Iago and Cassio.*)

---

287.   Tone down.

Iago. What! are you hurt, lieutenant?

Cassio. Ay; past all surgery.

Iago. Marry, heaven forbid!

Cassio. Reputation, reputation, reputation! O! I have lost my reputation. I have lost the immortal part of myself, and what remains is bestial. My reputation, Iago, my reputation!

Iago. As I am an honest man, I thought you had received some bodily wound; there is more offence in that than in reputation. Reputation is an idle and most false imposition;[288] oft got without merit, and lost without deserving: you have lost no reputation at all, unless you repute yourself such a loser. What! man; there are ways to recover the general again; you are but now cast in his mood,[289] a punishment more in policy[290] than in malice; even so as one would beat his offenceless dog to affright an imperious lion. Sue to him again, and he is yours.

Cassio. I will rather sue to be despised than to deceive so good a commander with so slight, so drunken and so indiscreet an officer. Drunk! and speak parrot![291] and squabble, swagger, swear, and discourse fustian[292] with one's own shadow! O thou invisible spirit of wine! if thou hast no name to be known by, let us call thee devil!

Iago. What was he that you followed with your sword? What hath he done to you?

Cassio. I know not.

Iago. Is 't possible?

Cassio. I remember a mass of things, but nothing distinctly; a quarrel, but nothing wherefore. O God! that men should put an enemy in their mouths to steal away their brains; that we should, with joy, pleasance,[293] revel, and applause, transform ourselves into beasts.

Iago. Why, but you are now well enough; how came you thus recovered?

Cassio. It hath pleased the devil drunkenness to give place to the devil wrath; one unperfectness shows me another, to make me frankly despise myself.

Iago. Come, you are too severe a moraler. As the time, the place, and the condition of this country stands, I could heartily wish this had not befallen, but since it is as it is, mend it for your own good.

Cassio. I will ask him for my place again; he shall tell me I am a drunkard! Had I as many mouths as Hydra,[294] such an answer would stop them all. To be now a sensible man, by and by a fool, and presently a beast! O strange! Every inordinate cup is unblessed and the ingredient[295] is a devil.

Iago. Come, come; good wine is a good familiar creature if it be well used; exclaim no more against it. And, good lieutenant, I think you think I love you.

---

288. Something external.   289. Dismissed because he is angry.   290. *I.e.,* more for the sake of the example, or to show his fairness.   291. *I.e.,* without thinking.   292. *I.e.,* nonsense.   293. Pleasure.   294. Many-headed snake in Greek mythology.   295. Contents.

Cassio. I have well approved it, sir. I drunk!

Iago. You or any man living may be drunk at some time, man. I'll tell you what you shall do. Our general's wife is now the general; I may say so in this respect, for that he hath devoted and given up himself to the contemplation, mark, and denotement of her parts and graces: confess yourself freely to her; importune her; she'll help to put you in your place again. She is of so free, so kind, so apt, so blessed a disposition, that she holds it a vice in her goodness not to do more than she is requested. This broken joint between you and her husband entreat her to splinter;[296] and, my fortunes against any lay[297] worth naming, this crack of your love shall grow stronger than it was before.

Cassio. You advise me well.

Iago. I protest, in the sincerity of love and honest kindness.

Cassio. I think it freely; and betimes in the morning I will beseech the virtuous Desdemona to undertake for me. I am desperate of my fortunes if they check me here.

Iago. You are in the right. Good-night, lieutenant; I must to the watch.

Cassio. Good-night, honest Iago! *(Exit.)*

Iago. And what's he then that says I play the villain?
When this advice is free I give and honest,
Probal[298] to thinking and indeed the course
To win the Moor again? For 'tis most easy
The inclining Desdemona to subdue
In any honest suit; she's fram'd as fruitful[299]
As the free elements. And then for her
To win the Moor, were 't to renounce his baptism,
All seals and symbols of redeemed sin,
His soul is so enfetter'd to her love,
That she may make, unmake, do what she list,
Even as her appetite shall play the god
With his weak function.[300] How am I then a villain
To counsel Cassio to this parallel[301] course,
Directly to his good? Divinity of hell!
When devils will the blackest sins put on,
They do suggest at first with heavenly shows,
As I do now; for while this honest fool
Plies Desdemona to repair his fortunes,
And she for him pleads strongly to the Moor,
I'll pour this pestilence into his ear
That she repeals[302] him for her body's lust;
And, by how much she strives to do him good,
She shall undo her credit with the Moor.

---

296. Bind up with splints.   297. Wager.   298. Provable.   299. Generous.
300. Faculties.   301. Purposeful.   302. *I.e.*, seeks to recall.

So will I turn her virtue into pitch,
And out of her own goodness make the net
That shall enmesh them all.

(*Re-enter Roderigo.*)

How now, Roderigo!

Roderigo. I do follow here in the chase, not like a hound that hunts, but one that fills up the cry.[303] My money is almost spent; I have been to-night exceedingly well cudgelled; and I think the issue will be, I shall have so much experience for my pains; and so, with no money at all and a little more wit, return again to Venice.

Iago. How poor are they that have not patience!
What wound did ever heal but by degrees?
Thou know'st we work by wit and not by witchcraft,
And wit depends on dilatory time.
Does 't not go well? Cassio hath beaten thee,
And thou by that small hurt hast cashiered Cassio.
Though other things grow fair against the sun,
Yet fruits that blossom first will first be ripe:
Content thyself awhile. By the mass, 'tis morning;
Pleasure and action make the hours seem short.
Retire thee; go where thou art billeted:
Away, I say; thou shalt know more hereafter:
Nay, get thee gone. (*Exit Roderigo.*) Two things are to be done,
My wife must move for Cassio to her mistress;
I'll set her on;
Myself the while to draw the Moor apart,
And bring him jump[304] when he may Cassio find
Soliciting his wife: ay, that's the way:
Dull not device by coldness and delay.   (*Exit.*)

Act III

SCENE 1. *Cyprus. Before the Castle.*

(*Enter Cassio, and some Musicians.*)

Cassio. Masters, play here, I will content your pains;[305]
Something that's brief; and bid 'Good-morrow, general.'   (*Music.*)

(*Enter Clown.*)

Clown. Why, masters, have your instruments been in Naples, that they speak i' the nose[306] thus?

---

303. Pack (hunting term).   304. At the exact moment.   305. Reward your efforts.
306. Naples was notorious for venereal disease, and syphilis was believed to affect the nose.

First Musician. How, sir, how?

Clown. Are these, I pray you, wind-instruments?

First Musician. Ay, marry, are they, sir.

Clown. O! thereby hangs a tail.

First Musician. Whereby hangs a tale, sir?

Clown. Marry, sir, by many a wind-instrument that I know. But, masters, here's money for you; and the general so likes your music, that he desires you, for love's sake, to make no more noise with it.

First Musician. Well, sir, we will not.

Clown. If you have any music that may not be heard, to 't again; but, as they say, to hear music the general does not greatly care.

First Musician. We have none such, sir.

Clown. Then put up your pipes in your bag, for I'll away.
Go; vanish into air; away! (*Exeunt Musicians.*)

Cassio. Dost thou hear, mine honest friend?

Clown. No, I hear not your honest friend; I hear you.

Cassio. Prithee, keep up thy quillets.[307] There's a poor piece of gold for thee. If the gentlewoman that attends the general's wife be stirring, tell her there's one Cassio entreats her a little favour of speech: wilt thou do this?

Clown. She is stirring, sir: if she will stir hither, I shall seem to notify unto her.

Cassio. Do, good my friend. (*Exit Clown.*)

(*Enter Iago.*)

In happy time, Iago.

Iago. You have not been a-bed, then?

Cassio. Why, no; the day had broke
Before we parted. I have made bold, Iago,
To send in to your wife; my suit to her
Is, that she will to virtuous Desdemona
Procure me some access.

Iago. I'll send her to you presently;
And I'll devise a mean to draw the Moor
Out of the way, that your converse and business
May be more free.

Cassio. I humbly thank you for 't. (*Exit Iago.*)
I never knew
A Florentine more kind and honest.[308]

(*Enter Emilia.*)

Emilia. Good-morrow, good lieutenant: I am sorry
For your displeasure,[309] but all will soon be well.

---

307. Quibbles.   308. Cassio means that not even a fellow Florentine could behave to him in a friendlier fashion than does Iago.   309. Disgrace.

The general and his wife are talking of it,
And she speaks for you stoutly: the Moor replies
That he you hurt is of great fame in Cyprus
And great affinity,[310] and that in wholesome wisdom
He might not but refuse you; but he protests he loves you,
And needs no other suitor but his likings
To take the safest occasion by the front[311]
To bring you in again.[312]

Cassio. Yet, I beseech you,
If you think fit, or that it may be done,
Give me advantage of some brief discourse
With Desdemona alone.

Emilia. Pray you, come in:
I will bestow you where you shall have time
To speak your bosom[313] freely.

Cassio. I am much bound to you. (*Exeunt.*)

SCENE 2. *A Room in the Castle.*

(*Enter Othello, Iago, and Gentlemen.*)

Othello. These letters give, Iago, to the pilot,
And by him do my duties to the senate;
That done, I will be walking on the works;
Repair there to me.

Iago. Well, my good lord, I'll do 't.

Othello. This fortification, gentlemen, shall we see 't?

Gentlemen. We'll wait upon your lordship. (*Exeunt.*)

SCENE 3. *Before the Castle.*

(*Enter Desdemona, Cassio, and Emilia.*)

Desdemona. Be thou assur'd, good Cassio, I will do
All my abilities in thy behalf.

Emilia. Good madam, do: I warrant it grieves my husband,
As if the case were his.

Desdemona. O! that's an honest fellow. Do not doubt, Cassio,

---

310. Family connection.   311. Forelock.   312. Restore you (to Othello's favor).
313. Heart, inmost thoughts.

But I will have my lord and you again
As friendly as you were.

Cassio.   Bounteous madam,
Whatever shall become of Michael Cassio,
He's never any thing but your true servant.

Desdemona.   I know 't; I thank you. You do love my lord;
You have known him long; and be you well assur'd
He shall in strangeness[314] stand no further off
Than in a politic[315] distance.

Cassio.   Ay, but, lady,
That policy may either last so long,
Or feed upon such nice[316] and waterish diet,
Or breed itself so out of circumstance,
That, I being absent and my place supplied,
My general will forget my love and service.

Desdemona.   Do not doubt[317] that; before Emilia here
I give thee warrant of thy place. Assure thee,
If I do vow a friendship, I'll perform it
To the last article; my lord shall never rest;
I'll watch him tame,[318] and talk him out of patience;
His bed shall seem a school, his board a shrift;[319]
I'll intermingle every thing he does
With Cassio's suit. Therefore be merry, Cassio;
For thy solicitor shall rather die
Than give thy cause away.[320]

(*Enter Othello, and Iago at a distance.*)

Emilia.   Madam, here comes my lord.

Cassio.   Madam, I'll take my leave.

Desdemona.   Why, stay, and hear me speak.

Cassio.   Madam, not now; I am very ill at ease,
Unfit for mine own purposes.

Desdemona.   Well, do your discretion.   (*Exit Cassio.*)

Iago.   Ha! I like not that.

Othello.   What dost thou say?

Iago.   Nothing, my lord: or if—I know not what.

Othello.   Was not that Cassio parted from my wife?

Iago.   Cassio, my lord? No, sure, I cannot think it,
That he would steal away so guilty-like,
Seeing you coming.

Othello.   I do believe 'twas he.

---

314. Aloofness.   315. *I.e.,* dictated by policy.   316. Slight, trivial.   317. Fear.
318. Outwatch him (*i.e.,* keep him awake) till he submits.   319. Confessional.
320. Abandon your cause.

Desdemona.   How now, my lord!
   I have been talking with a suitor here,
   A man that languishes in your displeasure.
Othello.   Who is 't you mean?
Desdemona.   Why, your lieutenant, Cassio. Good my lord,
   If I have any grace or power to move you,
   His present[321] reconciliation take;
   For if he be not one that truly loves you,
   That errs in ignorance and not in cunning,
   I have no judgment in an honest face.
   I prithee[322] call him back.
Othello.   Went he hence now?
Desdemona.   Ay, sooth; so humbled,
   That he hath left part of his grief with me,
   To suffer with him. Good love, call him back.
Othello.   Not now, sweet Desdemona; some other time.
Desdemona.   But shall 't be shortly?
Othello.   The sooner, sweet, for you.
Desdemona.   Shall 't be to-night at supper?
Othello.   No, not to-night.
Desdemona.   To-morrow dinner, then?
Othello.   I shall not dine at home;
   I meet the captains at the citadel.
Desdemona.   Why, then, to-morrow night; or Tuesday morn;
   Or Tuesday noon, or night; or Wednesday morn:
   I prithee name the time, but let it not
   Exceed three days: in faith, he's penitent;
   And yet his trespass, in our common reason,—
   Save that they say, the wars must make examples
   Out of their best,—is not almost[323] a fault
   To incur a private check.[324] When shall he come?
   Tell me, Othello: I wonder in my soul,
   What you could ask me, that I should deny,
   Or stand so mammering[325] on. What! Michael Cassio,
   That came a wooing with you, and so many a time,
   When I have spoke of you dispraisingly,
   Hath ta'en your part; to have so much to do
   To bring him in! Trust me, I could do much,—
Othello.   Prithee, no more; let him come when he will;
   I deny thee nothing.
Desdemona.   Why, this is not a boon;
   'Tis as I should entreat you wear your gloves,

---

321. Immediate.   322. Pray thee.   323. Hardly.   324. (Even) a private reprimand.   325. Shilly-shallying.

Or feed on nourishing dishes, or keep you warm,
Or sue to you to do a peculiar profit
To your own person: nay, when I have a suit
Wherein I mean to touch your love indeed,
It shall be full of poise[326] and difficult weight,
And fearful to be granted.

Othello. I will deny thee nothing:
Whereon, I do beseech thee, grant me this,
To leave me but a little to myself.

Desdemona. Shall I deny you? no: farewell, my lord.

Othello. Farewell, my Desdemona: I'll come to thee straight.

Desdemona. Emilia, come. Be as your fancies teach you;
Whate'er you be, I am obedient. *(Exit, with Emilia.)*

Othello. Excellent wretch![327] Perdition catch my soul,
But I do love thee! and when I love thee not,
Chaos is[328] come again.

Iago. My noble lord,—

Othello. What dost thou say, Iago?

Iago. Did Michael Cassio, when you woo'd my lady,
Know of your love?

Othello. He did, from first to last: why dost thou ask?

Iago. But for a satisfaction of my thought;
No further harm.

Othello. Why of thy thought, Iago?

Iago. I did not think he had been acquainted with her.

Othello. O! yes; and went between us very oft.

Iago. Indeed!

Othello. Indeed! ay, indeed; discern'st thou aught in that?
Is he not honest?

Iago. Honest, my lord?

Othello. Honest! ay, honest.

Iago. My lord, for aught I know.

Othello. What dost thou think?

Iago. Think, my lord!

Othello. Think, my lord!
By heaven, he echoes me,
As if there were some monster in his thought
Too hideous to be shown. Thou dost mean something:
I heard thee say but now, thou lik'dst not that,
When Cassio left my wife; what didst not like?
And when I told thee he was of my counsel
In my whole course of wooing, thou criedst, 'Indeed!'

---

326. Weight. 327. Here, a term of endearment. 328. Will have.

And didst contract and purse thy brow together,
As if thou then hadst shut up in thy brain
Some horrible conceit.[329] If thou dost love me,
Show me thy thought.

Iago.   My lord, you know I love you.

Othello.   I think thou dost;
And, for[330] I know thou art full of love and honesty,
And weigh'st thy words before thou givest them breath,
Therefore these stops[331] of thine fright me the more;
For such things in a false disloyal knave
Are tricks of custom, but in a man that's just
They are close delations,[332] working from the heart
That passion cannot rule.

Iago.   For Michael Cassio,
I dare be sworn I think that he is honest.

Othello.   I think so too.

Iago.   Men should be what they seem;
Or those that be not, would they might seem none!

Othello.   Certain, men should be what they seem.

Iago.   Why then, I think Cassio's an honest man.

Othello.   Nay, yet there's more in this.
I pray thee, speak to me as to thy thinkings,
As thou dost ruminate, and give thy worst of thoughts
The worst of words.

Iago.   Good my lord, pardon me;
Though I am bound to every act of duty,
I am not bound to[333] that all slaves are free to.
Utter my thoughts? Why, say they are vile and false;
As where's that palace whereinto foul things
Sometimes intrude not? who has a breast so pure
But some uncleanly apprehensions[334]
Keep leets and law-days,[335] and in session sit
With meditations lawful?

Othello.   Thou dost conspire against thy friend, Iago,
If thou but think'st him wrong'd, and mak'st his ear
A stranger to thy thoughts.

Iago.   I do beseech you,
Though I perchance am vicious in my guess,—
As, I confess, it is my nature's plague
To spy into abuses, and oft my jealousy[336]
Shapes faults that are not,—that your wisdom yet,

---

329. Fancy.   330. Because.   331. Interruptions, hesitations.   332. Secret (*i.e.,* involuntary, unconscious) revelations.   333. Bound with regard to.   334. Conceptions.   335. Sittings of the local courts.   336. Suspicion.

From one that so imperfectly conceits,
Would take no notice, nor build yourself a trouble
Out of his scattering and unsure observance.
It were not for your quiet nor your good,
Nor for my manhood, honesty, or wisdom,
To let you know my thoughts.

Othello.   What dost thou mean?

Iago.   Good name in man and woman, dear my lord,
Is the immediate jewel of[337] their souls:
Who steals my purse steals trash; 'tis something, nothing;
'Twas mine, 'tis his, and has been slave to thousands;
But he that filches from me my good name
Robs me of that which not enriches him,
And makes me poor indeed.

Othello.   By heaven, I'll know thy thoughts.

Iago.   You cannot, if my heart were in your hand;
Nor shall not, whilst 'tis in my custody.

Othello.   Ha!

Iago.   O! beware, my lord, of jealousy;
It is the green-ey'd monster which doth mock
The meat it feeds on: that cuckold[338] lives in bliss
Who, certain of his fate, loves not his wronger;
But, O! what damned minutes tells[339] he o'er
Who dotes, yet doubts; suspects, yet soundly loves!

Othello.   O misery!

Iago.   Poor and content is rich, and rich enough,
But riches fineless[340] is as poor as winter
To him that ever fears he shall be poor.
Good heaven, the souls of all my tribe defend
From jealousy!

Othello.   Why, why is this?
Think'st thou I'd make a life of jealousy,
To follow still the changes of the moon
With fresh suspicions? No; to be once in doubt
Is once to be resolved. Exchange me for a goat
When I shall turn the business of my soul
To such exsufflicate[341] and blown[342] surmises,
Matching thy inference. 'Tis not to make me jealous
To say my wife is fair, feeds well, loves company,
Is free of speech, sings, plays, and dances well;
Where virtue is, these are more virtuous:
Nor from mine own weak merits will I draw

---

337. Jewel closest to.   338. Husband of an adulterous woman.   339. Counts.
340. Boundless.   341. Spat out (?).   342. Fly-blown.

The smallest fear, or doubt of her revolt;
For she had eyes, and chose me. No, Iago;
I'll see before I doubt; when I doubt, prove;
And, on the proof, there is no more but this,
Away at once with love or jealousy!

Iago. I am glad of it; for now I shall have reason
To show the love and duty that I bear you
With franker spirit; therefore, as I am bound,
Receive it from me; I speak not yet of proof.
Look to your wife; observe her well with Cassio;
Wear your eye thus, not jealous nor secure:
I would not have your free and noble nature
Out of self-bounty[343] be abus'd; look to 't:
I know our country disposition[344] well;
In Venice they do let heaven see the pranks
They dare not show their husbands; their best conscience
Is not to leave 't undone, but keep 't unknown.

Othello. Dost thou say so?

Iago. She did deceive her father, marrying you;
And when she seem'd to shake and fear your looks,
She lov'd them most.

Othello. And so she did.

Iago. Why, go to,[345] then;
She that so young could give out such a seeming,
To seel her father's eyes up close as oak,
He thought 'twas witchcraft; but I am much to blame;
I humbly do beseech you of your pardon
For too much loving you.

Othello. I am bound to thee for ever.

Iago. I see, this hath a little dash'd your spirits.

Othello. Not a jot, not a jot.

Iago. I' faith, I fear it has.
I hope you will consider what is spoke
Comes from my love. But I do see you're mov'd;
I am to pray you not to strain my speech
To grosser issues nor to larger reach
Than to suspicion.

Othello. I will not.

Iago. Should you do so, my lord,
My speech should fall into such vile success
As my thoughts aim not at. Cassio's my worthy friend—
My lord, I see you're mov'd.

---

343. Innate generosity. 344. *I.e.,* that of Venice. 345. Colloquialism; here, something like "all right."

Othello. No, not much mov'd:
I do not think but Desdemona's honest.[346]
Iago. Long live she so! and long live you to think so!
Othello. And yet, how nature erring from itself,—
Iago. Ay, there's the point: as, to be bold with you,
Not to affect many proposed matches
Of her own clime,[347] complexion, and degree,[348]
Whereto, we see, in all things nature tends;
Foh! one may smell in such, a will most rank,
Foul disproportion, thoughts unnatural.
But pardon me; I do not in position[349]
Distinctly[350] speak of her, though I may fear
Her will, recoiling[351] to her better judgment,
May fall to match you with her country forms
And happily[352] repent.
Othello. Farewell, farewell:
If more thou dost perceive, let me know more;
Set on thy wife to observe. Leave me, Iago.
Iago. My lord, I take my leave. *(Going.)*
Othello. Why did I marry? This honest creature, doubtless,
Sees and knows more, much more, than he unfolds.
Iago (*returning*). My lord, I would I might entreat your honour
To scan this thing no further; leave it to time.
Although 'tis fit that Cassio have his place,
For, sure he fills it up with great ability,
Yet, if you please to hold him off awhile,
You shall by that perceive him and his means:
Note if your lady strain his entertainment[353]
With any strong or vehement importunity;
Much will be seen in that. In the mean time,
Let me be thought too busy[354] in my fears,
As worthy cause I have to fear I am,
And hold her free, I do beseech your honour.
Othello. Fear not my government.
Iago. I once more take my leave. *(Exit.)*
Othello. This fellow's of exceeding honesty,
And knows all qualities, with a learned spirit,
Of human dealings; if I do prove her haggard,[355]
Though that her jesses[356] were my dear heart-strings,
I'd whistle her off and let her down the wind,[357]

---

346. Chaste.   347. Country.   348. Social rank.   349. In definite assertion.
350. Specifically.   351. Reverting.   352. Perhaps.   353. Urge his re-welcome
(*i.e.,* to Othello's trust and favor).   354. Meddlesome.   355. Wild hawk.
356. Leather thongs by which the hawk's legs were strapped to the trainer's wrist.   357. I'd
let her go and take care of herself.

To prey at fortune. Haply, for I am black,
And have not those soft parts of conversation
That chamberers[358] have, or, for I am declin'd
Into the vale of years—yet that's not much—
She's gone, I am abus'd;[359] and my relief
Must be to loathe her. O curse of marriage!
That we can call these delicate creatures ours,
And not their appetites. I had rather be a toad,
And live upon the vapour of a dungeon,
Than keep a corner in the thing I love
For others' uses. Yet, 'tis the plague of great ones;
Prerogativ'd[360] are they less than the base;
'Tis destiny unshunnable, like death:
Even then this forked plague[361] is fated to us
When we do quicken.[362]
                Look! where she comes.
If she be false, O! then heaven mocks itself.
I'll not believe it.

(Re-enter Desdemona and Emilia.)

Desdemona.   How now, my dear Othello!
Your dinner and the generous[363] islanders
By you invited, do attend your presence.
Othello.   I am to blame.
Desdemona.   Why do you speak so faintly?
Are you not well?
Othello.   I have a pain upon my forehead here.[364]
Desdemona.   Faith, that's with watching; 'twill away again:
Let me but bind it hard, within this hour
It will be well.
Othello.   Your napkin[365] is too little:

(She drops her handkerchief.)

Let it alone. Come, I'll go in with you.
Desdemona.   I am very sorry that you are not well.

(Exeunt Othello and Desdemona.)

Emilia.   I am glad I have found this napkin;
This was her first remembrance from the Moor;
My wayward husband hath a hundred times
Woo'd me to steal it, but she so loves the token,

---

358. Courtiers; or (more specifically): gallants, frequenters of bed chambers.   359. Deceived.   360. Privileged.   361. *I.e.,* the cuckold's proverbial horns.   362. Are
conceived, come alive.   363. Noble.   364. Othello again refers to his cuckoldom.
365. Handkerchief.

For he conjur'd her she should ever keep it,
That she reserves it evermore about her
To kiss and talk to. I'll have the work ta'en out,[366]
And giv 't Iago:
What he will do with it heaven knows, not I;
I nothing but[367] to please his fantasy.[368]

(*Enter Iago.*)

Iago. How now! what do you here alone?
Emilia. Do not you chide; I have a thing for you.
Iago. A thing for me? It is a common thing—
Emilia. Ha!
Iago. To have a foolish wife.
Emilia. O! is that all? What will you give me now
    For that same handkerchief?
Iago. What handkerchief?
Emilia. What handkerchief!
    Why, that the Moor first gave to Desdemona:
    That which so often you did bid me steal.
Iago. Hath stol'n it from her?
Emilia. No, faith; she let it drop by negligence,
    And, to the advantage, I, being there, took 't up.
    Look, here it is.
Iago. A good wench; give it me.
Emilia. What will you do with 't, that you have been so earnest
    To have me filch it?
Iago. Why, what's that to you? (*Snatches it.*)
Emilia. If it be not for some purpose of import
    Give 't me again; poor lady! she'll run mad
    When she shall lack it.
Iago. Be not acknown on 't;[369] I have use for it.
    Go, leave me.   (*Exit Emilia.*)
    I will in Cassio's lodging lose this napkin,
    And let him find it; trifles light as air
    Are to the jealous confirmations strong
    As proofs of holy writ; this may do something.
    The Moor already changes with my poison:
    Dangerous conceits are in their natures poisons,
    Which at the first are scarce found to distaste,[370]
    But with a little act upon the blood,
    Burn like the mines of sulphur. I did say so:
    Look! where he comes!

---

366. Pattern copied.   367. *I.e.,* only want.   368. Whim.   369. You know nothing
about it.   370. Scarce can be tasted.

(*Enter Othello.*)

        Not poppy,[371] nor mandragora,[372]
        Nor all the drowsy syrups[373] of the world,
        Shall ever medicine thee to that sweet sleep
        Which thou owedst yesterday.

Othello. Ha! ha! false to me?

Iago. Why, how now, general! no more of that.

Othello. Avaunt! be gone! thou hast set me on the rack;
        I swear 'tis better to be much abus'd
        Than but to know 't a little.

Iago. How now, my lord!

Othello. What sense had I of her stol'n hours of lust?
        I saw 't not, thought it not, it harm'd not me;
        I slept the next night well, was free and merry;
        I found not Cassio's kisses on her lips;
        He that is robb'd, not wanting what is stol'n,
        Let him not know 't, and he's not robb'd at all.

Iago. I am sorry to hear this.

Othello. I had been happy, if the general camp,[374]
        Pioners[375] and all, had tasted her sweet body,
        So[376] I had nothing known. O! now, for ever
        Farewell the tranquil mind; farewell content!
        Farewell the plumed troop and the big wars
        That make ambition virtue! O, farewell!
        Farewell the neighing steed, and the shrill trump,
        The spirit-stirring drum, the ear-piercing fife,
        The royal banner, and all quality,
        Pride, pomp, and circumstance[377] of glorious war!
        And, O you mortal engines,[378] whose rude throats
        The immortal Jove's dread clamours counterfeit,
        Farewell! Othello's occupation's gone!

Iago. Is it possible, my lord?

Othello. Villain, be sure thou prove my love a whore,
        Be sure of it; give me the ocular proof;
        Or, by the worth of mine eternal soul,
        Thou hadst been better have been born a dog
        Than answer my wak'd wrath.

Iago. Is 't come to this?

Othello. Make me to see 't; or, at the least, so prove it,
        That the probation[379] bear no hinge nor loop
        To hang a doubt on; or woe upon thy life!

---

371. Opium.   372. A soporific.   373. *I.e.,* soporifics.   374. Whole army.
375. Lowest rank of manual laborers in the army.   376. As long as.   377. Pageantry.
378. Deadly artillery.   379. Proof.

Iago. My noble lord,—

Othello. If thou dost slander her and torture me,
Never pray more; abandon all remorse;
On horror's head horrors accumulate;
Do deeds to make heaven weep, all earth amaz'd;
For nothing canst thou to damnation add
Greater than that.

Iago. O grace! O heaven forgive me!
Are you a man! have you a soul or sense?
God be wi' you; take mine office. O wretched fool!
That liv'st to make thine honesty a vice.
O monstrous world! Take note, take note, O world!
To be direct and honest is not safe.
I thank you for this profit,[380] and, from hence
I'll love no friend, sith[381] love breeds such offence.

Othello. Nay, stay; thou shouldst be honest.

Iago. I should be wise; for honesty's a fool,
And loses that it works for.

Othello. By the world,
I think my wife be honest and think she is not;
I think that thou art just and think thou art not.
I'll have some proof. Her name, that was as fresh
As Dian's[382] visage, is now begrim'd and black
As mine own face. If there be cords or knives,
Poison or fire or suffocating streams,
I'll not endure it. Would I were satisfied!

Iago. I see, sir, you are eaten up with passion.
I do repent me that I put it to you.
You would be satisfied?

Othello. Would! nay, I will.

Iago. And may; but how? how satisfied, my lord?
Would you, the supervisor,[383] grossly gape on;
Behold her tupp'd?   ·

Othello. Death and damnation! O!

Iago. It were a tedious[384] difficulty, I think,
To bring them to that prospect; damn them then,
If ever mortal eyes do see them bolster[385]
More[386] than their own! What then? how then?
What shall I say? Where's satisfaction?
It is impossible you should see this,
Were they as prime[387] as goats, as hot as monkeys,

---

380. Lesson.   381. Since.   382. Diana's, the goddess of the moon.   383. Observer.   384. Laborious.   385. Lie together.   386. Other.   387. Lustful.

As salt as wolves in pride,[388] and fools as gross
As ignorance made drunk; but yet, I say,
If imputation, and strong circumstances,
Which lead directly to the door of truth,
Will give you satisfaction, you may have it.

Othello. Give me a living reason she's disloyal.

Iago. I do not like the office;
But, sith I am enter'd in this cause so far,
Prick'd to 't by foolish honesty and love,
I will go on. I lay with Cassio lately;
And, being troubled with a raging tooth,
I could not sleep.
There are a kind of men so loose of soul
That in their sleeps will mutter their affairs;
One of this kind is Cassio.
In sleep I heard him say, 'Sweet Desdemona,
Let us be wary, let us hide our loves!'
And then, sir, would he gripe[389] and wring my hand,
Cry, 'O, sweet creature!' and then kiss me hard,
As if he pluck'd up kisses by the roots,
That grew upon my lips; then laid his leg
Over my thigh, and sigh'd, and kiss'd; and then
Cried, 'Cursed fate, that gave thee to the Moor!'

Othello. O monstrous! monstrous!

Iago. Nay, this was but his dream.

Othello. But this denoted a foregone conclusion:[390]
'Tis a shrewd doubt,[391] though it be but a dream.

Iago. And this may help to thicken other proofs
That do demonstrate thinly.

Othello. I'll tear her all to pieces.

Iago. Nay, but be wise; yet we see nothing done;
She may be honest yet. Tell me but this:
Have you not sometimes seen a handkerchief
Spotted with strawberries in your wife's hand?

Othello. I gave her such a one; 'twas my first gift.

Iago. I know not that; but such a handkerchief—
I am sure it was your wife's—did I to-day
See Cassio wipe his beard with.

Othello. If it be that,—

Iago. If it be that, or any that was hers,
It speaks against her with the other proofs.

---

388. Heat.   389. Seize.   390. Previous consummation.   391. (1) Cursed, (2) Acute, suspicion.

Othello. O! that the slave had forty thousand lives;
One is too poor, too weak for my revenge.
Now do I see 'tis true. Look here, Iago;
All my fond love thus do I blow to heaven:
'Tis gone.
Arise, black vengeance, from the hollow hell!
Yield up, O love! thy crown and hearted throne
To tyrannous hate. Swell, bosom, with thy fraught,[392]
For 'tis of aspics'[393] tongues!

Iago. Yet be content.[394]

Othello. O! blood, blood, blood!

Iago. Patience, I say; your mind, perhaps, may change.

Othello. Never, Iago. Like to the Pontic sea,[395]
Whose icy current and compulsive course
Ne'er feels retiring ebb, but keeps due on
To the Propontic and the Hellespont,[396]
Even so my bloody thoughts, with violent pace,
Shall ne'er look back, ne'er ebb to humble love,
Till that a capable[397] and wide revenge
Swallow them up.   (*Kneels.*)
Now, by yond marble heaven,
In the due reverence of a sacred vow
I here engage my words.

Iago. Do not rise yet.   (*Kneels.*)
Witness, you ever-burning lights above!
You elements that clip[398] us round about!
Witness, that here Iago doth give up
The execution of his wit, hands, heart,
To wrong'd Othello's service! Let him command,
And to obey shall be in me remorse,[399]
What bloody business ever.[400]   (*They rise.*)

Othello. I greet thy love,
Not with vain thanks, but with acceptance bounteous,
And will upon the instant put thee to 't:
Within these three days let me hear thee say
That Cassio 's not alive.

Iago. My friend is dead; 'tis done at your request:
But let her live.

Othello. Damn her, lewd minx! O, damn her!
Come, go with me apart; I will withdraw.

---

392. Burden.   393. Poisonous snakes.   394. Patient.   395. The Black Sea.
396. The Sea of Marmara, The Dardanelles.   397. Comprehensive.   398. Encompass.
399. Probably a corrupt line; the meaning appears to be: "to obey shall be my solemn obligation."
400. Soever.

> To furnish me with some swift means of death
> For the fair devil. Now art thou my lieutenant.

Iago. I am your own for ever.

(Exeunt.)

SCENE 4. *Before the Castle.*

(Enter Desdemona, Emilia, and Clown.)

Desdemona. Do you know, sirrah,[401] where Lieutenant Cassio lies?[402]

Clown. I dare not say he lies any where.

Desdemona. Why, man?

Clown. He is a soldier; and for one to say a soldier lies, is stabbing.[403]

Desdemona. Go to;[404] where lodges he?

Clown. To tell you where he lodges is to tell you where I lie.

Desdemona. Can anything be made of this?

Clown. I know not where he lodges, and for me to devise[405] a lodging, and say he lies here or he lies there, were to lie in mine own throat.

Desdemona. Can you inquire him out, and be edified by report?

Clown. I will catechize the world for him; that is, make questions, and by them answer.

Desdemona. Seek him, bid him come hither; tell him I have moved my lord in his behalf, and hope all will be well.

Clown. To do this is within the compass of man's wit, and therefore I will attempt the doing it.

(Exit.)

Desdemona. Where should I lose that handkerchief, Emilia?

Emilia. I know not, madam.

Desdemona. Believe me, I had rather have lost my purse
> Full of cruzadoes;[406] and, but my noble Moor
> Is true of mind, and made of no such baseness
> As jealous creatures are, it were enough
> To put him to ill thinking.

Emilia. Is he not jealous?

Desdemona. Who! he? I think the sun where he was born
> Drew all such humours from him.

Emilia. Look! where he comes.

Desdemona. I will not leave him now till Cassio
> Be call'd to him.

(Enter Othello.)

How is 't with you, my lord?

---

401. Common form of address to inferiors.   402. Lives.   403. *I.e.*, is cause for stabbing.   404. Here apparently: "Come on!"   405. Invent.   406. Portuguese gold coins.

Othello. Well, my good lady. (*Aside*) O! hardness to dissemble.
How do you, Desdemona?

Desdemona. Well, my good lord.

Othello. Give me your hand. This hand is moist,[407] my lady.

Desdemona. It yet has felt no age nor known no sorrow.

Othello. This argues fruitfulness and liberal[408] heart;
Hot, hot, and moist; this hand of yours requires
A sequester[409] from liberty, fasting and prayer,
Much castigation, exercise devout;
For here 's a young and sweating devil here,
That commonly rebels. 'Tis a good hand,
A frank one.

Desdemona. You may, indeed, say so;
For 'twas that hand that gave away my heart.

Othello. A liberal hand; the hearts of old gave hands,
But our new heraldry[410] is hands not hearts.

Desdemona. I cannot speak of this. Come now, your promise.

Othello. What promise, chuck?[411]

Desdemona. I have sent to bid Cassio come speak with you.

Othello. I have a salt and sorry rheum offends me.
Lend me thy handkerchief.

Desdemona. Here, my lord.

Othello. That which I gave you.

Desdemona. I have it not about me.

Othello. Not?

Desdemona. No, indeed, my lord.

Othello. That is a fault.
That handkerchief
Did an Egyptian[412] to my mother give;
She was a charmer,[413] and could almost read
The thoughts of people; she told her, while she kept it,
'Twould make her amiable[414] and subdue my father
Entirely to her love, but if she lost it
Or made a gift of it, my father's eye
Should hold her loathed, and his spirits should hunt
After new fancies.[415] She dying gave it me;
And bid me, when my fate would have me wive,
To give it her. I did so; and take heed on 't;
Make it a darling like your precious eye;

---

407. A supposed symptom of a lustful nature.   408. With overtones of: too free, loose.
409. Separation.   410. *I.e.*, new heraldic symbolism (Othello means that the new way is not to give the heart together with the hand.)   411. Common term of endearment.
412. Gypsy.   413. Sorceress.   414. Lovable, desirable.   415. Loves.

To lose 't or give 't away, were such perdition
As nothing else could match.

Desdemona. Is 't possible?

Othello. 'Tis true; there 's magic in the web of it;
A sibyl,[416] that had number'd in the world
The sun to course two hundred compasses,
In her prophetic fury sew'd the work;
The worms were hallow'd that did breed the silk,
And it was dy'd in mummy[417] which the skilful
Conserv'd of maidens' hearts.

Desdemona. Indeed! is 't true?

Othello. Most veritable; therefore look to 't well.

Desdemona. Then would to heaven that I had never seen it!

Othello. Ha! wherefore?

Desdemona. Why do you speak so startingly and rash?

Othello. Is 't lost? is 't gone? speak, is it out o' the way?

Desdemona. Heaven bless us!

Othello. Say you?

Desdemona. It is not lost: but what an if[418] it were?

Othello. How!

Desdemona. I say, it is not lost.

Othello. Fetch 't, let me see 't!

Desdemona. Why, so I can, sir, but I will not now.
This is a trick to put me from my suit:
Pray you let Cassio be receiv'd again.

Othello. Fetch me the handkerchief; my mind misgives.

Desdemona. Come, come;
You'll never meet a more sufficient[419] man.

Othello. The handkerchief!

Desdemona. I pray, talk[420] me of Cassio.

Othello. The handkerchief!

Desdemona. A man that all his time
Hath founded his good fortunes on your love,
Shar'd dangers with you,—

Othello. The handkerchief!

Desdemona. In sooth, you are to blame.

Othello. Away! (*Exit.*)

Emilia. Is not this man jealous?

Desdemona. I ne'er saw this before.
Sure, there 's some wonder in this handkerchief;
I am most unhappy in the loss of it.

---

416. Prophetess.　　417. Drug (medicinal or magic) derived from embalmed bodies.
418. If.　419. Adequate.　420. Talk to.

Emilia.   'Tis not a year or two shows us a man;
      They are all but[421] stomachs, and we all but[421] food;
      They eat us hungerly, and when they are full
      They belch us. Look you! Cassio and my husband.

(*Enter Iago and Cassio.*)

Iago.   There is no other way; 'tis she must do 't:
      And, lo! the happiness;[422] go and importune her.
Desdemona.   How now, good Cassio! what 's the news with you?
Cassio.   Madam, my former suit: I do beseech you
      That by your virtuous means I may again
      Exist, and be a member of his love
      Whom I with all the office[423] of my heart
      Entirely honour; I would not be delay'd.
      If my offence be of such mortal kind
      That nor my service past, nor present sorrows,
      Nor purpos'd merit in futurity,
      Can ransom me into his love again,
      But to know so must be my benefit;
      So shall I clothe me in a forc'd content,
      And shut myself up in some other course
      To fortune's alms.
Desdemona.   Alas! thrice-gentle Cassio!
      My advocation is not now in tune;
      My lord is not my lord, nor should I know him,
      Were he in favour[424] as in humour alter'd.
      So help me every spirit sanctified,
      As I have spoken for you all my best
      And stood within the blank of[425] his displeasure
      For my free speech. You must awhile be patient;
      What I can do I will, and more I will
      Than for myself I dare: let that suffice you.
Iago.   Is my lord angry?
Emilia.   He went hence but now,
      And certainly in strange unquietness.
Iago.   Can he be angry? I have seen the cannon,
      When it hath blown his ranks[426] into the air,
      And, like the devil, from his very arm
      Puff'd his own brother; and can he be angry?
      Something of moment[427] then; I will go meet him;
      There's matter in 't indeed, if he be angry.
Desdemona.   I prithee, do so. (*Exit Iago.*) Something, sure, of state,[428]

---

421. Only ... only.   422. "What luck!"   423. Duty.   424. Appearance.
425. As the target for.   426. *I.e.,* his soldiers.   427. Important.   428. Public
affairs.

Either from Venice, or some unhatch'd[429] practice
Made demonstrable here in Cyprus to him,
Hath puddled[430] his clear spirit; and, in such cases
Men's natures wrangle with inferior things,
Though great ones are their object. 'Tis even so;
For let our finger ache, and it indues[431]
Our other healthful members even to that sense
Of pain. Nay, we must think men are not gods,
Nor of them look for such observancy[432]
As fits the bridal.[433] Beshrew me much, Emilia,
I was—unhandsome warrior as I am—
Arraigning his unkindness with[434] my soul;
But now I find I had suborn'd the witness,[435]
And he 's indicted falsely.

Emilia. Pray heaven it be state matters, as you think,
And no conception,[436] nor no jealous toy[437]
Concerning you.

Desdemona. Alas the day! I never gave him cause.

Emilia. But jealous souls will not be answer'd so;
They are not ever jealous for the cause,
But jealous for they are jealous; 'tis a monster
Begot upon itself, born on itself.

Desdemona. Heaven keep that monster from Othello's mind!

Emilia. Lady, amen.

Desdemona. I will go seek him. Cassio, walk hereabout;
If I do find him fit, I'll move your suit
And seek to effect it to my uttermost.

Cassio. I humbly thank your ladyship.   (*Exeunt Desdemona and Emilia.*)

(*Enter Bianca.*)

Bianca. Save you, friend Cassio!

Cassio. What make you from home?
How is it with you, my most fair Bianca?
I' faith, sweet love, I was coming to your house.

Bianca. And I was going to your lodging, Cassio.
What! keep a week away? seven days and nights?
Eight score eight hours? and lovers' absent hours,
More tedious than the dial eight score times?
O weary reckoning!

Cassio. Pardon me, Bianca,
I have this while with leaden thoughts been press'd;

---

429. Abortive or budding plot.   430. Muddied.   431. Brings, leads.   432. Attention.   433. Wedding.   434. To.   435. *I.e.,* caused my soul to bring in wrong charges.   436. Fancy, supposition.   437. Fancy.

But I shall, in a more continuate[438] time,
Strike off[439] this score of absence. Sweet Bianca,

(*Giving her Desdemona's handkerchief.*)

Take me this work out.
Bianca. O Cassio! whence came this?
This is some token from a newer friend;
To the felt absence now I feel a cause;
Is 't come to this? Well, well.
Cassio. Go to, woman!
Throw your vile guesses in the devil's teeth,
From whence you have them. You are jealous now
That this is from some mistress, some remembrance:
No, in good troth, Bianca.
Bianca. Why, whose is it?
Cassio. I know not, sweet; I found it in my chamber.
I like the work well; ere it be demanded,—[440]
As like enough it will,—I'd have it copied;
Take it and do 't; and leave me for this time.
Bianca. Leave you! wherefore?
Cassio. I do attend here on[441] the general,
And think it no addition,[442] nor my wish,
To have him see me woman'd.
Bianca. Why, I pray you?
Cassio. Not that I love you not.
Bianca. But that you do not love me.
I pray you, bring me on the way a little
And say if I shall see you soon at night.
Cassio. 'Tis but a little way that I can bring you,
For I attend here; but I 'll see you soon.
Bianca. 'Tis very good; I must be circumstanc'd.[443]   (*Exeunt.*)

Act IV

SCENE 1. *Cyprus. Before the Castle.*

(*Enter Othello and Iago.*)

Iago. Will you think so?
Othello. Think so, Iago!

---

438. Uninterrupted.   439. Cancel (i.e., make up for).   440. Asked for.
441. Wait for.   442. Advantage, credit.   443. Governed by circumstances.

Iago.   What!
  To kiss in private?
Othello.   An unauthoriz'd kiss.
Iago.   Or to be naked with her friend a-bed
  An hour or more, not meaning any harm?
Othello.   Naked a-bed, Iago, and not mean harm?
  It is hypocrisy against the devil:[444]
  They that mean virtuously, and yet do so,
  The devil their virtue tempts, and they tempt heaven.
Iago.   If they do nothing, 'tis a venial slip;
  But if I give my wife a handkerchief,—
Othello.   What then?
Iago.   Why, then, 'tis hers, my lord; and, being hers,
  She may, I think, bestow 't on any man.
Othello.   She is protectress of her honour too;
  May she give that?
Iago.   Her honour is an essence that 's not seen;
  They have it very oft that have it not:[445]
  But for the handkerchief,—
Othello.   By heaven, I would most gladly have forgot it:—
  Thou said'st,—O! it comes o'er my memory,
  As doth the raven[446] o'er the infected house,
  Boding to all,—he had my handkerchief.
Iago.   Ay, what of that?
Othello.   That's not so good now.
Iago.   What,
  If I had said I had seen him do you wrong?
  Or heard him say, as knaves be such abroad,[447]
  Who having, by their own importunate suit,
  Or voluntary dotage[448] of some mistress,
  Convinced or supplied them,[449] cannot choose
  But they must blab.
Othello.   Hath he said any thing?
Iago.   He hath, my lord; but be you well assur'd,
  No more than he 'll unswear.
Othello.   What hath he said?
Iago.   Faith, that he did—I know not what he did.
Othello.   What? what?
Iago.   Lie—
Othello.   With her?

---

444. *I.e.*, by not committing the sin which the situation invites.   445. *I.e.*, some unchaste women are thought chaste.   446. (1) A bad omen, (2) A carrier of the plague.   447. As there are some such in the world.   448. Foolish affection.   449. Overcome (their reluctance) or satisfied (their desires).

Iago. With her, on her; what you will.

Othello. Lie with her; lie on her! We say, lie on her, when they belie her. Lie with her! that's fulsome. Handkerchief,—confessions,—handkerchief! To confess, and be hanged for his labour. First, to be hanged, and then to confess: I tremble at it. Nature would not invest herself in such shadowing passion without some instruction.[450] It is not words that shake me thus. Pish! Noses, ears, and lips. Is it possible?—Confess!—Handkerchief!—O devil!

(Falls in a trance.)

Iago. Work on,
My medicine, work! Thus credulous fools are caught;
And many worthy and chaste dames even thus,
All guiltless, meet reproach. What, ho! my lord!
My lord, I say! Othello!

(Enter Cassio.)

How now, Cassio!

Cassio. What's the matter?

Iago. My lord is fallen into an epilepsy;[451]
This is his second fit; he had one yesterday.

Cassio. Rub him about the temples.

Iago. No, forbear;
The lethargy[452] must have his quiet course,
If not, he foams at mouth, and by and by
Breaks out to savage madness. Look! he stirs;
Do you withdraw yourself a little while,
He will recover straight; when he is gone,
I would on great occasion[453] speak with you.   *(Exit Cassio.)*
How is it, general? have you not hurt your head?

Othello. Dost thou mock me?[454]

Iago. I mock you! no, by heaven.
Would you would bear your fortune like a man!

Othello. A horned man's a monster and a beast.

Iago. There 's many a beast then, in a populous city,
And many a civil[455] monster.

Othello. Did he confess it?

Iago. Good sir, be a man;
Think every bearded fellow that's but yok'd
May draw[456] with you; there 's millions now alive
That nightly lie in those unproper[457] beds

---

450. I would not fall into such passion unless there were some real grounds for it.
451. Seizure, fit.   452. Coma.   453. Important matter.   454. Another allusion to the cuckold's horns.   455. Citizen.   456. *I.e.*, pull the burden of cuckolddom.
457. Not exclusively their own.

Which they dare swear peculiar;[458] your case is better.
O! 'tis the spite of hell, the fiend's arch-mock,
To lip[459] a wanton in a secure[460] couch,
And to suppose her chaste. No, let me know;
And knowing what I am, I know what she shall be.

Othello. O! thou art wise; 'tis certain.

Iago. Stand you awhile apart;
Confine yourself but in a patient list.[461]
Whilst you were here o'erwhelmed with your grief,—
A passion most unsuiting such a man,—
Cassio came hither; I shifted him away,
And laid good 'scuse upon your ecstasy;[462]
Bade him anon return and here speak with me;
The which he promis'd. Do but encave yourself,
And mark the fleers, the gibes, and notable scorns,
That dwell in every region of his face;
For I will make him tell the tale anew,
Where, how, how oft, how long ago, and when
He hath, and is again to cope[463] your wife:
I say, but mark his gesture. Marry, patience;
Or I shall say you are all in all in spleen,[464]
And nothing of a man.

Othello. Dost thou hear, Iago?
I will be found most cunning in my patience;
But—dost thou hear?—most bloody.

Iago. That's not amiss:
But yet keep time[465] in all. Will you withdraw?   (*Othello goes apart.*)
Now will I question Cassio of Bianca,
A housewife[466] that by selling her desires
Buys herself bread and clothes; it is a creature
That dotes on Cassio; as 'tis the strumpet's plague
To beguile many and be beguil'd by one.
He, when he hears of her, cannot refrain
From the excess of laughter. Here he comes:

(*Re-enter Cassio.*)

As he shall smile, Othello shall go mad;
And his unbookish[467] jealousy must construe
Poor Cassio's smiles, gestures, and light behaviour
Quite in the wrong. How do you now, lieutenant?

Cassio. The worser that you give me the addition[468]
Whose want[469] even kills me.

---

458. Exclusively their own.   459. Kiss.   460. *I.e.,* without suspicion of having a rival.
461. Bounds of patience.   462. Derangement, trance.   463. Close with.
464. Completely overcome by passion.   465. Maintain control.   466. Hussy.
467. Unpracticed, naive.   468. Title.   469. The want of which.

Iago.   Ply Desdemona well, and you are sure on 't.
   (*Speaking lower*) Now, if this suit lay in Bianca's power,
   How quickly should you speed!
Cassio.   Alas! poor caitiff![470]
Othello.   Look! how he laughs already!
Iago.   I never knew woman love man so.
Cassio.   Alas! poor rogue, I think, i' faith, she loves me.
Othello.   Now he denies it faintly, and laughs it out.
Iago.   Do you hear, Cassio?
Othello.   Now he importunes him
   To tell it o'er: go to; well said, well said.
Iago.   She gives it out that you shall marry her;
   Do you intend it?
Cassio.   Ha, ha, ha!
Othello.   Do you triumph, Roman?[471] do you triumph?
Cassio.   I marry her! what? a customer?[472] I prithee, bear some charity to my
   wit;[473] do not think it so unwholesome. Ha, ha, ha!
Othello.   So, so, so, so. They laugh that win.[474]
Iago.   Faith, the cry goes that you shall marry her.
Cassio.   Prithee, say true.
Iago.   I am a very villain else.
Othello.   Have you scored me?[475] Well.
Cassio.   This is the monkey's own giving out: she is persuaded I will marry
   her, out of her own love and flattery, not out of my promise.
Othello.   Iago beckons me;[476] now he begins the story.
Cassio.   She was here even now; she haunts me in every place. I was the other
   day talking on the sea-bank with certain Venetians, and thither comes this
   bauble,[477] and, by this hand, she falls me thus about my neck;—
Othello.   Crying, 'O dear Cassio!' as it were; his gesture imports it.
Cassio.   So hangs and lolls and weeps upon me; so hales[478] and pulls me; ha,
   ha, ha!
Othello.   Now he tells how she plucked him to my chamber. O! I see that
   nose of yours, but not the dog I shall throw it to.
Cassio.   Well, I must leave her company.
Iago.   Before me![479] look, where she comes.
Cassio.   'Tis such another fitchew![480] marry, a perfumed one.

(*Enter Bianca.*)

   What do you mean by this haunting of me?
Bianca.   Let the devil and his dam haunt you! What did you mean by that

---

470. Wretch.   471. *I.e.*, one who triumphs(?).   472. Courtesan, prostitute.
473. Give me credit for some sense.   474. "He who laughs last laughs longest"(?).
475. Wounded, defaced(?); or: settled my account(?).   476. Signals.   477. Plaything.
478. Hauls.   479. An exclamation of surprise.   480. Polecat, noted both for its strong smell
and for its lechery.

same handkerchief you gave me even now? I was a fine fool to take it. I must take out the work! A likely piece of work, that you should find it in your chamber, and not know who left it there! This is some minx's token, and I must take out the work! There, give it your hobby-horse;[481] wheresoever you had it I'll take out no work on 't.

Cassio. How now, my sweet Bianca! how now, how now!

Othello. By heaven, that should be[482] my handkerchief!

Bianca. An you'll come to supper to-night, you may; an you will not, come when you are next prepared[483] for. *(Exit.)*

Iago. After her, after her.

Cassio. Faith, I must; she 'll rail in the street else.

Iago. Will you sup there?

Cassio. Faith, I intend so.

Iago. Well, I may chance to see you, for I would very fain[484] speak with you.

Cassio. Prithee come; will you?

Iago. Go to; say no more. *(Exit Cassio.)*

Othello (*advancing*): How shall I murder him, Iago?

Iago. Did you perceive how he laughed at his vice?

Othello. O! Iago!

Iago. And did you see the handkerchief?

Othello. Was that mine?

Iago. Yours, by this hand; and to see how he prizes the foolish woman your wife! she gave it him, and he hath given it his whore.

Othello. I would have him nine years a-killing. A fine woman! a fair woman! a sweet woman!

Iago. Nay, you must forget that.

Othello. Ay, let her rot, and perish, and be damned to-night; for she shall not live. No, my heart is turned to stone; I strike it, and it hurts my hand. O! the world hath not a sweeter creature; she might lie by an emperor's side and command him tasks.

Iago. Nay, that's not your way.[485]

Othello. Hang her! I do but say what she is. So delicate with her needle! An admirable musician! O, she will sing the savageness out of a bear. Of so high and plenteous wit and invention!

Iago. She 's the worse for all this.

Othello. O! a thousand, a thousand times. And then, of so gentle a condition![486]

Iago. Ay, too gentle.[487]

Othello. Nay, that 's certain;—but yet the pity of it, Iago!
O! Iago, the pity of it, Iago!

Iago. If you are so fond over her iniquity, give her patent to offend; for, if it touch not you, it comes near nobody.

---

481. Harlot.   482. *I.e.*, I think that is.   483. Expected (Bianca means that if he does not come that night, she will never want to see him again).   484. Gladly.   485. Proper course.   486. So much the high-born lady.   487. *I.e.*, yielding.

Othello. I will chop her into messes.[488] Cuckold me!

Iago. O! 'tis foul in her.

Othello. With mine officer!

Iago. That 's fouler.

Othello. Get me some poison, Iago; this night: I 'll not expostulate with her, lest her body and beauty unprovide my mind again.[489] This night, Iago.

Iago. Do it not with poison, strangle her in her bed, even the bed she hath contaminated.

Othello. Good, good; the justice of it pleases; very good.

Iago. And for Cassio, let me be his undertaker;[490] you shall hear more by midnight.

Othello. Excellent good. (*A trumpet within.*) What trumpet is that same?

Iago. Something from Venice, sure. 'Tis Lodovico,
Come from the duke; and see, your wife is with him.

(*Enter Lodovico, Desdemona, and Attendants.*)

Lodovico. God save you, worthy general!

Othello. With all my heart, sir.

Lodovico. The duke and senators of Venice greet you.

(*Gives him a packet.*)

Othello. I kiss the instrument of their pleasures.

(*Opens the packet, and reads.*)

Desdemona. And what's the news, good cousin Lodovico?

Iago. I am very glad to see you, signior;
Welcome to Cyprus.

Lodovico. I thank you. How does Lieutenant Cassio?

Iago. Lives, sir.

Desdemona. Cousin, there 's fall'n between him and my lord
An unkind[491] breach; but you shall make all well.

Othello. Are you sure of that?

Desdemona. My lord?

Othello (*reads*). 'This fail you not to do, as you will'—

Lodovico. He did not call; he 's busy in the paper.
Is there division[492] twixt my lord and Cassio?

Desdemona. A most unhappy one; I would do much
To atone[493] them, for the love I bear to Cassio.

Othello. Fire and brimstone!

Desdemona. My lord?

Othello. Are you wise?

Desdemona. What! is he angry?

---

488. Bits.   489. Unsettle my intention.   490. Dispatcher.   491. Unnatural.
492. Estrangement.   493. Reconcile.

Lodovico.   May be the letter mov'd him;
      For, as I think, they do command him home,
      Deputing Cassio in his government.
Desdemona.   Trust me, I am glad on 't.
Othello.   Indeed!
Desdemona.   My lord?
Othello.   I am glad to see you mad.
Desdemona.   Why, sweet Othello?
Othello.   Devil!   (*Strikes her.*)
Desdemona.   I have not deserved this.
Lodovico.   My lord, this would not be believ'd in Venice,
      Though I should swear I saw 't; 'tis very much;
      Make her amends, she weeps.
Othello.   O devil, devil!
      If that the earth could teem with woman's tears,
      Each drop she falls[494] would prove a crocodile.[495]
      Out of my sight!
Desdemona.   I will not stay to offend you.   (*Going.*)
Lodovico.   Truly, an obedient lady;
      I do beseech your lordship, call her back.
Othello.   Mistress!
Desdemona.   My lord?
Othello.   What would you with her, sir?
Lodovico.   Why, I, my lord?
Othello.   Ay; you did wish that I would make her turn:
      Sir, she can turn, and turn, and yet go on,
      And turn again; and she can weep, sir, weep;
      And she 's obedient, as you say, obedient,
      Very obedient. Proceed you in your tears.
      Concerning this, sir,—O well-painted passion!—
      I am commanded home. Get you away;
      I 'll send for you anon. Sir, I obey the mandate,
      And will return to Venice. Hence! avaunt![496]   (*Exit Desdemona.*)
      Cassio shall have my place. And, sir, to-night,
      I do entreat that we may sup together;
      You are welcome, sir, to Cyprus. Goats and monkeys!   (*Exit.*)
Lodovico.   Is this the noble Moor whom our full senate
      Call all-in-all sufficient? is this the noble nature
      Whom passion could not shake? whose solid virtue
      The shot of accident nor dart of chance
      Could neither graze nor pierce?
Iago.   He is much chang'd.
Lodovico.   Are his wits safe? is he not light of brain?

---

494. Lets fall.   495. The crocodile's tears were supposed to be hypocritical.   496. Begone!

Iago. He 's that he is; I may not breathe my censure.
   What he might be, if, what he might, he is not,
   I would to heaven he were![497]
Lodovico.   What! strike his wife!
Iago.   Faith, that was not so well; yet would I knew
   That stroke would prove the worst!
Lodovico.   Is it his use?
   Or did the letters work upon his blood,
   And new-create this fault?
Iago.   Alas, alas!
   It is not honesty in me to speak
   What I have seen and known. You shall observe him,
   And his own courses[498] will denote him so
   That I may save my speech. Do but go after
   And mark how he continues.
Lodovico.   I am sorry that I am deceiv'd in him.   (*Exeunt.*)

SCENE 2.   *A Room in the Castle.*

(*Enter Othello and Emilia.*)

Othello.   You have seen nothing, then?
Emilia.   Nor ever heard, nor ever did suspect.
Othello.   Yes, you have seen Cassio and her together.
Emilia.   But then I saw no harm, and then I heard
   Each syllable that breath made up between them.
Othello.   What! did they never whisper?
Emilia.   Never, my lord.
Othello.   Nor send you out o' the way?
Emilia.   Never.
Othello.   To fetch her fan, her gloves, her mask, nor nothing?[499]
Emilia.   Never, my lord.
Othello.   That's strange.
Emilia.   I durst, my lord, to wager she is honest,
   Lay down my soul at stake: if you think other,
   Remove your thought; it doth abuse your bosom.
   If any wretch have put this in your head,
   Let heaven requite it with the serpent's curse!
   For, if she be not honest, chaste, and true,
   There 's no man happy; the purest of their wives
   Is foul as slander.

---

497. Another of Iago's gnomic speeches; perhaps approximately: "If now he is not himself, I wish
he would be what he could be!"   498.   Actions.   499.   Anything.

Othello.   Bid her come hither; go.   (*Exit Emilia.*)
   She says enough; yet she 's a simple[500] bawd
   That cannot say as much. This is a subtle whore,
   A closet lock and key of villanous secrets;
   And yet she 'll kneel and pray; I have seen her do 't.

(*Re-enter Emilia with Desdemona.*)

Desdemona.   My lord, what is your will?
Othello.   Pray, chuck, come hither.
Desdemona.   What is your pleasure?
Othello.   Let me see your eyes;
   Look in my face.
Desdemona.   What horrible fancy 's this?
Othello (*to Emilia*).   Some of your function,[501] mistress;
   Leave procreants alone and shut the door;
   Cough or cry 'hem' if any body come;
   Your mystery,[502] your mystery; nay, dispatch.   (*Exit Emilia.*)
Desdemona.   Upon my knees, what doth your speech import?
   I understand a fury in your words.
   But not the words.
Othello.   Why, what art thou?
Desdemona.   Your wife, my lord; your true
   And loyal wife.
Othello.   Come, swear it, damn thyself;
   Lest, being like one of heaven, the devils themselves
   Should fear to seize thee; therefore be double-damn'd;
   Swear thou art honest.
Desdemona.   Heaven doth truly know it.
Othello.   Heaven truly knows that thou art false as hell.
Desdemona.   To whom, my lord? with whom? how am I false?
Othello.   Ah! Desdemona; away, away, away!
Desdemona.   Alas, the heavy day!—Why do you weep?
   Am I the motive of these tears, my lord?
   If haply you my father do suspect
   An instrument of this your calling back,
   Lay not your blame on me; if you have lost him,
   Why, I have lost him too.
Othello.   Had it pleas'd heaven
   To try me with affliction, had he rain'd
   All kinds of sores and shames on my bare head,
   Steep'd me in poverty to the very lips,
   Given to captivity me and my utmost hopes,

---

500.   Simpleminded.   501.   To your duty, business.   502.   Trade.

I should have found in some part of my soul
A drop of patience; but, alas! to make me
The fixed figure for the time of scorn[503]
To point his slow and moving finger at;
Yet could I bear that too; well, very well:
But there, where I have garner'd[504] up my heart,
Where either I must live or bear no life,
The fountain from the which my current runs
Or else dries up; to be discarded thence!
Or keep it as a cistern for foul toads
To knot and gender in![505] Turn thy complexion there,[506]
Patience, thou young and rose-lipp'd cherubin;
Ay, there, look grim as hell!

Desdemona.   I hope my noble lord esteems me honest.

Othello.   O! ay; as summer flies are in the shambles,[507]
That quicken even with blowing. O thou weed!
Who art so lovely fair and smell'st so sweet
That the sense aches at thee, would thou hadst ne'er been born.

Desdemona.   Alas! what ignorant sin have I committed?

Othello.   Was this fair paper, this most goodly book,
Made to write 'whore' upon? What committed!
Committed! O thou public commoner![508]
I should make very forges of my cheeks,
That would to cinders burn up modesty,
Did I but speak thy deeds. What committed!
Heaven stops the nose at it and the moon winks,[509]
The bawdy wind that kisses all it meets
Is hush'd within the hollow mine of earth,
And will not hear it. What committed!
Impudent strumpet!

Desdemona.   By heaven, you do me wrong.

Othello.   Are not you a strumpet?

Desdemona.   No, as I am a Christian.
If to preserve this vessel for my lord
From any other foul unlawful touch
Be not to be a strumpet, I am none.

Othello.   What! not a whore?

Desdemona.   No, as I shall be sav'd.

Othello.   Is it possible?

Desdemona.   O! heaven forgive us.

Othello.   I cry you mercy,[510] then;

---

503. *I.e.,* the scornful world.   504. Stored.   505. Bunch up and procreate.
506. *I.e.,* change your color to suit the "cistern for foul toads."   507. Slaughterhouse.
508. Harlot.   509. Closes her eyes.   510. Beg your pardon.

I took you for that cunning whore of Venice
That married with Othello. You, mistress,
That have the office opposite to Saint Peter,
And keep the gate of hell!

(Re-enter Emilia.)

You, you, ay, you!
We have done our course; there's money for your pains.
I pray you, turn the key and keep our counsel.   (Exit.)

Emilia.   Alas! what does this gentleman conceive?[511]
How do you, madam? how do you, my good lady?
Desdemona.   Faith, half asleep.
Emilia.   Good madam, what 's the matter with my lord?
Desdemona.   With who?
Emilia.   Why, with my lord, madam.
Desdemona.   Who is thy lord?
Emilia.   He that is yours, sweet lady.
Desdemona.   I have none; do not talk to me, Emilia;
I cannot weep, nor answer have I none,
But what should go by water.[512] Prithee, to-night
Lay on my bed my wedding sheets: remember:
And call thy husband hither
Emilia.   Here is a change indeed!   (Exit.)
Desdemona.   'Tis meet I should be us'd so, very meet.
How have I been behav'd, that he might stick
The small'st opinion on my least misuse?[513]

(Re-enter Emilia, with Iago.)

Iago.   What is your pleasure, madam? How is it with you?
Desdemona.   I cannot tell. Those that do teach young babes
Do it with gentle means and easy tasks;
He might have chid me so; for, in good faith,
I am a child to chiding.
Iago.   What 's the matter, lady?
Emilia.   Alas, Iago, my lord hath so bewhor'd her,
Thrown such despite[514] and heavy terms upon her,
As true hearts cannot bear.
Desdemona.   Am I that name, Iago?
Iago.   What name, fair lady?
Desdemona.   Such as she says my lord did say I was.
Emilia.   He call'd her whore; a beggar in his drink
Could not have laid such terms upon his callat.[515]

---

511. Imagine.   512. Be conveyed by means of tears.   513. The least suspicion on my
slightest misconduct.   514. Abuse.   515. Slut.

Iago. Why did he so?

Desdemona. I do not know; I am sure I am none such.

Iago. Do not weep, do not weep. Alas the day!

Emilia. Has she forsook so many noble matches,
    Her father and her country and her friends,
    To be call'd whore? would it not make one weep?

Desdemona. It is my wretched fortune.

Iago. Beshrew [516] him for it!
    How comes this trick upon him?

Desdemona. Nay, heaven doth know.

Emilia. I will be hang'd, if some eternal villain,
    Some busy and insinuating rogue,
    Some cogging[517] cozening slave, to get some office,
    Have not devis'd this slander; I 'll be hang'd else.

Iago. Fie! there is no such man; it is impossible.

Desdemona. If any such there be, heaven pardon him!

Emilia. A halter pardon him, and hell gnaw his bones!
    Why should he call her whore? who keeps her company?
    What place? what time? what form? what likelihood?
    The Moor 's abus'd by some most villanous knave,
    Some base notorious knave, some scurvy fellow.
    O heaven! that such companions[518] thou'dst unfold,
    And put in every honest hand a whip
    To lash the rascals naked through the world,
    Even from the east to the west!

Iago. Speak within door.

Emilia. O! fie upon them. Some such squire he was
    That turn'd your wit the seamy side without,[519]
    And made you to suspect me with the Moor.

Iago. You are a fool; go to.

Desdemona. O good Iago,
    What shall I do to win my lord again?
    Good friend, go to him; for, by this light of heaven,
    I know not how I lost him. Here I kneel:
    If e'er my will did trespass 'gainst his love,
    Either in discourse of thought or actual deed,
    Or that mine eyes, mine ears, or any sense,
    Delighted them[520] in any other form;
    Or that I do not yet,[521] and ever did,
    And ever will, though he do shake me off
    To beggarly divorcement, love him dearly,
    Comfort forswear me! Unkindness may do much;

---

516. Curse.   517. Cheating.   518. Fellows (derogatory).   519. Outward.
520. Found delight.   521. Still.

And his unkindness may defeat[522] my life,
But never taint my love. I cannot say 'whore':
It does abhor me now I speak the word;
To do the act that might the addition earn
Not the world's mass of vanity could make me.

Iago.   I pray you be content, 'tis but his humour;
The business of the state does him offence,
And he does chide with you.

Desdemona.   If 'twere no other,—

Iago.   'Tis but so, I warrant.   (*Trumpets.*)
Hark! how these instruments summon to supper;
The messengers of Venice stay the meat:
Go in, and weep not; all things shall be well.

                                  (*Exeunt Desdemona and Emilia.*)

(*Enter Roderigo.*)

How now, Roderigo!

Roderigo.   I do not find that thou dealest justly with me.

Iago.   What in the contrary?[523]

Roderigo.   Every day thou daffest me[524] with some device, Iago; and rather, as it seems to me now, keepest from me all conveniency,[525] than suppliest me with the least advantage of hope. I will indeed no longer endure it, nor am I yet persuaded to put up[526] in peace what already I have foolishly suffered.

Iago.   Will you hear me, Roderigo?

Roderigo.   Faith, I have heard too much, for your words and performances are no kin together.

Iago.   You charge me most unjustly.

Roderigo.   With nought but truth. I have wasted myself out of my means. The jewels you have had from me to deliver to Desdemona would half have corrupted a votarist;[527] you have told me she has received them, and returned me expectations and comforts of sudden respect[528] and acquaintance, but I find none.

Iago.   Well; go to; very well.

Roderigo.   Very well! go to! I cannot go to, man; nor 'tis not very well: by this hand, I say, it is very scurvy, and begin to find myself fobbed[529] in it.

Iago.   Very well.

Roderigo.   I tell you 'tis not very well. I will make myself known to Desdemona; if she will return me my jewels, I will give over my suit and repent my unlawful solicitation; if not, assure yourself I will seek satisfaction of you.

Iago.   You have said now.[530]

---

522. Destroy.   523. *I.e.*, what reason do you have for saying that.   524. You put me off.   525. Favorable circumstances.   526. Put up with.   527. Nun.   528. Immediate consideration.   529. Cheated.   530. *I.e.*, "I suppose you're through?" (?); or: "Now you're talking" (?).

Roderigo. Ay, and said nothing, but what I protest intendment of doing.

Iago. Why, now I see there's mettle in thee, and even from this instant do build on thee a better opinion than ever before. Give me thy hand, Roderigo; thou hast taken against me a most just exception; but yet, I protest, I have dealt most directly in thy affair.

Roderigo. It hath not appeared.

Iago. I grant indeed it hath not appeared, and your suspicion is not without wit and judgment. But, Roderigo, if thou hast that in thee indeed, which I have greater reason to believe now than ever, I mean purpose, courage, and valour, this night show it: if thou the next night following enjoy not Desdemona, take me from this world with treachery and devise engines for[531] my life.

Roderigo. Well, what is it? is it within reason and compass?

Iago. Sir, there is especial commission come from Venice to depute Cassio in Othello's place.

Roderigo. Is that true? why, then Othello and Desdemona return again to Venice.

Iago. O, no! he goes into Mauritania, and takes away with him the fair Desdemona, unless his abode be lingered here by some accident; wherein none can be so determinate[532] as the removing of Cassio.

Roderigo. How do you mean, removing of him?

Iago. Why, by making him uncapable of Othello's place; knocking out his brains.

Roderigo. And that you would have me do?

Iago. Ay; if you dare do yourself a profit and a right. He sups to-night with a harlotry,[533] and thither will I go to him; he knows not yet of his honourable fortune. If you will watch his going thence,—which I will fashion to fall out between twelve and one,—you may take him at your pleasure; I will be near to second your attempt, and he shall fall between us. Come, stand not amazed at it, but go along with me; I will show you such a necessity in his death that you shall think yourself bound to put it on him. It is now high supper-time, and the night grows to waste; about it.

Roderigo. I will hear further reason for this.

Iago. And you shall be satisfied. *(Exeunt.)*

SCENE 3. *Another Room in the Castle.*

(Enter Othello, Lodovico, Desdemona, Emilia, and Attendants.)

Lodovico. I do beseech you, sir, trouble yourself no further.

Othello. O! pardon me; 'twill do me good to walk.

---

531. Devices against. 532. Effective. 533. Harlot.

Lodovico.   Madam, good–night; I humbly thank your ladyship.

Desdemona.   Your honour is most welcome.

Othello.   Will you walk, sir?

O! Desdemona,—

Desdemona.   My lord?

Othello.   Get you to bed on the instant; I will be returned forthwith; dismiss your attendant there; look it be done.

Desdemona.   I will, my lord.   (*Exeunt Othello, Lodovico, and Attendants.*)

Emilia.   How goes it now? He looks gentler than he did.

Desdemona.   He says he will return incontinent;[534]

He hath commanded me to go to bed,

And bade me to dismiss you.

Emilia.   Dismiss me!

Desdemona.   It was his bidding; therefore, good Emilia,

Give me my nightly wearing, and adieu:

We must not now displease him.

Emilia.   I would you had never seen him.

Desdemona.   So would not I; my love doth so approve him,

That even his stubbornness,[535] his checks[536] and frowns,—

Prithee, unpin me,—have grace and favour in them.

Emilia.   I have laid those sheets you bade me on the bed.

Desdemona.   All 's one.[537] Good faith! how foolish are our minds!

If I do die before thee, prithee, shroud me

In one of those same sheets.

Emilia.   Come, come, you talk.

Desdemona.   My mother had a maid call'd Barbara;

She was in love, and he she lov'd prov'd mad[538]

And did forsake her; she had a song of 'willow';

An old thing 'twas, but it express'd her fortune,

And she died singing it; that song to-night

Will not go from my mind; I have much to do

But to go hang my head all at one side,

And sing it like poor Barbara. Prithee, dispatch.

Emilia.   Shall I go fetch your night-gown?

Desdemona.   No, unpin me here.

This Lodovico is a proper man.

Emilia.   A very handsome man.

Desdemona.   He speaks well.

Emilia.   I know a lady in Venice would have walked barefoot to Palestine for a touch of his nether lip.

Desdemona (*sings*).

The poor soul sat sighing by a sycamore tree,

---

534. At once.   535. Roughness.   536. Rebukes   537. *I.e.*, it doesn't matter.
538. Wild.

Sing all a green willow;
Her hand on her bosom, her head on her knee,
    Sing willow, willow, willow:
The fresh streams ran by her, and murmur'd her moans;
    Sing willow, willow, willow:
Her salt tears fell from her, and soften'd the stones;—

Lay by these:—
    Sing willow, willow, willow:

Prithee, hie thee;[539] he 'll come anon.—

Sing all a green willow must be my garland.
    Let nobody blame him, his scorn I approve,—
Nay, that's not next. Hark! who is it that knocks?
Emilia. It is the wind.
Desdemona.
    I call'd my love false love; but what said he then?
        Sing willow, willow, willow:
    If I court moe[540] women, you 'll couch with moe men.

So, get thee gone; good-night. Mine eyes do itch;
Doth that bode weeping?
Emilia. 'Tis neither here nor there.
Desdemona. I have heard it said so. O! these men, these men!
    Dost thou in conscience think, tell me, Emilia,
    That there be women do abuse their husbands
    In such gross kind?
Emilia. There be some such, no question.
Desdemona. Wouldst thou do such a deed for all the world?
Emilia. Why, would not you?
Desdemona. No, by this heavenly light!
Emilia. Nor I neither by this heavenly light;
    I might do 't as well i' the dark.
Desdemona. Wouldst thou do such a deed for all the world?
Emilia. The world is a huge thing; 'tis a great price
    For a small vice.
Desdemona. In troth, I think thou wouldst not.
Emilia. In troth, I think I should, and undo 't when I had done. Marry, I would
    not do such a thing for a joint-ring,[541] nor measures of lawn,[542] nor for
    gowns, petticoats, nor caps, nor any petty exhibition;[543] but for the whole
    world, who would not make her husband a cuckold to make him a
    monarch? I should venture purgatory for 't.

---

539. Hurry.   540. More.   541. Ring made in separable halves.   542. Fine
linen.   543. Offer, gift.

Desdemona.   Beshrew me, if I would do such a wrong
        For the whole world.
Emilia.   Why, the wrong is but a wrong i' the world; and having the world for
        your labour, 'tis a wrong in your own world, and you might quickly make
        it right.
Desdemona.   I do not think there is any such woman.
Emilia.   Yes, a dozen; and as many to the vantage,[544] as
        Would store[545] the world they played for.
        But I do think it is their husbands' faults
        If wives do fall. Say that they slack their duties,
        And pour our treasures into foreign laps,
        Or else break out in peevish jealousies,
        Throwing restraint upon us; or say they strike us,
        Or scant[546] our former having[547] in despite;
        Why, we have galls,[548] and though we have some grace,
        Yet have we some revenge. Let husbands know
        Their wives have sense like them; they see and smell,
        And have their palates both for sweet and sour,
        As husbands have. What is it that they do
        When they change us for others? Is it sport?[549]
        I think it is; and doth affection breed it?
        I think it doth; is 't frailty that thus errs?
        It is so too; and have not we affections,
        Desires for sport, and frailty, as men have?
        Then, let them use us well; else let them know,
        The ills we do, their ills instruct us so.
Desdemona.   Good-night, good-night; heaven me such usage[550] send,
        Not to pick bad from bad, but by bad mend!   (*Exeunt.*)

Act V

SCENE 1.   *Cyprus. A Street.*

(*Enter Iago and Roderigo.*)

Iago.   Here, stand behind this bulk;[551] straight will he come:
        Wear thy good rapier bare, and put it home.
        Quick, quick; fear nothing; I 'll be at thy elbow.
        It makes us, or it mars us; think on that,
        And fix most firm thy resolution.
Roderigo.   Be near at hand; I may miscarry in 't.

---

544. Over and above.   545. Populate.   546. Reduce.   547. Allowance.
548. Spirits, temper.   549. Lust, sexual enjoyment.   550. Habits (?), treatment (?).
551. Jutting part of a wall.

Iago.   Here, at thy hand: be bold, and take thy stand.   (*Retires.*)
Roderigo.   I have no great devotion to the deed;
      And yet he has given me satisfying reasons:
      'Tis but a man gone: forth, my sword; he dies.
Iago.   I have rubb'd this young quat[552] almost to the sense,[553]
      And he grows angry. Now, whether he kill Cassio,
      Or Cassio him, or each do kill the other,
      Every way makes my gain: live Roderigo,
      He calls me to a restitution large
      Of gold and jewels that I bobb'd[554] from him,
      As gifts to Desdemona;
      It must not be: if Cassio do remain,
      He hath a daily beauty in his life
      That makes me ugly: and, besides, the Moor
      May unfold me to him; there stand I in much peril.
      No, he must die. But so;[555] I hear him coming.

(*Enter Cassio.*)

Roderigo.   I know his gait; 'tis he. Villain, thou diest!

(*Makes a pass at Cassio.*)

Cassio.   That thrust had been mine enemy indeed
      But that my coat is better than thou know'st;
      I will make proof of thine.

(*Draws, and wounds Roderigo.*)

Roderigo.   O! I am slain.

(*Iago from behind wounds Cassio in the leg, and exit.*)

Cassio.   I am maim'd for ever. Help, ho! murder! murder!   (*Falls.*)

(*Enter Othello, at a distance.*)

Othello.   The voice of Cassio: Iago keeps his word.
Roderigo.   O! villain that I am!
Othello.   It is e'en so.
Cassio.   O, help, ho! light! a surgeon!
Othello.   'Tis he: O brave Iago, honest and just!
      That hast such noble sense of thy friend's wrong;
      Thou teachest me. Minion,[556] your dear lies dead,
      And your unblest fate hies; strumpet, I come!
      Forth of my heart those charms, thine eyes, are blotted;
      Thy bed lust-stain'd shall with lust's blood be spotted.   (*Exit.*)

---

552. Pimple.   553. To the quick.   554. Swindled.   555. *I.e.,* that's the only way.
556. (Cassio's) darling, *i.e.,* Desdemona.

(Enter Lodovico and Gratiano, at a distance.)

Cassio.   What ho! no watch? no passage?[557] murder! murder!
Gratiano.   'Tis some mischance; the cry is very direful.
Cassio.   O, help!
Lodovico.   Hark!
Roderigo.   O wretched villain!
Lodovico.   Two or three groans: it is a heavy[558] night;
   These may be counterfeits; let 's think 't unsafe
   To come in to the cry[559] without more help.
Roderigo.   Nobody come? then shall I bleed to death.
Lodovico.   Hark!

(Re-enter Iago, with a light.)

Gratiano.   Here 's one comes in his shirt, with light and weapons.
Iago.   Who 's there? whose noise is this that cries on murder?
Lodovico.   We do not know.
Iago.   Did not you hear a cry?
Cassio.   Here, here! for heaven's sake, help me.
Iago.   What 's the matter?
Gratiano.   This is Othello's ancient, as I take it.
Lodovico.   The same indeed; a very valiant fellow.
Iago.   What are you here that cry so grievously?
Cassio.   Iago? O! I am spoil'd, undone by villains!
   Give me some help.
Iago.   O me, lieutenant! what villains have done this?
Cassio.   I think that one of them is hereabout,
   And cannot make away.
Iago.   O treacherous villains!
   (To Lodovico and Gratiano.) What are you there? come in, and
   give some help.
Roderigo.   O! help me here.
Cassio.   That 's one of them.
Iago.   O murderous slave! O villain!

(Stabs Roderigo.)

Roderigo.   O damn'd Iago! O inhuman dog!
Iago.   Kill men i' the dark! Where be these bloody thieves?
   How silent is this town! Ho! murder! murder!
   What may you be? are you of good or evil?
Lodovico.   As you shall prove us, praise us.
Iago.   Signior Lodovico?
Lodovico.   He, sir.

---

557.   Passer-by.   558.   Dark.   559.   Where the cry comes from.

Iago. I cry you mercy. Here 's Cassio hurt by villains.
Gratiano. Cassio!
Iago. How is it, brother?
Cassio. My leg is cut in two.
Iago. Marry, heaven forbid.
Light, gentlemen; I 'll bind it with my shirt.

(*Enter Bianca.*)

Bianca. What is the matter, ho? who is 't that cried?
Iago. Who is 't that cried!
Bianca. O my dear Cassio! my sweet Cassio!
O Cassio, Cassio, Cassio!
Iago. O notable strumpet! Cassio, may you suspect
Who they should be that have thus mangled you?
Cassio. No.
Gratiano. I am sorry to find you thus; I have been to seek you.
Iago. Lend me a garter. So. O! for a chair,
To bear him easily hence!
Bianca. Alas; he faints! O Cassio, Cassio, Cassio!
Iago. Gentlemen all, I do suspect this trash[560]
To be a party in this injury.
Patience awhile, good Cassio. Come, come.
Lend me a light. Know we this face, or no?
Alas! my friend and my dear countryman,
Roderigo? no: yes, sure, O heaven! Roderigo.
Gratiano. What! of Venice?
Iago. Even he, sir: did you know him?
Gratiano. Know him! ay.
Iago. Signior Gratiano? I cry you gentle pardon;
These bloody accidents must excuse my manners,
That so neglected you.
Gratiano. I am glad to see you.
Iago. How do you, Cassio? O! a chair, a chair!
Gratiano. Roderigo!

(*A chair brought in.*)

Iago. He, he, 'tis he,—O! that 's well said; the chair:
Some good men bear him carefully from hence;
I 'll fetch the general's surgeon. (*To Bianca.*) For you, mistress,
Save you your labour. He that lies slain here, Cassio,
Was my dear friend. What malice was between you?
Cassio. None in the world; nor do I know that man.
Iago (*to Bianca*). What! look you pale? O! bear him out o' the air—

---

560. *I.e.,* Bianca.

(Cassio and Roderigo are borne off.)

> Stay you, good gentlemen. Look you pale, mistress?—
> Do you preceive the gastness[561] of her eye?
> Nay, if you stare, we shall hear more anon.
> Behold her well; I pray you, look upon her.
> Do you see, gentlemen? nay, guiltiness will speak
> Though tongues were out of use.

(Enter Emilia.)

Emilia. 'Las! what 's the matter? what 's the matter, husband?
Iago. Cassio hath here been set on in the dark
> By Roderigo and fellows that are 'scaped:
> He 's almost slain, and Roderigo dead.
Emilia. Alas! good gentleman; alas! good Cassio!
Iago. This is the fruit of whoring. Prithee, Emilia,
> Go know of Cassio where he supp'd to-night.
> *(To Bianca.)* What! do you shake at that?
Bianca. He supp'd at my house; but I therefore shake not.
Iago. O! did he so? I charge you, go with me.
Emilia. Fie, fie, upon thee, strumpet!
Bianca. I am no strumpet, but of life as honest
> As you that thus abuse me.
Emilia. As I! foh! fie upon thee!
Iago. Kind gentlemen, let 's go see poor Cassio dress'd.[562]
> Come, mistress, you must tell 's another tale.
> Emilia, run you to the citadel,
> And tell my lord and lady what hath happ'd.
> Will you go on afore? *(Aside.)* This is the night
> That either makes me or fordoes[563] me quite.   *(Exeunt.)*

SCENE 2. *A Bedchamber in the Castle. Desdemona in bed asleep. A light burning.*

(Enter Othello.)

Othello. It is the cause,[564] it is the cause, my soul;
> Let me not name it to you, you chaste stars!
> It is the cause. Yet I 'll not shed her blood,
> Nor scar that whiter skin of hers than snow,
> And smooth as monumental alabaster.

---

561. Terror.   562. Bandaged.   563. Ruins.   564. *I.e.,* Desdemona's unchastity
(Othello means that the severity of the punishment is required by the nature of her sin.)

Yet she must die, else she 'll betray more men.
Put out the light, and then put out the light:
If I quench thee, thou flaming minister,[565]
I can again thy former light restore,
Should I repent me; but once put out thy light,
Thou cunning'st[566] pattern of excelling nature,
I know not where is that Promethean[567] heat
That can thy light relume.[568] When I have pluck'd the rose,
I cannot give it vital growth again,
It needs must wither: I 'll smell it on the tree. (*Kisses her.*)
O balmy breath, that dost almost persuade
Justice to break her sword! One more, one more.
Be thus when thou art dead, and I will kill thee,
And love thee after. One more, and this the last:
So sweet was ne'er so fatal. I must weep,
But they are cruel tears; this sorrow 's heavenly,
It strikes where it doth love. She wakes.

Desdemona.   Who 's there? Othello?

Othello.   Ay, Desdemona.

Desdemona.   Will you come to bed, my lord?

Othello.   Have you pray'd to-night, Desdemona?

Desdemona.   Ay, my lord.

Othello.   If you bethink yourself of any crime
Unreconcil'd as yet to heaven and grace,
Solicit for it straight.

Desdemona.   Alas! my lord, what may you mean by that?

Othello.   Well, do it, and be brief; I will walk by:[569]
I would not kill thy unprepared spirit;
No; heaven forfend![570] I would not kill thy soul.

Desdemona.   Talk you of killing?

Othello.   Ay, I do.

Desdemona.   Then heaven
Have mercy on me!

Othello.   Amen! with all my heart.

Desdemona.   If you say so, I hope you will not kill me.

Othello.   Hum!

Desdemona.   And yet I fear you; for you are fatal then
When your eyes roll so. Why I should fear I know not,
Since guiltiness I know not; but yet I feel I fear.

Othello.   Think on thy sins.

Desdemona.   They are loves I bear to you.

---

565. *I.e.*, the candle.   566. Most intricately wrought.   567. In Greek mythology the
demi-god Prometheus stole fire from the gods and gave it to man.   568. Relight.
569. Nearby.   570. Forbid.

Othello.   Ay, and for that thou diest.

Desdemona.   That death 's unnatural that kills for loving.
Alas! why gnaw you so your nether lip?
Some bloody passion shakes your very frame;
These are portents,[571] but yet, I hope, I hope
They do not point on me.

Othello.   Peace, and be still!

Desdemona.   I will so. What 's the matter?

Othello.   That handkerchief which I so lov'd and gave thee
Thou gav'st to Cassio.

Desdemona.   No, by my life and soul!
Send for the man and ask him.

Othello.   Sweet soul, take heed,
Take heed of perjury; thou 'rt on thy death-bed.

Desdemona.   Ay, but not yet to die.

Othello.   Yes, presently;[572]
Therefore confess thee freely of thy sin;
For to deny each article with oath
Cannot remove nor choke the strong conception[573]
That I do groan withal. Thou art to die.

Desdemona.   Then Lord have mercy on me!

Othello.   I say, amen.

Desdemona.   And have you mercy too! I never did
Offend you in my life; never lov'd Cassio
But with such general warranty[574] of heaven
As I might love; I never gave him token.

Othello.   By heaven, I saw my handkerchief in 's hand.
O perjur'd woman! thou dost stone[575] my heart,
And mak'st me call what I intend to do
A murder, which I thought a sacrifice:
I saw the handkerchief.

Desdemona.   He found it then;
I never gave it him. Send for him hither;
Let him confess a truth.

Othello.   He hath confessed.

Desdemona.   What, my lord?

Othello.   That he hath us'd thee.

Desdemona.   How? Unlawfully?

Othello.   Ay.

Desdemona.   He will not say so.

Othello.   No; his mouth is stopp'd:
Honest Iago hath ta'en order for 't.[576]

---

571. Omens.   572. At once.   573. Belief.   574. Permission.   575. Turn to stone.   576. Taken steps.

Desdemona.   O! my fear interprets. What! is he dead?

Othello.   Had all his hairs been lives, my great revenge
    Had stomach[577] for them all.

Desdemona.   Alas! he is betray'd and I undone.

Othello.   Out, strumpet! Weep'st thou for him to my face?

Desdemona.   O! banish me, my lord, but kill me not!

Othello.   Down, strumpet!

Desdemona.   Kill me to-morrow; let me live to-night!

Othello.   Nay, if you strive,—

Desdemona.   But half an hour!

Othello.   Being done, there is no pause.

Desdemona.   But while I say one prayer!

Othello.   It is too late.   (*He smothers her*)

Emilia (*within*).   My lord, my lord! what, ho! my lord, my lord!

Othello.   What noise is this? Not dead? not yet quite dead?
    I that am cruel am yet merciful;
    I would not have thee linger in thy pain.
    So, so.

Emilia (*within*).   What, ho! my lord, my lord!

Othello.   Who's there?

Emilia (*within*).   O! good my lord, I would speak a word with you!

Othello.   Yes; 'tis Emilia: by and by.[578] She 's dead.
    'Tis like[579] she comes to speak of Cassio's death;
    The noise was high. Ha! no more moving?
    Still as the grave. Shall she come in? Were 't good?[580]
    I think she stirs again: no. What 's best to do?
    If she come in she'll sure speak to my wife:
    My wife! my wife! what wife? I have no wife;
    O, insupportable! O heavy hour!
    Methinks it should be now a huge eclipse
    Of sun and moon, and that the affrighted globe
    Should yawn[581] at alteration.

Emilia (*within*).   I do beseech you
    That I may speak with you, O! good my lord.

Othello.   I had forgot thee: O! come in, Emilia:
    Soft, by and by: let me the curtains draw.
    Where art thou?   (*Unlocks the door.*)

(*Enter Emilia.*)

    What 's the matter with thee now?

Emilia.   O! my good lord, yonder 's foul murder done.

Othello.   What! now?

---

577. Appetite.   578. *I.e.,* "just a moment."   579. Likely.   580. Would that be wise.   581. Open up (as in an earthquake).

Emilia.   But now, my lord.

Othello.   It is the very error[582] of the moon;
  She comes more near the earth than she was wont,
  And makes men mad.

Emilia.   Cassio, my lord, has kill'd a young Venetian
  Call'd Roderigo.

Othello.   Roderigo kill'd!
  And Cassio kill'd?

Emilia.   No, Cassio is not kill'd.

Othello.   Not Cassio kill'd! then murder 's out of tune,
  And sweet revenge grows harsh.

Desdemona.   O! falsely, falsely murder'd.

Emilia.   Alas! what cry is that?

Othello.   That! what?

Emilia.   Out, and alas! that was my lady's voice:
  Help! Help, ho! help! O lady, speak again!
  Sweet Desdemona! O! sweet mistress, speak.

Desdemona.   A guiltless death I die.

Emilia.   O! who hath done this deed?

Desdemona.   Nobody; I myself; farewell:
  Commend me to my kind lord. O! farewell!   *(Dies.)*

Othello.   Why, how should she be murder'd?

Emilia.   Alas! who knows?

Othello.   You heard her say herself it was not I.

Emilia.   She said so; I must needs report the truth.

Othello.   She 's like a liar gone to burning hell;
  'Twas I that kill'd her.

Emilia.   O! the more angel she,
  And you the blacker devil.

Othello.   She turn'd to folly, and she was a whore.

Emilia.   Thou dost belie her, and thou art a devil.

Othello.   She was false as water.

Emilia.   Thou art rash as fire to say
  That she was false! O! she was heavenly true.

Othello.   Cassio did tup her; ask thy husband else.
  O! I were damn'd beneath all depth in hell
  But that I did proceed[583] upon just grounds
  To this extremity. Thy husband knew it all.

Emilia.   My husband!

Othello.   Thy husband.

Emilia.   That she was false to wedlock?

Othello.   Ay, with Cassio. Nay, had she been true,
  If heaven would make me such another world

---

582. Straying.   583. Had I not proceeded.

Of one entire and perfect chrysolite,[584]
I'd not have sold her for it.

Emilia. My husband!

Othello. Ay, 'twas he that told me first:
An honest man he is, and hates the slime
That sticks on filthy deeds.

Emilia. My husband!

Othello. What needs this iterance,[585] woman? I say thy husband.

Emilia. O mistress! villany hath made mocks with love.
My husband say that she was false!

Othello. He, woman;
I say, thy husband: dost understand the word?
My friend, thy husband, honest, honest Iago.

Emilia. If he say so, may his pernicious soul
Rot half a grain a day! he lies to the heart:
She was too fond of her most filthy bargain.[586]

Othello. Ha!

Emilia. Do thy worst:
This deed of thine is no more worthy heaven
Than thou wast worthy her.

Othello. Peace! you were best.[587]

Emilia. Thou hast not half the power to do me harm
As I have to be hurt. O gull! O dolt!
As ignorant as dirt! thou hast done a deed,—
I care not for thy sword; I'll make thee known,
Though I lost twenty lives. Help! help, ho! help!
The Moor has kill'd my mistress! murder! murder!

(*Enter Montano, Gratiano, Iago, and others.*)

Montano. What is the matter? How now, general!

Emilia. O! are you come, Iago? you have done well,
That men must lay their murders on your neck.

Gratiano. What is the matter?

Emilia. Disprove this villain if thou be'st a man:
He says thou told'st him that his wife was false.
I know thou didst not, thou 'rt not such a villain.
Speak, for my heart is full.

Iago. I told him what I thought, and told no more
Than what he found himself was apt and true.

Emilia. But did you ever tell him she was false?

Iago. I did.

Emilia. You told a lie, an odious damned lie;

---

584. Topaz.   585. Repetition.   586. *I.e.,* Othello.   587. You'd better be quiet.

Upon my soul, a lie, a wicked lie;
She false with Cassio! Did you say with Cassio?

Iago. With Cassio, mistress. Go to, charm[588] your tongue.

Emilia. I will not charm my tongue; I am bound to speak.
My mistress here lies murder'd in her bed.

All. O heavens forfend!

Emilia. And your reports have set the murder on.

Othello. Nay, stare not, masters; it is true, indeed.

Gratiano. 'Tis a strange truth.

Montano. O monstrous act!

Emilia. Villany! villany! villany!
I think upon 't, I think, I smell 't; O villany!
I thought so then;[589] I'll kill myself for grief.
O! villany, villany!

Iago. What! are you mad? I charge you, get you home.

Emilia. Good gentlemen, let me have leave to speak:
'Tis proper I obey him, but not now.
Perchance, Iago, I will ne'er go home.

Othello. O! O! O!   (Falls on the bed.)

Emilia. Nay, lay thee down and roar,
For thou hast kill'd the sweetest innocent
That e'er did lift up eye.

Othello. O! she was foul.   (Rises.)
I scarce did know you, uncle. There lies your niece,
Whose breath, indeed, these hands have newly stopp'd:
I know this act shows terrible and grim.

Gratiano. Poor Desdemona! I am glad thy father 's dead.
Thy match was mortal to him, and pure grief
Shore[590] his old thread in twain: did he live now,
This sight would make him do a desperate turn,
Yea, curse his better angel from his side,
And fall to reprobation.[591]

Othello. 'Tis pitiful; but yet Iago knows
That she with Cassio hath the act of shame
A thousand times committed; Cassio confess'd it:
And she did gratify[592] his amorous works
With that recognizance and pledge of love
Which I first gave her. I saw it in his hand:
It was a handkerchief, an antique token
My father gave my mother.

---

588. *I.e.,* into silence.   589. *Cf.* "I will be hang'd, if some eternal villain,/Some busy and insinuating rogue,/Some cogging cozening slave, to get some office,/Have not devis'd this slander; . . ." (IV, ii, p. 609). Emilia means, not that she guessed Iago's guilt, but that she rightly guessed the slanderer's motive.   590. Cut.   591. Damnation.   592. Reward.

624   LOVE AND HATE: DRAMA

Emilia. O heaven! O heavenly powers!

Iago. Come, hold your peace.

Emilia. 'Twill out, 'twill out; I hold my peace, sir? no;
    No, I will speak as liberal as the north;[593]
    Let heaven and men and devils, let them all,
    All, all, cry shame against me, yet I'll speak.

Iago. Be wise, and get you home.

Emilia. I will not.

(Iago threatens to stab Emilia.)

Gratiano. Fie!
    Your sword upon a woman!

Emilia. O thou dull Moor! that handkerchief thou speak'st of
    I found by fortune and did give my husband;
    For often, with a solemn earnestness,
    More than, indeed, belong'd to such a trifle,
    He begg'd of me to steal it.

Iago. Villainous whore!

Emilia. She give it Cassio! no, alas! I found it,
    And I did give 't my husband.

Iago. Filth, thou liest!

Emilia. By heaven, I do not, I do not, gentlemen.
    O murderous coxcomb![594] what should such a fool
    Do with so good a wife?

Othello. Are there no stones[595] in heaven
    But what serve for the thunder? Precious villain!

(He runs at Iago. Iago stabs Emilia.)

Gratiano. The woman falls; sure, he has kill'd his wife.   *(Exit Iago.)*

Emilia. Ay, ay; O! lay me by my mistress' side.

Gratiano. He 's gone; but his wife 's kill'd.

Montano. 'Tis a notorious[596] villain. Take you this weapon,
    Which I have here recover'd from the Moor.
    Come, guard the door without; let him not pass,
    But kill him rather. I'll after that same villain,
    For 'tis a damned slave.   *(Exeunt Montano and Gratiano.)*

Othello. I am not valiant neither,
    But every puny whipster[597] gets my sword.
    But why should honour outlive honesty?
    Let it go all.

Emilia. What did thy song bode, lady?
    Hark, canst thou hear me? I will play the swan,

---

593. *I.e.*, the north wind (?), the supposedly free-spoken people of north England (?).
594. Idiot.   595. *I.e.*, thunderbolts (to strike Iago down).   596. Notable.
597. *I.e.*, a small boy whipping a top.

And die in music:—

(*Sings*.) Willow, willow, willow.

Moor, she was chaste; she lov'd thee, cruel Moor;

So come my soul to bliss as I speak true;

So speaking as I think, I die, I die.   (*Dies*.)

Othello. I have another weapon in this chamber;

It is a sword of Spain, the ice-brook's temper.[598]

O! here it is. Uncle, I must come forth.

Gratiano (*within*). If thou attempt it, it will cost thee dear:

Thou hast no weapon, and perforce must suffer.

Othello. Look in upon me then, and speak with me,

Or, naked[599] as I am, I will assault thee.

(*Re-enter Gratiano.*)

Gratiano. What is the matter?

Othello. Behold! I have a weapon;

A better never did itself sustain

Upon a soldier's thigh: I have seen the day,

That with this little arm, and this good sword,

I have made my way through more impediments

Than twenty times your stop: but, O vain boast!

Who can control his fate? 'tis not so now.

Be not afraid, though you do see me weapon'd;

Here is my journey's end, here is my butt,[600]

And very sea-mark of my utmost sail.[601]

Do you go back dismay'd? 'tis a lost fear;

Man but a rush[602] against Othello's breast,

And he retires. Where should Othello go?

Now how dost thou look now? O ill-starr'd wench!

Pale as thy smock! when we shall meet at compt,[603]

This look of thine will hurl my soul from heaven,

And fiends will snatch at it. Cold, cold, my girl!

Even like thy chastity.

O! cursed, cursed slave. Whip me, ye devils,

From the possession of this heavenly sight!

Blow me about in winds! roast me in sulphur!

Wash me in steep-down gulfs of liquid fire!

O Desdemona! Desdemona! dead!

Oh! Oh! Oh!

(*Enter Lodovico, Montano, Cassio carried in a chair, and Officers with Iago, prisoner.*)

---

598. Tempered in icy water (or the reference may be to Innsbruck, famed for the quality of its steel, but this hardly fits "a sword of Spain").   599. Unarmed.   600. Goal, end, limit. 601. Destination of my farthest journey.   602. Wield but a reed.   603. On the day of judgment.

Lodovico.   Where is this rash and most unfortunate man?

Othello.   That's he that was Othello; here I am.

Lodovico.   Where is that viper? bring the villain forth.

Othello.   I look down towards his feet;[604] but that's a fable.
If that thou be'st a devil, I cannot kill thee.   (*Wounds Iago.*)
                                                                   (*Othello is disarmed.*)

Lodovico.   Wrench his sword from him.

Iago.   I bleed, sir; but not kill'd.

Othello.   I am not sorry neither; I'd have thee live;
For, in my sense,[605] 'tis happiness to die.

Lodovico.   O thou Othello! that wert once so good,
Fall'n in the practice[606] of a damned slave,[607]
What shall be said to thee?

Othello.   Why, any thing:
An honourable murderer, if you will;
For nought did I in hate, but all in honour.

Lodovico.   This wretch hath part confess'd his villany:
Did you and he consent in Cassio's death?

Othello.   Ay.

Cassio.   Dear general, I never gave you cause.

Othello.   I do believe it, and I ask your pardon.
Will you, I pray, demand that demi-devil
Why he hath thus ensnar'd my soul and body?

Iago.   Demand me nothing: what you know, you know:
From this time forth I never will speak word.

Lodovico.   What! not to pray?

Gratiano.   Torments will ope[608] your lips.

Othello.   Well, thou dost best.

Lodovico.   Sir, you shall understand what hath befall'n,
Which, as I think, you know not. Here is a letter
Found in the pocket of the slain Roderigo,
And here another; the one of them imports
The death of Cassio to be undertook
By Roderigo.

Othello.   O villain!

Cassio.   Most heathenish and most gross!

Lodovico.   Now here's another discontented paper,
Found in his pocket too; and this, it seems,
Roderigo meant to have sent this damned villain,
But that, belike,[609] Iago in the interim[610]
Came in and satisfied him.

Othello.   O the pernicious caitiff!

---

604. *I.e.,* for the Devil's cloven hoof.   605. The way I feel.   606. Plot, machination.
607. *I.e.,* Iago.   608. Open.   609. Most likely.   610. In the meantime.

How came you, Cassio, by that handkerchief
That was my wife's?
Cassio.   I found it in my chamber;
And he himself confess'd but even now
That there he dropp'd it for a special purpose
Which wrought to his desire.
Othello.   O fool! fool! fool!
Cassio.   There is besides in Roderigo's letter
How he upbraids Iago that he made him
Brave me upon the watch; whereon it came
That I was cast:[611] and even but now he spake,
After long seeming dead, Iago hurt him,
Iago set him on.
Lodovico.   You must forsake this room and go with us;
Your power and your command is taken off,
And Cassio rules in Cyprus. For this slave,
If there be any cunning cruelty
That can torment him much and hold him long,
It shall be his. You shall close prisoner rest,
Till that the nature of your fault be known
To the Venetian state. Come, bring him away.
Othello.   Soft you; a word or two before you go.
I have done the state some service, and they know 't;
No more of that. I pray you, in your letters,
When you shall these unlucky deeds relate,
Speak of me as I am; nothing extenuate,
Nor set down aught[612] in malice: then, must you speak
Of one that lov'd not wisely but too well;
Of one not easily jealous, but, being wrought,
Perplex'd[613] in the extreme; of one whose hand
Like the base Indian,[614] threw a pearl away
Richer than all his tribe; of one whose subdu'd[615] eyes
Albeit unused to the melting mood,
Drop tears as fast as the Arabian trees
Their med'cinable gum. Set you down this;
And say besides, that in Aleppo once,
Where a malignant and a turban'd Turk
Beat a Venetian and traduc'd the state,
I took by the throat the circumcised dog,
And smote him, thus.   (*Stabs himself.*)
Lodovico.   O bloody period![616]

---

611. Dismissed.   612. Anything.   613. Distracted.   614. The Folio reads "Iudean." Both readings denote the foolish infidel who fails to appreciate the treasure he possesses.   615. Overcome (by grief).   616. Ending.

Gratiano. All that's spoke is marr'd.
Othello. I kiss'd thee ere I killed thee; no way but this,

(Falling upon Desdemona.)

    Killing myself to die upon a kiss.   *(Dies.)*
Cassio. This did I fear, but thought he had no weapon;
    For he was great of heart.
Lodovico *(to Iago).* O Spartan dog!
    More fell[617] than anguish, hunger, or the sea.
    Look on the tragic loading of this bed;
    This is thy work; the object poisons sight;
    Let it be hid. Gratiano, keep the house,
    And seize upon the fortunes of the Moor,
    For they succeed on you. To you, lord governor,
    Remains the censure of this hellish villain,
    The time, the place, the torture; O! enforce it.
    Myself will straight aboard, and to the state
    This heavy act with heavy heart relate.   *(Exeunt.)*

Questions

1. *What motivates Iago to seek vengeance? Do you find his motives a convincing basis for his acts? Explain.* **2.** *What function does Roderigo serve in the play? Bianca? Emilia?* **3.** *Compare the speeches of Cassio and Iago in Act II, scene 1. What does the difference in language and style reveal about their characters?* **4.** *Othello crumbles in Act III, scene 3, as Iago creates the jealousy that destroys Othello's self-confidence and peace of mind. Is the rapidity of Othello's emotional collapse justified? Does his being black have anything to do with his emotional turmoil? Explain.* **5.** *Carefully determine how much time elapses between the arrival at Cyprus and the end of the action. Can you find narrated events that could not possibly have occurred within that time? Do the chronological inconsistencies disturb you? Explain.* **6.** *The first part of Act IV, scene 2 (until Othello exits), is sometimes called the "brothel" scene. What features of Othello's language and behavior justify that designation?* **7.** *Discuss the relationship between love and hate in this play.*

---

617. Grim, cruel.

The Misanthrope*

MOLIÈRE [1622–1673]

CHARACTERS

Alceste, *in love with Célimène*
Philinte, *Alceste's friend*
Oronte, *in love with Célimène*
Célimène, *Alceste's beloved*
Éliante, *Célimène's cousin*
Arsinoé, *a friend of Célimène's*
Acaste ⎫
            ⎬ *Marquesses*
Clitandre ⎭
Basque, *Célimène's servant*
A Guard *of the Marshalsea*
Dubois, *Alceste's valet*

The Scene throughout is in Célimène's house at Paris.

Act I

SCENE 1. *Philinte, Alceste*

Philinte. Now, what's got into you?
Alceste (*seated*). Kindly leave me alone.
Philinte. Come, come, what is it? This lugubrious tone . . .
Alceste. Leave me, I said; you spoil my solitude.
Philinte. Oh, listen to me, now, and don't be rude.
Alceste. I choose to be rude, Sir, and to be hard of hearing.
Philinte. These ugly moods of yours are not endearing;
     Friends though we are, I really must insist . . .
Alceste (*abruptly rising*). Friends? Friends, you say? Well, cross me off your list.
     I've been your friend till now, as you well know;
     But after what I saw a moment ago

---

*English version by Richard Wilbur.

I tell you flatly that our ways must part.
I wish no place in a dishonest heart.
Philinte.   Why, what have I done, Alceste? Is this quite just?
Alceste.   My God, you ought to die of self-disgust.
I call your conduct inexcusable, Sir,
And every man of honor will concur.
I see you almost hug a man to death,
Exclaim for joy until you're out of breath,
And supplement these loving demonstrations
With endless offers, vows, and protestations;
Then when I ask you "Who was that?" I find
That you can barely bring his name to mind!
Once the man's back is turned, you cease to love him,
And speak with absolute indifference of him!
By God, I say it's base and scandalous
To falsify the heart's affections thus;
If I caught myself behaving in such a way,
I'd hang myself for shame, without delay.
Philinte.   It hardly seems a hanging matter to me;
I hope that you will take it graciously
If I extend myself a slight reprieve,
And live a little longer, by your leave.
Alceste.   How dare you joke about a crime so grave?
Philinte.   What crime? How else are people to behave?
Alceste.   I'd have them be sincere, and never part
With any word that isn't from the heart.
Philinte.   When someone greets us with a show of pleasure,
It's but polite to give him equal measure,
Return his love the best that we know how,
And trade him offer for offer, vow for vow.
Alceste.   No, no, this formula you'd have me follow,
However fashionable, is false and hollow,
And I despise the frenzied operations
Of all these barterers of protestations,
These lavishers of meaningless embraces,
These utterers of obliging commonplaces,
Who court and flatter everyone on earth
And praise the fool no less than the man of worth.
Should you rejoice that someone fondles you,
Offers his love and service, swears to be true,
And fills your ears with praises of your name,
When to the first damned fop he'll say the same?
No, no: no self-respecting heart would dream
Of prizing so promiscuous an esteem;
However high the praise, there's nothing worse

Than sharing honors with the universe.
Esteem is founded on comparison:
To honor all men is to honor none.
Since you embrace this indiscriminate vice,
Your friendship comes at far too cheap a price;
I spurn the easy tribute of a heart
Which will not set the worthy man apart:
I choose, Sir, to be chosen; and in fine,
The friend of mankind is no friend of mine.

Philinte. But in polite society, custom decrees
That we show certain outward courtesies. . . .

Alceste. Ah, no! we should condemn with all our force
Such false and artificial intercourse.
Let men behave like men; let them display
Their inmost hearts in everything they say;
Let the heart speak, and let our sentiments
Not mask themselves in silly compliments.

Philinte. In certain cases it would be uncouth
And most absurd to speak the naked truth;
With all respect for your exalted notions,
It's often best to veil one's true emotions.
Wouldn't the social fabric come undone
If we were wholly frank with everyone?
Suppose you met with someone you couldn't bear;
Would you inform him of it then and there?

Alceste. Yes.

Philinte. Then you'd tell old Emilie it's pathetic
The way she daubs her features with cosmetic
And plays the gay coquette at sixty-four?

Alceste. I would.

Philinte. And you'd call Dorilas a bore,
And tell him every ear at court is lame
From hearing him brag about his noble name?

Alceste. Precisely.

Philinte. Ah, you're joking.

Alceste. *Au contraire:*
In this regard there's none I'd choose to spare.
All are corrupt; there's nothing to be seen
In court or town but aggravates my spleen.
I fall into deep gloom and melancholy
When I survey the scene of human folly,
Finding on every hand base flattery,
Injustice, fraud, self-interest, treachery. . . .
Ah, it's too much; mankind has grown so base,
I mean to break with the whole human race.

Philinte.   This philosophic rage is a bit extreme;
        You've no idea how comical you seem;
        Indeed, we're like those brothers in the play
        Called *School for Husbands*, one of whom was prey . . .
Alceste.   Enough, now! None of your stupid similes.
Philinte.   Then let's have no more tirades, if you please.
        The world won't change, whatever you say or do;
        And since plain speaking means so much to you,
        I'll tell you plainly that by being frank
        You've earned the reputation of a crank,
        And that you're thought ridiculous when you rage
        And rant against the manners of the age.
Alceste.   So much the better; just what I wish to hear.
        No news could be more grateful to my ear.
        All men are so detestable in my eyes,
        I should be sorry if they thought me wise.
Philinte.   Your hatred's very sweeping, is it not?
Alceste.   Quite right: I hate the whole degraded lot.
Philinte.   Must all poor human creatures be embraced,
        Without distinction, by your vast distaste?
        Even in these bad times, there are surely a few . . .
Alceste.   No, I include all men in one dim view:
        Some men I hate for being rogues; the others
        I hate because they treat the rogues like brothers,
        And, lacking a virtuous scorn for what is vile,
        Receive the villain with a complaisant smile.
        Notice how tolerant people choose to be
        Toward that bold rascal who's at law with me.
        His social polish can't conceal his nature;
        One sees at once that he's a treacherous creature;
        No one could possibly be taken in
        By those soft speeches and that sugary grin.
        The whole world knows the shady means by which
        The low-brow's grown so powerful and rich,
        And risen to a rank so bright and high
        That virtue can but blush, and merit sigh.
        Whenever his name comes up in conversation,
        None will defend his wretched reputation;
        Call him knave, liar, scoundrel, and all the rest,
        Each head will nod, and no one will protest.
        And yet his smirk is seen in every house,
        He's greeted everywhere with smiles and bows,
        And when there's any honor that can be got
        By pulling strings, he'll get it, like as not.
        My God! It chills my heart to see the ways

Men come to terms with evil nowadays;
Sometimes, I swear, I'm moved to flee and find
Some desert land unfouled by humankind.

Philinte. Come, let's forget the follies of the times
And pardon mankind for its petty crimes;
Let's have an end of rantings and of railings,
And show some leniency toward human failings.
This world requires a pliant rectitude;
Too stern a virtue makes one stiff and rude;
Good sense views all extremes with detestation,
And bids us to be noble in moderation.
The rigid virtues of the ancient days
Are not for us; they jar with all our ways
And ask of us too lofty a perfection.
Wise men accept their times without objection,
And there's no greater folly, if you ask me,
Than trying to reform society.
Like you, I see each day a hundred and one
Unhandsome deeds that might be better done,
But still, for all the faults that meet my view,
I'm never known to storm and rave like you.
I take men as they are, or let them be,
And teach my soul to bear their frailty;
And whether in court or town, whatever the scene,
My phlegm's as philosophic as your spleen.

Alceste. This phlegm which you so eloquently commend,
Does nothing ever rile it up, my friend?
Suppose some man you trust should treacherously
Conspire to rob you of your property,
And do his best to wreck your reputation?
Wouldn't you feel a certain indignation?

Philinte. Why, no. These faults of which you so complain
Are part of human nature, I maintain,
And it's no more a matter for disgust
That men are knavish, selfish and unjust,
Than that the vulture dines upon the dead,
And wolves are furious, and apes ill-bred.

Alceste. Shall I see myself betrayed, robbed, torn to bits,
And not . . . Oh, let's be still and rest our wits.
Enough of reasoning, now. I've had my fill.

Philinte. Indeed, you would do well, Sir, to be still.
Rage less at your opponent, and give some thought
To how you'll win this lawsuit that he's brought.

Alceste. I assure you I'll do nothing of the sort.

Philinte. Then who will plead your case before the court?

Alceste.   Reason and right and justice will plead for me.

Philinte.   Oh, Lord. What judges do you plan to see?

Alceste.   Why, none. The justice of my cause is clear.

Philinte.   Of course, man; but there's politics to fear. . . .

Alceste.   No, I refuse to lift a hand. That's flat.
       I'm either right, or wrong.

Philinte.   Don't count on that.

Alceste.   No, I'll do nothing.

Philinte.   Your enemy's influence
       Is great, you know . . .

Alceste.   That makes no difference.

Philinte.   It will; you'll see.

Alceste.   Must honor bow to guile?
       If so, I shall be proud to lose the trial.

Philinte.   Oh, really . . .

Alceste.   I'll discover by this case
       Whether or not men are sufficiently base
       And impudent and villainous and perverse
       To do me wrong before the universe.

Philinte.   What a man!

Alceste.   Oh, I could wish, whatever the cost,
       Just for the beauty of it, that my trial were lost.

Philinte.   If people heard you talking so, Alceste,
       They'd split their sides. Your name would be a jest.

Alceste.   So much the worse for jesters.

Philinte.   May I enquire
       Whether this rectitude you so admire,
       And these hard virtues you're enamored of
       Are qualities of the lady whom you love?
       It much surprises me that you, who seem
       To view mankind with furious disesteem,
       Have yet found something to enchant your eyes
       Amidst a species which you so despise.
       And what is more amazing, I'm afraid,
       Is the most curious choice your heart has made.
       The honest Éliante is fond of you,
       Arsinoé, the prude, admires you too;
       And yet your spirit's been perversely led
       To choose the flighty Célimène instead,
       Whose brittle malice and coquettish ways
       So typify the manners of our days.
       How is it that the traits you most abhor
       Are bearable in this lady you adore?
       Are you so blind with love that you can't find them?
       Or do you contrive, in her case, not to mind them?

Alceste. My love for that young widow's not the kind
That can't perceive defects; no, I'm not blind.
I see her faults, despite my ardent love,
And all I see I fervently reprove.
And yet I'm weak; for all her falsity,
That woman knows the art of pleasing me,
And though I never cease complaining of her,
I swear I cannot manage not to love her.
Her charm outweighs her faults; I can but aim
To cleanse her spirit in my love's pure flame.
Philinte. That's no small task; I wish you all success.
You think then that she loves you?
Alceste.   Heavens, yes!
I wouldn't love her did she not love me.
Philinte. Well, if her taste for you is plain to see,
Why do these rivals cause you such despair?
Alceste. True love, Sir, is possessive, and cannot bear
To share with all the world. I'm here today
To tell her she must send that mob away.
Philinte. If I were you, and had your choice to make,
Éliante, her cousin, would be the one I'd take;
That honest heart, which cares for you alone,
Would harmonize far better with your own.
Alceste. True, true: each day my reason tells me so;
But reason doesn't rule in love, you know.
Philinte. I fear some bitter sorrow is in store;
This love . . .

SCENE 2. *Oronte, Alceste, Philinte*

Oronte (*to Alceste*). The servants told me at the door
That Éliante and Célimène were out,
But when I heard, dear Sir, that you were about,
I came to say, without exaggeration,
That I hold you in the vastest admiration,
And that it's always been my dearest desire
To be the friend of one I so admire.
I hope to see my love of merit requited,
And you and I in friendship's bond united.
I'm sure you won't refuse—if I may be frank—
A friend of my devotedness—and rank.

(*During this speech of Oronte's, Alceste is abstracted, and seems un-*

aware that he is being spoken to. He only breaks off his reverie when Oronte says:)

It was for you, if you please, that my words were intended.

Alceste. For me, Sir?

Oronte. Yes, for you. You're not offended?

Alceste. By no means. But this much surprises me. . . .
The honor comes most unexpectedly. . . .

Oronte. My high regard should not astonish you;
The whole world feels the same. It is your due.

Alceste. Sir . . .

Oronte. Why, in all the State there isn't one
Can match your merits; they shine, Sir, like the sun.

Alceste. Sir . . .

Oronte. You are higher in my estimation
Than all that's most illustrious in the nation.

Alceste. Sir . . .

Oronte. If I lie, may heaven strike me dead!
To show you that I mean what I have said,
Permit me, Sir, to embrace you most sincerely,
And swear that I will prize our friendship dearly.
Giver me your hand. And now, Sir, if you choose,
We'll make our vows.

Alceste. Sir . . .

Oronte. What! You refuse?

Alceste. Sir, it's a very great honor you extend:
But friendship is a sacred thing, my friend;
It would be profanation to bestow
The name of friend on one you hardly know.
All parts are better played when well-rehearsed;
Let's put off friendship, and get acquainted first.
We may discover it would be unwise
To try to make our natures harmonize.

Oronte. By heaven! You're sagacious to the core;
This speech has made me admire you even more.
Let time, then, bring us closer day by day;
Meanwhile, I shall be yours in every way.
If, for example, there should be anything
You wish at court, I'll mention it to the King.
I have his ear, of course; it's quite well known
That I am much in favor with the throne.
In short, I am your servant. And now, dear friend,
Since you have such fine judgment, I intend
To please you, if I can, with a small sonnet

I wrote not long ago. Please comment on it,
And tell me whether I ought to publish it.

Alceste. You must excuse me, Sir; I'm hardly fit
To judge such matters.

Oronte. Why not?

Alceste. I am, I fear,
Inclined to be unfashionably sincere.

Oronte. Just what I ask; I'd take no satisfaction
In anything but your sincere reaction.
I beg you not to dream of being kind.

Alceste. Since you desire it, Sir, I'll speak my mind.

Oronte. *Sonnet. It's a sonnet. . . . Hope . . .* The poem's addressed
To a lady who wakened hopes within my breast.
Hope . . . this is not the pompous sort of thing,
Just modest little verses, with a tender ring.

Alceste. Well, we shall see.

Oronte. *Hope . . .* I'm anxious to hear
Whether the style seems properly smooth and clear,
And whether the choice of words is good or bad.

Alceste. We'll see, we'll see.

Oronte. Perhaps I ought to add
That it took me only a quarter-hour to write it.

Alceste. The time's irrelevant, Sir: kindly recite it.

Oronte (*reading*).

> *Hope comforts us awhile, 'tis true,*
> *Lulling our cares with careless laughter,*
> *And yet such joy is full of rue,*
> *My Phyllis, if nothing follows after.*

Philinte. I'm charmed by this already; the style's delightful.

Alceste (*sotto voce, to Philinte*). How can you say that? Why, the thing is frightful.

Oronte. *Your fair face smiled on me awhile,*
> *But was it kindness so to enchant me?*
> *'Twould have been fairer not to smile,*
> *If hope was all you meant to grant me.*

Philinte. What a clever thought! How handsomely you phrase it!

Alceste (*sotto voce, to Philinte*). You know the thing is trash. How dare you praise it?

Oronte. *If it's to be my passion's fate*
> *Thus everlastingly to wait,*
> *Then death will come to set me free:*
> *For death is fairer than the fair;*
> *Phyllis, to hope is to despair*
> *When one must hope eternally.*

Philinte.   The close is exquisite—full of feeling and grace.

Alceste (*sotto voce, aside*).   Oh, blast the close; you'd better close your face
>   Before you send your lying soul to hell.

Philinte.   I can't remember a poem I've liked so well.

Alceste (*sotto voce, aside*).   Good Lord!

Oronte (*to Philinte*).   I fear you're flattering me a bit.

Philinte.   Oh, no!

Alceste (*sotto voce, aside*).   What else d'you call it, you hypocrite?

Oronte (*to Alceste*).   But you, Sir, keep your promise now: don't shrink
>   From telling me sincerely what you think.

Alceste.   Sir, these are delicate matters; we all desire
>   To be told that we've the true poetic fire.
>   But once, to one whose name I shall not mention,
>   I said, regarding some verse of his invention,
>   That gentlemen should rigorously control
>   That itch to write which often afflicts the soul;
>   That one should curb the heady inclination
>   To publicize one's little avocation;
>   And that in showing off one's works of art
>   One often plays a very clownish part.

Oronte.   Are you suggesting in a devious way
>   That I ought not . . .

Alceste.   Oh, that I do not say.
>   Further, I told him that no fault is worse
>   Than that of writing frigid, lifeless verse,
>   And that the merest whisper of such a shame
>   Suffices to destroy a man's good name.

Oronte.   D'you mean to say my sonnet's dull and trite?

Alceste.   I don't say that. But I went on to cite
>   Numerous cases of once-respected men
>   Who came to grief by taking up the pen.

Oronte.   And am I like them? Do I write so poorly?

Alceste.   I don't say that. But I told this person, "Surely
>   You're under no necessity to compose;
>   Why you should wish to publish, heaven knows.
>   There's no excuse for printing tedious rot
>   Unless one writes for bread, as you do not.
>   Resist temptation, then, I beg of you;
>   Conceal your pastimes from the public view;
>   And don't give up, on any provocation,
>   Your present high and courtly reputation,
>   To purchase at a greedy printer's shop
>   The name of silly author and scribbling fop."
>   These were the points I tried to make him see.

Oronte. I sense that they are also aimed at me;
　　　　But now—about my sonnet—I'd like to be told . . .
Alceste. Frankly, that sonnet should be pigeonholed.
　　　　You've chosen the worst models to imitate.
　　　　The style's unnatural. Let me illustrate:
　　　　　　　　For example, *Your fair face smiled on me awhile,*
　　　　　　　　Followed by, *'Twould have been fairer not to smile!*
　　　　　　　　Or this: *such joy is full of rue;*
　　　　　　　　Or this: *For death is fairer than the fair;*
　　　　　　　　Or, *Phyllis, to hope is to despair*
　　　　　　　　　　When one must hope eternally!
　　　　This artificial style, that's all the fashion,
　　　　Has neither taste, nor honesty, nor passion;
　　　　It's nothing but a sort of wordy play,
　　　　And nature never spoke in such a way.
　　　　What, in this shallow age, is not debased?
　　　　Our fathers, though less refined, had better taste;
　　　　I'd barter all that men admire today
　　　　For one old love song I shall try to say:
　　　　　　　　If the King had given me for my own
　　　　　　　　Paris, his citadel,
　　　　　　　　And I for that must leave alone
　　　　　　　　Her whom I love so well,
　　　　　　　　I'd say then to the Crown,
　　　　　　　　Take back your glittering town;
　　　　　　　　My darling is more fair, I swear,
　　　　　　　　My darling is more fair.
　　　　The rhyme's not rich, the style is rough and old,
　　　　But don't you see that it's the purest gold
　　　　Beside the tinsel nonsense now preferred,
　　　　And that there's passion in its every word?
　　　　　　　　If the King had given me for my own
　　　　　　　　Paris, his citadel,
　　　　　　　　And I for that must leave alone
　　　　　　　　Her whom I love so well,
　　　　　　　　I'd say then to the Crown,
　　　　　　　　Take back your glittering town;
　　　　　　　　My darling is more fair, I swear,
　　　　　　　　My darling is more fair.
　　　　There speaks a loving heart. (*To Philinte.*) You're laughing, eh?
　　　　Laugh on, my precious wit. Whatever you say,
　　　　I hold that song's worth all the bibelots
　　　　That people hail today with ah's and oh's.
Oronte. And I maintain my sonnet's very good.
Alceste. It's not at all surprising that you should.

You have your reasons; permit me to have mine
For thinking that you cannot write a line.
Oronte.   Others have praised my sonnet to the skies.
Alceste.   I lack their art of telling pleasant lies.
Oronte.   You seem to think you've got no end of wit.
Alceste.   To praise your verse, I'd need still more of it.
Oronte.   I'm not in need of your approval, Sir.
Alceste.   That's good; you couldn't have it if you were.
Oronte.   Come now, I'll lend you the subject of my sonnet;
I'd like to see you try to improve upon it.
Alceste.   I might, by chance, write something just as shoddy;
But then I wouldn't show it to everybody.
Oronte.   You're most opinionated and conceited.
Alceste.   Go find your flatterers, and be better treated.
Oronte.   Look here, my little fellow, pray watch your tone.
Alceste.   My great big fellow, you'd better watch your own.
Philinte (*stepping between them*).   Oh, please, please, gentlemen!
This will never do.
Oronte.   The fault is mine, and I leave the field to you.
I am your servant, Sir, in every way.
Alceste.   And I, Sir, am your most abject valet.

SCENE 3.   *Philinte, Alceste*

Philinte.   Well, as you see, sincerity in excess
Can get you into a very pretty mess;
Oronte was hungry for appreciation. . . .
Alceste.   Don't speak to me.
Philinte.   What?
Alceste.   No more conversation.
Philinte.   Really, now . . .
Alceste.   Leave me alone.
Philinte.   If I . . .
Alceste.   Out of my sight!
Philinte.   But what . . .
Alceste.   I won't listen.
Philinte.   But . . .
Alceste.   Silence!
Philinte.   Now, is it polite . . .
Alceste.   By heaven, I've had enough. Don't follow me.
Philinte.   Ah, you're just joking. I'll keep you company.

Act II

Alceste.　Shall I speak plainly, Madam? I confess
　　　　Your conduct gives me infinite distress,
　　　　And my resentment's grown too hot to smother.
　　　　Soon, I foresee, we'll break with one another.
　　　　If I said otherwise, I should deceive you;
　　　　Sooner or later, I shall be forced to leave you,
　　　　And if I swore that we shall never part,
　　　　I should misread the omens of my heart.
Célimène.　You kindly saw me home, it would appear,
　　　　So as to pour invectives in my ear.
Alceste.　I've no desire to quarrel. But I deplore
　　　　Your inability to shut the door
　　　　On all these suitors who beset you so.
　　　　There's what annoys me, if you care to know.
Célimène.　Is it my fault that all these men pursue me?
　　　　Am I to blame if they're attracted to me?
　　　　And when they gently beg an audience,
　　　　Ought I to take a stick and drive them hence?
Alceste.　Madam, there's no necessity for a stick;
　　　　A less responsive heart would do the trick.
　　　　Of your attractiveness I don't complain;
　　　　But those your charms attract, you then detain
　　　　By a most melting and receptive manner,
　　　　And so enlist their hearts beneath your banner.
　　　　It's the agreeable hopes which you excite
　　　　That keep these lovers round you day and night;
　　　　Were they less liberally smiled upon,
　　　　That sighing troop would very soon be gone.
　　　　But tell me, Madam, why it is that lately
　　　　This man Clitandre interests you so greatly?
　　　　Because of what high merits do you deem
　　　　Him worthy of the honor of your esteem?
　　　　Is it that your admiring glances linger
　　　　On the splendidly long nail of his little finger?
　　　　Or do you share the general deep respect
　　　　For the blond wig he chooses to affect?
　　　　Are you in love with his embroidered hose?
　　　　Do you adore his ribbons and his bows?
　　　　Or is it that this paragon bewitches
　　　　Your tasteful eye with his vast German breeches?

Perhaps his giggle, or his falsetto voice,
Makes him the latest gallant of your choice?

Célimène. You're much mistaken to resent him so.
Why I put up with him you surely know:
My lawsuit's very shortly to be tried,
And I must have his influence on my side.

Alceste. Then lose your lawsuit, Madam, or let it drop;
Don't torture me by humoring such a fop.

Célimène. You're jealous of the whole world, Sir.

Alceste.   That's true,
Since the whole world is well-received by you.

Célimène. That my good nature is so unconfined
Should serve to pacify your jealous mind;
Were I to smile on one, and scorn the rest,
Then you might have some cause to be distressed.

Alceste. Well, if I mustn't be jealous, tell me, then,
Just how I'm better treated than other men.

Célimène. You know you have my love. Will that not do?

Alceste. What proof have I that what you say is true?

Célimène. I would expect, Sir, that my having said it
Might give the statement a sufficient credit.

Alceste. But how can I be sure that you don't tell
The selfsame thing to other men as well?

Célimène. What a gallant speech! How flattering to me!
What a sweet creature you make me out to be!
Well then, to save you from the pangs of doubt,
All that I've said I hereby cancel out;
Now, none but yourself shall make a monkey of you:
Are you content?

Alceste.   Why, why am I doomed to love you?
I swear that I shall bless the blissful hour
When this poor heart's no longer in your power!
I make no secret of it: I've done my best
To exorcise this passion from my breast;
But thus far all in vain; it will not go;
It's for my sins that I must love you so.

Célimène. Your love for me is matchless, Sir; that's clear.

Alceste. Indeed, in all the world it has no peer;
Words can't describe the nature of my passion,
And no man ever loved in such a fashion.

Célimène. Yes, it's a brand-new fashion, I agree:
You show your love by castigating me,
And all your speeches are enraged and rude.
I've never been so furiously wooed.

Alceste. Yet you could calm that fury, if you chose.

Come, shall we bring our quarrels to a close?
Let's speak with open hearts, then, and begin . . .

SCENE 2. *Célimène, Alceste, Basque*

Célimène.   What is it?
Basque.   Acaste is here.
Célimène.   Well, send him in.

SCENE 3. *Célimène, Alceste*

Alceste.   What! Shall we never be alone at all?
   You're always ready to receive a call,
   And you can't bear, for ten ticks of the clock,
   Not to keep open house for all who knock.
Célimène.   I couldn't refuse him: he'd be most put out.
Alceste.   Surely that's not worth worrying about.
Célimène.   Acaste would never forgive me if he guessed
   That I consider him a dreadful pest.
Alceste.   If he's a pest, why bother with him then?
Célimène.   Heavens! One can't antagonize such men;
   Why, they're the chartered gossips of the court,
   And have a say in things of every sort.
   One must receive them, and be full of charm;
   They're no great help, but they can do you harm,
   And though your influence be ever so great,
   They're hardly the best people to alienate.
Alceste.   I see, dear lady, that you could make a case
   For putting up with the whole human race;
   These friendships that you calculate so nicely . . .

SCENE 4. *Alceste, Célimène, Basque*

Basque.   Madam, Clitandre is here as well.
Alceste.   Precisely.
Célimène.   Where are you going?
Alceste.   Elsewhere.
Célimène.   Stay.
Alceste.   No, no.

Célimène. Stay, Sir.

Alceste. I can't.

Célimène. I wish it.

Alceste. No, I must go.
  I beg you, Madam, not to press the matter;
  You know I have no taste for idle chatter.

Célimène. Stay: I command you.

Alceste. No, I cannot stay.

Célimène. Very well; you have my leave to go away.

> **SCENE 5.** *Éliante, Philinte, Acaste, Clitandre, Alceste, Célimène, Basque*

Éliante (*to Célimène*). The Marquesses have kindly come to call.
  Were they announced?

Célimène. Yes. Basque, bring chairs for all.

  (*Basque provides the chairs, and exits.*)

  (*To Alceste.*) You haven't gone?

Alceste. No; and I shan't depart
  Till you decide who's foremost in your heart.

Célimène. Oh, hush.

Alceste. It's time to choose; take them, or me.

Célimène. You're mad.

Alceste. I'm not, as you shall shortly see.

Célimène. Oh?

Alceste. You'll decide.

Célimène. You're joking now, dear friend.

Alceste. No, no; you'll choose; my patience is at an end.

Clitandre. Madam, I come from court, where poor Cléonte
  Behaved like a perfect fool, as is his wont.
  Has he no friend to counsel him, I wonder,
  And teach him less unerringly to blunder?

Célimène. It's true, the man's a most accomplished dunce;
  His gauche behavior charms the eye at once;
  And every time one sees him, on my word,
  His manner's grown a trifle more absurd.

Acaste. Speaking of dunces, I've just now conversed
  With old Damon, who's one of the very worst;
  I stood a lifetime in the broiling sun
  Before his dreary monologue was done.

Célimène. Oh, he's a wondrous talker, and has the power
  To tell you nothing hour after hour:

If, by mistake, he ever came to the point,
The shock would put his jawbone out of joint.
Éliante (*to Philinte*).   The conversation takes its usual turn,
And all our dear friends' ears will shortly burn.
Clitandre.   Timante's a character, Madam.
Célimène.   Isn't he, though?
A man of mystery from top to toe,
Who moves about in a romantic mist
On secret missions which do not exist.
His talk is full of eyebrows and grimaces;
How tired one gets of his momentous faces;
He's always whispering something confidential
Which turns out to be quite inconsequential;
Nothing's too slight for him to mystify;
He even whispers when he says "good-by."
Acaste.   Tell us about Géralde.
Célimène.   That tiresome ass.
He mixes only with the titled class,
And fawns on dukes and princes, and is bored
With anyone who's not at least a lord.
The man's obsessed with rank, and his discourses
Are all of hounds and carriages and horses;
He uses Christian names with all the great,
And the word Milord, with him, is out of date.
Clitandre.   He's very taken with Bélise, I hear.
Célimène.   She is the dreariest company, poor dear.
Whenever she comes to call, I grope about
To find some topic which will draw her out,
But, owing to her dry and faint replies,
The conversation wilts, and droops, and dies.
In vain one hopes to animate her face
By mentioning the ultimate commonplace;
But sun or shower, even hail or frost
Are matters she can instantly exhaust.
Meanwhile her visit, painful though it is,
Drags on and on through mute eternities,
And though you ask the time, and yawn, and yawn,
She sits there like a stone and won't be gone.
Acaste.   Now for Adraste.
Célimène.   Oh, that conceited elf
Has a gigantic passion for himself;
He rails against the court, and cannot bear it
That none will recognize his hidden merit;
All honors given to others give offense
To his imaginary excellence.

Clitandre.   What about young Cléon? His house, they say,
　　Is full of the best society, night and day.
Célimène.   His cook has made him popular, not he:
　　It's Cléon's table that people come to see.
Éliante.   He gives a splendid dinner, you must admit.
Célimène.   But must he serve himself along with it?
　　For my taste, he's a most insipid dish
　　Whose presence sours the wine and spoils the fish.
Philinte.   Damis, his uncle, is admired no end.
　　What's your opinion, Madam?
Célimène.　　　　　　　　　　　Why, he's my friend.
Philinte.   He seems a decent fellow, and rather clever.
Célimène.   He works too hard at cleverness, however.
　　I hate to see him sweat and struggle so
　　To fill his conversation with bons mots.
　　Since he's decided to become a wit
　　His taste's so pure that nothing pleases it;
　　He scolds at all the latest books and plays,
　　Thinking that wit must never stoop to praise,
　　That finding fault's a sign of intellect,
　　That all appreciation is abject,
　　And that by damning everything in sight
　　One shows oneself in a distinguished light.
　　He's scornful even of our conversations:
　　Their trivial nature sorely tries his patience;
　　He folds his arms, and stands above the battle,
　　And listens sadly to our childish prattle.
Acaste.   Wonderful, Madam! You've hit him off precisely.
Clitandre.   No one can sketch a character so nicely.
Alceste.   How bravely, Sirs, you cut and thrust at all
　　These absent fools, till one by one they fall:
　　But let one come in sight, and you'll at once
　　Embrace the man you lately called a dunce,
　　Telling him in a tone sincere and fervent
　　How proud you are to be his humble servant.
Clitandre.   Why pick on us? *Madame's* been speaking, Sir,
　　And you should quarrel, if you must, with her.
Alceste.   No, no, by God, the fault is yours, because
　　You lead her on with laughter and applause,
　　And make her think that she's the more delightful
　　The more her talk is scandalous and spiteful.
　　Oh, she would stoop to malice far, far less
　　If no such claque approved her cleverness.
　　It's flatterers like you whose foolish praise
　　Nourishes all the vices of these days.

Philinte.   But why protest when someone ridicules
Those you'd condemn, yourself, as knaves or fools?
Célimène.   Why, Sir? Because he loves to make a fuss.
You don't expect him to agree with us,
When there's an opportunity to express
His heaven-sent spirit of contrariness?
What other people think, he can't abide;
Whatever they say, he's on the other side;
He lives in deadly terror of agreeing;
'Twould make him seem an ordinary being.
Indeed, he's so in love with contradiction,
He'll turn against his most profound conviction
And with a furious eloquence deplore it,
If only someone else is speaking for it.
Alceste.   Go on, dear lady, mock me as you please;
You have your audience in ecstasies.
Philinte.   But what she says is true: you have a way
Of bridling at whatever people say;
Whether they praise or blame, your angry spirit
Is equally unsatisfied to hear it.
Alceste.   Men, Sir, are always wrong, and that's the reason
That righteous anger's never out of season;
All that I hear in all their conversation
Is flattering praise or reckless condemnation.
Célimène.   But . . .
Alceste.   No, no, Madam, I am forced to state
That you have pleasures which I deprecate,
And that these others, here, are much to blame
For nourishing the faults which are your shame.
Clitandre.   I shan't defend myself, Sir; but I vow
I'd thought this lady faultless until now.
Acaste.   I see her charms and graces, which are many;
But as for faults, I've never noticed any.
Alceste.   I see them, Sir; and rather than ignore them,
I strenuously criticize her for them.
The more one loves, the more one should object
To every blemish, every least defect.
Were I this lady, I would soon get rid
Of lovers who approved of all I did,
And by their slack indulgence and applause
Endorsed my follies and excused my flaws.
Célimène.   If all hearts beat according to your measure,
The dawn of love would be the end of pleasure;
And love would find its perfect consummation
In ecstasies of rage and reprobation.

Éliante.   Love, as a rule, affects men otherwise,
        And lovers rarely love to criticize.
        They see their lady as a charming blur,
        And find all things commendable in her.
        If she has any blemish, fault, or shame,
        They will redeem it by a pleasing name.
        The pale-faced lady's lily-white, perforce;
        The swarthy one's a sweet brunette, of course;
        The spindly lady has a slender grace;
        The fat one has a most majestic pace;
        The plain one, with her dress in disarray,
        They classify as *beauté négligée;*
        The hulking one's a goddess in their eyes,
        The dwarf, a concentrate of Paradise;
        The haughty lady has a noble mind;
        The mean one's witty, and the dull one's kind;
        The chatterbox has liveliness and verve,
        The mute one has a virtuous reserve.
        So lovers manage, in their passion's cause,
        To love their ladies even for their flaws.
Alceste.   But I still say . . .
Célimène.   I think it would be nice
        To stroll around the gallery once or twice.
        What! You're not going, Sirs?
Clitandre and Acaste.   No, Madam, no.   .
Alceste.   You seem to be in terror lest they go.
        Do what you will, Sirs; leave, or linger on,
        But I shan't go till after you are gone.
Acaste.   I'm free to linger, unless I should perceive
        Madame is tired, and wishes me to leave.
Clitandre.   And as for me, I needn't go today
        Until the hour of the King's *coucher.*
Célimène (*to Alceste*).   You're joking, surely?
Alceste.   Not in the least; we'll see
        Whether you'd rather part with them, or me.

        SCENE 6.   *Alceste, Célimène, Éliante, Acaste, Philinte, Clitandre,
                Basque*

Basque (*to Alceste*).   Sir, there's a fellow here who bids me state
        That he must see you, and that it can't wait.
Alceste.   Tell him that I have no such pressing affairs.

Basque.   It's a long tailcoat that this fellow wears,
  With gold all over.
Cèlimène (*to Alceste*).   You'd best go down and see.
  Or—have him enter.

  SCENE 7.   *Alceste, Cèlimène, Éliante, Acaste, Philinte, Clitandre,
    Guard*

Alceste (*confronting the Guard*).   Well, what do you want with me?
  Come in, Sir.
Guard.   I've a word, Sir, for your ear.
Alceste.   Speak it aloud, Sir; I shall strive to hear.
Guard.   The Marshals have instructed me to say
  You must report to them without delay.
Alceste.   Who? Me, Sir?
Guard.   Yes, Sir; you.
Alceste.   But what do they want?
Philinte (*to Alceste*).   To scotch your silly quarrel with Oronte.
Celimene (*to Philinte*).   What quarrel?
Philinte.   Oronte and he have fallen out
  Over some verse he spoke his mind about;
  The Marshals wish to arbitrate the matter.
Alceste.   Never shall I equivocate or flatter!
Philinte.   You'd best obey their summons; come, let's go.
Alceste.   How can they mend our quarrel, I'd like to know?
  Am I to make a cowardly retraction,
  And praise those jingles to his satisfaction?
  I'll not recant; I've judged that sonnet rightly.
  It's bad.
Philinte.   But you might say so more politely. . . .
Alceste.   I'll not back down; his verses make me sick.
Philinte.   If only you could be more politic!
  But come, let's go.
Alceste.   I'll go, but I won't unsay
  A single word.
Philinte.   Well, let's be on our way.
Alceste.   Till I am ordered by my lord the King
  To praise that poem, I shall say the thing
  Is scandalous, by God, and that the poet
  Ought to be hanged for having the nerve to show it.

(*To Clitandre and Acaste, who are laughing.*)

By heaven, Sirs, I really didn't know
That I was being humorous.
Célimène.   Go, Sir, go;
Settle your business.
Alceste.   I shall, and when I'm through,
I shall return to settle things with you.

Act III

SCENE 1. *Clitandre, Acaste*

Clitandre. Dear Marquess, how contented you appear;
All things delight you, nothing mars your cheer.
Can you, in perfect honesty, declare
That you've a right to be so debonair?
Acaste. By Jove, when I survey myself, I find
No cause whatever for distress of mind.
I'm young and rich; I can in modesty
Lay claim to an exalted pedigree;
And owing to my name and my condition
I shall not want for honors and position.
Then as to courage, that most precious trait,
I seem to have it, as was proved of late
Upon the field of honor, where my bearing,
They say, was very cool and rather daring.
I've wit, of course; and taste in such perfection
That I can judge without the least reflection,
And at the theater, which is my delight,
Can make or break a play on opening night,
And lead the crowd in hisses or bravos,
And generally be known as one who knows.
I'm clever, handsome, gracefully polite;
My waist is small, my teeth are strong and white;
As for my dress, the world's astonished eyes
Assure me that I bear away the prize.
I find myself in favor everywhere,
Honored by men, and worshiped by the fair;
And since these things are so, it seems to me
I'm justified in my complacency.
Clitandre. Well, if so many ladies hold you dear,
Why do you press a hopeless courtship here?

Acaste. Hopeless, you say? I'm not the sort of fool
  That likes his ladies difficult and cool.
  Men who are awkward, shy, and peasantish
  May pine for heartless beauties, if they wish,
  Grovel before them, bear their cruelties,
  Woo them with tears and sighs and bended knees,
  And hope by dogged faithfulness to gain
  What their poor merits never could obtain.
  For men like me, however, it makes no sense
  To love on trust, and foot the whole expense.
  Whatever any lady's merits be,
  I think, thank God, that I'm as choice as she;
  That if my heart is kind enough to burn
  For her, she owes me something in return;
  And that in any proper love affair
  The partners must invest an equal share.

Clitandre. You think, then, that our hostess favors you?

Acaste. I've reason to believe that that is true.

Clitandre. How did you come to such a mad conclusion?
  You're blind, dear fellow. This is sheer delusion.

Acaste. All right, then: I'm deluded and I'm blind.

Clitandre. Whatever put the notion in your mind?

Acaste. Delusion.

Clitandre.   What persuades you that you're right?

Acaste. I'm blind.

Clitandre.   But have you any proofs to cite?

Acaste. I tell you I'm deluded.

Clitandre.   Have you, then,
  Received some secret pledge from Célimène?

Acaste. Oh, no: she scorns me.

Clitandre.   Tell me the truth, I beg.

Acaste. She just can't bear me.

Clitandre.   Ah, don't pull my leg.
  Tell me what hope she's given you, I pray.

Acaste. I'm hopeless, and it's you who win the day.
  She hates me thoroughly, and I'm so vexed
  I mean to hang myself on Tuesday next.

Clitandre. Dear Marquess, let us have an armistice
  And make a treaty. What do you say to this?
  If ever one of us can plainly prove
  That Célimène encourages his love,
  The other must abandon hope, and yield,
  And leave him in possession of the field.

Acaste. Now, there's a bargain that appeals to me;
With all my heart, dear Marquess, I agree.
But hush.

SCENE 2.   *Célimène, Acaste, Clitandre*

Célimène.   Still here?
Clitandre.   'Twas love that stayed our feet.
Célimène.   I think I heard a carriage in the street.
Whose is it? D'you know?

SCENE 3.   *Célimène, Acaste, Clitandre, Basque*

Basque.   Arsinoé is here,
Madame.
Célimène.   Arsinoé, you say? Oh, dear.
Basque.   Éliante is entertaining her below.
Célimène.   What brings the creature here, I'd like to know?
Alcaste.   They say she's dreadfully prudish, but in fact
I think her piety . . .
Célimène.   It's all an act.
At heart she's worldly, and her poor success
In snaring men explains her prudishness.
It breaks her heart to see the beaux and gallants
Engrossed by other women's charms and talents,
And so she's always in a jealous rage
Against the faulty standards of the age.
She lets the world believe that she's a prude
To justify her loveless solitude,
And strives to put a brand of moral shame
On all the graces that she cannot claim.
But still she'd love a lover; and Alceste
Appears to be the one she'd love the best.
His visits here are poison to her pride;
She seems to think I've lured him from her side;
And everywhere, at court or in the town,
The spiteful, envious woman runs me down.
In short, she's just as stupid as can be,
Vicious and arrogant in the last degree,
And . . .

SCENE 4. *Arsinoé, Célimène, Clitandre, Acaste*

Célimène.   Ah! What happy chance has brought you here?
   I've thought about you ever so much, my dear.
Arsinoé.   I've come to tell you something you should know.
Célimène.   How good of you to think of doing so!

(Clitandre and Acaste go out, laughing.)

SCENE 5. *Arsinoé, Célimène*

Arsinoé.   It's just as well those gentlemen didn't tarry.
Célimène.   Shall we sit down?
Arsinoé.   That won't be necessary.
   Madam, the flame of friendship ought to burn
   Brightest in matters of the most concern,
   And as there's nothing which concerns us more
   Than honor, I have hastened to your door
   To bring you, as your friend, some information
   About the status of your reputation.
   I visited, last night, some virtuous folk,
   And, quite by chance, it was of you they spoke;
   There was, I fear, no tendency to praise
   Your light behavior and your dashing ways.
   The quantity of gentlemen you see
   And your by now notorious coquetry
   Were both so vehemently criticized
   By everyone, that I was much surprised.
   Of course, I needn't tell you where I stood;
   I came to your defense as best I could,
   Assured them you were harmless, and declared
   Your soul was absolutely unimpaired.
   But there are some things, you must realize,
   One can't excuse, however hard one tries,
   And I was forced at last into conceding
   That your behavior, Madam, is misleading,
   That it makes a bad impression, giving rise
   To ugly gossip and obscene surmise,
   And that if you were more *overtly* good,
   You wouldn't be so much misunderstood.
   Not that I think you've been unchaste—no! no!
   The saints preserve me from a thought so low!

But mere good conscience never did suffice:
One must avoid the outward show of vice.
Madam, you're too intelligent, I'm sure,
To think my motives anything but pure
In offering you this counsel—which I do
Out of a zealous interest in you.

Célimène.   Madam, I haven't taken you amiss;
I'm very much obliged to you for this;
And I'll at once discharge the obligation
By telling you about *your* reputation.
You've been so friendly as to let me know
What certain people say of me, and so
I mean to follow your benign example
By offering you a somewhat similar sample.
The other day, I went to an affair
And found some most distinguished people there
Discussing piety, both false and true.
The conversation soon came round to you.
Alas! Your prudery and bustling zeal
Appeared to have a very slight appeal.
Your affectation of a grave demeanor,
Your endless talk of virtue and of honor,
The aptitude of your suspicious mind
For finding sin where there is none to find,
Your towering self-esteem, that pitying face
With which you contemplate the human race,
Your sermonizings and your sharp aspersions
On people's pure and innocent diversions—
All these were mentioned, Madam, and, in fact,
Were roundly and concertedly attacked.
"What good," they said, "are all these outward shows,
When everything belies her pious pose?
She prays incessantly; but then, they say,
She beats her maids and cheats them of their pay;
She shows her zeal in every holy place,
But still she's vain enough to paint her face;
She holds that naked statues are immoral,
But with a naked *man* she'd have no quarrel."
Of course, I said to everybody there
That they were being viciously unfair;
But still they were disposed to criticize you,
And all agreed that someone should advise you
To leave the morals of the world alone,
And worry rather more about your own.

They felt that one's self-knowledge should be great
Before one thinks of setting others straight;
That one should learn the art of living well
Before one threatens other men with hell,
And that the Church is best equipped, no doubt,
To guide our souls and root our vices out.
Madam, you're too intelligent, I'm sure,
To think my motives anything but pure
In offering you this counsel—which I do
Out of a zealous interest in you.

Arsinoé. I dared not hope for gratitude, but I
Did not expect so acid a reply;
I judge, since you've been so extremely tart,
That my good counsel pierced you to the heart.

Célimène. Far from it, Madam. Indeed, it seems to me
We ought to trade advice more frequently.
One's vision of oneself is so defective
That it would be an excellent corrective.
If you are willing, Madam, let's arrange
Shortly to have another frank exchange
In which we'll tell each other, *entre nous,*
What you've heard tell of me, and I of you.

Arsinoé. Oh, people never censure you, my dear;
It's me they criticize. Or so I hear.

Célimène. Madam, I think we either blame or praise
According to our taste and length of days.
There is a time of life for coquetry,
And there's a season, too, for prudery.
When all one's charms are gone, it is, I'm sure,
Good strategy to be devout and pure:
It makes one seem a little less forsaken.
Some day, perhaps, I'll take the road you've taken:
Time brings all things. But I have time aplenty,
And see no cause to be a prude at twenty.

Arsinoé. You give your age in such a gloating tone
That one would think I was an ancient crone;
We're not so far apart, in sober truth,
That you can mock me with a boast of youth!
Madam, you baffle me. I wish I knew
What moves you to provoke me as you do.

Célimène. For my part, Madam, I should like to know
Why you abuse me everywhere you go.
Is it my fault, dear lady, that your hand
Is not, alas, in very great demand?

If men admire me, if they pay me court
And daily make me offers of the sort
You'd dearly love to have them make to you,
How can I help it? What would you have me do?
If what you want is lovers, please feel free
To take as many as you can from me.

Arsinoé. Oh, come. D'you think the world is losing sleep
Over that flock of lovers which you keep,
Or that we find it difficult to guess
What price you pay for their devotedness?
Surely you don't expect us to suppose
Mere merit could attract so many beaux?
It's not your virtue that they're dazzled by;
Nor is it virtuous love for which they sigh.
You're fooling no one, Madam; the world's not blind;
There's many a lady heaven has designed
To call men's noblest, tenderest feelings out,
Who has no lovers dogging her about;
From which it's plain that lovers nowadays
Must be acquired in bold and shameless ways,
And only pay one court for such reward
As modesty and virtue can't afford.
Then don't be quite so puffed up, if you please,
About your tawdry little victories;
Try, if you can, to be a shade less vain,
And treat the world with somewhat less disdain.
If one were envious of your amours,
One soon could have a following like yours;
Lovers are no great trouble to collect
If one prefers them to one's self-respect.

Célimène.   Collect them then, my dear; I'd love to see
You demonstrate that charming theory;
Who knows, you might . . .

Arsinoé.   Now, Madam, that will do;
It's time to end this trying interview,
My coach is late in coming to your door,
Or I'd have taken leave of you before.

Célimène.   Oh, please don't feel that you must rush away;
I'd be delighted, Madam, if you'd stay.
However, lest my conversation bore you,
Let me provide some better company for you;
This gentleman, who comes most apropos,
Will please you more than I could do, I know.

SCENE 6.   *Alceste, Célimène, Arsinoé*

Célimène.   Alceste, I have a little note to write
      Which simply must go out before tonight;
      Please entertain *Madame;* I'm sure that she
      Will overlook my incivility.

SCENE 7.   *Alceste, Arsinoé*

Arsinoé.   Well, Sir, our hostess graciously contrives
      For us to chat until my coach arrives;
      And I shall be forever in her debt
      For granting me this little tête-a-tête.
      We women very rightly give our hearts
      To men of noble character and parts,
      And your especial merits, dear Alceste,
      Have roused the deepest sympathy in my breast.
      Oh, how I wish they had sufficient sense
      At court, to recognize your excellence!
      They wrong you greatly, Sir. How it must hurt you
      Never to be rewarded for your virtue!
Alceste.   Why, Madam, what cause have I to feel aggrieved?
      What great and brilliant thing have I achieved?
      What service have I rendered to the King
      That I should look to him for anything?
Arsinoé.   Not everyone who's honored by the State
      Has done great services. A man must wait
      Till time and fortune offer him the chance.
      Your merit, Sir, is obvious at a glance,
      And . . .
Alceste.   Ah, forget my merit; I am not neglected.
      The court, I think, can hardly be expected
      To mine men's souls for merit, and unearth
      Our hidden virtues and our secret worth.
Arsinoé.   *Some* virtues, though, are far too bright to hide;
      Yours are acknowledged, Sir, on every side.
      Indeed, I've heard you warmly praised of late
      By persons of considerable weight.
Alceste.   This fawning age has praise for everyone,
      And all distinctions, Madam, are undone.
      All things have equal honor nowadays,

And no one should be gratified by praise.
To be admired, one only need exist,
And every lackey's on the honors list.

Arsinoé.   I only wish, Sir, that you had your eye
On some position at court, however high;
You'd only have to hint at such a notion
For me to set the proper wheels in motion;
I've certain friendships I'd be glad to use
To get you any office you might choose.

Alceste.   Madam, I fear that any such ambition
Is wholly foreign to my disposition.
The soul God gave me isn't of the sort
That prospers in the weather of a court.
It's all too obvious that I don't possess
The virtues necessary for success.
My one great talent is for speaking plain;
I've never learned to flatter or to feign;
And anyone so stupidly sincere
Had best not seek a courtier's career.
Outside the court, I know, one must dispense
With honors, privilege, and influence;
But still one gains the right, foregoing these,
Not to be tortured by the wish to please.
One needn't live in dread of snubs and slights,
Nor praise the verse that every idiot writes,
Nor humor silly Marquesses, nor bestow
Politic sighs on Madam So-and-So.

Arsinoé.   Forget the court, then; let the matter rest.
But I've another cause to be distressed
About your present situation, Sir.
It's to your love affair that I refer.
She whom you love, and who pretends to love you,
Is, I regret to say, unworthy of you.

Alceste.   Why, Madam? Can you seriously intend
To make so grave a charge against your friend?

Arsinoé.   Alas, I must. I've stood aside too long
And let that lady do you grievous wrong;
But now my debt to conscience shall be paid:
I tell you that your love has been betrayed.

Alceste.   I thank you, Madam; you're extremely kind.
Such words are soothing to a lover's mind.

Arsinoé.   Yes, though she *is* my friend, I say again
You're very much too good for Célimène.
She's wantonly misled you from the start.

Alceste. You may be right; who knows another's heart?
　　　But ask yourself if it's the part of charity
　　　To shake my soul with doubts of her sincerity.
Arsinoé. Well, if you'd rather be a dupe than doubt her,
　　　That's your affair. I'll say no more about her.
Alceste. Madam, you know that doubt and vague suspicion
　　　Are painful to a man in my position;
　　　It's most unkind to worry me this way
　　　Unless you've some real proof of what you say.
Arsinoé. Sir, say no more: all doubts shall be removed,
　　　And all that I've been saying shall be proved.
　　　You've only to escort me home, and there
　　　We'll look into the heart of this affair.
　　　I've ocular evidence which will persuade you
　　　Beyond a doubt, that Célimène's betrayed you.
　　　Then, if you're saddened by that revelation,
　　　Perhaps I can provide some consolation.

Act IV

SCENE 1. *Éliante, Philinte*

Philinte. Madam, he acted like a stubborn child;
　　　I thought they never would be reconciled;
　　　In vain we reasoned, threatened, and appealed;
　　　He stood his ground and simply would not yield.
　　　The Marshals, I feel sure, have never heard
　　　An argument so splendidly absurd.
　　　"No, gentlemen," said he, "I'll not retract.
　　　His verse is bad: extremely bad, in fact.
　　　Surely it does the man no harm to know it.
　　　Does it disgrace him, not to be a poet?
　　　A gentleman may be respected still,
　　　Whether he writes a sonnet well or ill.
　　　That I dislike his verse should not offend him;
　　　In all that touches honor, I commend him;
　　　He's noble, brave, and virtuous—but I fear
　　　He can't in truth be called a sonneteer.
　　　I'll gladly praise his wardrobe; I'll endorse
　　　His dancing, or the way he sits a horse;
　　　But, gentlemen, I cannot praise his rhyme.
　　　In fact, it ought to be a capital crime
　　　For anyone so sadly unendowed

To write a sonnet, and read the thing aloud."
At length he fell into a gentler mood
And, striking a concessive attitude,
He paid Oronte the following courtesies:
"Sir, I regret that I'm so hard to please,
And I'm profoundly sorry that your lyric
Failed to provoke me to a panegyric."
After these curious words, the two embraced,
And then the hearing was adjourned—in haste.

Éliante. His conduct has been very singular lately;
    Still, I confess that I respect him greatly.
    The honesty in which he takes such pride
    Has—to my mind—its noble, heroic side.
    In this false age, such candor seems outrageous;
    But I could wish that it were more contagious.

Philinte. What most intrigues me in our friend Alceste
    Is the grand passion that rages in his breast.
    The sullen humors he's compounded of
    Should not, I think, dispose his heart to love;
    But since they do, it puzzles me still more
    That he should choose your cousin to adore.

Éliante. It does, indeed, belie the theory
    That love is born of gentle sympathy,
    And that the tender passion must be based
    On sweet accords of temper and of taste.

Philinte. Does she return his love, do you suppose?

Éliante. Ah, that's a difficult question, Sir. Who knows?
    How can we judge the truth of her devotion?
    Her heart's a stranger to its own emotion.
    Sometimes it thinks it loves, when no love's there;
    At other times it loves quite unaware.

Philinte. I rather think Alceste is in for more
    Distress and sorrow than he's bargained for;
    Were he of my mind, Madam, his affection
    Would turn in quite a different direction,
    And we would see him more responsive to
    The kind regard which he receives from you.

Éliante. Sir, I believe in frankness, and I'm inclined,
    In matters of the heart, to speak my mind.
    I don't oppose his love for her; indeed,
    I hope with all my heart that he'll succeed,
    And were it in my power, I'd rejoice
    In giving him the lady of his choice.
    But if, as happens frequently enough
    In love affairs, he meets with a rebuff—

If Célimène should grant some rival's suit—
I'd gladly play the role of substitute;
Nor would his tender speeches please me less
Because they'd once been made without success.

Philinte. Well, Madam, as for me, I don't oppose
Your hopes in this affair; and heaven knows
That in my conversations with the man
I plead your cause as often as I can.
But if those two should marry, and so remove
All chance that he will offer you his love,
Then I'll declare my own, and hope to see
Your gracious favor pass from him to me.
In short, should you be cheated of Alceste,
I'd be most happy to be second best.

Éliante. Philinte, you're teasing.

Philinte.   Ah, Madam, never fear;
No words of mine were ever so sincere,
And I shall live in fretful expectation
Till I can make a fuller declaration.

SCENE 2.   *Alceste, Éliante, Philinte*

Alceste. Avenge me, Madam! I must have satisfaction,
Or this great wrong will drive me to distraction!

Éliante. Why, what's the matter? What's upset you so?

Alceste. Madam, I've had a mortal, mortal blow.
If Chaos repossessed the universe,
I swear I'd not be shaken any worse,
I'm ruined. . . . I can say no more. . . . My soul . . .

Éliante. Do try, Sir, to regain your self-control.

Alceste. Just heaven! Why were so much beauty and grace
Bestowed on one so vicious and so base?

Éliante. Once more, Sir, tell us. . . .

Alceste.   My world has gone to wrack;
I'm—I'm betrayed; she's stabbed me in the back:
Yes, Célimène (who would have thought it of her?)
Is false to me, and has another lover.

Éliante. Are you quite certain? Can you prove these things?

Philinte. Lovers are prey to wild imaginings
And jealous fancies. No doubt there's some mistake. . . .

Alceste. Mind your own business, Sir, for heaven's sake.

(To Éliante.)

Madam, I have the proof that you demand
Here in my pocket, penned by her own hand.
Yes, all the shameful evidence one could want
Lies in this letter written to Oronte—
Oronte! whom I felt sure she couldn't love,
And hardly bothered to be jealous of.

Philinte.   Still, in a letter, appearances may deceive;
This may not be so bad as you believe.

Alceste.   Once more I beg you, Sir, to let me be;
Tend to your own affairs; leave mine to me.

Éliante.   Compose yourself; this anguish that you feel . . .

Alceste.   Is something, Madam, you alone can heal.
My outraged heart, beside itself with grief,
Appeals to you for comfort and relief.
Avenge me on your cousin, whose unjust
And faithless nature has deceived my trust;
Avenge a crime your pure soul must detest.

Éliante.   But how, Sir?

Alceste.   Madam, this heart within my breast
Is yours; pray take it; redeem my heart from her,
And so avenge me on my torturer.
Let her be punished by the fond emotion,
The ardent love, the bottomless devotion,
The faithful worship which this heart of mine
Will offer up to yours as to a shrine.

Éliante.   You have my sympathy, Sir, in all you suffer;
Nor do I scorn the noble heart you offer;
But I suspect you'll soon be mollified,
And this desire for vengeance will subside.
When some belovèd hand has done us wrong
We thirst for retribution—but not for long;
However dark the deed that she's committed,
A lovely culprit's very soon acquitted.
Nothing's so stormy as an injured lover,
And yet no storm so quickly passes over.

Alceste.   No, Madam, no—this is no lovers' spat;
I'll not forgive her; it's gone too far for that;
My mind's made up; I'll kill myself before
I waste my hopes upon her any more.
Ah, here she is. My wrath intensifies.
I shall confront her with her tricks and lies,
And crush her utterly, and bring you then
A heart no longer slave to Célimène.

SCENE 3. *Célimène, Alceste*

Alceste (*aside*).   Sweet heaven, help me to control my passion.
Célimène (*aside*).   Oh, Lord.

(*To Alceste*)

                  Why stand there staring in that fashion?
And what d'you mean by those dramatic sighs,
And that malignant glitter in your eyes?
Alceste.   I mean that sins which cause the blood to freeze
Look innocent beside your treacheries;
That nothing Hell's or Heaven's wrath could do
Ever produced so bad a thing as you.
Célimène.   Your compliments were always sweet and pretty.
Alceste.   Madam, it's not the moment to be witty.
No, blush and hang your head; you've ample reason,
Since I've the fullest evidence of your treason.
Ah, this is what my sad heart prophesied;
Now all my anxious fears are verified;
My dark suspicion and my gloomy doubt
Divined the truth, and now the truth is out.
For all your trickery, I was not deceived;
It was my bitter stars that I believed.
But don't imagine that you'll go scot-free;
You shan't misuse me with impunity.
I know that love's irrational and blind;
I know the heart's not subject to the mind,
And can't be reasoned into beating faster;
I know each soul is free to choose its master;
Therefore had you but spoken from the heart,
Rejecting my attentions from the start,
I'd have no grievance, or at any rate
I could complain of nothing but my fate.
Ah, but so falsely to encourage me—
That was a treason and a treachery
For which you cannot suffer too severely,
And you shall pay for that behavior dearly.
Yes, now I have no pity, not a shred;
My temper's out of hand; I've lost my head;
Shocked by the knowledge of your double-dealings,
My reason can't restrain my savage feelings;
A righteous wrath deprives me of my senses,
And I won't answer for the consequences.

Célimène.   What does this outburst mean? Will you please explain?
  Have you, by any chance, gone quite insane?

Alceste.   Yes, yes, I went insane the day I fell
  A victim to your black and fatal spell,
  Thinking to meet with some sincerity
  Among the treacherous charms that beckoned me.

Célimène.   Pooh. Of what treachery can you complain?

Alceste.   How sly you are, how cleverly you feign!
  But you'll not victimize me any more.
  Look: here's a document you've seen before.
  This evidence, which I acquired today,
  Leaves you, I think, without a thing to say.

Célimène.   Is this what sent you into such a fit?

Alceste.   You should be blushing at the sight of it.

Célimène.   Ought I to blush? I truly don't see why.

Alceste.   Ah, now you're being bold as well as sly;
  Since there's no signature, perhaps you'll claim . . .

Célimène.   I wrote it, whether or not it bears my name.

Alceste.   And you can view with equanimity
  This proof of your disloyalty to me!

Célimène.   Oh, don't be so outrageous and extreme.

Alceste.   You take this matter lightly, it would seem.
  Was it no wrong to me, no shame to you,
  That you should send Oronte this billet-doux?

Célimène.   Oronte! Who said it was for him?

Alceste.   Why, those
  Who brought me this example of your prose.
  But what's the difference? If you wrote the letter
  To someone else, it pleases me no better.
  My grievance and your guilt remain the same.

Célimène.   But need you rage, and need I blush for shame,
  If this was written to a *woman* friend?

Alceste.   Ah! Most ingenious. I'm impressed no end;
  And after that incredible evasion
  Your guilt is clear. I need no more persuasion.
  How dare you try so clumsy a deception?
  D'you think I'm wholly wanting in perception?
  Come, come, let's see how brazenly you'll try
  To bolster up so palpable a lie:
  Kindly construe this ardent closing section
  As nothing more than sisterly affection!
  Here, let me read it. Tell me, if you dare to,
  That this is for a woman . . .

Célimène.   I don't care to.
What right have you to badger and berate me,
And so highhandedly interrogate me?
Alceste.   Now, don't be angry; all I ask of you
Is that you justify a phrase or two . . .
Célimène.   No, I shall not. I utterly refuse,
And you may take those phrases as you choose.
Alceste.   Just show me how this letter could be meant
For a woman's eyes, and I shall be content.
Célimène.   No, no, it's for Oronte; you're perfectly right.
I welcome his attentions with delight,
I prize his character and his intellect,
And everything is just as you suspect.
Come, do your worst now; give your rage free rein;
But kindly cease to bicker and complain.
Alceste (*aside*).   Good God! Could anything be more inhuman?
Was ever a heart so mangled by a woman?
When I complain of how she has betrayed me,
She bridles, and commences to upbraid me!
She tries my tortured patience to the limit;
She won't deny her guilt; she glories in it!
And yet my heart's too faint and cowardly
To break these chains of passion, and be free,
To scorn her as it should, and rise above
This unrewarded, mad, and bitter love.

(*To Célimène.*)

Ah, traitress, in how confident a fashion
You take advantage of my helpless passion,
And use my weakness for your faithless charms
To make me once again throw down my arms!
But do at least deny this black transgression;
Take back that mocking and perverse confession;
Defend this letter and your innocence,
And I, poor fool, will aid in your defense.
Pretend, pretend, that you are just and true,
And I shall make myself believe in you.
Célimène.   Oh, stop it. Don't be such a jealous dunce,
Or I shall leave off loving you at once.
Just why should I *pretend?* What could impel me
To stoop so low as that? And kindly tell me
Why, if I loved another, I shouldn't merely
Inform you of it, simply and sincerely!
I've told you where you stand, and that admission
Should altogether clear me of suspicion;

After so generous a guarantee,
What right have you to harbor doubts of me?
Since women are (from natural reticence)
Reluctant to declare their sentiments,
And since the honor of our sex requires
That we conceal our amorous desires,
Ought any man for whom such laws are broken
To question what the oracle has spoken?
Should he not rather feel an obligation
To trust that most obliging declaration?
Enough, now. Your suspicions quite disgust me;
Why should I love a man who doesn't trust me?
I cannot understand why I continue,
Fool that I am, to take an interest in you.
I ought to choose a man less prone to doubt,
And give you something to be vexed about.

Alceste.   Ah, what a poor enchanted fool I am;
These gentle words, no doubt, were all a sham,
But destiny requires me to entrust
My happiness to you, and so I must.
I'll love you to the bitter end, and see
How false and treacherous you dare to be.

Célimène.   No, you don't really love me as you ought.

Alceste.   I love you more than can be said or thought;
Indeed, I wish you were in such distress
That I might show my deep devotedness.
Yes, I could wish that you were wretchedly poor,
Unloved, uncherished, utterly obscure;
That fate had set you down upon the earth
Without possessions, rank, or gentle birth;
Then, by the offer of my heart, I might
Repair the great injustice of your plight;
I'd raise you from the dust, and proudly prove
The purity and vastness of my love.

Célimène.   This is a strange benevolence indeed!
God grant that I may never be in need. . . .
Ah, here's Monsieur Dubois, in quaint disguise.

SCENE 4.   *Célimène, Alceste, Dubois*

Alceste.   Well, why this costume? Why those frightened eyes?
What ails you?

Dubois.   Well, Sir, things are most mysterious.

Alceste. What do you mean?

Dubois. I fear they're very serious.

Alceste. What?

Dubois. Shall I speak more loudly?

Alceste. Yes; speak out.

Dubois. Isn't there someone here, Sir?

Alceste. Speak, you lout!
Stop wasting time.

Dubois. Sir, we must slip away.

Alceste. How's that?

Dubois. We must decamp without delay.

Alceste. Explain yourself.

Dubois. I tell you we must fly.

Alceste. What for?

Dubois. We mustn't pause to say good-by.

Alceste. Now what d'you mean by all of this, you clown?

Dubois. I mean, Sir, that we've got to leave this town.

Alceste. I'll tear you limb from limb and joint from joint
If you don't come more quickly to the point.

Dubois. Well, Sir, today a man in a black suit,
Who wore a black and ugly scowl to boot,
Left us a document scrawled in such a hand
As even Satan couldn't understand.
It bears upon your lawsuit, I don't doubt;
But all hell's devils couldn't make it out.

Alceste. Well, well, go on. What then? I fail to see
How this event obliges us to flee.

Dubois. Well, Sir: an hour later, hardly more,
A gentleman who's often called before
Came looking for you in an anxious way.
Not finding you, he asked me to convey
(Knowing I could be trusted with the same)
The following message.... Now, what *was* his name?

Alceste. Forget his name, you idiot. What did he say?

Dubois. Well, it was one of your friends, Sir, anyway.
He warned you to begone, and he suggested
That if you stay, you may well be arrested.

Alceste. What? Nothing more specific? Think, man, think!

Dubois. No, Sir. He had me bring him pen and ink,
And dashed you off a letter which, I'm sure,
Will render things distinctly less obscure.

Alceste. Well—let me have it!

Célimène. What *is* this all about?

Alceste. God knows; but I have hopes of finding out.
How long am I to wait, you blitherer?

Dubois (*after a protracted search for the letter*).   I must have left it on your
    table, Sir.

Alceste.   I ought to . . .

Célimène.   No, no, keep your self-control;
    Go find out what's behind his rigmarole.

Alceste.   It seems that fate, no matter what I do,
    Has sworn that I may not converse with you;
    But, Madam, pray permit your faithful lover
    To try once more before the day is over.

Act V

SCENE 1.   *Alceste, Philinte*

Alceste.   No, it's too much. My mind's made up, I tell you.

Philinte.   Why should this blow, however hard, compel you . . .

Alceste.   No, no, don't waste your breath in argument;
    Nothing you say will alter my intent;
    This age is vile, and I've made up my mind
    To have no further commerce with mankind.
    Did not truth, honor, decency, and the laws
    Oppose my enemy and approve my cause?
    My claims were justified in all men's sight;
    I put my trust in equity and right;
    Yet, to my horror and the world's disgrace,
    Justice is mocked, and I have lost my case!
    A scoundrel whose dishonesty is notorious
    Emerges from another lie victorious!
    Honor and right condone his brazen fraud,
    While rectitude and decency applaud!
    Before his smirking face, the truth stands charmed,
    And virtue conquered, and the law disarmed!
    His crime is sanctioned by a court decree!
    And not content with what he's done to me,
    The dog now seeks to ruin me by stating
    That I composed a book now circulating,
    A book so wholly criminal and vicious
    That even to speak its title is seditious!
    Meanwhile Oronte, my rival, lends his credit
    To the same libelous tale, and helps to spread it!
    Oronte! a man of honor and of rank,
    With whom I've been entirely fair and frank;
    Who sought me out and forced me, willy-nilly,

To judge some verse I found extremely silly;
And who, because I properly refused
To flatter him, or see the truth abused,
Abets my enemy in a rotten slander!
There's the reward of honesty and candor!
The man will hate me to the end of time
For failing to commend his wretched rhyme!
And not this man alone, but all humanity
Do what they do from interest and vanity;
They prate of honor, truth, and righteousness,
But lie, betray, and swindle nonetheless.
Come then: man's villainy is too much to bear;
Let's leave this jungle and this jackal's lair.
Yes! treacherous and savage race of men,
You shall not look upon my face again.

Philinte.   Oh, don't rush into exile prematurely;
Things aren't as dreadful as you make them, surely.
It's rather obvious, since you're still at large,
That people don't believe your enemy's charge.
Indeed, his tale's so patently untrue
That it may do more harm to him than you.

Alceste.   Nothing could do that scoundrel any harm:
His frank corruption is his greatest charm,
And, far from hurting him, a further shame
Would only serve to magnify his name.

Philinte.   In any case, his bald prevarication
Has done no injury to your reputation,
And you may feel secure in that regard.
As for your lawsuit, it should not be hard
To have the case reopened, and contest
This judgment . . .

Alceste.   No, no, let the verdict rest.
Whatever cruel penalty it may bring,
I wouldn't have it changed for anything.
It shows the times' injustice with such clarity
That I shall pass it down to our posterity
As a great proof and signal demonstration
Of the black wickedness of this generation.
It may cost twenty thousand francs; but I
Shall pay their twenty thousand, and gain thereby
The right to storm and rage at human evil,
And send the race of mankind to the devil.

Philinte.   Listen to me. . . .

Alceste.   Why? What can you possibly say?
Don't argue, Sir; your labor's thrown away.

Do you propose to offer lame excuses
For men's behavior and the times' abuses?
Philinte.   No, all you say I'll readily concede:
This is a low, conniving age indeed;
Nothing but trickery prospers nowadays,
And people ought to mend their shabby ways.
Yes, man's a beastly creature; but must we then
Abandon the society of men?
Here in the world, each human frailty
Provides occasion for philosophy,
And that is virtue's noblest exercise;
If honesty shone forth from all men's eyes,
If every heart were frank and kind and just,
What could our virtues do but gather dust
(Since their employment is to help us bear
The villainies of men without despair)?
A heart well-armed with virtue can endure. . . .
Alceste.   Sir, you're a matchless reasoner, to be sure;
Your words are fine and full of cogency;
But don't waste time and eloquence on me.
My reason bids me go, for my own good.
My tongue won't lie and flatter as it should;
God knows what frankness it might next commit,
And what I'd suffer on account of it.
Pray let me wait for Célimène's return
In peace and quiet. I shall shortly learn,
By her response to what I have in view,
Whether her love for me is feigned or true.
Philinte.   Till then, let's visit Éliante upstairs.
Alceste.   No, I am too weighed down with somber cares.
Go to her, do; and leave me with my gloom
Here in the darkened corner of this room.
Philinte.   Why, that's no sort of company, my friend;
I'll see if Éliante will not descend.

SCENE 2.   *Célimène, Oronte, Alceste*

Oronte.   Yes, Madam, if you wish me to remain
Your true and ardent lover, you must deign
To give me some more positive assurance.
All this suspense is quite beyond endurance.
If your heart shares the sweet desires of mine,
Show me as much by some convincing sign;

And here's the sign I urgently suggest:
That you no longer tolerate Alceste,
But sacrifice him to my love, and sever
All your relations with the man forever.
Célimène.   Why do you suddenly dislike him so?
You praised him to the skies not long ago.
Oronte.   Madam, that's not the point. I'm here to find
Which way your tender feelings are inclined.
Choose, if you please, between Alceste and me,
And I shall stay or go accordingly.
Alceste (*emerging from the corner*).   Yes, Madam, choose; this gentleman's
demand
Is wholly just, and I support his stand.
I too am true and ardent; I too am here
To ask you that you make your feelings clear.
No more delays, now; no equivocation;
The time has come to make your declaration.
Oronte.   Sir, I've no wish in any way to be
An obstacle to your felicity.
Alceste.   Sir, I've no wish to share her heart with you;
That may sound jealous, but at least it's true.
Oronte.   If, weighing us, she leans in your direction . . .
Alceste.   If she regards you with the least affection . . .
Oronte.   I swear I'll yield her to you there and then.
Alceste.   I swear I'll never see her face again.
Oronte.   Now Madam, tell us what we've come to hear.
Alceste.   Madam, speak openly and have no fear.
Oronte.   Just say which one is to remain your lover.
Alceste.   Just name one name, and it will all be over.
Oronte.   What! Is it possible that you're undecided?
Alceste.   What! Can your feelings possibly be divided?
Célimène.   Enough: this inquisition's gone too far:
How utterly unreasonable you are!
Not that I couldn't make the choice with ease;
My heart has no conflicting sympathies;
I know full well which one of you I favor,
And you'd not see me hesitate or waver.
But how can you expect me to reveal
So cruelly and bluntly what I feel?
I think it altogether too unpleasant
To choose between two men when both are present;
One's heart has means more subtle and more kind
Of letting its affections be divined,
Nor need one be uncharitably plain
To let a lover know he loves in vain.

Oronte.   No, no, speak plainly; I for one can stand it.
    I beg you to be frank.
Alceste.   And I demand it.
    The simple truth is what I wish to know,
    And there's no need for softening the blow.
    You've made an art of pleasing everyone,
    But now your days of coquetry are done:
    You have no choice now, Madam, but to choose,
    For I'll know what to think if you refuse;
    I'll take your silence for a clear admission
    That I'm entitled to my worst suspicion.
Oronte.   I thank you for this ultimatum, Sir,
    And I may say I heartily concur.
Célimène.   Really, this foolishness is very wearing:
    Must you be so unjust and overbearing?
    Haven't I told you why I must demur?
    Ah, here's Éliante; I'll put the case to her.

      SCENE 3.   *Éliante, Philinte, Célimène, Oronte, Alceste*

Célimène.   Cousin, I'm being persecuted here
    By these two persons, who, it would appear,
    Will not be satisfied till I confess
    Which one I love the more, and which the less,
    And tell the latter to his face that he
    Is henceforth banished from my company.
    Tell me, has ever such a thing been done?
Éliante.   You'd best not turn to me; I'm not the one
    To back you in a matter of this kind:
    I'm all for those who frankly speak their mind.
Oronte.   Madam, you'll search in vain for a defender.
Alceste.   You're beaten, Madam, and may as well surrender.
Oronte.   Speak, speak, you must; and end this awful strain.
Alceste.   Or don't, and your position will be plain.
Oronte.   A single word will close this painful scene.
Alceste.   But if you're silent, I'll know what you mean.

      SCENE 4.   *Arsinoé, Célimène, Éliante, Alceste, Philinte, Acaste,*
                  Clitandre, Oronte

Acaste *(to Célimène).*   Madam, with all due deference, we two
    Have come to pick a little bone with you.

Clitandre (*to Oronte and Alceste*).   I'm glad you're present, Sirs; as you'll soon learn,
Our business here is also your concern.
Arsinoé (*to Célimène*).   Madam, I visit you so soon again
Only because of these two gentlemen,
Who came to me indignant and aggrieved
About a crime too base to be believed.
Knowing your virtue, having such confidence in it,
I couldn't think you guilty for a minute,
In spite of all their telling evidence;
And, rising above our little difference,
I've hastened here in friendship's name to see
You clear yourself of this great calumny.
Acaste.   Yes, Madam, let us see with what composure
You'll manage to respond to this disclosure.
You lately sent Clitandre this tender note.
Clitandre.   And this one, for Acaste, you also wrote.
Acaste (*to Oronte and Alceste*).   You'll recognize this writing, Sirs, I think;
The lady is so free with pen and ink
That you must know it all too well, I fear.
But listen: this is something you should hear.

"How absurd you are to condemn my lightheartedness in society, and to accuse me of being happiest in the company of others. Nothing could be more unjust; and if you do not come to me instantly and beg pardon for saying such a thing, I shall never forgive you as long as I live. Our big bumbling friend the Viscount . . ."

What a shame that he's not here.

"Our big bumbling friend the Viscount, whose name stands first in your complaint, is hardly a man to my taste; and ever since the day I watched him spend three-quarters of an hour spitting into a well, so as to make circles in the water, I have been unable to think highly of him. As for the little Marquess . . ."

In all modesty, gentlemen, that is I.

"As for the little Marquess, who sat squeezing my hand for such a long while yesterday, I find him in all respects the most trifling creature alive; and the only things of value about him are his cape and his sword. As for the man with the green ribbons . . ."

(*To Alceste.*) It's your turn now, Sir.

"As for the man with the green ribbons, he amuses me now and then with his bluntness and his bearish ill-humor; but there are many times indeed when I think him the greatest bore in the world. And as for the sonneteer . . ."

(*To Oronte.*) Here's your helping.

"And as for the sonneteer, who has taken it into his head to be witty, and insists on being an author in the teeth of opinion, I simply cannot be bothered to listen to him, and his prose wearies me quite as much as his poetry. Be assured that I am not always so well-entertained as you suppose; that I long for your company, more than I dare to say, at all these entertainments to which people drag me, and that the presence of those one loves is the true and perfect seasoning to all one's pleasures."

Clitandre.   And now for me.

"Clitandre, whom you mention, and who so pesters me with his saccharine speeches, is the last man on earth for whom I could feel any affection. He is quite mad to suppose that I love him, and so are you, to doubt that you are loved. Do come to your senses; exchange your suppositions for his; and visit me as often as possible, to help me bear the annoyance of his unwelcome attentions."

It's a sweet character that these letters show,
And what to call it, Madam, you well know.
Enough. We're off to make the world acquainted
With this sublime self-portrait that you've painted.
Acaste.   Madam, I'll make you no farewell oration;
No, you're not worthy of my indignation.
Far choicer hearts than yours, as you'll discover,
Would like this little Marquess for a lover.

> **SCENE 5.**   *Célimène, Éliante, Arsinoé, Alceste, Oronte, Philinte*

Oronte.   So! After all those loving letters you wrote,
You turn on me like this, and cut my throat!
And your dissembling, faithless heart, I find,
Has pledged itself by turns to all mankind!
How blind I've been! But now I clearly see;
I thank you, Madam, for enlightening me.
My heart is mine once more, and I'm content;
The loss of it shall be your punishment.

(*To Alceste.*)

Sir, she is yours; I'll seek no more to stand
Between your wishes and this lady's hand.

Arsinoé (*to Célimène*).   Madam, I'm forced to speak. I'm far too stirred
　　To keep my counsel, after what I've heard.
　　I'm shocked and staggered by your want of morals.
　　It's not my way to mix in others' quarrels;
　　But really, when this fine and noble spirit,
　　This man of honor and surpassing merit,
　　Laid down the offering of his heart before you,
　　How *could* you . . .
Alceste.　　　　　　　Madam, permit me, I implore you,
　　To represent myself in this debate.
　　Don't bother, please, to be my advocate.
　　My heart, in any case, could not afford
　　To give your services their due reward;
　　And if I chose, for consolation's sake,
　　Some other lady, 'twould not be you I'd take.
Arsinoé.   What makes you think you could, Sir? And how dare you
　　Imply that I've been trying to ensnare you?
　　If you can for a moment entertain
　　Such flattering fancies, you're extremely vain.
　　I'm not so interested as you suppose
　　In Célimène's discarded gigolos.
　　Get rid of that absurd illusion, do.
　　Women like me are not for such as you.
　　Stay with this creature, to whom you're so attached;
　　I've never seen two people better matched.

SCENE 7.   *Célimène, Éliante, Alceste, Philinte*

Alceste (*to Célimène*).   Well, I've been still throughout this exposé,
　　Till everyone but me has said his say.
　　Come, have I shown sufficient self-restraint?
　　And may I now . . .
Célimène.　　　　　　Yes, make your just complaint.
　　Reproach me freely, call me what you will;
　　You've every right to say I've used you ill.
　　I've wronged you, I confess it; and in my shame
　　I'll make no effort to escape the blame.

The anger of those others I could despise;
My guilt toward you I sadly recognize.
Your wrath is wholly justified, I fear;
I know how culpable I must appear,
I know all things bespeak my treachery,
And that, in short, you've grounds for hating me.
Do so; I give you leave.

Alceste.   Ah, traitress—how,
How should I cease to love you, even now?
Though mind and will were passionately bent
On hating you, my heart would not consent.

(*To Éliante and Philinte.*)

Be witness to my madness, both of you;
See what infatuation drives one to;
But wait; my folly's only just begun,
And I shall prove to you before I'm done
How strange the human heart is, and how far
From rational we sorry creatures are.

(*To Célimène.*)

Woman, I'm willing to forget your shame,
And clothe your treacheries in a sweeter name;
I'll call them youthful errors, instead of crimes,
And lay the blame on these corrupting times.
My one condition is that you agree
To share my chosen fate, and fly with me
To that wild, trackless, solitary place
In which I shall forget the human race.
Only by such a course can you atone
For those atrocious letters; by that alone
Can you remove my present horror of you,
And make it possible for me to love you.

Célimène.   What! *I* renounce the world at my young age,
And die of boredom in some hermitage?

Alceste.   Ah, if you really loved me as you ought,
You wouldn't give the world a moment's thought;
Must you have me, and all the world beside?

Célimène.   Alas, at twenty one is terrified
Of solitude. I fear I lack the force
And depth of soul to take so stern a course.

But if my hand in marriage will content you,
Why, there's a plan which I might well consent to,
And . . .

Alceste. No, I detest you now. I could excuse
Everything else, but since you thus refuse
To love me wholly, as a wife should do,
And see the world in me, as I in you,
Go! I reject your hand, and disenthrall
My heart from your enchantments, once for all.

      SCENE 8. *Éliante, Alceste, Philinte*

Alceste (*to Éliante*). Madam, your virtuous beauty has no peer;
Of all this world, you only are sincere;
I've long esteemed you highly, as you know;
Permit me ever to esteem you so,
And if I do not now request your hand,
Forgive me, Madam, and try to understand.
I feel unworthy of it; I sense that fate
Does not intend me for the married state,
That I should do you wrong by offering you
My shattered heart's unhappy residue,
And that in short . . .

Éliante. Your argument's well taken:
Nor need you fear that I shall feel forsaken.
Were I to offer him this hand of mine,
Your friend Philinte, I think, would not decline.

Philinte. Ah, Madam, that's my heart's most cherished goal,
For which I'd gladly give my life and soul.

Alceste (*to Éliante and Philinte*). May you be true to all you now profess,
And so deserve unending happiness.
Meanwhile, betrayed and wronged in everything,
I'll flee this bitter world where vice is king,
And seek some spot unpeopled and apart
Where I'll be free to have an honest heart.

Philinte. Come, Madam, let's do everything we can
To change the mind of this unhappy man.

Questions

*1. Is the reader meant to admire Alceste for his principled refusal to abide by the rules
of a complacent and superficial aristocratic society, or does Molière want us to laugh*

at Alceste's rigidity, his insistence on turning everything into a challenge? Explain. **2.** Contrast Philinte's attitudes with those of Alceste. Why, despite their differences, does Philinte remain loyal to Alceste? **3.** What bearing does the exchange between Célimène and Arsinoé at the end of Act III have on the theme of the play? **4.** What does Alceste's jealous love for Célimène tell us about his character and principles? **5.** Considering Alceste's own attitudes and the kind of society he is a part of, what explanation is there for his assertion (in Act I, scene 1), regarding his lawsuit, that "Reason and right and justice will plead for me"? **6.** What is Éliante's function in the play? **7.** Does the final scene of the play present a clear resolution of the issues? Explain.

love aNd hate

QUESTIONS FOR FURTHER ANALYSIS

1. Every story in this section incorporates some sexual element. Distinguish among the functions served by the sexual aspects of the stories.

2. Shakespeare's *Othello* and Molière's *The Misanthrope* both deal with hate as well as love. What differences in the definitions of love and hate emerge from the two plays? What changed plot elements would result in a comic Othello and a tragic Misanthrope? What do such speculative plot changes reveal concerning cultural attitudes about love and hate?

3. Faulkner's "Dry September" and Baldwin's "Going to Meet the Man" are both based on a lynching. What differences in treatment emerge? Is there evidence in the stories that enables a reader to determine the race of each writer?

4. Blake's "A Poison Tree," Browning's "Soliloquy in a Spanish Cloister," Dickinson's "Mine Enemy Is Growing Old", and Schramm's "Calamity" all seem to describe some aspects of hate. Are there clues to the origins of the hatred? What images predominate? Are the hatreds of different varieties?

5. An eighteenth-century dramatist wrote: "Love, like death, [is] a universal leveller of mankind." What does this mean? Which works, if any, in this section support the proposition?

6. Examine the works in this section in terms of the support they provide for the contention that love and hate are closely related emotions.

7. What images are characteristically associated with love in the prose and poetry of this section? What images are associated with hate? What insight, if any, does this use of figurative language provide into our cultural evaluations of nature?

8. Which works in this section treat love or hate in a way that corresponds most closely with your own experience or conception of those emotional states? Which contradicts your experience? Isolate, in each case, the elements in the work responsible for your response and discuss them in terms of their "truth" or "falsity."

THE PRESENCE OF DEATH

The inevitability of death is not implied in the Biblical story of creation; it required an act of disobedience before an angry God passed sentence of hard labor and mortality on mankind: "In the sweat of your face you shall eat bread till you return to the ground, for out of it you were taken; you are dust and to dust you shall return." These words, written down some 2,800 years ago, preserve an ancient explanation for a condition of life which yet remains persistently enigmatic—the dissolution of the flesh and the personality as accident or age culminates in death, the "undiscovered country, from whose bourn / No traveller returns." Though we cannot know what death is like, from earliest times men and women have attempted to characterize death, to cultivate beliefs about it. The mystery of it and the certainty of it make death, in every age, an important theme for literary art.

Beliefs about the nature of death vary widely. The ancient Jews of the Pentateuch reveal no conception of immortality. Ancient Buddhist writings describe death as a mere translation from one painful life to another in an ongoing expiation which only the purest can avoid. The Christians came to conceive of a soul, separate from the body, which at the body's death is freed for a better (or worse) disembodied eternal life. More recently in the western world, the history of the attitudes about death reflect the great ideological revolutions that affected all thought—the Copernican revolution, which displaced the earth from the center of the solar system; the Darwinian revolution, which exchanged for man, the greatest glory of God's creation, an upright primate with an opposable thumb whose days, like the dinosaur's, are likely to be numbered by the flux between the fire and ice of geological history; and the Freudian revolution, which robbed man of his proudest certainty, the conviction that he possessed a dependable and controlling rational mind. All these ideological changes serve to diminish man, to mock his self-importance, and, inevitably, to alter his conception of death.

But despite the impact of intellectual history, death remains invested with a special awe—perhaps because it infallibly mediates between all human differences. For the churchly, death, like birth and marriage, is the occasion for solemn ritual that reaffirms for the congregation its own communal life and the promise of a better life hereafter—though the belief in immortality does not eliminate sadness and regret. For those for whom there is no immortality, death is nonetheless a ceremonial affair, full of awe, for nothing human is so purely defined, so utterly important, as a life ended. Further, both the religious and the secular see death in moral terms. For both, the killer is hateful. For both, there are some deaths that are deserved, some

deaths that human weakness makes inevitable, some deaths that are out-
rageously unfair. For both, there are courageous deaths, which exalt the
community, and cowardly deaths too embarrassing to recognize.

Everyman and The Seventh Seal, though separated by almost six hundred years, both confront death from a Christian standpoint that distrusts,
even condemns, this-worldliness. But whereas for Everyman, death represents a perilous consummation for a life too thoughtlessly pleasurable, for the
Knight of the The Seventh Seal and his strange band of followers, death
comes, one feels, as a release from a dark and menacing world. And this conception of release from the prison of life animates much of the essentially
optimistic religious poetry of death—John Donne's sonnet "Death Be Not
Proud" is an outstanding example. Another view that establishes death as
the great leveler, bringing kings and emperors to that selfsame dust, reassures
the impoverished when they contrast their misery with the wealth of the
mighty.

That leveling aspect of death, apparent in such poems as Shirley's dirge
"The Glories of Our Blood and State" and the speech of Shakespeare's King
Richard, "And nothing we can call our own but death," leads easily and logically to the tradition wherein life itself is made absurd by the fact of death.
Macbeth declares finally, that life "is a tale / Told by an idiot, full of sound
and fury, / Signifying nothing." And the contemplation of suicide, which the
pain and absurdity of life would seem to commend, provokes such diverse
responses as Hamlet's speech, "To be, or not to be," Robinson's "The
Mill," and Maxine Kumin's suggestive sonnet "Will." Some rage against
death—Poe in Ligeia and Dylan Thomas in "Do Not Go Gentle into That Good
Night"; others caution a quiet resignation—Frost in "After Apple-Picking"
and Catherine Davis in her answer to Thomas, "After a Time." Much fine
poetry on death is elegiac; it speaks the melancholy response of the living to
the fact of death in such poems as Gray's "Elegy Written in a Country Churchyard," Housman's "To an Athlete Dying Young," Ransom's "Bells for John
Whiteside's Daughter," Roethke's "Elegy for Jane."

In short, literary treatments of death display immense diversity. In Tolstoy's The Death of Iván Ilých, dying leads to a redemptive awareness. In de
Maupassant's "Two Friends," the characters rise to a heroic acceptance of
death. In Malamud's tragicomic "Idiots First," the protagonist insists upon
and wins fair treatment from death, and in Cummings' "nobody loses all
the time," the comic lightens the weight of death. The circumstances of
death and the way one confronts it paradoxically lend to life its meaning and
its value.

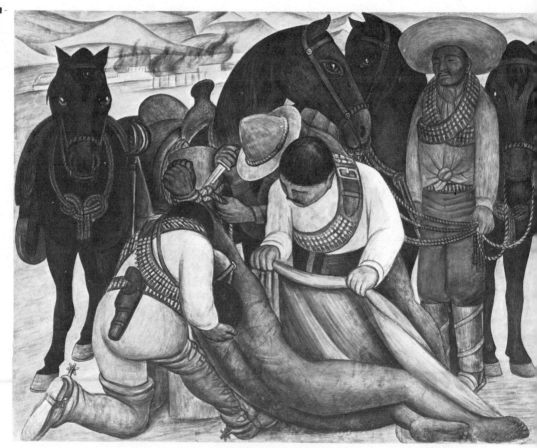

FICTION

Ligeia

EDGAR ALLAN POE [1809–1849]

And the will therein lieth, which dieth not. Who knoweth the mysteries of the will, with its vigor? For God is but a great will pervading all things by nature of its intentness. Man doth not yield himself to the angels, nor unto death utterly, save only through the weakness of his feeble will.—*Joseph Glanvill*

I cannot, for my soul, remember how, when, or even precisely where, I first became acquainted with the lady Ligeia. Long years have since elapsed, and my memory is feeble through much suffering. Or, perhaps, I cannot *now* bring these points to mind, because, in truth, the character of my beloved, her rare learning, her singular yet placid cast of beauty, and the thrilling and enthralling eloquence of her low musical language, made their way into my heart by paces so steadily and stealthily progressive that they have been unnoticed and unknown. Yet I believe that I met her first and most frequently in some large, old, decaying city near the Rhine. Of her family—I have surely heard her speak. That it is of a remotely ancient date cannot be doubted. Ligeia! Ligeia! Buried in studies of a nature more than all else adapted to deaden impressions of the outward world, it is by that sweet word alone—by Ligeia—that I bring before mine eyes in fancy the image of her who is no more. And now, while I write, a recollection flashes upon me that I have *never known* the paternal name of her who was my friend and my betrothed, and who became the partner of my studies, and finally the wife of my bosom. Was it a playful charge on the part of my Ligeia? or was it a test of my strength of affection, that I should institute no inquiries upon this point? or was it rather a caprice of my own—a wildly romantic offering on the shrine of the most passionate devotion? I but indistinctly recall the fact itself—what wonder that I have utterly forgotten the circumstances which originated or attended it? And, indeed, if ever that spirit which is entitled *Romance*—if ever she, the wan and the misty-winged *Ashtophet*[1] of idola-

---

1. A Phoenician fertility goddess.

trous Egypt, presided, as they tell, over marriages ill-omened, then most surely she presided over mine.

There is one dear topic, however, on which my memory fails me not. It is the *person* of Ligeia. In stature she was tall, somewhat slender, and, in her latter days, even emaciated. I would in vain attempt to portray the majesty, the quiet ease of her demeanor, or the incomprehensible lightness and elasticity of her footfall. She came and departed as a shadow. I was never made aware of her entrance into my closed study save by the dear music of her low sweet voice, as she placed her marble hand upon my shoulder. In beauty of face no maiden ever equalled her. It was the radiance of an opium-dream—an airy and spirit-lifting vision more wildly divine than the phantasies which hovered about the slumbering souls of the daughters of Delos.[2] Yet her features were not of that regular mould which we have been falsely taught to worship in the classical labors of the heathen. "There is no exquisite beauty," says Bacon, Lord Verulam, speaking truly of all the forms and *genera* of beauty, "without some *strangeness* in the proportion." Yet, although I saw that the features of Ligeia were not of a classic regularity—although I perceived that her loveliness was indeed "exquisite," and felt that there was much of "strangeness" pervading it, yet I have tried in vain to detect the irregularity and to trace home my own perception of "the strange." I examined the contour of the lofty and pale forehead—it was faultless—how cold indeed that word when applied to a majesty so divine!—the skin rivalling the purest ivory, the commanding extent and repose, the gentle prominence of the regions above the temples; and then the raven-black, the glossy, the luxuriant and naturally-curling tresses, setting forth the full force of the Homeric epithet, "hyacinthine!" I looked at the delicate outlines of the nose—and nowhere but in the graceful medallions of the Hebrews had I beheld a similar perfection. There were the same luxurious smoothness of surface, the same scarcely perceptible tendency to the aquiline, the same harmoniously curved nostrils speaking the free spirit. I regarded the sweet mouth. Here was indeed the triumph of all things heavenly—the magnificent turn of the short upper lip—the soft, voluptuous slumber of the under—the dimples which sported, and the color which spoke—the teeth glancing back, with a brilliancy almost startling, every ray of the holy light which fell upon them in her serene and placid yet most exultingly radiant of all smiles. I scrutinized the formation of the chin—and, here too, I found the gentleness of breadth, the softness and the majesty, the fullness and the spirituality, of the Greek—the contour which the god Apollo revealed but in a dream, to Cleomenes,[3] the son of the Athenian. And then I peered into the large eyes of Ligeia.

For eyes we have no models in the remotely antique. It might have

---

2. According to Greek mythology, the twins Apollo and Artemis were born on Delos, an island of the Cyclades. The reference here may be to the maidens, sworn to chastity, who attended Artemis.
3. An Athenian sculptor to whom the Venus de' Medici has been attributed.

been, too, that in these eyes of my beloved lay the secret to which Lord Verulam alludes. They were, I must believe, far larger than the ordinary eyes of
our own race. They were even fuller than the fullest of the gazelle eyes of the
tribe of the valley of Nourjahad.[4] Yet it was only at intervals—in moments of
intense excitement—that this peculiarity became more than slightly noticeable in Ligeia. And at such moments was her beauty—in my heated fancy
thus it appeared perhaps—the beauty of beings either above or apart from
the earth—the beauty of the fabulous Houri[5] of the Turk. The hue of the
orbs was the most brilliant of black, and, far over them, hung jetty lashes of
great length. The brows, slightly irregular in outline, had the same tint. The
"strangeness," however, which I found in the eyes, was of a nature distinct
from the formation, or the color, or the brilliancy of the features, and must,
after all, be referred to the *expression*. Ah, word of no meaning! behind
whose vast latitude of mere sound we intrench our ignorance of so much of
the spiritual. The expression of the eyes of Ligeia! How for long hours have I
pondered upon it! How have I, through the whole of a midsummer night,
struggled to fathom it! What was it—that something more profound than the
well of Democritus[6]—which lay far within the pupils of my beloved? What
was it? I was possessed with a passion to discover. Those eyes! those large,
those shining, those divine orbs! they became to me twin stars of Leda,[7]
and I to them devoutest of astrologers.

There is no point, among the many incomprehensible anomalies of
the science of mind, more thrillingly exciting than the fact—never, I believe,
noticed in the schools—that in our endeavors to recall to memory something
long forgotten, we often find ourselves *upon the very verge* of remembrance, without being able, in the end, to remember. And thus how frequently, in my intense scrutiny of Ligeia's eyes, have I felt approaching the
full knowledge of their expression—felt it approaching—yet not quite be
mine—and so at length entirely depart! And (strange, oh strangest mystery of
all!) I found, in the commonest objects of the universe, a circle of analogies
to that expression. I mean to say that, subsequently to the period when
Ligeia's beauty passed into my spirit, there dwelling as in a shrine, I derived,
from many existences in the material world, a sentiment such as I felt always
aroused, within me, by her large and luminous orbs. Yet not the more could
I define that sentiment, or analyze, or even steadily view it. I recognized it,
let me repeat, sometimes in the survey of a rapidly growing vine—in the contemplation of a moth, a butterfly, a chrysalis, a stream of running water. I
have felt it in the ocean; in the falling of a meteor. I have felt it in the glances
of unusually aged people. And there are one or two stars in heaven—(one

---

4. *The History of Nourjahad* (1767) by Frances Sheridan was an oriental romance familiar in
Poe's day.
5. One of the beautiful virgins, according to Moslem belief, given to those who attain Paradise.
6. Greek philosopher of the fifth century B.C. credited with the proverb, "Truth lies at the bottom of a well."
7. Castor and Pollux, named after the twin sons of Leda, are stars in the constellation Gemini.

especially, a star of the sixth magnitude, double and changeable, to be found near the large star in Lyra)[8] in a telescopic scrutiny of which I have been made aware of the feeling. I have been filled with it by certain sounds from stringed instruments, and not unfrequently by passages from books. Among innumerable other instances, I well remember something in a volume of Joseph Glanvill, which (perhaps from its quaintness—who shall say?) never failed to inspire me with the sentiment;—"And the will therein lieth, which dieth not. Who knoweth the mysteries of the will, with its vigor? For God is but a great will pervading all things by nature of its intentness. Man doth not yield him to the angels, nor unto death utterly, save only through the weakness of his feeble will."

Length of years and subsequent reflection, have enabled me to trace, indeed, some remote connection between this passage in the English moralist and a portion of the character of Ligeia. An *intensity* in thought, action, or speech, was possibly, in her, a result, or at least an index, of that gigantic volition which, during our long intercourse, failed to give other and more immediate evidence of its existence. Of all the women whom I have even known, she, the outwardly calm, the ever-placid Ligeia, was the most violently a prey to the tumultuous vultures of stern passion. And of such passion I could form no estimate, save by the miraculous expansion of those eyes which at once so delighted and appalled me—by the almost magical melody, modulation, distinctness, and placidity of her very low voice—and by the fierce energy (rendered doubly effective by contrast with her manner of utterance) of the wild words which she habitually uttered.

I have spoken of the learning of Ligeia; it was immense—such as I have never known in woman. In the classical tongues was she deeply proficient, and as far as my own acquaintance extended in regard to the modern dialects of Europe, I have never known her at fault. Indeed upon any theme of the most admired, because simply the most abstruse of the boasted erudition of the academy, have I *ever* found Ligeia at fault? How singularly—how thrillingly, this one point in the nature of my wife has forced itself, at this late period only, upon my attention! I said her knowledge was such as I have never known in woman—but where breathes the man who has traversed, and successfully, *all* the wide areas of moral, physical, and mathematical science? I saw not then what I now clearly perceive, that the acquisitions of Ligeia were gigantic, were astounding; yet I was sufficiently aware of her infinite supremacy to resign myself, with a child-like confidence, to her guidance through the chaotic world of metaphysical investigation at which I was most busily occupied during the earlier years of our marriage. With how vast a triumph—with how vivid a delight—with how much of all that is ethereal in hope—did I *feel*, as she bent over me in studies but little sought—but less known—that delicious vista by slow degrees expanding before me, down

---

8. The "large star" in the constellation Lyra is Vega, one of the brightest in the heavens. Near it but of lesser magnitude is Epsilon Lyrae, requiring a telescope to be seen.

whose long, gorgeous, and all untrodden path, I might at length pass onward to the goal of a wisdom too divinely precious not to be forbidden!

How poignant, then, must have been the grief with which, after some years, I beheld my well-grounded expectations take wings to themselves and fly away! Without Ligeia I was but as a child groping benighted. Her presence, her readings alone, rendered vividly luminous the many mysteries of the transcendentalism in which we were immersed. Wanting the radiant lustre of her eyes, letters, lambent and golden, grew duller than Saturnian lead.[9] And now those eyes shone less and less frequently upon the pages over which I pored. Ligeia grew ill. The wild eyes blazed with a too—too glorious effulgence; the pale fingers became of the transparent waxen hue of the grave; and the blue veins upon the lofty forehead swelled and sank impetuously with the tides of the most gentle emotion. I saw that she must die—and I struggled desperately in spirit with the grim Azrael.[10] And the struggles of the passionate wife were, to my astonishment, even more energetic than my own. There had been much in her stern nature to impress me with the belief that, to her, death would have come without its terrors; but not so. Words are impotent to convey any just idea of the fierceness of resistance with which she wrestled with the Shadow. I groaned in anguish at the pitiable spectacle. I would have soothed—I would have reasoned; but, in the intensity of her wild desire for life,—for life—*but* for life—solace and reason were alike the uttermost folly. Yet not until the last instance, amid the most convulsive writhings of her fierce spirit, was shaken the external placidity of her demeanor. Her voice grew more gentle—grew more low—yet I would not wish to dwell upon the wild meaning of the quietly uttered words. My brain reeled as I hearkened entranced, to a melody more than mortal—to assumptions and aspirations which mortality had never before known.

That she loved me I should not have doubted; and I might have been easily aware that, in a bosom such as hers, love would have reigned no ordinary passion. But in death only was I fully impressed with the strength of her affection. For long hours, detaining my hand, would she pour out before me the overflowing of a heart whose more than passionate devotion amounted to idolatry. How had I deserved to be so blessed by such confessions?—how had I deserved to be so cursed with the removal of my beloved in the hour of her making them? But upon this subject I cannot bear to dilate. Let me say only, that in Ligeia's more than womanly abandonment to a love, alas! all unmerited, all unworthily bestowed, I at length recognized the principle of her longing with so wildly earnest a desire for the life which was now fleeing so rapidly away. It is this wild longing—it is this eager vehemence of desire for life—*but* for life—that I have no power to portray—no utterance capable of expressing.

At high noon of the night in which she departed, beckoning me,

---

9. In ancient alchemy, Saturn is the technical term for lead.
10. The angel of death in Mohammedan and Hebrew mythology.

peremptorily, to her side, she bade me repeat certain verses composed by herself not many days before. I obeyed her.—They were these:

Lo! 'tis a gala night
    Within the lonesome latter years!
An angel throng, bewinged, bedight
    In veils, and drowned in tears,
Sit in a theatre, to see
    A play of hopes and fears,
While the orchestra breathes fitfully
    The music of the spheres.

Mimes, in the form of God on high,
    Mutter and mumble low,
And hither and thither fly—
    Mere puppets they, who come and go
At bidding of vast formless things
    That shift the scenery to and fro,
Flapping from out their Condor wings
    Invisible Woe!

That motley drama!—oh, be sure
    It shall not be forgot!
With its Phantom chased forever more,
    By a crowd that seize it not,
Through a circle that ever returneth in
    To the self-same spot,
And much of Madness and more of Sin
    And Horror the soul of the plot.

But see, amid the mimic rout,
    A crawling shape intrude!
A blood-red thing that writhes from out
    The scenic solitude!
It writhes!—it writhes!—with mortal pangs
    The mimes become its food,
And the seraphs sob at vermin fangs
    In human gore imbued.

Out—out are the lights—out all!
    And over each quivering form,
The curtain, a funeral pall,
    Comes down with the rush of a storm,
And the angels, all pallid and wan,
    Uprising, unveiling, affirm

That the play is the tragedy, "Man,"
    And its hero the Conqueror Worm.

"O God!" half shrieked Ligeia, leaping to her feet and extending her arms aloft with a spasmodic movement, as I made an end of these lines—"O God! O Divine Father!—shall these things be undeviatingly so?—shall this Conqueror be not once conquered? Are we not part and parcel in Thee? Who—who knoweth the mysteries of the will with its vigor? Man doth not yield him to the angels, *nor unto death utterly*, save only through the weakness of his feeble will."

And now, as if exhausted with emotion, she suffered her white arms to fall, and returned solemnly to her bed of death. And as she breathed her last sighs, there came mingled with them a low murmur from her lips. I bent to them my ear, and distinguished, again, the concluding words of the passage in Glanvill—"*Man doth not yield him to the angels, nor unto death utterly, save only through the weakness of his feeble will.*"

She died;—and I, crushed into the very dust with sorrow, could no longer endure the lonely desolation of my dwelling in the dim and decaying city by the Rhine. I had no lack of what the world calls wealth. Ligeia had brought me far more, very far more than ordinarily falls to the lot of mortals. After a few months, therefore, of weary and aimless wandering, I purchased, and put in some repair, an abbey, which I shall not name, in one of the wildest and least frequented portions of fair England. The gloomy and dreary grandeur of the building, the almost savage aspect of the domain, the many melancholy and time-honored memories connected with both, had much in unison with the feelings of utter abandonment which had driven me into that remote and unsocial region of the country. Yet although the external abbey, with its verdant decay hanging about it, suffered but little alteration, I gave way, with a child-like perversity, and perchance with a faint hope of alleviating my sorrows, to a display of more than regal magnificence within. —For such follies, even in childhood, I had imbibed a taste, and now they came back to me as if in the dotage of grief. Alas, I feel how much even of incipient madness might have been discovered in the gorgeous and fantastic draperies, in the solemn carvings of Egypt, in the wild cornices and furniture, in the Bedlam patterns of the carpets of tufted gold! I had become a bounden slave in the trammels of opium, and my labors and orders had taken a coloring from my dreams. But these absurdities I must not pause to detail. Let me speak only of that one chamber, ever accursed, whither, in a moment of mental alienation, I led from the altar as my bride—as the successor of the unforgotten Ligeia—the fair-haired and blue-eyed Lady Rowena Trevanion, of Tremaine.

There is no individual portion of the architecture and decoration of that bridal chamber which is not now visibly before me. Where were the souls of the haughty family of the bride, when, through thirst of gold, they permitted to pass the threshold of an apartment *so* bedecked, a maiden and a daughter so beloved? I have said that I minutely remember the details of the chamber—yet I am sadly forgetful on topics of deep moment—and here there was no system, no keeping, in the fantastic display, to take hold upon the memory. The room lay in a high turret of the castellated abbey, was pentagonal in shape, and of capacious size. Occupying the whole southern face of the pentagon was the sole window—an immense sheet of broken glass from Venice—a single pane, and tinted of a leaden hue, so that the rays of either the sun or moon, passing through it, fell with a ghastly lustre on the objects within. Over the upper portion of this huge window, extended the trellis-work of an aged vine, which clambered up the massy walls of the turret. The ceiling, of gloomy-looking oak, was excessively lofty, vaulted, and elaborately fretted with the wildest and most grotesque specimens of a semi-Gothic, semi-Druidical device. From out the most central recess of this melancholy vaulting, depended, by a single chain of gold with long links, a huge censer of the same metal, Saracenic in pattern, and with many perforations so contrived that there writhed in and out of them, as if endued with a serpent vitality, a continual succession of parti-colored fires.

Some few ottomans and golden candelabra, of Eastern figure, were in various stations about—and there was the couch, too—the bridal couch—of an Indian model, and low, and sculptured of solid ebony, with a pall-like canopy above. In each of the angles of the chamber stood on end a gigantic sarcophagus of black granite, from the tombs of the kings over against Luxor,[11] with their aged lids full of immemorial sculpture. But in the draping of the apartment lay, alas! the chief phantasy of all. The lofty walls, gigantic in height—even unproportionably so—were hung from summit to foot, in vast folds, with a heavy and massive-looking tapestry—tapestry of a material which was found alike as a carpet on the floor, as a covering for the ottomans and the ebony bed, as a canopy for the bed and as the gorgeous volutes of the curtains which partially shaded the window. The material was the richest cloth of gold. It was spotted all over, at irregular intervals, with arabesque figures, about a foot in diameter, and wrought upon the cloth in patterns of the most jetty black. But these figures partook of the true character of the arabesque only when regarded from a single point of view. By a contrivance now common, and indeed traceable to a very remote period of antiquity, they were made changeable in aspect. To one entering the room, they bore the appearance of simple monstrosities; but upon a farther advance, this appearance gradually departed; and step by step, as the visiter moved his station in the chamber, he saw himself surrounded by an endless succession of the ghastly forms which belong to the superstition of the Norman, or arise in the guilty slumbers of the monk. The phantasmagoric effect was vastly heightened by the artificial introduction of a strong continual current of wind behind the draperies—giving a hideous and uneasy animation to the whole.

---

11. The ancient site of Thebes, on the Nile in central Egypt.

In halls such as these—in a bridal chamber such as this—I passed, with the Lady of Tremaine, the unhallowed hours of the first month of our marriage—passed them with but little disquietude. That my wife dreaded the fierce moodiness of my temper—that she shunned me and loved me but little—I could not help perceiving; but it gave me rather pleasure than otherwise. I loathed her with a hatred belonging more to demon than to man. My memory flew back, (oh, with what intensity of regret!) to Ligeia, the beloved, the august, the beautiful, the entombed. I revelled in recollections of her purity, of her wisdom, of her lofty, her ethereal nature, of her passionate, her idolatrous love. Now, then, did my spirit fully and freely burn with more than all the fires of her own. In the excitement of my opium dreams (for I was habitually fettered in the shackles of the drug) I would call aloud upon her name, during the silence of the night, or among the sheltered recesses of the glens by day, as if, through the wild eagerness, the solemn passion, the consuming ardor of my longing for the departed, I could restore her to the pathways she had abandoned—ah, *could* it be forever?—upon the earth.

About the commencement of the second month of the marriage, the Lady Rowena was attacked with sudden illness, from which her recovery was slow. The fever which consumed her rendered her nights uneasy; and in her perturbed state of half-slumber, she spoke of sounds, and of motions, in and above the chamber of the turret, which I concluded had no origin save in the distemper of her fancy, or perhaps in the phantasmagoric influences of the chamber itself. She became at length convalescent—finally well. Yet but a brief period elapsed, ere a second more violent disorder again threw her upon a bed of suffering; and from this attack her frame, at all times feeble, never altogether recovered. Her illnesses were, after this epoch, of alarming character, and of more alarming recurrence, defying alike the knowledge and the great exertions of her physicians. With the increase of the chronic disease which had thus, apparently, taken too sure hold upon her constitution to be eradicated by human means, I could not fail to observe a similar increase in the nervous irritation of her temperament, and in her excitability by trivial causes of fear. She spoke again, and now more frequently and pertinaciously, of the sounds—of the slight sounds—and of the unusual motions among the tapestries, to which she had formerly alluded.

One night, near the closing in of September, she pressed this distressing subject with more than usual emphasis upon my attention. She had just awakened from an unquiet slumber, and I had been watching, with feelings half of anxiety, half of vague terror, the workings of her emaciated countenance. I sat by the side of her ebony bed, upon one of the ottomans of India. She partly arose, and spoke, in an earnest low whisper, of sounds which she *then* heard, but which I could not hear—of motions which she *then* saw, but which I could not perceive. The wind was rushing hurriedly behind the tapestries, and I wished to show her (what, let me confess it, I could not *all* believe) that those almost inarticulate breathings, and those very gentle variations of the figures upon the wall, were but the natural effects of that customary rushing of the wind. But a deadly pallor, overspreading her face, had proved to me that my exertions to reassure her would be fruitless. She appeared to be fainting, and no attendants were within call. I remembered where was deposited a decanter of light wine which had been ordered by her physicians, and hastened across the chamber to procure it. But, as I stepped beneath the light of the censer, two circumstances of a startling nature attracted my attention. I had felt that some palpable although invisible object had passed lightly by my person; and I saw that there lay upon the golden carpet, in the very middle of the rich lustre thrown from the censer, a shadow—a faint, indefinite shadow of angelic aspect—such as might be fancied for the shadow of a shade. But I was wild with the excitement of an immoderate dose of opium, and heeded these things but little, nor spoke of them to Rowena. Having found the wine, I recrossed the chamber, and poured out a gobletful, which I held to the lips of the fainting lady. She had now partially recovered, however, and took the vessel herself, while I sank upon an ottoman near me, with my eyes fastened upon her person. It was then that I became distinctly aware of a gentle foot-fall upon the carpet, and near the couch; and in a second thereafter, as Rowena was in the act of raising the wine to her lips, I saw, or may have dreamed that I saw, fall within the goblet, as if from some invisible spring in the atmosphere of the room, three or four large drops of a brilliant and ruby colored fluid. If this I saw—not so Rowena. She swallowed the wine unhesitatingly, and I forbore to speak to her of a circumstance which must, after all, I considered, have been but the suggestion of a vivid imagination, rendered morbidly active by the terror of the lady, by the opium, and by the hour.

Yet I cannot conceal it from my own perception that, immediately subsequent to the fall of the ruby-drops, a rapid change for the worse took place in the disorder of my wife; so that, on the third subsequent night, the hands of her menials prepared her for the tomb, and on the fourth, I sat alone, with her shrouded body, in that fantastic chamber which had received her as my bride.—Wild visions, opium-engendered, flitted, shadowlike, before me. I gazed with unquiet eye upon the sarcophagi in the angles of the room, upon the varying figures of the drapery, and upon the writhing of the parti-colored fires in the censer overhead. My eyes then fell, as I called to mind the circumstances of a former night, to the spot beneath the glare of the censer where I had seen the faint traces of the shadow. It was there, however, no longer; and breathing with greater freedom, I turned my glances to the pallid and rigid figure upon the bed. Then rushed upon me a thousand memories of Ligeia—and then came back upon my heart, with the turbulent violence of a flood, the whole of that unutterable woe with which I had regarded *her* thus enshrouded. The night waned; and still, with a bosom full of bitter thoughts of the one only and supremely beloved, I remained gazing upon the body of Rowena.

It might have been midnight, or perhaps earlier, or later, for I had taken no note of time, when a sob, low, gentle, but very distinct, startled me from my revery.—I *felt* that it came from the bed of ebony—the bed of death. I listened in an agony of superstitious terror—but there was no repetition of the sound. I strained my vision to detect any motion in the corpse—but there was not the slightest perceptible. Yet I could not have been deceived. I *had* heard the noise, however faint, and my soul was awakened within me. I resolutely and perseveringly kept my attention riveted upon the body. Many minutes elapsed before any circumstance occurred tending to throw light upon the mystery. At length it became evident that a slight, a very feeble, and barely noticeable tinge of color had flushed up within the cheeks, and along the sunken small veins of the eyelids. Through a species of unutterable horror and awe, for which the language of mortality has no sufficiently energetic expression, I felt my heart cease to beat, my limbs grow rigid where I sat. Yet a sense of duty finally operated to restore my self-possession. I could no longer doubt that we had been precipitate in our preparations—that Rowena still lived. It was necessary that some imme-diate exertion be made; yet the turret was altogether apart from the portion of the abbey tenanted by the servants—there were none within call—I had no means of summoning them to my aid without leaving the room for many minutes—and this I could not venture to do. I therefore struggled alone in my endeavors to call back the spirit still hovering. In a short period it was certain, however, that a relapse had taken place; the color disappeared from both eyelid and cheek, leaving a wanness even more than that of marble; the lips became doubly shrivelled and pinched up in the ghastly expression of death; a repulsive clamminess and coldness overspread rapidly the surface of the body; and all the usual rigorous stiffness immediately supervened. I fell back with a shudder upon the couch from which I had been so startlingly aroused, and again gave myself up to passionate waking visions of Ligeia.

An hour thus elapsed when (could it be possible?) I was a second time aware of some vague sound issuing from the region of the bed. I listened—in extremity of horror. The sound came again—it was a sigh. Rushing to the corpse, I saw—distinctly saw—a tremor upon the lips. In a minute afterward they relaxed, disclosing a bright line of the pearly teeth. Amazement now struggled in my bosom with the profound awe which had hitherto reigned there alone. I felt that my vision grew dim, that my reason wandered; and it was only by a violent effort that I at length succeeded in nerving myself to the task which duty thus once more had pointed out. There was now a partial glow upon the forehead and upon the cheek and throat; a perceptible warmth pervaded the whole frame; there was even a slight pulsation at the heart. The lady *lived;* and with redoubled ardor I betook myself to the task of restoration. I chafed and bathed the temples and the hands, and used every exertion with experience, and no little medical reading, could suggest. But in vain. Suddenly, the color fled, the pulsation ceased, the lips resumed the ex-pression of the dead, and, in an instant afterward, the whole body took upon itself the icy chilliness, the livid hue, the intense rigidity, the sunken outline, and all the loathsome peculiarities of that which has been, for many days, a tenant of the tomb.

And again I sunk into visions of Ligeia—and again, (what marvel that I shudder while I write?) *again* there reached my ears a low sob from the region of the ebony bed. But why shall I minutely detail the unspeakable horrors of that night? Why shall I pause to relate how, time after time, until near the period of the gray dawn, this hideous drama of revivification was repeated; how each terrific relapse was only into a sterner and apparently more irredeemable death; how each agony wore the aspect of a struggle with some invisible foe; and how each struggle was succeeded by I know not what of wild change in the personal appearance of the corpse? Let me hurry to a conclusion.

The greater part of the fearful night had worn away, and she who had been dead once again stirred—and now more vigorously than hitherto, although arousing from a dissolution more appalling in its utter hopelessness than any. I had long ceased to struggle or to move, and remained sitting rigidly upon the ottoman, a helpless prey to a whirl of violent emotions, of which extreme awe was perhaps the least terrible, the least consuming. The corpse, I repeat, stirred, and now more vigorously than before. The hues of life flushed up with unwonted energy into the countenance—the limbs relaxed—and, save that the eyelids were yet pressed heavily together, and that the bandages and draperies of the grave still imparted their charnel character to the figure, I might have dreamed that Rowena had indeed shaken off, utterly, the fetters of Death. But if this idea was not, even then, altogether adopted, I could at least doubt no longer, when, arising from the bed, tottering, with feeble steps, with closed eyes, and with the manner of one bewildered in a dream, the thing that was enshrouded advanced boldly and palpably into the middle of the apartment.

I trembled not—I stirred not—for a crowd of unutterable fancies connected with the air, the stature, the demeanor of the figure, rushing hurriedly through my brain, had paralyzed—had chilled me into stone. I stirred not—but gazed upon the apparition. There was a mad disorder in my thoughts—a tumult unappeasable. Could it, indeed, be the *living* Rowena who confronted me? Could it, indeed, be Rowena *at all*—the fair-haired, the blue-eyed Lady Rowena Trevanion of Tremaine? Why, *why* should I doubt it? The bandage lay heavily about the mouth—but then might it not be the mouth of the breathing Lady of Tremaine? And the cheeks—there were the roses as in her noon of life—yes, these might indeed be the fair cheeks of the living Lady of Tremaine. And the chin, with its dimples, as in health, might it not be hers?—but *had she then grown taller since her malady?* What inexpressible madness seized me with that thought? One bound, and I had reached her feet! Shrinking from my touch, she let fall from her head, unloosened, the ghastly cerements which had confined it, and there streamed forth into the rushing atmosphere of the chamber huge masses of long and dishevelled hair; *it was blacker than the raven wings of midnight!* And now slowly opened *the eyes* of the figure which stood before me. "Here then, at least," I shrieked aloud, "can I never—can I never be mistaken—these are the full, and the black, and the wild eyes—of my lost love—of the Lady—of the LADY LIGEIA."

Questions

1. Is this a story of serious moral and psychological meaning or merely a thriller? Defend your answer.   **2.** What do the patterns of color imagery contribute to the meaning? **3.** Contrast the attitude toward life expressed in the passage from Glanvill with that in Ligeia's poem.   **4.** How does the decor of the English abbey contribute to the unity of atmosphere in the story?

The Death of Ivan Ilych*

LEO TOLSTOY [1828–1910]

CHAPTER I

DURING an interval in the Melvínski trial in the large building of the Law Courts the members and public prosecutor met in Ivan Egorovich Shébek's private room, where the conversation turned on the celebrated Krasóvski case. Fëdor Vasrlievich warmly maintained that it was not subject to their jurisdiction, Iván Egórovich maintained the contrary, while Peter Ivánovich, not having entered into the discussion at the start, took no part in it but looked through the *Gazette* which had just been handed in.

"Gentlemen," he said, "Iván Ilých has died!"

"You don't say so!"

"Here, read it yourself," replied Peter Ivánovich, handing Fëdor Vasílievich the paper still damp from the press. Surrounded by a black border were the words: "Praskóvya Fëdorovna Golovíná, with profound sorrow, informs relatives and friends of the demise of her beloved husband Iván Ilých Golovín, Member of the Court of Justice, which occurred on February the 4th of this year 1882. The funeral will take place on Friday at one o'clock in the afternoon."

Iván Ilých had been a colleague of the gentlemen present and was liked by them all. He had been ill for some weeks with an illness said to be incurable. His post had been kept open for him, but there had been conjectures that in case of his death Alexéev might receive his appointment, and that either Vínnikov or Shtábel would succeed Alexéev. So on receiving the news of Iván Ilých's death the first thought of each of the gentlemen in that private room was of the changes and promotions it might occasion among themselves or their acquaintances.

"I shall be sure to get Shtábel's place or Vínnikov's," thought Fëdor Vasílievich. "I was promised that long ago, and the promotion means an extra eight hundred rubles a year for me besides the allowance."

"Now I must apply for my brother-in-law's transfer from Kalúga," thought Peter Ivánovich. "My wife will be very glad, and then she won't be able to say that I never do anything for her relations."

"I thought he would never leave his bed again," said Peter Ivánovich aloud. "It's very sad."

"But what really was the matter with him?"

"The doctors couldn't say—at least they could, but each of them said something different. When last I saw him I thought he was getting better."

---

*Translated by Aylmer Maude.

"And I haven't been to see him since the holidays. I always meant to go."

"Had he any property?"

"I think his wife had a little—but something quite trifling."

"We shall have to go to see her, but they live so terribly far away."

"Far away from you, you mean. Everything's far away from your place."

"You see, he never can forgive my living on the other side of the river," said Peter Ivánovich, smiling at Shébek. Then, still talking of the distances between different parts of the city, they returned to the Court.

Besides considerations as to the possible transfers and promotions likely to result from Iván Ilých's death, the mere fact of the death of a near acquaintance aroused, as usual, in all who heard of it the complacent feeling that "it is he who is dead and not I."

Each one thought or felt, "Well, he's dead but I'm alive!" But the more intimate of Iván Ilých's acquaintances, his so-called friends, could not help thinking also that they would now have to fulfill the very tiresome demands of propriety by attending the funeral service and paying a visit of condolence to the widow.

Fëdor Vasílievich and Peter Ivánovich had been his nearest acquaintances. Peter Ivánovich had studied law with Iván Ilých and had considered himself to be under obligations to him.

Having told his wife at dinner-time of Iván Ilých's death, and of his conjecture that it might be possible to get her brother transferred to their circuit, Peter Ivánovich sacrificed his usual nap, put on his evening clothes, and drove to Ivan Ilých's house.

At the entrance stood a carriage and two cabs. Leaning against the wall in the hall downstairs near the cloak-stand was a coffin-lid covered with cloth of gold, ornamented with gold cord and tassels, that had been polished up with metal powder. Two ladies in black were taking off their fur cloaks. Peter Ivanovich recognized one of them as Iván Ilých's sister, but the other was a stranger to him. His colleague Schwartz was just coming downstairs, but on seeing Peter Ivánovich enter he stopped and winked at him, as if to say: "Iván Ilých has made a mess of things—not like you and me."

Schwartz's face with his Piccadilly whiskers, and his slim figure in evening dress, had as usual an air of elegant solemnity which contrasted with the playfulness of his character and had a special piquancy here; or so it seemed to Peter Ivánovich.

Peter Ivánovich allowed the ladies to precede him and slowly followed them upstairs. Schwartz did not come down but remained where he was, and Peter Ivánovich understood that he wanted to arrange where they should play bridge that evening. The ladies went upstairs to the widow's room, and Schwartz with seriously compressed lips but a playful look in his eyes, indicated by a twist of his eye-brows the room to the right where the body lay.

Peter Ivánovich, like everyone else on such occasions, entered feeling uncertain what he would have to do. All he knew was that at such times it is always safe to cross oneself. But he was not quite sure whether one should make obeisances while doing so. He therefore adopted a middle course. On entering the room he began crossing himself and made a slight movement resembling a bow. At the same time, as far as the motion of his head and arm allowed, he surveyed the room. Two young men—apparently nephews, one of whom was a high-school pupil—were leaving the room, crossing themselves as they did so. An old woman was standing motionless, and a lady with strangely arched eyebrows was saying something to her in a whisper. A vigorous, resolute Church Reader, in a frock-coat, was reading something in a loud voice with an expression that precluded any contradiction. The butler's assistant, Gerásim, stepping lightly in front of Peter Ivánovich, was strewing something on the floor. Noticing this, Peter Ivánovich was immediately aware of a faint odour of a decomposing body.

The last time he had called on Iván Ilych, Peter Ivánovich had seen Gerásim in the study. Iván Ilých had been particularly fond of him and he was performing the duty of a sick nurse.

Peter Ivánovich continued to make the sign of the cross slightly inclining his head in an intermediate direction between the coffin, the Reader, and the icons on the table in a corner of the room. Afterwards, when it seemed to him that this movement of his arm in crossing himself had gone on too long, he stopped and began to look at the corpse.

The dead man lay, as dead men always lie, in a specially heavy way, his rigid limbs sunk in the soft cushions of the coffin, with the head forever bowed on the pillow. His yellow waxen brow with bald patches over his sunken temples was thrust up in the way peculiar to the dead, the protruding nose seeming to press on the upper lip. He was much changed and had grown even thinner since Peter Ivánovich had last seen him, but, as is always the case with the dead, his face was handsomer and above all more dignified than when he was alive. The expression on the face said that what was necessary had been accomplished, and accomplished rightly. Besides this there was in that expression a reproach and a warning to the living. This warning seemed to Peter Ivánovich out of place, or at least not applicable to him. He felt a certain discomfort and so he hurriedly crossed himself once more and turned and went out of the door—too hurriedly and too regardless of propriety, as he himself was aware.

Schwartz was waiting for him in the adjoining room with legs spread wide apart and both hands toying with his top-hat behind his back. The mere sight of that playful, well-groomed, and elegant figure refreshed Peter Ivánovich. He felt that Schwartz was above all these happenings and would not surrender to any depressing influences. His very look said that this incident of a church service for Iván Ilých could not be a sufficient reason for infringing the order of the session—in other words, that it would certainly not prevent his unwrapping a new pack of cards and shuffling them that evening while a footman placed four fresh candles on the table: in fact, there was no reason for supposing that this incident would hinder their spending the evening agreeably. Indeed he said this in a whisper as Peter Ivánovich passed him, proposing that they should meet for a game at Fëdor Vasílievich's. But apparently Peter Ivánovich was not destined to play bridge that evening. Praskóvya Fëdorovna (a short, fat woman who despite all efforts to the contrary had continued to broaden steadily from her shoulders downwards and who had the same extraordinarily arched eyebrows as the lady who had been standing by the coffin), dressed all in black, her head covered with lace, came out of her own room with some other ladies, conducted them to the room where the dead body lay, and said: "The service will begin immediately. Please go in."

Schwartz, making an indefinite bow, stood still, evidently neither accepting nor declining this invitation. Praskóvya Fëdorovna recognizing Peter Ivánovich, sighed, went close up to him, took his hand, and said: "I know you were a true friend to Iván Ilých . . ." and looked at him awaiting some suitable response. And Peter Ivánovich knew that, just as it had been the right thing to cross himself in that room, so what he had to do here was to press her hand, sigh, and say, "Believe me . . ." So he did all this and as he did it felt that the desired result had been achieved: that both he and she were touched.

"Come with me. I want to speak to you before it begins," said the widow. "Give me your arm."

Peter Ivánovich gave her his arm and they went to the inner rooms, passing Schwartz who winked at Peter Ivánovich compassionately.

"That does for our bridge! Don't object if we find another player. Perhaps you can cut in when you do escape," said his playful look.

Peter Ivánovich sighed still more deeply and despondently, and Praskóvya Fëdorovna pressed his arm gratefully. When they reached the drawing-room, upholstered in pink cretonne and lighted by a dim lamp, they sat down at the table—she on a sofa and Peter Ivánovich on a low pouffe, the springs of which yielded spasmodically under his weight. Praskóvya Fëdorovna had been on the point of warning him to take another seat, but felt that such a warning was out of keeping with her present condition and so changed her mind. As he sat down on the pouffe Peter Ivánovich recalled how Iván Ilých had arranged this room and had consulted him regarding this pink cretonne with green leaves. The whole room was full of furniture and knick-knacks, and on her way to the sofa the lace of the widow's black shawl caught on the carved edge of the table. Peter Ivánovich rose to detach it, and the springs of the pouffe, relieved of his weight, rose also and gave him a push. The widow began detaching her shawl herself, and Peter Ivánovich again sat down, suppressing the rebellious springs of the pouffe under him. But the widow had not quite freed herself and Peter Ivánovich got up again, and again the pouffe rebelled and even creaked. When this was all over she took out a clean cambric handkerchief and began to weep. The episode with the shawl and the struggle with the pouffe had cooled Peter Ivánovich's emotions and he sat there with a sullen look on his face. This awkward situation was interrupted by Sokolóv, Iván Ilých's butler, who came to report that the plot in the cemetery that Praskóvya Fëdorovna had chosen would cost two hundred rubles. She stopped weeping and, looking at Peter Ivánovich with the air of a victim, remarked in French that it was very hard for her. Peter Ivánovich made a silent gesture signifying his full conviction that it must indeed be so.

"Please smoke," she said in a magnanimous yet crushed voice, and turned to discuss with Sokolóv the price of the plot for the grave.

Peter Ivánovich while lighting his cigarette heard her inquiring very circumstantially into the price of different plots in the cemetery and finally decide which she would take. When that was done she gave instructions about engaging the choir. Sokólov then left the room.

"I look after everything myself," she told Peter Ivánovich, shifting the albums that lay on the table; and noticing that the table was endangered by his cigarette-ash, she immediately passed him an ashtray, saying as she did so: "I consider it an affectation to say that my grief prevents my attending to practical affairs. On the contrary, if anything can—I won't say console me, but—distract me, it is seeing to everything concerning him." She again took out her hand-kerchief as if preparing to cry, but suddenly, as if mastering her feeling, she shook herself and began to speak calmly. "But there is something I want to talk to you about."

Peter Ivánovich bowed, keeping control of the springs of the pouffe, which immediately began quivering under him.

"He suffered terribly the last few days."

"Did he?" said Peter Ivánovich.

"Oh, terribly! He screamed unceasingly, not for minutes but for hours. For the last three days he screamed incessantly. It was unendurable. I cannot understand how I bore it; you could hear him three rooms off. Oh, what I have suffered!"

"Is it possible that he was conscious all that time?" asked Peter Ivánovich.

"Yes," she whispered. "To the last moment. He took leave of us a quarter of an hour before he died, and asked us to take Volódya away."

The thought of the sufferings of this man he had known so intimately, first as a merry little boy, then as a school-mate, and later as a grown-up colleague, suddenly struck Peter Ivánovich with horror, despite an unpleasant consciousness of his own and this woman's dissimulation. He again saw that brow, and that nose pressing down on the lip, and felt afraid for himself.

"Three days of frightful suffering and then death! Why, that might suddenly, at any time, happen to me," he thought, and for a moment felt terrified. But—he did not himself know how—the customary reflection at once occurred to him that this had happened to Iván Ilých and not to him, and that it should not and could not happen to him, and that to think that it could would be yielding to depression which he ought not to do, as Schwartz's expression plainly showed. After which reflection Peter Ivánovich felt reassured, and began to ask with interest about the details of Iván Ilých's death, as though death was an accident natural to Iván Ilých but certainly not to himself.

After many details of the really dreadful physical sufferings Iván Ilých had endured (which details he learnt only from the effect those sufferings had produced on Praskóvya Fëdorovna's nerves) the widow apparently found it necessary to get to business.

"Oh, Peter Ivánovich, how hard it is! How terribly, terribly hard!" and she again began to weep.

Peter Ivánovich sighed and waited for her to finish blowing her nose. When she had done so he said, "Believe me . . ." and she again began talking and brought out what was evidently her chief concern with him—namely, to question him as to how she could obtain a grant of money from the government on the occasion of her husband's death. She made it appear that she was asking Peter Ivánovich's advice about her pension, but he soon saw that she already knew about that to the minutest detail, more even than he did himself. She knew how much could be got out of the government in consequence of her husband's death, but wanted to find out whether she could not possibly extract something more. Peter Ivánovich tried to think of some means of doing so, but after reflecting for a while and, out of propriety, condemning the government for its niggardliness, he said he thought that nothing more could be got. Then she sighed and evidently began to devise means of getting rid of her visitor. Noticing this, he put out his cigarette, rose, pressed her hand, and went out into the anteroom.

In the dining-room where the clock stood that Iván Ilých had liked so much and had bought at an antique shop, Peter Ivánovich met a priest and a few acquaintances who had come to attend the service, and he recognized Iván Ilých's daughter, a handsome young woman. She was in black and her slim figure appeared slimmer than ever. She had a gloomy, determined, almost angry expression, and bowed to Peter Ivánovich as though he were in some way to blame. Behind her, with the same offended look, stood a wealthy young man, an examining magistrate, whom Peter Ivánovich also knew and who was her fiancé, as he had heard. He bowed mournfully to them and was about to pass into the death-chamber, when from under the stairs appeared the figure of Iván Ilých's schoolboy son, who was extremely like his father. He seemed a little Iván Ilých, such as Peter Ivánovich remembered when they studied law together. His tear-stained eyes had in them the look that is seen in the eyes of boys of thirteen or fourteen who are not pure-minded. When he saw Peter Ivánovich he scowled morosely and shame-facedly. Peter Ivánovich nodded to him and entered the death-chamber. The service began: candles, groans, incense, tears, and sobs. Peter Ivánovich stood looking gloomily down at his feet. He did not look once at the dead man, did not yield to any depressing influence, and was one of the first to leave the room. There was no one in the anteroom, but Gerásim darted out of the dead man's room, rummaged with his strong hands among the fur coats to find Peter Ivánovich's and helped him on with it.

"Well, friend Gerásim," said Peter Ivánovich, so as to say something. "It's a sad affair, isn't it?"

"It's God's will. We shall all come to it some day," said Gerásim, displaying his teeth—the even, white teeth of a healthy peasant—and, like a man in the thick of urgent work, he briskly opened the front door, called the coachman, helped Peter Ivánovich into the sledge, and sprang back to the porch as if in readiness for what he had to do next.

Peter Ivánovich found the fresh air particularly pleasant after the smell of incense, the dead body, and carbolic acid.

"Where to, sir?" asked the coachman.

"It's not too late even now. . . . I'll call around on Fëdor Vasilievich."

He accordingly drove there and found them just finishing the first rubber, so that it was quite convenient for him to cut in.

CHAPTER II

IVÁN Ilých's life had been most simple and most ordinary and therefore most terrible.

He had been a member of the Court of Justice, and died at the age of forty-five. His father had been an official who after serving in various ministries and departments of Petersburg had made the sort of career which brings men to positions from which by reason of their long service they cannot be dismissed, though they are obviously unfit to hold any responsible position, and for whom therefore posts are specially created, which though fictitious carry salaries of from six to ten thousand rubles that are not fictitious, and in receipt of which they live on to a great age.

Such was the Privy Councillor and superfluous member of various superfluous institutions, Ilyá Epímovich Golovín.

He had three sons, of whom Iván Ilých was the second. The eldest son was following in his father's footsteps only in another department, and was already approaching that stage in the service at which a similar sinecure would be reached. The third son was a failure. He had ruined his prospects in a number of positions and was now serving in the railway department. His father and brothers, and still more their wives, not merely disliked meeting him, but avoided remembering his existence unless compelled to do so. His sister had married Baron Greff, a Petersburg official of her father's type. Iván Ilých was *le phénix de la famille*[1] as people said. He was neither as cold and formal as his elder brother nor as wild as the younger, but was a happy mean between them—an intelligent, polished, lively and agreeable man. He had studied with his younger brother at the School of Law, but the latter had failed to complete the course and was expelled when he was in the fifth class. Iván Ilých finished the course well. Even when he was at the School of Law he was just what he remained for the rest of his life: a capable, cheerful, good-natured, and sociable man, though strict in the fulfilment of what he considered to be his duty: and

---

1. The phoenix of the family, here meaning "rare bird" or "prodigy."

he considered his duty to be what was so considered by those in authority. Neither as a boy nor as a man was he a toady, but from early youth was by nature attracted to people of high station as a fly is drawn to the light, assimilating their ways and views of life and establishing friendly relations with them. All the enthusiasms of childhood and youth passed without leaving much trace on him; he succumbed to sensuality, to vanity, and latterly among the highest classes to liberalism, but always within limits which his instinct unfailingly indicated to him as correct.

At school he had done things which had formerly seemed to him very horrid and made him feel disgusted with himself when he did them; but when later on he saw that such actions were done by people of good position and that they did not regard them as wrong, he was able not exactly to regard them as right, but to forget about them entirely or not be at all troubled at remembering them.

Having graduated from the School of Law and qualified for the tenth rank of the civil service, and having received money from his father for his equipment, Iván Ilých ordered himself clothes at Scharmer's, the fashionable tailor, hung a medallion inscribed *respice finen*[2] on his watch-chain, took leave of his professor and the prince who was patron of the school, had a farewell dinner with his comrades at Donon's first-class restaurant, and with his new and fashionable portmanteau, linen, clothes, shaving and other toilet appliances, and a travelling rug, all purchased at the best shops, he set off for one of the provinces where, through his father's influence, he had been attached to the Governor as an official for special service.

In the province Iván Ilých soon arranged as easy and agreeable a position for himself as he had had at the School of Law. He performed his official tasks, made his career, and at the same time amused himself pleasantly and decorously. Occasionally he paid official visits to country districts, where he behaved with dignity both to his superiors and inferiors, and performed the duties entrusted to him, which related chiefly to the sectarians,[3] with an exactness and incorruptible honesty of which he could not but feel proud.

In official matters, despite his youth and taste for frivolous gaiety, he was exceedingly reserved, punctilious, and even severe; but in society he was often amusing and witty, and always good-natured, correct in his manner, and *bon enfant*, as the governor and his wife—with whom he was like one of the family—used to say of him.

In the provinces he had an affair with a lady who made advances to the elegant young lawyer, and there was also a milliner; and there were carousals with aides-de-camp who visited the district, and after-supper visits to a certain outlying street of doubtful reputation; and there was too some obsequiousness to his chief and even to his chief's wife, but all this was done with

---

2. "Regard the end."
3. A large sect, whose members were placed under many legal restrictions, which broke away from the Orthodox Church in the seventeenth century.

such a tone of good breeding that no hard names could be applied to it. It all came under the heading of the French saying: "*Il faut que jeunesse se passe.*"[4] It was all done with clean hands, in clean linen, with French phrases, and above all among people of the best society and consequently with the approval of people of rank.

So Iván Ilých served for five years and then came a change in his official life. The new and reformed judicial institutions were introduced, and new men were needed. Iván Ilých became such a new man. He was offered the post of Examining Magistrate, and he accepted it though the post was in another province and obliged him to give up the connexions he had formed and to make new ones. His friends met to give him a send-off; they had a group-photograph taken and presented him with a silver cigarette-case, and he set off to his new post.

As examining magistrate Iván Ilých was just as *comme il faut*[5] and decorous a man, inspiring general respect and capable of separating his official duties from his private life, as he had been when acting as an official on special service. His duties now as examining magistrate were far more interesting and attractive than before. In his former position it had been pleasant to wear an undress uniform made by Scharmer, and to pass through the crowd of petitioners and officials who were timorously awaiting an audience with the governor, and who envied him as with free and easy gait he went straight into his chief's private room to have a cup of tea and a cigarette with him. But not many people had then been directly dependent on him—only police officials and the sectarians when he went on special missions—and he liked to treat them politely, almost as comrades, as if he were letting them feel that he who had the power to crush them was treating them in this simple, friendly way. There were then but few such people. But now, as an examining magistrate, Iván Ilých felt that everyone without exception, even the most important and self-satisfied, was in his power, and that he need only write a few words on a sheet of paper with a certain heading, and this or that important, self-satisfied person would be brought before him in the role of an accused person or a witness, and if he did not choose to allow him to sit down, would have to stand before him and answer his questions. Iván Ilých never abused his power; he tried on the contrary to soften its expression, but the consciousness of it and of the possibility of softening its effect, supplied the chief interest and attraction of his office. In his work itself, especially in his examinations, he very soon acquired a method of eliminating all considerations irrelevant to the legal aspect of the case, and reducing even the most complicated case to a form in which it would be presented on paper only in its externals, completely excluding his personal opinion of the matter, while above all observing every prescribed

---

4. "Youth must have its fling."
5. "Proper."

formality. The work was new and Iván Ilých was one of the first men to apply the new Code of 1864.[6]

On taking up the post of examining magistrate in a new town, he made new acquaintances and connexions, placed himself on a new footing, and assumed a somewhat different tone. He took up an attitude of rather dignified aloofness towards the provincial authorities, but picked out the best circle of legal gentlemen and wealthy gentry living in the town and assumed a tone of slight dissatisfaction with the government, of moderate liberalism, and of enlightened citizenship. At the same time, without at all altering the elegance of his toilet, he ceased shaving his chin and allowed his beard to grow as it pleased.

Iván Ilých settled down very pleasantly in this new town. The society there, which inclined towards opposition to the Governor, was friendly, his salary was larger, and he began to play *vint*,[7] which he found added not a little to the pleasure of life, for he had a capacity for cards, played good-humouredly, and calculated rapidly and astutely, so that he usually won.

After living there for two years he met his future wife, Praskóvya Fëdorovna Míkhel, who was the most attractive, clever, and brilliant girl of the set in which he moved, and among other amusements and relaxations from his labours as examining magistrate, Iván Ilých established light and playful relations with her.

While he had been an official on special service he had been accustomed to dance, but now as an examining magistrate it was exceptional for him to do so. If he danced now, he did it as if to show that though he served under the reformed order of things, and had reached the fifth official rank, yet when it came to dancing he could do it better than most people. So at the end of an evening he sometimes danced with Praskóvya Fëdorovna, and it was chiefly during these dances that he captivated her. She fell in love with him. Iván Ilých had at first no definite intention of marrying, but when the girl fell in love with him he said to himself: "Really, why shouldn't I marry?"

Praskóvya Fëdorovna came of a good family, was not bad looking, and had some little property. Iván Ilých might have aspired to a more brilliant match, but even this was good. He had his salary, and she, he hoped, would have an equal income. She was well connected, and was a sweet, pretty, and thoroughly correct young woman. To say that Ivan Ilých married because he fell in love with Praskóvya Fëdorovna and found that she sympathized with his views of life would be as incorrect as to say that he married because his social circle approved of the match. He was swayed by both these considerations: the marriage gave him personal satisfaction, and at the same time it was considered the right thing by the most highly placed of his associates.

So Iván Ilých got married.

---

6. Judicial procedures were thoroughly reformed after the emancipation of the serfs in 1861.
7. A card game similar to bridge.

The preparations for marriage and the beginning of married life, with its conjugal caresses, the new furniture, new crockery, and new linen, were very pleasant until his wife became pregnant—so that Iván Ilých had begun to think that marriage would not impair the easy, agreeable, gay and always decorous character of his life, approved of by society and regarded by himself as natural, but would even improve it. But from the first months of his wife's pregnancy, something new, unpleasant, depressing, and unseemly, and from which there was no way of escape, unexpectedly showed itself.

His wife, without any reason—de gaieté de coeur as Iván Ilých expressed it to himself—began to disturb the pleasure and propriety of their life. She began to be jealous without any cause, expected him to devote his whole attention to her, found fault with everything, and made coarse and ill-mannered scenes.

At first Iván Ilých hoped to escape from the unpleasantness of this state of affairs by the same easy and decorous relation to life that had served him heretofore: he tried to ignore his wife's disagreeable moods, continued to live in his usual easy and pleasant way, invited friends to his house for a game of cards, and also tried going out to his club or spending his evenings with friends. But one day his wife began upbraiding him so vigorously, using such coarse words, and continued to abuse him every time he did not fulfil her demands, so resolutely and with such evident determination not to give way till he submitted—that is, till he stayed at home and was bored just as she was—that he became alarmed. He now realized that matrimony—at any rate with Praskóvya Fëdorovna—was not always conducive to the pleasures and amenities of life but on the contrary often infringed both comfort and propriety, and that he must therefore entrench himself against such infringement. And Iván Ilých began to seek for means of doing so. His official duties were the one thing that imposed upon Praskóvya Fëdorovna, and by means of his official work and the duties attached to it he began struggling with his wife to secure his own independence.

With the birth of their child, the attempts to feed it and the various failures in doing so, and with the real and imaginary illnesses of mother and child, in which Iván Ilých's sympathy was demanded but about which he understood nothing, the need of securing for himself an existence outside his family life became still more imperative.

As his wife grew more irritable and exacting and Iván Ilých transferred the centre of gravity of his life more and more to his official work, so did he grow to like his work better and became more ambitious than before.

Very soon, within a year of his wedding, Iván Ilých had realized that marriage, though it may add some comforts to life, is in fact a very intricate and difficult affair towards which in order to perform one's duty, that is, to lead a decorous life approved of by society, one must adopt a definite attitude just as towards one's official duties.

And Iván Ilých evolved such an attitude towards married life. He only required of it those conveniences—dinner at home, housewife, and bed—

which it could give him, and above all that propriety of external forms required by public opinion. For the rest he looked for light-hearted pleasure and propriety, and was very thankful when he found them, but if he met with antagonism and querulousness he at once retired into his separate fenced-off world of official duties, where he found satisfaction.

Iván Ilých was esteemed a good official, and after three years was made Assistant Public Prosecutor. His new duties, their importance, the possibility of indicting and imprisoning anyone he chose, the publicity his speeches received, and the success he had in all these things, made his work still more attractive.

More children came. His wife became more and more querulous and ill-tempered, but the attitude Iván Ilých had adopted towards his home life rendered him almost impervious to her grumbling.

After seven years' service in that town he was transferred to another province as Public Prosecutor. They moved, but were short of money and his wife did not like the place they moved to. Though the salary was higher the cost of living was greater, besides which two of their children died and family life became still more unpleasant for him.

Praskóvya Fëdorovna blamed her husband for every inconvenience they encountered in their new home. Most of the conversations between husband and wife, especially as to the the children's education, led to topics which recalled former disputes, and those disputes were apt to flare up again at any moment. There remained only those rare periods of amorousness which still came to them at times but did not last long. These were islets at which they anchored for a while and then again set out upon that ocean of veiled hostility which showed itself in their aloofness from one another. This aloofness might have grieved Iván Ilých had he considered that it ought not to exist, but he now regarded the position as normal, and even made it the goal at which he aimed in family life. His aim was to free himself more and more from those unpleasantnesses and to give them a semblance of harmlessness and propriety. He attained this by spending less and less time with his family, and when obliged to be at home he tried to safeguard his position by the presence of outsiders. The chief thing however was that he had his official duties. The whole interest of his life now centered in the official world and that interest absorbed him. The consciousness of his power, being able to ruin anybody he wished to ruin, the importance, even the external dignity of his entry into court, or meetings with his subordinates, his success with superiors and inferiors, and above all his masterly handling of cases, of which he was conscious— all this gave him pleasure and filled his life, together with chats with his colleagues, dinners, and bridge. So that on the whole Iván Ilých's life continued to flow as he considered it should do—pleasantly and properly.

So things continued for another seven years. His eldest daughter was already sixteen, another child had died, and only one son was left, a schoolboy and a subject of dissension. Iván Ilých wanted to put him in the School of Law, but to spite him Praskóvya Fëdorovna entered him at the High School. The daughter had been educated at home and had turned out well: the boy did not learn badly either.

CHAPTER III

So Iván Ilých lived for seventeen years after his marriage. He was already a Public Prosecutor of long standing, and had declined several proposed transfers while awaiting a more desirable post, when an unanticipated and unpleasant occurrence quite upset the peaceful course of his life. He was expecting to be offered the post of presiding judge in a University town, but Happe somehow came to the front and obtained the appointment instead. Iván Ilých became irritable, reproached Happe, and quarrelled both with him and with his immediate superiors—who became colder to him and again passed him over when other appointments were made.

This was in 1880, the hardest year of Iván Ilých's life. It was then that it became evident on the one hand that his salary was insufficient for them to live on, and on the other that he had been forgotten, and not only this, but that what was for him the greatest and most cruel injustice appeared to others a quite ordinary occurrence. Even his father did not consider it his duty to help him. Iván Ilých felt himself abandoned by everyone, and that they regarded his position with a salary of 3,500 rubles as quite normal and even fortunate. He alone knew that with the consciousness of the injustices done him, with his wife's incessant nagging, and with the debts he had contracted by living beyond his means, his position was far from normal.

In order to save money that summer he obtained leave of absence and went with his wife to live in the country at her brother's place.

In the country, without his work, he experienced *ennui* for the first time in his life, and not only *ennui* but intolerable depression, and he decided that it was impossible to go on living like that, and that it was necessary to take energetic measures.

Having passed a sleepless night pacing up and down the veranda, he decided to go to Petersburg and bestir himself, in order to punish those who had failed to appreciate him and to get transferred to another ministry.

Next day, despite many protests from his wife and her brother, he started for Petersburg with the sole object of obtaining a post with a salary of five thousand rubles a year. He was no longer bent on any particular department, or tendency, or kind of activity. All he now wanted was an appointment to another post with a salary of five thousand rubles, either in the administration, in the banks, with the railways, in one of the Empress Márya's Institutions,[8] or even in the customs—but it had to carry with it a salary of five thousand rubles and be in a ministry other than that in which they had failed to appreciate him.

---

8. A charitable organization founded in the late eighteenth century by the Empress Márya.

And this quest of Iván Ilých's was crowned with remarkable and unexpected success. At Kursk an acquaintance of his, F. I. Ilyín, got into the first-class carriage, sat down beside Iván Ilých, and told him of a telegram just received by the Governor of Kursk announcing that a change was about to take place in the ministry: Peter Ivánovich was to be superseded by Iván Semënovich.

The proposed change, apart from its significance for Russia, had a special significance for Iván Ilých, because by bringing forward a new man, Peter Petróvich, and consequently his friend Zachár Ivánovich, it was highly favourable for Iván Ilých, since Zachár Ivánovich was a friend and colleague of his.

In Moscow this news was confirmed, and on reaching Petersburg Iván Ilých found Zachár Ivánovich and received a definite promise of an appointment in his former Department of Justice.

A week later he telegraphed to his wife: "Zachár in Miller's place. I shall receive appointment on presentation of report."

Thanks to this change of personnel, Iván Ilých had unexpectedly obtained an appointment in his former ministry which placed him two stages above his former colleagues besides giving him five thousand rubles salary and three thousand five hundred rubles for expenses connected with his removal. All his ill humour towards his former enemies and the whole department vanished, and Iván Ilých was completely happy.

He returned to the country more cheerful and contented than he had been for a long time. Praskóvya Fëdorovna also cheered up and a truce was arranged between them. Iván Ilých told of how he had been fêted by everybody in Petersburg, how all those who had been his enemies were put to shame and now fawned on him, how envious they were of his appointment, and how much everybody in Petersburg had liked him.

Praskóvya Fëdorovna listened to all this and appeared to believe it. She did not contradict anything, but only made plans for their life in the town to which they were going. Iván Ilých saw with delight that these plans were his plans, that he and his wife agreed, and that, after a stumble, his life was regaining its due and natural character of pleasant lightheartedness and decorum.

Iván Ilých had come back for a short time only, for he had to take up his new duties on the 10th of September. Moreover, he needed time to settle into the new place, to move all his belongings from the province, and to buy and order many additional things: in a word, to make such arrangements as he had resolved on, which were almost exactly what Praskóvya Fëdorovna too had decided on.

Now that everything had happened so fortunately, and that he and his wife were at one in their aims and moreover saw so little of one another, they got on together better than they had done since the first years of marriage. Iván Ilých had thought of taking his family away with him at once, but the insistence of his wife's brother and her sister-in-law, who had suddenly become particularly amiable and friendly to him and his family, induced him to depart alone.

So he departed, and the cheerful state of mind induced by his success and by the harmony between his wife and himself, the one intensifying the other, did not leave him. He found a delightful house, just the thing both he and his wife had dreamt of. Spacious, lofty reception rooms in the old style, a convenient and dignified study, rooms for his wife and daughter, a study for his son—it might have been specially built for them. Iván Ilých himself superintended the arrangements, chose the wall-papers, supplemented the furniture (preferably with antiques which he considered particularly *comme il faut*), and supervised the upholstering. Everything progressed and progressed and approached the ideal he had set himself: even when things were only half completed they exceeded his expectations. He saw what a refined and elegant character, free from vulgarity, it would all have when it was ready. On falling asleep he pictured to himself how the reception-room would look. Looking at the yet unfinished drawing-room he could see the fireplace, the screen, the what-not, the little chairs dotted here and there, the dishes and plates on the walls, and the bronzes, as they would be when everything was in place. He was pleased by the thought of how his wife and daughter, who shared his taste in this matter, would be impressed by it. They were certainly not expecting as much. He had been particularly successful in finding, and buying cheaply, antiques which gave a particularly aristocratic character to the whole place. But in his letters he intentionally understated everything in order to be able to surprise them. All this so absorbed him that his new duties—though he liked his official work—interested him less than he had expected. Sometimes he even had moments of absent-mindedness during the Court Sessions, and would consider whether he should have straight or curved cornices for his curtains. He was so interested in it all that he often did things himself, rearranging the furniture, or rehanging the curtains. Once when mounting a step-ladder to show the upholsterer, who did not understand, how he wanted the hangings draped, he made a false step and slipped, but being a strong and agile man he clung on and only knocked his side against the knob of the window frame. The bruised place was painful but the pain soon passed, and he felt particularly bright and well just then. He wrote: "I feel fifteen years younger." He thought he would have everything ready by September, but it dragged on till mid-October. But the result was charming not only in his eyes but to everyone who saw it.

In reality it was just what is usually seen in the houses of people of moderate means who want to appear rich, and therefore succeed only in resembling others like themselves: there were damasks, dark wood, plants, rugs, and dull and polished bronzes—all the things people of a certain class have in order to resemble other people of that class. His house was so like the others that it would never have been noticed, but to him it all seemed to be quite exceptional. He was very happy when he met his family at the station and brought them to the newly furnished house all lit up, where a footman in a white tie opened the door into the hall decorated with plants, and when they went on into the drawing-room and the study uttering exclamations of delight. He conducted them everywhere, drank in their praises eagerly, and beamed with pleasure. At tea that evening, when Praskóvya Fëdorovna among other things asked him about his fall, he laughed, and showed them how he had gone flying and had frightened the upholsterer.

"It's a good thing I'm a bit of an athlete. Another man might have been killed, but I merely knocked myself, just here; it hurts when it's touched, but it's passing off already—it's only a bruise."

So they began living in their new home—in which, as always happens, when they got thoroughly settled in they found they were just one room short—and with the increased income, which as always was just a little (some five hundred rubles) too little, but it was all very nice.

Things went particularly well at first, before everything was finally arranged and while something had still to be done: this thing bought, that thing ordered, another thing moved, and something else adjusted. Though there were some disputes between husband and wife, they were both so well satisfied and had so much to do that it all passed off without any serious quarrels. When nothing was left to arrange it became rather dull and something seemed to be lacking, but they were then making acquaintances, forming habits, and life was growing fuller.

Iván Ilých spent his mornings at the law court and came home to dinner, and at first he was generally in a good humour, though he occasionally became irritable just on account of his house. (Every spot on the tablecloth or the upholstery, and every broken window-blind string, irritated him. He had devoted so much trouble to arranging it all that every disturbance of it distressed him.) But on the whole his life ran its course as he believed life should do: easily, pleasantly, and decorously.

He got up at nine, drank his coffee, read the paper, and then put on his undress uniform and went to the law courts. There the harness in which he worked had already been stretched to fit him and he donned it without a hitch: petitioners, inquiries at the chancery, the chancery itself, and the sittings public and administrative. In all this the thing was to exclude everything fresh and vital, which always disturbs the regular course of official business, and to admit only official relations with people, and then only on official grounds. A man would come, for instance, wanting some information. Iván Ilých, as one in whose sphere the matter did not lie, would have nothing to do with him: but if the man had some business with him in his official capacity, something that could be expressed on officially stamped paper, he would do everything, positively everything he could within the limits of such relations, and in doing so would maintain the semblance of friendly human relations, that is, would observe the courtesies of life. As soon as the official relations ended, so did everything else. Iván Ilých possessed this capacity to separate his real life from the official side of affairs and not mix the two, in the highest degree, and by long practice and natural aptitude had brought it to such a pitch that sometimes, in the manner of a virtuoso, he would even allow himself to let the human and official relations mingle. He let himself do this just because he felt that he could at any time he chose resume the strictly official attitude again and drop the human relation. And he did it all easily, pleasantly, correctly, and even artistically. In the intervals between the sessions he smoked, drank tea, chatted a little about politics, a little about general topics, a little about cards, but most of all about official appointments. Tired, but with the feelings of a virtuoso—one of the first violins who has played his part in an orchestra with precision—he would return home to find that his wife and daughter had been out paying calls, or had a visitor, and that his son had been to school, had done his homework with his tutor, and was duly learning what is taught at High Schools. Everything was as it should be. After dinner, if they had no visitors, Iván Ilých sometimes read a book that was being much discussed at the time, and in the evening settled down to work, that is, read official papers, compared the depositions of witnesses, and noted paragraphs of the Code applying to them. This was neither dull nor amusing. It was dull when he might have been playing bridge, but if no bridge was available it was at any rate better than doing nothing or sitting with his wife. Iván Ilých's chief pleasure was giving little dinners to which he invited men and women of good social position, and just as his drawing-room resembled all other drawing-rooms so did his enjoyable little parties resemble all other such parties.

Once they even gave a dance. Iván Ilých enjoyed it and everything went off well, except that it led to a violent quarrel with his wife about the cakes and sweets. Praskóvya Fëdorovna had made her own plans, but Iván Ilých insisted on getting everything from an expensive confectioner and ordered too many cakes, and the quarrel occurred because some of those cakes were left over and the confectioner's bill came to forty-five rubles. It was a great and disagreeable quarrel. Praskóvya Fëdorovna called him "a fool and an imbecile," and he clutched at his head and made angry allusions to divorce.

But the dance itself had been enjoyable. The best people were there, and Iván Ilých had danced with Princess Trúfonova, a sister of the distinguished founder of the Society "Bear my Burden."

The pleasures connected with his work were pleasures of ambition; his social pleasures were those of vanity; but Iván Ilých's greatest pleasure was playing bridge. He acknowledged that whatever disagreeable incident happened in his life, the pleasure that beamed like a ray of light above everything else was to sit down to bridge with good players, not noisy partners, and of course to four-handed bridge (with five players it was annoying to have to stand out, though one pretended not to mind), to play a clever and serious game (when the cards allowed it) and then to have supper and drink a glass of wine. After a game of bridge, especially if he had won a little (to win a large sum was unpleasant), Iván Ilých went to bed in specially good humour.

So they lived. They formed a circle of acquaintances among the best people and were visited by people of importace and by young folk. In their views as to their acquaintances, husband, wife and daughter were entirely agreed, and tacitly and unanimously kept at arm's length and shook off the various shabby friends and relations who, with much show of affection, gushed into the drawing-room with its Japanese plates on the walls. Soon these shabby friends ceased to obtrude themselves and only the best people remained in the Golovíns' set.

Young men made up to Lisa, and Petríshchev, an examining magistrate and Dmítri Ivanovich Petríshchev's son and sole heir, began to be so attentive to her that Iván Ilých had already spoken to Praskóvya Fëdorovna about it, and considered whether they should not arrange a party for them or get up some private theatricals.

So they lived, and all went well, without change, and life flowed pleasantly.

CHAPTER IV

THEY were all in good health. It could not be called ill health if Iván Ilých sometimes said that he had a queer taste in his mouth and felt some discomfort in his left side.

But this discomfort increased and, though not exactly painful, grew into a sense of pressure in his side accompanied by ill humour. And his irritability became worse and worse and began to mar the agreeable, easy, and correct life that had established itself in the Golovín family. Quarrels between husband and wife became more and more frequent, and soon the ease and amenity disappeared and even the decorum was barely maintained. Scenes again became frequent, and very few of those islets remained on which husband and wife could meet without an explosion. Praskóvya Fëdorovna now had good reason to say that her husband's temper was trying. With characteristic exaggeration she said he had always had a dreadful temper, and that it had needed all her good nature to put up with it for twenty years. It was true that now the quarrels were started by him. His bursts of temper always came just before dinner, often just as he began to eat his soup. Sometimes he noticed that a plate or dish was chipped, or the food was not right, or his son put his elbow on the table, or his daughter's hair was not done as he liked it, and for all this he blamed Praskóvya Fëdorovna. At first she retorted and said disagreeable things to him, but once or twice he fell into such a rage at the beginning of dinner that she realized it was due to some physical derangement brought on by taking food, and so she restrained herself and did not answer, but only hurried to get the dinner over. She regarded this self-restraint as highly praiseworthy. Having come to the conclusion that her husband had a dreadful temper and made her life miserable, she began to feel sorry for herself, and the more she pitied herself the more she hated her husband. She began to wish he would die; yet she did not want him to die because then his salary would cease. And this irritated her against him still more. She considered herself dreadfully unhappy just because not even his death could save her, and though she concealed her exasperation, that hidden exasperation of hers increased his irritation also.

After one scene in which Iván Ilých had been particularly unfair and after which he had said in explanation that he certainly was irritable but that it was due to his not being well, she said that if he was ill it should be attended to, and insisted on his going to see a celebrated doctor.

He went. Everything took place as he had expected and as it always does. There was the usual waiting and the important air assumed by the doctor, with which he was so familiar (resembling that which he himself assumed in court), and the sounding and listening, and the questions which called for answers that were forgone conclusions and were evidently unnecessary, and the look of importance which implied that "if only you put yourself in our hands we will arrange everything—we know indubitably how it has to be done, always in the same way for everybody alike." It was all just as it was in the law courts. The doctor put on just the same air towards him as he himself put on towards an accused person.

The doctor said that so-and-so indicated that there was so-and-so inside the patient, but if the investigation of so-and-so did not confirm this, then he must assume that and that. If he assumed that and that, then . . . and so on. To Iván Ilých only one question was important: was his case serious or not? But the doctor ignored that inappropriate question. From his point of view it was not the one under consideration, the real question was to decide between a floating kidney, chronic catarrh, or appendicitis. It was not a question of Iván Ilých's life or death, but one between a floating kidney and appendicitis. And that question the doctor solved brilliantly, as it seemed to Iván Ilých, in favour of the appendix, with the reservation that should an examination of the urine give fresh indications the matter would be reconsidered. All this was just what Iván Ilých had himself brilliantly accomplished a thousand times in dealing with men on trial. The doctor summed up just as brilliantly, looking over his spectacles triumphantly and even gaily at the accused. From the doctor's summing up Iván Ilých concluded that things were bad, but that for the doctor, and perhaps for everybody else, it was a matter of indifference, though for him it was bad. And this conclusion struck him painfully, arousing in him a great feeling of pity for himself and of bitterness towards the doctor's indifference to a matter of such importance.

He said nothing of this, but rose, placed the doctor's fee on the table, and remarked with a sigh: "We sick people probably often put inappropriate questions. But tell me, in general, is this complaint dangerous, or not? . . ."

The doctor looked at him sternly over his spectacles with one eye, as if to say: "Prisoner, if you will not keep to the questions put to you, I shall be obliged to have you removed from the court."

"I have already told you what I consider necessary and proper. The analysis may show something more." And the doctor bowed.

Iván Ilých went out slowly, seated himself disconsolately in his sledge, and drove home. All the way home he was going over what the doctor had said, trying to translate those complicated, obscure, scientific phrases into plain language and find in them an answer to the question: "Is my condition bad? Is it very bad? Or is there as yet nothing much wrong?" And it seemed to him that the meaning of what the doctor had said was that it was very bad. Everything in the streets seemed depressing. The cabmen, the houses, the passers-by, and the shops, were dismal. His ache, this dull gnawing ache that never ceased for a moment, seemed to have acquired a new and more serious significance from the doctor's dubious remarks. Iván Ilých now watched it with a new and oppressive feeling.

He reached home and began to tell his wife about it. She listened, but in the middle of his account his daughter came in with her hat on, ready to go out with her mother. She sat down reluctantly to listen to this tedious story, but could not stand it long, and her mother too did not hear him to the end.

"Well, I am very glad," she said. "Mind now to take your medicine regularly. Give me the prescription and I'll send Gerásim to the chemist's." And she went to get ready to go out.

While she was in the room Iván Ilých had hardly taken time to breathe, but he sighed deeply when she left it.

"Well," he thought, "perhaps it isn't so bad after all."

He began taking his medicine and following the doctor's directions, which had been altered after the examination of the urine. But then it happened that there was a contradiction between the indications drawn from the examination of the urine and the symptoms that showed themselves. It turned out that what was happening differed from what the doctor had told him, and that he had either forgotten, or blundered, or hidden something from him. He could not, however, be blamed for that, and Iván Ilých still obeyed his orders implicitly and at first derived some comfort from doing so.

From the time of his visit to the doctor, Iván Ilých's chief occupation was the exact fulfilment of the doctor's instructions regarding hygiene and the taking of medicine, and the observation of his pain and his excretions. His chief interests came to be people's ailments and people's health. When sickness, deaths, or recoveries, were mentioned in his presence, especially when the illness resembled his own, he listened with agitation which he tried to hide, asked questions, and applied what he heard to his own case.

The pain did not grow less, but Iván Ilých made efforts to force himself to think that he was better. And he could do this so long as nothing agitated him. But as soon as he had any unpleasantness with his wife, any lack of success in his official work, or held bad cards at bridge, he was at once acutely sensible of his disease. He had formerly borne such mischances, hoping soon to adjust what was wrong, to master it and attain success, or make a grand slam. But now every mischance upset him and plunged him into despair. He would say to himself: "There now, just as I was beginning to get better and the medicine had begun to take effect, comes this accursed misfortune, or unpleasantness . . ." And he was furious with the mishap, or with the people who were causing the unpleasantness and killing him, for he felt that this fury was killing him but could not restrain it. One would have thought that it should have been clear to him that this exasperation with circumstances and people aggravated his illness, and that he ought therefore to ignore unpleasant occurrences. But he drew the very opposite conclusion: he said that he needed peace, and he watched for everything that might disturb it and became irritable at the slightest infringement of it. His condition was rendered worse by the fact that he read medical books and consulted doctors. The progress of his disease was so gradual that he could deceive himself when comparing one day with another—the difference was so slight. But when he consulted the doctors it seemed to him that he was getting worse, and even very rapidly. Yet despite this he was continually consulting them.

That month he went to see another celebrity, who told him almost the same as the first had done but put his questions rather differently, and the interview with this celebrity only increased Iván Ilých's doubts and fears. A friend of a friend of his, a very good doctor, diagnosed his illness again quite differently from the others, and though he predicted recovery, his questions and suppositions bewildered Iván Ilých still more and increased his doubts. A homoeopathist diagnosed the disease in yet another way, and prescribed medicine which Iván Ilých took secretly for a week. But after a week, not feeling any improvement and having lost confidence both in the former doctor's treatment and in this one's, he became still more despondent. One day a lady acquaintance mentioned a cure effected by a wonder-working icon. Iván Ilých caught himself listening attentively and beginning to believe that it had occurred. This incident alarmed him. "Has my mind really weakened to such an extent?" he asked himself. "Nonsense! It's all rubbish. I mustn't give way to nervous fears but having chosen a doctor must keep strictly to his treatment. That is what I will do. Now it's all settled. I won't think about it, but will follow the treatment seriously till summer, and then we shall see. From now there must be no more of this wavering!" This was easy to say but impossible to carry out. The pain in his side oppressed him and seemed to grow worse and more incessant, while the taste in his mouth grew stranger and stranger. It seemed to him that his breath had a disgusting smell, and he was conscious of a loss of appetite and strength. There was no deceiving himself: something terrible, new, and more important than anything before in his life, was taking place within him of which he alone was aware. Those about him did not understand or would not understand it, but thought everything in the world was going on as usual. That tormented Iván Ilých more than anything. He saw that his household, especially his wife and daughter who were in a perfect whirl of visiting, did not understand anything of it and were annoyed that he was so depressed and so exacting, as if he were to blame for it. Though they tried to disguise it he saw that he was an obstacle in their path, and that his wife had adopted a definite line in regard to his illness and kept to it regardless of anything he said or did. Her attitude was this: "You know," she would say to her friends, "Iván Ilých can't do as other people do, and keep to the treatment prescribed for him. One day he'll take his drops and keep strictly to his diet and go to bed in good time, but the next day unless I watch him he'll suddenly forget his medicine, eat sturgeon—which is forbidden—and sit up playing cards till one o'clock in the morning."

"Oh, come, when was that?" Iván Ilých would ask in vexation. "Only once at Peter Ivánovich's."

"And yesterday with Shébek."

"Well, even if I hadn't stayed up, this pain would have kept me awake."

"Be that as it may you'll never get well like that, but will always make us wretched."

Praskóvya Fëdorovna's attitude to Iván Ilých's illness, as she expressed it both to others and to him, was that it was his own fault and was another of the annoyances he caused her. Iván Ilých felt that this opinion escaped her involuntarily—but that did not make it easier for him.

At the law courts too, Iván Ilých noticed, or thought he noticed, a strange attitude towards himself. It sometimes seemed to him that people were watching him inquisitively as a man whose place might soon be vacant. Then again, his friends would suddenly begin to chaff him in a friendly way about his low spirits, as if the awful, horrible, and unheard-of thing that was going on within him, incessantly gnawing at him and irresistibly drawing him away, was a very agreeable subject for jests. Schwartz in particular irritated him by his jocularity, vivacity, and *savoir-faire*, which reminded him of what he himself had been ten years ago.

Friends came to make up a set and they sat down to cards. They dealt, bending the new cards to soften them, and he sorted the diamonds in his hand and found he had seven. His partner said "No trumps" and supported him with two diamonds. What more could be wished for? It ought to be jolly and lively. They would make a grand slam. But suddenly Iván Ilých was conscious of that gnawing pain, that taste in his mouth, and it seemed ridiculous that in such circumstances he should be pleased to make a grand slam.

He looked at his partner Mikháil Mikháylovich, who rapped the table with his strong hand and instead of snatching up the tricks pushed the cards courteously and indulgently towards Iván Ilých that he might have the pleasure of gathering them up without the trouble of stretching out his hand for them. "Does he think I am too weak to stretch out my arm?" thought Iván Ilých, and forgetting what he was doing he over-trumped his partner, missing the grand slam by three tricks. And what was most awful of all was that he saw how upset Mikháil Mikháylovich was about it but did not himself care. And it was dreadful to realize why he did not care.

They all saw that he was suffering, and said: "We can stop if you are tired. Take a rest." Lie down? No, he was not at all tired, and he finished the rubber. All were gloomy and silent. Iván Ilých felt that he had diffused this gloom over them and could not dispel it. They had supper and went away, and Iván Ilých was left alone with the consciousness that his life was poisoned and was poisoning the lives of others, and that this poison did not weaken but penetrated more and more deeply into his whole being.

With this consciousness, and with physical pain besides the terror, he must go to bed, often to lie awake the greater part of the night. Next morning he had to get up again, dress, go to the law courts, speak, and write; or if he did not go out, spend at home those twenty-four hours a day each of which was a torture. And he had to live thus all alone on the brink of an abyss, with no one who understood or pitied him.

CHAPTER V

So one month passed and then another. Just before the New Year his brother-in-law came to town and stayed at their house. Iván Ilých was at the law courts and Praskóvya Fёdorovna had gone shopping. When Iván Ilých came home and entered his study he found his brother-in-law there—a healthy, florid man—unpacking his portmanteau himself. He raised his head on hearing Iván Ilých's footsteps and looked up at him for a moment without a word. That stare told Iván Ilých everything. His brother-in-law opened his mouth to utter an exclamation of surprise but checked himself, and that action confirmed it all.

"I have changed, eh?"

"Yes, there is a change."

And after that, try as he would to get his brother-in-law to return to the subject of his looks, the latter would say nothing about it. Praskóvya Fёdorovna came home and her brother went out to her. Iván Ilých locked the door and began to examine himself in the glass, first full face, then in profile. He took up a portrait of himself taken with his wife, and compared it with what he saw in the glass. The change in him was immense. Then he bared his arms to the elbow, looked at them, drew the sleeves down again, sat down on an ottoman, and grew blacker than night.

"No, no, this won't do!" he said to himself, and jumped up, went to the table, took up some law papers and began to read them, but could not continue. He unlocked the door and went into the reception-room. The door leading to the drawing-room was shut. He approached it on tiptoe and listened.

"No, you are exaggerating!" Praskóvya Fёdorovna was saying.

"Exaggerating! Don't you see it? Why, he's a dead man! Look at his eyes—there's no light in them. But what is it that is wrong with him?"

"No one knows. Nikoláevich (that was another doctor) said something, but I don't know what. And Leshchetítsky (this was the celebrated specialist) said quite the contrary . . ."

Iván Ilých walked away, went to his own room, lay down, and began musing: "The kidney, a floating kidney." He recalled all the doctors had told him of how it detached itself and swayed about. And by an effort of imagination he tried to catch that kidney and arrest it and support it. So little was needed for this, it seemed to him. "No, I'll go to see Peter Ivánovich again." (That was the friend whose friend was a doctor.) He rang, ordered the carriage, and got ready to go.

"Where are you going, Jean?" asked his wife, with a specially sad and exceptionally kind look.

This exceptionally kind look irritated him. He looked morosely at her.

"I must go to see Peter Ivánovich."

He went to see Peter Ivánovich, and together they went to see his friend, the doctor. He was in, and Iván Ilých had a long talk with him.

Reviewing the anatomical and physiological details of what in the doctor's opinion was going on inside him, he understood it all.

There was something, a small thing, in the vermiform appendix. It might all come right. Only stimulate the energy of one organ and check the activity of another, then absorption would take place and everything would come right. He got home rather late for dinner, ate his dinner, and conversed cheerfully, but could not for a long time bring himself to go back to work in his room. At last, however, he went to his study and did what was necessary, but the consciousness that he had put something aside—an important, intimate matter which he would revert to when his work was done—never left him. When he had finished his work he remembered that this intimate matter was the thought of his vermiform appendix. But he did not give himself up to it, and went to the drawing-room for tea. There were callers there, including the examining magistrate who was a desirable match for his daughter, and they were conversing, playing the piano and singing. Iván Ilých, as Praskóvya Fëdorovna remarked, spent that evening more cheerfully than usual, but he never for a moment forgot that he had postponed the important matter of the appendix. At eleven o'clock he said good-night and went to his bedroom. Since his illness he had slept alone in a small room next to his study. He undressed and took up a novel by Zola, but instead of reading it he fell into thought, and in his imagination that desired improvement in the vermiform appendix occurred. There was the absorption and evacuation and the re-establishment of normal activity. "Yes, that's it!" he said to himself. "One need only assist nature, that's all." He remembered his medicine, rose, took it, and lay down on his back watching for the beneficent action of the medicine and for it to lessen the pain. "I need only take it regularly and avoid all injurious influences. I am already feeling better, much better." He began touching his side: it was not painful to the touch. "There, I really don't feel it. It's much better already." He put out the light and turned on his side . . . "The appendix is getting better, absorption is occurring." Suddenly he felt the old, familiar, dull, gnawing pain, stubborn and serious. There was the same familiar loathsome taste in his mouth. His heart sank and he felt dazed. "My God! My God!" he muttered. "Again, again! And it will never cease." And suddenly the matter presented itself in a quite different aspect. "Vermiform appendix! Kidney!" he said to himself. "It's not a question of appendix or kidney, but of life and . . . death. Yes, life was there and now it is going, going and I cannot stop it. Yes. Why deceive myself? Isn't it obvious to everyone but me that I'm dying, and that it's only a question of weeks, days . . . it may happen this moment. There was light and now there is darkness. I was here and now I'm going there! Where?" A chill came over him, his breathing ceased, and he felt only the throbbing of his heart.

"When I am not, what will there be? There will be nothing. Then where shall I be when I am no more? Can this be dying? No, I don't want to!" He jumped up and tried to light the candle, felt for it with trembling hands, dropped candle and candlestick on the floor, and fell back on his pillow.

"What's the use? It makes no difference," he said to himself, staring with wide-open eyes into the darkness. "Death. Yes, death. And none of them know or wish to know it, and they have no pity for me. Now they are playing." (He heard through the door the distant sound of a song and its accompaniment.) "It's all the same to them, but they will die too! Fools! I first, and they later, but it will be the same for them. And now they are merry . . . the beasts!"

Anger choked him and he was agonizingly, unbearably miserable. "It is impossible that all men have been doomed to suffer this awful horror!" He raised himself.

"Something must be wrong. I must calm myself—must think it all over from the beginning." And he again began thinking. "Yes, the beginning of my illness: I knocked my side, but I was still quite well that day and the next. It hurt a little, then rather more. I saw the doctors, then followed despondency and anguish, more doctors, and I drew nearer to the abyss. My strength grew less and I kept coming nearer and nearer, and now I have wasted away and there is no light in my eyes. I think of the appendix—but this is death! I think of mending the appendix, and all the while here is death! Can it really be death?" Again terror seized him and he gasped for breath. He leant down and began feeling for the matches, pressing with his elbow on the stand beside the bed. It was in his way and hurt him, he grew furious with it, pressed on it still harder, and upset it. Breathless and in despair he fell on his back, expecting death to come immediately.

Meanwhile the visitors were leaving. Praskóvya Fëdorovna was seeing them off. She heard something fall and came in.

"What has happened?"

"Nothing. I knocked it over accidentally."

She went out and returned with a candle. He lay there panting heavily, like a man who has run a thousand yards, and stared upwards at her with a fixed look.

"What is it, Jean?"

"No . . . o . . . thing. I upset it." ("Why speak of it? She won't understand," he thought.)

And in truth she did not understand. She picked up the stand, lit his candle, and hurried away to see another visitor off. When she came back he still lay on his back, looking upwards.

"What is it? Do you feel worse?"

"Yes."

She shook her head and sat down.

"Do you know, Jean, I think we must ask Leshchetítsky to come and see you here."

This meant calling in the famous specialist, regardless of expense. He smiled malignantly and said "No." She remained a little longer and then went up to him and kissed his forehead.

While she was kissing him he hated her from the bottom of his soul and with difficulty refrained from pushing her away.

"Good-night. Please God you'll sleep."

"Yes."

CHAPTER VI

IVÁN Ilých saw that he was dying, and he was in continual despair.

In the depth of his heart he knew he was dying, but not only was he not accustomed to the thought, he simply did not and could not grasp it.

The syllogism he had learnt from Kiezewetter's Logic:[9] "Caius is a man, men are mortal, therefore Caius is mortal," had always seemed to him correct as applied to Caius, but certainly not as applied to himself. That Caius—man in the abstract—was mortal, was perfectly correct, but he was not Caius, not an abstract man, but a creature quite, quite separate from all others. He had been little Ványa, with a mamma and a papa; with Mitya and Volódya, and the toys, a coachman and a nurse, afterwards with Kátenka and with all the joys, griefs, and delights of childhood, boyhood, and youth. What did Caius know of the smell of that striped leather ball Ványa had been so fond of? Had Caius kissed his mother's hand like that, and did the silk of her dress rustle so for Caius? Had he rioted like that at school when the pastry was bad? Had Caius been in love like that? Could Caius preside at a session as he did? "Caius really was mortal, and it was right for him to die; but for me, little Ványa, Iván Ilých, with all my thoughts and emotions, it's altogether a different matter. It cannot be that I ought to die. That would be too terrible."

Such was his feeling.

"If I had to die like Caius I should have known it was so. An inner voice would have told me so, but there was nothing of the sort in me and I and all my friends felt that our case was quite different from that of Caius. And now here it is!" he said to himself. "It can't be. It's impossible! But here it is. How is this? How is one to understand it?"

He could not understand it, and tried to drive this false, incorrect, morbid thought away and to replace it by other proper and healthy thoughts. But that thought, and not the thought only but the reality itself, seemed to come and confront him.

---

9. Karl Kiezewetter (1766–1819), author of an outline of logic widely used in Russian schools at the time.

And to replace that thought he called up a succession of others, hoping to find in them some support. He tried to get back into the former current of thoughts that had once screened the thought of death from him. But strange to say, all that had formerly shut off, hidden, and destroyed, his consciousness of death, no longer had that effect. Iván Ilých now spent most of his time in attempting to re-establish that old current. He would say to himself: "I will take up my duties again—after all I used to live by them." And banishing all doubts he would go to the law courts, enter into conversation with his colleagues, and sit carelessly as was his wont, scanning the crowd with a thoughtful look and leaning both his emaciated arms on the arms of his oak chair; bending over as usual to a colleague and drawing his papers nearer he would interchange whispers with him, and then suddenly raising his eyes and sitting erect would pronounce certain words and open the proceedings. But suddenly in the midst of those proceedings the pain in his side, regardless of the stage the proceedings had reached, would begin its own gnawing work. Iván Ilých would turn his attention to it and try to drive the thought of it away, but without success. It would come and stand before him and look at him, and he would be petrified and the light would die out of his eyes, and he would again begin asking himself whether It alone was true. And his colleagues and subordinates would see with surprise and distress that he, the brilliant and subtle judge, was becoming confused and making mistakes. He would shake himself, try to pull himself together, manage somehow to bring the sitting to a close, and return home with the sorrowful consciousness that his judicial labours could not as formerly hide from him what he wanted them to hide, and could not deliver him from It. And what was worst of all was that It drew his attention to itself not in order to make him take some action but only that he should look at It, look it straight in the face: look at it and without doing anything, suffer inexpressibly.

And to save himself from this condition Iván Ilých looked for consolations—new screens—and new screens were found and for a while seemed to save him, but then they immediately fell to pieces or rather became transparent, as if It penetrated them and nothing could veil It.

In these latter days he would go into the drawing-room he had arranged—that drawing-room where he had fallen and for the sake of which (how bitterly ridiculous it seemed) he had sacrificed his life—for he knew that his illness originated with that knock. He would enter and see that something had scratched the polished table. He would look for the cause of this and find that it was the bronze ornamentation of an album, that had got bent. He would take up the expensive album which he had lovingly arranged, and feel vexed with his daughter and her friends for their untidiness—for the album was torn here and there and some of the photographs turned upside down. He would put it carefully in order and bend the ornamentation back into position. Then it would occur to him to place all those things in another corner of the room, near the plants. He would call the footman, but his daughter or wife would come to help him. They would not agree, and his wife would contradict him, and he would dispute and grow angry. But that was all right, for then he did not think about *It*. *It* was invisible.

But then, when he was moving something himself, his wife would say: "Let the servants do it. You will hurt yourself again." And suddenly *It* would flash through the screen and he would see it. It was just a flash, and he hoped it would disappear, but he would involuntarily pay attention to his side. "It sits there as before, gnawing just the same!" And he could no longer forget *It*, but could distinctly see it looking at him from behind the flowers. "What is it all for?"

"It really is so I lost my life over that curtain as I might have done when storming a fort. Is that possible? How terrible and how stupid. It can't be true! It can't, but it is!"

He would go to his study, lie down, and again be alone with *It*: face to face with *It*. And nothing could be done with *It* except to look at it and shudder.

CHAPTER VII

How it happened it is impossible to say because it came about step by step, unnoticed, but in the third month of Iván Ilých's illness, his wife, his daughter, his son, his acquaintances, the doctors, the servants, and above all he himself, were aware that the whole interest he had for other people was whether he would soon vacate his place, and at last release the living from the discomfort caused by his presence and be himself released from his sufferings.

He slept less and less. He was given opium and hypodermic injections of morphine, but this did not relieve him. The dull depression he experienced in a somnolent condition at first gave him a little relief, but only as something new, afterwards it became as distressing as the pain itself or even more so.

Special foods were prepared for him by the doctors' orders, but all those foods became increasingly distasteful and disgusting to him.

For his excretions also special arrangements had to be made, and this was a torment to him every time—a torment from the uncleanliness, the unseemliness, and the smell, and from knowing that another person had to take part in it.

But just through this most unpleasant matter Iván Ilých obtained comfort. Gerásim, the butler's young assistant, always came in to carry the things out. Gerásim was a clean, fresh peasant lad, grown stout on town food and always cheerful and bright. At first the sight of him, in his clean Russian peasant costume, engaged on that disgusting task embarrassed Iván Ilých.

Once when he got up from the commode too weak to draw up his trousers, he dropped into a soft armchair and looked with horror at his bare, enfeebled thighs with the muscles so sharply marked on them.

Gerásim with a firm light tread, his heavy boots emitting a pleasant smell of tar and fresh winter air, came in wearing a clean Hessian apron, the sleeves of his print shirt tucked up over his strong bare young arms; and refraining from looking at his sick master out of consideration for his feelings, and restraining the joy of life that beamed from his face, went up to the commode.

"Gerásim!" said Iván Ilých in a weak voice.

Gerásim started, evidently afraid he might have committed some blunder, and with a rapid movement turned his fresh, kind, simple young face which just showed the first downy signs of a beard.

"Yes, sir?"

"That must be very unpleasant for you. You must forgive me. I am helpless."

"Oh, why, sir," and Gerásim's eyes beamed and he showed his glistening white teeth, "what's a little trouble? It's a case of illness with you, sir."

And his deft strong hands did their accustomed task, and he went out of the room stepping lightly. Five minutes later he as lightly returned.

Iván Ilých was still sitting in the same position in the armchair.

"Gerásim," he said when the latter had replaced the freshly-washed utensil. "Please come here and help me." Gerásim went up to him. "Lift me up. It is hard for me to get up, and I have sent Dmítri away."

Gerásim went up to him, grasped his master with his strong arms deftly but gently, in the same way that he stepped—lifted him, supported him with one hand, and with the other drew up his trousers and would have set him down again, but Iván Ilých asked to be led to the sofa. Gerásim, without an effort and without apparent pressure, led him, almost lifting him, to the sofa and placed him on it.

"Thank you. How easily and well you do it all!"

Gerásim smiled again and turned to leave the room. But Iván Ilých felt his presence such a comfort that he did not want to let him go.

"One thing more, please move up that chair. No, the other one—under my feet. It is easier for me when my feet are raised."

Gerásim brought the chair, set it down gently in place, and raised Iván Ilých's legs on to it. It seemed to Iván Ilých that he felt better while Gerásim was holding up his legs.

"It's better when my legs are higher," he said. "Place that cushion under them."

Gerásim did so. He again lifted the legs and placed them, and again Iván Ilých felt better while Gerásim held his legs. When he set them down Iván Ilých fancied he felt worse.

"Gerásim," he said. "Are you busy now?"

"Not at all, sir," said Gerásim, who had learnt from the townsfolk how to speak to gentlefolk.

"What have you still to do?"

"What have I to do? I've done everything except chopping the logs for to-morrow."

"Then hold my legs up a bit higher, can you?"

"Of course I can. Why not?" And Gerásim raised his master's legs higher and Iván Ilých thought that in that position he did not feel any pain at all.

"And how about the logs?"

"Don't trouble about that, sir. There's plenty of time."

Iván Ilých told Gerásim to sit down and hold his legs, and began to talk to him. And strange to say it seemed to him that he felt better while Gerásim held his legs up.

After that Iván Ilých would sometimes call Gerásim and get him to hold his legs on his shoulders, and he liked talking to him. Gerásim did it all easily, willingly, simply, and with a good nature that touched Iván Ilých. Health, strength, and vitality in other people were offensive to him, but Gerásim's strength and vitality did not mortify but soothed him.

What tormented Iván Ilých most was the deception, the lie, which for some reason they all accepted, that he was not dying but was simply ill, and that he only need keep quiet and undergo a treatment and then something very good would result. He however knew that do what they would nothing would come of it, only still more agonizing suffering and death. This deception tortured him—their not wishing to admit what they all knew and what he knew, but wanting to lie to him concerning his terrible condition, and wishing and forcing him to participate in that lie. Those lies—lies enacted over him on the eve of his death and destined to degrade this awful, solemn act to the level of their visitings, their curtains, their sturgeon for dinner—were a terrible agony for Iván Ilých. And strangely enough, many times when they were going through their antics over him he had been within a hairbreadth of calling out to them: "Stop lying! You know and I know that I am dying. Then at least stop lying about it!" But he had never had the spirit to do it. The awful, terrible act of his dying was, he could see, reduced by those about him to the level of a casual, unpleasant, and almost indecorous incident (as if someone entered a drawing-room diffusing an unpleasant odour) and this was done by that very decorum which he had served all his life long. He saw that no one felt for him, because no one even wished to grasp his position. Only Gerásim recognized it and pitied him. And so Iván Ilých felt at ease only with him. He felt comforted when Gerásim supported his legs (sometimes all night long) and refused to go to bed, saying: "Don't you worry, Iván Ilých. I'll get sleep enough later on," or when he suddenly became familiar and exclaimed: "If you weren't sick it would be another matter, but as it is, why should I grudge a little trouble?" Gerásim alone did not lie; everything showed that he alone understood the facts of the case and did not consider it necessary to disguise them, but simply felt sorry for his emaciated and enfeebled master. Once when Iván Ilých was sending him away he even said straight out: "We shall all of us die, so why should I grudge a little trouble?"—expressing the fact that he did not think his work burdensome, because he was doing it for a dying man and hoped someone would do the same for him when his time came.

Apart from this lying, or because of it, what most tormented Iván Ilých was that no one pitied him as he wished to be pitied. At certain moments after prolonged suffering he wished most of all (though he would have been ashamed to confess it) for someone to pity him as a sick child is pitied. He longed to be petted and comforted. He knew he was an important functionary, that he had a beard turning grey, and that therefore what he longed for was impossible, but still he longed for it. And in Gerásim's attitude towards him there was something akin to what he wished for, and so that attitude comforted him. Iván Ilých wanted to weep, wanted to be petted and cried over, and then his colleague Shébek would come, and instead of weeping and being petted, Iván Ilých would assume a serious, severe, and profound air, and by force of habit would express his opinion on a decision of the Court of Cassation and would stubbornly insist on that view. This falsity around him and within him did more than anything else to poison his last days.

CHAPTER VIII

IT was morning. He knew it was morning because Gerásim had gone, and Peter the footman had come and put out the candles, drawn back one of the curtains, and begun quietly to tidy up. Whether it was morning or evening, Friday or Sunday, made no difference, it was all just the same: the gnawing, unmitigated, agonizing pain, never ceasing for an instant, the consciousness of life inexorably waning but not yet extinguished, that approach of that ever dreaded and hateful Death which was the only reality, and always the same falsity. What were days, weeks, hours, in such a case?

"Will you have some tea, sir?"

"He wants things to be regular, and wishes the gentlefolk to drink tea in the morning," thought Iván Ilých, and only said "No".

"Wouldn't you like to move onto the sofa, sir?"

"He wants to tidy up the room, and I'm in the way. I am uncleanliness and disorder," he thought, and said only:

"No, leave me alone."

The man went on bustling about. Iván Ilých stretched out his hand. Peter came up, ready to help.

"What is it, sir?"

"My watch."

Peter took the watch which was close at hand and gave it to his master.

"Half-past eight. Are they up?"

"No sir, except Vladímir Ivánich" (the son) "who has gone to school. Praskóvya Fëdorovna ordered me to wake her if you asked for her. Shall I do so?"

"No, there's no need to." "Perhaps I'd better have some tea," he thought, and added aloud: "Yes, bring me some tea."

Peter went to the door but Iván Ilých dreaded being left alone. "How can I keep him here? Oh yes, my medicine." "Peter, give me my medicine."

"Why not? Perhaps it may still do me some good." He took a spoonful and swallowed it. "No, it won't help. It's all tomfoolery, all deception," he decided as soon as he became aware of the familiar, sickly, hopeless taste. "No, I can't believe in it any longer. But the pain, why this pain? If it would only cease just for a moment!" And he moaned. Peter turned towards him. "It's all right. Go and fetch me some tea."

Peter went out. Left alone Iván Ilých groaned not so much with pain, terrible though that was, as from mental anguish. Always and for ever the same, always these endless days and nights. If only it would come quicker! If only *what* would come quicker? Death, darkness? . . . No, no! Anything rather than death!

When Peter returned with the tea on a tray, Iván Ilých stared at him for a time in perplexity, not realizing who and what he was. Peter was disconcerted by that look and his embarrassment brought Iván Ilých to himself.

"Oh, tea! All right, put it down. Only help me to wash and put on a clean shirt."

And Iván Ilých began to wash. With pauses for rest, he washed his hands and then his face, cleaned his teeth, brushed his hair, and looked in the glass. He was terrified by what he saw, especially by the limp way in which his hair clung to his pallid forehead.

While his shirt was being changed he knew that he would be still more frightened at the sight of his body, so he avoided looking at it. Finally he was ready. He drew on a dressing-gown, wrapped himself in a plaid, and sat down in the armchair to take his tea. For a moment he felt refreshed, but as soon as he began to drink the tea he was again aware of the same taste, and the pain also returned. He finished it with an effort, and then lay down stretching out his legs, and dismissed Peter.

Always the same. Now a spark of hope flashes up, then a sea of despair rages, and always pain; always pain, always despair, and always the same. When alone he had a dreadful and distressing desire to call someone, but he knew beforehand that with others present it would be still worse. "Another dose of morphine—to lose consciousness. I will tell him, the doctor, that he must think of something else. It's impossible, impossible, to go on like this."

An hour and another pass like that. But now there is a ring at the door bell. Perhaps it's the doctor? It is. He comes in fresh, hearty, plump, and cheerful, with that look on his face that seems to say: "There now, you're in a panic about something, but we'll arrange it all for you directly!" The doctor knows this expression is out of place here, but he has put it on once for all and can't take it off—like a man who has put on a frock-coat in the morning to pay a round of calls.

The doctor rubs his hands vigorously and reassuringly.

"Brr! How cold it is! There's such a sharp frost; just let me warm myself!" he says, as if it were only a matter of waiting till he was warm, and then he would put everything right.

"Well now, how are you?"

Iván Ilých feels that the doctor would like to say: "Well, how are our affairs?" but that even he feels that this would not do, and says instead: "What sort of a night have you had?"

Iván Ilých looks at him as much as to say: "Are you really never ashamed of lying?" But the doctor does not wish to understand this question, and Iván Ilých says: "Just as terrible as ever. The pain never leaves me and never subsides. If only something . . ."

"Yes, you sick people are always like that. . . . There, now I think I am warm enough. Even Praskóvya Fëdorovna, who is so particular, could find no fault with my temperature. Well, now I can say good-morning," and the doctor presses his patient's hand.

Then, dropping his former playfulness, he begins with a most serious face to examine the patient, feeling his pulse and taking his temperature, and then begins the sounding and auscultation.

Iván Ilých knows quite well and definitely that all this is nonsense and pure deception, but when the doctor, getting down on his knee, leans over him, putting his ear first higher then lower, and performs various gymnastic movements over him with a significant expression on his face, Iván Ilých submits to it all as he used to submit to the speeches of the lawyers, though he knew very well that they were all lying and why they were lying.

The doctor, kneeling on the sofa, is still sounding him when Praskóvya Fëdorovna's silk dress rustles at the door and she is heard scolding Peter for not having let her know of the doctor's arrival.

She comes in, kisses her husband, and at once proceeds to prove that she has been up a long time already, and only owing to a misunderstanding failed to be there when the doctor arrived.

Iván Ilých looks at her, scans her all over, sets against her the whiteness and plumpness and cleanness of her hands and neck, the gloss of her hair, and the sparkle of her vivacious eyes. He hates her with his whole soul. And the thrill of hatred he feels for her makes him suffer from her touch.

Her attitude towards him and his disease is still the same. Just as the doctor had adopted a certain relation to his patient which he could not abandon, so had she formed one towards him—that he was not doing something he ought to do and was himself to blame, and that she reproached him lovingly for this—and she could not now change that attitude.

"You see he doesn't listen to me and doesn't take his medicine at the proper time. And above all he lies in a position that is no doubt bad for him—with his legs up."

She described how he made Gerásim hold his legs up.

The doctor smiled with a contemptuous affability that said: "What's to be done? These sick people do have foolish fancies of that kind, but we must forgive them."

When the examination was over the doctor looked at his watch, and then Praskóvya Fëdorovna announced to Iván Ilých that it was of course as he pleased, but she had sent to-day for a celebrated specialist who would examine him and have a consultation with Michael Danílovich (their regular doctor).

"Please don't raise any objections. I am doing this for my own sake," she said ironically, letting it be felt that she was doing it all for his sake and only said this to leave him no right to refuse. He remained silent, knitting his brows. He felt that he was so surrounded and involved in a mesh of falsity that it was hard to unravel anything.

Everything she did for him was entirely for her own sake, and she told him she was doing for herself what she actually was doing for herself, as if that was so incredible that he must understand the opposite.

At half-past eleven the celebrated specialist arrived. Again the sounding began and the significant conversations in his presence and in another room, about the kidneys and the appendix, and the questions and answers, with such an air of importance that again, instead of the real question of life and death which now alone confronted him, the question arose of the kidney and appendix which were not behaving as they ought to and would now be attacked by Michael Danílovich and the specialist and forced to amend their ways.

The celebrated specialist took leave of him with a serious though not hopeless look, and in reply to the timid question Iván Ilých, with eyes glistening with fear and hope, put to him as to whether there was a chance of recovery, said that he could not vouch for it but there was a possibility. The look of hope with which Iván Ilých watched the doctor out was so pathetic that Praskóvya Fëdorovna, seeing it, even wept as she left the room to hand the doctor his fee.

The gleam of hope kindled by the doctor's encouragement did not last long. The same room, the same pictures, curtains, wall-paper, medicine bottles, were all there, and the same aching suffering body, and Iván Ilých began to moan. They gave him a subcutaneous injection and he sank into oblivion.

It was twilight when he came to. They brought him his dinner and he swallowed some beef tea with difficulty, and then everything was the same again and night was coming on.

After dinner, at seven o'clock, Praskóvya Fëdorovna came into the room in evening dress, her full bosom pushed up by her corset, and with traces of powder on her face. She had reminded him in the morning that they were going to the theatre. Sarah Bernhardt was visiting the town and they had a box, which he had insisted on their taking. Now he had forgotten about it and her toilet offended him, but he concealed his vexation when he remembered that he had himself insisted on their securing a box and going because it would be an instructive and aesthetic pleasure for the children.

Praskóvya Fëdorovna came in, self-satisfied but yet with a rather guilty air. She sat down and asked how he was but, as he saw, only for the sake of asking and not in order to learn about it, knowing that there was nothing to learn—and then went on to what she really wanted to say: that she would not on any account have gone but that the box had been taken and Helen and their daughter were going, as well as Petríshchev (the examining magistrate, their daughter's fiancé) and that it was out of the question to let them go alone; but that she would have much preferred to sit with him for a while; and he must be sure to follow the doctor's orders while she was away.

"Oh, and Fëdor Petróvich" (the fiancé) "would like to come in. May he? And Lisa?"

"All right."

Their daughter came in in full evening dress, her fresh young flesh exposed (making a show of that very flesh which in his own case caused so much suffering), strong, healthy, evidently in love, and impatient with illness, suffering, and death, because they interfered with her happiness.

Fëdor Petróvich came in too, in evening dress, his hair curled à la Capoul, a tight stiff collar round his long sinewy neck, an enormous white shirt-front and narrow black trousers tightly stretched over his strong thighs. He had one white glove tightly drawn on, and was holding his opera hat in his hand.

Following him the schoolboy crept in unnoticed, in a new uniform, poor little fellow, and wearing gloves. Terribly dark shadows showed under his eyes, the meaning of which Iván Ilých knew well.

His son had always seemed pathetic to him, and now it was dreadful to see the boy's frightened look of pity. It seemed to Iván Ilých that Vásya was the only one besides Gerásim who understood and pitied him.

They all sat down and again asked how he was. A silence followed. Lisa asked her mother about the opera-glasses, and there was an altercation between mother and daughter as to who had taken them and where they had been put. This occasioned some unpleasantness.

Fëdor Petróvich inquired of Iván Ilých whether he had ever seen Sarah Bernhardt. Iván Ilých did not at first catch the question, but then replied: "No, have you seen her before?"

"Yes, in *Adrienne Lecouvreur*."[10]

Praskóvya Fëdorovna mentioned some roles in which Sarah Bernhardt was particularly good. Her daughter disagreed. Conversation sprang up as to the elegance and realism of her acting—the sort of conversation that is always repeated and is always the same.

In the midst of the conversation Fëdor Petróvich glanced at Iván Ilých and became silent. The others also looked at him and grew silent. Iván Ilých was staring with glittering eyes straight before him, evidently indignant with them. This had to be rectified, but it was impossible to do so. The silence had to be broken, but for a time no one dared to break it and they all became afraid that the conventional deception would suddenly become obvious and the truth become plain to all. Lisa was the first to pluck up courage and break that silence, but by trying to hide what everybody was feeling, she betrayed it.

"Well, if we are going it's time to start," she said, looking at her watch, a present from her father, and with a faint and significant smile at Fëdor Petró-

---

10. A play by the French dramatist Eugène Scribe (1791–1861).

vich relating to something known only to them. She got up with a rustle of her dress.

They all rose, said good-night, and went away.

When they had gone it seemed to Iván Ilých that he felt better; the falsity had gone with them. But the pain remained—that same pain and that same fear that made everything monotonously alike, nothing harder and nothing easier. Everything was worse.

Again minute followed minute and hour followed hour. Everything remained the same and there was no cessation. And the inevitable end of it all became more and more terrible.

"Yes, send Gerasim here," he replied to a question Peter asked.

CHAPTER IX

H<small>IS</small> wife returned late at night. She came in on tiptoe, but he heard her, opened his eyes, and made haste to close them again. She wished to send Gerásim away and to sit with him herself, but he opened his eyes and said: "No, go away."

"Are you in great pain?"

"Always the same."

"Take some opium."

He agreed and took some. She went away.

Till about three in the morning he was in a state of stupefied misery. It seemed to him that he and his pain were being thrust into a narrow, deep black sack, but though they were pushed further and further in they could not be pushed to the bottom. And this, terrible enough in itself, was accompanied by suffering. He was frightened yet wanted to fall through the sack, he struggled but yet co-operated. And suddenly he broke through, fell, and regained consciousness. Gerásim was sitting at the foot of the bed dozing quietly and patiently, while he himself lay with his emaciated stockinged legs resting on Gerásim's shoulders; the same shaded candle was there and the same unceasing pain.

"Go away, Gerásim," he whispered.

"It's all right, sir. I'll stay a while."

"No. Go away."

He removed his legs from Gerásim's shoulders, turned sideways onto his arm, and felt sorry for himself. He only waited till Gerásim had gone into the next room and then restrained himself no longer but wept like a child. He wept on account of his helplessness, his terrible loneliness, the cruelty of man, the cruelty of God, and the absence of God.

"Why hast Thou done all this? Why hast Thou brought me here? Why, why dost Thou torment me so terribly?"

He did not expect an answer and yet wept because there was no answer and could be none. The pain again grew more acute, but he did not stir and did not call. He said to himself: "Go on! Strike me! But what is it for? What have I done to Thee? What is it for?"

Then he grew quiet and not only ceased weeping but even held his breath and became all attention. It was as though he were listening not to an audible voice but to the voice of his soul, to the current of thoughts arising within him.

"What is it you want?" was the first clear conception capable of expression in words, that he heard.

"What do you want? What do you want?" he repeated to himself.

"What do I want? To live and not to suffer," he answered.

And again he listened with such concentrated attention that even his pain did not distract him.

"To live? How?" asked his inner voice.

"Why, to live as I used to—well and pleasantly."

"As you lived before, well and pleasantly?" the voice repeated.

And in imagination he began to recall the best moments of his pleasant life. But strange to say none of these best moments of his pleasant life now seemed at all what they had then seemed—none of them except the first recollections of childhood. There, in childhood, there had been something really pleasant with which it would be possible to live if it could return. But the child who had experienced that happiness existed no longer, it was like a reminiscence of somebody else.

As soon as the period began which had produced the present Iván Ilých, all that had then seemed joys now melted before his sight and turned into something trivial and often nasty.

And the further he departed from childhood and the nearer he came to the present the more worthless and doubtful were the joys. This began with the School of Law. A little that was really good was still found there—there was light-heartedness, friendship, and hope. But in the upper classes there had already been fewer of such good moments. Then during the first years of his official career, when he was in the service of the Governor, some pleasant moments again occurred: they were the memories of love for a woman. Then all became confused and there was still less of what was good; later on again there was still less that was good, and the further he went the less there was. His marriage, a mere accident, then the disenchantment that followed it, his wife's bad breath and the sensuality and hypocrisy: then that deadly official life and those preoccupations about money, a year of it, and two, and ten, and twenty, and always the same thing. And the longer it lasted the more deadly it became. "It is as if I had been going downhill while I imagined I was going up. And that is really what it was. I was going up in public opinion, but to the same extent life was ebbing away from me. And now it is all done and there is only death."

"Then what does it mean? Why? It can't be that life is so senseless and horrible. But if it really has been so horrible and senseless, why must I die and die in agony? There is something wrong!"

"Maybe I did not live as I ought to have done," it suddenly occurred to him. "But how could that be, when I did everything properly?" he replied, and immediately dismissed from his mind this, the sole solution of all the riddles of life and death, as something quite impossible.

"Then what do you want now? To live? Live how? Live as you lived in the law courts when the usher proclaimed "The judge is coming!" "The judge is coming, the judge!" he repeated to himself. "Here he is, the judge. But I am not guilty!" he exclaimed angrily. "What is it for?" And he ceased crying, but turning his face to the wall continued to ponder on the same question: Why, and for what purpose, is there all this horror? But however much he pondered he found no answer. And whenever the thought occurred to him, as it often did, that it all resulted from his not having lived as he ought to have done, he at once recalled the correctness of his whole life and dismissed so strange an idea.

CHAPTER X

ANOTHER fortnight passed. Iván Ilých now no longer left his sofa. He would not lie in bed but lay on the sofa, facing the wall nearly all the time. He suffered ever the same unceasing agonies and in his loneliness pondered always on the same insoluble question: "What is this? Can it be that it is Death?" And the inner voice answered: "Yes, it is Death."

"Why these sufferings?" And the voice answered, "For no reason—they just are so." Beyond and besides this there was nothing.

From the very beginning of his illness, ever since he had first been to see the doctor, Iván Ilých's life had been divided between two contrary and alternating moods: now it was despair and the expectation of this uncomprehended and terrible death, and now hope and an intently interested observation of the functioning of his organs. Now before his eyes there was only a kidney or an intestine that temporarily evaded its duty, and now only that incomprehensible and dreadful death from which it was impossible to escape.

These two states of mind had alternated from the very beginning of his illness, but the further it progressed the more doubtful and fantastic became the conception of the kidney, and the more real the sense of impending death.

He had but to call to mind what he had been three months before and what he was now, to call to mind with what regularity he had been going downhill, for every possibility of hope to be shattered.

Latterly during that loneliness in which he found himself as he lay facing the back of the sofa, a loneliness in the midst of a populous town and surrounded by numerous acquaintances and relations but that yet could not have been more complete anywhere—either at the bottom of the sea or under the earth—during that terrible loneliness Iván Ilých had lived only in memories of the past. Pictures of his past rose before him one after another. They always began with what was nearest in time and then went back to what was most remote—to his childhood—and rested there. If he thought of the stewed prunes that had been offered him that day, his mind went back to the raw shrivelled French plums of his childhood, their peculiar flavour and the flow of saliva when he sucked their stones, and along with the memory of that taste came a whole series of memories of those days: his nurse, his brother, and their toys. "No, I mustn't think of that. . . . It is too painful," Iván Ilých said to himself, and brought himself back to the present—to the button on the back of the sofa and the creases in its morocco. "Morocco is expensive, but it does not wear well: there had been a quarrel about it. It was a different kind of quarrel and a different kind of morocco that time when we tore father's portfolio and were punished, and mamma brought us some tarts. . . ." And again his thoughts dwelt on his childhood, and again it was painful and he tried to banish them and fix his mind on something else.

Then again together with that chain of memories another series passed through his mind—of how his illness had progressed and grown worse. There also the further back he looked the more life there had been. There had been more of what was good in life and more of life itself. The two merged together. "Just as the pain went on getting worse and worse so my life grew worse and worse," he thought. "There is one bright spot there at the back, at the beginning of life, and afterwards all becomes blacker and blacker and proceeds more and more rapidly—in inverse ratio to the square of the distance from death," thought Iván Ilých. And the example of a stone falling downwards with increasing velocity entered his mind. Life, a series of increasing sufferings, flies, further and further towards its end—the most terrible suffering. "I am flying. . . ." He shuddered, shifted himself, and tried to resist, but was already aware that resistance was impossible, and again with eyes weary of gazing but unable to cease seeing what was before them, he stared at the back of the sofa and waited—awaiting that dreadful fall and shock and destruction.

"Resistance is impossible!" he said to himself. "If I could only understand what it is all for! But that too is impossible. An explanation would be possible if it could be said that I have not lived as I ought to. But it is impossible to say that," and he remembered all the legality, correctitude, and propriety of his life. "That at any rate can certainly not be admitted," he thought, and his lips smiled ironically as if someone could see that smile and be taken in by it. "There is no explanation! Agony, death. . . . What for?"

CHAPTER XI

ANOTHER two weeks went by in this way and during that fortnight an event occurred that Iván Ilých and his wife had desired. Petríshchev formally proposed. It happened in the evening. The next day Praskóvya Fëdorovna came into her husband's room considering how best to inform him of it, but that very night there had been a fresh change for the worse in his condition. She found him still lying on the sofa but in a different position. He lay on his back, groaning and staring fixedly straight in front of him.

She began to remind him of his medicines, but he turned his eyes towards her with such a look that she did not finish what she was saying; so great an animosity, to her in particular, did that look express.

"For Christ's sake, let me die in peace!" he said.

She would have gone away, but just then their daughter came in and went up to say good morning. He looked at her as he had done at his wife, and in reply to her inquiry about his health said dryly that he would soon free them all of himself. They were both silent and after sitting with him for a while went away.

"Is it our fault?" Lisa said to her mother. "It's as if we were to blame! I am sorry for papa, but why should we be tortured?"

The doctor came at his usual time. Iván Ilých answered "Yes" and "No", never taking his angry eyes from him, and at last said: "You know you can do nothing for me, so leave me alone."

"We can ease your sufferings."

"You can't even do that. Let me be."

The doctor went into the drawing-room and told Praskóvya Fëdorovna that the case was very serious and that the only resource left was opium to allay her husband's sufferings, which must be terrible.

It was true, as the doctor said, that Iván Ilých's physical sufferings were terrible, but worse than the physical sufferings were his mental sufferings which were his chief torture.

His mental sufferings were due to the fact that that night, as he looked at Gerásim's sleepy, good-natured face with its prominent cheek-bones, the question suddenly occurred to him: "What if my whole life has really been wrong?"

It occurred to him that what had appeared perfectly impossible before, namely that he had not spent his life as he should have done, might after all be true. It occurred to him that his scarcely perceptible attempts to struggle against what was considered good by the most highly placed people, those scarcely noticeable impulses which he had immediately suppressed, might have been the real thing, and all the rest false. And his professional duties and the whole arrangement of his life and of his family, and all his social and official interests, might all have been false. He tried to defend all those things to himself and suddenly felt the weakness of what he was defending. There was nothing to defend.

"But if that is so," he said to himself, "and I am leaving this life with the consciousness that I have lost all that was given me and it is impossible to rectify it—what then?"

He lay on his back and began to pass his life in review in quite a new way. In the morning when he saw first his footman, then his wife, then his daughter, and then the doctor, their every word and movement confirmed to him the awful truth that had been revealed to him during the night. In them he saw himself—all that for which he had lived—and saw clearly that it was not real at all, but a terrible and huge deception which had hidden both life and death. This consciousness intensified his physical suffering tenfold. He groaned and tossed about, and pulled at his clothing which choked and stifled him. And he hated them on that account.

He was given a large dose of opium and became unconscious, but at noon his sufferings began again. He drove everybody away and tossed from side to side.

His wife came to him and said:

"Jean, my dear, do this for me. It can't do any harm and often helps. Healthy people often do it."

He opened his eyes wide.

"What? Take communion? Why? It's unnecessary! However. . . ."

She began to cry.

"Yes, do, my dear. I'll send for our priest. He is such a nice man."

"All right. Very well," he muttered.

When the priest came and heard his confession, Iván Ilých was softened and seemed to feel a relief from his doubts and consequently from his sufferings, and for a moment there came a ray of hope. He again began to think of the vermiform appendix and the possibility of correcting it. He received the sacrament with tears in his eyes.

When they laid him down again afterwards he felt a moment's ease, and the hope that he might live awoke in him again. He began to think of the operation that had been suggested to him. "To live! I want to live!" he said to himself.

His wife came in to congratulate him after his communion, and when uttering the usual conventional words she added:

"You feel better, don't you?"

Without looking at her he said "Yes".

Her dress, her figure, the expression of her face, the tone of her voice, all revealed the same thing. "This is wrong, it is not as it should be. All you have lived for and still live for is falsehood and deception, hiding life and death from you." And as soon as he admitted that thought, his hatred and his agonizing physical suffering again sprang up, and with that suffering a consciousness of the unavoidable, approaching end. And to this was added a new sensation of grinding shooting pain and a feeling of suffocation.

The expression of his face when he uttered that "yes" was dreadful. Having uttered it, he looked her straight in the eyes, turned on his face with a rapidity extraordinary in his weak state and shouted:

"Go away! Go away and leave me alone!"

CHAPTER XII

FROM that moment the screaming began that continued for three days, and was so terrible that one could not hear it through two closed doors without horror. At the moment he answered his wife he realized that he was lost, that there was no return, that the end had come, the very end, and his doubts were still unsolved and remained doubts.

"Oh! Oh! Oh!" he cried in various intonations. He had begun by screaming "I won't!" and continued screaming on the letter "o".

For three whole days, during which time did not exist for him, he struggled in that black sack into which he was being thrust by an invisible, resistless force. He struggled as a man condemned to death struggles in the hands of the executioner, knowing that he cannot save himself. And every moment he felt that despite all his efforts he was drawing nearer and nearer to what terrified him. He felt that his agony was due to his being thrust into that black hole and still more to his not being able to get right into it. He was hindered from getting into it by his conviction that his life had been a good one. That very justification of his life held him fast and prevented his moving forward, and it caused him most torment of all.

Suddenly some force struck him in the chest and side, making it still harder to breathe, and he fell through the hole and there at the bottom was a light. What had happened to him was like the sensation one sometimes experiences in a railway carriage when one thinks one is going backwards while one is really going forwards and suddenly becomes aware of the real direction.

"Yes, it was all not the right thing," he said to himself, "but that's no matter. It can be done. But what *is* the right thing?" he asked himself, and suddenly grew quiet.

This occurred at the end of the third day, two hours before his death. Just then his schoolboy son had crept softly in and gone up to the bedside. The dying man was still screaming desperately and waving his arms. His hand fell on the boy's head, and the boy caught it, pressed it to his lips, and began to cry.

At that very moment Ivān Ilých fell through and caught sight of the light, and it was revealed to him that though his life had not been what it should have been, this could still be rectified. He asked himself, "What *is* the right thing?" and grew still, listening. Then he felt that someone was kissing his hand. He opened his eyes, looked at his son, and felt sorry for him. His wife came up to him and he glanced at her. She was gazing at him open-mouthed, with undried tears on her nose and cheek and a despairing look on her face. He felt sorry for her too.

"Yes, I am making them wretched," he thought. "They are sorry, but it will be better for them when I die." He wished to say this but had not the strength to utter it. "Besides, why speak? I must act," he thought. With a look at his wife he indicated his son and said: "Take him away . . . sorry for him . . . sorry for you too. . . ." He tried to add, "forgive me," but said "forego" and waved his hand, knowing that He whose understanding mattered would understand.

And suddenly it grew clear to him that what had been oppressing him and would not leave him was all dropping away at once from two sides, from ten sides, and from all sides. He was sorry for them, he must act so as not to hurt them: release them and free himself from these sufferings. "How good and how simple!" he thought. "And the pain?" he asked himself. "What has become of it? Where are you, pain?"

He turned his attention to it.

"Yes, here it is. Well, what of it? Let the pain be."

"And death . . . where is it?"

He sought his former accustomed fear of death and did not find it. "Where is it? What death?" There was no fear because there was no death.

In place of death there was light.

"So that's what it is!" he suddenly exclaimed aloud. "What joy!"

To him all this happened in a single instant, and the meaning of that instant did not change. For those present his agony continued for another two hours. Something rattled in his throat, his emaciated body twitched, then the gasping and rattle became less and less frequent.

"It is finished!" said someone near him.

He heard these words and repeated them in his soul.

"Death is finished," he said to himself. "It is no more!"

He drew in a breath, stopped in the midst of a sigh, stretched out, and died.

Questions

1. Why does Tolstoy begin the story immediately after Ilých's death and then move back to recount his life?   2. Is there any evidence that Ilých's death is a moral judgment—that is, a punishment for his life? Explain.   3. Why is Gerásim, Ilých's peasant servant, most sympathetic to his plight?   4. At the very end, Ilých achieves peace and understanding, and the questions that have been torturing him are resolved. He realizes that "though his life had not been what it should have been, this could still be rectified." What does this mean?

An Occurrence at Owl Creek Bridge

AMBROSE BIERCE [1842–1914?]

I

Aman stood upon a railroad bridge in northern Alabama, looking down into the swift water twenty feet below. The man's hands were behind his back, the wrists bound with a cord. A rope closely encircled his neck. It was attached to a stout cross-timber above his head and the slack fell to the level of his knees. Some loose boards laid upon the sleepers supporting the metals of the railway supplied a footing for him and his executioners—two private soldiers of the Federal army, directed by a sergeant who in civil life may have been a deputy sheriff. At a short remove upon the same temporary platform was an officer in the uniform of his rank, armed. He was a captain. A sentinel at each end of the bridge stood with his rifle in the position known as "support," that is to say, vertical in front of the left shoulder, the hammer resting on the forearm thrown straight across the chest—a formal and unnatural position, enforcing an erect carriage of the body. It did not appear to be the duty of these two men to know what was occurring at the centre of the bridge; they merely blockaded the two ends of the foot planking that traversed it.

Beyond one of the sentinels nobody was in sight; the railroad ran straight away into a forest for a hundred yards, then, curving, was lost to view. Doubtless there was an outpost farther along. The other bank of the stream was open ground—a gentle acclivity topped with a stockade of vertical tree trunks, loopholed for rifles, with a single embrasure through which protruded the muzzle of a brass cannon commanding the bridge. Midway of the slope between bridge and fort were the spectators—a single company of infantry in line, at "parade rest," the butts of the rifles on the ground, the barrels inclining slightly backward against the right shoulder, the hands crossed upon the stock. A lieutenant stood at the right of the line, the point of his sword upon the ground, his left hand resting upon his right. Excepting the group of four at the centre of the bridge, not a man moved. The company faced the bridge, staring stonily, motionless. The sentinels, facing the banks of the stream, might have been statues to adorn the bridge. The captain stood with folded arms, silent, observing the work of his subordinates, but making no sign. Death is a dignitary who when he comes announced is to be received with formal manifestations of respect, even by those most familiar with him. In the code of military etiquette silence and fixity are forms of deference.

The man who was engaged in being hanged was apparently about thirty-five years of age. He was a civilian, if one might judge from his habit, which was that of a planter. His features were good—a straight nose, firm mouth, broad forehead, from which his long, dark hair was combed straight back, falling behind his ears to the collar of his well-fitting frock-coat. He wore a mustache and pointed beard, but no whiskers; his eyes were large and dark gray, and had a kindly expression which one would hardly have expected in one whose neck was in the hemp. Evidently this was no vulgar assassin. The liberal military code makes provision for hanging many kinds of persons, and gentlemen are not excluded.

The preparations being complete, the two private soldiers stepped aside and each drew away the plank upon which he had been standing. The sergeant turned to the captain, saluted and placed himself immediately behind that officer, who in turn moved apart one pace. These movements left the condemned man and the sergeant standing on the two ends of the same plank, which spanned three of the cross-ties of the bridge. The end upon which the civilian stood almost, but not quite, reached a fourth. This plank had been held in place by the weight of the captain; it was now held by that of the sergeant. At a signal from the former the latter would step aside, the plank would tilt and the condemned man go down between two ties. The arrangement commended itself to his judgment as simple and effective. His face had not been covered nor his eyes bandaged. He looked a moment at his "unsteadfast footing," then let his gaze wander to the swirling water of the stream racing madly beneath his feet. A piece of dancing driftwood caught his attention and his eyes followed it down the current. How slowly it appeared to move! What a sluggish stream!

He closed his eyes in order to fix his last thoughts upon his wife and children. The water, touched to gold by the early sun, the brooding mists under the banks at some distance down the stream, the fort, the soldiers, the piece of drift—all had distracted him. And now he became conscious of a new disturbance. Striking through the thought of his dear ones was a sound which he could neither ignore nor understand, a sharp, distinct, metallic percussion like the stroke of a blacksmith's hammer upon the anvil; it had the same ringing quality. He wondered what it was, and whether immeasurably distant or near by—it seemed both. Its recurrence was regular, but as slow as the tolling of a death knell. He awaited each stroke with impatience and—he knew not why—apprehension. The intervals of silence grew progressively longer; the delays became maddening. With their greater infrequency the sounds increased in strength and sharpness. They hurt his ear like the thrust of a knife; he feared he would shriek. What he heard was the ticking of his watch.

He unclosed his eyes and saw again the water below him. "If I could free my hands," he thought, "I might throw off the noose and spring into the stream. By diving I could evade the bullets and, swimming vigorously, reach the bank, take to the woods and get away home. My home, thank God, is as yet outside their lines; my wife and little ones are still beyond the invader's farthest advance."

As these thoughts, which have here to be set down in words, were flashed into the doomed man's brain rather than evolved from it the captain nodded to the sergeant. The sergeant stepped aside.

II

PEYTON Farquhar was a well-to-do planter, of an old and highly respected Alabama family. Being a slave owner and like other slave owners a politician he was naturally an original secessionist and ardently devoted to the Southern cause. Circumstances of an imperious nature, which it is unnecessary to relate here, had prevented him from taking service with the gallant army that had fought the disastrous campaigns ending with the fall of Corinth, and he chafed under the inglorious restraint, longing for the release of his energies, the larger life of the soldier, the opportunity for distinction. That opportunity, he felt, would come, as it comes to all in war time. Meanwhile he did what he could. No service was too humble for him to perform in aid of the South, no adventure too perilous for him to undertake if consistent with the character of a civilian who was at heart a soldier, and who in good faith and without too much qualification assented to at least a part of the frankly villainous dictum that all is fair in love and war.

One evening while Farquhar and his wife were sitting on a rustic bench near the entrance to his grounds, a gray-clad soldier rode up to the gate and asked for a drink of water. Mrs. Farquhar was only too happy to serve him with her own white hands. While she was fetching the water her husband approached the dusty horseman and inquired eagerly for news from the front.

"The Yanks are repairing the railroads," said the man, "and are getting ready for another advance. They have reached the Owl Creek bridge, put it in order and built a stockade on the north bank. The commandant has issued an order, which is posted everywhere, declaring that any civilian caught interfering with the railroad, its bridges, tunnels or trains will be summarily hanged. I saw the order."

"How far is it to the Owl Creek bridge?" Farquhar asked.

"About thirty miles."

"Is there no force on this side the creek?"

"Only a picket post half a mile out, on the railroad, and a single sentinel at this end of the bridge."

"Suppose a man—a civilian and student of hanging—should elude the picket post and perhaps get the better of the sentinel," said Farquhar, smiling, "what could he accomplish?"

The soldier reflected. "I was there a month ago," he replied. "I observed that the flood of last winter had lodged a great quantity of driftwood against the wooden pier at this end of the bridge. It is now dry and would burn like tow."

The lady had now brought the water, which the soldier drank. He thanked her ceremoniously, bowed to her husband and rode away. An hour later, after nightfall, he repassed the plantation, going northward in the direction from which he had come. He was a Federal scout.

III

As Peyton Farquhar fell straight downward through the bridge he lost consciousness and was as one already dead. From this state he was awakened—ages later, it seemed to him—by the pain of a sharp pressure upon his throat, followed by a sense of suffocation. Keen, poignant agonies seemed to shoot from his neck downward through every fibre of his body and limbs. These pains appeared to flash along well-defined lines of ramification and to beat with an inconceivably rapid periodicity. They seemed like streams of pulsating fire heating him to an intolerable temperature. As to his head, he was conscious of nothing but a feeling of fulness—of congestion. These sensations were unaccompanied by thought. The intellectual part of his nature was already effaced; he had power only to feel, and feeling was torment. He was conscious of motion. Encompassed in a luminous cloud, of which he was now merely the fiery heart, without material substance, he swung through unthinkable arcs of oscillation, like a vast pendulum. Then all at once, with terrible suddenness, the light about him shot upward with the noise of a loud plash; a frightful roaring was in his ears, and all was cold and dark. The power of thought was restored; he knew that the rope had broken and he had fallen into the stream. There was no additional strangulation; the noose about his neck was already suffocating him and kept the water from his lungs. To die of hanging at the bottom of a river!—the idea seemed to him ludicrous. He opened his eyes in the darkness and saw above him a gleam of light, but how distant, how inaccessible! He was still sinking, for the light became fainter and fainter until it was a mere glimmer. Then it began to grow and brighten, and he knew that he was rising toward the surface—knew it with reluctance, for he was now very comfortable. "To be hanged and drowned," he thought, "that is not so bad; but I do not wish to be shot. No; I will not be shot; that is not fair."

He was not conscious of an effort, but a sharp pain in his wrist apprised him that he was trying to free his hands. He gave the struggle his attention, as an idler might observe the feat of a juggler, without interest in the outcome. What splendid effort!—what magnificent, what superhuman strength! Ah, that was a fine endeavor! Bravo! The cord fell away; his arms parted and floated upward, the hands dimly seen on each side in the growing light. He watched them with a new interest as first one and then the other pounced upon the noose at his neck. They tore it away and thrust it fiercely aside, its undulations resembling those of a water-snake. "Put it back, put it back!" He thought he shouted these words to his hands, for the undoing of the noose had been succeeded by the direst pang that he had yet experienced. His neck ached horribly, his brain was on fire; his heart, which had been fluttering faintly, gave a great leap, trying to force itself out at his mouth. His whole body was racked and wrenched with an insupportable anguish! But his disobedient hands gave no heed to the command. They beat the water vigorously with quick, downward strokes, forcing him to the surface. He felt his head emerge; his eyes were blinded by the sunlight; his chest expanded convulsively, and with a supreme and crowning agony his lungs engulfed a great draught of air, which instantly he expelled in a shriek!

He was now in full possession of his physical senses. They were, indeed, preternaturally keen and alert. Something in the awful disturbance of his organic system had so exalted and refined them that they made record of things never before perceived. He felt the ripples upon his face and heard their separate sounds as they struck. He looked at the forest on the bank of the stream, saw the individual trees, the leaves and the veining of each leaf—saw the very insects upon them: the locusts, the brilliant-bodied flies, the gray spiders stretching their webs from twig to twig. He noted the prismatic colors in all the dewdrops upon a million blades of grass. The humming of the gnats that danced above the eddies of the stream, the beating of the dragon-flies' wings, the strokes of the water-spiders' legs, like oars which had lifted their boat—all these made audible music. A fish slid along beneath his eyes and he heard the rush of its body parting the water.

He had come to the surface facing down the stream; in a moment the visible world seemed to wheel slowly round, himself the pivotal point, and he saw the bridge, the fort, the soldiers upon the bridge, the captain, the sergeant, the two privates, his executioners. They were in silhouette against the blue sky. They shouted and gesticulated, pointing at him. The captain had drawn his pistol, but did not fire; the others were unarmed. Their movements were grotesque and horrible, their forms gigantic.

Suddenly he heard a sharp report and something struck the water smartly within a few inches of his head, spattering his face with spray. He heard a second report, and saw one of the sentinels with his rifle at his shoulder, a light cloud of blue smoke rising from the muzzle. The man in the water saw the eye of the man on the bridge gazing into his own through the sights of the rifle. He observed that it was a gray eye and remembered having read that gray eyes were keenest, and that all famous marksmen had them. Nevertheless, this one had missed.

A counter-swirl had caught Farquhar and turned him half round; he was again looking into the forest on the bank opposite the fort. The sound of a clear, high voice in a monotonous singsong now rang out behind him and came across the water with a distinctness that pierced and subdued all other sounds, even the beating of the ripples in his ears. Although no soldier, he had frequented camps enough to know the dread significance of that deliberate, drawling, aspirated chant; the lieutenant on shore was taking a part in the morning's work. How coldly and pitilessly—with what an even, calm intonation, presaging, and enforcing tranquillity in the men—with what accurately measured intervals fell those cruel words:

"Attention, company! . . . Shoulder arms! . . . Ready! . . . Aim! . . . Fire!"

Farquhar dived—dived as deeply as he could. The water roared in his ears like the voice of Niagara, yet he heard the dulled thunder of the volley and, rising again toward the surface, met shining bits of metal, singularly flattened, oscillating slowly downward. Some of them touched him on the face and hands, then fell away, continuing their descent. One lodged between his collar and neck; it was uncomfortably warm and he snatched it out.

As he rose to the surface, gasping for breath, he saw that he had been a long time under water; he was perceptibly farther down stream—nearer to safety. The soldiers had almost finished reloading; the metal ramrods flashed all at once in the sunshine as they were drawn from the barrels, turned in the air, and thrust into their sockets. The two sentinels fired again, independently and ineffectually.

The hunted man saw all this over his shoulder; he was now swimming vigorously with the current. His brain was as energetic as his arms and legs; he thought with the rapidity of lightning.

"The officer," he reasoned, "will not make that martinet's error a second time. It is as easy to dodge a volley as a single shot. He has probably already given the command to fire at will. God help me, I cannot dodge them all!"

An appalling plash within two yards of him was followed by a loud, rushing sound, *diminuendo,* which seemed to travel back through the air to the fort and died in an explosion which stirred the very river to its deeps! A rising sheet of water curved over him, fell down upon him, blinded him, strangled him! The cannon had taken a hand in the game. As he shook his head free from the commotion of the smitten water he heard the deflected shot humming through the air ahead, and in an instant it was cracking and smashing the branches in the forest beyond.

"They will not do that again," he thought; "the next time they will use a charge of grape. I must keep my eye upon the gun; the smoke will apprise me—the report arrives too late; it lags behind the missile. That is a good gun."

Suddenly he felt himself whirled round and round—spinning like a top. The water, the banks, the forests, the now distant bridge, fort and men—all were commingled and blurred. Objects were represented by their colors only; circular horizontal streaks of color—that was all he saw. He had been caught in a vortex and was being whirled on with a velocity of advance and gyration that made him giddy and sick. In a few moments he was flung upon the gravel at the foot of the left bank of the stream—the southern bank—and behind a projecting point which concealed him from his enemies. The sudden arrest of his motion, the abrasion of one of his hands on the gravel, restored him, and he wept with delight. He dug his fingers into the sand, threw it over himself in handfuls and audibly blessed it. It looked like diamonds, rubies, emeralds; he could think of nothing beautiful which it did not resemble. The trees upon the bank were giant garden plants; he noted a definite order in their arrangement, inhaled the fragrance of their blooms. A strange, roseate light shone through the spaces among their trunks and the wind made in their branches the music of aeolian harps. He had no wish to perfect his escape—was content to remain in that enchanting spot until retaken.

A whiz and rattle of grapeshot among the branches high above his head roused him from his dream. The baffled cannoneer had fired him a random farewell. He sprang to his feet, rushed up the sloping bank, and plunged into the forest.

All that day he traveled, laying his course by the rounding sun. The forest seemed interminable; nowhere did he discover a break in it, not even a woodman's road. He had not known that he lived in so wild a region. There was something uncanny in the revelation.

By night fall he was fatigued, footsore, famishing. The thought of his wife and children urged him on. At last he found a road which led him in what he knew to be the right direction. It was as wide and straight as a city street, yet it seemed untraveled. No fields bordered it, no dwelling anywhere. Not so much as the barking of a dog suggested human habitation. The black bodies of the trees formed a straight wall on both sides, terminating on the horizon in a point, like a diagram in a lesson in perspective. Overhead, as he looked up through this rift in the wood, shone great golden stars looking unfamiliar and grouped in strange constellations. He was sure they were arranged in some order which had a secret and malign significance. The wood on either side was full of singular noises, among which—once, twice, and again, he distinctly heard whispers in an unknown tongue.

His neck was in pain and lifting his hand to it he found it horribly swollen. He knew that it had a circle of black where the rope had bruised it. His eyes felt congested; he could no longer close them. His tongue was swollen with thirst; he relieved its fever by thrusting it forward from between his teeth into the cold air. How softly the turf had carpeted the untraveled avenue—he could no longer feel the roadway beneath his feet!

Doubtless, despite his suffering, he had fallen asleep while walking, for now he sees another scene—perhaps he has merely recovered from a delirium. He stands at the gate of his own home. All is as he left it, and all bright and beautiful in the morning sunshine. He must have traveled the entire night. As he pushes open the gate and passes up the wide white walk, he sees a flutter of female garments; his wife, looking fresh and cool and sweet, steps down from the veranda to meet him. At the bottom of the steps she stands waiting, with a smile of ineffable joy, an attitude of matchless grace and dignity. Ah, how beautiful she is! He springs forward with extended arms. As he is about to clasp her he feels a stunning blow upon the back of the neck; a blinding white light blazes all about him with a sound like the shock of a cannon—then all is darkness and silence!

Peyton Farquhar was dead; his body, with a broken neck, swung gently from side to side beneath the timbers of the Owl Creek bridge.

Two Friends

GUY DE MAUPASSANT [1850-1893]

Paris was blockaded,—famished,—at her last gasp. The sparrows were becoming very rare upon the roofs, and the sewers were losing their population of rats. People ate anything they could get.

As he was trudging sadly along the exterior boulevard, one fine January morning, with his stomach empty,—his hands thrust into the pockets of his uniform trousers, M. Morissot, watchmaker by trade, stopped short in face of a man whom he recognized as a friend. It was M. Sauvage, whose acquaintance he had made while angling.

Before the war, every Sunday at dawn, M. Morissot used to start out with a bamboo fishing-rod in his hand, and a tin box strapped to his back. He would take the Argenteuil train, get out at Colombes, and walk to l'Ile Marante. On reaching this scene of his dreams he would at once begin fishing, and would keep on fishing until nightfall.

Every Sunday also he used to meet there a little pursy, jolly man,—M. Sauvage,—dry goods dealer in the Rue Notre Dame de Lorette,—another fanatical angler. They would often sit there a whole half-day, side by side,—line in hand and feet dangling over the current; and they had conceived a great friendship for one another.

Some days they did not talk. Occasionally they might drop a word or two; but they understood each other admirably well, without saying anything,—having similar tastes and identical ideas.

Of a spring morning, about ten o'clock, when the rejuvenated sun would be creating that light mist which flows away with the water, and would be pouring down on the backs of the two enthusiastic fishers the pleasant warmth of the new season—then would Morissot sometimes say to his neighbour "Hey!—this is fine, isn't it?" And M. Sauvage would answer: "Don't know of anything finer!" And that sufficed them for comprehending and esteeming each other.

Toward the end of an autumn day, when the sky, all ensanguined by sunset, would be flinging upon the water shapes of scarlet cloud,—would be purpling the whole river, setting fire to the heavens, reddening the faces of the two friends, and gilding the already fading foliage, as it trembled with the first shivers of winter,—then M. Morissot would look at M. Sauvage with a smile and say: "What a sight!" And M. Sauvage, delighted, would answer, without taking his eyes off his float: "This is better than the boulevard,—eh?"

*   *   *

The moment they recognized each other, they shook hands energetically,—quite affected to find themselves together under such a changed condition of affairs. M. Sauvage murmured with a sigh:

"Here's a nice state of things!" Morissot, very gloomy, groaned out: "And such weather!—to-day is the first fine day of the year."

The sky was, in fact, quite blue, and full of light.

They began to walk along, side by side, sad and dreamy. Morissot spoke again: "And that fishing,—eh?—what a fine time we had then!"

M. Sauvage asked:

"When shall we ever have such another?"

They entered a little café, and took an absinthe together: they then went out to walk about the boulevards again.

Morissot suddenly stopped: "Let's take another—eh?" M. Sauvage consented:—"Just as you like." And they went into another drinking-resort.

They felt quite dizzy when they came out, and trembled, as people do who have swallowed plenty of alcohol upon an empty stomach. It was pleasant outside. A mild breeze caressed their faces.

M. Sauvage, made quite tipsy by the warm air, stopped and said:

"Suppose we go, anyhow?"

"Go where?"

"Why, to fish, of course."

"But where?"

"Why, to our old place—the island. The French outposts are at Colombes. I know Colonel Dumoulin; he'll pass us through all right."

Morissot trembled with desire. "Good!" he cried:—"I'll go!" And they went off to get their fishing-tackle.

An hour later they were walking along the high-road, side by side. Then they reached the villa where the Colonel was. He smiled at their whim, and gave his consent at once. They walked on, provided with a written permit.

In a short time they passed beyond the outposts, traversed deserted Colombes, and found themselves at the edge of the little vineyards which slope down to the Seine. It was about eleven o'clock.

The village of Argenteuil in front of them seemed dead. The heights of Orgemont and Sannois dominated the landscape. The great plain which reaches to Nanterre was empty—perfectly bare,—with its naked cherry-trees and gray fields.

M. Sauvage, pointing to the heights, said: "The Prussians are there!" And a sense of uneasiness almost paralyzed the two friends as they gazed upon the deserted country.

"The Prussians!" They had never seen them; but they *felt them* there, as they had felt their presence for two long months around Paris,—ruining France, pillaging, massacring, starving-out the people,—invisible and omnipotent enemies. And a sort of superstitious terror blended itself with their hatred of those unknown and victorious people.

Morissot stammered:—"Say! . . . suppose, suppose we'd meet some of them?"

M. Sauvage replied, with that peculiar Parisian *gouaillerie*,—that spirit of jest which will crop out under any possible circumstances:

"Why, we'd just offer them some nice broiled fish."

Nevertheless they hesitated to go further on—feeling intimidated by the silence of the whole horizon.

At last M. Sauvage decided:—"Come, let us go—but prudently." And they descended a vineyard slope, bending down, crouching on all fours, taking advantage of every bush to screen themselves as they advanced, straining their ears, and looking anxiously around.

A narrow strip of bare land remained to cross in order to reach the river bank. They started at a run, and as soon as they got to the shore, they crouched down among the reeds.

Morissot put his ear to the ground in order to find out if somebody was not walking about in the neighbourhood. He could not hear anything. They were all alone,—quite by themselves.

They took courage and began to fish.

*   *   *

In front of them l'Ile Marante, now deserted, concealed them from observation from the further bank. The little restaurant was closed,—looked as if it had been closed for years and years.

M. Sauvage caught the first gudgeon;—M. Morissot the second; and then, moment by moment, they kept on lifting their lines, each time with some little silver creature quivering at the end of them—a really marvelous catch.

They carefully dropped the fish into a fishing-bag of strong close network, which lay in the shallow water at their feet. And a delicious joy penetrated them—such a joy as you feel on once more obtaining some loved pleasure of which you had been long deprived.

The kind sun poured down his warmth between their shoulders; they ceased to hear anything; they thought of nothing more; they ignored the rest of the world;—they simply fished!

But suddenly a deep sound that seemed to rise out of the ground made everything shake. The cannon were at work again.

Morissot turned his head, and above the slope he saw, high on the right, the great silhouette of Mont Valerien, bearing on its brow a white plume,—a puff of powder-smoke.

And immediately a second jet of smoke puffed out from the summit of the fortress;—a few seconds later, the detonation came to their ears.

Then other reports followed; and from time to time the mountain exhaled its breath of destruction, blew forth milky vapors, which rose in the clear sky to hang as a cloud above it.

M. Sauvage shrugged his shoulders:

"There they go!" he said.

Morissot, who was watching the feather on his float dipping again and again, was suddenly seized with the wrath that a peaceful man feels, against the people who were fighting thus; and he muttered between his teeth:

"What idiots!—to be killing one another like that!"

M. Sauvage answered:

"Worse than brutes."

And Morissot, who had just hooked a whitebait, exclaimed: "Just to think it will always be like that as long as there are governments!"

M. Sauvage interrupted him:

"The Republic would not have declared war—"

M. Morissot interrupted in his turn: "With kings there is foreign war; with a Republic, civil war."

And very calmly they proceeded to discuss politics,—unraveling great problems with the healthy reasoning of gentle and plainly educated men,—both agreeing on one point, that humanity would never be free. And Mont Valerien thundered on without a pause,—demolishing French houses with solid shot, braying out lives, crushing beings—putting an end to many dreams, many anticipated joys, many a hope of bliss;—opening in the hearts of wives and in the hearts of daughters, and in the hearts of mothers, dwelling far away in other lands, wounds that would never heal.

"Such is life!" declared M. Sauvage.

"Better say, such is death!" responded Morissot with a laugh.

But they suddenly started in terror,—feeling that somebody was walking behind them; and, turning round to look, they saw, right at their backs, four men,—four tall bearded men, armed, dressed like livery servants, and wearing flat caps, who were covering them with rifles.

The two fishing-lines slipped from their hands, and went floating down the river.

In an instant the two Parisians were seized, tied, dragged away, pitched into a boat, and taken to the island beyond.

And behind the house which they had imagined deserted, they saw a company of some twenty German soldiers.

A sort of hairy giant, who, seated a-straddle of a chair, was smoking a big porcelain pipe, asked them, in excellent French:

"Well, gentlemen, was the fishing good?"

Then a soldier threw down at the officer's feet the net-full of fish, which he had taken good care to bring along. The Prussian smiled: "Well, well!—I see you had pretty good luck. . . . But we have something else to talk about now. Listen to me, and don't feel uneasy.

"In my opinion, you are simply two spies sent to watch me. I take you, therefore, and have you shot at once. You were pretending to fish, just so as to conceal your real designs. You have fallen now into my hands. So much the worse for you;—war is war!

"But as you must have passed the outposts, you must also certainly have a password in order to get back. Give me that password, and I shall let you go!"

The two friends, standing side by side, with faces livid, and hands quivering a little from nervous excitement, answered not a word.

The officer resumed: "No one shall ever know; you can return home quietly. The secret will disappear with you. If you refuse, it's death—and that immediately. Choose!"

They remained motionless, without uttering a syllable.

The Prussian, always perfectly cool, pointed to the river, and continued:

"Think of it!—in five minutes you will be at the bottom of that water. In five minutes! You must have relatives."

And still Mont Valerien uttered its thunder.

The two fishers remained silent. The German gave orders in his own language. Then he moved his chair back, so as not to be too close to the prisoners; and twelve men took their places in line twenty paces off, with rifles at attention.

The officer spoke again.

"I give you one minute—not a second more."

Then he rose up suddenly, approached Morissot, led him away by the arm to a short distance, and said to him in a whisper: "Quick! tell me that password. You comrade will know nothing about it. I'll just pretend to have changed my mind, to take pity on you."

Morissot made no reply.

The Prussian led M. Sauvage away, and put the same question to him.

M. Sauvage made no reply.

The two friends found themselves side by side once more.

And the officer gave the word of command;—the soldiers brought up their rifles to a present.

Then the eyes of Morissot fell upon the net full of fish, lying there in the grass, a few steps away from him.

A beam of sunlight made the heap of fish glimmer, as they still quivered. And he felt weak for the first time. In spite of all his efforts, the tears rose to his eyes.

He stammered out:

"Goodby, M. Sauvage."

M. Sauvage replied:

"Goodby, M. Morissot."

They shook hands, shaking from head to foot with a trembling they could not master.

The officer gave the word,—"Fire!"

The twelve shots made only one report.

M. Sauvage fell all of a heap on his nose. Morissot, a taller man, swayed, twirled, and fell back across his comrade, with his face to the sky,—while thick gushes of blood escaped from his vest,—all burst in at the breast.

Again the German gave some orders.

His men scattered, and came back with ropes and some big stones, which they fastened to the feet of the two dead men. Then they carried them to the river-bank.

Mont Valerien still roared,—now coiffed with a mountain of smoke.

Two soldiers took Morissot by the head and by the legs;—two others lifted Sauvage in the same way. The corpses, strongly swung a moment, were flung far out in a curve, and fell, feet foremost, into the river,—the weight of the stones dragging down the feet first.

The water splashed, bubbled, quivered;—then calmed down, while two little waves broke against the shore.

A little blood floated away.

The officer, always serene, muttered: "The fishes' turn now!"

Then he walked back to the house.

And suddenly he perceived the net full of gudgeons in the grass. He lifted it, looked at it, smiled, and called out:

"Wilhelm!"

A soldier, wearing a white apron, ran out.

And the Prussian, flinging to him the catch of the two dead men, ordered:

"Cook for me these little things right off—fry them while they are still alive. They will make a delicious dish."

Then he resumed his pipe.

The Jilting of Granny Weatherall

KATHERINE ANNE PORTER [b. 1890]

SHE flicked her wrist neatly out of Doctor Harry's pudgy careful fingers and pulled the sheet up to her chin. The brat ought to be in knee breeches. Doctoring around the country with spectacles on his nose! "Get along now, take your schoolbooks and go. There's nothing wrong with me."

Doctor Harry spread a warm paw like a cushion on her forehead where the forked green vein danced and made her eyelids twitch. "Now, now, be a good girl, and we'll have you up in no time."

"That's no way to speak to a woman nearly eighty years old just because she's down. I'd have you respect your elders, young man."

"Well, Missy, excuse me." Doctor Harry patted her cheek. "But I've got to warn you, haven't I? You're a marvel, but you must be careful or you're going to be good and sorry."

"Don't tell me what I'm going to be. I'm on my feet now, morally speaking. It's Cornelia. I had to go to bed to get rid of her."

Her bones felt loose, and floated around in her skin, and Doctor Harry floated like a balloon around the foot of the bed. He floated and pulled down his waistcoat and swung his glasses on a cord. "Well, stay where you are, it certainly can't hurt you."

"Get along and doctor your sick," said Granny Weatherall. "Leave a well woman alone. I'll call for you when I want you. . . . Where were you forty years ago when I pulled through milk-leg and double pneumonia? You weren't even born. Don't let Cornelia lead you on," she shouted, because Doctor Harry appeared to float up to the ceiling and out. "I pay my own bills, and I don't throw my money away on nonsense!"

She meant to wave good-by, but it was too much trouble. Her eyes closed of themselves, it was like a dark curtain drawn around the bed. The pillow rose and floated under her, pleasant as a hammock in a light wind. She listened to the leaves rustling outside the window. No, somebody was swishing newspapers: no, Cornelia and Doctor Harry were whispering together. She leaped broad awake, thinking they whispered in her ear.

"She was never like this, *never* like this!" "Well, what can we expect?" "Yes, eighty years old. . . ."

Well, and what if she was? She still had ears. It was like Cornelia to whisper around doors. She always kept things secret in such a public way. She was always being tactful and kind. Cornelia was dutiful; that was the trouble with her. Dutiful and good: "So good and dutiful," said Granny, "that I'd like to spank her." She saw herself spanking Cornelia and making a fine job of it.

"What'd you say, Mother?"

Granny felt her face tying up in hard knots.

"Can't a body think, I'd like to know?"

"I thought you might want something."

"I do. I want a lot of things. First off, go away and don't whisper."

She lay and drowsed, hoping in her sleep that the children would keep out and let her rest a minute. It had been a long day. Not that she was tired. It was always pleasant to snatch a minute now and then. There was always so much to be done, let me see: tomorrow.

Tomorrow was far away and there was nothing to trouble about. Things were finished somehow when the time came; thank God there was always a little margin over for peace: then a person could spread out the plan of life and tuck in the edges orderly. It was good to have everything clean and folded away, with the hair brushes and tonic bottles sitting straight on the white embroidered linen: the day started without fuss and the pantry shelves laid out with rows of jelly glasses and brown jugs and white stone-china jars with blue whirligigs and words painted on them: coffee, tea, sugar, ginger, cinnamon, allspice: and the bronze clock with the lion on top nicely dusted off. The dust that lion could collect in twenty-four hours! The box in the attic with all those letters tied up, well she'd have to go through that tomorrow. All those letters—George's letters and John's letters and her letters to them both—lying around for the children to find afterwards made her uneasy. Yes, that would be tomorrow's business. No use to let them know how silly she had been once.

While she was rummaging around she found death in her mind and it felt clammy and unfamiliar. She had spent so much time preparing for death there was no need for bringing it up again. Let it take care of itself now. When she was sixty she had felt very old, finished, and went around making farewell trips to see her children and grandchildren, with a secret in her mind: This is the very last of your mother, children! Then she made her will and came down with a long fever. That was all just a notion like a lot of other things, but it was lucky too, for she had once for all got over the idea of dying for a long time. Now she couldn't be worried. She hoped she had better sense now. Her father had lived to be one hundred and two years old and had drunk a noggin of strong hot toddy on his last birthday. He told the reporters it was his daily habit, and he owed his long life to that. He had made quite a scandal and was very pleased about it. She believed she'd just plague Cornelia a little.

"Cornelia! Cornelia!" No footsteps, but a sudden hand on her cheek. "Bless you, where have you been?"

"Here, mother."

"Well, Cornelia, I want a noggin of hot toddy."

"Are you cold, darling?"

"I'm chilly, Cornelia. Lying in bed stops the circulation. I must have told you that a thousand times."

Well, she could just hear Cornelia telling her husband that Mother was getting childish and they'd have to humor her. The thing that most annoyed her was that Cornelia thought she was deaf, dumb, and blind. Little hasty glances and tiny gestures tossed around her and over her head saying. "Don't cross her, let her have her way, she's eighty years old," and she sitting there as if she lived in a thin glass cage. Sometimes Granny almost made up her mind to pack up and move back to her own house where nobody could remind her every minute that she was old. Wait, wait, Cornelia, till your own children whisper behind your back!

In her day she had kept a better house and had got more work done. She wasn't too old yet for Lydia to be driving eighty miles for advice when one of the children jumped the track, and Jimmy still dropped in and talked things over: "Now, Mammy, you've a good business head, I want to know what you think of this? . . ." Old Cornelia couldn't change the furniture around without asking. Little things, little things! They had been so sweet when they were little. Granny wished the old days were back again with the children young and everything to be done over. It had been a hard pull, but not too much for her. When she thought of all the food she had cooked, and all the clothes she had cut and sewed, and all the gardens she had made—well, the children showed it. There they were, made out of her, and they couldn't get away from that. Sometimes she wanted to see John again and point to them and say, Well, I didn't do so badly, did I? But that would have to wait. That was for tomorrow. She used to think of him as a man, but now all the children were older than their father, and he would be a child beside her if she saw him now. It seemed strange and there was something wrong in the idea. Why, he couldn't possibly recognize her. She had fenced in a hundred acres once, digging the post holes herself and clamping the wires with just a negro boy to help. That changed a woman. John would be looking for a young woman with the peaked Spanish comb in her hair and the painted fan. Digging post holes changed a woman. Riding country roads in the winter when women had their babies was another thing: sitting up nights with sick horses and sick negroes and sick children and hardly ever losing one. John, I hardly ever lost one of them! John would see that in a minute, that would be something he could understand, she wouldn't have to explain anything!

It made her feel like rolling up her sleeves and putting the whole place to rights again. No matter if Cornelia was determined to be everywhere at once, there were a great many things left undone on this place. She would start tomorrow and do them. It was good to be strong enough for everything, even if all you made melted and changed and slipped under your hands, so that by the time you finished you almost forgot what you were working for. What was it I set out to do? she asked herself intently, but she could not remember. A fog rose over the valley, she saw it marching across the creek swallowing the trees and moving up the hill like an army of ghosts. Soon it would be at the near edge of the orchard, and then it was time to go in and light the lamps. Come in, children, don't stay out in the night air.

Lighting the lamps had been beautiful. The children huddled up to her and breathed like little calves waiting at the bars in the twilight. Their eyes followed the match and watched the flame rise and settle in a blue curve, then they moved away from her. The lamp was lit, they didn't have to be scared and hang on to mother any more. Never, never, never more. God, for all my life I thank Thee. Without Thee, my God, I could never have done it. Hail, Mary, full of grace.

I want you to pick all the fruit this year and see that nothing is wasted. There's always someone who can use it. Don't let good things rot for want of using. You waste life when you waste good food. Don't let things get lost. It's bitter to lose things. Now, don't let me get to thinking, not when I am tired and taking a little nap before supper. . . .

The pillow rose about her shoulders and pressed against her heart and the memory was being squeezed out of it: oh, push down the pillow, somebody: it would smother her if she tried to hold it. Such a fresh breeze blowing and such a green day with no threats in it. But he had not come, just the same. What does a woman do when she has put on the white veil and set out the white cake for a man and he doesn't come? She tried to remember. No, I swear he never harmed me but in that. He never harmed me but in that . . . and what if he did? There was the day, the day, but a whirl of dark smoke rose and covered it, crept up and over into the bright field where everything was planted so carefully in orderly rows. That was hell, she knew hell when she saw it. For sixty years she had prayed against remembering him and against losing her soul in the deep pit of hell, and now the two things were mingled in one and the thought of him was a smoky cloud from hell that moved and crept in her head when she had just got rid of Doctor Harry and was trying to rest a minute. Wounded vanity, Ellen, said a sharp voice in the top of her mind. Don't let your wounded vanity get the upper hand of you. Plenty of girls get jilted. You were jilted, weren't you? Then stand up to it. Her eyelids wavered and let in streamers of blue-gray light like tissue paper over her eyes. She must get up and pull the shades down or she'd never sleep. She was in bed again and the shades were not down. How could that happen? Better turn over, hide from the light, sleeping in the light gave you nightmares. "Mother, how do you feel now?" and a stinging wetness on her forehead. But I don't like having my face washed in cold water!

Hapsy? George? Lydia? Jimmy? No, Cornelia, and her features were swollen and full of little puddles. "They're coming, darling, they'll all be here soon." Go wash your face, child, you look funny.

Instead of obeying, Cornelia knelt down and put her head on the pillow. She seemed to be talking but there was no sound. "Well, are you tongue-tied? Whose birthday is it? Are you going to give a party?"

Cornelia's mouth moved urgently in strange shapes. "Don't do that, you bother me, daughter."

"Oh, no, Mother, Oh, no. . . ."

Nonsense. It was strange about children. They disputed your every word. "No what, Cornelia?"

"Here's Doctor Harry."

"I won't see that boy again. He just left five minutes ago."

"That was this morning, Mother. It's night now. Here's the nurse."

"This is Doctor Harry, Mrs. Weatherall. I never saw you look so young and happy!"

"Ah, I'll never be young again—but I'd be happy if they'd let me lie in peace and get rested."

She thought she spoke up loudly, but no one answered. A warm weight on her forehead, a warm bracelet on her wrist, and a breeze went on whispering, trying to tell her something. A shuffle of leaves in the everlasting hand of God. He blew on them and they danced and rattled. "Mother, don't mind, we're going to give you a little hypodermic." "Look here, daughter, how do ants get in this bed? I saw sugar ants yesterday." Did you send for Hapsy too?

It was Hapsy she really wanted. She had to go a long way back through a great many rooms to find Hapsy standing with a baby on her arm. She seemed to herself to be Hapsy also, and the baby on Hapsy's arm was Hapsy and himself and herself, all at once, and there was no surprise in the meeting. Then Hapsy melted from within and turned flimsy as gray gauze and the baby was a gauzy shadow, and Hapsy came up close and said, "I thought you'd never come," and looked at her very searchingly and said, "You haven't changed a bit!" They leaned forward to kiss, when Cornelia began whispering from a long way off, "Oh, is there anything you want to tell me? Is there anything I can do for you?"

Yes, she had changed her mind after sixty years and she would like to see George. I want you to find George. Find him and be sure to tell him I forgot him. I want him to know I had my husband just the same and my children and my house like any other woman. A good house too and a good husband that I loved and fine children out of him. Better than I hoped for even. Tell him I was given back everything he took away and more. Oh, no, oh, God, no, there was something else besides the house and the man and the children. Oh, surely they were not all? What was it? Something not given back. . . . Her breath crowded down under her ribs and grew into a monstrous frightening shape with cutting edges; it bored up into her head, and the agony was unbelievable: Yes, John, get the doctor now, no more talk, my time has come.

When this one was born it should be the last. The last. It should have been born first, for it was the one she had truly wanted. Everything came in good time. Nothing left out, left over. She was strong, in three days she would be as well as ever. Better. A woman needed milk in her to have her full health.

"Mother, do you hear me?"

"I've been telling you—"

"Mother, Father Connolly's here."

"I went to Holy Communion only last week. Tell him I'm not so sinful as all that."

"Father just wants to speak to you."

He could speak as much as he pleased. It was like him to drop in and inquire about her soul as if it were a teething baby, and then stay on for a cup of tea and a round of cards and gossip. He always had a funny story of some sort, usually about an Irishman who made his little mistakes and confessed them, and the point lay in some absurd thing he would blurt out in the confessional showing his struggles between native piety and original sin. Granny felt easy about her soul. Cornelia, where are your manners? Give Father Connolly a chair. She had her secret comfortable understanding with a few favorite saints who cleared a straight road to God for her. All as surely signed and sealed as the papers for the new Forty Acres. Forever . . . heirs and assigns forever. Since the day the wedding cake was not cut, but thrown out and wasted. The whole bottom dropped out of the world, and there she was blind and sweating with nothing under her feet and the walls falling away. His hand had caught her under the breast, she had not fallen, there was the freshly polished floor with the green rug on it, just as before. He had cursed like a sailor's parrot and said, "I'll kill him for you." Don't lay a hand on him, for my sake leave something to God. "Now, Ellen, you must believe what I tell you. . . ."

So there was nothing, nothing to worry about any more, except sometimes in the night one of the children screamed in a nightmare, and they both hustled out shaking and hunting for the matches and calling, "There, wait a minute, here we are!" John, get the doctor now, Hapsy's time has come. But there was Hapsy standing by the bed in a white cap. "Cornelia, tell Hapsy to take off her cap. I can't see her plain."

Her eyes opened very wide and the room stood out like a picture she had seen somewhere. Dark colors with the shadows rising towards the ceiling in long angles. The tall black dresser gleamed with nothing on it but John's picture, enlarged from a little one, with John's eyes very black when they should have been blue. You never saw him, so how do you know how he looked? But the man insisted the copy was perfect, it was very rich and handsome. For a picture, yes, but it's not my husband. The table by the bed had a linen cover and a candle and a crucifix. The light was blue from Cornelia's silk lampshades. No sort of light at all, just frippery. You had to live forty years with kerosene lamps to appreciate honest electricity. She felt very strong and she saw Doctor Harry with a rosy nimbus around him.

"You look like a saint, Doctor Harry, and I vow that's as near as you'll ever come to it."

"She's saying something."

"I heard you, Cornelia. What's all this carrying-on?"

"Father Connolly's saying—"

Cornelia's voice staggered and bumped like a cart in a bad road. It rounded corners and turned back again and arrived nowhere. Granny stepped up in the cart very lightly and reached for the reins, but a man sat beside her and she knew him by his hands, driving the cart. She did not look in his face, for she knew without seeing, but looked instead down the road where the trees leaned over and bowed to each other and a thousand birds were singing a Mass. She felt like singing too, but she put her hand in the bosom of her dress and pulled out a rosary, and Father Connolly murmured Latin in a very solemn voice and tickled her feet. My God, will you stop that nonsense? I'm a married woman. What if he did run away and leave me to face the priest by myself? I found another a whole world better. I wouldn't have exchanged my husband for anybody except St. Michael himself, and you may tell him that for me with a thank you in the bargain.

Light flashed on her closed eyelids, and a deep roaring shook her. Cornelia, is that lightning? I hear thunder. There's going to be a storm. Close all the windows. Call the children in. . . . "Mother, here we are, all of us." "Is that you, Hapsy?" "Oh, no, I'm Lydia. We drove as fast as we could." Their faces drifted above her, drifted away. The rosary fell out of her hands and Lydia put it back. Jimmy tried to help, their hands fumbled together, and Granny closed two fingers around Jimmy's thumb. Beads wouldn't do, it must be something alive. She was so amazed her thoughts ran round and round. So, my dear Lord, this is my death and I wasn't even thinking about it. My children have come to see me die. But I can't, it's not time. Oh, I always hated surprises. I wanted to give Cornelia the amethyst set—Cornelia, you're to have the amethyst set, but Hapsy's to wear it when she wants, and, Doctor Harry, do shut up. Nobody sent for you. Oh, my dear Lord, do wait a minute. I meant to do something about the Forty Acres, Jimmy doesn't need it and Lydia will later on, with that worthless husband of hers. I meant to finish the altar cloth and send six bottles of wine to Sister Borgia for her dyspepsia. I want to send six bottles of wine to Sister Borgia, Father Connolly, now don't let me forget.

Cornelia's voice made short turns and tilted over and crashed. "Oh, Mother, oh, Mother, oh, Mother. . . ."

"I'm not going, Cornelia. I'm taken by surprise. I can't go."

You'll see Hapsy again. What about her? "I thought you'd never come." Granny made a long journey outward, looking for Hapsy. What if I don't find her? What then? Her heart sank down and down, there was no bottom to death, she couldn't come to the end of it. The blue light from Cornelia's lampshade drew into a tiny point in the center of her brain, it flickered and winked like an eye, quietly it fluttered and dwindled. Granny lay curled down within herself, amazed and watchful, staring at the point of light that was herself; her body was now only a deeper mass of shadow in an endless darkness and this darkness would curl around the light and swallow it up. God, give a sign!

For the second time there was no sign. Again no bridegroom and the priest in the house. She could not remember any other sorrow because this grief wiped them all away. Oh, no, there's nothing more cruel than this—I'll never forgive it. She stretched herself with a deep breath and blew out the light.

Questions

1. Characterize Granny. What facts do we know about her life? 2. Why, after sixty full years, does the jilting by George loom so large in Granny's mind? Are we to accept her own strong statements that the pain of the jilting was more than compensated for by the happiness she ultimately found with her husband John, her children, and her grandchildren? Explain. 3. Why does the author not present us with Granny's final thoughts in an orderly and sequential pattern? 4. Granny is revealed to us not only through her direct thoughts but also through the many images that float through her mind—the "fog" (p. 758), the blowing breeze (pp. 759 and 760), "a whirl of dark smoke" (p. 759), and others. What do these images reveal about Granny? 5. The final paragraph echoes Christ's parable of the bridegroom (Matthew 25:1–13). Why does Granny connect this final, deep religious grief with the grief she felt when George jilted her?

Idiots First

BERNARD MALAMUD [b. 1914]

THE thick ticking of the tin clock stopped. Mendel, dozing in the dark, awoke in fright. The pain returned as he listened. He drew on his cold embittered clothing, and wasted minutes sitting at the edge of the bed.

"Isaac," he ultimately sighed.

In the kitchen, Isaac, his astonished mouth open, held six peanuts in his palm. He placed each on the table. "One . . . two . . . nine."

He gathered each peanut and appeared in the doorway. Mendel, in loose hat and long overcoat, still sat on the bed. Isaac watched with small eyes and ears, thick hair graying the sides of his head.

"Schlaf," he nasally said.

"No," muttered Mendel. As if stifling he rose. "Come, Isaac."

He wound his old watch though the sight of the stopped clock nauseated him.

Isaac wanted to hold it to his ear.

"No, it's late." Mendel put the watch carefully away. In the drawer he found the little paper bag of crumpled ones and fives and slipped it into his overcoat pocket. He helped Isaac on with his coat.

Isaac looked at one dark window, then at the other. Mendel stared at both blank windows.

They went slowly down the darkly lit stairs, Mendel first, Isaac watching the moving shadows on the wall. To one long shadow he offered a peanut.

"Hungrig."

In the vestibule the old man gazed through the thin glass. The November night was cold and bleak. Opening the door he cautiously thrust his head out. Though he saw nothing he quickly shut the door.

"Ginzburg, that he came to see me yesterday," he whispered in Isaac's ear.

Isaac sucked air.

"You know who I mean?"

Isaac combed his chin with his fingers.

"That's the one, with the black whiskers. Don't talk to him or go with him if he asks you."

Isaac moaned.

"Young people he don't bother so much," Mendel said in afterthought.

It was suppertime and the street was empty but the store windows dimly lit their way to the corner. They crossed the deserted street and went on. Isaac, with a happy cry, pointed to the three golden balls. Mendel smiled but was exhausted when they got to the pawnshop.

The pawnbroker, a red-bearded man with black horn-rimmed glasses, was eating a whitefish at the rear of the store. He craned his head, saw them, and settled back to sip his tea.

In five minutes he came forward, patting his shapeless lips with a large white handkerchief.

Mendel, breathing heavily, handed him the worn gold watch. The pawnbroker, raising his glasses, screwed in his eyepiece. He turned the watch over once. "Eight dollars."

The dying man wet his cracked lips. "I must have thirty-five."

"So go to Rothschild."

"Cost me myself sixty."

"In 1905." The pawnbroker handed back the watch. It had stopped ticking. Mendel wound it slowly. It ticked hollowly.

"Isaac must go to my uncle that he lives in California."

"It's a free country," said the pawnbroker.

Isaac, watching a banjo, snickered.

"What's the matter with him?" the pawnbroker asked.

"So let be eight dollars," muttered Mendel, "but where will I get the rest till tonight?"

"How much for my hat and coat?" he asked.

"No sale." The pawnbroker went behind the cage and wrote out a ticket. He locked the watch in a small drawer but Mendel still heard it ticking.

In the street he slipped the eight dollars into the paper bag, then searched in his pockets for a scrap of writing. Finding it, he strained to read the address by the light of the street lamp.

As they trudged to the subway, Mendel pointed to the sprinkled sky.

"Isaac, look how many stars are tonight."

"Eggs," said Isaac.

"First we will go to Mr. Fishbein, after we will eat."

They got off the train in upper Manhattan and had to walk several blocks before they located Fishbein's house.

"A regular palace," Mendel murmured, looking forward to a moment's warmth.

Isaac stared uneasily at the heavy door of the house.

Mendel rang. The servant, a man with long sideburns, came to the door and said Mr. and Mrs. Fishbein were dining and could see no one.

"He should eat in peace but we will wait till he finishes."

"Come back tomorrow morning. Tomorrow morning Mr. Fishbein will talk to you. He don't do business or charity at this time of the night."

"Charity I am not interested—"

"Come back tomorrow."

"Tell him it's life or death—"

"Whose life or death?"

"So if not his, then mine."

"Don't be such a big smart aleck."

"Look me in my face," said Mendel, "and tell me if I got time till tomorrow morning?"

The servant stared at him, then at Isaac, and reluctantly let them in.

The foyer was a vast high-ceilinged room with many oil paintings on the walls, voluminous silken draperies, a thick flowered rug at foot, and a marble staircase.

Mr. Fishbein, a paunchy bald-headed man with hairy nostrils and small patent leather feet, ran lightly down the stairs, a large napkin tucked under a tuxedo coat button. He stopped on the fifth step from the bottom and examined his visitors.

"Who comes on Friday night to a man that he has guests, to spoil him his supper?"

"Excuse me that I bother you, Mr. Fishbein," Mendel said. "If I didn't come now I couldn't come tomorrow."

"Without more preliminaries, please state your business. I'm a hungry man."

"Hungrig," wailed Isaac.

Fishbein adjusted his pince-nez. "What's the matter with him?"

"This is my son Isaac. He is like this all his life."

Isaac mewled.

"I am sending him to California."

"Mr. Fishbein don't contribute to personal pleasure trips."

"I am a sick man and he must go tonight on the train to my Uncle Leo."

"I never give to unorganized charity," Fishbein said, "but if you are hungry I will invite you downstairs in my kitchen. We having tonight chicken with stuffed derma."

"All I ask is thirty-five dollars for the train ticket to my uncle in California. I have already the rest."

"Who is your uncle? How old a man?"

"Eighty-one years, a long life to him."

Fishbein burst into laughter. "Eighty-one years and you are sending him this halfwit."

Mendel, flailing both arms, cried, "Please, without names."

Fishbein politely conceded.

"Where is open the door there we go in the house," the sick man said. "If you will kindly give me thirty-five dollars, God will bless you. What is thirty-five dollars to Mr. Fishbein? Nothing. To me, for my boy, is everything."

Fishbein drew himself up to his tallest height.

"Private contributions I don't make—only to institutions. This is my fixed policy."

Mendel sank to his creaking knees on the rug.

"Please, Mr. Fishbein, if not thirty-five, give maybe twenty."

"Levinson!" Fishbein angrily called.

The servant with the long sideburns appeared at the top of the stairs.

"Show this party where is the door—unless he wishes to partake food before leaving the premises."

"For what I got chicken won't cure it," Mendel said.

"This way if you please," said Levinson, descending.

Isaac assisted his father up.

"Take him to an institution," Fishbein advised over the marble balustrade. He ran quickly up the stairs and they were at once outside, buffeted by winds.

The walk to the subway was tedious. The wind blew mournfully. Mendel, breathless, glanced furtively at shadows. Isaac, clutching his peanuts in his frozen fist, clung to his father's side. They entered a small park to rest for a minute on a stone bench under a leafless two-branched tree. The thick right branch was raised, the thin left one hung down. A very pale moon rose slowly. So did a stranger as they approached the bench.

"Gut yuntif" [Happy holiday], he said hoarsely.

Mendel, drained of blood, waved his wasted arms. Isaac yowled sickly. Then a bell chimed and it was only ten. Mendel let out a piercing anguished cry as the bearded stranger disappeared into the bushes. A policeman came running, and though he beat the bushes with his nightstick, could turn up nothing. Mendel and Isaac hurried out of the little park. When Mendel glanced back the dead tree had its thin arm raised, the thick one down. He moaned.

They boarded a trolley, stopping at the home of a former friend, but he had died years ago. On the same block they went into a cafeteria and ordered two fried eggs for Isaac. The tables were crowded except where a heavy-set man sat eating soup with kasha. After one look at him they left in haste, although Isaac wept.

Mendel had another address on a slip of paper but the house was too far away, in Queens, so they stood in a doorway shivering.

What can I do, he frantically thought, in one short hour?

He remembered the furniture in the house. It was junk but might bring a few dollars. "Come, Isaac." They went once more to the pawnbroker's to talk to him, but the shop was dark and an iron gate—rings and gold watches glinting through it—was drawn tight across his place of business.

They huddled behind a telephone pole, both freezing. Isaac whimpered.

"See the big moon, Isaac. The whole sky is white."

He pointed but Isaac wouldn't look.

Mendel dreamed for a minute of the sky lit up, long sheets of light in all directions. Under the sky, in California, sat Uncle Leo drinking tea with lemon. Mendel felt warm but woke up cold.

Across the street stood an ancient brick synagogue.

He pounded on the huge door but no one appeared. He waited till he had breath and desperately knocked again. At last there were footsteps within, and the synagogue door creaked open on its massive brass hinges.

A darkly dressed sexton, holding a dripping candle, glared at them.

"Who knocks this time of night with so much noise on the synagogue door?"

Mendel told the sexton his troubles. "Please, I would like to speak to the rabbi."

"The rabbi is an old man. He sleeps now. His wife won't let you see him. Go home and come back tomorrow."

"To tomorrow I said goodbye already. I am a dying man."

Though the sexton seemed doubtful he pointed to an old wooden house next door. "In there he lives." He disappeared into the synagogue with his lit candle casting shadows around him.

Mendel, with Isaac clutching his sleeve, went up the wooden steps and rang the bell. After five minutes a big-faced, gray-haired bulky woman came out on the porch with a torn robe thrown over her nightdress. She emphatically said the rabbi was sleeping and could not be waked.

But as she was insisting, the rabbi himself tottered to the door. He listened a minute and said, "Who wants to see me let them come in."

They entered a cluttered room. The rabbi was an old skinny man with bent shoulders and a wisp of white beard. He wore a flannel nightgown and black skullcap; his feet were bare.

"Vey is mir" [Woe is me], his wife muttered. "Put on shoes or tomorrow comes sure pneumonia." She was a woman with a big belly, years younger than her husband. Staring at Isaac, she turned away.

Mendel apologetically related his errand. "All I need more is thirty-five dollars."

"Thirty-five?" said the rabbi's wife. "Why not thirty-five thousand? Who has so much money? My husband is a poor rabbi. The doctors take away every penny."

"Dear friend," said the rabbi, "if I had I would give you."

"I got already seventy," Mendal said, heavy-hearted. "All I need more is thirty-five."

"God will give you," said the rabbi.

"In the grave," said Mendel. "I need tonight. Come, Isaac."

"Wait," called the rabbi.

He hurried inside, came out with a fur-lined caftan, and handed it to Mendel.

"Yascha," shrieked his wife, "not your new coat!"

"I got my old one. Who needs two coats for one body?"

"Yascha, I am screaming—"

"Who can go among poor people, tell me, in a new coat?"

"Yascha," she cried, "what can this man do with your coat? He needs tonight the money. The pawnbrokers are asleep."

"So let him wake them up."

"No." She grabbed the coat from Mendel.

He held on to a sleeve, wrestling her for the coat. Her I know, Mendel thought. "Shylock," he muttered. Her eyes glittered.

The rabbi groaned and tottered dizzily. His wife cried out as Mendel yanked the coat from her hands.

"Run," cried the rabbi.

"Run, Isaac."

They ran out of the house and down the steps.

"Stop, you thief," called the rabbi's wife.

The rabbi pressed both hands to his temples and fell to the floor.

"Help!" his wife wept. "Heart attack! Help!"

BERNARD MALAMUD   767

But Mendel and Isaac ran through the streets with the rabbi's new fur-lined caftan. After them noiselessly ran Ginzburg.

It was very late when Mendel bought the train ticket in the only booth open.

There was no time to stop for a sandwich so Isaac ate his peanuts and they hurried to the train in the vast deserted station.

"So in the morning," Mendel gasped as they ran, "there comes a man that he sells sandwiches and coffee. Eat but get change. When reaches California the train, will be waiting for you on the station Uncle Leo. If you don't recognize him he will recognize you. Tell him I send best regards."

But when they arrived at the gate to the platform it was shut, the light out.

Mendel, groaning, beat on the gate with his fists.

"Too late," said the uniformed ticket collector, a bulky, bearded man with hairy nostrils and a fishy smell.

He pointed to the station clock. "Already past twelve."

"But I see standing there still the train," Mendel said, hopping in his grief.

"It just left—in one more minute."

"A minute is enough. Just open the gate."

"Too late I told you."

Mendel socked his bony chest with both hands. "With my whole heart I beg you this little favor."

"Favors you had enough already. For you the train is gone. You shoulda been dead already at midnight. I told you that yesterday. This is the best I can do."

"Ginzburg!" Mendel shrank from him.

"Who else?" The voice was metallic, eyes glittered, the expression amused.

"For myself," the old man begged, "I don't ask a thing. But what will happen to my boy?"

Ginzburg shrugged slightly. "What will happen happens. This isn't my responsibility. I got enough to think about without worrying about somebody on one cylinder."

"What then is your responsibility?"

"To create conditions. To make happen what happens. I ain't in the anthropomorphic business."

"Whatever business you in, where is your pity?"

"This ain't my commodity. The law is the law."

"Which law is this?"

"The cosmic universal law, goddamit, the one I got to follow myself."

"What kind of a law is it?" cried Mendel. "For God's sake, don't you understand what I went through in my life with this poor boy? Look at him. For thirty-nine years, since the day he was born, I wait for him to grow up, but he don't. Do you understand what this means in a father's heart? Why don't you let him go to his uncle?" His voice had risen and he was shouting.

Isaac mewled loudly.

"Better calm down or you'll hurt somebody's feelings," Ginzburg said with a wink toward Isaac.

"All my life," Mendel cried, his body trembling, "what did I have? I was poor. I suffered from my health. When I worked I worked too hard. When I didn't work was worse. My wife died a young woman. But I didn't ask from anybody nothing. Now I ask a small favor. Be so kind, Mr. Ginzburg."

The ticket collector was picking his teeth with a match stick.

"You ain't the only one, my friend, some got it worse than you. That's how it goes in this country."

"You dog you." Mendel lunged at Ginzburg's throat and began to choke. "You bastard, don't you understand what it means human?"

They struggled nose to nose, Ginzburg, though his astonished eyes bulged, began to laugh. "You pipsqueak nothing. I'll freeze you to pieces."

His eyes lit in rage and Mendel felt an unbearable cold like an icy dagger invading his body, all of his parts shriveling.

Now I die without helping Isaac.

A crowd gathered. Isaac yelped in fright.

Clinging to Ginzburg in his last agony, Mendel saw reflected in the ticket collector's eyes the depth of his terror. But he saw that Ginzburg, staring at himself in Mendel's eyes, saw mirrored in them the extent of his own awful wrath. He beheld a shimmering, starry, blinding light that produced darkness.

Ginzburg looked astounded. "Who me?"

His grip on the squirming old man slowly loosened, and Mendel, his heart barely beating, slumped to the ground.

"Go." Ginzburg muttered, "take him to the train."

"Let pass," he commanded a guard.

The crowd parted. Isaac helped his father up and they tottered down the steps to the platform where the train waited, lit and ready to go.

Mendel found Isaac a coach seat and hastily embraced him. "Help Uncle Leo, Isaakil. Also remember your father and mother."

"Be nice to him," he said to the conductor. "Show him where everything is."

He waited on the platform until the train began slowly to move. Isaac sat at the edge of his seat, his face strained in the direction of his journey. When the train was gone, Mendel ascended the stairs to see what had become of Ginzburg.

Questions

1. *Can this story be read as a religious drama? In this connection, consider the rabbi, the only person who helps Mendel. His compassion and his indifference to material things reveal him as a man of God. What does the supernatural Ginzburg represent?* 2. *What is the significance of the fact that Isaac, for whom Mendel is determined to provide before death claims him, is an idiot?* 3. *How do the various episodes in this story establish Mendel's character and prepare the reader for the final, climactic confrontation between Mendel and Ginzburg?* 4. *Mendel wins his battle with Ginzburg. What does that victory signify?*

Patriotism*

YUKIO MISHIMA [1925–1970]

IN the twenty-eighth of February, 1936 (on the third day, that is, of the February Incident[1]), Lieutenant Shinji Takeyama of the Konoe Transport Battalion—profoundly disturbed by the knowledge that his closest colleagues had been with the mutineers from the beginning, and indignant at the imminent prospect of Imperial troops attacking Imperial troops—took his officer's sword and ceremonially disemboweled himself in the eight-mat room of his private residence in the sixth block of Aoba-chō, in Yotsuya Ward. His wife, Reiko, followed him, stabbing herself to death. The lieutenant's farewell note consisted of one sentence: "Long live the Imperial Forces." His wife's, after apologies for her unfilial conduct in thus preceding her parents to the grave, concluded: "The day which, for a soldier's wife, had to come, has come. . . ." The last moments of this heroic and dedicated couple were such as to make the gods themselves weep. The lieutenant's age, it should be noted, was thirty-one, his wife's twenty-three; and it was not half a year since the celebration of their marriage.

2

THOSE who saw the bride and bridegroom in the commemorative photograph—perhaps no less than those actually present at the lieutenant's wedding—had exclaimed in wonder at the bearing of this handsome couple. The lieutenant, majestic in military uniform, stood protectively beside his bride, his right hand resting upon his sword, his officer's cap held at his left side. His expression was severe, and his dark brows and wide-gazing eyes well conveyed the clear integrity of youth. For the beauty of the bride in her white over-robe no comparisons were adequate. In the eyes, round beneath soft brows, in the slender, finely shaped nose, and in the full lips, there was both sensuousness and refinement. One hand, emerging shyly from a sleeve of the over-robe, held a fan, and the tips of the fingers, clustering delicately, were like the bud of a moonflower.

After the suicide, people would take out this photograph and examine it, and sadly reflect that too often there was a curse on these seemingly flawless unions. Perhaps it was no more than imagination, but looking at the picture

---

*Translated by Geoffrey W. Sargeant.
1. On February 26, 1936, a long period of political turmoil culminated in an attempted coup led by young officers. Units commanded by the rebels seized and held central Tokyo for a number of days, and numerous high-ranking government officials, including Lord Privy Seal Saitō, were assassinated. The mutiny was crushed by loyal troops, and the leaders were executed.

after the tragedy it almost seemed as if the two young people before the gold-lacquered screen were gazing, each with equal clarity, at the deaths which lay before them.

Thanks to the good offices of their go-between, Lieutenant General Ozeki, they had been able to set themselves up in a new home at Aoba-chō in Yotsuya. "New home" is perhaps misleading. It was an old three-room rented house backing onto a small garden. As neither the six- nor the four-and-a-half mat room downstairs was favored by the sun, they used the upstairs eight-mat room as both bedroom and guest room. There was no maid, so Reiko was left alone to guard the house in her husband's absence.

The honeymoon trip was dispensed with on the grounds that these were times of national emergency. The two of them had spent the first night of their marriage at this house. Before going to bed, Shinji, sitting erect on the floor with his sword laid before him, had bestowed upon his wife a soldierly lecture. A woman who had become the wife of a soldier should know and resolutely accept that her husband's death might come at any moment. It could be tomorrow. It could be the day after. But, no matter when it came—he asked—was she steadfast in her resolve to accept it? Reiko rose to her feet, pulled open a drawer of the cabinet, and took out what was the most prized of her new possessions, the dagger her mother had given her. Returning to her place, she laid the dagger without a word on the mat before her, just as her husband had laid his sword. A silent understanding was achieved at once and the lieutenant never again sought to test his wife's resolve.

In the first few months of her marriage Reiko's beauty grew daily more radiant, shining serene like the moon after rain.

As both were possessed of young, vigorous bodies, their relationship was passionate. Nor was this merely a matter of the night. On more than one occasion, returning home straight from maneuvers, and begrudging even the time it took to remove his mud-splashed uniform, the lieutenant had pushed his wife to the floor almost as soon as he had entered the house. Reiko was equally ardent in her response. For a little more or a little less than a month, from the first night of their marriage Reiko knew happiness, and the lieutenant, seeing this, was happy too.

Reiko's body was white and pure, and her swelling breasts conveyed a firm and chaste refusal; but, upon consent, those breasts were lavish with their intimate, welcoming warmth. Even in bed these two were frighteningly and awesomely serious. In the very midst of wild, intoxicating passions, their hearts were sober and serious.

By day the lieutenant would think of his wife in the brief rest periods between training; and all day long, at home, Reiko would recall the image of her husband. Even when apart, however, they had only to look at the wedding photograph for their happiness to be once more confirmed. Reiko felt not the slightest surprise that a man who had been a complete stranger until a few months ago should now have become the sun about which her whole world revolved.

All these things had a moral basis, and were in accordance with the Education Rescript's[2] injunction that "husband and wife should be harmonious." Not once did Reiko contradict her husband, nor did the lieutenant ever find reason to scold his wife. On the god shelf below the stairway, alongside the tablet from the Great Ise Shrine,[3] were set photographs of their Imperial Majesties, and regularly every morning, before leaving for duty, the lieutenant would stand with his wife at this hallowed place and together they would bow their heads low. The offering water was renewed each morning, and the sacred sprig of *sasaki* was always green and fresh. Their lives were lived beneath the solemn protection of the gods and were filled with an intense happiness which set every fiber in their bodies trembling.

3

ALTHOUGH Lord Privy Seal Saitō's house was in their neighborhood, neither of them heard any noise of gunfire on the morning of February 26. It was a bugle, sounding muster in the dim, snowy dawn, when the ten-minute tragedy had already ended, which first disrupted the lieutenant's slumbers. Leaping at once from his bed, and without speaking a word, the lieutenant donned his uniform, buckled on the sword held ready for him by his wife, and hurried swiftly out into the snow-covered streets of the still darkened morning. He did not return until the evening of the twenty-eighth.

Later, from the radio news, Reiko learned the full extent of this sudden eruption of violence. Her life throughout the subsequent two days was lived alone, in complete tranquillity, and behind locked doors.

In the lieutenant's face, as he hurried silently out into the snowy morning, Reiko had read the determination to die. If her husband did not return, her own decision was made: she too would die. Quietly she attended to the disposition of her personal possessions. She chose her sets of visiting kimonos as keepsakes for friends of her schooldays, and she wrote a name and address on the stiff paper wrapping in which each was folded. Constantly admonished by her husband never to think of the morrow, Reiko had not even kept a diary and was now denied the pleasure of assiduously rereading her record of the happiness of the past few months and consigning each page to the fire as she did so. Ranged across the top of the radio were a small china dog, a rabbit, a squirrel, a bear, and a fox. There were also a small vase and a water pitcher. These comprised Reiko's one and only collection. But it would hardly do, she imagined, to give such things as keepsakes. Nor again would it be quite proper to ask specifically for them to be included in the coffin. It seemed to Reiko, as these thoughts passed through her mind, that the expressions on the small animals' faces grew even more lost and forlorn.

---

2. The Education Rescript was a code promulgated during the Meiji, the reign of Emperor Mutsuhito which lasted from 1867 to 1912. The period is regarded as an historic era in the development of modern Japan.
3. The Great Ise Shrine is the highest ranking shrine in Japan. The emperor's ancestors were buried there.

Reiko took the squirrel in her hand and looked at it. And then, her thoughts turning to a realm far beyond these childlike affections, she gazed up into the distance at the great sunlike principle which her husband embodied. She was ready, and happy, to be hurtled along to her destruction in that gleaming sun chariot—but now, for these few moments of solitude, she allowed herself to luxuriate in this innocent attachment to trifles. The time when she had genuinely loved these things, however, was long past. Now she merely loved the memory of having once loved them, and their place in her heart had been filled by more intense passions, by a more frenzied happiness. . . . For Reiko had never, even to herself, thought of those soaring joys of the flesh as a mere pleasure. The February cold, and the icy touch of the china squirrel, had numbed Reiko's slender fingers; yet, even so, in her lower limbs, beneath the ordered repetition of the pattern which crossed the skirt of her trim *meisen* kimono, she could feel now, as she thought of the lieutenant's powerful arms reaching out toward her, a hot moistness of the flesh which defied the snows.

She was not in the least afraid of the death hovering in her mind. Waiting alone at home, Reiko firmly believed that everything her husband was feeling or thinking now, his anguish and distress, was leading her—just as surely as the power in his flesh—to a welcome death. She felt as if her body could melt away with ease and be transformed to the merest fraction of her husband's thought.

Listening to the frequent announcements on the radio, she heard the names of several of her husband's colleagues mentioned among those of the insurgents. This was news of death. She followed the developments closely, wondering anxiously, as the situation became daily more irrevocable, why no Imperial ordinance was sent down, and watching what had at first been taken as a movement to restore the nation's honor come gradually to be branded with the infamous name of mutiny. There was no communication from the regiment. At any moment, it seemed, fighting might commence in the city streets where the remains of the snow still lay.

Toward sundown on the twenth-eighth Reiko was startled by a furious pounding on the front door. She hurried downstairs. As she pulled with fumbling fingers at the bolt, the shape dimly outlined beyond the frosted-glass panel made no sound, but she knew it was her husband. Reiko had never known the bolt on the sliding door to be so stiff. Still it resisted. The door just would not open.

In a moment, almost before she knew she had succeeded, the lieutenant was standing before her on the cement floor inside the porch, muffled in a khaki greatcoat, his top boots heavy with slush from the street. Closing the door behind him, he returned the bolt once more to its socket. With what significance, Reiko did not understand.

"Welcome home."

Reiko bowed deeply, but her husband made no response. As he had already unfastened his sword and was about to remove his greatcoat, Reiko moved around behind to assist. The coat, which was cold and damp and had lost the odor of horse dung it normally exuded when exposed to the sun, weighed heavily upon her arm. Draping it across a hanger, and cradling the sword and leather belt in her sleeves, she waited while her husband removed his top boots and then followed behind him into the "living room." This was the six-mat room downstairs.

Seen in the clear light from the lamp, her husband's face, covered with a heavy growth of bristle, was almost unrecognizably wasted and thin. The cheeks were hollow, their luster and resilience gone. In his normal good spirits he would have changed into old clothes as soon as he was home and have pressed her to get supper at once, but now he sat before the table still in his uniform, his head drooping dejectedly. Reiko refrained from asking whether she should prepare the supper.

After an interval the lieutenant spoke.

"I knew nothing. They hadn't asked me to join. Perhaps out of consideration, because I was newly married. Kanō, and Homma too, and Yamaguchi."

Reiko recalled momentarily the faces of high-spirited young officers, friends of her husband, who had come to the house occasionally as guests.

"There may be an Imperial ordinance sent down tomorrow. They'll be posted as rebels, I imagine. I shall be in command of a unit with orders to attack them. . . . I can't do it. It's impossible to do a thing like that."

He spoke again.

"They've taken me off guard duty, and I have permission to return home for one night. Tomorrow morning, without question, I must leave to join the attack. I can't do it, Reiko."

Reiko sat erect with lowered eyes. She understood clearly that her husband had spoken of his death. The lieutenant was resolved. Each word, being rooted in death, emerged sharply and with powerful significance against this dark, unmovable background. Although the lieutenant was speaking of his dilemma, already there was no room in his mind for vacillation.

However, there was a clarity, like the clarity of a stream fed from melting snows, in the silence which rested between them. Sitting in his own home after the long two-day ordeal, and looking across at the face of his beautiful wife, the lieutenant was for the first time experiencing true peace of mind. For he had at once known, though she said nothing, that his wife divined the resolve which lay beneath his words.

"Well, then . . ." The lieutenant's eyes opened wide. Despite his exhaustion they were strong and clear, and now for the first time they looked straight into the eyes of his wife. "Tonight I shall cut my stomach."

Reiko did not flinch.

Her round eyes showed tension, as taut as the clang of a bell.

"I am ready," she said. "I ask permission to accompany you."

The lieutenant felt almost mesmerized by the strength in those eyes. His words flowed swiftly and easily, like the utterances of a man in delirium, and it was beyond his understanding how permission in a matter of such weight could be expressed so casually.

"Good. We'll go together. But I want you as a witness, first, for my own suicide. Agreed?"

When this was said a sudden release of abundant happiness welled up in both their hearts. Reiko was deeply affected by the greatness of her husband's trust in her. It was vital for the lieutenant, whatever else might happen, that there should be no irregularity in his death. For that reason there had to be a witness. The fact that he had chosen his wife for this was the first mark of his trust. The second, and even greater mark, was that though he had pledged that they should die together he did not intend to kill his wife first—he had deferred her death to a time when he would no longer be there to verify it. If the lieutenant had been a suspicious husband, he would doubtless, as in the usual suicide pact, have chosen to kill his wife first.

When Reiko said, "I ask permission to accompany you," the lieutenant felt these words to be the final fruit of the education which he had himself given his wife, starting on the first night of their marriage, and which had schooled her, when the moment came, to say what had to be said without a shadow of hesitation. This flattered the lieutenant's opinion of himself as a self-reliant man. He was not so romantic or conceited as to imagine that the words were spoken spontaneously, out of love for her husband.

With happiness welling almost too abundantly in their hearts, they could not help smiling at each other. Reiko felt as if she had returned to her wedding night.

Before her eyes was neither pain nor death. She seemed to see only a free and limitless expanse opening out into vast distances.

"The water is hot. Will you take your bath now?"

"Ah yes, of course."

"And supper . . .?"

The words were delivered in such level, domestic tones that the lieutenant came near to thinking, for the fraction of a second, that everything had been a hallucination.

"I don't think we'll need supper. But perhaps you could warm some sake?"

"As you wish."

As Reiko rose and took a *tanzen* gown from the cabinet for after the bath, she purposely directed her husband's attention to the opened drawer. The lieutenant rose, crossed to the cabinet, and looked inside. From the ordered array of paper wrappings he read, one by one, the addresses of the keepsakes. There was no grief in the lieutenant's response to this demonstration of heroic resolve. His heart was filled with tenderness. Like a husband who is proudly shown the childish purchases of a young wife, the lieutenant, overwhelmed by affection, lovingly embraced his wife from behind and implanted a kiss upon her neck.

Reiko felt the roughness of the lieutenant's unshaven skin against her neck. This sensation, more than being just a thing of this world, was for Reiko almost the world itself, but now—with the feeling that it was soon to be lost forever—it had freshness beyond all her experience. Each moment had its own vital strength, and the senses in every corner of her body were reawakened. Accepting her husband's caresses from behind, Reiko raised herself on the tips of her toes, letting the vitality seep through her entire body.

"First the bath, and then, after some sake . . . lay out the bedding upstairs, will you?"

The lieutenant whispered the words into his wife's ear. Reiko silently nodded.

Flinging off his uniform, the lieutenant went to the bath. To faint background noises of slopping water Reiko tended the charcoal brazier in the living room and began the preparations for warming the sake.

Taking the *tanzen*, a sash, and some underclothes, she went to the bathroom to ask how the water was. In the midst of a coiling cloud of steam the lieutenant was sitting cross-legged on the floor, shaving, and she could dimly discern the rippling movements of the muscles on his damp, powerful back as they responded to the movement of his arms.

There was nothing to suggest a time of any special significance. Reiko, going busily about her tasks, was preparing side dishes from odds and ends in stock. Her hands did not tremble. If anything, she managed even more efficiently and smoothly than usual. From time to time, it is true, there was a strange throbbing deep within her breast. Like distant lightning, it had a moment of sharp intensity and then vanished without trace. Apart from that, nothing was in any way out of the ordinary.

The lieutenant, shaving in the bathroom, felt his warmed body miraculously healed at last of the desperate tiredness of the days of indecision and filled—in spite of the death which lay ahead—with pleasurable anticipation. The sound of his wife going about her work came to him faintly. A healthy physical craving, submerged for two days, reasserted itself.

The lieutenant was confident there had been no impurity in that joy they had experienced when resolving upon death. They had both sensed at that moment—though not, of course, in any clear and conscious way—that those permissible pleasures which they shared in private were once more beneath the protection of Righteousness and Divine Power, and of a complete and unassailable morality. On looking into each other's eyes and discovering there an honorable death, they had felt themselves safe once more behind steel walls which none could destroy, encased in an impenetrable armor of Beauty and Truth. Thus, so far from seeing any inconsistency or conflict between the urges of his flesh and the sincerity of his patriotism, the lieutenant was even able to regard the two as parts of the same thing.

Thrusting his face close to the dark, cracked, misted wall mirror, the lieutenant shaved himself with great care. This would be his death face. There must be no unsightly blemishes. The clean-shaven face gleamed once more with a youthful luster, seeming to brighten the darkness of the mirror. There was a certain elegance, he even felt, in the association of death with this radiantly healthy face.

Just as it looked now, this would become his death face! Already, in fact, it had half departed from the lieutenant's personal possession and had become the bust above a dead soldier's memorial. As an experiment he closed his eyes tight. Everything was wrapped in blackness, and he was no longer a living, seeing creature.

Returning from the bath, the traces of the shave glowing faintly blue beneath his smooth cheeks, he seated himself beside the now well-kindled charcoal brazier. Busy though Reiko was, he noticed, she had found time lightly to touch up her face. Her cheeks were gay and her lips moist. There was no shadow of sadness to be seen. Truly, the lieutenant felt, as he saw this mark of his young wife's passionate nature, he had chosen the wife he ought to have chosen.

As soon as the lieutenant had drained his sake cup he offered it to Reiko. Reiko had never before tasted sake, but she accepted without hesitation and sipped timidly.

"Come here," the lieutenant said.

Reiko moved to her husband's side and was embraced as she leaned backward across his lap. Her breast was in violent commotion, as if sadness, joy, and the potent sake were mingling and reacting within her. The lieutenant looked down into his wife's face. It was the last face he would see in this world, the last face he would see of his wife. The lieutenant scrutinized the face minutely, with the eyes of a traveler bidding farewell to splendid vistas which he will never revisit. It was a face he could not tire of looking at—the features regular yet not cold, the lips lightly closed with a soft strength. The lieutenant kissed those lips, unthinkingly. And suddenly, though there was not the slightest distortion of the face into the unsightliness of sobbing, he noticed that tears were welling slowly from beneath the long lashes of the closed eyes and brimming over into a glistening stream.

When, a little later, the lieutenant urged that they should move to the upstairs bedroom, his wife replied that she would follow after taking a bath. Climbing the stairs alone to the bedroom, where the air was already warmed by the gas heater, the lieutenant lay down on the bedding with arms outstretched and legs apart. Even the time at which he lay waiting for his wife to join him was no later and no earlier than usual.

He folded his hands beneath his head and gazed at the dark boards of the ceiling in the dimness beyond the range of the standard lamp. Was it death he was now waiting for? Or a wild ecstasy of the senses? The two seemed to overlap, almost as if the object of this bodily desire was death itself. But, however that might be, it was certain that never before had the lieutenant tasted such total freedom.

There was the sound of a car outside the window. He could hear the screech of its tires skidding in the snow piled at the side of the street. The sound of its horn re-echoed from near-by walls. . . . Listening to these noises he had the feeling that this house rose like a solitary island in the ocean of a society going as restlessly about its business as ever. All around, vastly and untidily, stretched the country for which he grieved. He was to give his life for it. But would that great country, with which he was prepared to remonstrate to the extent of destroying himself, take the slightest heed of his death? He did

not know; and it did not matter. His was a battlefield without glory, a battlefield where none could display deeds of valor: it was the front line of the
spirit.

Reiko's footsteps sounded on the stairway. The steep stairs in this old
house creaked badly. There were fond memories in that creaking, and many a
time, while waiting in bed, the lieutenant had listened to its welcome sound.
At the thought that he would hear it no more he listened with intense
concentration, striving for every corner of every moment of this precious time
to be filled with the sound of those soft footfalls on the creaking stairway. The
moments seemed transformed to jewels, sparkling with inner light.

Reiko wore a Nagoya sash about the waist of her *yukata*, but as the
lieutenant reached toward it, its redness sobered by the dimness of the light,
Reiko's hand moved to his assistance and the sash fell away, slithering swiftly to
the floor. As she stood before him, still in her *yukata*, the lieutenant inserted
his hands through the side slits beneath each sleeve, intending to embrace her
as she was; but at the touch of his finger tips upon the warm naked flesh, and
as the armpits closed gently about his hands, his whole body was suddenly
aflame.

In a few moments the two lay naked before the glowing gas heater.

Neither spoke the thought, but their hearts, their bodies, and their
pounding breasts blazed with the knowledge that this was the very last time. It
was as if the words "The Last Time" were spelled out, in invisible brushstrokes,
across every inch of their bodies.

The lieutenant drew his wife close and kissed her vehemently. As their
tongues explored each other's mouths, reaching out into the smooth, moist interior, they felt as if the still unknown agonies of death had tempered their
senses to the keenness of red-hot steel. The agonies they could not yet feel,
the distant pains of death, had refined their awareness of pleasure.

"This is the last time I shall see your body," said the lieutenant. "Let me
look at it closely." And, tilting the shade on the lampstand to one side, he
directed the rays along the full length of Reiko's outstretched form.

Reiko lay still with her eyes closed. The light from the low lamp clearly
revealed the majestic sweep of her white flesh. The lieutenant, not without a
touch of egocentricity, rejoiced that he would never see this beauty crumble
in death.

At his leisure, the lieutenant allowed the unforgettable spectacle to en-
grave itself upon his mind. With one hand he fondled the hair, with the other
he softly stroked the magnificent face, implanting kisses here and there where
his eyes lingered. The quiet coldness of the high, tapering forehead, the closed
eyes with their long lashes beneath faintly etched brows, the set of the finely
shaped nose, the gleam of teeth glimpsed between full, regular lips, the soft
cheeks and the small, wise chin . . . these things conjured up in the lieutenant's
mind the vision of a truly radiant death face, and again and again he pressed
his lips tight against the white throat—where Reiko's own hand was soon to
strike—and the throat reddened faintly beneath his kisses. Returning to the
mouth he laid his lips against it with the gentlest of pressures, and moved them

rhythmically over Reiko's with the light rolling motion of a small boat. If he closed his eyes, the world became a rocking cradle.

Wherever the lieutenant's eyes moved his lips faithfully followed. The high, swelling breasts, surmounted by nipples like the buds of a wild cherry, hardened as the lieutenant's lips closed about them. The arms flowed smoothly downward from each side of the breast, tapering toward the wrists, yet losing nothing of their roundness or symmetry, and at their tips were those delicate fingers which had held the fan at the wedding ceremony. One by one, as the lieutenant kissed them, the fingers withdrew behind their neighbor as if in shame. . . . The natural hollow curving between the bosom and the stomach carried in its lines a suggestion not only of softness but of resilient strength, and while it gave forewarning of the rich curves spreading outward from here to the hips it had, in itself, an appearance only of restraint and proper discipline. The whiteness and richness of the stomach and hips was like milk brimming in a great bowl, and the sharply shadowed dip of the navel could have been the fresh impress of a raindrop, fallen there that very moment. Where the shadows gathered more thickly, hair clustered, gentle and sensitive, and as the agitation mounted in the now no longer passive body there hung over this region a scent like the smoldering of fragrant blossoms, growing steadily more pervasive.

At length, in a tremulous voice, Reiko spoke.

"Show me. . . . Let me look too, for the last time."

Never before had he heard from his wife's lips so strong and unequivocal a request. It was as if something which her modesty had wished to keep hidden to the end had suddenly burst its bonds of constraint. The lieutenant obediently lay back and surrendered himself to his wife. Lithely she raised her white, trembling body, and—burning with an innocent desire to return to her husband what he had done for her—placed two white fingers on the lieutenant's eyes, which gazed fixedly up at her, and gently stroked them shut.

Suddenly overwhelmed by tenderness, her cheeks flushed by a dizzying uprush of emotion, Reiko threw her arms about the lieutenant's close-cropped head. The bristly hairs rubbed painfully against her breast, the prominent nose was cold as it dug into her flesh, and his breath was hot. Relaxing her embrace, she gazed down at her husband's masculine face. The severe brows, the closed eyes, the splendid bridge of the nose, the shapely lips drawn firmly together . . . the blue, cleanshaven cheeks reflecting the light and gleaming smoothly. Reiko kissed each of these. She kissed the broad nape of the neck, the strong, erect shoulders, the powerful chest with its twin circles like shields and its russet nipples. In the armpits, deeply shadowed by the ample flesh of the shoulders and chest, a sweet and melancholy odor emanated from the growth of hair, and in the sweetness of this odor was contained, somehow, the essence of young death. The lieutenant's naked skin glowed like a field of barley, and everywhere the muscles showed in sharp relief, converging on the lower abdomen about the small, unassuming navel. Gazing at the youthful, firm stomach, modestly covered by a vigorous growth of hair, Reiko thought of it as it was soon to be, cruelly cut by the sword, and she laid her head upon it, sobbing in pity, and bathed it with kisses.

At the touch of his wife's tears upon his stomach the lieutenant felt ready to endure with courage the cruelest agonies of his suicide.

What ecstasies they experienced after these tender exchanges may well be imagined. The lieutenant raised himself and enfolded his wife in a powerful embrace, her body now limp with exhaustion after her grief and tears. Passionately they held their faces close, rubbing cheek against cheek. Reiko's body was trembling. Their breasts, moist with sweat, were tightly joined, and every inch of the young and beautiful bodies had become so much one with the other that it seemed impossible there should ever again be a separation. Reiko cried out. From the heights they plunged into the abyss, and from the abyss they took wing and soared once more to dizzying heights. The lieutenant panted like the regimental standard-bearer on a route march. . . . As one cycle ended, almost immediately a new wave of passion would be generated, and together—with no trace of fatigue—they would climb again in a single breathless movement to the very summit.

4

WHEN the lieutenant at last turned away, it was not from weariness. For one thing, he was anxious not to undermine the considerable strength he would need in carrying out his suicide. For another, he would have been sorry to mar the sweetness of these last memories by overindulgence.

Since the lieutenant had clearly desisted, Reiko too, with her usual compliance, followed his example. The two lay naked on their backs, with fingers interlaced, staring fixedly at the dark ceiling. The room was warm from the heater, and even when the sweat had ceased to pour from their bodies they felt no cold. Outside, in the hushed night, the sounds of passing traffic had ceased. Even the noises of the trains and streetcars around Yotsuya station did not penetrate this far. After echoing through the region bounded by the moat, they were lost in the heavily wooded park fronting the broad driveway before Akasaka Palace. It was hard to believe in the tension gripping this whole quarter, where the two factions of the bitterly divided Imperial Army now confronted each other, poised for battle.

Savoring the warmth glowing within themselves, they lay still and recalled the ecstasies they had just known. Each moment of the experience was relived. They remembered the taste of kisses which had never wearied, the touch of naked flesh, episode after episode of dizzying bliss. But already, from the dark boards of the ceiling, the face of death was peering down. These joys had been final, and their bodies would never know them again. Not that joy of this intensity—and the same thought had occurred to them both—was ever likely to be reexperienced, even if they should live on to old age.

The feel of their fingers intertwined—this too would soon be lost. Even the wood-grain patterns they now gazed at on the dark ceiling boards would be taken from them. They could feel death edging in, nearer and nearer.

There could be no hesitation now. They must have the courage to reach out to death themselves, and to seize it.

"Well, let's make our preparations," said the lieutenant. The note of determination in the words was unmistakable, but at the same time Reiko had never heard her husband's voice so warm and tender.

After they had risen, a variety of tasks awaited them.

The lieutenant, who had never once before helped with the bedding, now cheerfully slid back the door of the closet, lifted the mattress across the room by himself, and stowed it away inside.

Reiko turned off the gas heater and put away the lamp standard. During the lieutenant's absence she had arranged this room carefully, sweeping and dusting it to a fresh cleanness, and now—if one overlooked the rosewood table drawn into one corner—the eight-mat room gave all the appearance of a reception room ready to welcome an important guest.

"We've seen some drinking here, haven't we? With Kanō and Homma and Noguchi . . ."

"Yes, they were great drinkers, all of them."

"We'll be meeting them before long, in the other world. They'll tease us, I imagine, when they find I've brought you with me."

Descending the stairs, the lieutenant turned to look back into this calm clean room, now brightly illuminated by the ceiling lamp. There floated across his mind the faces of the young officers who had drunk there, and laughed, and innocently bragged. He had never dreamed then that he would one day cut open his stomach in this room.

In the two rooms downstairs husband and wife busied themselves smoothly and serenely with their respective preparations. The lieutenant went to the toilet, and then to the bathroom to wash. Meanwhile Reiko folded away her husband's padded robe, placed his uniform tunic, his trousers, and a newly cut bleached loincloth in the bathroom, and set out sheets of paper on the living-room table for the farewell notes. Then she removed the lid from the writing box and began rubbing ink from the ink tablet. She had already decided upon the wording of her own note.

Reiko's fingers pressed hard upon the cold gilt letters of the ink tablet, and the water in the shallow well at once darkened, as if a black cloud had spread across it. She stopped thinking that this repeated action, this pressure from her fingers, this rise and fall of faint sound, was all and solely for death. It was a routine domestic task, a simple paring away of time until death should finally stand before her. But somehow, in the increasingly smooth motion of the tablet rubbing on the stone, and in the scent from the thickening ink, there was unspeakable darkness.

Neat in his uniform, which he now wore next to his skin, the lieutenant emerged from the bathroom. Without a word he seated himself at the table, bolt upright, took a brush in his hand, and stared undecidedly at the paper before him.

Reiko took a white silk kimono with her and entered the bathroom. When she reappeared in the living room, clad in the white kimono and with her face lightly made up, the farewell note lay completed on the table beneath the lamp. The thick black brushstrokes said simply:

"Long Live the Imperial Forces—Army Lieutenant Takeyama Shinji."

While Reiko sat opposite him writing her own note, the lieutenant gazed in silence, intensely serious, at the controlled movement of his wife's pale fingers as they manipulated the brush.

With their respective notes in their hands—the lieutenant's sword strapped to his side, Reiko's small dagger thrust into the sash of her white kimono—the two of them stood before the god shelf and silently prayed. Then they put out all the downstairs lights. As he mounted the stairs the lieutenant turned his head and gazed back at the striking, white-clad figure of his wife, climbing behind him, with lowered eyes, from the darkness beneath.

The farewell notes were laid side by side in the alcove of the upstairs room. They wondered whether they ought not to remove the hanging scroll, but since it had been written by their go-between, Lieutenant General Ozeki, and consisted, moreover, of two Chinese characters signifying "Sincerity," they left it where it was. Even if it were to become stained with splashes of blood, they felt that the lieutenant general would understand.

The lieutenant sitting erect with his back to the alcove, laid his sword on the floor before him.

Reiko sat facing him, a mat's width away. With the rest of her so severely white the touch of rouge on her lips seemed remarkably seductive.

Across the dividing mat they gazed intently into each other's eyes. The lieutenant's sword lay before his knees. Seeing it, Reiko recalled their first night and was overwhelmed with sadness. The lieutenant spoke, in a hoarse voice:

"As I have no second to help me I shall cut deep. It may look unpleasant, but please do not panic. Death of any sort is a fearful thing to watch. You must not be discouraged by what you see. Is that all right?"

"Yes."

Reiko nodded deeply.

Looking at the slender white figure of his wife the lieutenant experienced a bizarre excitement. What he was about to perform was an act in his public capacity as a soldier, something he had never previously shown his wife. It called for a resolution equal to the courage to enter battle; it was a death of no less degree and quality than death in the front line. It was his conduct on the battlefield that he was now to display.

Momentarily the thought led the lieutenant to a strange fantasy. A lonely death on the battlefield, a death beneath the eyes of his beautiful wife . . . in the sensation that he was now to die in these two dimensions, realizing an impossible union of them both, there was sweetness beyond words. This must be the very pinnacle of good fortune, he thought. To have every moment of his death observed by those beautiful eyes—it was like being borne to death on a gentle, fragrant breeze. There was some special favor here. He did not understand precisely what it was, but it was a domain unknown to others: a dispensation granted to no one else had been permitted to himself. In the radiant, bridelike figure of his white-robed wife the lieutenant seemed to see a vision of all those things he had loved and for which he was to lay down his life—the Imperial Household, the Nation, the Army Flag. All these, no less than the wife who sat before him, were presences observing him closely with clear and never-faltering eyes.

Reiko too was gazing intently at her husband, so soon to die, and she thought that never in this world had she seen anything so beautiful. The lieutenant always looked well in uniform, but now, as he contemplated death with severe brows and firmly closed lips, he revealed what was perhaps masculine beauty at its most superb.

"It's time to go," the lieutenant said at last.

Reiko bent her body low to the mat in a deep bow. She could not raise her face. She did not wish to spoil her make-up with tears, but the tears could not be held back.

When at length she looked up she saw hazily through the tears that her husband had wound a white bandage around the blade of his now unsheathed sword, leaving five or six inches of naked steel showing at the point.

Resting the sword in its cloth wrapping on the mat before him, the lieutenant rose from his knees, resettled himself cross-legged, and unfastened the hooks of his uniform collar. His eyes no longer saw his wife. Slowly, one by one, he undid the flat brass buttons. The dusky brown chest was revealed, and then the stomach. He unclasped his belt and undid the buttons of his trousers. The pure whiteness of the thickly coiled loincloth showed itself. The lieutenant pushed the cloth down with both hands, further to ease his stomach, and then reached for the white-bandaged blade of his sword. With his left hand he massaged his abdomen, glancing downward as he did so.

To reassure himself on the sharpness of his sword's cutting edge the lieutenant folded back the left trouser flap, exposing a little of his thigh, and lightly drew the blade across the skin. Blood welled up in the wound at once, and several streaks of red trickled downward, glistening in the strong light.

It was the first time Reiko had ever seen her husband's blood, and she felt a violent throbbing in her chest. She looked at her husband's face. The lieutenant was looking at the blood with calm appraisal. For a moment— though thinking at the same time that it was hollow comfort—Reiko experienced a sense of relief.

The lieutenant's eyes fixed his wife with an intense, hawk-like stare. Moving the sword around to his front, he raised himself slightly on his hips and let the upper half of his body lean over the sword point. That he was mustering his whole strength was apparent from the angry tension of the uniform at his shoulders. The lieutenant aimed to strike deep into the left of his stomach. His sharp cry pierced the silence of the room.

Despite the effort he had himself put into the blow, the lieutenant had the impression that someone else had struck the side of his stomach agonizingly with a thick rod of iron. For a second or so his head reeled and he had no idea what had happened. The five or six inches of naked point had vanished completely into his flesh, and the white bandage, gripped in his clenched fist, pressed directly against his stomach.

He returned to consciousness. The blade had certainly pierced the wall of the stomach, he thought. His breathing was difficult, his chest thumped violently, and in some far deep region, which he could hardly believe was a part of himself, a fearful and excruciating pain came welling up as if the ground had split open to disgorge a boiling stream of molten rock. The pain came suddenly nearer, with terrifying speed. The lieutenant bit his lower lip and stifled an instinctive moan.

Was this *seppuku*?—he was thinking. It was a sensation of utter chaos, as if the sky had fallen on his head and the world was reeling drunkenly. His will power and courage, which had seemed so robust before he made the incision, had now dwindled to something like a single hairlike thread of steel, and he was assailed by the uneasy feeling that he must advance along this thread, clinging to it with desperation. His clenched fist had grown moist. Looking down, he saw that both his hand and the cloth were drenched in blood. His loincloth too was dyed a deep red. It struck him as incredible that, amidst this terrible agony, things which could be seen could still be seen, and existing things existed still.

The moment the lieutenant thrust the sword into his left side and she saw the deathly pallor fall across his face, like an abruptly lowered curtain, Reiko had to struggle to prevent herself from rushing to his side. Whatever happened, she must watch. She must be a witness. That was the duty her husband had lain upon her. Opposite her, a mat's space away, she could clearly see her husband biting his lip to stifle the pain. The pain was there, with absolute certainty, before her eyes. And Reiko had no means of rescuing him from it.

The sweat glistened on her husband's forehead. The lieutenant closed his eyes, and then opened them again, as if experimenting. The eyes had lost their luster, and seemed innocent and empty like the eyes of a small animal.

The agony before Reiko's eyes burned as strong as the summer sun, utterly remote from the grief which seemed to be tearing herself apart within. The pain grew steadily in stature, stretching upward. Reiko felt that her husband had already become a man in a separate world, a man whose whole being had been resolved into pain, a prisoner in a cage of pain where no hand could reach out to him. But Reiko felt no pain at all. Her grief was not pain. As she thought about this, Reiko began to feel as if someone had raised a cruel wall of glass high between herself and her husband.

Ever since her marriage her husband's existence had been her own existence, and every breath of his had been a breath drawn by herself. But now, while her husband's existence in pain was a vivid reality, Reiko could find in this grief of hers no certain proof at all of her own existence.

With only his right hand on the sword the lieutenant began to cut sideways across his stomach. But as the blade became entangled with the entrails it was pushed constantly outward by their soft resilience; and the lieutenant realized that it would be necessary, as he cut, to use both hands to keep the point pressed deep into his stomach. He pulled the blade across. It did not cut as easily as he had expected. He directed the strength of his whole body into his right hand and pulled again. There was a cut of three or four inches.

The pain spread slowly outward from the inner depths until the whole stomach reverberated. It was like the wild clanging of a bell. Or like a thousand bells which jangled simultaneously at every breath he breathed and every throb of his pulse, rocking his whole being. The lieutenant could no longer stop himself from moaning. But by now the blade had cut its way through to below the navel, and when he noticed this he felt a sense of satisfaction, and a renewal of courage.

The volume of blood had steadily increased, and now it spurted from the wound as if propelled by the beat of the pulse. The mat before the lieutenant was drenched red with splattered blood, and more blood overflowed onto it from pools which gathered in folds of the lieutenant's khaki trousers. A spot, like a bird, came flying across to Reiko and settled on the lap of her white silk kimono.

By the time the lieutenant had at last drawn the sword across to the right side of his stomach, the blade was already cutting shallow and had revealed its naked tip, slippery with blood and grease. But, suddenly stricken by a fit of vomiting, the lieutenant cried out hoarsely. The vomiting made the fierce pain fiercer still, and the stomach, which had thus far remained firm and compact, now abruptly heaved, opening wide its wound, and the entrails burst through, as if the wound too were vomiting. Seemingly ignorant of their master's suffering, the entrails gave an impression of robust health and almost disagreeable vitality as they slipped smoothly out and spilled over into the crotch. The lieutenant's head drooped, his shoulders heaved, his eyes opened to narrow slits, and a thin trickle of saliva dribbled from his mouth. The gold markings on his epaulettes caught the light and glinted.

Blood was scattered everywhere. The lieutenant was soaked in it to his knees, and he sat now in a crumpled and listless posture, one hand on the floor. A raw smell filled the room. The lieutenant, his head drooping, retched repeatedly, and the movement showed vividly in his shoulders. The blade of the sword, now pushed back by the entrails and exposed to its tip, was still in the lieutenant's right hand.

It would be difficult to imagine a more heroic sight than that of the lieutenant at this moment, as he mustered his strength and flung back his head. The movement was performed with sudden violence, and the back of his head struck with a sharp crack against the alcove pillar. Reiko had been sitting until now with her face lowered, gazing in fascination at the tide of blood advancing toward her knees, but the sound took her by surprise and she looked up.

The lieutenant's face was not the face of a living man. The eyes were hollow, the skin parched, the once so lustrous cheeks and lips the color of dried mud. The right hand alone was moving. Laboriously gripping the sword, it hovered shakily in the air like the hand of a marionette and strove to direct the point at the base of the lieutenant's throat. Reiko watched her husband make this last, most heart-rending, futile exertion. Glistening with blood and grease, the point was thrust at the throat again and again. And each time it missed its aim. The strength to guide it was no longer there. The straying point struck the collar and the collar badges. Although its hooks had been unfastened, the stiff military collar had closed together again and was protecting the throat.

Reiko could bear the sight no longer. She tried to go to her husband's help, but she could not stand. She moved through the blood on her knees, and her white skirts grew deep red. Moving to the rear of her husband, she helped no more than by loosening the collar. The quivering blade at last contacted the naked flesh of the throat. At that moment Reiko's impression was that she herself had propelled her husband forward; but that was not the case. It was a movement planned by the lieutenant himself, his last exertion of strength. Abruptly he threw his body at the blade, and the blade pierced his neck, emerging at the nape. There was a tremendous spurt of blood and the lieutenant lay still, cold blue-tinged steel protruding from his neck at the back.

5

SLOWLY, her socks slippery with blood, Reiko descended the stairway. The upstairs room was now completely still.

Switching on the ground-floor lights, she checked the gas jet and the main gas plug and poured water over the smoldering, half-buried charcoal in the brazier. She stood before the upright mirror in the four-and-a-half-mat room and held up her skirts. The bloodstains made it seem as if a bold, vivid pattern was printed across the lower half of her white kimono. When she sat down before the mirror, she was conscious of the dampness and coldness of her husband's blood in the region of her thighs, and she shivered. Then, for a long while, she lingered over her toilet preparations. She applied the rouge generously to her cheeks, and her lips too she painted heavily. This was no longer make-up to please her husband. It was make-up for the world which she would leave behind, and there was a touch of the magnificent and the spectacular in her brushwork. When she rose, the mat before the mirror was wet with blood. Reiko was not concerned about this.

Returning from the toilet, Reiko stood finally on the cement floor of the porchway. When her husband had bolted the door here last night it had been in preparation for death. For a while she stood immersed in the consideration of a simple problem. Should she now leave the bolt drawn? If she were to lock the door, it could be that the neighbors might not notice their suicide for several days. Reiko did not relish the thought of their two corpses putrifying before discovery. After all, it seemed, it would be best to leave it open. . . . She released the bolt, and also drew open the frosted-glass door a fraction. . . . At once a chill wind blew in. There was no sign of anyone in the midnight streets and stars glittered ice-cold through the trees in the large house opposite.

Leaving the door as it was, Reiko mounted the stairs. She had walked here and there for some time and her socks were no longer slippery. About halfway up, her nostrils were already assailed by a peculiar smell.

The lieutenant was lying on his face in a sea of blood. The point protruding from his neck seemed to have grown even more prominent than before. Reiko walked heedlessly across the blood. Sitting beside the lieutenant's corpse, she stared intently at the face, which lay on one cheek on the mat. The eyes were opened wide, as if the lieutenant's attention had been attracted by something. She raised the head, folding it in her sleeve, wiped the blood from the lips, and bestowed a last kiss.

Then she rose and took from the closet a new white blanket and a waist cord. To prevent any derangement of her skirts, she wrapped the blanket about her waist and bound it there firmly with the cord.

Reiko sat herself on a spot about one foot distant from the lieutenant's body. Drawing the dagger from her sash, she examined its dully gleaming blade intently, and held it to her tongue. The taste of the polished steel was slightly sweet.

Reiko did not linger. When she thought how the pain which had previously opened such a gulf between herself and her dying husband was now to become a part of her own experience, she saw before her only the joy of herself entering a realm her husband had already made his own. In her husband's agonized face there had been something inexplicable which she was seeing for the first time. Now she would solve that riddle. Reiko sensed that at last she too would be able to taste the true bitterness and sweetness of that great moral principle in which her husband believed. What had until now been tasted only faintly through her husband's example she was about to savor directly with her own tongue.

Reiko rested the point of the blade against the base of her throat. She thrust hard. The wound was only shallow. Her head blazed, and her hands shook uncontrollably. She gave the blade a strong pull sideways. A warm substance flooded into her mouth, and everything before her eyes reddened, in a vision of spouting blood. She gathered her strength and plunged the point of the blade deep into her throat.

Questions

1. Despite the title and the political event that sets the plot in motion, this story focuses almost exclusively on the relationship between the hero and heroine, their love-making, and their ritual suicides. In what ways do the intensely psychological explorations of the story define and clarify the meaning of patriotism for Lieutenant Takeyama? **2.** *In the West, we tend to view the family—the relationship between husband and wife—as a private and personal matter that has little to do with public, political life. How do Lieutenant Takeyama and his wife view their relationship?* **3.** *Lieutenant Takeyama views "the urges of his flesh and the sincerity of his patriotism" as "two parts of the same thing." What does he mean by this?* **4.** *What does Mishima achieve by the opening paragraph? Why does he sacrifice suspense by recounting at the outset the major events and the story's outcome?* **5.** *What connections does the story establish between love and death?* **6.** *What is the significance of Reiko's deliberations as to whether or not she should leave the door bolt drawn?*

Edward

ANONYMOUS

1
"Why does your brand° sae° drap wi' bluid,   *sword/so*
        Edward, Edward,
Why does your brand sae drap wi' bluid,
        And why sae sad gang° ye, O?"   *go*
"O I ha'e killed my hawk sae guid,
        Mither, mither,
O I ha'e killed my hawk sae guid,
        And I had nae mair but he, O."

2
"Your hawke's bluid was never sae reid,°   *red*
        Edward, Edward,   10
Your hawke's bluid was never sae reid,
        My dear son I tell thee, O."
"O I ha'e killed my reid-roan steed,
        Mither, mither,
O I ha'e killed my reid-roan steed,
        That erst was sae fair and free, O."

3
"Your steed was auld, and ye ha'e gat mair,
        Edward, Edward,
Your steed was auld, and ye ha'e gat mair,
        Some other dule° ye drie,° O."   *grief/suffer*
"O I ha'e killed my fader dear,   21
        Mither, mither,
O I ha'e killed my fader dear,
        Alas, and wae° is me, O!"   *woe*

4

"And whatten penance wul ye drie for that,
     Edward, Edward?
And whatten penance wul ye drie for that,
     My dear son, now tell me O?"
"I'll set my feet in yonder boat,
     Mither, mither,   30
I'll set my feet in yonder boat,
     And I'll fare over the sea, O."

5

"And what wul ye do wi' your towers and your ha',
     Edward, Edward?
And what wul ye do wi' your towers and your ha',
     That were sae fair to see, O?"
"I'll let them stand tul they down fa',
     Mither, mither,
I'll let them stand tul they down fa',   39
     For here never mair maun° I be, O."   *must*

6

"And what wul ye leave to your bairns° and your wife,   *children*
     Edward, Edward?
And what wul ye leave to your bairns and your wife,
     Whan ye gang over the sea, O?"
"The warlde's° room, let them beg thrae° life,   *world's/through*
     Mither, mither,
The warlde's room, let them beg thrae life,
     For them never mair wul I see, O."

7

"And what wul ye leave to your ain mither dear,
     Edward, Edward?   50
And what wul ye leave to your ain mither dear,
     My dear son, now tell me, O?"
"The curse of hell frae° me sall° ye bear,   *from/shall*
     Mither, mither,
The curse of hell frae me sall ye bear,
     Sic° counsels ye gave to me, O."   *such*

1. *Why does the mother reject Edward's answers to her first two questions?* **2.** *Does the poem provide any clues as to the motive of the murder?* **3.** *What effects are achieved through the question-and-answer technique?* **4.** *Edward has murdered his father and then bitterly turns away from his mother, wife, and children. What basis is there in the poem for nevertheless sympathizing with Edward?*

Elegy, Written with His Own Hand in the Tower Before His Execution

CHIDIOCK TICHBORNE [1558?–1586]

My prime of youth is but a frost of cares,
　My feast of joy is but a dish of pain,
My crop of corn is but a field of tares°,   *weeds*
　And all my good is but vain hope of gain:
The day is past, and yet I saw no sun,
And now I live, and now my life is done.

My tale was heard, and yet it was not told,
　My fruit is fall'n, and yet my leaves are green,
My youth is spent, and yet I am not old,
　I saw the world, and yet I was not seen: *10*
My thread is cut, and yet it is not spun,
And now I live, and now my life is done.

I sought my death, and found it in my womb,
　I looked for life, and saw it was a shade,
I trod the earth, and knew it was my tomb,
　And now I die, and now I was but made:
My glass is full, and now my glass is run,
And now I live, and now my life is done.

1. *This poem is based primarily on a series of paradoxical metaphors. Explain the paradoxes in lines 1, 7, and 13.* **2.** *Is there progression and development in this poem or do the second and third stanzas merely repeat in different ways what has already been said in the opening stanza?*

from

Richard II

WILLIAM SHAKESPEARE [1564–1616]

And nothing can we call our own but death
And that small model of the barren earth
Which serves as paste and cover to our bones.
For God's sake, let us sit upon the ground
And tell sad stories of the death of kings:
How some have been deposed; some slain in war;
Some haunted by the ghosts they have deposed;
Some poison'd by their wives; some sleeping kill'd;
All murder'd: for within the hollow crown
That rounds the mortal temples of a king   10
Keeps Death his court,and there the antic sits,
Scoffing his state and grinning at his pomp,
Allowing him a breath, a little scene,
To monarchize, be fear'd and kill with looks,
Infusing him with self and vain conceit,
As if this flesh which walls about our life
Were brass impregnable, and humour'd thus
Comes at the last and with a little pin
Bores through his castle wall, and farewell king!

from

Macbeth

WILLIAM SHAKESPEARE [1564–1616]

She should have died hereafter;
There would have been a time for such a word.
To-morrow, and to-morrow, and to-morrow,
Creeps in this petty pace from day to day
To the last syllable of recorded time,
And all our yesterdays have lighted fools
The way to dusty death. Out, out, brief candle!
Life's but a walking shadow, a poor player
That struts and frets his hour upon the stage
And then is heard no more: it is a tale   10
Told by an idiot, full of sound and fury,
Signifying nothing.

1. *Examine the images in this meditation by Macbeth on the meaning of life (he has just received word that Lady Macbeth has died). Do they hold together or are they confusing; for example, how does the image of the candle (l. 7) relate to the images that precede and follow it?*

from

Hamlet

WILLIAM SHAKESPEARE   **[1564–1616]**

To be, or not to be, that is the question:
Whether 'tis nobler in the mind to suffer
The slings and arrows of outrageous fortune,
Or to take arms against a sea of troubles,
And by opposing end them. To die, to sleep—
No more; and by a sleep to say we end
The heartache, and the thousand natural shocks
That flesh is heir to. 'Tis a consumation
Devoutly to be wished—to die, to sleep—
To sleep, perchance to dream, ay there's the rub;   *10*
For in that sleep of death what dreams may come
When we have shuffled off this mortal coil°   *turmoil*
Must give us pause—there's the respect
That makes calamity of so long life.
For who would bear the whips and scorns of time,
Th' oppressor's wrong, the proud man's contumely,
The pangs of despised love, the law's delay,
The insolence of office, and the spurns
That patient merit of th' unworthy takes,   *19*
When he himself might his quietus° make   *settlement*
With a bare bodkin°? Who would fardels° bear,   *dagger/burdens*
To grunt and sweat under a weary life,
But that the dread of something after death,
The undiscovered country, from whose bourn°   *realm*
No traveller returns, puzzles the will,
And makes us rather bear those ills we have
Than fly to others that we know not of?
Thus conscience° does make cowards of us all;   *thought*
And thus the native hue of resolution
Is sicklied o'er with the pale cast of thought,   *30*
And enterprises of great pitch° and moment   *degree*
With this regard their currents turn awry
And lose the name of action.

1. *What does Hamlet conclude about man's fear of death? Does he view it as cowardly and ignoble?*   **2.** *Explain line 28.*

Death, Be Not Proud

JOHN DONNE [1572–1631]

Death, be not proud, though some have calléd thee
Mighty and dreadful, for thou art not so;
For those whom thou think'st thou dost overthrow
Die not, poor Death, nor yet canst thou kill me.
From rest and sleep, which but thy pictures be,
Much pleasure; then from thee much more must flow,
And soonest our best men with thee do go,
Rest of their bones, and soul's delivery.
Thou art slave to fate, chance, kings, and desperate men,
And dost with poison, war, and sickness dwell,   10
And poppy or charms can make us sleep as well
And better than thy stroke; why swell'st thou then?
One short sleep past, we wake eternally
And death shall be no more; Death, thou shalt die.

1. *Examine the various meanings of "sleep" in this sonnet. Does it have the same meanings in Hamlet's soliloquy?* **2.** *Why is Donne able to face death without that fear which Hamlet says all men feel in the face of death?*

The Glories of Our Blood and State

JAMES SHIRLEY [1596–1666]

The glories of our blood and state
Are shadows, not substantial things;
There is no armor against fate;
Death lays his icy hand on kings.
    Scepter and crown
    Must tumble down
And in the dust be equal made
With the poor crooked scythe and spade.

Some men with swords may reap the field
And plant fresh laurels where they kill,   10
But their strong nerves at last must yield;
They tame but one another still.
    Early or late
    They stoop to fate

And must give up their murmuring breath,
When they, pale captives, creep to death.

The garlands wither on your brow,
Then boast no more your mighty deeds;
Upon death's purple altar now
See where the victor-victim bleeds.   20
    Your heads must come
    To the cold tomb;
Only the actions of the just
Smell sweet and blossom in their dust.

1. *Explain the meaning of the "crooked scythe and spade" (l. 8).*   **2.** *What are "blood and state"?*   **3.** *Whom is the poet addressing in the final stanza?*

To a Mistress Dying

SIR WILLIAM DAVENANT   [1606–1668]

LOVER.   Your beauty, ripe and calm and fresh
              As eastern summers are,
           Must now, forsaking time and flesh,
              Add light to some small star.

PHILOSOPHER.   Whilst she yet lives, were stars decayed,
                    Their light by hers relief might find;
                 But death will lead her to a shade
                    Where love is cold and beauty blind.

LOVER.   Lovers, whose priests all poets are,
              Think every mistress, when she dies,   10
           Is changed at least into a star:
              And who dares doubt the poets wise?

PHILOSOPHER.   But ask not bodies doomed to die.
                    To what abode they go;
                 Since knowledge is but sorrow's spy,
                    It is not safe to know.

1. *State the differences between the positions of the Lover and the Philosopher. Are they contradictory?*   **2.** *Explain the meaning of line 15.*

Elegy Written in a Country Churchyard

THOMAS GRAY [1716–1771]

The curfew tolls the knell of parting day,
    The lowing herd wind slowly o'er the lea,
The plowman homeward plods his weary way,
    And leaves the world to darkness and to me.

Now fades the glimmering landscape on the sight,
    And all the air a solemn stillness holds,
Save where the beetle wheels his droning flight,
    And drowsy tinklings lull the distant folds;

Save that from yonder ivy-mantled tower
    The moping owl does to the moon complain   *10*
Of such, as wandering near her secret bower,
    Molest her ancient solitary reign.

Beneath those rugged elms, that yew tree's shade,
    Where heaves the turf in many a moldering heap,
Each in his narrow cell forever laid,
    The rude° forefathers of the hamlet sleep.   *untaught*

The breezy call of incense-breathing Morn,
    The swallow twittering from the straw-built shed,
The cock's shrill clarion, or the echoing horn,°   *hunter's horn*
    No more shall rouse them from their lowly bed.   *20*

For them no more the blazing hearth shall burn,
    Or busy housewife ply her evening care;
No children run to lisp their sire's return,
    Or climb his knees the envied kiss to share.

Oft did the harvest to their sickle yield,
    Their furrow oft the stubborn glebe° has broke;   *field*
How jocund did they drive their team afield!
    How bowed the woods beneath their sturdy stroke!

Let not Ambition mock their useful toil,
    Their homely joys, and destiny obscure;   *30*
Nor Grandeur hear with a disdainful smile
    The short and simple annals of the poor.

The boast of heraldry,° the pomp of power,   *noble birth*
    And all that beauty, all that wealth e'er gave,
Awaits alike the inevitable hour.
    The paths of glory lead but to the grave.

Nor you, ye proud, impute to these the fault,
    If Memory o'er their tomb no trophies° raise,   *memorial*
Where through the long-drawn aisle and fretted° vault   *decorated*
    The pealing anthem swells the note of praise.   40

Can storied° urn or animated bust   *inscribed*
    Back to its mansion call the fleeting breath?
Can Honor's voice provoke the silent dust,
    Or Flattery soothe the dull cold ear of Death?

Perhaps in this neglected spot is laid
    Some heart once pregnant with celestial fire;
Hands that the rod of empire might have swayed,
    Or waked to ecstasy the living lyre.

But Knowledge to their eyes her ample page
    Rich with the spoils of time did ne'er unroll;   50
Chill Penury repressed their noble rage,
    And froze the genial current of the soul.

Full many a gem of purest ray serene,
    The dark unfathomed caves of ocean bear:
Full many a flower is born to blush unseen,
    And waste its sweetness on the desert air.

Some village Hampden,¹ that with dauntless breast
    The little tyrant of his fields withstood;
Some mute inglorious Milton here may rest,
    Some Cromwell guiltless of his country's blood.   60

The applause of listening senates to command,
    The threats of pain and ruin to despise,
To scatter plenty o'er a smiling land,
    And read their history in a nation's eyes,

Their lot forbade: nor circumscribed alone
    Their growing virtues, but their crimes confined;
Forbade to wade through slaughter to a throne,
    And shut the gates of mercy on mankind,

---

1. John Hampden (1594–1643) championed the people against the autocratic policies of Charles I.

The struggling pangs of conscious truth to hide,
    To quench the blushes of ingenuous shame,   70
Or heap the shrine of Luxury and Pride
    With incense kindled at the Muse's flame.

Far from the madding crowd's ignoble strife,
    Their sober wishes never learned to stray;
Along the cool sequestered vale of life
    They kept the noiseless tenor of their way.

Yet even these bones from insult to protect
    Some frail memorial still erected nigh,
With uncouth rhymes and shapeless sculpture decked,
    Implores the passing tribute of a sigh.   80

Their name, their years, spelt by the unlettered Muse,
    The place of fame and elegy supply:
And many a holy text around she strews,
    That teach the rustic moralist to die.

For who to dumb Forgetfulness a prey,
    This pleasing anxious being e'er resigned,
Left the warm precincts of the cheerful day,
    Nor cast one longing lingering look behind?

On some fond breast the parting soul relies,
    Some pious drops the closing eye requires;   90
Even from the tomb the voice of Nature cries,
    Even in our ashes live their wonted fires.

For thee, who mindful of the unhonored dead
    Dost in these lines their artless tale relate;
If chance, by lonely contemplation led,
    Some kindred spirit shall inquire thy fate,

Haply some hoary-headed swain may say,
    "Oft have we seen him at the peep of dawn
Brushing with hasty steps the dews away
    To meet the sun upon the upland lawn.   100

"There at the foot of yonder nodding beech
    That wreathes its old fantastic roots so high,
His listless length at noontide would he stretch,
    And pore upon the brook that babbles by.

"Hard by yon wood, now smiling as in scorn,
    Muttering his wayward fancies he would rove,
Now drooping, woeful wan, like one forlorn,
    Or crazed with care, or crossed in hopeless love.

"One morn I missed him on the customed hill,
      Along the heath and near his favorite tree;   110
Another came; nor yet beside the rill,
      Nor up the lawn, nor at the wood was he;

"The next with dirges due in sad array
      Slow through the churchway path we saw him borne.
Approach and read (for thou canst read) the lay,
      Graved on the stone beneath yon aged thorn."

THE EPITAPH

Here rests his head upon the lap of Earth
      A youth to Fortune and to Fame unknown
Fair Science° frowned not on his humble birth,   learning
      And Melancholy marked him for her own.   120

Large was his bounty, and his soul sincere,
      Heaven did a recompense as largely send:
He gave to Misery all he had, a tear,
      He gained from Heaven ('twas all he wished) a friend.

No farther seek his merits to disclose,
      Or draw his frailties from their dread abode
(There they alike in trembling hope repose),
      The bosom of his Father and his God.

1. *Does this poem celebrate the advantages of obscurity and ignorance over fame,
wealth, and knowledge? Explain.*   **2.** *Why have the people Gray honors in this poem
lived and died in obscurity? Does the poet offer any suggestions for change? Explain.*   **3.**
Why would "Ambition mock their useful toil" (l. 29)?

When I Have Fears

JOHN KEATS   [1795–1821]

When I have fears that I may cease to be
      Before my pen has gleaned my teeming brain,
Before high-piléd books, in charact'ry,°   written symbols
      Hold like rich garners the full-ripened grain;
When I behold, upon the night's starred face,
      Huge cloudy symbols of a high romance,
And think that I may never live to trace
      Their shadows, with the magic hand of chance;
And when I feel, fair creature of an hour,

That I shall never look upon thee more,   10
  Never have relish in the faery° power   *magical*
     Of unreflecting love!—then on the shore
Of the wide world I stand alone, and think
Till Love and Fame to nothingness do sink.

1. *What consequences of death does the poet fear in each of the three quatrains?* **2.** *What value have Love and Fame in the face of death?*

Ode to a Nightingale

JOHN KEATS [1795–1821]

1

My heart aches, and a drowsy numbness pains
  My sense, as though of hemlock I had drunk,
Or emptied some dull opiate to the drains
  One minute past, and Lethe-wards² had sunk:
'Tis not through envy of thy happy lot,
  But being too happy in thine happiness—
    That thou, light-wingéd Dryad of the trees,
      In some melodious plot
  Of beechen green, and shadows numberless,
    Singest of summer in full-throated ease.   10

2

O, for a draught of vintage! that hath been
  Cooled a long age in the deep-delvéd earth,
Tasting of Flora³ and the country green,
  Dance, and Provençal song,⁴ and sunburnt mirth!
O for a beaker full of the warm South,
  Full of the true, the blushful Hippocrene,⁵
    With beaded bubbles winking at the brim,
      And purple-stainéd mouth;
  That I might drink, and leave the world unseen,
    And with thee fade away into the forest dim: 20

2. Towards Lethe, in Greek mythology the river in Hades which caused forgetfulness.
3. Roman goddess of flowers.
4. Provence, in southern France, renowned for its medieval troubadors.
5. In Greek mythology, the fountain of the Muses whose waters gave poetic inspiration.

3

Fade far away, dissolve, and quite forget
    What thou among the leaves hast never known,
The weariness, the fever, and the fret
    Here, where men sit and hear each other groan;
Where palsy shakes a few, sad, last gray hairs,
    Where youth grows pale, and specter-thin, and dies;
        Where but to think is to be full of sorrow
           And leaden-eyed despairs,
    Where Beauty cannot keep her lustrous eyes,
        Or new Love pine at them beyond tomorrow.   *30*

4

Away! away! for I will fly to thee,
    Not charioted by Bacchus⁶ and his pards,
But on the viewless wings of Poesy,
    Though the dull brain perplexes and retards:
Already with thee! tender is the night,
    And haply the Queen-Moon is on her throne,
        Clustered around by all her starry Fays;°   *fairies*
          But here there is no light,
    Save what from heaven is with the breezes blown
        Through verdurous glooms and winding mossy ways.   *40*

5

I cannot see what flowers are at my feet,
    Nor what soft incense hangs upon the boughs,
But, in embalmèd darkness, guess each sweet
    Wherewith the seasonable month endows
The grass, the thicket, and the fruit tree wild;
    White hawthorn, and the pastoral eglantine;
        Fast fading violets covered up in leaves;
          And mid-May's eldest child,
    The coming musk-rose, full of dewy wine,
        The murmurous haunt of flies on summer eves.   *50*

6

Darkling° I listen; and for many a time   *in darkness*
    I have been half in love with easeful Death,
Called him soft names in many a musèd rhyme,
    To take into the air my quiet breath;
Now more than ever seems it rich to die,
    To cease upon the midnight with no pain,
        While thou art pouring forth thy soul abroad
          In such an ecstasy!
    Still wouldst thou sing, and I have ears in vain—
        To thy high requiem become a sod.   *60*

---

6.   The god of wine, often represented in a chariot drawn by leopards ("pards").

7

Thou wast not born for death, immortal Bird!
    No hungry generations tread thee down;
The voice I hear this passing night was heard
    In ancient days by emperor and clown:
Perhaps the selfsame song that found a path
        Through the sad heart of Ruth,[7] when, sick for home,
            She stood in tears amid the alien corn;
                The same that ofttimes hath
    Charmed magic casements, opening on the foam
        Of perilous seas, in faery lands forlorn.   70

8

Forlorn! the very word is like a bell
    To toll me back from thee to my sole self!
Adieu! the fancy cannot cheat so well
    As she is famed to do, deceiving elf.
Adieu! adieu! thy plaintive anthem fades
        Past the near meadows, over the still stream,
            Up the hill side; and now 'tis buried deep
                In the next valley-glades:
    Was it a vision, or a waking dream?
        Fled is that music:—Do I wake or sleep?   80

1. *What does the nightingale represent?* **2.** *In stanza 6, Keats declares that the very moment at which the nightingale's song is most ecstatic would be the right moment to die; yet the realization that the nightingale's song would continue after his death jars him. Why?* **3.** *In what sense is the nightingale "not born for death" (l. 61)? Does this line imply that all men are born for death? Explain.* **4.** *In stanza 4, Keats says that he will reach the nightingale "on the viewless wings of Poesy." Why are the wings of poetry "viewless," and what is the connection between the nightingale and poetry?*

Nature

HENRY WADSWORTH LONGFELLOW [1807–1882]

As a fond mother, when the day is o'er,
    Leads by the hand her little child to bed,
    Half willing, half reluctant to be led,
    And leave his broken playthings on the floor,

---

7. The young widow in the Old Testament (Ruth, 2) who left her own people to live in a strange land, where she gleaned in the barley fields ("alien corn").

Still gazing at them through the open door,
    Nor wholly reassured and comforted
    By promises of others in their stead,
    Which, though more splendid, may not please him more;
So Nature deals with us, and takes away
    Our playthings one by one, and by the hand   10
    Leads us to rest so gently, that we go
Scarce knowing if we wish to go or stay,
    Being too full of sleep to understand
    How far the unknown transcends the what we know.

The Raven

EDGAR ALLAN POE [1809–1849]

Once upon a midnight dreary, while I pondered, weak and weary,
Over many a quaint and curious volume of forgotten lore,
While I nodded, nearly napping, suddenly there came a tapping,
As of some one gently rapping, rapping at my chamber door.
" 'Tis some visitor," I muttered, "tapping at my chamber door—
        Only this and nothing more."

Ah, distinctly I remember it was in the bleak December,
And each separate dying ember wrought its ghost upon the floor.
Eagerly I wished the morrow;—vainly I had sought to borrow
From my books surcease of sorrow—sorrow for the lost Lenore—   10
For the rare and radiant maiden whom the angels name Lenore—
        Nameless here for evermore.

And the silken sad uncertain rustling of each purple curtain
Thrilled me—filled me with fantastic terrors never felt before;
So that now, to still the beating of my heart, I stood repeating,
" 'Tis some visitor entreating entrance at my chamber door—
Some late visitor entreating entrance at my chamber door;—
        This it is and nothing more."

Presently my soul grew stronger; hesitating then no longer,
"Sir," said I, "or Madam, truly your forgiveness I implore;   20
But the fact is I was napping, and so gently you came rapping,
And so faintly you came tapping, tapping at my chamber door,
That I scarce was sure I heard you"—here I opened wide the door;—
        Darkness there, and nothing more.

Deep into that darkness peering, long I stood there wondering, fearing,
Doubting, dreaming dreams no mortals ever dared to dream before;
But the silence was unbroken, and the stillness gave no token,
And the only word there spoken was the whispered word, "Lenore!"
This I whispered, and an echo murmured back the word, "Lenore!"—
          Merely this and nothing more.   30

Back into the chamber turning, all my soul within me burning,
Soon again I heard a tapping somewhat louder than before.
"Surely," said I, "surely that is something at my window lattice;
Let me see, then, what thereat is, and this mystery explore—
Let my heart be still a moment and this mystery explore;—
          'Tis the wind and nothing more."

Open here I flung the shutter, when, with many a flirt and flutter,
In there stepped a stately raven of the saintly days of yore;
Not the least obeisance made he; not a minute stopped or stayed he;
But, with mien of lord or lady, perched above my chamber door—   40
Perched upon a bust of Pallas[8] just above my chamber door—
          Perched, and sat, and nothing more.

Then this ebony bird beguiling my sad fancy into smiling,
By the grave and stern decorum of the countenance it wore,
"Though thy crest be shorn and shaven, thou," I said, "art sure no craven,
Ghastly grim and ancient raven wandering from the Nightly shore—
Tell me what thy lordly name is on the Night's Plutonian[9] shore!"
          Quoth the raven, "Nevermore."

Much I marvelled this ungainly fowl to hear discourse so plainly,
Though its answer little meaning—little relevancy bore;   50
For we cannot help agreeing that no living human being
Ever yet was blessed with seeing bird above his chamber door—
Bird or beast upon the sculptured bust above his chamber door,
          With such name as "Nevermore."

But the raven, sitting lonely on the placid bust, spoke only
That one word, as if his soul in that one word he did outpour.
Nothing farther then he uttered—not a feather then he fluttered—
Till I scarcely more than muttered, "Other friends have flown before—
On the morrow *he* will leave me as my hopes have flown before."
          Then the bird said, "Nevermore."   60

Startled at the stillness broken by reply so aptly spoken,
"Doubtless," said I, "what it utters is its only stock and store,
Caught from some unhappy master whom unmerciful Disaster

---

8. In Greek mythology, the goddess of wisdom.
9. In Greek and Roman mythology, Pluto was the god of the dead.

Followed fast and followed faster till his songs one burden bore—
Till the dirges of his Hope that melancholy burden bore
        Of 'Never—nevermore.' "

But the raven still beguiling all my sad soul into smiling,
Straight I wheeled a cushioned seat in front of bird and bust and door;
Then, upon the velvet sinking, I betook myself to linking
Fancy unto fancy, thinking what this ominous bird of yore—   70
What this grim, ungainly, ghastly, gaunt, and ominous bird of yore
        Meant in croaking "Nevermore."

This I sat engaged in guessing, but no syllable expressing
To the fowl whose fiery eyes now burned into my bosom's core;
This and more I sat divining, with my head at ease reclining
On the cushion's velvet lining that the lamplight gloated o'er,
But whose velvet violet lining with the lamplight gloating o'er,
        She shall press, ah, nevermore!

Then, methought, the air grew denser, perfumed from an unseen censer
Swung by angels whose faint foot-falls tinkled on the tufted floor.   80
"Wretch," I cried, "thy God hath lent thee—by these angels he hath sent thee
Respite—respite and nepenthe[10] from thy memories of Lenore!
Quaff, oh quaff this kind nepenthe and forget this lost Lenore!"
        Quoth the raven, "Nevermore."

"Prophet!" said I, "thing of evil!—prophet still, if bird or devil!—
Whether Tempter sent, or whether tempest tossed thee here ashore,
Desolate, yet all undaunted, on this desert land enchanted—
On this home by Horror haunted,—tell me truly, I implore—
Is there—*is* there balm in Gilead[11]—tell me—tell me, I implore!"
        Quoth the raven, "Nevermore."   90

"Prophet!" said I, "thing of evil!—prophet still, if bird or devil!
By that heaven that bends above us—by that God we both adore—
Tell this soul with sorrow laden if, within the distant Aidenn,
It shall clasp a sainted maiden whom the angels name Lenore—
Clasp a rare and radiant maiden whom the angels name Lenore."
        Quoth the raven, "Nevermore."

"Be that word our sign of parting, bird or fiend!" I shrieked, upstarting—
"Get thee back into the tempest and the Night's Plutonian shore!
Leave no black plume as a token of that lie thy soul hath spoken!
Leave my loneliness unbroken!—quit the bust above my door!   100
Take thy beak from out my heart, and take thy form from off my door!"
        Quoth the raven, "Nevermore."

---

10. A drug thought by the Greeks to banish pain and sorrow.
11. A reference to the region of ancient Palestine that produced, according to the Old Testament (Jeremiah 8:22), an herb of great healing power.

And the raven never flitting, still is sitting, *still* is sitting
On the pallid bust of Pallas just above my chamber door;
And his eyes have all the seeming of a demon's that is dreaming,
And the lamp-light o'er him streaming throws his shadow on the floor;
And my soul from out that shadow that lies floating on the floor
        Shall be lifted—nevermore!

Growing Old

MATTHEW ARNOLD [1822–1888]

What is it to grow old?
Is it to lose the glory of the form,
The luster of the eye?
Is it for beauty to forego her wreath?
—Yes, but not this alone.

Is it to feel our strength—
Not our bloom only, but our strength—decay?
Is it to feel each limb
Grow stiffer, every function less exact,
Each nerve more loosely strung?   10

Yes, this, and more; but not
Ah, 'tis not what in youth we dreamed 'twould be!
'Tis not to have our life
Mellowed and softened as with sunset glow,
A golden day's decline.

'Tis not to see the world
As from a height, with rapt prophetic eyes,
And heart profoundly stirred;
And weep, and feel the fullness of the past,
The years that are no more.   20

It is to spend long days
And not once feel that we were ever young;
It is to add, immured
In the hot prison of the present, month
To month with weary pain.

It is to suffer this,
And feel but half, and feebly, what we feel.
Deep in our hidden heart
Festers the dull remembrance of a change,
But no emotion—none.   30

It is—last stage of all—
When we are frozen up within, and quite
The phantom of ourselves,
To hear the world applaud the hollow ghost
Which blamed the living man.

After Great Pain,
a Formal Feeling Comes

EMILY DICKINSON [1830–1886]

After great pain, a formal feeling comes—
The Nerves sit ceremonious, like Tombs—
The stiff Heart questions was it He, that bore,
And Yesterday, or Centuries before?

The Feet, mechanical, go round—
Of Ground, or Air, or Ought—
A Wooden way
Regardless grown,
A Quartz contentment, like a stone—

This is the Hour of Lead—   10
Remembered, if outlived,
As Freezing persons, recollect the Snow—
First—Chill—then Stupor—then the letting go—

1. *Is this poem about physical or psychic pain? Explain.* **2.** *What is the meaning of "stiff Heart" (l. 3) and "Quartz contentment" (l. 9)? Are they part of a larger pattern of images? Explain.*

I Heard a Fly Buzz—When I Died

EMILY DICKINSON [1830–1886]

I heard a Fly buzz—when I died—
The Stillness in the Room
Was like the Stillness in the Air—
Between the Heaves of Storm—

The Eyes around—had wrung them dry—
And Breaths were gathering firm
For that last Onset—when the King
Be witnessed—in the Room—

I willed my Keepsakes—Signed away
What portion of me be   10
Assignable—and then it was
There interposed a Fly—

With Blue—uncertain stumbling Buzz—
Between the light—and me—
And then the Windows failed—and then
I could not see to see—

Rest

CHRISTINA ROSSETTI   [1830–1894]

O Earth, lie heavily upon her eyes;
Seal her sweet eyes weary of watching, Earth;
Lie close around her: leave no room for mirth
With its harsh laughter, nor for sound of sighs.

She hath no questions, she hath no replies,
Hushed in and curtained with a blesséd dearth
Of all that irked her from the hour of birth;
With stillness that is almost Paradise.

Darkness more clear than noonday holdeth her,
Silence more musical than any song;   10
Even her very heart has ceased to stir.
Until the morning of Eternity
Her rest shall not begin nor end, but be;
And when she wakes she will not think it long.

1. *Does the speaker see the death of the girl as tragic? Explain.*   **2.** *What has been the girl's experience of life?*   **3.** *Explain the paradoxes of lines nine and ten.*

To an Athlete Dying Young

A. E. HOUSMAN   [1859–1936]

The time you won your town the race
We chaired you through the market place;
Man and boy stood cheering by,
And home we brought you shoulder-high.

Today, the road all runners come,
Shoulder-high we bring you home,
And set you at your threshold down,
Townsman of a stiller town.

Smart lad, to slip betimes away
From fields where glory does not stay   10
And early though the laurel grows
It withers quicker than the rose.

Eyes the shady night has shut
Cannot see the record cut,
And silence sounds no worse than cheers
After earth has stopped the ears:

Now you will not swell the rout
Of lads that wore their honors out,
Runners whom renown outran
And the name died before the man.   20

So set, before its echoes fade,
The fleet foot on the sill of shade,
And hold to the low lintel up
The still defended challenge cup.

And round that early laureled head
Will flock to gaze the strengthless dead
And find unwithered on its curls
The garland briefer than a girl's.

The Old Men Admiring
Themselves in the Water

WILLIAM BUTLER YEATS   [1865–1939]

I heard the old, old men say,
'Everything alters,
And one by one we drop away.'
They had hands like claws, and their knees
Were twisted like the old thorn-trees
By the waters.
I heard the old, old men say,
'All that's beautiful drifts away
Like the waters.'

1. Does this poem celebrate old age? **2.** What do the old men admire about themselves? Does the reader share that admiration? **3.** Compare the two statements of the old men (ll. 3–4; 8–9) paying particular attention to "drop away" in the first and "drifts away / like the waters" in the second. What does the difference between them suggest about mortality and time?

Sailing to Byzantium[12]

WILLIAM BUTLER YEATS [1865–1939]

1

That is no country for old men. The young
In one another's arms, birds in the trees
—Those dying generations—at their song,
The salmon-falls, the mackerel-crowded seas,
Fish, flesh, or fowl, commend all summer long
Whatever is begotten, born, and dies.
Caught in that sensual music all neglect
Monuments of unaging intellect.

2

An aged man is but a paltry thing,
A tattered coat upon a stick, unless   10
Soul clap its hands and sing, and louder sing
For every tatter in its mortal dress,
Nor is there singing school but studying
Monuments of its own magnificence;
And therefore I have sailed the seas and come
To the holy city of Byzantium.

3

O sages standing in God's holy fire
As in the gold mosaic of a wall,
Come from the holy fire, perne in a gyre,[13]
And be the singing-masters of my soul.   20
Consume my heart away; sick with desire
And fastened to a dying animal
It knows not what it is; and gather me
Into the artifice of eternity.

---

12. Capital of the ancient Eastern Roman Empire, Byzantium (modern Istanbul) is celebrated for its great art, including mosaics (in lines 17–18, Yeats addresses the figures in one of these mosaics). In *A Vision*, Yeats cites Byzantium as possibly the only civilization which had achieved what he called "Unity of Being," a state where "religious, aesthetic and practical life were one...."
13. I.e., whirl in a spiral motion. Yeats associated this motion with the cycles of history and the fate of the individual. Here he entreats the sages represented in the mosaic to take him out of the natural world described in the first stanza and into the eternal world of art.

4

Once out of nature I shall never take
My bodily form from any natural thing,
But such a form as Grecian goldsmiths make
Of hammered gold and gold enameling
To keep a drowsy Emperor awake;[14]
Or set upon a golden bough to sing   30
To lords and ladies of Byzantium
Of what is past, or passing, or to come.

1. *Examine the ways in which the imagery of bird and song are used throughout this poem.* **2.** *This poem incorporates a series of contrasts, among them "That" country and Byzantium, the real birds of the first stanza and the artificial bird of the final stanza. What others do you find?* **3.** *What are the meanings of "generations" (l. 3)?* **4.** *For what is the poet "sick with desire" (l. 21)?* **5.** *In what sense is eternity an "artifice" (l. 24)?*

Richard Cory

EDWIN ARLINGTON ROBINSON [1869–1935]

Whenever Richard Cory went down town,
We people on the pavement looked at him:
He was a gentleman from sole to crown,
Clean favored, and imperially slim.

And he was always quietly arrayed,
And he was always human when he talked;
But still he fluttered pulses when he said,
"Good-morning," and he glittered when he walked.

And he was rich—yes, richer than a king—
And admirably schooled in every grace: 10
In fine, we thought that he was everything
To make us wish that we were in his place.

So on we worked, and waited for the light,
And went without the meat, and cursed the bread;
And Richard Cory, one calm summer night,
Went home and put a bullet through his head.

---

14. "I have read somewhere," Yeats wrote, "that in the Emperor's palace at Byzantium was a tree made of gold and silver, and artificial birds that sang." The poet wishes to become an artificial bird (a work of art) in contrast to the real birds of the first stanza.

How Annandale Went Out

EDWIN ARLINGTON ROBINSON   [1869–1935]

"They called it Annandale—and I was there
To flourish, to find words, and to attend:
Liar, physician, hypocrite, and friend,
I watched him; and the sight was not so fair
As one or two that I have seen elsewhere:
An apparatus not for me to mend—
A wreck, with hell between him and the end,
Remained of Annandale; and I was there.

"I knew the ruin as I knew the man;
So put the two together, if you can,   10
Remembering the worst you know of me.
Now view yourself as I was, on the spot—
With a slight kind of engine. Do you see?
Like this . . . You wouldn't hang me? I thought not."

1. *Who is the speaker in this poem?*   **2.** *Annandale is the name of a man. Why is he referred to as "it" in line 1?*   **3.** *What is "a slight kind of engine" (l. 13)?*   **4.** *What has the speaker done?*

The Mill

EDWIN ARLINGTON ROBINSON   [1869–1935]

The miller's wife had waited long,
    The tea was cold, the fire was dead;
And there might yet be nothing wrong
    In how he went and what he said:
"There are no millers any more,"
    Was all that she had heard him say;
And he had lingered at the door
    So long that it seemed yesterday.

Sick with a fear that had no form
    She knew that she was there at last;   10
And in the mill there was a warm
    And mealy fragrance of the past.
What else there was would only seem
    To say again what he had meant;

And what was hanging from a beam
    Would not have heeded where she went.

And if she thought it followed her,
    She may have reasoned in the dark
That one way of the few there were
    Would hide her and would leave no mark: 20
Black water, smooth above the weir
    Like starry velvet in the night,
Though ruffled once, would soon appear
    The same as ever to the sight.

1. *What has happened to the miller?* **2.** *Explain lines 13–14.* **3.** *Explain the reference to the ruffled water in the final stanza.*

After Apple-Picking

ROBERT FROST [1874–1963]

My long two-pointed ladder's sticking through a tree
Toward heaven still,
And there's a barrel that I didn't fill
Beside it, and there may be two or three
Apples I didn't pick upon some bough.
But I am done with apple-picking now.
Essence of winter sleep is on the night,
The scent of apples: I am drowsing off.
I cannot rub the strangeness from my sight
I got from looking through a pane of glass   10
I skimmed this morning from the drinking trough
And held against the world of hoary grass.
It melted, and I let it fall and break.
But I was well
Upon my way to sleep before it fell,
And I could tell
What form my dreaming was about to take.
Magnified apples appear and disappear,
Stem end and blossom end,
And every fleck of russet showing clear.   20
My instep arch not only keeps the ache,
It keeps the pressure of a ladder-round.
I feel the ladder sway as the boughs bend.
And I keep hearing from the cellar bin
The rumbling sound
Of load on load of apples coming in.

For I have had too much
Of apple-picking: I am overtired
Of the great harvest I myself desired.
There were ten thousand thousand fruit to touch,   30
Cherish in hand, lift down, and not let fall.
For all
That struck the earth,
No matter if not bruised or spiked with stubble,
Went surely to the cider-apple heap
As of no worth.
One can see what will trouble
This sleep of mine, whatever sleep it is.
Were he not gone,
The woodchuck could say whether it's like his   40
Long sleep, as I describe its coming on,
Or just some human sleep.

1. *What does apple-picking symbolize?* **2.** *Why is the speaker uncertain, at the end, what kind of sleep is coming on him?*

'Out, Out-'[15]

ROBERT FROST [1874–1963]

The buzz-saw snarled and rattled in the yard
And made dust and dropped stove-length sticks of wood,
Sweet-scented stuff when the breeze drew across it.
And from there those that lifted eyes could count
Five mountain ranges one behind the other
Under the sunset far into Vermont.
And the saw snarled and rattled, snarled and rattled,
As it ran light, or had to bear a load.
And nothing happened: day was all but done.
Call it a day, I wish they might have said   10
To please the boy by giving him the half hour
That a boy counts so much when saved from work.
His sister stood beside them in her apron
To tell them 'Supper.' At the word, the saw,
As if to prove saws knew what supper meant,
Leaped out at the boy's hand, or seemed to leap—
He must have given the hand. However it was,
Neither refused the meeting. But the hand!

---

15.   The title is taken from the famous speech of Macbeth upon hearing that his wife has died (see p. 792).

The boy's first outcry was a rueful laugh,
As he swung toward them holding up the hand   20
Half in appeal, but half as if to keep
The life from spilling. Then the boy saw all—
Since he was old enough to know, big boy
Doing a man's work, though a child at heart—
He saw all spoiled. 'Don't let him cut my hand off—
The doctor, when he comes. Don't let him, sister!'
So. But the hand was gone already.
The doctor put him in the dark of ether.
He lay and puffed his lips out with his breath.
And then—the watcher at his pulse took fright.   30
No one believed. They listened at his heart.
Little—less—nothing!—and that ended it.
No more to build on there. And they, since they
Were not the one dead, turned to their affairs.

Tract

WILLIAM CARLOS WILLIAMS [1883–1963]

I will teach you my townspeople
how to perform a funeral—
for you have it over a troop
of artists—
unless one should scour the world—
you have the ground sense necessary.

See! the hearse leads.
I begin with a design for a hearse.
For Christ's sake not black—
nor white either—and not polished!   10
Let it be weathered—like a farm wagon—
with gilt wheels (this could be
applied fresh at small expense)
or no wheels at all:
a rough dray to drag over the ground.

Knock the glass out!
My God—glass, my townspeople!
For what purpose? Is it for the dead
to look out or for us to see
how well he is housed or to see   20
the flowers or the lack of them—
or what?
To keep the rain and snow from him?
He will have a heavier rain soon:

pebbles and dirt and what not.
Let there be no glass—
and no upholstery! phew!
and no little brass rollers
and small easy wheels on the bottom—
my townspeople what are you thinking of!   30

A rough plain hearse then
with gilt wheels and no top at all.
On this the coffin lies
by its own weight.

        No wreaths please—
especially no hot-house flowers.
Some common memento is better,
something he prized and is known by:
his old clothes—a few books perhaps—
God knows what! You realize   40
how we are about these things,
my townspeople—
something will be found—anything—
even flowers if he had come to that.
So much for the hearse.

For heaven's sake though see to the driver!
Take off the silk hat! In fact
that's no place at all for him
up there unceremoniously
dragging our friend out of his own dignity!   50
Bring him down—bring him down!
Low and inconspicuous! I'd not have him ride
on the wagon at all—damn him—
the undertaker's understrapper!
Let him hold the reins
and walk at the side
and inconspicuously too!

Then briefly as to yourselves:
Walk behind—as they do in France,
seventh class, or if you ride   60
Hell take curtains! Go with some show
of inconvenience; sit openly—
to the weather as to grief.
Or do you think you can shut grief in?
What—from us? We who have perhaps
nothing to lose? Share with us
share with us—it will be money
in your pockets.

        Go now
I think you are ready.

Bells for John Whiteside's Daughter

JOHN CROWE RANSOM [b. 1888]

There was such speed in her little body,
And such lightness in her footfall,
It is no wonder that her brown study°   reverie
Astonishes us all.

Her wars were bruited in our high window.
We looked among orchard trees and beyond,
Where she took arms against her shadow,
Or harried unto the pond

The lazy geese, like a snow cloud
Dripping their snow on the green grass,   10
Tricking and stopping, sleepy and proud,
Who cried in goose, Alas,

For the tireless heart within the little
Lady with rod that made them rise
From their noon apple-dreams, and scuttle
Goose-fashion under the skies!

But now go the bells, and we are ready;
In one house we are sternly stopped
To say we are vexed at her brown study,
Lying so primly propped.   20

Dulce et Decorum Est

WILFRED OWEN [1893–1918]

Bent double, like old beggars under sacks,
Knock-kneed, coughing like hags, we cursed through sludge,
Till on the haunting flares we turned our backs,
And towards our distant rest began to trudge.
Men marched asleep. Many had lost their boots,
But limped on, blood-shod. All went lame, all blind;
Drunk with fatigue; deaf even to the hoots
Of gas-shells dropping softly behind.

Gas! GAS! Quick, boys!—An ecstasy of fumbling,
Fitting the clumsy helmets just in time,   10
But someone still was yelling out and stumbling
And flound'ring like a man in fire or lime.—
Dim through the misty panes and thick green light,
As under a green sea, I saw him drowning.

In all my dreams before my helpless sight
He plunges at me, guttering, choking, drowning.

If in some smothering dreams, you too could pace
Behind the wagon that we flung him in,
And watch the white eyes writhing in his face,
His hanging face, like a devil's sick of sin,   20
If you could hear, at every jolt, the blood
Come gargling from the froth-corrupted lungs
Bitter as the cud
Of vile, incurable sores on innocent tongues,—
My friend, you would not tell with such high zest
To children ardent for some desperate glory,
The old lie: *Dulce et decorum est
Pro patria mori.*[16]

nobody loses all the time

E. E. CUMMINGS [1894–1962]

nobody loses all the time

i had an uncle named
Sol who was a born failure and
nearly everybody said he should have gone
into vaudeville perhaps because my Uncle Sol could
sing McCann He Was A Diver on Xmas Eve like Hell Itself which
may or may not account for the fact that my Uncle

Sol indulged in that possibly most inexcusable
of all to use a highfalootin phrase
luxuries that is or to   10
wit farming and be
it needlessly
added

my Uncle Sol's farm
failed because the chickens
ate the vegetables so
my Uncle Sol had a
chicken farm till the
skunks ate the chickens when

---

16. A quotation from the Latin poet Horace, "It is sweet and fitting to die for one's country."

my Uncle Sol   20
had a skunk farm but
the skunks caught cold and
died and so
my Uncle Sol imitated the
skunks in a subtle manner

or by drowning himself in the watertank
but somebody who'd given my Uncle Sol a Victor
Victrola and records while he lived presented to
him upon the auspicious occasion of his decease a
scrumptious not to mention splendiferous funeral with   30
tall boys in black gloves and flowers and everything and

i remember we all cried like the Missouri
when my Uncle Sol's coffin lurched because
somebody pressed a button
(and down went
my Uncle
Sol

and started a worm farm)

1. *Explain the title.*   **2.** *What is the speaker's attitude toward Uncle Sol?*

In Memory of W. B. Yeats
(D. JAN. 1939)

W. H. AUDEN   [b. 1907]

1
He disappeared in the dead of winter:
The brooks were frozen, the airports almost deserted,
And snow disfigured the public statues;
The mercury sank in the mouth of the dying day.
O all the instruments agree
The day of his death was a dark cold day.

Far from his illness
The wolves ran on through the evergreen forests,
The peasant river was untempted by the fashionable quays;
By mourning tongues   10
The death of the poet was kept from his poems.

But for him it was his last afternoon as himself,
An afternoon of nurses and rumors;
The provinces of his body revolted,

The squares of his mind were empty,
Silence invaded the suburbs,
The current of his feeling failed: he became his admirers.

Now he is scattered among a hundred cities
And wholly given over to unfamiliar affections;
To find his happiness in another kind of wood   20
And be punished under a foreign code of conscience.
The words of a dead man
Are modified in the guts of the living.

But in the importance and noise of tomorrow
When the brokers are roaring like beasts on the floor of the
      Bourse,°   stock exchange
And the poor have the sufferings to which they are fairly accustomed,
And each in the cell of himself is almost convinced of his freedom;
A few thousand will think of this day
As one thinks of a day when one did something slightly unusual.
O all the instruments agree   30
The day of his death was a dark cold day.

        2
    You were silly like us: your gift survived it all;
    The parish of rich women, physical decay,
    Yourself; mad Ireland hurt you into poetry.
    Now Ireland has her madness and her weather still,
    For poetry makes nothing happen: it survives
    In the valley of its saying where executives
    Would never want to tamper; it flows south
    From ranches of isolation and the busy griefs,
    Raw towns that we believe and die in; it survives,   40
    A way of happening, a mouth.

        3
    Earth, receive an honored guest;
    William Yeats is laid to rest:
    Let the Irish vessel lie
    Emptied of its poetry.

    In the nightmare of the dark
    All the dogs of Europe bark,
    And the living nations wait,
    Each sequestered in its hate;

    Intellectual disgrace   50
    Stares from every human face,
    And the seas of pity lie
    Locked and frozen in each eye.

    Follow, poet, follow right
    To the bottom of the night,

With your unconstraining voice
Still persuade us to rejoice;

With the farming of a verse
Make a vineyard of the curse,
Sing of human unsuccess   60
In a rapture of distress;

In the deserts of the heart
Let the healing fountain start,
In the prison of his days
Teach the free man how to praise.

1. *In what sense does a dead poet become "his admirers" (l. 17)?* **2.** *Why does Auden view the death of Yeats as a significant event?* **3.** *Is Auden's statement that "poetry makes nothing happen" (l. 36) consistent with the attitudes expressed in the final three stanzas?*

Elegy for Jane
MY STUDENT, THROWN BY A HORSE

THEODORE ROETHKE   [1908–1963]

I remember the neckcurls, limp and damp as tendrils;
And her quick look, a sidelong pickerel smile;
And how, once startled into talk, the light syllables leaped for her,
And she balanced in the delight of her thought,
A wren, happy, tail into the wind,
Her song trembling the twigs and small branches.
The shade sang with her;
The leaves, their whispers turned to kissing;
And the mold sang in the bleached valleys under the rose.

Oh, when she was sad, she cast herself down into such a pure depth,   10
Even a father could not find her:
Scraping her cheek against straw;
Stirring the clearest water.

My sparrow, you are not here,
Waiting like a fern, making a spiny shadow.
The sides of wet stones cannot console me,
Nor the moss, wound with the last light.

If only I could nudge you from this sleep,
My maimed darling, my skittery pigeon.
Over this damp grave I speak the words of my love: 20
I, with no rights in this matter,
Neither father nor lover.

Do Not Go Gentle into That Good Night

DYLAN THOMAS   [1914–1953]

Do not go gentle into that good night,
Old age should burn and rave at close of day;
Rage, rage against the dying of the light.

Though wise men at their end know dark is right,
Because their words had forked no lightning they
Do not go gentle into that good night.

Good men, the last wave by, crying how bright
Their frail deeds might have danced in a green bay,
Rage, rage against the dying of the light.

Wild men who caught and sang the sun in flight,   10
And learn, too late, they grieved it on its way,
Do not go gentle into that good night.

Grave men, near death, who see with blinding sight
Blind eyes could blaze like meteors and be gay,
Rage, rage against the dying of the light.

And you, my father, there on the sad height,
Curse, bless, me now with your fierce tears, I pray.
Do not go gentle into that good night.
Rage, rage against the dying of the light.

1. *What do wise, good, wild, and grave men have in common?*   **2.** *Why does the poet use the adjective "gentle" rather than the adverb "gently"?*   **3.** *What is the "sad height" (l. 16)?*

The Death of the Ball Turret Gunner

RANDALL JARRELL   [1914–1965]

From my mother's sleep I fell into the State,
And I hunched in its belly till my wet fur froze.

Six miles from earth, loosed from its dream of life,
I woke to black flak and the nightmare fighters.
When I died they washed me out of the turret with a hose.

1. *To what do "its" (ll. 2 and 3) and "they" (l.5) refer?* **2.** *Why is the mother described as asleep?*

Losses

RANDALL JARRELL   [1914–1965]

It was not dying: everybody died.
It was not dying: we had died before
In the routine crashes—and our fields
Called up the papers, wrote home to our folks,
And the rates rose, all because of us.
We died on the wrong page of the almanac,
Scattered on mountains fifty miles away;
Diving on haystacks, fighting with a friend,
We blazed up on the lines we never saw.
We died like aunts or pets or foreigners.   10
(When we left high school nothing else had died
For us to figure we had died like.)

In our new planes, with our new crews, we bombed
The ranges by the desert or the shore,
Fired at towed targets, waited for our scores—
And turned into replacements and woke up
One morning, over England, operational.
It wasn't different: but if we died
It was not an accident but a mistake
(But an easy one for anyone to make).   20
We read our mail and counted up our missions—
In bombers named for girls, we burned
The cities we had learned about in school—
Till our lives wore out; our bodies lay among
The people we had killed and never seen.
When we lasted long enough they gave us medals;
When we died they said, "Our casualties were low."
They said, "Here are the maps"; we burned the cities.

It was not dying—no, not ever dying;
But the night I died I dreamed that I was dead,   30
And the cities said to me: "Why are you dying?
We are satisfied, if you are; but why did I die?"

1. *Who is the speaker in this poem?* **2.** *Why are the deaths described as "not an accident but a mistake" (l. 19)?* **3.** *Explain the final stanza.*

Five Ways to Kill a Man

EDWIN BROCK [b. 1917]

There are many cumbersome ways to kill a man:
you can make him carry a plank of wood
to the top of a hill and nail him to it. To do this
properly you require a crowd of people
wearing sandals, a cock that crows, a cloak
to dissect, a sponge, some vinegar and one
man to hammer the nails home.

Or you can take a length of steel,
shaped and chased° in a traditional way,   *grooved*
and attempt to pierce the metal cage he wears.   10
But for this you need white horses,
English trees, men with bows and arrows,
at least two flags, a prince and a
castle to hold your banquet in.

Dispensing with nobility, you may, if the wind
allows, blow gas at him. But then you need
a mile of mud sliced through with ditches,
not to mention black boots, bomb craters,
more mud, a plague of rats, a dozen songs
and some round hats made of steel.   20

In an age of aeroplanes, you may fly
miles above your victim and dispose of him by
pressing one small switch. All you then
require is an ocean to separate you, two
systems of government, a nation's scientists,
several factories, a psychopath and
land that no one needs for several years.

These are, as I began, cumbersome ways
to kill a man. Simpler, direct, and much more neat
is to see that he is living somewhere in the middle   30
of the twentieth century, and leave him there.

After a Time

CATHERINE DAVIS [b. 1924]

After a time, all losses are the same.
One more thing lost is one thing less to lose;
And we go stripped at last the way we came.

Though we shall probe, time and again, our shame,
Who lack the wit to keep or to refuse,
After a time, all losses are the same.

No wit, no luck can beat a losing game;
Good fortune is a reassuring ruse: ·
And we go stripped at last the way we came.

Rage as we will for what we think to claim,   10
Nothing so much as this bare thought subdues:
After a time, all losses are the same.

The sense of treachery—the want, the blame—
Goes in the end, whether or not we choose, —
And we go stripped at last the way we came.

So we, who would go raging, will go tame
When what we have we can no longer use:
After a time, all losses are the same;
And we go stripped at last the way we came.

1. What difference in effect would occur if the refrain "After a time" were changed to "When life is done"? 2. What are the various meanings of "stripped" in line 3 and line 19? 3. Explain the meaning of "The sense of treachery" (l. 13). 4. Does this poem say that life is meaningless? Explain. 5. Compare this poem with Dylan Thomas' "Do Not Go Gentle into That Good Night."

Will

MAXINE KUMIN [b. 1925]

For love, for money, for reasons less than plain
one swims the Channel or the Hellespont,
masters mountains, in drought prays down the rain,
burns barns or bridges and hurries to the front.

God serves the choosy. They know what to want
and how to bear hope out to the edge of pain.
Nothing drops from them by accident.
But one, in a warm bath opening his vein
and leaning back to watch his act of will,
knows even the chestiest Leanders[17] drown,   10
the Alps have avalanches they can spill,
nor does the front line always shoot to kill;
and also knows, as the watered pulse runs down,
that would-be suicides are sometimes found.

1. *Explain the meaning of "God serves the choosy" (l. 5).*   **2.** *Does the poem provide any clues as to why the would-be suicide opens his veins? If so, why, as the last line seems to suggest, does he wish to be rescued before he dies?*

Relic

TED HUGHES   **[b. 1930]**

I found this jawbone at the sea's edge:
There, crabs, dogfish, broken by the breakers or tossed
To flap for half an hour and turn to a crust
Continue the beginning. The deeps are cold:
In that darkness camaraderie does not hold:
Nothing touches but, clutching, devours. And the jaws,
Before they are satisfied or their stretched purpose
Slacken, go down jaws; go gnawn bare. Jaws
Eat and are finished and the jawbone comes to the beach:
This is the sea's achievement; with shells,   10
Vertebrae, claws, carapaces, skulls.

Time in the sea eats its tail, thrives, casts these
Indigestibles, the spars of purposes
That failed far from the surface. None grow rich
In the sea. This curved jawbone did not laugh
But gripped, gripped and is now a cenotaph.°   *empty tomb*

1. *What is the "relic" of the title? What characteristic of nature does it symbolize?*   **2.** *What does "Continue the beginning" (l. 4) signify?*   **3.** *This poem is metrically quite irregular and thus difficult to scan. Further, there are only two pair of perfect rhymes (lines 4–5 and 15–16). Yet the poem is richly musical. Identify the poetic devices that generate the music.*

17.   According to legend Leander nightly swam the Hellespont (now called the Dardanelles) from Abydos to Sestos in Greece in order to visit his beloved Hero. On one occasion a storm came up and Leander drowned.

People

YEVGENY YEVTUSHENKO   [b. 1933]

No people are uninteresting.
Their fate is like the chronicle of planets.

Nothing in them is not particular,
and planet is dissimilar from planet.

And if a man lived in obscurity
making his friends in that obscurity
obscurity is not uninteresting.

To each his world is private,
and in that world one excellent minute.

And in that world one tragic minute.   10
These are private.

In any man who dies there dies with him
his first snow and kiss and fight.
It goes with him.

They are left books and bridges
and painted canvas and machinery.

Whose fate is to survive.
But what has gone is also not nothing:

by the rule of the game something has gone.
Not people die but worlds die in them.   20

Whom we knew as faulty, the earth's creatures.
Of whom, essentially, what did we know?

Brother of a brother? Friend of friends?
Lover of lover?

We who knew our fathers
in everything, in nothing.

They perish. They cannot be brought back.
The secret worlds are not regenerated.

And every time again and again
I make my lament against destruction.   30

DRAMA

Everyman

ANONYMOUS

CHARACTERS

God	**Cousin**	**Strength**
Messenger	**Goods**	**Discretion**
Death	**Good Deeds**	**Five Wits**
Everyman	**Knowledge**	**Angel**
Fellowship	**Confession**	**Doctor**
Kindred	**Beauty**	

Here Beginneth a Treatise how the High Father of Heaven Sendeth Death to Summon Every Creature to Come and Give Account of their Lives in this World, and is in Manner of a Moral Play.

Messenger.   I pray you all give your audience,
    And hear this matter with reverence,
    By figure[1] a moral play:
    The *Summoning of Everyman* called it is,
    That of our lives and ending shows
    How transitory we be all day.
    This matter is wondrous precious,
    But the intent of it is more gracious,
    And sweet to bear away.
    The story saith: Man, in the beginning
    Look well, and take good heed to the ending,
    Be you never so gay!
    Ye think sin in the beginning full sweet,

---

1. form

Which in the end causeth the soul to weep,
When the body lieth in clay.
Here shall you see how Fellowship and Jollity,
Both Strength, Pleasure, and Beauty,
Will fade from thee as flower in May;
For ye shall hear how our Heaven King
Calleth Everyman to a general reckoning:
Give audience, and hear what he doth say.   (Exit.)

(God speaketh:)

God.   I perceive, here in my majesty,
How that all creatures be to me unkind,
Living without dread in worldly prosperity:
Of ghostly[2] sight the people be so blind,
Drowned in sin, they know me not for their God;
In worldly riches is all their mind,
They fear not my righteousness, the sharp rod.
My law that I showed, when I for them died,
They forget clean,[3] and shedding of my blood red;
I hanged between two, it cannot be denied;
To get them life I suffered[4] to be dead;
I healed their feet, with thorns hurt was my head.
I could do no more than I did, truly;
And now I see the people do clean forsake me:
They use the seven deadly sins damnable,
As pride, covetise, wrath, and lechery
Now in the world be made commendable;
And thus they leave of angels the heavenly company.
Every man liveth so after his own pleasure,
And yet of their life they be nothing[5] sure:
I see the more that I them forbear
The worse they be from year to year.
All that liveth appaireth[6] fast;
Therefore I will, in all the haste,
Have a reckoning of every man's person;
For, and[7] I leave the people thus alone
In their life and wicked tempests,
Verily they will become much worse than beasts;
For now one would by envy another up eat;

---

2. spiritual
3. completely, altogether
4. allowed myself
5. not at all
6. becomes worse
7. if

Charity they do all clean forget.
I hoped well that every man
In my glory should make his mansion,
And thereto I had them all elect;
But now I see, like traitors deject,
They thank me not for the pleasure that I to them meant,
Nor yet for their being I them have lent.
I proffered the people great multitude of mercy,
And few there be that asketh it heartily.
They be so cumbered with worldly riches
That needs on them I must do justice,
On every man living without fear.
Where art thou, Death, thou mighty messenger?

(Enter Death.)

Death. Almighty God, I am here at your will,
Your commandment to fulfil.
God. Go thou to Everyman,
And show him, in my name,
A pilgrimage he must on him take,
Which he in no wise[8] may escape;
And that he bring with him a sure reckoning
Without delay or any tarrying.   *(God withdraws.)*
Death. Lord, I will in the world go run overall,[9]
And cruelly outsearch both great and small;
Every man will I beset that liveth beastly
Out of God's laws, and dreadeth not folly.
He that loveth riches I will strike with my dart,
His sight to blind, and from heaven to depart[10]—
Except that alms be his good friend—
In hell for to dwell, world without end.
Lo, yonder I see Everyman walking.
Full little he thinketh on my coming;
His mind is on fleshly lusts and his treasure,
And great pain it shall cause him to endure
Before the Lord, Heaven King.

(Enter Everyman.)

Everyman, stand still! Wither art thou going
Thus gaily? Hast thou thy Maker forgot?

---

8. manner
9. everywhere
10. separate

Everyman. Why askest thou?
  Wouldest thou wit?[11]
Death. Yea, sir; I will show you:
  In great haste I am sent to thee
  From God out of his majesty.
Everyman. What, sent to me?
Death. Yea, certainly.
  Though thou hast forgot him here,
  He thinketh on thee in the heavenly sphere,
  As, ere we depart, thou shalt know.
Everyman. What desireth God of me?
Death. That shall I show thee:
  A reckoning he will needs have
  Without any longer respite.
Everyman. To give a reckoning longer leisure I crave;
  This blind[12] matter troubleth my wit.
Death. On thee thou must take a long journey;
  Therefore thy book of count[13] with thee thou bring,
  For turn again thou cannot by no way.
  And look thou be sure of thy reckoning,
  For before God thou shalt answer, and show
  Thy many bad deeds, and good but a few;
  How thou hast spent thy life, and in what wise,
  Before the chief Lord of paradise.
  Have ado[14] that we were in that way,[15]
  For, wit thou well, thou shalt make none[16] attorney.
Everyman. Full unready I am such reckoning to give.
  I know thee not. What messenger art thou?
Death. I am Death, that no man dreadeth,[17]
  For every man I rest,[18] and no man spareth;
  For it is God's commandment
  That all to me shall be obedient.
Everyman. O Death, thou comest when I had thee least in mind!
  In thy power it lieth me to save;
  Yet of my good will I give thee, if thou wilt be kind:
  Yea, a thousand pound shalt thou have,
  And defer this matter till another day.

---

11. know
12. obscure
13. account
14. see to it
15. on that journey
16. have no
17. dreads no man
18. arrest

Death. Everyman, it may not be, by no way.

I set not by[19] gold, silver, nor riches.

Ne by pope, emperor, king, duke, ne princes;

For, and I would receive gifts great,

All the world I might get;

But my custom is clean contrary.

I give thee no respite. Come hence, and not tarry.

Everyman. Alas, shall I have no longer respite?

I may say Death giveth no warning!

To think on thee, it maketh my heart sick,

For all unready is my book of reckoning.

But twelve year and I might have abiding,

My counting-book I would make so clear

That my reckoning I should not need to fear.

Wherefore, Death, I pray thee, for God's mercy,

Spare me till I be provided of remedy.

Death. Thee availeth not to cry, weep, and pray;

But haste thee lightly[20] that thou were gone that journey,

And prove thy friends if thou can;

For, wit thou well, the tide abideth no man,

And in the world each living creature

For Adam's sin must die of nature.[21]

Everyman. Death, if I should this pilgrimage take,

And my reckoning surely make,

Show me, for[22] saint charity,

Should I not come again shortly?

Death. No, Everyman; and thou be once there,

Thou mayst never more come here,

Trust me verily.

Everyman. O gracious God in the high seat celestial,

Have mercy on me in this most need!

Shall I have no company from this vale terrestrial

Of mine acquaintance, that way me to lead?

Death. Yea, if any be so hardy

That would go with thee and bear thee company.

Hie[23] thee that thou were gone to God's magnificence,

Thy reckoning to give before his presence.

What, weenest[24] thou thy life is given thee,

And thy worldly goods also?

---

19. do not care for
20. quickly
21. as a natural thing
22. in the name of
23. hurry
24. think

Everyman. I had wend[25] so, verily.

Death. Nay, nay; it was but lent thee;
    For as soon as thou art go,
    Another a while shall have it, and then go therefro,[26]
    Even as thou hast done.
    Everyman, thou art mad! Thou hast thy wits five,
    And here on earth will not amend thy life;
    For suddenly I do come.

Everyman. O wretched caitiff, whither shall I flee,
    That I might scape this endless sorrow?
    Now, gentle Death, spare me till to-morrow,
    That I may amend me
    With good advisement.[27]

Death. Nay, thereto I will not consent,
    Nor no man will I respite;
    But to the heart suddenly I shall smite
    Without any advisement.
    And now out of thy sight I will me hie;
    See thou make thee ready shortly,
    For thou mayst say this is the day
    That no man living may scape away.   *(Exit Death.)*

Everyman. Alas, I may well weep with sighs deep!
    Now have I no manner of company
    To help me in my journey, and me to keep;
    And also my writing is full unready.
    How shall I do now for to excuse me?
    I would to God I had never be get![28]
    To my soul a full great profit it had be;
    For now I fear pains huge and great.
    The time passeth. Lord, help, that all wrought!
    For though I mourn it availeth nought.
    The day passeth, and is almost ago;[29]
    I wot not well what for to do.
    To whom were I best my complaint to make?
    What and I to Fellowship thereof spake,
    And showed him of this sudden chance?
    For in him is all mine affiance;[30]
    We have in the world so many a day
    Been good friends in sport and play.

---

25. thought
26. from it
27. reflection
28. been born
29. gone
30. trust

I see him yonder, certainly.
I trust that he will bear me company;
Therefore to him will I speak to ease my sorrow.
Well met, good Fellowship, and good morrow!

(Fellowship speaketh:)

Fellowship.   Everyman, good morrow, by this day!
    Sir, why lookest thou so piteously?
    If any thing be amiss, I pray thee me say,
    That I may help to remedy.
Everyman.   Yea, good Fellowship, yea;
    I am in great jeopardy.
Fellowship.   My true friend, show to me your mind;
    I will not forsake thee to my life's end,
    In the way of good company.
Everyman.   That was well spoken, and lovingly.
Fellowship.   Sir, I must needs know your heaviness;[31]
    I have pity to see you in any distress.
    If any have you wronged, ye shall revenged be,
    Though I on the ground be slain for thee—
    Though that I know before that I should die.
Everyman.   Verily, Fellowship, gramercy.
Fellowship.   Tush! by thy thanks I set not a straw.
    Show me your grief, and say no more.
Everyman.   If I my heart should to you break,[32]
    And then you to turn your mind from me,
    And would not me comfort when ye hear me speak,
    Then should I ten times sorrier be.
Fellowship.   Sir, I say as I will do indeed.
Everyman.   Then be you a good friend at need:
    I have found you true herebefore.
Fellowship.   And so ye shall evermore;
    For, in faith, and thou go to hell,
    I will not forsake thee by the way.
Everyman.   Ye speak like a good friend; I believe you well.
    I shall deserve it, and I may.
Fellowship.   I speak of no deserving, by this day!
    For he that will say, and nothing do,
    Is not worthy with good company to go;
    Therefore show me the grief of your mind,
    As to your friend most loving and kind.

---

31. sorrow
32. open

Everyman.   I shall show you how it is:
    Commanded I am to go a journey,
    A long way, hard and dangerous,
    And give a strait count, without delay,
    Before the high Judge, Adonai.[33]
    Wherefore, I pray you, bear me company,
    As ye have promised, in this journey.
Fellowship.   That is matter indeed. Promise is duty;
    But, and I should take such a voyage on me,
    I know it well, it should be to my pain;
    Also it maketh me afeard, certain.
    But let us take counsel here as well as we can,
    For your words would fear[34] a strong man.
Everyman.   Why, ye said if I had need
    Ye would me never forsake, quick[35] ne dead,
    Though it were to hell, truly.
Fellowship.   So I said, certainly,
    But such pleasures be set aside, the sooth to say;
    And also, if we took such a journey,
    When should we come again?
Everyman.   Nay, never again, till the day of doom.
Fellowship.   In faith, then will not I come there!
    Who hath you these tidings brought?
Everyman.   Indeed, Death was with me here.
Fellowship.   Now, by God that all hath bought,
    If Death were the messenger,
    For no man that is living to-day
    I will not go that loath journey—
    Not for the father that begat me!
Everyman.   Ye promised otherwise, pardie.[36]
Fellowship.   I wot well I said so, truly;
    And yet if thou wilt eat, and drink, and make good cheer,
    Or haunt to women the lusty company,[37]
    I would not forsake you while the day is clear,[38]
    Trust me verily.
Everyman.   Yea, thereto ye would be ready!
    To go to mirth, solace, and play,
    Your mind will sooner apply,
    Than to bear me company in my long journey.

---

33. Hebrew name for God
34. frighten
35. alive
36. by God
37. frequent the pleasant company of women
38. until daybreak

Fellowship. Now, in good faith, I will not that way.
   But and thou will murder, or any man kill,
   In that I will help thee with a good will.
Everyman. O, that is a simple advice indeed.
   Gentle fellow, help me in my necessity!
   We have loved long, and now I need;
   And now, gentle Fellowship, remember me.
Fellowship. Whether ye have loved me or no,
   By Saint John, I will not with thee go.
Everyman. Yet, I pray thee, take the labour, and do so much for me
   To bring me forward,[39] for saint charity,
   And comfort me till I come without the town.
Fellowship. Nay, and thou would give me a new gown,
   I will not a foot with thee go;
   But, and thou had tarried, I would not have left thee so.
   And as now God speed thee in thy journey,
   For from thee I will depart as fast as I may.
Everyman. Whither away, Fellowship? Will thou forsake me?
Fellowship. Yea, by my fay![40] To God I betake[41] thee.
Everyman. Farewell, good Fellowship; for thee my heart is sore.
   Adieu for ever! I shall see thee no more.
Fellowship. In faith, Everyman, farewell now at the ending;
   For you I will remember that parting is mourning.

(Exit Fellowship.)

Everyman. Alack! shall we thus depart indeed—
   Ah, Lady, help!—without any more comfort?
   Lo, Fellowship forsaketh me in my most need.
   For help in this world whither shall I resort?
   Fellowship herebefore with me would merry make,
   And now little sorrow for me doth he take.
   It is said, 'In prosperity men friends may find,
   Which in adversity be full unkind.'
   Now whither for succour shall I flee,
   Sith that[42] Fellowship hath forsaken me?
   To my kinsmen I will, truly,
   Praying them to help me in my necessity;
   I believe that they will do so,
   For kind[43] will creep where it may not go.
   I will go say, for yonder I see them.
   Where be ye now, my friends and kinsmen?

---

39. escort me
40. faith
41. commend
42. since
43. kinship, family

(Enter Kindred and Cousin.)

Kindred.   Here be we now at your commandment.
     Cousin, I pray you show us your intent
     In any wise, and do not spare.[44]
Cousin.   Yea, Everyman, and to us declare
     If ye be disposed to go anywhither;
     For, wit you well, we will live and die together.
Kindred.   In wealth and woe we will with you hold,
     For over his kin a man may be bold.[45]
Everyman.   Gramercy, my friends and kinsmen kind.
     Now shall I show you the grief of my mind:
     I was commanded by a messenger,
     That is a high king's chief officer;
     He bade me go a pilgrimage, to my pain,
     And I know well I shall never come again;
     Also I must give a reckoning strait,
     For I have a great enemy[46] that hath me in wait,
     Which intendeth me for to hinder.
Kindred.   What account is that which ye must render?
     That would I know.
Everyman.   Of all my works I must show
     How I have lived and my days spent;
     Also of ill deeds that I have used[47]
     In my time, sith life was me lent;
     And of all virtues that I have refused.
     Therefore, I pray you, go thither with me
     To help to make mine account, for saint charity.
Cousin.   What, to go thither? Is that the matter?
     Nay, Everyman, I had liefer[48] fast[49] bread and water
     All this five year and more.
Everyman.   Alas, that ever I was bore![50]
     For now shall I never be merry,
     If that you forsake me.
Kindred.   Ah, sir, what ye be a merry man!
     Take good heart to you, and make no moan.
     But one thing I warn you, by Saint Anne—
     As for me, ye shall go alone.
Everyman.   My Cousin, will you not with me go?

---

44. hold back
45. a man may freely command the services of his family
46. i.e., the Devil
47. practiced
48. rather
49. have nothing but
50. born

Cousin. No, by our Lady! I have the cramp in my toe.
    Trust not to me, for, so God me speed,
    I will deceive you in your most need.
Kindred. It availeth not us to tice.[51]
    Ye shall have my maid with all my heart;
    She loveth to go to feasts, there to be nice,[52]
    And to dance, and abroad to start:[53]
    I will give her leave to help you in that journey,
    If that you and she may agree.
Everyman. Now show me the very effect of your mind:
    Will you go with me, or abide behind?
Kindred. Abide behind? Yea, that will I, and I may!
    Therefore farewell till another day.   *(Exit Kindred.)*
Everyman. How should I be merry or glad?
    For fair promises men to me make,
    But when I have most need they me forsake.
    I am deceived; that maketh me sad.
Cousin. Cousin Everyman, farewell now,
    For verily I will not go with you.
    Also of mine own an unready reckoning
    I have to account; therefore I make tarrying.
    Now God keep thee, for now I go.   *(Exit Cousin.)*
Everyman. Ah, Jesus, is all come hereto?
    Lo, fair words maketh fools fain,[54]
    They promise, and nothing will do, certain.
    My kinsmen promised me faithfully
    For to abide with me steadfastly,
    And now fast away do they flee:
    Even so Fellowship promised me.
    What friend were best me of to provide?[55]
    I lose my time here longer to abide.
    Yet in my mind a thing there is:
    All my life I have loved riches;
    If that my Good[56] now help me might,
    He would make my heart full light.
    I will speak to him in this distress—
    Where art thou, my Goods and riches?

(Goods speaks from a corner:)

---

51. entice
52. wanton
53. rush
54. glad
55. to provide me with
56. goods, possessions

Goods. Who calleth me? Everyman? What! hast thou haste?
    I lie here in corners, trussed and piled so high,
    And in chests I am locked so fast,
    Also sacked in bags. Thou mayst see with thine eye
    I cannot stir; in packs low I lie.
    What would ye have? Lightly me say.

Everyman. Come hither, Good, in all the haste thou may,
    For of counsel I must desire thee.

Goods. Sir, and ye in the world have sorrow or adversity,
    That can I help you to remedy shortly.

Everyman. It is another disease that grieveth me;
    In this world it is not, I tell thee so.
    I am sent for, another way to go,
    To give a strait count general
    Before the highest Jupiter of all;
    And all my life I have had joy and pleasure in thee,
    Therefore, I pray thee, go with me;
    For, peradventure, thou mayst before God Almighty
    My reckoning help to clean and purify;
    For it is said ever among[57]
    That money maketh all right that is wrong.

Goods. Nay, Everyman, I sing another song.
    I follow no man in such voyages;
    For, and I went with thee,
    Thou shouldst fare much the worse for me;
    For because on me thou did set thy mind,
    Thy reckoning I have made blotted and blind,
    That thine account thou cannot make truly;
    And that hast thou for the love of me.

Everyman. That would grieve me full sore,
    When I should come to that fearful answer.
    Up, let us go thither together.

Goods. Nay, not so! I am too brittle, I may not endure;
    I will follow no man one foot, be ye sure.

Everyman. Alas, I have thee loved, and had great pleasure
    All my life-days on good and treasure.

Goods. That is to thy damnation, without leasing,
    For my love is contrary to the love everlasting;
    But if thou had me loved moderately during,
    As to the poor to give part of me,
    Then shouldst thou not in this dolour be,
    Nor in this great sorrow and care.

---

57. at times

Everyman.   Lo, now was I deceived ere I was ware,
And all I may wite[58] misspending of time.
Goods.   What, weenest thou that I am thine?
Everyman.   I had wend so.
Goods.   Nay, Everyman, I say no.
As for a while I was lent thee;
A season thou hast had me in prosperity.
My condition is man's soul to kill;
If I save one, a thousand I do spill.
Weenest thou that I will follow thee?
Nay, not from this world, verily.
Everyman.   I had wend otherwise.
Goods.   Therefore to thy soul Good is a thief;
For when thou art dead, this is my guise[59]—
Another to deceive in this same wise
As I have done thee, and all to his soul's reprief.[60]
Everyman.   O false Good, cursed may thou be,
Thou traitor to God, that hast deceived me
And caught me in thy snare!
Goods.   Marry, thou brought thyself in care,
Whereof I am glad;
I must needs laugh, I cannot be sad.
Everyman.   Ah, Good, thou hast had long my heartly love;
I gave thee that which should be the Lord's above.
But wilt thou not go with me indeed?
I pray thee truth to say.
Goods.   No, so God me speed!
Therefore farewell, and have good day.   (*Exit Goods.*)
Everyman.   O, to whom shall I make my moan
For to go with me in that heavy journey?
First Fellowship said he would with me gone;
His words were very pleasant and gay,
But afterward he left me alone.
Then spake I to my kinsmen, all in despair,
And also they gave me words fair;
They lacked no fair speaking,
But all forsook me in the ending.
Then went I to my Goods, that I loved best,
In hope to have comfort, but there had I least;
For my Goods sharply did me tell
That he bringeth many into hell.

---

58.   blame on
59.   practice
60.   shame

Then of myself I was ashamed,
And so I am worthy to be blamed;
Thus may I well myself hate.
Of whom shall I now counsel take?
I think that I shall never speed
Till that I go to my Good Deed.
But, alas, she is so weak
That she can neither go nor speak;
Yet will I venture on her now.
My Good Deeds, where be you?

(*Good Deeds speaks from the ground*:)

Good Deeds. Here I lie, cold in the ground;
Thy sins hath me sore bound,
That I cannot stir.
Everyman. O Good Deeds, I stand in fear!
I must you pray of counsel,
For help now should come right well.
Good Deeds. Everyman, I have understanding
That ye be summoned account to make
Before Messias, of Jerusalem King;
And you do by me,[61] that journey with you will I take.
Everyman. Therefore I come to you, my moan to make;
I pray you that ye will go with me.
Good Deeds. I would full fain, but I cannot stand, verily.
Everyman. Why, is there anything on you fall?
Good Deeds. Yea, sir, I may thank you of[62] all;
If ye had perfectly cheered me,
Your book of count full ready had be.
Look, the books of your works and deeds eke![63]
Behold how they lie under the feet,
To your soul's heaviness.
Everyman. Our Lord Jesus help me!
For one letter here I cannot see.
Good Deeds. There is a blind reckoning in time of distress.
Everyman. Good Deeds, I pray you help me in this need,
Or else I am for ever damned indeed;
Therefore help me to make reckoning
Before the Redeemer of all thing,
That King is, and was, and ever shall.
Good Deeds. Everyman, I am sorry of your fall,
And fain would I help you, and I were able.

---

61. as I advise
62. for
63. also

Everyman. Good Deeds, your counsel I pray you give me.
Good Deeds. That shall I do verily;
    Though that on my feet I may not go,
    I have a sister that shall with you also,
    Called Knowledge, which shall with you abide,
    To help you to make that dreadful reckoning.

    (*Enter Knowledge.*)

Knowledge. Everyman, I will go with thee, and be thy guide,
    In thy most need to go by thy side.
Everyman. In good condition I am now in every thing,
    And am wholly content with this good thing,
    Thanked be God my creator.
Good Deeds. And when she hath brought you there
    Where thou shalt heal thee of thy smart,[64]
    Then go you with your reckoning and your Good Deeds together,
    For to make you joyful at heart
    Before the blessed Trinity.
Everyman. My Good Deeds, gramercy!
    I am well content, certainly,
    With your words sweet.
Knowledge. Now go we together lovingly
    To Confession, that cleansing river.
Everyman. For joy I weep; I would we were there!
    But, I pray you, give me cognition
    Where dwelleth that holy man, Confession.
Knowledge. In the house of salvation:
    We shall find him in that place,
    That shall us comfort, by God's grace.

    (*Knowledge takes Everyman to Confession.*)

    Lo, this is Confession. Kneel down and ask mercy,
    For he is in good conceit[65] with God Almighty.
Everyman. O glorious fountain, that all uncleanness doth clarify,
    Wash from me the spots of vice unclean,
    That on me no sin may be seen.
    I come with Knowledge for my redemption,
    Redempt with heart and full contrition;
    For I am commanded a pilgrimage to take,
    And great accounts before God to make.
    Now I pray you, Shrift,[66] mother of salvation,
    Help my Good Deeds for my piteous exclamation.

---

64. pain
65. esteem
66. confession

Confession.   I know your sorrow well, Everyman.
　　Because with Knowledge ye come to me,
　　I will you comfort as well as I can,
　　And a precious jewel I will give thee,
　　Called penance, voider of adversity;
　　Therewith shall your body chastised be,
　　With abstinence and perseverance in God's service.
　　Here shall you receive that scourge of me,
　　Which is penance strong that ye must endure,
　　To remember thy Saviour was scourged for thee
　　With sharp scourges, and suffered it patiently;
　　So must thou, ere thou scape that painful pilgrimage.
　　Knowledge, keep him in this voyage,
　　And by that time Good Deeds will be with thee.
　　But in any wise be siker[67] of mercy,
　　For your time draweth fast; and ye will saved be,
　　Ask God mercy, and he will grant truly.
　　When with the scourge of penance man doth him[68] bind,
　　The oil of forgiveness then shall he find.
Everyman.   Thanked be God for his gracious work!
　　For now I will my penance begin;
　　This hath rejoiced and lighted my heart,
　　Though the knots be painful and hard within.
Knowledge.   Everyman, look your penance that ye fulfil,
　　What pain that ever it to you be;
　　And Knowledge shall give you counsel at will
　　How your account ye shall make clearly.
Everyman.   O eternal God, O heavenly figure,
　　O way of righteousness, O goodly vision,
　　Which descended down in a virgin pure
　　Because he would every man redeem,
　　Which Adam forfeited by his disobedience:
　　O blessed Godhead, elect and high divine,
　　Forgive my grievous offence;
　　Here I cry thee mercy in this presence.
　　O ghostly treasure, O ransomer and redeemer,
　　Of all the world hope and conductor,[69]
　　Mirror of joy, and founder of mercy,
　　Which enlumineth heaven and earth thereby,[70]
　　Hear my clamourous complaint, though it late be;

---

67. sure
68. himself
69. guide
70. besides

Receive my prayers, of thy benignity;
Though I be a sinner most abominable,
Yet let my name be written in Moses' table.
O Mary, pray to the Maker of all thing,
Me for to help at my ending;
And save me from the power of my enemy,
For Death assaileth me strongly.
And, Lady, that I may by mean of thy prayer
Of your Son's glory to be[71] partner,
By the means of his passion, I it crave;
I beseech you help my soul to save.
Knowledge, give me the scourge of penance;
My flesh therewith shall give acquittance:[72]
I will now begin, if God give me grace.

Knowledge. Everyman, God give you time and space!
Thus I bequeath you in the hands of our Saviour;
Now may you make your reckoning sure.

Everyman. In the name of the Holy Trinity,
My body sore punished shall be:
Take this, body, for the sin of the flesh!

(*Scourges himself.*)

Also thou delightest to go gay and fresh,
And in the way of damnation thou did me bring,
Therefore suffer now strokes and punishing.
Now of penance I will wade the water clear,
To save me from purgatory, that sharp fire.

(*Good Deeds rises from the ground.*)

Good Deeds. I thank God, now I can walk and go,
And am delivered of my sickness and woe.
Therefore with Everyman I will go, and not spare;
His good works I will help him to declare.

Knowledge. Now, Everyman, be merry and glad!
Your Good Deeds cometh now; ye may not be sad.
Now is your Good Deeds whole and sound,
Going upright upon the ground.

Everyman. My heart is light, and shall be evermore;
Now will I smite faster than I did before.

Good Deeds. Everyman, pilgrim, my special friend,
Blessed be thou without end;
For thee is preparate the eternal glory.

---

71. be
72. atonement

Ye have me made whole and sound,
Therefore I will bide by thee in every stound.[73]

Everyman.   Welcome, my Good Deeds; now I hear thy voice,
I weep for very sweetness of love.

Knowledge.   Be no more sad, but ever rejoice;
God seeth thy living in his throne above.
Put on this garment to thy behoof,[74]
Which is wet with your tears,
Or else before God you may it miss,
When ye to your journey's end come shall.

Everyman.   Gentle Knowledge, what do ye it call?

Knowledge.   It is a garment of sorrow:
From pain it will you borrow;[75]
Contrition it is,
That geteth forgiveness;
It pleaseth God passing well.

Good Deeds.   Everyman, will you wear it for your heal?

Everyman.   Now blessed be Jesu, Mary's Son,
For now have I on true contrition.
And let us go now without tarrying;
Good Deeds, have we clear our reckoning?

Good Deeds.   Yea, indeed, I have it here.

Everyman.   Then I trust we need not fear;
Now, friends, let us not part in twain.

Knowledge.   Nay, Everyman, that will we not, certain.

Good Deeds.   Yet must thou lead with thee
Three persons of great might.

Everyman.   Who should they be?

Good Deeds.   Discretion and Strength they hight,[76]
And thy Beauty may not abide behind.

Knowledge.   Also ye must call to mind
Your Five Wits as for your counsellors.

Good Deeds.   You must have them ready at all hours.

Everyman.   How shall I get them hither?

Knowledge.   You must call them all together,
And they will hear you incontinent.[77]

Everyman.   My friends, come hither and be present,
Discretion, Strength, my Five Wits,[78] and Beauty.

(*Enter Beauty, Strength, Discretion, and Five Wits.*)

---

73. always (or: in every attack)
74. advantage
75. take
76. are called
77. immediately
78. senses

Beauty.   Here at your will we be all ready.
  What will ye that we should do?
Good Deeds.   That ye would with Everyman go,
  And help him in his pilgrimage.
  Advise you, will ye with him or not in that voyage?
Strength.   We will bring him all thither,
  To his help and comfort, ye may believe me.
Discretion.   So will we go with him all together.
Everyman.   Almighty God, lofed[79] may thou be!
  I give thee laud that I have hither brought
  Strength, Discretion, Beauty, and Five Wits. Lack I nought.
  And my Good Deeds, with Knowledge clear,
  All be in my company at my will here;
  I desire no more to[80] my business.
Strength.   And I, Strength, will by you stand in distress,
  Though thou would in battle fight on the ground.
Five Wits.   And though it were through the world round,
  We will not depart for sweet ne sour.
Beauty.   No more will I unto death's hour,
  Whatsoever thereof befall.
Discretion.   Everyman, advise you first of all;
  Go with a good advisement and deliberation.
  We all give you virtuous monition
  That all shall be well.
Everyman.   My friends, harken what I will tell:
  I pray God reward you in his heavenly sphere.
  Now harken, all that be here,
  For I will make my testament
  Here before you all present:
  In alms half my good I will give with my hands twain
  In the way of charity, with good intent,
  And the other half still shall remain
  In queth,[81] to be returned there[82] it ought to be.
  This I do in despite of the fiend of hell,
  To go quit out of his peril
  Ever after and this day.
Knowledge.   Everyman, harken what I say:
  Go to priesthood, I you advise,
  And receive of him in any wise
  The holy sacrament and ointment together.

---

79. praised
80. for
81. bequest
82. where

Then shortly see ye turn again hither;
We will all abide you here.

Five Wits.   Yea, Everyman, hie you that ye ready were.
There is no emperor, king, duke, ne baron,
That of God hath commission
As hath the least priest in the world being;
For of the blessed sacraments pure and benign
He beareth the keys, and thereof hath the cure[83]
For man's redemption—it is ever sure—
Which God for our soul's medicine
Gave us out of his heart with great pine.
Here in this transitory life, for thee and me,
The blessed sacraments seven there be:
Baptism, confirmation, with priesthood good,
And the sacrament of God's precious flesh and blood,
Marriage, the holy extreme unction, and penance;
These seven be good to have in remembrance,
Gracious sacraments of high divinity.

Everyman.   Fain would I receive that holy body,
And meekly to my ghostly father I will go.

Five Wits.   Everyman, that is the best that ye can do.
God will you to salvation bring,
For priesthood exceedeth all other thing:
To us Holy Scripture they do teach,
And converteth man from sin heaven to reach;
God hath to them more power given
Than to any angel that is in heaven.
With five words[84] he may consecrate,
God's body in flesh and blood to make,
And handleth his Maker between his hands.
The priest bindeth and unbindeth all bands,
Both in earth and in heaven.
Thou ministers[85] all the sacraments seven;
Though we kissed thy feet, thou were worthy;
Thou art surgeon that cureth sin deadly:
No remedy we find under God
But all only[86] priesthood.
Everyman, God gave priests that dignity,
And setteth them in his stead among us to be;
Thus be they above angels in degree.

---

83. charge
84. i.e., *Hoc est enim corpus meum* (Lat. "For this is my body"; from the sacrament of the Eucharist)
85. administer
86. except

(Everyman goes to the priest to receive the last sacraments.)

Knowledge.   If priests be good, it is so,[87] surely.
   But when Jesus hanged on the cross with great smart,
   There he gave out of his blessed heart
   The same sacrament in great torment:
   He sold them not to us, that Lord omnipotent.
   Therefore Saint Peter the apostle doth say
   That Jesu's curse hath all they
   Which God their Saviour do buy or sell,
   Or they for any money do take or tell.[88]
   Sinful priests giveth the sinners example bad;
   Their children sitteth by other men's fires, I have heard;
   And some haunteth women's company
   With unclean life, as lusts of lechery:
   These be with sin made blind.
Five Wits.   I trust to God no such may we find;
   Therefore let us priesthood honour,
   And follow their doctrine for our souls' succour.
   We be their sheep, and they shepherds be
   By whom we all be kept in surety.
   Peace, for yonder I see Everyman come,
   Which hath made true satisfaction.
Good Deeds.   Methink it is he indeed.

   (Re-enter Everyman.)

Everyman.   Now Jesu be your alder speed![89]
   I have received the sacrament for my redemption,
   And then mine extreme unction:
   Blessed be all they that counselled me to take it!
   And now, friends, let us go without longer respite;
   I thank God that ye have tarried so long.
   Now set each of you on this rood[90] your hand,
   And shortly follow me:
   I go before there I would be; God be our guide!
Strength.   Everyman, we will not from you go
   Till ye have done this voyage long.
Discretion.   I, Discretion, will bide by you also.
Knowledge.   And though this pilgrimage be never so strong,[91]
   I will never part you fro.

---

87. i.e., "above angels in degree"
88. count
89. help to all of you
90. cross
91. hard, difficult

Strength.   Everyman, I will be as sure by thee
As ever I did by Judas Maccabee.[92]

(*Everyman comes to his grave.*)

Everyman.   Alas, I am so faint I may not stand;
My limbs under me doth fold.
Friends, let us not turn again to this land,
Not for all the world's gold;
For into this cave must I creep
And turn to earth, and there to sleep.
Beauty.   What, into this grave? Alas!
Everyman.   Yea, there shall ye consume, more and less.[93]
Beauty.   And what, should I smother here?
Everyman.   Yea, by my faith, and never more appear.
In this world live no more we shall,
But in heaven before the highest Lord of all.
Beauty.   I cross out all this; adieu, by Saint John!
I take my cap in my lap, and am gone.
Everyman.   What, Beauty, whither will ye?
Beauty.   Peace, I am deaf; I look not behind me,
Not and thou wouldest give me all the gold in thy chest.   (*Exit Beauty.*)
Everyman.   Alas, whereto may I trust?
Beauty goeth fast away from me;
She promised with me to live and die.
Strength.   Everyman, I will thee also forsake and deny;
Thy game liketh me not at all.
Everyman.   Why, then, ye will forsake me all?
Sweet Strength, tarry a little space.
Strength.   Nay, sir, by the rood of grace!
I will hie me from thee fast,
Though thou weep till thy heart to-brast.[94]
Everyman.   Ye would ever bide by me, ye said.
Strength.   Yea, I have you far enough conveyed.
Ye be old enough, I understand,
Your pilgrimage to take on hand;
I repent me that I hither came.
Everyman.   Strength, you to displease I am to blame;
Yet promise is debt, this ye well wot.
Strength.   In faith, I care not.
Thou art but a fool to complain;

---

92. Jewish religious and national leader against Syria in the 2nd century B.C. He told his men that "the success of war is not in the multitude: but strength cometh from heaven" (Apocrypha, I Maccabees, 3:19)
93. high and low
94. broke to pieces

You spend your speech and waste your brain.
Go thrust thee into the ground!   *(Exit Strength.)*

Everyman. I had wend surer I should you have found.
He that trusteth in his Strength
She him deceiveth at the length.
Both Strength and Beauty forsaketh me;
Yet they promised me fair and lovingly.

Discretion. Everyman, I will after Strength be gone;
As for me, I will leave you alone.

Everyman. Why, Discretion, will ye forsake me?

Discretion. Yea, in faith, I will go from thee,
For when Strength goeth before
I follow after evermore.

Everyman. Yet, I pray thee, for the love of the Trinity,
Look in my grave once piteously.

Discretion. Nay, so nigh will I not come;
Farewell, every one!   *(Exit Discretion.)*

Everyman. O, all things faileth, save God alone—
Beauty, Strength, and Discretion;
For when Death bloweth his blast,
They all run from me full fast.

Five Wits. Everyman, my leave now of thee I take;
I will follow the other, for here I thee forsake.

Everyman. Alas, then may I wail and weep,
For I took you for my best friend.

Five Wits. I will no longer thee keep;
Now farewell, and there an end.   *(Exit Five Wits.)*

Everyman. O Jesu, help! All hath forsaken me.

Good Deeds. Nay, Everyman; I will bide with thee.
I will not forsake thee indeed;
Thou shalt find me a good friend at need.

Everyman. Gramercy, Good Deeds! Now may I true friends see.
They have forsaken me, every one;
I loved them better than my Good Deeds alone.
Knowledge, will ye forsake me also?

Knowledge. Yea, Everyman, when ye to Death shall go;
But not yet, for no manner of danger.

Everyman. Gramercy, Knowledge, with all my heart.

Knowledge. Nay, yet I will not from hence depart
Till I see where ye shall become.

Everyman. Methink, alas, that I must be gone
To make my reckoning and my debts pay,
For I see my time is nigh spent away.
Take example, all ye that this do hear or see,
How they that I loved best do forsake me,
Except my Good Deeds that bideth truly.

Good Deeds. All earthly things is but vanity:
    Beauty, Strength, and Discretion do man forsake,
    Foolish friends, and kinsmen, that fair spake—
    All fleeth save Good Deeds, and that am I.
Everyman. Have mercy on me, God most mighty;
    And stand by me, thou mother and maid, holy Mary.
Good Deeds. Fear not; I will speak for thee.
Everyman. Here I cry God mercy.
Good Deeds. Short[95] our end, and minish our pain;
    Let us go and never come again.
Everyman. Into thy hands, Lord, my soul I commend;
    Receive it, Lord, that it be not lost.
    As thou me boughtest, so me defend,
    And save me from the fiend's boast,
    That I may appear with that blessed host
    That shall be saved at the day of doom.
    In manus tuas, of mights most
    For ever, *commendo spiritum meum.*[96]   *(He sinks into his grave.)*
Knowledge. Now hath he suffered that we all shall endure;
    The Good Deeds shall make all sure.
    Now hath he made ending;
    Methinketh that I hear angels sing,
    And make great joy and melody
    Where Everyman's soul received shall be.
Angel. Come, excellent elect spouse, to Jesu!
    Hereabove thou shalt go
    Because of thy singular virtue.
    Now the soul is taken the body fro,
    Thy reckoning is crystal-clear.
    Now shalt thou into the heavenly sphere,
    Unto the which all ye shall come
    That liveth well before the day of doom.

(Enter Doctor.)

Doctor. This moral men may have in mind.
    Ye hearers, take it of worth,[97] old and young,
    And forsake Pride, for he deceiveth you in the end;
    And remember Beauty, Five Wits, Strength, and Discretion,
    They all at the last do every man forsake,
    Save[98] his Good Deeds there doth he take.

---

95. shorten
96. into thy hands I commend my spirit (Luke, 23:46)
97. value it
98. unless

But beware, for and they be small
Before God, he hath no help at all;
None excuse may be there for every man.
Alas, how shall he do then?
For after death amends may no man make,
For then mercy and pity doth him forsake.
If his reckoning be not clear when he doth come,
God will say: 'Ite, maledicti, in ignem eternum.'[99]
And he that hath his account whole and sound,
High in heaven he shall be crowned;
Unto which place God bring us all thither,
That we may live body and soul together.
Thereto help the Trinity!
Amen, say ye, for saint charity.

Thus Endeth this Moral Play of Everyman.

Questions

1. *What does the dramatist's utilization of the allegorical mode within a timeless setting contribute to the meaning of the play?* **2.** *What difference, if any, would there be if God appeared at the end of the play rather than at the beginning?* **3.** *What thematic reasons are there for the order in which Everyman meets his various friends?* **4.** *Some commentators have seen* Everyman *as a psychological drama of great tension and suspense. Do you agree? Explain.*

---

99. depart, ye cursed, into everlasting fire (Matthew, 25:41)

The Seventh Seal*

INGMAR BERGMAN [b. 1918]

THE CAST

The squire	The witch	The church painter
Death	The knight's wife	Skat
Jof	The girl	The merchant
The knight	Raval	Woman at the inn
Mia	The monk	Leader of the soldiers
Lisa	The smith	The young monk

THE night had brought little relief from the heat, and at dawn a hot gust of wind blows across the colorless sea.

The knight, Antonius Block, lies prostrate on some spruce branches spread over the fine sand. His eyes are wide-open and bloodshot from lack of sleep.

Nearby his squire Jöns is snoring loudly. He has fallen asleep where he collapsed, at the edge of the forest among the wind-gnarled fir trees. His open mouth gapes toward the dawn, and unearthly sounds come from his throat.

At the sudden gust of wind the horses stir, stretching their parched muzzles toward the sea. They are as thin and worn as their masters.

The knight has risen and waded into the shallow water, where he rinses his sunburned face and blistered lips.

Jöns rolls over to face the forest and the darkness. He moans in his sleep and vigorously scratches the stubbled hair on his head. A scar stretches diagonally across his scalp, as white as lightning against the grime.

The knight returns to the beach and falls on his knees. With his eyes closed and brow furrowed, he says his morning prayers. His hands are clenched together and his lips form the words silently. His face is sad and bitter. He opens his eyes and stares directly into the morning sun which wallows up from the misty sea like some bloated, dying fish. The sky is gray and immobile, a dome of lead. A cloud hangs mute and dark over the western horizon. High up, barely visible, a sea gull floats on motionless wings. Its cry is weird and restless.

The knight's large gray horse lifts its head and whinnies. Antonius Block turns around.

---

*Translated by Lars Malmstrom and David Kushner.

Behind him stands a man in black. His face is very pale and he keeps his hands hidden in the wide folds of his cloak.

Knight. Who are you?
Death. I am Death.
Knight. Have you come for me?
Death. I have been walking by your side for a long time.
Knight. That I know.
Death. Are you prepared?
Knight. My body is frightened, but I am not.
Death. Well, there is no shame in that.

The knight has risen to his feet. He shivers. Death opens his cloak to place it around the knight's shoulders.

Knight. Wait a moment.
Death. That's what they all say. I grant no reprieves.
Knight. You play chess, don't you?

A gleam of interest kindles in Death's eyes.

Death. How did you know that?
Knight. I have seen it in paintings and heard it sung in ballads.
Death. Yes, in fact I'm quite a good chess player.
Knight. But you can't be better than I am.

The knight rummages in the big black bag which he keeps beside him and takes out a small chessboard. He places it carefully on the ground and begins setting up the pieces.

Death. Why do you want to play chess with me?
Knight. I have my reasons.
Death. That is your privilege.
Knight. The condition is that I may live as long as I hold out against you. If I win, you will release me. Is it agreed?

The knight holds out his two fists to Death, who smiles at him suddenly. Death points to one of the knight's hands; it contains a black pawn.

Knight. You drew black!
Death. Very appropriate. Don't you think so?

The knight and Death bend over the chessboard. After a moment of hesitation, Antonius Block opens with his king's pawn. Death moves, also using his king's pawn.

THE morning breeze has died down. The restless movement of the sea has ceased, the water is silent. The sun rises from the haze and its glow whitens. The sea gull floats under the dark cloud, frozen in space. The day is already scorchingly hot.

The squire Jöns is awakened by a kick in the rear. Opening his eyes, he grunts like a pig and yawns broadly. He scrambles to his feet, saddles his horse and picks up the heavy pack.

The knight slowly rides away from the sea, into the forest near the beach and up toward the road. He pretends not to hear the morning prayers of his squire. Jöns soon overtakes him.

Jöns (sings).   Between a strumpet's legs to lie
                  Is the life for which I sigh.

He stops and looks at his master, but the knight hasn't heard Jöns' song, or he pretends that he hasn't. To give further vent to his irritation, the squire sings even louder.

Jöns (sings).   Up above is God Almighty
                  So very far away,
                  But your brother the Devil
                  You will meet on every level.

Jöns finally gets the knight's attention. He stops singing. The knight, his horse, Jöns' own horse and Jöns himself know all the songs by heart. The long, dusty journey from the Holy Land hasn't made them any cleaner.

They ride across a mossy heath which stretches toward the horizon. Beyond it, the sea lies shimmering in the white glitter of the sun.

Jöns.   In Farjestad everyone was talking about evil omens and other horrible things. Two horses had eaten each other in the night, and, in the churchyard, graves had been opened and the remains of corpses scattered all over the place. Yesterday afternoon there were as many as four suns in the heavens.

The knight doesn't answer. Close by a scrawny dog is whining, crawling toward its master, who is sleeping in a sitting position in the blazing hot sun. A black cloud of flies clusters around his head and shoulders. The miserable-looking dog whines incessantly as it lies flat on its stomach, wagging its tail.

Jöns dismounts and approaches the sleeping man. Jöns addresses him politely. When he doesn't receive an answer, he walks up to the man in order to shake him awake. He bends over the sleeping man's shoulder, but quickly pulls back his hand. The man falls backward on the heath, his face turned toward Jöns. It is a corpse, staring at Jöns with empty eye sockets and white teeth.

The squire remounts and overtakes his master. He takes a drink from his waterskin and hands the bag to the knight.

Knight.   Well, did he show you the way?
Jöns.   Not exactly.
Knight.   What did he say?
Jöns.   Nothing.
Knight.   Was he a mute?

Jöns. No, sir, I wouldn't say that. As a matter of fact, he was quite eloquent.

Knight. Oh?

Jöns. He was eloquent, all right. The trouble is that what he had to say was most depressing. (*Sings*)

> One moment you're bright and lively,
> The next you're crawling with worms.
> Fate is a terrible villain
> And you, my friend, its poor victim.

Knight. Must you sing?

Jöns. No.

The knight hands his squire a piece of bread, which keeps him quiet for a while. The sun burns down on them cruelly, and beads of perspiration trickle down their faces. There is a cloud of dust around the horses' hoofs.

They ride past an inlet and along verdant groves. In the shade of some large trees stands a bulging wagon covered with a mottled canvas. A horse whinnies nearby and is answered by the knight's horse. The two travelers do not to stop to rest under the shade of the trees but continue riding until they disappear at the bend of the road.

IN his sleep, Jof the juggler hears the neighing of his horse and the answer from a distance. He tries to go on sleeping, but it is stifling inside the wagon. The rays of the sun filtering through the canvas cast streaks of light across the face of Jof's wife, Mia, and their one-year-old son, Mikael, who are sleeping deeply and peacefully. Near them, Jonas Skat, an older man, snores loudly.

Jof crawls out of the wagon. There is still a spot of shade under the big trees. He takes a drink of water, gargles, stretches and talks to his scrawny old horse.

Jof. Good morning. Have you had breakfast? I can't eat grass, worse luck. Can't you teach me how? We're a little hard up. People aren't very interested in juggling in this part of the country.

He has picked up the juggling balls and slowly begins to toss them. Then he stands on his head and cackles like a hen. Suddenly he stops and sits down with a look of utter astonishment on his face. The wind causes the trees to sway slightly. The leaves stir and there is a soft murmur. The flowers and the grass bend gracefully, and somewhere a bird raises its voice in a long warble.

Jof's face breaks into a smile and his eyes fill with tears. With a dazed expression he sits flat on his behind while the grass rustles softly, and bees and butterflies hum around his head. The unseen bird continues to sing.

Suddenly the breeze stops blowing, the bird stops singing, Jof's smile fades, the flowers and grass wilt in the heat. The old horse is still walking around grazing and swishing its tail to ward off the flies.

Jof comes to life. He rushes into the wagon and shakes Mia awake.

Jof. Mia, wake up, Wake up! Mia, I've just seen something. I've got to tell you about it!

Mia *(sits up, terrified).* What is it? What's happened?

Jof. Listen, I've had a vision. No, it wasn't a vision. It was real, absolutely real.

Mia. Oh, so you've had a vision again!

Mia's voice is filled with gentle irony. Jof shakes his head and grabs her by the shoulders.

Jof. But I did see her!

Mia. Whom did you see?

Jof. The Virgin Mary.

Mia can't help being impressed by her husband's fervor. She lowers her voice.

Mia. Did you really see her?

Jof. She was so close to me that I could have touched her. She had a golden crown on her head and wore a blue gown with flowers of gold. She was barefoot and had small brown hands with which she was holding the Child and teaching Him to walk. And then she saw me watching her and she smiled at me. My eyes filled with tears and when I wiped them away, she had disappeared. And everything became so still in the sky and on the earth. Can you understand . . .

Mia. What an imagination you have.

Jof. You don't believe me! But it was real, I tell you, not the kind of reality you see everyday, but a different kind.

Mia. Perhaps it was the kind of reality you told us about when you saw the Devil paint your wagon wheels red, using his tail as a brush.

Jof *(embarrassed).* Why must you keep bringing that up?

Mia. And then you discovered that you had red paint under your nails.

Jof. Well, perhaps that time I made it up. *(Eagerly)* I did it just so that you would believe in my other visions. The real ones. The ones that I didn't make up.

Mia. *(severely).* You have to keep your visions under control. Otherwise people will think that you're a half-wit, which you're not. At least not yet —as far as I know. But, come to think of it, I'm not so sure about that.

Jof *(angry).* I didn't ask to have visions. I can't help it if voices speak to me, if the Holy Virgin appears before me and angels and devils like my company.

Skat *(sits up).* Haven't I told you once and for all that I need my morning's sleep! I have asked you politely, pleaded with you, but nothing works. So now I'm telling you to *shut up!*

His eyes are popping with rage. He turns over and continues snoring where he left off. Mia and Jof decide that it would be wisest to leave the wagon. They sit down on a crate. Mia has Mikael on her knees. He is naked and squirms vigorously. Jof sits close to his wife. Slumped over, he still looks dazed and astonished. A dry, hot wind blows from the sea.

Mia.   If we would only get some rain. Everything is burned to cinders. We won't have anything to eat this winter.

Jof *(yawning).*   We'll get by.

He says this smilingly, with a casual air. He stretches and laughs contentedly.

Mia.   I want Mikael to have a better life than ours.

Jof.   Mikael will grow up to be a great acrobat—or a juggler who can do the one impossible trick.

Mia.   What's that?

Jof.   To make one of the balls stand absolutely still in the air.

Mia.   But that's impossible.

Jof.   Impossible for us—but not for him.

Mia.   You're dreaming again.

She yawns. The sun has made her a bit drowsy and she lies down on the grass. Jof does likewise and puts one arm around his wife's shoulders.

Jof.   I've composed a song. I made it up during the night when I couldn't sleep. Do you want to hear it?

Mia.   Sing it. I'm very curious.

Jof.   I have to sit up first.

He sits with his legs crossed, makes a dramatic gesture with his arms and sings in a loud voice.

Jof.   On a lily branch a dove is perched
                  Against the summer sky,
                  She sings a wondrous song of Christ
                  And there's great joy on high.

He interrupts his singing in order to be complimented by his wife.

Jof.   Mia! Are you asleep?

Mia.   It's a lovely song.

Jof.   I haven't finished yet.

Mia.   I heard it, but I think I'll sleep a little longer. You can sing the rest to me afterward.

Jof.   All you do is sleep.

Jof is a bit offended and glances over at his son, Mikael, but he is also sleeping soundly in the high grass. Jonas Skat comes out from the wagon. He yawns; he is very tired and in a bad humor. In his hands he holds a crudely made death mask.

Skat.   Is this supposed to be a mask for an actor? If the priests didn't pay us so well, I'd say no thank you.

Jof.   Are you going to play Death?

Skat.   Just think, scaring decent folk out of their wits with this kind of nonsense.

Jof. When are we supposed to do this play?

Skat. At the saints' feast in Elsinore. We're going to perform right on the church steps, believe it or not.

Jof. Wouldn't it be better to play something bawdy? People like it better, and, besides, it's more fun.

Skat. Idiot. There's a rumor going around that there's a terrible pestilence in the land, and now the priests are prophesying sudden death and all sorts of spiritual agonies.

Mia is awake now and lies contentedly on her back, sucking on a blade of grass and looking smilingly at her husband.

Jof. And what part am I to play?

Skat. You're such a damn fool, so you're going to be the Soul of Man.

Jof. That's a bad part, of course.

Skat. Who makes the decisions around here? Who is the director of this company anyhow?

Skat, grinning, holds the mask in front of his face and recites dramatically.

Skat. Bear this in mind, you fool. Your life hangs by a thread. Your time is short. (*In his usual voice*) Are the women going to like me in this getup? Will I make a hit? No! I feel as if I were dead already.

He stumbles into the wagon muttering furiously. Jof sits, leaning forward. Mia lies beside him on the grass.

Mia. Jof!

Jof. What is it?

Mia. Sit still. Don't move.

Jof. What do you mean?

Mia. Don't say anything.

Jof. I'm as silent as a grave.

Mia. Shh! I love you.

WAVES of heat envelop the gray stone church in a strange white mist. The knight dismounts and enters. After tying up the horses, Jöns slowly follows him in. When he comes onto the church porch he stops in surprise. To the right of the entrance there is a large fresco on the wall, not quite finished. Perched on a crude scaffolding is a painter wearing a red cap and paint-stained clothes. He has one brush in his mouth, while with another in his hand he outlines a small, terrified human face amidst a sea of other faces.

Jöns. What is this supposed to represent?

Painter. The Dance of Death.

Jöns. And that one is Death?

Painter. Yes, he dances off with all of them.

Jöns. Why do you paint such nonsense?

Painter. I thought it would serve to remind people that they must die.

Jöns. Well, it's not going to make them feel any happier.

Painter. Why should one always make people happy? It might not be a bad idea to scare them a little once in a while.

Jöns. Then they'll close their eyes and refuse to look at your painting.

Painter. Oh, they'll look. A skull is almost more interesting than a naked woman.

Jöns. If you do scare them . . .

Painter. They'll think.

Jöns. And if they think . . .

Painter. They'll become still more scared.

Jöns. And then they'll run right into the arms of the priests.

Painter. That's not my business.

Jöns. You're only painting your Dance of Death.

Painter. I'm only painting things as they are. Everyone else can do as he likes.

Jöns. Just think how some people will curse you.

Painter. Maybe. But then I'll paint something amusing for them to look at. I have to make a living—at least until the plague takes me.

Jöns. The plague. That sounds horrible.

Painter. You should see the boils on a diseased man's throat. You should see how his body shrivels up so that his legs look like knotted strings—like the man I've painted over there.

The painter points with his brush. Jöns sees a small human form writhing in the grass, its eyes turned upward in a frenzied look of horror and pain.

Jöns. That looks terrible.

Painter. It certainly does. He tries to rip out the boil, he bites his hands, tears his veins open with his fingernails and his screams can be heard everywhere. Does that scare you?

Jöns. Scare? Me? You don't know me. What are the horrors you've painted over there?

Painter. The remarkable thing is that the poor creatures think the pestilence is the Lord's punishment. Mobs of people who call themselves Slaves of Sin are swarming over the country, flagellating themselves and others, all for the glory of God.

Jöns. Do they really whip themselves?

Painter. Yes, it's a terrible sight. I crawl into a ditch and hide when they pass by.

Jöns. Do you have any brandy? I've been drinking water all day and it's made me as thirsty as a camel in the desert.

Painter. I think I frightened you after all.

Jöns sits down with the painter, who produces a jug of brandy.

THE knight is kneeling before a small altar. It is dark and quiet around him. The air is cool and musty. Pictures of saints look down on him with stony eyes. Christ's face is turned upward, His mouth open as if in a cry of anguish.

On the ceiling beam there is a representation of a hideous devil spying on a miserable human being. The knight hears a sound from the confession booth and approaches it. The face of Death appears behind the grill for an instant, but the knight doesn't see him.

Knight.   I want to talk to you as openly as I can, but my heart is empty.

Death doesn't answer.

Knight.   The emptiness is a mirror turned toward my own face. I see myself in it, and I am filled with fear and disgust.

Death doesn't answer.

Knight.   Through my indifference to my fellow men, I have isolated myself from their company. Now I live in a world of phantoms. I am imprisoned in my dreams and fantasies.
Death.   And yet you don't want to die.
Knight.   Yes, I do.
Death.   What are you waiting for?
Knight.   I want knowledge.
Death.   You want guarantees?
Knight.   Call it whatever you like. Is it so cruelly inconceivable to grasp God with the senses? Why should he hide himself in a mist of half-spoken promises and unseen miracles?

Death doesn't answer.

Knight.   How can we have faith in those who believe when we can't have faith in ourselves? What is going to happen to those of us who want to believe but aren't able to? And what is to become of those who neither want to nor are capable of believing?

The knight stops and waits for a reply, but no one speaks or answers him. There is complete silence.

Knight.   Why can't I kill God within me? Why does he live on in this painful and humiliating way even though I curse Him and want to tear Him out of my heart? Why, in spite of everything, is He a baffling reality that I can't shake off? Do you hear me?
Death.   Yes, I hear you.
Knight.   I want knowledge, not faith, not suppositions, but knowledge. I want God to stretch out his hand toward me, reveal Himself and speak to me.
Death.   But he remains silent.
Knight.   I call out to him in the dark but no one seems to be there.
Death.   Perhaps no one is there.
Knight.   Then life is an outrageous horror. No one can live in the face of death, knowing that all is nothingness.
Death.   Most people never reflect about either death or the futility of life.

Knight. But one day they will have to stand at that last moment of life and look toward the darkness.

Death. When *that* day comes . . .

Knight. In our fear, we make an image, and that image we call God.

Death. You are worrying . . .

Knight. Death visited me this morning. We are playing chess together. This reprieve gives me the chance to arrange an urgent matter.

Death. What matter is that?

Knight. My life has been a futile pursuit, a wandering, a great deal of talk without meaning. I feel no bitterness or self-reproach because the lives of most people are very much like this. But I will use my reprieve for one meaningful deed.

Death. Is that why you are playing chess with Death?

Knight. He is a clever opponent, but up to now I haven't lost a single man.

Death. How will you outwit Death in your game?

Knight. I use a combination of the bishop and the knight which he hasn't yet discovered. In the next move I'll shatter one of his flanks.

Death. I'll remember that.

Death shows his face at the grill of the confession booth for a moment but disappears instantly.

Knight. You've tricked and cheated me! But we'll meet again, and I'll find a way.

Death (*invisible*). We'll meet at the inn, and there we'll continue playing.

The knight raises his hand and looks at it in the sunlight which comes through the tiny window.

Knight. This is my hand. I can move it, feel the blood pulsing through it. The sun is still high in the sky and I, Antonius Block, am playing chess with Death.

He makes a fist of his hand and lifts it to his temple.

Meanwhile, Jöns and the painter have gotten drunk and are talking animatedly together.

Jöns. Me and my master have been abroad and have just come home. Do you understand, you little pictor?

Painter. The Crusade.

Jöns (*drunk*). Precisely. For ten years we sat in the Holy Land and let snakes bite us, flies sting us, wild animals eat us, heathens butcher us, the wine poison us, the women give us lice, the lice devour us, the fevers rot us, all for the Glory of God. Our crusade was such madness that only a real idealist could have thought it up. But what you said about the plague was horrible.

Painter. It's worse than that.

Jöns. Ah me. No matter which way you turn, you have your rump behind you. That's the truth.

Painter. The rump behind you, the rump behind you—there's a profound truth.

Jöns paints a small figure which is supposed to represent himself.

Jöns. This is squire Jöns. He grins at Death, mocks the Lord, laughs at himself and leers at the girls. His world is a Jöns-world, believable only to himself, ridiculous to all including himself, meaningless to Heaven and of no interest to Hell.

The knight walks by, calls to his squire and goes out into the bright sunshine. Jöns manages to get himself down from the scaffolding.

Outside the church, four soldiers and a monk are in the process of putting a woman in the stocks. Her face is pale and child-like, her head has been shaved, and her knuckles are bloody and broken. Her eyes are wide open, yet she doesn't appear to be fully conscious.

Jöns and the knight stop and watch in silence. The soldiers are working quickly and skillfully, but they seem frightened and dejected. The monk mumbles from a small book. One of the soldiers picks up a wooden bucket and with his hand begins to smear a bloody paste on the wall of the church and around the woman. Jöns holds his nose.

Jöns. That soup of yours has a hell of a stink. What is it good for?

Soldier. She has had carnal intercourse with the Evil One.

He whispers this with a horrified face and continues to splash the sticky mess on the wall.

Jöns. And now she's in the stocks.

Soldier. She will be burned tomorrow morning at the parish boundary. But we have to keep the Devil away from the rest of us.

Jöns (holding his nose). And you do that with this stinking mess?

Soldier. It's the best remedy: blood mixed with the bile of a big black dog. The Devil can't stand the smell.

Jöns. Neither can I.

Jöns walks over toward the horses. The knight stands for a few moments looking at the young girl. She is almost a child. Slowly she turns her eyes toward him.

Knight. Have you seen the Devil?

The monk stops reading and raises his head.

Monk. You must not talk to her.

Knight. Can that be so dangerous?

Monk. I don't know, but she is believed to have caused the pestilence with which we are afflicted.
Knight. I understand.

He nods resignedly and walks away. The young woman starts to moan as though she were having a horrible nightmare. The sound of her cries follows the two riders for a considerable distance down the road.

THE sun stands high in the sky, like a red ball of fire. The waterskin is empty and Jöns looks for a well where he can fill it.

They approach a group of peasant cottages at the edge of the forest. Jöns ties up the horses, slings the skin over his shoulder and walks along the path toward the nearest cottage. As always, his movements are light and almost soundless. The door to the cottage is open. He stops outside, but when no one appears he enters. It is very dark inside and his foot touches a soft object. He looks down. Beside the whitewashed fireplace, a woman is lying with her face to the ground.

At the sound of approaching steps, Jöns quickly hides behind the door. A man comes down a ladder from the loft. He is broad and thick-set. His eyes are black and his face is pale and puffy. His clothes are well cut but dirty and in rags. He carries a cloth sack. Looking around, he goes into the inner room, bends over the bed, tucks something into the bag, slinks along the walls, looking on the shelves, finds something else which he tucks in his bag.

Slowly he re-enters the outer room, bends over the dead woman and carefully slips a ring from her finger. At that moment a young woman comes through the door. She stops and stares at the stranger.

Raval. Why do you look so surprised? I steal from the dead. These days it's quite a lucrative enterprise.

The girl makes a movement as if to run away.

Raval. You're thinking of running to the village and telling. That wouldn't serve any purpose. Each of us has to save his own skin. It's as simple as that.
Girl. Don't touch me.
Raval. Don't try to scream. There's no one around to hear you, neither God nor man.

Slowly he closes the door behind the girl. The stuffy room is now in almost total darkness. But Jons becomes clearly visible.

Jöns. I recognize you, although it's a long time since we met. Your name is Raval, from the theological college at Roskilde. You are Dr. Mirabilis, Coelestis et Diabilis.

Raval smiles uneasily and looks around.

Jöns. Am I not right?

The girl stands immobile.

Jöns. You were the one who, ten years ago, convinced my master of the necessity to join a better-class crusade to the Holy Land.

Raval looks around.

Jöns. You look uncomfortable. Do you have a stomach-ache?

Raval smiles anxiously.

Jöns. When I see you, I suddenly understand the meaning of these ten years, which previously seemed to me such a waste. Our life was too good and we were too satisfied with ourselves. The Lord wanted to punish us for our complacency. That is why He sent you to spew out your holy venom and poison the knight.

Raval. I acted in good faith.

Jöns. But now you know better, don't you? Because now you have turned into a thief. A more fitting and rewarding occupation for scoundrels. Isn't that so?

With a quick movement he knocks the knife out of Raval's hand, gives him a kick so that he falls on the floor and is about to finish him off. Suddenly the girl screams. Jöns stops and makes a gesture of generosity with his hand.

Jöns. By all means. I'm not bloodthirsty. (*He bends over Raval*)

Raval. Don't beat me.

Jöns. I don't have the heart to touch you, Doctor. But remember this: The next time we meet, I'll brand your face the way one does with thieves. (*He rises*) What I really came for is to get my waterskin filled.

Girl. We have a deep well with cool, fresh water. Come, I'll show you.

They walk out of the house. Raval lies still for a few moments, then he rises slowly and looks around. When no one is in sight, he takes his bag and steals away.

Jöns quenches his thirst and fills his bag with water. The girl helps him.

Jöns. Jöns is my name. I am a pleasant and talkative young man who has never had anything but kind thoughts and has only done beautiful and noble deeds. I'm kindest of all to young women. With them, there is no limit to my kindness.

He embraces her and tries to kiss her, but she holds herself back. Almost immediately he loses interest, hoists the waterbag on his shoulder and pats the girl on the cheek.

Jöns. Goodbye, my girl. I could very well have raped you, but between you and me, I'm tired of that kind of love. It runs a little dry in the end.

He laughs kindly and walks away from her. When he has walked a short distance he turns; the girl is still there.

Jöns. Now that I think of it, I will need a housekeeper. Can you prepare good food? (*The girl nods*) As far as I know, I'm still a married man, but I have high hopes that my wife is dead by now. That's why I need a housekeeper. (*The girl doesn't answer but gets up*) The devil with it! Come along and don't stand there staring. I've saved your life, so you owe me a great deal.

She begins walking toward him, her head bent. He doesn't wait for her but walks toward the knight, who patiently awaits his squire.

THE Embarrassment Inn lies in the eastern section of the province. The plague has not yet reached this area on its way along the coast.

The actors have placed their wagon under a tree in the yard of the inn. Dressed in colorful costumes, they perform a farce.

The spectators watch the performance, commenting on it noisily. There are merchants with fat, beer-sweaty faces, apprentices and journeymen, farmhands and milkmaids. A whole flock of children perch in the trees around the wagon.

The knight and his squire have sat down in the shadow of a wall. They drink beer and doze in the midday heat. The girl from the deserted village sleeps at Jons' side.

Skat beats the drums, Jof blows the flute, Mia performs a gay and lively dance. They perspire under the hot white sun. When they have finished Skat comes forward and bows.

Skat. Noble ladies and gentlemen, I thank you for your interest. Please remain standing a little longer, or sit on the ground, because we are now going to perform a tragedia about an unfaithful wife, her jealous husband, and the handsome lover—that's me.

Mia and Jof have quickly changed costumes and again step out on the stage. They bow to the public.

Skat. Here is the husband. Here is the wife. If you'll shut up over there, you'll see something splendid. As I said, I play the lover and I haven't entered yet. That's why I'm going to hide behind the curtain for the time being. (*He wipes the sweat from his forehead*) It's damned hot. I think we'll have a thunderstorm.

He places his leg in front of Jof as if to trip him, raises Mia's skirt, makes a face as if he could see all the wonders of the world underneath it, and disappears behind the gaudily patched curtains.

Skat is very handsome, now that he can see himself in the reflection of a tin washbowl. His hair is tightly curled, his eyebrows are beautifully bushy, glittering earrings vie for equal attention with his teeth, and his cheeks are flushed rose red.

He sits out in back on the tailboard of the wagon, dangling his legs and whistling to himself.

In the meantime Jof and Mia play their tragedy; it is not, however, received with great acclaim.

Skat suddenly discovers that someone is watching him as he gazes contentedly into the tin bowl. A woman stands there, stately in both height and volume.

Skat frowns, toys with his small dagger and occasionally throws a roguish but fiery glance at the beautiful visitor.

She suddenly discovers that one of her shoes doesn't quite fit. She leans down to fix it and in doing so allows her generous bosom to burst out of its prison—no more than honor and chastity allow, but still enough so that the actor with his experienced eye immediately sees that there are ample rewards to be had here.

Now she comes a little closer, kneels down and opens a bundle containing several dainty morsels and a skin filled with red wine. Jonas Skat manages not to fall off the wagon in his excitement. Standing on the steps of the wagon, he supports himself against a nearby tree, crosses his legs and bows.

The woman quietly bites into a chicken leg dripping with fat. At this moment the actor is stricken by a radiant glance full of lustful appetites.

When he sees this look, Skat makes an instantaneous decision, jumps down from the wagon and kneels in front of the blushing damsel.

She becomes weak and faint from his nearness, looks at him with a glassy glance and breathes heavily. Skat doesn't neglect to press kisses on her small, chubby hands. The sun shines brightly and small birds make noises in the bushes.

Now she is forced to sit back; her legs seem unwilling to support her any longer. Bewildered, she singles out another chicken leg from the large sack of food and holds it up in front of Skat with an appealing and triumphant expression, as if it were her maidenhood being offered as a prize.

Skat hesitates momentarily, but he is still the strategist. He lets the chicken leg fall to the grass, and murmurs in the woman's rosy ear.

His words seem to please her. She puts her arms around the actor's neck and pulls him to her with such fierceness that both of them lose their balance and tumble down on the soft grass. The small birds take to their wings with frightened shrieks.

Jof stands in the hot sun with a flickering lantern in his hand. Mia pretends to be asleep on a bench which has been pulled forward on the stage.

Jof. Night and moonlight now prevail
Here sleeps my wife so frail . . .
Voice from the Public. Does she snore?

Jof. May I point out that this is a tragedy, and in tragedies one doesn't snore.
Voice from the Public. I think she should snore anyhow.

This opinion causes mirth in the audience. Jof becomes slightly confused and goes out of character, but Mia keeps her head and begins snoring.

Jof. Night and moonlight now prevail.
There snores—I mean sleeps—my wife so frail.
Jealous I am, as never before,
I hide myself behind this door.
Faithful is she
To her lover—not me.
He soon comes a-stealing
To awaken her lusty feeling.
I shall now kill him dead
For cuckolding me in my bed.
There he comes in the moonlight,
His white legs shining bright.
Quiet as a mouse, here I'll lie,
Tell him not that he's about to die.

Jof hides himself. Mia immediately ends her snoring and sits up, looking to the left.

Mia. Look, there he comes in the night
My lover, my heart's delight.

She becomes silent and looks wide-eyed in front of her.

The mood in the yard in front of the inn has, up to now, been rather lighthearted despite the heat.

Now a rapid change occurs. People who had been laughing and chattering fall silent. Their faces seem to pale under their sunbrowned skins, the children stop their games and stand with gaping mouths and frightened eyes. Jof steps out in front of the curtain. His painted face bears an expression of horror. Mia has risen with Mikael in her arms. Some of the women in the yard have fallen on their knees, others hide their faces, many begin to mutter half-forgotten prayers.

All have turned their faces toward the white road. Now a shrill song is heard. It is frenzied, almost a scream.

A crucified Christ sways above the hilltop.

The cross-bearers soon come into sight. They are Dominican monks, their hoods pulled down over their faces. More and more of them follow, carrying litters with heavy coffins or clutching holy relics, their hands stretched out spasmodically. The dust wells up around their black hoods; the censers sway and emit a thick, ashen smoke which smells of rancid herbs.

After the line of monks comes another procession. It is a column of men, boys, old men, women, girls, children. All of them have steel-edged scourges in their hands with which they whip themselves and each other, howling ecstatically. They twist in pain; their eyes bulge wildly; their lips are gnawed to shreds and dripping with foam. They have been seized by madness. They bite their own hands and arms, whip each other in violent, almost rhythmic outbursts. Throughout it all the shrill song howls from their bursting throats. Many sway and fall, lift themselves up again, support each other and help each other to intensify the scourging.

Now the procession pauses at the crossroads in front of the inn. The monks fall on their knees, hiding their faces with clenched hands, arms pressed tightly together. Their song never stops. The Christ figure on its timbered cross is raised above the heads of the crowd. It is not Christ triumphant, but the suffering Jesus with the sores, the blood, the hammered nails and the face in convulsive pain. The Son of God, nailed on the wood of the cross, suffering scorn and shame.

The penitents have now sunk down in the dirt of the road. They collapse where they stood like slaughtered cattle. Their screams rise with the song of the monks, through misty clouds of incense, toward the white fire of the sun.

A large square monk rises from his knees and reveals his face, which is red-brown from the sun. His eyes glitter; his voice is thick with impotent scorn.

Monk.   God has sentenced us to punishment. We shall all perish in the black death. You, standing there like gaping cattle, you who sit there in your glutted complacency, do you know that this may be your last hour? Death stands right behind you. I can see how his crown gleams in the sun. His scythe flashes as he raises it above your heads. Which one of you shall he strike first? You there, who stand staring like a goat, will your mouth be twisted into the last unfinished gasp before nightfall? And you, woman, who bloom with life and self-satisfaction, will you pale and become extinguished before the morning dawns? You back there, with your swollen nose and stupid grin, do you have another year left to dirty the earth with your refuse? Do you know, you insensible fools, that you shall die today or tomorrow, or the next day, because all of you have been sentenced? Do you hear what I say? Do you hear the word? You have been sentenced, sentenced!

The monk falls silent, looking around with a bitter face and a cold scornful glance. Now he clenches his hands, straddles the ground and turns his face upward.

Monk.   Lord have mercy on us in our humiliation! Don't turn your face from us in loathing and contempt, but be merciful to us for the sake of your son, Jesus Christ.

He makes the sign of the cross over the crowd and then begins a new song in a strong voice. The monks rise and join in the song. As if driven by some superhuman force, the penitents begin to whip themselves again, still wailing and moaning.

The procession continues. New members have joined the rear of the column; others who were unable to go on lie weeping in the dust of the road.

Jöns the squire drinks his beer.

Jöns.   This damned ranting about doom. Is that food for the minds of modern people? Do they really expect us to take them seriously?

The knight grins tiredly.

Jöns.   Yes, now you grin at me, my lord. But allow me to point out that I've either read, heard or experienced most of the tales which we people tell each other.

Knight (*yawns*).   Yes, yes.

Jöns.   Even the ghost stories about God the Father, the angels, Jesus Christ and the Holy Ghost—all these I've accepted without too much emotion.

He leans down over the girl as she crouches at his feet and pats her on the head. The knight drinks his beer silently.

Jöns (*contentedly*).   My little stomach is my world, my head is my eternity, and my hands, two wonderful suns. My legs are time's damned pendulums, and my dirty feet are two splendid starting points for my philosophy. Everything is worth precisely as much as a belch, the only difference being that a belch is more satisfying.

The beer mug is empty. Sighing, Jöns gets to his feet. The girl follows him like a shadow.

In the yard he meets a large man with a sooty face and a dark expression. He stops Jöns with a roar.

Jöns.   What are you screaming about?

Plog.   I am Plog, the smith, and you are the squire Jöns.

Jöns.   That's possible.

Plog.   Have you seen my wife?

Jöns.   No, I haven't. But if I had seen her and she looked like you, I'd quickly forget that I'd seen her.

Plog.   Well, in that case you haven't seen her.

Jöns.   Maybe she's run off.

Plog.   Do you know anything?

Jöns.   I know quite a lot, but not about your wife. Go to the inn. Maybe they can help you.

The smith sighs sadly and goes inside.

THE inn is very small and full of people eating and drinking to forget their newly aroused fear of eternity. In the open fireplace a roasting pig turns on an iron spit. The sun shines outside the casement window, its sharp rays piercing the darkness of the room, which is thick with fumes and perspiration.

Merchant. Yes, it's true! The plague is spreading along the west coast. People are dying like flies. Usually business would be good at this time of year, but, damn it, I've still got my whole stock unsold.

Woman. They speak of the judgment day. And all these omens are terrible. Worms, chopped-off hands and other monstrosities began pouring out of an old woman, and down in the village another woman gave birth to a calf's head.

Old Man. The day of judgment. Imagine.

Farmer. It hasn't rained here for a month. We'll surely lose our crops.

Merchant. And people are acting crazy, I'd say. They flee the country and carry the plague with them wherever they go.

Old Man. The day of judgment. Just think, just think!

Farmer. If it's as they say, I suppose a person should look after his house and try to enjoy life as long as he can.

Woman. But there have been other things too, such things that can't even be spoken of. (*Whispers*) Things that mustn't be named—but the priests say that the woman carries it between her legs and that's why she must cleanse herself.

Old Man. Judgment day. And the Riders of the Apocalypse stand at the bend in the village road. I imagine they'll come on judgment night, at sundown.

Woman. There are many who have purged themselves with fire and died from it, but the priests say that it's better to die pure than to live for hell.

Merchant. This is the end, yes, it is. No one says it out loud, but all of us know that it's the end. And people are going mad from fear.

Farmer. So you're afraid too.

Merchant. Of course I'm afraid.

Old Man. The judgment day becomes night, and the angels descend and the graves open. It will be terrible to see.

They whisper in low tones and sit close to each other. Plog, the smith, shoves his way into a place next to Jof, who is still dressed in his costume. Opposite him sits Raval, leaning slightly forward, his face perspiring heavily. Raval rolls an armlet out on the table.

Raval. Do you want this armlet? You can have it cheap.

Jof. I can't afford it.

Raval. It's real silver.

Jof. It's nice. But it's surely too expensive for me.

Plog. Excuse me, but has anyone here seen my wife?

Jof. Has she disappeared?

Plog. They say she's run away.

Jof. Has she deserted you?

Plog. With an actor.

Jof. An actor! If she's got such bad taste, then I think you should let her go.

Plog.   You're right. My first thought, of course, was to kill her.

Jof.   Oh. But to murder her, that's a terrible thing to do.

Plog.   I'm also going to kill the actor.

Jof.   The actor?

Plog.   Of course, the one she eloped with.

Jof.   What has he done to deserve that?

Plog.   Are you stupid?

Jof.   The actor! Now I understand. There are too many of them, so even if he hasn't done anything in particular you ought to kill him merely because he's an actor.

Plog.   You see, my wife has always been interested in the tricks of the theater.

Jof.   And that turned out to be her misfortune.

Plog.   Her misfortune, but not mine, because a person who's born unfortunate can hardly suffer from any further misfortune. Isn't that true?

Now Raval enters the discussion. He is slightly drunk and his voice is shrill and evil.

Raval.   Listen, you! You sit there and lie to the smith.

Jof.   I! A liar!

Raval.   You're an actor too and it's probably your partner who's run off with Plog's old lady.

Plog.   Are you an actor too?

Jof.   An actor! Me! I wouldn't quite call myself that!

Raval.   We ought to kill you; it's only logical.

Jof (*laughs*).   You're really funny.

Raval.   How strange—you've turned pale. Have you anything on your conscience?

Jof.   You're funny. Don't you think he's funny? (*To Plog*) Oh, you don't.

Raval.   Maybe we should mark you up a little with a knife, like they do petty scoundrels of your kind.

Plog bangs his hands down on the table so that the dishes jump. He gets up.

Plog (*shouting*).   What have you done with my wife?

The room becomes silent. Jof looks around, but there is no exit, no way to escape. He puts his hands on the table. Suddenly a knife flashes through the air and sinks into the table top between his fingers.

Jof snatches away his hands and raises his head. He looks half surprised, as if the truth had just become apparent to him.

Jof.   Do you want to hurt me? Why? Have I provoked someone, or got in the way? I'll leave right now and never come back.

Jof looks from one face to another, but no one seems ready to help him or come to his defense.

Raval.   Get up so everyone can hear you. Talk louder.

Trembling, Jof rises. He opens his mouth as if to say something, but not a word comes out.

Raval. Stand on your head so that we can see how good an actor you are.

Jof gets up on the table and stands on his head. A hand pushes him forward so that he collapses on the floor. Plog rises, pulls him to his feet with one hand.

Plog (*shouts*). What have you done with my wife?

The smith beats him so furiously that Jof flies across the table. Raval leans over him.

Raval. Don't lie there moaning. Get up and dance.
Jof. I don't want to. I can't.
Raval. Show us how you imitate a bear.
Jof. I can't play a bear.
Raval. Let's see if you can't after all.

Raval prods Jof lightly with the knife point. Jof gets up with cold sweat on his cheeks and forehead, frightened half to death. He begins to jump and hop on top of the tables, swinging his arms and legs and making grotesque faces. Some laugh, but most of the people sit silently. Jof gasps as if his lungs were about to burst. He sinks to his knees, and someone pours beer over him.

Raval. Up again! Be a good bear.
Jof. I haven't done any harm. I haven't got the strength to play a bear any more.

At that moment the door opens and Jöns enters. Jof sees his chance and steals out. Raval intends to follow him, but suddenly stops. Jöns and Raval look at each other.

Jöns. Do you remember what I was going to do to you if we met again?

Raval steps back without speaking.

Jöns. I'm a man who keeps his word.

Jöns raises his knife and cuts Raval from forehead to cheek. Raval staggers toward the wall.

THE hot day has become night. Singing and howling can be heard from the inn. In a hollow near the forest, the light still lingers. Hidden in the grass and the shrubbery, nightingales sing and their voices echo through the stillness.

The players' wagon stands in a small ravine, and not far away the horse grazes on the dry grass. Mia has sat down in front of the wagon with her son in her arms. They play together and laugh happily.

Now a soft gleam of light strokes the hilltops, a last reflection from the red clouds over the sea.

Not far from the wagon, the knight sits crouched over his chess game. He lifts his head.

The evening light moves across the heavy wagon wheels, across the woman and the child.

The knight gets up.

Mia sees him and smiles. She holds up her struggling son, as if to amuse the knight.

Knight. What's his name?
Mia. Mikael.
Knight. How old is he?
Mia. Oh, he'll soon be two.
Knight. He's big for his age.
Mia. Do you think so? Yes, I guess he's rather big.

She puts the child down on the ground and half rises to shake out her red skirt. When she sits down again, the knight steps closer.

Knight. You played some kind of show this afternoon.
Mia. Did you think it was bad?
Knight. You are more beautiful now without your face painted, and this gown is more becoming.
Mia. You see, Jonas Skat has run off and left us, so we're in real trouble now.
Knight. Is that your husband?
Mia (*laughs*). Jonas! The other man is my husband. His name is Jof.
Knight. Oh, that one.
Mia. And now there's only him and me. We'll have to start doing tricks again and that's more trouble than it's worth.
Knight. Do you do tricks also?
Mia. We certainly do. And Jof is a very skillful juggler.
Knight. Is Mikael going to be an acrobat?
Mia. Jof wants him to be.
Knight. But you don't.
Mia. I don't know. (*Smiling*) Perhaps he'll become a knight.
Knight. Let me assure you, that's no pleasure either.
Mia. No, you don't look so happy.
Knight. No.
Mia. Are you tired?
Knight. Yes.
Mia. Why?
Knight. I have dull company.
Mia. Do you mean your squire?
Knight. No, not him.
Mia. Who do you mean, then?
Knight. Myself.
Mia. I understand.

Knight. Do you, really?

Mia. Yes, I understand rather well. I have often wondered why people torture themselves as often as they can. Isn't that so?

She nods energetically and the knight smiles seriously.

     Now the shrieks and the noise from the inn become louder. Black
figures flicker across the grass mound. Someone collapses, gets up and runs.
It is Jof. Mia stretches out her arms and receives him. He holds his hands in
front of his face, moaning like a child, and his body sways. He kneels. Mia
holds him close to her and sprinkles him with small, anxious questions: What
have you done? How are you? What is it? Does it hurt? What can I do? Have
they been cruel to you? She runs for a rag, which she dips in water, and
carefully bathes her husband's dirty, bloody face.

     Eventually a rather sorrowful visage emerges. Blood runs from a bruise
on his forehead and his nose, and a tooth has been loosened, but otherwise
Jof seems unhurt.

Jof. Ouch, it hurts.

Mia. Why did you have to go there? And of course you drank.

Mia's anxiety has been replaced by a mild anger. She pats him a little harder
than necessary.

Jof. Ouch! I didn't drink anything.

Mia. Then I suppose you were boasting about the angels and devils you
consort with. People don't like someone who has too many ideas and
fantasies.

Jof. I swear to you that I didn't say a word about angels.

Mia. You were, of course, busy singing and dancing. You can never stop
being an actor. People also become angry at that, and you know it.

Jof doesn't answer but searches for the armlet. He holds it up in front of Mia
with an injured expression.

Jof. Look what I bought for you.

Mia. You couldn't afford it.

Jof (*angry*). But I got it anyhow.

The armlet glitters faintly in the twilight. Mia now pulls it across her wrist.
They look at it in silence, and their faces soften. They look at each other,
touch each other's hands. Jof puts his head against Mia's shoulder and sighs.

Jof. Oh, how they beat me.

Mia. Why didn't you beat them back?

Jof. I only become frightened and angry. I never get a chance to hit back.
I can get angry, you know that. I roared like a lion.

Mia. Were they frightened?

Jof. No, they just laughed.

Their son Mikael crawls over to them. Jof lies down on the ground and pulls his son on top of him. Mia gets down on her hands and knees and playfully sniffs at Mikael.

Mia.   Do you notice how good he smells?

Jof.   And he is so compact to hold. You're a sturdy one. A real acrobat's body.

He lifts Mikael up and holds him by the legs. Mia looks up suddenly, remembering the knight's presence.

Mia.   Yes, this is my husband, Jof.

Jof.   Good evening.

Knight.   Good evening.

Jof becomes a little embarrassed and rises. All three of them look at one another silently.

Knight.   I have just told your wife that you have a splendid son. He'll bring great joy to you.

Jof.   Yes, he's fine.

They become silent again.

Jof.   Have we nothing to offer the knight, Mia?

Knight.   Thank you, I don't want anything.

Mia (*housewifely*).   I picked a basket of wild strawberries this afternoon. And we have a drop of milk fresh from a cow . . .

Jof. . . . that we were *allowed* to milk. So, if you would like to partake of this humble fare, it would be a great honor.

Mia.   Please be seated and I'll bring the food.

They sit down. Mia disappears with Mikael.

Knight.   Where are you going next?

Jof.   Up to the saints' feast at Elsinore.

Knight.   I wouldn't advise you to go there.

Jof.   Why not, if I may ask?

Knight.   The plague has spread in that direction, following the coast line south. It's said that people are dying by the tens of thousands.

Jof.   Really! Well, sometimes life is a little hard.

Knight.   May I suggest . . . (*Jof looks at him, surprised*) . . . that you follow me through the forest tonight and stay at my home if you like. Or go along the east coast. You'll probably be safer there.

Mia has returned with a bowl of wild strawberries and the milk, places it between them and gives each of them a spoon.

Jof.   I wish you good appetite.

Knight.   I humbly thank you.

Mia.   These are wild strawberries from the forest. I have never seen such large ones. They grow up there on the hillside. Notice how they smell!

She points with a spoon and smiles. The knight nods, as if he were pondering some profound thought. Jof eats heartily.

Jof. Your suggestion is good, but I must think it over.

Mia. It might be wise to have company going through the forest. It's said to be full of trolls and ghosts and bandits. That's what I've heard.

Jof (*staunchly*). Yes, I'd say that it's not a bad idea, but I have to think about it. Now that Skat has left, I am responsible for the troupe. After all, I have become director of the whole company.

Mia (*mimics*). After all, I have become director of the whole company.

Jöns comes walking slowly down the hill, closely followed by the girl. Mia points with her spoon.

Mia. Do you want some strawberries?

Jof. This man saved my life. Sit down, my friend, and let us be together.

Mia (*stretches herself*). Oh, how nice this is.

Knight. For a short while.

Mia. Nearly always. One day is like another. There is nothing strange about that. The summer, of course, is better than the winter, because in summer you don't have to be cold. But spring is best of all.

Jof. I have written a poem about the spring. Perhaps you'd like to hear it. I'll run and get my lyre. (*He sprints toward the wagon*)

Mia. Not now, Jof. Our guests may not be amused by your songs.

Jöns (*politely*). By all means. I write little songs myself. For example, I know a very funny song about a wanton fish which I doubt that you've heard yet.

The knight looks at him.

Jöns. You'll not get to hear it either. There are persons here who don't appreciate my art and I don't want to upset anyone. I'm a sensitive soul.

Jof has come out with his lyre, sits on a small, gaudy box and plucks at the instrument, humming quietly, searching for his melody. Jöns yawns and lies down.

Knight. People are troubled by so much.

Mia. It's always better when one is two. Have you no one of your own?

Knight. Yes, I think I had someone.

Mia. And what is she doing now?

Knight. I don't know.

Mia. You look so solemn. Was she your beloved?

Knight. We were newly married and we played together. We laughed a great deal. I wrote songs to her eyes, to her nose, to her beautiful little ears. We went hunting together and at night we danced. The house was full of life . . .

Mia.   Do you want some more strawberries?

Knight (*shakes his head*).   Faith is a torment, did you know that? It is like loving someone who is out there in the darkness but never appears, no matter how loudly you call.

Mia.   I don't understand what you mean.

Knight.   Everything I've said seems meaningless and unreal while I sit here with you and your husband. How unimportant it all becomes suddenly.

He takes the bowl of milk in his hand and drinks deeply from it several times. Then he carefully puts it down and looks up, smiling.

Mia.   Now you don't look so solemn.

Knight.   I shall remember this moment. The silence, the twilight, the bowls of strawberries and milk, your faces in the evening light. Mikael sleeping, Jof with his lyre. I'll try to remember what we have talked about. I'll carry this memory between my hands as carefully as if it were a bowl filled to the brim with fresh milk. (*He turns his face away and looks out toward the sea and the colorless gray sky*) And it will be an adequate sign—it will be enough for me.

He rises, nods to the others and walks down toward the forest. Jof continues to play on his lyre. Mia stretches out on the grass.

   The knight picks up his chess game and carries it toward the beach. It is quiet and deserted; the sea is still.

Death.   I have been waiting for you.

Knight.   Pardon me. I was detained for a few moments. Because I revealed my tactics to you, I'm in retreat. It's your move.

Death.   Why do you look so satisfied?

Knight.   That's my secret.

Death.   Of course. Now I take your knight.

Knight.   You did the right thing.

Death.   Have you tricked me?

Knight.   Of course. You fell right in the trap. Check!

Death.   What are you laughing at?

Knight.   Don't worry about my laughter; save your king instead.

Death.   You're rather arrogant.

Knight.   Our game amuses me.

Death.   It's your move. Hurry up. I'm a little pressed for time.

Knight.   I understand that you've a lot to do, but you can't get out of our game. It takes time.

Death is about to answer him but stops and leans over the board. The knight smiles.

Death.   Are you going to escort the juggler and his wife through the forest? Those whose names are Jof and Mia and who have a small son.

Knight. Why do you ask?
Death. Oh, no reason at all.

The knight suddenly stops smiling. Death looks at him scornfully.

IMMEDIATELY after sundown, the little company gathers in the yard of the inn. There is the knight, Jöns and the girl, Jof and Mia in their wagon. Their son, Mikael, is already asleep. Jonas Skat is still missing.

Jöns goes into the inn to get provisions for the night journey and to have a last mug of beer. The inn is now empty and quiet except for a few farmhands and maidens who are eating their evening meal in a corner.

At one of the small windows sits a lonely, hunched-over fellow, with a jug of brandy in his hands. His expression is very sad. Once in a while he is shaken by a gigantic sob. It is Plog, the smith, who sits there and whimpers.

Jöns. God in heaven, isn't this Plog, the smith?
Plog. Good evening.
Jöns. Are you sitting here sniveling in loneliness?
Plog. Yes, yes, look at the smith. He moans like a rabbit.
Jöns. If I were in your boots, I'd be happy to get rid of a wife in such an easy way.

Jöns pats the smith on the back, quenches his thirst with beer, and sits down by his side.

Plog. Are *you* married?
Jöns. *I!* A hundred times and more. I can't keep count of all my wives any longer. But it's often that way when you're a traveling man.
Plog. I can assure you that *one* wife is worse than a hundred, or else I've had worse luck than any poor wretch in this miserable world, which isn't impossible.
Jöns. Yes, it's hell *with* women and hell *without* them. So, however you look at it, it's still best to kill them off while it's most amusing.
Plog. Women's nagging, the shrieking of children and wet diapers, sharp nails and sharp words, blows and pokes, and the devil's aunt for a mother-in-law. And then, when one wants to sleep after a long day, there's a new song—tears, whining and moans loud enough to wake the dead.

Jöns nods delightedly. He has drunk deeply and talks with an old woman's voice.

Jöns. Why don't you kiss me good night?
Plog (*in the same way*). Why don't you sing a song for me?
Jöns. Why don't you love me the way you did when we first met?
Plog. Why don't you look at my new shift?
Jöns. You only turn your back and snore.
Plog. Oh hell!

Jöns. Oh hell. And now she's gone. Rejoice!

Plog (*furious*). I'll snip their noses with pliers, I'll bash in their chests with a small hammer, I'll tap their heads ever so lightly with a sledge.

Plog begins to cry loudly and his whole body sways in an enormous attack of sorrow. Jöns looks at him with interest.

Jöns. Look how he howls again.

Plog. Maybe I love her.

Jöns. So, maybe you love her! Then, you poor misguided ham shank, I'll tell you that love is another word for lust, plus lust, plus lust and a damn lot of cheating, falseness, lies and all kinds of other fooling around.

Plog. Yes, but it hurts anyway.

Jöns. Of course. Love is the blackest of all plagues, and if one could die of it, there would be some pleasure in love. But you almost always get over it.

Plog. No, no, not me.

Jöns. Yes, you too. There are only a couple of poor wretches who die of love once in a while. Love is as contagious as a cold in the nose. It eats away at your strength, your independence, your morale, if you have any. If everything is imperfect in this imperfect world, love is most perfect in its perfect imperfection.

Plog. You're happy, you with your oily words, and, besides, you believe your own drivel.

Jöns. Believe! Who said that I believed it? But I love to give good advice. If you ask me for advice you'll get two pieces for the price of one, because after all I really am an educated man.

Jöns gets up from the table and strokes his face with his hands. The smith becomes very unhappy and grabs his belt.

Plog. Listen, Jöns. May I go with you through the forest? I'm so lonely and don't want to go home because everyone will laugh at me.

Jöns. Only if you don't whimper all the time, because in that case we'll all have to avoid you.

The smith gets up and embraces Jöns. Slightly drunk, the two new friends walk toward the door.

When they come out in the yard, Jof immediately catches sight of them, becomes angry and yells a warning to Jöns.

Jof. Jöns! Watch out. That one wants to fight all the time. He's not quite sane.

Jöns. Yes, but now he's just sniveling.

The smith steps up to Jof, who blanches with fear. Plog offers his hand.

Plog. I'm really sorry if I hurt you. But I have such a hell of a temper, you know. Shake hands.

Jof gingerly proffers a frightened hand and gets it thoroughly shaken and squeezed. While Jof tries to straighten out his fingers, Plog is seized by great good will and opens his arms.

Plog. Come in my arms, little brother.
Jof. Thank you, thank you, perhaps later. But now we're really in a hurry.

JOF climbs up on the wagon seat quickly and clucks at the horse.

The small company is on its way toward the forest and the night.

It is dark in the forest.

First comes the knight on his large horse. Then Jof and Mia follow, sitting close to each other in the juggler's wagon. Mia holds her son in her arms. Jöns follows them with his heavily laden horse. He has the smith in tow. The girl sits on top of the load on the horse's back, hunched over as if asleep.

The footsteps, the horses' heavy tramp on the soft path, the human breathing—yet it is quiet.

Then the moon sails out of the clouds. The forest suddenly becomes alive with the night's unreality. The dazzling light pours through the thick foliage of the beech trees, a moving, quivering world of light and shadow.

The wanderers stop. Their eyes are dark with anxiety and foreboding. Their faces are pale and unreal in the floating light. It is very quiet.

Plog. Now the moon has come out of the clouds.
Jöns. That's good. Now we can see the road better.
Mia. I don't like the moon tonight.
Jof. The trees stand so still.
Jöns. That's because there's no wind.
Plog. I guess he means that they stand *very* still.
Jof. It's completely quiet.
Jöns. If one could hear a fox at least.
Jof. Or an owl.
Jöns. Or a human voice besides one's own.
Girl. They say it's dangerous to remain standing in moonlight.

Suddenly, out of the silence and the dim light falling across the forest road, a ghostlike cart emerges.

It is the witch being taken to the place where she will be burned. Next to her eight soldiers shuffle along tiredly, carrying their lances on their backs. The girl sits in the cart, bound with iron chains around her throat and arms. She stares fixedly into the moonlight.

A black figure sits next to her, a monk with his hood pulled down over his head.

Jöns. Where are you going?
Soldier. To the place of execution.

Jöns. Yes, now I can see. It's the girl who has done it with the Black One. The witch?

The soldier nods sourly. Hesitantly, the travelers follow. The knight guides his horse over to the side of the cart. The witch seems to be half conscious, but her eyes are wide open.

Knight. I see that they have hurt your hands.

The witch's pale, childish face turns toward the knight and she shakes her head.

Knight. I have a potion that will stop your pain.

She shakes her head again.

Jöns. Why do you burn her at this time of night? People have so few diversions these days.

Soldier. Saints preserve us, be quiet! It's said that she brings the Devil with her wherever she goes.

Jöns. You are eight brave men, then.

Soldier. Well, we've been paid. And this is a volunteer job.

The soldier speaks in whispers while glancing anxiously at the witch.

Knight (*to witch*). What's your name?

Tyan. My name is Tyan, my lord.

Knight. How old are you?

Tyan. Fourteen, my lord.

Knight. And is it true that you have been in league with the Devil?

Tyan nods quietly and looks away. Now they arrive at the parish border. At the foot of the nearby hills lies a crossroads. The pyre has already been stacked in the center of the forest clearing. The travelers remain there, hesitant and curious.

The soldiers have tied up the cart horse and bring out two long wooden beams. They nail rungs across the beams so that it looks like a ladder. Tyan will be bound to this like an eelskin stretched out to dry.

The sound of the hammering echoes through the forest. The knight has dismounted and walks closer to the cart. Again he tries to catch Tyan's eyes, touches her very lightly as if to waken her.

Slowly she turns her face toward him.

Knight. They say that you have been in league with the Devil.

Tyan. Why do you ask?

Knight. Not out of curiosity, but for very personal reasons. I too want to meet him.

Tyan. Why?

Knight. I want to ask him about God. He, if anyone, must know.

Tyan. You can see him anytime.

Knight. How?

Tyan. You must do as I tell you.

The knight grips the wooden rail of the cart so tightly that his knuckles whiten. Tyan leans forward and joins her gaze with his.

Tyan. Look into my eyes.

The knight meets her gaze. They stare at each other for a long time.

Tyan. What do you see? Do you see *him*?

Knight. I see fear in your eyes, an empty, numb fear. But nothing else.

He falls silent. The soldiers work at the stacks; their hammering echoes in the forest.

Tyan. No one, nothing, no one?

Knight (*shakes his head*).   No.

Tyan. Can't you see him behind your back?

Knight (*looks around*).   No, there is no one there.

Tyan. But he is with me everywhere. I only have to stretch out my hand and I can feel his hand. He is with me now too. The fire won't hurt me. He will protect me from everything evil.

Knight. Has he told you this?

Tyan. I know it.

Knight. Has he said it?

Tyan. I know it, I know it. You must see him somewhere, you must. The priests had no difficulty seeing him, nor did the soldiers. They are so afraid of him that they don't even dare touch me.

The sound of the hammers stops. The soldiers stand like black shadows rooted in the moss. They fumble with the chains and pull at the neck iron. Tyan moans weakly, as if she were far away.

Knight. Why have you crushed her hands?

Soldier (*surly*).   We didn't do it.

Knight. Who did?

Soldier. Ask the monk.

The soldiers pull the iron and chains. Tyan's shaven head sways, gleaming in the moonlight. Her blackened mouth opens as if to scream, but no sound emerges.

They take her down from the cart and lead her toward the ladder and the stake. The knight turns to the monk, who remains seated in the cart.

Knight. What have you done with the child?

Death turns around and looks at him.

Death. Don't you ever stop asking questions?

Knight. No, I'll never stop.

The soldiers chain Tyan to the rungs of the ladder. She submits resignedly, moans weakly like an animal and tries to ease her body into position.

When they have fastened her, they walk over to light the pyre. The knight steps up and leans over her.

Jöns. For a moment I thought of killing the soldiers, but it would do no good. She's nearly dead already.

One of the soldiers approaches. Thick smoke wells down from the pyre and sweeps over the quiet shadows near the crossroads and the hill.

Soldier. I've told you to be careful. Don't go too close to her.

The knight doesn't heed this warning. He cups his hand, fills it with water from the skin and gives it to Tyan. Then he gives her a potion.

Knight. Take this and it will stop the pain.

Smoke billows down over them and they begin to cough. The soldiers step forward and raise the ladder against a nearby fir tree. Tyan hangs there motionlessly, her eyes wide open.

The knight straightens up and stands immobile. Jöns is behind him, his voice nearly choked with rage.

Jöns. What does she see? Can you tell me?
Knight (*shakes his head*). She feels no more pain.
Jöns. You don't answer my question. Who watches over that child? Is it the angels, or God, or the Devil, or only the emptiness? Emptiness, my lord!
Knight. This cannot be.
Jöns. Look at her eyes, my lord. Her poor brain has just made a discovery. Emptiness under the moon.
Knight. No.
Jöns. We stand powerless, our arms hanging at our sides, because we see what she sees, and our terror and hers are the same. (*An outburst*) That poor little child. I can't stand it, I can't stand it . . .

His voice sticks in his throat and he suddenly walks away. The knight mounts his horse. The travelers depart from the crossroads. Tyan finally closes her eyes.

THE forest is now very dark. The road winds between the trees. The wagon squeaks and rattles over stones and roots. A bird suddenly shrieks.

Jof lifts his head and wakes up. He has been asleep with his arms around Mia's shoulders. The knight is sharply silhouetted against the tree trunks.

His silence makes him seem almost unreal.

Jöns and the smith are slightly drunk and support each other. Suddenly Plog has to sit down. He puts his hands over his face and howls piteously.

Plog. Oh, now it came over me again!

Jöns. Don't scream. What came over you?

Plog. My wife, damn it. She is so beautiful. She is so beautiful that she can't be described without the accompaniment of a lyre.

Jöns. Now it starts again.

Plog. Her smile is like brandy. Her eyes like blackberries . . .

Plog searches for beautiful words. He gestures gropingly with his large hands.

Jöns (*sighs*). Get up, you tear-drenched pig. We'll lose the others.

Plog. Yes, of course, of course. Her nose is like a little pink potato; her behind is like a juicy pear—yes, the whole woman is like a strawberry patch. I can see her in front of me, with arms like wonderful cucumbers.

Jöns. Saints almighty, stop! You're a very bad poet, despite the fact that you're drunk. And your vegetable garden bores me.

They walk across an open meadow. Here it is a little brighter and the moon shimmers behind a thin sky. Suddenly the smith points a large finger toward the edge of the forest.

Plog. Look there.

Jöns. Do you see something?

Plog. There, over there!

Jöns. I don't see anything.

Plog. Hang on to something, my friends. The hour is near! Who is that at the edge of the forest if not my own dearly beloved, with actor attached?

The two lovers discover the smith and it's too late. They cannot retreat. Skat immediately takes to his heels. Plog chases him, swinging his sledge and bellowing like a wild boar.

For a few confusing moments the two rivals stumble among the stones and bushes in the gray gloom of the forest. The duel begins to look senseless, because both of them are equally frightened.

The travelers silently observe this confused performance. Lisa screams once in a while, more out of duty than out of impulse.

Skat (*panting*). You miserable stubbleheaded bastard of seven scurvy bitches, if I were in your lousy rags I would be stricken with such eternal shame about my breath, my voice, my arms and legs—in short, about my whole body—that I would immediately rid nature of my own embarrassing self.

Plog (*angry*). Watch out, you perfumed slob, that I don't fart on you and immediately blow you down to the actor's own red-hot hell, where you can sit and recite monologues to each other until the dust comes out of the Devil's ears.

Then Lisa throws herself around her husband's neck.

Lisa. Forgive me, dear little husband. I'll never do it again. I am so sorry and you can't imagine how terribly that man over there betrayed me.

Plog. I'll kill him anyway.

Lisa. Yes, do that, just kill him. He isn't even a human being.

Jöns. Hell, he's an actor.

Lisa. He is only a false beard, false teeth, false smiles, rehearsed lines, and he's as empty as a jug. Just kill him.

Lisa sobs with excitement and sorrow. The smith looks around, a little confused. The actor uses this opportunity. He pulls out a dagger and places the point against his breast.

Skat. She's right. Just kill me. If you thought that I was going to apologize for being what I am, you are mistaken.

Lisa. Look how sickening he is. How he makes a fool of himself, how he puts on an act. Dear Plog, kill him!

Skat. My friends, you have only to push, and my unreality will soon be transformed into a new solid reality. An absolutely tangible corpse.

Lisa. Do something then. Kill him.

Plog (*embarrassed*). He has to fight me, otherwise I can't kill him.

Skat. Your life's thread now hangs by a very ragged shred. Idiot, your day is short.

Plog. You'll have to irritate me a little more to get me as angry as before.

Skat looks at the travelers with a pained expression and then lifts his eyes toward the night sky.

Skat. I forgive all of you. Pray for me sometimes.

Skat sinks the dagger into his breast and slowly falls to the ground. The travelers stand confused. The smith rushes forward and begins to pull at the actor's hands.

Plog. Oh dear, dear, I didn't mean it that way! Look, there's no life left in him. I was beginning to like him, and in my opinion Lisa was much too spiteful.

Jof leans over his colleague.

Jof. He's dead, totally, enormously dead. In fact, I've never seen such a dead actor.

Lisa. Come on, let's go. This is nothing to mourn over. He has only himself to blame.

Plog. And I have to be married to *her*.

Jöns. We must go on.

Skat lies in the grass and keeps the dagger pressed tightly to his breast. The travelers depart and soon they have disappeared into the dark forest on the other side of the meadow. When Skat is sure that no one can see him, he sits up and lifts the dagger from his breast. It is a stage dagger with a blade that pushes into the handle. Skat laughs to himself.

Skat. Now that was a good scene. I'm really a good actor. After all, why shouldn't I be a little pleased with myself? But where shall I go? I'll wait until it becomes light and then I'll find the easiest way out of the forest. I'll climb up a tree for the time being so that no bears, wolves or ghosts can get at me.

He soon finds a likely tree and climbs up into its thick foliage. He sits down as comfortably as possible and reaches for his food pouch.

Skat (*yawns*). Tomorrow I'll find Jof and Mia and then we'll go to the saints' feast in Elsinore. We'll make lots of money there. (Yawns) Now, I'll sing a little song to myself:

I am a little bird
Who sings whate'er he will,
And when I am in danger
I fling out a pissing trill
As in the carnal thrill.

(*Speaks*) It's boring to be alone in the forest tonight. (*Sings*) The terrible night doesn't frighten me . . .

He interrupts himself and listens. The sound of industrious sawing is heard through the silence.

Skat. Workmen in the forest. Oh, well! (*Sings*) The terrible night doesn't frighten me . . . Hey, what the devil . . . it's *my* tree they're cutting down.

He peers through the foliage. Below him stands a dark figure diligently sawing away at the base of the tree. Skat becomes frightened and angry.

Skat. Hey, you! Do you hear me, you tricky bastard? What are you doing with my tree?

The sawing continues without a pause. Skat becomes more frightened.

Skat. Can't you at least answer me? Politeness costs so little. Who are you?

Death straightens his back and squints up at him. Skat cries out in terror.

Death. I'm sawing down your tree because your time is up.
Skat. It won't do. I haven't got time.
Death. So you haven't got time.
Skat. No, I have my performance.
Death. Then it's been canceled because of death.
Skat. My contract.
Death. Your contract is terminated.
Skat. My children, my family.
Death. Shame on you, Skat!
Skat. Yes, I'm ashamed.

Death begins to saw again. The tree creaks.

Skat. Isn't there any way to get off? Aren't there any special rules for actors?
Death. No, not in this case.
Skat. No loopholes, no exceptions?

Death saws.

Skat. Perhaps you'll take a bribe.

Death saws.

Skat. Help!

Death saws.

Skat. Help! Help!

The tree falls. The forest becomes silent again.

Night and then dawn.
    The travelers have come to a sort of clearing and have collapsed on the moss. They lie quietly and listen to their own breathing, their heartbeats, and the wind in the tree tops. Here the forest is wild and impenetrable. Huge boulders stick up out of the ground like the heads of black giants. A fallen tree lies like a mighty barrier between light and shadow.
    Mia, Jof and their child have sat down apart from the others. They look at the light of the moon, which is no longer full and dead but mysterious and unstable.
    The knight sits bent over his chess game. Lisa cries quietly behind the smith's back. Jöns lies on the ground and looks up at the heavens.

Jöns. Soon dawn will come, but the heat continues to hang over us like a smothering blanket.
Lisa. I'm so frightened.
Plog. We feel that something is going to happen to us, but we don't know what.
Jöns. Maybe it's the day of judgment.
Plog. The day of judgment . . .

Now something moves behind the fallen tree. There is a rustling sound and a moaning cry that seems to come from a wounded animal. Everyone listens intently, all faces turned toward the sound.
    A voice comes out of the darkness.

Raval. Do you have some water?

Raval's perspiring face soon becomes visible. He disappears in the darkness, but his voice is heard again.

Raval. Can't you give me a little water? (*Pause*) I have the plague.
Jöns. Don't come here. If you do I'll slit your throat. Keep to the other side of the tree.
Raval. I'm afraid of death.

No one answers. There is complete silence. Raval gasps heavily for air. The dry leaves rustle with his movements.

Raval.   I don't want to die! I don't want to!

No one answers. Raval's face appears suddenly at the base of the tree. His eyes bulge wildly and his mouth is ringed with foam.

Raval.   Can't you have pity on me? Help me! At least talk to me.

No one answers. The trees sigh. Raval begins to cry.

Raval.   I am going to die. I. I. *I!* What will happen to me! Can no one console me? Haven't you any compassion? Can't you see that I . . .

His words are choked off by a gurgling sound. He disappears in the darkness behind the fallen tree. It becomes quiet for a few moments.

Raval (*Whispers*).   Can't anyone . . . only a little water.

Suddenly the girl gets up with a quick movement, snatches Jöns' water bag and runs a few steps. Jöns grabs her and holds her fast.

Jöns.   It's no use. It's no use. I know that it's no use. It's meaningless. It's totally meaningless. I tell you that it's meaningless. Can't you hear that I'm consoling you?

Raval.   Help me, help me!

No one answers, no one moves. Raval's sobs are dry and convulsive, like a frightened child's. His sudden scream is cut off in the middle.

Then it becomes quiet.

The girl sinks down and hides her face in her hands. Jöns places his hand on her shoulder.

THE knight is no longer alone. Death has come to him and he raises his hand.

Death.   Shall we play our game to the end?
Knight.   Your move!

Death raises his hand and strikes the knight's queen. Antonius Block looks at Death.

Death.   Now I take your queen.
Knight.   I didn't notice that.

The knight leans over the game. The moonlight moves over the chess pieces, which seem to have a life of their own.

Jof has dozed off for a few moments, but suddenly he wakens. Then he sees the knight and Death together.

He becomes very frightened and awakens Mia.

Jof.   Mia!

Mia.   Yes, what is it?

Jof.   I see something terrible. Something I almost can't talk about.

Mia.   What do you see?

Jof.   The knight is sitting over there playing chess.

Mia.   Yes, I can see that too and I don't think it's so terrible.

Jof.   But do you see who he's playing with?

Mia.   He is alone. You *mustn't* frighten me this way.

Jof.   No, no, he isn't alone.

Mia.   Who is it, then?

Jof.   Death. He is sitting there playing chess with Death himself.

Mia.   You mustn't say that.

Jof.   We must try to escape.

Mia.   One can't do that.

Jof.   We must try. They are so occupied with their game that if we move very quietly, they won't notice us.

Jof gets up carefully and disappears into the darkness behind the trees. Mia remains standing, as if paralyzed by fear. She stares fixedly at the knight and the chess game. She holds her son in her arms.

Now Jof returns.

Jof.   I have harnessed the horse. The wagon is standing near the big tree. You go first and I'll follow you with the packs. See that Mikael doesn't wake up.

Mia does what Jof has told her. At the same moment, the knight looks up from his game.

Death.   It is your move, Antonius Block.

The knight remains silent. He sees Mia go through the moonlight toward the wagon. Jof bends down to pick up the pack and follows at a distance.

Death.   Have you lost interest in our game?

The knight's eyes become alarmed. Death looks at him intently.

Knight.   Lost interest? On the contrary.

Death.   You seem anxious. Are you hiding anything?

Knight.   Nothing escapes you—or does it?

Death.   Nothing escapes me. No one escapes from me.

Knight.   It's true that I'm worried.

He pretends to be clumsy and knocks the chess pieces over with the hem of his coat. He looks up at Death.

Knight.   I've forgotten how the pieces stood.

Death (laughs contentedly).   But I have not forgotten. You can't get away that easily.

Death leans over the board and rearranges the pieces. The knight looks past him toward the road. Mia has just climbed up on the wagon. Jof takes the horse by the bridle and leads it down to the road. Death notices nothing; he is completely occupied with reconstructing the game.

Death.   Now I see something interesting.
Knight.   What do you see?
Death.   You are mated on the next move, Antonius Block.
Knight.   That's true.
Death.   Did you enjoy your reprieve?
Knight.   Yes, I did.
Death.   I'm happy to hear that. Now I'll be leaving you. When we meet again, you and your companions' time will be up.
Knight.   And you will divulge your secrets.
Death.   I have no secrets.
Knight.   So you know nothing.
Death.   I have nothing to tell.

The knight wants to answer, but Death is already gone.

A murmur is heard in the tree tops. Dawn comes, a flickering light without life, making the forest seem threatening and evil. Jof drives over the twisting road. Mia sits beside him.

Mia.   What a strange light.
Jof.   I guess it's the thunderstorm which comes with dawn.
Mia.   No, it's something else. Something terrible. Do you hear the roar in the forest?
Jof.   It's probably rain.
Mia.   No, it isn't rain. He has seen us and he's following us. He has overtaken us; he's coming toward us.
Jof.   Not yet, Mia. In any case, not yet.
Mia.   I'm so afraid. I'm so afraid.

The wagon rattles over roots and stones; it sways and creaks. Now the horse stops with his ears flat against his head. The forest sighs and stirs ponderously.

Jof.   Get into the wagon, Mia. Crawl in quickly. We'll lie down, Mia, with Mikael between us.

They crawl into the wagon and crouch around the sleeping child.

Jof.   It is the Angel of Death that's passing over us, Mia. It's the Angel of Death. *The Angel of Death, and he's very big.*
Mia.   Do you feel how cold it is? I'm freezing. I'm terribly cold.

She shivers as if she had a fever. They pull the blankets over them and lie closely together. The wagon canvas flutters and beats in the wind. The roar outside is like a giant bellowing.

THE castle is silhouetted like a black boulder against the heavy dawn. Now the storm moves there, throwing itself powerfully against walls and abutments. The sky darkens; it is almost like night.

Antonius Block has brought his companions with him to the castle. But it seems deserted. They walk from room to room. There is only emptiness and quiet echoes. Outside, the rain is heard roaring noisily.

Suddenly the knight stands face to face with his wife. They look at each other quietly.

Karin. I heard from people who came from the crusade that you were on your way home. I've been waiting for you here. All the others have fled from the plague.

The knight is silent. He looks at her.

Karin. Don't you recognize me any more?

The knight nods, silent.

Karin. You also have changed.

She walks closer and looks searchingly into his face. The smile lingers in her eyes and she touches his hand lightly.

Karin. Now I can see that it's you. Somewhere in your eyes, somewhere in your face, but hidden and frightened, is that boy who went away so many years ago.
Knight. It's over now and I'm a little tired.
Karin. I see that you're tired.
Knight. Over there stand my friends.
Karin. Ask them in. They will break the fast with us.

They all sit down at the table in the room, which is lit by torches on the walls. Silently they eat the hard bread and the salt-darkened meat. Karin sits at the head of the table and reads aloud from a thick book.

Karin. "And when the Lamb broke the seventh seal, there was silence in heaven for about the space of half an hour. And I saw the seven angels which stood before God; and to them were given seven trumpets. And another . . ."

Three mighty knocks sound on the large portal. Karin interrupts her reading and looks up from the book. Jöns rises quickly and goes to open the door.

Karin. "The first angel sounded, and there followed hail and fire mingled with blood, and they were cast upon the earth; and the third part of the trees was burnt up and all the green grass was burnt up."

Now the rain becomes quiet. There is suddenly an immense, frightening silence in the large, murky room where the burning torches throw uneasy shadows over the ceiling and the walls. Everyone listens tensely to the stillness.

Karin. "And the second angel sounded, and as it were a great mountain burning with fire was cast into the sea; and a third part of the sea became blood..."

Steps are heard on the stairs. Jöns returns and sits down silently at his place but does not continue to eat.

Knight. Was someone there?
Jöns. No, my lord. I saw no one.

Karin lifts her head for a moment but once again leans over the large book.

Karin. "And the third angel sounded, and there fell a great star from heaven, burning as it were a torch, and it fell upon the third part of the rivers and upon the fountains of waters; and the name of the star is called Wormwood..."

They all lift their heads, and when they see who is coming toward them through the twilight of the large room, they rise from the table and stand close together.

Knight. Good morning, noble lord.
Karin. I am Karin, the knight's wife, and welcome you courteously to my house.
Plog. I am a smith by profession and rather good at my trade, if I say so myself. My wife Lisa—curtsy for the great lord, Lisa. She's a little difficult to handle once in a while and we had a little spat, so to say, but no worse than most people.

The knight hides his face in his hands.

Knight. From our darkness, we call out to Thee, Lord. Have mercy on us because we are small and frightened and ignorant.
Jöns. (*bitterly*): In the darkness where You are supposed to be, where all of us probably are ... In the darkness You will find no one to listen to Your cries or be touched by Your sufferings. Wash Your tears and mirror Yourself in Your indifference.
Knight. God, You who are somewhere, who *must* be somewhere, have mercy upon us.
Jöns. I could have given you an herb to purge you of your worries about eternity. Now it seems to be too late. But in any case, feel the immense triumph of this last minute when you can still roll your eyes and move your toes.
Karin. Quiet, quiet.
Jöns. I shall be silent, but under protest.
Girl (*on her knees*). It is the end.

JOF and Mia lie close together and listen to the rain tapping lightly on the wagon canvas, a sound which diminishes until finally there are only single drops.

They crawl out of their hiding place. The wagon stands on a height above a slope, protected by an enormous tree. They look across ridges, forests, the wide plains, and the sea, which glistens in the sunlight breaking through the clouds.

Jof stretches his arms and legs. Mia dries the wagon seat and sits down next to her husband. Mikael crawls between Jof's knees.

A lone bird tests its voice after the storm. The trees and bushes drip. From the sea comes a strong and fragrant wind.

Jof points to the dark, retreating sky where summer lightning glitters like silver needles over the horizon.

Jof. I see them, Mia! I see them! Over there against the dark, stormy sky. They are all there. The smith and Lisa and the knight and Raval and Jöns and Skat. And Death, the severe master, invites them to dance. He tells them to hold each other's hands and then they must tread the dance in a long row. And first goes the master with his scythe and hourglass, but Skat dangles at the end with his lyre. They dance away from the dawn and it's a solemn dance toward the dark lands, while the rain washes their faces and cleans the salt of the tears from their cheeks.

He is silent. He lowers his hand.

His son, Mikael, has listened to his words. Now he crawls up to Mia and sits down in her lap.

Mia (*smiling*).   You with your visions and dreams.

Questions

1. *What is the nature of the knight's quest? Do you admire him for the seriousness and single-mindedness of his quest? What is the knight's own judgment on the result of his lifelong pursuit?* **2.** *In contrast to the knight, his squire Jöns is an agnostic and hedonist who believes that the meaning of life is to be found in living. Does a comparison of the actions of the two men suggest which one is more humane?* **3.** *How does the milk and wild strawberries scene help define the theme?* **4.** *How does the comic subplot of Skat, Plog the blacksmith, and his faithless wife relate to the theme?* **5.** *Why do Jof, Mia, and their child survive? Has Bergman prepared us for this ending, or does it come as a surprise?* **6.** *Can you suggest why Bergman, a twentieth-century artist concerned with modern man, set his drama in the Middle Ages?*

THE PRESENCE Of dEATH

QUESTIONS

1. In *Everyman*, Tolstoy's "The Death of Iván Ilých," Bergman's *The Seventh Seal*, and Donne's sonnet, "Death Be Not Proud," death and dying are considered from a religious viewpoint. Do these works develop a similar attitude toward death, or do the attitudes they develop differ crucially?

2. State the argument against resignation to death made in Thomas' "Do Not Go Gentle into That Good Night." State the argument of Catherine Davis' reply, "After a Time." What other works in this section support each position?

3. Read chapters 8–10 in The Revelation of St. John the Divine in the New Testament. The opening of the "seventh seal" is described there, along with the consequences of that event. Does the allusive title of Bergman's screenplay enhance or detract from the story line? Are the knight and his friends "saved" or "damned" at the end? Does the religious conception of a man facing death developed in *Everyman* differ from or support the conception developed in *The Seventh Seal?*

4. Although Gray's "Elegy Written in a Country Churchyard," Housman's "To an Athlete Dying Young," Ransom's "Bells for John Whiteside's Daughter," Auden's "In Memory of W. B. Yeats," and Roethke's "Elegy for Jane" employ different poetic forms, they all embody a poetic mode called *elegy*. Define *elegy* in terms of the characteristic tone of these poems. Compare the elegiac tone with the tone of such poems as Poe's "The Raven," Thomas' "Do Not Go Gentle into That Good Night," and Shakespeare's speech from *Richard II*. How do they differ?

5. What figurative language in the prose and poetry of this section is commonly associated with death itself? With dying? Contrast the characteristic imagery of this section with the characteristic imagery of love poetry. What might the differences indicate about the way we perceive man in nature?

6. Yevtushenko, in his poem "People," writes, "Not people die but worlds die in them." Illustrate the meaning of this line with a discussion of Bierce's "An Occurrence at Owl Creek Bridge," Katherine Anne Porter's "The Jilting of Granny Weatherall," and Robinson's poem "The Mill."

7. Are there works in this section that illustrate the first four of Edwin Brock's "Five Ways to Kill a Man?" Explain the fifth way. What works lend support to that method?

APPENDICES

The Poet and His Craft

One of the discoveries a student of poetry quickly makes is that a good poem grows in richness and subtlety with rereading and close scrutiny. We grasp the theme of the poem perhaps on first reading, but on further reading and analysis, we discover that a particular word is charged with more meaning than we had thought or that an image relates to other parts of the poem in ways the first reading did not reveal. The excitement that comes from discovering something new and enriching in a poem is one of the great pleasures of studying poetry. Soon, however, the excitement is dampened for many readers as they inevitably begin to ask themselves: Did the poet really intend to put this or that into the poem, or are we just demonstrating a cleverness and super-subtlety that would surprise the poet as much as it disquiets us?

The question cannot be answered with direct evidence because most poets do not give us statements about their intentions in writing a particular poem. But many poets have left records, in the form of notebooks and journals, of early versions of their poems. An examination of these early versions shows very clearly that most finished poems are the result of painstaking and often protracted revision as the poet searches for the right word, the right phrase, the right sequence of image and idea to embody his theme. That poets work with such care and calculation suggests a general answer to our question: What we find in a good poem is more likely than not the result of the poet's skill, assuming that we are attending to the whole poem and not just free associating from some part of it.

A comparison of the draft versions with the final versions of the three poems below provides a fascinating glimpse into the process of poetic creation. A careful consideration of why particular changes were made will probably make for a fuller understanding of the final version. But more important for our purposes here, your analysis will be an exercise in close and subtle reading firmly grounded in different versions. While the reasons you offer for changes will be speculative and not subject to any kind of definitive proof, the poet did make these changes for *some* reason. Thus, although we can rarely, if ever, know what the poet intended, our detailed knowledge of how poems get written makes equally clear that what we find in a poem is probably the result of the poet's skill, not chance or our clever imaginings.

In the draft versions, variants and deletions are indicated by brackets. Line numbers in the questions refer to the final version.

LONDON   (WILLIAM BLAKE, 1757–1827)

I wander through each chartered[1] street,
Near where the chartered Thames does flow
And mark in every face I meet
Marks of weakness, marks of woe.

In every cry of every man,
In every infant's cry of fear,
In every voice; in every ban,
The mind-forged manacles I hear:

How the chimney-sweeper's cry
Every blackening church appalls,   10
And the hapless soldier's sigh
Runs in blood down palace-walls.

But most, through midnight streets I hear
How the youthful harlot's curse
Blasts the new-born infant's tear,
And blights with plagues the marriage-hearse.

LONDON   (NOTEBOOK VERSION, 1793)

I wander thro' each dirty street,
Near where the dirty Thames does flow,
And [see] mark in every face I meet
Marks of weakness, marks of woe.

In every cry of every man
In [every voice of every child]
      every infant's cry of fear
In every voice, in every ban
The [german] mind forg'd [links I hear] manacles I hear.

[But most] How the chimney sweeper's cry
[Blackens o'er the churches' walls]
Every black'ning church appalls,   10
And the hapless soldier's sigh
Runs in blood down palace walls.

[But most the midnight harlot's curse
From every dismal street I hear,
Weaves around the marriage hearse
And blasts the new born infant's tear.]

But most [from every] thro' wintry streets I hear
How the midnight harlot's curse
                                                    20

---

1.   Preempted by the state and leased out under royal patent.

Blasts the new born infant's tear,
And [hangs] smites with plagues the marriage hearse.

But most the shrieks of youth I hear
But most thro' midnight & . . . .
How the youthful . . .

1. *How does the change from "dirty" to "chartered" (ll. 1–2) help establish the theme of the poem?* **2.** *Suggest why Blake changed "see" to "mark" in line 3.* **3.** *Would it have made any significant difference if Blake had retained "In every voice of every child" as line 6? Explain.* **4.** *Look up the meaning and derivation of "appalls" and then consider what Blake achieves by the revision of line 10.*

THE LAST LAUGH   (WILFRED OWEN, 1893–1918)

'O Jesus Christ! I'm hit,' he said; and died.
Whether he vainly cursed, or prayed indeed,
The Bullets chirped—In vain! vain! vain!
Machine-guns chuckled,—Tut-tut! Tut-tut!
And the Big Gun guffawed.

Another sighed,—'O Mother, mother! Dad!'
Then smiled, at nothing, childlike, being dead.
    And the lofty Shrapnel-cloud
    Leisurely gestured,—Fool!
    And the falling splinters tittered.   10

'My Love!' one moaned. Love-languid seemed his mood,
Till, slowly lowered, his whole face kissed the mud.
    And the Bayonets' long teeth grinned;
    Rabbles of Shells hooted and groaned;
    And the Gas hissed.

LAST WORDS   (EARLY VERSION)

"O Jesus Christ!" one fellow sighed.
And kneeled, and bowed, tho' not in prayer, and died.
    And the Bullets sang "In Vain,"
    Machine Guns chuckled "Vain,"
    Big Guns guffawed "In Vain."

"Father and mother!" one boy said.
Then smiled—at nothing, like a small child; being dead.
    And the Shrapnel Cloud
    Slowly gestured "Vain,"
    The falling splinters muttered "Vain."   10

"My love!" another cried, "My love, my bud!"
Then, gently lowered, his whole face kissed the mud.
    And the Flares gesticulated, "Vain."

The Shells hooted, "In Vain,"
And the Gas hissed, "In Vain."

1. *What does Owen achieve in dramatic effect by the revision of the first two lines?* **2.** *How do the changes of the exact rhymes of the first version to the half rhymes of the final version affect the meaning of the poem?* **3.** *What insights into the revision of of line 7 are provided by scanning the poem?* **4.** *Suggest why Owen abandoned the "In Vain" motif in the final version.* **5.** *Examine the changes in verbs. What effect do the changes have on the tone of the poem?*

THE SECOND COMING   (WILLIAM BUTLER YEATS, 1865–1939)

Turning and turning in the widening gyre°   spiral
The falcon cannot hear the falconer;
Things fall apart; the center cannot hold;
Mere anarchy is loosed upon the world,
The blood-dimmed tide is loosed, and everywhere
The ceremony of innocence is drowned;
The best lack all conviction, while the worst
Are full of passionate intensity.

Surely some revelation is at hand;
Surely the Second Coming is at hand;   10
The Second Coming! Hardly are those words out
When a vast image out of *Spiritus Mundi*[2]
Troubles my sight: somewhere in sands of the desert
A shape with lion body and the head of a man,
A gaze blank and pitiless as the sun,
Is moving its slow thighs, while all about it
Reel shadows of the indignant desert birds.
The darkness drops again; but now I know
That twenty centuries of stony sleep
Were vexed to nightmare by a rocking cradle,   20
And what rough beast, its hour come round at last,
Slouches towards Bethlehem to be born?

THE SECOND COMING (FIRST FULL DRAFT)

Turning and turning in the wide gyre [widening gyre]
The falcon cannot hear the falconer
[Things fall apart, the centre has lost]
Things fall apart—the centre cannot hold
[Vile] Mere anarchy is loose there on the world
The blood stained flood [dim tide] is loose and anarchy
[The good are wavering and intensity]
The best [lose] lack all conviction while the worst
Are full of passionate intensity.

---

2. The Soul or Spirit of the Universe, which Yeats believed constituted a fund of racial images and memories.

Surely some revelation is at hand
[The cradle at Bethlehem has rocked must leap anew]
[Surely the great falcon must come]
[Surely the hour of the second birth is here]
[Surely the hour of the second birth has struck]
[The second Birth! Scarce have those] words been spoken
The second [Birth] coming. [Scarce have the words been spoken]
[Before the dark was cut as with a knife]
And new intensity rent as it were cloth
And a [stark] lost image out of spiritus mundi
Troubles my sight. [A waste of sand]—A waste of desert sand
A shape with lion's body & with and the head [breast and head] of a man
[An eye] A gaze blank and pitiless as the sun
[Move with a slow slouching step]
Moves its slow [feet] thighs while all about its head
[An angry crowd of desert]
[Fall] [Run] shadows of the [desert birds they] indignant desert birds
The darkness drops again but now I know
[For] That twenty centuries of [its] stony sleep
[Were vexed & all but broken by the second]
Were vexed to nightmare by a rocking cradle
[And now at last]
[And now at last knowing its hour come round]
And what [at last] [wild thing] rough beast its hour come round at last
        knowing the hour [come round]
[It slouches towards Bethlehem to be born]
It has set out for Bethlehem to be born
It has set out for Bethlehem to be born
[Is slouching] towards Bethlehem to be born
Slouches towards Bethlehem to be born

1. *Can you suggest why "Reel" (l. 17) is a better word than "Fall" or "Run?"* **2.** *After many trials, Yeats decided on "The Second Coming" rather than "The Second Birth" for line 10. Can you suggest why (aside from number of syllables) Yeats decided as he did?* **3.** *Examine the changes Yeats made in the description of the sphinx (ll. 14–16). Does the description in the final version represent an improvement over that of the draft version? Why?* **4.** *In the draft version of line 19, Yeats used the pronoun "its" to modify "stony sleep," making clear that these words refer to the sphinx. Does the deletion of the pronoun in the final version weaken the poem by making "stony sleep" ambiguous? Explain.*

Reading Fiction

An author is a god, creator of the world he describes. That world has a limited and very special landscape. It is peopled with men and women of a particular complexion, of particular gifts and failings. Its history, almost always, is determined by the tight interaction of its people within its narrow geography. Everything that occurs in a work of fiction—every figure, every tree, every furnished room and crescent moon and dreary fog—has been *purposely* put there by its creator. When a story pleases, when it moves its reader, he has responded to that carefully created world. The pleasure, the emotional commitment, the human response are not results of analysis. The reader has not registered in some mental adding machine the several details that establish character, the particular appropriateness of the weather to the events in the story, the marvelous rightness of the furnishings, the manipulation of the point of view, the plot, the theme, the style. He has recognized and accepted the world of the author and has been delighted (or saddened or made angry) by what happens in it.

But how does it come about that readers recognize the artificial worlds, often quite different from their own, that authors create? And why is it that readers who recognize some fictional worlds effortlessly are bewildered and lost in other fictional worlds? Is it possible to extend the boundaries of readers' recognition? Can more and more of the landscapes and societies of fiction be made available to that onlooking audience?

The answer to the first of these questions is easy. Readers are comfortable in literary worlds that, however exotic the landscapes and the personalities that people it, incorporate moral imperatives which reflect the value system in the readers' world. Put another way, much fiction ends with its virtuous characters rewarded and its villains punished. This we speak of as poetic justice. Comedies, and most motion pictures of the recent past, end this way. But such endings are illustrations of poetic justice, and *poetic* seems to suggest that somehow such endings are ideal rather than "real." Not much experience of life is required to recognize that injustice, pain, frustration, and downright villainy often prevail, that the beautiful young girl and the strong, handsome hero do not always overcome all obstacles, marry, and live happily ever after, that not every man is strong and handsome nor every woman beautiful. But readers, knowing that, respond to tragic fiction as well—where virtue is defeated, where obstacles prove too much for the men and women, where ponderous forces result in defeat, even death. Unhappy outcomes are painful to contemplate, but it is not difficult to recognize the world in which they occur. That world is much like our own. And unhappy outcomes serve to emphasize the very ideals which we have established in this world as the aims and goals of human activity. Consequently, both the "romantic" comedies that gladden with justice and success and the "realistic" stories that end in defeat provide readers with recognizable and available emotional worlds, however exotic the settings and the characters in those stories might be.

If we look at fiction this way, the answer to the question "Why is it that some readers are bewildered and lost in some fictional worlds?" is clearly implied. Some fictional worlds *seem* to incorporate a strange set of moral imperatives. Readers are not altogether certain who are the virtuous characters and who are the villains, nor even what constitutes virtue and evil. Sometimes tragic oppositions in a fictional world that brooks no compromise puzzle readers who live in a world where compromise has become almost a virtue. Sometimes, particularly in more recent fiction that reflects the ever widening influence of psychoanalytic theory, the landscape and the behavior of characters is designed to represent deep interiors, the less-than-rational hearts and minds of characters. Those weird interiors are not part of the common awareness of readers; the moral questions raised there are not the same moral questions that occupy most of our waking hours. Such fictional worlds (those of Franz Kafka, for example) are difficult to map, and bewildered readers may well reject these underworlds for the sunshine of the surfaces they know more immediately.

Studying Literature

It might be useful to distinguish between three different kinds of discussion that take literature for a subject. Literary *history* attends to the consequences for literature of the passing of time. Certain forms that were popular in medieval times—the religious allegory, for instance—have waned in popularity and importance. Certain authors have been measurably influenced by their predecessors. Certain features of Elizabethan culture and belief illuminate passages in Shakespeare's plays. Most of the footnotes in this book provide readers with historical information (the meaning of an archaic word, perhaps, the characteristics of some half-forgotten Greek god, or an allusion to an earlier literary work). Sometimes such information liberates the enduring life of old stories for new readers. Literary *criticism*, on the other hand, attends to the *value* of a work. It is good? Bad? Minor? Major? Criticism itself has a history: taste changes over the years; standards of judgment change; cultural forces contribute to critical judgments. But, though information about the history of criticism may help you understand why an author did what he did, it will not significantly help you make your own critical judgment. The story must finally speak for itself to you—no amount of historical justification can really enliven a dead work for a new reader. Unconcerned with both history and criticism, literary *theory* attends to the *craft* of literature. How does the author manipulate language (the substance of all literature—and the only substance) in order to create a world which affects his readers? Over many years of incessant examination of literature, observers have noted that certain techniques, certain characteristic uses of language, occur again and again—so frequently that it is useful to name them. Literary theory makes particular use of these observations in its discussion of *form* and the features on which form depends. Note that theoretical discussions frequently trespass on the discipline of psychology. Theoreticians and critics frequently speak of the *effect* on readers of an author's craft—his images, his clever symbols, his vision of mortality, his colors and shapes. But it is a dangerous business to assert that certain combinations of words will generate, invariably, the same complex emotional response. What are we to make of the spectacle of two critics, or two teachers, testifying that the same story affects them quite differently? Is one of them wrong? Are both of them wrong, perhaps? Perhaps! But we do the best we can, and we use all the varieties of human experience that both authors and critics and theoreticians share in an attempt to respond significantly to significant fiction.

Fiction and Reality

Why do people read fiction (or go to movies)? The question is not so easy to answer as one might suppose. The first response is likely to have something to do with "amusement" or "entertainment." But you have doubtless read stories and novels (or seen movies) that end tragically. Is it accurate to say that they were amusing or entertaining? Is it entertaining to be made sad or to be made angry by the defeat of "good" people? Or does the emotional impact of such stories somehow enlarge our own humanity? Fiction teaches its readers by providing them a vast range of experience that they could not acquire otherwise. Especially for the relatively young, conceptions of love, of success in life, of war, of malignant evil and cleansing virtue are learned from fiction—not from life. And herein lies a great danger, for literary artists are notorious liars and their lies frequently become the source of people's convictions about human nature and human society.

To illustrate, a huge number of television series based on the exploits of the FBI, or the Hawaiian police force, or the dedicated surgeons at the general hospital, or the young lawyers always end with a capture, with a successful (though dangerous) operation, with justice triumphant. But, in the real world, police are able to resolve only about 10 percent of reported crime, exotic disease ravages, and we have long since learned that economic and political power often extends into the courtroom. The very existence of such television drama bespeaks a sort of yearning that things should be different; their heroes are heroic precisely in that they regularly overcome those obstacles that we all experience, and that, alas, we do not overcome.

Some writers, beginning about the middle of the nineteenth century, were particularly incensed at the real damage which a lying literature promotes, and they devoted their energies to exposing and counteracting the lies of the novelists, particularly those lies that formed attitudes about what constituted human success and happiness. Yet that popular fiction, loosely called escapist, is still most widely read for reasons that would probably fill several studies in social psychology. It needs no advocate. The fiction in this book, on the other hand, has been chosen largely because it does not lie about life—at least it does not lie about life in the ordinary way. And the various authors employ a large variety of literary methods and modes in an effort to illuminate the deepest wells of human experience. Consequently, many of these stories do not retail high adventure (though some do), since an adventurous inner life does not depend on an incident-filled outer life. Some stories, like Toomer's "Theater," and Melville's "Bartleby the Scrivener" might almost be said to be about what does not happen, rather than what does—not-happening being as much incident, after all, as happening.

All fiction attempts to be interesting, to involve the reader in situations, to force some aesthetic response from him—most simply put, in the widest sense of the word, to entertain. Some fiction aspires to nothing more —Poe's "Ligeia," "a tale of effect," might fall into this category. Other fiction seeks, as well, to establish some truth about the nature of man—Melville's "Bartleby the Scrivener" and Daniel's "Hands" ask the reader to perceive the inner life of central figures. Some fiction seeks to explore the relationships among men—Faulkner's "Dry September," Toomer's "Theater," and Lawrence's "The Horse Dealer's Daughter" depend for their force on the powerful interaction of one character with another. Still other fiction seeks to explore the connection between men and society—Harlan Ellison's "Repent, Harlequin! Said the Ticktockman" and Wright's "The Man Who Lived Underground" acquire their force from the implied struggle between men seeking a free and rich emotional life and the tyrannically ordering society that would sacrifice their humanity to some ideal of social efficiency.

We have been talking about that aspect of fiction which literary theorists identify as *theme.* Theorists also talk about plot, characterization, setting, point of view, and conflict—all terms naming aspects of fiction that generally have to do with the author's technique. Let us here deal with one story— James Joyce's "Araby." Read it. Then compare your private responses to the story with what we hope will be helpful and suggestive remarks about the methods of fiction.

The Methods of Fiction

One can perceive only a few things simultaneously and can hardly respond to everything contained in a well-wrought story all at once. When he has finished the story, the reader likely thinks back, makes readjustments, and reflects on the significance of things before he reaches that set of emotional and intellectual experiences that we have been calling *response.* Most readers of short stories respond first to what may be called the *tone* of the opening lines. Now tone is an aspect of literature about which it is particularly difficult to talk, because it is an aura—a shimmering and shifting atmosphere that depends for its substance on rather delicate emotional responses to language and situation. Surely, before the reader knows anything at all about the plot of "Araby," he has experienced a tone.

> North Richmond Street, being blind, was a quiet street except at the hour when the Christian Brothers' School set the boys free. An uninhabited house of two storeys stood at the blind end, detached from its neighbors in a square ground. The other houses of the street, conscious of decent lives within them, gazed at one another with brown imperturbable faces.

Is the scene gay? Vital and active? Is this opening appropriate for a story that goes on to celebrate joyous affirmations about life and living? Hopefully, you answer these questions negatively. Why? Because the dead end street is described as "blind," because the Christian Brothers' School sounds much like a prison (it sets the boys free), because a vacant house fronts the dead end, because the other houses, personified, are conscious of decent lives within (a mildly ironic description—*decent* suggesting ordinary, thin-lipped respectability rather than passion or heroism), because those houses gaze at one another with "brown imperturbable faces"—*brown* being nondescript, as opposed, say, to scarlet, gold, bright blue, and *imperturbable faces* reinforcing the priggish decency within.

Compare this opening from Faulkner's "Dry September":

> Through the bloody September twilight, aftermath of sixty-two rainless days, it had gone like fire in a dry grass—the rumor, the story, whatever it was. Something about Miss Minnie Cooper and a Negro.

The tone generated by "bloody twilight," "rainless days," "fire in a dry grass" is quite different from the blind, brown apathy of "Araby." And unsurprisingly, Faulkner's story involves movement to a horrifying violence. "Araby," on the other hand, is a story about the dawning of awareness in the mind and heart of the child of one of those decent families in brown and blind North Richmond Street. Tone, of course, permeates all fiction, and it may change as the narrative develops. Since short stories generally reveal change, the manipulation of tone is just one more tool used in the working of design.

Short stories, of course, are short, but this fact implies some serious considerations. In some ways, a large class of good short fiction deals with events that may be compared to the tip of the proverbial iceberg. The events animating the story represent only a tiny fraction of the characters' lives and experiences; yet, that fraction is terribly important and provides the basis for wide understanding both to the characters within the story and to its readers. In "Araby," the plot, the connected sequence of events, may be simply stated. A young boy who lives in a rather drab, respectable neighborhood develops a crush on the sister of one of his playmates. She asks him if he intends to go to a charity fair that she cannot attend. He resolves to go and purchase a gift for her. He is tormented by the late and drunken arrival of his uncle who has promised him the money he needs. When the boy finally arrives at the bazaar, he is disappointed by the difference between his expectation and the actuality of the almost deserted fair. He perceives some minor events, overhears some minor conversation and finally "saw [himself] as a creature driven and derided by vanity." Yet this tiny stretch of experience out of the life of the boy introduces him to an awareness about the differences between imagination and reality, between his romantic infatuation and the vulgar reality all about him. We are talking now about what is called the *theme* of the story. Emerging from the workaday events that constitute its plot is a general statement about intensely idealized childish "love," the shattering recognition of the false sentimentality that occasions it, and the enveloping vulgarity of adult life. The few pages of the story, by detailing a few events out of a short period of the protagonist's life, illuminate one aspect of the loss of innocence that we all endure and that is always painful. In much of the literature in the section on innocence and experience, the protagonists learn painfully the moral complexities of a world that had once seemed uncomplicated and predictable. That education does not always occur, as in "Araby," at an early age, either in literature or life.

Certainly theme is a centrally important aspect of prose fiction, but "good" themes do not neccessarily ensure good stories. One may write a wretched story with the same theme as "Araby." What, then, independent of theme, is the difference between good stories and bad stories? Instinctively you know how to answer this question. Good stories, to begin with, are interesting; they present characters you care about; however fantastic, they are yet somehow plausible; they project a moral world you recognize. One of the obvious differences between short stories and novels requires that story writers develop character rapidly and limit the number of developed characters. Many stories have only one fleshed character; the other characters are frequently two-dimensional projections or even stereotypes. We see their surface only, not their souls. Rarely does a short story have more than three developed characters. Again, unlike novels, short stories usually work themselves out in restricted geographical setting, in a single place, and within a rather short period of time.

We often speak of character, setting, plot, theme, and style as separate aspects of a story in order to break down a complex narrative into more manageable parts. But it is important to understand that this analytic process of separating various elements is something we have done to the story—the story (if it is a good one) is an integrated whole. The closer we examine the separate elements, the clearer it becomes that each is integrally related to the others.

It is part of the boy's character that he lives in a brown imperturbable house in North Richmond Street, that he does the things he does (which is, after all, the plot), that he learns what he does (which is the theme), and that all of this characterization emerges from Joyce's rich and suggestive style. Consider this paragraph:

> Her image accompanied me even in places the most hostile to romance. On Saturday evenings when my aunt went marketing I had to go to carry some of the parcels. We walked through the flaring streets, jostled by drunken men and bargaining women, amid the curses of labourers, the shrill litanies of shop-boys who stood on guard by the barrels of pigs' cheeks, the nasal chanting of street-singers, who sang a come-all-you about O'Donovan Rossa, or a ballad about the troubles in our native land. These noises converged in a single sensation of life for me: I imagined that I bore my chalice safely through a throng of foes. Her name sprang to my lips at moments in strange prayers and praises which I myself did not understand. My eyes were often full of tears (I could not tell why) and at times a flood from my heart seemed to pour itself out into my bosom. I thought little of the future. I did not know whether I would ever speak to her or not or, if I spoke to her, how I could tell her of my confused adoration. But my body was like a harp and her words and gestures were like fingers running upon the wires.

This paragraph furthers the plot. But it suggests much more. The boy thinks of his friend's sister even when he carries parcels for his aunt during the shopping trips through a crowded and coarse part of town. In those coarse market streets the shop-boys cry shrill "litanies," the girl's name springs to his lips in strange "prayers and praises," and the boy confesses a confused "adoration." Further, he bears "his chalice safely through a throng of foes." Now the words *litanies, prayers, praises, adoration* all come from a special vocabulary that is easy to identify. It is the vocabulary of the church. The *chalice* and the *throng of foes* comes from the vocabulary of chivalric romance, which is alluded to in the first line of the quoted paragraph. Taken together, Joyce evokes a sort of holy chivalry that characterizes the boy on this otherwise altogether ordinary shopping trip. This paragraph suggests to the careful reader that the boy has cast his awakening sexuality in a mold that mixes the disparate shapes of the heroic knight, winning his lady by force of arms, and the ascetic penitent, adoring the holy virgin, mother of god.

Playing the word game, of course, can be dangerous. But from the beginning of this story to its end, a certain religious quality shimmers. That now-dead priest of the story's second paragraph had three books (at least). One is a romantic chivalric novel by Sir Walter Scott; one is a sensational account of the adventures of a famous rogue; one is what a priest might be expected to have at hand—an Easter week devotional guide. That priest who read Scott novels might have understood the boy's response—that mixture of religious devotion and romance. Shortly after the shopping trip, the boy finally speaks to the girl, and it is instructive to see her as he does. He stands at the *railings* and looks up (presumably) at her, she bowing her head towards him. "The light from the lamp opposite our door caught the white curve of her neck, lit up her hair that rested there and, falling, lit up the hand upon the railing. It fell over one side of her dress and caught the white border of a petticoat, just visible as she stood at ease." Skip the petticoat, for a moment. Might the description of Mangan's sister remind the careful reader of quite common sculptured representations of the Virgin Mary? But the petticoat! And the white curve of her neck! This erotic overlay characterizes the boy's response. The sexuality is his own; the chivalry, the religious adoration, comes from the culture in which he is immersed—comes from Scott, the ballads sung in the market place, the "Arab's Farewell to his Steed" sung by the boy's uncle. And it is the culture that so romanticizes and elevates the boy's yearning.

He finally gets to Araby—"the word called to him through the silence in which his soul luxuriated and cast an Eastern enchantment over him." His purpose is to serve his lady—to bring her something from that exotic place. What he finds is a weary-looking man guarding a turnstile, the silence that pervades a church after a service, and two men counting money on a salver (that tray is called a *salver* by design). And in this setting he overhears the courtship of a young lady by two gentlemen:

> "O, I never said such a thing!"
> "O, but you did!"
> "O, but I didn't!"
> "Didn't she say that?"
> "Yes, I heard her."
> "O, there's a . . . fib!"

This is Araby, this is love in a darkened hall where money is counted. Is it any wonder that the boy, in the moment of personal illumination that Joyce calls an epiphany, sees himself as a creature driven and derided by vanity?

"Araby" is a careful, even a delicate story. Nothing much happens—what does occur largely in the boy's perception and imagination. The story focuses on the boy's confusion of sexual attraction with the lofty sentiments of chivalry and religion. The climax occurs when he confronts the darkened, money-grubbing fair and the utterly banal expression of the sexual attraction between the gentlemen and the young lady. The result is a sudden deflation of the boy's ego, his sense of self, as he recognizes his own delusions about the nature of love and the relationship between men, women, heroism, god, and money.

We would like to conclude with a discussion of one feature of fiction that sometimes proves troublesome to developing readers. Often the events of a story, upon which much depends, puzzle or annoy readers. Why does that fool do that? Why doesn't X simply tell Y the way he feels and then the tragedy would be averted? In a sense, such responses reflect the intrusion of a reader into the world of the story. The reader, a sensible and sensitive person, understands some things about life after all and is oppressed by the characters' inability to understand at least as much. Characters choose to die when they might with a slight adjustment live. They risk danger when with a slight adjustment they might proceed safely. They suffer the pain of an unfortunate marriage when with a little trouble they might be free to live joyously. If the "whys" issuing from the reader are too insistent, too sensible, then the story must fail, at least for that reader. But many "whys" are not legitimate. Many are intrusions of the reader's hindsight, the reader's altogether different cultural and emotional fix. Henry James urged that the author must be allowed his *donnée*, his "given." He creates the society and the rules by which it operates within his own fictional world. Sometimes his creation is so close to the reader's own world that it is hardly possible to object. Black readers will recognize the inner life of Wright's man who lived underground even if the events are bizarre. Those who have grown up in a small southern town will recognize the atmosphere of Faulkner's "Dry September" and Baldwin's "Going to Meet the Man." But few readers of this book know 1895 Dublin and Irish middle-class society, which plays a brooding role in "Araby" (as it does in almost all of Joyce's work). None know the futuristic world of Harlan Ellison's Harlequin. In every case, we must finally imagine those worlds. If we cannot, the events that take place in them will be of no consequence. If those worlds are unimaginable, then the stories must fail. If they too much strain belief or remain too foreign to the reader's heart, they must likewise fail. But all response to fiction depends on the reader's acquiescence to the world of the author and his perceptions of the moral consequences of acts and attitudes in that world. At best, that acquiescence will provide much pleasure as well as emotional insight into his own existence.

Reading Poetry

For many people, the question "What is poetry?" is irrelevant if not irreverent. The attempt to answer such a question leads to abstract intellectual analysis, the very opposite of the emotional pleasure one seeks in a good poem. Why does it matter what poetry is so long as readers enjoy poems? Doesn't the attempt to define the nature of poetry lead to technical analysis of poetic devices so that study, finally, destroys pleasure?

These are valid issues that touch on very real dangers. If the study of poetry bogs down in theoretical or historical issues and the study of a poem becomes a mere exercise in the identification and discussion of poetic devices, the reader may well find that reading a poem is more effort than pleasure. He may begin to feel like the many nineteenth-century poets who complained that science, in laying bare the laws of nature, robbed the universe of its ancient awe and mystery. Walt Whitman, for example, describes such a feeling in his poem, "When I Heard the Learn'd Astronomer."

> When I heard the learn'd astronomer,
> When the proofs, the figures, were ranged in columns before me,
> When I was shown the charts and diagrams, to add, divide,
>   and measure them,
> When I sitting heard the astronomer where he lectured with
>   much applause in the lecture-room,
> How soon unaccountable I became tired and sick,
> Till rising and gliding out I wander'd off by myself,
> In the mystical moist night-air, and from time to time,
> Look'd up in perfect silence at the stars.

The distinction implicit in Whitman's poem between the mind (intellectual knowledge) and the heart (emotion and feeling) is very old, but still a useful one. All of us have no doubt felt at some time that the overexercise of the mind interfered with our capacity to feel. Compelled to analyze, dissect, categorize, and classify, we finally yearn for the simple and "mindless" pleasure of unanalytical enjoyment, the pleasure of sensuous experience. But man derives pleasure in a variety of ways, and while we needn't assert a *necessary* connection between understanding and pleasure, understanding can enhance pleasure. The distinction between the mind and the heart is, after all, a fiction or metaphor that cannot be pushed too far before it breaks down. Readers may very well enjoy Dylan Thomas' "Fern Hill" without understanding Thomas' use of symbolism or color or religious imagery. But understanding that symbolism and imagery will certainly deepen the pleasure derived from the poem.

We don't mean to suggest by all this that every poem needs to be studied in detail or that it is possible to say in the abstract what kind and amount of study will be rewarding. Some poems are straightforward, requiring little by way of analysis; others, dense and complex, seem to yield little without some study. But study of even the simplest poems can be rewarding. (Consider the effect of the special vocabulary implied by such words as "arrayed," "imperially," "crown," and "glittered" in Edwin Arlington Robinson's "Richard Cory.") On the other hand, it is possible to be moved on first reading by the tone and quality of such complex poems as Leonard Cohen's "Suzanne" and T. S. Eliot's "The Love Song of J. Alfred Prufrock" even though they are difficult to understand immediately.

As to our original question—What is poetry?—we cannot offer anything like a definitive and comprehensive answer. Poetry is a form of writing that often employs rhyme, a regular rhythm, unusual word order, and an intense or heightened language. This formal definition will serve about as well as any although it is by no means comprehensive, as any collection of poems will readily demonstrate. Up to about a century ago, poetry was governed by rather precise and often elaborate rules and conventions; if a poem did not use rhyme, it certainly was characterized by rhythmic regularity, or meter. Further, there existed a long tradition of poetic types (epic, elegaic, tragic, satiric, etc.), each with quite specific rules and characteristics. While these traditions still retain some force, the old notion that these forms are part of the natural scheme of things has been largely abandoned. No one nowadays equates painting with photographic realism or music with the diatonic scale, and no one insists that the form of writing we call poetry must exhibit a combination of fixed characteristics.

Consider poetry from a different angle and ask not what poetry is but rather what functions it serves. Poetry fulfills some deep and abiding need of man, for no culture we know of has been without it. We know also that in ancient societies, before the advent of science and technology in the modern sense, the arts were not divided by types nor differentiated from science. In ancient tribal societies, poetry, dance, sculpture, and painting might all be parts of a tribal ceremony designed to propitiate the gods and thereby ensure a full harvest or a successful hunt. Poetry, then, was part of a primitive (we would now label it "superstitious") science that defined and helped control the external world. Though one can only guess in these matters, it is probably safe to assume that in such a primitive society the inner emotional world of the individual was not sharply distinguished from the outer world of nature. Nature and the gods who controlled it might be harsh and unpredictible, and the function of ritual was to control and appease these gods (to ensure rain, for example). But ritual also nurtured and strengthened the individual's communal spirit and conditioned his feelings about the arduous work that the life of the tribe required.

The conditions of our lives are, of course, vastly different. We operate within an enormous industrialized society that developed over the centuries because men abandoned primitive explanations of the universe and sought others. One result of that development was a continuing differentiation and specialization of human endeavors, as science broke away from art and both divided into separate if related disciplines. Science became astronomy, biology, physics, and the like, while art became poetry, drama, painting, and sculpture. And it was modern science, not poetry or the other arts, that produced profound and measurable changes in man's life. Poetry might movingly and memorably remind us of the sorrow of unrequited love or the ravages of growing old, but science created a technology that produced undreamed of material wealth and power.

Is the very persistence of poetry evidence that it serves some important function, however obscure? On the other hand, maybe poetry is merely a vestigial organ of evolution that, like the appendix, continues to exist even though it has outlived its usefulness. Certainly, the historical process we have sketched here seems to involve a gradual diminution in the importance men attach to poetry.

It would be misleading, of course, to suggest that the scientist and the poet exist in separate worlds. But the differences between them are important. The truth that science seeks is the truth of physical reality. Social sciences such as psychology, sociology, and economics have attempted to demonstrate that human behavior can be understood in terms of a set of definite and quantifiable mechanisms. And, though no one would assert that science has achieved final answers, it is clear that the spectacular discoveries of science have left many, Walt Whitman among them, with the feeling that man's importance in the universe has diminished. Further, modern physical science has uncovered a disturbing indeterminateness and asymmetry in the universe that have far-reaching philosophical implications not only for science but for society as a whole. As the old scientific verities crumble, so, too, do the old social verities.

Science may describe and educate us about the outer world and its inexorable laws with as rigorous an objectivity and neutrality as it can achieve. It may explain to us that in a naturalistic world death comes to all living creatures or that sunsets result from certain physical phenomena; but it is silent on the terror of death and its human or emotional meaning or on the beauty of a sunset. To understand those emotions, to give them form and meaning, we turn to poetry—we read it and, perhaps, even write it. For poetry, so to speak, educates our emotions and our feelings, allows us to learn who we are and to articulate what we feel.

We might wonder whether such an assertion makes sense. What we feel, we feel. We don't need a poem to tell us that. Not so. Often we don't know what we feel except in a vague and inarticulate way. A powerful poem articulates and thereby clarifies. Further, a poem may even deepen feelings. Andrew Marvell's poem "To His Coy Mistress" may well help the reader understand his own feelings about physical love and mortality. The outrageous absurdity of a young person cut down by death when his life has barely begun is objectified by Robert Frost's "Out, Out—" and John Crowe Ransom's "Bells for John Whiteside's Daughter." The confusion that often attends the powerful emotion generated by love and death is arrested by the poet who provides order.

Poetry at its highest and most general level is a form of communication, a means of defining, affirming, and deepening its reader's humanity. This is not to say that one should approach poetry solemnly, expecting always to be loftily enlightened. Poetry is a complex form of communication that provides pleasure in various ways. One may, for instance, look upon a poem as a kind of game in which the poet skillfully works within a set of self-imposed rules—rhyme, meter, and stanzaic pattern—and delights in clever rhymes, as when Byron rhymes "intellectual" with "henpecked you all" or "maxim" with "tax 'em." Anyone familiar with Plato's theory that everything in our world is an imperfect replica of an ideal heavenly form will appreciate the beauty and condensed brilliance of William Butler Yeats' lines from "Among School Children":

> Plato thought nature but a spume that plays
> Upon a ghostly paradigm of things.

Some will discover in poetry, as children often do in nursery rhymes, the pleasure of rhythm, meter, and sound—the musical aspects of poetry. The pleasures of poetry range from the loftiest insights and discoveries to memorable lines and clever rhymes.

A discussion of the major techniques and devices of poetry will provide some suggestions about how to approach poems and also furnish tools and a vocabulary for analyzing and discussing them. Keep in mind that a tool is not an end in itself but the means to an end. The end is fuller understanding and, thereby, deeper enjoyment of poetry.

The Words of Poetry

It is not unusual to hear some great and original philosopher, sociologist, or economist referred to as a mediocre writer. Yet, while one may judge the writing poor, he may at the same time recognize and honor the originality and significance of the idea conveyed. Such a distinction cannot be made in poetry. If a poem is written poorly, it is a poor poem. "In reading prose," Ralph Waldo Emerson said, "I am sensitive as soon as a sentence drags; but in poetry, as soon as one word drags." *Where* a poem arrives is inseparable from *how* it arrives. Everything must be right in a poem, every word. "The correction of prose," said Yeats, "is endless, a poem comes right with a click like a closing box."

"Poetry is heightened language" means, among other things, that the poet strives for precision and richness in the words he uses, and "precision" and "richness" are not contradictory for the poet. Words have dictionary or denotative meanings as well as associative or connotative meanings; they also have histories and relationships with other words. The English language is rich in synonyms, groups of words whose denotative meanings are roughly the same but whose connotations vary widely (portly, stout, fat; horse, steed, courser; official, statesman, politician). Many words are identical in sound and often in spelling but different in meaning (forepaws, four paws; lie down! you lie!). The meanings of words have changed in the course of time, and the poet may consciously select a word whose older meaning adds a dimension to his poem (astonished = turned to stone). There are, of course, no rules that can be given to a reader for judging a poet's effectiveness and skill in the handling of words (or anything else, for that matter). All we can do is look at particular works for examples of how a good poet manipulates words.

In a moving and passionate poem on his dying father, "Do Not Go Gentle into That Good Night," Dylan Thomas pleads with his father not to accept death passively but rather to "Rage, rage against the dying of the light." He then declares in the following stanzas that neither "wise men" nor "good men" nor "wild men" accept death quietly. And neither, Thomas says, do "grave men," punning on *grave* in its meaning of both "serious" and "burial place." William Blake's poem about the inhumane jobs children were forced into in eighteenth-century England, "The Chimney Sweeper" begins:

> When my mother died I was very young,
> And my Father sold me while yet my tongue
> Could scarcely cry "'weep! 'weep! 'weep!"
> So your chimneys I sweep, and in soot I sleep.

"'Weep," a clipped form of "sweep," is what the boy cries as he walks a street looking for work, but *weep* clearly evokes the tears and sorrow of the mother's death and the sadness of the small boy's cruel life. And this is only part of Blake's skillful handling of words. "Cry" is also an effective pun, the precise word to describe how the boy seeks work while simultaneously reinforcing the emotional meaning of *weep*.

Henry Reed's "Naming of Parts" develops a contrast between the instructions a group of soldiers are receiving on how to operate a rifle (in order to cause death) and the lovely world of nature (which represents life and beauty). In the fourth stanza, bees are described as "assaulting and fumbling the flowers." "Fumbling," with its meaning of awkwardness and nervous uncertainty, may strike us as an arresting and perhaps puzzling word at first. Yet anyone who has watched a bee pollinating a flower will find the word extremely effective. In addition, of course, *fumbling* is a word often used to describe the actions of human beings caught up in sexual passion—a connotation precisely appropriate to the poet's purposes, since pollination is, in a sense, a sexual process. Furthermore, these various interpretations of *fumbling* contrast powerfully with the cold, mechanical precision of the death-dealing instruments the recruits are learning how to use. The next line of Reed's poem exhibits yet another resource of words: "They call it easing the Spring." The line is an exact repetition of a phrase used two lines earlier except *Spring* is now capitalized. While *Spring* retains its first meaning as part of the bolt action of the rifle, the capitalization makes it the season of the year when flowers are pollinated and the world of nature is reborn. With a mere typographical device, Reed has charged a single word with the theme of his poem. These few illustrations will suggest how sensitive the poet is to words and how much more pleasure the reader will find in poems if he develops the same sensitivity.

Sometimes meanings are not inherent in the isolated words but created in the poet's use of the word. A tree is a tree and a rose is a rose. A tree is also Yeats' "great-rooted blossomer" in "Among School Children" and something quite different in William Blake's "A Poison Tree"; a rose is specially defined in Robert Burns' "A Red, Red Rose" and Edmund Waller's "Go, Lovely Rose." In these poems, because *tree* and *rose* are given such rich and varied meaning and are so central to the poems' development and meaning, they exceed mere connotation and become images that, finally, are symbolic.

Imagery

The world is revealed to us through our senses—sight, sound, taste, touch, and smell. And while some philosophers and psychologists might challenge the statement, it seems pretty clear that much, if not all, of our knowledge is linked to sensory experience. *Imagery* is the representation in poetry of sensory experience, one of the means by which the poet creates a world that we all know and share. Or, put another way, imagery allows the poet to create a recognizable world by drawing upon a fund of common experiences. Bad poetry is often bad because the imagery is stale ("golden sunset," "the smiling sun," "the rolling sea") or so skimpy that the poem dissolves into vague and shadowy and meaningless abstractions.

A good poet never loses touch with the sensory world. The invisible, the intangible, the abstract are anchored to the visible, the tangible, the concrete. Andrew Marvell begins his poem "To His Coy Mistress" with an elaborate statement of how he would court his beloved if their lives were measured in centuries rather than years. In the second stanza, he describes the reality:

> But at my back I always hear
> Time's wingéd chariot hurrying near;
> And yonder all before us lie
> Deserts of vast eternity.
> Thy beauty shall no more be found,
> Nor, in thy marble vault, shall sound
> My echoing song; then worms shall try
> That long-preserved virginity,
> And your quaint honor turn to dust,
> And into ashes all my lust:
> The grave's a fine and private place,
> But none, I think, do there embrace.

Time, eternity, honor, and *lust* are all vague abstractions. But Marvell joins each to a sensuous image that gives to the abstraction an extraordinary sharpness and power: Time is a winged *chariot,* eternity a sequence of *deserts,* honor turns to *dust* and lust to *ashes.*

Any analysis of the imagery of a poem will soon reveal that our definition of imagery as the representation of sensory experience needs to be qualified. One of the primary functions of language is to bring meaning and order into our lives, and poetry is the most intense use of language. We will find, therefore, that the images in poetry tend to be charged with meanings. A rose may be only a rose, but it becomes much more in Burns' and Waller's poems. Imagery, then, is closely related to, perhaps inseparable from, *figurative* language, the language which *says* one thing and *means* another.

The difference between good and bad poetry often turns on the skill with which imagery (or figurative language) is used. Marvell's images are striking, fresh, and powerful, nicely suited to his purposes. When Robert Frost in his poem "Birches" compares life to "a pathless wood," the image strikes us as natural and appropriate (the comparison of life to a path or road is a common one, as is a wood or forest to a state of moral bewilderment). We are accustomed to the imagery of birds, flowers, and sunsets in love poems, but when John Donne in "A Valediction: Forbidding Mourning" describes the relationship between himself and his beloved in terms of a drawing compass, the image may seem jarring or even ludicrous. Such a bold and daring comparison is a kind of challenge. The poet intends not only to surmount the reader's feeling that the image is strange but to develop it with such skill that the reader will accept it as natural and appropriate. And as Donne elaborates the comparison through various stages and concludes it (and the poem) with the brilliantly appropriate image of the completed circle, we recognize that he has successfully met the challenge.

Figurative Language

Figurative language is the general phrase we use to describe the many devices of language that allow us to speak nonliterally, to say one thing and mean another. Any attempt to communicate an emotion will very quickly utilize figurative language. When Robert Burns compares his love to a red rose, he does so not because he is unable to find the literal language he needs but because what he wants to say can only be expressed in figurative language. (Literal language might be used by a scientist to describe the physiological state of someone in love, but that is not what interests Burns). The world of emotions, feelings, attitudes remains shadowy and insubstantial until figurative language gives it form and substance.

Consider, for example, these familiar old sayings: "The grass is always greener on the other side of the fence"; "A rolling stone gathers no moss"; "A bird in the hand is worth two in a bush"; "The early bird catches the worm." While these sayings unquestionably make sense in literal terms (the grass you see from a distance looks greener than the grass under your feet), the meaning of these phrases to a native speaker of English is clearly non-literal. When we use them we are not speaking about grass or rolling stones or birds; we are making general and highly abstract observations about human attitudes and behavior. Yet strangely these generalizations and abstractions are embodied in concrete and sensuous imagery. Try to explain what any one of these expressions means and you will quickly discover that you are using many more words and much vaguer language than the expression itself. Indeed, this is precisely what happens when you attempt to paraphrase—that is, put into your own words—the meaning of a poem. Like poetry, these sayings rely on the figurative use of language.

Since poetry is an intense and heightened use of language that explores the world of feeling, it uses more varied figurative devices than does ordinary language. One of the most common figurative devices, *metaphor*, where one thing is called something else, occurs frequently in ordinary speech. "School is a rat race," we say, or "She's a bundle of nerves," and the meaning is perfectly clear—too clear, perhaps, because these metaphors are by now so common and unoriginal they have lost whatever vividness they may once have had. But when Macbeth declares that "[Life] is a tale / Told by an idiot, full of sound and fury, / Signifying nothing" or Chidiock Tichborne begins the poem on his short life the night before his execution with "My prime of youth is but a frost of cares,/My feast of joy is but a dish of pain," we have metaphors that compel readers to confront certain painful aspects of life.

Simile is closely related to metaphor. But where metaphor says that one thing *is* another, simile says that one thing is *like* another, as in Burns' "O My luve's like a red, red rose" and Frost's "life is too much like a pathless wood." The distinction between simile and metaphor, while easy enough to make technically, is often difficult to distinguish in terms of effects. Frost establishes a comparison between life and a pathless wood and keeps the two even more fully separated by adding the qualifiers "too much." Burns' simile maintains the same separation and, in addition, since it occurs in the opening line of the poem, eliminates any possible confusion the reader might momentarily experience about the subject of the poem if the line read, "O My love is a red, red rose." The reader can test the difference in effect between simile and metaphor by changing a metaphor into a simile or a simile into a metaphor to see if the meaning of the poem is thereby altered.

The critical vocabulary useful in discussions of poetry includes several additional terms, all of which name particular figures of speech: *metonymy, synecdoche, personification, hyperbole, understatement, paradox.* These terms are defined and illustrated in the Glossary of Literary Terms. But, though there may be a certain academic pleasure in recognizing the figures a poet uses, naming a figure of speech will never explain its effectiveness. The reader must, finally, perceive the usefulness of figures and respond emotionally to the construction of language that the poet creates in order to touch his reader's nerves.

Symbol

A *symbol* is anything that stands for or suggests something else. In this sense, most words are symbolic: the word *tree* stands for an object in the real world. When we speak of a symbol in poetry, however, we usually mean something more precise. In poetry, a symbol is an object or event that suggests more than itself. It is one of the most common and most powerful devices available to the poet, for it allows him to convey economically and simply a wide range of meanings.

It is useful to distinguish between two kinds of symbols, *public symbols* and *contextual symbols.* Public symbols are those objects or events that history has invested with rich meanings and associations. In a sense, then, a public symbol is a ready-made symbol. Yeats utilizes such a symbol in his poem "No Second Troy," assuming that his readers will be familiar with the Trojan War of antiquity which was brought about by the legendary beauty of Helen of Troy. Helen herself is a public symbol of dazzling beauty, and although Yeats does not mention her name in the poem, he clearly associates the woman of the poem with Helen. Another public symbol is found in E. E. Cummings' "i sing of Olaf glad and big." Olaf refuses to kiss the flag that symbolizes those values which Olaf rejects.

When a poet uses a public symbol, he is drawing from what he assumes is a common and shared fund of knowledge and tradition. If Yeats' reader is unaware of the symbolic meaning with which history has invested the Trojan War, it is doubtful that the poem will have much meaning for him. The poem's use of the terms "courage," "nobleness," and "beauty like a tightened bow" cannot be fully understood by readers unfamiliar with the story of Helen's beauty and its epic consequences. Nor does Olaf's refusal to kiss the flag have much meaning unless we immediately recognize that flag as a symbol of nationalism and unquestioning patriotism.

In contrast to public symbols, contextual symbols are objects or events that are symbolic by virtue of the poet's handling of them in a particular poem —that is, by virtue of the context. Consider, for example, the opening lines of Robert Frost's "After Apple-Picking":

> My long two-pointed ladder's sticking through a tree
> Toward heaven still,
> And there's a barrel that I didn't fill
> Beside it, and there may be two or three
> Apples I didn't pick upon some bough.

The apple tree is a literal tree, but as one reads through the poem, it becomes clear that the apple tree also symbolizes the speaker's life with a wide range of possible meanings (do the few apples he hasn't picked symbolize the hopes, dreams, aspirations that even the fullest life cannot satisfy?).

Amy Lowell's "Patterns" is rich in symbols. The speaker is an aristocratic lady whose life and most vital emotions are kept in rigid control by a series of patterns that the society she lives in has imposed on her. She describes herself as walking in her elegant gown down the garden paths laid out in precise patterns. Her gown is real; the path is a real path. But it very quickly becomes apparent that the patterned paths and her elegant gown are symbolic of the narrowly restricted and oppressive life her deepest feelings are at war with. They are the visible manifestation, the symbols, of the trap in which she is caught. She weeps when she notices "The daffodils and squills / Flutter in the breeze / As they please" because the flowers symbolize a freedom she knows she will never have.

The paths and flowers in Amy Lowell's poem are clear and easily recognizable examples of contextual symbols. However, contextual symbols by their very nature tend to present more difficulties than public symbols, because recognizing them depends on a sensitivity to everything else in the poem. In T. S. Eliot's dense and difficult poem "The Love Song of J. Alfred Prufrock," the speaker twice says, "In the room the women come and go / Talking of Michelangelo," a couplet that is baffling at first because it seems to have no clear relationship to what precedes and follows it. But as one reads through the poem, he begins to see that Prufrock is a man, like the young woman in Amy Lowell's poem, trapped in a life of upper-class superficialities and meaninglessness. The women discussing Michelangelo symbolize this dilettantish and arid life from which Prufrock desperately wishes to escape. Prufrock reminds himself that he will have time "To prepare a face to meet the faces that you meet," and Eleanor Rigby, in John Lennon and Paul McCartney's song, is described as "wearing the face that she keeps in a jar by the door." In both poems, that face is a symbol of a lonely existence in a society where people play elaborate games in order to conceal from others their real emotions and feelings.

A final word on symbols. If a reader fails to recognize a symbol, he has missed an important part of the poem's meaning. On the other hand, one of the pitfalls of reading poetry is that some readers become so intent on finding symbols they tend to forget that an object must first have a literal meaning before it can function as a symbol. Or, put in terms of our earlier definition, an object or event is itself before it is something else.

The setting of "After Apple-Picking" is an orchard, and the setting of "Patterns" the paths of a manorial garden. As we begin to understand the theme of each poem, we come to recognize the symbolic meanings these objects gradually take on. But there are no rules that will allow a reader to identify symbols. If you do not know what Troy symbolizes and have never heard of Helen of Troy, you will not discover the meanings of these public symbols by repeated and intensive readings of the poem; like unfamiliar words, you must look up (or be told of) their significance. On the other hand, the recognition of contextual symbols often depends on careful and sensitive reading. Readers may very well disagree on whether or not something should be taken as a symbol. When this occurs, one can only consider whether the symbolic reading adds meanings that are consistent with other elements in the poem. Is the fly in Emily Dickinson's "I Heard a Fly Buzz—When I Died" a symbol or merely an insect? Your answer will depend on what you see as the theme of the poem.

Music

The *music* of poetry, by which we mean the poetic use of all the devices of sound and rhythm inherent in language, is at once central to the poetic effect and yet the most difficult to account for. We can discuss the ways in which figurative language works with some clarity because we are using words to explain words. Anyone who has ever tried to explain the effect a piece of music had on him (or who has read music criticism) will be familiar with the problem of describing a nonverbal medium with words.

The possible musical effects of language are complex. The terms we have to describe various musical devices deal only with the most obvious and easily recognizable patterns. *Alliteration, assonance, consonance, caesura, meter, onomatopoeia, rhythm,* and *rhyme* (all of them defined in the Glossary) are the key traditional terms for discussing the music of poetry. Along with the other terms already introduced, they are an indispensable part of the vocabulary one needs to discuss poetry. But the relationship between sound and sense can be perceived nicely in a celebrated passage from Alexander Pope's poem "An Essay on Criticism," in which the meaning of each line, first a condemnation of mechanical bad verse, then an illustration of well-managed verse, is ingeniously supported by the musical devices:

> These[1] equal syllables alone require,
> Though oft the ear the open vowels tire;
> While expletives their feeble aid do join;
> And ten low words oft creep in one dull line:

---

1. Bad poets.

While they ring round the same unvaried chimes,
With sure returns of still expected rhymes;
Where 'er you find "the cooling western breeze,"
In the next line, it "whispers through the trees";
If crystal streams "with pleasing murmurs creep,"
The reader's threatened (not in vain) with "sleep";
Then, at the last and only couplet fraught
With some unmeaning thing they call a thought,
A needless Alexandrine[2] ends the song
That, like a wounded snake, drags its slow length along.

*   *   *

True ease in writing comes from art, not chance,
As those move easiest who have learned to dance.
'Tis not enough no harshness gives offense,
The sound must seem an echo to the sense:
Soft is the strain when Zephyr gently blows,
And the smooth stream in smoother numbers flows;
But when loud surges lash the sounding shore,
The hoarse, rough verse should like the torrent roar:
When Ajax[3] strives some rock's vast weight to throw,
The line too labors, and the words move slow;
Not so, when swift Camilla[4] scours the plain,
Flies o'er the unbending corn, and skims along the main.

When Pope speaks of open vowels, the line is loaded with open vowels. When Pope condemns the use of ten monosyllables, the line contains ten monosyllables. When Pope urges that the sound should echo the sense and speaks of the wind, the line is rich in sibilants that hiss, like the wind. When he speaks of Ajax striving, the combination of final consonants and initial sounds slow the line; when he speaks of Camilla's swiftness, the final consonants and initial sounds form liaisons that are swiftly pronounceable.

Or, consider the opening lines of Wilfred Owen's poem "Dulce et Decorum Est," describing a company of battle-weary soldiers trudging toward their camp and rest:

Bent double, like old beggars under sacks,
Knock-kneed, coughing like hags, we cursed through sludge.

These lines are dominated by a series of harsh, explosive consonant sounds (b, d, k, g) that reinforce the meaning of the lines (a description of tired World War I soldiers). More specifically, the first two syllables of each line are heavily stressed, which serves to slow the reading. And, finally, while the poem ultimately develops a prevailing meter, the meter is only faintly suggested in these opening lines, through the irregular rhythms used to describe a weary stumbling march.

---

2. Twelve-syllable line.
3. A Greek warrior celebrated for his strength.
4. A swift-footed queen in Virgil's *Aeneid*.

Let us remember, then, that analysis of musical (or for that matter any other) devices can illuminate and enrich our understanding of poetry. But let us also remember that analysis has its limitations. Dylan Thomas once remarked:

> You can tear a poem apart to see what makes it technically tick and say to yourself when the works are laid out before you—the vowels, the consonants, the rhymes, and rhythms—"Yes, this is it. This is why the poem moves me so. It is because of the craftsmanship." But you're back where you began. The best craftsmanship always leaves holes and gaps in the works of the poem so that something that is not in the poem can creep, crawl, flash, or thunder in.

Reading Drama

Plays are fundamentally different from other literary forms. Unlike stories and poems, almost all plays are designed to be performed, not to be read. Consequently, the audial and the visual aspects of the drama, which should be at least as important as its dialogue, are left altogether to the imagination of the reader (with the aid of some meager stage directions). Great effort is invested in such matters as costuming, set design, lighting effects, and stage movement by the director and his staff; all of that effort is lost to the reader who must somehow contrive to supply imaginatively some of those dramatic features not contained on the printed page.

As much as possible, the way to read a play is to imagine that you are its director. Hence you will concern yourself with creating the set and the lighting. You will see people dressed so that their clothes give support to their words. You will think about timing—how long between events and speeches—and blocking—how the characters move as they interact on stage. Perhaps the best way to confront the literature of the stage, to respond most fully to what is there, is to attempt to produce some scenes in class or after class. If possible, attend the rehearsals of plays in production on the campus. Nothing will provide better insight into the complexities of the theater than attending a rehearsal where the problems are encountered and solved.

As an exercise, read the opening speeches of any of the plays here and make decisions. How should the lines be spoken (quietly, angrily, haltingly)? What should the characters do as they speak (remain stationary, look in some direction, traverse the stage)? How should the stage be lit (partially, brightly, in some color that contributes to the mood of the dialogue and action)? What should the characters who are not speaking do? What possibilities exist for conveying appropriate signals solely through gesture and facial expression—signals not contained in the words you read?

Staging

Since plays are written to be staged, the particular kind of theater available to the dramatist is often crucial to the structure of the play. The Greek theater of Dionysius in Athens, for which Sophocles wrote, was an open-air amphitheater seating about 14,000 people. The skene, from which actors entered, was fixed, though it might have had painted panels to suggest the scene. Consequently, there is no scene shifting in *Antigone*. All the dialogue and action take place in the same location before the skene building, which represents the Palace of Creon. Important things happen elsewhere, but the audience is informed of these events by messenger. Three deaths occur, but none in sight of the audience, partly as a matter of taste and partly because the conditions of the Greek stage prevented the playwright from moving the action inside the palace or to that terrifying mausoleum where both Antigone and her betrothed chose death before submission. Later dramatists, writing for a more flexible stage and a more intimate theater, were able to profit from the intensely dramatic nature of murder and suicide, but the Greeks, almost invariably, chose to tell, rather than show, the most gripping physical events in their stories.

Further, an outdoor theater of vast dimensions implies obvious restrictions on acting style. Facial expression can play no important role in such a theater, and, in fact, the actors of Sophoclean tragedy wore masks, larger than life and probably equipped with some sort of megaphone device to aid in voice projection. Those voices were denied the possibility of subtle variety in tone and expression, and the speeches were probably delivered in rather formal declamatory style. The characters wore special built-up footwear which made them larger than life. In addition to these limitations, Sophocles had as well to write within the formal limitations imposed by the Athenian government, which made available only three principal actors, all male, as the cast (exclusive of the chorus) for each play. Consequently, there are never more than three players on stage at once, and the roles are designed so that each actor takes several parts—signified by different masks. Yet, despite the austerity of production values, the unavoidable clumsiness of fortuitous messengers appearing at all the right moments, and the sharply restricted dramatis personae, among the few Greek plays that have survived are some still universally regarded as superlatively fine dramatic representations of tragic humanity.

Until recently we thought we had a clear conception of what Shakespeare's stage looked like. Scholarship has raised some doubts about this conception, but though we no longer accept the accuracy of the reconstruction shown here, we still have a good enough understanding of the shape of the playing area to re-create roughly the staging of a Shakespearean play. That staging was altogether different from the Greek. Though both theaters were open air, the enclosure around the Elizabethan stage was much smaller, and the audience capacity limited to something between 2,000 and 3,000. As in classical drama, men played all the roles, but they no longer wore masks, and the jutting stage made for great intimacy. Hence the actors' art expanded to matters of facial expression, and the style of speech and movement was certainly closer than was Greek style to what we might loosely call realism. Shakespeare has Hamlet caution the actors: "suit the action to the word, the word to the action, with this special observance, that you o'erstep not the modesty of nature: for anything so overdone is from the purpose of playing, whose end, both at first and now, was and is, to hold as 't were, the mirror up to nature...." But the characteristic matter of Shakespearean tragedy certainly did not lend itself to a modern realistic style. Those great speeches are written in verse; they frequently are meant to augment the rather meager set design by providing verbal pictures to set the stage; they are much denser in texture, image, and import than is ordinary speech.

The Globe Theatre

Interior of the Swan Theatre, London, 1596

Interior of the Globe Theatre in the days of Shakespeare

A French theatre during Moliere's management

The Greek theatre at Epidaurus

These characteristics all serve to distinguish the Shakespearean stage from the familiar realism of most recent theater and film.

The Elizabethan stage made possible a tremendous versatility for the dramatist and the acting company. Most of the important action was played out on the uncurtained main platform, jutting into the audience and surrounded on three sides by spectators. The swiftly moving scenes followed each other without interruption, doubtless using different areas of the stage to signify different locations. There was some sort of terrace or balcony one story above the main stage, and there was an area, at the back of the main protruding stage that could be curtained off when not in use. Although Shakespeare's plays are usually divided into five separate acts in printed versions, they were played straight through, without intermission, much like a modern motion picture.

Though more versatile and intimate than the Greek stage, the Elizabethan stage had limitations which clearly influenced the playwright. Those critical imperatives of time, place, and action (i.e., the time represented should not exceed one day, the location should be fixed in one place, and the action should be limited to one cohesive story line—one plot), the so-called "unities" that Aristotle discovered in the drama of Sophocles, may well reflect the physical conditions of the Greek theater. Elizabethan dramatists largely ignored them, and in *Othello* we move from Venice to Crete, from the fortifications of the island to the city streets to Desdemona's bedchamber. Certainly some props were used to suggest these locations, but nothing comparable to the furniture of Ibsen's stage. Instead, the playwright often wove a sort of literary scenery into the speeches of the characters. For example, in *Othello*, Roderigo has occasion to say to Iago, "Here is her father's house; I'll call aloud." The second act of *Othello* opens with some gentlemen at "an open place near the quay." Notice the dialogue:

> **Montano.** What from the cape can you discern at sea?
> **First Gentleman.** Nothing at all: it is a high-wrought flood;
> I cannot, 'twixt the heaven and the main,
> Descry a sail.
> **Montano.** Methinks the wind hath spoke aloud at land;
> A fuller blast n'er shook our battlements.
> If it hath ruffian'd so upon the sea,
> What ribs of oak, when mountains melt on them,
> Can hold the mortise?

There is no sea, of course, and Elizabethan technology was not up to a wind machine. The men are, doubtless, looking off stage and creating the stormy setting through language. An open-air theater which played in daylight had few techniques for controlling lighting, and speeches had to be written to supply the effect:

> But look, the morn, in russet mantle clad,
> Walks o'er the dew of yon high eastern hill.

Further, the company had not the resources to place armies on the stage;

hence, a speaker in *King Henry V* boldly invites the audience to profit from imagination:

> Piece out our imperfections with your thoughts;
> Into a thousand parts divide one man,
> And make imaginary puissance;
> Think, when we talk of horses, that you see them
> Printing their proud hoofs i' the receiving earth.
> For 'tis your thoughts that now must deck our kings.

Molière's theater in the Petit-Bourbon Palace, built about twenty-five years after Shakespeare's death, was a forerunner of the common "box stage" on which so much recent drama is acted. Essentially, this stage is a box with one wall removed so that the audience can see into the playing area. Such a stage lends itself to realistic settings. Since the stage is essentially a room, it can easily be furnished to look like one. If street scenes are required, painted backdrops provide perspective and an accompanying sense of distance. Sets at an angle to the edge of the stage might be constructed. The possibilities for scenic design allowed by such a stage soon produced great set designers, and the structure of such a stage led to the development of increasingly sophisticated stage machinery, which in turn freed the dramatist from the physical limitations imposed by earlier stages. Although Molière preferred, generally, to use a single set (*The Misanthrope* is set at the home of Célimène), by Ibsen's time the versatility of the box stage enabled the father of modern drama to write elaborately detailed stage settings for the various locations in which the drama unfolds. Further, the furnishing of the stage in Ibsen's plays sometimes functions symbolically to convey visually the choking quality of certain bourgeois life-styles.

None of the historical stages have passed into mere history. The modern theater, in its vitality, still uses the Greek theater at Epidaurus, insists upon constructing approximations of the Elizabethan stage for its Shakespeare festivals, still employs with ever increasing inventiveness the box stage of Molière and Ibsen. Early in the twentieth century, some plays were produced in the "round," the action taking place on a stage in the center of the theater with the audience on all sides. A number of theaters were built that incorporated a permanent in-the-round arrangement. But versatility has become so important to the modern production designer that some feel the very best theater is simply a large empty room (with provisions for technical flexibility in the matter of lighting) that can be rearranged to suit the requirements of specific productions. This ideal of a "theater space" that can be freely manipulated has become increasingly attractive—some have been constructed—since it frees the dramatist and the performance from limitations built into permanent stage design.

Drama and Society

The history of dramatic literature (like the history of literature in general) provides evidence for another kind of history as well—the history of changing attitudes, changing values, and even changing taste. In ancient Greece, in Elizabethan England when Shakespeare wrote his enduring tragedies, right up to the end of the eighteenth century, certain expectations controlled the nature of tragedy. Those expectations were discussed by Aristotle as early as 335 B.C.; they involved the fall of a noble figure from a high place. Such tragedy reflects important cultural attitudes. It flourished in conjunction with a certain sort of politics and certain notions about human nature. The largest part of an audience of several thousand Athenians in the fifth century B.C. was certainly not itself noble. Neither was Shakespeare's audience at the Globe Theater in London. That audience, much as a modern audience, was composed of tradesmen, artisans, petty officials, and, in Greece, even slaves. Why then were there no tragedies in which the central figure was a store-keeper, a baker or butcher, a traveling salesman?

There have been many attempts to answer this difficult question, and those answers tend to make assumptions about the way individuals see them-selves and their society. If the butcher down the street dies, well, that is sad, but after all rather unimportant to the society. If the king falls, however, the society itself is touched, and a general grief prevails that makes possible sweeping observations about the chancy conditions of life. A culture always elevates some of its members to the status of culture heroes—often by virtue of the office they hold. Even now, societies are collectively moved, and moved profoundly, by the death of a president, a prime minister—a Kennedy, a de Gaulle, a Churchill—when they are not nearly so moved by immense disasters such as killing storms or earthquakes or civil wars. But things have changed, and most rapidly within the last 150 years or so.

Simply stated, new cultural values, new attitudes about human nature have developed, especially since the advent of industrialism and since Freud began publishing his systematic observations about the way men's minds interact with their bodies. The result has been an increasing humanization of those who used to be heroes and an increasing realization of the capacity for heroism in those who are merely bakers and butchers. Thus Henrik Ibsen, frequently referred to as the father of modern drama, can compel a serious emotional response from his audience over the tribulations of a small-town doctor in An Enemy of the People. And Arthur Miller can write an immensely successful tragedy on the life and death of a loud-mouthed traveling salesman named Willie Loman (and that last name may not be altogether accidental). These plays succeed in spite of their commonplace heroes because, as a so-ciety, we can now accept the experiences of ordinary people as emblems of our own. Perhaps we can because political institutions in the modern republics and in the socialist countries have, at least theoretically, exalted the common man and rejected political aristocracy. Certainly the reasons for the change are complex. But it remains true that neither Sophocles nor Shakespeare could have written An Enemy of the People.

Comedy, on the other hand, which features protagonists who over-come obstacles and rise to higher positions, has from earliest times dealt with the common people. Moreover, when the comic dramatist extended his wit to the powerful, he courted danger, as Molière discovered when Tartuffe was banned in seventeenth-century France as offensive to the established church. The same shift in attitudes that made possible a hero like Ibsen's Dr.

Stockmann in serious drama has made possible the satirical baiting of Christian charity in Shaw's *Major Barbara*. Earlier satire was directed against abuse —corrupt lawmakers, hypocritical churchmen. It was never directed against an ideal like Christian charity. Current attitudes about human nature and society permit the exaltation of the common people *and* the ridicule of exalted ideals.

Dramatic Irony

Dramatic irony allows the audience to know more than the characters do about their own circumstances. Consequently, that audience *hears more* (the ironic component) than do the characters who speak. Shakespeare's *Othello* provides an excellent illustration of the uses of dramatic irony. At the end of Act II, Cassio, who has lost his position as Othello's lieutenant, asks Iago for advice on how to regain favor. Iago, who, unknown to Cassio, had engineered Cassio's disgrace, advises him to ask Desdemona, Othello's adored wife, to intervene. Actually this is good advice; ordinarily the tactic would succeed, so much does Othello love his wife and wish to please her. But Iago explains, in a soliloquy to the audience, that he is laying groundwork for the ruin of all the objects of his envy and hatred—Cassio, Desdemona, and Othello:

> . . . for while this honest fool
> Plies Desdemona to repair his fortunes,
> And she for him pleads strongly to the Moor,
> I'll pour this pestilence into his ear
> That she repeals him for her body's lust;
> And, by how much she strives to do him good,
> She shall undo her credit with the Moor.
> So will I turn her virtue into pitch,
> And out of her own goodness make the net
> That shall enmesh them all.

Of course Desdemona, Cassio, and Othello are ignorant of Iago's enmity. Worse, all of them consider Iago a loyal friend. But the audience knows Iago's design, and that knowledge provides the chilling dramatic irony of Act III, scene 3.

When Cassio asks for Desdemona's help, she immediately consents, declaring, "I'll intermingle everything he does with Cassio's suit." At this, the audience, knowing what it does, grows a little uneasy—that audience, after all, rather likes Desdemona and doesn't want her injured. As Iago and Othello come on stage, Cassio, understandably ill at ease, leaves at the approach of the commander who has stripped him of his rank, thus providing Iago with a magnificent tactical advantage. And as Cassio leaves, Iago utters an exclamation and four simple words that may rank among the most electrifying in all of English drama:

Ha! I like not that.

They are certainly not very poetic words; they do not conjure up any telling images; they do not mean much either to Othello or Desdemona. But they are for the audience the intensely anticipated first drop of poison. Othello hasn't heard clearly:

What dost thou say?

Maybe it all will pass, and Iago's clever design will fail. But what a hiss of held breath the audience expels when Iago replies:

Nothing, my lord: or if—I know not what.

And Othello is hooked:

Was not that Cassio parted from my wife?

The bait taken, Iago beings to play his line:

Cassio, my lord? No, sure, I cannot think it,
That he would steal away so guilty-like,
Seeing you coming.

And from this point on in the scene, Iago cleverly and cautiously leads Othello. He assumes the role of Cassio's great friend—reluctant to say anything that might cast suspicion on him. But he is also the "friend" of Othello and cannot keep silent his suspicions. So honest Iago (he is often called *honest* by the others in the play), apparently full of sympathy and kindness, skillfully brings the trusting Othello to emotional chaos. And every word they exchange is doubly meaningful to the audience, which perceives Othello led on the descent into a horrible jealousy by his "friend." The scene ends with Othello visibly shaken and convinced of Desdemona's faithlessness and Cassio's perfidy:

Damn her, lewd minx! O, damn her!
Come, go with me apart; I will withdraw,
To furnish me with some swift means of death
For the fair devil. Now art thou my lieutenant.

To which Iago replies:

I am your own for ever.

Now, all of Iago's speeches in this scene operate on the audience through dramatic irony. The tension, the horror, the urge to cry out, to save Cassio, Desdemona, and Othello from the devilish Iago—all the emotional tautness in the audience results from irony, from knowing what the victims do not know. The play would have much less force if the audience did not know Iago's intentions from the outset and did not anticipate as he bends so many innocent events to his own increasingly evil ends. Note that dramatic irony is not limited to the drama; poetry, sometimes (as in William Blake's "The Chimney Sweeper"), and fiction, often (as in Joseph Conrad's "The Secret Sharer"), make use of this technique. But dramatic irony is the special tool of the dramatist, well suited to produce an electric tension in a live audience that overhears the interaction of people on stage.

Drama and Belief

Scholarly ordering that identifies the parts of drama and discusses the perceptive distinctions made by Aristotle among its parts can help you confront a play and understand how your responses were triggered by the playwright, the designers of the play, and the performers. But such analysis cannot substitute for the emotional experience produced by successful drama—your deepest responses have to do with states of mind, not with the three dramatic unities. Plays, no less than other art forms, address themselves to that incredibly complex melange of belief, attitude, intellect, and awareness that comprises a human psyche. As in *Antigone*, sometimes the play torments its audience by imposing on a courageous central character a duty that must be performed and must end in tragic death. Sometimes, as in *Major Barbara*, the play mocks widely held cultural values—the virtue of charity and the nobility of devoting oneself to Christian good works—and compels the audience to reexamine some of its fundamental values. If, as humans, we did not share the capacity for possessive love as well as jealousy, with all its terror, all its threat to self-esteem, then the tragedy of *Othello* would be incomprehensible.

While plays operate from within elaborate social and cultural constructions, response to dramatic art depends to a large extent on the condition of the responder's psyche, the state of mind he brings to the performance (or the reading). And that state of mind almost certainly changes with experience and, perhaps, with mood or preoccupation. A confirmed atheist may be indifferent to the religious dogma of *Everyman* but still be moved by the anonymous medieval dramatist's powerful vision of death. For a number of reasons, that same atheist may find himself engrossed by the powerful dramatic values in Ingmar Bergman's modern morality play *The Seventh Seal*. Though atheist, our hypothetical viewer is steeped in the tradition emanating from the Book of Revelations in the New Testament. He has frequently seen or read of death personified—that grim reaper. He discovers in Bergman's squire a character who puts forward his own skeptical view with wit and vigor. If he sees the film, he must be struck with the effect of what Aristotle called spectacle—those lowering leaden skies, the black and whiteness of things, the flagellants attempting to scourge themselves free of some God-sent plague, the burning of a beautiful young witch in the name of God, the relentless pursuit by Death, a figure of some strength, understanding, and wit himself. So, despite disbelief in God, in personifications of death, or in the validity of the Christian experience, the audience is nonetheless moved by the drama that is believable within its own well-known context.

Film

For all the versatility modern technology has given the modern dramatist in lighting, sound effects, scenery, and the like, a play, finally, is fundamentally static—locked in place upon a narrow stage, seen from a vantage point that never changes, dependent on dialogue and stage business for all its effects. If motion pictures were made by filming a performance with a stationary camera, then films would be no more than plays permanently recorded. But films are not made that way. While the film bears some obvious relationships to plays, the differences in technique and range are so significant that one must recognize that film is truly an art form itself, as distinguishable from plays as plays are from novels.

Consider some of the distinctive features of the film. It can take its audience anywhere and provide constantly changing vantage points (thus sharing something of the omniscient point of view available to the novelist). It can look up or look down. It can move close in, focus on a single sinister eye, or move out to watch the whole earth circle slowly below. It will, characteristically, in the time consumed by a typical scene in a play, combine scores of different shots lasting from one to fifteen seconds—long shots of characters in a room, middle shots of one character listening to another talk, closeups of a head alone grimacing expressively. Through the use of fade technique, the film can change time and place instantly. Perhaps most significantly, the film can, somewhat like the novel, provide with comparative ease a great deal of descriptive material—a long shot of the whole village in which the hero's house lies or a raging, ominous sea. The dramatist most often cannot. Again, through the use of close-up, the film can comment, like the novelist. But the effect of a single watching, malevolent eye occupying almost the entire screen has no counterpart in the dramatist's or novelist's art.

These distinguishing techniques of the film point to the unique and crucial characteristic that distinguishes it from novel and play: the film is overwhelmingly and flexibly visual. For this reason film scripts are almost always very difficult to read. Not only is a shooting script distractingly cluttered with camera directions, but, more significantly, the narrative development and meaning conveyed through visual imagery is lost in print. While we would not want to suggest that there are not important differences between reading a play and seeing it performed (plays *are* written to be produced), it is nonetheless true that plays have always enjoyed wide success as literary pieces for reading, because they can be understood and enjoyed as a purely verbal art form. If the dramatist feels that the printed version of his play loses significant meanings or coherence, he can make up for the loss by adding or expanding stage directions (note the elaborate and novelistic stage directions of Shaw's *Major Barbara*).

This is the remedy employed by Ingmar Bergman for his screenplay *The Seventh Seal*. The very first clause, "The night had brought very little relief from the heat," establishes a fact novelistically. Indeed, much of the power of *The Seventh Seal* as a literary document is attributable to Bergman's skill as a writer. The entire opening passage is a skillful evocation in words of the scene evoked visually in the film with equal power. But Bergman clearly knows that the writer's art differs from the filmmaker's, and so he tells us, as he cannot in the film, that "the morning sun ... wallows up from the misty sea like some bloated, dying fish." Bergman employs this kind of purely verbal technique throughout the descriptive prose passages, but only sparingly. For the most part, the prose passages *describe* what the film *shows*.

As successful as the printed screenplay is in describing what the film shows, we must recognize that we are ultimately dealing with a translation, with all the loss of power that translations usually involve. The dialogue, set down on paper and strung together and fleshed out by descriptive passages, captures everything except the overwhelmingly visual quality that is unique to the film, with its almost infinite possibilities for varying movement, point of view, clarity, time, and place. While the screenplay of *The Seventh Seal*, then, is a powerful work in its own right, the film is even more powerful. And comparison of the two will teach the reader much about the film as art.

Three Critical Approaches: Formalist, Sociological, Psychoanalytic

Literary criticism has to do with the *value* of literature, its goodness or badness, not with the history of literature or the theory of literature. Because value judgments tend to be highly subjective, lively, and sometimes even acrimonious, debates among literary critics accompany their diverse responses to and judgments of the same work. The judgment a literary critic makes about a story or poem is bound to reflect his own cherished values. The truth of a work of art is, obviously, very different from the truth of a mathematical formula. Certainly one's attitudes toward war, religion, sex, and politics are irrelevant to the truth of a formula but quite relevant to his judgment of a literary work.

Yet, any examination of the broad range of literary criticism reveals that groups of critics (and all readers, ultimately, are critics) share certain assumptions about literature. These shared assumptions govern the way the critic approaches a work, the elements he tends to look for and emphasize, the details he finds significant or insignificant, and, finally, his overall judgment of the value of the work. In order to illustrate diverse critical methodologies, we have examined two of the works in this anthology—Matthew Arnold's poem, "Dover Beach," and Nathaniel Hawthorne's short story, "My Kinsman, Major Molineux"—from three different critical positions: the formalist, the sociological, and the psychoanalytic. We have selected these three critical positions not because they are the only ones (there are others), but because they represent three major and distinctive approaches of literary criticism that may help readers formulate their own responses to a work of literature.

We do not suggest that one approach is more valid than the others nor that the lines dividing the approaches are always clear and distinct. Readers will, perhaps, discover one approach more congenial to their temperament, more "true" to their sense of the world, than another. Again, they may find that some works seem to lend themselves to one approach, other works to a different approach. More likely, they will find themselves utilizing more than one approach in dealing with a single work. What the reader will discover in reading the three analyses of the Arnold poem and the Hawthorne story is not that they contradict one another, but that, taken together, they complement and enrich his understanding and enjoyment of these works.

Formalist Criticism

While the formalist critic would not deny the relevance of sociological, bio-graphical, and historical information to a work of art, he insists that the func-tion of criticism is to focus on the work itself as a verbal structure and to dis-cover the ways in which the work achieves (or does not achieve) unity. The job of criticism is to show how the various parts of the work are wedded to-gether into an organic whole. That is to say, we must examine the *form* of the work, for it is the form that is its meaning. Put somewhat oversimply, the for-malist critic views a work as a timeless aesthetic object; we may find what-ever we wish in the work as long as what we find is demonstrably in the work itself.

Dover Beach

From the perspective of the formalist critic, the fact that Matthew Arnold was deeply concerned with how man could live a civilized and enjoy-able life under the pressures of modern industrialization or that Arnold ap-pears to have suffered in his youth an intense conflict between sexual and spiritual love may be interesting but ought not to be the focal points in an analysis of his poetry. After all, the historian is best equipped to reconstruct and illuminate Matthew Arnold's Victorian England, and it is the biographer's and psychologist's job to tell us about his personal life. A critic of "Dover Beach" who speculates on these matters is doing many things, perhaps quite interesting things, but he is not giving us a description of the work itself.

"Dover Beach" (p. 525) is a dramatic monologue, a poem in which a speaker addresses another person at a particular time and place. In the opening lines, Arnold skillfully sets the scene, introduces the image of the sea that is to dominate the poem, and establishes a moment of tranquility and moonbathed loveliness appropriate to a poem in which a man addresses his beloved. The beauty of the scene is established through visual images that give way, beginning with line 9, to a series of auditory images that undermine or bring into serious question the atmosphere established by the opening eight lines. In this contrast between visual and auditory imagery, a contrast that is developed through the entire poem, Arnold embodies one of the poem's major themes: appearance differs from reality.

In the second stanza, the "eternal note of sadness" struck in the final line of the first stanza is given an historical dimension and universalized by the allusion to Sophocles, the great Greek tragedian of fifth-century B.C. Athens. We become aware that the sadness and misery the speaker refers to are not the consequences of some momentary despair or particular historical event but are rather perennial, universal conditions of man's mortal life. Indeed, the allusion to Sophocles and the Aegean extends the feeling not only over centuries of time but over an immense geographical area, from the southern Aegean to the northern Atlantic.

The third stanza develops further the dominant sea imagery. But the real, literal seas of the earlier stanzas now become a metaphor for faith, per-haps religious faith, which once gave unity and meaning to man's life but now has ebbed away and left man stranded, helpless, bereft of virtually any defenses against sadness and misery. The "bright girdle furled," suggesting a happy and universal state, turns into a "roar" down the "naked shingles [i.e., pebble beaches] of the world."

The poet, therefore, turns, in the final stanza, to his beloved, to their love for each other as the only possible hope, meaning, and happiness in such a world. And his words to her echo the imagery of the opening lines with the important difference that the controlling verb *is* of the opening lines, denoting the actual and the real, is now replaced by the verb *seems*. The beautiful world is an illusion that conceals the bleak truth that the world provides no relief for man's misery. This grim realization leads to the powerful final image which compares man's life to a battle of armies at night. We have moved from the calm, serene, moon-bathed loveliness of the opening scene to an image of violence in a dark world where it is impossible to distinguish friend from foe or indeed even to understand what is happening.

"Dover Beach," then, is a meditation upon the irremediable pain and anguish of human existence, in the face of which the only possibility for joy and love and beauty is to be found in an intimate relationship between two human beings. The depth of the speaker's sadness is emphasized by his powerful evocation in the opening lines of the beauty of the scene. The first eight lines move with a quiet ease and flow with liquids and nasals, a movement enhanced by the balancing effect of the caesuras. In lines 9 to 14, the sounds also echo the sense, for now the sounds are much harsher and most of the lines are broken irregularly by more than one caesura. The dominant l, m, n sounds of the first eight lines give way to a pattern of hard g's, plosive t's and b's.

We have already noted that the dominant image of the poem, the key to the poem's structure, is the sea. It is the real sea the speaker describes in the opening stanza, but when it sounds the "eternal note of sadness," the sea becomes symbolic. In the second stanza, the speaker is reminded of another real sea, the Aegean, which he associates with Sophocles, and the developing unity is achieved, not only at the literal level (Sophocles listening to the Aegean parallels the speaker's listening to the northern sea) but at the symbolic level (Sophocles perceived the ebb and flow of human misery as the speaker perceives the eternal note of sadness). The third stanza further develops the sea image but presents something of a problem, for it is not altogether clear what the speaker means by "Faith." If he means religious faith, and that seems most likely, we face the problem of determining what period of history Arnold is alluding to. "Dover Beach" establishes two reference points in time—the present and fifth-century B.C. Athens—that are related to each other by negative auditory images. Since the function of the lines about the Sea of Faith is to provide a sharp contrast to the present and fifth-century Athens (the visual image of "a bright girdle furled" associates the Sea of Faith with the opening eight lines), the time when the Sea of Faith was full must lie somewhere between these two points or earlier than the fifth century. Since a formalist critic deals only with the work *itself* and since there appears to be nothing elsewhere in the poem that will allow us to make a choice, we might conclude that these lines weaken the poem.

For the formalist critic, however, the final stanza presents the most serious problem. Most critics of whatever persuasion agree that they are moving and memorable lines, poignant in the speaker's desperate turning to his beloved in the face of a world whose beauty is a deception, and powerful in their description of that world, especially in the final image of ignorant armies clashing by night. But what, the formalist critic will ask, has become of the sea image? Is it not strange that the image which had dominated the poem throughout, has given it its unity, is in the climactic stanza simply dropped? On the face of it, at least, we, as formalist critics, would have to conclude that the abandonment of the unifying image in the concluding stanza is a serious structural weakness, lessened perhaps by the power of the images that replace it, but a structural weakness nonetheless. On the other hand, a formalist critic might commend the poet for his effective alternation of visual and auditory imagery throughout the poem. The first four lines of the final stanza return to visual images of an illusory "good" world (controlled by *seems*, as we have already noted) and concludes with a simile that fuses a sombre vision of darkness and night, with the harsh auditory images of *alarms* and *clashes*.

My Kinsman, Major Molineux

This rather strange story by Hawthorne may be summarized easily. After an opening paragraph in which Hawthorne comments on the harsh treatment of colonial governors appointed by the British crown at the hands of the people of the Massachusetts Bay Colony, we meet an eighteen-year-old boy named Robin who crosses the ferry one night into an unnamed town. He is the second son of a country minister and has been sent to town to seek out his powerful kinsman, Major Molineux, who, presumably, will use his influence to help the boy make his way in the world. Strangely, the boy is unsuccessful in locating the residence of his kinsman. Worse, he is mocked and threatened by the several people he accosts and is almost seduced by a pretty harlot. Finally, he is told to wait in a certain spot, and shortly a boisterous procession, led by a man with a face painted half red and half black, passes. The procession conducts an open cart in which his kinsman, Major Molineux, tarred and feathered, is being led out of the town and into exile. The boy joins in the laughter at the plight of his once powerful relative but soon decides (his prospects blasted) to return home. A kindly bystander urges him to stay and make his way in the world without the help of his kinsman.

The formalist critic would note that the story is about a young man's initiation into the rude adult world where he must make his own way unprotected by a sheltering family. That world is at best morally ambiguous and at worst menacingly hostile. The transformation in Robin from a self-confident but ignorant grown child to a self-doubting but aware young adult is conveyed through a series of events culminating in a violent climax. Those events, and the atmosphere surrounding them, make for a story that creates, through irony, a mounting suspense released for Robin and the reader with explosive suddenness. Hawthorne's considerable skill in creating that suspense and his method for releasing it are fundamental to the successful embodiment of the *theme*. Naive Robin, a "good child," becomes experienced Robin, more sober and more aware of the evil aspect of the human condition.

The story opens with an apparently superfluous preface in which Hawthorne tells his readers that royal governors in Massachusetts Bay (that is, governors appointed by the English crown rather than elected by the people) were treated roughly, even if they were fair and lenient. The discussion is to serve as "a preface to the following adventures, which chanced upon a summer night, not far from a hundred years ago [approximately 1732]." Hawthorne concludes that opening paragraph: "The reader, in order to avoid a long and dry detail of colonial affairs, is requested to dispense with an account of the train of circumstances that had caused much temporary inflammation of the popular mind." Now it is an article of faith for the formalist critic that no part of a literary work is superfluous. Art is *organic*. All its parts are essential to the whole. The reader may remain ignorant of some particular events that caused some particular social inflammation, but he cannot go on to the adventures of that summer night without some expectation that they will have something to do with the politics of colonial Massachusetts. If this prefatory paragraph is really superfluous, then it constitutes a flaw in the work. If it is not, we shall have, finally, to understand its function in the story.

The narrative begins with an account of the arrival of an eighteen-year-old country-bred youth on his first visit to town, at nine o'clock of a moonlit evening. All of the details provided in this second paragraph are significant and repay close reading. A young man from the country on his first visit to town, dressed humbly but serviceably, with brown curly hair, well-shaped features, and bright cheerful eyes describes an agreeable character. His physical description is pleasing. He is doubtless rather innocent (being country-bred and on his first visit to town). But he arrives at night and remains hidden in darkness until illuminated by some light-giving source. The moonlight alone doesn't suffice, and we require the help of the boatman's lantern to see him.

The manipulation of the light and the darkness in the story is crucial. As Robin walks about the town looking for the lodging of his kinsman Major Molineux, he encounters six different people. The first, a rather dignified old man, is stopped by Robin "just when the light from the open door and windows of a barber's shop fell upon both their figures." The second encounter is within the inn, where there is light. The third encounter is with the harlot who is discerned by Robin as "a strip of scarlet petticoat, and the occasional sparkle of an eye, as if the moonbeams were trembling on some bright thing." We will see those moonbeams trembling on something altogether different later on. The fourth encounter, like the first two, ends with a threat from the sleepy watchman who carried a lantern. The fifth encounter is with the demonic man with the parti-colored face who "stepped back into the moonlight" when he unmuffled to Robin.

Now for all the local illumination that surrounds the threats, the temptation, and the final promise to Robin that his kinsman would soon be by, Robin remains in the dark. He does not understand why his questions generate such fierce threats from the elderly gentleman, the innkeeper, the watchman, and the demonic man. He sees the harlot in her parlor but doubts (quite rightly) her words and, finally, frightened a bit by the watchman, resists her seduction. The sixth encounter differs from the rest. The kindly stranger dimly sees Robin in the darkness—a literal and metaphorical darkness—and joins him. What of all this?

When the climactic moment occurs, when the procession arrives, it is lit by a dense multitude of torches "concealing, by their glare, whatever object they illuminated." This is rather a strange statement. When there is at last adequate light, the very glare conceals—and conceals what Robin must discover. Yet again, when the demonic leader of the procession fixes his eyes on Robin, "the unsteady brightness of the [torches] formed a veil which he could not penetrate." Finally, as the cart stops before Robin, "the torches blazed the brightest, there the moon shone out like day, and there, in tar-and-feathery dignity, sat his kinsman, Major Molineux!"

The orchestration of the light and darkness in the story becomes a metaphor for Robin's condition. Throughout, he is blind, despite the light. Rebuffs and laughter repeatedly greet his reiterated simple question, and in every case Robin—being, as he says, a "shrewd" youth—rationalizes the responses so that he can accept them without loss of self-esteem. The old man who threatens him is a "country representative" who simply doesn't know how powerful his kinsman is. The innkeeper who expels him is responding to Robin's poverty. The grinning demonic man with face painted half red, half black generates the ejaculation "Strange things we travellers see!" And Robin engages in some philosophical speculations upon the weird sight, which "settled this point shrewdly, rationally, and satisfactorily." In every case, however, Robin's rationalizations are wrong. As "shrewd" as he is, he constantly misunderstands because he is optimistic and self-confident. The reality would shatter both his optimism and his confidence. Despite the lighted places in the darkness, the places where the fate of his kinsman is hinted, he remains in the dark. At the climax, as the light becomes brighter and brighter, it does not illuminate but rather conceals by glare, forming an impenetrable veil through which he cannot see. Finally, when the torches blaze the brightest and the moon shines out like day, Robin sees! Presumably, now, he understands correctly the events of that long night.

But what is it that Robin understands? The question might be put another way. What is it that from the outset Robin doesn't understand? He is a good-looking "shrewd" lad with a powerful relative who expects the people he meets to behave with kindness and civility. A country youth, a minister's son, his experience of the world is limited. As the night wears on, the reader perceives Robin doggedly refusing to recognize that some sinister, evil action is afoot. Robin doesn't accept the existence of evil—everything can be explained in some rational way. With the temptation by the lovely harlot, Robin discovers within himself a sinfulness he might indignantly deny—and he does, after all, resist the temptation. But his weakness might be the beginning of wisdom, because Robin must discover that the human condition is not simple—it is complex. As he waits by the church, he peers into the window and notices the "awful radiance" within; he notices that a solitary ray of moonlight dares to rest upon the open page of the Bible. He wonders whether "that heavenly light" was "visible because no earthly and impure feet were within the walls?" And the thought makes him shiver with a strong loneliness. The implication that humans are inevitably impure grows strong.

This notion is driven home by the cryptic exchange between Robin and the kindly stranger when a great shout comes up from the still distant crowd. Robin is astonished by the numerous voices which comprise that one shout, and the stranger replies, "May not a man have several voices, Robin, as well as two complexions?" The notion that a man may have several voices has never occurred to Robin. In his attempt to deal with the strange sight of the man with two complexions, Robin rationalizes. But he does not learn from the evidence of his senses that man is complex, has different, even conflicting aspects. The stranger tries to teach him this truth—a man has many voices. Robin responds rather fatuously, thinking of the pretty harlot, "Perhaps a man may; but Heaven forbid that a woman should!" What does he mean? Doubtless he wishes to believe that the harlot was indeed the Major's housekeeper, that she told the truth, spoke with one voice, and was not the embodiment of a sort of satanic evil attempting to entrap him. All in all, Robin's view of the world from the outset is simplistic. And that view encourages him in his optimistic confidence. The stranger tells him that the world is not simple—that each man speaks with many voices, that many aspects comprise the human condition. The heavenly radiance enters only into an empty church, unsoiled by impure human feet. But Robin still does not understand.

The procession approaches. Grotesque sounds—"tuneless bray," the "antipodes of music," "din"—announce the rout. Laughter dominates, and the light grows brighter and brighter. But still Robin does not understand. There sits his kinsman in tar-and-feathery dignity. Their eyes meet in an anguished and humiliating recognition. And Robin laughs.

That laughter is the outward symbol of his understanding. He has learned of human complexity. He has learned that he too contains a satanic aspect. His innocent optimism, based on an unreal conception of man, is altered to experienced doubt based on a new understanding of the complexity and the universality of that evil aspect of humanity symbolized by the behavior of the mob and the wild abiding laughter that infects even Robin.

The story is based on colonial history. The opening paragraph serves to remind us of the literal level on which the story operates. Mobs did roam the streets of Boston, did disguise themselves as Indians, did tar and feather and expel crown officers. But our attention is directed to a young, inexperienced boy. Finally, we must ask what has happened. How is Robin changed by his experiences? The images of darkness and light, the temptation scene, the moonlit church, the mob, and Robin's response to it all weave together into a single cord, the strands of which guide him to a new awareness both of himself and of his world.

Sociological Criticism

In contrast to the formalistic critic, who maintains that the proper job of criticism is to approach each work of art as a self-contained aesthetic object and to attempt to illuminate its inherent structure and unity, the sociological critic asserts that since all men are the products of a particular time and place, we can never fully understand a work without some understanding of the social forces that molded the author and all that he did and thought. The sociological critic feels that the formalistic critic's attempt to view a work as timeless denies the fundamental and self-evident fact that authors do not (and cannot) divest themselves of all the shaping forces of their history and environment. Consequently, the critic must look to those forces if he is to understand a man's works.

Dover Beach

To understand "Dover Beach," we must, according to the sociological critic, know something about the major intellectual and social currents of Victorian England and the way in which Arnold responded to them. By the time Arnold was born in 1822, the rapid advances in technology that had begun with the Industrial Revolution of the eighteenth century were producing severe strains on the social and intellectual fabric. The ancient rural, agrarian economy was giving way to the new urban industrial economy, and the transition was long and painful. The new economy was creating a new merchant middle class whose growing wealth and power made it increasingly difficult for the upper classes to maintain exclusive political power. The passage of the celebrated Reform Bill of 1832, extending suffrage to any man who owned property worth at least ten pounds in annual rent, shifted political power to the middle class. It was not until 1867 that the franchise was extended to the lower classes. The intervening years were marked by severe social crises: depression, unemployment, rioting. Indeed, during these critical years when England was attempting to cope with the new problems of urban industrialism, the agitation and rioting of the lower classes created genuine fears of revolution (Englishmen remembered very clearly the French Revolution of 1789).

The ferment was no less intense and disruptive in the more rarified world of intellectual and theoretical debate. While it would be erroneous to assume that pre-industrial England was a world of idyllic stability, there can be little doubt that it was comparatively more settled and that the pace of change was much slower than during the nineteenth century. Perhaps the greatest stabilizing force in pre-industrial England was religion. It offered men answers to the ultimate questions of human existence and, on the basis of those answers, justification and authority for the temporal order—kingship (or political control by a small aristocracy), sharp class distinctions, and the like. The technology that made industrialism possible grew out of the scientific discoveries and methodologies that challenged some of man's fundamental assumptions and faith. Specific scientific discoveries seemed to undermine the old religious faith (for example, Darwin's *The Origin of Species*, published in 1859); the scientific approach of skepticism and empirical investigation led to numerous studies of the Bible not as a sacred text of infallible truth but as an historical text that arose out of a particular time and place in the history of man. Close examination of the Bible itself resulted in discoveries of inconsistencies and contradictions as well as demonstrable evidence of its temporal rather than supernatural origin.

Matthew Arnold, born into a substantial middle-class family and educated at England's finest schools, established himself early as an important poet and as one of the leading social critics of the period. In much of his poetry and his voluminous prose writings, Arnold addressed himself to the critical questions of his time. The old values, particularly religious, were crumbling under the onslaught of new ideas; Arnold recognized that a simple reactionary defense of the old values was not possible (even if one still believed in them). Unless some new system of values could be formulated, society was likely to, at worst, fall into anarchy or, at best, offer the prospect of an arid and narrow life to individual men. And since the destiny of the nation was clearly devolving into the hands of the middle class, Arnold spent much of his career attempting to show the middle class the way to a richer and fuller life.

For an understanding of "Dover Beach," however, Arnold's attempt to define and advance cultural values is less important than his confrontation with the pain and dilemma of his age. Caught in what he called in one of his poems "this strange disease of modern life," Arnold found that modern discoveries made religious faith impossible, and yet he yearned for the security and certainty of his childhood faith. In his darker and more despairing moments, it seemed to him that with the destruction of old values the world was dissolving into chaos and meaninglessness. In these moments, he saw himself as "wandering between two worlds, one dead, / The other powerless to be born."

"Dover Beach" expresses one of those dark moments in Arnold's life— a moment shared by many of Arnold's contemporaries and modern readers as well, who, in many ways, instinctively understand the mood and meaning of the poem because the realities to which it responds are still very much with us. Simply stated, it is a poem in which the speaker declares that even in a setting of the utmost loveliness and tranquility (a sociological critic might very well here discuss the opening lines in much the same way a formalistic critic does) the uncertainty and chaos of modern life cannot for long be forgotten or ignored. For uncertainty and chaos so permeate the life and consciousness of the speaker that everything he sees, everything he meditates upon, is infected. The scene of silent loveliness described in the opening lines turns into a grating roar that sounds the eternal note of sadness.

In the second stanza, the speaker turns to ancient Greece and its greatest tragic playwright in an effort to generalize and thereby lessen and defend against the overwhelming despair he feels. If the confusion and chaos of modern life are part of the eternal human condition, then perhaps it can be borne with resignation. Yet the third stanza seems to deny this possibility, for it suggests that at some other time in man's history Christian faith gave meaning and direction to life but now that faith is no longer available.

Trapped in a world where faith is no longer possible, the speaker turns in the final stanza—turns with a kind of desperation because no other possibilities seem to exist—to his beloved and their relationship as the only chance of securing from a meaningless and grim life some fragment of meaning and joy. Everything else, he tells her, everything positive in which man might place his faith, is a mere "seeming." The real world, he concludes, in a powerful and strikingly modern image, is like two armies battling in darkness. Whether or not the final image is an allusion to a particular historical battle (as many critics have suggested), it is a graphic image to describe what modern life seemed to a sensitive Victorian who could see no way out of the dilemma.

For the sociological critic, then, an understanding of "Dover Beach" requires some knowledge of the major stresses and intellectual issues of Victorian England, because the poem is a response to and comment upon those issues by one of the great Victorian poets and social critics. Our description of those issues and Arnold's ideas is extremely sketchy and selective; it merely illustrates the approach a sociological critic might take in dealing with the poem. Nevertheless, the sketchiness of the presentation raises important questions about sociological criticism: Where does the sociological critic stop? How deep and detailed an understanding of the times and the writer's relationship to the period is necessary to understand the work? The formalistic critic might charge that the sociological critic is in constant danger of becoming so immersed in sociological matters (and even biography) that he loses sight of the work he set out to investigate. The danger, of course, is a real one, and the sociological critic must be mindful, always, that his primary focus is art, not sociology, history, or biography; the extent of his sociological investigations will be controlled and limited by the work he is attempting to illuminate. To this charge, the sociological critic might very well respond (perhaps in pique) that the formalistic critic becomes so preoccupied with matters of structure and unity that his criticism becomes arid and apparently divorced from all the human concerns that make people want to read poems in the first place. The sociological critic would agree with the comment made by Leon Trotsky, the Russian Marxist revolutionary, in his book on *Literature and Revolution:*

> The methods of formal analysis are necessary, but insufficient. You may count up the alliterations in popular proverbs, classify metaphors, count up the number of vowels and consonants in a wedding song. It will undoubtedly enrich our knowledge of folk art, in one way or another; but if you don't know the peasant system of sowing, and the life that is based on it, if you don't know the part the scythe plays, and if you have not mastered the meaning of the church calendar to the peasant, of the time when the peasant marries, or when the peasant women give birth, you will have only understood the outer shell of folk art, but the kernel will not have been reached.

As a final note, a few remarks need to be made on a special form of sociological criticism, namely, ideological (i.e., Marxist, Christian, etc.) criticism. While the sociological critic differs from the formalistic critic in his approach to literature, the sociological critic tends to share with the formalistic critic the view that works of art are important in their own right and do not need to be justified in terms of any other human activity or interest. The Marxist critic, on the other hand, while sharing many of the assumptions and the approaches of the sociological critic, carries the approach an important step further. The Marxist critic sees literature as one activity among many that are to be studied and judged in terms of a larger and all-encompassing ideology. He holds that one cannot understand the literature of the past unless he understands how it reflects the relationship between economic production and social class. And since the Marxist sees his duty—indeed, the duty of all responsible and humane people—as not merely to describe the world but to change it in such a way as to free the oppressed masses of the world, he will not be content merely to illuminate a work, as does the sociological critic, or to demonstrate its aesthetic unity and beauty, as does the formalist critic. The Marxist critic will judge contemporary literature by the contribution it makes to bringing about revolution or in some way making the masses of workers (the proletariat) more conscious of their oppression and, therefore, more equipped to struggle against the oppressors.

The Marxist critic might describe "Dover Beach" very much as the sociological critic, but he would go on to point out that the emotion Arnold expresses in the poem is predictable, the inevitable end product of a dehumanizing, capitalistic economy in which a small class of oligarchs is willing, at whatever cost, to protect and increase its wealth and power. Moreover, the Marxist critic, as a materialist who believes that man makes his own history, would find Arnold's reference to "the eternal note of sadness" a mystic evasion of the real sources of his alienation and pain; Arnold's misery can be clearly and unmystically explained by the socioeconomic conditions of his time. It is Arnold's refusal to face this fact which leads him to the conclusion typical of a bourgeois artist-intellectual who refuses to face the truth; the cure for Arnold's pain cannot be found in a love relationship, because relationships between people, like everything else, are determined by socioeconomic conditions. The cure for the pain which he describes so well will be found in the world of action, in the struggle to create a socioeconomic system that is just and humane. "Dover Beach," then, is both a brilliant evocation of the alienation and misery caused by a capitalistic economy and a testimony to the inability of a bourgeois intellectual to understand what is responsible for his feelings.

My Kinsman, Major Molineux

"MY Kinsman, Major Molineux" presents a nocturnal world, viewed largely from the point of view of its young hero, where nothing makes sense to him. It appears to be an allegoric or symbolic world, a dreamlike world where everything seems to mean something else. Robin searches for the meaning to the strange behavior of townsmen he accosts, for some key which will unlock the mystery. The sociological critic also searches for the key, and he finds it in the opening paragraph of the story, the paragraph that in any short story is crucial in setting the stage for the action about to unfold.

That paragraph, the sociological critic would note, is not a part of the narrative itself but is rather a straightforward summary of the historical situation in the American colonies prior to the Revolutionary War. We are given this summary, Hawthorne tells us, "as a preface to the following adventures." No critic, of whatever persuasion, can ignore that paragraph. In contrast to the actual story, the opening paragraph is clear and straightforward: on the eve of the Revolution, the bitterness and hostility of the colonists toward the mother country had become so intense that no colonial administrators, even those who were kindest in exercising their power, were safe from the wrath of the people. It is in the context of this moment of American history, when there occured a "temporary inflammation of the popular mind," that the story of Robin's search for his kinsman must be read and interpreted. For "My Kinsman, Major Molineux" is an examination of and comment upon the American colonies as they prepared to achieve, by violence if necessary, independence from the increasingly intolerable domination of England.

We are introduced to Robin as he arrives in town, an energetic, likable, and innocent young man who has left the secure comfort of his rural family to commence a career. He is on the verge of manhood and independence, filled with anticipation and promise, as well as apprehension, as he confronts an uncertain future. But Robin, unlike most young men in his position, has the advantage of a wealthy cousin who has offered to help the young man establish himself. The story narrates Robin's polite and reasonable inquiries as to where Major Molineux resides and the bafflingly rude and hostile responses of the townspeople.

The mystery is Major Molineux, or, rather, the hostility his name evokes. For the reader, at least, the mystery begins to dispel when he learns that the major, an aristocratic and commanding figure, represents inherited wealth and civil and military rank—in short, the authority and values of the mother country. To Robin, fresh from the simple and nonpolitical world of his pastoral home, Major Molineux is a real person, his cousin, whose aid he seeks. To the townsman, on the other hand, Molineux is a symbol of the hated mother country in a political struggle that is turning increasingly ugly.

This difference between what Major Molineux means to Robin and what he means to the townspeople is prepared for at the very outset of the narrative. Robin has left the morally simplistic and nonpolitical world of his country home and arrived in the town seething with revolutionary fervor. The country is the past, America's past; the town is the present, the place where America's future will be decided. As Robin wends his way through the metropolis vainly searching for his kinsman, Hawthorne skillfully weaves into the narrative details suggestive of the political theme. Robin, we are told, enters the town "with as eager an eye as if he were entering a London city." Before entering the tavern, "he beheld the broad countenance of a British hero swinging before the door." Once in the tavern, he observes a group of men who look like sailors drinking punch, which, Hawthorne tells us, "the West India trade had long since made a familiar drink in the colony." More significantly, this episode ends when the innkeeper, in response to Robin's inquiry about his cousin, merely points to a poster offering a reward for a runaway, "bounden servant," and ominously advises Robin to leave. The suggestion is clear—anyone seeking Major Molineux must be a willing bond servant (bond servitude being a form of limited slavery used by England to help populate the American colonies) and, therefore, an enemy of the revolutionaries.

Robin continues his wanderings, his confusion deepening, until a stranger he accosts tells him that Major Molineux will soon pass by the very spot where they are standing. As Robin waits, his thoughts drift to his country home and family. In a dreamlike state, he dwells upon the warmth and security of the life he has left, the sturdy simplicity of a happy family bound together by a gentle and loving clergyman father. The dream ends abruptly, however, when Robin, attempting to follow his family into their home, finds the door locked. After an evening of "ambiguity and weariness," it is natural that Robin's thoughts should turn back to his home. It is just as natural that his dream should end as it does, for Robin has begun the journey to manhood and independence from which there is no turning back. Although he is not fully aware of the fact, he shares a good deal with the townsmen who have so baffled and angered him. The world of manhood and independence is the complex and ambiguous world where political battles are fought out, and Robin, like America itself, is set upon a course of action from which there is no turning back. The simplicities of an older, rural America, where authority is vested in a gentle father and the Scriptures or figures of authority like

Major Molineux, must inevitably yield to the ambiguities of the metropolis, where the future will be decided.

That future, Robin's and the nation's, is dramatically embodied in the climactic episode, when Robin finally finds his kinsman. Tarred and feathered, Major Molineux sits in the midst of a garish and riotous procession, led by a man whose face is half red and half black. This man, Hawthorne tells us, is the personification of war and its consequences:

> The single horseman, clad in a military dress, and bearing a drawn sword, rode onward as the leader, and, by his fierce and variegated countenance, appeared like war personified; the red of one cheek an emblem of fire and sword; the blackness of the other betokened the mourning that attends them.

The strange Indian masquerade of those in the procession is a clear allusion to the disguise of the rebellious participants in the Boston tea party. The incomprehensible words addressed to Robin earlier by various townspeople are clearly passwords arranged to identify the conspirators against established authority.

The meaning of the night's events begins to dawn on Robin as he joins in the laughter of the throng as it wildly celebrates the demise of Major Molineux, whom Hawthorne compares to "some dead potentate, mighty no more, but majestic still in his agony." The entire scene, the entire story which this scene brings to a climax, gives Robin's laughter a crucial meaning. In joining in the the laughter of the throng, Robin identifies himself with the political goals of the revolutionaries. But more than that, in so doing he begins, finally, to see that his personal relationship, both to his home and his uncle, are parallel with and inseparable from the relationship of the colonies to its past and the mother country. Robin's joy in seeing his dignified and powerful uncle a scorned captive of the townsmen is intensely personal, the joy a young man feels, ambivalent though it may be, when he is released from the bonds of an authority figure. But the meaning of that authority figure, as the story makes clear, cannot be separated from the political theme, as Robin himself now recognizes.

Such a reading is not meant to imply that "My Kinsman, Major Molineux" is a simple story, a kind of allegory, which embodies in dramatic action a straightforward set of abstract ideas. It is, rather, a story revealing how complex a particular historical event is. That Hawthorne himself had equivocal feelings about the event is made clear by his description of the major, whose dignity and majestic bearing the utmost humiliation cannot altogether extinguish. This fact, together with the unflattering way the townspeople are presented throughout, suggests that Hawthorne viewed the event itself, at least in part, as the victory of mob rule over dignified and settled authority.

At any rate, the procession past, the tension released, Robin turns to the friendly citizen and asks directions back to the ferry. Defeated in his purpose, shaken by and perhaps not yet fully comprehending the extraordinary events of the evening, he decides to return to his family. But the kindly stranger urges Robin to stay. "Perhaps," he says, "as you are a shrewd youth, you may rise in the world without the help of your kinsman, Major Molineux." The stranger's comment is an appropriate conclusion to the story, for it appeals to Robin as a man, as an American man who must achieve independence through his own efforts, however difficult and ambiguous the struggle. Robin must make his way without the aid of his wealthy and powerful uncle, just as America must make its way without the aid of the mother country. However problematical that freedom is, however dangerous and frightening, it is the inescapable price that real independence exacts.

Psychoanalytic Criticism

Psychoanalytic criticism always proceeds from a set of principles which describe the inner life of *all* men and women. Though there is now a great diversity of conviction about the nature of inner life and how to deal with it, certainly all analysts, and all psychoanalytic critics, assume that the development of the psyche in humans is analogous to the development of physique. Doctors can provide charts indicating physical growth stages, and analysts can supply similar charts, based on generations of case history, indicating stages in the growth of the psyche. Obviously the best psychoanalytic critic is a trained analyst, but few analysts engage in literary criticism. Most of that criticism is performed by more or less knowledgeable amateurs, and much of that criticism is based on a relatively few universal principles set down by Sigmund Freud which describe the dominating human drives and the confusions they produce. We must examine those principles.

First among them is the universality of the Oedipus complex. Freud contends that everyone moves through a psychic history which at one point, in early childhood, involves an erotic attachment to the parent of the opposite sex and an accompanying hostility and aggression against the parent of the same sex, who is seen as a rival in the jealous struggle. Such feelings, part of the natural biography of the psyche, pass or are effectively controlled in most cases. But sometimes, the child grown to adulthood is still strongly gripped by that Oedipal mode, which then may result in neurotic or even psychotic behavior. A famous lengthy analysis of Shakespeare's *Hamlet* argues that Hamlet is best understood as gripped by Oedipal feelings which account for his difficulties and his inability to act decisively, and the Laurence Olivier film of *Hamlet* presents such an interpretation. But how could Shakespeare create an Oedipal Hamlet when Freud was not to be born for some two and half centuries? Freud did not invent the Oedipus complex—he simply described it. It was always there, especially noticeable in the work of great literary artists who in every era demonstrate a special insight into the human condition. At one point in Sophocles' *Oedipus Rex*, written about 430 B.C., Jocasta the queen says to her son-husband, "Have no more fear of sleeping with your mother: / How many men, in dreams have lain with their mothers / No reasonable man is troubled by such things." And the situation of Oedipus, and the awareness of Jocasta, provide for Freud the very name for the psychic phase he detects.

Paralleling the Oedipal phase in the natural history of the psyche is the aggressive phase. This psychic feature urges physical and destructive attacks on those who exercise authority, that is, those in a position to control and to deny the primal desires of each of us. For the young, the authority figure is frequently the father. For the more mature, that authority figure may be the policeman, the government official, the office manager. As far back as the Hebrew Bible story of the Tower of Babel and the old Greek myths in which the giant Titans attack their father Zeus (much as Zeus himself attacked his father Chronos), there appears evidence of the rebellion against the father-authority figure. Freud views that aggressive hostility as another ever present component of the developing psyche. But, in the interest of civilization and the advantages which organized society provides, that aggressiveness must be controlled. The mechanisms of control are various. Early on comes the command to honor one's father and mother. The culture demands of its members that they love and revere their parents. What, then, of the frequent hostility which children feel toward those parents who punish them and deny them the freedom they seek? That hostility is often the occasion of guilt—one is supposed to love not hate his parents—and the guilt can be severe as the child (or adult) detects the variance between his desires and his "duty." Such guilt feelings sometimes generate behavior that effectively punishes. The punishment may be internal—may take the form of psychotic withdrawal or psychosomatic illness. Or the guilt may generate external behavior that requires punishment at the hands of society. In any case, the psychoanalytic critic is constantly aware that the author and/or his characters suffer and resuffer a primal tension that results from the conflict of his psychic aggressions with his social obligations.

Dover Beach

"DOVER Beach" is richly suggestive of the fundamental psychic dilemma of man in civilization. And since man in civilization is, by definition, discontent because his social duties require him to repress his primal urges, it is not surprising that the opening visual images of the poem which create a lovely and tranquil scene—calm sea, glimmering cliffs, a tranquil bay, sweet night air—are quickly modified by the ominous "only" that begins the seventh line of the poem. That *only*, in the sense of "in contrast," is addressed to a lady who has been called to the window to see the quiet and reassuring scene. No reassurance, finally, remains, as the images shift to an auditory mode:

> Listen! you hear the grating roar
> Of pebbles which the waves draw back, and fling,

Further, the land is "moon-blanched," a color with an emotional tone quite different from the earlier glimmering cliffs and fair moon. The tone is strangely changed, the emotional impact of "roar" and "blanched" suggesting something quite different from the serenity of the opening image, and the second stanza closes with the sounds of the surf bringing "the eternal note of sadness in."

Why should sadness be an *eternal* note? And why is the visual imagery largely pleasing while the auditory imagery is largely ominous? The answers to these two questions provide the focus for a psychoanalytic reading of the poem.

The "eternal note of sadness" (an auditory image) represents Arnold's recognition that, however sweet the night air and calm the sea, the central human experience is sadness. At the point in the poem where that sadness is recognized, the poet recalls the great Greek tragedian Sophocles who heard that same note of sadness over 2,000 years ago. (It is, after all, an eternal sadness.) For Sophocles, the sadness brings to mind the "turbid ebb and flow of human misery." Now Sophocles' greatest and best known tragedy, *Oedipus Rex*, ends with the chorus pointing out that no man should count himself happy until at the moment of his death he can look back over a life without pain. Fate, as it afflicted Oedipus, afflicts us all. And the fate of Oedipus provided Freud with the name of that psychic mode through which we all pass. We would all be guilty of parental murder and incest were it not for the necessity to repress those urges in order to construct a viable society. The unacceptable passions are controlled by guilt. We may not commit murder or incest on pain of punishment. We may not even desire to commit murder or incest on pain of possible psychic punishment. The dilemma, the guarantee of guilt or the guarantee of discontent, defines that eternal note of sadness which the poet hears.

We might go further. There is agreement that in infancy and very early childhood the tactile and the visual senses are most important. Somewhat later the auditory sense increases in importance. Consequently, the child recognizes security—certitude, peace, help for pain—tactilely and visually, in the warmth and the form of the omnipresent and succoring mother. Later, through his ears comes the angry "no!" When discipline and painful interaction with others begin, he experiences the auditory admonition which frustrates his desires. It is immensely interesting to the psychoanalytic critic that in "Dover Beach" the tranquilities are visual but the ominous sadness is auditory—the "roar" which brings in the "note" of sadness, the "roar" of the retreating sea of faith, the "night-wind," the "alarms," the "clash by night."

We need to look at the opening lines of the final stanza. Certainly the principal agency developed by society to enforce the morality it required was religion. Ancient religious teaching recognized those very primal urges that Freud systematically described and made them offenses against God. Faith, then, became the condition that made society possible; religious injunction and religious duty served as a sort of cultural superego, a mass conscience, that not only controlled human aggression but substituted for it a set of ideal behavior patterns that could guarantee a set of gratifying rewards for humanity. Hence the poet recalls:

> The Sea of Faith
> Was once, too, at the full, and round earth's shore
> Lay like the folds of a bright girdle furled.

This is a strange image. Surely the emotional tone of "the folds of a bright girdle furled" is positive—that bright girdle is a "good" thing, not an ominous thing. Yet, that girdle (i.e., a sash or belt worn round the waist) is restrictive. It is furled (i.e., rolled up, bound) around the land. In short, the Sea of Faith contains, limits, strictly controls the land. In the context of the poem, that containment is a good thing, for without the restricting Sea of Faith the world, despite appearances,

> Hath really neither joy, nor love, nor light,
> Nor certitude, nor peace, nor help for pain.

Without strong religious faith, acting as a cultural superego, the primal aspects of men are released—aggression and lust come to dominate human activity:

> And we are here as on a darkling plain
> Swept with confused alarms of struggle and flight,
> Where ignorant armies clash by night.

A certain confusion persists. On the one hand, the Sea of Faith serves a useful function as an emblem of the superego (loosely, the conscience), the name Freud gives to the guilt-inducing mechanism that incessantly "watches" the ego to punish it for certain kinds of behavior. When it is at the full, ignorant armies, presumably, do not clash by night. On the other hand, the superego as associated with auditory imagery is ominous. It reverberates with the painful experience of frustration. Finally, however, the usefulness of the Sea of Faith is illusory. The note of sadness is eternal. Sophocles, long before the foundation of Christianity, heard it. What emerges from the poem's images, understood psychoanalytically, is a progression from a mild note of sadness (frustrated desires) to alarms and clashes (threatening uncontrolled aggressive desires). The calm sea, the fair moon, the world is like a land of dreams—illusory and without substance. Sadness, struggle, and flight are real.

We need to deal with the girl to whom the poet speaks; we need to understand his relationship to her. The quest for that understanding involves another psychoanalytic principle, another set of images, and a reconsideration of the image of the Sea of Faith.

In earliest infancy, the ego, the sense of self, is not yet formed. The infant child considers the mother, particularly the mother's breast, as part of himself. A gradual and a painful recognition must occur in which the child is dissociated from the mother. The process begins with the birth trauma. In the womb, the child is utterly safe, never hungry, never cold. After birth, there are discomforts. But for a time the mother and her nourishing breast are so much present that the infant does not distinguish where he ends and the other, the mother, begins. But this state of affairs does not continue, and the infant becomes increasingly dissociated. Slowly he learns what is "him" and what is not, what he can control by will (moving his arm, say) and what he cannot (his mother's availability). In short, he learns the borders of his being, the edges of his existence.

Images of borders and edges constantly recur in the poem. Such images may be taken as emblems of dissociation—that is, symbols of the separation between the warm nourishing mother and the child. Consequently, they are symbols of painful dissatisfaction. The Sea of Faith that

> . . . round earth's shore
> Lay like the folds of a bright girdle furled

seems, on the other hand, much like that warm, encompassing mother who, to the infant, was a part of himself. But dissociation occurs, and the distressed poet perceives that comforting entity withdrawing, retreating "down the vast edges drear / And naked shingles of the world." He has an edge and can no longer reside safely in close association with the source of comfort and security.

Instantly the poet turns to the girl and says

> Ah, love, let us be true
> To one another!

He perceives his companion not erotically as a love object but as the source of security, as a replacement for the withdrawing emblematic mother. He offers his "love" a mutual fidelity not to reassure her of his committment but to assure himself of hers. He wishes to dissolve the edges of his ego and associate, as in infancy, with his "mother." Such an association will protect him from a world in which "ignorant armies clash by night."

My Kinsman, Major Molineux

THE story opens with the crossing of a river into an unnamed town after dark. If one takes a psychoanalytic stance, the mysterious opening nicely symbolizes a sort of spiritual journey into mysterious realms. More specifically, the opening suggests an inward journey into the dark recesses of the human spirit. Robin has to confront the psychic confusion resulting from the conflict between the civilized and the psychological response to paternal authority. Robin takes his journey to discover and deal with the paternal figure that is identified in his mind with safety and security, his powerful kinsman, Major Molineux. From a psychoanalytic point of view, it is reasonable to point out that Robin has at least two fathers, since his kinsman, if Robin ever finds him, will serve a paternal function. Some critics suggest that every male Robin encounters serves as a surrogate father. Note that the men Robin meets, with one exception, all act threateningly, all offer to punish him, all assume a position of authority, and, hence, all in some respect are paternalistic. The one exception, the kindly stranger who joins Robin in his watch and who urges him to make his own way without the aid of a paternalistic power is in some ways himself a kind of unreal, idealized father figure, who, though kindly and helpful, requires no price for his help.

From the psychoanalytic point of view, the story is precisely about the price required of young men by their fathers. The price, of course, is not coin. It is behavior. Robin must behave as authority wishes, not as Robin wishes. In return, he will be secure—but almost certainly discontent. Perhaps, deeper than consciousness, Robin feels the pinch of such an economy and unwittingly seeks to avoid payment. After all, the story runs its course as Robin seeks directions to the house of his kinsman. But a kind of haunting inefficiency constantly disrupts his search. Early he realizes that he should have asked the ferryman to take him to Major Molineux. But he didn't. He stops an old gentleman by seizing hold of his coat—rather curious behavior to an elderly stranger. And the stranger's response to the youth's behavior is an angry threat. That threat provokes the first round of recurrent laughter from the loungers in the barber shop. And the threat frightens Robin. Next he becomes "entangled in a succession of crooked and narrow streets," a set of literal streets near the waterfront (but also a lovely metaphor for the human psyche), where he is attracted to an inn. There he receives his second rebuff from the innkeeper, another threat, and is followed out into the street by more laughter.

Robin responds to this rebuff with considerable anger, thinks violent thoughts, but continues to pursue his quest in a most curious way. He walks up and down the main street of the town hoping to run into his kinsman. Actually he is thrilled by the rich and exotic shopwindows and strollers. It is reasonable to assert that at this point, regardless of his rationalization, Robin is not at all seeking his kinsman. He is, for once, doing what he wishes to do. He is enjoying himself, free from any paternal interference. Remarkably, as he gawks along the exotic street, he hears the distinctive cough of the old gentleman he first encountered, the gentleman who threatened him with the stocks, the gentleman who proclaimed, "I have—hem, hem—authority." Robin responds by declaring "Mercy on us!" and ducking around a corner to avoid meeting him. Strange, this, passing strange. Stranger still that just around that corner which provides the escape from authority, Robin chances upon a half-opened door through which he could discern "a strip of scarlet petticoat, and the occasional sparkle of an eye."

This encounter is quite different from the others which occur both before and after. That red petticoat and sparkling eye belong to a vivacious and devastatingly attractive lady. A harlot, to be sure, but awfully attractive. She tells Robin, in response to his standard question, that Major Molineux is asleep within (an outrageous lie which Robin can't help but doubt), and she takes him by the hand "and the touch was light, and the force was gentleness, and though Robin read in her eyes what he did not hear in her words, yet the slender-waisted woman in the scarlet petticoat proved stronger than the athletic country youth. She had drawn his half-willing footsteps nearly to the threshold" when the watchman appeared. The girl hastily withdraws, and Robin is once again warned by authority of punishment for bad behavior.

The frightened youth does not realize until the watchman has turned the corner that *he* would certainly know the whereabouts of his kinsman, Major Molineux, but his tardy shouted request to the vanished watchman is answered only by more vague laughter. Why didn't Robin ask for directions immediately? Well, he was about to sin against the paternal authority which generally represses and most particularly represses the sexual instincts of sons. The psychoanalytic critic might go even further here in explaining the sources of Robin's guilty demeanor before the watchman whose appearance is fantastically coincidental. (Is he the ever present psychic "watchman" who cries "guilty" at even our ego-gratifying *thoughts* when they violate the "law"?) The desirable girl in the scarlet petticoat says that Major Molineux cohabits with her. Her eyes and her behavior invite Robin to a sexual encounter which he, however nervously, welcomes. If Major Molineux is a surrogate father for Robin, is not the lovely scarlet lady a surrogate mother? And is not an Oedipal situation developed? For students not familiar with principles of pscyhoanalytic criticism, this will seem a rather wild reading. But reserve judgment. Consider how the story ends. Then, perhaps, the Oedipal feature will not seem bizarre.

Now events move rapidly. Robin, brought to his "senses" by the intrusion of the watchman, remembers that he is a "good" boy and rejects the lovely beckoning arm. But he is upset and feeling violent. He intends to succeed in his quest, even if it means clubbing someone with his stout oak cudgel. The next man he meets, mysteriously muffled, is forced to answer—and answer he does. The muffling, dropped, reveals a hideous, satanic face painted half red and half black. Certainly that painting is a disguise. But this man, we later discover, is the leader of the mob which destroys Major Molineux's power and dignity and, as such, represents a certain aspect first of the community but also of each man in it, particularly of Robin. An old-fashioned Freudian would have no trouble identifying him as Robin's embodied *id*, the name given by Freud to the insistent selfish, lustful, and aggressive aspect of man's psyche, just as he would have no trouble earlier identifying the intrusive watchman as Robin's *superego*. Our awful demonic parti-colored citizen tells Robin to wait where he is and within an hour he will surely meet his kinsman, Major Molineux.

Robin waits and experiences some dreams which are almost hallucinations. He is standing by a church and notices the graves. Perhaps the major is already dead and will appear to haunt him. Wouldn't it be nice to be at home, safe in his family circle? And he is there, but when he seeks to follow his family into the house, the door is closed and locked in his face. It is a normal dream for a frightened young man the first time away from home. But in the context of the story, this dream acts as a metaphor for Robin's expulsion from the safety of home. Even if he would submit again to the "father" in return for security, the opportunity is denied. One father only remains for him—his kinsman, Major Molineux (who may be dead). It is his home that Robin must seek for shelter from all the perils of independence. But the price is the same —submission and repression. The rioters draw near, the tumult grows loud, the torches cast a great light into the darkness—some revelation is at hand. And the light reveals the demonic man on horseback with a drawn sword leading a riotous procession around a cart in which the powerful, gray, dignified, upright, fatherly Major Molineux sits trembling and humiliated. All the figures Robin encountered during the story return—old "hem-hem," the laughing innkeeper, the saucy harlot. And all laugh. But Robin's laugh is louder than all the rest! For the psychoanalytic critic, that laugh cannot be interpreted other than as the laugh of exultant release from the tyranny of the father, of established authority, and the prospect of independent activity free of stifling inner guilt.

The psychoanalytic critic might go further. He might call attention to the drawn sword held by the embodied id and remark on the relationship between that phallic symbol and the thwarted desire of Robin in the encounter with the harlot. Certain figures which recur throughout the history of literature (and in dreams and psychiatric case histories) are accepted by

Freudian critics as symbols of the sexual and aggressive aspects of the human condition. Such deep reading, like all deep reading, is perilous. Yet to the reader well versed in the premises of psychoanalysis and the universal symbols behind which the mind conceals its primal nature, the bold analysis enriches the literary art.

Did Hawthorne deliberately design the psychoanalytic structure of "My Kinsman, Major Molineux"? A difficult question. He certainly did not incorporate an embodied superego and id. He never heard of those psychic abstractions. He certainly did not incorporate by design a phallic sword suggesting that Robin's sexual freedom is obtained through Major Molineux's exile. But, the psychoanalytic critic responds, Hawthorne, as a sensitive artist, perceives the deep struggle between desire and duty, between primal urge and social restraint. And that struggle he incorporates. As for the drawn sword, he had no idea of its psychic significance. He would be appalled by the modern psychoanalytic response. But, for the analyst, that does not in the least contradict the modern conviction that universal symbols, however unconscious, struggle to the surface in all art. That psychoanalytic critic would admire Hawthorne's "My Kinsman, Major Molineux" for effectively and accurately portraying the rite of passage of young Robin from innocence to experience, from repressed childhood to independent manhood.

Glossary of Literary Terms

Alexandrine See Meter.

Allegory A form of symbolism in which ideas or abstract qualities are represented as characters in a narrative and dramatic situation, resulting in a moral or philosophic statement.

> *Everyman*, p. 829
> Ingmar Bergman, *The Seventh Seal*, p. 854

Alliteration The repetition within a line or phrase of the same initial consonant sound.

> Death, thou shalt die.—John Donne, "Death, Be Not Proud," l. 14, p. 794
> And mouth with myriad subtleties–Paul Laurence Dunbar, "We Wear the Mask," l.5, p. 330

Allusion A reference, explicit or indirect, to something outside the work itself. The reference is usually to some famous person, event, or other literary work.

> Did their Catullus walk that way?—William Butler Yeats, "The Scholars," l. 12, p. 327
> W. H. Auden, title of "The Unknown Citizen," p. 341

Ambiguity A phrase, statement, or situation that may be understood in two or more ways. As a literary device, it is used to enrich meaning or achieve irony.

> my Uncle Sol imitated the
> skunks in a subtle manner
>
> or by drowning himself in the watertank—E.E. Cummings, "nobody loses all the time," ll. 24–26, p. 819

Anapest See Meter.

Antistrophe See Strophe.

Apostrophe A direct address to a person who is absent or to an abstract or inanimate entity.

> How oft, in spirit, have I turned to thee,
> O sylvan Wye! thou wanderer through the woods—William Wordsworth, "Lines Composed a Few Miles Above Tintern Abbey," ll. 55–56, p. 83
> Christina Rossetti, "Rest," p. 808
> John Donne, "Death, Be Not Proud," p. 794

Archetype Themes, images, and narrative patterns that are universal and thus embody some enduring aspects of man's experience. Some of these themes are the death and rebirth of the hero, the underground journey, and the search for the father.

Assonance The repetition of vowel sounds in a line, stanza, or sentence.

> His lesions are legion—Gwendolyn Brooks, "The Children of the Poor," Stanza 11, l. 17, p. 347
> W. H. Auden, *from* "Five Songs," p. 533

Ballad A narrative poem, originally of folk origin, usually focusing upon a climactic episode and told without comment. The most common form is a quatrain of alternating four- and three-stress iambic lines, with the second and fourth lines rhyming. Typically the ballad will employ a *refrain*—that is, the last line of each stanza will be identical (or virtually identical), but each repetition somehow advances the story.

> "Edward," p. 789
> "Bonny Barbara Allan," p. 505

Blank Verse   Lines of unrhymed iambic pentameter.

> William Shakespeare, speech from *Hamlet,* p. 793
> William Wordsworth, "Lines Composed a Few Miles Above Tintern Abbey," p. 82

Cacophony   The use of harsh and discordant language. *Compare* Euphony.

> Is perjured, murderous, bloody, full of blame,
> Savage, extreme, rude, cruel, not to trust—William Shakespeare, Sonnet 129, ll. 3–4, p. 510

Caesura   A strong phrasal pause within a line of verse.

> There is a loveliness exists.
> Preserves us.//Not for specialists.—W.D. Snodgrass, "April Inventory," ll. 59–60, p. 110

Carpe Diem   Latin, meaning "seize the day." A work, generally a lyric poem, in which the speaker calls the attention of his auditor (often a young girl) to the shortness of life and youth and then urges her to enjoy life while there is time.

> Andrew Marvell, "To His Coy Mistress," p. 518
> Robert Herrick, "Corinna's Going A-Maying," p. 514

Catharsis   One of the key concepts in *The Poetics* of Aristotle by which he attempts to account for the fact that representations of suffering and death in drama paradoxically leave the audience feeling relieved rather than depressed. According to Aristotle, a tragic hero arouses in the viewer feelings of "pity and fear," pity because he is a man of great moral worth and fear because the viewer sees himself in the hero.

Central Intelligence   *See* Point of View.

Comedy   In drama, situations that are designed to delight and amuse rather than concern or sadden. Comic heroes rise in the course of the action from a low to a higher position. *Compare* Tragedy.

Conceit   A figure of speech that establishes an elaborate parallel between unlike things.

> John Donne, "A Valediction: Forbidding Mourning," ll. 25–36, p. 513

Connotation   The associative and suggestive meanings of a word in contrast to its literal meaning. *Compare* Denotation.

Consonance   Repetition of the final consonant sounds in stressed syllables.

> That night when joy began
> Our narrowest veins to flush,
> We waited for the flash
> Of morning's levelled gun—W.H. Auden, *from* "Five Songs," ll. 1–4, p. 533

Couplet   A pair of rhymed lines.

> Cease then, nor ORDER imperfection name:
> Our proper bliss depends on what we blame.—Alexander Pope, *from* "An Essay on Man," ll. 1–2, p. 322

Dactyl   *See* Meter.

Denotation   The literal, dictionary definition of a word. *Compare* Connotation.

Diction   The choice of words in a work of literature, generally applied to indicate such distinctions as abstract or concrete, formal or colloquial, literal or figurative.

Didactic   A work whose primary and avowed purpose is to teach or to persuade the reader of the truth of some philosophical, religious, or moral statement or doctrine.

Dimeter   *See* Meter.

Dramatic Distance   In fiction, the point of view which enables the reader to know more than the narrator of the story.

Dramatic Irony   *See* Irony.

Elegy   Usually a poem lamenting the death of a particular person, but often used to describe meditative poems on the subject of man's mortality.

> W. H. Auden, "In Memory of W. B. Yeats," p. 819
> Thomas Gray, "Elegy Written in a Country Churchyard," p. 796

End-rhyme   *See* Rhyme.

End-stopped Line   A line of verse that constitutes a complete logical and grammatical unit. A line of verse that does not constitute a complete syntactic unit is designated *run-on*. Thus in the opening lines of Browning's "My Last Duchess":

> That's my last Duchess painted on the wall,
> Looking as if she were alive. I call
> That piece a wonder, now: . . .

The opening line is end-stopped, while the second line is run-on, because the direct object of *call* "runs on" to the third line.

English Sonnet   *See* Sonnet.

Epode   *See* Strophe.

Euphony   Sounds that are pleasing to the ear. *Compare* Cacophony.

> Wallace Stevens, "Peter Quince at the Clavier," ll. 1–9, p. 101

Figurative Language   A general term covering the many ways in which language is used nonliterally. *See* Hyperbole, Irony, Metaphor, Metonymy, Paradox, Simile, Symbol, Synecdoche, Understatement.

First-person Narrator   *See* Point of View.

Foot   *See* Meter.

Free Verse   Poetry that does not adhere to the metric regularity of traditional verse and that is usually unrhymed.

> Walt Whitman, "Out of the Cradle Endlessly Rocking," p. 87

Hexameter   *See* Meter.

Hubris   In Greek tragedy, overweening pride usually exhibited in a character's defiance of the gods. Creon, in Sophocles' *Antigone,* is guilty of hubris.

Hyperbole   Exaggeration; overstatement. *Compare* Understatement.

> on freeways fifty lanes wide—Lawrence Ferlinghetti, "In Goya's Greatest Scenes," l. 28, p. 349
> Robert Burns, "A Red, Red Rose," p. 520

Iamb   *See* Meter.

Imagery   Language that embodies an appeal to the senses: sight, sound, smell, taste, or touch.

> Thom Gunn, "Innocence," last two stanzas, p. 110
> William Shakespeare, Sonnet 18, "Shall I compare thee to a summer's day?" p. 509
> William Shakespeare, Sonnet 130, "My mistress' eyes are nothing like the sun," p. 511

Robert Frost, "Birches," p. 99
Wallace Stevens, "Peter Quince at the Clavier," p. 101

Internal Rhyme   *See* Rhyme.

Irony   Language in which the intended meaning is different from or opposite to the literal meaning. Verbal irony includes overstatement (hyperbole), understatement, and opposite statement.

> Had it any been but she,
>   And that very face,
> There had been at least ere this
>   A dozen dozen in her place.—Sir John Suckling,   "Out upon It!"
>   p. 518

> The grave's a fine and private place,
> But none, I think, do there embrace.—Andrew Marvell, "To His Coy
>   Mistress," ll. 31–32, p. 519

> Was he free? Was he happy? The question is absurd:
> Had anything been wrong, we should certainly have heard.—W. H. Auden,
>   "The Unknown Citizen," ll. 28–29, p. 342

Dramatic irony occurs when a reader knows things a character is ignorant of or when the speech and action of a character reveal him to be different from what he believes himself to be.

William Blake, "The Chimney Sweeper," p. 79
Robert Browning, "My Last Duchess," p. 86
William Shakespeare, *Othello,* Act III, Scene 3, p. 578

Italian Sonnet   *See* Sonnet.

Lyric   Originally, a song accompanied by lyre music. Now, a relatively short poem expressing the thought or feeling of a single speaker.

Christina Rossetti, "A Birthday," p. 527

Metaphor   A figurative expression consisting of two elements in which one element is provided with special attributes by being equated with a second unlike element.

Chidiock Tichborne, "Elegy," p. 791
A wren, happy, tail into the wind,

• • •

> If only I could nudge you from this sleep,
> My maimed darling, my skittery pigeon—Theodore Roethke, "Elegy for
>   Jane," ll. 5, 18–19, p. 821

Meter   Refers to recurrent patterns of accented and unaccented syllables in verse. A metrical unit is called a *foot,* and there are four basic accented patterns. An *iamb,* or *iambic foot,* consists of an unaccented syllable followed by an accented syllable (before, tŏdáy). A *trochee,* or *trochaic foot,* consists of an accented syllable followed by an unaccented syllable (fúnnў, phántŏm). An *anapest,* or *anapestic foot,* consists of two unaccented syllables followed by an accented syllable (in the line "Ĭf ĕv̆│er̆ўthĭng háp│pĕns thăt cán't│bĕ dóne," the second and third metrical feet are anapests). A *dactyl,* or *dactyllic foot,* consists of a stressed syllable followed by two unstressed syllables (sýllăblĕ, métrĭcăl). One common variant, consisting of two stressed syllables, is called a *spondee,* or *spondaic foot* (dáybréak, moónshíne).
    Lines are named by virtue of the number of metrical feet they contain.

one foot	monometer
two feet	dimeter
three feet	trimeter
four feet	tetrameter
five feet	pentameter
six feet	hexameter (An iambic hexameter line is an *Alexandrine*.)

Here are some examples of various metrical patterns:

Tŏ eăch|hĭs súff|erĭngs: áll|ăre mén,   iambic tetrameter
    Cŏndemńed|ălike|tŏ groán;   iambic trimeter
Ońce ŭp|on ă|mídnĭght|dreăry,|whĭle Ĭ|pońdeřed|wéak ănd|wéaŗy,
            trochaic octómeter (with a spondee in the third foot)
Ĭs this|the reǵ|iŏn, this|the soíl,|the clíme,   iambic pentameter
Fóllŏw ĭt|uttěrlȳ,   dactyllic dimeter
Hópe bě|yońd hope:·   dimeter line—trochee and spondee

Metonymy   A figure of speech in which a word stands for a closely related idea. In the expression "the pen is mightier than the sword," *pen* and *sword* are metonymies for written ideas and military force respectively.

Free hearts, free foreheads—you and I are old—Alfred, Lord Tennyson, "Ulysses," l. 49, p. 324

They are sick of the palette and fiddle-bow—William Butler Yeats, "Lapis Lazuli," l. 2, p. 97

Monometer   *See* Meter.

Near Rhyme   *See* Rhyme.

Octave   *See* Sonnet.

Ode   Usually a long, serious poem on exalted subjects, often in the form of an address.
John Keats, "Ode to a Nightingale," p. 800

Off Rhyme   *See* Rhyme.

Omniscient Narrator   *See* Point of View.

Onomatopoeia   Language that sounds like what it means. Words like *buzz, bark,* and *hiss* are onomatopoetic. Also, sound patterns that reinforce the meaning over one or more lines may be designated onomatopoetic.

Is lust in action; and till action, lust
Is perjured, murderous, bloody, full of blame—William Shakespeare, Sonnet 129, ll. 2–4, p. 510

Wallace Stevens, "Peter Quince at the Clavier," stanza one, p. 101

Opposite Statement   *See* Irony.

Overstatement   *See* Hyperbole.

Paradox   A statement that seems self-contradictory or absurd but is, somehow, valid.

And death shall be no more; Death, thou shalt die—John Donne, "Death, Be Not Proud," l. 14, p. 794

Chidiock Tichborne, "Elegy," p. 791

William Butler Yeats, "Lapis Lazuli," p. 97

Pentameter   *See* Meter.

Persona   Literally "mask." The term is used to describe a narrator in fiction (Sherwood Anderson's "I Want to Know Why") or the speaker in a poem (Robert Browning's "My Last Duchess"). The persona's views are different from the author's views.

Personification   The attribution of human qualities to nature, animals, or things.
>   Edmund Waller, "Go, Lovely Rose!" p. 516
>   John Donne, "Death, Be Not Proud," p. 794

Petrarchan Sonnet   *See* Sonnet.

Plot   A series of actions in a story or a drama which bear a significant relationship to each other. E. M. Forster illuminates the definition: " 'The King died, and then the Queen died,' is a story. 'The King died and then the Queen died of grief,' is a plot."

Point of View   The person or intelligence a writer of fiction creates to tell the story to the reader. The major techniques are:

>   *First person,* where the story is told by someone, often though not necessarily the principal character, who identifies himself as "I."
>>   Sherwood Anderson, "I Want to Know Why," p. 57

>   *Third person,* where the story is told by someone (not identified as "I") who is not a participant in the action and who refers to the characters by name or as "he," "she," and "they."
>>   Petronius, "The Widow of Ephesus," p. 461

>   *Omniscient,* a variation on the third person, where the narrator knows everything about the characters and events, can move about in time and place as well as from character to character at will, and can, whenever he wishes, enter the mind of any character.
>>   Leo Tolstoy, "The Death of Iván Ilých," p. 700

>   *Central intelligence,* another variation on the third person, where narrative elements are limited to what a single character sees, thinks, and hears.
>>   Richard Wright, "The Man Who Lived Underground," p. 267

Quatrain   A four-line stanza that may incorporate various metrical patterns.
>   "Bonny Barbara Allan," p. 505
>   Thomas Gray, "Elegy Written in a Country Churchyard," p. 796

Refrain   *See* Ballad.

Rhyme   The repetition of the final stressed vowel sound and any sounds following (debate, relate; pelican, belly can) produces perfect rhyme. When rhyming words appear at the end of lines, the poem is *end-rhymed.* When rhyming words appear within one line, the line contains *internal rhyme.* When the correspondence in sounds is imperfect (heaven, given; began, gun), *off rhyme,* or *near rhyme,* is produced.
>   Internal rhyme: Edgar Allan Poe, "The Raven," p. 803
>   Off rhyme: W. H. Auden, *from* "Five Songs," p. 533

Rhythm   The alternation of accented and unaccented syllables in language. A regular pattern of alternation produces *meter.* Irregular alternation of stressed and unstressed syllables produces *free verse.*

Run-on Line   *See* End-stopped Line.

Satire   Writing in a comic mode that holds a subject up to scorn and ridicule, often with the purpose of correcting human vice and folly.
>   E. E. Cummings, "the Cambridge ladies who live in furnished souls," p. 339
>   W. H. Auden, "The Unknown Citizen," p. 341
>   Robert Frost, "Departmental," p. 335
>   Harlan Ellison, " 'Repent, Harlequin!' Said the Ticktockman," p. 310

Scansion   The process of analyzing the metrical or rhythmical pattern of a poem.
>   Th' expense|of spir|it in|a waste|of shame

Ĭš lust|iñ ác|tiŏn,‖añd tĭll ác|tiŏn, lúst
Ĭš pér|jure̊d, múr|derŏus, blood|y̆, fúll|oĭ bláme,
Sávăge,|extréme,|rude, cru|ĕl, nót|tŏ trúst:

In this excerpt from one of Shakespeare's sonnets, the dominant meter is iambic pentameter, but variations occur in every line. A strong caesura occurs in the middle of the second line.

Sestet *See* Sonnet.

Shakespearean Sonnet *See* Sonnet.

Simile A figurative expression in which an element is provided with special attributes through a comparison with something quite different. The words *like* or *as* create the comparison, e.g. "My love is like a red, red rose," "As virtuous men pass mildly away . . . so let us melt, and make no noise."

> John Donne, "A Valediction: Forbidding Mourning," p. 513
> Henry Wadsworth Longfellow, "Nature," p. 802

Soliloquy A dramatic convention in which an actor, alone on the stage, speaks his thoughts aloud.

> William Shakespeare, speeches from *Hamlet*, p. 793, and *Macbeth*, p. 792

Sonnet A lyric poem of fourteen lines, usually of iambic pentameter. The two major types are the Petrarchan (or Italian) and Shakespearean (or English). The *Petrarchan sonnet* is divided into an octave (the first eight lines, rhymed abbaabba) and a sestet (the final six lines, usually rhymed cdecde or cdcdcd). The *Shakespearean sonnet* consists of three quatrains and a concluding couplet, rhymed abab cdcd efef gg.

> William Shakespeare, Sonnets, pp. 509–511
> Henry Wadsworth Longfellow, "Nature," p. 802

Spondee *See* Meter.

Stanza The grouping of the lines of a poem in a recurring pattern of meter, rhyme, and number of lines. Among the most common are the *couplet* and the *quatrain*.

Stream of Consciousness The narrative technique of some modern fiction which attempts to reproduce the full and uninterrupted flow of a character's mental process, in which ideas, memories, and sense impressions may intermingle without logical transitions. A characteristic of this technique is the abandonment of conventional rules of syntax and punctuation.

> Katherine Anne Porter, "The Jilting of Granny Weatherall," p. 756

Strophe In Greek tragedy, the unit of verse the chorus chanted as it moved to the left in a dance rhythm. The chorus sang the *antistrophe* as it moved to the right and the *epode* while standing still.

Symbol A thing or an action that embodies more than its literal, concrete meaning.

> Alastair Reid, "Curiosity," p. 107
> J. Peter Meinke, "Advice to My Son," p. 111

Synecdoche A figure of speech in which a part is used to signify the whole.

> Bald heads forgetful of their sins—William Butler Yeats, "The Scholars," l. 1, p. 326

Synesthesia In literature, the description of one kind of sensory experience in terms of another. Taste might be described as a color or a song.

> John Keats, "Ode to a Nightingale," stanza two, p. 800

Tetrameter *See* Meter.

Theme The moral proposition that a literary work is designed to advance. The theme of Milton's *Paradise Lost* is to "justify the ways of God to men." The theme of Joseph Conrad's "The Secret Sharer" might be briefly stated: The recognition of complex moral ambiguities is essential to maturity.

Third-person Narrator *See* Point of View.

Tone The attitude embodied in the language a writer chooses. The tone of a work might be sad, joyful, ironic, solemn, playful.

> Compare: Matthew Arnold, "Dover Beach," p. 525, with Anthony Hecht, "The Dover Bitch," p. 534.

Tragedy The dramatic representation of serious and important actions which turn out badly for the chief character. Aristotle saw tragedy as the fall of a noble figure from a high position as the result of a flaw in his character. *Compare* Comedy.

Trimeter *See* Meter.

Trochee *See* Meter.

Understatement A figure of speech that represents something as less important than it really is. *Compare* Hyperbole.

> Much the same smile? This grew; I gave commands;
> Then all smiles stopped together. . . .—Robert Browning, "My Last Duchess," ll. 45–46, p. 87

Recordings and Films

The catalogs of the following companies and agencies list a surprisingly comprehensive set of recordings (on records, tapes, and cassettes) of early poetry read by performers and recent poetry read by poets. Several of the plays included in this anthology have also been recorded.

Caedmon Records, 505 Eighth Ave., New York, N.Y. 10018: offers recordings of Arthur Miller's adaptation of *An Enemy of the People, The Misanthrope, Othello, Major Barbara,* and *Antigone*

The Library of Congress, Music Division, Recording Laboratory, Washington, D. C. 20540: features modern poetry

Superintendent of Documents, U.S. Government Printing Office, Washington, D. C. 20402: Write for the catalog of the Library of Congress Tapes Archives (there is a small charge). The catalog lists a great number of taped poetry readings.

Spoken Arts, Inc., 59 Locust Ave., New Rochelle, N.Y. 10801

Catalogs listing films that bear on the teaching of poetry may be obtained from: NET Film Service, Indiana University, Audio Visual Center, Bloomington, Ind. 47401; Encyclopaedia Britannica Educational Corp., 425 N. Michigan Ave., Chicago, Ill. 60611; McGraw-Hill/Contemporary Films, 330 West 42nd Street, New York, N.Y., 10036.

Sixteen mm. films of works in this anthology available for rental:

Major Barbara and *The Seventh Seal,* from Janus Films, 745 5th Ave., New York, N.Y. 10022

Othello (Russian version, English dialogue), from Audio/Brandon, 1619 North Cherokee, Los Angeles, Calif. 90028

Othello (Olivier version), from Warner Bros. Film Rental, 4000 Warner Blvd., Burbank, Calif.

Bartleby, from Encyclopaedia Britannica, Educational Corp., 425 Michigan Ave., Chicago, Ill. 60611

An Occurrence at Owl Creek Bridge, from Contemporary Films/McGraw-Hill, 330 W. 42nd St., New York, N.Y. 10036

Face to Face ("The Secret Sharer" and "The Bride Comes to Yellow Sky"), from Willoughby-Peerless Film Library, 415 Lexington Ave., New York, N.Y. 10017

Index of Authors and Titles